THE VISION OF GOD

THE VISION OF GOD

THE CHRISTIAN DOCTRINE OF THE
SUMMUM BONUM

KENNETH E. KIRK

'visne ergo attendere quæ apud alios interim comperi divinarum scripturarum egregios tractatores, quid de visione Dei senserint, ne forte sufficiant desiderio tuo, quamvis ea forsitan noveris? pauca ergo ista attende, si placet.' —S. AUGUSTINE, *ep.* 147. 6 (17)

HARPER TORCHBOOKS ❧ The Cloister Library
Harper & Row, Publishers, New York

TO MY MOTHER

THE VISION OF GOD

Printed in the United States of America.

All rights reserved.

This book was originally published in 1931 by Longmans, Green and Co., Ltd., London and New York, with a second edition in 1932. It is here reprinted by arrangement.

First HARPER TORCHBOOK edition published 1966 by
Harper & Row, Publishers, Incorporated
49 East 33rd Street
New York, N.Y. 10016

The Library of Religion and Culture
General Editor: Benjamin Nelson

TABLE OF CONTENTS.

LECTURE III.

FORMALISM.

LECTURE IV.

RIGORISM.

LECTURE V.

THE REPLY TO RIGORISM (I.—DISCIPLINE).

LECTURE VI.

THE REPLY TO RIGORISM (II.—DOCTRINE).

LECTURE VII.

CONFUSION AND ORDER.

LECTURE VIII.

LAW AND PROMISE.

ADDITIONAL NOTES.

INDICES.

PRINCIPAL ABBREVIATIONS.

ALKG. : H. Denifle and F. Ehrle, *Archiv für Litteratur und Kirchengeschichte des Mittelalters* (Berlin and Freiburg, 1885-1900,).

ARW. : *Archiv für Religionswissenschaft* (Freiburg and Leipzig, 1898-   ).

Aquinas, *CG.* ; *ST.* : S. Thomas Aquinas, *Summa contra Gentiles ; Summa Theologica.*

Boll., *AS.* : *Acta Sanctorum Bollandiana* (Antwerp and Brussels, 1643-1794).

Bousset, *KC.* ; *RJ.* : W. Bousset, *Kyrios Christos* (2nd edn., Göttingen, 1921) ; *Die Religion des Judentums* (3rd edn., Tübingen, revised by H. Gressmann, 1926—now vol. xxi of *HNT.*).

Bremond, *HLSR.* : H. Bremond, *Histoire Littéraire du Sentiment Religieux en France depuis la fin des Guerres de Religion jusqu'à nos Jours* (vols. i-viii published, Paris, 1914-   ).

CE. : C. G. Herberman and others, *The Catholic Encyclopædia* (17 vols., New York, 1907-1922).

C. Med. H. : J. B. Bury and others, *The Cambridge Mediæval History* (vols. i-vi published, 1911-   ).

C. Mod. H. : Lord Acton and others, *The Cambridge Modern History* (14 vols., 1907-1912).

CSEL. : *Corpus Scriptorum Ecclesiasticorum Latinorum* (Vienna, 1866-   ).

Clemen, *RGENT.* : C. Clemen, *Religionsgeschichtliche Erklärung des Neuen Testaments* (2nd edn., Giessen, 1924).

DAC. : J. Hastings, *A Dictionary of the Apostolic Church* (1918).

DALC. : F. Cabrol and H. Leclerq, *Dictionnaire d'Archéologie Chrétienne et de Liturgie* (Paris, 1907-   ).

DB. : H. Denzinger and C. Bannwart, SJ., *Enchiridion Symbolorum, Definitionum et Declarationum de Rebus Fidei et Morum* (15th edn., Freiburg, 1922).

DCB. : W. Smith and H. Wace, *A Dictionary of Christian Biography* (4 vols., 1877-1887).

DCG. : J. Hastings, *A Dictionary of Christ and the Gospels* (1906).

DHGE. : A. Baudrillart and others, *Dictionnaire d'Histoire et de Géographie Ecclésiastiques* (Paris, 1912-   )

DTC. : A. Vacant and E. Mangenot, *Dictionnaire de Théologie Catholique* (Paris, 1903-   ).

Dar.-Sagl. : C. Daremberg and E. Saglio, *Dictionnaire des Antiquités Grecques et Romaines* (5 vols. in 10, Paris, 1877-1919).

ERE. : J. Hastings, *An Encyclopædia of Religion and Ethics* (13 vols., 1908-1926).

GCSS. : *Die Griechischen Christlichen Schriftsteller der ersten drei Jahrhunderte* (Berlin and Leipzig, 1897-   ).

HDB. : J. Hastings, *A Dictionary of the Bible* (5 vols., 1898-1904.

HNT. : H. Lietzmann and others, *Handbuch zum Neuen Testament* (2nd and 3rd edns., Tübingen, 1923-   ).

Hef.-Lecl. : H. Leclerq, *Histoire des Conciles d'après les docmuents originaux par Charles Joseph Hefele, nouvelle traduction francaise . . . corrigée et augmentée* (Paris, 1907-   ). A greatly enlarged and annotated rendering of the 2nd edn. (1873-1890) of Hefele-Hergenröther, *Conciliengeschichte.*

JE. : I. Singer and others, *The Jewish Encyclopædia* (12 vols., New York, 1901-1903).

JTS. : *The Journal of Theological Studies* (1899-).

LNP-NF. : H. Wace and P. Schaff, *A Select Library of the Nicene and Post-Nicene Fathers*, new series (14 vols., 1890-1900).

MGH. : G. H. Pertz, T. Mommsen and others, *Monumenta Germaniæ Historica* (1826-).

MPL. : J. P. Migne, *Patrologiæ cursus completus, series latina* (Paris, 1844-1865).

MPG. : J. P. Migne, *Patrologiæ cursus completus, series græca* (Paris, 1857-1866).

PRE. . J. J. Hertzog and A. Hauck, *Realencyclopädie für protestantische Theologie und Kirche* (3rd edn., Leipzig, 1896-1913).

PW. : G. Wissowa, *Paulys Realencyclopädie der Classischen Altertumswissenschaft*, neue bearbeitung (Stuttgart, 1894-).

Pourrat, *SC.*: P. Pourrat, *La Spiritualité chrétienne* (4 vols., Paris, 1917-1928)

Reitzenstein, *HMHL.* ; *HMR.* : R. Reitzenstein, *Historia Monachorum und Historia Lausiaca, eine Studie zur Geschichte des Mönchtums* (Göttingen, 1916) ; *Die Hellenistischen Mysterienreligionen* (3rd edn., Leipzig, 1927).

Rosweyde, i, ii : H. Rosweyde, SJ., *Vitæ Patrum sive Historiæ Eremeticæ libri decem* (Antwerp, 1615 , reprinted in *MPL.* as vols. 73, 74).

SNT. : W. Bousset and W. Heitmüller, *Die Schriften des Neuen Testaments* (4 vols., 3rd edn., Göttingen, 1917).

TU. : O. v. Gebhardt and A. Harnack, *Texte und Untersuchungen zur Geschichte der altchristlichen Literatur* (Leipzig, 1883-).

Wendland, *HRK.* : P. Wendland, *Die Hellenistich-Römische Kultur in ihren Beziehungen zu Judentum und Christentum* (3rd edn., Tübingen, 1912—now vol. i, part 2, of *HNT.*).

PREFACE.

I.

THE history of the Christian doctrine of the *summum bonum*, or of 'man's last end,' as it is not too happily called in technical theology, has never been written in full. The present book, in which movements of vast importance for Christianity are dismissed, as often as not, in a single paragraph, whilst many great names receive no more than cursory mention in the footnotes, makes no claim to supply the deficiency. I have been content simply to review a few outstanding episodes in the history of the doctrine, with the purpose of illustrating the different interpretations, legitimate and illegitimate, to which it has been subjected.

Even this limited aim has had to suffer further restriction. The traditional Christian formula, that the purpose of human life is to see God, opens up a vast field of metaphysical enquiry into the nature of the divine essence, and the modes, conditions, and limits of its communicability to men—how vast, even when restricted to the sphere of Christian theology, may be inferred, for example, from Dr. O'Mahony's admirable recent exposition of S. Thomas' discussions.[1] Questions of this character I have left almost entirely untouched, thinking it better to attempt to fill up a gap in Anglican moral theology, to which I have drawn attention elsewhere,[2] by concentrating upon the ethical implications of the doctrine.

It is suggested, therefore, in the chapters which follow, that the doctrine 'the end of life is the vision of God' has throughout been interpreted by Christian thought at its best as implying in practice that the highest prerogative of the Christian, in this life as well as hereafter, is the activity of *worship* ; and that nowhere except in this activity will he find

[1] J. E. O'Mahony, *The Desire of God in the Philosophy of S. Thomas Aquinas* (Cork University Press, 1929) ; and cp. *infra*, pp. 106, 305.
[2] *Conscience and its Problems*, pp. xviii, xix.

the key to his ethical problems. As a practical corollary it follows that the principal duty of the Christian moralist is to stimulate the spirit of worship in those to whom he addresses himself, rather than to set before them codes of behaviour. Both interpretation and corollary, however, although they spring direct from the genius of the New Testament, have in the course of history been obscured from time to time by accidental causes. Thus the doctrine of the vision of God has sometimes been set forward in such a way as to suggest that the primary purpose of life is to achieve ' religious experience,' and in its narrowest forms has even confined authentic religious experience to moments of ecstatic exhilaration. Again the word ' worship,' at all events, in English use, is normally confined to what is more properly called *public* worship, whilst ' prayer ' is often thought of as no more than *petitionary* prayer ; thus we tend to overlook the truth that worship (sometimes called also ' contemplation,' the ' prayer of simplicity,' or the ' prayer of union ') should be the culminating moment and the invariable concomitant even of the humblest act of private prayer. Further, it must be agreed that, for various reasons, Christianity has often forgotten this primary supernaturalism of its charter, and has allowed itself to be presented as a moral system among other moral systems, with the religious element reduced to little more than an emotional tinting of its ethical scheme. Despite these accidental variations, the unanimity of Christian moralists on the point of cardinal importance is sufficiently striking, and it has been one part of my purpose to exhibit it.

The first lecture, therefore, reviews the antecedents of the doctrine of the vision of God as the end for man in Jewish and pagan thought, and notices the dominance in such circles of the passion for religious ' experience.' Lecture II, though in large part concerned with another problem to which reference will be made in a moment, shows the New Testament writers as a whole insisting upon the primacy of worship, and deprecating, at the same time, the tendency to make ' experience ' the test of its reality or worth. Lecture III contrasts with this central Christian doctrine the attempt to substitute moralism for religion by throwing the weight of emphasis upon the promulgation and enforcement of codes of Christian behaviour. Lectures IV and V, though the historical sequence dictated that they too should in the main be occupied with subsidiary questions, illustrate the contention that the great monastic founders and legislators were in the true line of succession from the New Testament, in respect of the emphasis they laid upon contemplative prayer. Lecture VI deals with a few of the wider theological connexions of the conception, particularly in Clement of Alexandria, Augustine, and Bernard of Clairvaux ; Lecture VII with its orderly formulation in theory by the Victorines and S. Thomas, and in the practice of prayer, as arising from loving meditation upon the person of Jesus, by Ignatius of Loyola and S. Francis de Sales. Finally, in Lecture VIII, modern deviations, both Catholic and Protestant, from the traditional doctrine are passed under review, and some, at least, of the criticisms to which the tradition has been and can be subjected are considered.

The changes and chances to which the doctrine of the primacy of the vision of God has been exposed in the progress of the Christian Church are bound up with the history of three institutions—the codification of moral precepts, the exercise of corporate discipline, and the organization of asceticism in the monastic movement. Behind these three tendencies, which I have summarily represented (pp. 3-8) as aspects of the problem of *discipline* in its widest sense, lie three modes of thought— ' formalism,' ' institutionalism ' and ' rigorism '—whose relations with the central ethical *motif* of Christianity seemed to require investigation. This will account for the intrusion into the main theme of the book of episodes from the history of the canon law, in its pre-scientific phase, of penance, and of monasticism, and the moral principles or theories bound up with them. I have not thought it necessary to carry these accounts beyond the stage at which the institutions in question reached a certain degree of stability, and have tried to confine any extended or detailed treatment to points and problems on which information does not appear at present to be readily accessible to English readers. Thus, apart from the special points dealt with in the additional notes, the earlier stages in the history of codification and of penance occupy some part of Lectures III, IV and V ; whilst the beginnings of Christian rigorism are dealt with in Lecture II, its first blossoming into monasticism in Lecture IV, and its incorporation into the full Christian tradition in Lecture V. The final section of Lecture VIII contains some concluding reflections on these three subjects.

II.

To return for a moment to the main theme of the book. It must be obvious that the doctrine that worship is the Christian's first and paramount duty, though it receives lip-service in every branch of the Church, is not one which goes unquestioned at the present day. The criticisms which, consciously and unconsciously, have borne and still bear heavily upon it, I have attempted to consider in the last lecture ; but subsidiary discussions are incorporated at other points where, for one reason or another, they appeared specially appropriate. Taken as a whole, therefore, the line of argument which underlies the lectures may be set out as follows :—

The primary question of all formal ethics (if once it is agreed that man is sufficiently endowed with liberty of choice to entitle us to speak of ' ethics ' at all) is the definition of the *summum bonum*. Is it best defined in terms of ' happiness ' (reward) or in terms of ' virtue ' (duty) ? Christian moral theology has evolved the answer, in general terms, that whilst happiness (conceived either as present communion with God, or as future beatitude, or in that sense in which virtue is spoken of as ' its own reward ') is indeed the reward of virtue, yet the more a man's conduct is determined by his desire to achieve the reward, and by no other desire, the less he deserves the name of Christian (*infra*, pp. 142, 452 f., 458-460, 489 f.).[1] For such a doctrine, which on the one hand rejects emphatically all forms of hedonism, but refuses to lend itself to the extremes of Quietism on the other (pp. 145, 461-463, 554), the words ' disinterestedness ' or ' unselfishness,' difficult though they are to define (pp. 552-554), express the ideal of Christian character. It is, further, of the essence of Christian ethics that no form of ' self-centredness ' can truly be called disinterested ; and under the name of ' self-centredness ' is condemned not merely naked egoism of a worldly kind, nor even the quest for beatitude (present or future) in addition, but any kind of preoccupation with one's own soul and its successes and failures in the moral life or the service of its fellow-men (*infra*, pp. 97, 132-134, 198, 447, 554 f.). This last point is one of crucial importance : for it is here that the divergence between Christianity and moralism pure and simple, between ' gospel ' and ' law,' has its starting-point (pp. 135, 203, 204). Christianity has known for

[1] For a complete survey of the subject it would of course have been necessary to trace the history of the idea of happiness (εὐδαιμονία, *beatitudo*, *felicitas*) through pre-Christian and Christian thought. I have been able to do no more than indicate, in brief notes, one or more phases of that history. That the purpose of the gospel is to offer men happiness, on conditions which have no value of their own except as making access to that beatitude possible, has no doubt at all times been a commonplace of vulgar Christianity. I hope I have frankly admitted this, and have recognized in addition that rightly or wrongly such a point of view can find some justification in the writings of no less a person (for example) than S. Augustine, if not in the gospel record itself (*infra*, pp. 141 f., 551). Little, however, would be gained for the history of Christian thought about ethics by compiling an anthology of eudæmonistic sentiments from different centuries ; what is important at any period is the manner and degree in which eudæmonism has been tempered by the ideal of disinterestedness.

centuries what psychology has discovered in recent years—
that the introvert is of all others the type of character most
remote from the ethical ideal.

The first practical question for Christian ethics is, therefore,
How is disinterestedness, unselfishness, to be attained ? Once
grant that moralism, or formalism, cannot bring the soul nearer
to it, and there remains only one way—the way of worship.
Worship lifts the soul out of its preoccupation with itself and
its activities, and centres its aspirations entirely on God (pp. 448-
451). In saying this, we must be careful to confuse worship
neither with the quest for ' religious experience ' (pp. 103, 104,
203, 271, 444, 489-491), nor with the employment of devout
thoughts to stimulate moral effort (' ascéticisme '—pp. 440,
441), for both these counterfeits of worship lend themselves
only too readily to egocentrism. To the criticism that the
effort to set oneself to worship must be as egocentric as any
other, it can fairly be replied that the spirit of worship, being
universally and congenitally diffused among men, requires no
antecedent efforts ; it is something which *comes upon* the soul,
not which is achieved *by it* (pp. 464-466).

When once it is recognized that worship is the key to disinterestedness, the effort to conform to codes and standards of
behaviour falls into its proper place. It is, on the one hand,
an activity which the worshipping soul finds itself compelled
to undertake so that its worship may flow more freely ; on the
other, an invariable outcome of all true worship, in so far as
the latter inevitably strives to render its environment more
harmonious with the Ideal of which it has caught glimpses.
Self-discipline and service, therefore, are to be thought of both
as the antecedents and the consequents of worship ; and so
long as they retain these subordinate but wholly necessary
positions, the disinterestedness of worship overflows upon them,
and (in M. Bremond's fine phrase) ' disinfects them from egoism '
(*infra*, p. 96). It is, I believe, to some such scheme as this that
the great paradoxes with which our Lord Himself, and after
Him S. Paul, invested the idea of ' law ' bear witness ; and the
following chapters will have failed of their main purpose if
they do not suggest that Christian thought at its best has
always returned to the same cardinal principle.

III

In preparing the book for publication I have restored to
the text passages which considerations of time made it impossible to deliver from the University pulpit : some further
passages have been added, together with the appended notes

dealing with points of detail. My obligations to modern
writers will be sufficiently evident from the footnotes ; if any
remain unacknowledged the oversight is unintentional. It has
proved impracticable, in the case of patristic and scholastic
writers, to append the original text of passages cited in translation ; but I have tried to make verification easy by detailed
references, wherever necessary, to standard editions.

One inconsistency in quotation must be confessed. Many
modern foreign books are available in English translation : in
some such cases I have cited direct from the published English
version ; in other cases have made my own rendering from
the original. The choice has been determined by personal
convenience alone ; the usage in respect of each book is (I
believe) consistent ; and the footnotes should make it clear—
always in the first and often in subsequent citations—whether
references are to the pages of the original or to the translation.
In the case of M. Bremond's ' Histoire Littéraire du Sentiment
Religieux ' I have referred readers, for the first volume, to the
admirable translation by K. L. Montgomery ; [1] for the remaining volumes to the as yet untranslated original.

There are one or two books (notably Batiffol's ' Études
d'Histoire et de Théologie Positive,' and Cumont's ' Religions
Orientales ') of which I have only learnt at a very late stage
that the editions I happened to be using were not the most
recent. In the case of Cumont I have revised the references,
and I hope that they now conform in every case to the paging
of his attractive new edition (the fourth) : but I have not been
able to make any use of the wealth of new material he has
collected in the notes. For Batiffol's ' Études ' I have retained the references to the fifth edition. In the majority of
cases these will serve for the seventh and latest edition as well,
the paging remaining in general the same. But two sections
of the fifth edition (pp. 195-222, 327-342), which, despite the
author's modest disclaimer (seventh edition, p. xxv), are still
of importance, are omitted in the seventh, and to these I have
found it necessary to refer more than once. The new material
in the seventh edition (pp. 194-224, 337-362) deals with
S. Augustine's teaching on penance ; such allusions to it as
seemed necessary I have made in the footnotes to additional
note O, where the same problem is considered. The minor
variations between the fifth and the seventh editions as a whole
I have not been able to notice, except in two cases (Origen,
infra, p. 226 ; and Victor of Cartenna, *infra*, p. 507).

[1] S.P.C.K., 1928- . The translation of the second volume has now
appeared, but it came too late for me to use it.

IV.

It is impossible to mention by name the very many friends by whose advice, correction, warnings and encouragement I have profited in the preparation of the book. My special thanks are due to the Rev. J. S. Bezzant, Fellow of Exeter College, and to the Rev. Austin Farrer, Chaplain-elect of S. Edmund Hall, who discharged the heavy duty of reading the proofs ; and to Miss A. R. Stuart, lecturer in Church History at S. Christopher's College, Blackheath, who undertook the even more irksome task of compiling the indices. I have also to acknowledge the courtesy of Archdeacon Charles and the Delegates of the Oxford University Press, for allowing me to quote passages from their edition of the 'Apocrypha and Pseudepigrapha' ; and to the same Delegates and the Jowett Trustees, as also to the Editors of the Loeb Classical Library, for similar permissions as regards Jowett's translation of the Dialogues of Plato, and Mr. Gaselee's edition of Apuleius' 'Metamorphoses' respectively. To the compositors and readers of the Aberdeen University Press I owe both an apology for submitting to them a manuscript so full of detailed references, and an acknowledgment of the care and patience with which they have overcome its difficulties.

This leaves me with two final obligations to discharge. The one is due to Messrs. Longmans, Green & Co., who have allowed me to add so large a book to the three other 'Studies in Moral Theology' which they have published in the last ten years. If these studies should contribute anything of value towards the revival of moral theology in the Church of England, no small part of the credit will be due to the initiative of Messrs. Longmans, who in the difficult years immediately following the war took the risk of publishing a book on a neglected subject by an unknown writer, and allowed (and indeed encouraged) him to persevere in work of the same character.

The other acknowledgment is of a peculiarly personal character. By what was for me the most fortunate of accidents, the syllabus of the original lectures fell into the hands of M. Henri Bremond shortly after they had been delivered. That any member of Cardinal Newman's University and College should receive courteous treatment from the most discerning of his modern interpreters, will cause no surprise ; but M. Bremond's kindness went much further than this. Disregarding the hesitations, inconsistencies, and imperfections in which the lectures then abounded and still abound, he professed to discern (what I hope is indeed the truth) that the opinions

I had attempted to put forward had affinities with his own illuminating critiques of the abiding tendencies in religious thought ; and with the most generous of gestures opened the way to an interchange of views whose value to myself it would be impossible to over-estimate. Despite the vast claims which the publication of his great 'Histoire' and its subsidiary studies makes upon his time, he has shown himself throughout more than willing to answer questions, give advice, and draw attention to investigations and points of view which would otherwise have escaped my notice. I have availed myself very freely of his kind interest : have adopted no small part of his terminology : and have throughout the lectures incorporated references to his books at points where his clear and penetrating exposition seemed likely to throw light on my own obscurities. The pages which follow challenge no comparison with his majestic and finished treatment of religious thought : but if they serve no other purpose than to make his writings better known in England I shall at least be able to feel that I have repaid some trifling part of the debt which I owe to him.

K. E. K.

Oxford,
Michaelmas, 1930.

NOTE TO SECOND EDITION.

In this edition I have corrected a number of misprints, and added a few illustrative references; but no alteration of material importance has been made, except in one respect. A kindly and illuminating criticism published by Abbot Butler in *The Downside Review* for October, 1931, convinced me that I had unintentionally misrepresented his views on 'acquired' and 'infused' contemplation. I have therefore amended the phraseology of a number of sentences between pages 528 and 534, in the hope thereby of removing the false impression conveyed by the first edition. At the same time, I discovered that a paragraph of my own on page 412 might lead to misunderstanding; an explanatory footnote has been added at that point.

Several reviewers have called attention to the omission of any reference to Malebranche and his doctrine of *vision en Dieu*. The omission can only be forgiven if it is agreed that a consideration of Malebranche belongs rather to that metaphysical treatment of the subject which, on page ix of the Preface, I disclaimed any intention of undertaking in the present volume.

K. E. K.

Whitsuntide, 1932.

LECTURE 1.

THE VISION OF GOD AND THE PROBLEM OF DISCIPLINE.

S. Matth. v. 8—'Blessed are the pure in heart, for they shall see God.'

I. THE VISION OF GOD.

Beati mundo corde, quoniam ipsi Deum videbunt.—The development of Christian thought and teaching about conduct is inseparably bound up with the history of these words—the sixth of the beatitudes as recorded by S. Matthew. In the earliest days of the new religion no one could have foretold that this would be the case. Christianity advanced to its assault upon the civilized world equipped with a vocabulary of extraordinary wealth and possibilities, gathered from very different sources, and increasing in complexity as time went on. Many decades were to elapse before the key-phrases in doctrine, in philosophy, in liturgy, and in ethics made good their footing against vast numbers of competing formulæ. But the thought of the *vision of God* as the goal of human life, and the determinant, therefore, of Christian conduct, came rapidly to its own. Before the first of our extant creeds had assumed its present shape—before any dominant liturgical form had emerged from the primitive fluidity of worship—before so much as the bare terminology of the great Christological controversies had entered the new vocabulary—before it was certain whether 'the Word' or 'the Son of God' should be the crowning title of the Risen Lord—before even the propriety of speaking of the Godhead as a Trinity had become apparent—before the Church had passed a single one of these milestones in her history, the first of a great line of post-apostolic theologians had declared : 'The glory of God is a living man ; and the life of man is the vision of God.' [1]

Thenceforward, as we shall see, there was little question as to the fact. Christianity had come into the world with a double purpose, to offer men the vision of God, and to call them to the pursuit of that vision. But there were many questions of interpretation. The idea of seeing God could have very different

[1] Iren., *adv. haer.*, iv, 20. 7 :—'gloria enim Dei vivens homo; vita autem hominis visio Dei.'

I

implications, both as to the goal and as to the mode of its attainment. Men's varying conceptions of God, and of His relation to the created universe, brought new influences of every kind to bear upon it, and none without effect. So it comes about that the simple words of this beatitude have in their day called men into the desert, have drawn them into the cloister, have made of them saints and solitaries, martyrs and missionaries. They have bred errors and schisms past man's power to number; they have beckoned to the forbidden labyrinths of magic and astrology; they have led a Pope himself to the verge of formal heresy; they have been tied with the bands of orthodoxy, only to break their chains and witness again to the freedom of the gospel. They have torn men from the study of philosophy and the love of family and friends; again they have sent them to school with Aristotle and Plato, and have taught them to look for God in the sanctities of the Christian home. Under their influence some have learnt to hate the beauties of nature and of life, whilst others have been inspired to embrace those beauties perhaps too rashly. The age-long drama centred upon the interpretation of the words is too complex to be treated fully within the compass of a single volume, but perhaps enough has been said to prove how engrossing is the theme. For the history of the phrase is the history of Christian ethics itself.

The Christian of to-day, no less than his predecessors, is concerned with this question of *interpretation*. To ' see God ' implies something which we constantly and yet vaguely speak of as ' religious experience '; and, even if we do not question that such ' experience ' may indeed be objective experience of a living God, we are at a loss to know which, among all the varied manifestations it assumes, is its truest and highest form. But the Christian of to-day, far more than his predecessors, is concerned with the question of *fact* as well. Modern interpreters of Christian ethics more commonly build their systems upon some other of the great New Testament doctrines—the Fatherhood of God, for example; the brotherhood of man; or the primacy of the Kingdom. The reason is self-evident. They are not convinced that the vision of God—' religious experience,' let us say, even in its fullest and highest form—is the true goal to set before the Christian. Is it not too self-centred an ideal to spring from the religion of self-denial? Is it not too narrow—ignoring, as it appears to do, the worth of all types of experience except one, even though that be the highest—to be worthy of a Lord to Whom no type of human experience was indifferent? Is it not—for the vast majority of non-mystical, commonplace men and women, tied down to secular occupations—an ideal at once uninspiring and unrealizable? Is not ' service ' a higher goal than ' experience,' and to give more blessed than to receive? These doubts lie very near the surface of modern thought about morals; it cannot be time wholly wasted to ask what answer history gives to them. We are concerned, in fact, with the fundamental problem of ethics—'What is man's true end?'

We can, however, approach the enquiry with other hopes as well. Clear grasp of an ideal or first principle must serve to illuminate subordinate problems. In proportion as we learn more about the Christian ideal for life—in proportion as we can say whether 'the vision of God' does or does not express it adequately —so we shall be able to understand better the several duties and virtues of the Christian. No attempt will be made, in these lectures, to carry this secondary enquiry through to its end. But to reduce the scope of investigation, and at the same time to reach clearer definition as to men's meaning when they spoke (or speak) of seeking purity of heart that they might see God, it will be of advantage to have in mind certain particular problems of special relevance and importance. Each one will have his own preference in such a matter ; for my own part, I believe that we shall find something of what we require if we ask what the history of the vision of God has to tell us about the problem of *discipline*—using that pregnant word in its widest sense.

II. THE PROBLEM OF DISCIPLINE.

'The legacy of mediæval Christianity to later ages,' it has been well said, 'was the problem of authority . . . (but) beyond the problem of authority lay the still greater problem of discipline— the task of finding some harmony between the Christian view of things and the life of the ordinary man.'[1] 'Christians,' the writer at once goes on to say,—

'Christians, it is unnecessary to add, did not create the problem, which is involved in the art of conscious living ; but they revealed it in all the bewildering amplitude of the conflict between order and freedom, between obedience to Christ and submission to His Church.'[2]

We may hold in suspense for a moment our judgment upon that last phrase, which contrasts *Christ* and the *Church* as the recipients of obedience ; but the rest is true enough. The problems of authority and discipline *are* indeed involved in the art of conscious living, and are bound to arise wherever men dwell together in society. Yet it is of the genius of Christianity in general, and of mediæval Christianity in particular, to have focussed upon them rays of such unprecedented brightness that no detail of their complexity has contrived to evade attention. Why it should have fallen to the lot of Christianity, more than to that of any other religion,—and to the Middle Ages, more than to any other period,

[1] F. M. Powicke in *The Legacy of the Middle Ages* (Oxford, 1926), pp. 23, 27.
[2] *Ib.*, p. 23.

—to have done the world this service or disservice, is a matter
worthy of more than passing notice ; but it must stand over for
the present. Our immediate task is to discover the principal
forms in which the problem of discipline manifests itself.

(a) The Problem of Institutionalism.

The first and most obvious line of thought is suggested by
Professor Powicke in the stimulating essay from which I have
already ventured to quote. To him ' the history of the Church is
the record of the gradual and mutual adaptation of Christianity
and paganism to each other.' [1] By ' paganism ' he understands
a ' state of acquiescence, or merely professional activity, unaccompanied by sustained religious experience and inward discipline.' [2]
Using the word so understood in this connexion, he has already
both abandoned his original definition, and shown that it envisaged no more than half his real meaning. For it is not merely
the pagan within the Church, but the saint as well, who creates the
problem. ' Submission to the Church ' may be contrasted not only
with obedience to pagan impulses, but also (as in the second
sentence quoted above) [3] with ' obedience to the claims of Christ,'
or of conscience. The history of the Church becomes for us now a
' gradual and mutual adaptation ' of Christianity on the one hand
and both paganism *and saintliness* on the other—each conceived as
being within the Church.

This then is the first variant of the general problem of discipline
—we may call it the problem of *corporate discipline,* or *institutionalism.* It opens up a whole series of subordinate but important
questions. What demands shall the Church make upon her
members, either saintly or pagan respectively, or both saintly and
pagan together ; and by what methods shall she attempt to secure
conformity to her demands with the minimum of friction and
loss ? Again, what is she to do if one of her ministers or members
refuses to comply with her demands ; or if the principles of conduct which, in all good faith, he chooses for himself and commends
to others contradict those which she has evolved in her experience,
or believes herself to hold as of divine institution ? Is he to be
left to go his own way, and to lead others with him ? Or is the
Church to bring pressure to bear upon him, and if so at what point
and in what measure ?

A moment's reflection will remind us how much this problem
of corporate discipline, or institutionalism, presses especially in
the Church of England, regaining as she is, after a long forgetfulness, her sense of corporate and independent spiritual responsibility. For the Church of England—more perhaps than for
other churches—this ' legacy ' of the problem of discipline has
become an embarrassing heirloom. She has experimented with

---

[1] F. M. Powicke in *The Legacy of the Middle Ages* (Oxford, 1926), p. 31.
[2] *Ib.,* p. 30.   [3] *Supra,* p. 3.

rigidity; she has experimented with tolerance. She has mortgaged her autonomy to the State; and in the last few years has tentatively and timidly received a fraction of it back again, only to find that the gift thus granted carries with it as many burdens as reliefs. She has taken up the unaccustomed responsibility of legislation, and has dealt with notable arrears; she has even entered upon the supremely difficult task of official theological restatement. But that other supremely difficult work of plainly setting forth and reiterating her moral demands she has scarcely made up her mind to face; and she has taken only the most tentative steps to overhaul the machinery by which those demands, if and when formulated, shall be not merely commended but also made effective. We approach the question of discipline, therefore, as members of a Church specially called to the task of evolving out of confusion such moral order or cohesion as may be conformable to the mind of Christ.

(b) The Problem of Formalism.

Even so, however, the question of discipline has scarcely been opened out in all its fullness. A second aspect is revealed by another of Professor Powicke's dexterous phrases. He speaks of the 'pagan' as one who is destitute of 'inward discipline'; and in those two words brings to light a new problem more germane, perhaps, to the present enquiry than to his own. Pagan and saint jostle one another not merely in the visible Church; they are to be found at issue, with greater or less intensity of struggle, in every Christian soul. The best of us is half a pagan still; the worst of us is not without some trace of saintliness. In the visible Church, no doubt, the saint is often more of a rebel than the pagan; and the pagan will loyally burn him for a schismatic at the command of the hierarchy. But in the human heart the position is reversed. Here that which is saintly—the 'higher' self—if it reckons with the Church outside at all, will always be found allied with her against the paganism of the soul—the 'lower' impulses which for the moment we may call sinful. At first sight, the correspondence between the Church's demands and those of saintliness in the heart is often so slight as to be negligible. In such a case the higher self finds in the actual Church an ally of little moment. Even so, however, the dissentient rarely contrasts the Church's demands with a private code of his own. He appeals from the actual to the ideal Church, and on the point at issue conceives himself allied to that greater and wider Church of eternity whose precepts, if they could ever be embodied in an actual code, would be identical in every respect with the mind of Christ. In so far as any Christian recognizes the corporate aspect of Christianity at all, he will derive comfort and strength from the reflection that the demands he lays upon himself of his own free will are also demands which the Church (actual or ideal) lays upon him by virtue of her divine commission.

Thus the problem of discipline is not merely a problem between the Church and the individual ; it is at the same time a problem between the individual and himself. Further, it is the same problem in a new form. Once again, it divides itself into two main questions—' What demands am I, as a Christian, to make upon myself ? ' and, ' What methods shall I employ to secure the triumph of these demands over the complex unruliness of my soul ? ' The methods by which the Church attempts (rightly or wrongly) to secure compliance with her code comprise the whole circuit of organization, jurisdiction and canon law. The methods by which the individual attempts to discipline himself are identical with the round of religious observances, and moral restraints and excitations, which of his own freewill he adopts. This disciplinary machinery, whether of the Church or the individual, will always be found to vary in character with the code to which it is subsidiary ; if the ideal form of the latter could be discovered, the true lineaments of the former would not be far to seek. Clearly, then, if the problem of discipline is indeed the legacy of the Christian past to the Church of to-day, we shall only enter upon our inheritance in its fullness according as we ask and answer the question, ' What is the true Christian code of moral behaviour ? '

It is at this point that the second variant of the problem of discipline presents itself. We have used the words ' code ' and ' discipline ' ; but it is natural to ask whether those words have any valid place in the vocabulary of Christianity. Even in the form of *self-discipline*—the application of constraint to one's own instincts, emotions and aspirations—discipline may appear to some as a conception foreign to the genius of Christianity. ' Surely,' it may be said, ' Christianity is not regulated but spontaneous ; not legalised but free ; not a code, but the living of a life dedicated to God and penetrated by His grace ? What else is the message of Christ, the promise of the Spirit ? What other meaning can we attach to S. Paul's great indictment of the law ? '

From this point of view *any* tendency to live the moral life by rule, to anticipate or solve its problems by casuistry,[1] to bring its natural impulsive growth under the control of law and reason, must appear the merest ethical pedantry—a reversion to the ideal of the scribes and Pharisees which it was Christ's first mission to attack. The modern mind is perhaps partisan in this matter. It welcomes spontaneity, and rejects suggestions of discipline and regulation. Yet it would be absurd to maintain that the ideal of ordered self-discipline has *no* place in the Christian life ; a study of the development of Christian thought about ethics may well

---

[1] I use the word ' casuistry ' throughout these lectures without any sinister implications, wishing to denote thereby simply the application of general principles to particular ' cases ' or problems. See my *Conscience and its Problems*, pp. 106 ff.

help us nearer to an understanding of the true place of this element
—the element which in perverted instances we call 'formalist'—
in the determination of conduct. This second question, therefore,
may be termed the question of *formalism*.

(c) The Problem of Rigorism.

Finally, we may take into our survey a third question; one
which—with only a slight misuse of technical language—can be
called the problem of *rigorism*.[1] If life is to be disciplined at all,
of what fashion shall the discipline be? Amid all the variations
of ethics which have sheltered under the name of 'Christian,' two
in particular stand out in marked contrast. On the one hand there
have been teachers and sects who have prescribed for their adherents, and individuals who have prescribed for themselves, a life
of rigorous self-denial, self-mortification, and other-worldliness.
Not that such a life is always regardless of the active duties of
society, nor that it must lead, in every case, to the extreme of
eremitic solitude; but that it tends to test the worth of every
action by its cost to the giver, and the degree to which it requires
him to mortify his own affections and enforce a caveat against
his natural instincts, rather than by its value to the receiver.
Puritanism, asceticism, rigorism—whatever we choose to call it—
here is a well-marked type of thought and practice which in all
ages has appealed to the self-abnegation and cross of our Redeemer
as its final example and justification. Perhaps it finds fewer
sponsors and adherents at the present day than it has done at other
epochs; but that fact alone would not justify us in eliminating it
from the Christian scheme. It claims, or has often claimed, to
represent the sole ideal of life worthy of the name of Christian;
and even if it be non-suited in that plea it may still retain a claim
to stand for *something* without which—even if only in combination
with other elements—no Christian life can be complete.

Against this rigorist other-worldliness must be arrayed a 'this-
worldly' code of ethics, which also appeals for its sanctions to
the gospel. This *humanist*[2] code, if we may so call it, bids us

---

[1] In technical moral theology, 'rigorism' is the name of a system of
thought which forbids the Christian ever to take the benefit of the doubt,
however 'probable' the doubt may be (*Conscience and its Problems*, pp. 260-
263); it was condemned by Pope Alexander VIII. In ethics as a whole,
however, the use of the word as a synonym for systematic and extreme
asceticism is so universal among writers of all schools of thought as to make
any protest against this wider employment pedantic.

[2] I follow M. Henri Bremond, as in many other respects, so in this
use of the word 'humanist.' In vol. i, c. i, of his *Histoire Littéraire du
Sentiment Religieux en France* (the volume, entitled *L'Humanisme Dévot*, has
now been translated, London, S.P.C.K., 1928), he says (E. tr., p. 9): 'The
common spring [of all humanism] is that curiosity and sympathy which
incline us towards all manifestations of activity and all aspects of human
history; a tendency moral rather than literary. . . . "Moral" here implies
nothing of asceticism. Education, civilization, yes; but for the sheer

enjoy life in due moderation, and realize the highest possibilities of every instinct and factor in the complex organism of personality. It prescribes positive social virtues as the ideal, and seeks to set up a new Jerusalem by steady evolution out of the existing world-order. It finds goodness in embracing the world and its joys, not in flight from them ; it looks for God in His creation, instead of seeking Him by spurning what He has made. On this reading of the Christian message we need not dwell in detail at the moment. It is familiar to the modern mind ; it is engrained, we might almost say, in the modern temperament. Within the womb of the Christian Church these two children—rigorism and humanism— have striven for the mastery from the moment of their conception ; and to the fortunes of that fierce battle no student of Christian ethics can be indifferent. Here are two tendencies pointing towards codes of very different types. Which of them is Christian and which non-Christian ; or better still, if *both* are Christian, how are they to be harmonized in a single code of conduct ?

(d) Two Further Considerations.

(i) The second and third of the problems just reviewed direct attention to two further considerations of a preliminary character which may fitly be noticed at this stage. The first is this. For-malism, as we have defined it hitherto,—the demand for a definite rule of life—has rigorism as one of its branches ; the Puritan is as much disposed to live by rule as any other.[1] But formalism has other branches too. There are other types of code beside the rigorist ; other rules of life beside the crucifixion of earthly affections. To these other rules of life, and to one variant of them in particular, the name of formalism is often appropriated. In this restricted sense, ' formalism ' stands for a type of code not so much heroically ascetic, as detailed and meticulous—a code which delights to prescribe duties, not necessarily of an arduous

---

pleasure of them. . . . The fundamental doctrine of humanism is simple. It is an accepted axiom that a man feels little interest in that which he holds contemptible. The humanist does not consider humanity contemptible. He whole-heartedly takes the part of human nature ; even when he sees it miserable and impotent, he excuses and defends it and raises it.' M. Bremond sharply distinguishes 'humanism' from naturalism or paganism (*ib.*, p. 12, and see *infra*, pp. 304 ff.) ; but he also recognises two humanisms—'Christian' and 'devout,' the former ' eternal,' the latter ' flamboyant ' (*ib.*, p. 9). The former is distinctive of the Middle Ages and the present day ; the latter of the Renaissance and the Counter-Reformation. ' *Humani nil alienum* is their motto. It is the motto of eternal humanism ; but for us as for the Middle Ages it is a motto of humility, of toleration of humanity in the ten-derest sense of the word. . . . For the Renaissance, however, *Humani nil alienum* is a watchword of battle and of hope, a promise and a shout of victory. Nothing which human faculty can attain is beyond ourselves. To be a man, is not that enough ? To be a man is to be a thing of splendour ' (*ib.*, p. 8). On p. 6, M. Bremond defends his thesis (which I have tried to illustrate below in chapters vi and vii) that there was a genuine Christian humanism prior to the Renaissance.

[1] Indeed, in some respects, *more* than any other ; see *infra*, p. 234.

kind, for every conjuncture of life, and to leave little, if anything, to the autonomy of the individual conscience. Rabbinism is, of course, the outstanding example of this type. And if 'formalism' be taken in this narrow sense it no longer comprehends rigorism, but is opposed to it.

That this is so may be seen by a comparison of the temperamental affinities of rigorism and formalism respectively. Rigorism is the natural correlative of the evangelistic spirit ; the spirit which cries, 'Save yourselves from this untoward generation.' It expresses itself in negations ; it calls for a final breach with the world and its entanglements. It sees no gradations between the sheep who are saved and the goats who are lost—the children of light, and the children of this world ; if a man is not to be numbered among the one, then without question he must belong to the other. Formalism, on the other hand, even if it be brought up in the most puritan of schools, exhibits the temper not so much of the evangelist as of the pastor. The sheep may be in the fold, but they are at best frail and wayward ; the fence has to be maintained around them, and hedged about with cautions, rules and prohibitions. Saved they may be, but their salvation must be made doubly sure.

Whenever, therefore, the Christian Church has found herself faced by a predominantly pagan world, from which she has conceived it her mission to snatch elect souls as brands from the burning, she has displayed the rigorist temper, stiffening her terms of communion, both for the postulant and for the member, so that none may be admitted to or retained in the society except such as can face the fires of persecution. Whenever, on the contrary, her prime interest has been to watch over the needs of a nominally Christian flock, she has tended to formalism of this rabbinic type, and in addition has commonly used the expedient of casuistry so to extend her purview as to enclose within the fold every soul which by stretch of charity could be called Christian at all. Some at least of the ethical phenomena which appear in Christian history do not therefore arise out of the void. They are created by the impact of circumstance upon temperament, calling into prominence at one time those in the Church who are by nature fitted to become evangelists and martyrs, at another those whom God has specially equipped to be pastors and stewards.

(ii) This leads at once to the second and last of these preliminary considerations. It is not only with temperaments of different kinds that different ethical tendencies have their affinities. The whole of a man's intellectual outlook upon life—his creed, his faith—is to some extent bound up with his behaviour. If we know how he conceives of God we shall have a clue to his probable conduct ; his conduct illumines—to some extent at least—not merely the genuineness but even the type of his creed. Nor can conduct or creed be separated from experience. If there is such a thing as experience of God—and it is difficult to believe that the

word 'God' stands throughout history for no more than a form
without content—then it is bound to have reactions both with
creed and conduct. Thought about God must in the end correspond with experience of God; and experience of God will be
modified and interpreted in harmony with intellectual presuppositions as to His nature. Even in ordinary life we often see only
what we expect to see.

So too with morality. The intellectual, the ethical, and the
empirical elements in religion are not so many water-tight and
distinct compartments. In any one human soul their mutual
compatibility may often be incomplete, but their basic tendency is
always towards a diapason of testimony. There is no reason why
we should spend time upon this truth; it is one whose importance
has been fully emphasized by Baron von Hügel. For our purposes
it is enough to notice that variations in ethics will often be appre-
ciated at their true value only when their theological and empirical
implications have been taken into account. We must not be surprised if what is primarily an ethical enquiry leads at times into
the byways of Christian doctrine or of religious psychology.

.   .   .   .

The problem of discipline—articulated into its three subordinate problems of institutionalism, formalism and rigorism—
touches the matter of Christian ethics at every point. Of these
three constituent problems, the last two are urgent for each of
us as individuals; the first appears no less urgent the moment we
realize our responsibilities as members in one body. The Christian
Church has had a vast experience of all three problems; has known
the dangers of leaving them unsolved and the disasters of solving
them amiss. Time after time, as these dangers or disasters manifested themselves, her statesmen and theologians have reviewed
the problems again in the light of the vision of God which they
have accepted as the keynote and the test of all the principles of
Christian life. The solutions they offered have varied in different
generations, as their conceptions of the beatific vision and all
that it implies have varied too. It is by noticing the most apparent
of these variations, examining their causes and recording their
results, that Christians of to-day may in their turn take up the
task transmitted to them. The starting-point is the same for all—
'Blessed are the pure in heart, for they shall see God.'

III. THE VISION OF GOD—JEWISH ANTICIPATIONS.

(a) The Old Testament.

The Church, we have said, went out into the world with a
double purpose—to offer men the vision of God and to call them
to pursue that vision. The world was not unprepared for the
message; indeed, it was the one message for which the whole world,

Jew and Greek alike, was waiting. To the Jew at least it could not fail to call up a whole vast series of theophanies, stretching back to the dawn of his national history. The earliest of his written records proclaimed that Jacob had seen God face to face and lived;[1] so too had Abraham and Moses.[2] Isaiah had beheld the Lord high and lifted up in His temple in the year that King Uzziah died;[3] Amos and Micah both hint at a similar vision.[4] Ezekiel had seen Jahweh in His chariot leave the doomed temple at Jerusalem, and in His chariot return.[5] Micaiah the son of Imlah had been present at a session of the heavenly court.[6]

The attitude, however, of Old Testament writers towards this possibility of seeing God was not unequivocal. Whatever experience the phrase embodied for them was hedged about with cautions and reservations. To some it seemed that no man could see God and live, apart from ' an exceptional manifestation of the divine favour ';[7] the fatality attaching to the vision of God was occasionally extended even to the hearing of His voice,[8] or the seeing of His angel.[9] Levi as a tribe disappeared from the roll-call of the nation ; the cause assigned by the Rabbis was that they had looked upon the face of God.[10] Others again,—later writers, in the main, like Jesus the son of Sirach [11]—held that the vision of God was impossible, at all events in this life. In general, however, it was agreed to regard Moses as specially favoured. So in the story of the insubordination of Aaron and Miriam, Jahweh says :—

' Hear now My words ; if there be a prophet among you, I the Lord will make Myself known unto him in a vision, I will speak with him in a dream. My servant Moses is not so ; he is faithful in all Mine house ; with him will I speak mouth to mouth, even manifestly, and not in dark speeches ; and the form of the Lord shall he behold.' [12]

---

[1] Gen. 32^{30}—(by the Jahwist writer, usually supposed to have written in the ninth century, B.C.). Hence *Peniel,* ' the Face of God '; but the name of the place may have been derived from some physical feature (S. R. Driver in *Westminster Commentaries, ad loc.*).

[2] Gen. 12^7, 18^1 (cp. Ex. 6^3) ; Ex. 33^{11} ; Num. 12^{6-8} ; Dt. 34^{10}.   [3] Is. 6^1.

[4] Am. 7^7—' Thus he showed me : and behold the Lord stood by a wall made by a plumb-line '; 9^1—' I saw the Lord standing beside the altar '; Mic. 1^{1-3}.

[5] Ezk. $10^{18, 19}$, $11^{22, 23}$, $43^{4, 7}$; cp. I. Abrahams, *The Glory of God,* pp. 76, 77—the ten stages by which, according to the Talmud, the Shekinah withdrew from the sanctuary.

[6] 1 Kgs. 22^{19}.

[7] C. F. Burney, *The Book of Judges,* p. 193, on Jud. 6^{22}. Cp. Gen. 32^{30}; Ex. 19^{21}, 33^{20}; Jud. 13^{22}; Is. 6^5.

[8] Ex. 20^{19} ; Dt. 4^{33}, 5^{24-26}.   [9] Jud. 6^{22}.

[10] H. L. Strack and P. Billerbeck, *Kommentar zum N. T. aus Talmud und Midrash,* i, p. 214 (Tanchuma on Ex. 33^{20}).

[11] Ecclus. 43^{31}—' Who hath seen Him that he may tell thereof ? ' (But the verse is possibly a gloss.) On the doctrine of the inaccessibility of God in later Judaism, I. Abrahams, *The Glory of God,* pp. 39 ff.

[12] Num. 12^{6-8}.

The stories of Hagar,[1] and of the elders of Israel at Sinai,[2] were emended so as to avoid the implication that Jahweh had been seen by other eyes than those of the leader of His people. One extremist even cast the story of Moses into such a form that he too was denied the full vision.[3]

What then of the other visions recorded—the visions of the prophets and patriarchs? Different expedients were adopted to secure that—while the divine element in them should not be lost —the implication of seeing God face to face might be evaded. ' The prophets saw through a dark glass,' the Mischnah says,[4] thus laying down the principle ; ' Moses alone through a clear one.' Trances and dreams, as the passage from Numbers reminds us, were exploited to this end ;—not, indeed, without reason, for the experience which lies behind the phrase is at all events for primitive races not incompatible with these conditions. Devices of a more literary character were employed as well. In the patriarchal stories, the cloud and the pillar of fire were introduced to reveal, and at the same time to veil, the presence of Jahweh. His angel or the captain of His host might take His place. His voice might suffice where His appearance dared not be thought of. The writing prophets adopted expedients of a less materialistic character. Ezekiel concentrates his attention on the mystic chariot, its furniture and ministers ; Isaiah on the ' glory ' of the Lord which filled the temple. The same instinct of reverence which led the Jew to avoid pronouncing the sacred Name led him to deny that any man living could see God, even though—as in the case of the prophets—he himself was conscious of so intimate a relationship with Jahweh as to believe himself constituted His mouthpiece and messenger to the people.

Another influence tended, in a similar way, to banish all reference to the vision of God from the sacred text, and therewith to banish from the minds of men the hope that such a consummation was a possibility. In the older, simpler days any ceremonial visit to the local sanctuary, with its sacred pillar, stone or tree, had been

---

[1] Gen. 16[13, 14]—' And she called the name of the Lord that spake unto her, Thou art (RV. marg., ' Or, *Thou God seest me*') a God that seeth (RV. marg., ' Heb. *El roi, that is, God of seeing*') : for she said, Have I even here looked after Him that seeth me ? Wherefore the well was called Beer-lahai-roi ' (RV. marg., ' *The well of the living one that seeth me*'). The difficulty of the phrase, ' Have I even looked after Him that seeth me ? ' is obvious ; and no reason is given for the title ' the living one ' in the name of the well. Wellhausen conjectures that the question originally ran, ' Have I even seen [God and lived] after [my] seeing ? ' in which case ' a God of seeing ' meant ' a God Who is seen,' and the name of the well was, ' He that seeth Me liveth' (Driver, *Genesis, ad loc.*). The further suggestion (Michaelis and Wellhausen) that the original name of the spot was ' antelope's jawbone' (A. S. Peake, *Commentary on the Bible, ad loc.*) does not affect the question.

[2] Ex. 24[9]—' Then went up Moses, and Aaron, Nadab, and Abihu, and seventy of the elders of Israel : and they saw the God of Israel.' LXX, however, to avoid the implication, renders the last sentence, ' they saw the place where the God of Israel stood.'

[3] Ex. 33[20].   [4] Quoted, Strack-Billerbeck, *op. cit.*, iii, p. 453.

spoken of as a pilgrimage ' to see God.' The instructed believer
might retain the phrase for occasional use without fear of idolatrous
associations ; to the psalmists it becomes at times little more than
a devout periphrasis, tinged with archaic modes of thought, for
visiting the temple. So if the true reading in the 17th Psalm [1]
be (as in our Revised Version) ' As for me, let me behold Thy face
in righteousness ; let me be satisfied, when I awake, with Thy
likeness,' it is not necessary to see more in the passage than a
pious hope that the writer will be present at the daily morning
sacrifice. In the 24th Psalm [2] the connexion is even clearer.
Who is the true worshipper of Jahweh ? Who is morally fit to be
present at the celebration of the cultus ? ' He that hath clean
hands and a pure heart ; who hath not lifted up his soul unto
vanity, and hath not sworn deceitfully. He shall receive a blessing
from the Lord, and righteousness from the God of his salvation.
This is the generation of them that seek after Him, *that seek Thy
face*, O God of Jacob.' So too in the 27th Psalm :—' One thing I
asked of the Lord, that will I seek after, that I may dwell in the
house of the Lord all the days of my life, *to behold the beauty* of the
Lord, and to enquire in His temple.' [3] It would be presumptuous
to insist that here we are dealing with mere survival-formulæ ;
but the possibility must at least be reckoned with. No more may
be meant than mere outward attendance at divine worship.

But even with this attenuated meaning the phrase had dangerous connotations. Spiritual sight and physical sight are easily
confused ; an idolatrous mind might readily be led by the words
to confound the visible place and symbols of Jahweh's habitation
with the invisible God himself. Throughout the sacred texts,
therefore, editors developed the habit of substituting the phrase
' appear before Jahweh ' or ' be seen by Jahweh ' for the phrase
' see Jahweh.' The substitution is easily detected by Hebraists
by means of the grammatical peculiarities of the amended sentences ; [4] comparison of the Authorized with the Revised Version
often enables the English reader to guess at it for himself. In

---

[1] Verse 15 (marg.). RV. text has ' I shall behold.'

[2] Verses 3-6.

[3] Verse 4—RV. marg., ' to consider His temple.' ' To meditate, or
contemplate, in His temple ' is an even more probable rendering (A. Maclaren,
The Book of Psalms, i, p. 263, *ad loc.*).

[4] The principal passages concerned are Ex. 23[15], 34[20] ; Is. 1[12] ; Ps. 42[2].
The substitution could in most cases be effected by an alteration of the vowel
points. Other passages where the change is suspected are Ex. 23[17], 34[23], [24] ;
Dt. 16[16], 31[11] ; 1 Sam. 1[22]. The words ' see My face,' ' see the face of
Yahweh ' (but *not*, apparently, the phrase ' see Yahweh '), adapt the usual
phrase for admission into the presence of a monarch (as in 2 Sam. 3[13], 14[28], [32] ;
2 Kgs. 25[19] ; cp. Gen. 43[3]) to the ceremonial visit to the shrine. See S. R.
Driver, *The Book of Exodus* (Cambridge Bible for Schools, 1911), p. 243
(on Ex. 23[15]). Fr. Nötscher, '*Das Angesicht Gottes Schauen*' (1924), p. 90,
considers that the idea of the fatality of the vision motived these substitu-
tions, as well as the feeling of reverence. It is difficult, however, to see the
connexion of thought.

the 11th Psalm [1] the Authorized Version gives the words, ' The righteous Lord loveth righteousness ; His countenance doth behold the upright ' ; the Revisers restored the older and truer reading, ' The upright shall behold His face.' In the 42nd Psalm [2] the words ' When shall I come to see God ' were altered to ' When shall I come and appear before God ' ; in the 84th for ' They see God, even God, in Sion ' was substituted, ' Every one of them appeareth before God in Sion.' [3] Frequent passages in the historical books exhibit the same phenomenon.

When, therefore, the Old Testament canon closed, various influences had combined to dim the hope of the individual Jew that he should see God. There might indeed be a vision after death—' apart from his flesh ' Job hoped against hope to see his Maker.[4] Nor was it doubted that prophets had seen the Lord in the past ; and, although prophecy was dead,[5] if a prophet like Moses were to appear again, he might expect to receive the same manifestation of divine approval as had been vouchsafed to Moses.[6] Dreams and visions—though they could perhaps no longer give even a glimpse of Jahweh's personality,—brought the devout believer into nearer relationship with Him, just as the temple still stood as a place where He might be sought.[7] The lamp has burnt very low. But it is not extinguished ; one feature remains constant, as the psalmists show. If there is anyone at all who shall see God, either in this life or the next, it shall be the upright. Righteousness is the condition of the vision if it has a condition at all. For the Jew who doubted whether purity of heart was worth striving for with such an uncertain reward the gospel offered its unqualified promise, ' Blessed are the pure in heart, for they *shall* see God.'

---

[1] Verse 7.

[2] Verse 2. With all this may be compared S. Paul's reserve, Gal. 4[9]— ' Now that ye have come to know God, or rather *to be known of God*.'

[3] Verse 7. The true reading is supported by LXX and Pesh.

[4] Job 19[26, 27]. Here the LXX provides a meaningless translation, which however excludes all idea of seeing God.

[5] 1 Macc. 4[46], 9[27], 14[41] ; Ps. 74[9]. In Zech. 13 the mere *profession* of the prophetic gift is treated as hypocrisy (verse 3) ; and even the true prophets (if any arise) shall conceal their genius (verses 4, 5).

[6] Dt. 18[15-18]. Note also Job 42[5]—a claim unique in the O. T.

[7] Mr. Stacy Waddy's remarkable *Homes of the Psalms* (S.P.C.K., 1928) came to my notice too late for me to use it in the text of this chapter. But it suggests that we must not make too much of the pessimism about the possibility of the vision of God which can be discovered in Jewish thought. Mr. Waddy emphasizes the fact that the vision was at once the setting (*op. cit.*, pp. 120-131), and—in the form of a fire-theophany—the climax (*ib.*, pp. 144-153) of the temple liturgy. This view he illustrates by countless references in the Psalter ; and adds the further fact that the Psalter, and *all that it implied*, was taken over for synagogue use from the temple services. It follows from this that the thought of ' seeing God,' whether in temple or synagogue, whether by the fire-symbol or *solâ reverentiâ*, may have dominated the Jewish worshipper's mind to a far greater extent than I have allowed. I am profoundly happy to have this opportunity of mentioning Mr. Waddy's inspiring and illuminating book.

(b) The Apocalyptists.

The evangelical assurance did not stand altogether alone. Wilhelm Bousset has clearly proved that the apocalyptic school of Jewish theology, which blossomed with the beginning of Maccabean revolt, employed something more than a bizarre literary device.[1] Whatever we may think of the trance-visions which initiated the prophecies of Isaiah and Ezekiel—and perhaps, as some modern scholars suggest,[2] of all other prophets as well—it is clear that they were not a phenomenon confined to the great men of the Old Testament. In certain families at least a traditional prescription was handed down for the attainment of such visions —the *ma'ase merkaba*, or 'chariot-lore,' which would give the devotee an experience akin to Ezekiel's.[3] Where such conventional methods were employed, the results could not fail to be in some measure conventional too ; and this we find to be the case. But it seems certain that, however much traditional formulæ influenced the literary presentation of their message, some at least of the apocalyptists believed themselves to be recording actual experiences of their own. And what is most significant about these experiences is that they find their culminating point in just such a vision of God as Ezekiel had enjoyed.

We need scarcely remind ourselves of the first vision of this apocalyptic kind—that in the book of ' Daniel.'[4] The writer, a Jew, writhing under the oppressions of Antiochus,—

> ' beheld till thrones were placed, and One that was ancient of days did sit ; His raiment was white as snow, and the hair of His head like pure wool ; His throne was fiery flames, and the wheels thereof burning fire. A fiery stream issued and came forth from before Him ; thousand thousands ministered unto Him, and ten thousand times ten thousand stood before Him ; the judgment was set and the books were opened.'

[1] W. Bousset, *RJ.*, pp. 394-395 :—' Despite the widespread belief that immediate contact of the human spirit with the divine was no longer possible . . . ecstatic experiences, the effect of the Spirit of God, still occurred in pious circles. In almost every Apocalypse " pneumatic " experiences are predicated of the heroes of old in an emphatic and detailed manner. . . . Such descriptions would scarcely have been possible if the authors had had no acquaintance with ecstasy.' Cp. *ib.*, pp. 396, 397 ; and the instances of ecstasy and prophecy among Jews of the hellenistic period, pp. 397, 398.

[2] E.g. T. H. Robinson, *Prophecy and the Prophets*, pp. 36, 40-46.

[3] The allusion is of course to Ezekiel's ' chariot '-visions (Ezk. 1^{15-26}, 10^{9-20}) ; but the conception of a supernatural chariot taking the soul up to heaven (as in the case of Elijah, 2 Kgs. 2^{11}) is widespread (A. Dieterich, *Eine Mithras-Liturgie* [3], pp. 183, 184). Rabbinic references to the *ma'ase merkaba*, Bousset, *RJ.*, pp. 356, 500 ; R. H. Charles, *Apocrypha and Pseudepigrapha*, i, p. 505. The earliest reference is probably Ecclus. 49^8— ' Ezekiel saw a vision, and described the different beings of the chariot.'

[4] Dan. $7^{9, 10}$.

Later apocalyptists were not content with so abrupt a translation to the court of heaven ; they prefaced it with an account of the soul's flight through the three (or in the later tradition, the seven) inferior heavens.[1] But the vision is the same. ' I saw the appearance of the Lord's face,' writes a hellenistic Jew of the beginning of the Christian era,—[2]

> ' like iron made to glow in fire, and brought out, emitting sparks—and it burns. Thus I saw the Lord's face ; but the Lord's face is ineffable, marvellous and very awful, and very, very terrible ; and who am I to tell of the Lord's unspeakable being, and of His very wonderful face ? '

Physical phenomena are experienced in translations of this character.[3] The visionary is carried away like a leaf by the whirlwind.[4] His ' whole body is relaxed ' ; his ' spirit is transfigured ' ; he ' cries with his voice, with the spirit of power.' [5] Mysteries that cannot be uttered are revealed—the mysteries of

---

[1] On this *himmelfahrt* or *himmelsreise* of the soul see especially W. Bousset in *ARW.*, iv (1901), pp. 136-169, 229-273 ; *RJ.*, pp. 501, 519. A. Dieterich (*Eine Mithras-Liturgie* [3], pp. 179-205 ; cp. also pp. 253-255), while admitting the Jewish mythology of the *himmelfahrt*, attributes the similar doctrines in the mysteries and in gnosticism to specifically Greek sources. He denies all possibility of a Babylonian (Iranian) origin (p. 190). C. Clemen, however (*RGENT.*, p. 151), carries the Greek doctrine back to earlier Oriental sources (cp. Cumont, *Les Religions Orientales* [4], p. 264). Traces of the conception in the New Testament are to be found certainly in 2 Cor. 12[2 ff.] ; possibly also in Hebr. 4[14] (' a great high-priest *who hath passed through the heavens* '), and 1 Tim. 3[16] (' seen of angels '—i.e. during His return through the heavenly spheres to the Father). The imagined adventures of the soul after death and actual ecstatic experiences were of course held to be analogous with each other. Further references, F. Cumont, *Les Religions Orientales* [4], pp. 116 f., 264 ff. ; R. Reitzenstein, *Poimandres*, p. 81 ; P. Wendland, *HRK.* (index, *s.v.* ' Himmelfahrt ') ; H. Lietzmann in *HNT.* on 2 Cor. 12[4] (ix, p. 151). On the three or seven heavens, R. H. Charles, *Apocrypha and Pseudepigrapha*, ii, pp. 304 ff.—on Test. Levi, 2[7 ff.], where the original three heavens have been worked up to include seven ; cp. also 4 Ezra 7[81 ff.] (quoted *infra*).—For mediæval examples cp. G. Grupp, *Kulturgeschichte des Mittelalters* [2], i, p. 258 ; ii, pp. 370-373.

[2] Slav. Enoch 22[1] (Charles, *Apocrypha and Pseudepigrapha*, ii, p. 442). This occurs in the tenth heaven.

[3] Cp. Dan. 4[19] (LXX)—' He feared, and a trembling seized him, and his visage was changed, and his head shook.' RV., as Hebrew, is much less detailed.

[4] Slav. Enoch 21[5] (Charles, *op. cit.*, ii, p. 442)—' And Gabriel caught me up as a leaf caught up by the wind, and placed me before the Lord's face ' ; cp. 1 Enoch 39[3] (Charles, *op. cit.*, ii, p. 210)—' And in those days a whirlwind carried me off from the earth, and set me down at the end of the heavens.'

[5] 1 Enoch 71[11] (Charles, ii, pp. 236, 237) ; cp. 60[3] (*ib.*, p. 224)—' And a great trembling seized me, and fear took hold of me, and my loins gave way, and dissolved were my reins, and I fell upon my face ' ; Ascension of Isaiah, 6[10-12] (ed. R. H. Charles, 1900, p. 45)—' He became silent, and his mind was taken up from him, and he saw not the men that stood before him, though his eyes indeed were open. Moreover his lips were silent, and the mind in his body was taken up from him. But his breath was in him ; for he was seeing a vision.' The passage occurs in the Christian section of the *Ascension*, which dates perhaps from the first century A.D. (*ib.*, p. xlv).

creation in particular,[1] and of the stellar orders.[2] The unutterable chant of the heavenly choir is heard close at hand, as S. Paul heard it,[3] together with the prayers of the saints.[4] But the very conditions under which the writers lived demanded that the vision should primarily be one of judgment upon the enemies of the Lord and His people. The punishment of the angels who fell, and of men who have ' denied the Lord of Spirits,'[5] is indicated throughout with a wealth of dramatic imagery. Here is introduced a notable thought. What, after all, could be more terrible for the wicked than to look upon the face of the Most High ? So the third Parable of Enoch [6] insists that the ' kings and the mighty,' who are to be punished, must look the Son of Man in the face :—

> ' And they shall be terrified,
> And they shall be downcast of countenance,
> And pain shall seize them
> When they see that Son of Man
> Sitting on the throne of His glory . . .
> (And) that Lord of Spirits will so press them
> That they shall hastily go forth from His presence,
> And their faces shall be filled with shame
> And the darkness grow deeper on their faces.'

Another writer [7] makes the souls of the wicked pass through six successive circles of ever-increasing torment ; in the last and seventh circle their doom is

[1] E.g. Slav. Enoch 23[1]—' He [the Archangel Pravnil] was telling me all the works of heaven, earth and sea, and all the elements, their passages and goings, and the thunderings of the thunders, the sun and moon, the goings and changes of the stars, the seasons, years, days, and hours, the risings of the wind, the numbers of the angels and the formation of their songs, and all human things, the tongue of every human song and life, the commandments, instructions, and sweet-voiced singing, and all things that it is fitting to learn.' In the following chapters (24-32) the account of creation is given in great detail.

[2] Slav. Enoch 3-21.

[3] E.g. Slav. Enoch 20[4]—' All the heavenly troops . . . go to their places in joy and felicity, singing songs in the boundless light with small and tender voices, gloriously serving Him ' ; cp. 2 Cor. 12[4].

[4] 1 Enoch 39[5].   [5] ib., 38[2].   [6] ib., 62[5, 10].

[7] 2 (4) Ezra 7[81-87]. The six earlier stages are (1) remorse ; (2) recognition of the irrevocability of the past ; (3) vision of the reward laid up for the righteous ; (4) vision of the torment reserved for sinners ; (5) vision of the guardian angels who watch over the repose of the righteous ; (6) recognition of the inevitability of their own punishment. Archdeacon Charles says of this passage (op. cit. ii, p. 587) : ' These descriptions [he includes the " seven ways " of the righteous, infra, p. 18, n. 1], which are psychological in character, apparently portray the emotional experiences of the soul, through which it passes during the entire period of the intermediate state. In its subtle delineation of the soul-life the whole section is remarkable, and by the elevation and refinement of its conceptions affords a striking contrast to similar descriptions in other parts of the apocalyptic literature (e.g. 1 En. 22).'—The source from which the section is drawn (the ' Salathiel-apocalypse ') is late—probably about A.D. 100 ; but the material used may, of course, be older.

' to pine away for shame and be consumed with confusion and withered with fear, in that they see the glory of the Most High, before Whom they have sinned in life, and before Whom they are destined to be judged in the last times.'

Not in this life, perhaps, but certainly after death, man is destined to see God ; and how terrible may that vision be !

With the righteous it is very different. For them there is an ascending ladder of six joys, crowned by a seventh, ' which exceeds all the aforesaid,' in which they

> ' Rejoice with boldness,
> Are confident without confusion,
> Are glad without fear ;

for they are hastening to behold the face of Him Whom in life they served, and from Whom they are destined to receive their reward in glory.' [1]

They shall ' stand near the Lord and be His ministers and declare His mysteries ' ; [2] they ' shall dwell with the righteous angels, and have a resting-place with the holy.' [3] ' There I wished to dwell,' exclaims one of our writers after such a vision of Paradise, ' and my spirit longed for that dwelling-place.' [4] We need not wonder therefore that for the perfect enjoyment of the eternal vision—nay even for a temporary glimpse of it here —righteousness is once again insisted upon as an invariable condition. It is because of his ' rectitude and chastity from his youth ' that Ezra is rewarded with his apocalypse.[5] Enoch brings back with him from heaven moral instructions for his sons ; [6]—in fact, this writer is outstanding among ancient moralists, for he insists that men shall be punished even for unkindness to animals.[7] One passage, however, in the so-called ' 4th Book of Ezra ' is remarkable for the contrast it draws between the amplitude of the reward and the strictness of the path by which alone it can be attained. There is a ' sea which is broad and vast,' but it is reached only through a channel ' so narrow as to be like a river.'

---

[1] 2 (4) Ezra 7⁹⁸. The six preceding stages of the righteous are (1) consciousness of victory over the evil *yetser ;* (2) vision of the punishment of the ungodly ; (3) consciousness of having kept the Law ; (4) consciousness of the peace of heaven ; (5) joy at having escaped what is corruptible ; (6) joy at their coming radiance.

[2] Test. Levi 2¹⁰.   [3] 1 Enoch 39⁵.

[4] *Ib.*, 39⁸.   [5] 2 (4) Ezra 6³².

[6] Slav. Enoch 44-46 ; cp. especially 45³—' When the Lord demands bread, or candles, or flesh, or any other sacrifice, then that is nothing ; but God demands pure hearts, and with all that only tests the heart of man.'

[7] Slav. Enoch 58⁶—' As every soul of man is according to number, similarly beasts will not perish, nor all souls of beasts which the Lord created, till the great judgment ; and they will accuse man if he feed them ill.' An interesting note on the belief in the survival of animals, in Charles, *ad loc.* (*op. cit.*, ii, p. 464).

There is a ' builded city which lies on level ground, and it is full of all good things ; but its entrance is narrow and lies on a steep, having fire on the right hand and deep water on the left ' ; and between them there is only one path lying —a path so narrow that ' it can contain only one man's footstep at once.' [1] Here is the very echo of our Lord's own words, ' Strait is the gate and narrow is the way which leadeth unto life, and few there be that find it.' [2]

(c) Rabbinic Theology.

It is natural and usual enough to draw a contrast between the picturesque fantasies of apocalyptic and the prosaic and laboured prudential maxims of the scribes and Pharisees. But the boundary between the two cannot be traced with absolute distinctness ; even the Rabbis had their visionary moments.[3] Of four of them, but only four, it was told that they too had penetrated into Paradise ; [4] and to three of the four the vision was fatal. ' Ben Asai saw and died '—so the midrash ran—' Ben Somah saw and was struck down ' (that is to say, as Bousset interprets it, ' with madness ') ; ' Acher ' (the notorious heretic) ' laid waste the garden,' by theosophical fantasies resulting from his mental loss of balance ; ' only Rabbi Akiba came away in peace.' Here is a trace of ecstatic experience in an environment where we should least expect it.

In general, however, the Rabbis deferred the full beatific vision to the days of Messiah, or at all events to the hour of death. Of the former they were careful to say that God would not reveal His full majesty in one dazzling vision, ' for were He to manifest it at once, all men would die.' In a beautiful midrash [5] on the prophecy of Isaiah xxxv, 1, 2, Jahweh's unveiling of Himself is spoken of as gradual :—

' He reveals Himself by slow degrees. First He makes the mountains rejoice ; then the wilderness laughs ; next it blossoms ; last it borrows the glory of Lebanon ; and then shall they see the glory of Jahweh, the majesty of our God.'

[1] 2 (4) Ezra 7[4-9].

[2] Mt. 7[14]. Charles (op. cit., ii, p. 559) cites a number of other resemblances in thought and diction between ' Ezra ' and the New Testament, but concludes that they exhibit ' nothing which suggests direct dependence.' Of eternal life, as contrasted with the narrow way which leads to it, Ezra says (7[13])—' The ways of the future world are broad and safe, and yield the fruit of immortality.'

[3] Bousset, RJ., pp. 355 ff. ; G. F. Moore, Judaism, i, pp. 411, 413, 434-436.

[4] Tract. Chagiga, 14b, quoted Bousset, in SNT., ii, p. 216 (on 2 Cor. 12[2]) ; G. F. Moore, op. cit., i, p. 413. Bousset, RJ., p. 356, gives instances of other Rabbis who were alleged to have penetrated the heavens. Id., ARW., iv (1901), p. 153—the rabbinic exercises prescribed as preliminaries for a himmelfahrt.

[5] Tanchuma B. (Strack-Billerbeck, op. cit., i, p. 213).

In the hour of death, on the other hand, there would be no such tempering of the wind. ' At the time of his death,' it was said of Rabbi Jochanan ben Zakkai—

> ' He lifted up his voice and wept :—" Were I going only to greet the face of a king of flesh and blood, his anger (were he angry with me) would be for this world only ; his chains—if he cast me in prison—only for this world. If he killed me I should die to this world only, and perchance I could soothe him with words or bribe him with gold. But now I go to greet the face of the King of kings, the Holy One (blessed be He !)—and if *He* be angry His wrath embraces both this world and the world to come ; and *Him* I may in no wise move with words nor bribe with gold." ' [1]

Of the wicked the same Rabbi Jochanan said :—[2]

> ' In the last hour these rebels against God shall see the presence (*Shekinah*) and hear the words, " Come and look upon the face of the King against Whom you have rebelled ; He shall exact punishment of you." But the righteous,' he added, ' shall see the face of God in their last hour, and hear the words, " Come and see the countenance of the King Whom ye have served,—He shall give you your reward." '

Once again we observe the close connexion of righteousness with the vision. To some of the Rabbis it seemed enough that the punishment of the unrighteous should consist in nothing other than loss of the vision.[3] When the righteous man dies, on the other hand, ' the shout goes up : Make way for the righteous, for he goeth from place to place till he see the countenance of the Shekinah.' [4] On the text of Isaiah lxvi, 23 (' All flesh shall come to worship before Me ') the question arose, ' Why " all *flesh* " and not " all *Israel* " ? ' To this it was replied, with an appropriate reference to a passage in Ezekiel,[5] ' He whose stony heart has become *flesh* is worthy to look upon the face of the *Shekinah*.' [6] Often enough, again, the conception of righteousness was given a characteristically rabbinic turn. It was a commonplace that the

---

[1] Aboth R. Nathan, 25 (Strack-Billerbeck, i, p. 207).
[2] Strack-Billerbeck, i, p. 209 (midrash on Ps. 22) ; cp. Mt. 25[31] (Parable of Sheep and Goats).
[3] Sota 42a. R. Jirmeja b. Abba enumerated four classes of sinners who should not be allowed to greet the *Shekinah*—mockers, flatterers, liars and slanderers (Strack-Billerbeck, i, p. 211).
[4] Midrash on Ps. 11[7] (Strack-Billerbeck, i, p. 209).
[5] Ezk. 11[19].
[6] Pesiqtha Rabbathi i (2a), Strack-Billerbeck, i, p. 214. (The German editors regard this as the nearest approach to ' Blessed are the pure in heart ' in all rabbinic literature.) Similarly, Is. 33[17]—' Thine eyes shall see the King in his beauty '—was taken as a blessing upon those mentioned two verses previously (verse 15—' he that shutteth his eyes from looking upon evil '),—*ib.*

giving of alms—even of a halfpenny to a beggar—would be rewarded by the vision of God ; and to this end the words of Psalm
xvii, 15 (' I shall behold Thy face in righteousness ') were interpreted in the not impossible sense of ' With an alms shall I behold
Thy face.' [1] By a similar use of artificial exegesis the commandment as to the fringes of the orthodox Jewish gown [2] gained a
specious importance. The wearing of these fringes made the
believer peculiarly worthy of the vision of God ; for the ' blue of
the tassel reminds us of the sea,' it was said, ' and the sea of the
sky, and the sky of the throne of Glory.' [3]

This leads on to one of the distinctive features in rabbinic
teaching about the vision. If it is to be attained at all, whether
in this world or the next, it will be attained by the study and
observance of the Law. So the beatific vision is pressed into the
service of the Torah, and becomes the sanction of that aristo-
cratically intellectual life of study which was the Pharisaic ideal.
' He who haunts the synagogue and the schoolhouse '—' he who
busies himself with the Torah '—these are the men to whom the
Presence will manifest itself.[4] Narrow though the conception is,
it has yet enough in common with Aristotle's praise of the ' life
of contemplation ' [5] to make it worthy of notice ; and centuries
later the two will find a counterpart among the ethical theories
of the Schoolmen. But at this point, it is clear, the Rabbi who
sought his vision in meticulous examination and comparison of the
sacred text, and the apocalyptist who hoped to attain it by supernatural manifestation in the ecstasy of a trance, part company
finally and for ever.

The late Dr. Abrahams noted two further distinctive characteristics of rabbinic teaching on this subject. Of the periphrases
employed by the Rabbi to avoid pronouncing the name of Jahweh, three were pre-eminent—the ' Word,' the ' Glory,' and the
' Presence ' (' Shekinah ').[6] Of these the ' Word ' was used by the
Targums for the invisible presence, as the ' Glory ' for the visible

---

[1] Baba Bathra 10a, and commonly (Strack-Billerbeck, i, p. 207). Scriptural
grounds for the doctrine that the wicked should see God at death were found
in Ps. 22²⁹, ' All they that go down to the dust shall bow before Him,' and in
Ex. 33²⁰, ' Man shall not see Me and live ' (sc. ' but in death he shall see Me ').
[2] Num. 15³⁹.
[3] Strack-Billerbeck, i, p. 211 ; ii, p. 315. The Jew does not appear to
have known the blue mantle, worn for example by Zeus as the sky-god
(A. B. Cook, Zeus, i, pp. 33, 56-62) ; but the idea is similar.
[4] Strack-Billerbeck, i, p. 207. ' The synagogue and the schoolhouse '
were referred to (it was supposed) in the ' gates ' and ' doors ' of Prov. 8³⁴, ³⁵.
Another aphorism was, ' To greet the face of the learned is as though one
greeted the Shekinah.' Similarly the midrash on Ps. 105⁴ (' Seek ye the Lord
and His strength (= Torah, Law), seek His face evermore ')—' Wouldest
thou see the face of the Shekinah in this world ? Then busy thyself with the
Torah in the land of Israel.' Ps. 84⁷ (' They go from strength to strength
. . . ') was rendered ' They go from synagogue to schoolhouse ' (Strack-
Billerbeck, i, p. 214).
[5] Additional Note B, infra, p. 475.
[6] Cp. Bousset, RJ., pp. 315 ff. ; G. F. Moore, Judaism, i, pp. 434-438.

presence of God. Both, however, were superseded in popularity by the term ' Shekinah,' and it is in connexion with ' Shekinah ' that the vision is most commonly mentioned. But ' Shekinah ' stood for *both* the visible and the invisible presence—it ' applied to both as a continuous religious experience . . . to spasmodic and continuous, to local and universal, to earthly and heavenly, to visible and invisible, manifestations of the holy spirit.'[1] By this usage therefore, the Rabbis made ' the glory of God the possession, within the reach, if not within the grasp, of all simple souls, at all stages of their pilgrimage, in the terrestrial as well as in the celestial sphere.'[2] The vision transcends all limits of time and space, and is ours for the asking, even here and now.

Finally, Dr. Abrahams notices that the vision was commonly thought of as corporate. ' The glory was present at the study of the law . . . but the Rabbis preferred at least two to study together . . . they had an antipathy to the monastic cell and its solitary occupant.'[3] So much was this the case, that the wickedness of the many could impede the attainment of the one. Thus a heavenly voice was heard in the upper chamber of Beth Gorian in Jericho : ' There is one here '—the reference is to Hillel—' fit that the Shekinah should rest on him ; but the generation is unworthy.'[4] The thought is one with which the greatest Christian writers were not unfamiliar ; but one which the world often forgot, and that to its gravest loss.

It would be premature at this stage to ask what types of religious experience underlay language of the kind we have been considering ; or to attempt to discover the conception of God and the ethical framework with which it was bound up. I content myself at this point with one further quotation from rabbinic sources, which shows how vividly devout reflection illuminated the idea. ' A king,' so runs the parable,[5]—

> ' went into his garden to speak to his gardener, but the gardener hid himself from him. Then said the king, "Why hidest thou from me ? See I am even as thou."—So too shall God walk with the righteous in the earthly Paradise after the resurrection ; and they shall see Him and quake before Him. Then shall He say unto them, " Fear not ; for lo !—I am even as ye." '

---

[1] I. Abrahams, *The Glory of God*, pp. 51 ff.

[2] *Ib.*, p. 58. Dr. Abrahams contrasts unfavourably with this rabbinic doctrine the less optimistic views of Philo, Maimonides, and the mediæval Hebrew poets, who all ' inscribe over this life's gate a caution not to approach the throne.'

[3] *Ib.*, p. 82. Note, however, that, as Dr. Abrahams says, the doctrine was not universal; ' the mystics redressed the balance,' and insisted upon solitude.

[4] *Ib.*, p. 84.

[5] Siphra on Lev. 26[12] (Strack-Billerbeck, i, p. 212).

IV. THE VISION OF GOD—PAGAN ANTICIPATIONS.

(a) Plato.

It is a far cry from the virtuosity of Jewish synagogues and schoolrooms to the banks of Ilissus, hard by the spot ' where Boreas carried off Orithyia.' There, on a summer day some four hundred years before the birth of Christ, with ' the air full of summer sights and sounds,' and ' the agnus castus high and clustering in the fullest blossom and the greatest fragrance,' Socrates and Phædrus sat under the waving branches of a plane tree, ' on grass like a pillow gently sloping to the head,' and talked about love.[1] But the thought of love brought to their minds just such another theophany as that of law brought to the Rabbi. Once again divinity rides in its chariot through the heavens,[2] ' and there are many ways to and fro along which the blessed gods are passing, every one doing his own work; he may follow who will and can, for jealousy has no place in the celestial choir.'[3] This is the lower heaven; but Socrates' fancy is not content with anything below the highest. He continues :—

> ' Of the heaven which is above the heavens what earthly poet ever did or ever will sing worthily ? It is such as I will describe ; for I must dare to speak the truth, when truth is my theme. There abides the very being with which true knowledge is concerned ; the colourless, formless, intangible essence visible only to mind, the pilot of the soul. . . . Every soul which is capable of receiving the food proper to it rejoices at beholding reality . . . she beholds justice, and temperance, and knowledge absolute, not in the form of generation or of relation, which men call existence, but knowledge absolute in existence absolute.'[4]

In this supersensual world those who are to be born as human beings wheel and manœuvre the chariots of their souls. First among them come the philosophers, and the sight to which they attain is unforgettable :—

> ' There was a time when with the rest of the happy band they saw beauty shining in brightness—we philosophers following in the train of Zeus ; others in company with other gods ; and then we beheld the beatific vision and were initiated into a mystery which may be truly called most blessed, celebrated by us in our state of innocence, before we had any experience of evils to come, when we were admitted to the sight of apparitions innocent and simple and calm and happy which

[1] Plato, Phædrus, 229A, 230B (Jowett's translation, vol. i, pp. 433 ff.—The quotations in the text are drawn from this translation).
[2] Ib., 246E.   [3] Ib., 247A.   [4] Ib., 247C-E.

we beheld shining in pure light ; pure ourselves, and not yet enshrined in that living tomb which we carry about, now that we are imprisoned in the body, like an oyster in his shell.'[1]

Others are less skilful or less fortunate than the philosopher. They fail to dominate the passionate steed which, with its more noble and pliant brother, makes up their team.[2] These only ' rise and fall, and see and again fail to see.'[3] Others, though ' longing after the upper world ' and following, ' are carried round below the surface.' Their horses plunge and trample one another underfoot, are lamed and have their wings broken, so that the charioteer cannot attain to the mysteries of true Being. But according to their pre-natal fortunes in the pursuit of the vision, so is their state in this world. ' Those who have seen most ' become philosophers, musicians and artists ; lower in the scale are righteous monarchs, statesmen and politicians ; lowest of all, yokels, sophists and tyrants.[4]

We can follow the destiny of the ' philosopher ' or ' true lover,' as Plato conceives it. He has seen ' beauty in heaven ' shining in company with celestial forms ; and when he comes to earth he finds her here as well, ' shining in clearness through the clearest aperture of sense.'[5] And so in this world too the philosopher

' is always, according to the measure of his abilities, clinging to the recollection of those things in which God abides, and in beholding which He is what He is. And he who employs aright these memories is ever being initiated into perfect mysteries and alone becomes truly perfect. . . . He forgets earthly interests and is rapt in the divine . . . and when he sees the beauty of earth, is transported with the recollection of the true beauty.'[6]

So we learn the relation between the vision of God and the highest earthly love. ' Love is a madness which is a divine gift ' like prophecy and poetry ; ' and the madness of love is the greatest of heaven's blessings.'[7] For true love, as distinct from mere casual attraction, consists in seeing in the loved one the traces of real beauty there ;[8] in behaving towards the beloved ' after the manner of God,' and desiring that the object of one's affections should ' have a soul like Zeus.'[9] ' They seek a love who is to be made like him whom they serve,' says Socrates,—

---

[1] Plato, *Phædrus*, 250B, C. The 'beatific vision' is Jowett's rendering of μακαρίαν ὄψιν τε καὶ θέαν εἶδον. Note especially the final sentence, which is commonly taken as a metaphor from initiation by the unveiling of illuminated statues or pictures in the mysteries (*infra*, p. 28, n. 3).

[2] *Ib.*, 254A.   [3] *Ib.*, 248A.   [4] *Ib.*, 248D, E.
[5] *Ib.*, 250D.   [6] *Ib.*, 249C, D.   [7] *Ib.*, 245B.
[8] *Ib.*, 251A.   [9] *Ib.* 252E.

' and when they have found him, they themselves imitate their god, and persuade their love to do the same, and educate him into the manner and nature of the god as far as they each can, for no feelings of envy or jealousy are entertained by them towards their beloved, but they do their utmost to create in him the greatest likeness of themselves and of the god whom they honour.' [1]

We notice here the intimate union which Plato has descried between the vision of God, the love of God, the imitation of God and the spiritual well-being of our fellow-men. The same colloca-tion of ideals is to meet us in Christianity, and it is scarcely fair at this stage to insist that with Plato the fellow-man upon whom the philosopher expends his care is a consciously selected ' loved one,' whilst S. John instils ' love of the brethren ' as a whole, and our Lord the even wider ideal of love of the neighbour. Plato himself would have been the last to deny progress in moral insight to his philosophers. Their vision of God is far more than a vague and static reminiscence from a mythical pre-natal state. Though Plato, at one stage of his career, seems to have cared little enough for the concept of immortality,[2] this agnosticism passed away. Difficult though it may be to reconcile the doctrine of personal survival with that of the Ideas,[3] there is no doubt that, to his own satisfaction

---

[1] Plato, *Phædrus*, 253 B, C. I subjoin the following beautiful passage from 252A, which, though it refers primarily to human love, is rightly described by Jowett with the words ' fruitio dei '—' This is the sweetest of all pleasures at the time, and is the reason why the soul of the lover will never forsake his beautiful one, whom he esteems above all ; he has forgotten mother and brethren and companions, and he thinks nothing of the neglect and loss of his property ; the rules and proprieties of life, on which he formerly prided himself, he now despises, and is ready to sleep like a servant, wherever he is allowed, as near as he can to his desired one, who is the object of his worship, and the physician who can alone assuage the greatness of his pain.'

[2] ' Not only does [Plato] make his Socrates go to his death without the most distant approach to a belief in the undying vitality of his soul, but also in the first sketch of his Ideal State—a sketch made while the influence of the Socratic view of life still prevailed with him—the belief in immortality is omitted and even excluded '—E. Rohde, *Psyche*[8], E. tr. (by W. B. Hillis, 1925), p. 464. Rohde (*op. cit.*, pp. 477, 478) gives reasons for regarding Bks. II to V, 471C ; VIII, IX (in great part), and X, 608c to end, of the *Republic*, as this ' first sketch ' (Bks. V, 471C-VII fin. ; IX, 580D to 588A ; and X (to 608c) being ' an afterthought not originally included in the plan of the whole book, and not anticipated in the beginning of it,' in which ' the indestructibility of the soul is implied in its sublimest form '). Thus *Republic*, II, 363C, D, is a gentle satire on the popular (poetical) realistic doctrine of the joys of the righteous after death, put into the mouth of Adeimantus, and neither rebuked nor corrected by Socrates ; whilst 364B, C, and 366,A, B contain a much more serious attack, if not on the doctrine of immortality embodied in the mystery cults, at least upon the professions of the mysteries and their hierophants to supply eternal happiness on easy terms. The pro-gramme set out in the sequel ignores the question of immortality, and seeks to find the true worth of ' justice ' irrespective of its possible rewards either in the next world or the present one.

[3] E. Rohde, *op. cit.*, pp. 468, 484 (n. 43) ; cp. E. Zeller, *Plato and the Older Academy* (E. tr.), pp. 397-404. Plato's acceptance of the doctrine of metempsychosis does not concern us here.

at least, he achieved it. And the pure soul, ' once it has put off the folly of the body,' shall see the whole truth of itself, even though to no other is this possible, ' for only the pure may touch the pure.' [1] Even on earth the philosopher, by his traffic in divine things, is made divine and immortal ; [2] and at death his soul enters ' the divine, the pure, the eternally self-identical,' and as a disembodied mind remains for ever with ' that which is its kin.' [3]

In the "Symposium," therefore, Plato designedly traces the progress of the philosopher, the true lover, from the point at which he has left him in the " Phædrus." [4] Beginning in youth with the love of beautiful forms, he easily passes to the stage at which beauty of mind is seen to be higher and better than beauty of physical appearance alone. ' So, though a virtuous man have little comeliness, we are content to love and tend him ' for the beauty of his soul. Thence we pass to deeper and more universal beauties still—the beauty of institutions, laws and sciences. The heavenly pilgrimage, as the " Phædrus " has already told us, is not without its temptations, struggles, and bitter failures,[5] nor has Plato any illusions on this head. But he bids his disciples press forward unremittingly :—

' Drawing towards and contemplating the vast sea of beauty [the philosophic soul] will create many fair and noble thoughts and notions in boundless love of wisdom, . . . until at last the vision is revealed to him of a single science, which is the science of beauty everywhere. . . . He who ascending under the influence of true love begins to perceive *that* beauty, is not far from the end. And the true order of going, or being led by another, to the things of love, is to begin from the beauties of earth and mount upwards for the sake of that other beauty, using these as steps only, and from one going on to two, and from two to all fair forms : from fair forms to fair practices, and from fair practices to fair notions, until from fair notions he arrives at the notion of absolute Beauty, and at last knows what the essence of Beauty is. This . . . is that life above all others which man should live . . . holding converse with the true Beauty, simple and divine. . . . In that communion only, beholding Beauty with the eye of the mind, he will be enabled to bring forth, not images of beauty, but reality . . . and bringing forth and nourishing true virtue, to become the friend of God and be immortal, if mortal man may. Would that be an ignoble life ? ' [6]

[1] Plato, *Phædo*, 67A, B.
[2] Plato, *Rep.*, 500D ; *Symp.*, 212A ; *Tim.*, 90C ; *Soph.*, 210B.
[3] Plato, *Phædo*, 83E-84B.   [4] Plato, *Symp.*, 210A ff.
[5] Plato, *Phædrus*, 254.
[6] Plato, *Symp.*, 210D-212A (Jowett's translation, i, p. 581).

(b) The Mysteries.

These aspirations of the Platonic philosopher for supernatural experience of God found an echo among thousands to whom philosophy could never be more than a closed book. In these wider circles the yearning for the vision was endorsed and encouraged in the fullest measure by the organized cults of the Hellenic world, whether in official or private hands—cults which, dating from remote antiquity and lasting to the fourth century of our era, supplied the mysticisms [1] of Plato, of Philo, and of successive generations of Christian theologians, with many of their most inspiring terms.

The mysteries of Eleusis may serve us as an example.[2] In the ' greater mysteries,' on the 16th or 17th of Boedromion, the older initiates and the new initiands passed in procession along the sacred way, to the cry of ' Mystics, to the sea!'; the catechumens and their offerings were bathed in the surf. There followed the days of public sacrifice, procession, and festival; the climax for the ' mystic ' himself was yet to come. The 22nd and 23rd of the month were his peculiar privilege—the ' mystic nights,'[3] the *pannuchides*, or all-night ceremonial. Of what took place we only catch glimpses. There was a long wait in the gloom outside the darkened temple—' the gate of heaven, the house of God where the good God dwells alone.'[4] Then the glow of light, as lamps were lit within; the doors were flung wide, and the hierophant with his blazing torches ushered the devotees into the sanctuary.[5] Here took place the *epopteia*, the *theia thea*, the *autopsia*, the *horasis*;[6] and in a sacred drama ' the most beautiful sights of the world '[7] were seen. What these ' sights ' were we shall probably never

---

[1] I use the words ' mystic ' and ' mysticism ' throughout to denote a type of religious thought which believes personal intercourse with the divine to be possible to man (whether it advocates sacramental methods or not), as distinct from what Johannes Weiss (*Das Urchristentum*, pp. 351, 352, 355, 361) calls ' Lord-Slave ' or ' I-and-Thou ' religion, in which God (Christ) and the believer are strongly differentiated, and the only relationship conceived to exist between them is that of God commanding and man obeying or disobeying. (See also A. E. J. Rawlinson (ed.), *Essays on the Trinity and Incarnation*, pp. 198, 227.)

[2] L. R. Farnell, *Cults of the Greek States*, iii, pp. 126-198; Dar. Sagl., ii, pp. 544 ff.; W. R. Halliday, *Pagan Background of Early Christianity*, c. viii; P. E. Foucart, *Les Mystères d'Éleusis, pass.*

[3] Aristoph., *Ran.*, 371 ; Sopater, *Dist. Quæst.* (p. 121, ed. Walz.).

[4] Hippolytus, *Philosophoumena*, v, 8 (*fin.*) (the passage also in R. Reitzenstein, *Poimandres*, p. 96). Reitzenstein regards this sentence as a Gnostic-Christian addition to the original pagan text which Hippolytus is working upon.

[5] Claudian, *de rapt. Pros.*, i, 7-11.

[6] See G. Anrich, *Das antike Mysterienwesen* (1894), pp. 30, 33 ; G. P. Wetter, *ΦΩΣ* (1915), pp. 15 ff., 27 ff. Wetter's theory is that the illumination of the telesterion was itself regarded as an epiphany of the god, and so the central moment of the ' mystery ' (p. 30).

[7] [Plato], *Epinomis*, 986D.

know for certain.[1] There is some evidence that in the ' lesser
mysteries ' in the spring Demeter's search for Persephone was represented, and in the ' greater mysteries ' the nuptials of Zeus and
Demeter and the birth of Plutus their son.[2]   Excavations at Eleusis
show that little if any use was made of mechanical devices to heighten
whatever scenic effect there was ; [3] and a passage in Hippolytus [4] has
been taken to mean that the climax of the initiation was no more than
the unveiling, in silence, of a sacred cornstalk—' a great and perfect spark from the ineffable.' It is possible that more prurient
sights were offered to the votary's eyes.[5] Other evidence points
simply to ritual dancing in the midst of light and movement—' the
sound of flutes, a dazzling light, myrtle groves and happy groups

---

[1] Farnell, *op. cit.*, iii, pp. 173 ff. On the ' shock ' caused by the *epopteia*,
Halliday, *op. cit.*, pp. 257, 270, 271 (quotations from Proclus).

[2] P. Foucart, *Les Mystères d'Éleusis* (1914), p. 478 ; Farnell, iii, pp. 176 ff.
—the conclusion as to the *hieros gamos* is based on Tert., *ad. nat.* ii, 7—' cur
rapitur sacerdos Cereris, si non tale Ceres passa est,' and Asterius (fourth
century) *encom. martyr.* (Farnell, iii, p. 356) ; the nativity of Plutus on
Hippol., *Philosoph.*, v. 8 :

> ' The queen hath borne a holy son,
> Brimo hath given birth to Brimos.'

Other references, Dar. Sagl., ii, pp. 578, 579. Loisy, *Les Mystères Païens*,
pp. 65, 70 ff., strains this slender evidence to its fullest extent ; Farnell
is much more balanced. What constituted the central *secret* act of the
Attis-Cybele rite is unknown ; though there is plenty of evidence for the
public ritual (e.g. Cumont, *op. cit.*, p. 54, etc.). On the basis of ὑπὸ τὸν
παστὸν ὑπέδυν (Clem. Al., *Protr.*, ii, 15 ; but Firm. Mat., *de err.*, 18, gives
' I have become an initiate of Attis ') another *hieros gamos* has been suspected (Loisy, p. 109 ; Dieterich, *Mithras-Liturgie*[3], p. 126 ; Hepding, *Attis*,
p. 193). So, too, of the Sabazios-cult, Dieterich, p. 123. In Mithraism, the
central rite was a sacred meal, perhaps accompanied by a sacrifice (Loisy,
p. 197). On the ' mystic marriage ' idea generally, cp. W. R. Inge, *Christian
Mysticism*, pp. 369-372 ; A. Harnack, *History of Dogma*, ii, p. 295; iii,
pp. 129-131 ; v, p. 28 ; E. Underhill, *Mysticism*, pp. 162-167, 509-512;
F. Heiler, *Das Gebet*, pp. 331-341; R. Reitzenstein, *HMR.*, pp. 35 ff.,
245-252; W. Bousset, *KC.*, pp. 204, 205; A. Dieterich, *Mithras-Liturgie*[3],
pp. 121-134, 244-248 (the last especially important); and *infra*, pp. 354, 355.

[3] Farnell, iii, p. 181 ; cp. for Mithra, Cumont, *Textes et Monuments*,
i, p. 65. Halliday, pp. 297-299, thinks more was possible in the way of stage
effects than is commonly supposed. Certainly statues (Cumont, *Religions*[4],
pp. 87, 240), pictures (Dieterich, *Mithras-Liturgie*, p. 86), and lighting
effects (Bousset, *KC.*, pp. 165, 343 ; G. P. Wetter, ΦΩΣ, pp. 7 ff.), played
a large part.

[4] *Philosoph.*, v, 8 (Reitzenstein, *Poimandres*, p. 95). The corn-stalk
was, of course, symbolical of resurrection (cp. Jn. 12[23, 24]) ; Attis also was
identified with it (Hipp., *Philosoph.*, *ut supr.*).

[5] This has been inferred (Loisy, *Les Mystères Païens*, p. 111, contrast
Dieterich, *Mithras-Liturgie*, p. 103) on the basis of ἐκερνοφόρησα in the
formula (Attis-Cybele) in Clem. Alex., *Protrept.*, ii, 15, which a scholiast on
Plato (Farnell, iii, p. 357, n. 219e ; Dieterich, *op. cit.*, p. 217) attaches to the
Eleusinian cult ; and on ἔλαβον ἐκ κίστης, ἐργασάμενος (Lobeck *et al.*: ἐγγευ-
σάμενος ; the Latin version of Arnobius, *adv. nat.*, v, 26, throws no light
on the word) ἀπέθεμην εἰς κάλαθον καὶ ἐκ καλάθου εἰς κίστην, *ib.*, ii, 21 (Dieterich,
op. cit., pp. 125, 245 ; Loisy, *op. cit.*, p. 68, contrast Farnell, iii, pp. 185, 186).
The whole chapter in the *Protrepticus* is an attack on the lubricity of the
mysteries.

of men and women, the initiates.' [1] 'At first,' so Plutarch tells us [2]—

> 'there are wanderings and laborious circuits, and journey-ings through the dark, full of misgivings where there is no consummation; then before the very end come terrors of every kind, shivers and trembling and sweat and amazement. After this a wonderful light meets the wanderer—he is admitted into pure meadow-lands where are songs and dances to temper the majesty of the sacred words, and holy apparitions.' [3]

But of whatever nature the revelation may have been, the mystic went out again as an *epoptes*—'one who has seen '—pledged of course to secrecy touching the details of his experience; inspired, as reliable authorities assert, if not actually pledged, to newness of life; [4] comforted as to the uncertain future; [5] and perhaps

---

[1] Aristophanes, *Ran.*, 154 ff.

[2] Describing by analogy his conception of the vision which awaits the pure soul after death—a pendant to his account of the punishment of sinners (the myth of Thespesius, *de ser. num. vind.*, c. 22)—but this last betrays too many conventional literary features to warrant Halliday (p. 260) in speaking of ' echoes of an initiate's experiences.'

[3] Stobaeus, *Flor.*, 120, 28 (Meineke, iv, p. 107). Stobaeus attributes the passage to ' Themistius '; it was identified by Wyttenbach and Lobeck (Foucart, *Les Mystères d'Éleusis*, pp. 393, 394). An English version in A. O. Prickard, *Selected Essays of Plutarch*, p. 215. Another interesting Plutarch passage is *de prof. in virt.*, 10 (comparison of philosophic progress with initiation)—' First of all the initiates shout and hurl themselves about and jostle one another; but when the rites are performed, the mystery enacted, they are terrified and silent.' Details of the ' mystery ' are ' we enter the temple, see the great light, put on the new robe.' On the ' shouts and cries' of the initiates, and their religious significance, Dieterich, *Eine Mithras-Liturgie*, pp. 40-42, 228; on the ' silence,' *ib.*, pp. 42, 43, 229 (and refs. there); G. Mensching, *Das Heilige Schweigen*, pp. 70-72, 86; J. Kroll, *Die Lehren des Hermes Trismegistus*, pp. 335 ff.; H. Koch, *Pseudo-Dionysius Areopagita*, pp. 123 ff.

[4] Cicero, *de legg.*, ii, 14, 36—' Many glorious and divine things has your Athens produced and contributed to our existence; but none is better than these mysteries, which have raised us from the state of savagery to that of civilized humanity. They have taught us the rudiments, the first prin-ciples of life; they have given us a rule as well of happy living as of hopeful dying '; *in Verr.*, ii, 5, 72—' From the rites of Ceres and Libera men and states have derived the first beginnings of life and nutriment, of morals, of laws, of kindliness, of humanity'; Diod. Sic., *Hist.*, v, 49, 6 (of the Samothracian mysteries)—' They say that those who take part in them become nobler, juster, better in every way.' Andocides, *de myst.*, 31, ' assumes that those who have been initiated would take a juster and sterner view of moral guilt and innocence ' (so Farnell, iii, p. 191; but Rohde, *Psyche* [8] (E. tr.), p. 235, rejects this interpretation, and is to be pre-ferred). Rohde (*ib.*, and p. 228) perhaps states an extreme view when he says, ' There can hardly have been any question of moral influence in the mysteries'; a more balanced view, Farnell, iii, pp. 191, 192; A. D. Nock in (ed. A. E. J. Rawlinson) *Essays on the Trinity and Incarnation*, pp. 70-72.

[5] Cp. the phrase (from the mysteries of Sabazios), ' I have escaped the worse, I have found the better ' (Demosth., *de Corona*, 259)—also used in Athenian wedding-hymns (refs. Dieterich, *Mithras-Liturgie* [3], p. 215). In the Isis-mysteries the initiates cried, ' We have found, we rejoice together'

possessed of an indefectible consciousness of immortality.[1] All this the vision could do.

In the less official cults of the Empire the initiate was vouchsafed an experience even more emotional and intense. For a time at least it seems that he played the part of the priest, perhaps even of the deity himself.[2] His preliminary ascetic preparations were more severe, and he might carry the sacerdotal tonsure all his life to witness to his dedication.[3] The XIth book of Apuleius' "Metamorphoses" is our chief authority here. Lucius, the ass restored to human form, 'sees the goddess' in no less than three different ways ; sometimes in contemplation of her sacred statue, sometimes in dreams at night, and at the culminating point

(ref. *ib.*, p. 216). In the Attis-mysteries the priest cried (Firm. Mat., *de err. prof. rel.*, 22) :—

> ' Rejoice, ye mystics, for the God is saved ;
> So shall we too be saved from all our woes.'

So also Aristophanes, *Ran.*, 745, uses *epopteuein* quite generally for ' to be happy.'

[1] For the belief, as to which there can be no doubt, see the quotations from the Homeric *Hymn to Demeter* (lines 480 ff.), Sophocles (*Frag.*, 719 Dindorf, 753 Nauck, 837 Pearson) and others, Lobeck, *Aglaoph.*, pp. 69 ff. ; Farnell, iii, pp. 343, 344 ;—similarly the Orphic mysteries, Rohde, *op. cit.*, pp. 344, 358 ;—Attis-Cybele, Hepding, p. 203 ; Mithra (' renatus in aeternum '), Cumont, *Religions*[4], pp. 147 f. The problem lies in the question, *how* was immortality supposed to be guaranteed ? Was it (1) by ' indefectible grace ' (the phrase used in this connexion, Dar. Sagl., ii, p. 580) or ' identification with the god,' and if so, by (a) the rite as a whole, (b) by the ' baptisms ' and sacred meals ?—or (2) by *symbolical exercises*—the initiate having his fears removed by a dress-rehearsal of the passage of his soul through the heavenly spheres ?—or (3) by *spiritual consolation*—the initiate reminded that the cult-god had passed through the pangs of death and been restored to ' life ' ? (1(a)) or (2) seem probable, in view of the superstition of the Græco-Roman world—Foucart (*op. cit.*, pp. 392 ff., 420 ff. ; cp. 457, 474) supports (2), and Cumont, p. 220 (n. 49) seems to suggest that the two ideas belong to the Egyptian and the Asiatic cycles of theology respectively. In any case, the well-known Orphic tablets, or the passage from the ' Gospel of Philip,' quoted by Reitzenstein, *HMHL.*, p. 99, show how important it was to know how to address the heavenly bodies correctly. (1(b)) can scarcely be sustained, despite its popularity, in view of the secondary character assumed by lustrations and meals in the mysteries (see H. A. A. Kennedy, *St. Paul and the Mystery Religions*, pp. 69, 70). (3) seems antecedently unlikely ; yet it is Plutarch's theory, *de Is. et Os.*, 27—' Isis instituted holy mysteries in which images, allegories and action should recall the sufferings of other days ; to instil piety and encouragement in men and women suffering the same distresses.' Loisy (p. 142) regards this interpretation as ' superficial and inexact,' the offspring of Plutarch's ' intellectualist tendency ' ; but it is not actually contradicted by any explicit evidence about the mysteries. We shall probably never know what conscious soteriology underlay the Oriental mystery rites, any more than we know it of the Hebrew sacrificial system (W. P. Paterson, in *HDB.*, iv, pp. 340-342) ; perhaps—as also possibly with the Hebrews—there was none, and any interpretation, from the most ' intellectualist ' to the most grossly superstitious, was equally valid. (Further references in *Theology*, xi, p. 335 (Dec. 1925).)

[2] Reitzenstein, *HMR.*, pp. 22, 43 ; Rohde, *Psyche*[8] (E. tr.), pp. 258-260 ; Hepding, *Attis*, p. 196 ; A. D. Nock (*ut supr.*), pp. 105 f.

[3] Apuleius, *Met.*, xi. 30.

of his initiation in the mystic ritual of the shrine.[1] Of his first vision, when as the unhappy beast he is still lying under the full moon on the seashore, he speaks as follows (I quote from the Elizabethan translation of William Adlington) :—[2]

> 'Whenas I had ended this oration, discovering my plaints to the goddess, I fortuned to fall again asleep upon that same bed ; and by-and-by (for mine eyes were but newly closed) appeared to me from the midst of the sea a divine and venerable face, worshipped even of the gods themselves. Then, by little and little, I seemed to see the whole figure of her body, bright and mounting out of the sea and standing before me ; wherefore I purpose to describe her divine semblance, if the poverty of my human speech will suffer me, or her divine power give me a power of eloquence rich enough to express it.'[3]

Then follows a long and detailed description, based no doubt upon the conventional features and ornaments of the statue which later he came to love so well and leave so mournfully ; and then the goddess speaks, revealing herself as the divinity ' adored throughout all the world, in diverse manners, in variable customs, and by many names,' and promises him his liberty and restoration to fortune.

Of his initiation itself—after he has become a man once more, dedicated himself to the ' holy war,' and taken up the ' voluntary yoke of service,'[4]—he writes in the often-quoted words :—

> ' Thou wouldst peradventure demand, thou studious reader, what was said and done there : verily I would tell thee if it were lawful for me to tell, thou wouldst know if it were convenient for thee to hear ; but both thy ears and my tongue should incur the like pain of rash curiosity. Howbeit I will not long torment thy mind, which peradventure is somewhat religious and given to some devotion. Listen therefore and believe it to be true. Thou shalt understand that I approached near unto hell, even to the gates of Proserpine, and after that I was ravished throughout all the elements, I returned to my proper place : about midnight I saw the sun brightly shine, *I saw likewise the gods celestial and the gods infernal*, before whom I presented myself and worshipped them. Behold now I have

---

[1] For the statue, *Met.*, xi, 18, 19, 20, 24 ; for the dreams, *ib.*, 19, 26, 29, 30 ; for the initiatory rite. the citation above. Cp. also Lucius' farewell vow (*ib.*, 25)—' I will carry Thy divine visage and most holy presence for ever in my heart.'

[2] Conveniently republished, with a new recension of the text (based on Helm) by S. Gaselee, in the Loeb Classical Library (1915).

[3] *Met.*, xi, 3.

[4] *Ib.*, 15 ; on the phrases used, Reitzenstein, *HMR.*, pp. 192 ff., 214. For parallels to the ' yoke ' Reitzenstein quotes Ecclus. 51^{26}, Mt. 11^{29} ; for the Christian ' service ' and ' soldier ' cp. 2 Cor. 10^4, 1 Tim. 1^{18}, 2 Tim. $2^{3, 4}$.

told thee, which although thou hast heard, yet it is necessary that thou conceal it.' [1]

Further visions follow, and—to Lucius' surprise and cost—two further initiations in Rome.[2]   Then in the last chapter [3] of the book comes the climax of it all. ' Finally after a few days the great God Osiris appeared in my sleep, which is the more powerful god of the great gods, the highest of the greater, the greatest of the highest, and the ruler of the greatest.' The revelation given by this ' more powerful of the great gods ' is singularly inept, and warns us how difficult it must have been for the ancient world to keep upon the highest planes of religious exaltation for long ; it concerns nothing more than Lucius' future success as a pleader in the Roman courts.[4]   But not even this can blunt very much the sonorous dignity with which the writer proclaims this last and highest of his visions—*deus deum magnorum potior ; et majorum summus et summorum maximus et maximorum regnator Osiris.*[5]

---

[1] Apuleius, *Met.*, xi, 23.   The experience was no doubt supposed to confer immortality, though Isis' promise (xi, 6) seems to be conditioned not so much by the initiation as by the devout life which Lucius is to lead. Nothing in the text justifies Reitzenstein's suggestion that the ' traditio ad instar voluntariae mortis ' (xi, 21) refers to the bath taken (*ib.*, 23) before the initiation (*HMR.*, pp. 221, 231 ff.) or has any particular relation to baptism ; the *whole rite* is a ' voluntary death.' (When Firmicus Maternus, *de err. prof. rel.*, 18, speaks of the Attis-initiand as ' homo moriturus,' it seems unreasonable to regard this as having any reference to the rite at all ; it is simply that a ' mortal ' man is entering upon a ceremony from which he hopes to receive immortality.)   We must not stress the evidence for the rite being an initiation into immortality, or ' rebirth,' more than it deserves.   Whatever may be true of the Mithraic ' renatus in aeternum ' (*CIL.*, vi, 510, 736), the ' renatus quodam modo ' of Apuleius (xi, 16, 21) refers, in its first appearance, to Lucius' restoration to human form ; in its second to the recovery of health, by Isis' mediation, of those initiated on their (supposed) deathbeds. (A similar extension of life ' beyond the limits set by fate ' is promised to Lucius, on conditions, xi, 6 ; cp. the prayer in 25.)   On the morning following his initiation, Lucius emerges from the temple ' with twelve stoles and in a religious habit '—an ' embroidered vestment of fine linen ' which is described in detail—carrying a lighted torch and with a garland of flowers (xi, 24). This *may* perhaps typify a spiritual rebirth ; the gorgeous robe *may* designate him as an ' incarnation of the world-god ' (Reitzenstein, *HMR.*, p. 228) ; and the ' people crowding to see him ' *may* be an act of worship, as also perhaps in the case of the initiate by taurobolium, Prudentius, *Peristephan.*, x. 1046 ff. (Hepding, *Attis*, p. 66).   But all these are at best precarious inferences from the text.   Still, the conception of immortality as conferred by the Isis-Osiris cult is too well established to need further authentication (see F. Cumont, *Les Religions Orientales* [4], pp. 91, 92).   On this passage in general, see further Reitzenstein in *ARW.*, vii (1904), pp. 406 ff. ; M. Dibelius, *Die Isis-weihe bei Apuleius* (*Sitz.-Ber. Akad Heidelb.*, 1917).

[2] *Met.*, xi, 28, 29.   [3] *Ib.*, 31.

[4] Mr. A. D. Nock kindly sends me a suggestion to the effect that there is here no anticlimax ; Osiris assigns to Lucius his life's work.

[5] For the so-called ' Mithras-Liturgy,' which presents points of similarity to Lucius' initiation, *infra*, p. 473, Additional Note A.   Other visions of the underworld, or overworld, and the relation between the two, Dieterich, *Eine Mithras-Liturgie* [2], pp. 179 ff. ; Rohde, *op. cit.*, pp. 236, 237, 240.

(c) The Philosophers.

Whether because of the vitality of the Platonic tradition, or as a by-product of the mysteries, there were throughout the Empire in the first Christian centuries groups and individuals who claimed the vision of God for themselves, offered it to others, and proclaimed its supremacy as the goal of life for all. Popular thought —influenced no doubt by the semi-astrological speculations of Posidonius and others [1]—conceived the soul after death as haunting the æther round the universe ; and (as many funeral inscriptions testify) there was a vivid hope that in this environment the disembodied spirit would ' see the gods ' [2]—a phrase which often, perhaps, meant no more than ' watching the stars go round.' [3]

Even the most academic philosophers were not untouched by it. Aristotle himself had chosen as his title for the philosopher's career a phrase which could not but suggest the atmosphere of the mysteries—the philosophic life is one of ' seeing.' [4] Latin writers translated his ' life of seeing ' (bios theoretikos) by a word (contemplatio) whose religious associations, though different, were even more obvious. In each case the choice seems to have been deliberate ; other terms, devoid of mystical significance, were ready to hand. And Aristotle had moments, if no more, in which he explicitly invested the high pursuit of philosophic truth with a religious colouring. The ' highest branch of contemplation,' he said, ' is theology,' and the philosophic ideal is the ' worship and contemplation of God.' [5] It is not strange that, with such a loophole left open for the admission of religious aspirations into the purview of philosophic investigation, even the most unpromising systems should betray some trace of the quest for the vision of God.

Epicureanism in the Græco-Roman world was a synonym with atheism. Gods (if gods it had) were untouched by any kinship or sympathy with men ; it knew and desired no destiny except

---

[1] On Posidonius († 51 B.C.), his philosophy and influence, see E. Bevan, Stoics and Sceptics, c. 4 ; W. Warde Fowler, Religious Experience of the Roman People, pp. 382 ff.; Dieterich, op. cit., p. 202 ; E. Norden, Vergil : Aeneis, Buch VI, pp. 20 ff. ; Schmekel, Philosophie der mittleren Stoa (1892), pp. 85-154, 238-290. K. Reinhardt, Poseidonios (1921), pp. 2, 164, 472, etc., though fully emphasizing the importance of Posidonius, recognizes that he was not the only syncretistic philosopher of the period ; cp. Id., Kosmos u. Sympathie (1926), pass.

[2] On the souls in the æther, Rohde, Psyche [8], p. 517; on ' seeing the gods,' the inscriptions, ib., p. 572 ; generally Cumont, After Life in Roman Paganism, esp. pp. 121, 207, 212.

[3] Bevan, Stoics and Sceptics, p. 111, where the relevant passages from Seneca (ad Marc. de consol., 25) and Cicero (Tusc. disp., i, 44, 45 (19, 20) ; de rep., vi, 16 (Scipio's dream)) are given in the original ; A. D. Nock, ut supr., p. 142 (with further refs.) ; J. Kroll, Hermes Trismegistus, pp. 368 ff.

[4] See Note B, " Aristotle and the Contemplative Life," infra, p. 475.

[5] Aristotle, Met., v, 1 (1026a, 19) ; Eth. Eud., vii, 15 (1249b, 16 ff.). For the Nicomachean Ethics, see infra, p. 475 ; and for an illuminating note on this element in Aristotle, A. E. Taylor, St. Thomas Aquinas as a Philosopher, pp. 22-24.

extinction for the soul at death. Yet Lucretius, the great poet of
the Epicurean school, could find a value for the practice of religion ;
and he casts it in terms of the vision. ' Unless you reject,' he
says, ' all unworthy conceptions of the gods . . . you will be unable
to welcome with tranquil mind the herald-images of their divine
nature which come from the sacred statues in the shrine.' [1] The
doctrine here may be, as Warde Fowler asserts,[2] one of a ' purely
subjective ' self-culture by the means of examples known to be
wholly imaginary ; but it is significant that it should be expressed
in terms amenable to the needs of a more objective religion.

Stoicism, again, was in essence a purely pantheistic system,
knowing no destiny for the individual soul except absorption in the
Soul of the Universe. But here, as is well-known, a variety of
influences encouraged and enabled the later Stoics without intolerable inconsistency to import a strong theistic tendency into their
creed, and to speak of knowing, apprehending, imitating, serving
and worshipping God. ' The materialistic *Anima Mundi*,' as Sir
Samuel Dill says, becomes with the Roman Stoics ' the infinitely
benign Creator, Providence and Guardian ; the Father and almost
the Friend of men.' [3] A curious piece of sophistry enabled them
to tolerate the growing superstition of divination,[4] and the practice
was interpreted, if not as ' seeing God,' at least as ' seeing into '
God's purposes. At the same time, the desire to believe in the
survival and progress of the soul after death produced something
certainly amounting to a strong hope, if not to faith itself ; [5] and
the ground was thus cleared for the incorporation of ideas with
which we are now becoming familiar.

---

[1] Lucretius, *de rer. nat.*, vi, 68 ff.

[2] W. Warde Fowler, *Religious Experience of the Roman People*, p. 360.

[3] S. Dill, *Roman Society from Nero to Marcus Aurelius*, p. 390 ; cp.
Halliday, *op. cit.*, pp. 174, 175 ; A. Bonhöffer, *Epiktet u. das N. Test.*, p. 342.

[4] Kinship with the divine enables man to share in the divine *foresight*
(' providentia '), hence *divinatio*, aptly so-called, is possible to the godlike
man ; Dill, *op. cit.*, pp. 439, 440, with reference to Plutarch ; Bevan, *op.
cit.*, p. 115. Cp. Cicero, *de div.*, i, 64, 110, 115 ; *Tusc. disp.*, i, 27 (66)—
the three 'divine ' qualities of the soul are ' praeterita tenere,' ' *futura
providere* ' and ' praesentia complecti ' (from the ' Consolatio '). The Sibyl
prophesies by virtue of her ' divinity and communion with the immortals '
(Pliny, *Nat. Hist.*, vii, 33 (119) (Rohde, p. 316)). See also W. Scott, *Hermetica*, ii, pp. 364, 365, with illustrations there.

[5] The main influence was once again Posidonius, mediating the older
Orphic and Platonic faith through neo-Pythagorean (South Italian) channels.
Panaetius, his immediate teacher, ' rejected Plato's doctrine of the immortality of the soul ' (Cicero, *Tusc. disp.*, i, 32 (79)). For Cicero see again
the passage from the ' Consolatio ' quoted *Tusc. disp.*, i, 27 (66) :—' [The
soul, like] everything that has feeling, wisdom, life, activity, is heavenly
and divine, and therefore must be immortal ' ; also the letters to Atticus
after Tullia's death, *ad Att.*, xii, 18 ff. Lact., *Inst.*, i, 15, 20, quotes
another fragment of the ' Consolatio ' in which Tullia is said now ' to dwell
in the company of the gods.'—For the problem of Seneca's attitude to the
question of immortality, contrast Dill, *op. cit.*, pp. 514 ff., with Rohde, *op. cit.*,
p. 520 ; also J. B. Lightfoot, *Philippians*, p. 323—on this subject Seneca is
' both timid and capricious.'—Plutarch's views epitomized, Dill, pp. 520-528,
cp. *ib.*, p. 416.

The intensity and conviction with which these ideas are expressed varies with temperamental differences. From Marcus Aurelius [1] little enough can be quoted ; his wistful pessimism stood in the way of supernatural desires. With Epictetus, similarly, an unruffled joy and peace in the virtuous life made both mystical aspirations and future hopes almost superfluous ; [2] nevertheless, a religious strain from time to time imparts a warmer colour to his tranquil creed. God has made man ' to see Himself and His works ; and not to see alone, but also to proclaim them.' [3] He is not far from any one of us ; ' when we close the doors and all within is dark, let us never say we are alone—for God is within as well, our guardian angel.' [4] Only by ' looking to God ' can we cast out the vices of the soul ; [5] and so even Epictetus asserts that the reward of a good life is to see God after death :—' Brethren, await your God. For when He gives the sign, and releases you from this service, then ye shall go to Him . . . and if ye are so disposed then, short and easy is the time of your sojourn here.' [6]

But it is in the emotional outpourings of Seneca, Epictetus' predecessor by a generation and more, that the clearest examples of this surrender of philosophy to religion are to be found. With him theism is all but a firm conviction ; [7] and though he will not commit himself to an absolute belief in personal immortality, ' the Platonic vision of God—nay a higher vision of the Creator, the pitiful and loving Guardian, the Giver of all good, the Power which draws us to Himself, who receives us at death and in whom is our eternal beatitude,' are promised to the faithful soul.[8] Our

---

[1] Marcus Aurelius, though he is prepared to discuss as open questions various problems as to *what* exactly happens to the soul at death, is unhesitating on the main point. He neither needs nor longs for survival after death. ' Death put Alexander of Macedon and his stable-boy on a par. Either they were received into the seminal principles of the universe, or were alike dispersed into atoms ' (vi, 24) ; ' As in the amphitheatre monotonous repetition makes the spectacle pall, so it is with the experience of life. Everything is one monotonous round. How long ? How long ? Think ever of the dead. . . . What matters it to them ? ' (vi, 46, 47). Cp. x, 31 on the nothingness of life ; xii, 5, on the apparent irony that ' men who have kept close communion with the divine by holy acts and sacred ministries ' should be ' utterly extinguished ' at death. In iii, 3 he seems to admit the possibility of ' another life,' but it is only to prove that his contention, death is not to be feared, can be accepted by a believer in immortality. Similarly, viii, 58.

[2] Dill, *op. cit.*, p. 359—a pleasant sketch of Epictetus' philosophy; *ib.*, p. 504, his attitude to the question of immortality. More scientific and extremely illuminating is A. Bonhöffer's list (*Epiktet u. das N. Test.*, pp. 268 f., 274 ff.) of New Testament words which do not occur in Epictetus. The ethical distance of Epictetus from Christianity is marked by the absence of ἀγάπη and ἀγαπάω.

[3] *Diss.*, i, 6, 19.

[4] *Diss.*, i, 14, 13, cp. ii, 14, 11. Rohde, p. 514, has an important note on this *agathos daemon* which played a prominent part in Græco-Roman religion. Cp. Dill, *op. cit.*, pp. 425-433, 439. To the Platonists and to Maximus of Tyre, the demons were all good ; Xenocrates, and above all, Plutarch, developed the doctrine of the existence of *evil* demons.

[5] *Diss.*, ii, 16, 46.   [6] *Diss.*, i, 9, 16.

[7] Dill, *op. cit.*, pp. 331, 332, 513.   [8] *Ib.*, p. 305, and references there.

life here is but a ' prelude to a longer and better life elsewhere ';
we shall ' break through the clouds which have beset us, and with
self-congratulation see clearly with no feeble vision ';[1] and the
vision will purge away the taints of the flesh, and give communion
with the spirits of the blessed.[2] It is no accident that Seneca,
more succinctly than any other non-Christian writer, sets down
what is almost a paraphrase of the gospel promise :—' The mind
unless it is pure and holy cannot apprehend God.'[3]

More eclectic thinkers than those who professed the older ortho-
doxies could and did allow themselves a far greater scope. Ælius
Aristides, the rhetorician, an older contemporary of Marcus
Aurelius, is one such person.[4] A supernatural voice had said to
him, ' Withdraw thy spirit from all that is everyday and commonplace ; set thy mind on things which are above ; enter into
communion with God and rise above thy mortal self.'[5] Thenceforward his life was a series of visions, in which various deities
(but especially Asclepius, his patron) appeared to him, and granted
him certainty of his own future distinction,[6] and even (on occasion)
effective prescriptions for the cure of his physical ailments.[7]
Maximus of Tyre, a far more famous person, elevated the quest of
the vision of God into a veritable ascetic theology :—

' God—eye cannot see Him, words cannot name Him, flesh
and blood cannot touch Him, ear cannot hear Him ; within
the soul only that which is most fair, most pure, most intelligible, most ethereal, most honourable, can contemplate Him
because it is like Him, can hear Him because of their kinship.
. . . The soul holds herself erect and strong, she gazes at the
pure light (of the Godhead) ; she wavers not, turns not her
glance to earth, but closes her ears and directs her eyes and
all her other senses within. She forgets the troubles and
sorrows of earth, its joys and honours, its glory and its shame ;
and submits to the guidance of pure reason and strong love.
For reason points the road that must be followed, and love
drives the soul forward, making the rough places smooth by
its charm and constancy. And as we approach heaven and
leave earth behind, the goal becomes clear and luminous—
that is a foretaste of God's very self. On the road we learn
His nature better; but when we reach the end we see Him.'[8]

---

[1] Seneca, *Ep.* 102, 22 ; 79, 12 ; cp. 73, 15 ; 102, 26-28.
[2] *Ep.* 26, 5 ; cp. *ad Marc. consol.*, 24, 25.   [3] *Ep.* 87, 21.
[4] On him A. Boulanger, *Aelius Aristide* (1923) ; cp. Halliday, *op. cit.*,
pp. 83, 270.
[5] Boulanger (*op. cit.*), p. 178 (Aristides, *Diss. Sacr.*, iv (Keil, 1, 62)).
[6] Boulanger, pp. 133, 207.
[7] *Ib.*, pp. 130 f., 202 f. ; on Aristides' descriptions of his ecstasies, and his
use of mystery-terminology, *ib.*, p. 179 ; his visions of the other world, *ib.*,
p. 202.
[8] Maximus Tyrius, *Diss.*, xi, 9, 10 (ed. Hobein = Duebner, xvii ; Heinsius, i).
In xvii, 12 ff. he deals with the subject of ' seeing God in His works,' which,
however, he regards as the lower stage of the ' vision.'

Even Celsus, the rationalist, was not untouched with the same spirit.[1] M. Lebreton is right in setting this doctrine or quest in the forefront of the tendencies of the day. The whole truth is enshrined, as he appositely says,[2] in Justin Martyr's 'Dialogue with Trypho.'

In this dialogue, after defining philosophy as 'the highest of possessions, and most honourable before God, to Whom it alone leads us and commends us,'[3] Justin describes his own spiritual pilgrimage. From his first instructor—a Stoic—he obtained no knowledge of God,—'for he did not know himself, and said such instruction was unnecessary.' With the Peripatetic philosopher, to whom he next turned for guidance, he differed on the question of remuneration, and they parted company after a few days. A Pythagorean refused to lead him on to the 'contemplation of what is honourable and good in essence,' until he had fitted himself for the task by preliminary studies in music, astronomy, and geometry. 'So I bethought me that I would seek out the Platonists; for their fame was great,' Justin continues, 'and with them I progressed daily. The perception of immaterial things quite overpowered me, and the contemplation of the Ideas gave my mind wings . . . and I expected forthwith to see God—for that is the end of Plato's philosophy.'[4] On one of his solitary walks in a field by the sea he fell into converse with an old man, who after a few preliminary exchanges put the question, 'Is it possible for the mind of man to see God at any time, if it is uninstructed by the Holy Spirit?'[5] Justin, fortified with Platonic quotations, replies without hesitation, 'Yes, if the mind is pure'; and bases his confidence on the essential kinship between the human and the divine. He adds, however, that the vision is most possible only when the soul has been set free from the body. To this the old man counters with a disparaging criticism of Pythagoras and Plato, who 'know nothing about these things';[6] and insists with a wealth of argument that the soul is mortal, and therefore has no kinship with God; and that the duration of its life is wholly dependent upon the divine will.

But the old man is no sceptic, except as to the scope and value of philosophy. His purpose is to turn Justin's mind from the philosophers to the prophets; and in this he proves successful, though Justin suppresses much of his argument. But the conclusion is clear. 'Straightway a flame was kindled in my soul,' the apologist concludes;[7]—

[1] Origen, *c. Cels.*, vi, 3 (fin.).—Celsus, quoting Plato, *ep.* 7 (for authenticity see A. E. Taylor, *Plato*, p. 15), says that the 'highest good cannot be described in words, but after we have for a long while dwelt in association with it, it is suddenly kindled like a light in the soul, as though a fire sprang forth; and henceforward it feeds its own flame.' Origen accepts the statement, but points out that it scarcely coheres with the superstitious practices which Celsus champions.

[2] J. Lebreton, *Histoire du dogme de la Trinité*, ii, pp. 76-78.
[3] Justin, *Dial.*, 2.   [4] *Ib.*
[5] *Ib.*, c. 4.   [6] *Ib.*, c. 6.   [7] *Ib.*, c. 8.

'and a love of the prophets and of the friends of Christ possessed me. . . . If then you have any concern for yourself, if
you look for salvation, if you believe in God, . . . you may
come to know the Christ of God, and so being made perfect,[1]
live the life of the blessed.'

V. PHILO AND THE HERMETICA.

(a) Philo of Alexandria.

The long development we have been tracing culminates in two
amazing collections of documents—one Jewish, the other pagan—
the works of Philo, and the Hermetic books. If ever there was a
Jew with a soul athirst for God, it was Philo of Alexandria, whose
lifetime overlapped that of most of the characters in the New
Testament. Despite the strongest admiration both for Platonic
philosophy and for 'Chaldean' astrology,[2]—despite his constant
borrowing of thoughts from Stoicism[3] and of metaphors from the
pagan mysteries,[4]—his ruling passion was identical with that of the
greatest figures of his race. And however much he dressed his
teaching about God in the cold abstractions of metaphysical
definition, it was for communion with the *personal*, living God that
he yearned. Bousset, rightly divining his dominant interest, calls
him ' the first *theologian* worthy of the name ';[5] but rightly adds
that among strictly monotheistic theologians he is the first mystic,
too, whilst in circles where monotheism was not yet the rule ' no
mysticism reached the height of Philo's desire for union with the
living, All-Highest God.'[6] To see God was his aim, and he thought
of this vision as a ' vision of peace '; for ' God alone is perfect
peace.'[7]

Philo is well aware that physical sight cannot attain the
vision ; only the ' eye of the soul ' can see God.[8] Of the quest
for the vision he speaks as follows :—

[1] Τελείῳ γενομένῳ—this might mean either ' having become perfect,'
' being initiated ' (metaphor from the mysteries), or ' being baptized ' (by
analogy with mystery initiations). Unless Justin has forgotten that he is
addressing a Jew, the first seems the most suitable meaning.

[2] For Plato see (e.g.) *q. omn. prob. lib.*, 2 (13) ; Mangey, ii, p. 447 ; CW.,
vi, 4 ; *de fug. et inv.*, 11 (63) ; M., i, p. 555 ; CW., iii, p. 144, etc. For the
' Chaldeans ' see *de migr. Abr.*, 32 (178) ; M., i, p. 464 ; CW., ii, p. 303 (but
he attacks their pantheism and fatalism ; *ib.*, cp. *QRDH.*, 20 (97) ; M., i, 486 ;
CW., iii, 22). (References throughout are paragraphed as in L. Cohn u.
P. Wendland, *Philonis Alex. opera quae supersunt* (1896-) ; references to
Mangey's edition are designated M.)

[3] J. Drummond, *Philo Judaeus*, ii, p. 63, gives an exhaustive list of
Philo's periphrases for ' God,' which shows clearly his indebtedness to Stoic-
Platonic thought.

[4] A full list of these, Bousset, *RJ.*, pp. 450, 451 ; cp. *KC.*, p. 167.

[5] Bousset, *RJ.*, p. 445 ; cp. Lebreton, *Dogme de la Trinité*, i, p. 172.

[6] *RJ.*, p. 452.

[7] *de somn.*, ii, 38 (250-253) (M., i, p. 692 ; CW., iii, p. 299).

[8] *de conf. ling.*, 20 (92) (M., 1, p. 418 ; CW., ii, p. 246) ; cp. *mut. nom.*, 1 (3)
(M., i, p. 578 ; CW., iii, p. 156).

'It is the characteristic of him who would see God not to leave the holy warfare without his crown, but to persevere till he reaps the prize of victory. And what crown could be more verdant or welcome to the victorious soul than to see Him Who is with accurate vision ? It is a worthy conflict that lies before the 'ascetic' soul—to win eyes for the clear vision of Him Whom alone it is worth man's while to see.' [1]

We scarcely need to be told, in a note upon Deut. xix, 5 ('He shall flee unto one of these cities (of refuge) and live'), that 'to take sanctuary with Him Who is, is life eternal, but to flee away from Him is death.' [2] So vital a truth is it to Philo that 'to know God is the highest happiness, and life of immortal span,' that he can call it a 'necessary doctrine of philosophy,' [3] though, as will appear, it was not from philosophy that he had learnt it.

With this thought uppermost in his mind Philo searched the scriptures. There he found the name 'Israel' for his people, and his faith was confirmed ; for 'Israel' meant to him 'seeing God.' [4] Etymologically, no doubt, he was wrong ; [5] but his interpretation had a justification in tradition. It was at Penuel, where he saw God face to face, that Jacob received his new name. The whole of Old Testament history [6]—indeed the whole history of his race— at once appeared to Philo in a new light, and he set himself to rewrite it. 'All Jews are sons of one father '—that is to say of 'Israel,' the 'seer.' [7] Their title, 'sons of Israel,' means 'hearers of him who saw' [8]—'hearing being the most honourable thing next to seeing.' Israel's destiny as a nation is—not so much to be saved in the 'day of the Lord,' as—to see God. How seriously Philo took this doctrine of the special privilege of his kindred may be inferred from the important historical tract in which he describes the criminal tyranny of Caligula, the persecution of the Jews in Alexandria, and his own mission to Rome. To those who are despondent about God's care for the nation he replies that, despite all appearances, they are still God's peculiar people, because they have the vision—

---

[1] *mut. nom.*, 12 (81) (M., i, p. 590; CW., iii, p. 171). Here also we are told that 'Israel' means 'seeing God.'

[2] *de fug. et inv.*, 15 (78) (M., i, p. 557 ; CW., iii, p. 126).

[3] *spec. leg.*, i, 16 (345) (M., ii, p. 264 ; CW., v, p. 84).

[4] *Supra*, n. 1 ; cp. *de ebr.*, 20 (82) (M., i, p. 369 ; CW., ii, p. 185) ; *de fug. et inv.*, 38 (208) (M., i, p. 577 ; CW., iii, p. 154)—(a model little homily on Hagar's flight from Sarah) ; *de conf. ling.*, 28 (146) (M., i, p. 427 ; CW., ii, p. 257) *et pass.*

[5] 'Israel' means 'God perseveres' ; it is taken in Gen. 32²⁸ as the equivalent of 'perseveres with God,' and given to Jacob as the result of the encounter at Penuel. (See e.g. *HDB.*, ii, p. 530, *s.v.* 'Jacob.')

[6] Philo's special interest, however, was the Pentateuch—five-and-a-half pages of Mangey's indices are occupied with his Pentateuchal references ; less than half a page with references to other parts of the Old Testament.

[7] *conf. ling.*, 11 (41) (M., i, p. 411 ; CW., ii, p. 237) on Gen. 42¹¹.

[8] *Ib.*, 28 (148) (M., i, p. 427 ; CW., ii, p. 257).

'which seems to me worth more than all wealth, private or public. For if the sight of elders or teachers, magistrates or parents, moves to reverence and modesty and zeal for a pure life, how great a support for virtue in our souls shall *we* find, who have learnt to pass beyond all things created, and to see That Which is Uncreated and Divine, the Highest Good, the Happy and the Blessed—nay, to say sooth, That Which is Better than the best, Fairer than the fairest, more Blessed than the most blessed, Happier than the happiest—aye, more Perfect, if it may be, than any words such as these.' [1]

We have no need for surprise that, buoyed up by such a faith as this, he undertook the dangerous and uncongenial task of pleading his nation's cause at the imperial court. [2]

Philo is so commonly called a universalist in theology that it seemed worth while to insist upon this element of almost fanatical nationalism in his thought. But it is true enough that he has a wider message, and appears to invite men of every creed or none to join the *horatikon genos*—' the race of them that see.' He does not confine the privilege to Jewry. ' Knowledge of the vision ' was the ' true magic ' of the Chaldean sages; [3] the Therapeutæ— the ' race of seers ' *par excellence*—are confined to no one land, though Egypt is their headquarters. Israel, therefore, is typical of those who seek the vision everywhere, whoever they may be. It is for them Philo writes, to encourage them to ' aim at the vision of Him who is, to go beyond the visible sun, and never to leave the road that leads to perfect happiness '; to tell them of the ' divine love,' which—unlike ' mere habit or exhortation or monition '—can ' inspire them with the frenzy of Bacchæ or Korybantes, till they reach the vision they desire.' [4]

Philo has no doubts as to the stages by which the vision is to be secured. First of all must come the rigorous practice of virtue —the ' askesis,' or training, of the warrior of God. At this first stage he wavers, to some extent, between two ideals of the truly virtuous life. One such ideal of ' askesis,' and at first sight much the more potent in his thought, is that of detachment—of asceticism strictly so-called. This ascetic interest of his is not without

[1] *de leg. ad Caium*, i (4, 5) (M., ii, p. 546 ; CW., vi, p. 156).

[2] In one passage already mentioned Philo busies himself with the obvious question, How come the Jews to enjoy this exceptional privilege of the vision ? The answer he suggests is that they are more akin to the divine Reason, Logos or Word than other men, and so more able to see Him as He sees Himself. The argument, however, is almost lost in allegory. ' We are all sons of the one man—Israel ' he quotes, and then goes on to say that Israel was not mortal, but ' the Immortal Man of God—who being the Word of the Unseen must be himself immortal.' ' He is the first-born Word, the eldest of the angels, the archangel of many names, the Beginning and the Name of God, the Word and the archetypal Man. . . . And even if we are not yet worthy to be called sons of God yet are we sons of His most holy and eternal image, the Word ' (*conf. ling.*, 28 (146, 147) ; *ut sup.*).

[3] *de spec. leg.*, iii, 18 (100) (M., ii, p. 316 ; CW., v, p. 178).

[4] *de vit. cont.*, 2 (12) (M., ii, p. 473 ; CW., vi. p. 49).

its problems ;[1] but clearly he respected the Essenes for their
retirement from the world (though he still treats them as representative of the ' active ' life) ;[2] idolized the Therapeutæ, who by
retirement had won to ' vision '; and at times himself sought the
desert and its solitudes with a zeal which could at least stir him
to temporary eremitism.[3] He allies himself wholeheartedly with
those who call the body a tomb, or carcase, or prison house ;[4]
and urges the soul to escape from bondage to the body by the
practice of self-mortification.

But his real thought, it may be suggested, is wider. No one
mode of life has the monopoly of the vision of God. Under Philo's
long-drawn-out sentences and paragraphs there can be discerned
something very much akin to that simple purity of heart which in
the gospel is the only prerequisite of the beatific vision. He makes
much of the cardinal virtues of Greek ethics, but even that vigorous
scheme is too rigid for him. On the passage ' Come up unto the
Lord, thou and Aaron,'[5] he comments as follows :—

> ' Go up, O soul, to the vision of Him Who is—go up, *quietly,
> reasonably, willingly, fearlessly, lovingly.* . . . For these are the
> spear-bearing powers of the mind that is worthy to reign, and
> they should escort and accompany their king. It is dangerous
> for the soul to go up to the vision of Him Who is, by itself
> alone, not knowing the path, and in ignorance and temerity ;
> for ignorance and excess of daring breed great transgressions.'[6]

This ideal of purity can be expressed, also, in terms of citizenship and kinship :—

> ' We must begin our search,' says Philo, ' by being citizens
> of the universe—citizens of no mean city—enrolled in the
> greatest and most perfect citizenship. . . . He who is kith and
> kin with the Monarch of the city, since the divine spirit is poured
> out upon him in fullest measure, tries in every word and deed
> to please his royal Father. He follows His footprints in the
> paths—or rather highways—which the virtues carve out,

---

[1] *Infra*, p. 486.

[2] *de vit. cont.*, I (1) (M., ii, p. 471 ; CW., vi, p. 47).

[3] *leg. all.*, ii, 21 (85) (M., i, pp. 81, 82 ; CW., i, p. 107)—' I have often left
my relations, my friends, my home, and have sought the desert, to see something worth the seeing.' But he adds that sometimes this has proved
of no avail, whilst sometimes he has found God in a crowd. The passage is
singularly beautiful. On the limits of Philo's asceticism, *infra*, pp. 486, 487.

[4] On the doctrine in general, see Rohde, *Psyché*, index, *s.v.* σῶμα—σῆμα ;
Philonic references, Bousset, *RJ.*, p. 422 ; *infra*, pp. 47, 86, 482, 487.

[5] Ex. 24¹.

[6] *migr. Abr.*, 31 (169) (M., i, p. 462 ; CW., ii, p. 301). The adverbs are
definitely non-ascetic : εὐαρμόστως, λογικῶς, ἑκουσίως, ἀφόβως, ἀγαπητικῶς. A
note on δορυφόροι, or ψυχοπομποί, the supernatural escort of the soul to the
other world, in J. Kroll, *Die Lehren des Hermes Trismegistus* (1914),
p. 270.

wherein only those souls may walk who find their true end in imitating the God who begat them.' [1]

Or we may think of it in terms of sacrifice :—

' Offer up all thy powers as a sacrifice to Him from Whom all corporeal composition, all true understanding and utterance come. . . . Look upwards then ; confute the blind and vulgar herd, who think they see but are darkened indeed, preferring evil to good, injustice to justice, passion to tranquillity ("eupatheia"), what is mortal to what is immortal. . . . Only the clean ("asteioi") can see.' . . . ' We should receive God's gifts for God's use rather than our own, and dedicate them all to Him, keeping our stewardship holy and undefiled ; we should think of nothing except God and His powers, speak naught except, with unfettered lips, the praise of the Father of all in hymns and psalms and anthems. . . . This is the happy life.' [2]

These first steps in the practice of virtue, however, superhuman and exalted though they may seem to be, are no more than the following of 'customary' doctrine to Philo. Only when the soul as a result is enfranchised does it become a soul indeed—one capable of seeing God. Here Philo's hellenic leanings show themselves at their fullest. The virtuous soul must advance by *philosophy* to a ' self-taught wisdom ' [3] of its own. The doctrine seems forbidding enough ; it becomes more human as we realize that by ' philosophy ' Philo means what later ages called ' meditation ' upon God and His works—something, that is to say, in essence open to the capacities even of the meanest. The path of ' philosophy ' is no narrow gate for the select few; it is a ' royal road,' a ' broad highway,' [4] for all who choose to tread it.

' It is useful,' we are told, ' if not to attain to perfect virtue, at least for citizenship, to know the ancient and Ogygian doctrines, to search out time-honoured reports of noble deeds which historians and poets have handed down.' [5] Philo has much to say of this life of meditation. He calls it communion with the Logos, the ' firstborn son ' of God; [6] or knowing God by images. [7] But in relation to the true knowledge of God all that we gain by philosophy— ' profound gift ' as it is—is as a voice in the darkness compared

---

[1] *mund. op.*, 50 (144) (M., i, pp. 34 f.; CW., i, p. 50). Actually the passage refers to Adam in his innocence, the archetype of all who take as their goal ' the imitation of God who made them.' Adam dwelt in the society of the ' powers ' of God—some incorporeal, some corporeal (' as, for example, the stars '—the ' first citizens ' of the city of God).

[2] *QRDH.*, 15 (76, 77) (M., i, p. 483 ; CW., iii, p. 18) ; 22 (110) (M., i, p. 488; CW., iii, p. 26). Note the use of *eupatheia*, where a strict Stoic, for example, would have said *apatheia*.

[3] *det. pot. ins.*, 9 (30) (M., i, p. 197; CW., i, p. 265) ; *sacr. Ab. et Cain*, 22 (78) (M., i, p. 178 ; CW., i, p. 234).

[4] *deus immut.*, 30 (143) (M., i, p. 294 ; CW., ii, p. 86).

[5] *sacr. Ab. et Cain*, 22 (78) (M., i, p. 178 ; CW., i, p. 234).

[6] *quod a deo somn.*, 19 (M., i, p. 638).   [7] *Ib.*

to vision in the full light of day.[1] Philosophy is at best conjectural; if it initiates us into anything at all, it is into the 'lower mysteries' alone.[2] But there are higher mysteries to which the pure in heart are summoned.[3] Even while we busy our minds with 'the ancient and Ogygian doctrines'

> 'sometimes a sudden gleam of self-taught wisdom shines through upon us, beyond all hope and expectation. It opens the sealed eyes of the soul; we *see* wisdom now, no longer hear it alone. Vision, the swiftest of the senses, replaces hearing, the slower; why therefore vex the ears with words any more? . . . When God quickens these seedlings of self-taught wisdom in the soul, we may pack away and erase the things we have learnt—nay, they fade back into oblivion of their own motion. The associate or friend or pupil of God—whatever we choose to call him—has no more need for the guidance of mere mortals.' [4]

We are very near now to the vision of God, in which He is seen 'not as a body is inferred from its shadow'—not as Bezaleel saw, who worked from copies of the heavenly things—but with the eyes of Moses in the mount. For when Moses said, 'Show me now Thy ways that I may know Thee,' [5] his meaning was, 'Show me Thyself not by heaven, or earth, or water, or air, or sight created —let me not see Thy shape mirrored in aught else, but in Thyself'; [6] and his prayer was granted. M. Lebreton, in his sympathetic study of Philo, makes much of the fact that our writer at times treats the vision of God as something not certainly to be attained even by the pure in heart, at all events in this life.[7] The fact cannot be

---

[1] *quod a deo somn.*, 19 (M., i, p. 638).

[2] *de Abr.*, 24 (122) (M., ii, p. 19; CW., iv, p. 28). The lower mysteries, in which 'we cannot comprehend That which is by Its own nature, but need some other, and recognize It as creator and ruler through Its works'; with them are contrasted the 'higher mysteries' in which the mind, 'now utterly purified,' 'reaches to the Idea itself, unmixed, uncompounded, wholly self-existent.' Similarly *leg. all.*, iii, 33 (100) (M., i, p. 107; CW., i, p. 135).

[3] Note his use of formulæ (invitation and warning) obviously drawn from pagan liturgies. Thus *de fug. et inv.*, 16 (85) (M., i, p. 558; CW., iii, p. 127)— 'Ho! mystics and hierophants of our holy rites, away—away with the promiscuous mob of foul and sin-stained souls! Away with their greedy ears, their lips unsealed, fit instruments of their undoing, wherewith they lust for the telling of all things, even of what is forbidden!' Similarly, *de cher.*, 12 (42) (M., i, p. 146; CW., i, p. 180)—'Guard well your ears, or depart, ye worshippers! We are to impart a holy secret to initiates worthy of the holiest. . . . But none shall be admitted to our holy rites who is bound by incurable sin. . . . Now the beginning of the mystery is this. . . .'

[4] *sacr. Ab. et Cain*, 22, 23 (78, 79) (M., i, p. 178; CW., i, p. 234).

[5] Ex. 33¹³. But Philo quotes from the LXX, 'Show me now Thyself, that I may see Thee clearly,' which enables him to make his point much more effectively.

[6] *leg. all.*, iii, 33 (101) (M., i, p. 107; CW., i, p. 135).

[7] Lebreton, *op. cit.*, i, pp. 185, 186. But M. Lebreton is primarily concerned with Philo as a theologian, and does less than justice to his mystical convictions. Cp. also E. Fascher, *Deus Invisibilis* ('Marburger Theologische Studien,' vol. i), p. 60.

denied , indeed it is the occasion of one of Philo's bravest utterances :—

> ' Whether by seeking thou shalt find God is uncertain, for
> to many He has not made Himself known, and their labour
> seemed without reward. Yet even the bare search avails to
> the attainment of good ; high aspirations, even though they
> fail, bring joy to those who pursue them. . . . So the good
> man, fleeing from himself, strives for the knowledge of the One
> unceasingly. He runs a straight race, and fights a good fight
> triumphantly.' [1]

But in general Philo is far more optimistic ; he has, indeed, a
theology and theodicy in one which give him grounds for optimism.
The natural soul of man was not ' capable of seeing its Creator,'—

> ' but when God perceived how fruitful it would be to the crea-
> ture to know his Maker (for this is the sublimity of all joy and
> blessedness) He breathed into it some spark of His divinity
> from above, which, working invisibly, sealed with its impress
> the soul invisible, . . . so that it no longer received mortal but
> immortal thought. . . . And now it comprehends the very
> bounds of earth and sea, of air and heaven ; yet stays not
> there. The universe itself seems too narrow for its soaring
> ambition. Further it penetrates in its striving, to grasp the
> incomprehensible nature of God, if it can.' [2]

Man, therefore, was made of kindred stuff to God ; like must
infallibly turn to like, and rest not till it finds it. As to the nature
of the vision, Philo is quite definite. It is an *ecstasy*, akin to that
of the Bacchæ or Korybantes of paganism, or the prophetic frenzies
of the Old Testament. [3] In a famous passage he writes of his own
experience :—

> ' I am not ashamed to confess that which has befallen me a
> thousand times. I have set myself down, according to my
> wont, to write upon the principles of philosophy. I have seen

---

[1] *leg. all.*, iii, 15 (47) (M., i, p. 96 ; CW., i, p. 123).

[2] *det. pot. ins.*, 24 (89) (M., i, p. 208 ; CW., i, p. 278). Philo continues :—
' How is it possible that this tiny mind of man, confined by the narrow bonds
of brain-membrane or of heart, can grasp the vast expanse of heaven and
universe ?   Only if it be an integral portion of the blessed soul of God.   For
nothing divine is separable ; there is continuity throughout. So the mind
is continuous with Perfection in the universe ; and when it beholds the universe, it expands to the very bounds of all, without breaking, so elastic are
its powers.'

[3] *QRDH.*, 14 (69) (M., i, p. 482 ; CW., iii, p. 16)—' Therefore, my soul, if
thou art seized with a longing for the good gifts of God, leave not only *fatherland*—the body, and *kindred*—the senses, and *father's house*—the power of
speech, but flee from thyself as well. Go forth from thyself in an ecstasy,
like the Bacchæ, etc.'   The whole passage is important for its use of ' ecstatic' language. So, too, of the Therapeutæ, *de vit. cont.*, 2 (12) (M., ii,
p. 473 ; CW., vi, p. 49).   On the neo-Platonic ecstasy generally, H. Koch,
Pseudo-Dionysius Areopagita, pp. 136 ff.

clearly what I wished to say. Yet my mind has remained
blank and sterile ; and I have abandoned the attempt, cursing
the impotence of my mind, but amazed at the might of Him
Who is, Who at His will doth open and close the womb of the
soul. At other times, coming empty-handed to my work, I
have suddenly been filled. In some strange way ideas have
poured in upon me from above like rain or snow. A Bacchic
frenzy has filled me with ecstasy ; I knew no more the place
where I sat, my company, myself—nay, even what I said or
wrote. A flow of exposition comes upon me at such seasons, a
delectable light, and vision of the keenest ; problems become
crystal clear, as though I saw their every detail with my physical
sight. Then is revealed to me That Which is most worthy to
be seen and contemplated and loved—the perfect Good, which
changes the soul's bitterness to honey—the most savoury of
all condiments, which makes even unnutritious foods to be
healthful.' [1]

Philo's ecstasies, like those of some Christian mystics, savour
at times of heterodoxy. He claims for himself that in such a condition he has from time to time added to the corpus of revealed truth,[2]
just as of the Therapeutæ he asserts that ' some from their dreams
have enunciated famous dicta of divine philosophy.' [3] It would
be cruel to insist upon these traces of superstition, error and self-
hallucination ; we shall do better to turn to one last aspect of his
teaching. Dr. Edersheim, in an attempt to show Philo's inferiority to Christian thought, could say that in his system ' faith is
not yet required for approach to God.' [4] No statement more
flatly opposed to the facts could very well be imagined. The truth
is put succinctly by Bousset :—' Apart from Isaiah, Philo is the first
great psychologist of faith.' [5] Like S. Paul, his younger contemporary, Philo seizes upon the great text of Genesis xv, 2 (' Abraham
believed God ') and, in an epigrammatic moment very rare with
him, calls it ' the shortest of sentences, the greatest of achievements '.[6] So he proceeds to his Hymn of Faith :—

> ' Faith is the only true and certain good—yea, faith in God ;
> —the consolation of life, the fulfilment of the highest hopes,
> the death-blow to evils, the purveyor of benefits, the end of

---

[1] *migr. Abr.*, 7 (34 f.) (M., i, p. 441 ; CW., ii, p. 275). Note ὑπὸ κατόχης
ἐνθέου κορυβαντᾶν (*infra*, p. 494) ; and cp. *de somn.*, i, 60 (M., i, p. 630; CW.,
iii, p. 218) :—' He that knoweth not himself, knoweth Him Who is.'
[2] Thus of the two great ' powers ' of God, *cher.*, 9 (27) (M. i, p. 143 ; CW.,
i, p. 176) ; of the world being governed by necessity and God alone free,
de somn., ii, 38 (252) (M., i, p. 692 ; CW., iii, p. 298).
[3] *de vit. cont.*, 3 (26) (M., ii, p. 475 ; CW., vi, p. 53).
[4] *DCB.*, iv, p. 384.
[5] *RJ.*, p. 447. Judaistic anticipations, *ib.*, pp. 194 ff. Lebreton, i, p. 174,
supports Bousset, but does not emphasize the point. Reitzenstein, *HMR.*,
pp. 234 ff., admits that the *word* is rare in contemporary paganism, but professes to find trace of the *idea*.
[6] *de Abr.*, 45 (262) (M., ii, p. 38 ; CW., iv, p. 57).

unhappiness, the knowledge of piety, the assurance of bliss, the progress of a soul which in all things rests assured upon God, the Author of all, Who can do everything, but wills only what is best.   It is faith alone which makes our path secure.' [1]

The desire for the living God—the certainty that the pure in heart shall see Him—the conviction that faith alone can lead us to His presence—we may set aside everything else that Philo chose to say, if we bring away from him these great convictions which certainly lay nearest to his heart.   By his laborious and often confused philosophizing of the Logos doctrine he has won his way into our text-books ; but it is his passion for God which must always make him dear to the heart of the Christian Church.

(b) *The Hermetic Books.*

Of all the pagan documents which date from the beginning of our era the most mysterious, and at the same time the most intense in the desire of seeing God which they express, are those bound up in the so-called ' Corpus Hermeticum.'   In their present form they are not earlier than the fourth century, but undoubtedly they embody an older tradition.   Their place of origin was Egypt ; and though the different tracts (and even sometimes one and the same tract, in its present form) embody varying theological ideas, there is yet a unity which characterizes them all.   Thus Scott, their latest editor, can say with justice, ' If one were to try to sum up the Hermetic teaching in one sentence, I can think of none that would serve the purpose better than the sentence, " Blessed are the pure in heart, for they shall see God." ' [2]

What the mysteries did for the eye, the Hermetic tracts professed to do for the ear.   By word of mouth, by exhortation, by instruction, rather than by ornate ceremonial or solemn theurgy, they proposed to bring men to the vision of God.[3]   Reitzenstein [4] is inclined to regard them as an offshoot, or refinement, of the mysteries, which gradually shed their external trappings and so appeared in the new form of theosophy.   The relationship is not impossible, and it enables Reitzenstein to read back into the mysteries many of the nicer theologisms of the Hermetic books, and so hypothetically to fill out some of the puzzling blanks in

---

[1] *de Abr.*, 45 (262) (M., ii, p. 38 ; CW., iv, p. 57).

[2] W. Scott, *Hermetica* (Oxford, 1924), i, p. 14.

[3] The title of one of the Hermetic tractates (now extant in a Latin translation (' Asclepius ') only) was ' Logos Teleios ' (so Lactantius and Lydus, Scott, iii, p. 1 ; cp. also *Tract.* ix, 1 (Scott i, p. 179)).   This has been taken to mean ' a revelation which initiates ' (H. A. A. Kennedy, *St. Paul and the Mystery Religions*, p. 132 ; Reitzenstein, *HMR.*, pp. 47, 242, 339), and if so might well be the title of every tractate ; Scott (iii, pp. 1, 2), however, gives reasons for supposing that it means no more than ' crowning discourse.'

[4] *HMR.*, pp. 37, 64, 242 ff.

our knowledge of the older system.[1]   But when we remember the
reaction of Philo, the devout Jew, to pure Platonism, it is not clear
that the Hermetic writers owe any more to the mysteries than he
did.   Like him they borrowed their terminology freely enough,
but otherwise they present us simply with an eclectic combination
of Platonic and Oriental doctrines.

The agent by whom esoteric knowledge of the Godhead was
conveyed to followers of this way of life was, in Greek, Hermes, in
Egyptian, Thot, the messenger of the gods.   The message derived
from him was passed on to disciples by the anonymous writers of
the several tracts.   It consisted often enough, as with the apocalyptists, of elaborate instructions on creation and the birth of the
universe, and accounts of the soul's flight after death through the
seven spheres to the eighth and perfect heaven ;[2] or of equally
elaborate meditations on the nature of the Godhead.   'What
would you hear and see and perceive and learn and know ?' says
the teacher to the disciple.   The reply is, 'I would fain know the
things that are, and understand their nature, and know God.'[3]
The instructions given vary in the different tractates.   Sometimes,
in language which constantly reminds us of Philo, the disciple is
told to 'flee the world' and all its snares ; to lift himself out of the
tomb of the body.   'There is nothing good on earth ; there is
nothing bad in heaven,' runs one extract ;[4] and again,—

'We must hate the body to be able to love ourselves. . . .
There are two sorts of things, the corporeal and the incorporeal.
What is mortal is of the first sort ; what is immortal is of the
second . . . and no man can choose both of these.   But
the choice of the better is glorious, for it saves a man from
perdition and shows piety towards God ; whilst the choice of
the worse is perdition to man and an offence towards God.'[5]

The body is a filthy garment, a prop of evil, a bond of corruption, a living death, an animate corpse, a robber in the house.[6]

[1] Similarly, data from magical incantations and astrological formulæ are
employed by Bousset, Reitzenstein, and Dieterich to make up a 'theology'
of the mysteries (infra, pp. 53, 54).   In general, Dr. A. E. J. Rawlinson's
criticism of this procedure (New Testament Doctrine of the Christ, pp. 67, 68)
is essentially valid.
[2] Corp. Herm., i, 24-26 (Scott, i, pp. 126-128).   In quoting from Scott's
text throughout, I have held myself free to ignore the many corrections
which—often with comparatively little justification—he has introduced.
His meticulous apparatus criticus makes it easy to see the MSS. text behind
his emendations.   I have not adhered to the exact words of Scott's translations.
[3] Ib., i, 3 (Scott, i, p. 115).
[4] Stobaeus, Ecl., i, 41, 1 (Scott, i, p. 428).
[5] Corp. Herm., iv, 6, 7 (Scott, i, pp. 152, 154).   Note also the 'intensely
pessimistic' document (Scott, ii, p. 169), Tractate vi, which insists that there
is nothing 'good' in either the world or man ; what is called 'good' being
merely 'that which is not evil beyond measure' (§ 3).
[6] Ib., vii, 2 (Scott, i, p. 172).   For this sôma-sêma thought, cp. supra,
p. 41 ; and Scott, ii, p. 186.

Although few if any detailed ascetic precepts are given,[1] the general tone of the tracts lends itself more readily to rigorism than to humanism. Congruous with this is a second characteristic. It will appear in later chapters that in so far as ascetic precepts—doctrines of self-mortification and world-flight—are based upon the philosophical presupposition that nature and its phenomena are evil, God—if He is to be found at all—will be found in the unnatural, the extraordinary, the abnormal. This also at times is a Hermetic doctrine ; prior to receiving the vision the worshipper must look for God not in the ordinary processes of nature, but in ' dreams at night and signs in the daytime—in divination by the flight of birds and the entrails of beasts, in inspiration, in the (whispering of) the oak trees.' [2]

Very often, however, there are passages of real beauty, in which all creation is spoken of as giving its witness to God. ' The world is not indeed evil, though it is not as good as God is.' [3] ' It is not difficult, my son,' one writer says,[4]

> ' to contemplate God in thought, or even to see Him. Look at the arrangement of the universe and its orderliness. Look at the necessity which governs all that is presented to our sight, and the providence shown in what has been and in what came to be. Look at the material world filled to the brim with life, and see this great God in movement in all things—in all fair and noble gods and spirits and men. . . . '

' Is God in matter, then, father ? ' asks the disciple ; and the answer runs, ' Why, what is matter, my son, that you should assign a place to it (apart from God) ? . . . This God, my son, I bid you worship and adore. And there is but one way to worship God—to abstain from evil.'

Similar in intention is the following passage :—[5]

> ' Think that for you nothing is impossible. Deem that you too are immortal and that you are able to grasp all things in your thought, to know every craft and way of science. Find your home in the haunts of every living creature. Make yourself higher than all heights and lower than all depths. . . . Think that you are not yet begotten, that you are in the womb, that you are young, that you are old, that you are dead, that you are beyond the grave. Grasp in your mind all this at once—all times and places, all substances and qualities and magnitudes together ; then you can apprehend God. But if you shut up your soul in your body, and abase yourself, and say, ' I know nothing, I can do nothing ; I am afraid of earth

[1] Cp. J. Kroll, *Die Lehren des Hermes Trismegistus*, p. 348.
[2] *Corp. Herm.*, xii (ii), 19 (Scott, i, p. 234) ; cp. *infra*, pp. 213, 214.
[3] *Ib.*, x, 10 (Scott, i, p. 194).
[4] *Ib.*, xii (ii), 21, 22 (Scott, i, p. 236).
[5] *Ib.*, xi (ii), 20 ff. (Scott, i, pp. 220, 222).

and sea, I cannot mount to heaven ; I know not what I was nor what I shall be '—then what have you to do with God ? . . . It is the height of evil not to know God ; but to be capable of knowing Him, to wish and hope to know Him, is the road which leads straight to the good. It is an easy road to travel. Everywhere God will come to meet you. Everywhere He will appear to you—at places and times at which you look not for it ; in your waking hours and in your sleep, when you journey by water and by land, in the night-time and in the day-time, when you are speaking and when you are silent. For there is nothing which is not God. And do you say God is invisible ? Speak not so. . . .—Who is more manifest than God ? For this very purpose has He made all things, that through all things you may see Him. This is God's goodness, this His clemency, that He manifests Himself in all things.' [1]

From the beginning to end of the ' Corpus ' purity of heart and moral rectitude are represented as essential conditions of seeing God. ' Like can only be seen by like,' therefore we must ' become equal ' with God :—[2]

> ' There is but one way to worship God, my son, and it is to be devoid of evil.' [3] ' [If you would be born again], you must cleanse yourself from the irrational torments of matter . . . ignorance, incontinent desires, injustice, covetousness, deceitfulness, envy, fraud, rashness, vice. . . . When God has had mercy on a man all these depart from him, and thus is the Rebirth accomplished. Then is reason built up in you, cleansed by the power of God—knowledge of God has come, joy, continence, endurance, justice, unselfishness, truth.' [4]

Self-knowledge is the first step towards knowledge of God,[5] for without self-knowledge progress is impossible. In a passage reminiscent both of Plato's ' Republic ' and of the psalmists, but still more of the New Testament, a Hermetic writer discerns the deep truth that the goodness which characterizes those alone who see God must bring upon them the hatred of the evil-disposed. ' To be righteous is to see God . . . but those who have the vision

---

[1] Scott, in his important and illuminating note on this passage (ii, pp. 303-305), does less than justice to the writer. ' He has nothing to say,' he insists, ' about the brotherhood of man, or the love of one's neighbour. For him, as for most of the Hermetists, human society hardly exists, and the only human relation recognized is that between teacher and pupil. The individual man stands solitary, face to face with the universe at large.' But surely the instructions to identify oneself in mind with ' the babe, the young and the old ' imply a doctrine of sympathy with mankind ?

[2] *Corp. Herm.*, xi (ii), 20*b* (Scott, i, p. 220).
[3] *Ib.*, xii (ii), 23 (Scott, i, p. 238).
[4] *Ib.*, xiii, 7 ff. (compressed) (Scott, i, pp. 242, 244).
[5] *Ib.*, i, 19, 21 (Scott, i, p. 124).

are called mad and laughed at—hated, despised, and put to death.'[1]
For so arduous a journey towards God the prelude must be a
rebirth; 'no one can be saved until he has been born again.'[2]
In a highly allegorical passage this experience is spoken of in terms
which seem to imply some knowledge of the Christian rite of baptism. The soul is bathed in a spiritual laver;[3] and a heavenly
messenger proclaims, 'Wash yourselves in this laver if ye can'
(or perhaps 'will'), 'believing that ye shall ascend to Him from
Whom it came.'[4] Occasional passages of a pessimistic kind suggest
that the vision of God is not possible in this life, even to such reborn
souls. It is when the soul after death has entered the eighth and
highest sphere of the heavens—and not till then—that it

> 'sings together with those who dwell there, hymning the
> Father . . . and with them in turn mounts up to the Father,
> giving itself up to the Powers and itself becoming a Power, and
> so enters into God.'[5]

But in general the tone of the Hermetists, like that of Philo, is
optimistic. 'Man is more immortal' (i.e. as Scott[6] suggests,
'divine') 'than aught else that lives, for he can receive God and
hold intercourse with God.'[7] Even in this life, after receiving the
vision, he can be, 'in comparison with others, as an immortal God
in comparison with mortal man.'[8] For the vision of God 'has
a power of its own, it takes possession of those who have caught
a glimpse of it, and draws them on as a magnet draws iron.'[9]
The vision itself is commonly accompanied by ecstatic experiences.[10] 'He who has apprehended the beauty of the Good can
apprehend nothing else,' we are told,—

---

[1] *Corp. Herm.*, ix, 4a (Scott, i, p. 180).
[2] *Ib.*, xiii, 1 (Scott, i, p. 238). Cp. Jn. 3³. Scott (ii, p. 373) gives an
exhaustive list of the periphrases for 'rebirth' in the Hermetists. For the
conception in contemporary paganism cp. Dieterich, *Eine Mithras-Liturgie*³,
pp. 135 ff., 162 f., 166; Reitzenstein, *HMR.*, pp. 40, 262 f.
[3] *Ib.*, iv, 4 (Scott, i, p. 150).
[4] *Ib.* Scott (ii, p. 143), rightly rejecting Reitzenstein's view of the importance of 'baptisms' in the mystery cults, is nevertheless guilty of slight
perversity in refusing to see any idea of 'consecration' ('initiation') in this
passage.
[5] *Ib.*, i, 26 (Scott, i, p. 128). Scott (ii, pp. 238, 241) reads the same doctrine into x, 4b, 6; but wrongly (*infra*, pp. 51, n. 1; 52, n. 1).
[6] Scott, ii, p. 364. The writer has just said that all things are in a sense
immortal.
[7] *Corp. Herm.*, xii (ii), 18 (Scott, i, p. 234).
[8] *Ib.*, iv, 5 (Scott, i, p. 152).
[9] *Ib.*, iv, 11 (Scott, i, p. 156).
[10] On the ecstatic as a sign of communion with God, *supra*, pp. 15, 19, 44,
infra, pp. 104, 195 ff., 373 ff.; and generally cp. Rohde, *op. cit.*, pp. 255, 259,
270 (n. 24), 274, 275 (nn. 46-52), 316 (n. 63), 328 (n. 109); Halliday, *op. cit.*,
pp. 270, 271; Reitzenstein, *HMR.*, pp. 289, 290; *Poimandres*, pp. 200-206;
Dieterich, *op. cit.*, p. 98; W. James, *Varieties of Religious Experience*,
pp. 379-422; R. H. Thouless, *Psychology of Religion*, pp. 230-232, 249-251.

' he who has seen it can see naught else ; he cannot hear speech
of any other matter. He cannot move his limbs at all ; he
forgets all bodily sensations and movements, and is still. But
the beauty of the good bathes his mind in light, and takes all
his soul up to itself, and draws it out from the body and
changes the whole man into [true] being. For a soul may
not become divine while it abides in a human body ; it
must [be drawn out of the body in ecstasy and so] behold
God, and therewith become divine.' [1]

In two tractates a dramatic attempt is made to express the
emotions of the actual moment of vision. The first of these is
frankly ecstatic. ' Father,' the disciple cries,—

' God has given me a new being,[2] and I perceive things now not
with bodily eyesight but by the working of the mind. I am
in heaven and in earth, in water and in air ; I am in beasts and
plants. I am a babe in the womb, and one that is not yet
conceived, and one that has been born ; I am present
everywhere. Father, I see the whole, and myself in the Mind.'

The teacher recognizes in these experiences the authentic signs
of the vision. ' This is the Rebirth, my son, no longer to see with
tri-dimensional limitations . . .,' he replies ; ' you have become
a God, and the son of the One, as I am.' [3]

In another tractate,[4] however, remarkable both for its psychological insight and its religious tone, ecstasy is treated as emphatically *not* the test of the vision. ' Father,' the disciple cries once
more, ' you have given me my fill of this good and most beautiful
sight ; and my mind's eye is almost blinded by the splendour of
the vision.' The teacher remains unmoved. ' Nay,' he says,—

' the vision of God is not a thing of fire, as are the sun's rays.
It does not blaze down upon us, and force us to close our eyes.
It shines forth much or little according as he who gazes on it
is able to receive the inflow. . . . It cannot harm us, it is
full of all immortal life. Even those, who are able to imbibe
somewhat more of that vision than others can, are again and
again lulled into blind sleep by the body ; but anon they attain
to the full fruition of that most lovely sight, as did Uranos and
Cronos, our ancestors. . . . For the moment we are too weak

[1] *Corp. Herm.*, x, 6 (Scott, i, p. 190). The text is corrupt, but although
Reitzenstein (*HMR.*, p. 289) emends differently, he reaches the same sense
as Scott. There is no need to suggest, as Scott does (ii, pp. 238, 241, 242),
that the reference here is to death rather than to ecstasy (*infra*, p. 52, n. 1).

[2] So Scott, i, p. 246 ; but the text is corrupt, and we should probably
render (with Reitzenstein, *Poimandres*, p. 343), ' God has given me stedfastness.'

[3] *Corp. Herm.*, xiii, 11-14 (Scott, i, pp. 246, 248 ; Reitzenstein, *Poimandres*, pp. 344, 345).

[4] *Ib.*, x, 4*b*, 5 (Scott, i, pp. 188, 190).

to see that sight, and we have not strength to open our mortal eyes and to behold the beauty of the good, that incorruptible beauty which no tongue can tell.' [1]

There are two suggestions here which—as will appear at a later stage—are of exceptional importance for any doctrine of the vision of God.   The first is, that it is continuous (though not identical) with normal experiences—proportioned, as we may say, to natural insight and development.   The second is, that it is not indefectible, but intermittent ; it carries with it no certainty of irresistible grace.   Of both these principles we shall have to speak again.

Several of the passages just quoted are instances of one of the most significant features in the Hermetic texts ; a feature which, whilst not absolutely new, receives an emphasis unequalled in any other of the writings we have reviewed.   Celsus [2] knew of impostors who claimed to be ' God or the son of God ' ; Simon Magus, in New Testament history, may have made such a claim.[3]   With the Hermetists the claim becomes a commonplace.   The famous phrase, ' Thou hast deified us by the vision,' is now admitted by its discoverer to depend upon a mistaken reading of the original ; [4] but

[1] The train of thought is difficult, for after a transitional sentence (' Then only will you see it, when you cannot speak of it ; for the knowledge of it is deep silence, and suppression of the senses ') the passage goes on to the ' ecstatic ' description (§ 6) quoted above, pp. 50 f., (' He who has apprehended,' etc.).   It would appear that the pupil has experienced an emotional crisis which he wrongly supposes to be the vision ; the teacher warns him of his mistake, pointing out that the vision is not commonly vouchsafed to beginners in full measure, but as they are able to receive it ; and then goes on to describe the full experience of the faithful soul, which has learnt to overcome the soporific influences of the body.—The reference to Uranos and Cronos is, of course, to deification.   Scott, by taking this as a reference to death, making νῦν δε mean ' in this life,' inserting without warrant ἀπολύθεντες τοῦ σώματος in § 5, and insisting that the poetic description of ecstasy in § 6 must be a prosaic description of a corpse (' can see nothing else,' etc.), infers the doctrine that the vision is only possible after death.   But this is forced and unnecessary.

[2] Origen, c. Cels., vii, 9 ; cp. generally A. D. Nock in Essays on the Trinity and Incarnation, p. 97 ; A. E. J. Rawlinson, New Testament Doctrine of the Christ, p. 70 ; E. Underhill, Mysticism, pp. 500-509 ; G. P. Wetter, ' Der Sohn Gottes,' p. 4, et pass. ; Reitzenstein, HMR., pp. 262-265, 312-316, Poimandres, pp. 222 ff. ; E. Norden, Agnostos Theos, pp. 188 ff. ; W. Bauer on Jn. 1[34] in HNT., vi, pp. 34, 35 ; A. Dieterich, Eine Mithras-Liturgie, pp. 157 ff.

[3] Justin, Apology, i, 26—' After Christ's ascension into heaven the devil put forward certain men who said that they themselves were gods . . . such as was the Samaritan, Simon.'   Further references, Wetter, op. cit., pp. 6, 8, etc., and generally E. Meyer, Ursprung u. Anfänge des Christentums, ii, pp. 278 ff.

[4] The phrase occurs in the conclusion of the Logos Teleios (' Asclepius '), as found in a Greek papyrus fragment, and first printed by Reitzenstein (ARW., vii, p. 393 ; HMR. (first edition, p. 114) in the form ἐν σώμασιν ἡμᾶς ὄντας ἀπεθέωσας τῇ σεαυτοῦ θέᾳ (so quoted by Bousset, KC., pp. 166, 343).   The last word, however, was purely conjectural, as Reitzenstein now admits (HMR.[3], p. 286) ; he now reads χάριτι ; Eitrem, δυνάμει or θελήσει ; Scott suggests αἰωνιότητι or αἰωνίῳ ζωῇ.   Scott's suggestions are nearest the Latin version, but too long for the lacuna in the papyrus (Scott, i, pp. 376, 377 iii, p. 292).

many other examples remain. ' He that is born by that birth is another (person) ; he is a god and son of God ' ;[1] ' This is the good end for them that have gnosis, to become divine.'[2] ' Wherewith shall I sing to Thee ? ' cries the soul that has seen God, ' Am I my own or have I anything of my own ? Am I other than Thou ? Thou art whatsoever I am, and whatsoever I say.'[3] Reitzenstein, Bousset and Johannes Weiss have been at pains to show that this audacious and indeed blasphemous thought is not confined to the Hermetic texts. Magical fragments dating from the same period illustrate the same tenet. ' Come to me, Lord Hermes, as babes to their mothers' wombs,' is an example frequently quoted ; and when the prayer is answered the suppliant can say, ' I know Thee, Hermes ; and thou knowest me. I am thou and thou art I. . . . Thy name is mine and mine is thine ; I am thy image.'[4] He is now ' armed with a magic soul ' and has ' a nature equal to God's.'[5] A prayer for an infant runs : ' Come into the soul of this child, that it may be moulded into (thine) immortal form in strong imperishable light.'[6] In reproducing this sentiment, the Hermetists show themselves children of their own time ; but they show also that no phrase seemed to them too exaggerated to express the richness of their spiritual experience.

.   .   .   .

It would be possible to trace the desire for the vision of God and the conviction of its possibility back from the many writers, Jewish and pagan, whom we have considered, to far more primitive sources—back, for example, as Graf-Baudissin[7] has traced it, to Babylonian, Accadian, and Egyptian ancestry—back, further still,

---

[1] *Corp. Herm.*, xiii, 2 (Scott, i, p. 240).

[2] *Ib.*, i, 26 (Scott, i, p. 128). Scott quite wilfully brackets the last word θεωθῆναι.

[3] *Ib.*, v, 11 (Scott, i, p. 164). On the Hermetic doctrine of the *natural* divinity of all men (*theoi thnêtoi*), J. Kroll, *Die Lehren des Hermes Trismegistos*, pp. 317 ff.

[4] Reitzenstein, *Poimandres*, pp. 20, 21 (from Kenyon, *Greek Papyri*, i, p. 116).

[5] Reitzenstein, *HMR.*, p. 187 (from Wessely, *Denkschrift d. Wiener Akademie* (1888), pp. 48 ff.).

[6] *HMR.*, pp. 44, 45 (from Kenyon, *op. cit.*, i, p. 102). Cp. also the prayer from the Leyden papyrus, *Poimandres*, pp. 15-17—' Come to me from the four winds, O Almighty One, that hast breathed spirit into men to life. . . . Come into my mind and my intelligence for the whole span of my life, and fulfil every wish of my heart. For Thou art I, and I am Thou; whatever I say, let it be fulfilled. For I have thy name as an amulet in my heart . . . '; *ib.*, p. 19, an incantation (from Wessely), ' I command thee, enter into me, and show me concerning such-an-one.' Further (gnostic) examples, *HMR.*, p. 291 ; cp. also the ' Mithras-liturgy,' *infra*, pp. 473 ff., and Dieterich, *Eine Mithras-Liturgie*, p. 240 ; neo-Platonic, H. Koch, *Pseudo-Dionysius Areopagita*, pp. 190 ff.

[7] *ARW.*, xviii (1915), pp. 173 ff. ; cp. also Fr. Nötscher, ' *Das Angesicht Gottes Schauen*,' esp. pp. 62 ff. On pp. 80 ff., Nötscher collects the evidence for the employment of the idea in Accadian proper names, e.g. ' May-I-see-Bêl-in-his-temple,' ' I-shall-see-Bêl,' etc. A general review of the idea of ' seeing God ' in ethnic religions, Dieterich, *op. cit.*, p. 408.

to the desert-storms and lightning flashes in which Semitic nomads thought to recognize the appearance of their deity; or to the most elementary notions of traffic with the divine through dreams and trances which present themselves in ethnic religion. But the passages already reviewed suffice to exhibit the bewildering divergences of theology and ethics which accompany the doctrine of the beatific vision in its more representative forms. Little would be gained by exploring non-Christian examples further. We cannot, of course, accept at their face value each and all of the witnesses who have come before us. The most generous appreciation of Philo, or the apocalyptists, or the mysteries, or the ' Hermetica,' must admit that here and there at least they may have been the victims of illusion—it was not always God with whom they had communion, when they thought they saw Him. Sometimes (again to say the least) they may have been misled by pathological obsessions or by diseased fancies of their own ; sometimes they merely reproduce the conventional jargon of contemporary theosophies ; sometimes their apprehension of God may have been distorted by unworthy thoughts about Him, by a mistaken method of approach, or—worst of all—by unclean living. We shall be in a better position to estimate the respective worth of different types of thought about the vision and the road which leads to it, as we learn more of the history of the doctrine in its Christian development.

What is clear so far is that Christianity came into a world tantalized with the belief that some men at least had seen God, and had found in the vision the sum of human happiness ; a world aching with the hope that the same vision was attainable by all. Men came into the Church assured that there, if anywhere, they would ' see God ' ; and they brought with them all the diverse conceptions of theology and conduct with which the thought was invested in non-Christian circles. Their quest was primarily a selfish one ; their motive to secure for themselves, either here or hereafter, an all-absorbing religious experience. For reasons which will become clearer as we proceed, the Church undertook the amazing task of transforming this self-centred cult of the divine into an ideal of disinterested worship and service. In doing so, she altered the entire emphasis of the doctrine of the vision of God ; but the doctrine itself—purified, ennobled, and brought into coherence— was too precious to be thrown aside. Thus the stage was set for a new and epoch-making development of religion and ethics, in which these various conceptions and experiences of pre-Christian pioneers should influence the distinctively Christian ethos and inheritance, and by them be influenced in turn ; and the end of that development is not yet in sight.

LECTURE II.

THE NEW TESTAMENT.

2 Cor. iv. 6—' It is God, that said *Light shall shine out of darkness*, Who shined in our hearts to give the light of the knowledge of the glory of God, in the face of Jesus Christ.'

I. Rigorism and Eschatology in the Teaching of Jesus.

NEW Testament theology has scarcely as yet recovered from the shock administered to it by Johannes Weiss and Albert Schweitzer some twenty-five to thirty years ago.[1] The normal interpretation of the life and teaching of our Lord was at that time stereotyped in a convention whose complacent self-sufficiency it is easy enough now to decry and to condemn, though in its day it exercised a curiously specious fascination. The message of the gospel—so theologians persuaded themselves—was to all intents and purposes identical with that of nineteenth century civilization; a message of hard work, good fellowship, self-realization, and general kindliness;—a *humanist*[2] message in fact. The duty of the Christian was to surround himself with an aura of tact and generosity, and so to make the lives of his less fortunate neighbours run more smoothly. As with the message, so also with the person of the Redeemer—it found its significance primarily as manifesting in actual fact the life thus adumbrated in the gospel. In England, so much stress had been laid on the Incarnation, as sanctifying all the common things of life, that the Cross, in which they are all renounced, was in danger of being forgotten. For Germany, Harnack's " What is Christianity? " is evidence enough of the dominant mode of thought.

Against this whole theological outlook, with its this-worldly interpretation of the gospel and its humanitarian Jesus, Weiss and

---

[1] J. Weiss, *Die Predigt Jesu vom Reiche Gottes*, 1892, 2nd edition, 1900 ; A. Schweitzer, *Von Reimarus zu Wrede*, 1906 (E. tr., *The Quest of the Historical Jesus*, W. Montgomery, 1910) ; 2nd edition, *Geschichte der Leben-Jesu-Forschung*, 1913. Dr. F. A. M. Spencer has cited a number of long passages from Weiss (in translation) in his *Theory of Christ's Ethics*, pp. 31-35, which give a fair indication of the scope and tenour of the original. Dr. Spencer himself advances the interesting theory that our Lord's teaching was originally humanist, but that He abandoned it first for a ' redemptive ' and then for an ' apocalyptic ' message (*op. cit.*, p. 44) because ' the world refused to pay heed ' (p. 41). I doubt if this theory recognizes the rigorist element in our Lord's teaching as fully as it deserves.

[2] *Supra*, p. 7.

Schweitzer declared war. The lines of their attack are well known. They insisted primarily upon the ' eschatological fixed idea ' [1] of Jesus,—His apparently constant expectation of an apocalyptic coming of the kingdom of God either in His own lifetime, or (this perhaps at a later stage of His ministry) immediately after His death—the death itself being the means of releasing the pent-up forces of salvation. They insisted, secondly, upon the element of rigorism, renunciation, and self-crucifixion in our Lord's teaching. Weiss underlines this rigorist element to such an extent as to exclude from the gospel-message everything of a different character. ' The transcendental character of Jesus' expectation,' he writes, [2]

' consists precisely in this—that the state and all other earthly institutions, conditions and benefits, as belonging to the present age, shall either not exist at all in the coming kingdom, or shall exist only in a sublimated form. Hence Jesus cannot preach a special ethic of the kingdom of God, but only an ethic which in this world makes man free from the world and prepared to enter into the kingdom. That is why His ethic is of so completely negative a character ; it is, in fact, not so much an ethic as a penitential discipline.'

Schweitzer is at once more fair-minded and more subtle. He recognizes in the teaching of our Lord what Weiss had ignored—an element which set apparent store by earthly well-being, human relationships, and civic order. But he denies to it anything approaching its face-value. The current estimate of this world and its benefits, he suggested, was from time to time adopted by Jesus simply and solely because He had reached in their regard a condition of such complete indifference, such Stoic apathy, that He was not concerned even to correct the misapprehensions of His contemporaries. The paradox is driven home with full consciousness of its gravity. In Jesus' teaching, asks Schweitzer,—

' are not earthly goods emptied of any essential value, in such a way that joy in the world and indifference to the world were simply the final expression of an ironic attitude which had been sublimated into pure serenity ? ' [3] ' His acceptance of the world is but the last expression of the completeness with which He rejects it.' [4]

---

[1] A. Schweitzer, *op. cit.* (E. tr.), p. 300, n. All quotations are from this translation.

[2] Summarized, Schweitzer, p. 239.

[3] *Ib.*, p. 247. The German runs :—' Ob diese nicht an sich entwertet werden so, dass Weltfreudigkeit und Weltsorglosigkeit nur die Errungenschaft einer zur reiner Heiterkeit hindurchgedrungenen Ironie sind.'

[4] *Ib.*, p. 248 ; similarly, p. 247—' All present goods serve only to support life and render possible an undistracted attitude of waiting in pious hope . . . and are therefore not thought of as *gains* ' (if they are thought of in any other way than as hindrances) ' but purely as a gift of God to be cheerfully and freely enjoyed as a foretaste of those blessings which the elect are to enjoy in the future divine dispensation.'

That this is the true point of view Schweitzer attempts to substantiate by the assertion that ' it has at its disposal inexhaustible reserves of world-renouncing, world-contemning sayings ; whilst the few utterances, which might possibly be interpreted as expressing a purely positive joy in the world, desert and go over to the enemy, because they textually and logically belong to the other set of sayings.' [1] Schweitzer will not even accept Bousset's mitigated doctrine that ' for Jesus this world's goods are not evil, but are only to be given a secondary place.' [2] ' The teaching of the historical Jesus,' he concludes, ' was purely and exclusively world-renouncing.' [3]

We noticed at an earlier stage that in the history of Christian ethics the phenomenon of *rigorism*,—the ideal of a consistent renunciation not merely of the ways of the world but of the joys and interests and ideals of the world as well (however innocent and laudable in themselves they may appear to be),—is of primary importance and difficulty. It is the merit of Weiss and Schweitzer, whatever their defects, to have brought theology back to the consciousness that this problem lies enshrined in all its fullness in the heart of Jesus' teaching. The Son of Man shall come as a householder, no doubt ; and to the householder it is of importance that every talent he has left behind him should have been put out to use, and every servant supplied with nurture fitted to his needs. But He shall come as a reaper as well ; and the reaper cares little what he destroys so that the grain be gathered in—the beauty of the fields is nothing to him, and vanishes with the coming of sickle, fan and fire. The world-accepting principles of Jesus are easy for us to embody in our code ; the stark element of world-renunciation is supremely difficult, and we are only too ready to make shift with any expedient that will eliminate it. What has been gained for theology by the German eschatological school of enquiry is the general sense that renunciation, if it is to be eliminated from Christianity at all, cannot be eliminated from the historic teaching of the Lord.

It is not altogether clear at first sight why Schweitzer should bring the apocalyptic and the rigorist elements in our Lord's teaching into such close relationship. Sometimes he suggests that self-humiliation and self-denial are, in Jesus' mind, attributes so pleasing to God, that none but those who have practised them are worthy of a place in the kingdom.[4] At other times it would appear that asceticism of this character, with the voluntary seeking out and

---

[1] Schweitzer, *op. cit.*, p. 247—similarly (p. 248) Schweitzer explains away all passages which speak of the kingdom as already present.

[2] *Ib.*, p. 247.   [3] *Ib.*, p. 249.

[4] *Op. cit.*, p. 364—' For the loftier stations ' in the kingdom of God ' it is necessary to have proved oneself in persecution and suffering ' ; similarly, p. 353 (where, incidentally, Schweitzer would reject the words ' are worthy of ' in the text above)—' In their being poor in spirit, in their meekness, in their love of peace, it is made manifest that they are predestined to the kingdom.'

enduring of tribulation and martyrdom on the part of Jesus and
His disciples, were thought of as the ' Messianic woes ' which would
usher in the kingdom.[1]   In general, however, the relation seems
to be treated as something deeper still.   It is of the essence of
apocalyptic to despair of this world's order—to think that even
the things that are best in it, its highest ideals, its noblest impulses,
are dross and dust in the sight of God.   For Him no course is
possible except to sweep away all that exists, and introduce a new
world wholly other from that which now is.   And therefore (we
should suppose) those who would inherit the new world must
dissociate themselves entirely from the present one, adopting an
attitude of uncompromising hostility towards the body, the mind,
the emotions,—towards all that cements or beautifies social intercourse,—and pinning their hope wholly and entirely upon the kingdom which by the unmediated and catastrophic activity of God is
soon to be.[2]

This can be put more simply, if we say that both apocalyptic
and asceticism are *dualist* in tone, and that it is natural therefore to
expect to find them in conjunction. ' Dualism ' is without doubt
a word more easy to use than to expound.[3] It expresses a *temper*,
rather than a principle of thought ; the temper which is prepared
to acquiesce in the apparent contradictions of experience as though
they were ultimate and insuperable.   Contrasted with it are two
other tempers—the ' monistic,' if we may be allowed the word,
which is prepared to ignore, if not to deny, the contradictions
altogether in the interests of unity ; and the ' synthetic,' which
recognizes the contradictions as such, and yet cannot rest happy
so long as they are unreconciled.   God and the universe, mind and
matter, the one and the many, good and evil, soul and body,
eternity and time, freedom and order—these are some of the
antinomies presented to us in experience.   Dualism says, ' Let it
be so ; we cannot reconcile them ; we must find the best escape
from a problem which has no solution.   Good and evil, mind and
matter, God and the universe, soul and body—there is no common
term in any of these pairs of antitheses.   Matter and mind cannot
in the end coexist ; the universe is incapable of redemption.   If
mind is to survive, it must escape from matter ; if God is to
survive, the universe must perish ; if the soul is to see God, the
body must be annihilated.'

Wherever, then, we find a doctrine of anything *irredeemable*—
anything which has to be swept away before God's purposes can be

---

[1] *Op. cit.*, pp. 370, 386 f.   Cp. also the same writer's *Mystery of the
Kingdom, pass.*, especially pp. 74-76, 97-104.

[2] Criticism has rightly fastened upon this point as the central one in
Schweitzer's theory ; but he does not emphasize it as much as might be
expected.   Thus, though he employs the phrase ' interimsethik ' on pp. 352,
364 (E. tr.), the remark (p. 247), ' Jesus' attitude towards earthly goods
was wholly conditioned by eschatology,' may perfectly well apply to the
theories mentioned in the preceding notes.

[3] Cp. *infra*, p. 212, n. 3.

secured—we are in the presence of dualistic thought. On such a basis apocalyptic, with its despair of the existing world-order, is dualist beyond a doubt. Wherever, again, the earnest-minded seeker after God is found expressing relentless opposition towards whole classes of phenomena, interests, and worldly goods as such, and not merely towards the possibility of their misuse—wherever, in fact, ascetic rigorism is regarded as the only mode of salvation —there is to be seen dualism in practice.[1] We have therefore a perfect logical right to expect apocalyptic imagery and ascetic practices to go hand in hand—nothing could very well be more natural or appropriate. So Schweitzer seems to understand the situation. In his view, each of these two elements in our Lord's message reinforces the other, by pointing back to the dualist basis common to them both. Nothing is allowed to mar the seamless robe of the Saviour's teaching : it is coherent—and coherent in a rigorist sense—in all its parts.

Nevertheless, as applied at least to the Jewish background of the teaching of Jesus, the suggested systematization breaks down. In this matter, as in so many others, religion refused to be bound by logic. In the whole range of Jewish apocalyptic there is little or nothing of an ascetic character. Once or twice ascetic practices are mentioned as the condition of the apocalyptic trance ; it is because of his continence that ' Ezra ' is vouchsafed his vision,[2] and ' Enoch ' receives his manifestations before marriage.[3] In the ' Martyrdom of Isaiah ' [4] the prophet and his companions retire to the wilderness naked, or clothed at best with garments of hair, and eat nothing but wild herbs. But this, again, appears to be no more than self-discipline for the sake of revelations. John the Baptist, it is commonly supposed, led an ascetic life and revived the expectations of apocalyptic. This, however, is the picture of S. Mark's gospel alone (followed by S. Matthew) ; our other authorities water down any such connexion as there may have been between the two facts. In S. Luke,[5] John's teaching to the soldiers

---

[1] It seems scarcely necessary at this point to emphasize the fact that the idea of asceticism as self-training—the harmonizing of instincts rather than their extirpation—is not in any sense dualistic ; otherwise all asceticism would have to be condemned *sans phrase*. Dualist and non-dualist asceticism may look exactly the same in outward appearance. It is only by considering the system of thought, as a whole, to which any set of ascetic practices belongs that we have a sound basis for criticism. Thus our main question is, How far does the genuinely *Christian* system of thought require asceticism, and to what end ?

[2] 2 (4) Ezra 6^{32} (probably about A.D. 100).

[3] 1 Enoch 83^2. But Charles (*ad loc.*) notices the curious fact that, although these *dreams* occurred before marriage, the *bodily translations* apparently took place afterwards. The absurdity is probably due to editorial oversight. Chapter 108, with its praise of those ' who love God and loved neither gold nor silver nor any of the good things which are in the world, but gave over their bodies to torture ; who, since they came into being, longed not after earthly food, but regarded everything as a passing breath, and lived accordingly,' is a later (? Essene) addition.

[4] Mart. Is. 2$^{10, 11}$ (first century A.D.). [5] Lk. 4$^{10-14}$.

and the publicans assumes the unbreaking continuance of the present world-order ; Josephus [1] does not emphasize the asceticism of the Baptist and his followers, and takes no notice at all of any eschatological element in his teaching. The Essenes [2] and Therapeutæ [3] undoubtedly practised asceticism of a perhaps not very

---

[1] *Ant.*, xviii, 5, 2 (Whiston—' He commanded the Jews to exercise virtue both as to justice toward one another, and piety towards God, and so to come to baptism '). The word translated ' exercise ' (ἐπασκοῦσι) *might* refer to ascetic practices, but John would hardly have exhorted the Jews as a whole to these. If ἀλλῶν (so most MSS.) is read three lines later, the passage implies an antithesis between the original hearers (perhaps the ascetic sect) and a later audience ; but one MSS. reads λαῶν, and the Latin *per-plurima multitudo*, and Niese suggests ἀνθρώπων, all of which readings eliminate the antithesis. In any case, the reference is very slight, and nothing is said either of asceticism or eschatology in connexion with John himself. The (presumably) spurious Slavonic version of the *Jewish War* (summarized H. St. J. Thackeray, *Selections from Josephus*, p. 189 ; translated K. Lake and F. J. Foakes-Jackson, *Beginnings of Christianity*, part i, vol. i, pp. 433-435), on the other hand, adds numerous ascetic traits to the gospel account of John, but curiously enough brings him into conflict with the Essenes.

[2] The article ' Essener,' in Pauly-Wissowa, Supplement iv (1924), coll. 386-430, now supersedes earlier discussions ; but the accounts in J. B. Lightfoot, *Colossians*, pp. 347-417, and Bousset, *RJ.*, pp. 456 ff., are still very important. Cp. also *DALC.*, ii, coll. 3059-3063. Any estimate of the institutions and ideas of the Essenes must reckon with the fact that practically the only sources of information are Philo and Josephus ; the former strongly under the influence of hellenistic thought, the latter at all events a keen apologist for his people to the gentile world. They might both, therefore, have coloured (even if they did not exaggerate) the Essene asceticism to assimilate it to conventional philosophic deas and practices, and have watered down such apocalyptic eschatology, if any, as the Essenes accepted. Taking them as a whole, their *asceticism* showed itself in communism, simplicity of life, celibacy (though a branch of them allowed and even enjoined matrimony—Josephus, *BJ.*, ii, 160 f.), vegetarianism (this is a doubtful inference from *BJ.*, ii, 143, where we are told that their excommunicates, being bound by oath not to take food from any but members of their order, and having lost the privilege of communal support, attempted to sustain life by eating grass), a three-year novitiate, a solemn oath of admission, manual work, a daily ceremonial washing and a common (? sacramental) meal. The *purpose* of their asceticism has been variously interpreted (see esp. H. Strathmann, *Geschichte d. frühchrist. Askese*, i, pp. 91 ff.), as extreme Pharisaic formalism, as neo-Pythagorean preparation for immortality, as self-training for prophetic revelations, and as cult-asceticism, based on the old conception of a holy priesthood. The last seems most probable, especially if, with Bousset, we hold that for them the bath and religious meal took the place of the temple sacrifices, which they certainly eschewed (on the apparent contradiction between Philo and Josephus here see Lake and Foakes-Jackson, *Beginnings of Christianity*, I, i, p. 92). Their *eschatology* (*BJ.*, ii, 154-157) appears to have been a simple doctrine of the immortality of the soul, with rewards and punishments in the future life, but no apocalyptic features.

[3] The latest account of the Therapeutæ is Bousset, *RJ.*, pp. 465 ff. ; see also F. C. Conybeare, *Philo about the Contemplative Life* (1895), and *infra*, p. 491. Philo says they existed throughout the world, but especially in Egypt ; he calls their life ' contemplative ' as contrasted with the ' active ' life of the Essenes. Bousset (*loc. cit.*) has emphasized the differences between their mode of life and that of the Essenes perhaps unduly ; the principal features seem to have been that the Therapeutæ were less cœnobitic, and more addicted to study, than the Essenes. For our purposes we need not consider them further. Cp. also E. Meyer, *Ursprung u. Anfänge des Christentums*, ii, pp. 368-371.

advanced character, but they appear to have had no particular apocalyptic interests ; whilst of the doctrinal outlook of Bannus,[1] the strange hermit friend of Josephus, we know nothing. Only in the so-called Zadokite fragment from Damascus are asceticism and eschatology linked together ; but this document lies apart from the main stream of Judaism, and its asceticism is not strongly marked.[2] Bousset himself, who held as strongly as anyone the theory of the dependence of asceticism upon apocalyptic, found himself constrained to admit the predominantly non-ascetic character even of late Jewish ethics ; and apologized for it by the assertion that Judaism ' was not so dominated by the eschatological motive as was primitive Christianity.' [3]

Judaism, in fact, was too deeply committed to the doctrine of the goodness of all God's creation, and the divine authority for peopling the world and reaping the fruits of the earth, to admit any large element of asceticism or self-mortification into its constitution, even when it thought of the coming Day of the Lord. ' A man will have to give account on the judgment-day,' so ran a famous saying, ' of every good thing which he refused to enjoy when he might have done so.' [4] Poverty was regarded as the natural concomitant of sin, wealth of righteousness.[5] Fasts,[6] penitential

---

[1] Josephus, *Vita*, 2, where Bannus' ascetic life is described. Strathmann, p. 73, calls Bannus a ' unique phenomenon in Judaism,' but with Elijah and Elisha and the Baptist before him, this is absurd.

[2] See R. H. Charles, *Apocrypha and Pseudepigrapha*, ii, pp. 785 ff. (' Fragments of a Zadokite Work '), Lake and Foakes-Jackson, *op. cit.*, pp. 97-101 ; Bousset, *RJ.*, pp. 15, 16, and literature there cited. Beyond the fact that they kept a strict Sabbath-law, formed a closely-knit order, and called their quarters ' camps ' (' Fragment ' 9[1]) there is little enough to be said of them on the score of asceticism. They undoubtedly held very definite Messianic expectations. The fragment has affinities with the Book of Jubilees and the Testament of Levi, but neither of these works has any ascetic interest.

[3] Bousset, *RJ.*, p. 423 ; cp. p. 428.

[4] G. F. Moore, *Judaism*, ii, p. 265.

[5] Strathmann, *op. cit.*, pp. 25-29 :—another rabbinic saying : ' There is nothing worse than poverty in this world ; it is the worst of all evils.' Warnings against the *danger* and *worry* of riches are, of course, common, e.g. Prov. 15[16], 23[4, 5] ; I Enoch 94[8], 98[2, 3], 100[6], etc., but this is prudence, not asceticism. The normal view is given in the story of Jehuda (Strathmann, p. 28)—he sold half a field and gave the proceeds to a collection in support of the learned ; in ploughing the other half he came across a buried treasure. M. Hughes, *Ethics of Jewish Apocryphal Literature*, pp. 78 f., notices that a certain idealization of poverty emerges in the Pharisaic literature of the first century B.C. (e.g. the *Psalms of Solomon*), dating from the period when the Sadducees were generally rich and the Pharisees poor ; and this no doubt is reflected in the gospels, especially S. Luke (*infra*, p. 73).

[6] Cp. particularly the curious custom of ' fasting for rain ' to which some of the Rabbis were addicted ; particularly Onias, the Circle-Drawer, who marked a circle round himself and never left it till rain came in answer to his prayer. Even then he remained fasting within his circle until it fell at the rate at which he wanted it (Strathmann, p. 68). Fasting as an accompaniment of or preliminary to prayer was naturally very common. But R. Joshua thought any form of self-mortification a decline from virtue ; and explicitly condemned excessive prayer and fasting (*ib.*, p. 37 ; and cp. *Jewish Encyclopædia*, ii, pp. 166-168, *s.v.* ' Fasting ').

discipline, mourning customs, of course, there were; but even these were to be practised in moderation. The great disaster of the fall of Jerusalem might have seemed to call for unusual manifestations of grief; but even here optimism triumphed. Rabbi Joshua ben Chananja would not allow it to divert the ordinary course of life more than a hair's breadth. ' Whitewash your houses as before,' he said, ' leaving only a small piece bare, in memory of Jerusalem; prepare your meals as before, omitting just one slight dainty in memory of Jerusalem; let your women adorn themselves as before, leaving off just one trinket for Jerusalem's sake.' [1]

It was noticed as an extraordinary eccentricity of R. ben Azzai [2] that, although he taught that the man who neglected to beget children was dishonouring the image of God, he himself remained unmarried in order to be free for the undisturbed study of the law. His reply to Rabbi Eleazar's accusation of inconsistency is at best an apology which justifies only by pleading special circumstances. ' What shall I do ? ' he answered; ' My soul hangs upon the law; let others maintain the race.'

A further result of the prevalently world-accepting outlook of the Jews, which was peculiarly effective in preventing any intrusion of asceticism by the natural route of apocalyptic, was the doctrine of the resurrection of the body. The body, as created by God, is not a thing to be condemned. God shall redeem it, and the righteous shall enjoy bodily well-being in Paradise. But—if so—Paradise must be furnished with all that makes for bodily well-being. So far from being the utter antithesis of this present life, it represented the full realization of all that in this life men count good. Certain limitations to this conception were admitted; but the admissions were not made in the ascetic interest. It was a rabbinic commonplace, for example, that in the world to come there would be neither marrying nor giving in marriage, nor buying nor selling; [3] but the reasons of these restrictions are not far to seek. Once the Day of the Lord has come and the number of the elect is made up, history has reached its goal; and where there is no more history there can be no further place for the propagation of the species. Trade and commerce, again, are the exigencies of a world in which the goods of nature do not come unasked to the hand of every receiver; the profusion of the Messianic kingdom will be such that everyone can have his fill of good things without labour or organi-

---

[1] Strathmann, p. 35.

[2] Strack-Billerbeck, i, p. 807; though the exaltation of matrimony often went hand in hand with a very low estimate of women. E. Bevan, *Jerusalem under the High Priests*, pp. 62, 63, puts together the evidence from Ben Sira; Strathmann, pp. 17-24, gives rabbinic examples. Note particularly R. Jochanan—' There is only one Scripture which records that God spake to a woman (Sarah). He did indeed speak to Eve, but only to say, "I will greatly multiply thy sorrow"'; and R. Beri—' How much circumlocution must God endure when He hears the prayers even of a pious woman!' There is a slight emphasis on the virtue of continued widowhood in Judith 9[4], 16[22], which has its echo in Luke 2[38] f, 1 Tim. 5[9, 10].

[3] Strack-Billerbeck, i, p. 210.

zation. Super-terrestrial the joys of Paradise may be—non-terrestrial they emphatically are not; and with such an eschatology there is little ground for any strong movement towards asceticism.

It seems scarcely possible, therefore, to cite the eschatology of Judaism as a theological basis for the ascetic element in Jesus' teaching.[1] That the eschatological outlook influenced His ethics profoundly, we shall discover; [2] but the rigorist strain to be found there did not result from this influence. In so far as they suggested such a chain of causation, Weiss and Schweitzer spoke without the book. The conclusion is of the first importance, since it tends to increase rather than to diminish the urgency of the question which they raised. The ascetic outlook of the gospels is seen to stand out of any recognizable relation with contemporary Judaism. The passages about turning the other cheek, about taking no thought for the morrow, about laying up no treasure on earth, about forsaking parents and possessions, about bearing the cross, are foreign to the genius of the race.[3] The spirit which pervades them constitutes an erratic block in the teaching of Jesus whose provenance—other than in His direct intuition of supernatural truth—must for the moment remain unknown. And therefore we are finally prohibited from treating it, as many have been tempted to do, as a mere conventional borrowing of current ideas which can be discarded by the critic as soon as they are recognized.

Weiss and Schweitzer, in fact, rendered paramount service to the work of New Testament exegesis by their emphasis upon the

---

[1] The conclusion is put much more forcibly (but not more forcibly than it deserves) by R. Bultmann, one of the pioneers of the *formgeschichtliche* school of synoptic interpretation, but who also shows himself under the influence of the circle of ideas associated with the name of Karl Barth. In his remarkable study, *Jesus* (1926—one of a series entitled *Die Unsterblichen*), he says (p. 117): 'Social ideals and hopes could perfectly well be associated with eschatology; Jewish apocalyptic gives ample evidence of that.' Then, though recognizing to the full (*infra*, pp. 65 f.) the rigorist element in our Lord's teaching, he adds, 'Neither in His attack upon legalism nor in the demands of the Sermon on the Mount is any allusion made to the threat of a coming end of the world. . . . This is no *interimsethik*.' I doubt whether there is a single clear instance in the gospels of the association of world-renouncing ethics with eschatological teaching; certainly in one case of pronounced eschatology—the parable of the sheep and the goats—the ethical principles enunciated assume the excellence of temporal well-being in a very high degree.

[2] *Infra*, p. 142.

[3] Schweitzer is uneasily conscious of this, and so postulates (p. 366) that in 'the Baptist, Jesus and Paul' Jewish eschatology took a stride forward to its 'culminating manifestation.' *Op. cit.*, p. 246—'Jewish eschatology' is normally an 'effort of strongly eudæmonistic popular religion'; *ib.*, p. 366—'"Jewish eschatology" is an eschatology with a great gap in it . . . the true historian will describe the eschatology of the Baptist, of Jesus and of Paul in order to explain Jewish eschatology'; *ib.*, p. 368—with Jesus and the Baptist 'instead of literary artifice speaking out of a distant imaginary past, there now enter into the field of eschatology men—living, active men. It was the only time when that ever happened in Jewish eschatology.' There is much truth in this; but it does not account in the slightest for the emergence of other-worldliness in Jesus' teaching.

sterner sides of our Lord's thought.[1] Among the most characteristic sayings of Jesus are some at least which demand uncompromising renunciation of this life and its blessings. There is
indeed a distinction which must be drawn here. However much
the ascetic element is emphasized by Jesus, it is certainly not
generalized into any one unvarying rule of life for all. The rigorist
spirit, rather than specified ascetic *practices*, is the most He can
be said to have demanded of His contemporaries. But so much
He certainly demanded. We have already noticed a connexion
between this rigorist spirit and what we ventured to call the *evange-*
listic temper—the temper, that is to say, which classifies men remorselessly into the two groups of the saved and the lost ; which
ignores the *nuances* of character and the blending of good and bad
observable in nature, society, and man ; which calls for the abandonment of compromise, of diplomacy, of tolerance, of patience.
It is of the first significance that modern writers of the most diverse
points of view insist—even, as it may be thought, to an undue and
unjustified extent—on some such ' intolerance ' as integral to the
teaching of Jesus.

So, for example, though Bishop Gore reminds us that Jesus
did not proclaim ' asceticism as generally understood,'[2] and
qualifies his conclusion by the reminder that He was dealing primarily
with contemporary conditions as He found them, he speaks in no
uncertain terms of the character of the Lord's message. The
Sermon on the Mount, he says,

> ' is a proclamation of unworldliness in its extremest form. It
> is the poor, or those who have no care at all for wealth, those
> whose concessiveness or submissiveness to injustice knows
> no limit, and who have no desire for place or power or dis-
> tinction, and those who take up their burden of misery most
> readily, who are to enjoy the blessings of the kingdom. These
> negative characteristics—expressing an extreme renunciation
> of " the world " and all its normal desires—are constantly

---

[1] This is not the place at which to consider the problem created by the
apocalyptic element in our Lord's teaching. No doubt a certain amount of
it, perhaps a good deal, can be shown to be later accretion (cp. B. H. Streeter
in W. Sanday (ed.), *Oxford Studies in the Synoptic Problem*, pp. 425-426).
For the rest, Schweitzer is far from representing our Lord (as he is commonly supposed to do) as a deluded fanatic in this matter (see his final chapter)
—any more than he is prepared to accept the world-renouncing principles as
ultimate (*op. cit.*, pp. 249, 283, 284). Perhaps nothing more is possible than
to appeal, with Schweitzer, from the ' historical Jesus ' to the ' spirit of
Jesus ' (p. 399), and to insist that His eschatological view was ' grounded in
dogma ' (p. 399). I take this to mean that our Lord had certain dogmatic
convictions which, for His time and to His contemporaries, He could only
express in terms of apocalyptic ; though I should add as a possibility that
they may *never* perhaps be expressible except in those terms. And I should
be inclined to suggest that ' theocentrism ' (*infra*, pp. 96, 97) is the word
which best sums up these convictions.

[2] C. Gore, H. L. Goudge, A. Guillaume (edd.), *New Commentary on Holy
Scripture* (1928), part iii (The New Testament), pp. 287, 288.

emphasized. . . . We are bound in honesty to recognize the extreme demand for renunciation, or detachment from all the normal interests and claims of society, as not only an element, but a most prominent element in our Lord's teaching, though we occasionally detect more conciliatory features also.'

And again, of our Lord's teaching as a whole :—[1]

' There are two ways in which a teacher of truth can approach mankind. He may make the best of society and human nature as it is, and seek to improve it and insinuate reform without suggesting the necessity for any marked break with the past. Or he may proclaim that existing society is on the way to utter ruin, and demand a fresh start, a new birth, a radical reform. *The latter is the method of Jesus.*'

The judgment of Professor Bultmann tallies with that of Dr. Gore. His profound and thoughtful study of the teaching of Jesus runs along the following lines. The apocalyptic message of the gospel implies that ' here and now ' every man stands in a moment of decision, and must decide, once and for all, for God or against Him.[2] Jesus was no ' dualist ' indeed—that is, He had no *metaphysical* doctrine of the radical badness of the world, of ' matter,' the senses, or the body.[3] Evil for Him was in the will alone.[4] But if a human will was anything but wholly devoted to the service of God—if it had reserves, hesitations, doubts and difficulties— then it was *wholly* evil, and the man whose soul it expressed was *wholly* a sinner, *wholly* doomed to damnation. Taking the comparison of the old and the new law in the Sermon on the Mount as his text, Bultmann comments as follows :—[5]

' The decisive demand in all these sentences is this—whatever good is to be done, must be done *completely*. Whoever does less than the complete good, with reservations,—whoever merely obeys the letter of the law, and that when he is forced to it,—has done no good at all. To refrain from murder, but leave anger unconquered, means that a man has not learnt that he must make the *complete* decision. To refrain from adultery, but retain lust at heart, means that he does not understand the command against adultery as a demand for *complete* purity. . . . Jesus regards action as a function of the *whole* man, and treats it from the point of view of decision— either this or that. Half-decision is abomination.'

[1] *New Commentary on Holy Scripture*, p. 292.
[2] Bultmann, *Jesus*, pp. 31 (the great *Either—Or*) ; 32 (the call for decision) ; 40, 77 (complete obedience or submission) ; 81, 83, 84, 121 (decision here and now at every moment), etc. Cp. also P. E. More, *The Christ of the New Testament*, pp. 136-142, on the rejection of the spirit of compromise in our Lord's teaching.
[3] Bultmann, p. 47 ; hence (pp. 92-97) there is no formulation of specific ascetic rules in our Lord's teaching.
[4] *Ib.*, p. 46.   [5] *Ib.*, p. 86.

Or again :—[1]

> 'There are no relative standards in Jesus' teaching ; everything is absolute. At the moment of decision we are concerned with an absolute " Either—Or." The good which is demanded is not a relative good, which may be superseded by something better at a higher stage—it is the will of God. A man's decision at such a moment does not entitle us to say that he is rising to higher things, or falling to lower. It marks him out either as wholly righteous or as wholly a sinner—and to be a sinner does not mean that he merely stands on a relatively lower moral stage. It means that he has been rejected by God.'

It follows from this that, according to Bultmann, human nature, earthly society and the like, are in Jesus' teaching wholly evil—for we are not allowed to think that for the gospel ethics anything can be merely neutral or indifferent.[2] And this is stated explicitly—' Jesus knows nothing of human ideals, of the development of natural capacities, of any worth in man as such. . . . The *only thing of value* in man is the attitude he adopts in the moment of decision.' [3]

Similarly, Dr. Bultmann denies that Jesus ever thought of the kingdom of God as something embryonically present in human nature and society, to be brought to realization by steady progress from strength to strength.[4] There is nothing good at all except in perfection. All else is wholly evil, and out of evil no good can come, unless by direct divine intervention, which produces perfection immediately. ' But at the same time ' is a phrase that has no parallel in the Lord's vocabulary : ' Either—or ' is His motto.[5] In the parables of the seed growing secretly, the mustard seed, the leaven, there is no reference (so Bultmann insists, against most other interpreters) to the slow but saving efficacy of grace in the human heart. The first deals only with the supernatural character of conversion, brought about by no human means : the second and third illustrate the overwhelming and tremendous power of the coming kingdom.[6]

It is unprofitable to quarrel about the bare meaning of words. If Bultmann chooses to deny the title ' dualist ' to a system of thought which can see nothing at all but evil except where there is conscious *and complete* obedience to the will of God, we must leave him to his own strange terminology. The vital point is this. The passages just instanced are absolutely true in so far as they express the sterner side of Jesus' thought. But His teaching has another side. An array of texts could be quoted which endorse the legitimacy of earthly joys and ideals, and proclaim or imply the permanent

---

[1] Bultmann, p. 81.
[2] *Ib.*, p. 74.
[3] *Ib.*, pp. 51, 52, 105.
[4] *Ib.*, p. 35 ; cp. pp. 37, 97-100.
[5] *Ib.*, pp. 31, 49, 50.
[6] *Ib.*, pp. 36, 38.

value of natural beauty, domestic happiness and civil order.[1] The very employment of parables from nature and human life implies a real community of character between the earthly type and its heavenly archetype. Even 'evil' parents, Jesus says, give good gifts to their children, and in so doing evince the presence of a divine spark within. The Lord Who would have us forgive to seventy times seven betrays by that same demand the conviction that no sinner is utterly lost before the day of judgment—there must still be some possibility for good in a soul to which forgiveness still can have a meaning. The spirit of a *pastor*—the spirit of making allowances and discriminations, the spirit of tolerance, the patience which can overlook constant lapses and still find something to love in the sinner who has fallen time and again, the optimism which seeks for goodness and messages from heaven even in the most humble and everyday surroundings—this, no less than the evangelistic temper, is a spirit which we must ascribe to the Jesus of the gospels.

It is essential for Christian ethics that it should attempt to find the truth about this amazing conjunction of the two ideals of rigorism and humanism in our Lord's outlook. The two points of view lie side by side in the gospel ; neither can be eliminated, yet no clue to their reconciliation is expressed. It may in the end appear that asceticism—although not in itself a necessary or actual development from apocalyptic—is indeed based upon a deep theological dualism whose importance is only emphasized (as Schweitzer suggests) by the fact that apocalyptic, embodying the same dualistic principle, is conjoined with it in the gospels. This principle again may show itself so intractable as to render impossible any synthesis between it and the admitted humanism of much of Jesus' teaching. If that prove to be the case, the Christian moralist will have forced upon him the invidious task of deciding which of the two elements

---

[1] Bultmann disposes of these in drastic fashion. He collects (p. 147) the passages which betray ' a childlike belief in providence and a naive optimistic outlook upon nature and the world.' They comprise the ' lilies of the field ' (Lk. 12$^{22-31}$, Mt. 6$^{25-32}$), the ' two sparrows ' (Mt. 10$^{29-31}$, Lk. 12$^{6, 7}$), the sun and rain sent to good and bad alike (Mt. 5^{45}). He is inclined to think them spurious ; but assuming that they are not he holds, as the result of an intricate and delicate analysis, that they exhibit no deep enjoyment or appreciation of the marvels of nature (p. 150), but rather imply an utter acceptance, without question, of God's will, and so fall into line with that demand for implicit, unquestioning obedience which he regards as the heart of Jesus' message (p. 158). There was no need, however, for any special discussion of these passages ; Bultmann (p. 80) holds that Jesus could have enunciated *no* general principles of conduct (ascetic or world-embracing (p. 98)), since the only thing that matters is decision in the ' here and now ' of a particular crisis. And as each such crisis (that is, in fact, each moment of life) is absolutely distinct and unique (p. 81), not till the moment comes will any man be in a position to know what form God's will for him will take (pp. 83, 98). Bultmann's theory, like Schweitzer's, is a notable and inevitable reaction against nineteenth-century liberalism ; but both theories, stimulating though they certainly are, dehumanize the gospel story to an extent which makes it virtually unrecognizable.

is to be attributed to the Lord Himself, and which discarded as an alien excrescence. These questions lie at the very heart of Christian ethics, but any attempt to solve them must come at the end rather than at the beginning of enquiry. We shall be in a better position to return to the problem when we have considered what Christian theology has had to say about it in the process of its development. That the phenomenon set going two streams of interpretation in the Church from the very outset—one which found in loyal acceptance and temperate use of the things of this world its ideal for life, and one which demanded their uncompromising renunciation—is sufficiently clear from the data of the New Testament itself. It is to be seen at work even in the transmission and interpretation of the words of the Lord.

II. New Testament Variations.

(a) The Synoptists.

An illustration of the diversity of ethical views in the synoptic tradition presents itself in connexion with the story of the young man with great possessions. As the narrative stands in S. Mark's gospel, it shows clear traces of editorial revision in the interests of the less rigorist view. The significant verses [1] run as follows in the Revised Version :—

> (x, 23) ' And Jesus looked round about and saith unto His disciples, How hardly shall they that have riches enter into the kingdom of God. (24) And the disciples were amazed at His words. But Jesus answereth again and saith unto them, Children how hard it is for them that trust in riches to enter into the kingdom of God. (25) It is easier for a camel to go through a needle's eye, than for a rich man to enter into the kingdom of God. (26) And they were astonished exceedingly, saying unto Him, Then who can be saved ? '

Even on the surface the words ' for them that trust in riches ' present a difficulty. The context, if they are removed, implies throughout that the *mere possession of riches* is a disability or barrier for entrance into the kingdom. This phrase, however, modifies the meaning, and throws the emphasis upon *trust in* rather than upon *possession of* riches. Yet the following verses ignore the mitigation. Verse 25 insists once again upon the danger of mere possession ; verse 26 raises the disciples' amazement to the highest possible pitch. We are led inevitably to consider the words ' for them that trust in riches ' to be an insertion ; and this doubt as to their authenticity becomes a certainty that they are spurious when it is seen

---

[1] Mk. 10[23-26].

that neither Matthew nor Luke take any notice of them ;[1] whilst the most authoritative texts of Mark itself read simply in their place, ' How hard it is to enter into the kingdom of God.'[2]

The history of the text is obvious. The words ' for them that trust in riches ' did not originally stand there. Whatever the intention of the passage as originally written, there were those in the Church who interpreted it to mean that the mere possession of riches debarred a man finally from the kingdom ; and the insertion in the text (maladroit though it is) was designed to modify the severity of the doctrine. Matthew was faced by the same difficulty, but dealt with it in a different way. He introduced a conception not unknown elsewhere in the New Testament, which was to have a dramatic and far-reaching influence upon Christian thought, life, and organization—that of the ' double standard' in ethics. If the young man would *enter into life* he is to keep the commandments (without, apparently, surrendering his riches) ; but if he *would be perfect and have treasure in heaven*, he must sell all that he has and follow Christ. Riches are still a barrier, and the better course is to be rid of them ; but they are not an impenetrable barrier, and some degree of beatitude may be reached even by those who retain them.[3]

The Lucan version adds a further point of interest by taking

[1] Mt. 19[23-25] ; Lk. 18[24-26]. S. Luke will not allow the disciples even to be ' astonished ' at the depreciation of riches. He removes the astonishment altogether, and attributes the final exclamation ('Who can be saved ? ') to a vague ' they that heard it,' for whom he has prepared the way by removing the ' disciples ' from verse 24 as well. This is characteristic of the asceticism of the third gospel (*infra*, p. 73).

[2] אBk all read simply, ' How hard it is to enter into the kingdom of God.' D also felt a difficulty about the text, and transposed verses 24 and 25. This does not help matters—rather the reverse, in fact : it attaches the ' exceeding astonishment ' directly to the ' trust in riches ' (instead of to the ' needle's eye ' interposition), and it makes the Lord definitely water down His pronouncement, whereas the R.V. text, after introducing the mitigation, reverts to the original rigorist conception. Even the reading of אBk, however, cannot be original ; for further considerations see additional note C, *infra*, p. 479.

[3] On the double standard generally, *infra*, pp. 239 ff. Another Matthæan example is Mt. 5[19], ' Whosoever therefore shall break one of these least commandments, and shall teach men so, shall be called least *in the kingdom of heaven :* but whosoever shall do and teach them, he shall be called great in the kingdom of heaven.' This again would appear to be a Matthæan addition to the source, as it breaks the context. B. S. Easton, *The Gospel before the Gospels*, p. 108, may be right in saying, ' The " two levels of salvation " doctrine is foreign to the teaching of Jesus,' but is it true to add, ' and it reflects a controversy that did not exist in His lifetime ' ? In so far as the ' controversy ' referred to is that between Jewish Christians (who kept even the ' least commandments ') and Gentile converts (who did not), Dr. Easton's statement is acceptable; but it is not certain that S. Matthew had this controversy in view at all. It is more probable that (as in the case of the rich young man) he is simply ' lightening the yoke ' for ' babes in Christ,' but at the same time reminding them of the fuller requirements of the Christian law. Cp. also Mt. 19[10-12] on celibacy. The *New Commentary* (Gore, Goudge and Guillaume) is to the point as regards Mt. 19[10-12, 17-21], but not to be followed on 5[19].

no notice whatever of the problem.   It accepts the rigorist interpretation without hesitation and in all its fulness.[1]   This is all the
more important, because it is at least arguable that one of Luke's
sources emanated from a school which thought of poverty and
poverty alone as worthy of commendation.   From this source,
also, came presumably the story of the rich man and Lazarus,
which suggests that the rich man's torments in Hades arise from
no other cause than that he has received ' good things ' in his lifetime, whilst Lazarus is comforted solely because of the ' evil things '
he has suffered.   We are so accustomed to import into the story
the idea of moral worth and its opposite, that it is difficult to realize
how little the text says upon the point.[2]

Similarly, whatever may have been the process of transmission
which gave us two versions of the beatitudes,[3] it is well-known that
the Matthæan ' Blessed are the poor in spirit ' is paralleled in the
Lucan sermon by ' Blessed are ye poor,' [4] and is there accompanied
by an appropriate ' Woe ' against the rich.   The antithesis between
the two versions points to the same phenomenon as before.   Either
the ' poor in spirit ' is the earlier, in which case some writer, who
held material poverty a higher condition than material wealth,
deleted the ' in spirit ' ; or ' Blessed are the poor' was the original
form, and ' in spirit' was added by a moralist who wished to
eliminate the purely ascetic interpretation.   Whichever be the
case, it is clear evidence of a divergence of views upon the problem
of riches.

[1] And also (12^{33}—' Sell that ye have and give alms ') makes it a general
rule for all disciples (? the Twelve—or ministers of the gospel—see *infra*,
p. 73)—a passage for which Mt. has no exact parallel, though he seems to
be aware of it, and to reproduce it in a much modified form in 6^{19-20} (Mt. 6^{21}
corresponds with Lk. 12^{34}) in the same connexion.   The *Gospel according
to the Hebrews* (*infra*, p. 160) also accepts the rigorist interpretation of
the ' rich young man ' by equating the command, ' Sell all that thou hast,'
with the commandment, ' Thou shalt love thy neighbour.'   After the Lord's
words, ' the rich man began to scratch his head, and it pleased him not.   And
the Lord said unto him :   " How sayest thou, I have kept the law and the
prophets ?   For it is written in the law, Thou shalt love thy neighbour as
thyself.   And lo, many of thy brethren, sons of Abraham, are clad in filth,
dying for hunger, and thine house is full of many good things, and naught
at all goeth out of it unto them." '   Then follows the ' needle's eye ' saying,
addressed to Simon (Pseudo-Origen *in Mt.*—M. R. James, *Apocryphal New
Testament*, p. 6).   This reads both like a protest against Matthew (which
was used by the *Gospel according to the Hebrews*) and a moralization of
the parable of the Rich Man and Lazarus in Luke.

[2] Lk. 16^{19-31}.   I do not for a moment deny the legitimacy of moralizing
the parable (see end of last note for an early instance) ; but it seems quite
clear that, as S. Luke records it, he lost a very obvious opportunity (to say
the least) for such moralization, which he would scarcely have failed to take,
had he wished to do so.

[3] On this question, B. H. Streeter, *The Four Gospels*, pp. 250-254.   For
reasons given in the text (pp. 71-73) I hesitate to accept Canon Streeter's
not very fully argued conclusion (p. 289) that Lk. here preserves the more
original form of the *sayings*, though I do not dissent from the hypothesis
that the *sermon* circulated at a very early date in two widely different forms.

[4] Mt. 5^3, Lk. 6^{20} ; cp. Lk. 6^{24}—' Woe unto you that are rich ! for ye have
received your consolation.'

It is instructive, however, to consider the problem of the beatitudes a little further. It may of course be urged that the Lucan ' poor ' is no more than the technical Old Testament term for the ' pious,' identical in meaning with the ' poor in spirit ' of the first gospel.[1] This interpretation, however, falls to the ground, and that for two reasons. In the first place, the ' rich ' of verse 24 are contrasted with the ' poor,' and as the former must be thought of in the strictly literal sense, it would weaken the parallel to interpret the ' poor ' simply as ' spiritually poor.' Again, in a subsequent beatitude, Matthew reads, ' Blessed are they that hunger and thirst after righteousness, for they shall be filled,' whilst Luke has, ' Blessed are ye that hunger now, for ye shall be filled ' [2]—a sentence which can refer to nothing except physical hunger. It is hard to resist the conclusion already suggested, that whichever of our two contrasted versions represents the original utterance of Jesus most closely, it was deliberately modified in a variant tradition either in a rigorist or in a liberal sense.

That it was S. Luke in person to whom the modification is due, and that it represents a genuine demand for severe asceticism on the part at all events of the ministers of the gospel, seems probable from another consideration. On the surface the Lucan version might be taken as no more than a word of consolation—appropriate enough from the pen of a practical and experienced Christian missionary—for those hearers of the gospel who, in the slums and ghettoes of the Orient, must have suffered only too often from actual poverty and physical hunger. But this interpretation of the change of text is ruled out by a consideration of its position in the gospel. Both in Matthew and in Luke the original ' great sermon ' (whose outline is still clearly recognizable) is presented with considerable literary modification, not necessarily in all its details the work of the evangelists. But the *setting* of the sermon must in each case be attributed to the evangelist, and the difference between the two is remarkable. Matthew breaks off from his Marcan original at the first point where a mention of formal preaching is to be found in his source.[3] At this place he at once inserts the sermon,[4] giving it a mountain setting from a later section of Mark.

---

[1] See e.g. *HDB.*, iv, pp. 19, 20, for an account of the O.T. usage.

[2] Mt. 5⁶; Lk. 6²¹.

[3] There is indeed an earlier reference to preaching in Mk. (1¹⁴, ¹⁵) which Mt. reproduces (4¹⁷). But he did not insert the sermon here, either because the vague ' preaching the gospel ' and the message of repentance did not give him sufficient authority for a formal exposition of Christian duty at this point ; or because he naturally wished to have some of the Twelve present at the sermon, and so postponed it until four of them had been called.

[4] Mk. 1²¹ (after the call of the Four)—' And they go into Capernaum : and straightway on the sabbath day He entered into the synagogue and taught.' Then follow the healing of the demoniac and of Simon's wife's mother, the healing at evening, the retirement in the morning, and (verse 30), ' He went into their synagogues throughout all Galilee, preaching and casting out devils.' Mt. eliminates the references to Capernaum and the events there, and building

His purpose is clear : the new law is to be given by the new Law-giver upon a new Sinai.   Luke, on the other hand, brings the ser-mon into relation with the Marcan account of the call of the twelve ; [1] explicitly states that it was addressed to the disciples ; [2] presents the beatitudes in the second person and not the third ; and lays particular emphasis on the solemn preliminaries of the scene. Jesus retires to a mountain to pray, spends the whole night in prayer with God,[3] calls His immediate followers to Him at day-break, and from their number selects twelve whom He names apostles.[4]   He then descends to a level spot where a great crowd is gathered,[5] and here, lifting up His eyes on His disciples, addresses the beatitudes specifically and directly to them in the presence of the multitude.   To achieve this *mise-en-scène* the evangelist has to make a curious and at first sight meaningless transposition of two tiny sections of Mark ; [6] and throughout the passage—so long as he follows the Marcan original—he varies the details in a manner whose significance only becomes apparent when the resultant picture is viewed as a whole.[7]

But as to the meaning of that picture there can be no two opinions.   Luke has artificially adjusted his material so as to present an ideal description of the first Christian ordination service. The whole setting is liturgical ; the retirement and prayer of the officiant, the solemn selection of the ordinands from a number of

on the ' synagogue ' of Mk. 1[21] inserts immediately after the call of the Four his version of Mk. 1[30] (Mt. 4[23])—' And Jesus went about in all Galilee, teaching in their synagogues and preaching the gospel of the kingdom.'   To compensate for the miracles he has left out he now expands the ' casting out devils ' of Mk. into a general statement about healing, and proceeds at once to the sermon.   This, however, must not be in a synagogue—it is a new law, and must be given from a new Sinai ; and it must have an audience worthy of it.   He therefore collects the first really impressive crowd he can find in Mk. (Mk. 3[7, 8] ; Mt. 4[25]) and assembles them round the first mountain (Mk. 3[13]—' and He goeth up into a mountain ' (actually to choose the Twelve) ; Mt. 5[1]—' and seeing the multitudes He went up into the mountain ') and his stage is set.   It seems clear that the sermon in Q must already have had a mountain-context, for both Mt. and Lk. take pains to fit it to a mountain-context in Mk. ; and though Mt.'s reason for doing so is obvious (see above) and was probably also Q's, there is no particular reason why Lk. should have done so—his ordination scene would have been complete without the mountain.

[1] Call of the Twelve (Mk. 3[13-19]), Lk. 6[12-16] ; the sermon, Lk. 6[20] ff.

[2] Lk. 6[20]—' He lifted up His eyes on His disciples, and said ' ; contrast the much vaguer Mt. 5[2]—' He opened His mouth and taught them, saying.'

[3] Lk. 6[12].   [4] Lk. 6[13].

[5] Lk. 6[17-19].   This is, of course, the same ' crowd ' that Matthew has used ; luckily for both the later evangelists it stood in the immediate context of a mountain in Mark.

[6] The crowd in Mark (3[7-12]) comes before the mountain and the call of the Twelve (3[13-19]) ; Lk. reverses the order.   It would be inconvenient only to select the ordinands after the congregation has gathered for the ordination.

[7] He *adds* the night-long prayer, the ' selection ' (ἐκλεξάμενος) of the Twelve, and the level place ; he *cuts out* the reference to the Twelve ' casting out demons ' (Mk. 3[15]), the seashore and the boat (naturally enough—Matthew eliminates them too), all references but one to the healing of sick in the crowd, the recognition of Jesus by the demoniacs, and His rebuke.

eligible candidates in the early morning, their due commission and formal exhortation in the face of the congregation. No Christian community throughout the world could have failed to witness a similar scene. From this emerges one definite conclusion. S. Luke regards the beatitudes as addressed directly to the apostles and their potential successors in the Christian ministry. He insists that they (who were not actually ' poor ' or ' hungry ' before their call) must *make* themselves poor and hungry in the literal sense for the gospel's sake ; and he does so because the strictly ascetic life appears to him to be the only possible life, at all events for the ministers of the gospel.[1]

The alleged ' Ebionism ' of the third gospel, which has so often been denied,[2] seems therefore to have a very real basis in fact. It is wholly consistent with what we have just noticed that S. Luke should be the only evangelist to insist that a man must *hate* his father and mother and wife and children—and his own soul also— before he can be a disciple of Christ.[3] It is not inconsistent that

[1] It may be urged against this that the ' Woes ' are also expressed in the second person, and would appear therefore to be addressed to the disciples exclusively. But this fits the picture well—the disciples are warned against the temptations of riches and the like. And the last ' woe ' is appropriate *only* to ministers of the gospel (Lk. 6^{26}) : ' Woe unto you when all men shall speak well of you ! for in the same manner did their fathers *unto the false prophets.*' The sermon goes on (as many ordination sermons do) to address the congregation as a whole (v. 27, ' But I say unto you which hear ') on general topics of Christian duty.

[2] See e.g. A. Plummer, *The Gospel according to St. Luke* (ICC.), pp. xxv, xxvi, 179, 180. Two points made by Dr. Plummer *against* the ' Ebionism ' of the third gospel tell much more strongly *for* it : (*a*) In the parable of the sower, according to Mt. (13^{22}) and Mk. (4^{19}) it is only the ' *deceitfulness* of riches ' which chokes the good seed ; in Lk. (8^{14}) it is ' riches ' as such, however used. (*b*) It is true that Mt. and Mk. ' tell us that Joseph of Arimathea was a man of rank ' (Mk. 15^{43} : εὐσχήμων ; though this word ' in vulgar Greek was used to mean "rich"' (Rawlinson, *ad loc.*, but contrast Moulton-Milligan, *Vocabulary of New Testament Greek, s.v.*)) ' and wealth (Mt. 27^{57}). Luke is much more explicit than they are about his goodness and rectitude (23$^{50, 51}$).' This, Dr. Plummer adds, ' does not look like a prejudice against the rich ' ; but he fails to observe that S. Luke has definitely eliminated the statement that Joseph was rich (he is neither εὐσχήμων nor πλούσιος). Is this because Luke thought no rich man was capable of such charity—or because he wished to suppress what from his point of view was a slur on Joseph's character ? Whatever the reason, it suggests that ' a prejudice against the rich ' motived the suppression.

[3] Lk. 14^{26}. Note also that in the two passages about leaving one's family for Christ's sake (Mt. 10^{37}, Lk. 14^{26} ; Mk. 10^{29}, Mt. 19^{29}, Lk. 18^{29}) Luke on each occasion says that the *wife* must be abandoned with the other relatives—a feature which occurs in neither of the other evangelists. (Some secondary versions insert ' or wife ' in Mk. 10^{29}, Mt. 19^{29}, by assimilation with Luke, but there can be no doubt that this is wrong.) In the second passage the next words, ' who shall not receive manifold more ' (Lk. 18^{30} ; Mk. 10^{30}— ' an hundred-fold ' ; the texts of Mt. waver between the two), with or without the addition of ' in this time ' (which Mt. omits), must have emphasized the impropriety of mentioning the ' wife ' in the catalogue—an impropriety which was seized upon by Julian the Apostate (' Shall ye then also receive wives an hundred-fold ? '—Theophylact, quoted by E. Klostermann, *Das Markusevangelium* (*HNT.*, iii, p. 118)). In spite of this, Luke in his

S. Luke should omit the passage about cutting off the hand and foot *if it offend* (a passage which seems to have occurred both in Mark and Q) ; [1] for to the genuine ascetic his renunciations are absolute, and not conditional upon failure to make due use of what God has given. It is wholly consistent that the beatitudes should be followed—in this gospel only, not in Matthew—by the uncompromising ' woes ' to the rich and prosperous : a doom with which they are threatened not because of any misuse of their riches, but by virtue of possession and possession alone—' Ye have received your reward.' It is consistent that Luke alone should state both of the sons of Zebedee, and of Levi, that they left *all* to follow Jesus.[2]

(b) S. James.

The same uncompromising hostility to riches is to be seen—and that in curious company—in the Epistle of S. James, where indeed it rings almost as a reminiscence of S. Luke :—

> ' Go to, now, ye rich, weep and howl for the miseries that are coming upon you. Your riches are corrupted and your garments are moth-eaten. Your gold and your silver are rusted ; and their rust shall be for a testimony against you, and shall eat your flesh as fire. Ye have laid up your treasure in the last days.' [3]

The passage is badly adjusted to its context. There were rich men in the church to which the letter was written ; but hitherto the writer has merely urged that their presence should not be distinguished by special attentions such as would by contrast ' dishonour ' the poor,[4] though a stricter view is latent in the sweeping words, ' Do not the rich oppress you, and themselves drag you before the judgment seats ? Do they not blaspheme the honourable name by the which ye are called ? ' There were merchants in the church, whose trade monopolized their interest and attention ; but although reminding them that they are ' a vapour that appeareth for a little time and then vanisheth away ' [5]—a phrase which

ascetic fervour has at all events not followed Mark in removing the impropriety (if it stood there in a common source—possibly Q), and in all probability has actually introduced it by inserting the word in a passage where it had no place.—F. C. Burkitt, *Gospel History and its Transmission,* pp. 211 ff., argues definitely for the ' Ebionism ' of Lk.

[1] Mk. 9⁴³⁻⁴⁸ ; Mt. 18⁸⁻⁹. The probability that the passage occurred in Q is inferred from the fact of a doublet in Mt. 5²⁹. It may, however, have been in one of Mt.'s special sources.

[2] Lk. 5¹¹, ²⁸. [3] Jas. 5¹⁻³.

[4] *Ib.,* 2¹⁻⁷—or does the passage refer to rich heathen who came as visitors to the synagogue (so Hollmann and Bousset, *SNT.,* iii, p. 230) ? In that case the ' rich oppressors ' of vv. 6, 7 may be heathen too ; and this seems probable in view of the ' blasphemy of the Name ' in v. 7. But why should only the *rich* heathen blaspheme the Name ? The whole thought of the epistle is too disordered to offer any hope of answering these questions.

[5] Jas. 4¹⁴.

might easily have lent itself to a whole-hearted condemnation of all worldly interests,—he contents himself with urging that their business plans and policies should always be regarded as conditional upon the Lord's will.[1] Even the three verses of outspoken doom quoted a moment ago are half retracted in the sequel ; it appears that it is only the rich who ' keep back the hire of labourers by fraud,' who ' nourish their hearts in a day of slaughter,' who have ' condemned and killed the righteous,' [2] who are denounced. The general tenour of the épistle is therefore liberal and humanist ; it is all the more noticeable that an unconditional denunciation of the rich as a class should have been allowed to stand, even in one passage, in stark unmitigated severity.

(c) S. Paul.

It is not in connexion with riches that the ascetic spirit betrays itself in S. Paul. The Corinthian parody of the eucharist was only possible in a church where private possessions were recognized as the rule at least for the more fortunate in the community ; and among all the far-reaching administrative measures which S. Paul takes to deal with the church there, he makes no attempt even to limit the income or expenditure of the Christian. He contemplates that the Lord will so prosper individual believers that at the week's end they will be able to set something by for the needs of others less fortunate.[3] Anything approaching the luxury of the pagan world around was no doubt wholly foreign to his conception of the Christian life ; but there is no attack upon riches as such, no exaltation of holy poverty. If traces of asceticism are to be found in his epistles, they occur in connexion with the question of marriage rather than with that of poverty.

Once more we need not go beyond the New Testament to find in primitive Christianity a strain of thought which looked askance at marriage and family life. Our Lord's phrase about those who made themselves eunuchs for the kingdom of heaven's sake had far-reaching effects ; [4] and He Himself remained unmarried. S. Luke included the wife among the list of persons whom the disciple must ' hate,' or ' leave,'—a very sinister addition to the Marcan source.[5] The great procession of the redeemed in the Apocalypse is characterized by the words : ' These are they that are not defiled with women ' ; and as though the author wished to make it clear that he excluded not merely the sexually irregular but also the legally married from the company, he adds at once, ' for they are virgins.' [6] So strongly is Canon Charles moved by this phrase, that he regards the verse as an interpolation by an editor whom he is not afraid to call a ' shallow-brained fanatic and celibate.' [7]

---

[1] Jas. 4[15].   [2] Jas. 5[4-6].
[3] 1 Cor. 16[2].   [4] Mt. 19[12].
[5] *Supra*, p. 73, n. 3.   [6] Rev. 14[4].
[7] R. H. Charles, *Revelation of St. John* (*ICC.*), i, p. lv.

To such extremes S. Paul will not go. He recognizes that it is legitimate for himself to ' lead about a wife, a sister,' ' even as the rest of the apostles, and the brethren of the Lord, and Cephas.' [1] But the seventh chapter of the first Corinthian letter is devoted to a steady vindication of celibacy as against marriage. Here indeed we meet at first sight with a definitely eschatological reference. It is ' by reason of the present distress ' that virginity is commended ; the ' time is shortened,' ' the fashion of this world passeth away.' [2] Even the married must be as though they are celibate ; those that use the world as not using it to the full.[3] But the eschatology is only incidental. Other reasons are advanced which do not depend for their validity (whatever that may be) upon any imminence of the Lord's coming. Marriage brings tribulation in the flesh,[4] and is full of cares ; [5] its consequent effect is to divert the Christian from the whole-hearted attempt to ' please God,' [6] to be holy both in body and in spirit,[7] to attend upon the Lord without distraction.[8] The best that can be said of marriage is that it is a remedy against fornication—it is better to marry than to burn ; [9] and a drastic remedy the apostle must count it if it involves so many dangers of its own.[10]

There is little here of what we have called the liberal, or humanist, spirit in Christian ethics. There is little sense of the dignity of Christian wedlock, or its potentialities for bringing new virtues to light. There is no such recognition of the pure and innocent beauty of little children as rings through the gospel ; [11] the joys and privileges of family life are wholly ignored. This steady indifference to all that is best—nay all that is positively good—in marriage can be seen on inspection to colour the apostle's views on all the relationships of life. It is sometimes suggested that as S. Paul advanced in years, and the hope of the Lord's coming failed, he

---

[1] 1 Cor. 9[5].   [2] 1 Cor. 7[26, 29, 31].

[3] 1 Cor. 7[29, 31].—' As not abusing it,' for ὡς μὴ καταχρώμενοι, is of course an entire misrepresentation of A.V. and R.V. See Moulton-Milligan, *Vocabulary*, *s.v.*

[4] 1 Cor. 7[28]. Note for S. Paul's use of *sarx* (*infra*, pp. 89 ff.), that ' tribulation in the flesh ' is here an *evil* thing ; mortification of the ' flesh ' is not always to be welcomed.

[5] 1 Cor. 7[33].   [6] 1 Cor. 7[32].   [7] 1 Cor. 7[34].

[8] 1 Cor. 7[35].   [9] 1 Cor. 7[2, 9].

[10] It would appear from verse 29 that S. Paul is urging complete abstinence from intercourse even upon the married, and thus gives his sanction to a practice widely followed in the early Church on ascetic grounds (*infra*, pp. 187, 236). But the words are not definite, and in verse 5 he is certainly using the weight of his authority (though no doubt gently) *against* any such attempts at Corinth. For the suggestion, now widely accepted, that verses 36 to 38 refer to an early example of the practice of *virgines subintroductæ*, and its dangers, see H. Lietzmann, *ad loc.*, in *HNT.*, ix, pp. 36, 37, with references there ; and K. Lake, *Earlier Epistles of St. Paul*, pp. 184-191. The suggestion appears to have originated with C. Weiszäcker ; see his *Apostolic Age* (E. tr.), ii, pp. 371, 372.

[11] F. C. Burkitt, *Gospel History and its Transmission*, pp. 285 ff., shows that this unevangelic indifference to children goes much further than the Pauline epistles alone in early Christian thought.

became more sympathetic in outlook ; and the attempt is made
to build a positive system of Christian ethics on the ' household
code,' or ' table of domestic duties '[1] sketched in the epistles to
Ephesus and Colossæ. But the suggestion over-simplifies the
curiously involved truth. Closer inspection shows that S. Paul's
whole attitude as expressed in these passages, from beginning to
end, is tinged (if no more) by a fundamental apathy towards this
present world, with all its interests, order, progress, and joys.[2]

No one has put this conclusion more incisively than Johannes
Weiss. He addresses himself to the famous ' household code,'
and his dissection leaves it a very cold and forbidding skeleton.
Of the words, ' Husbands love your wives,'[3] he writes :—[4]

> ' The direct command undoubtedly envisages " love " in the
> highest and most Christian sense. But the context as a whole
> is on a lower plane. When wives are merely commanded to
> " be in subjection "[5] to their husbands, and husbands " not
> to be bitter against them,"[6] children merely " to obey their
> parents " and fathers " not to provoke them " that they be not
> discouraged,[7] we are regrettably far from the ideal of the Chris-
> tian household. . . . The grudging words fall short even of the
> ideal of family life in classical paganism. Above all there is
> no recognition of the fact that, even without any high ethical
> or religious motive, the normal domestic affections ordinarily
> produce moral results of real importance. There is no joy in
> that finest flower of civilization—that ideal transformation of a
> natural relationship which the spirit of Christian love made
> possible. . . . In this matter S. Paul shows himself a Christian
> indeed, but a Christian dominated by eschatology;[8] an Oriental,
> an ascetic, a hermit, who has never experienced the joys of
> family life, and perhaps even lacks all capacity for the experi-
> ence.'

So too with the State. We are bidden to be ' in subjection to
the higher powers ; for the powers that be are ordained of God.'[9]
But the words and their context are ' devoid of any warmth of
civic feeling.' S. Paul indeed ' shares the gratitude of the Roman
provincial who sees in the Emperor the guardian of peace, the
principle of order against chaos.'[10] But his social interest goes no
further ; once even he permits himself to speak of the Roman

---

[1] On the ' household codes ' (haustafeln), infra, pp. 121, 125.

[2] As with Schweitzer's representation of our Lord's teaching, supra, p. 56.

[3] Col. 3[19] (cp. Eph. 5[25], and on the theological expansion here, infra,
p. 125).

[4] Das Urchristentum, pp. 454, 455.

[5] Col. 3[18] ; cp. Eph. 5[22].

[6] Col. 3[19].   [7] Col. 3[21] ; cp. Eph. 6[4].

[8] Despite this reference to eschatology (as also in the footnote on p. 455,
where S. Paul's ' apathy ' is distinguished from Epictetus's and Aristippus's
on the same grounds) Weiss has just made it clear (p. 453) that he does not
regard eschatology as the determining factor in this aspect of S. Paul's thought.

[9] Rom. 13[1].   [10] J. Weiss, op. cit., p. 461.

judicial authorities as ' the ungodly.' [1]   Again, he has no sense of the joy and privilege of labour :—

> ' Work to him is never a source of delight.   It is a necessity imposed upon us by circumstance ; its colour is of the soberest. . . . He does not sanction that idealization of work as a duty of citizenship which the world needs so much.   He is apathetic towards all the interests of the everyday social life.' [2]

No less marked is this ethical inertia of S. Paul in relation to the problem of slavery.   It is not only that he fails to catch the essential injustice of the institution ; such a failure was to be expected.   It is that, accepting the institution as he does, he omits altogether to regulate it by Christian principles.   Thus the slave, Johannes Weiss reminds us,[3] is not required by S. Paul either to respect or to honour his master, still less to love him :—

> ' In the nature of things all that could be expected to result from this would be a formally correct and efficient obedience— nothing very gratifying to the master in the circumstances. In practice, no doubt, Christian slaves did far more than this. . . . But we find in S. Paul little recognition of the fact that the welfare of the master and household is an ideal laid upon the servant by God—the condition is not moralized.   And, on the other hand, nothing more is demanded of the master than that he should "render unto his servants that which is just and equal"[4]—a dictate of general humanitarianism which falls very far short of what a Christian master might do.   The possibility that the new ethic (quite apart from the question of Christian brotherhood) should permeate all the relationships of life is at all events never mentioned, although in practice it may often

---

[1] 1 Cor. 6[1] ; and even when he speaks of the Empire as the defence against anti-Christ, he goes no further than to call it τὸ κατέχον—ὁ κατέχων (2 Thess. 2[6, 7]).

[2] J. Weiss, *op. cit.*, p. 463, with reference to 1 Cor. 7[30] and 2 Thess. 3[10-12]. Weiss notes in passing that S. Paul, in consequence of this outlook, gives no attention to what was the great problem of Stoic ethics before him and Christian ethics after him—that of the ' fair price.'   (See my *Conscience and its Problems*, pp. 144, 198-202.)   Yet it must have troubled his converts not a little.   There are some interesting and surprising reflections on this whole subject from the liberal Protestant point of view in Harnack's *What is Christianity ?* pp. 120-126.

[3] *Op. cit.*, p. 460 ; Col. 3[22], Eph. 6[5].—This is not to say that S. Paul did not give utterance to a sentiment which ultimately (though after many centuries) affected the question of slavery profoundly—' There can be neither bond nor free . . . for ye are all one in Christ Jesus ' (Gal. 3[28] ; cp. Weiss, pp. 456, 457, for the contrast between this and the superficially identical Stoic thought).

[4] Col. 4[1], Eph. 6[9].   Notice how the ' Two Ways ' (*infra*, p. 111) has Christianized S. Paul's doctrine of the slave's duty.   *He* draws a distinction between ' serving men ' and ' serving Christ ' (Col. 3[23], Eph. 6[6, 7]) ; the ' Two Ways ' drops this distinction, and taking up the hint of Eph. 6[5] (which is contradicted by its context) explicitly identifies ' the master ' and God in the strongest terms : *Did.* 4[11], ' Ye slaves be subject to your masters as to a type of God ' (cp. *Barnabas* 19[7]).

enough unconsciously have had this effect. In general, S. Paul evinces a definite coolness towards the world ; the thought that we can only serve the world by a loving self-consecration towards it remains unuttered.'[1]

Admittedly we are here tracing out only one thread in the many-coloured pattern of S. Paul's thought. But it suggests that there were moments when he was prepared to pass beyond rigorism to that extreme of indifference which, based on rigorism, ends in its antithesis. The phenomenon is most noticeable in the later history of gnosticism.[2] The rigorist selects in the universe certain activities, circumstances or emotions which he regards as wholly evil, and against them he inaugurates his ethical crusade. But why draw the line at any particular point ? Why not assume that *all* activities, circumstances and emotions except one in particular (call it prayer, or contemplation, or communion with God, or what you will) are alike evil ? Then you reach a moral indifferentism in which there is no distinction between black and white—in which all whites except the selected one are equally black. So long as you are present in the body you are absent from the Lord ; and as mere presence in the body is itself the greatest of evils, it matters not what you do with the body. Whether you honour it or dishonour it is all one—you are occupying yourself with the body in either case ; and to be occupied with the body at all is the crowning infamy in which there cannot be degrees of more and less.

We shall find something of this character explicit in the practice of some at least of the gnostic sects. In S. Paul it betrays itself only as a possibility ; but the door is not barred against it. Very significant in this matter is his treatment of slavery and freedom. 'Wast thou called being a bond-servant ? ' he says ;[3] 'Care not for it '—and that is well said. The next sentence however is crucial. In the text of the Revised Version it reads, 'But if thou canst become free, use it rather '[4]—where the ' it ' seems to mean the opportunity of freedom. But the R.V. margin renders, ' Nay, *even* if thou canst become free, use it rather '; where the ' it ' obviously refers to slavery. The meaning must be, 'There is nothing to choose between slavery and freedom. Neither has any bearing on the question of God's purposes. The matter is not one that

---

[1] With this may be compared an interesting passage in R. Bultmann, *Der Stil der Paulinischen Predigt*, p. 91. After an exhaustive enumeration of S. Paul's metaphors as compared with those of contemporary pagan diatribes (*infra*, p. 119), he says : ' Practically all S. Paul's metaphors have parallels in the diatribes; on the other hand many of the most characteristic metaphors of the diatribes are absent from S. Paul. That he uses no theatrical analogies is not surprising. But it is remarkable that he has no metaphors from animal life or children's games, and no nautical metaphor. The most extraordinary fact of all is that he never employs the picture of the physician ' (we may contrast our Lord's teaching with all this). . . . ' It is perhaps mere accident . . . but as far as we can judge from his metaphors he seems to have had no eyes for all the motley life that went on around him.'

[2] *Infra*, p. 216.　　　　[3] 1 Cor. 7[21].　　　　[4] 1 Cor. 7[21].

concerns Him ; it is not worth while to take the slightest step to embrace the offered opportunity.' Modern commentators are practically agreed that this is the real meaning of the passage ;[1] if so, what a depth of apathy as to this world's goods does it not reveal ?

It is possible therefore that even that ' depreciation of hyper-ascetic experiments ' for which Johannes Weiss commends S. Paul [2]—his opposition to the rigorist who, like Ezra, would command mixed marriages to be broken ; [3] his caveat against marriages in name alone,[4] and against the curious practice of ' spiritual marriages ' at Corinth [5]—is not in itself a sign of liberalism in the apostle. It may be no more than the extreme of apathy in another form. Asceticism and non-asceticism are equally irrelevant to the Christian. Any preoccupation with the flesh—even with the purpose of crucifying it—is in itself evil. Virtuosity in self-mortification stands equally condemned with temperate self-discipline and with undisciplined licence ; all three are foreign to the real goal of life, which is spiritual experience and nothing more. S. Paul does not say this ; it is merely a hint of something of which he might prove capable—certainly of a point of view which the gnostics did not find it impossible to read into his words.

The preceding paragraphs have stated the case for rigorism in S. Paul's epistles at its highest.[6] At its lowest it is still something to be reckoned with ; at its highest it is very formidable indeed. But even at its highest it does not stand alone. There is another strain of completely opposite tendency with which it can be matched. We may hold that the two together form a consistent ethical system, and that their apparent contradictions are no more than the chimeras of an unjust and perverse criticism ; or we may hold that there was a genuine inconsistency in the apostle's own thought. In either case we are faced with the same problem as presented itself in connexion with the teaching of our Lord ; and once again we must relegate it to a later stage. For that S. Paul's epistles, in spite of all that has been said, are a storehouse of Christian humanism, of warm social morality, cannot be gainsaid. The love which he hymns so lyrically in 1 Cor. xiii, the catalogues of virtues in Galatians v and Philippians iv, the spiritual armour of Ephesians vi—these are things which cannot be exercised or realised in any eremitic passivity. They are essentially social and positive ; but at the very least they are as distinctively Pauline as anything else in the corpus of his writings.

Even in relation to the body and its needs—always the first victim to suffer at the hands of rigorist principles—S. Paul is no convinced dualist. He disciplines his body, and brings it into

---

[1] H. L. Goudge in *Westminster Commentary, ad loc.*, remains doubtful.
[2] *Das Urchristentum*, p. 455. Weiss adds that this was ' against S. Paul's own inclinations.'
[3] 1 Cor. 7[12-16].   [4] 1 Cor. 7[3-5].   [5] 1 Cor. 7[36-38] (*supra*, p. 76).
[6] What may be said on the other side can be inferred from (e.g.) A. C. McGiffert, *Apostolic Age*, p. 136 ; A. Sabatier, *The Apostle Paul*, p. 164.

subjection ; [1] but he does not regard it as something against which the Christian must war to the end. God has a care for the body ; the body has a part to play in the divine economy. It is ' for the Lord ' as the ' Lord is for the body.' [2] It can be made a ' living sacrifice, holy, acceptable to God,' [3] and ' a temple of the Holy Spirit.' [4] Its members may be used as weapons of righteousness [5]—part of the same armoury, we may say, as the ' helmet of salvation ' and the ' sword of the spirit.' Most surprising of all,—though redemption from the *flesh* is no doubt to S. Paul, the goal of the Christian life, the body—transformed and glorified indeed, but still the body—shall share in this deliverance. [6]

Again, if we have seen rigorism raising its head even in that ' table of household duties ' which has so often been thought to embody the full Christian code of this-world morality, we must be equally ready to recognize a striking piece of genuinely humanist feeling where we should least of all expect it. In the heart of the ' apathetic ' passage to which allusion has already been made stands a phrase of extraordinary importance. ' Let each man abide in that calling wherein he was called . . . Brethren, let each man, wherein he was called, therein abide with God ' is the R.V. rendering. [7] The words ' call ' and ' calling ' here obviously have two meanings. There is the ' call ' to be a Christian, and the ' calling ' (as we say), or worldly avocation, already being followed when the call to Christianity comes. It would have suited S. Paul's purpose, we might have thought, to have said, ' Let each man remain in the circumstances, conditions, profession, or status, in which he was when he was converted.' But he has a deeper meaning than that. Quite deliberately he places these secular conditions and circumstances—this profession or status in which a man happens to be at the time of his conversion—on the same spiritual level as that conversion itself. Each is a ' call ' or ' calling ' direct from God. To express this the apostle is forced to use the Greek word *klēsis* in an entirely new sense ; for no strict parallel to the use of ' calling ' for secular ' avocation '—a usage so familiar to us in modern English—can be found in contemporary literature. [8] The inference

---

[1] 1 Cor. 9[27].

[2] 1 Cor. 6[13] ; cp. also *ib.*, 7[34]—one can be ' holy ' in body as well as in spirit.

[3] Rom. 12[1].   [4] 1 Cor. 6[19].   [5] Rom. 6[13].   [6] Phil. 3[21].

[7] 1 Cor. 7[20], [24]—ἕκαστος ἐν τῇ κλήσει ᾗ ἐκλήθη, ἐν ταύτῃ μενετω . . . ἕκαστος ἐν ᾧ ἐκλήθη, ἀδελφοί, ἐν τούτῳ μενέτω παρὰ Θεῷ.

[8] Weiss, *op. cit.*, p. 459, is inclined to rob S. Paul of the credit due to him for this conception, and holds that he was anticipated by the Stoics. Bonhöffer, however (*Epiktet und das Neue Testament*, pp. 37 ff.) shows clearly that in the passage on which Weiss relies (which, incidentally, is from Epictetus, and therefore at least sixty years later than S. Paul) κλῆσις always implies ' a dangerous or critical conjuncture ' in which a man finds himself, and in which God calls upon him to play the man. He maintains emphatically, therefore, that the Stoic κλῆσις is neither a *general* call to a new life (p. 37), nor a ' calling ' (vocation) in our modern sense (p. 208). He will not allow us, however, to take the κλῆσις of 1 Cor. 7[20], [24] as a ' calling ' or ' vocation,' and refers it to God's general calling of man to salvation ; but

is as amazing as it is inevitable. This 'Oriental,' this 'ascetic,' this Puritan who stands aloof from the everyday life of the world —it is to him we owe the great Christian truth that the most ordinary and secular employment can and should be regarded as a mission directly laid upon us by the Omnipotent God Himself.

(d) The Fourth Gospel.

That juxtaposition of the two strains of thought—the rigorist and the humanist—which we have been tracing through the New Testament, is to be seen in its most paradoxical form in the Fourth Gospel. It has become, indeed, a commonplace of Johannine exegesis. ' The gospel,' Dr. Lock says,[1] ' holds in equal poise sides of truth and life which are often placed in opposition to one another.' It is ' pervaded from end to end,' in Professor Scott's words, ' by one grand antinomy.' [2] A Jewish writer is betrayed into calling it epigrammatically [3] ' the gospel of Christian love and Jew-hatred.' More fully, but with ample justification, Dean Inge writes :—

> ' The intense ethical dualism of the Fourth Gospel is an-
> other perplexing phenomenon to those who look for philo-
> sophical consistency in a religious treatise. . . . Although the
> Logos is the immanent cause of all life, so that "without Him
> nothing whatever came into being," the " darkness " in which
> the light shines is no mere absence of colour, but a positive
> malignant thing, a rival kingdom which has its own subjects
> and its own sphere. . . . The writer is not careful to draw the
> line between the ethical dualism, which was part of his religious
> experience, and the metaphysical dualism which would have
> subverted the foundations of his intellectual experiences.' [4]

the five lines which he devotes to the passage (p. 208) show that he has no appreciation of its niceties.   Moulton-Milligan, *Vocabulary, s.v.*, seems also to miss its significance.

[1] Gore-Goudge-Guillaume, *New Commentary*, iii (New Testament), p. 240; though Dr. Lock is not here referring to the ethical problem.

[2] E. F. Scott, *The Fourth Gospel*, p. 12.

[3] *Jewish Encyclopædia*, ix, p. 251.

[4] *DCG.*, i, p. 889.—It follows from this, as Dean Inge rightly suggests, that the dualism of the Fourth Gospel is *empirical* through and through ; it contradicts the whole theological Logos-doctrine which is the author's dearest thought. ' The sources of this ethical dualism may be found partly in the spiritual struggles of an intensely devout nature, but to a greater extent, probably, in the furious antagonism of Judaism to nascent Christianity' (Inge, *loc. cit.*)—but *not* in ' John's ' theological outlook. (So also Bousset, *KC.*, p. 182—' John's *practical* dualism is more pronounced than Paul's, his theoretical dualism, on the other hand, is much less strongly expressed.')   Hence the ethical dualism in the Fourth Gospel is in a sense *accidental ;* it may have affinities with fundamental Christian thoughts, but it was only by the accident of circumstance that the writer was led to em-phasize it.   Had his life and environment been otherwise, there might have been no dualism in his teaching at all.   It is because of this that accusations of dualism against the New Testament are commonly directed against S. Paul (*infra*, p. 88), and only in a minor degree against the Fourth Gospel.   (Curi-ously enough W. Bauer, *HNT.*, vi, p. 240, takes the exactly opposite view;

The contrast, however, is not merely one between ethical dualism and philosophical monism, as Dr. Inge appears to suggest. It is equally marked and equally perplexing if we consider the ethical sphere alone. Neither the Fourth Gospel nor the allied epistles give even so much sanction to specific ascetic practices as could be drawn from particular passages in the Synoptists and the Pauline corpus. It is possible to say of the author that the ' idea of asceticism is not so much foreign as repulsive to him.'[1] Yet his hostile use of the term ' cosmos ' (' the world ') would lend his authority to every degree of rigorist excess ; and it was this fact, no doubt, as much as any other, which made his work the favourite gospel of different gnostic sects.[2]

At first sight, the ' world ' in the Johannine writings,—meaning, beyond all doubt, the sum-total of humanity,[3] apart from the Church of the redeemed—appears as something wholly evil. Without Christ it is ' darkness ' and not light.[4] It has refused to know the Word, its creator.[5] Its ruler is Satan, and it appears to tolerate his rule with equanimity—so that both together are destined to suffer the same fate.[6] Everything that is ' in the world,' being lust of flesh and lust of eyes and vainglory of life, is of the world, and not of God.[7] The world has given birth to the false prophets who are of anti-Christ's part ; they speak ' of the world ' and the world heareth them.[8] Christ cannot or will not pray for it ;[9] and its hatred is focussed upon Him[10] and His disciples.[11]

The ethical complement of all this—the *verso* of the new commandment that Christians should love one another—is provided by the injunction, ' Love not the world, neither the things that are in the world. If any man love the world, the love of the Father is not in him.'[12] The business of the Christian appears to be not to ' save,' but to ' overcome ' the world.[13] The command seems absolute and unconditioned ; the most extreme and anti-social of ascetics could shelter himself behind it, and defend his practices as no more than its literal fulfilment. It is therefore with real surprise that the reader comes across other passages in which the world, so far from being treated as irrevocably opposed to God, is

the author of the Fourth Gospel is a dualist through and through,—he only adopts mystical and metaphysical monism, without inner conviction, as the framework of his thought. Bauer suggests no reason for this curious procedure.)

[1] H. L. Jackson, *Problem of the Fourth Gospel*, p. 91.

[2] E.g. Valentinus made special use of the Prologue to the Fourth Gospel ; see [Clem. Alex.], *Excerp. ex Theod.*, 6, 7 ; cp. Irenæus, *haer.*, i, 8, 5 ; Tert., *de praescr.*, 38 ; and cp. V. H. Stanton, *The Gospels as Historical Documents*, i, pp. 64-69, 205.

[3] Cp. Jn. 7^4, 14^{19}, 17^6, [18].   [4] Jn. 1^9, 8^{12}.

[5] Jn. 1^{10}—' the world knew Him not.'

[6] Jn. 12^{31}—' the prince of this world,' cp. 14^{30}, 16^{11}; 1 Jn. 5^{19}—' the whole world lieth in the evil one'; Jn. 12^{31} and 16^{11}—both the 'world' and 'the prince of this world' are 'judged.'

[7] 1 Jn. 2^{16}.   [8] 1 Jn. $4^{1, 3-5}$.   [9] Jn. 17^9.

[10] Jn. 7^7, 15^{18}.   [11] Jn. $15^{18, 19}$, 17^{14}; 1 Jn. 3^{13}.

[12] 1 Jn. 2^{15}.   [13] 1 Jn. $5^{4, 5}$.

spoken of as under His peculiar favour and love. The Christian, we have just heard, is *not* to love the world ; but *God* so loved it that He gave His only-begotten Son, that the world should be saved through Him.[1] 'The life of the world' is God's especial interest,—to give life to the world is the purpose of the Son's coming.[2] And there is no braver confession of faith than that of the despised Samaritans : 'We have heard for ourselves, and know that this is indeed the Saviour *of the World.*'[3]

So perplexed have critics been by these last sentences, with their pointed contrast to the evangelist's general attitude about the 'world,' that they have resorted to desperate shifts to explain them away. They suggest for example that 'John' is not in these passages 'speaking his own mind ; his own mind is expressed in 1 Jn. iv. 9—God sent His Son into the world that *we* (not *it*) might live through Him.'[4] 'Saviour of the world,' again (we are told) is merely a hackneyed title taken over from Græco-Roman emperor-worship or the cults of heathen gods ;[5] the author uses it in no more than this conventional sense. It is difficult to take these suggestions seriously. 'Cosmos' is one of the evangelist's key-words ; if he attributes to it two antithetically opposed meanings, we must give full weight to the fact. It can point in one direction only. Dualism and monism were both at work in his mind ; as with the other writers in the New Testament, so with him—perhaps the greatest of them all.[6] Even his most fundamental conceptions were bound to show traces of both these opposite interpretations of the universe.[7]

---

[1] Jn. 3[16, 17], cp. 1[29], 12[47] ; 1 Jn. 2[2].　　[2] Jn. 6[33, 51].　　[3] Jn. 4[42].

[4] W. Bauer on Jn. 3[16] (*HNT.*, vi, p. 54 ; cp. *ib.*, p. 18, for Hermetic and other parallels).

[5] Id. on Jn. 4[42] (*HNT.*, vi, p. 71), cp. Bousset, *KC.*, pp. 241-244; A. Deissmann, *Light from the Ancient East*[4] (E. tr., 1927), pp. 363-365 ; A. D. Nock, in Rawlinson (ed.) *Essays on the Trinity and Incarnation*, pp. 87-94 ; where full references and illustrations are given. Note particularly Mr. Nock's conclusion, p. 93 : 'The application of the title *Soter* to Jesus is not in origin connected with non-Jewish religious use of the word.'

[6] Cp. also the way in which throughout the gospel 'the Jews' without differentiation are treated as a community finally hostile to the Church (e.g. Jn. 2[18, 20]; 5[10, 15, 16, 18]; 7[1, 13, 35]; 8[22, 48, 52, 57]; 19[7, 12, 31]; 20[19]) and yet 'salvation is of the Jews' (4[22])—well commented on by E. F. Scott, *Fourth Gospel*, pp. 74-77.

[7] It would be tedious to spend time drawing out the evidence for the remaining books of the New Testament. Of Hebrews more must be said (*infra*, pp. 159 ff.). The Apocalypse, with its clarion-call to martyrdom, is defiantly rigorist; but the peaceful and almost pastoral feeling of the last two chapters exhibits a different temper. For the Pastoral Epistles we may quote F. Koehler's comment on 1 Tim. 5[23] (*SNT.*, ii, p. 429) : 'This personal warning to Timothy covers a reminder to the leaders of the community not to allow a disproportionate enthusiasm for total abstinence from wine to assume the appearance of sanctioning ascetic tendencies (cp. 4[3]). But the recommendation of wine *for medical purposes* (only) is a half-hearted concession to asceticism, though it does not force the author to contradict his fundamental principle (4[4]: " Every creature of God is good, and nothing is to be rejected "). Thus he manages to evade the crucial question, how far the use of wine as a beverage is legitimate ; but it is certain that he would not condemn its enjoyment in moderation.' Koehler regards this as typical of the writer's 'sober and practical' attitude in general.

III. The Origin of New Testament Rigorism.

All the New Testament evidence, therefore, conspires to enforce a single conclusion—that in apostolic Christianity there may be discovered both a strong leaning towards humanism and a strong leaning towards rigorism. We are faced once more with the problem, Is the rigorist strain, whose claim to a substantive place in Christian ethics the modern world would be so slow to allow, indigenous in our religion, or is it an alien intrusion? As with the gospels, so here, there are those who are not slow to set down the presence of asceticism in the apostolic age to the eschatological motive, with the implication that, if eschatology be discounted or ' transmuted,' asceticism need not trouble us further.

So of primitive Christianity in general G. Volkmar has said :—[1]

' With the expectation of the Parousia, marriage and the bringing-up of children came to be regarded as superfluous, and were consequently thought of as signs of an absorption in earthly interests which was out of harmony with the near approach to the goal of those hopes.'

Similarly Professor Troeltsch :—[2]

' Art and science are unknown in the circles within which the gospel rises . . . State and law are on the downward grade. Work and property are dangerous if they go beyond the care for the day. The gospel loves the poor . . . but it neither formulates nor solves any social problems, for the days of society are numbered, and the day of God's kingdom is at hand. Let us all possess the world as though we possessed it not. But the heralds of this gospel shall go further—they are to make themselves eunuchs for the kingdom of heaven, and to give all their possessions to the poor, so that, as shining patterns of a readiness for every sacrifice, they may proclaim the great message through the cities of Israel until He comes.'

The conclusion here suggested is as ill-founded as it was in the case of the teaching of our Lord. It depends almost wholly upon the isolated and momentary phenomenon of communism in the primitive Church at Jerusalem ; [3] and on S. Paul's eschatological allusions in the Corinthian discussion of marriage and virginity. Neither of these pieces of evidence will bear the strain to which it is subjected. For the second, we have already seen that S. Paul's argument is substantially independent of it ; and we may agree with Johannes Weiss, who has already been quoted so often, that in S. Paul's other-worldliness ' the temporal note—the contrast

---

[1] Quoted, Schweitzer, *Quest of the Historical Jesus*, p. 227.
[2] Quoted F. von Hügel, *Essays and Addresses on the Philosophy of Religion*, i, pp. 158, 159.
[3] Acts 2[44, 45], 4[32-35].

between this æon and the next—shades off imperceptibly into the transcendental—the contrast between the earthly and the heavenly.'[1] Its tone is 'religious,' not 'eschatological.'[2] Of the former we may say, both that the incident is probably exaggerated by the author of Acts, and that in any case it was extremely short-lived; despite the apocalyptic interests of the moment S. Paul strongly deprecates the attempt to introduce a similar system (or want of system) at Thessalonica.[3] Other-worldliness in the New Testament is in the main independent of eschatology.

But may it not have another and even more insidious source— a source no less foreign to the genius of Christianity, but far more difficult to discover and eradicate? The pioneers of the *religions-geschichtliche* school of theology in Germany—notably Wilhelm Bousset and Richard Reitzenstein—have thought as much. To them, as is well-known, it has seemed necessary to comprehend the entire religious phenomena of the Graeco-Roman world, Christianity included, under a single formula; though in Bousset's theory the formula is more capable of analysis into separate, self-existent elements, both on the pagan and on the Christian side, than Reitzenstein seems to allow. The formula is as follows. Hellenism, now for many centuries subject to the influence of oriental dualism,[4] was gripped by a deep disquietude, showing itself in a distrust of matter, the body, and the passions as being under the dominance of evil and 'Heimarmené,' or fate, personified by the astral bodies. From this complex tyranny of evil, release was desired; and release was possible. Over against evil stands God, and in some men at least there is a spark of divine nature[5] capable of return to God. That return might be spoken of in many ways—as a rebirth, a new life, a becoming God ('apotheosis') or 'becoming in God' ('enthousiasmos'), a possession of or possession by the divine spirit, a reception of knowledge ('gnosis') or illumination ('photismos'), a 'seeing God' or spiritual marriage. But whatever it might be called, the man who achieved it, or to whom it was vouchsafed, entered into a distinct and clearly marked category different from that of ordinary men—the category of the 'pneumatikoi,' or spiritual persons; of the 'teleioi,' the 'perfect ones' or 'initiates.' Many nostrums were hawked about the spiritual market-place by which this new experience might be attained—mysteries, private and public, astrological and magical runes, ritual or verbal initiations. The hierophants naturally

---

[1] *Das Urchristentum*, p. 438.
[2] *Ib.*—Weiss's choice of words in which to express the contrast is awkward; but the meaning is clear.
[3] 2 Thess. 3[6-12].
[4] The main instruments in popularizing this dualism in the west were of course Orphism, and the *Phædo* of Plato. For Orphism, see *infra*, p. 482; for Plato, cp. *Phædo*, 64-68, 79-84, 97-100.
[5] Gnostic phrases for this divine spark are conveniently collected by Bousset, *KC.*, p. 195.

looked askance at their rivals; the postulants—as naturally—attempted one remedy after another as each was found to fail.[1]

Asceticism, though not necessarily either long-protracted or highly rigorous, was no doubt a constant feature of these initiations. But it is not on this fact that Bousset and Reitzenstein lay stress, for as a rule the asceticism involved was of a specifically 'cultus' character.[2] It involved prohibitions ('Touch not, taste not, handle not') of a kind which Christianity not merely discounted, but openly reprobated. Its dominant motif was that of ceremonial 'cleanness' or 'uncleanness.' New Testament rigorism, if not dominated by, is at all events bound up with ethical associations—such and such things are to be avoided because they 'lust against the Spirit,' or are 'displeasing to God.' Pagan asceticism, on the contrary, is directed towards securing that the ritual shall be validly performed. No doubt the idea of 'pleasing the god' is implicit here as well, but it is not primary. No attempt, therefore, to prove an immediate connexion between Christian and non-Christian asceticism, a direct imitation of the latter by the former, can have much hope of success.

But there may be an indirect or mediate connexion which unites the two, despite their superficial diversity. They may both spring from a common theological root. Such a hypothesis might, for example, lay hold on the idea of 'pleasing God,' and finding this common to both systems, show that it led by natural transitions to the prohibitions on either side. But even this is unnecessary. If it can be shown that New Testament Christianity shared in the alleged fundamental dualism of contemporary paganism, and accepted its conception of whole classes of phenomena, activities, and impulses irrevocably antipathetic to the divine purposes in the universe—a category of being incapable of redemption, and fitted only to destruction—then we should have at hand something potent enough to account for all the asceticism in the New Testament, and far more besides. Asceticism—complete flight from the world, complete mortification of the body—would now be the only way to God; and if the New Testament were found to develop this inference more consistently than paganism, that would only prove Christianity to be the fine flower of hellenistic religious thought. It is the primacy of such a dualist strain in the New Testament that modern German theology claims to have established.

We must note the exact extent of the claim. It is not that S. Paul and S. John have certain ideas, phrases, striking turns of thought, in common with this alleged pagan dualism. That would be natural enough, but it would prove nothing whatever; a man

---

[1] The general *religionsgeschichtliche* formula, as summarized above, is built up upon the evidence of which instances have been given (*supra*, pp. 47, 53); cp. also *infra*, pp. 208 ff., also additional notes D and G. Reference to the principal modern authorities are given on the appropriate pages, and need not be recapitulated here.

[2] On cultus-asceticism in general, *infra*, p. 480, additional note D.

may borrow freely of his opponent's armoury without surrendering what is individual to himself. For the 'mystery-hypothesis' to hold good, it must be proved that the *dominant* theological conceptions in New Testament Christianity are dualistic; nothing less will serve the purpose of the argument. On the other hand, it is not necessary for such proof that we should have a full knowledge of contemporary pagan aspirations and practices—such knowledge, of course, is wholly impossible at the present day. If it could be shown that New Testament thought as a whole is capable of a consistently dualistic interpretation, and that the writers made steady choice of a vocabulary which to the contemporary world could have none other than a dualistic connotation, the case would be sufficiently established. Reitzenstein's single all-pervading syncretistic pagan theology may be a philologist's dream; but so long as dualistic phrases are found widespread in the pagan world, and S. Paul (for example) can be convicted of using them with full consciousness of the meaning that would be put upon them, and without any effort to evade the imposition of that meaning, the work would have been done. New Testament Christianity might perhaps be a *new* version of paganism, but pagan in essentials it would still remain.

In relation to S. Paul, with whom we are primarily concerned, Bousset starts at the most obvious point—the apostle's sharp antithesis between 'spirit' and 'flesh.'[1] That this antithesis is a dominant note of his soteriology is not to be denied; but is it as certainly dualist as we are asked to believe? The answer appears to be definitely in the negative. Even on Bousset's own statement of his theory it soon became evident that there was no such rooted dualism between 'flesh' and 'spirit' in contemporary thought as he suggested. The term 'sarkikos' ('fleshly') for the completely unilluminated occurs only in the *later* literature of gnosticism;[2] whilst in S. Paul himself, and indeed in many other first and second century writers, the dualism is very far from absolute.[3] Such antithesis as the apostle draws between the terms is wholly explicable as the development of a Jewish psychology which is very far from lending itself to rigorism.

That S. Paul uses the terms 'flesh' and 'spirit' in opposition to one another is self-evident. So also is the fact that of the two 'flesh' has an evil connotation, 'spirit' a good one. 'I know that in me, that is, in my flesh, dwelleth no good thing,' says the apostle;[4] he can speak of a 'flesh of sin,'[5] and the 'mind of the flesh' is 'death.'[6] So far as can be seen the emphasis he laid on

---

[1] Bousset, *KC.*, pp. 120-134.
[2] Bousset admits this implicitly, by his failure to quote any exact philological parallels from S. Paul's contemporaries (*KC.*, pp. 130-134).
[3] This is first allowed explicitly by Reitzenstein (*HMR.*, pp. 70, 340; *infra*, p. 92); Bousset is obviously not aware of it.
[4] Rom. 7¹⁸.   [5] Rom. 8³.
[6] Rom. 8⁶, ⁷; cp. Gal. 5¹⁹—the 'works of the flesh.'

this contrast was original.[1] But the vital question is a different one. Is the ' sarx,' the ' flesh,' in S. Paul's psychology a principle so evil that it is incapable of redemption ? that it must be extirpated, annihilated, before man can be saved ? If so, then it is clear that there is something *positive* in human nature—not a flaw, or failure, or weakness, but a recognized psychological disposition or tendency akin to the primitive instincts and part of the original human endowment—which is inherently evil, and against which unremitting war must be waged.

One fact is certain at the outset. To S. Paul the ' flesh ' is somehow bound up with the body and its needs.[2] In Rom. vii, 23, it is implicitly identified with ' the members ' ; [3] in Rom. viii, 10, he speaks of the ' body ' in language which shows that here at least it is a synonym for the ' flesh,' which occurred to him so naturally that he did not see its inappropriateness.[4] In 2 Cor. x, 2, 3, he uses the phrase ' to walk in the flesh '—which would naturally with him mean to ' live sinfully '—in the simple sense of ' living in a body,' and finds himself accordingly compelled to speak of ' warring after the flesh ' where he would normally have said ' walk after the flesh.' [5] These facts are in themselves significant. The body,

---

[1] So H. de Witt Burton, in his exhaustive review of the evidence up to and including the time of S. Paul (*Spirit, Soul, and Flesh*, Chicago, 1918) :—(p. 172) ' Neither in non-Jewish nor in Jewish writers does *sarx* seem to have acquired any ethical significance . . . though like *sôma* it is spoken of in disparagement as compared with the soul. . . . It is nowhere used to express the notion that matter is the source or cause of moral evil ' ; (p. 175) in the magic texts *sarx* has no distinctive meaning ; (p. 177) in the Hermetica *sarx* is very infrequently used.

[2] As constantly in the Old Testament, *HDB.*, iv, p. 165 ; Burton, *op. cit.*, p. 192.

[3] The ' law in the members ' is evidently the ' law of sin ' to which the flesh is subject (Rom. 7[25]). Cp. also Col. 3[5].

[4] ' If Christ is in you, *the body* is dead because of sin, but the spirit is life because of righteousness.' The antithesis is a difficult one, and the interpretation ' body ' = ' flesh ' is not the only one. Sanday and Headlam, *ad loc.*, refer back to 5[12] (' death passed unto all men, for that all sinned ') and take the words to mean ' the body is *mortal*.' But this would require θνητόν for νεκρόν (as in 8[11]) ; and in any case S. Paul does not begin to speak of physical death till verse 11. Cp. also the ' works of the *body* ' in 8[13].

[5] ἐν σαρκὶ γὰρ περιπατοῦντες οὐ κατὰ σάρκα στρατευόμεθα. Again a curious choice of words. S. Paul constantly uses περιπατεῖν, with ἐν, κατὰ, or the simple dative ; but *always* (except here) in an ethical sense (e.g. with ἐν, Rom. 6[4] ; 2 Cor. 4[2] ; Eph. 2[2, 10], 5[2] ; Col. 2[6], 3[7], 4[5] ; with κατὰ, Rom. 8[4], 14[15] ; 1 Cor. 3[3], 10[2] ; with dative, 2 Cor. 12[18], Gal. 5[16]). There is therefore an epigrammatic tendency in his use of it here in a physical sense. Why did he not drive the epigram home by repeating the περιπατεῖν in an ethical sense—ἐν σαρκὶ περιπατοῦντες οὐ κατὰ σάρκα περιπατοῦμεν (a perfectly possible sentence, for on the whole he uses κατὰ σάρκα more commonly than ἐν σαρκὶ when he wishes to convey an ethical implication) ? By avoiding this form of sentence he seems almost to evade the issue, for the rebellious Corinthians have accused him directly of περιπατεῖν κατὰ σάρκα (2 Cor. 10[2]). The reminiscence of the text in *Ep. ad Diognet.* 5[8] (ἐν σαρκὶ τυγχάνουσιν, ἀλλ' οὐ κατὰ σάρκα ζῶσιν) is nearer the form we should have expected ; and, although its innovations may be due merely to lapse of memory, it shows how little S. Paul's actual turn of phrase commended itself. But none of this affects the fact that he can on occasion use ἐν σαρκὶ (even where the περιπατεῖν of the context suggests ethical ideas) in a wholly neutral sense, and as a mere equivalent for ἐν σώματι.

as we have seen, was to S. Paul redeemable ; and though he never asserts that the 'flesh' can be redeemed—such a suggestion, as will appear, would have been impossible on his vocabulary—its association with the body makes it probable that he cannot regard it as wholly evil.

The probability is confirmed by other evidence. Although S. Paul's 'flesh' stands in direct relation to the body and its needs, its meaning is not thereby exhausted. In Phil. iii, 3-7, speaking of 'confidence in the flesh,' he enumerates as the grounds of this confidence his Israelitish birth, his tribal origin from Benjamin, his untainted Hebraism, his circumcision on the eighth day, his Pharisaic upbringing, the persecuting zeal with which he upheld the law, and his legal blamelessness. On the evidence of this text Dr. Burton concludes[1] that 'sarx' means to S. Paul 'the whole of his personality and possessions except that which comes through a distinct personal religious experience'; elsewhere he expands the statement to add that the 'sarx' 'may even specifically include whatever excellent powers, privileges, etc., come by heredity.'[2] In other uses of the word the reference to the body is even slighter. In 2 Cor. i, 17, S. Paul mentions 'fickleness' as an example of 'fleshly purposes'; although 'fickleness' is a psychological impulse as nearly independent of physical promptings as any impulse could be. So too are some at least of the 'works of the flesh' in Gal. v, 19-23. The 'infirmity of the flesh' among the Roman Christians which forced the apostle to speak to them 'after the manner of men' has no connexion with the body.[3] The 'fleshly wisdom' of 2 Corinthians[4] appears to be no more than a tendency to speculation ; the Colossian ascetics, whose life was one continued mortification of the body, are on that account—so it would seem—paradoxically accused of having 'fleshly minds.'[5]

These varied meanings of the word in S. Paul suggest at first

---

[1] *Op. cit.*, p. 193.

[2] *Ib.*, p. 186. Cp. *ib.*, p. 194, ' The *sarx* can do much, though it is the *pneuma* only that can produce the true, the perfect.' Although I accept Dr. Burton's conclusion without reserve, I must admit that many of the texts which he cites in its support on p. 186 do not appear to me to contribute anything of value to the argument.

[3] Rom. 6[19]. The ' infirmity of the flesh ' has sometimes been interpreted as ' moral hindrances which prevent the practice of Christianity,' but its principal meaning here must surely be ' defective apprehension of spiritual truth ' (so Sanday and Headlam, *ad loc.*). ' I speak after the manner of men,' again, might mean either, the use of a crude or ' common ' (so Sanday and Headlam) illustration, or ' an illustration drawn from human relationships ' (Lietzmann in *HNT.*, *ad loc.*). Actually S. Paul's very happy phrase covers all these different *nuances* :—' I use an illustration drawn from this human relationship of slavery. It is crude and inappropriate, for it is absurd to speak seriously of being " enslaved " to righteousness. You, however, would not understand more spiritual language, because your moral immaturity makes you still feel the life of Christianity to be an oppressive burden.'

[4] 2 Cor. 1[12]—the phrase refers back to the ' wisdom of this world ' or ' human wisdom ' of 1 Cor. 2[6, 13], with which the ' words taught by the Spirit ' (*ib.*) are contrasted.

[5] Col. 2[18-23].

sight that his usage of it is not consistent.[1]   Here, however, we may apply the principle already employed in respect of the Fourth Gospel. ' Sarx ' is one of the great keywords of Pauline theology ; and though the apostle might use outlying terms in various senses, it is incredible that he should have any vagueness about one of his most central conceptions.   We must attempt therefore to summarize his uses of the term in some all-inclusive phrase.

It is customary among scholars who do not accept the extremer views we have been considering to define S. Paul's ' flesh,' following Old Testament usage, as ' human nature in its weakness.' [2]   But the passages just quoted show that this definition is too narrow. A better suggestion is that of Dr. Laidlaw—' Flesh is what nature evolves ; spirit what God in His grace bestows ' ; [3]—though even here we must interpret ' nature ' as covering both heredity and environment.   This provides a basis for a definite conclusion on the main question.   There is not a word in the passage just quoted from Philippians to suggest that these gifts of nature, by heredity and environment, are anything but good in themselves ; and yet they are ' of the flesh.'   In what sense then can the ' flesh ' be evil ? The answer is clear.   S. Paul has indeed two meanings for the word, but they are very closely connected.   It implies, first, those factors in a man's character, possessions or surroundings which, though they are good in themselves, it is *possible for him to misuse* or misapply ; it implies, in the second place, the *tendency to misuse them* which, apart from grace, is the normal and indeed inevitable tendency of life.[4]   But even this latter tendency is in itself no more than a potentiality.   Not until *sin* enters in does the flesh become positively evil ; *then* it is defiled [5] with a defilement from which we

---

[1] So Burton, *op. cit.*, p. 197—' Where the two terms (" flesh " and " spirit ") stand in antithesis . . . in S. Paul, it is by no means always the same meanings that are contrasted.'
[2] Sanday and Headlam, *Epistle to the Romans*, p. 169, cp. p. 181 ; G. B. Stevens, *Theology of the New Testament*, pp. 341, 342, cp. p. 347.
[3] *HDB.*, iv, p. 166.
[4] Cp. G. B. Stevens, *op. cit.*, p. 347—' Metaphysically considered, the flesh is neutral ; empirically considered it is sinful.'   Dr. Stevens' admirable discussion seems to have one fault only, that it assumes too close an identification of ' body ' and ' flesh ' in S. Paul's thought (see *supra*, p. 90).
[5] So also can the ' spirit ' be defiled, 2 Cor. 7¹ ; a passage which has always proved a difficulty to those who regard *pneuma* in S. Paul as the wholly divine element entering into the Christian from without.   Marcion was the first to see it, and substituted ' blood ' for ' spirit ' (Tert., *adv. Marc.*, v, 12—or was this Tertullian's own text ?   In *de pud.* 15 he gets it right.)   Lietzmann (*HNT.*, *ad loc.*) hesitatingly suggests that ' flesh and spirit ' here is a popular expression for body and soul, but does not deal very happily with the problem which would be created by S. Paul saying, ' cleanse yourselves from bodily defilement.'   He would obviously welcome a suggestion that the sentence is a non-Pauline interpolation, though he does not see his way to making it explicitly himself.   The passage proves that we can no more take S. Paul's *pneuma* as something wholly divine, than we can take his *sarx* as something wholly evil ; and thus weakens still further the case for S. Paul's ' gnosticism.' It is noteworthy again that 2 Cor. 7⁵ refers back *verbatim* to 2¹³ (' had no relief '), and that there is therefore a complete identification between ' relief for the flesh ' in the one, and ' relief for the spirit ' in the other.   Here again

can and must cleanse ourselves. But that which can be defiled is
not in itself defilement; and this alone proves that S. Paul did
not regard ' what nature evolves '—whether within the man or
around him—as wholly evil.

So much as this is admitted by Reitzenstein, the protagonist—as
Bousset was not [1]—of the strictly philological method in theology.
After a somewhat misleading reference to Ignatius [2] which need
not delay us, he proceeds to argue that S. Paul employs the
adjective ' fleshly ' explicitly of those who, though still ' babes,'
are nevertheless ' babes *in Christ*.' [3] And although he will not
admit that in the ' perfect ' or ' spiritual ' man any trace of the
' flesh ' remains, the force of this passage constrains him to the
conclusion that ' flesh ' and ' spirit ' are not mutually exclusive,
because ' flesh ' and ' fleshly ' are ' not as yet terminological usages
permanently stamped as the currency in which such mutually
exclusive opposition is to be expressed.' [4] The concession, though
grudging, is important; Reitzenstein admits that S. Paul can
discern a ' spiritual ' colouring even in the ' flesh '—it is not wholly
doomed to perdition.

Reitzenstein, however, is none the less insistent on the alleged
dualism of S. Paul's theology; but he reaches his conclusion by a

Lietzmann is so distressed by the equation as to toy with the idea of interpolation (*HNT*., ix, p. 131). Note further that in 2 Cor. 3[3] S. Paul uses
' hearts of flesh ' in Ezekiel's sense (Ezk. 11[19], 36[26]) as opposed to ' stone ';
here again 'fleshly' comes near to meaning 'spiritual,' though the metaphor
is too involved to allow of an exact equation.

[1] Cp. Bousset, *KC*., p. 135—' The decisive factor must be the great
positive agreements, *not the terminology*.'

[2] *HMR*., p. 326—' For Ignatius, *pneuma* and *sarx* are the two great
complementary antitheses '—that is true, as everyone agrees; cp. especially
Ign., *Eph*. 8[2]. But Reitzenstein does *not* say, either that to Ignatius the
' flesh ' is so little a wholly evil thing that Christ can actually be called
sarkikos as well as *pneumatikos* (*Eph*., 7[2], cp. *Smyrn*., 12), or that the central
thought of the whole of Ignatius' theology is (not the supersession of ' flesh '
by ' spirit,' but) the harmonizing of flesh and spirit in love through the grace
of Christ (see e.g. *Eph*., 8, 10; *Magn*., 1, 13; *Rom*., inscr.; *Phil*., inscr.;
Trall., inscr.; 12). This is all the more surprising as Reitzenstein actually
quotes *Eph*. 7[2]. What is clear is that for Ignatius the *sarx*, though opposed
in some sense to the spirit, is far more amenable to spiritual influence than
in S. Paul's usage. Bousset, *KC*., p. 218, faces the facts about Ignatius much
more fairly than Reitzenstein.

[3] 1 Cor. 3[1,3] (*HMR*., p. 340). The word used in 3[1] is *sarkinoi*, not *sarkikoi*,
but from Rom. 7[14] it is clear that S. Paul makes no difference between the
two.

[4] *HMR*., p. 340—' Es (i.e. the word *sarkinos*) schliesst das *pneuma*
offenbar nicht voll aus, weil es eben nicht wie *psychikos*, einer festgeprägten
und *auf dem ausschliesslichen Gegensatz berechneten* Terminologie entnommen
ist.' (Italics as in the original.) Reitzenstein (*ib*.) only reaches this conclusion by assuming that S. Paul could not call them *psychikoi*, because they
were already baptized, and must therefore be distinguished strictly from the
(presumably unbaptized) *psychikoi* of 2[14]. I see no ground whatever for this
assumption, and there is nothing in the text to suggest that *psychikos* and
sarkikos (or *sarkinos*) in 2[14], 3[1,3] are anything but synonymous. But it is
significant that, on whatever grounds, Reitzenstein should hold that the
position which makes *sarx* in S. Paul wholly evil is untenable.

different route. Abandoning the contrast between 'flesh' and
'spirit' he fixes upon a second antithesis—that between the illuminated as 'pneumatikos' ('spiritual'), and the unilluminated as
'psychikos' ('natural'); and maintains that in the New Testament,
as in gnosticism, it connotes a completely rigorist dualism.   Here
for a moment we seem to be on firmer ground—'psychikos' in the
earliest 'gnostic' sources may perhaps denote the wholly unspiritual
man 'whose end is destruction,'[1] and Reitzenstein, by emending
the text, can even quote a parallel from the curious heathen document commonly known as the 'Mithras liturgy.'[2]   But at this point
a great gulf appears.   S. Paul only uses the word 'psychikos' in
two passages in the whole compass of his letters,[3] and apart from
this he is aware of no such radical opposition between 'pneuma'
and 'psyché' as we are asked to infer.[4]   Nor is the interpretation
of the passages in question by any means bound down to the dualism
which is attributed to them.[5]   It is surely obvious that the occurrence of a single word on two occasions only cannot by any sober
criticism be regarded as sufficient evidence for fathering upon the
apostle an entire system of thought of a highly contentious and
radical character.

Critical irresponsibility could hardly be expected to go further;
and yet in the case of S. John it has done so.   Starting from the
evangelist's deep interest in the vision of God as the goal of life,
Bousset assigns to him as his dominant thought the conception of
the deification or apotheosis of the Christian by means of the vision.[6]
That such a conception was common enough in the Hermetic literature, for instance, and that these texts have other points of kinship
with the Fourth Gospel, goes without saying; and for the moment
we may allow that the idea is dualist and ascetic in principle.   But
this cannot obviate the crucial fact that S. John never uses the
word *apotheosis*, or any word even remotely akin to it.[7]   'Eternal

---

[1] But see additional note E, *infra*, p. 487.

[2] See additional notes A and E, *infra*, pp. 473, 487.

[3] 1 Cor. 2^{14}, 15^{44-46}.

[4] S. Paul only uses the word *psyché* thirteen times.   Three times it means
simply 'person' or 'living being'; five times 'animate existence'; four
times at least the 'higher spiritual life'—something closely akin to *pneuma*
(2 Cor. 12^{15}, Eph. 6^6, Phil. 1^{27}, Col. 3^{23}).   In one case (1 Thess. 2^8) it might
have either the second or the third meaning.   This is surely decisive.

[5] In 1 Cor. 2^{14} *psychikos* must mean 'unilluminated,' but carries no connotation of moral evil with it.   In 15^{44-46} (the contrast between the 'natural'
and the 'spiritual' (resurrection) body), *sôma psychikon* means 'a body
adapted to be the vehicle of ordinary animate life,' as distinct from *sôma
pneumatikon*—'one adapted to be the vehicle of a purely spiritual (= invisible,
heavenly) life.'

[6] Bousset, KC., pp. 164-176—'Vergottung durch Gotteschau.'

[7] Bousset admits disingenuously (*KC.*, p. 168)—'*Apart from a single passage in the first Epistle*, the Johannine literature never speaks of the deification of the believer.'   The passage referred to is 1 Jn. 3^2: 'Beloved, now are
we children of God, and it is not yet made manifest what we shall be.   We
know that, if He shall be manifested, *we shall be like Him;* for we shall see
Him even as He is'!

life ' is his phrase ; and it is utterly unworthy of serious scholarship to suggest that the phrase ' eternal life ' cannot be employed without the implication of ' deification.' [1] If any inference at all is to be drawn from a comparison between the Fourth Gospel and the ' Hermetica,' it is that the former was deliberately planned to substitute for the theory of ' deification ' as the end of life a conception of a wholly different character. The means may perhaps be the same ; the goal is absolutely distinct.

IV. The Vision of God in the New Testament.

It seems impossible, therefore, to hold that New Testament theology borrowed anything of importance from the alleged dualism of the pagan world around it. The ancestry of the ascetic element in the New Testament has yet to be discovered ; and the problem of its legitimacy within the Christian scheme of life as a whole is no nearer solution than before. There for a moment we must leave the paradox, until the history of Christian asceticism shall have given us more material for a judgment. Another question, equally relevant to the subject, presents itself. Within a few generations of the apostles' day, rigorism will be found making a determined bid to capture the whole machinery of discipline, and to oust humanism altogether from the Church. Why was that attack delayed for nearly a hundred years, if it could appeal to the authority of scripture ?

No doubt it may have made such an attempt, but have been defeated by the exercise of apostolic authority. There are indications of this in the epistle to the Colossians and the Pastorals. But against a tendency so powerful and relentless as asceticism was about to prove, authority can make little headway except with a backing of strong principle. Such a principle the apostolic writers had ; it is to be found in their significant development of the doctrine of seeing God.

(a) The Teaching of Jesus.

Our Lord had promised the vision of God as a guerdon to the pure in heart. It is extraordinary—especially in view of the prominence which the thought had attained in contemporary religion, and the high relief into which New Testament theology was about to throw it—that the sentence seems to stand without even an echo in the synoptic tradition. But this judgment is at best superficial. In actual fact the idea of the vision dominates both our Lord's teaching and the synoptic presentation of His life.[2] Ideas are not conveyed by words alone ; emphasis often serves

---

[1] Bousset insists upon this suggestion (*KC.*, p. 169), basing it wholly and solely upon the fact that the Latin translation of the Hermetic ' Asclepius' renders ἀπεθέωσας by ' aeternitati fueris consecrare dignatus.'

[2] I must dissent entirely from Bultmann's statement (*Jesus*, pp. 46, 95, 96, 141) that ' there is no mysticism in the teaching of Jesus.'

to express them even better than direct enunciation. And the moment we seek to discover the *emphasis* of the Lord's work and teaching, as the Synoptists record them, the truth becomes evident. The whole emphasis of Jesus' teaching is laid upon the character of God and the nature of His Kingdom.

It has become the custom latterly to say that Jesus added little or nothing to the Jewish doctrine of God. Even the ' Fatherhood of God,' there is reason to suppose, was more widely accepted and more generously understood by His contemporaries than was once thought to be the case.[1] The statement is contentious, as all such statements must be ; probably it is exaggerated as well. Mr. H. G. Wood, following Dr. Moffatt's ' Theology of the Gospels,' has reason on his side when he says :—[2]

> ' The sense of the nearness and the reality of the God of love is Jesus' gift to man. This sense of nearness is expressed in His use of the term " Abba " in addressing His Father. Negatively, it is apparent in the abandonment of the customary terms of address of Jewish piety, and in the absence of the adjective " holy." Moffatt points out that Jesus uses the term " holy " in relation to God only once in the four gospels. The word implied a sense of distance that was untrue to the experience of Jesus.'

Happily we are not required to discuss whether our Lord's teaching about God was or was not a ' new teaching ' to pious Jews. What is important is that it was specifically and above all a *teaching about God*. He came ' preaching the good news of God.'[3] That He spoke also of the kingdom of God makes no difference to this fact : for if anything is certain as the result of modern research, it is that the kingdom, in Jesus' thought, whether it means ' realm ' or ' kingship,' is wholly bound up with the character of God. It is something in which *He* is to come—not a state of things prepared for His coming by human effort.[4] It is true, of course, that Jesus also spoke, and that constantly, of the character and behaviour necessary for those who would ' inherit,' ' enter into,' or ' possess ' the kingdom ; and that in so doing He purified, simplified, and breathed new life into the ethical code of Judaism. This is no more than to say that, like all great teachers, He spoke both of God and of man, or preached both doctrine and ethics. But whereas contemporary Judaism laid all the stress on *man*—that is to say on ethics, on what man has to do to fulfil the will of God—it

---

[1] C. G. Montefiore, *The Old Testament and After*, pp. 201-206 ; Id. in Lake and Foakes-Jackson, *Beginnings of Christianity*, I, i, pp. 39, 47 ff. ; *ib.*, p. 288 ; Bultmann, *Jesus*, pp. 176-178 ; Bousset, *RJ.*, pp. 377, 378. For reservations see Bousset, *loc. cit.* ; G. Dalman, *Words of Jesus* (E. tr.), pp. 189-194.

[2] A. S. Peake, *One-Volume Commentary on the Bible*, p. 664.

[3] Mk. 1[14] ; Mt. 4[23] ; Lk. 4[43].

[4] Cp. Bultmann, *op. cit.*, pp. 35, 37.

is surely true to say that by contrast the emphasis of Jesus' teaching
is upon *God*, rather than upon man—upon what God has done, is
doing, and shall do for His people.

So He tells of the divine Fatherhood which watches over the
lilies, the ravens, and the sparrows ; which sends rain upon the just
and the unjust alike ; which understands men's needs and gives
to them liberally ; which is patient and long-suffering. He tells
of a God always ready to welcome the prodigal, to search for the
lost sheep, or to give in His pleasure the kingdom to His flock ; and
of a heaven where there is infinite joy over the sinner that repents.
God sees in secret and shall reward openly ; God sows His seed far
and wide with a lavish hand, and reveals His innermost truths to
babes and sucklings. There is another side to the picture ; but it
is still a picture of God, though it represents Him—whenever the
time shall come that there is no more space for repentance—as a
Judge before whom there is no excuse. For all the ethical teaching
in the gospel, it seems impossible to deny that Jesus' primary thought
and message was about God, and that human conduct in his mind
came in a second and derivative place.

This means to say that Jesus, though He spoke little about
'seeing God,' brought God more vividly before the spiritual eyes
of His contemporaries than any other has ever done. He *gave* a
vision of God where others could only *speak* of it. It is worth while
to consider for a moment the importance of this factor in His
teaching. There must be both ethics and doctrine in every gospel
presented to men. But the moment ethics predominates over
doctrine—the moment, that is, that the thought of man ousts the
thought of God from the place of primary honour—the whole
purpose of a gospel is undone, whether the gospel be Christian or
any other. Ethics, or teaching about man and the conduct proper
to him, centres a man's thoughts upon himself ; and the end of
self-centredness is unethical and unevangelical alike. It is bound
to result—as S. Paul so clearly showed—either in spiritual pride or
in spiritual despair : and by neither of these roads can a man find
his true destiny. The path of purity, humility, and self-sacrifice
is only possible to the man who can *forget* himself, can ' disinfect
himself from egoism ' ; [1] whose mind is centred not upon himself,
but at least upon his fellows and their needs, and at most and at
best upon God and his neighbour seen through the eyes of God.
We cannot by thinking add a cubit to our stature : still less can we,
by thinking about *ourselves* and our conduct, achieve that self-
forgetfulness or self-sacrifice which is the hall-mark of the saints. [2]

[1] H. Bremond, *Histoire Littéraire du Sentiment Religieux en France*,
vii, p. 15.

[2] The conviction that the purpose of religion is to annihilate ' anthropocentrism ' or ' egocentrism ' (Bremond, *op. cit.*, vii, p. 16), and to render
life ' theocentric,' has revived with startling intensity in the last generation.
In Germany it has taken a primarily intellectualist form, and shows itself
(in the work of Karl Barth and Eric Schaeder, for example, and Bultmann
so far as he is influenced by them) as a demand for a new orientation in

There is another side to this truth, of course. It would be absurd to say that self-criticism and self-examination play no part in the making of saintliness.[1] But the essential fact about religion in its relation to ethics is this—that self-examination and self-criticism are dangerous in the highest degree unless the soul is already reaching out in self-forgetfulness to something higher and better than itself. Self-centredness, even in the morally earnest, is the greatest snare in life : ' God-centredness ' the only true salvation. We shall recur to this matter more fully at a later stage ;[2] in the meantime it throws a flood of light upon the whole of the New Testament. It makes it clear why Jesus spoke first and foremost of God, and only in the second place of man and his conduct. And it gives a reason why the Church fixed upon the single text in the beatitudes about seeing God, and elevated it into the summary of all that it had to give to men.

(b) The Synoptists.

The framework of all three synoptic gospels is that supplied by S. Mark ; and the watershed of S. Mark's gospel is the double peak of the confession of Peter and the Transfiguration.[3] To these connected events the whole of the earlier history of the gospel, with its gradual unveiling of our Lord's Messiahship, leads up ; with these events a new act opens in the drama—the act which is to find its climax on Calvary. It is significant enough that the central point of the gospel is a vision of the divinity breaking through the humanity of Jesus. The fact would become more significant still if for a moment we assume—with some modern scholars [4]— that the Transfiguration originally stood *before* S. Peter's confession

metaphysics or theology. In France, and above all in M. Bremond's great *Histoire*, it is principally interested in ethics, and so ultimately concentrated on the problem of prayer, in which the tension between ' religious ' and ' ethical ' practice is seen at its height. For this reason I shall have to revert continually to M. Bremond's epoch-making contribution, not merely to the history, but also to the philosophy (one might almost say the ' apologetics '), of religion. Readers who have not time to enjoy at length the infinite delights of the eight volumes of the *Histoire* which have been published so far, will find the most significant passages in vol. iii, pp. 23-42 ; vol. iv, pp. 336-353, 359-381 ; vol. vii, pp. 5-47, 144-162. Cp. *infra*, pp. 133 f., 203 f., 441 ff., and 489, additional note F.

[1] So the ' method of S. Sulpice ' (Bérulle and Olier) analyses prayer into the three stages of contemplation, communion, and *co-operation*. The order is important, if not all-important (Bremond, *op. cit.*, iii, p. 116).

[2] *Infra*, pp. 445-451.

[3] Dr. Rawlinson's edition of *S. Mark* (Westminster Commentaries) is an outstanding contribution to English scholarship, but it is doubtful whether he has proved his main contention (p. xx) that ' attempts to treat the Marcan arrangement of the gospel materials as supplying an outline, in chronological order, of the course of events are profoundly mistaken.' However, even if it be true that ' it is just the framework and the arrangement of the materials in our gospels which ought to be set down to the account of the Evangelists ' (*ib.*, p. xxi), it would only emphasize the doctrinal significance of the position assigned to the Transfiguration.

[4] Loisy, Schweitzer, P. E. More, and others.

in the narrative, and was indeed its cause.　But most significant of
all is the obvious truth that here, more than anywhere else in the
archetypal gospel, Christian imagination has from the very earliest
period loaded the original occurrence with devout embellishment.

The wealth of allusive material in the account of the Transfiguration has long been the despair of commentators, as well as the
whetstone of their ingenuity.　The successive phrases point to
associations not merely with other incidents in the gospel-narrative,
but with Old Testament and New Testament passages alike.　The
presence of Moses and Elijah, for example, can be explained in
various manners ; and each explanation, considered in its turn, has
about it an appropriateness which for the moment suggests that
it must be the dominant one.　Moses and Elijah represent the Law
and the Prophets respectively.　They are the two Old Testament
figures to whom (with Enoch) tradition assigned a translation to
heaven analogous to the Ascension.[1]　Each was expected to appear
as a forerunner of the Messiah.[2]　Each had received his crowning
revelation of the character of God on a mountain-height ; [3] and at
such a time Moses' face, at least, had shone, transfigured by the rare
experience.[4]　That Moses and Elijah are also the two witnesses of
the Apocalypse is of course self-evident.[5]　Moreover, Messianic
expectation was bound up with the hope of a ' prophet like unto
Moses,' and the ' Unto him ye shall hearken,' to which the Deutero-
nomic prophecy leads up, [6] is echoed by the ' Hear Him ' of the
Voice at the Transfiguration.

Similarly, this same Voice at the Transfiguration re-echoes also
the Voice heard at the Baptism : ' Thou art my beloved Son ' ; [7]

---

[1] Elijah, 2 Kgs. 2[11] ;　Moses, the apocryphal *Assumption of Moses* (first
century A.D.)—but the conception as regards Moses is not rabbinic (Strack-
Billerbeck, i, pp. 753-758).　Cp. 2 (4) Esdras 6[26]—' the men who have been
taken up, who have not tasted death from their birth,' and Box's note, *ad loc.*,
in Charles, *Apocr. and Pseudep.*, ii, p. 576.

[2] Moses, Dt. 18[15, 18] ; Elijah, Mal. 4[5].　In the LXX of Malachi, verse 4
(' Remember ye the law of Moses ') came *after* verses 5, 6 (' I will send you
Elijah . . .') ;　this may account for the order of the two names in Mk. 9[4],
which Mt. and Lk. rearrange into the natural historical sequence.　The ' two
witnesses ' of Rev. 11[3-11] are of course the same ; verses 5, 6a refer to Elijah ;
verse 6b to Moses.　Various secondary authorities for the text of Mk. 9[4],
Lk. 9[31] give this ' witness ' as the explicit reason for their presence at the
Transfiguration (A. Loisy, *Les Évangiles Synoptiques*, ii, p. 34).　A variant
tradition, preserved by Tertullian (*de an.*, 50), made Enoch the companion of
Elijah ;　but the many associations favouring Moses were too strong to allow
of effective competition (Rawlinson, *S. Mark*, pp. 117, 118, for further
references).

[3] Elijah, 2 Kgs. 19[8-18] ;　Moses, Ex. 24-31—for Moses also notice the
presence of three ' disciples ' (Aaron, Nadab and Abihu), Ex. 24[1] ; the preparatory six days, Ex. 24[16] ；　the entry into the cloud, 24[18] ；　and the uproar
at the descent from the mountain, Ex. 32[17, 18].

[4] Ex. 34[33-35].　It is curious that whereas Mt. (17[2]) and Lk. (9[29]) mention
the ' shining ' or ' change ' of Jesus' face, Mark is silent on the subject.
Streeter, *Four Gospels*, pp. 315, 316, suggests on MS. evidence that a word
or words to this effect have dropped out of the Marcan text.

[5] *Supra*, n. 2.　　　　　　　　　　[6] Dt. 18[15].

[7] Mk. 1[11]. Mt. 3[17], Lk. 3[22] (Mt. has ' This is ' for ' Thou art ').

and provokes the question—which is even more pressing with reference to the account of the Baptism—whether these manifestations of divine approval were primarily addressed to Jesus Himself, or to the bystanders. If to the bystanders—in this case the three prince-apostles, Peter, James and John [1]—to which of their doubts or questionings was it a special response ? Was it a final vindication of their faith against the wild fancies of the mob —Jesus is indeed neither Elijah nor ' the prophet,' [2] since both Elijah and Moses are present with Him, discernibly distinct ? Is it a more general endorsement of S. Peter's confession ? Is it a guarantee that the sufferings of the Christ, just predicted by our Lord Himself for the first time, shall have an issue even more glorious than those which crowned the trials of Moses and Elijah ; or is it a first fulfilment of the prophecy of Jesus which immediately precedes it in the narrative, that some of those there present should not taste of death till they saw the kingdom of God coming in power ? [3]

That so many lines of association should radiate outward from a single episode suggests as a high probability that even in its earliest surviving form (the Marcan account) it has already been subjected to some degree of literary or semi-literary elaboration. Other factors point to the same possibility. Moses and Elijah may have been originally, perhaps, anonymous figures ; [4] the scene is then in close relationship with the accounts of the Resurrection morning, [5]

---

[1] Or (Bousset, *SNT.*, i, p. 155) to Peter alone. The grounds on which Bousset suggests this are too complicated to be considered here.

[2] Jn. 1[21], [25]. The emphatic ὁ προφήτης (*the* prophet *par excellence*) must refer to ' the prophet like Moses ' of Dt. 18[15], [18]. It is true that this suggestion comes from the Fourth Gospel, but it has its analogy in Mk. 8[28] (' one of the prophets '), and indeed gives the latter passage the necessary precision.

[3] So interpreted as early as the *Excerpta Theodoti*, § 4 : ' So Peter and James and John saw, and then fell asleep.'

[4] Bousset, *SNT.*, i, p. 156—based, curiously enough, on the assertion that ' despite all attempts at explanation, the presence and significance of Moses and Elijah remain enigmas ' ; cp. R. Bultmann, *Geschichte der Synoptischen Tradition*, p. 157, who produces a parallel from the *Apocalypse of Peter* (English translation in M. R. James, *Apocryphal New Testament*, p. 508).

[5] Thus in the Akhmîm fragments of the *Gospel of Peter* the theophany from the *Apocalypse of Peter* is inserted as a post-Resurrection appearance of the Lord (M. R. James, *op. cit.*, pp. 90, 505). Hence Bultmann, Loisy and others think the Transfiguration narrative was originally a Resurrection appearance which Mark has ante-dated ; E. Meyer, *Ursprung u. Anfänge*, i, p. 152 (cp. Harnack, cited Klostermann, *HNT.*, iii, p. 97) thinks it is in its original position, and regards it as the source of the Resurrection and post-Resurrection narratives (p. 156 ; cp. *ib.*, iii, p. 216). The most probable explanation would appear to be a variation of Klostermann's. The two celestial figures belong to the Transfiguration, but have influenced the Resurrection and Ascension narratives ; though the latter, as narratives, are independent of the former. The process is clearly traceable in S. Luke. He alone supplies a subject of conversation for Moses and Elijah (the ' exodus ' which Jesus is to accomplish in Jerusalem, Lk. 9[31]) ; and it is not unnatural that he should suppose them to have been interested in witnessing the outcome of their predictions. So Mk.'s single ' young man ' (Mk. 16[5])

with its two angels; and of the Ascension, with the 'two men in
white raiment.' Some critics, without necessarily denying an
original historical basis, have found traces of literary craftsmanship
of an even more elaborate kind. The supernatural drama is cut
into two, as everyone is aware, by the strange human episode of
Peter's interjection. This episode, it has been suggested, marks
the junction between two originally parallel accounts of the Transfiguration; that which comes second in the text, with the cloud
and the voice,[1] taking the familiar form of a characteristic Jewish
theophany, whilst the metamorphosis and glistening robe of the
earlier part of the incident betray touches of Greek thought.[2]

It is to this last possibility that Professor Bacon has devoted
special attention. He regards S. Peter's gauche ejaculation about
the three tabernacles neither as a genuine survival of the original
tradition, nor as an editorial insertion to conceal an unsightly
junction, but as an integral part of the first (or hellenistic) version
of the Transfiguration-story. To him the essence of the incident
lies in the contrast between the 'metamorphosis' which Jesus
underwent, and the earthly 'skené' (tabernacle) in which Peter
foolishly would have Him remain.[3] The two terms are part of the
currency of hellenistic Christianity. To S. Paul, the converted
Christian undergoes a 'metamorphosis' of soul which renders his
mortal body, or 'tabernacle,' less and less adequate as a vehicle of
this transformed and spiritual soul, more and more irksome to him
for the brief period during which he has still to wear it. 'We that
are in this tabernacle do groan,' 'longing to be clothed upon with
our habitation which is from heaven'—'a house not made with
hands' (as Peter's booths would have been), 'eternal in the heavens'[4]
—a 'spiritual body,' as he calls it elsewhere,[5] which being no longer
of flesh is adequate to the needs of the man who is no more fleshly,
but spiritual through and through.

This truth (Professor Bacon suggests) that the transformed
Christian, like the transformed Christ, can no longer find himself at
home in the earthly tabernacle which satisfied him when he walked
after the flesh, is, in S. Mark, revealed to the disciples at the moment

becomes 'two men' in shining (or white) raiment in Lk. 24[4] (the Resurrection), and Acts 1[10] (the Ascension). Lk. significantly uses the same phrase
in each of the three cases—'Behold, two men.' The Fourth Gospel (20[12])
takes the 'two' from Lk.; explicitly makes them angelic (cp. Mt. 28[2, 3]);
and says that they were 'seated' (as Mk. 16[5], Mt. 28[2]).

[1] The cloud is the 'Shekinah'; the voice a 'Bath-Qol' (for references,
Rawlinson, S. Mark, pp. 10, 120).

[2] Klostermann, loc. cit.

[3] B. W. Bacon, The Gospel of Mark, p. 254:—'As Origen already saw,
this suggestion of Peter's to prepare tabernacles for the glorified is the equivalent of his proposal that Jesus reject the cross in the previous story. . . .
Not in earthly tabernacles of corruptible flesh is the deliverance of the Christ
to be accomplished, but in bodies of incorruptible glory, " our house which
is from heaven." ' (Bacon's reference is presumably to Origen, comm. in
Mt., xii, 40 (MPG., xiii, col. 1076).)

[4] 2 Cor. 5[1-4].   [5] 1 Cor. 15[44].

when they gaze upon the glorified Jesus.[1] Similarly in the hellenistic teaching of S. Paul:—it is the vision of the Lord ' seen as in a
mirror ' which transforms the Christian ' into the same image from
glory to glory,' [2] and thereby reveals to him his discontent with the
earthly house of his tabernacle. Surely, Professor Bacon argues,
whatever the original nucleus of the narrative may have been, it
must have been subjected to the influence of Pauline theology
before it reached its present form ? [3]

The reader may form his own opinion as to these various suggestions. One conclusion, however, seems inevitable. Before the
earliest gospel assumed its present shape, the Church had fixed
upon the Transfiguration as the central moment of the Lord's
earthly life. It had surrounded that moment with a glamour of
allusion and allegorism so complex that it cannot now with any
certainty be analysed into its constituent elements. And it had
done this as though to remind itself that the *whole* gospel, from beginning to end, must be read and regarded as one great vision of
God in Christ, akin to the vision given to the favoured three on the
Mount of Transfiguration.

(c) S. Paul.

What is implicit in the synoptic gospels becomes explicit when
we turn to S. Paul.   The goal of life for the Christian is ' to gain
Christ, to be found in Him, to *know* Him, with the power of His resurrection and the fellowship of His sufferings.' [4] . . . 'Not that
I have already obtained,' S. Paul adds at once,

> ' or am already made perfect ; but I press on if so be that I may
> apprehend ; seeing that also I was apprehended by Christ
> Jesus. Brethren, I count not myself yet to have apprehended ;
> but one thing I do, forgetting the things which are behind and
> stretching forward to the things which are before, I press on
> towards the goal unto the prize of the upward calling of God in
> Christ Jesus.' [5]

' Knowing,' ' apprehending,' ' gaining ' God, then, or God in
Christ, is the goal or prize of the Christian life—' whilst we are
at home in the body we are absent from the Lord ; we walk by faith
and not by sight.' [6] But S. Paul has always an inexpugnable
tendency to bring the Christian hope out of the future into the
present. Eschatology holds out the promise of a day of the Lord
in which the forces of evil shall be overcome, and this was the

---

[1] Bacon, *op. cit.*, pp. 258, 259.   [2] 2 Cor. 3[18] ; *infra*, pp. 103 f.
[3] Further refinements of criticism, Bacon, *loc. cit.*; C. Clemen, *RGENT.*,
pp. 242-244.
[4] Phil. 3[8-10].   [6] Phil. 3[12-14] (as RV. marg.).
[6] 2 Cor. 5[6]—on εἶδος as ' sight,' see Lietzmann, *HNT., ad loc.* Cp.
Rom. 8[24]—' By hope were we saved, but hope that is seen is not hope, for
who hopeth for that which he seeth ? '

outlook of the primitive Church. S. Paul asserts triumphantly that they are *already* overcome ; death has lost its sting, the grave its victory ; the reign of law is terminated ; sin is annulled, the flesh crucified. The resurrection of Jesus corroborated the Jewish hope that the righteous should rise again 'in that day' ; S. Paul diverts attention to a resurrection of the soul which is possible here and now—a rising from dead works. This is no mere psychological idiosyncrasy of the apostle's. It is a conviction—shared, as we shall see, by others of his fellowship—springing from direct experience of all that Christianity means. On this basis, reinforced no doubt by his own experience of visions and revelations of the Lord, he asserts emphatically that we *have already seen* God. 'It is God, that said, Light shall shine out of darkness, Who shined in our hearts to give the light' (better, as RV. marg., ' illumination ') ' of the knowledge of the glory of God in the face of Jesus Christ.' [1]

To describe this vision he uses a pregnant and vivid analogy. ' Now we see in a mirror, in a riddle, but then face to face ; now I know in part ; but then I shall know fully even as also I have been known fully ' [2] he says, in what is without doubt the most exalted passage of his writings. The words have been a *casus belli* between two of the greatest modern theologians, in a controversy which has raged over the whole field of ' gnosis ' and ' gnosticism ' ; [3] but there can be no serious doubt as to their meaning. S. Paul is not here depreciating the vision of God which we already possess. It is ' in a riddle ' certainly, but it is still something to be prized above all earthly possessions. It is not yet as full and glorious as it will one day be ; but very full and very glorious it still is. Nor is the passage altogether unique in the epistles. There is another which inevitably challenges comparison with it ; for in this second passage S. Paul again uses the analogy of the mirror. It occurs at the end of a context in which, with a free use of allegory, he is contrasting Christian emancipation with Jewish bondage. [4] The contrast is used to assert, in parenthesis, that rightly interpreted the letter of scripture must—as being ' glorious '—conform to the spirit of Christianity. But the Jews had not dared to gaze directly on Moses' face, and so could not interpret the scriptures rightly ; the Christians *have* dared to gaze on—what ? S. Paul's answer is

---

[1] 2 Cor. 4⁶. The aspirations of the mystery-cults and gnostic devotees referred to above (pp. 27, 54. 86) were commonly concentrated upon this culminating boon of ' illumination ' (*photismos*). See especially G. P. Wetter, $\Phi\Omega\Sigma$, pp. 46 ff.

[2] 1 Cor. 13¹² (RV. as marg.).

[3] See *infra*, pp. 208-212 ; and on this particular question cp. Harnack, *Sitzungsb. d. Berl. Akad.* (1911), pp. 149-165 ; Reitzenstein, *HMHL.*, pp. 239, 252 f. The point at issue is unimportant ; it concerns merely the degree of imperfection implied by ' in a riddle.' Harnack's view (*loc. cit.*, p. 156) that it is ' worthless ' is obviously too extreme ; nor is it strengthened by his entirely unsupported assertion (p. 150) that S. Paul's ' mirror ' has no connexion with the mirrors of *Wisdom* and *Od. Sol.* (*infra*, p. 103). This would seem highly improbable.

[4] 2 Cor. 3⁷⁻¹⁸.

not quite clear. At first it is 'the Lord,' and this 'Lord' is 'the Spirit'; and 'where the Spirit of the Lord is [1] there is liberty.' Then he continues, 'We all with unveiled face reflecting as a mirror (*or* RV. marg. ' beholding as in a mirror ') the glory of the Lord, are transformed into the same image from glory to glory, even as from the Lord the Spirit.' [2]

Discussion centres round the word 'katoptrizomenoi'—does it mean '*reflecting as*' a mirror, or '*beholding as in*' a mirror? In a sense it matters little; the mirror must 'see' that which it reflects. But the illustrations collected by Reitzenstein seem to point to the conclusion that God, or rather the 'glory' of God, is the glass.[3] If this is so the metaphor can be followed out in various directions. God is seen as 'mirrored'—either in Christ, or in His 'glory,' or (as in S. James) [4] in the perfect law of liberty. Again the mirror of God, brought near to the human soul, illuminates it so that a man can know himself better. This is the obvious point of S. James' analogy, and is borne out by well-known passages in the 'Odes of Solomon' and a fragment of Zosimus.[5] We have every right to infer that the same idea is latent in S. Paul's thought as well; for he too, like S. James, employs the idea of the *law*, the instrument of self-knowledge, in the immediate context [6]—a fact which in itself points towards the rejection of the interpretation 'reflecting as in a mirror.'

[1] Or, by the very simple emendation of κυρίου to κύριον, 'where the Spirit is Lord.'

[2] 2 Cor. 3[18].

[3] Reitzenstein, *HMR.*, p. 358; *HMHL.*, pp. 243-251, 262; further passages, Lietzmann, *HNT.*, ix, pp. 67, 113, 114; Clemen, *RGENT.*, p. 333. The most interesting passages are *Wisd.* 7[26]—' She is . . . an unspotted mirror of the working of God'; *Od. Sol.* 13, 1—'Behold, our mirror is the Lord'; 1 *Clem.*, xxxvi, 2—' By Him (Jesus) we behold as in a glass (ἐνοπτρι-ζόμεθα) His immaculate and most excellent visage'; Philo, *de dec.*, 105 (M., ii, p. 198; CW., iv, p. 293)—' As in a mirror the mind perceives God acting and creating and guiding His universe'; Id., *Leg. All.*, iii, 101 (*supra*, p. 43); *Acts of John*, 95 (M. R. James, *op. cit.*, p. 253)—' A mirror am I to thee that perceivest Me; a door am I to thee that knockest at Me ') ; [Cyprian] *de mont. Sin. et Sion*, 13 (from an apocryphal 'Epistle of John ')—' Ye see Me in yourselves as one of you sees himself in water or a mirror'; *Corp. Herm.*, xvii (as emended by Scott, *Hermetica*, i, p. 272), etc.

[4] Jas. 1[23-25].

[5] Reitzenstein, *HMHL.*, p. 247, from Berthelot, *La Chimie au Moyen Âge*, ii, pp. 260 ff.—a magic mirror made for Alexander the Great, with ethical as well as magical properties; for 'when a man looks into it, it prompts him to examine himself and purify himself, from his head to the tips of his nails.' Again, 'the mirror represented the divine spirit; when the soul looked at itself therein, it saw all its own faults and revolted from them' (Berthelot, p. 262). Other phrases are equally important—the man who looks in the mirror 'becomes himself spirit,' 'becomes a perfect man,' etc. (*ib.*, pp. 262, 263).

[6] The intention of the passage (2 Cor. 3[7-19]) may be expressed as follows. The law is not so much abrogated as spiritually interpreted in the Christian dispensation; and when 'the Spirit is (thus) lord' in exegesis 'there is liberty.' Cp. Reitzenstein, *HMHL.*, p. 250; *HMR.*, pp. 319 (an analogous passage in Philo); 384 (S. Paul's attack on a *non-ethical* 'gnosis' in 1 Cor. 13).

Once more—and here S. Paul makes dexterous and effective use of one of the oldest pieces of ethnic superstition—the mirror is a *magic* mirror. Such mirrors, and their alleged magical properties, were well-known to his readers.[1] But this of which S. Paul speaks is different from theirs. It does not foretell the future, as theirs were supposed to do. It does not reveal to a man the face of his destined bride ; it does not repel the assaults of demons ; still less does it steal the beauty or wither the health of those who gaze into it. The new Christian experience, the vision of God, is a magic mirror both because, as we have seen, it enhances a man's knowledge of himself, and *because by a mystical process it transforms him into the image of God,* ' as from the Lord the Spirit.' In this sense, *man* also becomes a mirror and reflects the likeness of God. It is clear now why S. Paul has used the ' mirror ' analogy. ' Seeing God ' would not convey this rich variety of meaning ; ' seeing God as a mirror,' or ' seeing God as mirrored in His glory,' is the phrase he needs for fullness of self-expression.

We must notice two other points in S. Paul's teaching about the vision of God to which the Christian presses forward. Whatever else is meant by this ubiquitous phrase of ' seeing ' or ' knowing ' God, it certainly refers to some kind of inward or subjective experience. We have seen already how in much pagan thought such a subjective experience—as, for example, ecstasy—was taken as constituting the *whole* end of human endeavour ; we shall see the same idea obtruding itself from time to time with disastrous results in the history of the Church. Such an attitude M. Bremond aptly calls ' panhedonist,'[2] and no reflection is needed to convince us of the dangers which follow in its train. Once again a man's thoughts and ideals converge upon himself—not this time on his behaviour, but on the changing and treacherous emotional content of his consciousness. *Without* an experience of a particular kind, he supposes himself to be deserted by God, void of religion, and without hope in the world ; *with* that experience (or with something which he mistakes for it) he may only too easily regard everything else—morality, self-discipline, love of the brethren—as irrelevant and superfluous.

It is possible, of course, that this danger can only be eliminated by deposing the thought of religious experience, and the vision of God, altogether from the primary position which it has held in traditional Christianity. That suggestion we must consider later. S. Paul took a different path ; but even so he set his face rigidly against any such perversions of the truth as those we have been considering. He insists that ' experience ' in itself is of less importance than two other things :—the love by which it is conditioned on the human side ; and God's loving care for man, which alone makes it possible, on the other. It is not so much that we come to

---

[1] See *ERE.*, viii, 695-697, *s.v.* ' Mirror.'
[2] Bremond, *HLSR.*, vii, p. 17 ; further consideration in detail, *infra*, pp. 196 ff. ; and additional note F, p. 489.

'know' God that matters, but that God has always 'known' us—
the end of life is at best to know God as we have *always* been known
by Him.[1] This epigram, it is to be noticed, comes at the conclusion
of a chapter in which throughout the superiority of love to 'gnosis'
is emphasized. So also of conversion : it is not so much knowing
God as being known by Him.[2] The most explicit passage of all
marshals the two thoughts for a direct attack upon the Corinthian
pride in 'gnosis' :—[3]

> 'We know that we have " gnosis." " Gnosis " puffeth up,
> but *love* edifieth. If any man thinketh that he hath known
> aught, he knoweth not yet as he ought to know. But—*if any
> man love God, he is already known by Him.*'

There are very many Christians who, without depreciating
'mystical experience,' shrink from claiming it for themselves,
because it seems something too high for them. They shrink even
from looking for it, lest—falling into some emotional self-halluci-
nation—they mistake the false for the true. The impulses are
laudable and salutary, though religion would be a colder thing than
it is if it had nothing more to offer. But at least S. Paul sets us
on a safe road when he insists that in 'seeing God'—whatever that
phrase may mean in its fullness—the emotional experience here and
now is secondary, and is never to be made the final test of genuine
Christianity. What *matters* is that a man should have the right
attitude—should love his God and his neighbour. If he preserves
this attitude, he may rest assured that (however much he doubts
whether he 'knows' God) he himself is 'known' by God with a
knowledge in which love, and providence, and the desire to give all
that can be given, are equally compounded.

(d) The Fourth Gospel.

If there is some slight hesitation in S. Paul as to the possibility
of receiving the vision of God in this life, it has disappeared altogether in the fourth evangelist. 'His gospel is a perpetual theophany.'[4] The prelude to the first epistle would come even more
fitly if it stood as a footnote to the gospel :—

> 'That which was from the beginning, that which we have
> heard, that which we have seen with our eyes, that which we

---

[1] 1 Cor. 13[12] (*supra*, p. 102).
[2] Gal. 4[9]; cp. 1 Cor. 8[3]—'if any man loveth God, the same is known of
Him.' J. Weiss, *Urchristentum*, p. 187, develops the thought very happily,
although, with his general tendency to deny S. Paul any *personal* mystical
experience, he suggests rather too readily that the idea is borrowed ; the
pagan parallels are given by E. Norden, *Agnostos Theos*, p. 287. (Cp. *supra*,
p. 14, n. 2.)
[3] 1 Cor. 8[2]. I take it for granted that *gnosis* here means 'mystic illumination '—an experience for which the title of ' seeing God ' was claimed.
See *infra*, pp. 208-212.
[4] A. Loisy, *Quatrième Évangile*, p. 104.

beheld and our hands handled, concerning the Word of Life
(and the Life was manifested and we have seen, and bear witness, and declare unto you the Life, the eternal Life which was
with the Father and was manifested unto us) : that which we
have seen and heard, declare we unto you also, that ye also may
have fellowship with us.'[1]

Heitmüller puts the fact succinctly :—

' The gospel is to show by what means Christians saw the
divine majesty of the Logos—by His miracle-working power,
His supernatural knowledge, His physical inviolability, the
spiritual efficacy of His preaching, and—not least of all—by
His voluntary suffering and death, and His resurrection. The
contrast with Paul and the Synoptists is remarkable. Paul
also knows of a divine Majesty of Jesus, but he predicates it
of the *risen* Lord, and will not ascribe it to the earthly Jesus ;
the Synoptists are prepared to maintain that even His nearest
intimates caught only a fleeting glimpse of the divine Majesty
of the Messiah, and that only once before the Resurrection, on
the Mount of Transfiguration.'[2]

It is true of course that the author of the Fourth Gospel reminds
his readers that ' no man hath seen God at any time ' ;[3] but in
the sense in which he here uses the words the vision of God is
at all times impossible.[4] Again, he looks forward to a day in which

----

[1] 1 Jn. 1[1-3]. This passage, with Jn. 1[14], is commonly taken as evidence
that the author claimed to have been an eyewitness of the historic ministry
of Jesus. But is any such personal claim really involved ? The ' we '
surely implies that he is speaking of the corporate witness of the Church.

[2] *SNT.*, iv, pp. 45, 46 ; but Heitmüller exaggerates S. Paul's ' indifference ' to the historic Jesus.

[3] Jn. 1[18], 6[46] ; 1 Jn. 4[12] ; cp. 1 Tim. 1[17], 6[16], Col. 1[15], Heb. 11[27] ; non-
Christian parallels, Bauer, *HNT.*, vi, p. 27.

[4] A clear distinction must be drawn between (i) the doctrine that God
is not ' visible ' to the *physical eye*, which is of course a commonplace, and
(ii) the doctrine that He is not ' visible ' to the ' *eye* ' *of intelligence*, i.e.
cannot be inferred from His works in creation and providence, but is to be
' seen ' only by the illuminate in a non-rational, ecstatic moment of ' faith.'
The second is the ' gnostic ' doctrine in its most extreme form. It gained
some of its currency through the ambiguity of the words ' visible ' and
' invisible,' which enabled it to use every text denying the *physical* visibility
of God to support the doctrine that He could be known only by faith, and
not at all by *reason*. To this ' gnostic ' position the New Testament gives
little if any support. The Logos doctrine involves the conviction that God
is truly intelligible (though not of course *wholly* intelligible) from His works.
S. Paul shares this conviction (Rom. 1[19, 20]), though, as Bonhöffer (*Epiktet
u. d. N.T.*, pp. 149-153) has pointed out, he prefers not to emphasize it.
Of course, the N.T. writers set faith, communion, the mystic experience,
' the Spirit,' alongside reason as a mode of apprehending God—I think we
may say that they give them priority ; but they enrich at the same time the
field of evidence on which reason can draw, by adding the O.T. revelation,
and the person of the historic Jesus, as sign-posts pointing clearly to the
nature of God. (See further, ' Summary,' *infra*, p. 110 ; and for the gnostics,
pp. 210, 211). The extraordinary popularity of texts affirming the invisibility of God and the things of God may be illustrated by the wide diffusion

' we shall see Him as He is '[1]—implying that as yet we do not see Him as He is ; but here what is implied is only a difference of degree and not of kind—the *uninterrupted* vision of the future will give a clearer knowledge of the nature of God than any which to-day is within our grasp. Beyond this, however, there is no need to make exceptions. The Word, which in the beginning was with God and was God, ' became flesh, and we beheld His glory ' (i.e. His manifest presence)—' the glory as of the only-begotten from the Father, full of grace and truth.'[2] ' He that hath seen Me hath seen the Father,'[3] the Lord proclaims ; and again, ' One who is God, only-begotten, Which is in the bosom of the Father, He hath declared Him.'[4] To the Jews ' who believe not Him Whom the Father sent,' and who therefore ' have not His word abiding in them,' it is said, ' Ye have neither heard His voice at any time, nor seen His form '[5]—a reproof obviously administered by the Christian Church to the synagogue. But everyone that beholdeth the Son and believeth on Him shall have eternal life, and be raised up at the last day.[6] And finally, the vision of God makes the Christian like the Father [7] (as in S. Paul's mirror analogy) ; and resemblance to Him is shown in mutual love, for God is love.[8]

It would be foolish to suggest that ' to see God ' was the only formula used by S. Paul or the fourth evangelist for the plenitude of Christian experience, here or hereafter. Many others recur to the mind at once—phrases which by their resemblance to those current in contemporary paganism witness clearly to a community of vocabulary, and would go far to corroborate a community of thought were it possible to establish, as Bousset and Reitzenstein have attempted to do, any resemblance in fundamentals between Christianity and the mysteries. But the vision of God is the thought to which S. Paul recurs in some at least of his most exalted moments, and it cannot be denied that it dominates S. John. And there is a notable unanimity in what they have to say about this vision.

of the sentence from a lost Apocalypse quoted by S. Paul, 1 Cor. 2[9] (affinities with Is. 64[4])—' Things which eye saw not and ear heard not,' etc. (Lietzmann, *HNT.*, ix, p. 13 ; add further references from Bauer, *HNT.*, vi, p. 4). Cp. generally, E. Fascher, *Deus Invisibilis, pass.*

[1] 1 Jn. 3[2]; cp. Fascher, *op. cit.*, pp. 70-77.

[2] Jn. 1[14]. Here also the contrast between *skênê* and *doxa* (cp. *supra*, p. 100) :—*although* the Word was ' in a tabernacle ' (and so veiled) among us, *nevertheless* His ' glory ' shone through. For the ' glory ' of God, *supra*, p. 32.

[3] Jn. 14[7, 9] ; cp. 12[45], 17[21].

[4] Jn. 1[18]—on the reading μονογενὴς Θεός, which is to be preferred to ὁ μονογενὴς υἱός, see Westcott, Bauer and others, *ad loc.*

[5] Jn. 5[37, 38] (εἶδος = μορφὴ Θέου = Christ).

[6] Jn. 6[40].   [7] 1 Jn. 3[2].

[8] 1 Jn. 4[12, 16]—a passage which echoes S. Paul's thought that loving service is higher than ' mystical experience ' (*supra*, p. 105) ; cp. Jn. 14[21], 17[21] ; 1 Jn. 2[3, 4], 3[23, 24], and Bauer's note on Jn. 17[21] (*HNT.*, vi, p. 200). Similarly Rev. 22[3, 4].

That unbroken personal intercourse with the divine is the end for which man was created; that a foretaste of this experience is possible even in this life;[1] that to receive it depends upon moral rectitude and issues in increase of personal holiness—these are the pillars of the conception.   Two further facts emerge with absolute clearness.   S. Paul indeed appeals to his personal visions, and vindicates his apostleship by the cry, 'Have I not seen the Lord'?[2]   But apart from these two sentences—in each of which he is replying to a challenge addressed directly and specifically to himself—he conforms to what is also the uniform usage of S. John. The vision is always a *corporate* one.   'We' is the word used throughout.   This implies that the experience of the Church makes up for deficiencies on the part of the individual; even those who have *not* seen are blessed, the Fourth Gospel asserts, because they share in the Church's belief.[3]   It implies, further, that any alleged experience of the individual must be tested and over-ruled by this corporate vision of the Church.   And it implies, finally, that it is only by holding to the unity of the Church, and cementing it by mutual deference and communal uniformity, that the vision can be secured. Bousset is surely wrong in suggesting that S. Paul, starting from a 'corporate mysticism' common to the mysteries and himself, conferred a distinctive character on Christianity by individualizing the mystic experience;[4] it was the mysteries—especially the later private mysteries—and gnosticism which individualized.   S. Paul's thought—and even more, if that were possible, S. John's—is corporate through and through.   Once more we come back to the cardinal belief that what matters, for the individual Christian, is not that he should have such and such 'experiences' here and now; but that he should be standing in the right attitude towards God and the Christian fellowship.

In the second place, the vision of God expresses itself throughout in terms of the historic Christ—the revelation of God is 'in the face of Jesus Christ,'[5] and he that has seen Him has seen the Father.   The whole purpose of S. John, in throwing his meditations into the form of a gospel, is to emphasize this fact, and no more need be said about it.   But it is often suggested that S. Paul, at least, was so enthralled by the thought of the exalted Christ that he ignored the historic Jesus.   No more specious perversion of the

---

[1] In view of the passages cited above, it seems ridiculous to say (Graf-Baudissin, *ARW.*, xviii (1915), pp. 219 ff.; Fr. Nötscher, '*Das Angesicht Gottes Schauen*,' p. 172) that 'the "vision of God" in the New Testament is a privilege reserved almost exclusively for the future life'; still more, to add (Nötscher, p. 180) that 'this marks a great advance.'   The statements could only have a shadow of verisimilitude if by 'seeing' God were meant *physical* vision alone (*supra*, p. 106, n. 4); and even then they would be untrue, for it is impossible to suppose that New Testament writers conceived the risen saints (with their 'spiritual bodies,' 1 Cor. 15^{44}) to have physical vision.

[2] 2 Cor. 12$^{1-4}$; 1 Cor. 9^1.   [3] Jn. 20^{29}.
[4] Bousset, *KC.*, pp. 104-110.   [5] 2 Cor. 4^6.

truth could be conceived.[1] S. Paul *is* engrossed in the thought of the exalted Christ ; but he understands His nature, even in His exaltation, wholly in terms of His earthly life. It is absurd to pretend that one who could idealize the virtue of love in words which so exactly describe the Lord's intercourse with men and women upon earth, or could quite incidentally embrace in one all-inclusive epigram—' though He was rich He became poor for your sakes ' [2]—the whole course of the earthly life as well as the whole purpose of the Incarnation, was indifferent to what had happened in Galilee and Jerusalem. Merely to notice that the great hymn to the exalted Jesus in Philippians ii, 9-11 follows closely upon the writer's fullest exposition of the Lord's incarnate life, should prove a final barrier to superficial speculations of this character.

What then must be inferred from these notes of the vision of God, as conceived by S. Paul and S. John, as to the character and conduct of those for whom the experience is reserved ? Theirs must be a social life—not necessarily ' social,' that is to say, in the narrower sense of direct activity of personal service ; but social in so far as its aims, methods and ideals are always tested by, and adjusted to, the aims, methods and ideals of the Church. In the second place, they may despise and condemn nothing which Jesus did not despise and condemn on earth. How carefully the apostolic writers observed these two conditions may be seen, once more, from S. Paul's crucial chapter on marriage. So long as he is dealing with divorce he is on firm ground ; he has a definite precept of the Lord's to guide him, and he says emphatically, ' I give charge—yet not I, but the Lord.' [3] The question of mixed marriages is different. Where one partner has become a Christian, whilst the other remains a heathen, he is prepared to allow the former either to remain with or to depart from the other as circumstances decide. Either way the ruling could be considered a lax one. To allow the mixed marriage to continue might be to defile the integrity of the Christian community ; to allow—still more to insist—that it should be broken could be regarded as inimical in principle to the primary character of marriage as ordained by God. The apostle, therefore, speaks with a hesitation strikingly at variance with his previous dogmatism : ' To the rest say I, not the Lord.' [4]—' Concerning virgins,' again, he has ' no commandment of the Lord ' ; he is prepared ' to give a judgment ' ($\gamma\nu\acute{\omega}\mu\eta$, ' an opinion ') but nothing further.[5] So important is it that authoritative sanction should be given to nothing which might even possibly be more lax, or more rigorous, than the Master Himself would have allowed.

Asceticism was at most only one of the tendencies in the teaching of Jesus. In conformity with the principles just noticed, it might

---

[1] Cp. R. J. Knowling, *Witness of Epistles*, pp. 291-348, and *Testimony of S. Paul, pass.*, for the apostle's ' concealed ' references to the earthly ministry of our Lord.

[2] 2 Cor. 8[9].   [3] 1 Cor. 7[10].
[4] 1 Cor. 7[12].   [5] 1 Cor. 7[25].

perhaps be countenanced in some of its extremer forms in individual
cases, provided that the ascetic did not sever himself from the over-
ruling communion and teaching of the Church. It could not for
a moment, in those severer forms, be regarded as obligatory on
every member of the community. Claims of this sweeping character came very shortly to be pressed with the utmost vehemence
upon the Church ; claims wholly at issue with the Christian doctrine of the vision of God as we have just seen it taking shape. The
same claims were no doubt pressed even within the lifetime of the
apostles ; it need not surprise us that, so long as their conception
of the vision and its requirements held the field, the claims could
no sooner have been stated than their incongruity with the Christian tradition must have been manifest. Not until the first balanced
rapture of the new religion lost its grip upon the Church could
uncompromising asceticism hope to make substantial headway.

SUMMARY.

It may be convenient at this point to summarize briefly the different
conceptions of the vision of God which have come before us in the last
two chapters ; but it must be insisted that such a summary can be
approximate only, and that to force a writer strictly into one class
or another will be to rob him of the niceties (and perhaps also of the
contradictions) in his thought. (1) The most primitive view is that
God is *physically visible* in this life, though to see Him is death (older
stages of the O.T.). (2) God is *physically invisible;* but metaphori-
cally visible (i.e. knowable), that is, *His character can be inferred from
His ' works '* (Rabbis and philosophers—but most representatives of
both schools are touched by the next conception too). (3) God is
comprehensible to reason, from His works, but *still more knowable by
' faith,' or mystic and ecstatic experience* (many representatives among
the philosophers ; also Philo and *Hermetica* in their best moments).
(4) The N.T. position is analogous to (3), but enriches it (*a*) by *adding
the O.T. revelation and the person of Jesus* as sources of rational knowledge of the character of God ; (*b*) by stabilizing the vague concept of
' mystical experience ' in the far richer and more definite experience
of *communion with Christ in the Spirit.* As to the relation between
' reason ' and ' faith,' the N.T. writers insist upon no one point of
view, and so leave the way open for further developments. (5) Most
representatives of (2) to (4) insist that *moral affinity with God* is essential to the vision ; the N.T. suggests that it is *more important* than
' experience.' (6) The ' gnostic ' position (apocalyptists, mysteries,
Philo and *Hermetica* at times, and cp. *infra*, pp. 213 f.)—God *wholly
incomprehensible* to human reason, but *' knowable ' by non-rational
methods* (dreams, trances, initiations, ecstasies, etc.). (7) Most schools
of thought insist that God will be far more ' knowable ' in the next
life than in this, but we shall come across ' naturalist ' writers (e.g.
Aetius, *infra*, p. 306) who deny even this.

LECTURE III.

FORMALISM.

Gal. i. 6—' I marvel that ye are so soon removed from Him That called you into the grace of Christ unto another gospel.'

I. THE BEGINNINGS OF CODIFICATION.

S. PAUL'S indignant wonder was evoked by the reversion of a small province of the Christian Church to the legalist spirit of Jewish religion. Had he lived half-a-century or a century later, his cause for amazement would have been increased a hundredfold. The example of the Galatians might be thought to have infected the entire Christian Church; writer after writer seems to have little other interest than to express the genius of Christianity wholly in terms of law and obedience, reward and punishment. The mysterious document known as ' Didaché ' (' The Teaching of the Twelve Apostles,' or, as the subtitle has it, ' The Teaching of the Lord through the Twelve Apostles to the Heathen ') is as clear an example of this tendency as could be desired.

Long before the discovery of the ' Didaché,' it was generally recognized by ecclesiastical historians that behind some of the most noteworthy documents of early Christianity must lie a common original, perhaps actually with the name ' Apostolic Teaching ' or something akin thereto; and that part at least of this document must be a section on the ' two ways ' of life—the virtuous and the vicious. In 1882 a Continental scholar [1] of considerable ingenuity put together and published a reconstruction of this hypothetical document, calling it, after Rufinus,[2] ' The Two Ways, or, the Judgment of Peter.' A year later, Bryennios, Metropolitan of Nicomedia, published for the first time a text of the ' Didaché ' from a manuscript in the Jerusalem monastery of the Greek quarter of Constantinople. It was at once seen, not merely how exact and brilliant had been the reconstruction of the ' Duæ Viæ,' but also that—though the ' Didaché ' as we now have it could not be regarded as in every way the original of the later documents,—it

---

[1] Krawutzscky, *Über das altkirchliche Unterrichtsbuch*, in *Theol. Quartalschrift*, lxiv (1882), pp. 359-445.

[2] *Comm. in Symb. Ap.*, 38, but Rufinus has confused it with Hermas (' libellus qui dicitur Pastoris sive Hermæ, qui appellatur Duæ Viæ vel Judicium Petri ') unless an ' et is ' has fallen out after ' Hermæ '; cp. Jerome, *de virr. ill.*, i; Athanasius, *Fest. Ep.*, 39.

marked at all events a stage nearer to the source than any hitherto known.[1]

> 'There are two ways,' the 'Didaché' begins abruptly,[2] 'one of life, and one of death ; and there is much difference between the two ways. The way, then, of life is this : first, thou shalt love God Who made thee ; second, thou shalt love thy neighbour as thyself ; and whatsoever thou wouldest not have done to thyself, do not thou either to another.'

Here follows a mosaic of sentences from the great sermon in the first and third gospels, which may be an addition to the original text ; [3] and a curious passage about almsgiving which will come before us at a later stage.[4] The 'Didaché' then proceeds :—[5]

> 'And the second commandment of the doctrine' (that is to say, of the way of life) 'is this :—Thou shalt not kill, thou shalt not commit adultery, sodomy nor fornication, thou shalt not steal, thou shalt not use magic, thou shalt not traffic with drugs, nor procure abortion, nor kill the new-born child. Thou shalt not covet they neighbour's goods, thou shalt not forswear thyself, thou shalt not bear false witness, thou shalt not slander, thou shalt not bear malice. Thou shalt not be double-minded nor double-tongued ; for a double tongue is a snare of death. Thy word shall not be false nor empty, but fulfilled in deed. Thou shalt not be covetous, nor extortionate, nor a hypocrite, nor spiteful, nor arrogant. Thou shalt not take evil counsel against thy neighbour. Thou shalt hate no man ;

---

[1] It seems unnecessary here to enter upon a discussion of the relationship between *Didaché* and the allied texts. A useful bibliography is included in C. Bigg, *Doctrine of the Twelve Apostles* (translation ; new edition by A. J. Maclean, 1922), pp. xxxvii, xxxviii ; to which should be added the articles in *HDB.*, v, pp. 438 ff. ; *JE.*, iv, pp. 585-587 ; *DAC.*, i, pp. 296 ff.; R. Knopf, *Die Lehre der Zwölf Apostel*, in *HNT.: Ergänzungsband* (further bibliography); B. H. Streeter, *The Primitive Church*, pp. 279-287. In spite of the arguments of Bigg (*op. cit.*), and J. A. Robinson, *Barnabas, Hermas, and Didaché*, pp. 85-103, there seems little doubt that the book must be dated not later than the earliest years of the second century. Its place of origin is certainly Syria. Streeter's theory that it is a semi-official manifesto from the church of Antioch to more backward churches in the *hinterland* is interesting, but does not affect our present purpose.

[2] *Did.*, i[1, 2].

[3] *Ib.*, i[3–5]. The passage begins with the curious phrase, ' Now the teaching of these words is this '—i.e. it represents itself as an expansion of i[1, 2], as indeed it is. This passage (i[3–6]) does not occur in any other ' Two Ways ' document before the Apostolic Constitutions (vii, 1-32), nor in the Latin fragments from Melk and Munich (see for Latin texts J. Schlecht, *Die Apostellehre* (1901), pp. 16, 17). It is scarcely likely that it would have been omitted by anyone who knew it ; it seems probable therefore *either* that the other writers (and the Didachist as well) used an earlier (? Jewish) ' Two Ways ' ; *or* that the passage was interpolated into *Did.* at a relatively late date. On the possibility of such interpolation, Streeter, *Primitive Church*, pp. 281-283.

[4] *Did.*, i[5, 6] ; *infra.* p. 131.   [5] *Ib.*, 2[1] ff.

but some thou shalt rebuke,[1] and for some thou shalt pray, and some thou shalt love more than thy soul.'

After this free version of the decalogue, here used to exemplify and expand the second commandment of the ' way of life,' the Didachist proceeds to ' hedge about the law.' He tabulates the chief causes of sin, and shows how great offences spring from small beginnings.[2] ' My child,' he says,

' flee from all evil and from all that is like it.   Be not wrathful, for wrath guideth to murder ; nor a zealot, nor contentious, nor quick to anger ; for from all these things murders are begotten. My child, be not lustful, for lust guideth to fornication ; nor a filthy talker, nor one of high looks ; for from all these things adulteries are begotten.   My child, be not an augur, for it guideth to idolatry, nor an enchanter, nor a mathematician'

---

[1] The text here is doubtful.   The *Ap. Ch. Order* adds ' on some thou shalt have mercy ' after ' some thou shalt rebuke.' *Ap. Const.*, vii, 5, can have read (or allowed to stand) nothing more than, ' Thou shalt hate no man, but some thou shalt rebuke' (without the rest of the sentence).   The Latin fragment, on the other hand, has simply, ' Thou shalt hate no man, and some thou shalt love more than thy soul.'   The only parallel in *Barnabas* is 19[5], ' Thou shalt love thy neighbour more than thine own soul ' ; but he may also have read, ' Thou shalt hate no one ' in his original, and omitted it because he wished to conclude his ' Way of Life ' with the emphatic, ' To the last thou shalt hate evil ' (or even, in the inferior text, ' the evil one ') in 19[11]. Biblical parallels are Lev. 19[17, 18]—' Thou shalt not hate thy brother in thine heart ; thou shalt surely rebuke thy neighbour (ἐλέγξεις) . . . thou shalt love thy neighbour as thyself '—and Jude [22, 23], ' And on some have mercy (*v.l.* (A, C) : ἐλέγχετε, "rebuke ") who are in doubt' (*or* ' making a distinction') ' [some] saving [with fear], snatching them from the fire ; and on some have mercy in fear, hating even the garment spotted from the flesh' (for variations see *infra*, p. 162).—I suggest that the Latin represents the pre-*Didaché* original (which alone would be suited for a catechumen about to enter the Church—the Didachist, for example, intended to deal with ' rebuking ' when he came to the catechumen's future responsibilities, 4[3]). Under the influence of Lev., and possibly Jude, the οὓς μὲν ἐλέγξεις came into the tradition (primarily as a moral precept), but was later taken as a disciplinary ordinance (cp. Mt. 18[15], 1 Tim. 5[20], 2 Tim. 4[2], Tit. 1[9, 13], 2[15], *Did.*, 15[3], *infra*, pp. 149, 153, 166) of ' convicting' obstinate sinners.   The Didachist then recalled (perhaps by direct recollection, for it is possible that he knew the Johannine literature—(cp. 10[5] with 1 Jn. 4[18] ; 7[1] with Jn. 4[10], 7[38] ; 9[4] with Jn. 11[52] ; 10[2] with Jn. 17[11]) the distinction between sins unto death, and sins not unto death for which one may ' pray ' (1 Jn. 5[16, 17]), and inserted a sentence about this too (for which *Ap. Ch. Ord.* gives an equivalent paraphrase).   He thus reaches a three-fold division—(1) those convicted of grave sin and presumably permanently excommunicated ; (2) those under discipline for ' forgiveable ' sin ; and (3) those in full membership of the Church, who are to be ' loved more than one's own soul '—incidentally revealing himself as a supporter of the more liberal school of thought in the matter of discipline.   But, of course, the insertion is inappropriate at this point of the ' Two Ways.' (Knopf, *ad loc.*, recognizes a somewhat similar division, but takes ' those who are to be prayed for ' somewhat incongruously as the hardened sinners.)   *Ap. Const.*, vii (or an intermediate editor) disliked the implied laxity, and cut out everything after ' rebuke,' as though to say : ' Hate no one ; but have no sentimental weakness about excommunicating them if they deserve it.'

[2] *Did.*, 3[1–6].

(but he means an ' astrologer '), ' nor a purifier ' (one who prac-
tises heathen lustrations), ' nor do thou consent to look on these
things : for from all these things idolatry is begotten. My
child, be not a liar, for the lie guideth to theft ; nor a lover of
money, nor vainglorious ; for from all these things thefts are
begotten,' and so forth.[1]

There follows a list of Christian virtues,[2] succeeded by a passage
on special duties.[3] First of these is respect for the ministers of the
gospel—' My child, night and day shalt thou remember him that
speaketh to thee the word of God, and thou shalt honour him as the
Lord, for where the Lordship is spoken of, there is the Lord.'
Another of the documents which employs the ' Two Ways ' adds
to this the duty of supporting the minister with ' perishable and
temporal food ' (in contrast to the ' spiritual meat and drink '
which he purveys) ;[4] a third [5] has a reference to ' remembering the
day of judgment,' whose importance will appear. The catechumen
is to ' seek out the faces of the saints '—that is, to attend public
worship—daily, in order ' to rest on their words.' It is contemplated that he will rise to a position of authority in the Church ; he
is ' to set at peace them that strive, to judge justly, and not to
regard persons when he rebukes for transgressions.' [6] Once again

[1] There is more than a suggestion in this passage of the seven capital or
' root ' sins ; cp. *infra*, p. 201. Since Barnabas has no parallel to this section
it would appear to be a detached instruction (of considerable psychological
power and insight) which was not in the original ' Two Ways.'

[2] A confused little passage (3^{7-10}), composed partly of positive and partly
of negative precepts ; but known to *Barnabas*, and so from the original ' Two
Ways.'

[3] *Did.*, 4^{1-13}.

[4] *Ap. Ch. Ord.*, 12 (*JTS.*, iii (1901), p. 67).

[5] *Barnabas*, 19^{10} (in place of the sentence ' where the Lordship is . . . ';
and with ' love ' instead of ' remember night and day ' for the duty towards
ministers). Knopf suggests that Barnabas substitutes the ' day of judgment '
for this sentence ' out of false modesty ' ; Maclean thinks that he disliked as
an exaggeration the injunction to remember the preacher *by night* as well as
by day, but substituted the day of judgment as something that might fitly
be remembered at all times. The addition at this point is inept.

[6] *Did.*, $4^{2, 3}$. The writer adds, ' Thou shalt not be double-minded,
whether it shall be or no ' (4^4). *Ap. Ch. Ord.* and *Ap. Const.*, vii, add ' in
thy prayers.' In Herm., *Vis.*, iii, 4^3, ' double-mindedness ' refers to those
who are doubtful ' whether *these things* shall be '—i.e. as to the certainty of
' salvation ' (inclusion in the tower) ; which must have particular reference
to the salvation of sinners who ' repent while the tower is in building ' (*Vis.*,
iii, 5^4). Herm., *Mand.*, ix, *pass.*, uses the word (*dipsychia*) of ' doubting in
prayer ' on the basis that the Lord ' will not hear a sinner ' (ix, 1), and in
view of the general subject of the book and evidence in this mandate itself,
we may assume that the particular boon for which the sinner prays, but is
doubtful whether he will receive, is restoration to the state of salvation on
repentance. This explains the purpose of the sentence in *Did.*, 4^4—the
ecclesiastical judge is to judge justly, and to convict fearlessly ; but, if he
decides that a sin is forgiveable and so ' to be prayed for ' (*Ap. Ch. Ord.* and
Ap. Const. rightly) he is not to doubt that God has mercy in such cases.
He is reinforcing the message of 1 Jn. 5^{16} against such hesitations as even
Jude [23] (' on some have mercy *with fear* ') expresses (*infra*, pp. 161, 162).

the author reverts to the importance of almsgiving,[1] after which he inserts a table of domestic duties, emphasizing the true behaviour of a Christian parent towards his children, slaves and maid-servants, and the duties of slaves towards their masters.[2] The ' way of life ' is then closed with an injunction not to add or remove anything from the commandments of the Lord ; and with a sentence which has been the occasion of much debate : ' Thou shalt confess thy sins in the church, and shalt not come to thy prayer in an evil conscience.'[3]

Then follows the way of death :—[4]

> ' The way of death is this ; first of all it is wicked and full of curse ; murders, adulteries, lusts, fornications, thefts, idolatries, sorceries, traffic in drugs, ravenings, false witnessings, hypocrisies, a double heart, guile, arrogance, malice, self-will, covetousness, filthy talking, jealousy, boldness, pride, boasting.'

The list of abstract sins is followed by a detailed description of sinners in the concrete ; and the ' way of death ' closes with the prayer (probably not in the original) [5]—' May ye be delivered, my children, from all these.' ' See that no man lead thee astray from this way of the doctrine, for he teacheth thee without our God,' says the writer ; and there in all probability the original tract of the ' Two Ways ' ended. But the ' Didaché ' does not end here. After two sentences which revive the Matthæan doctrine of the double standard,[6] it passes on to ecclesiastical regulations affecting baptism, fasting, the eucharist, and the ministry ; and concludes with an apocalyptic epilogue.

The ' Didaché ' is commonly dated about the year A.D. 100. To the same date or thereabout must be assigned a document very different in style and purpose—the so-called ' Epistle of Barnabas.'[7]

---

[1] *Did.*, 4[5-8]; *infra*, pp. 131, 139.   [2] *Ib.*, 4[9-11] ; *infra*, pp. 119, 129, 135.
[3] *Ib.*, 4[12, 13] ; *infra*, p. 172, n.   [4] *Ib.*, 5[1-61].
[5] *Ib.*, 5[2 fin.]. Not in *Barn.* ; and the sudden intrusion of the second person plural, into a passage which (up to 6[3]) is entirely addressed to one reader in the singular, is suspicious.
[6] *Ib.*, 6[2, 3], see *supra*, p. 69 ; *infra*, pp. 239 ff.
[7] For composition and date of *Barnabas* see e.g. Harnack, *Chronologie der Altchristl. Lit.*, i, pp. 410-428 ; H. Windisch, *Der Barnabasbrief* (in *HNT. : Ergänzungsband*, iii, pp. 408-413). It is commonly agreed that *Did.* represents an earlier form of the ' Two Ways ' than Barnabas, and that Barnabas has ' rearranged ' the material and so ' brought it into confusion ' (Bigg-Maclean, *Teaching of the Twelve Apostles*, pp. ix, x, xiv ; Windisch, *op. cit.*, pp. 204 ff. ; J. A. Robinson, *Barnabas, Hermas and Didaché*, pp. 16, 72—but Robinson regards Barnabas as nearer the original). But Barnabas is not really in confusion at all. In the ' way of death,' though the order in the catalogues differs, there is nothing to choose between the two writers. In the ' way of life ' (apart from the probably interpolated sections) *Did.* has the following order : (i) the evangelical summary of the Decalogue (*Did.*, 1[2]) ; (ii) a meditation on the ten commandments, or possibly on the ' second commandment ' of the summary, love to one's neighbour (2[1-7]) ; (iii) ecclesiastical duties (4[1-4]) and almsgiving (4[5-8]) ; (iv) the ' domestic code ' (4[9-11]). Barnabas, on the other hand, decides to group most of his

Yet 'Barnabas' knows and incorporates the 'Two Ways,' which he calls the ways of light and darkness, over which preside respectively the angels of God and of Satan.[1] Barnabas explicitly proclaims himself a 'teacher'[2] of those to whom he writes. He has indeed 'doctrines' to communicate[3]—doctrines as to the divine sonship of Christ, His life, His cross and resurrection. This he does through a series of *testimonia* drawn from the Old Testament, and interpreted by 'gnosis'—which here means allegorism—in an anti-Jewish sense. Even the 318 servants of Abraham are made to typify Jesus.[4] But the greater part of his 'teaching,' even in the passages not dependent upon the 'Two Ways,' is ethical; and justification by works is his theme.

At the very outset he proclaims three 'sentences' ('dogmata') of the Lord[5]:—'The hope of life is the beginning and end of our faith; righteousness in judgment is the beginning and end; and love in joy and gladness is the proof of works of righteousness.' True 'knowledge,' therefore—he uses the word 'gnosis' here in a very specialized sense[6]—is knowledge of the will of God.[7] On this he insists again and again. For him, as for Justin and Tertullian later, Christ is the new lawgiver;[8] as Windisch, his latest editor says,[9] 'in essence he leaves the Jewish theory of salvation unchanged.' Quite apart from the catalogues of virtues and vices in the 'Two Ways' section, he enumerates at the very beginning of his exposition the characteristics which alone can ensure salvation.[10] They include godliness, hating the errors of the present world, restraint of soul, avoidance of sinners, avoidance of idleness (ματαιότης), church-going and striving to keep the commandments of God.

material round the two commands of the evangelical summary, and so we have (i) love to God, expanded (*Barn.*, 19²⁻⁵ᵇ); (ii) love to one's neighbour (19⁵ᶜ⁻⁹ᵃ); (iii) ecclesiastical duties and almsgiving, rearranged (19⁹ᵇ⁻¹²); the material of the 'domestic code' being redistributed between (i) and (ii). I am inclined to think the *Did.* order the more original, because of the 'domestic code'; if so Barnabas has sacrificed this to secure his own arrangement. He has not been conspicuously successful in distinguishing duties towards God from duties towards man, but that is always a difficult thing to do. On the other hand, there is method even in his rearrangement —note particularly the attempt to group the 'neighbours' by age (19⁵— the unborn child, infants, boys and girls, full-grown persons). In any case, to accuse him of 'confusion' is misleading.

[1] *Barnabas*, 18¹.
[2] *Ib.*, 1⁴. The document, of course, is in no sense a genuine letter.
[3] *Ib.*, 1⁶.   [4] *Ib.*, 9⁷⁻⁹.
[5] *Ib.*, 1⁶. The text is very uncertain (see e.g. Windisch, *ad loc.*), but the significant fact is that 'righteousness' has twice intruded into a passage obviously based on the evangelical triad of faith, hope and love. There is some literary connexion with Ign., *Eph.*, 14¹. The Latin version of Barnabas compresses drastically and meaninglessly.
[6] He also uses it, in a sense more akin to his contemporaries, of allegorical interpretation of the prophets (1⁵, ⁷) and the Old Testament generally (6⁹, 9⁸, 10¹⁰, 13⁷, 14⁷).
[7] *Barn.*, 18¹, 21⁵; cp. 5⁴.
[8] *Ib.*, 2⁶; cp. Justin, *Dial.*, 18; Tert., *adv. Jud.*, 3—'nova lex'; *de præscr. hær.*, 13 (in the 'regula fidei').
[9] *Op. cit.*, p. 340.   [10] *Barn.*, 4¹⁻², ¹⁰, ¹¹.

Again and again he emphasizes the certainty of the judgment, the reward of the righteous and the punishment of the wicked ; again and again he insists upon the paramount importance of the fear of the Lord. In his anxiety to set before his readers the full knowledge of what is required of them, he takes up even the food-regulations of the old dispensation,[1] and interprets them allegorically (with some interesting and remarkable sidelights on the natural history of his day) of the vices which the Christian is to avoid as carefully as the Jew eschews his unclean meats.

With the two documents just quoted it is natural and usual to compare a third, dating from much the same period—the earliest known Christian homily or sermon, commonly called the second epistle of Clement.[2] 'Brethren,' the preacher begins, 'we ought so to think of Jesus Christ as of God '—and that is well said. But the dominant interest betrays itself in the next words—'that is, as of the Judge of quick and dead.'[3] From this sentence the whole tenour of the sermon develops itself directly. Gratitude is mentioned as well as fear as a motive for obedience to the commandments ;[4] but obedience to the commandments and doing the will of God, serving Him and fighting a good fight, are phrases which recur at the shortest possible intervals throughout the text. Almost alone among his contemporaries he appears to be ignorant of the 'Two Ways' (both Ignatius and Hermas know of them) ;[5] but he is as capable as they are of compiling lists of virtues. 'Let us confess God by our works, brethren,' he says ; ' by loving one another, by avoidance of fornication, slander and envy, by temperance, mercy and godliness ; by mutual sympathy and freedom from avarice. By these works and not by their opposites will we confess Him.'[6] Apart from a single doctrinal passage which is very much of a digression—an attack on those who deny the resurrection of the flesh [7]—the whole sermon partakes of this

[1] Barn., 10.
[2] On this, J. B. Lightfoot, Apostolic Fathers : I. St. Clement of Rome, ii, pp. 191-210 ; R. Knopf in HNT. : Ergänzungsband, i, pp. 151-153. That it is a sermon is clear from 17³, 'when we go home,' and 19¹, ' I read you an exhortation.' Its place of origin is usually supposed to be Corinth or Rome ; its date not later than A.D. 150. Streeter, Primitive Church, pp. 243-247, argues on no very convincing grounds for Alexandria.
[3] 2 Clem., 1¹.   [4] Ib., 1⁸⁻⁵.
[5] Ign., Magn., 5—' These two are set before us simultaneously,—death and life ; and everyone shall go to his own place'; Herm., Mand., vi, 1²⁻⁵— ' The path of righteousness is straight, but the path of unrighteousness is crooked ; walk in the straight path and avoid the crooked,' etc. Cp. also Ps.-Clem. Hom., vii, 7, 8 ; xx, 2 ; Recogn., viii, 54. (It is true that 2 Clement uses the phrase ' dead gods,' which also occurs Did. 6³ ; but this comes after the ' Two Ways ' section, and there were numerous scriptural passages (esp. Wisd. 15¹⁷) which might have suggested the phrase independently to both writers).
[6] 2 Clem., 4², ³.
[7] 2 Clem., 9¹⁻⁵—but even here the principal interest lies in the fact that we shall be judged in the flesh. There is also a fanciful and confused doctrinal passage in c. 14, in which from the conception ' the male is Christ, the female is the Church ' is derived (how ?) the formula, ' The Church is the flesh and

discursive ethical character; if anything distinguishes it, it is a reiterated insistence upon repentance which suggests an almost morbid preoccupation with sin. The sermon ends, as it began, with a reminder of the day of judgment, and a promise of reward, future, if not immediate, for the righteous.

The three documents just reviewed are among the earliest of our post-apostolic literary survivals. They are clear evidence of what was obviously the principal ethical interest of the period—the interest in codification. They are part of that process to which Harnack has given the name of the 'hellenization' or 'secularization,'[1] of Christianity, and of which, in the doctrinal sphere, he regards the gnostics as the principal agents.[2] There is a certain paradox in using the adjective 'hellenistic' of a group of writings which includes so Judaistic a document as 'Didaché.' But the paradox is only superficial. Both the Jewish and the Greek worlds at the beginning of the Christian era were demanding clear, authoritative, and easily-remembered instruction on ethical questions; and Christianity, in codifying its principles of conduct, did no more than follow a well-beaten track. It would have followed the same track, perhaps, if it had remained a purely Jewish or semi-Jewish sect. Yet the need would have been less urgent, for in the main it could have depended upon the enveloping Jewish code,[3] simplifying and purifying it, no doubt, but adding few new duties of its own. The breach with Judaism, however, forced the Church to stand alone against the pagan world. It had to be prepared not merely to keep its own members together, but to answer the ethical questions of earnest heathen enquirers. The main impetus towards codification came, therefore, from contact with the Greek world; and the Church adopted the method already in use in the Jewish diaspora of throwing its ethical teaching into well-recognized moulds. How far any particular writer actually used Jewish or Greek models—how far, in fact, any Jewish model had already assimilated itself to Greek usage—is a problem of secondary importance.

Christ the spirit'; which in its turn is cited, unnecessarily, to support the obvious maxim, 'Guard the flesh that ye may partake of the Spirit.' The whole passage, as the author naively says (15[1]), is 'no small counsel concerning abstinence,' and is probably composed of semi-gnostic aphorisms which are introduced as already familiar to the readers (14[2], 'I ween you are not ignorant '). 'Clement,' like Hermas, had Encratite leanings (cf. *infra*, p. 187); in this, as in his childlike self-conceit (15[1]), his weird excursion into theology, and his emphasis upon judgment, repentance, and ' healing,' his affinities with Hermas are noticeable.

[1] *Hist. of Dogma* (E. tr.), ii, pp. 4, 5, 7, etc.; cp. i, pp. 49-51, 170 ff.; C. Luthardt, *History of Christian Ethics*, p. 109.

[2] Harnack, i, pp. 226, 227. What Harnack dislikes, and describes by the names of ' secularization ' or ' hellenization,' is the *systematizing* of Christianity, which in the theological sphere meant the importing of methods and terms from Greek philosophy. How far he is right in accusing the gnostics of this (though he only accuses them of doing precipitately what the Church did gradually) must be considered later (*infra*, pp. 208-212).

[3] This point is well put, C. Weizsäcker, *Apostolic Age*, ii, p. 351.

Three main devices were employed in this early formalizing of Christian ethics—the metaphor of the ' Two Ways,' the use of catalogues of virtues and vices, and the systematic arrangement of domestic duties in what may be called ' household codes.'[1] All three were known both to Hellenism and to Judaism. In the Greek world they characterized the popular Stoic and Cynic diatribes which were the rhetorical stock-in-trade of itinerant evangelists—' elastic combinations of treatise and sermon, of monologue and dialogue '[2] which lent themselves to the most diverse themes. The conception of the ' Two Ways,' for example, is an obvious one ; yet it has an interesting history in Greek thought, being derived apparently from the ' antitheses' with which Heraclitus, five centuries before Christ, attempted to wake his contemporaries from their complacent acceptance of conventional ethical standards.[3] Antithesis remained to the end a favourite device in the diatribes ; but the specific form of the ' Two Ways' achieved a popularity of its own. It occurs in ethical connexions in Xenophon, Hesiod, Theognis, Virgil and Plutarch,[4]—so much so that Lactantius[5] could say of the ' ways ' in question—' Quas et poetæ in carminibus et philosophi in disputationibus suis induxerunt.'

Similarly with the catalogue[6]—which, indeed, is only one of several convenient artifices adopted by orators, good and bad alike,

---

[1] Other 'household codes' of this period, besides that in *Didaché* which *Barnabas* has used, will be found in 1 *Clem.*, 1[3]—a brief resumé of the code in use at Corinth, mentioning its instructions to young men and to wives (perhaps 1[2]—the sobriety, hospitality, ' gnosis,' incorruptibility, obedience to rulers and deference to presbyters, of the Corinthians themselves—belongs to this as well) ; *ib.*, 21[6] (duties towards rulers, elders, juniors ; duties of the young, of wives, of children—a passage which pleased Clement of Alexandria so much that he quoted it *in extenso, Strom.*, iv, 17, 108) ; Pol., *ad Phil.*, 4, 5 (duties of wives, children, widows, deacons, young men, virgins, presbyters) ; Ignat., *ad Pol.*, 4, 5 (duties towards widows and slaves; church-going ; duties of slaves, duties of wives, husbands, ascetics, etc.).

[2] J. Weiss, *Das Urchristentum*, p. 317.   Strictly speaking, the word ' diatribe ' should be confined to rhetorical dialogue, and ' paraenesis ' used for ethical instruction as a whole.   On the diatribe generally, E. Norden, *Antike Kunstprosa*, pp. 129 ff. ; A. D. Nock in (ed.) A. E. J. Rawlinson, *Essays on the Trinity and Incarnation*, pp. 145, 146 ; R. Bultmann, *Der Stil der Paulinischen Predigt u. die Kynisch-stoische Diatribe*, pp. 1-64; P. Wendland, *Die Hellenistisch-Römische Kultur*, pp. 75-81, 92 ff. ; S. Dill, *Roman Society from Nero to Marcus Aurelius*, pp. 346 ff. ; W. M. Edwards in (ed.) J. U. Powell and E. A. Barber, *New Chapters in the History of Greek Literature*, second series, pp. 88-100.

[3] So E. Norden, *Kunstprosa*, pp. 16 ff., 508 f.

[4] References, Knopf, *HNT.*: *Ergänzungsband*, i, p. 4; Windisch, *ib.*, iii, p. 196 ; Clemen, *RGENT.*, p. 227 ; C. Taylor, ' The Two Ways in Hermas and Xenophon,' *Journal of Phil.*, 1893, pp. 243 ff. (on Xen., *Mem.*, ii, 1, 21-34—Prodicus' fable of Herakles).

[5] *Div. Inst.*, vi, 3 ff.—a very elaborate ' Two Ways ' passage.

[6] Other catalogues in second-century Christian writers, Hermas, *Mand.*, v, 2[4], vi, 2, viii, 3-5 ; *Sim.*, vi, 5[5], ix, 15[2,3]; Pol., *ad Phil.*, 2[2], 4[3]; Aristides, *Apol.*, 15 ; Justin, *Apol.*, i, 14-17.   A specially good note on the subject in Lietzmann, *Römerbrief (HNT.*, iii, 1), pp. 34, 35 ; with texts from Diog. Laert., Philo, and *Corp. Herm.*, *ib.*, pp. 127-129. Cp. also Bultmann, *Stil*, pp. 19, 71, 72.

when they are gravelled for lack of matter. The Orphic ethical instruction was given in catalogue-form ; [1] so also was that of the Pythagoreans. Iamblichus preserves a double catalogue of Lysis, the Pythagorean [2] :—from ' akrasia ' (intemperance) proceed unlawful unions, destructions, intoxication, unnatural pleasures, and ' very many lusts ' ; from ' greed ' come theft, burglary, parricide, sacrilege, poisonings, and the vices akin to them. A popular gambling game was played with counters like draughtsmen, on each of which was inscribed the name of a separate vice ; and a sufficient variety of these counters has been discovered to parallel all but one of the sins enumerated in one of S. Paul's great catalogues (I Cor. vi, 9-10). [3] Comic dramatists found such lists of vices convenient for the more scurrilous parts of their dialogue ; sorrowing relatives employed corresponding catalogues of virtues for funeral inscriptions. [4] The Stoics tabulated all passions under the four great heads of ' grief,' ' fear,' ' desire,' and ' pleasure.' [5] A specially ambitious catalogue of the evils which follow a life of pleasure is compiled by Philo ; he has succeeded in bringing together a hundred and forty-seven adjectives (without a single conjunction) descriptive of the man who becomes pleasure's slave. [6]

No less popular were the ' household codes.' [7] Diogenes Laertius traces one of these as far back as Pythagoras—it dealt with duties towards the gods, heroes, the aged, parents, friends, and the law. [8] Stobaeus preserves extensive fragments from Hierocles of another,

[1] E. von Dobschütz, *Christian Life in the Primitive Church*, E. tr., p. 407.

[2] Iamblichus, *de vit. Pyth.*, xvii, 18 ; von Dobschütz, *op. cit.*, p. 407.

[3] A. Deissmann, *Light from the Ancient East* [4] (E. tr.), p. 316—' the vices greatly preponderate on the counters that have been preserved ' ; further catalogue-references, Clemen, *RGENT.*, pp. 134, 135, 347 (a remarkable comparison between the virtues demanded of a good general by Onosander, and those required of bishops and presbyters in the Pastorals) ; E. Zeller, *Stoics, Epicureans and Sceptics* (E. tr.), pp. 255, 256.

[4] Deissmann, *op. cit.*, pp. 317, 318.

[5] See e.g. J. von Arnim, *Stoic. Vet. Fragm.*, i, pp. 51, 52 ; iii, pp. 92-96. Andronicus subdivided ' desire ' into twenty-seven categories ; pleasure into five ; fear into thirteen ; grief into twenty-five (*ib.*, pp. 96-100). Many further catalogues, *ib.*, pp. 101-132.

[6] Philo, *de sacr. Ab. et Cain*, 32 (M., ii, pp. 268, 269; CW., i, pp. 214, 215), also printed Lietzmann, *HNT.*, iii, i, p. 128. The passage (§§ 20-32) is ultimately based upon a ' two-ways ' contrast between Virtue and Pleasure ; several minor catalogues are also included.

[7] I have used the phrase ' household ' or ' domestic code ' to translate the expressive German *Haustafel*, which has now become a technical term. The word was apparently first used by Luther as a title for the simple scheme of duties which he appended to his Shorter Catechism (see B. J. Kidd, *Documents of the Continental Reformation*, pp. 220-222) ; the Reformers then used it in the chapter-headings of their translations of the Bible. The latest investigator thinks that Luther's *Haustafel* goes back for its contents to Gerson and the mediæval Penitentials (K. Weidinger, *Die Haustafeln* (1928), p. 2). An interesting sixteenth-century *Haustafel* of the Russian Church (including instructions on the Christian method of chastising an erring wife) is summarized by W. H. Frere, *Links in the Chain of Russian Church History*, p. 75.

[8] Diog. Laert., viii, 22 ff. (E. tr., C. D. Yonge (Bohn), 1901, p. 347) ; cp. also Sen., *ep.* 94, 4, on Cleanthes' approval of household codes.

in which duties towards parents, brothers, wife, children and slaves were dealt with.[1] Dio Chrysostom, Cicero, Marcus Aurelius and Epictetus tabulate duties, virtues and vices in accordance with the same scheme ;[2] so do Seneca, Horace and Polybius. It is true that no coherent or fully developed exposition of a household code survives from classical antiquity : but enough has been recovered to show that the tabulation was well-known, and that it must have been used as a skeleton to be clothed by individual moralists according to their personal preferences or the needs of the audience.[3]

Although, however, contact with the Greek world continually helped to popularize these artifices among Christian writers, the direct influence of the Old Testament and Palestinian rabbinic teaching cannot be overlooked. Codification is after all a natural instinct with moralists of every period and every clime. Certainly it was common enough among the Jews. Of catalogues of virtues and sins it is almost unnecessary to speak. They are found throughout the Old Testament ; and Lietzmann's attempt to show that the early Christian catalogues reflect Greek rather than Jewish influence is supported by evidence too vague to be convincing.[4] Rendel Harris[5] has drawn an ingenious parallel between the ' Didaché' catalogue of vices, S. Paul's catalogue in Rom. i, 29, and the enumeration of sins used by the pious Jew for his confession on the Day of Atonement ; and is inclined to infer from their resemblance a lost alphabetical Jewish catalogue of sins from which they are all derived. This hypothesis, again, is too insecure to command general acceptance ; but it is at least interesting as showing that, apart from all Greek influence, the Jewish background of early Christian thought would have sufficed to mature the catalogue style.[6]

The same is true of the ' household codes.' Here the best examples come undoubtedly from the Judaism of the Dispersion. The scheme occurs repeatedly in Philo ;[7] in one passage he goes into considerable detail :—[8]

> ' The fifth commandment, as to honouring parents, contains in an allegory many necessary precepts—for old and young, for rulers and ruled, for benefactors and beneficiaries, for slaves and masters. ' Parents ' stand for all in a position of authority—elders, rulers, benefactors and masters ; ' children ' for all in an inferior station—the young, subjects, beneficiaries, slaves. Hence the commandment implies many

---

[1] Weidinger, pp. 27-34, 41, 42 ; Clemen, p. 342.
[2] Weidinger, pp. 34-38.
[3] *Ib.*, pp. 38, 39.
[4] *HNT.*, iii, 1, p. 35 ; cp. Bonhöffer's criticism of Bultmann, *Epiktet u. das N.T.*, p. 179.
[5] *Teaching of the Apostles*, pp. 82-86.
[6] Other Jewish catalogues, Bousset, *RJ.*, p. 421.
[7] Weidinger, pp. 25, 26.
[8] *de dec.*, 165 ff. (M., ii, p. 207 ; CW., iv, p. 305).

other injunctions—that the young should reverence the old,
the old supervise the young ; subjects obey their rulers, and
rulers consider the subjects' interests. Beneficiaries should
aim at repaying favour for favour ; benefactors should refrain
from looking for return as though they were moneylenders.
Servants should exhibit an obedience which expresses love
towards the master ; masters should show themselves gentle
and meek, and so redress the inequality of status between
themselves and their slaves.'

A poem falsely attributed to Phocylides, which is almost certainly the composition of an Alexandrian Jew,[1] develops the ' household code ' to even greater length, and indeed makes of it a fully
articulated tract. But although these codes receive their fullest
treatment in non-Palestinian Judaism, the material of which they
are compounded is native. Joshua ben Sira deals exhaustively
with the duties of various members of a family towards one another,[2]
though he never brings them together into a single tabulation.
Similar material can be quoted from rabbinic sources.[3] It is
curious that the obvious gathering together of such fragments
into a systematic whole never took place in Palestine. But the
natural tendency of the Hebrew moralist was to elaborate single
apophthegms by parallelism or antithesis ; and this would to some
extent preclude their codification on the basis of a more fully-
developed reciprocal plan.[4]

The ' Two Ways,' finally, appear to be more Jewish even than
Greek. According to Bousset the idea is originally eschatological,[5]
and certainly its dramatic employment in the apocryphal ' Apocalypse of Peter ' supports the theory.[6] Probably the original document which underlies the early chapters of ' Didaché ' was a Jewish
proselyte-catechism.[7] But the ' Two Ways ' recur continually
throughout the Old Testament and in later Jewish writings. References to them are found in the first psalm (the whole psalm

---

[1] Weidinger, p. 23 ; see Harnack, *Geschichte der Altchristl. Lit.*, pp.
863, 864 ; *Chronologie*, i, p. 589.

[2] E.g. Ecclus. 7[18-35] (duties towards friends, wife, children (especially
daughters), parents, priests, the poor, the sick) : 9[1-9] (various kinds of
ladies and the behaviour appropriate towards each) ; 33[24-31] (treatment of
servants) ; 41[17-24] (behaviour towards different classes) ; cp. Job 31 (list of
duties towards various classes).

[3] Strack-Billerbeck, i, pp. 705 ff. (parents and children) ; cp. Bousset,
RJ., pp. 426, 427.

[4] Similarly, the ' domestic codes ' disappeared from Christian literature
at a very early date, probably because the exigencies of the Church in her
conflicts, both internal and external, demanded more detailed handling of
the specific problems of the moment from preachers and writers. (Other
reasons suggested by Weidinger, pp. 75-79, seem too fanciful to be accepted.)

[5] *RJ.*, pp. 276, 413.

[6] Its employment in the full text of the *Apocalypse* is implied in the
last sentence of the Inferno (§ 34, M. R. James, *Apocryphal New Testament*,
p. 510 : ' These were they that forsook the way of God ').

[7] See C. Taylor, *Teaching of the Twelve Apostles*, pp. 18-22.

being, in the words of a recent scholar, ' no more than a variation
on the theme, " the Lord knoweth the way of the righteous ; but
the way of the ungodly shall perish " ') ; in Jeremiah, Proverbs,
the books of the Maccabees and of Enoch ; in Philo of Alexandria,
and in rabbinic teaching.[1] The idea is to be seen more fully developed than elsewhere in the ' Testaments of the xii Patriarchs '—
a Chasidic document of the second century B.C. which Canon Charles
regards as the nearest approach to Christian ethics in the whole of
Jewish literature.[2]

Thus the ' Testament of Levi ' (xix, 1) says : ' Choose for yourselves either the light or the darkness ; either the law of the Lord
or the works of Beliar'; the ' Testament of Judah ' (xx, 1) : ' Two
spirits wait upon man, the spirit of truth and the spirit of deceit.'
Most important of all is the ' Testament of Asher.' ' Two ways,'
the writer begins,[3] ' hath God given to the sons of men, and two
inclinations, and two kinds of action and two modes, and two issues.
Therefore all things are by twos, one over against another. For
there are two ways of good and evil ; and with these are the two
inclinations in our breasts, discriminating them.'

At this point the ethical instinct of the writer reveals itself ;
and in its originality and insight it certainly marks him out as a
moralist of the very highest rank. For that reason we may consider
him a little further. He adverts to the danger of thinking that the
' two ways ' classification will enable us to pass moral judgments
automatically and out of hand. Few actions fall exclusively into
one category or the other ; life is too complex to be easily comprehended by such simple formulations.

Most things are ' double-faced,' he asserts ; [4] nevertheless this
does not exempt from the duty of decision and judgment. Reflection will show in the end (however difficult the process) that the
' whole is good,' or ' the whole is bad.' Of this he proceeds to give
instances :—[5]

> ' There is a man that loveth him that worketh evil because
> he would prefer even to die in evil for his sake ; and concerning
> this it is clear that it hath two aspects, but the whole is an evil
> work. Though indeed there is love, yet it is wicked, as it con-
> cealeth what is evil ; now this thing seemeth good in name ;
> but the end of the action tendeth unto evil.'

[1] Ps. 1[6] ; Jer. 21[8] (' the way of life and the way of death ') ; Prov. 4[18, 19]
(' the path of the righteous,' ' the way of the wicked ') ; 4 Macc. 14[5] (' the
road to immortality ') ; 1 En. 94[1–4] (' paths of righteousness and unrighteousness,' ' path of violence and path of peace '), cp. 91[19] ; 2 En. 30[15] (' light and
darkness ') ; for Philo see Windisch (*HNT.*, *Erg.-band*) on *Barn.*, 18[1]; *Pirké
Aboth*, 2[1] ; Jochanan ben Zakkai (' way to Eden and way to Gehinnom '
Bousset, *RJ.*, p. 276).
[2] Charles, *Apocr. and Pseudep.*, ii, p. 282.
[3] *Test. Asher*, 1[3]. Canon Charles (*ad loc.*) notes that this is the first
appearance of the good *yetzer* in Jewish thought ; the evil *yetzer* had appeared earlier.
[4] *Ib.*, 4[3].   [5] *Ib.*, 2[3, 4].

Or again—

> ' Many in killing the wicked do two works, of good and evil ;
> but the whole is good, because he hath uprooted and destroyed
> that which is evil. One man hateth the " merciful-unjust "
> man or the " fasting-adulterer " ' (two types of hypocrite
> which the author has just mentioned in parenthesis) ; ' this too
> hath a twofold aspect, but the whole work is good, because he
> followeth the Lord's example, in that he accepteth not the
> seeming good as the genuine good. Another desireth not to
> see a good day with them that riot, lest he pollute his body
> and defile his soul ; this too is double-faced, but the whole is
> good. . . . They walk in zeal for the Lord, and abstain from
> what God also hateth and forbiddeth by His commandments,
> warding off the evil from the good.' [1]

We shall go far before we meet with any such nicety of ethical
discrimination as this. The passage is salutary for every practical
moralist. It emphasizes one at least of the dangers of the primitive
Christian codification of virtues and vices—its tendency to judge
by externals and in the mass, without due consideration of circumstances. It emphasizes, as well, the imperative need for a sane
casuistry to supplement the limitations of moral codes. We have
only to review the simple cases proposed by ' Asher ' and ask
ourselves in each instance, after the problem is stated, ' Will he say
" the end is evil," or " the end is good " ? ' to see how clearly he
recognizes the dangers of a too facile intuitionism.

But there is a third reason why the passage is important.
Casuistry has its dangers, as well as codification—the danger in
particular that the broad moral distinctions which we know to be
universally valid should be whittled away and forgotten in a maze
of argument and subdivision. It is only tolerable, therefore, where
there is also a rigorous and tenacious hold upon first principles.
This is the lesson with which ' Asher ' concludes his illuminating
excursion into casuistry :—

> ' Ye see, my children, there are two in all things—one
> against the other, the one hidden by the other. In wealth
> [is hidden] covetousness, in conviviality drunkenness, in
> laughter grief, in wedlock profligacy. . . . *Yet it may never
> be said that truth is a lie, nor right wrong ;* for all truth is
> under the light, even as all things are under God.' [2]

II. Codification in the New Testament.

In the first lecture I ventured to give to this tendency to regulate
and codify morality the name of ' formalism '; and to suggest that,

---

[1] *Test. Asher*, 4³⁻⁵. ' Desiring not to see a good day ' is of course evil ;
but to avoid association ' with them that riot ' is good ; hence this state of
mind (not unusual in mixed gatherings) is ' two-faced.'
[2] *Ib.*, 5¹⁻³.

the more it runs to casuistry, the more it is distinctive of the
pastoral rather than of the missionary side of the Church's life.
But the Church was pastoral from the first, and the formalist tendency which dominates ' Didaché,' ' Barnabas,' and pseudo-Clement
is represented also in the New Testament, though here it is only
one of many different lines of approach.   It will help us to ap-
preciate the lights and shadows of this curiously perplexing phenomenon—for perplexing formalism is in very many respects—to
observe it in its evangelic and apostolic context.

The ' Two Ways ' are represented in the synoptic teaching of
Jesus by a direct reference in the first gospel, faintly echoed by
S. Luke [1]—the broad and the narrow way ; whilst approximations
to the thought occur in the parables of the Sheep and the Goats, the
Wheat and the Tares, the Drag Net, the Ten Virgins, the Rich
Man and Lazarus, and the Two Houses.   It assumes a very peculiar
form in the opening to S. Luke's version of the great sermon (the
Beatitudes and Woes) ; for what are contrasted here are not ways
of life, but external conditions.   The three notable duties of prayer,
fasting end almsgiving are catalogued in S. Matthew's version of
the sermon ; where also the canons of the New Law are set out
in parallel with those of the Old which they at once fulfil and
supersede.   Catalogues of sins are to be found in the invective
against the Pharisees, and the list of things which ' proceed out of
the heart ' in S. Mark ; [2] whilst the Matthæan Beatitudes provided
a catalogue of virtues which rightly captured the imagination of
Christendom.   And all of this is so Judaic in form, whichever gospel
it comes from—though nothing at once so simple and so piercing
has ever been quoted from contemporary rabbinism—that we
cannot hesitate for a moment to refer the teaching given by the
Synoptists in all its main outlines back to the Lord Himself.

There are no formal ' household codes ' in the gospels ; but
the epistles are singularly rich in them.   In the last chapter we
examined that which occurs in the epistle to the Colossians,[3] and
recognized that it bore throughout a rigorist tinge.   To a certain
extent this may be due to a general dependence upon some Stoic
archetype, for apart from the repeated but almost formal references
to ' the Lord ' [4] there are no specifically Christian sentiments in the
passage.   The code in Ephesians is an almost verbal echo of that
in Colossians [5]—both deal with the relationships of husband and
wife, parents and children, masters and slaves.   But in the Ephesian
code the writer has made a determined attempt to base his teaching
about marriage upon the mystic union between Christ and His
Church.[6]   In the Petrine code [7] the usual order is reversed.   The
writer starts with the duties of slaves, which leads him astray

---

[1] Mt. 7[13, 14] ; cp. Lk. 13[24].
[2] Mk. 7[21, 22] ; a shorter list in the parallel, Mt. 15[19].
[3] Col. 3[18]-4[1], *supra*, pp. 77-79.
[4] Col., 3[18, 20, 22, 23].
[5] Eph. 5[22]-6[9].
[6] *Ib.*, 5[23, 25-32].
[7] I Pet. 2[18]-3[7].

into a general exhortation to Christian patience,[1] supported by a beautiful and well-known reference to the sufferings of Jesus. On coming back to his theme, he leaves on one side the duties of masters and the reciprocal relationships of parents and children; [2] proceeds at once to the behaviour of wives, and concludes with that of husbands. The code is preceded by a catalogue of the virtues of a Christian citizen which is closely akin to Romans xiii,[3] just as the reference to Christian wives and heathen husbands [4] perhaps points back to S. Paul's discussion in 1 Cor. vii, 12-16.

In 1 Timothy a very elaborate code of the duties of different classes towards the Church, rather than towards one another, includes men, women, bishops, deacons and their wives, widows, elders and slaves; [5] but its outlines are blunted by the intrusion of doctrinal and personal parentheses. The passage about women's dress may depend on the same source as the code in 1 Peter.[6] A similarly elaborated code is that in Titus ii, 1-10.[7] Other hortatory passages in the New Testament, such as those in Hebrews (ch. xiii), 1 Thess. v, 12-22, and the epistle of S. James, pass from point to point, as do the household codes, but have a wider range than the latter, and therefore cannot fairly be quoted as examples.

A comparison of these 'household codes' in the New Testament provokes a further reflection. The epistle to the Colossians would read more continuously if the household code were detached.[8]

---

[1] 1 Pet. 2[19-25].

[2] The reasons for these omissions can only be guessed. If, as is often supposed, the first part of the epistle is an address to (adult) candidates for baptism, the instructions to children would naturally be out of place. This, however, does not account for the omission of the duties of parents to children, which would, in fact, be peculiarly appropriate. But we are witnessing here the first stage in the disintegration of the household codes (*supra*, p. 122, n. 4). The writer's primary interest is the behaviour of Christians under harsh treatment, particularly of Christian inferiors under the supervision of heathen superiors. So he deals (2[13-16]) with the behaviour of Christians in general towards (pagan) governors (many critics consider this section itself to be part of the 'code'); then with the behaviour of Christian slaves towards (? heathen) masters; and finally proceeds to the behaviour of Christian wives towards pagan husbands who 'hear not the word' (3[1]). 'Be subject' (2[13, 18], 3[1]), 'behaviour' (2[12], 3[1, 2]), 'well-doing' (2[14, 15, 20]; contrast 'evil-doing,' 2[12, 14]) are his key-words as regards the Christians; 'beholding' (*epopteuein*, 2[12], 3[2]) the attitude of their superiors. The writer has therefore used the 'code' merely as a conventional form into which to cast teaching dealing with a particular problem: the duties of (Christian) husbands come in at the end (3[7]), not altogether appropriately, in deference to the 'code'-form.

[3] 1 Pet. 2[13-17]; Rom. 13[1-7].   [4] 1 Pet. 3[1, 2].

[5] 1 Tim. 2[8-15], 3[1-13], 5[1]-6[2]—the *haustafel* is becoming a *gemeindetafel* (Weidinger, p. 68). Here again the code is prefixed (as in 1 Pet. 2[13-17]) with a reminder of the duties of citizenship, beautifully expressed in terms of intercession (2[2]).

[6] 1 Tim. 2[9, 10]; pagan parallels, Weidinger, p. 65.

[7] Prefixed by the duties of bishops, 1[5-9]; with a reminder as to citizenship appended, 3[1].

[8] This will easily be seen if 3[12-17], 4[2-6], are read continuously as one passage.

There is nothing to suggest that it is an addition to the Pauline text, but it has all the appearance of being originally an independent unit of teaching incorporated by S. Paul himself at this point. The same is true of the Ephesian code.[1] Of the code in 1 Peter Weiszäcker says that it too ' has been inserted in the body of the letter, the junctions being perfectly discernible '; other commentators are uncertain on the point.[2] Although, therefore, we are not in a position to say with confidence that a separate domestic code existed in the early Church for the instruction of catechumens, and was used as a convenient basis for expansion by different writers, it cannot be denied that the evidence points in this direction.

The catalogue-style, again, is a favourite with the apostolic writers. S. Paul has no less than five great catalogues of vices variously constituted and arranged, and several minor ones ; [3] he counters them with lists of virtues [4] of a similar elasticity. His frequent reference to τὸ καλόν or τὸ ἀγαθόν,[5] as a summary of ethics, show that for him and his readers the conventional Greek articulation of καλοκαγαθία was neither unfamiliar nor unacceptable. It is, furthermore, a suggestion not without great plausibility that the list of theological virtues itself is not so much a contribution of S. Paul to Christianity, as a rudimentary catalogue which he found in circulation, and adopted for his purposes. It underlies several passages in the epistles ; and S. Paul has raised it to immortal rank by a lightning-flash of genius. But the manner of its employment in 1 Cor. xiii provokes the question of its origin. ' Now abideth faith, hope, and love, these three,' he writes, but the greatest of these is love.' [6] The emphatic τὰ τρία ταῦτα—' this well-known triad'—suggests at once a popular formula. So also does the curiously unnecessary intrusion of faith and hope into the climax of a chapter devoted to the praise of love. And the fact that

---

[1] Here, similarly, we may pass easily from the general exhortations of 5^{15-21} to those of $6^{10\,ff}$. The code, however, has been prepared for by a *general* ' subjecting yourselves,' in 5^{21}, which enables the writer to dispense with a verb in 5^{22}, as though he were proceeding merely to give instances of ' subjection ' (cp. p. 126, n. 2, *supra*, on 1 Pet.). But the ' code ' does not really fit in with this general exhortation, for husbands, parents and masters could not very well be told to ' subject ' themselves to wives, children and slaves. The writer's attempt at introduce the code naturally is not, therefore, as fortunate as might at first sight appear.

[2] Weiszäcker, *Apostolic Age*, ii, p. 392 ; but as critics disagree whether the ' code ' begins at 2^{11}, 2^{13}, or 2^{18}, this ' junction ' is not so ' discernible ' after all.

[3] Rom. 1^{29-31} ; 1 Cor. $5^{10,\,11}$; 2 Cor. 12^{20} ; Gal. 5^{19-21} ; Col. $3^{5,\,8}$; cp. also 1 Cor. $6^{9,\,10}$; Eph. 4^{31}, 5^{3-5} ; 1 Tim. $1^{9,\,10}$; 2 Tim. 3^{2-4} ; 1 Pet. 2^1.

[4] 1 Cor. 13^{4-7} ; 2 Cor. 8^7 ; Gal. $5^{22,\,23}$; Eph. 4^{32} ; Phil. 4^8 ; Col. 3^{12-15} ; cp. 1 Tim. 3^{2-5} ; Tit. 2^2 ; Jas. 3^{17} ; 1 Pet. $3^{8,\,9}$; 2 Pet. 1^{5-7}. Weidinger (p. 51) points out Stoic elements in the ' Philippians ' catalogue.

[5] τὸ καλόν, Rom. $7^{18,\,21}$; 2 Cor. 13^7 ; Gal. 6^9 ; 1 Th. 5^{21} ; τὸ ἀγαθόν, Rom 2^{10}, 7^{13}, 12^9, ^{21}, 13^3, 14^{16}, 15^2, 16^{19} ; Gal. 6^{10} ; Eph. 4^{28} ; 1 Th. 5^{15} ; Philem. ^{14}.

[6] 1 Cor. 13^{13} ; other references to the three, Rom. 5^{1-5} ; Col. 1^{3-5} ; Thess. 1^3, 5^8 ; Heb. 10^{22-24} (RV.) ; 1 Pet. $1^{21,\,22}$.

elsewhere S. Paul traverses [1] what here he appears to state, that faith and hope, like love, will ' abide,' seems clear evidence that only their official catalogue-connexion with love entitles them on this one occasion to share love's characteristic of endurance. It is not unreasonable to suppose that the trinity of virtues appears at this somewhat inappropriate point because it was a trinity peculiarly familiar to S. Paul's readers.

Weiss and Harnack, therefore, are to some extent justified in thinking that we have here a Christian formula of the most primitive period. Even more suggestive is a conjecture made by Reitzenstein, and followed by Lietzmann, [2] which supplies a reason why the formula should occur especially in the epistle to the Corinthians rather than elsewhere. They have produced evidence—of a suggestive though not indeed of a conclusive character—for the currency, particularly in gnostic circles, either of a threefold formula of ' faith, *knowledge* ("gnosis") and love,' or a fourfold formula, ' faith, hope, knowledge and love.' One of the failings of the Corinthians in S. Paul's sight was their over-estimation of ' gnosis,' or spiritual knowledge, and their unspiritual pride in their supposed possession of it. He attacks these pretensions to a special revelation, under its other name of ' sophia ' (wisdom), throughout the first two chapters of the epistle ; and in dealing with a question analogous to that which evokes the hymn of love he says ironically, ' We know that we all have " gnosis " ' ; and adds ' " Gnosis " puffeth up but love edifieth.' [3] What could be more natural and effective, therefore, than that at the culminating point of the whole epistle,

---

[1] 2 Cor. 5⁷—while *we are absent from the Lord* ' we walk by faith, and not by sight ' ; Rom. 8²⁴—' Hope that is seen is not hope ; for who hopeth for that which he seeth ? ' (reading with RV. and WH. ὃ . . . τίς ; *al.* ὃ . . . τις, τί και :—' for what a man seeth, why doth he yet hope for ? ' (RV. marg.)—the meaning is the same). Harnack (*Sitzungsbericht d. Berlin. Ak.* (1911), p. 152) assumes that ' abideth ' in 1 Cor. 13¹³ has a different sense in the case of ' faith ' and ' hope ' from that which it has in the case of ' love.' The former ' abide ' in so far as they are transmuted into something higher than, and yet continuous with, themselves (whereas the charismata—*gnosis* and the like—are to be ' done away ' with altogether) ; the latter (love) ' abides ' in its own right. This attempt at interpretation only emphasizes the difficulty. The further suggestion (p. 156, cp. p. 152) that love itself is only a stage (νῦνι, 1 Cor. 13¹³, = ' in our present earthly existence ') and will be superseded by ' seeing face to face,' would make the whole passage meaningless.

[2] Reitzenstein, *HMHL.*, pp. 100-102, 242-244 ; *HMR.*, pp. 383-392 ; Lietzmann, *HNT.*, ix, p. 69. The evidence quoted comprises Porphyry, *ad Marcell.*, 24—' faith, truth (= *gnosis*), love, hope ' ; Clem. Alex., *Strom.*, iii, 10, 69—' *gnosis*, faith, love ' ; vii, 7, 46 ; 10, 55 ; 10, 57, an ascending scale of ' faith, *gnosis*, love ' ; and passages from Philo and the *Oracula Chaldaica*, with the usual references to the Mandæan fragments. That at all events a three-fold formula was common in Christian circles, and that ' hope ' was the variable member, may safely be inferred from e.g. Tit. 2², ' faith, love, patience ' ; cp. 2 Thess. 1⁴ ; Ign., *ad Pol.*, 6² ; similarly 1 Tim. 6¹¹, in the middle of a six-fold formula, and 2 Tim. 3¹⁰, another six-fold formula, but differently divided. See also A. D. Nock in A. E. J. Rawlinson, *Essays on the Trinity and Incarnation*, pp. 140, 141.

[3] 1 Cor. 8¹⁻³.

after insisting that the possession of 'all "gnosis"' is 'nothing' without love [1] and that its destiny is to be 'brought to nought,' [2] he should take their favourite catalogue and point it against them, with 'gnosis' either ignominiously omitted, or even more ignominiously replaced by what they would consider so elementary a virtue as hope ?

It is not only in his ethical passages that S. Paul exhibits a predilection for the catalogue-style. We need scarcely remind ourselves of the wonderful close of the eighth chapter of Romans :—

> 'Who shall separate us from the love of Christ ? Shall tribulation, or anguish, or persecution, or famine, or nakedness, or peril, or sword ? . . . Nay, in all these things we are more than conquerors through Him That loved us. For I am persuaded that neither death, nor life, nor angels, nor principalities, nor things present, nor things to come, nor powers, nor height, nor depth, nor any other creature, shall be able to separate us from the love of God which is in Christ Jesus our Lord.'

Other catalogues of considerable emotional power describe the humiliations of an apostle's life,[3] the sufferings of the Christian,[4] the changes and chances of his own missionary career.[5] This recalls another characteristic of formalism—its affinities with rhetoric. Rhetoric has its uses in life ; but in theology and ethics it is a very real danger.[6] It may lead either to unreal exaggerations or to refined abstractions ; and when virtues and sins have to be seen in their true proportions and proper perspective, neither exaggeration nor abstraction is desirable. The denunciations of a popular preacher lose force as they lose touch with life ; Gehazi may have felt as much resentment as repentance when the two talents of silver and two changes of raiment, which his fraud extracted from the willing Naaman, were generalized by Elisha into a wholesale misappropriation of money and garments and oliveyards and vineyards and sheep and oxen and menservants and maidservants.[7] Realism, rather than romanticism, has the more lasting effect in exhortation and rebuke.

Weiss, Norden, Wendland and others have thoroughly in-

---

[1] 1 Cor. 13[2].   [2] 1 Cor. 13[8].

[3] 1 Cor. 4[9-13] (cp. 2 Cor. 4[8-10]) ; Lietzmann and Weiss (ad loc.), supported by Wendland (HRK., p. 357), see in this the reflection of a popular Stoic figure—' the wise man a spectacle for gods and men' (cp. Bultmann, Stil, p. 71). Bonhöffer's criticism, though important, is not decisive (Epiktet u. das NT., p. 170 ; cp. Clemen, RGENT., p. 318).

[4] 2 Cor. 6[3-10].   [5] 2 Cor. 11[22-29].

[6] This is well brought out by Weidinger (op. cit., pp. 3, 4, 14, 15) who points out the absurdities that arise if every catalogue in the epistles is to be considered as having a personal reference to the readers (were the 'aged women' of Tit. 2[3] more 'subject to much wine' than the 'aged men' of 2[2] ?) Cp. also R. Thamin, Un Problème Morale dans l'Antiquité, p. 336 : 'C'est en morale que le romantisme et la fantaisie sont surtout dangereux.'

[7] 2 Kgs. 5[26].

vestigated this rhetorical element in apostolic Christianity. I adduce one example only of its effects upon ethics. The New Testament writers have an occasional fondness for associations of negative terms—whether in the form of verbs (with ἀπο-) expressing abstention from, or nouns and adjectives expressing absence of, sin.[1] An example occurs in the description of the ideal bishop in the epistle to Titus, where—before his positive characteristics are touched upon—nine negative qualifications of himself or his children are mentioned.[2] But whereas in the New Testament the negative virtues are balanced, if not more than balanced, by the positive ones, in the Apostolic Fathers the case is otherwise.[3] This had a double effect. It gave a strong impetus to the dualistic tendency which found its ultimate expression in rigorist asceticism ; whilst at the same time it encouraged the ordinary Christian to be content with a tepid ideal of blamelessness—of being void of offence— rather than to aspire to a life of positive well-doing and progress.

III. The Dangers of Formalism.

Nevertheless, New Testament formalism—even in the Pastoral Epistles, where catalogue succeeds catalogue in almost unbroken sequence—is something far less stultifying than that of the post-apostolic writers. The latter are moving on the path which leads towards a purely formal churchmanship of correct external observance. To estimate the extent of this decline, whose character should be sufficiently obvious from the quotations already given, we may observe four outstanding facts.

(a) In the first place, the reaction against the *spirit* of Judaism, which dominates the New Testament, is deteriorating into mere opposition to the *institutions* of Judaism. When ' Didaché,' on the subject of fasting, says, ' Let not your fasts be with the hypocrites ; for they fast on the second and fifth days of the week ' (Monday and Thursday—this being the Jewish practice), ' but do ye fast on the fourth and on Friday,'[4] it is clear that our Lord's great effort to purify the whole conception of fasting has degenerated into a sectarian wrangle about dates. When ' Barnabas ' uses the Mosaic law as a framework within which to interpret the Christian code, he is obviously a Jew in essentials, though a fanatical anti-Semite in externals.[5] When ' Clement ' says, ' Almsgiving is good

---

[1] Rom. 1[31] (absence of *virtues*) ; Phil. 2[15] ; 2 Tim. 3[2, 3] ; 1 Pet. 1[4] (of the Christian inheritance).

[2] Tit. 1[6, 7] ; in the parallel passage, 1 Tim. 3[2, 3] (as also in the Onosander parallel, *supra*, p. 120, n. 3), the negative characteristics are divided out among the positive requirements.

[3] E. von Dobschütz, *Christian Life in the Primitive Church*, p. 405, —e.g. Pol., *ad Phil.*, 6 ; and cp. *Did.* (and *Barn.*) above, pp. 112, 113.

[4] *Did.*, 8[1]—a good note on the early Christian ' station days,' Bigg-Maclean, *ad loc.*

[5] So Lightfoot, *Apostolic Fathers : Clement*, p. 503 : ' Barnabas ' treats the Law and the Prophets ' with a degree of respect which would have satisfied the most devout rabbi.'

as repentance for sin; fasting is better than prayer, and alms-giving than either . . . for almsgiving is a relief from sin,'[1] he is reproducing a specifically Jewish sentiment[2] which in later Christianity will go hand in hand with the doctrine of merit and works of supererogation, and the practice of commutation of penance.[3] 'Didaché' and 'Barnabas' are at one with 'Clement' on this point. A difficult passage in 'Didaché' says, 'Give to everyone that asketh thee, and ask it not again. . . . Blessed is he that giveth according to the commandment, for he is guiltless.'[4] There is here, no doubt, a reference to the maxim, 'It is more blessed to give than to receive' (for the text goes on to show that unworthy dependence upon the alms of others is culpable); but the words are at the same time a formalist parody of 'Charity covereth a multitude of sins.' The Christian should even be uneasy (so the 'Didaché' suggests) if a beneficiary for his almsgiving is slow to appear; 'Let thine alms sweat in thine hand until thou know to whom to give them,' it quotes from an unknown source.[5] Commentators have sometimes taken this as a warning against indiscriminate almsgiving;[6] but no such warning can be paralleled in

---

[1] 2 Clem., 16[4]. He quotes 1 Pet. 4[8] as his authority—'love' has degenerated into 'almsgiving.'

[2] Bousset, RJ., pp. 140, 141, 180, 424.

[3] See especially Cyprian, de op. et el., cc. 2 ff.—' Alms and faith cleanse from sin'; de orat. dom., 33—alms compel God to listen to prayer (' merita nostri operis ') ; Ambrose, de el. et jej., 20 (76)—' Thou hast money ; redeem thy sins. God is not to be bought, but thou canst be bought ; thou art sold under sin—buy thyself back with works, buy thyself with money. Money is cheap, but mercy is precious ; cp. Id., comm. in Phil., iv, 18 ; and infra, p. 139. The proof text was Lk. 11[41] (Vulg.)—' facite eleemosynam, et ecce omnia vobis munda sunt.'

[4] Did., 1[5]. The sequel is a warning against ' unworthy receiving.' The passage comes in the Christian ' interpolation ' in Didaché, and is not found in Barnabas. It occurs, however, in Hermas, in a variant and more intelligible form (Mand., ii, 4). There the warning against unworthy receiving comes first, and the point of the saying as to ' giving ' is made clear both by its form (' he that giveth is blameless ') and by the addition ' for he maketh no distinction to whom he giveth or not.' But as Streeter (The Primitive Church, pp. 281-283) has shown, this need not argue any dependence of Did. upon Hermas. The passage about unworthy receiving occurs also in an apocryphal saying of the Lord recorded by Clem. Alex. (fragment ; cp. also Didascalia, iv, 3 and Ap. Const., iv, 3, all quoted in A. Resch, Agrapha[2] (TU., xv. (1906)), pp. 194-196). It seems clear that when Didaché ' improves ' upon the form of the passage as given in Hermas by representing almsgiving as not merely ' blameless ' but also ' blessed,' he is influenced by the idea that almsgiving makes amends for deficiency in other virtues. Hermas is simply making a virtue of indiscriminate charity as such ; Didaché, though not averse to this idea, is emphasizing its prudential value as well. Similarly Did., 4[6]—' If thou have ought in thy hands, thou shalt give a ransom for thy sins,' explained by further injunctions to almsgiving, 4[7, 8], and the promise of reward from the μισθοῦ καλὸς ἀνταποδότης, 4[7]. ' Giving according to the commandment ' occurs also in Did., 13[5, 7]. For Barnabas, see 19[10, 11], where in spite of rearrangement the ideas of ' giving ' and ' working for the ransom of thy sins ' are still held in close connexion.

[5] Did., 1[6]—' Concerning this also it has been said, etc.'

[6] J. V. Bartlet in HDB., v, pp. 445, 446 ; C. Taylor, in Journal of Philology, xix (1891), pp. 148-172.

Christian literature before the end of the second century,[1] although Lucian's ' Peregrinus ' shows how necessary it was.[2] The anxiety implied in the words must surely be an anxiety to be giving—it matters not to whom—rather than an anxiety as to the worthiness of the recipient.

(*b*) In these and similar respects our writers show that they are no longer alert to the characteristic dangers of Judaism, which were exactly the dangers that formalist codification tends to foster. What those dangers are may be seen from the New Testament. That the best of the Jews were no doubt aware of them is nowadays fully admitted. In the ' Similitudes of Enoch,' a Pharisaic work, there is only one mention of the ' law ' from beginning to end ; [3] and the ' Testaments of the xii Patriarchs '—which for the first time in history unite the two commands of ' love for God ' and ' love for one's neighbour ' [4]—contain passages which, as has already been mentioned, Dr. Charles rightly regards as standing on a plane as high as the highest in New Testament morality. It is clear, therefore, that the invective against the Pharisees in the gospels, and S. Paul's great attack, not so much on the Jewish law as on the spirit of law in itself, hold good in a wider sphere than that of anti-Jewish controversy. That legally-expressed codes tend to place preponderant emphasis upon correct behaviour, to the relative disregard of purity of motive, and to substitute punctiliousness for piety,[5] is the kernel of our Lord's teaching about the law. It is noticeable that the code most certainly to be attributed to Him—the beatitudes in their Matthæan form—is a table not of actions but of *dispositions*, of the virtues from which right action will habitually spring. S. Paul, in the same way, is convinced that blamelessness ' as touching the law ' [6] is nothing to be proud of. His catalogues, also, are mainly catalogues of dispositions rather than of actions. It is only with the Apostolic Fathers that actions and dispositions are wholly confused,—actions right and wrong pushing

---

[1] The earliest seems to be Clem. Alex., *ap.* Anastas. Sin., *Quæst.*, 14 : (*GCSS.*, ' Clemens,' iii, p. 225 ; *MPG.*, lxxxix, col. 465) :—' We must give alms, but with discrimination (μετὰ κρισέως) and to the worthy only. . . . For as the farmer sows not on every soil but only on that which is good, that he may have his harvest, so we should scatter the seeds of our charity upon devout and spiritual persons, to reap a reward in their prayers.' The motive here is not very disinterested, and the almost outspoken contrast with the Parable of the Sower is suggestive. The earlier injunctions to indiscriminate charity seem less un-Christian than this : but it is not a question of indiscriminate charity, in our sense of the phrase, with Clement at all. Cp. Ecclus. 12[1, 2], to which Clem. Alex. refers.

[2] Lucian, *de morte Peregrini*, 13.

[3] 1 En. 60[6]—so M. Hughes, *Ethics of Jewish Apocryphal Literature*, p. 75 ; but even here Charles (*ad loc.*) notes that ' law ' may = ' divine judgment,' in which case no reference to *the* law is intended.

[4] *Test. Dan*, 5[3] ; *Test. Iss.*, 5[2], 7[6].

[5] Cp. R. Thamin, *Un Problème Morale*, p. 340—' ces dévots dont la ponctualité est toute la pieté.'

[6] Phil. 3[6].

their way more and more into the foreground of the code,[1] and obedience and conformity taking the place of enthusiastic loyalty as the basis of Christian life.

It might be suggested, however, that this danger is so easy to eliminate as to be unworthy of further discussion. Once ensure that an ethical codification, in so far as any is needed, shall be a code of virtues and dispositions (as indeed it sometimes is even with the Apostolic Fathers), rather than of external actions,—shall conform, that is to say, to the New Testament models,—and the work is done. This, however, is a fallacy of superficial optimism. There is another danger inherent in all codes, which reaches its acme in the codification of virtues or motives. It is the danger noticed in the last chapter—the danger of ' anthropocentrism '.[2] If my aim in life is to attain a specified standard, or to live according to a defined code, I am bound continually to be considering myself, and measuring the distance between my actual attainment and the ideal. It is impossible by such a road to attain the self-forgetfulness which we believe to be the essence of sanctity.

The self-centredness resulting from a life lived according to rule may be manifested in different ways. If a man has set himself no very exalted standard, or is so little versed in self-knowledge as to believe himself to have attained his ideal, the result is a self-centred complacency. If, on the other hand, he is in earnest about the moral life, and does not connive at his own failures, he will be hard put to it to avoid the danger of scrupulosity, with the attendant and even greater evil of despair. Scrupulosity is the natural companion of codes of *actions*. It embodies a spirit which Christianity, in its criticism of the Jews, designated by the name of ' cautiousness '—'eulabeia'; and which was undoubtedly enhanced by the characteristically Jewish delight in constant elaborations of the code. The Jews are the ' cautious ones '—the ' eulabeis.' They will do nothing without authority. For fear of doing wrong they will refrain from action altogether until they are assured that what they contemplate is right, ' lest haply they be found fighting against God.' [3] Gamaliel's plea for a *laissez-faire* policy towards the apostles, which he enforced with this warning, was just such a piece of caution. It is to him, again, that we owe the significant maxim, ' Get thee an authority ; and give not [even] the tithe by guesswork.' And however earnest-hearted the scrupulous man

---

[1] A very remarkable example of this substitution of *actions* for *thoughts* as the subject of moral judgments, is instanced by K. Holl, *Enthusiasmus u. Bussgewalt*, p. 246, from *Conc. Neo-Caes.*, c. 4—' If a man lusteth after a woman and plan to possess her, and his lust faileth of its object, *it would seem that he has been saved by grace.*' Contrast Mt. 5[28].

[2] On M. Bremond's use of this phrase, and its implications, *supra*, pp. 96, 97. In *HLSR.*, vii, p. 16, he expresses himself ready to accept 'egocentrism' as a synonym for all purposes. I may add that for the attitude which I am calling ' formalism ' M. Bremond uses the slightly misleading word ' ascéticisme ' (*ib.*, vii, p. 17) ; here again he is prepared to regard ' moralisme ' as the equivalent (*ib.*, vii, p. 26). Cp. *infra*, pp. 436 f., 440 f.

[3] See my *Conscience and its Problems*, pp. 134, 135.

may be, his activities are bound to be self-centred. The question uppermost in his mind is always, ' Am I doing right ? '

But what is often no more than an unworthy timidity with codes of actions or duties, may become a psychological obsession with codes of dispositions or virtues. We can, in considerable measure, control our actions ; but dispositions are at best susceptible only to a painfully slow influence by habitual attempts at regulation. The hope of future success is continually daunted, if not extinguished, by present experience of failure. This is the real burden of S. Paul's attack on the law. In the seventh chapter of Romans, which must surely be a piece of autobiography,[1] it is significant that S. Paul selects as his example the only command in the decalogue which is exclusively concerned with dispositions—' Thou shalt not covet.'[2] His gravamen is complex. By the law comes the consciousness of sin—the knowledge of what covetousness is, and that it is wrong. This, though it must dishearten us by the light it throws on evil hitherto undiscovered in the heart, is not in itself disastrous. By the law, again, the evil disposition is stirred into active revolt against its threatened extirpation—' sin revives,' and ' through the commandment works in me all manner of covetousness.'[3] This accentuates the conflict, but simplifies it ; an enemy in the open may be less terrible in the end than one concealed. But S. Paul has not yet exposed his basic accusation. The law—*any* law—is powerless to alter the dispositions of the heart. There is a different law in the members, warring against the law of the mind, and to all appearance carrying the day.[4] Virtue is not conferred by mere knowledge of what is right. On the contrary, the more penetrating the law is in its illumination of the depths of personality, the more it results simply in exposing the ineluctable security with which sin is entrenched, and so in ministering to despair—that most self-centred of all emotions.[5] This Pauline doctrine, based on the truest apprehensions of human psychology, is wholly ignored by or unknown to the Apostolic Fathers, who thus again betray the limitations of their outlook. They rejoice in law, without recognizing either its moral inadequacy or its psychological menace.

(c) A self-righteous complacency—a self-conscious scrupulosity—a self-centred despair—one or other of these is the inevitable result of a religion whose special emphasis is upon law. They are not so flatly un-Christian as is self-seeking egoism ; yet it was not to foster such emotions that the Church went out into the world. It is small wonder then that S. Paul, for example, sets grace over against the law, faith against works, the spirit against the letter, the

---

[1] But contrast A. E. J. Rawlinson, *New Testament Doctrine of the Christ*, pp. 88, 89.
[2] Rom. 7[7]. [3] Rom. 7[8, 9]. [4] Rom. 7[23].
[5] P. Batiffol, *Études d'Histoire et de Théologie Positive*, p. 49, has put together from Hermas and Irenæus several examples of this despair as it manifested itself in the early Church.

vision of God against the tables of stone. The vision of God, we remember, is a mirror which transforms the soul into which its light is flashed ; it bestows eternal life and likeness to the Father. It, and it alone, can confer self-forgetfulness upon the receiver.[1] Man's first duty (in a sense his only duty) is to be receptive—to wait for this transforming or renewing energy of God. Only as he receives it will law be of real use to him, in laying open the channels along which the stream of new life is to flow. Whatever metaphor the New Testament may be using of this primary bond set up between God and the soul—the Spirit, or grace, or the indwelling Christ, or the vision—the doctrine is still the same. The distinctively Christian life begins with a new relationship (not, be it noticed, new belief in the possibility of that relationship alone—'faith' in that low sense in which the devils also believe), though a relationship which can in some measure be expressed in knowledgeable forms. Once the relationship has been established, the field is open for human effort and activity ; and the lines along which effort can best be exercised can now fitly be laid down in terms of law.[2]

To the last, therefore, the formalist element is secondary—and rightly so—in the New Testament. Even the epistle of S. James, with its purely intellectualist conception of faith and its strong emphasis on works, sees that the beginning of the Christian life is something very different from a mere acceptance of law and doctrine, though it cannot speak of this new condition in other than legal terms—we begin our new life by initiation into the perfect law of liberty.[3] With the sub-apostolic writers the pendulum swings in the opposite direction, and this constitutes the third ground of criticism against them. 'Didaché' is practically devoid of any reference to grace received, or continuing experience of God. Its eucharistic prayer has a brief allusion to 'life and knowledge' given through Jesus ; but little more may be involved here than in the parallel Jewish table-prayers which refer to the natural life and knowledge of the law.[4] Later comes a more definite allusion to

---

[1] This can be said unhesitatingly, without prejudice to the question whether the *quest* for the vision, or (what sometimes amounts to the same thing) the propounding of the vision as the true goal of life, is not more dangerously self-centred even than legalism. (*Supra*, pp. 3, 104 ; *infra*, pp. 198 f., 442 ff.)

[2] It will perhaps be convenient to anticipate here conclusions, relevant to this matter, which will be dealt with more fully later :—(a) this new relationship is expressed, on the human side, by the attitude of *worship* (*infra*, pp. 204 f;, 271 ff., 449) ; (b) it is not attained by human effort, otherwise it would itself be subject to a 'law of works' (*infra*, pp. 463 ff.) ; (c) but is imposed upon man from the outset by the very conditions of his existence (*infra*, pp. 464 f.) ; although (d) it is reached most fully by the 'vision of God in the face of Jesus Christ' (*infra*, p. 467).

[3] Jas. 1[25].

[4] *Did.*, 9[3] ; the Jewish parallel in Oesterley and Box, *Religion and Worship of the Synagogue*[2], pp. 375, 376. The Jewish prayer is in fact more outspoken in gratitude than *Didaché*.

spiritual meat and drink, and life eternal,[1] but even if we take this
sacramentally, as the context seems to require, it is jejune enough.
Beyond this the tract is wholly legal.

Pseudo-Clement enumerates at the outset the manifold goodness of God for which we should show gratitude—but whereas
much is said about the new external status of the Christian which
God has made known to us there is little reference to any new
inner principle of life. ' He hath given us light,' the sermon says
—and as this is its only reference to illumination, it is probably purely
intellectualist—' He hath spoken to us as sons ; hath preserved us
from falling, . . . shown us the folly of idolatry (that living death),
of error and ignorance, hath given us a hope of salvation, and called
us from not-being into being.' [2] Here is knowledge of God's activities, but little communion with God. ' Barnabas ' has a wider
and richer vocabulary ; he speaks more than once of ' renewal
through forgiveness,' [3] of the indwelling of Christ in the Christian,[4]
of newness of life ; [5] but he lacks that sense of childlike dependence
upon and of personal intercourse with God which is so characteristic
of New Testament religion.   Most remarkable of all perhaps is the
definite and formal list of gifts already received from God in the
genuine epistle of Clement. ' How blessed and wonderful are the
gifts of God, beloved,' he writes ; [6] ' Life in immortality, joy in
righteousness, boldness in truth, trust in faith, temperance in
sanctification. These we know already.' The list is possibly taken
from some liturgical source ; but although it is full of the sense of
Christian joy and emancipation, nothing is said of any distinctive
source of that joy. It could all arise out of knowledge of a new
law less irksome and more inspiring than the old, though (as
further experience would show) not on that account exempt from
the fundamental defects of law.

In all this there is practically no reference either to seeing God
or receiving the Spirit, to being in Christ or enshrining an indwelling Lord. Salvation from the doom impending upon sinners
is the principal hope the writers set before the Christian. The
vision is indeed referred to by Clement,[7] and that with the mirror
analogy. But it occurs in a context which suggests that he is
simply repeating traditional material ; and the gift of the Spirit,
to which he also alludes, is apparently a reward of good works,
rather than a source of them—the ' conscientia bona sequens '
of the Stoics.[8] We must not belittle the relief and exaltation which

---

[1] *Did.*, 10[3].   [2] *2 Clem.*, 1[4-7] (compressed).
[3] *Barn.*, 5[1], 6[11], 8[3], 16[8].   [4] *Barn.*, 4[11], 6[15], 16[7-10].
[5] *Barn.*, 6[11], 11[1], 16[8], etc.   [6] *1 Clem.*, 35[1, 2].
[7] *1 Clem.*, 36[2]—an expressive passage (*supra*, p. 103, n. 3).
[8] *1 Clem.*, 2[2]. He has been enumerating the virtues exhibited by the
Corinthians in the past, and proceeds : ' *and so* there hath been given to
you all a deep and abundant peace, and an insatiable desire of doing good,
and ye have all received a full outpouring of the Holy Spirit '—i.e. the
Spirit is the reward, rather than the source, of good works. It is to be
noticed that Clement appears to have a very high opinion of the value of

even the mere conception of Christianity as a new law—a law at last in correspondence with the deeper demands of conscience—brought to the world; but we cannot view without alarm this growing tendency to think of its message as exhausted in these terms.

(*d*) The tendency to exaggerate the idea of Christianity as a new law; to substitute obedience for faith; to exalt the precepts above the grace of God; to speak, as Clement does, of the ' traditional' canon of morality, and to fill in its outlines with Old Testament examples, and maxims drawn from both Testaments alike, has further implications. By thrusting into the background the primary feature of redeeming grace it alters the whole balance of New Testament theology. The thought of God still dominates our post-apostolic writers, but He is no longer conceived of as a Father Whose loving purposes are the true and only canon of the law, and Whose abiding and inspiring presence is the perpetual instrument of its fulfilment. He is now thought of primarily as Lawgiver and as Judge. In the sub-apostolic literature these Judaic features receive new prominence. There is a vast increase in the titles of God, but they are all titles which emphasize these aspects only—titles which bring God back into line with the conception of the Oriental despot. He is now δεσπότης as well as κύριος.[1] If he is called ' Father' at all, it is always in connexion with some other epithet—' Founder' or ' Ruler' for choice; he is King, All-Highest (ὕψιστος), All-Holy (πανάγιος), All-Seeing (πανεπόπτης). His natural providence is more emphasized than His supernatural dispensations. ' In this literature,' it has been said, ' the person of Christ is overshadowed and set into the background by the person of the divine ruler.'[2]   And in so far as Christ

---

gnosis (1², 36², 40¹, 41⁴, 48⁵), which would seem to ally him with a non-formalist school of thought. R. Knopf (*HNT. Ergänz.-b.*, i, pp. 112, 113) takes this merely to mean (as undoubtedly with Barnabas, *supra*, p. 116, n. 6) the allegorical interpretation of the Old Testament. This is possible, for in three of the above-mentioned passages an Old Testament citation, with explanation, stands in the immediate context. I doubt, however, if it fully explains Clement's use of the word. It seems more likely that he employs it in a complimentary and ingratiating fashion. The Corinthians still, as in S. Paul's day, pride themselves on their *gnosis;* and in order to secure a hearing for his unpalatable message he decides to humour them in this respect. In 1² it is definitely *their* (alleged) *gnosis* which is praised; in 36², 40¹, 41⁴ *gnosis* is something which ' we' possess (a polite way of saying it is something which *they* claim); in 48⁵ the over-valuation of *gnosis* is gently deprecated—even if a man has it, and so appears to be ' great,' he should all the more ' think humble thoughts.' There is therefore no evidence that Clement *himself* thought highly of it.

[1] δεσπότης for God (or Christ) occurs only six times in the entire New Testament; in 1 *Clement* alone it is used at least twenty-five times. The details in Bousset, *KC.*, pp. 220, 292, and for late Judaism, *RJ.*, pp. 312, 316. Particularly important is the passage 1 *Clem.*, 59-61 (almost certainly the great intercession from the Roman liturgy of his day) which is dominated throughout by these conceptions.

[2] Bousset, *KC.*, p. 292.

Himself appears, He too comes primarily in the guise of Lawgiver and Judge.[1]

What then has the believer to hope for where God is thought of in these terms? In this life little, except the temporary relief which comes with the substitution of a simple for an elaborate code of rules. In the next life, reward (or at all events forgiveness and freedom from punishment) in the day of judgment. The only motives left for a Christian life are, in Tertullian's phrase, 'fear and hope—eternal fire and eternal life.'[2] Thoughts of this character are bound together into a closely-knit system in the sub-apostolic writings. Communion with God, present and future, is relegated into the background; salvation and recompense become the main objects of the Christian's desire. It is in this particular, especially, that apocalyptic showed itself a *damnosa hereditas;* there, as here, the only rationale for obedience was the hope of future reward. The law does not carry its sanctions in itself; it makes no appeal to the progressive response of conscience. It is an arbitrary rule set out by an arbitrary ruler, to be obeyed without question, comprehension, or assent, and to be crowned by the promised guerdon.

The issue towards which such a system leads is the triumph of complete irrationalism in ethics. If obedience for the sake of reward is all that matters, the inherent ethical value of the action performed is indifferent. So long as it is commanded it is right, and it is right for no other reason than that it is commanded. 'A corpse doth not really make unclean,' said Jochanan ben Zakkai, 'nor water clean; but God hath said, This is My law'[3]—and so the command must be obeyed. Ritual and moral commands now stand on the same footing; they are equally parts of the system, and there is no choice between them. Religion is sublimated into etiquette, although an etiquette attended by formidable sanctions.[4] Excess of ceremonial observance will make up for a defect of active morality. Congenial, or at all events simple, duties will provide a substitute for irksome and complex ones; a surplus of simple duties correctly performed will avail in the rainy day even for premeditated derelictions. This is the theory of the relief of sins by alms to which allusion has already been made; and it stands on the threshold of the doctrine of merit and works of supererogation.[5]

---

[1] Detailed exposition, Bousset, *KC.*, pp. 299-303.

[2] Tert., *de pud.*, 1. Harnack, *Hist. Dogm.*, v, pp. 18-20, has made a very full collection of the principal formalist ideas in Tertullian.

[3] Bousset, *RJ.*, p. 130; cp. pp. 373-375.

[4] So, for example, the extraordinary perversion of ethical values in *Pirkê Aboth*, 3⁹—'He who walks in the way and studies, and interrupts his study, to say "How beautiful is this tree," or "How beautiful is that ploughed field," the Scripture reckons it unto him as though he had made himself guilty of his own soul.' Generally cp. E. Schürer, *Jewish People in the Time of Christ* (E. tr.), II, ii, § 28, pp. 94 ff.; R. Bultmann, *Jesus*, pp. 64-68.

[5] For the treasury of merit and works of supererogation in Judaism, see Bousset, *RJ.*, pp. 198, 392; M. Hughes, *Ethics of Jewish Apocryphal Literature*, pp. 55, 80, 116, 130, 132; Charles, *Apocr. and Pseudep.*, ii, p. 587 n.; and for the theoretical problem involved, *infra*, pp. 522 f.

How deeply these thoughts fought their way into Christianity is easy to see. The treasury of merit is to be found as early as Ignatius ; [1] and the story of the palace, built in heaven by alms given (unwillingly and unintentionally) to the poor on earth, is the most romantic episode in the ' Acts of Thomas.' [2] Tertullian says openly, ' If we do well, we merit of God, and He becomes our debtor ' ; [3] Cyprian, Victorinus, Hilary and Jerome all echo the sentiment.[4] Financial need and real generosity enhanced the insistence on almsgiving as a substitute for all virtue in the early Church ; even Augustine reproduces the doctrine.[5] Ambrose says markedly, ' Thou hast alms ; ransom thy sins. God cannot be bought, but thou canst be bought off ; buy thyself off with money.' [6]

There is no need to dwell upon the disastrous results of such tendencies and ideas. Amiable, harmless and even beneficent though the habit of codification may sometimes be, the issue to which it leads if unchecked is wholly un-Christian. In it a defective theology and a defective experience of God combine with an unintelligent misapprehension of the essence of morality and a stereotyped ethical code to undo the entire work of revelation. Whether the root cause of the evil lies in the theological, the religious or the ethical sphere, it is often impossible to say ; but the three go hand-in-hand throughout history to produce all that is commonly condemned under the name of legalism. The vision of God is fading ; and as it fades the characteristic dangers of Judaism come back, only thinly disguised by a veneer of Christian phrases. The process initiated by the ' Didaché ' will be taken up by the Church Orders, the Councils of successive centuries, the rescripts of the ' servant of the servants of God,' the Penitential Books, until it finds its completion in the *Corpus Juris Canonici*—a monument of industry indeed, but a monument alike in conception and execution almost wholly of this world. By progressive codification Christianity (in Eduard Meyer's [7] appropriate phrase) is becoming ' mechanized,' as though it were a modern army ; the Church is all but completely assimilated to the model of secular society.[8]

---

[1] In the extraordinary metaphor from the Roman army (*ad Pol.*, 6²)— ' Earn bounty-money by good works, that you may have a handsome creditbalance to draw (on the day of your discharge).'   See Lightfoot's note, *ad loc.*

[2] *Acts of Thomas*, Act 2 ; M. R. James, *Apocryphal New Testament*, pp. 371-375 ; a similar anecdote in Pallad., *Hist. Laus.*, 6.

[3] *de pœn.*, 2.

[4] Cyprian, *de op. et el.*, 26—by good works the Christian ' makes God his debtor ' ; ' God will never fail to reward our merits ' (cp. *ib.*, 9, 17, 23) ; Hilary, *in ps.*, ii, 16—' merit' the result of free will; xci, 10—the works which ' earn ' the eternal Sabbath ; Hieron., *adv. Jov.*, ii, 32, 33.

[5] Aug., *serm.* 60. 10 (10)—' Almsgiving availeth much for the washingaway of sin ' ; *serm.* 86. 2 (2)—4 (4).

[6] Ambrose, *de el. et jej.*, 20, *supra*, p. 131, n. 3.

[7] E. Meyer, *Ursprung u. Anfänge*, iii, p. 322.

[8] Harnack has dealt very fully with the inner meaning of this process, *Hist. Dogm.*, ii, pp. 71-93 ; v, pp. 24-28, 262-272 (Gregory the Great). It must be remembered that the process was parallel to, and affected by, a similar ' mechanization ' of secular society dating at least from the period

IV. The Motive of Reward in the Gospels.

The last paragraphs have brought us to the threshold of a difficult and perplexing problem. After all, it may be said, the thought of judgment and recompense is common in the post-apostolic writers ; but is it not also true that the conception of reward and punishment dominates the whole of the synoptic presentation of ethics ? [1] If any tendency in Christianity has the undoubted warrant of our Lord's teaching, so far as it is recoverable, is it not this one ? And if it is proved to be an authentic feature of our Lord's teaching, does it not carry with it an implicit endorsement of every one of those sub-apostolic characteristics which we have just deplored ?

At first sight it would undoubtedly appear that the ethics of the synoptic gospels are dominated throughout by the idea of recompense. Each of the beatitudes receives its sanction in a promise ; many of the parables are parables of judgment. The charges and promises to the disciples—' If any man would be first, he shall be last of all,' [2]—' There is no man that hath left house, or brethren, or sisters, or mother, or father, or children, or lands, for My sake, and for the gospel's sake, but he shall receive a hundredfold now in this time, houses, and brethren, and sisters, and mothers

---

of Diocletian. See P. Vinogradoff in *Cambridge Mediæval History*, i, pp. 549 ff., where the resultant development of legislation is described in a manner which makes clear the close analogy between the ecclesiastical and the secular evolution. On the ecclesiastical development, *ib.*, pp. 179 ff. (C. H. Turner) ; on Pelagian formalism, C. Luthardt, *History of Christian Ethics*, pp. 222, 223 ; H. Reuter, *Augustinische Studien*, pp. 38-44 ; and on the way in which ' obedience ' steadily came to the fore almost as the monastic virtue *par excellence*, and found its apotheosis in the Military Orders of the Middle Ages, and the Jesuits after the Reformation, H. B. Workman, *Evolution of the Monastic Ideal*, pp. 268 f.

[1] And, indeed, the New Testament generally. For S. Paul, reference may be made to Rom. 2[5-9], 14[10-12] ; I Cor. 3[14, 15] ; 2 Cor. 5[10] ; Gal. 6[8] ; Col. 3[25] ; I Thess. 4[6] ; 2 Thess. 1[8, 9].—The Fourth Gospel, Jn. 3[19], 5[29], 8[24], 9[39], 12[31, 48], 16[11].—Hebrews, 2[2, 3], 6[7, 8], 10[27-31, 35], 11[6], etc. But in S. Paul, at least, there are indications, akin to those in the Synoptists, that the recompense-motive was not unaffected by his doctrine of the grace of God. On the one hand, as I have pointed out elsewhere (*Essays Catholic and Critical*, pp. 271, 272), he is quite definitely reluctant to use the phrase, ' the wrath of God,' and prefers the impersonal ' wrath.' On the other hand, he does not care to speak of God ' rewarding ' the righteous. Thus (Rom. 6[23]) he avoids the obvious parallelism, ' The wages of sin is death, the wages of righteousness is eternal life,' and twists the second member by introducing the new contrast, ' the gift of God.' (Cp. Rom. 4[4]—the idea of ' reward ' belongs only to the non-Christian scheme of justification by works.) ' Reward ' appears in I Cor. 3[8, 14], 9[17] ; but in the last of these passages no more may be meant than ' preaching the gospel is its own reward ' ; in the two former (as Deissmann, *Light from Ancient East*[4], p. 314) S. Paul may merely be ' borrowing a bit of good old workshop morality,' and using it as ' the concrete illustration of a popular preacher.' But should even popular preachers use concrete illustrations fundamentally at variance with their main doctrines ? Von Hügel regards passages like these as constituting simply the ' traditional layer ' of Pauline teaching (*Mystical Element*, ii, p. 158).

[2] Mk. 9[35].

and children, and lands, with persecutions ; and in the world to come eternal life '[1]—tell the same story. Even the most fundamental and far-reaching precepts of Christian duty are commended by the hope of recompense. Thus of charity :—'When thou makest a feast, bid the poor, the maimed, the lame, the blind, and thou shalt be blessed, because *they* have not wherewith to recompense thee ; for *thou shalt be recompensed* in the resurrection of the just '[2]— 'Sell all that thou hast and distribute to the poor, and *thou shalt have treasure* in heaven.'[3] Of humility :—'When thou art bidden to a feast, go and sit down in the lowest place ; that when he that hath bidden thee cometh, he may say to thee, Friend, go up higher ; *then shalt thou have glory* in the presence of all that sit at meat with thee. . . . He that humbleth himself *shall be exalted.*'[4] Of watchfulness and prayer :—'Watch ye at every season, making supplication, that *ye may prevail to escape all those things* that shall come to pass, and to stand before the Son of Man.'[5] 'Blessed is that servant whom his lord when he cometh shall find so doing ; of a truth I say unto you that *he will set him over all that he hath.*'[6] Of loving enemies :—'Love your enemies and do them good . . . and *your reward shall be great.*'[7] Of forgiveness :—'If ye forgive men their trespasses, your heavenly Father *will also forgive you.*'[8] Of secret piety :—'Thy Father which seeth in secret *shall recompense thee.*'[9] If ever moral pronouncements were dominated by the motive of recompense—if ever mercenary considerations, albeit of a spiritual kind, have held the centre of the stage—if ever purely external sanctions, hopes and fears were summoned to the aid of virtue—if ever, in short, a system of ethics was *self-centred* in its hopes and aspirations—surely, it might be said, it is so with the gospels. Whatever can be urged against the sub-apostolic writers can be urged with greater force against the evangelists ; 'Clement,' 'Barnabas' and 'Didaché' are only drawing legitimate deductions from the precepts of the highest authority of all.

The problem here presented cannot either be ignored or minimized. The main tendency of Jesus' teaching, as we saw at an earlier stage, was to help men to forget themselves by focussing all their aspirations upon God and the kingdom of God, and upon the needs of men as seen with the eyes of God. Consistent with and consequent upon this purpose, which the Lord expressed by speaking about God in such a way that hearts could not but be drawn to Him, come those demands for service in the gospel to which *no* promise or hint of reward is attached. The negative form of the great summons is no less authentic than the positive ; but it has a very different tenour : 'If any man cometh unto Me and hateth not his own father and mother and wife and children and brethren and sisters, yea and his own life also '—(then, *not* ' he shall lose his reward,' but)—'*he cannot be My disciple.* Whosoever doth not

---

[1] Mk. 10[29, 30]. [2] Lk. 14[13 14]. [3] Lk. 18[22].
[4] Lk. 14[10, 11]; cp. Lk. 18[14]. [5] Lk. 21[36]. [6] Lk. 12[43, 44].
[7] Lk. 6[35]. [8] Mt. 6[14]. [9] Mt. 6[4, 18].

bear his own cross and come after Me cannot be My disciple. . . . Whosoever he be of you that renounceth not all that he hath, he cannot be My disciple.' [1]   No recompense of peace and happiness is held out to the three aspirants to merely conditional discipleship. ' The foxes have holes and the birds of the heaven have nests, but the Son of Man hath not where to lay His head,' is said to the first. ' Leave the dead to bury their own dead, but go thou and publish abroad the kingdom of God,' and ' No man having put his hand to the plough and looking back is fit for the kingdom of God,' are the answers to the other two.[2]   Here and in similar passages the disinterestedness of Christian discipleship is emphasized as fully as it well can be.   In flat contradiction to this doctrine of ethical disinterestedness, or self-forgetfulness, are the passages from which we started.   The two strains of thought appear to contradict and neutralize one another beyond all hope of reconciliation ; and the ' mercenary ' sayings are at least as prominent as the others.

It is not without plausibility then that Christianity has so constantly been condemned as ' self-seeking ' or ' particularist ' ; and that the gospel has been represented as assuring the individual of his own salvation, and hinting at no more.[3]   If it has proved impossible to eliminate the apocalyptic element from the gospels, here is a factor even more difficult to ignore ; it is so deeply embedded that nothing would be left of Jesus' teaching if the references to reward and punishment were struck out as unauthentic.[4]   Nor is the problem made any easier by suggesting that the teaching of Jesus had its esoteric and exoteric sides, its higher and lower stages ; that He appealed to a ' hierarchy of motives,' and accepted as a temporary measure some of the less ethical conventions of His day (as for example this exploitation of the motive of reward) in the belief that His emphasis on higher truths would gradually wean men from the lower.   There is here no question of ' higher ' and ' lower ' at all.   We are concerned with wholly conflicting modes of thought—' self-centredness ' and ' self-forgetfulness ' ; ' self-centredness ' and ' God-centredness.'   ' God-centredness ' cannot be evolved from self-centredness ; the self-centred soul must undergo conversion to the roots before it can find a new centre in God. The slightest condonation of self-centredness is no less than treason to the ideal of self-forgetfulness ; and it is hard to believe that the

---

[1] Lk. 14[26, 27, 33].   [2] Lk. 9[57-62] ; cp. Mt. 8[19-22].
[3] The criticisms of Spinoza, Leibnitz, Kant, Simmel, A. E. Taylor, and others are ably summarized by von Hügel, *Mystical Element*, ii, pp. 174-181 ; G. F. Barbour, *Philosophical Study of Christian Ethics*, pp. 212-215.
[4] The connexion between apocalyptic and the idea of recompense is far closer than that between apocalyptic and asceticism ; nothing short of a consistent predestinarianism could banish ' recompense ' and yet retain a meaning in apocalyptic.   Thus, whatever cause made necessary the retention of the apocalyptic outlook by our Lord made inevitable His employment of the recompense-conception.   In this sense apocalyptic may fairly be said to have influenced His ethics (*supra*, p. 63).   But it does not account for His reiterated emphasis upon reward and punishment even in non-apocalyptic passages ; for this some other motive must be sought.

Lord—whatever He may have done in matters of less significance
—could for a moment have compromised on a matter so vital as
this. To accept such a solution, in fact, would be to acquiesce in
the belief not that Jesus contracted, for the moment, the scope of
His demands, but that He popularized them by appealing to false
motives ; that He accommodated and betrayed the purity of the
gospel in its most sacred aspects to win adherents ; that He debased
the divine currency in the traffic of God with man.

Nor, again, does it appear that much will be gained by suggesting
that the gospel emphasis on the rewards of virtue amounts to no
more than the proclamation that virtue is its own reward, and that
apart from a virtuous life *no* reward, *no* true happiness, that is to
say, is possible. This indeed would explain much that is difficult
in the recorded teaching of Jesus. It is obvious that the rewards
He holds out to men are such as will only appeal to the virtuous—
are rewards, in fact, which the man who leads a Christian life attains
progressively in proportion as he leads that life, and by virtue of
his leading that life. The life of self-forgetfulness *is* its own reward ; in it ' the reward is the congenital equivalent of the deed '—
the two are ' organically connected.' [1] Into such a scheme all our
Lord's sayings, I believe, will fit appropriately ; but the scheme
does not explain why the ' reward ' sayings bulk so largely. It *is*
true that the virtuous life is the only one which will bring lasting
happiness ; but that does not justify us in commending it *because*
it brings that happiness. To do so is to appeal to self-interest once
again, and self-interest and self-centredness are identical.

No solution of the difficulty [2] is possible unless we recognize
that our Lord's proclamation of reward is widely different from that
commonly attributed to Him by those who most impugn this aspect
of His teaching. In one of the most inspiring passages of his greatest
book, Baron von Hügel dealt very fully with this point ; and
although his conclusion (unless I mistake it) appears to me to be
unacceptable,[3] we cannot do better than follow him in his exegesis

---

[1] F. von Hügel, *Mystical Element*, ii, pp. 154, 155.

[2] For the sake of clarity I repeat that the ' difficulty ' here discussed is
simply, Assuming disinterestedness to be the Christian ideal, how comes it
that the idea of recompense bulks so largely in the gospels ? We are not
concerned *here* with two other questions, equally important, which must be
considered at a later stage, viz. :—(*a*) Is complete disinterestedness in any
sense a possible or realizable ideal (the Pure Love controversy, *infra*, pp.
451 ff.) ? ; and (*b*) Is not the traditional doctrine, that the end of man
is the vision of God, with its apparent implication that his primary duty is
to seek and acquire a particular experience, from first to last an *interested*
doctrine, and therefore incompatible with the true Christian ethos ? (*infra*,
pp. 442 ff.).

[3] For von Hügel seems to adopt the ' hierarchy of motives ' explanation.
Jesus appears at first sight to have ' taken over quite unchanged ' the entire
Jewish or formalist ' scheme and its spirit.' ' Yet we can follow the
delicate indications of the presence, and the transitions to the expression,
of the deeper apprehension and truth ' (*op. cit.*, ii, p. 154). Curiously enough,
however, Baron von Hügel does not seem to discuss the problem presented
by the presence of the ' unchanged Jewish scheme ' and the ' deeper apprehension and truth ' within the same system of teaching. We can only
guess, therefore, at the solution he would propose.

of the texts. He points out, for example, how Jesus constantly promised reward only to those who were prepared to follow and obey Him from some other motive.[1] Even in the great summons this is the case. ' For My sake and the gospel's ' is to be the motive of the Christian's renunciations ; if he renounces the joys and associations of this world *merely* for the sake of blessedness in the next, his blessedness will be forfeit. It is only those who did good in complete unconsciousness, not merely that it would be rewarded, but even that they were doing good at all, who were set on the right hand, and entered into the joy of the Lord.[2] So too the cup of cold water is to be given *in the name of a disciple*, the prophet to be received *in the name of a prophet*, the righteous man *in that of a righteous man* [3]—the motive of the action must be desire to honour the disciple, the prophet, the righteous man, with the honour which is their due, and not to secure reward. Here, as elsewhere, our Lord was building on rabbinic models ; [4] but the Jewish sayings which no doubt He had in mind emphasized by illustration just that excellence and desirability of the reward which He Himself passed over as unworthy of mention.

Again, Baron von Hügel points to the bewildering rejection of all human conceptions of merit in the divine assessment of reward.[5] There is, in our Lord's teaching, no exact apportionment of higher reward for greater effort—the prodigal and the labourers of the eleventh hour are blessed beyond all their deserts, as compared with the elder son and those who had borne the burden and heat of the day. S. Luke records a saying of Jesus which makes all heart-burning about these two parables superfluous. ' We are *all* un-profitable servants '—even the best of us has done nothing which deserves reward.[6] Reward, in fact, is not reward, but grace.[7]

These sidelights—if we may so call them—upon our Lord's completely novel evaluation of the traditional ' reward ' material make it clear that He employed the idea in a manner and for a purpose wholly His own. As interpreted by Him, it could fit into no existing ethical scheme. Its resemblance with the teaching of apocalyptic or of rabbinic legalism is purely superficial. If it is to be harmonized at all with His dominant requirement of disinterestedness, that conception itself must be examined a little more closely. At once a distinction suggests itself. The true Christian is self-

---

[1] von Hügel, *Mystical Element*, ii, p. 157 ; and cp. for a similar treatment of the problem, G. F. Barbour, *Philosophical Study of Christian Ethics*, pp. 231-247.

[2] Mt. 25[31-46].   [3] Mt. 10[40-42], 18[5] ; Mk. 9[37, 41] ; Lk. 9[48], 10[16].

[4] Strack-Billerbeck, *Kommentar, ad locc.*, for examples.

[5] von Hügel, *op. cit.*, ii, pp. 155, 156.

[6] Lk. 17[10]. This although elsewhere, as Baron von Hügel points out, the third gospel ' works up the Parable of the Talents, with its only approximate relation between the deeds and their rewards, into the Parable of the Pounds with its mathematically symmetrical interdependence between quantities of the merit and those of this merit's reward' von Hügel, *op. cit.*, ii, p. 157).

[7] von Hügel, ii, p. 155.

forgetful ; but no one can become a true Christian by the *pursuit*
of self-forgetfulness. Once again that would be to fall into the
all-pervading danger of legalism ; to seek for salvation by measuring
oneself against a standard—the standard this time of disinterestedness, unselfishness, altruism, or whatever we care to call it. The
calculated practice of self-sacrifice is as self-centred as any other
occupation ; not as gross, indeed, as naked egoism ; not as superficial as formalism and the quest for reward in heaven ; not as
seductive as what we have called ' panhedonism ' ; but self-centred
none the less. There is no official road to altruism. To *refuse* to
think of reward, to set oneself deliberately to *ignore* the idea of
reward, is as unevangelical, though not as immoral, as to practice
virtue for the sake of reward. It is as much a quest for merit as
the most mercenary bargaining with God ; it leads to a scrupulosity
even more morbid that that of the ' cautious ' Jew. It turns the
mind from God, and forces it back upon the self and its own
successes and failures.[1] *As a practical maxim for life*, the phrase,
' The first concern of ethical thought should be for the purity of
moral motive,'[2] is a profoundly dangerous guide.

It is possible, then, to see in our Lord's constant references to
reward—guarded as they are against all thoughts of corresponding
merit—a great warning to those who (knowing self-forgetfulness to
be the ideal of Christian sanctity) seek it by way of continual self-
scrutiny and self-discipline. They have to learn not to enquire
into their own motives in their own strength, but, fixing their
thoughts upon God, to wait till His light piercing into the soul reveals (like the mirror) whatever there is in need of correction. Even
so, they must strive to correct it not so much by any effort of their
own will, as by turning to God once more, to allow Him to correct
it by that infusion of power which the new contemplation of His
nature brings in its train. If they find themselves thinking, from
time to time, of Christianity as a fount of blessedness, or virtue as
a source of joy, they must not allow the presence of such interested
emotion in the heart to lead them astray into a campaign against
it. If this is true—and the world has seen too much of exaggerated
disinterestedness and conscious self-sacrifice to make it possible
to doubt it—our Lord's method of expressing the truth was at once
appropriate, original, and inspiring. He gave the thought of reward a baffling prominence in His teaching that men should learn
not to be afraid of it. They were not to make reward their goal ;
but neither were they to be so shocked at the idea, if and when it
presented itself, as to immerse themselves in studied attempts at
self-forgetfulness.[3] Leaving behind thoughts both of reward and
of disinterestedness as equally self-centred, they were to look forward to that true self-forgetfulness which cannot be acquired by

[1] See *infra*, pp. 451 ff., on the ' Pure Love ' controversy.
[2] G. F. Barbour, *Philosophical Study of Christian Ethics*, p. 224.
[3] Cp. S. Bernard's famous ' non sine præmio diligitur Deus, etsi absque
præmii intuitu diligendus ' (*de dil. Deo*, 7 (17 ff.)) ; and *infra*, p. 462, n. 4.

human effort, but comes only to those whose hearts are set on God.[1]

V. DISCIPLINE IN THE NEW TESTAMENT.

Few if any of these deep purposes of Jesus survive in the sub-apostolic writers. In formalism, as they presented it, we find New Testament thoughts perverted in character, and deprived of those cognate doctrines and points of view without which their influence is bound to be one-sided and detrimental. It is only fair to notice that in these primitive documents the tendency has not assumed its full proportions, nor indeed manifested its real dangers. One of the foremost students of the period has stated a satisfactory case for a general and progressive rise of the moral standard within the Church during the first century of its existence.[2] He bases this conclusion on a comparison of the later catalogues of sins with the earlier. ' The thought,' he says,[3]

'always turns from the gross form of heathen sin to what is inward. Moral judgment must have advanced, ripened and become fixed where this is done so plainly. . . . A Christian

---

[1] The interpretation suggested in the text above has points of agreement with the stimulating discussion of the same question in R. Bultmann's *Jesus* (pp. 74-76). Bultmann notices the paradox to which von Hügel also has drawn attention :—' Jesus promises reward to those who obey without thought of reward.' He continues :—' But He never surrenders the concept of reward, and by this means draws a further sharp distinction between His teaching and idealist ethics. He knows nothing of doing " good for its own sake " ; the thought that every good action carries its own worth within itself ' [virtue its own reward] ' is alien to Him. For this thought expresses once more the humanistic ethical ideal, with its assertion of the worth of human personality. But according to Jesus, human personality is incapable of acquiring any worth of itself ; only in so far as a man is obedient does God reward him, giving him more than he had before. . . . Similarly, Jesus' teaching is sharply opposed to the particular ascetic view which exalts self-mortification as the type of behaviour which God demands from men. God *does* demand self-denial and sacrifice. But He is no selfish tyrant. His demands connote not death, but life, for men—behind the demand is the promise.' Thus the gospel-emphasis upon reward implies that neither self-realization nor self-sacrifice can be set before man as the final determinant of conduct. With this statement we may express absolute agreement. What Bultmann does not seem to consider, however, are the *grounds on which* conscience is bound to assent to this outcome of Jesus' teaching ; these grounds appear to lie in the inherently egocentric character of all formalism, whether it takes ' self-realization ' or ' self-sacrifice ' as its shibboleth (*supra*, pp. 133 f.).

[2] E. von Dobschütz, *Christian Life in the Primitive Church* (E. tr.), pp. 187, 203, 209, 248-250, 350.

[3] *Ib.*, p. 209. With this may be compared such rapturous descriptions of the Christian brotherhood as *Ep. ad Diogn.*, 5-7 ; Aristides, *Apol.*, 15 (*Texts and Studies*, i (1893), pp. 48, 49) ; Tert., *Apol.*, 39, 45 ; Justin, *Apol.*, i, 7-13. Further corroborative evidence is furnished by the triviality of the Montanist demands, and the weakness of Lucian's and Celsus's attacks on the moral side of Christianity. The general ethical condition of second-century Christianity is well set out by Harnack, *Expansion of Christianity* (E. tr.), i, pp. 181-249, 258-272.

custom has been developed and lies like a wall round the individual members of the community, separating them absolutely from everything pagan.'

The observation is acute and noteworthy, though not beyond criticism ; the same writer, by the same canons, established the same degree of advance between the epistles to the Colossians and to the Ephesians [1]—a conclusion only tenable on the assumption that the latter epistle is both non-Pauline, and noticeably later in date than that to Colossæ.

It is only natural that formalism should at first have proved a cause of moral advance.   As a means of personal discipline it is not merely unexceptionable, but of the highest value, provided always that—true to the New Testament demand—it is kept in subordination to the living experience of the living God which is the heart of Christianity.   Further, codification of principles goes hand in hand with corporate discipline : and even corporate discipline is an agency for good as long as it is exercised for pastoral and remedial purposes—to strengthen, that is to say, and to co-operate with, the personal self-discipline of the individual.   But corporate discipline can have a very different side.   If it is employed not *pastorally* but *penally*—not to strengthen the weak and restore the falling, but to exclude them—the moral code, however carefully and truthfully expressed, becomes an instrument of tyranny which dragoons the many into purely outward observance, and breaks the heart of the spiritual genius who needs freedom from restraint to realize the gifts which God has given him.   And because the Church soon began to forget that its charter was simply and solely to help men to be pure in heart that they might see God, it sowed for itself in its exercise of discipline a harvest of evils of almost inconceivable gravity.

Communal discipline is impossible without accredited agents and workable machinery.   The Church was early in developing both. The growth of the hierarchy is a problem outside our present sphere ; all we need notice is the new attitude towards it which is becoming evident in the Apostolic Fathers.   The bishop holds a place in the Ignatian epistles which has rarely been his at any later time.   His authority is the authority of Christ.[2]   Neither asceticism nor marriage is to be undertaken except with his approval.[3] ' No such language ' (as that in which Ignatius insists upon the importance of obedience) ' had been used in the Church before,' wrote Dr. Bigg ; [4] ' at any rate it is not in any previous document now

---

[1] von Dobschütz, *op. cit.*, p. 187.

[2] See e.g. Ign., *ad Eph.*, 6^1 ; *Magn.*, 3^1 ; *Trall.*, 2^1, 3^1, etc.

[3] Ign., *ad Pol.*, 5^2—taking the difficult ἐὰν γνωσθῇ πλέον (*al.* πλὴν) τοῦ ἐπισκόπου, ἔφθαρται (with Lightfoot) to mean that the would-be ascetic must communicate his vow to the bishop, though to no one else.   The other rendering, ' if he become better known than the bishop,' is absurd ; why should fame up to the bishop's level (but no further) be allowed to a man to whom all boasting is forbidden ?

[4] C. Bigg, *Origins of Christianity*, pp. 107, 108.

extant ; and nothing was added to it afterwards.' How ' Barnabas '
and ' Didaché ' join in exalting the authority of the ministry has
already been indicated.[1] ' Woe is me ! that I did not believe Thee
nor obey the presbyters ! ' shall be the sinner's cry (so pseudo-
Clement asserts) in the day of judgment.[2] The Roman Clement
particularly goes out of his way to liken the ministry to the Jewish
hierarchy ; [3] and draws a long parallel between the discipline of the
Roman army and that which he would like to see observed in the
Church.[4] The first quarter of the second century did not elapse
before the agents of corporate discipline were fully established in
office. Long before that time, also, the machinery of discipline was
ready to hand.[5]

(a) The Discipline of the Synagogue.

Penance and excommunication were the instruments of discipline inherited by the Church from Judaism.[6] In origin, they
were essentially penal. They look back to the ḥerêm, or death-ban,
of the earliest codes, according to which the offender—and often his
family and associates as well—suffered the extreme penalty, and
all his goods were destroyed.[7] Time and circumstance, however,
brought a significant change, and a pastoral element crept into the
system. The first indication of the new practice is in the book of
Ezra.[8] The Jewish authorities are still in a position to ' ban,'
or confiscate, the goods of the offender ; he himself, however, is
not as in the older practice, put to death, but excluded from the
community. The later system devised further temporal penalties,
—fines, stripes,[9] exclusion from office, imprisonment—sometimes

---

[1] *Supra*, p. 114.   [2] 2 *Clem.*, 17[5].
[3] 1 *Clem.*, 40, 43.   [4] 1 *Clem.*, 37.
[5] On this whole development, in addition to Bigg, Harnack and von
Dobschütz (*opp. citt.*), cp. B. H. Streeter, *The Primitive Church, pass.*;
C. H. Turner in *Cambridge Mediæval History*, i, pp. 143 ff. ; R. Sohm,
Kirchenrecht, i, pp. 81 ff., 157 ff., etc.
[6] On this, see *ERE.*, iv, pp. 720 ff. (*s.v.* ' Discipline (Jewish) ') ; *Jewish
Encyclopædia*, i, pp. 560 ff. (*s.v.* ' Anathema ') ; ii, pp. 487-489 (*s.v.* ' Ban ') ;
G. F. Moore, *Judaism*, i, pp. 521, 526 ; Strack-Billerbeck, *Kommentar z.
N.T.*, iv, pp. 293-333 ; *HDB.*, i, pp. 534, 535 (*s.v.* ' Curse '), 800, 801 (*s.v.*
' Excommunication '). N.T. references to Jewish excommunication, Lk. 6[22];
Jn. 9[22], 12[42], 16[2]. On Essene excommunication, and its terrible consequences, Josephus, *BJ.*, ii, 8. 8, 9.
[7] Lev. 27[28]; Dt. 2[34], 3[6], 13[8-11]; Josh. 6[17], 7[11-26], etc. Ḥerêm meant
' set apart,' and so could signify either ' devoted to the Lord ' or ' accursed,'
and the idea passed freely from one sense to the other. So, too, of ἀνατίθημι
in Greek; but here there were two noun-forms. The LXX translators used
the earlier form (ἀνάθημα) in its ordinary Greek sense of ' consecrated '
(cp. Lk. 21[5]), keeping the new (dialect) form, ἀνάθεμα, for the ' ban.' In this
they were generally followed by N.T. writers; but MSS. variations are frequent. Cp. Moulton-Milligan, *Vocab.*, *s.vv.* ; Sanday and Headlam, *Romans*,
p. 228.
[8] Ezra 10[8].
[9] Hence S. Paul's ' forty stripes save one,' 2 Cor. 11[24]. The passage is
sometimes quoted to show S. Paul's personal loyalty to the Jewish law.

additional to, sometimes in substitution for, spiritual discipline and excommunication. At times, no doubt, the authorities were sufficiently strong to exercise these powers by *force majeure*. At other times they must have required voluntary acceptance by the penitent ; but whether his submission were voluntary or compulsory, he was always allowed a hope of return if he showed genuine penitence.

Excommunication itself had three grades, distinguished both by duration (this varied as between the Babylonian and the Palestinian practice), and by severity. Under the lightest punishment (the *nezîfa*), which in Babylon lasted one day, in Palestine seven, the offender was confined to his house, and allowed to take part neither in business nor in pleasure.[1] *Niddûi*, the second grade, lasted for either seven or thirty days. In this all social intercourse, except with his family, was forbidden to the sinner. He was required to wear mourning costume and walk barefoot, and neither to bathe nor cut his hair. He might attend the synagogue services, but was not reckoned to belong to the congregation. In the last and severest grade, the *herêm*, or ' ban' itself, the social and religious ostracism hitherto imposed upon the offender alone was extended to all about him. His wife was excluded from worship, his children from school. Only the bare necessities of life might be purveyed to him ; and if he died impenitent he was buried without funeral rites of any kind. In addition, supernatural forces were expected to visit him with punishment both temporal and eternal. This is shown by the formula of excommunication, solemnly pronounced with blowing of horns and extinguishing of candles. ' In the name of God,' the sentence ran, ' and of the tribunal of heaven and earth, we solemnly ban and excommunicate such an one, the sinner. May all the curses of the law rest upon his head, and this excommunication cling to the two hundred and forty-eight members of his body.' Yet terrible though the punishment was, it was not final ; the offender might still repent and recant, and his repentance if sincere secured for him readmission to the blessings of the covenant.[2]

But the apostle does not say that on any or all of these occasions he suffered willingly ; and although at this period no doubt the Jewish authorities could not expect the civil arm to support them in the infliction of physical punishment, it is quite possible that the local Gallio might turn a blind eye to the use of force, and resistance prove impossible.

[1] Strack-Billerbeck, iv, p. 293, do not regard the ' nezîfa' as an excommunication, but only as a ' censure.'

[2] G. F. Moore, *Judaism*, i, pp. 521, 526 ; *Jewish Encyclopædia*, i, p. 560 ; Strack-Billerbeck, iv, p. 328. The lack of centralization in Judaism made it possible for any rabbi to excommunicate any other ; the result must have been a considerable amount of confusion. Was it on this account that the attempt to transfer the ministry of discipline in the Church from the hands of the bishop to those of the priest met with such strenuous resistance (*infra*, pp. 280 f.) ?

(b) The Commission to Bind and Loose.

The first and fourth gospels gave ample warrant to the Church for incorporating this Jewish system of discipline into its own code.[1] Mt. xviii, 15 ff.—a curiously composite passage—records a general commission presumably addressed to the leaders of the community : ' What things soever ye shall bind on earth shall be bound in heaven, and what things soever ye shall loose on earth shall be loosed in heaven.' Loisy points out acutely that the evangelist has inserted this commission in a section dealing originally with private forgiveness of personal injuries.[2] The textual connexion makes it clear, therefore, that we must interpret ' bind and loose '—in this passage at all events—of the granting and refusal of reconciliation ;. and that commentators who understand it merely (on the basis of rabbinic parallels) as ' forbid and allow ' are wide of the mark.[3]

Further—and this comment also is due to Loisy—the evangelist has altered his original to make the passage refer to a question with which he was specially preoccupied (witness the parables of the Wheat and Tares and the Drag Net), that of sin within the community of which the community as a whole is not aware—*secret* as distinct from open sin. Whereas the original (Q) ran, ' If thy brother sin rebuke him, and if he repent forgive him,' Matthew wrote : ' If thy brother sin, *go tax him with it*—denounce him— between thyself and himself alone. If he hear thee, thou hast

---

[1] Though, of course, the practice was in vogue long before the gospels were published, and may have influenced their record of the commission. Excommunication is perhaps the only Christian institution for which modern German scholarship has not found, to its own satisfaction, a pagan origin, though even in this matter Reitzenstein (*HMR.*, p. 164, n. 1) hints at an ecclesiastical discipline among the Mandæans. The general practice of pagan cults was apparently to warn offenders and ' unclean ' of various types, either by inscriptions or public pronouncement, not to approach the mysteries under pain of vengeance from the god ; but to allow, if not to commend, expiatory rites such as would make them ' clean ' again. (See e.g. *HMR.*, pp. 137-145, 160-165.) This, however, bears no analogy to any general action of the community against the individual, such as we have in ecclesiastical discipline.

[2] A. Loisy, *Les Évangiles Synoptiques, ad loc.* The inference is based on the parallel Lk. 17[3, 4], which corresponds to Mt. 18[15], 18[21b]—the intervening verses being the Matthæan insertion. That it was originally *personal injury* with which the passage dealt is clear from the ' against me ' of Mt. 18[21a] (' against thee,' Lk. 17[4]), which led inferior authorities to insert ' against thee ' into Mt. 18[15] (as in RV. text).

[3] For the rabbinic usage see Strack-Billerbeck, i, pp. 738 ff. Weiss-Bousset (*SNT.*, i, p. 333) interpret the phrase by reference to pagan magical spells (cp. the Isis inscription quoted by Klostermann, *HNT.*, iv, p. 141, —' Whatsoever things I shall bind, none is able to loose '). In any case the point is immaterial ; if a member of the community insisted on doing what was forbidden, or *tabu*, the only possible course would be to exclude him. A much more vital problem is, how far would the passage justify the inference that the divine condemnation or forgiveness would be coterminous with the action of the Church (*infra*, p. 225) ?

gained a brother.'[1]   Failing this (and here begins Matthew's addition to the original saying) witnesses are to be summoned, whose presence is expected to act as a further incitement to repentance. If this expedient fails, the ' Church ' is to be told.[2] Here, then, is a system in which not only is secret (as distinct from open and notorious) sin proper matter for discipline ; but, rather than that it should go unvisited, any individual member of the Church who is cognizant of it is to act as delator. So far, therefore, discipline is pastoral,—its purpose is to ' gain a brother '; but its exercise is to be of the most meticulous character imaginable. Public interference in the private life of the members of the community could scarcely go further.

Following upon this brief account, or model, of procedure in cases of occult sin comes the logion about ' binding and loosing,' which again was not in Q. The next sentence of the original passage would have fitted in well here—it is the merciful instruction to be prepared to forgive till seventy times seven.[3] But Matthew holds it in reserve for a moment, and interpolates from an unknown source the saying about corporate prayer :—[4]

> ' If two of you shall agree on earth as touching anything they shall ask, it shall be done for them of My Father which is in heaven ; for where two or three are gathered together in My Name, there am I in the midst of them.'

These words may have been drawn into their present context because, like the ' binding and loosing ' saying, they too embody a parallel between earth and heaven ; or again because corporate prayer follows not unnaturally on corporate discipline. But it is at least possible that there is a closer connexion, and that we are still in the realm of procedure. In that case the prayer referred to will be the corporate intercession of the congregation on behalf of the offender, and a practice which endured for many centuries in the Church is then found to have its roots in the New Testament.[5] Matthew concludes by returning to the injunction about repeated forgiveness ;[6] which by virtue of his interpolations now achieves

---

[1] Note the substitution of ἔλεγξον (the word for the official process, *infra*, p. 153 ; RV., weakly, ' show him his fault ') for the vaguer ἐπιτίμησον ; the injunction to secrecy ; and the ' thou hast gained thy brother,' which changes the centre of interest from the question of forgiveness to that of Church membership (in Q the important point is that the offender should be forgiven ; in Mt. that he should be brought to a better state of mind).
[2] Mt. 18[16, 17].   [3] Lk. 17[4]—' seven times.'
[4] Mt. 18[19]—possibly *two* sayings, for something very like the second half occurs in the Oxyrhyncus *Logoi* (no. 10—E. White, *Sayings of Jesus*, p. 35).
[5] On prayer for penitents, F. E. Brightman in H. B. Swete, *Early History of the Church and the Ministry*, pp. 367, 372, and *supra*, p. 114, n. 6 ; on the petition of the laity *to the bishop* for the readmission of the offender, *ib.*, p. 373.
[6] He introduces this by a question from Peter, which is not found in Q. The Petrine reference, in a slightly different form, reappears in the *Gospel according to the Hebrews* (*infra*, p. 160 ; M. R. James, *Apocryphal New*

very great importance. It insists that the Church—though she is to treat the impenitent sinner as a ' heathen and publican '—must allow him constant opportunities of reconciliation, should he desire it ; and that even though he may relapse into sin not once but many times after a first forgiveness.[1]

The promise that what is bound or loosed on earth shall be bound and loosed in heaven is also inserted by S. Matthew—in the second person singular—in his account of S. Peter's confession at Cæsarea Philippi.[2] It is difficult to say which of the two versions—the apostolic or the Petrine commission—is the more original. The former perhaps is to be preferred, both as borne out by the evidence of the Fourth Gospel, and as being the less obviously unworkable of the two at the date at which the gospel was composed—for whatever S. Peter may have done at Jerusalem he cannot have had exclusive exercise of discipline in the Church at large.[3] In this Petrine account, the promise is bound up with the gift of the keys, which must refer to the first admission of believers to the privileges of the kingdom—that is to baptism. In that case ' binding and

---

Testament, p. 6). It is possible that this reference is a picturesque addition by the evangelist to show that he intended the injunction to repeated forgiveness to apply both to this commission (18[18]), and to the identical commission to Peter (16[19]).

[1] The Johannine version of the saying (Jn. 20[23]) adds little to the Matthæan logion. It gives precision to the ' loosing ' by explicitly mentioning ' forgiveness,' and that perhaps not without some personal qualms for the writer, who nowhere else speaks of the ' forgiveness of sins ' in his gospel (contrast 1 Jn. 1[9], 2[12]). But it is wholly in line with the Johannine doctrine of the infallibility of believing prayer (14[13, 14], 15[7], 16[23, 24]) which reappears in a similar connexion in 1 Jn. 5[16]. Thus the stark ' magical ' impression which the passage makes at first sight is relieved by its setting within the sphere of the Church's confidence in God's answers to her intercession.

[2] Mt. 16[19].

[3] For the priority of the Petrine reference might be urged (a) *the sequence of thought :* Peter, rock, gates (set in the rock), keys, binding and loosing ; (b) the *Aramaisms* of all these metaphors ; (c) the possible *topographical* reference (Inmisch, in *ZNTW.*, xvii (1916), pp. 18 ff.)—the Jordan-cliff near Philippi, with the temple of Augustus at the top and the grotto of Pan below (see A. E. J. Rawlinson, *S. Mark*, p. 112, for details of the locality). Against these arguments could be urged (a) the sequence of thought is too slipshod to be more than accidental (e.g. ' rock ' does not naturally call up ' gates ' ; keys do not ' bind,' they lock, etc.) ; (b) the Aramaisms may have caused the logia to come together; (c) the topographical reference, though it may bear on verse 18, has no relationship to verse 19. Thus there is nothing to prevent 18[18] being the original logion (in the plural—addressed to the Church, or her authorities, as a whole) ; it may have been turned into the singular and inserted into an (? Aramaic) poem in honour of Peter by some enthusiast of the Church at Antioch, and there incorporated as a whole in his gospel by Matthew, who however showed some historical sense by recording also the isolated logion in the plural. (For the relation of the First Gospel to the Church of Antioch, see Streeter, *The Four Gospels*, pp. 500-511 ; for the repute in which S. Peter was held there, *ib.*, 511-516.) The further question raised by Harnack on the basis of a possible variant: ' The gates of hell shall not prevail against *thee* ' (*Sitzungsber. d. Berl. Ak.* (1918), pp. 637 ff. ; cp. Loisy, *Les Évangiles Synoptiques*, ii, p. 13) does not concern us; it is criticized by P. Batiffol, *Catholicism and Papacy* (E. tr.), pp. 56-65 (incorporating further criticism by Kattenbusch), and E. Meyer, *Ursprung u. Anfänge*, i, p. 112.

loosing' *here* must mean 'refusing to admit' and 'admitting' respectively ; and the reference throughout the passage is not to penance at all (except to baptismal penance), but to the part played by Peter in deciding whether Gentiles should or should not be admitted to the Church.   We can learn nothing more from it as to the exercise of post-baptismal discipline.[1]

(c) S. Paul at Corinth.

Of the exercise of excommunication in the New Testament period there are ample instances.   Constant references occur to ' rejecting,' ' withdrawing from,' ' convicting,' or ' not receiving ' dissidents.[2]   But a new and significant feature begins to appear. The majority of writers give no hint that the pastoral exercise of

---

[1] Canon Streeter, *Primitive Church*, pp. 59, 60, has drawn attention to the connexion of thought between Mt. 16¹⁹ (αἱ κλεῖς τῆς β. τῶν οὐρανῶν), 23¹³ (κλείετε τὴν β. τῶν οὐρ.—the woe against the Pharisees), and Lk. 11⁵² (—the parallel woe against the lawyers, ἤρατε τὴν κλεῖδα τῆς γνωσέως).   He suggests, in consequence, that the ' keys of the kingdom ' are the ' knowledge ' which entitles S. Peter to ' expound the moral law,' and that ' binding and loosing ' has therefore its rabbinic sense of ' allow and disallow.'   The point is unimportant, for as I have pointed out above (p. 150, n. 3), ' allowing and disallowing ' would be of little use unless backed by the sanction of exclusion.   This Canon Streeter implicitly admits when (p. 60) he speaks of Peter's commission as the right ' to decide how much of the law the members of the Church shall be *required to observe* '—a *disciplinary* commission, in effect.   But it would be interesting to know whether the *gnosis* in the Lucan passage is the *key which unlocks*, or *that which is unlocked* (= the kingdom).   The parallel passage suggests the latter.   In that case, S. Luke is ' hellenizing ' drastically.   Mt. undoubtedly has the passage in its more original form ; it is natural to speak of entering a *kingdom* (Mt.), unnatural to speak of ' entering ' *gnosis* (Lk.).   By substituting *gnosis*, therefore, for the kingdom, Luke has made a large concession to incipient gnosticism. The case is even worse if *gnosis* is the key ; what early Christian (except always the recalcitrant Corinthians)—above all, what companion of S. Paul —would dare to call *gnosis* the key to the kingdom of God ?

[2] ἐκκλίνειν ἀπό, Rom. 16¹⁷ ; ἐξαίρειν, 1 Cor. 5¹³ ; ἀφορίζειν, 2 Cor. 6¹⁷ (cp. Lk. 6²², Gal. 2¹²) ; ἐλέγχειν, Eph. 5¹¹, 1 Tim. 5²⁰, 2 Tim. 4², Tit. 1⁹, ¹³, 2¹⁵, Jude²² (cp. Mt. 18¹⁵, and *supra*, pp. 113, 151) ; παραιτεῖσθαι, Tit. 3¹⁰ (elsewhere in non-disciplinary senses) ; στέλλεσθαι ἀπό, 2 Thess. 3⁶ ; μὴ συναναμίγνυσθαι, 2 Thess. 3¹⁴ ; μὴ λάμβανειν εἰς οἶκον, χαίρειν μὴ λέγειν, 2 Jn.¹⁰ ; μὴ ἐπιδεχέσθαι, ἐκβάλλειν, 3 Jn.¹⁰.   The earlier (admonitory) stages are expressed by ἐπιτιμᾶν, 2 Tim. 4² (where there is a descending order of severity, ἔλεγξον, ἐπιτίμησον, παρακάλεσον) ; νουθετεῖν, 1 Thess. 5¹⁴ ; 2 Thess. 3¹⁵ ; Tit. 3¹⁰ ; παρακαλεῖν, 1 Tim. 5¹, 2 Tim. 4².   ἐλέγχειν, ' convict,' represents the conclusion of the judicial process ; see Moulton-Milligan, *Vocabulary, s.v.*, and cp. Jn. 3²⁰, 8⁴⁶, 16⁸. On Eph. 5¹¹, and the possibly non-disciplinary meaning of the word there, see J. Armitage Robinson, *Ephesians, ad loc.*   Of *procedure* little if anything can be said, apart from the ' first and second admonition ' of Mt. 18¹⁸ and Tit. 3¹⁰ ; and the requirement of more than one witness, at all events in the case of presbyters, 1 Tim. 5¹⁹.   The *restoration* of offenders to communion is perhaps referred to by the term καταρτίζειν (Gal. 6¹).   It was probably mediated officially by the laying-on of hands, as in later practice ; this gives a simple meaning, particularly appropriate to the context (which is mainly concerned with discipline), to the otherwise difficult passage, 1 Tim. 5²², ' Lay hands hastily on no man ; neither be partaker of other men's sins.'   On confession of sin, *infra*, p. 171, n. 4.

discipline is to fall into the background, and be replaced by the penal. One, however,—the author of the epistle to the Hebrews—insists emphatically on the permanent exclusion of grave offenders from all hope of salvation ; others betray an uneasy sense that there are *some* sins which admit of this treatment alone. We know little enough of the dates of our documents, and less still of the antiquity of material or ideas which they incorporate ; and we have always to reckon with the possibility of local variations in disciplinary as in theological outlook. It is impossible, therefore, to trace any ' development ' in this matter ; nothing can be done except to observe and record tendencies as they appear.

Among the most important incidents are those connected with the Church at Corinth. The situation envisaged in S. Paul's second epistle is as follows. Friction of some kind had arisen between the apostle and his correspondents, and he had written them a severe letter,[1] which roused them to a grief which he calls a ' godly grief ' or ' grief to repentance.'[2] The news makes S. Paul rejoice, 'not merely,' he says, ' on account of him that did the injury, nor on account of him that was injured, but on account of the manifestation to yourselves in the sight of God of your earnest zeal for me.'[3] Two quarrels are involved, one between ' the injured ' and ' the injurer,' and the other between the community and S. Paul ; the latter, it is clear, has been healed by a change of mind on the part of the community. The reference to the other quarrel—the ' injured ' and the ' injurer '—is evidence that S. Paul had taken up some judicial attitude in this quarrel, from which the community had formerly dissented, but to which it now agrees.

So much for the past. But S. Paul has also an injunction for the future, which (although it appears in a different context) cannot but refer to the same incident :—[4]

> ' If any hath caused sorrow, he hath caused sorrow not to me but in part (that I press not too heavily)[5] to you all. Sufficient to such an one is this punishment which was inflicted by the many ; so that contrariwise ye should rather forgive him and comfort him, lest by any means such a one should be swallowed up with his overmuch sorrow. Wherefore I beseech you to confirm your love toward him. . . . To whom ye forgive anything, I forgive also ; for what I also have forgiven, if I have forgiven anything, for your sakes have I forgiven it in the person (*mg.* ' presence ') of Christ, *that no advantage may be gained over us by Satan.*'

---

[1] 2 Cor. 2[4], 7[8]. On the identification of this letter, in whole or part, with 2 Cor. 10-13 (which in that case must be detached from 2 Cor. 1-9), see K. Lake, *Earlier Epistles of S. Paul*, pp. 155-164.

[2] 2 Cor. 7[10, 11].   [3] 2 Cor. 7[12].   [4] 2 Cor. 2[5-11].

[5] A mitigating phrase to suggest, first, that a minority were not ' grieved ' (cp. the majority, who *were*, verse 6) ; and second, that this fact is, in all the circumstances, of no consequence.

It is not actually certain from this that the ' injured person ' of the previous passage is S. Paul himself, and the injury an offence offered to him, though the conjecture is highly probable. But it appears certain that the point at issue had been concentrated into a personal struggle between S. Paul and an individual in the Church of Corinth. The majority of the community had first associated themselves with the latter, had then veered to S. Paul's side and put the malignant under discipline ; the apostle is now pleading with them to relax the discipline and restore the penitent to communion.[1]

The word ' Satan '[2] connects this incident with another in the first epistle from which modern commentators usually dissociate it.[3] A case of incest[4] has occurred at Corinth, and the Church, so far from ' mourning so that the offender might be removed from among them,' is puffed up. ' But I verily,' the apostle goes on,[5]

> ' being absent in body but present in spirit, have already, as though I were present, judged him that hath so wrought this thing, in the name of our Lord Jesus, ye being gathered together, and my spirit, with the power of our Lord Jesus, *to deliver such a one unto Satan for the destruction of the flesh,* that the spirit may be saved in the day of the Lord Jesus.'

The details of the picture are obscure ; but it seems certain that S. Paul has determined that the offender shall be punished, and calls upon the community to execute the sentence in full assembly and

---

[1] The relaxing of discipline at his request will show that they are now 'obedient *in all things* ' (2[9]), and not merely in inflicting the penalty. This involves interpreting ἔγραψα (2[9]) as an epistolary aorist (' I write this present letter,' cp. 1 Cor. 5[11]), which presents no difficulties, and gives point to the εἰς πάντα. But it cannot be said with certainty that he is not here referring to the severe letter. As for the ' injurer ' and the ' injured ' (7[12]), they *might* be the ' son ' and ' father ' of 1 Cor. 5[1] ; but it seems fairly certain that the ' father ' was dead before the son committed the offence (*infra*, n. 4), and cannot now be an 'injured' person whose injury demands redress. It is therefore natural to take S. Paul as the ' injured,' and to identify the ' injurer ' with ' him who has grieved—not me, but you all ' (2[5]). On most theories this opponent (who has ' caused grief,' 2 Cor. 2[5]) could be *either* the ' son,' or a partisan, or—if the two incidents are disconnected—some entirely different person. On the theory expounded above, however, S. Paul's opponent must be the son, because it is the son who has been ' delivered over to Satan,' and now is to be released.

[2] Almost as decisive a link is that between ἐν προσώπῳ Χριστοῦ (2 Cor. 2[10]) and ἐν τῷ ὀνόματι τοῦ Κυρίου Ἰησοῦ . . . τῇ δυνάμει τοῦ Κυρίου ἡμῶν Ἰησοῦ (1 Cor. 5[4])—the anathema must be raised with the same solemn formula employed when it was pronounced. The presence of *two* such links as these can scarcely be explained away as mere coincidence.

[3] 1 Cor. 5[1-13].

[4] ' Marriage ' with a step-mother was forbidden both by Jewish and Roman law. That the father was dead is inferred from the γυναῖκα ἔχει, which seems to imply a permanent relationship, and from the absence of reference (except the very unlikely ἀδικηθέντος of 2 Cor. 7[12]) to him. The enactments on the subject are collected by von Dobschütz, *Christian Life in the Primitive Church*, pp. 387-389.

[5] 1 Cor. 5[3-5].

with due solemnity. That he has himself already ' delivered the sinner over to Satan,' as he does elsewhere with Hymenæus and Alexander,[1] is implied throughout.

But what does ' to deliver over to Satan ' mean ? Many interpreters take it to imply no more than ' excommunication '—explaining that Satan is the lord of the whole world except the redeemed oasis of the Church ; and that to ' deliver one over to Satan ' is thus to expel him from the Church. To this suggestion there are two fatal difficulties. It does not explain why such a terrible and solemn phrase should here be used for excommunication, when elsewhere (except in the passage from the Pastorals to which reference has just been made) quite simple and inconspicuous words are sufficient. Nor does it explain the words ' for destruction of the flesh,' which indeed on this theory become hopelessly obscure. For if ' being handed over to Satan ' means expulsion from the Church *and nothing more*, then the destruction of the flesh can be nothing except death (this being the only kind of destruction common to all those without the Church) ; and therefore even those in the Church are in this respect equally in Satan's power, and phrase and threat alike are wholly without meaning.[2]

It is hard to resist the conclusion that something more drastic than simple excommunication is in S. Paul's mind. This can only be an anathema [3] or curse,[4] intended to afflict the offender with a visible and wasting disease (' the destruction of the flesh '), ending (if the curse be not previously removed) in a miserable death. Such a curse, uttered at a distance by S. Paul, might well seem of doubtful efficacy, unless seconded by similar action, combined with excommunication, on the part of the sinner's immediate Church-fellowship. S. Paul therefore calls upon them to associate themselves with his curse by drastic and solemn action of their own.

[1] 1 Tim. 1[20]. We may be allowed perhaps to assume the authenticity of the passage for our present purpose.

[2] Lietzmann (*HNT.*) and Bousset (*SNT.*), *ad loc.*, and von Dobschütz, *op. cit.*, p. 390, advance the strange theory that ' the destruction of the flesh ' means, in effect, the liberation of the spirit from the ' bondage of the flesh ' in the usual Pauline sense, thus giving the man a chance of salvation. Two objections suggest themselves—(*a*) Why should Satan lend himself to a plan so fatal to his purpose ? (*b*) Why should the offender be thus specially assisted towards a consummation for which all Christians long ?

[3] In the later sense of the word, for in the N.T. ' anathema ' (Ac. 23[14], Rom. 9[3], 1 Cor. 12[3], 16[22], Gal. 1[8, 9]) always appears to mean ' cursed by God ' rather than ' cursed by man.' Note that *faute de mieux* S. Paul would be content with mere excommunication even in this case (1 Cor. 5[13]). Bingham, *Antiq.*, xvi, ii, 15, interprets the ' delivery to Satan ' as ' the infliction of bodily vexation and torments by the ministry of Satan,' and notes that this is the almost unanimous interpretation of the Fathers.

[4] So Ramsay, *Expository Times*, x (1898-1899), p. 59—' It cannot have been unknown to Paul that he was here using a form of words similar to the curses by which the Corinthians had formerly been accustomed to consign their enemies to destruction by the powers of the world of death ' (quoted *DAC.*, i, p. 382—*s.v.* ' Excommunication '). Good pagan examples of such curses in Deissmann, *Light from the Ancient East* [4] (E. tr.), pp. 301-303.

The curse, however, is *conditional*,[1]—its main purpose is to secure the sinner's 'salvation in the day of the Lord.' Salvation is only possible of course if he repents ; but if he repents the curse can be raised. Indeed *not* to raise it would be ' to give Satan an advantage ' [2]—he could continue to wreak his torments on one who no longer deserved or needed them. This consideration, together with the repetition of the name Satan—a name only used by S. Paul in moments of special stress,—combines with other arguments of lesser weight to link together the incidents of the first and second epistle. Ignoring for a moment the criticisms to which the suggestion may be exposed, we may reconstruct the course of events as follows.

The curse is pronounced by S. Paul, and the fact communicated to the Corinthian Church. The latter, however, refuse to associate themselves with the apostle's action, and remain in communion with the sinner. Perhaps in a hurried visit to Corinth, ignored by the Acts [3] (which throw no light whatever on this incident), during which he met with further defiance from the offender and his friends, certainly in the 'severe letter,' S. Paul calls upon the Church to comply with his demand. The majority now show themselves more docile—this is admitted by all theories alike—and all theories alike have to conjecture the reason. No doubt the apostle's adjurations had weight with them ; but it is at least possible that a sudden accident or illness afflicting the offender, or even a pathological condition induced in him by fear of the curse, led them to suppose that the latter has not been ineffective, and to withdraw themselves hurriedly from possible contagion. The offender himself expresses repentance, and S. Paul promptly lifts the curse ' that Satan may gain no advantage ' ; calling upon the Church at the same time to readmit the penitent to communion.[4]

Although this hypothesis meets difficulties which on any other remain unsolved, it is bound to raise objections as well. It will be

---

[1] On ' conditional ' curses see *ERE.*, iv, p. 372 (*s.v.* ' Cursing and Blessing ').

[2] 2 Cor. 2[11].

[3] On this visit most commentators are agreed : the evidence for it, K. Lake, *Earlier Epistles of S. Paul*, pp. 145, 149-154.

[4] E. von Dobschütz, *op. cit.*, pp. 46-49, 389-392, advances a theory somewhat similar to the above, mainly on the grounds that without combining the incidents of the two epistles, the first remains without a conclusion, the second without a beginning (p. 392). He assumes, however, that the curse *fails* of its effect (p. 48) but that the sinner repents, and that S. Paul, putting the two facts together—' the manifested repentance of the sinner and its divine acceptance revealed in the non-fulfilment of the curse ' (p. 49, cp. p. 391)—decides that ' there is nothing left to do but to concur with the divine acknowledgment ' (p. 49), and so raises the curse. This view seems to me defective. It finds no reason for the change of mind of the Corinthians, or for the repentance of the sinner (who would more likely have been confirmed in his sin by the failure of the curse) ; it ignores the psychological effect that the curse might be expected to produce on superstitious minds ; it overlooks the connexion between the use of the names ' Christ ' and ' Satan ' in the two incidents ; and it lays no stress upon the matter of Satan's ' advantage.' I therefore prefer the suggestion made in the text.

said that no such barbaric and unspiritual idea as that of the curse could hold ground in S. Paul's mind, and that there is no evidence for anathemas of this character (as distinct from or additional to excommunication) in the early Church. Neither objection is well founded. Many ethnic survivals remain even in the writings of S. Paul ; and the incidents of the withered fig tree, of Ananias and Sapphira, and of Simon Magus,[1] show that the cursing of offenders, with intent to cause physical harm or death, was not a wholly uncongenial conception to New Testament writers. Conditional curses, designed to produce just such a moral reformation as is S. Paul's intention here, are common in the Apocryphal Acts. Thus in the Vercelli ' Acts of Peter ' an adulteress, Rufina, presents herself at the Holy Eucharist. S. Paul says to her, ' Behold, Satan shall trouble thine heart and cast thee down in the sight of all them that believe. . . . But if thou repent of thine act, He is faithful that is able to blot out thy sin and set thee free from this sin.' Rufina is stricken then and there with paralysis, but the compiler is principally interested in the long sermon which he attributes to the apostle on this occasion ; and he forgets to give any account of the sinner's fate.[2] In the ' Acts of Thomas ' a case of very similar character is described.[3]

That the anathema, or curse combined with excommunication, ranked alongside excommunication as a more severe form of remedial discipline in the early Church, is more difficult to establish. From the sixth to the twelfth century it certainly had this char-

---

[1] The sequence of thought in the Simon Magus incident (Acts 8[20-24]) is identical with that of ' Corinthians '—' Thy silver perish *with thee*. . . . *Repent therefore*. . . . Pray ye for me to the Lord, *that none of the things which ye have spoken come upon me*.' In the case of Elymas (Acts 13[11]) the words employed by S. Paul are thrown into the form of a statement, not of an imprecation, but we can scarcely doubt that a ' curse ' is to be understood ; there is again a ray of hope in the ' for a season '—the curse will be raised when Elymas ceases to oppose the missionaries.

[2] M. R. James, *Apocryphal New Testament*, pp. 304, 305.

[3] *Acta Thomæ*, 51-52—a young man who has murdered his paramour (though not altogether from an evil motive) is similarly stricken with paralysis on approaching the Eucharist : on repentance he is healed, and (53-57) the girl also is raised from the dead and gives a graphic description of hell (M. R. James, *op. cit.*, pp. 388-392). Cp. *ib.*, pp. 367, 368—a recalcitrant cup-bearer is cursed with the words, ' My God will forgive thee in the life to come this iniquity, but in this world thou shalt show forth His wonders, and even now shall I behold this hand that hath smitten me dragged by dogs.' Shortly afterwards the cup-bearer is killed by a lion, and a black dog enters the banqueting-hall carrying his dismembered hand in his jaws. Here there is no suggestion that repentance will secure remission of the temporal penalty ; but in compensation the offender receives an explicit promise of forgiveness in the next world. Further instances of a similar kind, James, *op. cit.*, p. 317 (*Acts of Peter*, 15—a child of seven months curses Simon Magus with dumbness ' until the sabbath ') ; p. 247—an angel curses a young man with the words, ' Die that thou mayest live ' ; he is raised from a state of coma by John and expresses deep penitence for his sin. A particularly terrible and exhaustive curse on an unrepentant sinner, *Acts of John*, 84 ; the offender dies, and John says, ' Thou hast thy child, O devil ' (*op. cit.*, pp. 249, 250).

acter; Martène gives a series of terrible curses [1] pronounced upon recalcitrant sinners, which however usually end with some such phrase as, ' If however he repent and reform, then may God avert all these ills from him, and we are prepared to receive him back and to pray for him.' This exactly corresponds to the practice and theory which appear to underlie the incidents at Corinth. From the twelfth century onwards, the ' anathema ' is merely a synonym for the greater excommunication, solemnly pronounced with bell, book and candle. But the usage of the first five centuries is elusive. Evidence can be quoted in favour of the theory that anathema is in this period the same as excommunication, and conveys no idea of a temporal curse in addition. The latest authorities however are inclined to the opinion that the sixth-century practice ' did not create the distinction, but merely continued with a stricter organization an earlier tradition of ecclesiastical discipline.' [2]

(d) The Epistle to the Hebrews.

S. Paul, therefore, even in his most drastic exercise of discipline, allowed for the possibility of the offender's repentance and consequent restoration. The same is true of John the Seer; though we might have expected a mind imbued with apocalyptic to adopt a more rigorous attitude. The church of Ephesus has left her first love; the church of Pergamum tolerates the Balaamites and Nicolaitans; the church of Thyatira is defiled by the woman Jezebel; the church of Sardis has a name that it liveth but is dead; the church of Laodicea is neither hot nor cold—but any and all of them may repent and do the first works,[3] and be saved. Even the woman Jezebel herself has been given space for repentance, though hope seems to be at an end for her now.[4] No doubt the warnings addressed to these churches are warnings of divine, not human, punishment; but we cannot doubt that John would use such means as were in his power to express the divine attitude by

---

[1] E. Martène, de ant. eccl. rit., iii, 4 (Antwerp, 1763; ii, pp. 322 ff.). The second Council of Tours (A.D. 567). can. 24, makes a clear distinction between excommunication and anathema—' non solum excommunicatus sed etiam anathematizatus.' Hefele-Leclerq, iii, p. 191, understand this simply of the distinction between the lesser and the greater excommunication (infra, p. 508); but most authorities are against them, Labbe and Cossart, ad loc., infer a prayer for ' temporal ' punishment as well as spiritual. Similarly Conc. Meldens. (Meaux, A.D. 845), c. 56; but CJC., c. 106, C. XI, q. 3; c. 23, C. XI, q. 3; c. 10, X, ii, 1, show that the distinction has disappeared by the twelfth century. On the whole subject, see DALC., i, coll. 1926-1940; D.Th.C., i, coll. 1167-1171.

[2] Villieu-Magnin-Amanieu, Dictionnaire du Droit Canon, i, coll. 512-516. So possibly the imprecations pronounced against Arius (Socr., HE., i, 37) and Hermogenes (ib., vii, 12).

[3] Rev. 2⁵, ¹⁶, ²⁵, 3³, ¹⁹.

[4] Rev. 2²¹⁻²³: ' I gave her time that she should repent, and she willeth not to repent of her fornication.' This seems to imply that her chance has gone; but she may be included in the hope of amnesty offered to her accomplices in v. 22. Verse 23 seems a final doom: ' I will kill her children with death.'

ecclesiastical action. His cry throughout, however, is a cry of 'Repent' to the sinful, not one of 'Exclude them' to the righteous.

In the midst of so much mercy, the epistle to the Hebrews strikes a discordant note. Three times in succession the author asserts in different phrases that, if those who have tasted of the heavenly gift fall away, it is impossible to renew them again to repentance. The earth which beareth thorns and briers is rejected and nigh unto a curse—(a curse this time which no repentance can avail to lift)—its end is to be burnt.[1] Commentators have vainly attempted to mitigate the severity of these passages ;[2] but their implications and assertions are too plain to be avoided. The discipline contemplated by 'Hebrews,' in some cases of grave sin at least, is the exercise of purely penal excommunication, with no hope of reconciliation for the offender, even if he appears to men to be repentant.

The rigorism of 'Hebrews,' however, did not go unchallenged even in its birthplace. The epistle is Alexandrian in tone from beginning to end, and in the Jewish-Christian community at Alexandria there was current another document which was of profound influence in the early Church, though only fragments of it survive to-day. This was the so-called 'Gospel according to the Hebrews'—a version or adaptation of S. Matthew's gospel.[3] As though in defiance of the epistle, it takes up the Matthæan saying

---

[1] The passages are (a) Hebr. 6[4-8] ; (b) Hebr. 10[26-31] ; (c) Hebr. 12[16, 17]. The key-phrases are 'it is impossible to renew them again to repentance' (6[6]) ; 'there remaineth no more a sacrifice for sins' (10[26]) ; 'he found no place of repentance' (12[17]).

[2] The most recent mitigating interpretations are those of Dr. Nairne (*Epistle to the Hebrews: Cambridge Bible for Schools*, new edition). His general standpoint is clear—the coming crisis (the Roman invasion of Palestine, confused with the end of the world) will take away all opportunities of second thoughts—'in the coming disturbances you may die or you may be involved in an inextricable tangle of evil' (p. lxxxix, cp. p. lxxxvii). But 6[4] is interpreted, in the commentary, of a *psychological* inability to repent : 'if you fall away . . . it is impossible to start you again fair and fresh in the recovered simplicity of childhood's mind' (p. 40). On 12[17] Dr. Nairne merely says, 'The phrase ("found no place of repentance") had wide applications, and may not have conveyed to the first readers the theological hopelessness it suggests here to us.' The suggested interpretation of 10[26] is very obscure ; since 'a sacrifice for sin' is an O.T. term, the passage appears to be taken as meaning 'the whole of the old law with its technical sin offerings is gone by' (p. 80). It is therefore an *argumentum ad hominem* addressed to readers who (as Dr. Nairne supposes) are in danger of sliding back into Judaism. But as they would certainly not have any tendency to do so if they believed 'the old law' to have passed away, the argument would have been a singularly ineffective one—too ineffective, one would have thought, for a mind as keen as that of the author of 'Hebrews.'

[3] On the controversies which surround this mysterious document see *DAC.*, i, pp. 489-494, and M. R. James, *Apocryphal New Testament*, p. 1, with literature there cited. Where so much is utterly uncertain, I am not of course committed to the Alexandrian origin either of the Epistle or the 'Gospel.' But the contrast between them is interesting, and *may* be significant of a controversy in Alexandria analogous to that in which Hermas played so decisive a part at Rome.

about 'seventy-times seven,' and repeats it with a significant addition :—[1]

'"If thy brother have sinned . . . and make thee amends, seven times in a day receive thou him." Simon His disciple said unto Him, "Seven times in a day?" The Lord answered and said, "Yea, I say unto thee, unto seventy times seven. *For in the prophets also, after they were anointed with the Holy Spirit, matter of sin was found.*"'

The rigorist practice of refusing reconciliation to grave sinners was bound up, as will appear later, with a doctrine of irresistible grace—the immediate and indefectible perfecting of the Christian by the Spirit at his conversion. The 'Gospel of the Hebrews' sets its face not merely against the practice but against the doctrine too. *Even* ' *in the prophets* ' (and so much more in the ordinary Christian), and that *after* they had received the Holy Spirit, sin was found ; how tender, therefore, must not the Church be with the lapses of every-day believers !

(e) *The Sin unto Death.*

An echo of the rigorism of the epistle to the Hebrews is found in the first epistle of S. John,[2] but examination of the passage shows that the writer himself is in the main pleading on the liberal side :—

'If any man see his brother sinning a sin not unto death, he shall ask, and He shall give him life for them that sin not unto death. There is a sin unto death : I say not that he should ask concerning that. All unrighteousness is sin, and there is a sin not unto death.'

The passage as a whole deals with the 'boldness' with which the Christian may approach God in prayer.[3] Evidently the writer—who is about to say that 'whosoever is begotten of God sinneth not'[4]— is *doctrinally* of the same mind as those who believe that the Christian who sins is no Christian at all. But this comes into conflict with his doctrine of the efficacy of believing prayer ; and the latter is even dearer to him than the former. There *is* a sin unto death,[5] he admits ; and for that he cannot encourage his readers to pray. But he hedges this piece of pessimism about with the reiterated

---

[1] Hieron., *dial. c. Pel.*, iii, 2 (M. R. James, *op. cit.*, p. 6). 'Matter of sin' is Dr. James' rendering of Jerome's 'sermo peccati.' F. C. Burkitt, *Gospel History and its Transmission*, p. 342, regards this ('Gospel to the Hebrews') account of the incident as more authentic than the canonical versions.

[2] 1 Jn. 5[16, 17].

[3] 1 Jn. 5, verses 14, 15; for the same doctrine in the Fourth Gospel, *supra,* p. 152, n. 1.

[4] Verse 18.

[5] There is of course a reference here to the sins punishable by death under the Old Law, as also to the 'sin with a high hand,' for which no sacrifice could atone, Num. 15[30, 31].

6

assertion that there is *also* a sin not unto death, for which prayer will avail. It is this latter point that he wishes to press home, and not the former. Whatever his theory may be, in practice he relies upon the mercy of God, and commends it to the Church.[1]

(f) The sin against the Holy Spirit.

The Synoptists also know of an unforgivable sin—the sin against the Holy Spirit. It is incorporated in the Marcan version (followed by Matthew in this respect) of a passage common both to Mark and Q ;[2] in Q it appears (in a different form) to have been a detached logion without context.[3] The Marcan version is completely intelligible and admirably fitted to the context. ' People were saying, " He is beside Himself " ' ; and scribes from Jerusalem directly accused Him of casting out devils by Beelzebub the prince of the devils.[4] After ridiculing this suggestion with the parables of the divided kingdom, the divided house, and the strong man armed, Jesus attacks His opponents directly :—

[1] The extraordinary confusion of the text in Jude [22, 23] shows that various hands have been at work in the attempt to define an attitude on the question of discipline. But the $\dot{\epsilon}\nu$ $\phi\dot{o}\beta\omega$ $\sigma\dot{\omega}\zeta\epsilon\tau\epsilon$, or $\dot{\epsilon}\lambda\epsilon\hat{a}\tau\epsilon$ $\dot{\epsilon}\nu$ $\phi\dot{o}\beta\omega$, which remains in every version, shows how doubtful the writer and his correctors were as to the legitimacy of reconciliation in some, and perhaps many, cases. The general impression is one of less reliance on the mercy of God than in 1 Jn. or Hermas.

[2] Mk. 3^{20-35} ; Mt. $12^{22-32, 46-50}$; Lk. 11^{14-23}. That the passage occurred in Q also is shown by the presence in the same context of the dumb (Matthew : ' and blind ') demoniac (Mt. $12^{22, 23}$, Lk. 11^{14}) ; of the passage, ' If I by Beelzebub, etc.' (Mt. $12^{27, 28}$, Lk. $11^{19, 20}$) ; of the logion, ' He that is not with Me is against Me, and he that gathereth not with Me scattereth' (Mt. 12^{30}, Lk. 11^{23}) ; of the problem of the sign from heaven (Mt. 12^{38-42}, Lk. 11^{29-32}) ; and of the parable of the unclean spirit (Mt. 12^{43-45}, Lk. 11^{24-26}) —none of which occur in Mk.—Both Mt. and Lk. omit Mk.'s introduction (Mk. $3^{20, 21}$—the crowd,—' and when His friends heard of it, they went out to lay hold on Him, for they were saying, " He is beside Himself " ') probably because it seemed derogatory to the Lord ; but both respect his conclusion (Mk. 3^{31-35}—' My mother and My brethren ')—Mt. by retaining it at the end of his additions from Q ; Lk. (11^{27}) by substituting the analogous incident, ' Blessed is the womb that bare Thee, etc.' (He preferred to employ the ' mother and brethren ' saying as an appropriate conclusion to the Parable of the Sower (Lk. 8^{19-21}), which followed the Beelzebub incident in his Marcan source).

[3] Lk. 12^{10}—as Matthew does not record it in the parallel passage (the address to the twelve, Mt. 9^{35}-10^{40}), I am inclined to doubt whether it stood there originally. It is not too happily adjusted to its Lucan context, which refers to confession of Christ in persecution ($12^{4-9, 11-12}$) and would read more continuously without it. But it is sufficiently related in thought to verse 9 (' he shall be denied before the angels of God ') to have given Lk. a reason for inserting it here. He seems to have inserted other material at the same point (Lk. 12^{2-9} = Mt. 10^{26-33} ; Lk. 12^{51-53} = Mt. 10^{34-36}), all of it of a rather fortuitous kind.

[4] The whole incident, again, is appropriately fitted into the story of $o\dot{i}$ $\pi a\rho$' $a\dot{v}\tau o\hat{v}$ (' His people ') who came to ' get hold ' of Him ($\kappa\rho a\tau\hat{\eta}\sigma a\iota$), because ' people were saying " He is mad " ' ($\dot{\epsilon}\lambda\epsilon\gamma o\nu$ $\gamma\dot{a}\rho$ $\ddot{o}\tau\iota$ $\dot{\epsilon}\xi\dot{\epsilon}\sigma\tau\eta$)—Mk. $3^{20, 21}$. The conclusion of this incident, with the same house (implied in $\ddot{\epsilon}\xi\omega$, verse 31) and crowd as in verse 20, comes in verses 31-35. In between the two points Mark has inserted the Beelzebub affair and our Lord's reply.

' Verily I say unto you, All their sins shall be forgiven unto the sons of men, and their blasphemies wherewith soever they shall blaspheme. But whosoever shall blaspheme against the Holy Spirit hath never forgiveness, but is guilty of an eternal sin.'

To this Mark adds the explanatory note, 'Because they said, "He hath an unclean spirit." '[1] Nothing could be clearer. Any accusation against Jesus that He is in league with the powers of evil is a blasphemy against the Holy Spirit, and as such is unforgivable, both on earth and in heaven. But the Q version of the saying is more difficult. It runs (Lk. xii, 10) :—

' Everyone who shall speak a word against the Son of Man, it shall be forgiven him : but unto him that blasphemeth against the Holy Spirit, it shall not be forgiven.'

At first sight this would appear to imply the very reverse of the Marcan saying—blasphemy against Jesus (the Son of Man) is *not* blasphemy against the Holy Spirit, and is forgivable. It is generally agreed, however, that this is at all events not the *original* meaning of the logion. ' Son of man,' as is well known, was in Aramaic a simple periphrasis for ' man,' although Jesus (following ' Daniel ' and ' Enoch ') used it in the specific and perhaps esoteric sense of ' Messiah.' Thus the original meaning of the Q version may well have been, ' Evil-speaking against man is forgivable; evil-speaking against the Spirit is not.'[2] But it cannot have retained this meaning at the date at which the first and third gospels were put on paper, for by that time ' Son of Man ' could point to nobody except Jesus. To Matthew and Luke the words can only have meant, ' Blasphemy against Jesus is forgivable : blasphemy

---

[1] Mk. 3[30]. Not strictly accurate ; what had been said was, ' He is beside Himself ' (' mad '), ' He hath Beelzebub,' and ' In the prince of the devils he casteth out devils.' This slight discrepancy suggests that even Mk. knew the logion originally only as a disconnected unit, with no setting except a vague ' People were saying, "He hath an unclean spirit " ' ; a consideration reinforced by the probability that the logion was not combined with the Beelzebub incident in Q (since Lk. does not record it there). If so, the inspiration which prompted Mk. to bring the logion into connexion with the Beelzebub incident, and the whole thus put together into connexion with the ' He is beside Himself ' story, was a peculiarly happy one.

[2] What was the original form of the logion—the parent of both the Marcan and the Q versions ?—Possibly the Lucan (i.e. Q) version, with the meaning assigned to it in the text above ; Mk. then omits ' against the Son of Man ' because he took it to mean ' blasphemy against Jesus is permissible '; alters the arrangement; and inserts ' to the sons of men ' because he has a recollection of ' son of man ' in the passage somewhere. Or, again, the original may have been ' blasphemy shall be forgiven to a son of man ' (= a man), which proved generally objectionable as suggesting that *the* Son of Man could blaspheme and need forgiveness; Mk. therefore altered to the plural, Q (under the influence of the controversy alluded to in the text) to ' speaking *against* the Son of Man.'

against the Spirit is not '—and Matthew goes so far as to incorporate them in this form in the original Marcan story.[1]

On what grounds, then, should Matthew and Luke have retained a statement so derogatory to the person of Jesus ? Commentators have exercised their ingenuity on the problem to small effect. According to some [2] the distinction is a Christological one—evil-speaking against the humanity of Jesus is allowable, blasphemy against His divinity is not. This suggestion appears to be frankly nonsensical : but if it has any meaning at all it could only have arisen in the atmosphere of the fourth century, not in that of the first. According to others,[3] the contrast is between the ' distant Messiah in heaven ' (who may be spoken against), and the ' Spirit present in the Church on earth '—another interpretation which seems wholly foreign to the spirit of the New Testament. More popular and more plausible are the psychological explanations ; [4] ' momentary petulance,' ' want of thought,' ' honest conviction,' ' mistaken judgments ' are forgivable ; ' intellectual laziness,' ' moral insincerity,' ' hardened cynicism,' ' wilful rejection ' are not. But these and similar solutions appear to be modernizations which have no relation to the actual text. If it were to have this meaning we should have expected it to be expressed by a strong differentiation in the words used for the respective attitudes of the two classes of offenders. No such differentiation is observable.[5] The only contrast expressed is between the Son of Man and the Spirit, who (on this view) are to all intents and purposes identical, and require no differentiation.[6]

We must look further, therefore, for an explanation. Is it possible that here, as elsewhere, there is an echo of the conflict between rigorism and humanism in discipline ? The Marcan form of the logion lent itself very easily to rigorism. ' Blasphemy against the Holy Spirit ' was a vague phrase, and could be used to exclude sinners of very many kinds from communion, and that for life. But another

---

[1] He conflates the two rather dexterously (Mt. 12[31, 32]—Roman type shows words from Mark, italics words from Q, capitals words peculiar to Mt.) : —' Every sin and blasphemy shall be forgiven unto men ; but the blasphemy against the Spirit shall not be forgiven. *And whosoever shall speak a word against the Son of Man, it shall be forgiven him ; but whosoever* SHALL SPEAK *against the Holy Spirit it shall not be forgiven him,* NEITHER IN THIS world NOR IN THAT WHICH IS TO COME.'

[2] Wellhausen, Loisy, *ad loc.*, and apparently H. B. Swete on Mk. 3[28].

[3] Bousset (*SNT.* on Mt. 12[32]).

[4] H. G. Wood (Peake, *One Volume Commentary*, p. 686) ; C. H. Turner, C. Gore (*New Commentary : N.T.*, pp. 62, 225) ; J. Massie (*HDB.*, i, p. 305) ; J. Denney (*DCG.*, i, p. 733) ; J. C. Lambert (*ib.*, ii, p. 786).

[5] Lk. has ' speak a word ' of the sin against the Son of Man, ' blasphemeth ' of that against the Spirit. It does not seem probable that he intends the two phrases to be taken in different senses, but even if he does they can refer only to outward action, not to psychological attitude.

[6] For these ' psychological ' explanations to be borne out by the text, we should require a differentiation between *attitudes towards the Godhead* as such ; differentiations between *the persons in the Godhead* (which is what we actually find) are for explanations of this character wholly irrelevant.

form of the saying was current (whether originally spoken by our Lord, or arising by accident, or by pious invention, no one can tell) which reduced rigorism to the smallest possible limits. There *was* indeed an unforgivable sin—that could not be denied; but even blasphemy against the Son of Man was excluded from the category, still more all lesser sins. Here, then, was a message of hope for sinners: they were not to be unduly oppressed by the danger of incurring permanent excommunication. Those who popularized the logion in the Q version were willing to open the gates of forgiveness even to blasphemers against the Name.[1]

VI. DISCIPLINE AT ROME.

Unfortunately for the Church, the rigorist view of the epistle to the Hebrews predominated for many generations, and poisoned the whole atmosphere of Christian ethics. There is a moment's breathing space, it is true. S. Ignatius of Antioch speaks

---

[1] A very different view as to the prevalence and principles of discipline in the New Testament from that expressed here will be found in Bishop Creighton's remarkable Hulsean Lectures, *Persecution and Tolerance*, ch. ii. Bishop Creighton admits that sinners were 'punished' for 'moral offences' (pp. 56-58), that 'false teachers' are 'not to be received or welcomed by the faithful' (p. 54), and that the 'Church must preserve its purity by separating from offenders' (p. 59). But in general he maintains that there was no 'persecution' (i.e. 'punishment for erroneous opinions as such,' p. 46) in the New Testament. I suspect that there is here little more than ambiguity in the use of words. Neither 'punishment' nor 'erroneous' is defined; and no distinction is made between 'holding' and 'teaching' false opinions. Thus if 'punishment' means 'retaliation' (the vindictive 'eye for an eye' spirit) we may agree that there is none of it in the New Testament. But if it means 'inflicting pain on occasion of offence,' then 'separation,' 'not welcoming,' 'not receiving,' are *all* punishments, for they can all cause pain. So too can words; and it is therefore no support to the argument to say 'no weapons were used but words' (p. 49). 'Persuasion' and 'compulsion' (p. 81) merge imperceptibly into one another. Similarly the distinction between 'moral offences' and 'erroneous opinion' is an exceedingly difficult one to maintain; in which category does an 'erroneous opinion on moral questions' fall, particularly when it is acted upon? Finally, no one is 'punished' for 'holding' false opinions in the New Testament; but for the simple reason that no one ever has been or can be at any time. It is impossible to tell what opinions a man holds unless and until he begins to publish them; and the moment he begins to publish them he has begun to 'teach' as well as to 'hold.' Bishop Creighton adds a remarkable argument to the effect that the apostles' action in 'punishing' (on the rare occasions when they punished) 'affords no precedent for subsequent times'; because the 'punishment came from God and required no human intervention,' 'the offence . . . was beyond the ken of human judgment' (p. 58), and 'the action of the apostles was declaratory of God's purpose' (p. 55). Unless this simply means that the apostles never did more than interpret the significance of a 'miracle of judgment' after it occurred (a view which the text of the N.T. scarcely warrants), it says no more of N.T. discipline than could be said, with the same degree of justice (whatever that may be), of ecclesiastical discipline at all times; and therefore these three characteristics in themselves could scarcely make the apostles' action 'no precedent.' A more balanced view of the idea of discipline will be found in J. N. Figgis, *Churches in the Modern State*, p. 115; W. Temple, *Church and Nation*, p. 167. Cp. my *Conscience and Its Problems*, p. 223.

encouragingly of the reconciliation of penitent sinners, without any hint of limitation.[1]   Clement of Rome, again, esteems and quotes the epistle to the Hebrews, but he utterly ignores its doctrine of irremissible sins.   His epistle is concerned with disorders in the church of Corinth ; and so far the Roman community has devised no means of giving expression to its demands upon its sister-church other than that of friendly exhortation.   Clement undoubtedly urges the offenders to submit to formal discipline, but there is no suggestion that it may involve permanent exclusion from the Church.[2] The ' Pastor ' of Hermas, however, another Roman document certainly composed and published by the year 140, and possibly many years earlier,[3] shows how these things were dealt with at Rome itself.

[1] Ign., *ad Phil.*, 3[2], 8[1].   *Did.*, 15[3], is no less merciful in outlook—' Convict one another ' (ἐλέγχετε ἀλλήλους—a curiously delicate phrase, for the injunction is addressed to the presbyters and deacons whom he has just mentioned, and the ' one another ' of course refers to offenders only ; cp. next note ; and *infra*, p. 172, n.) ' not in anger, but in peace, as ye have it in the gospel. And everyone that behaveth amiss, let no man speak to him, nor let him hear any word from you, *until he repent.*' Similarly, *Did.*, 14[2] ; Polycarp, *ad Phil.*, 11[4].—On the modified liberalism in discipline which appears to underlie *Didaché* as a whole, *supra*, pp. 113, 114, footnotes.'

[2] In view of the respect in which, as his own quotations show, ' Hebrews ' was esteemed at Rome, and the controversy in which Hermas was about to play so prominent a part, Clement's complete silence as to any divergence of view on the question of irremissible sin is remarkable. Although the rigorist passages of Hebrews would have suited him well in the sterner rebukes at the end of his epistle, he avoids all quotation from them.   Is it possible that he was a protagonist on the liberal side ?   Hermas assumes that he will not hesitate to forward the liberal message to foreign churches (*Vis.*, II, 4[3]).   The actual references to formal discipline in his epistle seem to be these : 57[1, 2]—' Submit yourselves to the presbyters, and accept chastisement (παιδεία) to repentance (μετάνοια = (?) penance in a formal sense), bending the knees of your hearts.   Learn to submit . . . ' ;   56[2]— ' Let us accept chastisement . . . the monitions (νουθέτησεις) which we address to one another ' (the same delicacy as in Jas. 5[16], *Did.*, 15[3], *supra*, n. 1) ' are good and profitable.'   The Church is told to pray for the offender, 56[1].   Most remarkable however is the suggestion as to a penance, 54[2]—the offender should be prepared to say, ' I will depart, I will go where ye will, I will do whatever the majority require.'   This appears to refer to actual banishment, for Clement promises that, if the offenders show such meekness, ' every place will receive them ' ; and adds the rather inapposite quotation, ' for the earth is the Lord's and the fulness thereof ' (54[3]).   It is possible, of course, as Knopf, *ad loc.*, suggests, that the dissidents at Corinth were wandering prophets, who would not find moving-on too great a hardship, and would be content if they took with them such letters of commendation as would secure their being ' received ' in ' every place.'   But it is more likely that Clement has dropped into rhetoric—he is urging willingness to accept (probably temporary) exclusion from the community, and such penitential exercises as the ' majority ' impose ; and just as he is about to illustrate this by literary and historical examples (c. 55—not by any means all cases of voluntary exile) he suggests ' even if it came to banishment, God would look after you.'

[3] The latest discussion of the date of Hermas is Streeter, *Primitive Church*, pp. 203-213 ; but it should be modified bv Dibelius' cautions (*HNT.* : *Ergänzungsband*, iv, pp. 422, 423) against taking the reference to Clement as a contemporary too literally.

Hermas is a formalist to the backbone. Before the first of his visions he thinks of God mainly as Creator and Ruler ; [1] the operations of nature and providence are the main source of his knowledge.[2] Even at that time he is preoccupied with the question of sin and punishment : [3] he moves throughout in an atmosphere of recompense. Of personal experience of God he knows little, even in his visions. The Holy Spirit speaks indeed in the prophets ; but in so far as ' holy spirit ' can be predicated of the ordinary Christian, something very different from the Spirit of the New Testament is meant—Hermas' ' holy spirit ' can be defiled and tainted.[4] He delights in catalogues ; [5] and he is the first Christian writer to personify the virtues and vices as bevies of young women.[6] He can even commit himself to the amazing sentence :—' The Son of God who is preached throughout the world is the Law ' ; [7] and he alternates between the two besetting dangers of the formalist— spiritual pride and spiritual despair. The problem of discipline, therefore, must have been specially congenial to him in all its branches, and he handles it with true enthusiasm.

The dominant view at Rome is clear from his book : grave sinners are to be excluded from the Church without any hope of readmission.[8] So deep-rooted is this general conviction that Hermas is only prepared to question it by virtue of what seems to him (or what he represents to be) a special divine revelation.[9] Nor does his questioning amount to more than the suggestion of a temporary mitigation for a special emergency. The Church is threatened by a renewed outbreak of persecution.[10] She is reduced in numbers,

---

[1] *Vis.*, I, 1[3, 6], etc.   [2] *Vis.*, I, 1[3], 3[4].

[3] *Vis.*, I, 1[3, 5, 7-9], 2[1], 3[1] ; he is blamed for it by the old lady, *Vis.*, III, 1[6].

[4] *Mand.*, III, 2—Christians receive a πνεῦμα ἄψευστον, but they can make it ψευδές ; V, 1[2, 3]—the holy spirit that dwells in the Christian can be ' darkened ' and ' defiled.'

[5] E.g. *Mand.*, V, 2[3, 4] ; VI, 2[3, 5] ; VIII, 3, 5, 8-10 ; XI, 8, 12 ; XII, 3[1] ; *Sim.*, VI, 5[5], etc.

[6] The Virtues, *Vis.*, III, 8[2, 5] ; *Sim.*, IX, 15[2] ; the Vices, *Sim.*, IX, 15[3].

[7] *Sim.*, VIII, 3[2].

[8] *Mand.*, IV, 3[1, 2]. Hermas : ' I have heard that there is no other penance ' (μετάνοια) ' after that when we went down into the water and received forgiveness of our sins ' : The shepherd : ' Thou hast heard aright ; for so it is.' Cp. also *Sim.*, IX, 18[2]—even those who sin before ' knowing God ' are condemned to (physical) death ; those who sin after ' knowing God ' shall ' be punished doubly and shall die eternally ' ; *Mand.*, IV, 1[8]—' for the servant of God there is only one repentance ' (this, however, may refer to post-baptismal penance). The *heretics* of *Sim.*, VIII, 6[5], who ' do not allow the servants of God to repent,' are not of course these ultra-orthodox rigorists, but libertines with gnostic affinities.

[9] Batiffol, *Études d'Histoire* [5], etc., i, p. 57. The ' liberals ' in discipline seem to have favoured this device—cp. Elkesai (*infra*, p. 169), and John the Seer (*supra*, p. 159), whose messages of mercy are similarly embedded in a ' revelation ' (Rev. 1[1, 10], etc.). Does this imply that they were conscious of setting themselves against the stream ?

[10] *Vis.*, II, 2[7]—' the great tribulation which is coming ' ; cp. the message to Maximus, ' Behold, tribulation cometh ; if it seem fit to thee, deny again,' *ib.*, 3[3] ; *Vis.*, IV, the beast ; *Sim.*, VI, 2, 3 (probably, but it might refer to the trials of life in general). Batiffol rightly calls Hermas' proposal a ' kind of a jubilee.'

—for many who apostatized in the last persecution have been ex-communicated, and may not be readmitted, under the prevalent theory of discipline.[1] But that is not all. Within the Church itself, hypocrisy, laxity, and worldliness are rampant : she is in no spiritual condition to resist the fires of persecution.[2] What can be done ? ' Purge out the evil leaven,' say extremists ; but that is just what Hermas dare not contemplate. The application of the discipline in vogue would result in such drastic pruning, that the few branches lett would fall an easy prey to the imperial exe-cutioners.

So Hermas elects, with many hesitations and some genuine obscurities, for a limited modification of the existing order. A new moral impetus is needed to face the coming storm ; and like Samuel of old, he calls the whole congregation to a period of peni-tence and humiliation before God.[3] To the apostates and other excommunicates he offers what has hitherto been denied them—one more chance, but one alone. Grave sinners within the Church he calls to open penance, with the threat that after this opportunity nothing awaits them except the penalty of permanent excommuni-cation.[4] But from all others—even the ' all but righteous '[5]—he demands open penance as well ; they are to some degree associates in the graver sins of their fellows, and a piece of moral discipline for the lesser sins of which they have been guilty will do them no harm. Only a very few are exempt—those who confessed bravely in the last persecution, those who are transcendently saintly,[6] and the godly clergy.[7] By a curious and unexplained coincidence, a

---

[1] The excommunicate apostates ; *Vis.*, II, 2[8] ; III, 5[5] (they are thrown away from the tower, but wish to ' repent,' and if they repent, will be useful to the building), 7[2] ; *Sim.*, VIII, 6[4] ; IX, 19[1], etc.

[2] *Vis.*, III, 6, 9 ; *Sim.*, VIII, 6, 7, etc., and the descriptions of Hermas' ' wife ' and ' family,' probably typical of the Church as a whole—*Vis.*, II, 2, 3[1].

[3] This *period* of penance is hinted at frequently in the earlier part of the book ; but—as containing the vital message—it receives most stress at the end (*Sim.*, VI, 3[6] ; VII, 4-7 ; VIII, IX), where it dominates the whole thought of the writer.

[4] *Vis.*, II, 2[4, 5] ; III, 5[5] ; *Mand.*, IV, 3[3-6] ; *Sim.*, VIII, IX.

[5] *Vis.*, III, 6[4] ; *Sim.*, VIII, 10.

[6] *Vis.*, III, 5[2-4]. Curiously enough, he includes in this list those ' who are young in the faith and are faithful.' Does he mean that they have not yet had time to sin ? Further descriptions of those who appear to be exempt, *Sim.*, IX, 24, 25, 27-31.

[7] *Vis.*, III, 5[1]— ' Apostles, bishops, teachers and deacons who have walked in godly sobriety,' and so forth. Hermas' language might be taken to imply that all the Roman clergy were godly ; but the rest of the book makes it clear that this was not the case. Why then does he dissociate good *clergy* from the other godly people of whom penitence is not required ? Presumably because of the greater responsibilities of the clergy, which entitle them to ' go into the tower ' before laymen, even though the latter are as good. The responsibilities are emphasized : they have ' watched and taught and laboured in saintly and sober fashion for the elect of God.' Does Hermas expect the bad clergy to do penance ? He does not say ; but it has to be borne in mind that from early (though perhaps not from the earliest) times, the punishment for a guilty cleric was not penance, but

similar general amnesty was offered to all sinners in Eastern Christendom by Hermas' mysterious contemporary, the Parthian heresiarch Elkesai—though in this case it needed the appearance of an angel 96 miles high and broad in proportion, to invest the message with divine authority.[1]

The concession suggested by Hermas is put forward, it will be seen, wholly out of thought for the Church as an institution. He shows little interest in the well-being and moral advancement of the individual. It never occurs to him that if one reconciliation of the sinner to the Church after baptism be allowed no question of principle can stand in the way of repeated reconciliations where they may—unhappily—be needed. Such a suggestion would defeat his whole purpose, which is to brace the Church here and now for the coming trial, not to suggest to the weakling that there is always mercy. In another direction, too, the concession is limited. It is not available indefinitely, but only to an 'appointed day,' whose date Hermas does not exactly indicate.[2] Once the appointed day is past, there is no further opportunity of repentance. Those who have not responded before that day, together with all upon whom the axe of discipline falls thereafter, will be treated as permanently excluded from the Church.[3] Yet with all these reservations, Hermas remains the great sub-apostolic figure who first pointed out to the Church the way back from the severity of ' Hebrews ' to a more pastoral conception and exercise of discipline. The concession for which he pleaded may seem a very grudging one, but some one had to plead for it first ; and Hermas' success is the beginning of that development whereby the Church adapted for public use the rule of ' seventy times seven ' which Christ ordained for the forgiveness of private injuries.

There are innumerable problems connected with Hermas. It is not even certain, within fifty years or so, when he lived or wrote ;[4] and there is no evidence as to the particular persecutions which called for the publication of his book. It may be asked, further, how far the setting of his message, his visions, and the allusions to his family have any basis in fact, and how far they are conscious literary embellishments. At first sight his very artlessness appears

---

deposition. On the complicated problems involved in this matter of clerical deposition see especially P. Batiffol, *Études d'Histoire* [5], etc., i, pp. 103-107, 129-130, 169-177 ; B. Poschmann, *Abendländische Kirchenbusse*, pp. 172-203 ; J. Tixeront, *Histoire des Dogmes*, iii, pp. 410-412 ; *DTC.*, svv., ' Déposition,' ' Dégradation.' The deposed cleric was admitted to lay-communion, sometimes at once, sometimes after excommunication and (? life-long) penance ; often he retired, or was relegated, to a monastery. Temporary suspension, with or without excommunication, begins to appear locally in the sixth century. Batiffol's suggestion that it was Callistus who substituted deposition for penance in the case of clerics is scarcely borne out by the evidence ; but from beginning to end the whole question is beset with difficulties.

[1] Hippol., *Philos.*, ix, 13[2].

[2] *Infra*, p. 170, n. 2.

[3] A further limitation—the amnesty applies only to those already baptized ; new converts cannot claim its privileges : *Mand.*, IV, 3[3].

[4] *Supra*, p. 166, n. 3.

to preclude any possibility of fiction ; yet the opening incident of the book is sufficiently reminiscent of the amatory romances of his own day to suggest that he was not incapable of borrowing or inventing a picturesque situation if occasion seemed to demand it.[1] Again, what is to be thought of his complete silence as to *venial* sins—those everyday sins which, in the later practice of the Church, were not regarded as material for the severe discipline of penance ? Surely the sins of the ' all but righteous ' are of this character, and yet they have to be confessed.   Does it follow, then, that failure to confess them will involve excommunication ; and that further lapse, even though into venial sin alone, will be visited with permanent exclusion from the Church ?   Hermas supplies no answer to the question he has raised.   It can only be assumed that although venial sin has to be confessed *now* (as part of that general expression of humiliation before God for which the special occasion calls) it will not have to be confessed in future when conditions are more normal, nor will it constitute a ground for excommunication.

But perhaps the most important problem of all concerns the ' appointed day.'   Did Hermas really believe in it himself ?   He makes no attempt to fix it down in any way ; indeed, as the book progresses—its composition is obviously interrupted at various points by gaps of considerable duration—the ' appointed day ' still remains as remote as ever.[2]   Is it, perhaps, just another fiction

---

[1] The point is well and fully argued by Dibelius, *HNT. Ergänzungsband*, iv, pp. 425-429 ; cp. also pp. 618, 619.   He also suggests reasons for thinking that Hermas' family was—to say the least—not as black as he paints it, and may have been entirely allegorical, pp. 445, 446.   His arguments have a good deal of cogency, and put many of the problems of the book in a new light.

[2] In *Vis.*, II, $2^{4, 5, 8}$; III, 2^2, the ' appointed day ' seems for all practical purposes to be ' to-day '—i.e. the day on which Hermas receives the message, or rather on which he publishes it.   Even here there is of course a slight uncertainty, for different Christians will receive the message on different days.   But in *Vis.*, III, as a whole, Christians have already been divided up into classes with regard to penance, and there is a definite gap before ' the building of the tower is finished ' $(4^{2, 3})$ during which period repentance is still possible.   In *Sim.*, VIII, the proclamation of the message is evidently typified by the planting of the branches (2^8) ;   a time elapses (a ' few days,' 4^1), and even then we only have an intermediate visit of the Shepherd and Hermas ; for though some have already repented $(6^6, 7^5, 8^2, 9^2, 10^1, 10^3)$ there is yet time for others to repent $(6^6, 7^2, 8^{3, 4}, 9^4, 10^2)$.   In *Vis.*, IV, $2^5, 3^6$ the event to which attention is drawn is the ' great tribulation ' to come, and it seems clear that this has taken the place of the ' appointed day.'   The tribulation is presumably the expected, but still future, persecution, but there are eschatological traces about it which suggest that Hermas is thinking of it as the ' last day ' of the world.   In *Sim.*, IX, 7^7, the period between the proclamation (the visit of the ' Lord,' 6, 7) and the appointed day (the visit of the Shepherd and Hermas, and the completion of the tower, 7^7-10) is typified by the ' two days ' of 7^7 ; but the whole circumstances are eschatological, and the appointed day can be nothing but the end of the world.   There is indeed a slight inconsistency *here :* in the explanation of the parable (given on the ' appointed day ') the stones are divided into those who are (psychologically ?) incapable of repentance $(19^1, 26^5)$, *those who can yet repent* $(19^{2, 3}, 20^4, 21^4, 22^4, 23^5, 26^{2, 8})$ and those who have already repented $(22^3, 23^2, 26^8)$.   We have reverted, in fact, without

—designed, this time, both to conciliate the champions of severer discipline, and to frighten the laggards? If so, Hermas is legislating not for a single occasion but for perpetuity. He has grasped the fact that the Church's discipline is too penal—though how much too penal it is he does not recognize; and under cover of the special emergency is seeking to introduce a permanent mitigation. In any case, consciously or unconsciously, he was curiously successful in anticipating the course of events which actually took place.[1]

Between the time of the 'Pastor' and that of Tertullian (there is little clear evidence for the intervening years [2]) the Church gave permanent effect to Hermas' proposal: so much of the genuinely Christian and pastoral element was readmitted into a discipline which in the Roman communion had hitherto been vindictive only. Yet the new policy had to pay a price for its victory. Hermas proposed one post-baptismal reconciliation for *all* grave sins without exception (Tertullian has some hard words to say about him on this score); the Church excluded even from this strictly limited amnesty the three mortal sins of apostasy, adultery and homicide.[3] For them no reconciliation was allowed, though the sinner might be encouraged to submit to life-long discipline in the hope that God would forgive after death that from which the Church dared not absolve during life. For all other sins, one reconciliation only: for relapsing sinners no further hope on earth.[4]

notice, to the point of view of an intermediate visit, further borne out by the constant exhortations to repentance and stedfastness, and the explicit statement (32[1]) that the 'tower is still a-building.' For similar inconsistencies in *Sim.*, VIII, and the possibility that Hermas is here adding a liberalizing conclusion to an earlier rigorist parable, see Dibelius, *op. cit.*, pp. 587-589.

[1] Two further refinements of Hermas' teaching may be noted: (a) From time to time he refers to sinners who 'cannot repent' or 'have no repentance possible'—although apparently the appointed day has not come. Thus *Vis.*, III, 6[1], 7[2]; *Sim.*, VIII, 6[4], 8[2]; *Sim.*, IX, 19[1], 26[5]. They are variously described as 'apostates, traitors, and blasphemers,' 'working the works of the heathen,' 'sons of lawlessness,' 'lascivious,' 'those who have denied from the heart'; but in general the suggestion is *not* that by divine fiat they are excluded from the general amnesty. It is rather that they are as individuals psychologically incapable of repentance. This is clearly a sop to the rigorists; the offer of second penance will not encourage laxity, because there is no chance of the worst sinners taking advantage of it. (b) But Hermas hints at a further divine concession to the liberals as well. There is *some* hope left even for those who fail to repent before the appointed day, or who fall a second time. They can 'lie near the tower' (*Vis.*, III, 5[5]) 'in another and inferior place' (*ib.*, 7[7]); similarly in *Sim.*, VIII, 6[4], 7[3], 8[3], are mentioned sinners whose slowness at repentance has excluded them from the tower, but who may still 'dwell within the walls.' This *may* refer to purgatory, but is more probably an anticipation of that life-long penance without communion which even Tertullian as a Montanist will recommend to 'mortal' sinners, and which was customary later for relapsed penitents (*infra*, pp. 225, 506). In any case, Hermas is definitely suggesting that the divine mercy cannot be bound by ecclesiastical decisions.

[2] Such evidence as there is, is summarized *infra*, p. 224.

[3] *Infra*, p. 223.

[4] The question of 'confession' in relation to the discipline of penance will concern us later, *infra*, pp. 286 ff. In the meantime we may notice that

Of the principal effects of this terrible system, in which formalism and rigorism join hands, more will be said in the next chapter. Here only one point need be noticed. We have glanced at two simultaneous developments : the one, that steady elaboration of the Christian code by which more and more offences were disentangled from one another and placarded as grave sin ; the other, that by which the disciplinary weapon of penance and excommunication was brought into effective and tyrannical use—a use entirely different from that to which it is normally put in the New Testament. What resulted from the convergence of these two movements ? First of all, as was suggested above, a wholly wrong attitude towards ethical principles or maxims. Less and less are they thought of as means to secure the purity of life which achieves, and the energy of service which retains and attests, the vision of God. More and more they become mere conditions of membership in a society where external conformity will be rewarded with assured salvation. Attention is concentrated upon law rather than upon life ; actions become more important than motives ; obedience takes the place

---

the New Testament and the Apostolic Fathers urge the confession of sins on occasion from the pastoral point of view. It is, for example, the prerequisite of John's baptism (Mk. 1^5, Mt. 3^6), and presumably was required for Christian baptism as well, being covered by the ' repentance ' of Acts 2^{38}, 3^{19}. It thus became the root from which grew the later ' renunciation of the devil' (Brightman in Swete, *Church and Ministry*, p. 343).—A voluntary confession on the part of some ' who already believed ' is mentioned in Acts 19^{18}, and something of the same kind happened at Corinth (2 Cor. 7^{11}). 1 Jn. 1^9 makes confession a condition of forgiveness, but does not say whether to God or to man ; Jas. 5^{16} recommends ' confession to one another,' but whether as a condition of obtaining physical restoration to health, or as a spiritual counsel, is not clear ($\iota a\theta\hat{\eta}\tau\epsilon$ is ambiguous). I am inclined to think the ' one another ' to be a delicate euphemism for ' the presbyters ' (cp. *Did.*, 15^3, 1 *Clem.*, 56^2, *supra*, p. 166, and Acts 19^{38}, for similar circumlocutions) ; in that case we have a definite injunction to something very like sacramental confession, but nothing is said as to discipline. Clement of Rome knows of a corporate confession of sin before the liturgy (1 *Clem.* 60^{1-3}) ; it may be this to which *Didaché* refers in 4^{14} : ' Thou shalt confess thy transgressions *in Church*, and shalt not come to thy prayer in an evil conscience ' (*Barn.*, 19^{12} and *Ap. Const.*, vii, 14, omit the ' in Church '). Similarly *Did.*, 14^1—' On the Lord's day of the Lord come together and break bread and give thanks ($\epsilon\dot{\upsilon}\chi a\rho\iota\sigma\tau\dot{\eta}\sigma a\tau\epsilon$), having first confessed your sins ' (MS. $\pi\rho\sigma\epsilon\xi\sigma\mu\sigma\lambda\sigma\gamma\eta\sigma\dot{a}\mu\epsilon\nu\sigma\iota$; but read $\pi\rho\sigma\epsilon\xi\sigma\mu\sigma\lambda$.). Other (general) references to the confession of sins are 1 *Clem.*, $51^{1,3}$, 52^1, 2 *Clem.*, 8^3, 13^1, 16^1. In none of these is confession *to men* indicated, although in 1 *Clement* the idea of discipline lies of course in the background. In none of them, on the other hand, is it ruled out ; for 1 *Clem.*, 52^1 (' The Lord desires nothing of anyone except that confession be made *to Him* ') merely implies that confession to men is not universally obligatory ; and 56^1 (' That they may submit, not unto us, but unto the will of God '), in the same way, means that the only *motive* for confession should be the ' fear of the Lord.' What is clear is that, quite apart from all question of discipline, confession to God (which did not exclude the assistance of man in hearing the confession) was constantly urged upon the primitive Christian. It thus provided a permanent background of thought and practice from which sacramental ' confession ' could emerge later when disciplinary penance broke down (*infra*, pp. 286 ff.). For ' congregational' confessions in the Middle Ages see H. C. Lea, *Auricular Confession and Indulgences*, i, p. 206.

of communion with God as the mainspring of the Christian life ; outward submission rather than inward spontaneity is what is expected of the believer.

In the second place, those lesser sins for which the code did not prescribe the discipline of penance are steadily ignored by all but the most saintly. We should anticipate as the result of these developments an immediate deterioration of the moral standard of the community, with a widespread dominance of hypocrisy and purely formalist observance. Later centuries were to witness phenomena of just this character springing from just this cause ; Jerome frames a terrible indictment against the Roman Christendom of his day. But the first and second centuries are relatively free from such a catastrophe : a high standard of Christian conduct is still in general observance. The reason is not far to seek. A new danger—delayed, as was suggested in the last chapter, but delayed for a time alone, by the apostolic doctrine of the vision of God—forced itself into the cognizance of the Church ; a danger which by its more spiritual character created graver problems, and at the same time rallied formalism for a time to the standard and service of Christian spirituality. That danger was the incoming tide of rigorism.

LECTURE IV.

RIGORISM.

Acts xv. 10—'Now therefore why tempt ye God, to put a yoke upon the necks of the disciples, which neither our fathers nor we were able to bear?'

I. THE BEGINNINGS OF MONASTICISM.

THE steady development of formalism in the self-organizing Christian Church, to which the last lecture was devoted, had the deepest possible effect upon the *character* of the Christian code. It decided once for all, in fact (and the decision was epoch-making), that a code there should be, enforced by the corporate action of the whole community, and not a mere catena of edifying and instructive sentiments. On the *content* of the code it had a lesser influence, but one which, though it may fairly be called accidental, was fraught with grave dangers. Actions and external conformity, rather than motives and inner acceptance, tended to become the distinguishing characteristics of the Christian; and ceremonial and moral precepts of very diverse character were in process of welding into a single homogeneous whole. In such conditions, it was only too natural that those factors which distinguished Christian morality from contemporary social standards should be relegated to the background, their places being taken by duties which would cause no effort to the worldling, and evoke no mockery from his friends. An almost mechanical rule of almsgiving for example, supplanted in many minds all other precepts as the primary duty of the Christian, and the one which availed more than any other to secure his salvation.[1] The result of this whole process may be seen in Jerome's disturbing picture of Christian Rome in the fourth century.

With many other satirists, ancient and modern alike, Jerome fixes on widows as the victims of his scorn. He pictures these Christian ladies parading the city in their sedans, gaily dressed and buxom to the view, with trains of eunuchs before them—as though they were looking for husbands, rather than mourning them.[2] He

---

[1] *Supra*, p. 131; and for the worldliness of Eastern Christians cp. Joan. Chrysost., *adv. opp. vit. mon.*, iii, 7, etc.

[2] Hieron., *ep.* 22, 16 (ed. Vall. = *MPL.*, xxii—all references are to this edition).

describes their salons, filled with obsequious clergy, each of whom, on taking his leave, receives a delicate contribution from the lady— ostensibly, no doubt, for the needs of his parish, but actually, Jerome suggests, a *pourboire* in recognition of his polite attentions.[1] The levée over, he concludes, the widow who claims the homage due to those who are ' widows indeed,' relaxes over an immoderate supper, and so to bed—' to dream of the apostles.' [2] All harmless enough perhaps : but purely formal—so much official widowhood, with no attempt to realize the ideal which the Church still set before the widows as a recognised class ; [3] so much conventional alms- giving, with no care for the destination at which the gifts arrive ; a mechanical act of recollection at bedtime, so that you may ' dream of the apostles '—and that is all.

As with the widows, so with the clergy. They are placarded as scented fops ; curled and oiled Assyrian bulls, their fingers heavy with jewels,—tiptoeing gingerly across the muddy streets from one suspicious assignation to another ; [4] newsmongers and charlatans, who by the broadest of hints secure as perquisites any trifle of lace or marqueterie that tickles their fancy in the houses that they visit.[5] Everywhere there is luxury, only thinly dis- guised by the fact that the money is spent on *pièces de dévotion*. Parchments are dyed purple, gold is melted into lettering, manu- scripts are decked with jewels, while ' Christ lies at the door, naked and dying.' [6] Even charity itself is regulated by rule. ' Only the other day,' Jerome writes, ' I saw the noblest lady in Rome giving alms at S. Peter's—with her own hand too, that she might appear more religious—a coin to each of the poor.' An old woman ' full of years and rags, ran forward to receive a second dole ; but when her turn came she received not a penny—only a blow heavy enough to draw blood from her guilty veins.' [7]

Jerome himself had a very different ideal, of which he may fairly be called the first great literary champion. He is the most rhetorical of western rigorists ; hence his satirical condemnation of contemporary scandals is to be accepted only with reserve. But its vehemence is evidence—as striking as could be wished—of the

---

[1] Hieron., *ep.* 22, 16.

[2] *Ib.*, ' post coenam dubiam, apostolos somniant.' The reference in the ' coena dubia ' is to Terence, *Phormio*, 342.

[3] ' Widows ' were both a responsibility and a grade in the early Church. References to the support of widows as a primary duty, not merely of the individual Christian but also of the community as a whole, are innumerable. Distinct from these general beneficiaries of Christian charity were (a) the ' order ' of Church widows as a kind of ecclesiastical officials, for which special qualifications were required (1 Tim. 5[9, 10]) and special duties established; and (b) the ' order ' of widows as an ascetic class, ' vowed ' to widowhood as virgins were to celibacy. See generally *DCA.*, ii, pp. 2033 ff. ; A. Harnack, *Expansion of Christianity* (E. tr.), i, pp. 197, 198.

[4] Hieron., *ep.* 22, 28.

[5] *Ib.*, cp. also *ep.* 52 (ad *Nepotianum*—a rule of life for clergy) for instances of clerical depravity.

[6] *Ib.*, 32.   [7] *Ib*

spirit which was most influential in hindering that growth of laxity which is almost inevitable where codification has gone fast and far. The 'sternness of the gospel'[1] is a phrase in which Jerome sums up his whole message. Consider his picture of that which seemed to him the ideal Christian life, as he himself had lived it for a time :—

> ' I dwelt in the desert, in the vast solitude which gives the hermit his savage home, parched by the burning sun. . . . Sackcloth disfigured my unshapely limbs, and my skin from long neglect became as black as the Ethiopian's. Tears and groans were every day my portion ; if drowsiness chanced to overcome my struggles against it, my bare bones, which hardly held together, clashed against the ground. Of my food and drink I say nothing : for even in sickness the solitaries have nothing but cold water, and to eat one's food cooked is looked upon as self-indulgence. . . . My face was pale and my frame chilled with fasting. . . . I do not blush to avow my abject misery ; rather I lament that I am not now as then I was.'[2]

To his correspondent, a noble Roman lady, he commends a life as like this as is possible in the metropolis ; one which will reproduce its rigours without drawing attention to eccentricities laudable in the desert, but ostentatious in the city :—[3]

> ' Avoid wine as you would avoid poison ' (8) ;—' an empty stomach and fevered lungs are indispensable for the preservation of chastity ' (11) ;—' let your companions be women pale and thin with fasting ; rarely go out of the house ' (17) ;—' nightly water your couch with your tears ' (18) ;—' give away your property ; it is now no longer yours ' (31) ;—' what saint has ever won his crown without contending for it ? ' (39).

Eustochium, the Roman virgin, was allowed by Jerome to remain at home and practise asceticism in her mother's house.[4]

---

[1] ep. 77, 3, ' evangelii vigor.' Jerome actually uses the phrase of the prohibition against the marriage of divorced persons ; but it has a wider application.

[2] ep. 22, 7. The passage gives a vivid account of the psychological temptations inevitable in the hermit's life. In a later paragraph of the letter (§ 30) occurs the famous story of Jerome's vision of his judgment by God (' Ciceronianus es, non Christianus '), and his solemn renunciation of all such traffic.

[3] ep. 27. With the whole of this letter to Eustochium should be compared the much later one (ep. 130) to Demetrias.

[4] The starting-point of the ascetic movement in the West—apart from such sporadic manifestations as are mentioned below—was the visit of Athanasius with his two Egyptian companions, Ammon and Isidore, to Rome in A.D. 339, which inspired Marcella to a life of domestic asceticism (Hieron., ep. 127, 5 (Vallarsi)). It was not till ' many years after ' that ' first Sophronia, and then others, followed Marcella's example ' (ib.). Of the two monks, Isidore showed himself very much the more affable (on Ammon, Socr., HE., iv, 23 ; per contra, Isidore, Pallad., Hist. Laus., 1, 4), and the fact that his sisters were at the head of a community of seventy nuns (Palladius, ut sup.) was no doubt Marcella's particular inspiration. Marcellina, sister of Ambrose, professed virginity in A.D. 352 (Ambrose,

The priest Heliodorus, on the other hand, is bidden to break away even from that slender compromise with the world :—

> ' Should your little nephew hang on your neck, pay no regard to him. Should your mother with ashes on her hair, and garments rent, show you the breasts at which she nursed you, heed her not. Should your father prostrate himself on the threshold, trample him underfoot and go your way. With dry eyes fly to the standard of the cross. In such cases cruelty is the only true kindness. . . . The love of God and the fear of hell will easily break such bonds.' [1]

Fabiola, one of the austere circle of Roman matrons to whom Jerome acted as spiritual guide, found this letter so congenial to her ardent spirit as to learn it by heart.[2] Elsewhere Jerome draws a picture of the ' breaking of the bonds '—the departure of the widow Paula from her orphaned children when she set out for the desert :—

> ' The sails were set, and the strokes of the oars carried the vessel into the deep. On the shore the little Toxotius stretched forth his hands in entreaty ; while Rufina, now grown up, with silent sobs besought her mother to wait till she should be married. But still Paula's eyes were dry, as she turned them heavenwards. She overcame her love for her children by her love for God.' [3]

Other examples of a quite unnatural renunciation of all domestic affection were well known and applauded in Jerome's circle.[4] ' My prayer,' cried the same famous Paula, ' is that I may die a beggar, not leaving a penny to my daughter, and wrapped in a borrowed shroud.' [5] So successfully did she thus subordinate

---

de virg., iii, 1). H. Leclerq (*DALC.*, ii, col. 3177) identifies with her the Marcellina who in A.D. 384 was a member of Marcella's colony on the Aventine (Hieron., *ep.* 45, 7). To the same community belonged Asella, perhaps Marcella's sister (Hieron., *ep.* 24, 4), who devoted herself to asceticism from her twelfth year (*ib.*). Paula and Eustochium joined the colony, under Jerome's influence, in or about A.D. 382 (Hieron., *ep.* 127, 5). Melania the elder, at first Jerome's friend, later (on account of her championship of Rufinus) to be called ' as black in perfidy as in name ' (Hieron., *ep.* 133, 3), was a member of the saint's earlier ascetic community at Aquileia (A.D. 370-373) ; Melania the younger, her granddaughter, healed the breach by attaching herself to Jerome and Paula's institutions at Bethlehem in 414. For the rapid spread of the movement in the West after A.D. 380, Leclerq in *DALC.*, ii, coll. 3180 ff.

[1] *ep.* 14, 2, 3. The whole letter is important. Cp. Cass., *Inst.*, v, 32, *Coll.*, xxiv, 9, 13, for similar inhuman renunciations ; and contrast Chrys., *de sac.*, i, 5, where his mother's tears have the effect of retaining Chrysostom in secular life. A sane principle is enunciated by Palladius, *Hist. Laus.*, 6 :—' It is quite possible for a man without neglecting his soul to be influenced by godly consideration for the temporal needs of his kinsfolk ; but when a man subordinates his whole soul to the interests of his kin, he comes under condemnation, reckoning his soul " unto vanity." '

[2] *ep.* 77, 9.   [3] *ep.* 108, 6.

[4] References for further examples, O. Zöckler, *Kritische Geschichte der Askese*, pp. 228, 229.

[5] Hieron., *ep.* 108, 15.

domestic responsibility to indiscriminate charity that, in Jerome's
words, 'she obtained her wish at last ; and died, leaving her daughter overwhelmed with a mass of debt.'[1]   Even Jerome had been
startled by her altruistic prodigality, perhaps because he himself
was one of the creditors on whom she drew.[2]   But he asserts
quite roundly that he was wrong in urging caution ; and it is with
the utmost complacency that he adds, 'These debts Eustochium
still owes ; and indeed cannot hope to pay off by her own exertions.
Only the mercy of Christ can free her from them.'[3]

Apathy towards a death in the family always excited Jerome's
warmest approval ; where the death was that of a wife or husband
he asked for unstinted rejoicing.   Blaesilla, Paula's daughter and
Eustochium's sister, lost her husband after seven months of married
life.   'Unhappy girl,' Jerome writes, his morbid taste for epigram
unblunted even by this tragedy; 'You have lost, at one and the
same time, the crown of virginity and the joys of wedlock.'   Still,
the occasion demands a word of comfort ; and he bids her 'take
heart and rejoice' because she has now, 'as a widow,' the opportunity of exercising 'chastity of the lower order.'[4]   Three months'
asceticism under Jerome's guidance brought her to her grave ; and
Paula her mother suffered a severe rebuke for showing excessive
grief ; for what Jerome would be prepared to condone in an 'average
Christian woman' is intolerable in a recluse.   'The Lord is my
witness,' he adds, 'that I address you now as though I were standing
at His judgment seat. . . . Yours are detestable tears, sacrilegious
tears, the tears of an unbeliever.'[5]

As an example of better things he quotes Melania, a lady with
whom he afterwards quarrelled bitterly.   Before her dead husband
had been laid in the tomb, she lost at one stroke two of her sons :—

> 'Would you not suppose that in her frenzy she would have
> unbound her hair, and rent her clothes, and torn her breast ?
> Yet not a tear fell from her eyes.   Motionless she stood there ;
> then casting herself at the feet of Christ she smiled, as though
> she held Him with her hands.   "Henceforth, Lord," she said,
> "I will serve Thee more readily, for Thou has freed me from
> a great burden."'[6]

The lawyers, in short, were not the only party in the primitive
Church.   Over against them were ranged the martyrs and ascetics ;
and though occasionally—as in the cases of Marcion and Tertullian
—both schools of thought coalesced to produce systems full of the
most sinister possibilities, in general they were opposed.   The lawyer

---

[1] Hieron., *ep.* 108, 15.
[2] *ep.* 66, 14.   Jerome's funds supplied the material for Paula's convent
at Bethlehem.
[3] *ep.* 108, 15.   [4] *ep.* 22, 15.   [5] *ep.* 39, 5.
[6] *Ib.*, 4.   But the story is a pious invention—a much more natural
account of Melania's bereavement and its consequences is given by Paulinus
of Nola (*ep.* 29, 8 f. ; *MPL.*, lxi, col. 316).

may not have set himself deliberately to conciliate the world, though his preoccupation with codification and casuistry made that result almost inevitable.   But the martyr defied the world, and the ascetic anathematized it ; and their influence in the Church stultified to some extent the dangerous tendencies of formalism.   Not till the cessation of persecution in the fourth century deprived the Church of her opportunities of martyrdom, whilst new developments, in organization and theology alike, circumscribed the activities of asceticism, did the real summer of worldly Christianity set in.

Reitzenstein holds, with some justice, that the confessors and martyrs of the early Church claimed and received the honour due to supermen.[1]   His further conclusion that the mere fact of suffering for the Name was regarded as final evidence of a special outpouring of the Spirit upon them, and that they thereby became in a semi-official sense ' pneumatikoi,' or ' spiritual persons,' independent of and superior to the hierarchy, is more questionable.   Nor has Reitzenstein proved his case that primitive monasticism arose from a desire to emulate the heroism of the confessor, and so to achieve an equal position of spiritual autocracy, by substituting the anchorite's cell for the dungeon, and the horrors of the wilderness for the pangs of torture.   Domestic asceticism, as we shall see, was well known in the Church before persecution became widespread. Nevertheless, the heroic endurance of the confessor may well have stimulated the more eager among those who had not suffered for the Name to emulate him in mortifying the flesh ; whilst his high renown and even higher claims [2] suggested to men of baser mould the possibility of achieving, even at the cost of some discomfort, the like position.   It is at all events a suggestive fact that the beginnings of the monastic movement coincide with the period of the last persecutions.

At the end of the second century of the Christian era Tertullian could say categorically, ' Among us are no Brahman or Indian gymnosophists, no forest hermits or anchorites ; nay, we are mindful of all that we owe to God our Maker, and condemn no enjoyment of what He has made.' [3]   The dictum is surprising in view of the writer's known attitude towards imperial institutions, marriage, culture and the blessings of civilization.   But it shows at least that nothing approaching a systematic over-valuation of asceticism was yet known in the Church.   A hundred years later the situation had

---

[1] For Reitzenstein's theory as a whole see *infra*, additional note G, pp. 495 ff.

[2] The claim of the confessors to decide authoritatively that a lapsed Christian might (and must) be readmitted to communion, is well known. The principal documents, from S. Cyprian's correspondence, are collected in O. D. Watkins, *History of Penance*, pp. 143-167.

[3] Tert., *apol.*, 42.   He adds, ' We abjure neither forum nor market-place nor baths nor books nor factories nor inns nor fairs nor the exchange.   We sojourn with you in the world ; we sail with you, war with you, farm with you,' etc.   For the sentiment cp. *ep. ad Diognet.*, 5¹—' Christians are distinguished from their fellow-men neither by dwelling-place nor by speech nor by manners ' ; *ep. Barnab.*, 4¹⁰—' Do not lead a solitary life in retirement, as though you were already justified.'

altered profoundly. It was probably about A.D. 270[1] that Antony, a boy of eighteen, just orphaned by the death of his parents, was moved to think of the 'apostolic life,' and to contrast it with his own comfortable existence. Twice at the reading of the gospel in Church there came what seemed to him a personal message :—the first said, ' Go and sell all that thou hast ' ; the second, ' Take no thought for the morrow.' To give effect to the message was not difficult. In the very neighbourhood of his Egyptian home-village were groups of ascetics attempting to hold aloof from the world in spirit if not in person. With their approval, therefore, and perhaps on their advice, he disposed of all his possessions to the poor, and established his sister (for whom he had been left responsible) in a home for virgins.[2]

The neighbouring Christians, like-minded with himself, were edified by his proceedings, and spoke of him as Theophiles—the friend of God. But he himself was dissatisfied. First of all he withdrew to the tombs outside the village, and there established himself ; later to a ruined hill-fort in the wilderness, where nourishment was passed in to him only once in six months. Here he remained for twenty years in solitude, whilst round his retreat grew up a band of imitators and disciples—numbered certainly by hundreds, perhaps even by thousands.[3] There followed a brief interlude of six or seven years, during which he directed his disciples in the hermit-life ; then came his final withdrawal into the solitude of the inner wilderness, which he never left again.

Fasting, poverty, celibacy, solitude, are the means of renunciation attributed to Antony. Prayer, with such minimum of physical labour as would suffice to secure the bare necessities of life, was his occupation. What was their purpose ? Athanasius' biography of the Father of the Monks has often been attacked as unauthentic ; the existence of Antony himself has been denied. But not even Weingarten, the most destructive critic in this matter, is prepared to date the document later than the 'sixties of the fourth

---

[1] The date is fixed by reference to his death, at the age of 105, in A.D. 356—evidence for this summarized A. Robertson, *Athanasius* (*LNP-NF.*), p. 218, n. 16. The statements of Abbot Piamun in Cassian, *Coll.*, xviii, 5, 6, to the effect that a regulated cœnobitic life *preceded* the anchorite experiments of ' Paul and Antony ' in the history of the Church, must be regarded as a pious fiction, based probably on the exaggeration of such early phenomena as the Hierakian group (*infra*, p. 184), and heightened by the dogmatic conception, which certainly obtained in Schenoudi's institution, among the friends of Cassian, and (probably through Cassian's influence) in Gaul in the fifth century, that anchoritism was a higher form of asceticism than cœnobitism, which might be allowed to the successful ' athlete ' after he had undergone a preliminary discipline in the cœnobium (*infra*, pp. 201, 525).

[2] Ath., *Vit. Ant.*, 3—not necessarily nor probably a fully organized convent ; perhaps only an orphanage, or ' simple refuge ' (H. Leclerq, *DALC.*, ii, col. 3181), such as that at Tortona (' monasterium ') early in the fourth century, which the bishop Innocent founded for his sister Innocentia (Boll., *AS.*, Apr. ii, p. 484—the fuller description quoted by Leclerq is from Ughelli's *Italia Sacra* only, and apparently without earlier authority).

[3] *Vit. Ant.*, 14.

century.[1] The sermon which occupies chapters 16-43 of the 'Vita'
is evidence, therefore, for the views of that century on the purpose
of the eremitic life ; and the absence of any sign of controversial
motive is clear proof that the same views had been current for long
enough.[2]

Of the vision of God the sermon says nothing ; but this, though
at first surprising, is no argument against its authenticity. Athanasius knew—none better—that the beatific vision is the goal of life :
the fine peroration to the ' de Incarnatione ' is full of it. We are
to search the scriptures, to learn more of the 'second glorious and
truly divine appearance of Christ to us.' For that search ' an
honourable life is needed, and a pure soul, and the virtue which is
according to Christ,'—just as we must prepare ourselves if we wish
to ' see the light of the sun,' or make a journey to ' see a city or
country.' Such a life will enable the Christian to 'receive what is
laid up for the saints in the kingdom of heaven ; which "eye hath
not seen, nor ear heard, nor hath entered into the heart of man." ' [3]
The whole argument of the ' Contra Gentes ' turns on the same
doctrine ; the soul is in its own nature destined for and capable of
the direct beatific vision,—it has no need of heathen idols as a poor
substitute.[4]

Furthermore, Athanasius lays special stress upon the relation
between asceticism and the vision. In his first festal letter
(A.D. 329) he writes of the Lenten abstinence :—

> ' That which I am about to say is wonderful ; yea, it is of
> those things which are very miraculous ; yet not far from the
> truth, as ye may be able to learn from the sacred writings.
> That great man, Moses, when fasting, conversed with God, and
> received the law. The great and holy Elijah, when fasting,
> was thought worthy of divine visions, and at last was taken up
> like Him Who ascended into heaven. And Daniel when fasting,
> although a very young man, was entrusted with the mystery,
> and he alone understood the secret things of the King and was
> thought worthy of divine visions . . . [So] the contemplation
> of God, and of the Word which is from Him, suffices to nourish

---

[1] Weingarten, *Ursprung des Mönchtums*, p. 15. What can be said
against the authenticity and historicity of the treatise will be found summarized in H. M. Gwatkin, *Studies of Arianism*, pp. 102-107 ; spirited and
on the whole successful defences on both points, O. Zöckler, *Askese und
Mönchtum*, i, pp. 188-192 ; A. Robertson, *Athanasius* (*LNP-NF.*), pp.
188-193.

[2] Cp. K. Holl, *Enthusiasmus und Bussgewalt*, p. 141.

[3] Ath., *de Inc.*, 57.

[4] Note esp. *c. gent.*, 2—' God made man able to see and know the Real
by likeness to Jesus Christ '; ' giving him an apprehension of His own
eternal nature '; ' association with God '; ' the pure soul sees the Father's
image, the Son, the Word, above all corporeal vision, and is rapt in amazement '; ' the clean soul sees ' (or ' reflects ') ' God as in a mirror'; 4—loss
of the vision in the terrestrial Paradise the cause of the Fall ; 8—' the mirror
in the soul by which we see what the soul ought to see ' (cp. 30) ; 20-27,
35-38, the witness of nature to God ; 40-44, the Word seen in the universe.

> those who hear, and stands to them in the place of all food. . . .
> Wherefore, my beloved, having our souls nourished with this
> divine food, with the Word, according to the will of God, and
> fasting bodily in things external, let us keep this great and
> saving feast as becomes us.' [1]

If then the sermon says nothing of the beatific vision, the
reason may well be that Antony himself was reticent about it.
This seems to be the case. Athanasius says of Antony that he
' eagerly endeavoured to make himself fit to appear before God, to
become pure in heart, and ever ready to submit to His counsel and
to Him alone.' [2] The hermit, therefore, seems to have thought of
the vision as the end of life ; but its fruition is reserved till after
death. To prepare for this vision is the object of his asceticism.
On the other hand, he asserts and expects that ' *visions of holy
ones* ' will be the reward of asceticism here and now. The visions
recorded of him are of that crude kind of clairvoyance so common in
romantic hagiography ; but the experiences to which his sermon
points are of a far higher order. And obviously they are the most
precious thing in his life.

The sermon is in the main a warning against, and an exposition
of, the wiles employed by demons in their assaults upon the hermits. [3]
The first demonic suggestion (naturally enough) is that of sinful
thoughts (c. 23). The second attack—if this fails—can easily be
recognized, from Antony's description, as the insinuation of phobias
such as would be likely to arise in the complete loneliness of the
desert (cc. 23 ff.)—especially if the hermit's imagination were nur-
tured, to some extent, on such realistic descriptions of hell as occur
with repellent frequency in Christian apocalyptic writings. Thirdly,
the demons attempt to ' gain the hearer's confidence ' by foretelling
the future—that is, we must suppose, to lead him off into necro-
mantic practices. Any such ambition of prescience on the part of
the hermit Antony strongly condemns (cc. 31-33) ; and by contrast he describes the visions which the Christian can entertain
without fear :—

> ' The vision of the holy ones is not fraught with distraction.
> . . . It comes so quietly and gently that immediately joy,
> gladness and courage arise in the soul. For the Lord Who is
> our joy is with them, the power of God the Father. The

---

[1] Ath., *ep. fest.*, i, 6, 7 (A. Robertson, *Athanasius* (*LNP-NF.*, iv)
p. 508).
[2] Ath., *Vit. Ant.*, 7 ; cp. also c. 14—Antony comes out of his cave ' as
an inspired initiate from a sanctuary ' ; c. 34—' the pure soul is clear-
sighted, and can see more and further than the demons ' ; c. 60, after
Antony's vision of Amon, ' they marvelled at his purity of heart.'
[3] On Antony's demonic visitants, *Vit. Ant.*, cc. 4, 8, 9 ; for Pachomius,
Vit. Pac., 17 (Rosweyde, *MPL.*, lxxiii, coll. 240, 241). Some very happy
observations on the humorous element in monastic demonology will be found
in H. Bremond's introduction to J. Bremond, *Les Pères du Désert* (1923),
pp. xxvi-xxx ; cp. *ib.*, pp. xxxi-xxxv, on stories of the hermits and animals.

thoughts of the soul remain unruffled and undisturbed, so that, as in a flash of light, it beholds by itself those who appear.   The love of all that is divine and of the things to come possesses it, and willingly it would be wholly joined with them, if it could depart along with them.   But if, being men, some fear the vision of the good, those who appear immediately take fear away ; as Gabriel did to Zacharias, as the angel did who appeared to the women at the holy sepulchre. . . .

' Such then is the nature of the vision of the holy ones. . . . Whenever therefore ye have seen aught and are afraid, if your fear is immediately taken away and in the place of it comes joy unspeakable, cheerfulness, courage, renewed strength, calmness of thought and all those things I named before, boldness and love towards God, take heart and pray.   For joy and calmness of soul reveal the holiness of him who is present.' [1]

Here, in the climax of Antony's sermon, all the features of the New Testament doctrine are reproduced, with just the one personal peculiarity that his experience takes the form rather of ' visions of the holy ones ' than of the vision of God.   The goal of life is to achieve communion with the holy.   It can be attained in measure and from time to time even in this life.   Its condition is purity of heart ; its issue an enhancement of all the highest virtues of the soul.   We may question whether an asceticism as rigorous as Antony's was necessary—some will be disposed to ask whether it was even valid ; but if he has departed from the true Christian development in any respect at all, it is in this matter of the means alone.   As far as the end of the process is concerned, he is at one with the apostles.

It is not clear that Antony originated anything new in Christian asceticism, except perhaps—and this only for Egypt—that physical withdrawal from the world which Tertullian denied to be a Christian characteristic.[2]   Jerome composed a life of ' Paul the first hermit,' and ascribed to him a desert-residence of ninety years from A.D. 250-340.   But even in the author's own day the work was suspected as a pious fiction ; and one of the most level-headed of modern writers on primitive monasticism, Otto Zöckler, can do no more than point to the suggestive fact that the Decian persecution drove many Egyptian Christians into the wilderness.[3]   Paul may have been one of these ; but a compulsory flight and a voluntary acceptance of desert life are two very different things, and Zöckler's attempted vindication of Paul leaves Antony's originality unimpaired.

If in this one respect, however—and it is one whose importance, in the light of subsequent history, cannot well be over-estimated—

[1] Ath., *Vit. Ant.*, 35, 36 ; cp. *ib.*, 43.   In 36 *fin.* the visions are explicitly compared to Abraham's vision of God.

[2] It is not without significance that to Antony was attributed the famous maxim, ' the fish to the sea, the monk to the mountain,' *Vit. Ant.*, 85.

[3] See O. Zöckler, *Askese u. Mönchtum*, pp. 183, 184.

Antony was the originator of a new idea in Christianity, in other matters he did no more than follow a well-beaten track.[1] In Egypt itself two leaders of third-century asceticism are known by name, apart from Origen, whose personal predisposition in this direction did not apparently go so far as to make him the founder of an ascetic school. Of Pierius, an Alexandrian presbyter in the second half of the third century, little is recorded, except that he combined and advocated a life of complete poverty with one of philosophic culture.[2] But his contemporary, Hieracas, actually gathered a group of ascetics of both sexes at Leontopolis,—'none came to him,' says Epiphanius, 'save virgins, solitaries, celibates and widows.' Marriage of course was forbidden—Hieracas regarded the command of virginity as the distinctive condition which separated the New Covenant from the Old. It is more than probable that the Hieracians developed into a heretical sect with gnostic tendencies; the relationship between gnosticism and asceticism, as will appear, has always been a close one.[3]

For Syria in the third century two pieces of evidence are available. The pseudo-Clementine 'Letters to Virgins' are addressed to a body of wandering ascetics, bound to virginity, and presumably to poverty and homelessness as well.[4] The members (if we may so call them) of this fellowship were both male and female ; and it is clear from the warnings addressed to them that their vow of celibacy required practical reinforcement by a rigorous segregation of the sexes. They did not wholly withdraw from worldly intercourse, but their nomad life (apparently based on a nomad rule)

[1] At the same time we must agree with K. Holl (*Enthusiasmus u. Bussgewalt*, p. 146) that Antony substituted the idea of 'sanctification of the entire personality' for the 'isolated ascetic maxims' of his predecessors.

[2] Pierius is commemorated in the martyrologies on Nov. 4th. Eusebius, *HE.*, vii, 32, 27, says that he was 'distinguished for his life of extreme poverty and philosophic learning, was exceedingly diligent in the contemplation and exposition of divine things, and in public discourses in the Church.' Jerome (*de vir. ill.*, 76) adds that he was known as 'Origenes junior'; and quotes (*ep.* 49, 3) from his commentary on 1 Cor. 7[7] the words, 'In saying this Paul plainly preaches celibacy.' (The passage is interesting ; Jerome is defending himself against the indignation roused by his attack on Jovinian (*infra*, p. 238), and contrasts his own 'moderation' with Pierius' exaggeration.) Photius (*Cod.*, 119) says that he was head of the catechetical school, and suffered martyrdom ; also that his views on the Holy Spirit were less than orthodox.

[3] Practically the only authority for Hieracas and his followers is Epiphanius (*haer.*, 67) ; minor references are given in *DCB.*, iii, pp. 24, 25 (*s.v.*). Hieracas supported himself by calligraphy, at which he was expert, until his ninetieth year.

[4] These two letters (in a Syriac text) were discovered and published by Wetstein in 1752. A Latin version is contained in F. X. Funk, *Opera Patrum Apostolicorum*, ii, pp. 1-27 ; an English translation in the volume *The Writings of Methodius, etc.* (Ante-Nicene Christian Library), pp. 367-395. They are fully discussed by Harnack, *Sitzungsbericht der berl. Ak. d. Wissensch.* (1891), pp. 361-385. Other wandering communities were the Remoboth (Hieron., *ep.* 22, 34), Sarabaitae (Cassian, *Coll.*, xviii, 7), or 'gyrovagi' (Benedict, *Regula*, prol., where they are distinguished from the 'Sarabaites'). Their reputation was wholly unenviable.

forbade them to settle down, and even the occasional nights they spent in civilized communities were hedged about with ascetic restrictions. The male ascetic must select for his nightly dwelling, if possible, the house of a celibate like himself: failing that, one in which the householder was content to seclude his women-folk for the occasion. If the village to which he came was empty of male inhabitants, he must beg a lodging for the night from the eldest and most honourable woman there; if nightfall found him in a spot where one woman dwelt alone, he must flee from her as from a snake or a sin. All this of intercourse with Christians —in a heathen village the ascetic must be wise as a serpent and gentle as a dove, and specially on his guard against performing any Christian rites in public, ' that the name of the Lord be not blasphemed.'

Regulations of this kind are so formal as to suggest a somewhat academic origin: the pseudo-Clementine brotherhood was perhaps neither so imposing nor so numerous as the writer wished to imply. But Syria knew of other ascetic confraternities. One such, calling itself the ' Sons of the Covenant,' must have been an institution of some antiquity when Aphraates delivered his sixth homily to its address in or about A.D. 337;[1] ' Daughters of the Covenant' was the name of a corresponding society of women. Living in the midst of the world, the ' Sons of the Covenant' ' dwelt by themselves and not with the daughters of Eve '; Moses, Joshua, Elijah, Elisha, and the Baptist, are held up before their eyes as examples of celibates.

One step further back in the story of Christian asceticism brings us to Origen, whose personal practice was ascetic in the extreme;[2] and whose theory of asceticism was as fully developed as that of the ' Vita Athanasii,' the ' Banquet ' of Methodius,[3] or of Jerome himself. Celibacy to him stood almost in the same rank of saintliness as martyrdom;[4] and he insisted that earthly possessions should be reduced to the minimum.[5] ' When a man has learnt to despise the vanity of this world,' he writes, ' and has realized the perishable nature of the things that are passing away; when he has reached

---

[1] The homilies are published in a German translation in *TU.*, iii, 2 (1888); English translation in *LNP-NF.*, vol. xiii (*Gregory the Great*, part ii; *Ephraim Syrus, Aphraat*), pp. 362-375 (selected homilies only, but including the sixth); summaries in Zöckler, *Askese u. Mönchtum*, p. 182; and Leclerq, *DALC.*, ii, coll. 3139-3142. F. C. Burkitt (*Early Eastern Christianity*, pp. 125-142) argues that the Sons and Daughters of the Covenant were, up to Aphraates' time, the entire baptized Christian community, no married person being admitted to baptism. Thus the ' Sons of the Covenant ' did not become an ascetic group *within* the wider Christian community until the second half of the fourth century (*ib.*, p. 130). For the controversy on the point between R. H. Conolly and Dr. Burkitt, see *JTS.*, vi (1905), pp. 522-539; vii (1906), pp. 10-15. On the whole the evidence seems too slight to warrant so drastic a conclusion.

[2] Eus., *HE.*, vi, 3, 9-12.   [3] *Infra*, p. 187.

[4] *comm. in Rom.*, 9, 1 (*MPG.*, xiv, col. 1205).

[5] *hom. in Lev.*, 15, 2 (*GCSS.*, ' Origenes,' vi, p. 487).

the point of renouncing the world and all that is in it—then at length
he comes to contemplate and desire the things that are not seen but
are eternal.'[1]

Origen is the first Christian writer who can be quoted in direct
evidence for the lifelong vow of celibacy, to be taken, a century
later, with full liturgical celebration in the face of the Church.[2]   But
the widespread recognition of and reverence for celibates, male and
female, as a class, show that the vow must have been taken at a
much earlier date.   Even for Ignatius celibacy is a status to be
entered upon as solemnly as marriage, and both require the
bishop's consent.[3]   The ' cosmic mystery of the Church,' mentioned
by ' Didaché' in ambiguous language, which the true prophet is to
' handle aright,' ' without teaching others to do as he does,' is best
interpreted as a reference to deliberate and sustained virginity.[4]
The ' mystery ' is that the soul, like the Church, is the bride of
Christ, and therefore must avoid all earthly espousals ; but although the ' true prophet ' will conform to this mystery himself,
he will not impose it upon others.   The primitive homily known as
the second epistle of Clement is full of counsels of celibacy,[5] and

---

[1] *comm. in Cant., prol. (GCSS.,* 'Origenes,' viii, p. 78) ; cp. *hom. in
Lev.,* 11, 1.   Other passages illustrative of Origen's ascetic teaching will be
found in W. B. Bornemann, *In investiganda monachatus origine quibus de
causis ratio habenda sit Origenis,* pp. 18-22 (on poverty) ; 22-29 (on celibacy) ;
29-33 (on contemplation) ; 34-38 (on retirement).   Unfortunately the only
copy of this book to which I have had access lacks its annotations ; hence
it is all but impossible to verify its very numerous quotations.   On p. 40
Bornemann cites an interesting passage (*hom.* xv, 15 *in Mt.* 19 (*MPG.,*
xiii, coll. 1297-1300)) in which Origen quotes Acts 4[32 ff.], 5[1-10] in illustration
of Mt. 19[21], and suggests that rich Christians should be prepared, at the
bishop's request, to surrender their wealth, and invite others to join them
in a community where they will have all things in common.   This is a very
early anticipation of coenobitism.

[2] *in Lev. hom.,* 3, 4 ; the point is discussed at some length by Leclerq,
DALC., ii, coll. 3082, 3083 ; but he promises fuller treatment in the article
Vierges, which has not yet appeared.   The article ' Virgins ' in *DCA.,* ii,
pp. 2019-2022, is still useful ; cp. also H. Koch, *Virgines Christi, TU.,* xxxi
(1906).   The earliest explicit reference to a public ceremony appears to be
Basil, *ep.* 46, 2—the profession was made ' before God, angels and men.'
But the vow is constantly mentioned in the third and fourth centuries (for
references see authorities as above) ; and as early as Cyprian (*ep.* 62) canonical penalties were inflicted for its infringement.

[3] Ign., *ad Pol.,* 5[2]—The words ' if it be known further than the bishop '
imply that the bishop *must* be informed of the fact, as with espousals (*ib.*).
But on the alternative rendering of the clause, cp. *supra,* p. 147, n. 3.

[4] *Did.,* 11[11].   The ' mystery ' of the Church is that she is the ' unspotted '
or virgin bride of Christ (cp. 2 Cor. 11[2], Eph. 5[30], 2 *Clem.,* 14) ; this 'heavenly'
mystery has its ' worldly ' (' cosmic ') realization in the celibacy of believers.
So Harnack, Zöckler, Knopf.   A full discussion in H. Weinel, *Die Wirkungen
des Geistes u. der Geister,* pp. 131-138.

[5] I assume that this is the interpretation to be put upon the ' keep pure
the flesh ' of 2 *Clem.,* 8[4, 6], 9[3], 14[3], 15[1], cp. also 6[9], 7[6], 12[5].   For the phrase
Lightfoot adduces *Act. Paul. et Thecl.,* 5, 12, where the meaning is unmis-
takable.   So also is 1 *Clem.,* 38[2] (' He that is pure in the flesh, let him not
boast, knowing that it is Another who bestoweth his continence upon him ')
—the same thought as Ign., *ad Pol.,* 5[2].

Hermas himself has Encratite leanings.[1] In Justin's day there were many who for sixty or seventy years from their adolescence had remained celibate for Christ's sake ; only a few years later Athenagoras repeats Justin's statement, adding that the pledge (if we may call it a pledge) of celibacy is undertaken ' in the hope of a closer union with God.' [2] For Tertullian and Hippolytus, at the beginning of the third century, the ' continentes ' are as clearly marked a class as the clergy.[3]

The spirit of these domestic precursors of the monks may be learnt, as clearly as anywhere, from the writings of a contemporary of Antony's—Methodius, Bishop of Patara (or, less probably, Tyre) at the turn of the third and fourth centuries.[4] Plato and asceticism were his two greatest enthusiasms ; he honoured the first, and exalted the second, in a ' Symposium ' of ten virgins, who gather at a garden-banquet—(the garden furnished with scenery from the ' Phædrus ')—to praise not love but celibacy. The dialogue wavers between realism and allegorism in a confusing fashion. The virgins reach the garden of Virtue (Areté), their hostess, by a rough, steep and arduous path, typifying their asceticism. At the gate they receive what Antony would call ' a vision of a holy one '—a tall and beautiful woman walking along quietly, and gracefully clothed in a shining robe, as white as snow. ' Her beauty was something indescribable and divine ; modesty blended with majesty blooms in her face.' [5]

After this frankly allegorized opening, the story becomes realist again. Each of the virgins takes her turn in praising chastity. The book is stilted, its outlook narrow ; whole pages are plagiarized directly from Plato.[6] The teaching is rigorist in the extreme. One virgin, specially interested to find a place for the married in the kingdom of heaven, has a hard task of it with her fellows ; her

---

[1] See especially the emphasis upon ἐγκράτεια in Vis., I, 2[4]; II, 3[2]; III, 8[4] ; Mand., I[2] (in Mand., VIII, the conception is very much wider). Cp. also Vis., II, 2[3]—' thy wife who is also to be thy sister,' a clear reference to connubial abstinence (not contradicted by the ' remember thy wife' of Mand., IV, 1[1], which is simply a reminiscence of popular parænesis) ; and above all, Sim., IX, 11[3], which approves, at all events for allegorical purposes, of the dangerous practice of virgines subintroductæ (supra, p. 76).

[2] Justin, apol., 15 (cp. also 29) ; Athen., leg., 33. In both these passages the practice of second marriages is also condemned; similarly Tert., de monog., 15.

[3] Tert., apol., 9, 19 ; de pat., 13 ; de cult. fem., ii, 9 ; ad ux., i, 6 ; Hipp., fragm. in Prov. (MPG., x, col. 628), where the ' seven divine orders ' are enumerated as the prophets, apostles, martyrs, priests, ascetics, saints, and righteous. For Ebionite asceticism see PRE., v, pp. 125-128 ; DTC., iv, coll. 1987-1995 ; DALC., iv, coll. 1703-1709.

[4] Methodius was an active assailant of Origenistic doctrines, though according to Socrates (HE., vi, 13) he ended by expressing warm approval of their author. There was at all events no difference between them as regards asceticism.

[5] Method., Symp., prol.

[6] Especially Symp., viii, 1-3, which is wholly dependent upon the Phædrus—see the parallels in A. Jahn, Methodius Platonizans (1865), pp. 46-54.

arguments are criticized with a severity which suggest that the author, though he felt bound to state them, could barely find it in his heart to make them his own.[1]   Little is said of any experience of God in this life.   The end of virginity is to attain ' likeness to God,' to ' escape from corruption,' or to enter upon a ' spiritual marriage ' in the next world.[2]   One of the virgins ventures to derive ' parthenia ' (virginity) from ' partheia ' (wholly divine),[3] and so to make deification the goal of life.   With all this, however, there is an extraordinary spirit of joy and spontaneous exaltation [4] throughout the book, which rings true to the New Testament ; and a real emphasis upon moral excellence, though of a slightly negative character.

In a tiny fragment of Socratic dialogue, with which the ' Banquet ' closes, a new question is introduced—Is it better to be naturally free from sinful temptations, or to have them yet resist them manfully ?   The former condition seems at first to win the higher praise :—

> ' These are they whom God makes gods in the beatitudes ; they who believe in Him without doubt.   And He says that they shall look upon God with confidence, because they bring in nothing that darkens or confuses the eye of the soul for the beholding of God.'

Despite this, Methodius selects for the highest praise those who remain pure against grievous temptation.   They are the best pilots of their own soul, the best physicians, the best builders, the best athletes.   The man who struggles most successfully against the solicitations of passion is the man who most deserves to see God with confidence.[5]

We may return from this brief review of the practice and theory of Antony's precursors to Antony himself.   His one great innovation, as we have seen, was to complete the ascetic's detachment from the world by drawing him into the desert.   The novelty had results of epoch-making significance.   Ascetics henceforth did not merely form a class ; they became class-conscious.   The free associations of hermits in the lauras of lower Egypt or the Nitrian desert, and still more the organization of the cœnobitic system in upper Egypt by Pachomius,[6] made it possible to develop asceticism into

---

[1] Method., *Symp.*, ii and iii.

[2] See *Symp.*, i, 5 ; iv, 2 ; iv, 5 ; vi, 5, etc.

[3] *Symp.*, viii, 1 (*v.l.*, ' partheia ')—this is a device to make virginity the antecedent condition of that communion with God spoken of in the *Phædrus*.

[4] Cp. particularly the hymn, xi, 2, with its refrain, ' I keep myself pure for Thee, my Bridegroom ; and with flaming torch come forth to meet Thee.'

[5] Method., *Symp.*, xi, 3.

[6] *Infra*, pp. 258-262.   It must not be inferred, however, that the older type of domestic asceticism did not live on.   It is to be found in a particularly attractive form in Gaul in the fifth century, as in the ' Little Gidding ' which Sulpicius Severus, with his mother-in-law, Bassula, established at Primuliacum.   Even at Nola, Paulinus' wife Therasia resided with

an art and even a virtuosity. Companionship in austerities bred competition ; austerity itself, in Zöckler's effective phrase,[1] gave place to atrocity.

It would be superfluous to tell again at length the mournful story of exaggerated self-outrage which became the ideal, if not the rule, of fourth and fifth century monasticism, or to quote once more Jerome's bloodthirsty summons for greater and even greater mortifications. Here, as everywhere, painstaking German scholars have accumulated, sorted, and docketed the available facts.[2] In diet the hermit might set himself to avoid all flesh or cooked food, or to live wholly on grass, raw grain, beans or peas. He might extend his Lenten discipline until he passed the whole year with only one meal a day, or accustomed himself to fast the whole week except on Saturdays and Sundays. He might eschew natural food altogether, and attempt to meet bodily hunger in the strength of the Eucharist alone.[3] He might spend the night or many nights in succession, half-submerged in a stream or slough, or by other expedients plan to procure sleeplessness over a long period. There were anchorites to whom the very possession of a cell, however humble, was unworthy of the follower of Christ ; some took refuge in holes in the ground, or open cisterns, others stood day and night under the open sky exposed to all the rigours of heat and cold alike. The Stylites of northern Syria adopted the pillar-asceticism of the votaries of Atargatis (Dea Syria) ;[4] their vigils were relieved

him in his ' monastery ' (see e.g. Paul., *ep.* 31, 1) ; and they were at least not wholly indifferent to the amenities of life. It is with considerable diffidence that Sulpicius (*ep.* 3) sends to Nola the amateur cook whose ravages in search of vegetables and fuel he deplores ; and Paulinus is commendably grateful (perhaps in consequence of the amateur's failings) when another cook, Victor, arrives, who combines skill in the kitchen with an aptitude for valeting (Paulinus, *ep.* 23[3-10]). Cp. also the home-life of Vectius, Sid. Ap., *ep.* 4.

[1] O. Zöckler, *Askese u. Mönchtum*, p. 7 — ' die Austerität erscheint gesteigert zur Atrozität.'

[2] Despite their age, Zöckler's two books (*Kritische Geschichte* and *Askese u. Mönchtum*) remain the fullest summaries of the details ; what follows in the text above can easily be verified by reference to the relevant sections of his analytical tables of contents. I doubt whether Dom Butler's attempt (*C. Med. Hist.*, i, p. 527) to distinguish between the ' natural ' mortifications of the Egyptian monks, and the ' unnatural ' ones of the Syrian, can be regarded as wholly successful. Is it more ' unnatural ' to stand upon a pillar than to go unwashed for sixty years, as did Melania, or Silvania (Pallad., *Hist. Laus.*, 55, 1) ?—For Palladius I quote throughout from Butler's text (*Texts and Studies*, vi, 1904) ; English translation by W. Lowther Clarke, 1918.

[3] Reitzenstein makes great use of this dependence upon *himmelspeise* alone, in support of his theory of the origins of Christian monasticism (*infra*, pp. 495 ff.), see esp. *HMHL.*, pp. 121-127, 155, 156. Here the Christian examples are fully examined, but no pagan parallels adduced.

[4] So H. Strathmann, *Geschichte d. frühchr. Askese*, p. 247. H. Delehaye, *Les Saints Stylites* (1923), pp. clxxvii-clxxxi, denies all relationship between the Christian and the pagan phenomenon ; this however seems improbable in view of the common locality. For the φαλλοβάται see Lucian, *de dea Syria*, c. 29 ; and for the suppression of an attempt to import the practice into the West, Gregory of Tours, *Hist.*, viii, 15.

by the knowledge that statuettes commemorative of their exploits commanded a ready sale even in the streets of distant Rome.[1] Further mortifications were achieved by the wearing of iron chains and heavy weights.

Even an assumed idiocy might be employed,—not as David employed it to save his life, but to save the soul by the additional ill-usage it would bring to the apparent sufferer. Of such a kind was the famous Cinderella of Tabennesi, who ' feigned madness and possession by a demon.'[2] The other nuns, Palladius tells us with relish,

' detested her so much that they would not even eat with her, and this she herself preferred. She would wander about in the kitchen,[3] and do every menial work : and she was, as they say, the " monastery sponge," fulfilling in fact the words of Scripture :—" If anyone seem to be wise among you in this world, let him become foolish that he may be wise." . . . None of the 400 sisters ever saw her eating during the years of her life. She never sat at table nor partook of a piece of bread : but wiping up the crumbs from the tables and washing the kitchen pots, she was content with what she thus obtained. Never did she insult anyone nor grumble nor talk either little or much, although she was cuffed and cursed and execrated.'

It was not till a famous anchorite by divine guidance visited the convent that her true holiness was recognized ; and so intolerable did she find her consequent change of status that she promptly disappeared from all human society for good. Exaggerated and fictitious some of these stories may possibly be : but they must have originated in the diseased fancy, if not of any ascetic who actually put them into practice, at all events of writers who thought it reputable to enhance a monastic hero's renown by crediting him or her therewith.

How diseased that fancy could be is shown by another trait in the picture. Self-discipline is meaningless to a Christian except as an instrument to develop the life of prayer. But many of the fourth and fifth-century hermits made prayer itself primarily an instrument of discipline, and that of the crudest kind ; the daily or weekly record, in this particular, of the athletes of Christ was

[1] Theodoret, *Hist. Rel.* (*Philotheus*), 26. A further advantage of this form of asceticism was that the Stylite could always avoid answering awkward enquiries by saying that the wind was in the wrong direction and made it impossible to distinguish the words (Holl, *Enthusiasmus, etc.*, p. 204, from Eustathius of Thessalonica).

[2] Pallad., *Hist. Laus.*, 34.

[3] Weingarten (*op. cit.*), p. 52, rather unnecessarily suggests that ' she is in the kitchen ' was a polite euphemism for ' she is feeble-minded.' This, however, is impossible in view of the καλοῦσιν, which requires a noun (or its equivalent) as object—μίαν ἔχομεν σαλὴν ἔνδον ἐν τῷ μαγειρίῳ· οὕτω γὰρ καλοῦσιν τὰς πασχούσας. The οὕτω refers back to the σαλήν—a late and rare word, whose meaning might be unknown to Palladius' readers.

noticed as sedulously as the scores of modern competitors in more mundane conflicts. Moses, the reformed Ethiopian bandit, who converted four other robbers to the faith by the simple expedient of carrying them bound together on his back, and depositing them in the nearest church, achieved his fifty prayers a day ; [1] the younger Macarius maintained a record of one hundred a day for more than sixty years.[2] Paul, a hermit of the Sketic desert, improvised the first known rosary by carrying with him 300 pebbles, with which to reckon the 300 prayers which were his daily toll ; but lost heart when news reached him of a neighbouring virgin who accomplished seven hundred a day, in spite of fasting five days in the week.[3]

Another extraordinary example of the perverse outlook of primitive monachism in some respects is to be seen in connexion with the Eucharist. Canon Hannay [4] has collected instances in which the early hermits are represented not merely as lacking, but even as avoiding, the reception of Holy Communion. ' I do not need the communion,' said one of them, ' for I have seen Christ Himself to-day.' To another the devil appeared in the form of a venerable abbot, with the words : ' We profit nothing sitting in our cells, because we receive not the body and blood of Christ. Let us go to a church where there is a priest, and there receive the sacrament.' The hermit resisted the temptation for a time, but then yielded ; his going was the first step in a downward course which ended in fornication.[5] The spirit survived even into the days of monastic organization—Macarius himself told Palladius that he had never given the oblation to Mark the ascetic, although the latter was present when the mysteries were celebrated. A mediating position between the theory that the ascetic could safely dispense with communion (on which the original incident must be based), and the theory that the Eucharist is necessary for salvation (which is obviously that of the narrator), is conveyed by the miraculous termination of the anecdote :—' An angel gives it to him from off the altar : I behold only the fingers of him who gives it.' [6]

Canon Hannay maintains that the tendency behind these incidents is based on no principle ; all that is in question is an accident of eremitism. ' It is not to be supposed,' he says, ' that there was any hostility to the Church or any contempt for the Church's

---

[1] Palladius, *Hist. Laus.*, 19.   [2] *Ib.*, 20.

[3] *Ib.*, 20.—A gentle touch of irony shows how much Pachomius (*infra*, p. 258) disapproved of this sort of rivalry. The younger Macarius visited his monastery at Tabennesi in disguise, and created extreme discontent among the brethren by outmatching all their ascetic attainments. Pachomius, divinely enlightened as to his identity, thanked him for putting them all to shame, and added, ' Now go your way, *for you have edified us sufficiently* ' (*Hist Laus.*, 18).

[4] J. O. Hannay, *Spirit and Origin of Christian Monasticism*, pp. 115-117, with references there.

[5] Hannay's reference is incomplete ; the anecdote occurs in *Vit. Patr.*, v, 6, 24 (*MPL.*, lxviii, coll. 898-900).

[6] Pallad., *Hist. Laus.*, 18 ; see also Reitzenstein, *HMHL.*, pp. 189, 193.

means of grace. Simply we must conceive that S. Antony and
others followed a divine call, expecting to find, in the way on which
God led them, all that the Church's ordinances gave to others.'[1]
Reitzenstein, on the other hand, in the interests of a theory of which
more deserves to be said,[2] would insist upon a strenuous opposition
between the hermit and the Church :—the hermit is 'pneumatikos'
—a spiritual person—and as such is superior to all Church ordinances and institutions of any kind whatever.

It is doubtful whether the evidence points to either of these
conclusions. Reitzenstein's general theory is expugnable on many
different grounds ; whilst Hannay minimizes the fact that the
reception of the sacrament was regarded as a temptation to be
avoided. It is difficult not to think that here we have, in effect,
nothing but another paradoxical application of the ascetic principle. Asceticism demands that we deny ourselves all good things
of life : the Eucharist is a good thing : therefore we shall achieve
merit by abstaining from it. There must have been monks who
regarded all Church life as a luxury from which they were bound
to debar themselves. When Cassian repeats the well-known saying,
'Before all things the monk ought to avoid women and bishops,'[3]
we are not listening (as Reitzenstein[4] ingeniously supposes) to a
warning against that spiritual pride which the expert feels so readily
when consulted by prelates, nor even to an eddy of the conflict
between the hierarchy and the monks. The co-ordination of the
two parts of the sentence implies a similar motive in both :—the
Church is a family, and as with the natural family all participation
in its life is to be given up by the monk for Christ's sake.

II. Monasticism and the Vision of God.

It is time to sum up our impressions of rigorism as it exhibited
itself in the deserts of Egypt and Syria. Of its fundamental purpose
more than a hint has already been visible in Origen, Antony and
Methodius—it was to see God.[5] 'What are you doing in this barren

---

[1] Hannay, *op. cit.*, p. 117.   [2] *Infra*, additional note G, pp. 495 ff.
[3] Cassian, *Inst.*, xi, 17. Cassian himself took the second part of the
sentence to mean 'we should avoid being ordained if possible'; and confesses
'with shame' that he had been unable to 'escape the hands of the bishop'
—an unkind cut at Chrysostom, who ordained him deacon (presumably
against his will) at Constantinople about A.D. 401 (Cass., *de Inc.*, vii, 31). But
this is not to say that he had rightly understood the original purport of the
epigram.
[4] *HMHL.*, p. 191.
[5] In addition to the passages quoted on various pages above, I subjoin
the following :—Origen, *de princ.*, I, i. 1—the end of life is 'to see thoroughly
the truth of all things,' or 'to come to know God Himself who is called the
truth'; i. 5, 6—the vision of God compared to seeing the sun ; i. 9—'seeing
God' is 'understanding and knowing Him with the mind'; 6. 3—the end
is to reach 'what is invisible and eternal'; *c. Cels.*, vi, 5—the vision of
God as the Platonic 'light suddenly kindled in the soul'; vi, 66—the answer
to Celsus' question 'How shall I know God?'—'Everyone is in the light who
follows the radiance of the Word . . . Celsus will not find any *Christian*

spot ? ' said a huntsman, whose pack had led him far afield, to the hermit Macedonius. ' I too am a huntsman,' was the answer; ' I am hunting for my God, and yearn to capture and enjoy Him. Him I desire to see, and never will I rest from this my gallant hunting.' [1]

The ' Spiritual Homilies ' of S. Macarius of Egypt are among the most authoritative sources for the spirit of primitive monasticism, even if they do not go back in their present form to the saint himself.[2] Their central doctrine, repeated innumerable times, may be inferred from the following passage :—

> ' This is a thing that everyone ought to know—that we have eyes within, deeper than these eyes ; and a hearing deeper than this hearing.   As the eyes of sense behold and recognize the face of a friend or loved one, so the eyes of the true and faithful soul, spiritually illuminated with the light of God, behold and recognize the true Friend. . . . The soul is smitten with passionate love for God, and so directed into all virtues by the Spirit.   It possesses an unbounded, unfailing love for the Lord for Whom it longs.' [3]

saying to him, How will you show me God ? ' (cp. 67-69) ; vii, 33-39 (the same subject) ; in Jn., tr. xix, 22—' Beyond this visible world of earth and sky there is a spiritual and invisible country whose aspect the pure in heart shall see.   And seeing it, they learn to seek after it, so as to see God Himself as His nature is to be seen.'—Nilus, de orat. 35—' Prayer is the ascent of the mind to God'; Aphraates, Hom., iv, 18—' Prayer is colloquy with God'; Vit. Barl. et Jos., c. 17 (Rosweyde, MPL., lxxiii, coll. 507-509)—Barlaam's sermon on the vision of God : Vit. S. Mariæ Ægypt., c. 2 (ib., col. 673)—Zosimas deemed worthy of spiritual vision because, besides being pure in heart, he had given himself to asceticism ; Hist. Laus. (long recension), c. 43 (Rosweyde, MPL., lxxiii, coll. 1146, 1147)—Abbot John's sermon on seeing God ('Where the mind is distracted with secular cares, it cannot see God ') ; Rufinus, Hist. Mon., 1 (MPL., xxi, col. 397—more of the same sermon)—' If we come before God with pure consciences we shall see Him in so far as He can be seen in this life ' (and further considerations on the invisibility of God) ; Theodoret, Hist. Rel., 26—Simeon Stylites adopts his ascetic life in order to ' see God ' ; and on the bios theorêtikos, as the essence of the monastic movement, Reitzenstein, HMHL., pp. 114, 115, 119, 120 ; J. Bremond, Les Pères du Désert, pp. 445-455 ; K. Holl, Enthusiasmus u. Bussgewalt, pp. 148 ff., 182 ff. ; C. Butler, Benedictine Monachism, pp. 78-82.

[1] Theodoret, Hist. Rel., 13 (MPG., lxxxii, col. 1404).   It is well known that many of the apophthegms attributed to the Egyptian monks recur in different sources.   Much criticism remains to be done on the question of the affiliation of the various documents involved, and the brilliant work of Preuschen, Butler and Reitzenstein on the Historia Monachorum and Historia Lausiaca, of Ladeuze on the Vita Pachomii, and of Bousset on the Apophthegmata Patrum serves to bring out in high relief the complexity of the synoptic problem involved.

[2] On the doubts raised by Villecourt and Wilmart see G. L. Marriott in JTS., xxii (1921), pp. 259-262 ; A. J. Mason, Spiritual Homilies of S. Macarius, p. xliii.   There is a brief but interesting note on Macarius' use of the Cophetua-motif in his doctrine of the soul as the bride of Christ, in Harnack, Hist. of Dogma (E. tr.), iii, p. 130.   Other sides of his teaching are admirably summarized in E. Underhill, The Mystic Way, pp. 315-330.

[3] Macarius, Hom., xxviii, 5.

And again :—

> ' Christians behold as in a mirror the good things of eternity.
> . . . The sight of an earthly king is an object of desire to all
> men. Everyone in his capital longs to catch even a glimpse of
> his beauty, the magnificence of his apparel, the glory of his
> purple, the excellence of his pearls, the comeliness of his diadem,
> his retinue of honourable men. . . . Thus carnal men desire to
> see the glory of the earthly king. But what of those, upon whom
> has fallen the dew of the Spirit of life in the Godhead, smiting
> their hearts with a divine passion for Christ their heavenly
> King ? How much more are they bound fast to that beauty, to
> the ineffable glory, the unspeakable comeliness, the unimagin-
> able wealth of Christ, the true eternal King, . . . and desire to
> obtain those unspeakable blessings which by the Spirit they see
> in a mirror ? ' [1]

Other motives of course operated : William James has faithfully
enumerated the six great psychological impulses which lead to
asceticism.[2] Perhaps, therefore, only the greatest hermits could
consciously express the real reason why they crucified the flesh and
fled the world. Perhaps some even among the greatest had a lower
and more limited conception of that experience, which we have
so far called ' seeing God,' than had S. Paul and S. John. That
visions of an ecstatic character, analogous to those of the apocalyp-

---

[1] Macarius, *Hom.*, v, 4, 5 ; cp. i, 2 ; ii, 5—the eye of the soul ; iv, 12—the
' friends of God see the good things of heaven, the inexpressible delights and
infinite riches of the Godhead ' ; iv, 13—a beautiful passage on the various
ways in which God allows Himself to be seen ; xxx, 4—variant of the mirror-
analogy : as a portrait painter must look at the king whom he is painting, so
' Christ, the Good Artist, for those who believe Him and gaze continually on
His own image the heavenly man ' ; xxxiv,
1—the beatific vision after death. On the vision of God in general, xiv, 1 ;
xvii, 4 ; xxv, 5 ; xxxviii, 2 ; xlvi, 5 ; on the spiritual marriage, iv, 6, 7 ;
xii, 5 ; xv, 1 ff. ; xxv, 8 ; xxvii, 2, 3 ; xlvii, 17 ; deification, xv, 35 ; xvii,
1.—A good illustration of Macarius' happy sense of analogy is xviii, 4, 5—
the pastor who attempts to teach without himself being full of the experience
of God is like a beggar giving a feast with borrowed plate and linen, who
has to return it all to the lender, and is found naked. It is to be noted that
although the homilies are explicitly addressed to ascetics, there is very little
of the rigorist tone about them.

[2] W. James, *Varieties of Religious Experience*, pp. 296, 297. The six
causes are : (1) ' organic hardihood, disgusted with too much ease ' ; (2)
' love of purity, shocked by whatever savours of the sensual ' ; (3) ' love
towards God, delighting to make sacrifices to Him ' ; (4) ' pessimistic feelings
about the self, combined with theological beliefs concerning expiation ' ;
(5) ' in psychopathic persons, a sort of obsession or fixed idea which comes on
as a challenge and must be worked off '—(James does not give any clear
example of his meaning here, but presumably this is identical with ' the
passion of self-contempt wreaking itself on the poor flesh' (p. 304)) ; (6)
' genuine perversions of the bodily sensibility, in consequence of which normally pain-giving stimuli are actually felt as pleasures.' (' Masochism ' had
not yet become a technical phrase in popular psychology in 1902, when
Varieties was published.) From the instances given above it might be
suggested that ' the competitive spirit ' should be added to the other six as
a seventh cause of asceticism.

tists, represented to many the culminating point of religious exaltation is clear from frequent allusions, though even here critics
have emphasized the fact too much.   There is a delightful and instructive story in the ' Apophthegmata '[1] of a heathen priest, who
came to visit Abbot Olympius at Scete :—

> ' When he perceived the life of the monks, he said to me,'
> (Olympius narrates), '"With a life of this kind do ye receive no
> visions from your God ? " " No," said I to him.   Then said the
> priest to me, "From us as we minister to our god he conceals
> nothing, but reveals to us his mysteries.   And ye—after ye
> have endured so many labours and sleepless nights and days of
> silence and mortifications—say ye, ' We see nothing ' ?   Why
> then, if ye see nothing, evil must be the thoughts of your heart
> that separate you from your God ; and therefore He revealeth
> not to you His mysteries."   So I went and reported his words to
> the elders ; and they were amazed and said, "So indeed it is.
> Unclean thoughts do indeed separate God from man."'

The visions here mentioned must be, of course, of a mantic
character.   Others of a similar kind are constantly recorded.   One
visionary fasts for forty days in the desert to obtain assurance that
the Monophysites are heretics and the Catholics orthodox.   At the
end of the time Christ appears to him as a child with gleaming face,
and says, ' Thou art well where thou art ' ; at the same moment
the monk is miraculously transported to the doors of the orthodox
Church.[2]   Another, who had committed himself to the opinion that
Melchizedek was the Son of God, was taxed by Cyril of Alexandria
on the point.   The hermit, after waiting upon God for three days,
saw in a vision a procession of the patriarchs, with Melchizedek
duly included among them ; he came joyfully to the bishop and
admitted his error.[3]   Visions of heaven, hell, angels, and cosmology
are frequent.[4]   Remarkable for its mingling of superstition with
true simplicity is the story of Anuph, whose dying apologia takes
this form :—

> ' From the day when I first confessed my Redeemer under
> persecution, never an untrue word has passed my lips.   Never
> have I allowed earthly desire to dim my spiritual longings.

---

[1] Cotelier, *Ecclesiæ Græcæ Monumenta* (Paris, 1677), i, p. 583.

[2] *Ib.*, pp. 703, 704.   There is a pleasant touch in the story, in that it
all arose out of the universal popularity of Phocas, its hero.   Orthodox
and heretics were equally anxious to see him in the way of salvation ; and
each warned him, in a very friendly but very perplexing manner, against the
spiritual dangers of consorting with the other party.

[3] *Ib.*, pp. 423, 424.   Here again a pleasant incident :—Cyril did not
challenge the old man directly, but ' knowing him to be a miracle-worker
($\sigma\eta\mu\epsilon\iota o\phi\acute{o}\rho os$) and that God always revealed to him what he asked,' feigned
personal doubts on the subject, and asked the monk to pray for a vision
whereby to resolve them.   Church history would have taken a happier
course if Cyril had always exercised the same tact.

[4] Reitzenstein has collected large numbers of these ; see *HMHL.*, pp.
24, 80, 90, 91, 119, 129, 130, 144, 174, 175, etc.

But God's grace has never failed me, and I have needed naught from earth. Angels have given me all the sustenance I craved. Nothing that happens upon earth hath God kept hid from me. His light glows ever in my heart, it keeps me in waking ; and my longing ever to gaze upon Him drives sleep far from me. So he leaveth His angel by my side, and he showeth me whatsoever is virtuous in the world. The light of my understanding faileth not ; and whatsoever I ask of God in prayer, forthwith I receive it. Often showeth He me the hosts of angels that stand before Him ; often I behold the glorious company of the righteous, the martyrs and the monks,—such as had no purpose but to honour and praise God in singleness of heart. And therewith I behold Satan and his angels delivered to eternal torments, whilst the righteous for their part enjoy eternal bliss.' [1]

Sometimes, therefore, the hermit who set out, consciously or unconsciously, to see God, contented himself with visions of a lower order—revelations of the future, or apocalyptic flights through heaven and hell. Sometimes, again,—and this is of special importance for later developments of mystical aspiration,—he found his heart's desire in a purely ecstatic experience whose differentia was that its content could not be expressed in words ; or even in a cataleptic condition characterized simply and solely by complete failure of consciousness.[2] Cassian—in many respects a monastic reformer of real insight—was in danger of constant error on this point. He describes the sublimer kind of prayer as ' a flame of fire,'

' transcending all human thoughts, and distinguished—I will not say by no sound of the voice—but by no movement of the tongue, nor utterance of words. It is a prayer which the mind, enlightened by the infusion of heavenly light, confines within no stilted human speech, but pours forth richly in an accumulation of thoughts, as from a copious fountain, and ineffably utters to God, expressing in the shortest possible time such great things as the mind when it returns to itself cannot easily utter or relate.' [3]

A full description of such an experience is given in the nineteenth ' Collation,' from the lips of Abbot John :—

[1] Rufinus, *Hist. Mon.*, 10. This is that Anuph, who daily for a week threw stones at a statue, and every evening begged its pardon. Questioned as to the meaning of this strange behaviour, he replied that the statue was typical of the true monk—it neither showed annoyance when injured, nor refused to pardon (!) the offender. (Rosweyde, *MPL.*, lxxiii, coll. 804, 955, 1057.)

[2] Cp. E. Underhill, *Mystic Way*, p. 287, on ' the psychological method by which the contemplative stops the wheel of imagination, empties the field of consciousness, abstracts himself one by one from visible things, etc. '; and *infra*, pp. 302 f., on the ' negative way.'

[3] Cassian, *Coll.*, ix, 25 ; cp. *ib.*, 15, on the ' fourth kind of prayer,' and 18, where this prayer is (rightly) justified by appeal to the ' Lord's prayer.'

' I was often caught up into such an ecstasy as to forget that
I was clothed with the burden of a weak body. My soul on a
sudden forgot all external notions and entirely cut itself off from
all material objects, so that neither eyes nor ears performed
their proper tasks. And my soul was so filled with devout
meditations and spiritual contemplation that often in the
evening I did not know whether I had taken any food, and on
the next day was very doubtful whether I had broken my fast
yesterday.' [1]

We have met with this tendency to regard *ecstasy* as the goal
of all human endeavour at an earlier stage—in Philo, for example,
the pagan mysteries, and the Hermetic books.[2] The aspiration was
one which so shrewd an observer as S. Paul found it necessary to
correct.[3] Both in the chapter in which *love* is set above all ' knowledge of mysteries,' and in the account of his own ' visions and
revelations of the Lord ' of which it is ' not expedient ' for him to
glory, he strenuously set his face against this over-valuation of
ecstatic experience. His caveat was justified on three grounds at
least :—

(*a*) It was, in the first place, a warning against limiting the modes
of operation of God's condescension towards men. If we once
grant that ' personal experience of God ' is possible,[4] we shall not
be disposed to deny that some at least of those who claim to have
' seen,' or ' known,' or ' held communion ' with God have really
done so—least of all if they make that claim with due humility
and reticence, and manifest the fruits of their experience in lives of
self-forgetful service.[5] Nor can it be denied that all such experience of God is in some sense ' ecstatic '—that is to say, that at
such times the mind is wholly concentrated upon Him Who is
present to it, and thereby relegates all thoughts of self into the
background.[6] This does not mean, of course, that every ' ecstatic '

---

[1] *Coll.*, xix, 4 ; cp. also Climacus, *Scala*, xxvi (*MPG.*, lxxxviii, col. 1065)
on the 'ecstasy which in effulgence of light puts the soul in a secret and
ineffable manner in the presence of Christ.'

[2] *Supra*, pp. 44, 50.   [3] *Supra*, p. 104.

[4] See *supra*, pp. 9, 10 ; and *infra*, p. 464.

[5] On this concept of ' self-forgetfulness,' or ' disinterestedness,' as a mark
of truly Christian behaviour, *supra*, p. 133 ; *infra*, pp. 554 ff.

[6] This is the same as to say that there is an element of ' passivity ' about
the experience—not that the soul actively strives to make itself passive
before God (that is at best a method by which a semblance of passivity is
sometimes acquired—cp. E. Underhill on the ' negative way,' *supra*, p. 196,
n. 2), but that it actually *is* passive, or purely recipient, so far as is possible
to the living being. James (*Varieties*, p. 381) describes the condition in the
words, ' when the characteristic sort of consciousness once has set in, the
mystic feels as if his own will were in abeyance, and indeed sometimes as if
he were grasped and held by a superior power.' I doubt, however, whether
the ' feels as if ' has a valid place in this description. To be able to record a
feeling about oneself, there and then, implies the possibility of an activity of
will which is *not* present in the highest states described by the mystics, nor
indeed in the absorptions of quite ordinary life. What happens at times
when we are, as we say, ' engrossed ' (and that not necessarily in the presence

experience is an experience of God ; there are ecstasies of evil as well as of good.   Nor does it imply that ' ecstatic conditions ' in the narrower sense—visions, automatisms, loss of consciousness and the like—are *even at best*[1] anything more than occasional and irrelevant concomitants of this experience of God.   We can reject without hesitation any suggestion that communion with God is only possible when phenomena of this kind are experienced.

(*b*) In the second place, if true religion is always theocentric and self-forgetful, it is necessary to insist that the systematic quest of ecstasy, or of any other form of ' experience,' merely for the gratification which will be derived therefrom, is irreligious.   Such a quest, for which we have already noticed M. Bremond's title of ' panhedonism,'[2] turns the seeker's mind back upon himself and his own states of consciousness, and so induces once again just that self-centredness which it is the whole purpose of religion to annihilate.   If by thinking of our own *conduct* we cannot achieve self-forgetfulness, no more can we by thinking of our own *experiences*. Hence the Christian who ' feels no joy,' as we say, in his religion, is not *on that account alone* to vary his course by a hair's breadth. Absence of joy may indeed be a sign of something gravely amiss in the moral sphere ; on the other hand, it may be no more than a transient psychological condition.   In either case, to turn aside

---

or thought of God), is surely that will *is* in abeyance, and we *are* grasped and held by (an abnormal, if not) a ' superior ' power ; later, when we reflect upon what has passed, we feel that we *have been* so grasped and held, and that the will *was* at the time in abeyance.   The characteristic, that is to say, of ecstasy, absorption, or ' passivity,' is that it is not *at the moment* reflectively and consciously self-registering.   On the other hand, as James rightly points out (*loc. cit.*, and pp. 478-485), such a state is not ' interruptive ' ; it is not a trance, catalepsy, or total loss of consciousness (as in a dreamless sleep or anæsthesia), of such a character that ' there may be no recollection of the phenomenon, and it may have no significance for the subject's usual inner life, to which, as it were, it makes a mere interruption.'   If any Christian has ever regarded such a total vacancy of consciousness as in any sense experience of God, he must surely have been utterly at fault.   What James says of ' mystical states ' is true of ' religious experience ' in every sense of the phrase—it is ' never merely interruptive.   *Some memory of its content always remains*, and a profound sense of its importance.   It modifies the inner life of the subject between the times of its recurrence.'   I have italicized the words ' some memory,' etc., because they alone are of primary importance.   It is when this ' memory ' is tested in more normal moments by the *lex orandi et credendi* that its value (or, as Miss Underhill says, *Mysticism*, p. 323 (cp. p. 431), its ' life-enhancing quality '—for what constitutes an ' enhancement ' is decided by comparison with the Christian ethical tradition), if any, as ' religious ' experience is decided.   On the whole subject of ' passivity,' and the distinction of true ' passivity ' from ' quietism,' F. von Hügel, *Mystical Element of Religion*, ii, pp. 132-139 ; E. Underhill, *Mysticism*, pp. 378-391.   Cp. also W. R. Inge, *Philosophy of Plotinus*, ii, pp. 154-156 ; and on the Hesychiasts, and the doctrine of the ' Uncreated Light,' Holl, *op. cit.*, pp. 38-45, 211 ff.

[1] ' Even at best '—because whereas a ' vision,' may, and in a saintly person probably will, connote experience of God, total loss of consciousness —mere ' interruption '—cannot possibly do so (see previous note, with references there).

[2] *Supra*, p. 104 ; and see *infra*, p. 489, additional note F.

from the admitted course of duty to capture, or recapture a *feeling*, however rare and gratifying, cannot be other than wrong.[1]

(c) Finally, it is wholly Christian to insist that in the saintly life the self-forgetfulness of ecstasy (if we may so phrase it) must go hand-in-hand with a self-forgetfulness of service [2]—the service, that is to say, of God, and of His whole creation in Him.   We are not in a position yet to ask more definitely about the relation between these two aspects of sanctity ; nor have we attempted to analyse the supremely difficult concept of self-forgetfulness.[3]   But unless an alleged experience of God brings with it a call to disinterested action of some kind or another—unless there is reaction, response, reciprocity—we shall scarcely be able to avoid the conclusion that something is amiss.   More than this need not be said at the present stage ; we have here criteria enough by which to test the aspirations and achievements of the monks of Egypt.

There are many unguarded phrases in the records of primitive monasticism which prove that even its greatest representatives were at best only half alive to the principles just considered.   When Antony, for example, is quoted [4] with the warmest approval as saying, ' That is not a perfect prayer wherein the monk is cognizant of himself or the words with which he prays,' what may perhaps be a characteristic of some true prayers [5] is being made the test of *all* true prayer, and we are on very dangerous ground.   And when, in the next ' Collation,' Cassian introduces the phrase ' prayer without images,' [6] and characterizes it as a condition in which the mind is void of ' every image of the divinity, every memory of things said, every picture of things done, every impress or experience of any kind,' [7] we have reached the threshold of a point of view from which spiritual vacancy and spiritual fulness are almost indistinguishable.   The idea of this ' most perfect prayer '—' the ecstasy of

---

[1] We might perhaps plead a modest exception in cases where it is sought to recapture a feeling for the stimulating moral effects it has been found to induce.   But even here the ambition would have to be deprecated.   To depend upon anything so transient, arbitrary, and irresponsible as a recurrent feeling or ' experience' as the mainstay of life, is obviously a counsel of despair.

[2] The connexion between the two (i.e. that they are both self-forgetful) is well indicated by S. Francis de Sales when he speaks of the truly Christian life (in which both the ' natural' and the ' supernatural' requirements of God are observed) as ' the true ecstasy of the will,' or the ' ecstasy of action and operation ' (*Love of God*, vii, cc. 5, 6).

[3] *Infra*, pp. 445-451, on priority of worship ; pp. 555 ff. on concept of self-forgetfulness.

[4] *Coll.*, ix, 31.

[5] I have said ' may perhaps be a characteristic,' because it is commonly impossible to decide whether any given mystic is wholly and at all times free from the aberrations of ' quietism ' (as distinct from a doctrine of true ' passivity '—see above, p. 197, n. 6, with references to Underhill and von Hügel).   Much apparently quietist language (such as this phrase of Antony's) may be no more than an unskilful attempt to describe passivity.   In that case, it is indeed describing a characteristic of *some* true prayers ; but even so it is highly dangerous to attempt to make it a test of *all* true prayer.

[6] Cassian, *Coll.*, x, 11.   [7] *Ib.*, x, 5.

the soul,' ' the ravishing of the spirit to God ' [1]—as the goal of all
human endeavour occurs again and again in Macarius and John
Climacus. At such times, Macarius says,

> ' the soul leaves herself, as it were, and is transported into
> heavenly regions. All earthly cares are buried in oblivion.
> The spirit is captivated by things divine—things infinite and in-
> comprehensible—marvels which cannot be expressed in human
> words : and at the last it breaks out in longing, " Oh, that my
> soul might leave the earth, and soar away with my prayer ! " ' [2]

On the other hand, it is important to notice that in many
passages these primitive writers on the monastic ideal seem to have
envisaged just the dangers we have had under consideration. We
have only to read a very few pages of Cassian, or the ' Apophthegmata,' for example, to learn how constantly the saintliest of the
monks proclaimed that even the anchorite is called upon to exercise the virtue of brotherly love.[3] They themselves never hesitated
to put the stores of their spiritual experience at the disposal of every
earnest enquirer. The advice they give is not confined to the
realm of prayer alone ; it extends over the whole range of Christian
charity and helpfulness. Among the acquaintances made by
Cassian in Egypt was the Abbot Joseph, one of the greatest psychologists and casuists of the early centuries. His joy at the mutual
friendship of Germanus and Cassian, whose tour is the framework
of the ' Collations,' expresses itself in a discourse on that subject
which deserves to be immortal. He has observed and estimated
every kind of human affection, has found them all good, has noted
with kind but critical eye the dangers to which each is exposed.
Here are a few of his aphorisms :—

> ' Tolerance is generally a sign of strength, pertinacity a sign
> of weakness ' ; [4]—' the strong ought always to bear with the
> weak, but the weak do not always allow themselves to be borne
> with ' ; [5]—' a feigned patience often excites to anger more
> keenly than bitter words ' ; [6]—' this is " true love set in order "
> which, while it hates no one, yet loves some more than others by
> reason of their deserts ; and while it loves all in general, singles
> out some for itself to embrace with special affection ' ; [7]—' an
> opportune apology cures our own evil feelings.' [8]

[1] Climacus, *Scala*, xxviii (*MPG.*, lxxxviii, col. 1131).
[2] Macarius, *Hom.*, viii, 1 (*MPG.*, xxxiv, col. 527) ; cp. Cassian, *Coll.*, ix,
15, 25.
[3] This statement is not rendered untrue by the fact that the monks
divested themselves of domestic ties and responsibilities. Every Christian
finds himself bound by the restricted conditions of human life to limit in
some degree or other the sphere within which he sets himself to do good.
The monks may have chosen the wrong limits, and exercised them to the
wrong degree ; but we cannot say in consequence that they were blind to
the demands of brotherly love.
[4] Cass., *Coll.*, xvi, 23.   [5] *Ib.*, 26.   [6] *Ib.*, 18.
[7] *Ib.*, 14.   The reference is to Cant. 2⁴ (Vulg.).   [8] *Ib.*, 15.

These are but a few sentences from a discourse of twenty-eight chapters, but the whole is worthy of Cassian's closing eulogy, ' Thus much the blessed Joseph discoursed with us in his spiritual talk on friendship, and fired us with a more ardent desire to preserve the love of our fellowship as a lasting one.' [1]

Nesteros, another of Cassian's Egyptian friends, is emphatic that the ' contemplative science '—which we should call the quest for the vision of God,—must be preceded by the ' active science,' the ' ordering of one's life in virtue.' [2] He does not for a moment pretend that desert-asceticism is the only road to success in this ' active ' preliminary to the vision. Some are anchorites, indeed ; but some prefer the convent. Some preside over a guest house with open-handed hospitality ; some give themselves to nursing, teaching or works of charity. For all of these benevolent activities he has a word of praise.[3] But throughout the course, in ' active ' and ' contemplative ' spheres alike, self-love is the great danger which besets the Christian, and impedes both virtue and vision. With singular psychological insight, therefore, the monks examined the soul to find the ' root sins '—or ' primary impulses,' as we should say,—from which the rank vegetation of self-love springs in all its horrible variety,[4] not forgetting at the same time that *in themselves* these ' impulses are not by nature blameworthy, but given to man for useful and beneficent purposes.' [5] It would

---

[1] Cass., *Coll.*, xvi, 28. Cp. also Apollonius of Nitria, who made himself physician to the five thousand monks in his neighbourhood (Pall., *Hist. Laus.*, 13) ; and Moses, the converted robber (*ib.*, 19), who went out of his way to fill the water-pots of older monks secretly by night.

[2] *Ib.*, xiv, 2, ' actualis scientia ' (*infra*, p. 250) ; cp. i, 9, 10 ; ix, 3-5.

[3] *Ib.*, xiv, 4.—Cp. the story of the two brothers (Pall., *Hist. Laus.*, 14), one of whom bestowed all his goods in charity and retired to the desert ; whilst the other ' parted with nothing,' but endowed and continued to administer an almshouse. Each is equally praised. (The second brother ' made himself a monastery '—μοναστήριον. Reitzenstein, *HMHL.*, p. 45, suggests that this means an ' oratory in a private house ' (as in Philo). This is possible, and gives an added point to the anecdote ; but it cannot be accepted as certain.)

[4] I have dealt to some extent with the scheme of the seven (or eight) ' capital ' sins in *Some Principles of Moral Theology*, pp. 265-268 (and references there). Cp. also Hannay, *Spirit and Origin of Christian Monasticism*, pp. 135, 136 ; O. Zöckler, *Askese u. Mönchtum*, pp. 253-256. Research into the antecedents of this classification (as distinct from mere catalogues of sins) might produce interesting results. As T. B. Strong (*Christian Ethics*, p. 260) has pointed out, five of the seven occur in a sevenfold list in Origen. But *Didaché*, 3[1-6], is obviously intended as a fivefold list of roots of sin (note the five recurrences of ' my child ' marking the divisions), and comprises anger, lust, superstition, lying (including ' avarice ' in the same section), murmuring (including ' self-will ' (' pride ') in the same section). Earlier still, *Test. XII. Patriarchs* (Reuben, 2[1, 2], 3[1-8]) has as its ' seven spirits of evil,' lust, gluttony, anger (' fighting '), obsequiousness (' deceit '), pride, lying (' jealousy,' ' deceit '), injustice (' rapacity '). A further point of interest is, at what stage and under what influences, did ' envy ' gain a place in the list ? It does not occur in the enumerations of Evagrius, Nilus or Cassian (except perhaps in the disguise of ' tristitia,' cp. Aquinas, *ST.*, i, 2 ; q. 84, a. 4) ; but there is no doubt about it in Gregory (*Mor. in Job*, xxxi, 45).

[5] Cass., *Inst.*, vii, 3. In this passage we see a very high example of moral and ethical discernment struggling to the birth. First of all, Cassian

be easy to fill a volume with quotations proving how well the monks knew that purity of heart is both the condition and the result of contemplation, and that purity of heart is bound up with active service of others. ' This is true purity,' says S. Macarius, ' when you see the sinful and the sick, to have compassion on them and be tender-hearted to them . . . despising no one, judging no one, abhorring no one, making no distinctions.' [1]

Again, Antony's warnings against the hallucinations called up by demonic visitants are clear evidence that not *every* ecstatic condition was regarded as bringing the Christian nearer to his goal. By their fruits they were to be known. One story of such a hallucination shows also that, sometimes at least, the true monk laid little store by these experiences. The devil, disguised as an angel of light, appeared to an aged solitary with the words, ' I am the angel Gabriel, and God has sent me to you.' ' You are wrong,' replied the monk, ' God must have sent you to some one else ; I am not worthy of so high an honour.' [2] A large part of the monastic campaign against spiritual pride, as the worst of all sins, was directed to the address of those who thought the miraculous (including, we must suppose, miraculous visions and experiences) to be the highest possession of the Christian. That ecstasy was not everything, and that it had its dangers, seems therefore to have been generally allowed. One story—and that a specially emphatic one—insists that the presence of God does not depend upon any emotional apprehension. Antony, so the legend goes, at the height of a prolonged conflict with demons, looked up and saw the Lord in a glory of dazzling light. The demons vanished in terror, and all

---

definitely exempts ' covetousness ' from the list of impulses which may be ' useful and beneficent '—i.e. he has not yet recognized the importance of what modern psychology calls the ' acquisitive instinct.' (He also exempts ' envy ' (*Inst.*, vii, 5) in the same way, but ' envy ' is not yet with him explicitly one of the ' eight '—*supra*, p. 201, n. 4.) Secondly, he only predicates this ' useful and beneficent ' character explicitly of four of his *capitalia*— ' gluttony ' and ' fornication ' (= the ' carnal impulses,' *Inst.*, vii, 3), ' anger ' and ' sorrow '—what we should call respectively ' hunger and thirst,' the ' sexual instinct,' ' pugnacity,' and ' self-abasement.' Of the remainder (acedia, vain-glory, and pride) he is not prepared to make such an explicit statement. But, thirdly, he *does* assert it of them implicitly. The four which are definitely said to be ' useful and beneficent ' are obviously only quoted as examples (*Inst.*, vii, 3), and of all ' the incitements to sin ' except covetousness he says they are ' congenital with us, deeply rooted in our flesh, almost coeval with our birth, prior to our discernment of good and evil ' (*Inst.*, vii, 1) ; they are ' implanted in us by the Creator ' and only ' abused ' by our free-will (*ib.*, vii, 4). (In *Coll.*, v, 3, ' gluttony ' is quoted as the example of ' natural,' covetousness of ' unnatural ' impulses ; in v, 8, anger is said to be natural ; v, 12, vain-glory is at least in one respect ' useful '; the others are not distinguished in this respect, although the *Collation* is wholly concerned with the *octo principalia*.) Cassian's hesitations are a measure of the extraordinary originality of the view which he was attempting to put forward, and which modern knowledge so cordially endorses.

[1] Macarius, *Hom.*, xv, 8 ; generally, on this subject, Holl, *op. cit.*, pp. 153-155.

[2] *verb. sen. interpr. Pelag.*, xv, 68 (= Rosweyde, v ; *MPL.*, lxxiii, col. 965).

the saint's sufferings were forgotten.   But he cried to the vision :—
' Where wert Thou, my Lord and my Master ?   Why camest Thou
not before, to assuage my torments ?'   Then a voice answered him :—
' Antony, *I was here throughout thy struggles*, but I wished to observe
thee.   Now I know that thou didst resist bravely, and gavest not
place to the adversary ; and I will always be with thee, and will
make thy name famous throughout the earth.' [1]

Occasionally, indeed, passages may be found which suggest
doubts (if no more) on the most fundamental of our problems—the
legitimacy of the quest for ' experiences ' at all.   Cassian was
unhesitatingly of the opinion that spiritual ' dryness ' might be
as much a divine visitation as any degree of joy.[2]   Macarius [3]
on one occasion set himself to remain for five days ' in the most
intimate of unions with God ' :—

> ' To my soul I said : " Beware not to come down from
> heaven.   There thou hast the Angels and Archangels and all
> the celestial powers.   There thou hast thy God, the Creator of
> all.   Set up thy rest, then, there ; and come not down from
> heaven." '

The result was disastrous.   The saint experienced a demonic
assault so terrible that after three days he relaxed his attempt.
He gives two reasons for his retreat ; fear of the devil, and God's
desire to save him from spiritual vanity.   Neither suggests directly
that the attempt itself was misjudged.   Yet the very fact that the
failure is found to be in accordance with God's will indicates, at
all events, a suspicion on the monk's part that ambitions such as
this are dangerous.   From that suspicion it is, after all, only a step
to the conviction that the attainment or retention of a particular
state of consciousness is a wrong ambition for the Christian.

With all this, it can fairly be said that the monks made a great
positive contribution to Christianity by allotting to *prayer* the
primacy among Christian activities.[4]   Not that they belittled the
activities of a charitable life (so much we have seen), nor excluded
them from their purview.   But prayer stood first in rank.   If I
interpret this phenomenon aright, it is indeed of crucial importance.
It marks the point at which, rightly or wrongly, Christian ethics took

[1] Athan., *Vit. Ant.*, 10.

[2] Cass., *Coll.*, iv, 4.   Two reasons are assigned : (*a*) to bring home to the
Christian that ' the purity of heart granted to him by the divine visitation '
is wholly of God's free gift, and so to prevent his being ' puffed up,' as though
it were his own attainment ; (*b*) as a test of zeal and earnestness ; cp. *ib.*,
c. 6.   In this short passage Cassian anticipates the entire harmonious teaching of the great Christian mystics with a clearness of insight which leaves
nothing to be desired.

[3] Pallad., *Hist. Laus.*, 18.

[4] Cp. Cass., *Coll.*, i, 8—' Is it not clear that the Lord [in the incident
of Mary and Martha] sets man's chief good in *theoria*, that is to say, in the
contemplation of God ?   Wherefore all other virtues—necessary, useful, excellent though they be—must take second place ; they are exercised and
acquired for this one end alone.'

a divergent road from that of moralism pure and simple.[1] It
implies that for final self-forgetfulness the whole attention of the
soul must be centred upon the most absorbing, inspiring, and perfect of objects. Action, it is true, can be (and should be) directed
towards God, as well as prayer ; and action may often be as selfless
as prayer.[2] But the immediate end even of self-forgetful action is
always the well-being of some other and lesser person or thing than
God, and the lesser ends may fail to evoke the full disinterestedness
which attends upon the greater. Prayer, however—that is to say,
the full round of prayer, consummated in thanksgiving, praise, and
worship—is directed to God alone ; and so prepares the way for
a self-forgetfulness which, when it comes, shall be sustained by the
thought of God—the most enduring, most inexhaustible, thought
of which the mind is capable. To a mind so occupied, more than
to any other, there must surely come such peace, harmony and
inspiration, as will fit it to deal with all the emergencies and relationships of life as the saint should deal with them.

The thought may be illustrated from Abbot Isaac's second
Conference on prayer. It is worth while to notice how, though the
passage contains scarcely a single non-scriptural phrase, it is no
mere cento of familiar quotations. The whole has been recast in
the reality of personal religion. Isaac is speaking of the goal of
human life, and says :—

' Then will be perfectly fulfilled the prayer of our Saviour,
in which He prayed for His disciples to the Father, saying "That
the love wherewith Thou lovedst Me may be in them, and they
in Us " ;[3] and again, " That they all may be one ; as Thou,
Father, art in Me and I in Thee, that they also may be in Us."
For that perfect love of God, wherewith He first loved us, shall
pass into the depth of our hearts as well. . . . And this will
come about when God shall be all our love, and every desire
and wish and effort, every thought of ours, and all our life and
words and breath. . . . This, I say, is the end of all perfection,
that the mind purged from all carnal desires may duly be
lifted towards spiritual things, until the whole life and all the
thoughts of the heart become one continuous prayer.'[4]

[1] For fuller discussion see *infra*, pp. 445-451 ; and cp. W. R. Inge,
Philosophy of Plotinus, ii, p. 176, on a similar ' parting of the ways ' in neo-
Platonism.

[2] Conversely, of course, prayer—even if it consists in no more than
quieting the soul in the hope of receiving spiritual edification—is action of a
sort. ' Orare est laborare ' is therefore *always* true ; ' laborare est orare '
is true just in so far as activity partakes on any occasion of the selflessness of
truly Christian prayer. M. Bremond (*HLSR.*, vii, pp. 68-70) emphasizes this
as the fundamental thought of S. Francis de Sales. Nevertheless, a distinction between prayer and action in general is necessary, and universally
recognized. Further on the subject, *infra*, pp. 448, 449.

[3] A slight misquotation ; the last words of Jn. 17[26] are ' and I in them.'
The ' they in Us ' comes from verse 21, which Cassian is about to quote.

[4] Cass., *Coll.*, x, 7.

Further, the prayer set before the monk is prayer directed neither to a pagan nor to an unknown God, but to the God Whose creative and redeeming activities have been newly illuminated by the truth that He is love, as revealed in Jesus.[1] Wide as the purview of the vision of God must be, its focus is the Incarnation. This ensures, even more than before, that only the purest thoughts and aspirations shall take the place of those thoughts of self whose expulsion from the mind is a condition of Christian saintliness. How wide and yet how definitely focussed upon God in Christ a Christian's prayer should be, is beautifully put by Abbot Moses in Cassian's first Conference :—

' The contemplation of God is manifold. We see Him when we consider His incomprehensible Being—a thing which still lies hid in the hope of the promise. We see Him when we consider the greatness of His creation, His justice, and the aid of His daily providence. We see Him when with pure minds we consider what He has done with His saints in every generation ; when with trembling heart we admire the power with which He governs, directs, and rules all things ; the vastness of His knowledge, and that eye of His from which no secrets are hid. . . . We see Him as we gaze in unbounded admiration on that ineffable mercy of His, which with unwearied patience endures countless sins ; on the call with which by no merit of ours, but by His own free grace, He receives us ; on the numberless opportunities of salvation which He grants ; . . . *above all on the economy of the Incarnation which He undertook to save us,* extending the marvels of His sacraments to all nations.'[2] ·

In prayer, then, more than anywhere else, the monk believed that he would find that completeness of self-forgetful tranquillity which most of all should issue in self-sacrificing activity of service. He caught a glimpse of another fundamental truth as well :—that the mind in prayer must be directed upon God alone, and not upon the psychological results that are to be secured thereby. Prayer is a contemplation of God, not of oneself nor of one's subjective and transient emotions.[3] If he sometimes mistook other ecstasies for the ecstasy of Christian prayer ; if he sometimes treasured subjective experience too much ; if sometimes, in giving prayer priority over action, he undervalued or ignored altogether the principle that true contemplation must go hand-in-hand with Christian service—

[1] M. Bremond, *HLSR.*, iii, pp. 43 ff., has insisted upon the prime importance of Bérulle in reviving this aspect of genuinely Christian mysticism in post-Tridentine Catholicism; cp. also P. Pourrat, *La Spiritualité Chrétienne,* iii, pp. 502-506 ; and *infra,* pp. 354-356, on S. Bernard.

[2] Cass., *Coll.,* i, 15.

[3] W. R. Inge, *Philosophy of Plotinus,* ii, p. 150, has a suggestive sentence on ' the spiritual self-importance ' of some mystics, ' which makes them enjoy retailing their inner joys and miseries '—and, we might add, enjoy contemplating them as well.

these are lapses that may be forgiven him. On the great fundamental questions of Christian ethics in the widest sense, Cassian,
Macarius, and the hermits on whose experience they drew, expressed the genius of New Testament Christianity with an intuition
for which the Church must always be grateful.

How are we to judge this doctrine of the primacy of prayer,
contemplation, the vision of God, in the Christian life ? The final
decision must be postponed to the last lecture ; but we can take
the matter a step forward even here. Few who have thought
about prayer at all will dare to say that the monks were wholly
mistaken, either as to the object of their search, or in the choice
of means. If we hesitate to endorse this judgment, a hint of
S. Bernard's [1] will suggest a profitable line of approach. We have
only to think of the contemplation of God in terms of *worship*, and
apply to the understanding of it our own experience of corporate
worship.[2] As the worship of the Church proceeds through its ordered
stages of confession, praise, thanksgiving, reading of scripture and
intercession (stages which correspond closely to the practice of
prayer as given in Cassian's ' Conferences '), we all experience from
time to time—though perhaps rarely—moments which can fairly
be called ecstatic. At such moments the worshipper is lifted out
of himself into a higher and better atmosphere, which leaves traces
for good in his soul when it returns to its normal lower level. He

---

[1] Bernardus Clarevall., *de consid.*, i, 7 (8)—' Do you ask what piety is ?
It is to find time for consideration ' (' vacare considerationi '—see *infra*,
p. 372, for Bernard's use of ' consideration '). ' You may say that my definition differs from his who defined piety as the worship of God ' (' cultus Dei '
—the reference is apparently to Job 28²⁸, which in the LXX reads Ἰδοὺ ἡ
θεοσέβειά ἐστιν σοφία). ' There is no difference :—consider well, and you will
see that I have expressed his meaning in my words, though perhaps only in
part. For what is more pertinent to worship than that which the Psalm
commends, " Be still and know that I am God " (Ps. 46¹⁰) ? And this stands
first among the parts of consideration.'

[2] The comparison would have been welcome to Cassian—in fact, he
seems throughout to be challenging it himself. In *Coll.*, ix, 26, he definitely
selects the mystical experience which occasionally comes during the recitation of the office in public worship (note the ' modulation of a brother's voice ')
as the first example of the heights to which a contemplative may hope to rise
(cp. *Inst.*, ii, 10). Hence the whole of books ii and iii of the *Institutes* are
devoted to the ordering of the canonical hours of prayer ; whilst *Coll.*, x, 11
deals with the spirit in which the psalms should be sung ; and ix, 18-24
applies the same principle to the recitation of the Lord's Prayer. Cp. also
C. Butler, *Benedictine Monachism*, pp. 70-74, 299, 302, 312, 388, 389, 399,
on the place of vocal prayer in relation to contemplation, particularly in
reference to the Benedictine tradition ; and H. Bremond, *HLSR.*, iii, pp.
115-134 (cp. *Philosophie de la Prière*, pp. 52, 53) on the principles of Bérulle
and the ' French school ' (note especially p. 118, n. 2—' The purpose of the
liturgy is to fulfil the first duty of the Christian—to worship God in His
infinite majesty. . . . Bérulle shows his originality not least of all by insisting that private devotion—prayer, or (in short) the inner life as a whole
—should be consecrated to the same duty, a duty of which the public liturgy
and official prayers of the Church had imperceptibly been allowed to obtain
a monopoly.' The contrast is between Berullan and Jesuit piety, the latter
having tended more and more to interpret private prayer in the narrow
sense of the ' practice of virtue ' alone—*infra*, pp. 436-438, 450).

would be a fool and worse who attended public worship merely to experience such exaltations, without any wish or intention of drawing from them strength to live a better life. But no one who has experienced them—and this is all that matters for the moment—is without some understanding of what the monks called contemplation, the mystics the ' way of union,' and the New Testament ' seeing God.'

Not that an act of worship is vain and useless if it fails to bring the consummation of self-forgetfulness. Contemplation, as a human activity, is not so much ' looking *at* God ' as ' looking *towards* God.' If the Christian in worship, public or private, looks toward God with all the strength he possesses, he has done his part, and may rest assured that in some way or another—though not necessarily through any type of experience with which the words of others have made him familiar—God will respond to his advances. To expect a response of one *particular* kind is to doubt the resources of God [1] ; to expect a response of an *emotional* kind is, once again, to be looking at oneself and not at God. And neither of these attitudes has any place in Christian prayer.

III. THE GNOSTICS.

I have tried to set side by side—though in the barest of outlines only—the bathos and the exaltations of the ascetic spirit as it expressed itself in primitive monasticism ; on the one hand, the depraved aberrations of morbid self-annihilation by which it was so often dominated, on the other the high ideal of the vision of God towards which it strove. The least that can be said of the monastic outlook in this period is that—dimly, if no more—it envisaged some of the most important principles of the Christian way of life. But the fundamental principle adopted by the monks must still remain in question. They held it for certain that asceticism of the most rigorous kind was the normal road to the vision ; [2] and we are not yet in a position to pass judgment on this view. But at least we can discern that, sometimes at all events, in the early centuries, the connexion of asceticism with the vision of God was dominated and determined by a false conception of God ; and this will help us when we come to consider whether or no *all* ascetic practices are equally so determined.

When everything is said that can be said in depreciation of the eremitic tendency, one thing remains true. The monks rarely seem to have thought exclusively of themselves as the only Christians, or of the monastic life as the only road to salvation—though

---

[1] Cassian allows fully both for different forms of divine ' call ' (*Coll.*, iii, 4), and for different methods of approach to the consummation of ' contemplation' (*ib.*, ix, 26).

[2] On the importance of allowing for differences of climate and century in forming an estimate of these primitive austerities, J. Bremond, *Les Pères du Désert*, pp. 155, 156.

Athanasius' letter to Amun,[1] and the restraints imposed by the
Council of Gangra,[2] suggest that some at least had tendencies in
this direction. Monasticism was a challenge, but not an ultimatum.
The ultimatum—the deliberate attempt to stamp the entire
Christian code with the seals of celibacy, fasting and poverty—
came to the Church from another quarter. What by the monk
was voluntarily assumed, the gnostics (or at all events the
earlier gnostics, for in course of time they became more accommo-
dating) sought to impose compulsorily ; and if their attempt
had been successful rigorism would have reigned supreme in the
Church.

The bitterest of recent academic quarrels in theology is that
which is still raging in Germany on the subject of gnosticism. It
has been provoked, as have so many other developments, by the
incursion of exact and detailed philology—armed with a vast new
body of evidence drawn, in the main, from the papyri and similar
sources—into a sphere in which hitherto it had shown comparatively
little interest. Till a generation ago the view of Harnack held the
day. Gnosticism was a speculative movement, and consisted in
the introduction into Christianity of the principles of neo-Platonism.
The gnostics were the first Christian philosophers : they precipitated the ' acute secularising or hellenising ' of the gospel.[3] They
found Christianity ' a practical philosophy without any philosophic
system : this they endeavoured to provide.'[4] ' Gnosticism,' says
one of Harnack's most eminent disciples, ' is in the first place *intellectualism*—one-sided over-valuation of knowledge at the expense
of moral activity.'[5]

The rigour of these judgments is sometimes mitigated. ' We
should do great injustice to the gnostics,' the last-quoted writer
proceeds, ' to treat them as mere intellectualists, barren of practical
morality. Many of them bestowed a great deal of thought upon

---

[1] Ath., *ep.* 48. The letter is no more than a defence of the legitimacy
of married life in the Church ; its significance lies in the fact that it is addressed to a superior among the Nitrian monks, and hints very broadly
that ' malicious questions ' of this character have been raised in the ' flock
under his charge.'

[2] For the Council of Gangra, see *infra*, p. 265.

[3] Harnack, *History of Dogma*[3] (E. tr.), i, p. 226 (*supra*, p. 118). The
only thing which in Harnack's opinion separates the gnostics from orthodox
theologians is the ' acuteness ' (i.e. ' rapidity ') with which they carried
through a process which (to Harnack's regret) was bound to happen anyhow ;
together with their rejection of the Old Testament. The divergence between
Harnack and (say) Bousset can be concentrated in the latter's insistence
that what the gnostics introduced into Christianity was not the ' hellenic '
but the ' hellenistic ' point of view (*KC.*, pp. 184 f.)—i.e. not the spirit
of pure Greek philosophy, but that of the Oriental theosophies which by the
first century had wholly taken its place everywhere except perhaps in
limited Stoic circles. Harnack (E. tr.), i, pp. 230-233, shows a good deal
of confusion on the point.

[4] E. von Dobschütz, *Christian Life in the Primitive Church*, p. 276 ; cp.
Harnack, *Dogmengeschichte* (fourth German edition), i, pp. 249, 260.

[5] E. von Dobschütz, p. 254.

morals.' [1]   In spite of this concession, however, it will not be wrong to say that, according to the older view, gnosticism was a peculiarly *Christian* movement, in so far as it insisted upon the distinctively Christian doctrine of redemption ; [2] but a movement which betrayed a profound disloyalty to the Judaic origin and spirit of the gospel first by attempting to explain the fact of redemption at all ; and then by offering an explanation based upon the fundamental tenet of neo-Platonic dualism. To Harnack, the principal gravamen against the gnostics is not so much that they philosophized in a dualistic spirit (though that is serious) : it is that they philosophized at all. Their offence, as he conceives it, is only mitigated to a slight degree by the fact that the Church (though in a lesser measure) was guilty of it too.

There are points of minor importance in the philologists' reply to Harnack.[3]   It matters comparatively little, for example, whether the main gnostic interest was doctrinal or ethical—the fact is, as both sides admit, that they had a deep interest in problems of both kinds. It is not of any particular importance to urge, as Bousset

---

[1] von Dobschütz, p. 258. We may notice the much stronger statement of E. de Faye, *Gnostiques et Gnosticisme* (2nd edn. 1925), p. 475 :—' Even in the greatest teachers the *bios gnostikos* is more important than *gnosis*.'

[2] E.g. Harnack, *Hist. of Dogma* (E. tr.), i, p. 230. Bousset, *KC.*, p. 201, shows reasons why they were bound to weaken in their attachment to pure soteriology.

[3] Some of the main *acta* of the controversy are the following : (*a*) Harnack's original position can be studied in the third German edition of his *Dogmengeschichte* (1893) (E. tr. *History of Dogma*, 1894), or his *What is Christianity ?* (E. tr. 1901), pp. 209, 210 ; (*b*) The philologists' theory: G. Anrich, *Das Antike Mysterienwesen* (1894), pp. 67, 80 ff. ; W. Anz, *Ursprung des Gnosticismus* (1897) ; R. Reitzenstein, *Poimandres* (1904), pp. 156-160, 306-308 ; W. Bousset, *Hauptprobleme der Gnosis* (1907) ; (*c*) Harnack's reply is contained in the fourth edition of his *Dogmengeschichte* (1909), i, pp. 45 f., 249 ff., and in numerous articles in periodicals ; Reitzenstein, *HMHL.*, pp. 215-219, has collected Harnack's most biting phrases ; de Faye, *Gnostiques et Gnosticisme* [3], pp. 515-520, instances cases where Harnack has modified his views under pressure from the other side ; (*d*) the full ' philologist ' position is put by W. Bousset, articles ' Gnosis ' and ' Gnostiker ' in *PW.*, vii (1912), and *Kyrios Christos* (1st edn. 1913 ; 2nd 1921), especially c. 6 ; E. Norden, *Agnostos Theos*, pp. 56-115; R. Reitzenstein, *Die Hellenistischen Mysterien-Religionen* (1st edn. 1910), esp. pp. 112-159; 3rd edn. (1926), pp. 284-333; Id., *Historia Monachorum u. Historia Lausiaca* (1916), esp. c. 10 ; cp. also W. R. Inge, *Philosophy of Plotinus*, i, pp. 103-108 ; E. de Faye, *Gnostiques et Gnosticisme* (2nd edn. 1923) occupies a mediating position. The general position of the principal contestants may be gauged from the fact that Harnack describes the philologists as the ' new romantics ' (*Dogmengeschichte* [4], i, p. 45), whilst Reitzenstein retorts by classing him among the ' older rationalists ' (*HMHL.*, p. 216). For ' Essene ' gnosticism, J. B. Lightfoot, *Epistle to the Colossians*, pp. 71-111, 384-387 ; art. ' Essener,' in *PW.*, Supplement IV., coll. 386-430. On the *Minîm*, or supposed Jewish gnostics, M. Friedländer, *Der Vorchristliche jüdische Gnosticismus* (1898) *pass.* ; cp. Harnack, *Geschichte d. altchristl. Lit.*, i, p. 144. Strathmann, *Frühchristliche Askese*, pp. 102 ff., suggests restraint in accepting Friedländer's conclusions, which he regards as scarcely covered by the evidence. Cp. also *ERE.*, viii, pp. 657-659, *s.v.* ' Minîm,' which makes the Minîm converts from Judaism to Christianity—too simple a solution for the facts.

does with some vigour,[1] that the form of neo-Platonism familiar to the gnostic was an Orientalized one ; and that strictly speaking 'hellenic' philosophy and 'dualism' are contradictions in terms.[2] It is an irrelevance to notice that Harnack's complaint against the gnostics for philosophizing is met by the philologists' reply that they never philosophized at all. But it matters a great deal that— as modern investigations into the mystery-religions show—the idea of redemption, so far from being peculiarly Christian, should be recognized as of world-wide extent at the beginning of our era. This means nothing less than that gnosticism is not in essence Christian at all ; it is simply another name for the whole system of syncretistic religious thought which underlies, according to the philologist, the mysteries, the Hermetic sects, the astrological and magical cults of the Empire, and in addition (so the most extreme critics would have us believe) [3] the whole of Pauline and Johannine thought, and all Christian theology, orthodox or heretical, of the early centuries—everything in fact except that tendency towards hierarchical organization which alone is left to the Church as its peculiar prerogative, and the naturalist outlook which still survived in the later Stoics and to some extent in Plotinus.[4] A dualistic theology, an ascetic system of ethics, an ecstatic experience of God, and a hope of redemption from the evil dominance of the flesh— these, according to the more recent writers, constitute gnosticism ; and the minor variations which make of it a mystery religion, a neo-Pythagorean coterie, a Christian theology, or a monastic theory, introduce nothing new of any material importance.[5]

The first test-problem is of course the meaning of the word

---

[1] Bousset, *KC.*, p. 184.

[2] So for example Norden insists that the proposition 'God is invisible' is hellenic, whilst the superficially identical 'God is unknowable' is wholly Oriental. The possibility of the latter imperceptibly grafting itself on to the former, despite their fundamental difference, is obvious ; Norden sees the beginning of the process in Philo (*Agnostos Theos*, pp. 84-86). Cp. on the same point, Bousset, *Hauptprobleme*, pp. 84-91 ; and *supra*, p. 106, n. 4.

[3] Wrongly, of course, because as has been argued above, the 'dualism' of S. Paul and the Fourth Gospel is strongly tempered and balanced by monism.

[4] Thus Plotinus, Bousset, *KC.*, pp. 184-186. By allowing exceptions of this kind, the philologists might come to terms with Harnack and de Faye ; for Harnack is prepared to admit that gnosticism was 'strongly dualist in its two lower stages' so long as he may believe that it was 'monistic on the top-floor' (*Dogmengeschichte* [4], i, p. 261) ; and de Faye will allow that Bousset and Reitzenstein are right as concerns the later gnostics, and makes reservations only in respect of the earlier ones (*Gnostiques et Gnosticisme* [2], pp. 445-449, 519). On the other hand, Bousset (*PW.*, vii, coll. 1524, 1531) is prepared to admit that the later, or at all events the greater, gnostics had philosophical interests. On the problem of why the gnostics were attracted to Christianity in particular, which is still unsolved (for we can scarcely take seriously the suggestion (above, p. 208) that the absence of any intellectual interest in Christianity offered them a free field for speculation) see the observations of Bousset, *PW.*, vii, coll. 1525, 1529 ; and de Faye, *op. cit.*, pp. 462, 463.

[5] So, explicitly, Reitzenstein, *HMR.*, p. 303.

' gnosis.' Here the philologists seem to have it all their own way.[1]
' The gnostics,' says Wendland, ' were not philosophers : " gnosis "
is not discursive intellectual knowledge, but " seeing God " and
" knowing mysteries," which are attained by personal intercourse
with God, and revelations.' [2] The range of material analysed in
pursuit and support of this conclusion covers the Hermetic literature, Philo, the magic papyri, neo-Pythagoreanism, and the surviving fragments of Christian gnosticism. The latter is of course
crucial ; but the result of the investigation seems in any case
certain. ' Gnosis ' is ' gnosis Theou,' ' horasis,'' epopteia,' spiritual
vision. It is the very opposite of ' philosophia,' or discursive speculation, which was the ideal of the Greek sages ; it came into being
first because philosophy was proving fruitless.[3] In the earlier
gnostic thought it is not contrasted, but identified, with faith.[4] It
is closely connected with the reception of the Spirit, illumination,
deification and the beatific vision. The gnostic and the ' pneumatikos ' are identical ; they alone are free.[5] ' Gnosticism can
best be called a theosophy,' says Bousset ; [6] ' " Gnosis " is the world
of visions, ecstasies, secret revelations and their mediums, of apocalyptic literature and secret tradition.' Its object is to make known
' what we were and what we have become; whence we were and where
we have been placed; whither we speed and whence we are ransomed;
what is birth and what is re-birth.' [7] But the knowledge was not

---

[1] The matter is fully discussed in all the books mentioned *supra*, p. 209.
The clearest exposition is that of Norden ; the widest ground is covered by
Reitzenstein, especially in the latest edition of *HMR*.

[2] Wendland, *HRK*., p. 166 ; on Posidonius' influence in this connexion,
ib., p. 170.

[3] If Norden's investigation of the word ἀγνωστός is to be accepted, a
serious point arises, in that the gnostics must have used γνῶσις and its
compounds in two senses :—(a) God is ἄγνωστος (unknowable) by means of
philosophy (Norden, pp. 69 ff.) ; the testimony of nature, and even of prophecy, can only lead to the demiurge (Norden, pp. 74, 85) ; (b) But He is
γνωστός by means of γνῶσις—emphatically *not* philosophic speculation. In
(b), γνῶσις and γνωστός refer to the *reverse* of philosophy ; in (a) the com-
pound ἀ-γνώστος refers to philosophic speculation. Strictly speaking, the
word γνῶσις covers too much. To the question ' How is γνῶσις θεοῦ possible ? ' the gnostics answered: ' Not by philosophy.' But they should
not have gone on to say ' γνῶσις θεοῦ is only possible by γνῶσις ' (an absurd
tautology), but rather, ' γνῶσις θεοῦ is only possible by ἐποπτεία ' (or some
such phrase). However as ἐποπτεία and the like were in their opinion the
only ways of coming to a γνῶσις θεοῦ, they rather naturally arrogated the
word γνῶσις to this manner of approach to God alone.

[4] So Bousset, *PW*., vii, col. 1521 (from Liechtenhahn, *Die Offenbarung im
Gnosticismus* (1901)).—The distinction between γνῶσις and πίστις dates from
the later period at which room was found for the ' vulgar catholic ' in
the gnostic system, by recognizing him as a *tertium quid* between the ' pneumatikos ' and the ' sarkikos ' (*infra*, p. 217). ' Faith ' was then assigned
to him as his distinctive virtue.

[5] On this, the cardinal point of Reitzenstein's theory of the origin of
Christian monasticism, see *infra*, p. 495, n. 2.

[6] *KC*., p. 190 ; with reference to Liechtenhahn, *ut sup*.

[7] [Clem. Al.] *Excerpta ex Theodoto*, 78 (*MPG*., ix, col. 696). It is on this
passage, curiously enough, that Bousset bases his admission that the later
gnostics were ' at all events half philosophers ' (*PW*., vii, col. 1524).

imparted to all and sundry. Even to a *bonâ fide* enquirer, Tertullian says, the hierophant would reply with stern face and frowning brow, ''Tis too deep a matter.'[1]   The spirit of gnosticism was always esoteric, always mysterious and secretive.

The terminologies of ' Christian ' gnosticism and the theosophies of contemporary paganism are beyond all question identical ; so is their general outlook upon God, the universe, man and his destiny.   Gnosticism, therefore, is not so much an endemic disease of Christianity (as Harnack would suggest), as an epidemic of the whole of contemporary thought.   Its true offence is not that it philosophized, but rather that it rejected philosophy in favour of esoteric revelations.   If it has special affinities with Paulinism, it is not because it consciously laid hold of the Pauline doctrine of redemption as the peg on which to hang its neo-Platonic philosophy. It is because Paul himself, with his alleged dualistic doctrine of redemption, was (on the theory under consideration) the first Christian gnostic ; and in any case offered, by his contrast of ' spirit ' and ' flesh,' something sufficiently dualist on casual inspection to warrant the gnostic in claiming kinship with him.   At this point all schools of thought find agreement once more.   Whatever they think of S. Paul, whatever they regard as the relation between Christian gnosticism and contemporary paganism, whether they treat gnosticism itself as in essence philosophical or evangelistic—they do not hesitate to assert its overwhelming dualism both in theology and ethics.[2]   This is its special significance for us. If we accept—as I think we are bound to do—the philologist's contention that the aim of the gnostics was not to think about the problems of the universe, but to see God, then it is clear that they interpreted that vision and all that appertained to it in a very special sense, which demands further consideration.

Dualism, as was said at an earlier stage,[3] is a temper which accepts

---

[1] Tert., *adv. Val.*, 1.   The whole passage is a fine example of Tertullian's withering irony.

[2] Harnack, as noted above (p. 210, n. 4), makes a reservation in favour of a ' top-storey ' monism among the gnostics ; but in general admits their dualism as freely as any other scholar.

[3] *Supra*, p. 58.   It may be added here that it is not necessary for the principles of good and evil recognized by any system of thought to be *coequal*, before it can be regarded as dualist.   So long as the evil principle is organic to the system, and therefore incapable of surrendering to the redemptive activity of the good, the extent of its sway is irrelevant.   Something in the long run is bound to be lost.   The Christian view of evil, unless I am mistaken, regards it as *functional*—a disease of the will which can be cured— and so escapes fundamental dualism.   M. de Faye (p. 154), starting from Tertullian's dialectical exposure of Marcion's fallacy in *adv. Marc.*, i, 2-7, insists that without ' deux principes suprêmes égaux et semblables,' ' deux dieux suprêmes qui se partagent le tout, et dont les forces égales permettraient la lutte,' there is no true dualism.   The weakness of this is not so much that it enables de Faye to deny the alleged dualism of Marcion, but that it practically eliminates dualism from history ; for any system which supposes that the victory of the good (or for that matter of the evil) will end the chapter is on that account rendered non-dualist—the two forces are not ' equal ' ; one is ' superior ' to the other.   Only a system in which the two

the contradictions of experience as ultimate ; and consequently sees no victory for the divine except in the annihilation of the human, no escape for spirit except by the destruction of matter. It regards the evil in the world as an organic rather than a functional disease ; the tainted ' organs ' cannot be healed or purified, therefore they must be extirpated. Few of the gnostics carried the logic of their dualism to the full. Clement of Alexandria says of Basilides that he ' deified the devil ' ; [1] and if we accept this statement at its face value it can only mean that he attributed equal power to the devil with God. But the other gnostic sects all made some effort to posit a common term between the oppositions they recognized. The Valentinian aeons, the Syrian demiurge, represent attempts to bridge the unbridgeable gulf between God and creation ; the doctrine of the gnostic soul as the divine spark imprisoned in the world of matter [2] is another such philosophic olive-branch. Nevertheless, though there may be a slender thread of monism running through their explanations of how things came to be, and how the soul subsists in the body despite their mutual incompatibility, there is no hope that either thought or life can avail to reduce the dualism. The unity—shadowy enough at most—that can dimly be observed is transitory. The world and the flesh are irredeemable : at best we may hope that God will redeem the soul from them both. The eschatology of the gnostics is even more defiantly dualist than their cosmology and psychology.

The effects of such a system are obvious. In theology it leads to the doctrine of the ' unnatural God '—a God so radically unlike the world of nature that He will least be found in any process that

were maintained in absolute equilibrium throughout time and eternity alike —a process without end or meaning—could then be dualist. The keynote of what we ordinarily mean by the word is not that the evil force is *equal* to the good, but that it is *irredeemable*.

[1] Clem., *Strom.*, iv, 12, 85. De Faye (p. 40) attempts to mitigate the rigour of the phrase, and the older school of interpreters (e.g. Mansel, *Gnostic Heresies*, pp. 158, 165) tends to regard Basilides' system as peculiarly pantheist. But the language which Hippolytus (*Phil.*, vii, 21 ; *GCSS.*, ' Hippolytus,' iii, p. 197) puts in his mouth about the non-existent God making a non-existent world out of non-existent matter has a dangerously dualist ring ; and if (with most critics) we reject Irenæus's account of his system (Iren., *haer*, i, 24. 3), and assume that he eschewed any doctrine of emanations, he becomes the most dualist of them all, with the single exception of Marcion. On the fragments of the *Acta Archelai et Manetis*, and the dualism they ascribe to Basilides, Bousset, *Hauptprobleme*, pp. 92-96 ; *PW.*, vii, coll. 1507, 1508 ; de Faye, p. 40. An impartial modern account of the main gnostic systems is very badly needed. Hilgenfeld, Mansel, and the various articles in *DCB.*, though all invaluable, are out of date ; the Germans tend to treat the gnostics as a homogeneous block without assigning them individual personalities ; and de Faye, though he has surveyed the whole field, is wayward and subjective, and tends to paraphrase the evidence to suit his purposes, rather than to set it out dispassionately. In this connexion E. Meyer's chivalrous attempt to reinstate Simon Magus as the archgnostic (*Ursprung u. Anfänge*, iii, pp. 277 ff.) deserves special notice. Cp. also J. Weiss, *Urchristentum*, p. 588, and *PRE.*, xviii, pp. 351-361 (*s.v.*).

[2] *Supra*, p. 86, n. 5. On the ' mediating ' gnostic systems, Bousset, *Hauptprobleme*, pp. 119 ff., and on the imprisoned soul, *ib.*, pp. 361-369.

can be called natural. The normal is the evil : only the supremely abnormal is divine. Religion is the reverse of all that is natural. 'Unless ye make the male with the female neither male nor female; the right to be the left, and the left right,' says a constantly recurring gnostic proverb; [1] 'what is above to be below and what is below to be above ; what is before to be behind and what is behind to be before, ye shall not enter the kingdom of heaven. For the whole world is turned the wrong way, and every soul therein.'

It is one thing to think of God as a mirror, another to count heaven a spiritual looking-glass-country. Yet this seems to be the gnostic ideal. It has an immediate effect upon the concept of religious experience. Only those passages of life can witness to contact with divinity which are least akin to man's intercourse with man : trances, ecstasies, visions, and all the apparatus of theurgy become the standard of communion with God. It· has a similar though twofold effect upon ethics. To the mystic it means that communion can only come by way of the temporary annihilation of all sense-perception and experience : to the formalist, that God will only reward those who have crucified all natural desires and instincts. Asceticism is the inevitable outcome in either case.

The immediate opponent of God, and of the soul in so far as it was a spark of the divine, in the gnostic system, was matter—especially as exemplified in the human body. That the body was a prison-house, or tomb, to the soul, was an old Oriental belief which had long been held by Orphics and Pythagoreans alike, and had met with a responsive echo in Plato himself. [2] The doctrine found a new popularity in the theosophies of the early Christian centuries. Philo and the Hermetica, as we have seen, accepted it with alacrity. Even 'the philosopher Plotinus,' so his biographer tells us, 'was as one who is ashamed of his body'; [3] and despite his normally liberal outlook he was sufficiently pessimistic about the worth of earthly existence to refuse to keep his own birthday. [4] Notions of this kind become a gnostic commonplace. The only function that this body 'made of dust' can perform is to 'sustain the things that are without profit '—' things that vanish away '—' wealth, possessions, raiment, beauty.' [5] Marriage is the union of corruptibles, a 'foul and polluted way of life.' [6] Eating and drinking is slavery of the belly. There is nothing beautiful or innocent or desirable in children. [7] They beget rapacity and fraud in their parents : they themselves are for the most part sickly, infectious, or weak-

---

[1] It occurs in varying forms in 2 *Clement* and Clement of Alexandria (in each case as a quotation), the *Acts of Peter*, the *Acts of Thomas*, and the *Acts of Philip* (M. R. James, *Apocryphal New Testament*, pp. 11, 335, 429, 450). I have taken the liberty of making a conflate version.

[2] See additional note D, *infra*, p. 482 ; and cp. the *Phædo* references cited above, p. 86.

[3] Porphyry, *Vit. Plot.*, 1.   [4] *Ib.*, 2.

[5] *Act. Thom.*, 37 (M. R. James, *Apocryphal New Testament*, p. 383).

[6] *Act. Thom.*, 124 ; *Act. Andr.*, 5 (James, *op. cit.*, pp. 419, 352).

[7] *Act. Thom.*, 12 (James, *op. cit.*, p. 369).

witted : if they grow up they become murderers, knaves and rogues. No aspect of terrestrial existence has anything good in it.

The majority of the gnostic sects, therefore, were defiantly ascetic. ' Breaking away from nature,' it has been said, ' was their parole.'[1] Saturnilus, Tatian and the apocryphal Acts and Gospels all condemn marriage, often in the most scathing terms. The apostles in these early romances—the ' Sunday afternoon literature' (as they have been called) ' of the ancient Church'[2]— glory in parting bride from bridegroom on the wedding-night, or breaking up unions that have endured for years.[3] Most striking is the way in which the gnostics dared even to rewrite the beatitudes in the ascetic interest :—

> ' Blessed are the pure in heart, for they shall see God.
>
> ' Blessed are they that keep the flesh chaste, for they shall become the temple of God.
>
> ' Blessed are they that abstain (or ' the continent '), for unto them shall God speak.
>
> ' Blessed are they that have renounced this world, for they shall be well-pleasing unto God.
>
> ' Blessed are they that possess their wives as though they had them not, for they shall inherit God. . . .
>
> ' Blessed are the bodies of the virgins, for they shall be well-pleasing unto God and shall not lose the reward of their continence (chastity), for the word of the Father shall be unto them a word of salvation in the day of His Son, and they shall have rest world without end.'[4]

So too of poverty. ' Possession is sin ; and even involuntary loss is deliverance from sin,'[5] is the watch-word of the Clementine Homilies. Herbs are prescribed as the gnostic's diet throughout the apocryphal Acts, and even these must be enjoyed as sparingly as possible. ' Despise all temporal things, and hasten to overtake my soul as it wings its ways towards heaven,' are the last words ascribed to the apostle Andrew ;[6] whilst ' Flesh and blood cannot inherit the kingdom of God ' was the favourite gnostic quotation

---

[1] Von Dobschütz, op. cit., p. 258. Cp. Bousset, PW., vii, col. 1518, on the specially dualistic system of Saturnilus.

[2] C. H. Turner, Study of the New Testament (1920), p. 12.

[3] The evidence is too extensive to be quoted ; it will be found, for example, in Batiffol, Études d'Histoire et de Théologie Positive, pp. 50 ff. ; DCB., s.v. ' Encratites' ; M. R. James, Apocryphal New Testament, index, s.v. ' Marriage,' etc. One of the rare exceptions is the so-called Questions of Bartholomew, which takes a reasonable view of first and even of second marriages, though it outspokenly condemns a third (M. R. James, op. cit., p. 181).

[4] Acts of Paul, i, 5 (M. R. James, p. 273).

[5] Clem. Hom., xv, 9 ; cp. also Acts of Thomas, 28, 36, 88, 117, 136, etc.

[6] Acts of Andrew (M. R. James, p. 361) from the Epitome of Gregory of Tours. Dr. James notes (p. 349) how Gregory has altered the original text of the Acts so as to make a story which condemned marriage in toto merely censure the marriage of cousins, and to allow of the insertion of the phrase ' We do not forbid or shun marriage ; it is a divine institution ' (p. 340).

from the New Testament.[1]   None but the ascetic can achieve the vision of God, either in this life or the next.

That this was the dominant ethical principle of gnosticism is not contradicted by the well-known fact that certain schools of thought permitted, and indeed encouraged, the most flagrant licentiousness.   Different motives operated to this result.   The Cainites, according to the account of Irenæus and Epiphanius, acting on the assumption that the demiurge, the god of the Old Testament, is the opponent of all that is good, openly set themselves to infringe all precepts attributable to him.[2]   Others, such as Carpocrates and Epiphanes, took wider grounds.   Of them Dr. Bigg says, that they taught that ' God made the world and the devil made law ' ; [3] and Dean Mansel with special reference to Epiphanes, who died at the age of seventeen, aptly remarks : [4] ' This precocious philosopher was certainly not overburdened with modesty on account of his youth : indeed his philosophy was of that kind which a forward boy might be very apt at learning and teaching.'   Neander sums up the whole of this curious paradox as follows :—

> ' When the gnostics had once started on the principle that the whole of this world is the work of a finite, ungodlike spirit, . . . and that the loftier natures, who belong to a far higher world, are held in bondage by it, they easily came to the conclusion that everything external is a matter of perfect indifference to the inner man.   Nothing of a loftier nature can there be experienced ; the outward man may indulge in every lust, provided only that the tranquillity of the inner man is not thereby disturbed in its meditation.   The best way to show contempt of, and to bid defiance to, this wretched alien world, was not to allow the mind to be affected by it in any situation. Men should mortify sense by indulging in every lust, and still preserving their tranquillity of mind unruffled.' [5]

Irenæus, followed by Eusebius, suggests that licentiousness was not merely allowed and encouraged by the Carpocratians, but practically enjoined : it was the only ladder back to the heavenly sphere.[6]

---

[1] Bousset, *KC.*, p. 193.

[2] Clem. Alex., *Strom.*, vii, 17, 108 ; Iren., *haer.*, i, 31, etc.   It is to Irenæus that the accusation of immorality against the Cainites is principally due. Cp. generally E. de Faye, *Gnostiques et Gnosticisme*, pp. 353-377, on the ' anti-biblical gnostics.'

[3] C. Bigg, *Origins of Christianity*, p. 142.   The main source is Clem. Alex., *Strom.*, iii, 2, 1-9 ; for the Carpocratians, Iren., *haer.*, i, 25.   E. de Faye, *Gnostiques et Gnosticisme*, pp. 413-418, thinks that Carpocrates and Epiphanes themselves were purely heathen, and that the sect owed its existence to another (unknown) heresiarch of the same name as the former ; but he allows their licentiousness, and finds its source in dualism.   On p. 480, however, he withdraws the concession ; the ' licentious ' gnostics were simply ' debauchees who sought to justify their behaviour by an appeal to specious theories.'   [4] H. L. Mansel, *Gnostic Heresies*, p. 121.

[5] Neander, *Ch. Hist.*, ii, p. 26 ; quoted Mansel, *Gnostic Heresies*, p. 135.

[6] Iren., *haer.*, i, 25. 4 ; Eusebius, *HE.*, iv, 7.   Irenæus finds the theological basis for this in the doctrine of transmigration ; Eusebius in that of escape from the ' cosmic powers.'

Antinomianism of this character was an eccentricity which could have little appeal for Christendom. Asceticism, the other legitimate child of gnostic principles, was a different matter ; it had affinities both with the New Testament and with incipient monasticism. In the main, however, as has often been noticed, the gnostics founded no churches ; nor did they make any effort to seize the reins of discipline in the Catholic body. Indeed they could not consistently have done so. A Church can exist only where men are to be rescued from an evil world, or shepherded after rescue. But the gnostic dualism precluded both the possibility of rescue and the need of shepherding. A man is either ' gnostikos,' ' pneumatikos '—that is to say, in the way of salvation ; or ' sarkikos,' ' psychikos,' ' hylikos,' that is, so compounded of material elements as to be doomed to destruction. If the latter he is incapable of rescue ; if the former, he has within himself the ' gnosis ' which will save without external interference.[1] All that was needed was to preach the gospel of ' gnosis,' so that the unconscious gnostic might wake up to his happy destiny.

Here again we must not generalize too much. A curious sequence of accidents, combined with the desire to conciliate the ordinary Catholic by putting him in a category distinct from that of the doomed ' hylikos,' led the Valentinians to recognize a middle class between the gnostic and the fleshly man—and to this class, to which the title ' psychic ' was now reserved, a modified degree of beatitude was allotted.[2] Nor was the idea of ' spiritual progress ' wholly ignored ; [3] ' gnosis ' might be a ' way ' as well as a status. But this conception is secondary and unimportant ; in general gnosticism is wholly determinist. The ' invisible Church of the elect ' is already made up ; what need then of any visible Church ?

[1] On this dualistic anthropology of the gnostics, and its resemblance to Pauline predestinarianism, Bousset, *KC.*, pp. 197-200. Its origin must have been purely empirical ; there were those who, despite the preaching of the gnostics, remained untouched by higher things—the natural inference was that they were void of the divine spark. Interesting pagan parallels, Reitzenstein, *HMR.*, pp. 252-262.

[2] On this development Bousset, *KC.*, p. 198 ; *Hauptprobleme*, pp. 361 ff. Bousset regards its origin as simply the desire to conciliate the Catholics. But Reitzenstein, *HMR.*, p. 326, whilst admitting this influence, draws attention (a) to the normal tripartite psychology of ' body, soul and spirit,' to which anthropological distinctions might imperceptibly come to conform ; (b) to the natural tendency of all religions to recognize ' proselytes ' as a third class between ' believers ' and ' unbelievers ' ; and (c) to philological ambiguities (some gnostics held a dualism of *pneumatikoi* and *psychikoi* (p. 325), others one of *pneumatikoi* (or even *psychikoi*) and *sarkikoi* (*somatikoi*— pp. 309 ff.) ; and the Greek language could never tolerate the assigning of a wholly evil sense to *psyché ;* hence the desirability of a compromise. On the philological question, see additional note E, *infra,* p. 487 .

[3] Bousset, *KC.*, p. 202, on the ' rationalistic and Platonizing ' traits in some gnostic teaching (cp. *Hauptprobleme*, p. 277) ; Reitzenstein, *HMR.*, p. 295, *gnosis* as a ' way.'

IV. MARCION, TERTULLIAN AND MONTANUS.

In this matter of ecclesiastical organization, as in other respects, Marcion formed an interesting exception. ' He founded churches,' Tertullian says, ' as wasps build nests.' [1] Around his figure has raged one of the many skirmishes in the great gnostic battle : Harnack regards him as profoundly anti-gnostic, Bousset as typically gnostic.[2] The difference is partly due to the different views on the nature of gnosticism to which allusion has been made : partly to the idiosyncrasies of Marcion's own system. In respect of dualism he is *plus royaliste que le roi*. He will not tolerate any of the theosophical expedients by which some of the gnostics sought to clothe the nakedness of their opposition between good and evil. On the other hand, he is more obsequiously scriptural than any other,—if that can be called a scriptural system which begins by racking the scriptures on the Procrustean bed of an exaggerated Paulinism. The dualism of all others which seemed to him to matter was that between the gospel and the Old Testament. He will not allow to the Christian revelation any preparation in Jewish prophecy, nor to Christ even so much as his Jewish descent. Judaism is wholly natural, Christianity wholly supernatural ; Marcion's gospel begins with the thunderbolt of an unknown Christ appearing out of the void in the synagogue at Nazareth.[3] If ever we should have expected ethical lawlessness to flourish, it would have been on this ground : it is one of the paradoxes of Marcion that he took the less logical course, and insisted on a rigid asceticism as legalist in its way as anything in the Old Testament.[4] It followed the usual lines in respect of marriage and diet ; but its rigour is evident in the fact that married persons were not even accepted as candidates for baptism.[5]

Marcion did not draw the dividing line between good and evil through the middle of the human race, with the consequent inevitable separation of the gnostics from the fleshly. The line was drawn rather between Christ—or, to be exact, the spiritual principle in Christ—on the one hand, and all else that is on the other. All men therefore lie equally under the shadow of the law and the God of the Old Testament. None is more apt for salvation than the rest. Hence follow several consequences. Faith—though a very non-Pauline faith—is preferred once again to gnosis ; it is a fact of life that some at least believe themselves to be lacking in any form of

---

[1] Tert., *adv. Marc.*, iv, 5.

[2] For this controversy see additional note H, *infra*, p. 503 ; and cp. W. Bousset, *Hauptprobleme der Gnosis*, pp. 109 ff.

[3] Tert., *adv. Marc.*, iv, 7 ; cp. *ib.*, iv, 11—' All things happen of a sudden with Marcion.'

[4] E. de Faye, *op. cit.*, pp. 170, 171, though scarcely alive to the full importance of this paradox, is unconsciously influenced by it when he advances the theory that Marcion was primarily an ascetic moralist, who allowed his theology to reinforce his ethical rigorism.

[5] Tert., *adv. Marc.*, i, 29.

religious experience, but all are capable of that obedient acceptance of a system which in the second century passed for ' faith.' And a Church has a function after all ; its business is to bring the gospel of redemption to all and sundry. Marcion is the least mystical of gnostics. His is a religion for the plain man, and every man to him is a plain man. All need his gospel, but none are incapable of receiving it ; and because it is a new gospel—Tertullian is continually taunting him with the fact—the existing Church cannot proclaim it. A Marcionite Church is necessary, and Marcion founds it in full consciousness that he is declaring war not merely on Catholicism, but also on all the humane elements in Catholic morality. Asceticism is demanded of all without exception.

The doctrine of the ' unnatural God ' depends for its exact form upon the interpretation of the words ' natural ' and ' unnatural.' The gnostics as a whole defined the ' unnatural,' that is to say the divine, in terms of ecstasy and abnormal religious experience, with their closely allied phenomena of magic and divination. Marcion's dividing line traversed theirs directly. Personal religious experience is wholly set aside as a test of the divine ; that and all else, except a narrow revelation of the divine love in Jesus, is stamped as devilish. Everything in the world must be abjured except the superhuman theophany of Christ. Tertullian, Marcion's great critic, believes also—though not so consistently nor so wholeheartedly—in the unnatural God. He admits (and he is here on genuinely Christian ground), indeed he asserts as against Marcion, the revelation of God in nature.[1] But the obvious conclusion—the conclusion which for example Clement of Alexandria elaborated with a large-hearted humanity—that philosophy is a *præparatio evangelica* as genuine as Old Testament revelation, he emphatically rejects. ' What kinship has the Christian with philosophy ? ' he exclaims in a well-known passage ; ' the child of God with the child of Greece ? the candidate for life with the candidate for honour ? the enemy of error with its friend ? the guardian of truth with its thief ? '[2]

With philosophy Tertullian brackets the whole Roman world— its education, its amusements, its administrative, civil and military services, its religious aspirations. All are of the devil ; the Christian must shun them as he values his soul. His test of a creed is its ' ineptitude ' ; of a certainty, its ' impossibility.'[3] Interested in theology he is, as Marcion is not ; firmly committed—at all events in his orthodox days—to the traditional deposit, again in opposition to Marcion's critical rationalism ; yet neither of these divergences,

---

[1] The second book of *adv. Marc.* is devoted to this theme ; see esp. cc. 3, 4, 12, etc. It is not to be denied that in this assertion of the goodness of all nature Tertullian has taken a very long step away from the doctrine of the unnatural God. But he certainly failed, in general, to follow out the principles thus recognized.

[2] Tert., *apol.*, 46. For the sentiment generally cp. *apol.*, 22 ; *de test. an.*, 1 ; *de spect.*, 2 ; *de praescr. haer.*, 7, *de an.*, 2, 3, etc.

[3] *de carne Christi*, 5.

nor any other, is really fundamental. The controversy between
Tertullian and Marcion, in fact, turns on a point which, in view of
their essential identity of outlook, is of complete unimportance.
Both are dualists to the core; the only question is, Shall the Old
Testament lie within or without the boundary which separates
irrevocably the things of the next world from the things of this?
The true answer to the question—the answer, There is no such irre-
vocable division; behind the greatest diversity there must be at
least some principle of unity—passes them both by. In all that
matters they are one.

Tertullian, therefore, is all but as rigorist as Marcion. He
abates a little of his opponent's emphasis on fasting; he is not
quite so sweeping in his condemnation of marriage :—' We do not
reject matrimony,' he says, ' we only refrain from it.' [1]   In all
else he is utterly ascetic. ' The sacrifices that are pleasing to God,'
he declares, ' are the torturing of the soul, fasting, a harsh and
unpleasing diet, and all the other mortifications that go therewith.' [2]
It was only natural, therefore, that when a new reforming schism
came his way he should join it. There is little apparent reason
why he should have abominated Marcion and embraced Montanism ;
his main interest was ethical, and ethically the two seem to have
been identical. Possibly the romantic mysticism of Montanism
awoke an echo in his soul which the Marcionite realism could not
evoke. Perhaps he preferred a heresy which, so far from sub-
tracting the Old Testament from the New, made a specious pretence
of adding a third dispensation to them both.[3] At all events, about
the fiftieth year of his age, he deserted Catholicism for the ' new
prophecy ' of Montanus.

In Montanism, Reitzenstein suggests, all the main features of
syncretistic gnosticism recur.[4] The non-Montanist, like the non-
gnostic, is called ' psychikos '; asceticism is the way to obtain the
indwelling spirit ; visions and revelations are the keynote of all
that is divine. The German writer, however, ignores the fact that
Montanism, unlike the gnostic sects, was a highly organized Church
—formalism has come to the aid of rigorism, and the Montanist
clergy are the first duly salaried ecclesiastics in Christian history.[5]
Montanism, in fact, represents a middle way between the gnostics

---

[1] *adv. Marc.*, i, 29.

[2] *de es. carn.*, 8 ; cp. *de pud.*, 1—true modesty consists not in the discipline (' moderatio '), but in the extermination (' ejuratio ') of the appetites.

[3] Cp. E. Gebhart, *Mystics and Heretics in Italy* (E. tr. of *L'Italie
Mystique*), p. 71—' One of the most original and most tenacious ideas of the
first Christian society was that nothing, in the religious state of the world,
was yet definitive ; that revelation had by no means said its last word.'
Gebhart shows how this conception revived in the work and writings of
Scotus Eriugena (p. 77), Amalric of Chartres (p. 78), and Joachim of Flora
(p. 79). The passage quoted from Amalric (p. 77) has a wholly Montanist
ring. Both Montanism and these later heresies started from the promise of
the Comforter in the Fourth Gospel.

[4] Reitzenstein, *HMHL.*, p. 230.

[5] Eus., *HE.*, v, 18. 2.

and Marcion.   On the basis of the bizarre revelations accorded to
its founder and his female accomplices it laid claim to mystical
experience, and apparently its hierarchy was selected from among
those who could give evidence of similar charismata.   But the individual Montanist was not allowed the freedom of the individual
gnostic.   He might be more than ' psychic,' but he must pay to
his spiritual superiors the same deference which was demanded of
the mere ' psychic ' in the Catholic Church ; and in the West, at
least, Montanism tended to lose its interest in revelations, and to
concentrate upon discipline.[1]

Marriage was grudgingly allowed, but apart from this rigorism
was once again not merely commended but enjoined.   For, if we
may trust Tertullian, ethical austerity was the main substance of
Montanist visions, after the first days of new doctrinal revelation
were over.   Even the length of the maidens' veils was regulated
by celestial interpositions ; one easy-mannered lady was slapped by
an angel on the bare neck for ignoring the divine requirements in
this respect.[2]   The Paraclete has revealed in their fullness the *real*
demands of God upon man in the matter of conduct.   Even Christ
had tempered the wind to the shorn lamb, but the time is now ripe
for advance.   ' Hardness of heart reigned among men till Christ
came,' says Tertullian ; ' thereafter weakness of flesh till the day
of the Paraclete ' ;[3] as Christ would not condone the hardness of
men's hearts, so the Paraclete has no mercy for the weakness of the
flesh.   ' Righteousness,' he writes elsewhere, ' was once no more
than a hope ' (in pre-Mosaic days, that is) ; ' the law and the prophets
brought it to the birth ; with the gospel it reached its youth ; the
Paraclete is giving it the strength of maturity.'[4]   ' Christ had
introduced a new law,' so Dr. Bigg paraphrases the Montanist gospel,
' but sparingly and with reserve, out of compassion for the weakness
of mankind.   Now the time had come for a great forward movement, and the whole counsel of God must be declared with unflinching severity.'[5]

V. RIGORIST DISCIPLINE.

It would be tempting and indeed necessary to a full account of
the subject to take under review the manifestations of rigorism
which lingered on even in Catholic minds—such as those of Ambrose
and Augustine—for centuries, and to compare with the excesses
which we have passed under review the strange phenomenon of
Manicheeism,[6] which represented the extreme dualistic wing of

---

[1] F. Loofs, *Leitfaden der Dogmengeschichte* ⁴, p. 174, from Tert., *de virg.
vel.*, 1.
[2] *de virg. vel.*, 17—cp. the whole treatise ; also *de cult. fem.* (which may
however belong to Tertullian's Catholic days).
[3] *de monog.*, 14.   [4] *de virg. vel.*, 1.
[5] C. Bigg, *Origins of Christianity*, p. 185.
[6] Epiphanius, *haer.*, lxvi.   For modern views, see F. C. Burkitt, *Religion
of the Manichees*, 1925.

gnosticism; together with the various rigorist revivals, both
Catholic and heretical, of the middle ages. Little however would
be gained for the understanding of the rigorist temper; and a
third form in which it manifested itself remains to be considered.[1]
In one respect Marcion's pity for mankind, sunk beneath the yoke
of the God of the Old Testament, made him less rigorous either than
Montanus, Tertullian, or indeed the majority of Catholics of his
day. By enforced asceticism he secured—as did so many others
of his period—a complete severance of that which he conceived to
be the Church from the world. But isolation once secured has
still to be maintained; and the problem of relapse into sin is
a difficult one—for relapsing sinners in effect join together once
again the two things—the Church and the world—which discipline
has sundered. Hermas, it will be recalled, on a special occasion
and in the most tentative and hesitating fashion, allowed one reconciliation to those who lapsed from baptismal purity; Marcion
was more generous. With a pastoral instinct strangely alien to his
otherwise rigorist outlook, he refused to expel his converts from the
communion if they lapsed. They might be readmitted on repentance,
and that more than once; it is an eccentricity which does not
affect the question that rebaptism rather than absolution was the
means of reconciliation employed.[2]

The general Catholic view on reconciliation in the second century
is fairly clear from Tertullian. Penance was not required for
minor sins; [3] reconciliation (though not penance) [4] was refused to

---

[1] The majority of the texts here cited are conveniently printed in full in
O. D. Watkins, *History of Penance*, vol. 1, though the most modern editions
have not always been used. The selection of texts given in the second
volume (for the mediæval period) is not by any means as exhaustive or
satisfactory as that in the first. P. Batiffol, *Études d'Histoire et de Théologie
Positive* [5], i, pp. 45-222, 327-349, and B. Poschmann, *Die Abendländische
Kirchenbusse*, are among the most recent discussions—both of them invaluable. The whole history of penance is made extraordinarily difficult to
unravel by the ambiguity of the technical terms employed. Thus μετάνοια,
pœnitentia, may mean either (a) 'repentance,' (b) the course of penitential
exercises and the status of penitent, or (c) the course *together with* reconciliation at its conclusion. Similarly *exomologesis* may be either (a) confession
to God, (b) consultation of the bishop or priest as to the need for public
penance, (c) overt admission of guilt by public application for and admission
to, the status of penitent, or, as numerous texts in Cyprian suggest (see
Brightman in H. B. Swete, *Early History of the Church and the Ministry*,
p. 372), (d) a similar overt admission *at the end* of the course of penance,
preliminary to reconciliation. By a slight but natural extension of meaning
it can also stand (e) for the course of penance as a whole, with or without
reconciliation. Other terms of a vaguer kind, such as ἐλέγχειν (*supra*,
pp. 113, 151, 153) and *corripere* may also have technical meanings. In these
circumstances many details will always remain doubtful. For further discussions, *infra*, pp. 504 ff., additional note I.
[2] Epiphan., *hær.*, xlii, 3. 6 (*GCSS.*, 'Epiphanius,' ii, p. 98).
[3] An inference mainly based upon *de pud.*, 19; but on the difficulties of
interpretation here see *infra*, p. 515, additional note J.
[4] *Infra*, p. 225. But some African bishops appear to have refused
'penance,' as well as reconciliation, to these classes of sinners—Cyprian,
ep. 55. 21 (Hartel's numeration will be used in all references to Cyprian)
'in totum pœnitentiæ locum contra adulteria clauserunt.' It is true that

murderers, adulterers, and apostates; for the intermediate class of grave sins [1] one reconciliation after due penance was allowed. The classical passage dates from his orthodox days. After alluding to the complete forgiveness of all sins at baptism, he adds:—

> ' I shrink from mentioning a second (or rather, final) hope, for to treat of any further opportunity of repentance seems almost to suggest another chance of sin. Still . . . though the great gate of forgiveness has been barred and bolted at baptism' (he calls baptism ' sera,' the bar), ' second penance waits in the vestibule to open a postern door once more to those who knock. But once more only, for it is the second time; never again, if this once fails. Surely this once is enough; it is a mercy wholly undeserved. . . . The postern (therefore) is narrow and hard to pass' (he alludes in no encouraging terms to the inconveniences of exomologesis), ' . . . but the alternative is hell.' [2]

In this account of second penance, which he also calls the ' plank in the shipwreck,' [3] there is no mention of any unforgivable sins; and it has been suggested that the selection of the three sins *par excellence* as wholly irremissible is a heretical refinement which he

---

pœnitentiæ locum may be used either for admission to penitential status *alone*, or for admission to that status *with the prospect of reconciliation* when the ' exercises ' are satisfactorily completed. Cyprian *may* merely mean that the bishops in question refused *reconciliation*, but the ' in totum ' suggests something more than this. (On the ambiguity, *supra*, p. 222, n. 1.)

[1] Sometimes called ' modica,' ' leviora ' (Tert., *de pud.*, 1 ; 18) or ' minora ' (Cyprian, *ep.* 16. 2) to distinguish them from the irremissible sins. Cyprian (*ep.* 17. 3) speaks of them as ' not committed against God '; similarly Tertullian (*de pud.*, 21) says of ' mortal ' sins that they are committed against God and His temple. Origen similarly (*de orat.*, 28) recognizes a distinction between ' sins committed against ourselves, which each of us can remit '; sins remitted by ' spiritual men ' ' as the apostles ' (he appears to have some sympathy with the claim of monks and perhaps even confessors to remit sins) ; and ' incurable ' sins which even the spiritual man ' retains.' For Origen's curious distinction between ' *culpa* mortalis ' (? = ' graviora crimina,' *ib.*) which can admit of one penance, and ' *crimen* mortale ' (which *presumably* cannot) ; and the further distinction between these and the ' communia '' quæ semper pœnitentiam recipiunt ' (presumably, *here*, of private repentance before God with restitution towards the victim), (*in Lev. hom.*, xv, 2 (*GCSS.*, ' Origenes,' vi, p. 489)), see O. D. Watkins, *History of Penance*, pp. 98, 138.

[2] Tert., *de pœn.*, 7, 9, 12. On the inconveniences of penance, *infra*, pp. 227 f.

[3] *Ib.*, c. 4. Strictly speaking, this refers to penance or penitence as a whole, for the distinction between baptismal and post-baptismal remission has yet to be made (cc. 6, 7), but in c. 12 he speaks of baptism and penance as ' two planks.' The ' *second* plank ' is mentioned in this connexion by Jerome, *ep.* 130. 9. Second penance (μετάνοια—the context shows clearly that an official act is concerned) is also mentioned at this period by Clem. Alex., *Strom.*, ii, 13. Clement goes on to condemn συνεχεῖς καὶ ἐπάλληλοι μετάνοιαι . . . τὸ πολλάκις μετανοεῖν. This must be a condemnation of attempts to have recourse to official penance more than once after baptism ; for there would be no point in condemning penitence as such ; renewed *sin* could be condemned, but in that case why refer to μετάνοια at all ? It would seem that the practice of repeated penances was being urged at Alexandria, and the relative mildness of Clement's language suggests that there was no very authoritative guidance from the leaders of the Church.

first learnt in his Montanist days.[1] But his calm assumption, later, that Callistus is innovating suggests that this is not the case ; and, with a ' postern ' so narrow that none can pass through it without difficulty it is at least likely that *some* will not be able to get through at all. We may assume, therefore, that even as a Catholic Tertullian held that certain sins were irremissible on earth ; and that in so doing he was not going beyond tradition.[2]

Sporadic instances of mitigation in one direction or another are to be found. Under Pope Hyginus (*c.* A.D. 135), the heretic Cerdon repeatedly confessed his heresy and was repeatedly reconciled, only to fall again.[3] Dionysius of Corinth, forty years later, urged on the churches of Pontus that penitents ' who wished to return after any kind of lapse, whether moral or heretical, should be received back.'[4] About the same time the confessors of Vienne, through Irenæus, approached Pope Eleutherus with a request that he should raise the Catholic ban against the Montanists ,[5] he or one of his immediate successors (possibly Zephyrinus) actually took this step, but was over-persuaded by Praxeas.[6] But the outcry raised by Callistus' action only a few years later makes it clear that the rigour of the law was in general fully maintained.

Adulterers, apostates and murderers, therefore, were normally excluded from the Church without hope of readmission. A

---

[1] So Brightman, in (ed. H. B. Swete), *Early History of the Church and the Ministry*, p. 374 ; d'Alès, *L'Édit de Calliste*, pp. 152-154, 177-180, 197 ff. ; P. de Labriolle, *Tertullien, de pæn., de pud.*, p. xv ; G. Rauschen, *Florileg. Patrist.*, x, pp. 6, 7 ; G. Esser, *Die Bussschriften Tertullians*, pp. 11, 19, 28 ; contrast Batiffol, *Études d'Histoire, etc.*[5], i, pp. 328 ff. (the theory as stated by Esser and criticized by Funk), *ib.*, pp. 340 ff. (d'Alès' theory).

[2] Similarly, Origen, *de orat.*, 28, 8, knows of ' incurable sins,' and says that ' the sacrifice is not to be offered for them ' (an Old Testament metaphor), though he admits that this view is not universal. Tertullian's main object here being to move men to penitence, it is natural that he should not insist closely upon its limitations.

[3] Iren., *adv. haer.*, iii, 4. 3 ; similarly Tertullian, *de praescr.*, 30—Valentinus and Marcion were ' semel et iterum ejecti.' Clement's story of the apostle John and the brigand (*Quis Div. Salv.*, 42) is another case of the reconciliation of a person guilty of an ' irremissible ' sin ; but apostles may have been thought to have special privileges in the matter. We cannot infer that Clement would have approved of it as a general thing.

[4] Eus., *HE.*, iv, 23. 6. Dionysius was a stern opponent of Marcionism, and it is possible that he is urging his correspondents in Pontus (Marcion's home) to be *at least* as liberal as the Marcionites in readmitting offenders. For his liberalism in another matter he suffered a delicate but definite reproof from Pinytus, bishop of Cnossos (*ib.*).

[5] So H. B. Swete, *JTS.*, iv (1903), p. 325, and this certainly reproduces the tone of Eusebius' very vague statement (*HE.*, v, 3, 4). But A. C. McGiffert, *Eusebius* (Nicene and Post-Nicene Library), p. 219, and Salmon (*DCB.*, iii, p. 937) hold that the confessors were protesting against the reconciliation with Montanism. Duchesne, *Early History of the Church* (E. tr.), i, pp. 201, 202, is doubtful. The confessors of Vienne certainly went so far as to readmit apostates of their own body, as Hermas proposed at Rome, in the hope that they would do better a second time (Eus., *HE.*, v, 1. 45, 46 ; 2. 5).

[6] Tert., *adv. Prax.*, i. Swete (*ut sup.*) thinks this refers to Zephyrinus ; Duchesne (*ut sup.*) says ' it could hardly have been anyone but Eleutherus.'

further refinement of cruelty which occasionally emerges is the
suggestion that these three sins, which the Church will not remit
on earth, will not be remitted even by God Himself in heaven.
Such an inference was no doubt within the strict letter of the com
mission (as it was supposed to be) to bind and loose ; what was
bound upon earth would remain bound in heaven. Batiffol[1]
generalizes too widely when he says, ' The Church did not hold
offenders guilty of the three capital sins to be lost eternally ; but
for the general edification she decided that they must negotiate
with God direct for their reconciliation.' It is true that even as a
Montanist Tertullian argues that penance in the case of the irremissible sins is valuable because God may remit them though the
Church will not.[2] But he is not clear on the point ; he speaks of
a class of sin (including the irremissible ones) ' quorum exorator non
erit Christus ' ;[3] and although this may simply mean that Christ
will not obtain pardon for these sins *on earth*, it is a curiously strong
phrase to employ for the purpose.[4] Cyprian too suggests, though
not quite in the same connexion, that the divine forgiveness is
in all cases coterminous with reconciliation given here upon earth.[5]
' I entreat you, brethren,' he writes to the apostates who are being
given their unexpected second chance, ' each confess his own sin
while he is yet in the world ; while his confession may still be
received, while the satisfaction and remission made by the ministers
is acceptable with the Lord.' Similarly an anonymous writer, who
may be ' Ambrosiaster,' asserts roundly that no sin which has not
been remitted on earth can be remitted in heaven ;[6] but whether

---

[1] *Études d'Histoire, etc.*, p. 80.

[2] *de pud.*, 3. Tertullian's imaginary disputant says, ' Penance will be
useless if absolution (' venia '—see additional note J, p. 515) is lacking.'
He replies : God can forgive even ' mortal sin ' (' mortalia '—the first
use of the term) ; and so the penitent may think of his case as ' remitted
to God.' His repentance ' sows the seeds of pardon with God, it prepares
its fruit, it will not fail of its reward, it is not in vain ' (cp. also *ib.*, 18).
Tertullian can even go further—' the Church ' (though he makes it clear
that for him this means the true Church—i.e. the Montanists) ' has the
power of forgiving sins,' but (in the case of the ' irremissibilia ') the Spirit
(in the Church) says, ' I will not do so, lest they sin again.' Thus even the
irremissible sins are remissible *per se ;* it is expediency, not principle, which
leads the Church to refuse absolution for them (*de pud.*, 21). This power
of the Church, in the case of mortal sin, the Novatians later even went so
far as to deny (Pacian, *ep.* 3). An early instance of this lifelong penance is
apparently the case of the deacon's wife in Irenæus, *adv. haer.*, i, 13. 5. Of
the other women mentioned in the same chapter as doing penance, nothing
is said as to its duration. That lifelong penance for the three ' irremissibilia '
was known at Rome is clear from *de pud.*, 5 ; Tertullian there describes
the idolater, the homicide and the adulterer standing by the Church door
—Callistus ' damns ' the first two once for all (' semel damnas '), but ' welcomes ' their ' colleague.'

[3] *de pud.*, 19.   [4] *Infra*, p. 515, additional note J.

[5] Cyprian, *de laps.*, 29.

[6] [Aug.] *contra Novatianum* (= *Quæstiones Veteris et Novi Testamenti*,
n. 102) ; on the date of this treatise, O. D. Watkins, *op. cit.*, pp. 215, 216.
Leo the Great will not allow a penitent who has died without reconciliation
to be prayed for (*ep.* 167. 8) ; but a milder sentiment comes in with the

he is speaking his own mind or arguing from Novatian's premisses is not altogether clear.

The details of Callistus' famous 'edict,' together with the degree of authority which it claimed, are all uncertain ; it is not even proved that the anonymous bishop of Rome whom Tertullian pillories is Callistus himself.[1] The 'edict,' as given by Tertullian, professes to offer reconciliation to penitents guilty of adultery after baptism ; [2] Hippolytus—whose quarrel with Callistus was more personal in character—says that he offered absolution from sins of every kind, and adds that the measure was purely partisan.[3] If the incidents referred to are the same, Tertullian's account must be preferred (though a reference in Origen [4] might conceivably support Hippolytus) ; the whole argument of ch. 5 of the 'de Pudicitia' falls to the ground, and the Novatianist schism is inexplicable, if Cornelius had been anticipated by Callistus in offering reconciliation to penitent apostates.

Callistus won the day against his rigorist opponents, but only on the point in question. 'By the middle of the third century,' says Dr. Brightman,[5] 'the rigorist attitude towards the remission of sins of the flesh had disappeared in Africa and Italy. Even Novatian did not adopt it ; . . . although later on the Novatianist sect enlarged its programme and denied the right of the Church to absolve any mortal sin.' [6] The next problem to arise—in very practical form, thanks to the persecuting zeal of the Emperor Decius,

synods of Vaison (A.D. 442), can. 2, and II. Arles (A.D. 443 or 452), can. 12, in Gaul, in the case of worthy penitents whose sudden death has deprived them of reconciliation (Hefele-Leclerq, ii, pp. 445, 466).

[1] See A. d'Alès, L'Édit de Calliste, pp. 1-3. [2] de pud., 1.

[3] Hipp., Philos., ix, 12. 20.

[4] de orat., 28. 10; cp. supra, p. 224, n. 2. H. B. Swete, JTS., iv (1903), p. 331, takes this as a direct reference to Callistus ; similarly Döllinger, Hippolyt u. Kallist, pp. 254 ff., and Harnack, Hist. of Dogma, ii, p. 111 n. Batiffol, Études d'Histoire[5], p. 109, argues on the other side ; and although in the seventh edition he has changed his general view of Origen's position (p. 110), it does not affect this point.

[5] Swete, Church and Ministry, p. 375 ; cp. Cyprian, of some of his predecessors (ep. 55. 21) and his own practice (ib., 20). So also Clem. Alex., Strom., ii, 23. 147, of the penitent adulteress, apparently allowed penance.

[6] Cyprian, ep. 55. 26—Novatian offers adulterers 'penance '—this must mean penance with absolution, for in § 27 it is equated with 'communicare.' But the evidence of [Aug.] contra Nov. (ut sup.) contradicts it—'fornication ought not to be forgiven, according to Novatian.' Novatian apparently offered apostates lifelong penance without reconciliation. Cp. Cyprian, ep. 55. 28, 29—Cyprian reprobates the practice as a counsel of despair ; [Aug.], contra Nov.—' poenitentia quidem predicata est, non tamen remissio '; Socr., Hist. Eccl., i, 10, of Acesius, 'a Novatianist bishop,' with whose rigorism on this point Constantine was so surprised that he said, 'Place a ladder, Acesius, and climb up alone into heaven '—but Acesius was refusing reconciliation (though allowing penance) to all who committed 'mortal sin' after baptism. Ambrose, de pœnit., i, 3 (10), however, says that Novatian thought that no one should be admitted to penance, even without reconciliation ; whilst contemporary Novatianists absolve in cases of minor sins, and admit penance, without reconciliation, for grave ones (ib., i. 11 (52)). Pacian, ep. 3. 1 (MPL., xiii, col. 1063) gives as two Novatianist propositions, 'no penance after baptism,' and 'no forgiveness for mortal sin.'

—was that of apostasy. By this time the rigorists have stiffened. In Batiffol's words,[1] 'Callistus only raised controversies, Cornelius provoked a schism.' Rather than admit the new humanitarianism, which offered reconciliation to penitent apostates, Novatian and his friends accepted exile from the Church, and feeling was sufficiently strong to keep the schism alive for four centuries.[2] The third irremissible sin held its ground longer still ; it was not till the Council of Ancyra (A.D. 314) that the penitent murderer might hope for reconciliation—and only then at the point of death.[3] Meanwhile there were parts of the Christian world in which rigorism gained its local victories in this same matter ; the extraordinary Spanish Council of Elvira, in 306, tabulates no less than nineteen sins for which communion (and therefore reconciliation) is to be refused to the penitent even on his deathbed.[4]

In other directions, too, rigorism more than held its ground. The rule of one reconciliation only for grave sins is never relaxed during the Imperial period.[5] All grave sinners—however secret their offence may be—are expected to come forward for open penance. Further, the desire to keep the Church unspotted from the world led to a stiffening of the details of penitential discipline which must have deterred the vast majority of sinners from making any advance towards reconciliation. There is no doubt as to this result ; by the beginning of the fifth century—though many sinners are reconciled on their deathbeds—scarcely anyone does penance except those who, for notorious sins, are compelled to it by physical constraint. Exclusion from the Church was a solemn and humiliating function ; so was admission thereafter to the official status of a penitent under discipline, as well as the final reconciliation. Even in Tertullian's day, as a famous passage in the ' de Pœnitentia ' shows, the discipline was cruel not only in itself but in its publicity ; Jerome's account of Fabiola's penance is no less final evidence.[6]

---

[1] Batiffol, *Études d'Histoire*, p. 111.

[2] The last mention of the Novatianists in history appears to be *Conc. Trull.* (Quinisext, A.D. 692), can. 95 (Hefele-Leclerq, iii, p. 574), repeating *Conc. Constant.* (A.D. 381), can. 7 (*ib.*, ii, p. 36).

[3] *Conc. Anc.*, can. 22.

[4] For the Council of Elvira, and the refusal of death-bed penance, see *infra*, additional note I, p. 511.

[5] For expedients devised to mitigate the severity of this rule, *infra*, p. 278 ; and, generally, for this and the following paragraphs, see additional note I, p. 504.

[6] Tert., *de pœn.*, 9, 10 ; Jerome, *ep.* 77 ; cp. also the penance of Natalius (Eus., *HE.*, v, 28. 12). Further evidence from Cyprian, *de laps.*, 35 ; Sozomen, *HE.*, vii, 16 (Rome in the fifth century) ; Cæsarius Arel. ([Aug.], *app. serm.*, 104. 7) ; Pacian, *parænesis*, 10, etc. The required austerities comprised fasting in sackcloth and ashes, constant prayer with tears and groaning, prostration before the faithful, who were begged to add their prayers to those of the penitent, etc. They were allowed to be present during part of the mass (the East) or all of it (in the West), in the narthex or porch of the Church ; but not of course to communicate (details, Brightman, *ut sup.*, p. 367). This is severe enough, but humane ; barbarism only came into penance with the conversion of the northern races, who transformed into a torture what the Latins used as a discipline (*infra*, p. 285, n. 2).

Later the severity increased to an almost unbelievable degree. Not only before, but even after his reconciliation, the penitent suffered every kind of temporal penalty—so much so that entry into a monastery came to be a recognized (and even preferable) alternative to penance,[1] and evasion by suicide was not unknown.[2] The offender might not enter the ranks of the clergy ; [3] he might not marry, or, if married, cohabit with his wife ; he was forbidden to undertake military service or commercial enterprise ; public office, festivals, and civic occasions were all debarred.[4] In the fifth century, the attempt was made to extract from him a public confession of the details of his offence—an attempt promptly suppressed by S. Leo [5] in language which makes it certain (against an opinion still held among historians) that the practice was generally unknown in the early Church.

At the same time the penance itself was prolonged to inordinate lengths.[6] The Council of Elvira added to the severity we have already noticed by refusing reconciliation except *in articulo mortis* in the case of five other sins.[7] The laxity of Peter of Alexandria, who is known to have limited the duration of the penances he imposed for apostasy to a maximum of four years,[8] is said by Epiphanius to have shocked half his diocese into schism.[9] S. Basil suggests a penance of thirty years for unwitting offences against the seventh commandment ; [10] eleven years for unpremeditated homicide ; [11] twenty for wilful murder [12] (even this, however, is a relaxation of the rule of Ancyra) ; and life-long penance for apostasy.[13] There were loyalist minds in Southern Gaul who refused absolution

---

[1] ' Conversio ' ; *infra*, additional note I, p. 509.

[2] *Conc.* 16 *Tolet.* (A.D. 693), c. 4.

[3] Siricius (A.D. 384-398), *ep.* 1. *ad Himerium*, 14 (MPL., xiii, col. 1145); Innocent I. (A.D. 402-417), *ep.* 39 *ad ep. Apul.* (MPL., xx, col. 606). Curiously enough, as Poschmann (pp. 67, 68) notices, the renown obtained by worthy penitents was such that bishops naturally turned to them as the most likely candidates for holy orders. So Pope Hormisdas (A.D. 517) insists that *not even penitents* are to be ordained priest without passing through the minor orders. Cp. Poschmann, pp. 100, 101, 147, 148.

[4] Siricius, *ut sup.*, 5 ; Leo, *ep.* 167. 10-12 ; *Conc.* 2 *Arel.* (A.D. 443), c. 21 ; *Conc.* 3 *Aurel.* (A.D. 538), c. 4. Further instances Poschmann, pp. 98-100, 166. Morinus (*de pœn.*, v, 20) and others point out that there is no evidence for rigorism of this character before the fourth century ; Poschmann's hesitations on the subject (*op. cit.*, p. 58) seem unnecessary. The last actual canon on the subject appears to be *Conc.* 2 *Barcinon.* (A.D. 599), c. 4, in which anyone who has received the ' benedictio pœnitentiæ ' is classed with professed nuns as equally debarred from matrimony. On Leo's mitigations of these severities, *infra*, pp. 278, 506.

[5] *Infra*, additional note I, p. 510.

[6] But the bishop was normally empowered to remit part of the sentence in view of extenuating circumstances ; *infra*, additional note I. p. 508.

[7] *Conc. Illib.*, cann. 3, 9, 10, 13, 47 ; further Roman and Spanish instances, Poschmann, pp. 30 ff., 152.

[8] *ep. can.* (A.D. 306), c. 3 (Routh, *Reliquiæ Sacræ*, IV., pp. 25, 26).

[9] Epiphan., *hær.*, 68. 3—but the ground assigned by Epiphanius is Peter's leniency in general towards apostates.

[10] *ep.* 188 (*canonica*, i), c. 7.

[11] *Ib.*, c. 11.

[12] *ep.* 217 (*canonica*, iii), c. 56.

[13] *ep.* 217, c. 73.

altogether to those who deferred any attempt at penance until the approach of death.[1] Better counsels prevailed at times, as for instance in some of the Church Orders, which are content with penances of so short a duration as five or seven weeks; [2] but in general it is the penal and not the pastoral aspect of the system which is to the fore. What a recent writer has said of the first two centuries, that the Church was more concerned with her prerogative of binding than with that of loosing, can without exaggeration be extended to the first five.[3]

VI. THE SINLESSNESS OF THE CHRISTIAN.

The development just sketched is no more than an eddy of the great rigorist movement, but it shares all its characteristic features. Once again a line of demarcation is drawn down the middle of the phenomena of life, one side of the frontier being wholly the province of God and the other that of the devil; and all attempts to recognize a middle term, a neutral zone, a bridge or medium of transition between the two are stamped as un-Christian. Any pretending Christian who commits 'mortal,' or who relapses into 'grave,' sin is adjudged no Christian at all. The connexion between this disciplinary rigorism and the gnostic systems is not merely ethical; they stand in the closest doctrinal relationship as well. The doctrine of the 'unnatural' God—the God whose presence and operation is to be discerned only in the miraculous, the abnormal, the unheard-of—dominates them both. Its influence in the case of the gnostic we have already seen; the rigorist in discipline showed himself of the same school of thought when he insisted, in effect, that only those could be called Christians upon whom God had miraculously conferred the grace of perfect sinlessness.

This amazing doctrine of the actual sinlessness of the true Christian—the doctrine of an automatically irresistible infusion of grace—meets us continually in the early centuries. It betrays itself to some extent in the beautiful yet slightly complacent passages in which Aristides, Justin, Tertullian, and the author of 'ad Diognetum' describe the spotless purity of contemporary Christian society [4]—passages which, when all is said that can be said for the moral superiority of the Church over the surrounding world in the first three centuries, are clearly in advance of the facts. But it shows itself in explicit statements as well, and that even in orthodox writers. 'The spiritual man cannot do what is fleshly,' occurs in Ignatius' letter to the Ephesians: so do the words, 'No

[1] *Infra*, additional note I, p. 512.
[2] So *Didascalia* and *Ap. Const.*, Brightman, *op. cit.*, p. 370. On the possibility that Fabiola's penance lasted for one day only, Poschmann, p. 35.
[3] Watkins, *op. cit.*, p. 213.
[4] *Supra*, p. 146, n. 3. On the whole subject cp. also *ERE.*, ix, pp. 728-737 (*s.v.* 'Perfection ').

man sins who professes faith.'¹ The Christian, says Justin, must
be 'anamartetos'—beyond the possibility of sin.² According to
the 'Didascalia' it is inconceivable that 'once having gone down
into the water of baptism (the Christian) will again do the abominable
and impure works of the heathen and depraved.'³ Origen knows
of people who assert, 'If a man believes, he does not sin ; if he
sins, it is proof that he does not believe ' ; and again, ' The moment
a man begins to be holy, he can no longer sin : and thenceforth
he must be reckoned without sin.'⁴ Sentiments such as these he
deplored ; yet he himself, writing of the true 'pneumatikos,' could
say :—

> 'Happy those who, needing the Son of God, *need Him no
> more as a Physician of the soul's diseases, a Pastor or Redeemer*,
> but only as Wisdom and Word and Righteousness or some such
> other Grace as befits men who, *being perfect*, can claim the
> highest titles.'⁵

Clement's true gnostic, or ideal Christian, is throughout spoken
of as sinless ; and the language is too vivid to allow us to suppose
that the writer is merely depicting a perfection after which we are
to strive, without hope of attaining it on earth.⁶ The gnostic
' has already become a God ' ; he is ' perfect in righteousness ' ; his
soul is ' virgin of evil ' ; ' by his rectitude he makes up for the
absence of the apostles' ; he is ' assimilated to God the Saviour,
and as far as is possible to man is made perfect as the Father in
Heaven.'⁷ The picture is drawn in full detail :—

> ' Not even were God to allow the gnostic with impunity to
> do what is forbidden ;—not even if he were promised a reward
> for doing wrong, even the reward of the blessed ;—not even if he
> were persuaded that God could be blind to what he did (a thing
> impossible) ;—not even so could he so much as wish to do what
> is contrary to right reason.'⁸

Macarius knew of people who said that after baptism ' evil is
no more at liberty to pasture in the heart,' and that ' the Lord
condemned sin by the cross so that it is no longer within.' He

---

¹ Ign., *ad Eph.* 8², 14².

² Justin, *apol.*, 44. On the history of the word, which, except for Jn. 8⁷, is
not used in N.T., see H. Windisch, *Taufe und Sünde*, p. 396. He suggesst
that Justin adopted the pagan word as a deliberate challenge—' The Greeks
have the idea, but we Christians have the fact ! ' (*ib.*, p. 397). This is perhaps a little daring ; the word occurs three times in the LXX.

³ *Didasc.* 5 (tr. M. D. Gibson, p. 26).

⁴ *in Rom.*, ii, 7 (*MPG.*, xiv, col. 879) ; *hom. in Num.*, x, 1 (*GCSS.*,
' Origenes,' vii, p. 68).

⁵ *in Jn.* i, 20, 124 (*GCSS.*, ' Origenes,' iv, p. 25).

⁶ Though (as Windisch rightly points out, *op. cit.*, p. 467) Clement
reckons himself among the sinners.

⁷ E.g. *Strom.*, iv, 23. 149 ; vii, 12. 77 ; vi, 12. 104 ; and generally compare C. Bigg, *Christian Platonists of Alexandria*, pp. 123-127 ; H. Windisch,
Taufe u. Sünde, pp. 443-456.

⁸ *Strom.*, iv, 22. 146.

found it necessary to deal with such questions as ' Is it possible for a man who has a gift of grace to fall ? ' [1] or ' Can a man bound over to the Holy Spirit, and inebriated with heavenly things, be liable to turn to evil ? ' [2] Jovinian, of whom we shall hear more, was accused of holding the same views—a curious fact, when his generally humanistic outlook is taken into account.[3] The doctrine had gnostic and pagan parallels. Basilides, according to Clement of Alexandria, held that all sins were unpardonable except those of ignorance, clearly implying that the gnostic was incapable of conscious transgressions.[4] The Valentinians insisted that the ' pneumatikoi ' could not be damned whatever they might do.[5] The Manichees regarded themselves as beyond the reach of sin ; only the ' race of darkness ' was sinful.[6]

The idea of an immediate metamorphosis of the soul by reception of divine grace was common in the Græco-Roman world,[7] though immortality rather than moral perfection was the result usually attributed to it. If, as is sometimes supposed [8] (though in the face of all the probabilities), Apuleius' whole novel is an allegory whose explanation is reached in the religious passages of the last book, his hero's transformation from an ass to a man is symbolical of such a belief. Seneca experienced something of the kind, though he was too prudent to claim sinlessness as the result—' It is not so much an improvement as a transfiguration that I have undergone,' he writes to Lucilius ; [9] 'not that I have escaped from everything that ought to be changed . . . but that I see the faults which formerly I knew not of. . . . This sudden transformation of mine I would fain relate to thee.' In any case the picture of the superman— the ' divine man ' or ' son of god '—was so common in the Imperial period that the moralist must naturally have added sinlessness to its characteristics.[10] It even reached the extreme of

---

[1] Macar., *Hom.*, xv, 14, 16 ; cp. vii, 14 ; xvii, 8 ; xxvii, 9-13.

[2] *Ib.*, xv, 36.

[3] Hieron., *adv. Jovin.*, i, 3. From ii, 1, however, it appears that Jovinian rashly elaborated his proposition with the even more temerarious statement that the baptized cannot be *tempted*.

[4] Clem. Alex., *Strom.*, iv, 24. 153.

[5] Iren., *hær.*, i, 6. 2.

[6] Cæsar. Arel. [Aug.], *append. serm.*, 253. 2.

[7] On this cp. references *supra*, pp. 51-53 ; further, A. E. J. Rawlinson (ed.), *Essays on the Trinity and Incarnation*, pp. 186, 187, 228-234.

[8] E.g. Reitzenstein, *HMR.*, p. 262.

[9] Seneca, *ep.* 6. 1. For other pagan conversions cp. S. Dill, *Roman Society from Nero to Marcus Aurelius*, p. 347 ; E. Zeller, *Stoics, Epicureans and Sceptics* (E. tr.), p. 258.

[10] Slight traces of such a development are quoted by G. P. Wetter, ' *Der Sohn Gottes*,' pp. 37, 38. Probably, however, it was rare ; and that for a curious reason. The idea of ' metamorphosis ' is of course often superstitious, and would therefore be most readily received by the uneducated. But Christianity was the only *ethical* movement in the Empire (the mystery cults being in the main non-ethical) which spread widely amongst the uneducated ; only, therefore, in Christianity did the idea of *ethical metamorphosis* take deep root. We must not forget, however, the ' virtue cannot be lost ' of some of the Stoics (E. Zeller, *Stoics, Epicureans and Sceptics*, p. 277).

belief in the apotheosis of the devotee in this life—a doctrine which, verbally at least, more than one great Christian writer was ill-advised enough to reproduce.[1]

In Judaism also the doctrine was not unknown. The author of the 'Epistle of Barnabas' says quite naturally, 'When He renewed us through the remission of sins, He made us a new creature, and gave us the souls of children. . . . See, we have been recreated, as He saith by another prophet:—" I will take away their stony heart and give them a heart of flesh." '[2]   He is falling back upon the old apocalyptic doctrine that the end shall be like the beginning, and that the inhabitants of the kingdom of God shall be like the first denizens of the garden of Eden—or like the patriarchs, of whom rabbinic theology predicated sinlessness.   But, following the customary practice of S. Paul, he has ante-dated this eschatological sinlessness, and asserts it of the Christian here and now. Even this is not specifically Christian—the Rabbis had done as much. 'When the greater part of a man's life has been lived without sin, he shall not sin thereafter,' was one of their sayings ; and again, 'If a man resist temptation once or twice he shall not sin thereafter.'   Of certain Rabbis themselves it was told that they had lived wholly without sin.[3]

Certainly a one-sided interpretation of S. Paul would more than justify primitive Christians in the belief.   It has frequently been noted [4] that however fully he may lament his past sins, he himself has little consciousness of sin in the present.   And often enough he seems to expect the same of his converts.   They are free from sin (Rom. vi, 18, 22) ; dead to sin (vi, 11) ; they are not in the flesh but in the Spirit (viii, 9) ; they walk not after the flesh but after the Spirit (viii, 4) ; they have been reconciled, to be presented holy and without blemish and unreprovable before God (Col. i, 21, 22).   'If any man is in Christ, he is a new creation ; the old things are passed away ; behold, they are become new' (2 Cor. v, 17).[5]   Sentences such as these could of course be countered with

---

[1] A catena of Christian passages can be made up from the references in A. Robertson, *Athanasius* (*LNP-NF.*), p. 65, n. 5 ; Harnack, *Hist. of Dogma*, index, *s.v.* 'Deification' ; W. R. Inge, *Christian Mysticism*, Appendix C, pp. 356-368. Cp. *infra*, pp. 237, 337, n. 5, 339, 370, n. 8, 452, n. 2.

[2] *Barn.*, 6. 11 ; 6. 14.   The reference is to Ezk. 11[19], 36[26].   On the Jewish evidence for this belief, and its eschatological connexions, H. Windisch, *Taufe u. Sünde*, pp. 8-50.

[3] Strack-Billerbeck, *Kommentar*, i, pp. 814-816.   Cp. also *Test. XII. Patriarchs : Issachar* 7[1]—' I am a hundred and twenty-six years old, and am not conscious of committing any sin ' (another version of the text softens the arrogance of the statement by adding the words ' unto death ') ; *Zebulon*, 1[4]. [5]—' I am not conscious that I have sinned all my days ; nor yet do I remember that I have done any iniquity, except the sin of ignorance ' (here, too, a variant reading has ' save in thought ' after ' days ').

[4] I have collected references to statements to this effect by writers of different schools of thought in Rawlinson, *Essays on the Trinity and Incarnation*, p. 230, n. 1.   On its importance as a factor in Christian ethics, *infra*, p. 545, additional note R, *Augustinism*.

[5] On the parallel doctrine of the epistle to the Hebrews and the first epistle of S. John, *supra*, p. 161.

the greatest ease by others in which the Christian is called upon
to work out his own salvation with fear and trembling; and the
reconciliation between the two strains of thought is bound up with
the reconciliation between the world-renouncing and the world-
embracing elements in S. Paul's ethics. But taken apart from
the context of his full teaching, they would easily support a
doctrine of Christian sinlessness here and now.

It is improbable, however, that the ultimate source of the
doctrine of sinlessness, as it revealed itself in Christianity, with its
rigorist concomitants in ethics and discipline, is to be found in the
teaching either of S. Paul, or of Judaism, or of contemporary
paganism. Its origin was genuinely empirical. Sudden conversions,
resulting in an apparently complete and effortless cessation, if not
from *all* sins, at least from one or more besetting temptations, are
perhaps a rarer phenomenon under the conditions of modern Western
civilization than in less sophisticated epochs or continents. But
they do occur, as every student of religious psychology knows;
and there have been times when they have occurred plentifully.
There is no reason to suppose that the dawn of Christianity was not
such a time;[1] or that the contrast which S. Paul loves to draw
between the present purity and the past infamy of his converts
is based on anything less than fact. And if so, there was sufficient
empirical ground for the doctrine that *some* Christians at least,
under the influence of the Holy Spirit and the enthusiasm of conversion, passed through a change so sudden and so far-reaching as
to make them in effect, if perhaps only for a moment, new and
sinless men.

But, as before in the matter of the vision of God, to translate
what is true of *some* Christians into a final criterion of sincerity to
be applied to *all* Christians without exception, is to fall victim to
a most dangerous fallacy. This, however, was the course taken,
not indeed by the Church at large, but by many enthusiasts within
the Church. The Christian who was not here and now sinless was
adjudged no Christian at all. It is the doctrine of the unnatural
God making a new appearance. In no department of conscious
life is perfection normally achieved except as the result of long and
disciplined effort, of alternate success and failure, of tedious advance
retarded by constant checks, hesitations and reverses. Even in the
early Church there were innumerable *proficientes* whose progress
towards sinlessness must at best have been painfully slow. To
assume, therefore, that the only convincing sign of the presence
of divine grace shall be an immediate and compulsory moralization
of the whole personality would be to assume that God acts in the
moral life in a way wholly in contrast to man's efforts and achievements in that life, and wholly diverse from the processes of nature
elsewhere. Such a view introduces the ideas of magic into the

---

[1] Cp. P. Batiffol, *Études d'Histoire, etc.*, p. 46:—' Sans doute, il n'était
pas impossible au baptisé de garder toute sa vie cette pureté baptismale . . .
En thèse, cette fidelité était normale.'

sphere of all others in which they are most fatally devastating, and throws Christianity back upon perhaps the most tragic and superstitious of all possible errors.

The tragedy happened none the less. Christian discipline in the first four centuries was dominated by ' the favourite black-and white theory,' as it has been well called, ' of the narrow-minded revivalist.' [1] Far more than any Judaistic formula of earlier days, it attempted to put a yoke on the neck of the disciples heavier than they were able to bear. Formalist in operation—for it shows no interest in the communion of the Christian with God—it is fully rigorist in temper ; and therefore ranks with gnosticism and the aberrations of primitive monasticism as a factor in the whole great problem which the Church was called upon to face. Easy enough to state, the problem was extraordinarily difficult to solve. It is simply this—Is rigorism in all its manifestations wholly un-Christian ; or can some test be discovered to separate what is Christian in it from what is pagan, and some machinery devised to prevent the latter from intruding and encroaching upon the former ?

---

[1] H. Windisch, *Taufe u. Sünde*, p. 289. The combination of formalism and rigorism to be noticed in the first four centuries of the history of Christian discipline (see above, and also earlier, ch. iii, pp. 160, 164, 172) has very deep roots. Baron von Hügel (*Essays and Addresses*, i, p. 179) with unerring discrimination drew particular attention to Troeltsch's observations on the point. The essence of Catholicism is the distinction between nature and the supernatural, and yet the correlation of the two within one system of divine operation (*op. cit.*, p. 176 ; cp. *infra*, pp. 304, 379). Hence ' the essence of Christian supernaturalism consists in the elevation of the creature above this creature's co-natural limitations, to God's own supernature, to participation in His nature '—i.e. in the doctrine of the vision of God as the end for man. Thus formalism (which, as we have seen, tends to ignore the doctrine of the vision of God) has no secure anchor in the truly Catholic scheme. But what Troeltsch calls the ' sect-type,' with its ' hostility to the world ' (i.e. organized or propagandist rigorism), and its consequent abandonment of the correlation of ' nature ' and ' supernature ' within a single scheme of divine providence, *cannot* logically express its ideal in terms of the raising of the natural to the supernatural, i.e. in terms of the vision of God. ' [Its] ideal is without the character of a mystical supernature, of the elevation of man's essence in itself. . . . And since such mystical beatitude, as the crown of the system of stages, falls all but entirely away for the sects, the conception of Law now takes up an all-dominating position. . . . Thus in lieu of the institution of Grace and Redemption, the conception of Law becomes the centre of the sect theology.' This very profound observation accounts for many of the most difficult phenomena in Christian history—in particular, for the relatively early disappearance of mystical rigorism (gnosticism and primitive Montanism) as compared with the stubborn survival of formalist rigorism (Marcionism, later Montanism, Novatianism, Donatism, etc.).

LECTURE V.

THE REPLY TO RIGORISM.

(I.—DISCIPLINE.)

Mt. xi. 29, 30.—' Take My yoke upon you, and learn of Me ; for I am meek
and lowly in heart ; and ye shall find rest unto your souls. For My
yoke is easy, and My burden is light.'

I. RIGORISTS AND HUMANISTS.

IN the ' Verba Seniorum ' there is an often-quoted story of
S. Macarius of Alexandria.[1] He was warned by a heavenly voice
that he had not yet achieved the holiness of two women who
dwelt in the neighbouring city. Hurriedly seeking them out,
he enquired of them the manner of life they lived. At first
they demurred to the question—' Most holy father,' they protested, ' what kind of life is ours for you to ask about ? But
the saint persisted, and in the end they said :—' We are not indeed
related, but as it happened we married two brothers. For fifteen
years we have lived together without a quarrel, without even a
sharp word passing between us. We both desired to leave our
husbands and enter a convent ; but they would not allow it. So
we vowed that until the day of our death we would hold no worldly
talk with one another, but converse only about spiritual things.'
Then said Macarius, ' Truly virginity matters nothing, nor marriage ;
there is no difference between the monastic life and the secular.
It is the motive alone which God observes ; and He gives the spirit
of life to all alike.'

Anecdotes of this character recur throughout the records of
early Egyptian monasticism. Often however they have significant
variations. Sometimes the worldling held up as an example to
the monk is told that he lacks one thing more only—to break with

---

[1] Rosweyde, iii, 97 (*MPL.*, lxxiii, col. 778) ; another version, *ib.*, vi, 3,
17 (col. 1014). Cp. the analogous sentiment in the *Apophthegmata* (Cotelier,
i, p. 575)—' Are not all professions equal ? . . . Whatsoever thou seest thy
soul to desire according to God, that do.' Stories with the same general
moral, Rosweyde (*MPL.*, lxxiii), coll. 785, 1038 ; Cotelier, i, pp. 348, 432-433
(an added ascetic trait here, in the confession of celibate marriage ?) ; Pall.,
Hist. Laus., 14 (*supra*, p. 201, n. 3 ; the two brothers) ; Rufinus, *HM.*, 16
(Paphnutius) (*MPL.*, xxi, coll. 435-439 ; *MPG.*, xxxiv, coll. 1164-1171) ;
Cassian, *Coll.*, xiv, 7.

the world and become a monk himself.[1] Sometimes, again, the
worldling has anticipated one or more of the essential characteristics of monasticism—by giving away all his goods,[2] for example,
or by living a life of secret celibacy under the outward semblance
of marriage.[3] Reitzenstein has employed these variations to
support his own special theory of the origins of Christian asceticism,[4]
and in that respect I do not think we can follow him. But in one
point he is, I believe, absolutely right. Stories of this type were
not put into currency without ulterior purpose. They reflect
varying aspects of the long struggle of Christianity against the
menace of rigorism.

The struggle, indeed, was carried on largely by anecdote on
either side. The following tale recorded by Sulpicius Severus,[5]
whatever its original basis in fact, must have been used as a riposte
to stories (such as that of Macarius) which tended, however slightly,
to exalt the secular life and its spiritual achievements. A young
soldier, so the story ran, of good family and large estate, became a
monk, leaving behind him a wife and little son in the world :—

> ' But by and by, the thought ' (' *proceeding from the devil* '
> adds the chronicler at once) ' entered his mind that it would be
> better to return to his native land and be the means of saving his
> only son and his wife. This surely would be more acceptable to
> God than if, content with his own salvation, he should impiously
> neglect the salvation of his friends.'

Yielding to this diabolic suggestion, the monk started on his
journey with ' an unhappy obstinacy ' on which the arguments of
his godly friends made no impression. His fate was terrible and
dramatic. A demon took possession of him, and for two years
he had to be kept under restraint as a raving lunatic—' a well-
deserved punishment,' we are told, ' that he whom faith could not
restrain should now be restrained by chains.' ' In this way,' the
story concludes,

> ' he was himself corrected and therewith became a warning to
> others, that the shadow of a spurious righteousness should
> not delude us, nor fickle pliability induce us with unprofitable
> inconsistency to forsake a course on which we have once
> entered.'[6]

---

[1] So Reitzenstein (*HMHL.*, p. 35) takes the ' do not neglect thy soul '
of *Hist. Mon.*, 16 (*MPL.*, xxi, col. 436 ; *MPG.*, xxxiv, col. 1169) ; cp. *ib.*,
the head-man of the village, and the merchant ; where the facts are indis-
putable.

[2] The merchant in the Greek *Hist. Mon.*, 16 (*MPG.*, xxxiv, col. 1170).

[3] E.g. Eucharistus (Cotelier, col. 433) ; the head-man of the village,
Hist. Mon., 15 ; the old countryman, Cassian, *Coll.*, xiv, 7.

[4] Reitzenstein, *HMHL.*, pp. 34-49 ; *infra,* pp. 495 ff. ; additional note G.

[5] *Dial.*, i, 22 (*MPL.*, xx, col. 107).

[6] A similar moral in Cassian, *Coll.*, xxiv, 13 ; illustrated by Macarius'
story of the barber who discovered that the value of his earnings depended
upon the cost of living.

The controversial motive is obvious in every line of this anecdote.

There was, as we have seen, an element in the early Church which pressed for every Christian to become an encratite—to adopt, that is to say, the extreme of rigorism. Nowhere in early Christianity is the opposite position championed—the position which would represent monastic asceticism as untrue in all cases to the spirit of Christ. Rightly or wrongly, such opinions could scarcely be expected in view of much that was contained in the New Testament. It was not often, even, that anyone ventured to echo Macarius' outspoken adaptation of S. Paul's words, ' Circumcision is nothing and uncircumcision is nothing, but the keeping of the commandments of God,' or to draw out the full inference that monasticism is at best a vocation among other vocations, and that the secular life is as capable of high virtue and of the vision of God as the cloistered. One or two writers, however, who dared to perpetrate such statements are known to us by name—Helvidius, for example, Jovinian, and Vigilantius in the fourth century. But they received short shrift ; and their executioner in each case was S. Jerome.

Helvidius, a Roman Christian, had put marriage on the same plane as celibacy[1] in a treatise of about the year A.D. 383 which had as its main theme the denial of the perpetual virginity of the mother of the Lord. Jerome had not as yet developed to the extreme of his fanatical asceticism; and compared with his later treatises, the ' contra Helvidium ' is mild and almost friendly, although (or perhaps, because) his opponent was personally unknown to him. Jovinian, whose faith in the sinlessness of Christians has already been mentioned, received more drastic treatment. All that remains of his opinions are the few sentences quoted by Jerome in his reply (A.D. 393), but enough is preserved to make his position clear. Although a solitary himself, and refusing to marry, he lived the life of ordinary men ;[2] and his three fundamental propositions (apart from his views on post-baptismal sinlessness) were these—(1) ' Virgins, widows and married women, if they have been baptized and are equal in other respects (i.e. in ordinary moral conduct), are of equal merit ' ; (2) ' there is no difference between abstinence from food and its reception with thanksgiving ' ; (3) ' there is one and the same reward in heaven for all who have kept their baptismal vow '—i.e. whether married or celibate.[3] To the virgins he appealed :—

> ' I do you no wrong. You have chosen the unmarried life on account of the present distress ; you determined on this

[1] Hieron., *de perp. virg. adv. Helvid.*, 22. Nothing more is certainly known of Helvidius, though Gennadius (*de vir ill.*, 33) implies that he had Arian and even pagan leanings.

[2] Id., *adv. Jov.*, i, 40—Jovinian as the dog returning to its vomit.

[3] *Ib.*, i, 3 (the second proposition of the four which Jerome mentions was that on post-baptismal sinlessness).

course in order to be holy in body and spirit. But be not puffed up; you and your married sisters are members of the same Church.'[1]

Jerome replies in a treatise which is venomous, coarse, inconsistent and diffuse. Its only virtue is that it preserves an otherwise unknown passage of Theophrastus describing the inconveniences of marriage in humorous and even rollicking vein.[2] The saint's rancour did not desert Jovinian even in death. Jerome pursues him with the Parthian shot—' He did not breathe out his life; he hiccoughed it up in the midst of pork and peacocks,'[3]—attributing to his opponent a life of gluttony of which there is no other reason to suspect him. Even the friends at whose request Jerome wrote found his style too mordant for their taste. They tried to suppress the treatise; but its author, whilst thanking them for their pains, and even taking opportunity at the same time to mitigate the effect of his tirade a little, makes the incident an occasion for the expression of further views of the same kind.[4]

The success of his counterblast against Jovinian encouraged Jerome to persevere in controversy of this character—' if he was bad-tempered, at any rate he did not waste his time.'[5] Only a few years later Vigilantius—a more interesting figure than Jovinian, —came under the lash. He was a self-made man, obviously of real distinction of character; for he commanded the friendship of Sulpicius Severus, of Paulinus of Nola, and for a time, of Jerome himself.[6] The first sign of actual rupture[7] shows itself in a letter from Jerome which taxes Vigilantius on two counts: he has accused Jerome himself of Origenist heresy; and he has been guilty of the

---

[1] Hieron., *adv. Jov.*, i, 5 fin. [2] *Ib.*, i, 47.
[3] Id., *c. Vigil.* 1.
[4] Id., *epp.* 48, 49. Jovinian was condemned by a synod at Rome, under Siricius, about the year A.D. 390, at the instance of Jerome's friend Pammachius. The heresiarch and his partisans proceeded to Milan in the hope of appealing successfully to Theodosius; the attempt was frustrated by Ambrose, who secured their condemnation in his own synod (Ambrose, *ep.* 42). It was after these decisions that Pammachius, presumably because the heresy was still spreading (cp. Ambrose, *ep.* 63. 7—Sarmatio and Barbatianus) sent Jovinian's tracts to Jerome. Like Helvidius, Jovinian also denied the perpetual virginity of the mother of Jesus.
[5] L. Duchesne, *Early History of the Church* (E. tr.), ii, p. 447.
[6] Vigilantius was the son of an inn-keeper of Comminges. For his friendship with Sulpicius and Paulinus, see Paulinus, *ep.* 5. 11; Hieron., *ep.* 58. 11; 61. 3. All that is known of him is well put together by A. Réville, *Vigilance de Calagurris* (Paris, 1902).
[7] But there were earlier incidents. Vigilantius had apparently shown terror during an earthquake at Bethlehem to such an extent as to rouse Jerome's contempt (*c. Vigil.*, 11); he seems to have sided with Rufinus in the great controversy (Hieron., *apol.*, iii, 19); and he left Bethlehem under suspicious circumstances (Hieron., *ep.* 109. 2), although Jerome was sufficiently friendly still to entrust him with a letter to Paulinus (*ep.* 58. 11). But within a very short time he received from Jerome the letter referred to in the text above (*ep.* 61), in which what may have been no more than incautious expressions of opinion are mercilessly pilloried. The incidents are usually dated about A.D. 395-396.

almost unpardonable blasphemy—for Jerome suggests that even God will find it difficult to condone it—of misinterpreting ' the mountain from which the stone was cut without hands ' in Daniel ii. 34, 35.[1] Ten years later Vigilantius committed his crowning offence. He was, it would appear, a common-sense Christian, apt to test every institution and doctrine by its effect on conduct ; and to deprecate as superfluous, if not as evil, whatever failed to satisfy that test. His book may have been ill-advised, but it touched some tender spots. He attacked the excessive cult of relics, and the invocation of saints and martyrs ; the irregularities which were only too common in connexion with vigils by the martyrs' tombs ; the formalist sending of alms to Jerusalem as an act of piety, when elsewhere the poor were left starving ; and finally the pretensions of monks and virgins. Unfortunately for our knowledge of his arguments, Jerome thought a single night's labour enough for the composition of his reply.[2] It was enough, and more than enough, for the torrent of vulgar abuse which did duty for argument on this occasion ; but not enough to allow Jerome to quote Vigilantius on every point. Day must have been breaking when he reached the malignant's views on asceticism, for he has only time just to mention them [3] before he brings his invective to a close. No more than this is known of Vigilantius ; but there is no evidence that he was synodically condemned, as Jovinian had been a few years earlier.[4]

Although, however, the Church of the fourth century was not prepared for so strong a doctrine as that of Helvidius, Jovinian and Vigilantius, she was quite clear that her doors must remain open to men and women who lived ' in the world,' though they failed even to adopt that domestic asceticism which had prevailed in the first two centuries, and, under Jerome's auspices, was meeting with some popularity in Rome. The extremist must be made to face the facts. It is all very well for the Pharisee, in a verbal flourish, to say, ' This people that knoweth not the law is accursed,' but in a calm hour he must at least admit that some of them are more accursed than others ; and that to be only half-accursed is to be half-blessed. It is impossible to draw the line that separates the Church from the world, the sheep from the goats, the wheat from the tares, so as to exclude grades of merit on the one side, and grades of guilt on the other. The moon is not so bright as the sun, but still it shines ; silver is not as precious as gold, but it is worth more than base lead. A place must be found in the Church for virtuous

---

[1] Hieron., *ep.* 61. 4—' Christ's church has never heard such blasphemy ! '

[2] Id., *c. Vigil.*, 17. Jerome had already outlined his reply to Vigilantius in a letter to the priest Riparius (*ep.* 109), in which he asked for copies of his opponent's treatise.

[3] *c. Vigil.*, 15, 16.

[4] Further contemporary opposition to monasticism, of a very violent character, can be inferred from the riots at Rome on the occasion of Blæsilla's funeral, Hieron., *ep.* 39. 5 (' The monks to the Tiber ! ') ; and from the treatise *adv. opp. vit. mon.*, which Chrysostom felt himself obliged to write.

married life—inferior to celibacy, if you wish ; but still on a wholly
different plane from unbridled lust.

Arguments such as these recur endlessly not only in Jerome [1]
(who indeed forgets them whenever he conveniently can), but in
all the Fathers without exception.[2]   They do not settle the true
question—actually (as will appear) they evade it—the question
whether there can be distinctions of spiritual status as well as of
personal worth and achievement in Christ's Church.   But they *do*
settle the immediate practical question.   They find a valid and
sure place in the Church for the earnest Christian who cannot
disentangle himself from worldly affairs ; and they deter the
curious from enquiring too closely into the more special privileges,
if any, reserved for the monk.

So grew up the extraordinarily perplexing phenomenon of a
double moral standard in Catholicism—a lower and a higher grade
of Christian achievement—the distinction between counsels and
precepts, the religious and the secular vocations, the contemplative and active lives.   There can be no doubt that the distinction
saved Christianity.   It reconciled every extremist who was prepared
to face the facts at all, and so retained within the Church that
witness to Christian otherworldliness so greatly needed at a time of
acute secularization.   But it left the Christian moralist with the
curiously elusive problem—How far, if at all, is the distinction thus
expressed of any ultimate validity ? [3]

That it could be found in scripture was a matter as to which
none of the Fathers had any doubt whatever.   The Matthæan
version of the story of the young man who had great possessions,

---

[1] E.g. *adv. Jov.*, i, 3, 9, 12, 40, etc.   But Jerome's real view is expressed,
for example, in the famous epigram (*ep.* 22. 20), ' I praise marriage and
wedlock, but only because they beget celibates ;   I gather roses from thorns,
gold from the earth, pearls from the shell.'   Still more biting are *adv. Jov.*,
i, 7—' If it is "good for a man not to touch a woman " (1 Cor. 7[1]), it is bad
to touch one ;   there is no opposite to goodness but badness ' ;   ' a thing
which is only allowed because there may be something worse can have only
a slight degree of goodness ' ;   ' if we abstain from conjugal intercourse, we
honour our wives ;   if we do not abstain, well—the opposite of honour is
insult ! '—Tertullian, though he enunciated the most beautiful of all patristic
sentiments on the happiness of Christian married life (*ad ux.*, ii, 9), and
even as a Montanist defended the institution against Marcion (*adv. Marc.*, i,
29 ; cp. *de an.*, 27—also from his Montanist days), was capable of judgments
as severe.   He could call women the ' gate of the devil ' and the ' destroyers
of God's image ' (*de cult. fem.*, i, 1) ;   could regard the difference between
marriage and fornication as ' purely legal ' (*de exh. cast.*, 9), and while he is
bound to admit that S. Peter was married, he denies that the reference in
1 Cor. 9[5] is to ' wives ' whom the apostles ' led about '—they were ' ministering women ' (*de mon.*, 8).   Further references of the same character from
patristic and mediæval times in G. Grupp, *Kulturgeschichte des Mittelalters*[2],
iv, pp. 26 ff., 39 ff., 54 ff. ; G. G. Coulton, *Five Centuries of Religion*, i, pp.
174-181, 444, 445.

[2] *Infra*, p. 241, n. 2.   On the liberalism of the *Canons of Hippolytus*
and the *Egyptian Church Order* in this matter, see A. J. Maclean in *ERE.*,
iii, p. 493, *s.v.* ' Chastity.'

[3] For an important estimate of the ' double-standard ' doctrine by Canon
J. O. Hannay, and other points involved, see *infra*, p. 517, additional note K.

with its distinction between 'having eternal life' and 'being perfect,'[1] lent itself very readily to the argument. The relative inferiority of Leah to Rachel, of Martha to Mary, and of Peter to the beloved disciple, was noticed and brought into account. The many mansions in the Father's house were supposed to indicate degrees of reward; just as the thirty-fold, sixty-fold, and hundred-fold of the parable, and the gold, silver, precious stones, wood, hay and stubble of S. Paul indicated different degrees of merit.[2] S. Paul's distinction between 'permission' and 'command' was grasped as early as Tertullian's time—'We may with more impunity,' says the African Father, 'reject advice than injunction.'[3] Origen, in a fanciful moment, supposed that the unprofitable servants who did all that was commanded of them *but no more*, were matched by *profitable* servants who 'added to the precepts' and did more than they were commanded.[4] Finally Optatus of Milevis opened up a path which was to lead farther than he could ever have guessed, by exploiting the parable of the Good Samaritan with its 'quodcumque supererogaveris' in the same interest. S. Paul is the 'stabularius'—the innkeeper; he has spent in his teaching the 'two pence' of the Old and New Testaments entrusted to him: but more is still required. On his own independent authority, therefore, he

---

[1] E.g. Origen, *in Mt.*, xv, 12 (*MPG.*, xiii, coll. 1285 ff.); Ambrose, *de off.*, 1, 11; cp. *supra*, p. 69. It is a quite extraordinary instance of the liberality of Clement of Alexandria's outlook that he could compose a whole treatise (*Quis Dives Salvetur*) on this incident without ever mentioning the two lives, or alluding to asceticism. He makes no use of the Matthæan distinction which, although he is aware of it (c. 10), he regards as in essence irrelevant (c. 6—'Our Lord and Saviour was asked a question most appropriate to Him—the Life respecting life, . . . the Perfect respecting the perfect rest,' i.e. it is the *same* question in another form; cp. *ib.*, c. 8—the young man is '*imperfect* (ἀτελῆς) as touching *eternal life*.')

[2] Patristic references to the doctrine are of course innumerable; a good selection in Hannay, *Spirit and Origin of Christian Monasticism*, pp. 288-291. To his references I add the following:—Method., *Conviv.*, ii, 1; Joann. Chrys., *adv. opp. vit. mon.*, iii, 5 (moon and stars); Origen, *frag.*, 80, *in Jn* (*GCSS.*, 'Origenes,' iv, p. 547—Mary and Martha, cp. Aug., *de bon. conj.*, 8 (8); *Serm.*, 104. 3 (4); 169. 14 (17); 179. 3 (3); Greg. Magn., *Mor.*, vi, 61; *in Ezk.*, ii, 2, 9, 10; Isidor. Pel., *ep.* iii, 351); Cyprian, *de hab. virg.*, 23 (the many mansions); Aug., *c. Faust. Man.*, xxii, 52 (Leah and Rachel); Cyril Hier., *Cat.*, iv, 25 (gold and silver). Jerome (*ep.* 48. 2, 3) has almost all of these analogies. Sulp. Severus records (*Dial.*, ii, 10) a pithy but distressing metaphor of Martin of Tours—whilst fornication is like a field that has been rooted up by swine, marriage is compared to one that is cropped by cattle, and virginity to one still intact. Further references to the doctrine are Origen, *c. Cels.*, i, 26; vii, 48; viii, 55; Tert., *ad ux.*, i, 3, 4, 8; *de exh. cast.*, 9; *de monog.*, 3; *de virg. vel.*, 17; Athan., *ep.* 48; Greg. Naz., *carm.*, ii, 1-3 (*MPG.*, xxxvii, coll. 521-640); Chrysost., *de virg.*, 10, etc.; Ambrose, *de virg.*, i, 6 (24), 7 (35); *de vid.*, 12 (72), 13 (81), 14 (83); Aug., *de bon. conj.*, 23 (28, 29); *de mor. eccl. cath.*, 35 (79); *de sanct. virg.*, 14 (14), 18 (18); *de op. mon.*, 5 (6), 6 (7); *de civ. Dei*, xvi, 36; *enchir.*, 121.

[3] Tert., *ad ux.*, i, 3; ii, 1. The text is uncertain, but the meaning clear.

[4] Origen, *in Rom.*, iii, 3 (*MPG.*, xiv, col. 933). Of the things which can thus be 'added to the precepts' he mentions only virginity, and the repudiation of a salary (1 Cor. 9^14, 15) by ministers of the gospel. To the same effect, though not quite so definitely, Ambrose, *de vid.*, 12 (74).

gives counsels ' of supererogation ' to the life of virginity ; but makes it clear that this is something additional to the precepts received from Scripture.[1] Augustine and Fulgentius [2] unravelled this tangled metaphor of Optatus, and the doctrine of works of supererogation was fairly launched. With such a wealth of scriptural support, and harmonizing, as it did, with the immediate needs of the situation, the new theory achieved a success which in all the circumstances need cause no surprise.

II. THE TWO LIVES.

Nevertheless, the doctrine of the two lives,—the secular and the religious, the active and the contemplative, the married and the celibate,—was involved in an ambiguity fraught with very serious consequences—an ambiguity, moreover, which persists, in spite of a clear protest by Irenæus,[3] throughout the patristic and mediæval periods. The fact has escaped a majority of the historians of Christian ethics, and its neglect has vitiated much of their criticism in consequence. Two lines of thought (or three, if we count a compromise to be noticed later) may be seen running side-by-side under cover of the same distinction—one innocuous and of great practical value, the other of much more questionable character. That there was a difference between the active and the contemplative lives, and that the latter was the ' higher ' of the two, was agreed

---

[1] Opt., *de schism. Don.*, vi, 4. The reference is purely incidental. The Donatists had compelled Catholic virgins to do penance and to submit to reconsecration ; Optatus is at pains to emphasize the ' voluntary' character of the vow of celibacy, and thereby to make the case against the Donatists stronger still. The date of the treatise is about A.D. 366.

[2] Aug., *de sanct. virg.*, 30. (In *de op. mon.*, 5 (6), S. Paul's decision to ' work with his own hands ' becomes the excess expenditure.) Fulgent., *ad mon.*, ii, 13 (*MPL.*, lxv, col. 192)—little more than a verbal reproduction of Optatus. For a similar use of the ' double-standard ' in Plato and Aristotle, cp. e.g. H. Sidgwick, *History of Ethics*, pp. 42, 47, 57 ; and in Judaism, Bousset, *RJ.*, pp. 416, 417.

[3] Iren., *hær.*, iv, 11. 4—an attack, all the more effective for being incidental, on ' those who pretend to observe more than is commanded.' Irenæus reverts to the question by treating, in iv, 12. 5, of the incident of the Rich Young Man. Although he is commenting on the *Matthæan* version (*supra*, p. 69), he very significantly omits all reference to the antithesis between ' entering into life ' and ' being perfect,' on which the double-standard theory in its invalid form was so often based. Instead he draws attention to the order in which the law is recited (Mt. 19[18, 19]), with the fifth commandment at the end of the citation from the decalogue (so in Mk. 10[19]), and the addition (Mt. only) of ' Thou shalt love thy neighbour as thyself.' These precepts, he says, form an ' ascending scale,' and are given to *all* (here we have the valid theory fully expressed). Probably, he adds, the young man had *not* kept the commandments properly, and so the Lord adds the ' Sell all thou hast ' to ' expose his covetousness.' He quotes Mt. 19[21] in full (apart from the reference to treasure in heaven), and says that to those who obey it is promised ' the reward of the apostles.' This might seem at first to imply the invalid theory. But the implication is at once cancelled by the paraphrase, ' to do away with former covetousness by good works, and follow Christ ' ; by the lack of any restriction of this injunction to a particular class ; and by the instance of Zacchaeus, who, though he only gave away *half* his goods, is yet quoted as having fulfilled its requirements.

on all hands. But of what nature was the distinction, and why is 'contemplation' higher than 'action'?

There were those who tended to regard the distinction as one of *degree* only. The Christian life is a life of progress. It passes through its stages ;[1] its end is contemplation or the vision of God, and this is the 'highest' stage. All that comes below is the preparatory discipline of the 'active life '—a discipline meaningless and incomplete unless it ends in the vision. That is the one line of thought; the second is quite different. The two lives differ not in degree, but in *kind ;* the 'contemplative' life aims at vision, the 'active' at some other and lower goal. By the grace of God even the man 'in the world' can attain salvation if he brings forth fruits worthy of repentance ; but the highest rewards are for ever closed to him. He has turned his back upon the nobler course.

To understand the confusion caused by these two versions of the 'double-standard' theory, and the reason why the invalid version finally supplanted the valid one, to the despair of all sane moralists, we must examine them rather more closely.

(*a*) The *valid* theory, which made the 'active' life a stage on the road towards 'contemplation,' involved three great principles. *First*, the vision of God is open to all men—not perhaps equally (that may depend upon temperamental conditions), but at all events adequately. A secular environment or vocation is no final barrier. *Second*, all men are called to it ; if they refuse to follow the vision,— if they are content to rest in a lower stage,—they have not lived up to the level demanded of them. *Third*, the race is a long one ; the rigorist conception of the Christian becoming perfect in a moment is an idle and dangerous fiction. We must not daunt the immature Christian by laying on him too heavy a burden at once. He must take his life by stages, achieving what is possible here and now, and not attempting the higher flights till he has exercised himself in the lower ones. The immediate duties (e.g. the 'active life ') rank as 'precepts' to be obeyed at once ; the ulterior aims may be held in reserve as 'counsels' for the present, which will become, we may hope, precepts or immediate duties by-and-by.[2]

---

[1] I have pointed out elsewhere (*Some Principles of Moral Theology*, pp. 51, 126), that such a systematic division into stages is psychologically unsound ; in reality the successive 'stages' are concurrent 'tendencies' of which some have the greater prominence in the beginnings of the Christian life, others after progress has been made. On the 'periodicity '—if one may so call it—of the higher stages of spiritual experience (a common theme with all mystical writers), cp. e.g. Greg. Magn., *Hom. in Ezk.*, ii, 2. 12 ; *Mor.*, v, 11-27 ; viii, 50 ; x, 13-19 ; xxiv, 10-12, etc. See further, *infra*, pp. 250, n. 3 ; 252 ; and W. Shewring and J. McCann, *The Golden Epistle of Abbot William*, pp. xxxviii, 63.

[2] Well put by R. Thamin, *Un Problème Moral dans l'Antiquité*, p. 333 :— ' Les castes en morale ne sont pas fermées. Plusieurs ont tout ce qu'ils peuvent faire de se tenir dans les limites d'une morale bourgeoise et d'une sagesse vulgaire. Au-dessus d'eux est la législation plus subtile de l'honneur, et ses exigences plus délicates. C'est un idéal qui n'est pas le leur, *mais qui pourrait le devenir* . . . Ce sont là les degrés de la hiérarchie en morale, et il n'a été dit à personne : tu n'iras pas plus loin.' Cp. also Harnack, *History*

Despite constant intrusions from the invalid theory which has yet to be examined, these principles may be traced continuously through the writings of the greatest of the Fathers. That the vision is open to all, and that all are called to it, is emphatically asserted by Clement of Alexandria,[1] Augustine [2] and Gregory the Great.[3] As Dom Cuthbert Butler has well pointed out, the great Pope's principal expositions of contemplation and the contemplative life were delivered, ' not in conferences to his monks, but in public sermons preached in the Lateran basilica to mixed congregations of all comers.' [4] Similarly with eastern Christianity. S. Basil,[5] it has been well said,

' refuses to draw a hard and fast line between monks and other Christians. He teaches that all Christian life must be ascetic. There is a question of the degree of its asceticism between the life of a monk and that of a married man. There is no question that both lives are lived on the same principle. " God," he says, " has permitted man to live in one of two ways, either as married or as monks. But it must not be supposed that those who are married are therefore free to embrace the world. *The evangelic*

of Dogma (E. tr.), v, p. 75 :—' The last stage reached by the advanced Christian, who has passed through a rich experience, is a *refinement* to him who is in process of development. But a refined piety or morality is always pernicious, for it no longer starts at the point of duty and conscience.'

[1] See references, C. Bigg, *Christian Platonists of Alexandria*, pp. 119, 120 ; J. Tixeront, *Histoire des Dogmes*, i, p. 273 ; and *infra*, pp. 314, 315.

[2] The Augustinian passages well presented by C. Butler, *Western Mysticism* [2], pp. 227 ff. Note especially the long quotation from *Tr. in Jn.*, 124. 5, *ib.*, p. 228, where the wholly preparatory character of the ' active ' life is insisted upon. Cp. also *de cons. evang.*, i, 5 (8)—the ' active ' life is that ' whereby we journey' ('quâ itur '); contemplation is that ' whereby we reach journey's end' ('quâ pervenitur '); and especially *de civ. Dei*, xix, 19—' No one should busy himself so much [with his neighbour's welfare] as to abandon the quest for the vision of God . . . lest that sweetness be withdrawn from us and the obligation of charity overwhelm us.' It is to be noticed that Dom Butler, who insists that in S. Gregory the contemplative life is ' optional ' (see *infra*, p. 523, additional note L) finds the same doctrine in S. Augustine (p. 249—' The active life is necessary for all, whereas the contemplative is not necessary '). I can find no justification for this allegation ; indeed the passage to which Dom Butler refers in support, and which he summarizes on pp. 230-232 (*c. Faust. Man.*, xxii, 52-58), so far from confirming the contention, explicitly denies it. The active life is necessary for all, S. Augustine says, ' not for its own sake,' but as the *necessary preparatory discipline for contemplation* (c. 53); ' the contemplative life is *loved*, the active only *tolerated* for its sake ' (c. 54). That being so, the active life is only necessary because the contemplative life, to which it leads, here or hereafter, *is a prior necessity*. In the interests of the invalid theory, Dom Butler attributes it to S. Augustine in passages where it has no place whatever.

[3] On S. Gregory and the contemplative life, Butler, *Western Mysticism*, pp. 245-273 ; *Benedictine Monachism*, pp. 96-100. Dom Butler has no doubt that in S. Gregory's opinion it is ' open to all . . . no state or condition of life being debarred' (*Western Mysticism*, pp. 269, 270). On his view that it is ' optional ' (p. 249), *infra*, p. 523, additional note L.

[4] *Western Mysticism*, p. 270.

[5] J. O. Hannay, *Spirit and Origin of Christian Monasticism*, p. 188.

renunciation is their ideal too, for the Lord's words were spoken to those who were in the world as well as to the apostles : ' What I say unto you I say unto all ' ... " [1]

'One great aim of S. Basil's ascetic teaching,' Canon Hannay continues, 'was to connect the monastic life with that of ordinary Christians, and to place both alike beside the great standard of evangelic teaching. . . . [He taught the monks] that their way of life was no new kind of Christian life, no special and exclusive expression of the gospel spirit, but only a faithful following-out of common principles. "This," he says, "is the goal of Christianity, the imitation of Christ in the measure of His humanity as far as the vocation of *each man* permits." [2] "The law which bids us love God more than father, mother or self, more than wife and children, is as binding in wedlock as in celibacy." ' [3]

His brother Gregory of Nyssa is almost as explicit :—

' Our view of marriage is this,' he says, ' that *while the pursuit of heavenly things should be every man's first care,* yet if he can use the advantage of marriage with sobriety and moderation he need not despise this form of self-dedication.' [4]

Again, Christian perfection is not attained in a moment. It is a matter of progress. In the visible organization of the Church this doctrine of stages of progress was symbolized by the difference between the catechumen and the baptized ; but it was susceptible of more pliant treatment than that alone. It provides the key to the science of pastoral guidance—at one and the same moment to make the individual feel that he has already achieved much (or rather that much has been already achieved in him), thereby stimulating his hope of further advance ; and equally to remind him that there are higher stages—far higher stages—to which he must still reach out. Reveal the full demands of Christ in a single instant, and you are as likely to dismay as to encourage ; unveil them gradually, leading on to the next stage as each stage in turn is seen and firmly occupied, and you will hearten and encourage.

It will be recognized at once how congenial this method was to S. Paul, S. Peter, and even the rigorist author of the epistle to the Hebrews. They distinguished clearly between the ' babes in Christ ' and the fully grown ; between the early duties and simple doctrines appropriate to the first stages—the ' milk of the word,' and the

---

[1] Basil, *de renunt. saeculi (MPG.,* xxxi, coll. 628, 629).
[2] Id., *Reg. Fus. Tract.,* 43 (*MPG.,* xxxi, col. 1028).
[3] Id., *de ren. saec. (ubi supra).*
[4] Greg. Nyss., *de virg.,* 8 (*MPG.,* xlvi, col. 356). Similarly Chrysostom, *adv. cpp. vit. mon.,* iii, 13—' the Scriptures would have all men live the "monastic" life, even though they be married' (the context shows that the reference is not to marriage in name alone) ; cp. Id., *in Mt. hom.,* vii, 7 (*MPG.,* lvii, coll. 81, 82).

'meat' of the gospel reserved for the mature.[1]   An irreducible minimum of doctrine and precept was set before the beginner—a statement of truths to be held and of sins to be put off at the very outset.   Beyond that, and progressively to be attained, lay the deeper truths, the higher ideals and aspirations, of Christian holiness in the future.   Even in this form, no doubt, the doctrine has its dangers.   However low the minimum be placed, it must at least be appreciably higher than the world's standard, so that the veriest beginner has advanced a little from his unconverted state, and feels a moral stimulus in his new environment.   Again, both for the beginner and for the Church, the minimum itself must always be advancing, and the range of precept continually widening.   The temptations against which we find ourselves in some way proof, and in every way bound to struggle, should be more in number as time goes on.   In the third place, and no less important, the minimum must never be allowed to become other than a minimum.   Once it becomes a norm—so that any advance beyond it is regarded either as unnecessary, or as a work of supererogation or as the prerogative of an élite alone—what has been a valuable piece of pastoral machinery becomes a vital danger, leading either to complete moral stagnation, or to the doctrine of merit with all its attendant evils.

It would be too idealistic to say that early Christianity avoided these three dangers altogether.   When Hermas, for example, says,[2] 'If thou do any good thing beyond the commands of God, thou shalt gain for thyself a more abundant glory, and be more honoured by God than otherwise,' it is obvious that sinister perversions are already intruding into the theory.   But on the whole it is true that, consciously or unconsciously, the Church attempted to apply the doctrine wisely and well.   Her standard was well in advance of that of contemporary society.   Her record of moral achievement could be written by the apologists in terms that sound almost as a boast of sinlessness; and whatever libels fanatical mob-hatred might trump up against her, her sternest and most discerning critics, such as Celsus and Lucian, could find little to object to except a tendency to indiscriminate almsgiving and a taint of social inferiority.   Again, if we accept Professor von Dobschütz's strongly

---

[1] I Cor. 3$^{1-3}$, 13^{11}, I Pet. 2^2; Hebr. 5^{11}-6^1. (Tertullian actually suggests that this was S. Paul's reason for allowing marriage at all—he was legislating for the ' inexperience of a new and just rising church ' (de mon., II).   But Tertullian, as a Montanist, was committed to the principle of development in the moral code (cp. supra, p. 221) ; hence the idea need not be regarded as an original one of his own).   Similarly of the method of our Lord, the quotation from Is. 42^3 (' a bruised reed shall he not break,' etc.) in Mt. 12^{20} (cp. Lk. 3^{18} from Is. 61^1).   These passages, of course, stand in sharp contrast to the rigorist element in New Testament teaching, with its demand for a clean cut from all pagan associations (supra, pp. 9, 65), and thus provide another example of the contradiction which runs right through all Christian ethics.

[2] Hermas, Sim., V, 3. 3 ; cp. Mand., IV, 4. 2—second marriages are not sinful, but there is ' more honour and great glory before God ' for those who do not enter into them.

expressed opinion that the Christian moral standard in the first two centuries definitely advanced hand-in-hand with Christian moral achievement, it implies that the Church clearly marked and avoided the second of the dangers we have mentioned. As for the third danger—there was one factor in the life of the early centuries which must have finally prevented any earnest Christian from resting on his achievement, and thinking that he had done as much as could be asked of him. That was the factor of martyrdom. We have only to remember Ignatius' longing for the martyr's crown, and Hermas' full recognition that he is not as yet even a confessor, to understand how little grounds for moral complacency the Church allowed to anyone whose faith and endurance had not been tested by the fires of persecution.

It is in the sense of this valid theory that we can understand some of the earliest assertions of the double standard which meet us in Christian history. The first, perhaps, outside the New Testament, is the phrase in ' Didaché ' which comes in the conclusion of the section on the ' Two Ways.' Little doubt can exist as to the author's purpose in saying at this point, ' If thou canst bear the whole yoke of the Lord thou shalt be perfect ; if not, bear as much as thou canst.' [1] The full display of all the virtues of the ' Way of Life ' and all the vices of the ' Way of Death ' may be only too daunting for the newly converted Christian ; who is sufficient for a programme so extensive as this ? Not to lower his ideals, but to strengthen his resolution, the writer says, in effect, ' Choose out of this code I have given you such immediate duties to be discharged, and virtues to be manifested, as by the grace of God you feel your moral strength sufficient for. Do not ignore the remainder, nor yet be downhearted at their number ; hold them in reserve for the moment, to be adopted as immediate and practical goals when you have made sure your footing on the lower step.' [2]

Hermas, always original, preaches the same doctrine in a complicated parable whose purpose was not very clear even to himself. It begins as a commentary on the idea of true fasting ; it widens out into a description of moral progress as a whole ; it culminates— with a daring of which the writer is wholly conscious and more than half-afraid—in an extraordinary excursion into Christology which fully justifies his anxiety. In itself it is the simple story of a slave, commanded to do a piece of work, who exceeded his orders, and after completing the first task went on to other duties of his own discovering ; adding still further to his merits by sharing with his

---

[1] *Did.*, 6[2, 3].

[2] On one question the writer particularizes (*ib.*)—' Concerning meats, bear what thou canst ; but [in any case] keep far from meats sacrificed to idols.'

[3] *Sim.*, V. Note particularly 2[7]—' He has kept My commandment, and has done a good work besides.' That Hermas had originally in mind an ascending order of precepts and counsels is to be inferred from the ' first of all ' of 3[6] ; only when the precepts there summarized have been fulfilled, are the supreme ascetic exercises commended.

fellow-slaves the reward which he alone had earned. Stripped of its doctrinal trappings (which fit it badly enough) the apologue provides a beautiful and clear example for the Christian life. 'Start with the most necessary duties and do them well,' it may be paraphrased, 'but do not rest content with what you have achieved. Pass on at once to further efforts, and never think that you have reached the point at which you can cry "Enough."'

To be of real service such a doctrine must be adaptable to the needs of different churches and different individuals. No hard and fast list of counsels and precepts will meet the case. The influence of this principle is clearly visible in the early centuries. The line of demarcation between the lower and the higher stage is continually fluctuating. In 'Didaché' the commands, or precepts, of the way of life include blessing them that hate, prayer for enemies, fasting for persecutors (a curious elaboration of the gospel formula), and rejection of fleshly lusts. Then comes the counsel : ' But if any man strike thee on the right cheek turn to him the other, *and thou shalt be perfect.*' [1] To Clement of Alexandria the lower stages are marked out by faith, fear and hope, obedience to authority, discipline, control of passions. The higher stage, to which he says emphatically all men and women alike are called, is the life of righteousness and knowledge, of serene and reasonable convictions, of glad and spontaneous moral activity. The life of love issues in the life of freedom.[2] Origen enumerates the virtues of the lower stage, which he calls ' anointing the feet of the Lord,' or the ' work of penitents,' as almsgiving, deeds of mercy, visiting the sick, humility, kindliness, tolerance ; beyond and above them comes the work of saints by which the Master's head is anointed—eagerness in chastity, fasting and prayer.[3] S. Ambrose's version (reinforced for him by a parallel Stoic doctrine) [4] is quite different. In the lower grade

---

[1] *Did.*, I[3, 4].—In *ep. Barn.*, I[5], the stages appear to be *pistis* and *gnosis* respectively.

[2] See C. Bigg, *Christian Platonists of Alexandria*, pp. 118-120, for details.

[3] Origen, *in Mt. comm. ser.*, 77 (*MPG.*, xiii, col. 1726).

[4] S. Ambrose distinguishes between ' media ' and ' perfecta officia,' *de off.*, i, 11 ; cp. iii, 2. He drew the distinction from Cicero, *de off.*, i, 3. 8 ; iii, 3. 14 ; just as Cicero drew it from Panætius. The doctrine was a refinement upon the rigidity of the founders of the Stoic school ; to them the slightest dereliction from the ideal was fatal—' a foot below the water meant drowning, as much as a mile ' (Plut., *not. comm.*, 10. 4 ; cp. Sen., *ep.* 85, and generally on this aspect of Stoic ethics, R. Thamin, *Un Problème Moral*, pp. 6 ff. ; E. Bevan, *Stoics and Sceptics*, p. 71). Later, however, alongside the καθήκοντα τέλεια, or κατορθώματα (*officia perfecta*)—the ' perfect duties ' which only the wise man could perform,—they recognized the καθήκοντα μέσα (Stob., *Ecl.*, ii, 85. 13 (von Arnim, iii, p. 134) ; cp. Cic., *de off., ubi sup.*). Dr. Bevan has rightly insisted (*Stoics and Sceptics*, pp. 72-74), that to confine the meaning of *kathēkonta* to these lower duties or achievements, as is commonly done, is to misuse the Stoic terminology. But in view of the Stobæus passage just cited, in which marriage, politics, and so forth are spoken of as μέσα, his further conclusion that they are not to be regarded as a ' lower order of duties framed by the Stoics as a concession to human weakness ' (p. 74) is open to question. It would seem rather that the later Stoics verged on the ' invalid ' theory and regarded marriage and the like

stand the commandments of the decalogue; in the higher, evangelical poverty, love of enemies, prayer for false accusers and ' treating the poor as fellow-sharers in the blessings of grace and nature.' Flexibility of this character is all to the good.

The doctrine of progress was applied to all the various problems of the Christian life. It underlay. for example, the distinction between venial and mortal sin.[1] This indeed passed through a period of formalism ; but the moral earnestness of the Schoolmen, building on the genius of Abailard,[2] rescued it from its degradation. It is clearly a distinction capable of profitable use in the hands of a wise pastor. The despondent Christian, overburdened with sins of every kind, finds immediate relief if he comes under the influence of a priest who is able to analyse his difficulties, segregate the greater dangers from the less, and say, ' Here are your besetting sins. Begin by avoiding them with the utmost care ; once that battle has been won, you may turn to the conquest of the others.' Everything depends upon the emphasis and the direction in which the distinction is employed. It may help the man who is in little danger of mortal sin to look upwards, making the eradication even of venial sin his final ambition ; such a result is evidence that the doctrine has been put to wise and fruitful use. Or it may help him to look downward, and rest complacently on the fact that he is not as other men are ; that leads direct to Pharisaism and spiritual stagnation. In any case the doctrine itself is not evil ; it is a true statement of fact and nothing more. It takes its usefulness or harmfulness from the livery which from time to time it is caused to wear.

Exactly the same considerations apply to other and later variations of the doctrine of the double standard, which need not delay us—the doctrine of attrition and contrition,[3] for example ; and

as debarring from the practice of perfect virtue, but not as excluding the possibility of modified goodness. They had, at all events, no objection to the conception of the προκόπτοντες, or *proficientes* (Sen., *ep.* 75), who, though not perfect, were to be praised because they were striving after perfection— i.e. the ' valid ' theory. See further E. Zeller, *Stoics, Sceptics and Epicureans* (E. tr., pp. 248, 270 f.) ; A. Schmekel, *Die Philosophie der mittleren Stoa,* pp. 214 f., 358 ff. ; S. Dill, *Roman Society from Nero to Marcus Aurelius,* p. 315 ; A. Bonhöffer, *Epiktet u. d. N.T.,* pp. 17-19, 352 ; J. von Arnim, *Stoicorum Vet. Fragmenta,* iv, index, *s.vv.* καθῆκον, κατόρθωμα.

[1] The distinction was of course forced upon the Church by the controversies on penance (e.g. *supra,* p. 170 ; *infra,* pp. 297, 515, 540) ; but it had wider uses. Rigorist objections to the doctrine were expressed not merely in Stoicism, but also by Jovinian, in support of his theory of the equality of all states of life (Hieron., *adv. Jov.,* ii, 30. 31). Augustine's pagan friend Nectarius revived the Stoic principle of the equality of all sins in a somewhat half-hearted way, on the occasion of the riots of Calama (Aug., *ep.* 103. 4) ; Augustine's reply, inviting him to deny the distinction between mice and elephants, or flies and eagles, is a fine piece of controversial writing (Aug., *ep.* 104. 4 (13, 14)). On Luther's condemnation of the distinction, H. Denifle, *Luther u. Luthertum,* i, pp. 479-484.

[2] *Infra,* pp. 297, 540. S. Basil has some interesting remarks on the dangers of the distinction, *de jud. Dei,* 7 (*MPG.,* xxxi, col. 669), *RBT.,* 293.

[3] See *Some Principles of Moral Theology,* pp. 65, 66, 249, with references there ; further references M. Prümmer, *Manuale Theologiæ Moralis,* iii, pp. 238-241.

the distinction between lower and higher ways of loving God with which the Jesuits made great play.[1] More important is the form which the double, or rather the multiple, standard took in connexion with the idea of prayer, or (more generally) of the life appropriate to the vision of God. As originally expressed, two stages of 'prayer' were supposed to lie before the Christian. These were the active and the contemplative stages. 'Spiritual knowledge is twofold,' says Abbot Nesteros in Cassian's fourteenth 'Collation,'

'active (πρακτική) and contemplative (θεωρητική). The first comes about by the improvement of conduct and purification from sin ; the second consists in the contemplation of things divine and the knowledge of most sacred thoughts. We cannot reach this contemplative wisdom without first acquiring the practical ; . . . for the vision of God is not open to any who does not shun the stains of sin. . . . How can anyone who has not succeeded in understanding the nature of his faults, nor tried to eradicate them . . . attain to the mysteries of spiritual and heavenly things which mark the higher stage of contemplation ?'[2]

Other versions of the thought enumerate the stages in greater detail. Abbot Isaac, in the ninth Collation, has a fourfold ladder, fancifully based on the four divisions of prayer (1 Tim. ii. 1) in the Pastoral Epistles.[3] The first stage is that of Christians who, though converted, are still 'tormented by the arrows of sin ' ; the second, of those who have gained some real and stable love for the higher

---

[1] See e.g. Döllinger-Reusch, *Moralstreitigkeiten*, i, pp. 78 (*effective* and *affective* love) ; 285, 343 (*amor concupiscentiæ vel spei* and *amor benevolentiæ*), and cp. *ib.*, pp. 293, 294. The modern version, current in all Roman Catholic handbooks of moral theology, is between *intensive* and *appreciative* love. For the condemnation of the most lax views on the subject see Denzinger-Bannwart, *Enchiridion*[15], nn. 1101, 1155-1157, 1289.

[2] Cass., *Coll.*, xiv, 1-3—he uses 'actualis' of the active life. Cp. also *Coll.*, i, 3, 4—the 'end' is the kingdom of heaven ; the immediate goal is purity of heart ; and the interesting *sorites* of *Inst.*, IV, 43, reminiscent of *Wisd.* 6[17-20], 2 Pet. 1[6, 7] :—the fear of the Lord, compunction of heart, renunciation ('nuditas et contemptus '), humility, the mortification of desire, the uprooting of faults, the budding of virtues, purity of heart, and so, finally, the perfection of apostolic love.

[3] Cass., *Coll.*, ix, 9-25 : 'Supplications, prayers, intercessions and thanksgivings.' The first three are to all intents and purposes synonyms, whether in Greek, the Vulgate, or English, but Isaac gives them respectively the meanings of prayer for forgiveness, promise of amendment, and intercession, and so represents the four as successive activities suitable to four successive stages of progress in the spiritual life (c. 15). Nevertheless he repeatedly insists, in accordance with a principle noticed above (p. 243, n. 1), that they are not successive in any mutually exclusive sense ; they are 'useful to all men in all stages of their development (c. 15) ; they can and should from time to time 'be offered together in the fervour of a single prayer' (c. 17), as in the Lord's Prayer (c. 18). Notice how throughout the passage the life of prayer is thought of far more in terms of activity than of experience (*supra*, p. 197).

life ; the third, of those who have brought this love to some degree of fruition in a life of active service ; the fourth, of those who ' with a clean conscience and a pure heart can dwell upon God's providence and mercy, and be transported by the fervent prayer with God which passes man's tongue to express.' [1] When these four stages have been achieved, there is still one ' even more sublime to be attained,' ' which is brought about by the contemplation of God alone, and a fervent love, the mind throwing itself into love for God and addressing Him most familiarly as its own Father.' [2]

S. Benedict knows twelve stages of ' humility,' at the end of which we attain to the perfect love of God which casteth out all fear.[3] But the dominant formula became in time that of a life in three stages—purification, illumination, and union with God, or contemplation.[4] To this S. Gregory the Great approximates when he enumerates three other such stages (the subjection of the flesh, the discipline of the mind, the attainment of contemplation).[5] It does not matter very much which of these or similar formulations a Christian takes as the chart of his pilgrimage ; what is of interest is that here, if anywhere, we have the doctrine of stages of progress in its least questionable and most fruitful form.

---

[1] Cass., *Coll.*, c. 15.　　[2] *Ib.*, c. 18 ; cp. c. 25.

[3] Benedict, *Regula* 7—summarized, C. Butler, *Benedictine Monachism*, pp. 51, 52. A simpler scheme in the Rule of Columbanus (c. 4—also selected from Cassian) :—(1) renunciation ; (2) purification from sin ; (3) perfect love to God (Holsten-Brockie (1759), *Cod. Reg.*, i, p. 171). Other interesting examples are Clem. Alex., *Strom.*, v, 11, 71 (purification and contemplation —the lesser and greater mysteries) ; iv, 22, 135 (fear, hope, love = the characteristics of slaves, hirelings, and servants ; cp. Basil, *RFT.*, prooem., 3 ; Cass., *Coll.*, xi, 6-8) ; Macarius, *Hom.*, viii, 4 (twelve stages) ; Augustine, *de nat. et grat.*, 70 (84) (four stages of love—' caritas inchoata, provecta, magna, perfecta ') ; *de doctr. Christ.*, ii, 7 (9-11), *de quant. an.*, 33 (70-76) (seven stages of the soul's ascent, but differently conceived—in *de doctr. Christ.* they are (1) fear, (2) piety, (3) knowledge, (4) fortitude, (5) prudence, (6) purification, (7) vision ; in the neo-Platonic *de quant. an.* (1) animal life, (2) life of sense, (3) reason, (4) moral sense and effort, (5) desire for God, (6) perseverance, (7) vision) ; Johan. Climac., *Scala Paradisi, pass.* (thirty stages) ; Bernardus Clarevall., *de dilig. Deo*, 8-10 ; *ep.* 11, 8 (four stages of loving God).

[4] See *Some Principles of Moral Theology*, p. 50, with references there. The doctrine of the ' threefold way ' can be clearly traced in Plotinus (see W. R. Inge, *Philosophy of Plotinus*, ii, pp. 165-168) ; Iamblichus and Proclus (see H. Koch, *Pseudo-Dionysius*, pp. 175, 183) ; and pseudo-Dionysius (*ib.*, pp. 174-178, 183, 184). In Dionysius, however, the doctrine is still applied *within* the sphere of contemplation only. According to P. Pourrat, whose investigation of the historical connexions involved is so far the most exhaustive, the same is true of Gallus, abbot of Verceil (fl. c. A.D. 1200), to whom later Western mysticism particularly owes its Dionysian trend (P. Pourrat, *Spiritualité Chrétienne*, iii, pp. 15, 16 ; cp. M. de Wulf, *Mediæval Philosophy* [5] (E. tr., 1926), i, p. 214). The first to transfer the schematization to the ' general and normal development of the Christian life ' were S. Bonaventura (Pourrat, *op. cit.*, iii, p. 16 ; cp. ii, pp. 267-269), and his contemporary Hugo de Balma (*ib.*, iii, pp. 17, 18 ; cp. ii, p. 477). Cp. also F. Heiler, *Das Gebet*, pp. 309-317, especially the highly schematic tabulation on pp. 312, 313.

[5] Greg. Magn., *Mor. in Hiob*, vi, 56.

Gregory the Great's formulation of the doctrine is peculiarly interesting and important. Though based entirely on S. Augustine, it has an originality of its own which entitles it to rank as the culminating example of patristic teaching on the subject. Gregory delights in describing the joys of the vision of God ; but he insists on emphasizing the constant need for works of the active life—the life of discipline and service—as well. For him there is, strictly speaking, no such thing as a purely contemplative life at all. The strict idea of successive, clearly demarcated stages is, in fact, a simplification of the actual truth. There are at best moments, or periods, of contemplation which are achieved or experienced intermittently in the active life, thereby mingling both action and contemplation in a single 'mixed life.' Two reasons are given for this. First of all, the necessary labours of the day press even when the amenities of life are reduced to a minimum, and are a definite distraction from contemplation. In the second place, the love for God and our neighbour which is kindled in contemplation is of such a sort that it must find expression in the positive virtues of the active life.

'The active life,' says Gregory,[1]

'is this :—to give bread to the hungry, to teach the ignorant, to correct the erring, to rebuke the proud, to tend the sick, to give to all as they need, to care for one's dependents. Contemplation is, while retaining all one's love for God and our neighbour, to rest from action and cleave only to desire for the Maker, with a mind which has dismissed all cares and is aglow with the vision of its Creator.'

'We cannot stay long in contemplation,' he says elsewhere.[2] 'We can only glance at eternity through a mirror, by stealth, and in passing ; . . . we have to return to the active life, and occupy ourselves with good works. But good works help us again to rise to contemplation, and to receive nourishment of love from the vision of Truth. . . . Then, once more moving back to the life of service, we feed on the memory of the sweetness of God, strengthened by good deeds without, and by holy desires within.'

If I have interpreted this strain of thought aright, it would seem to be in essence wholly true to the New Testament. It offers the vision of God to all ; it calls all to the search for the vision ; the ideal is an obligation laid upon the married as upon the monk. Purity of heart is still the first and fundamental condition of seeing God. It allows for the rigorist element in the New Testament by insisting that self-discipline and renunciation are of the essence of the active life ; but it sets a bar against rigorist excesses by asserting that the Christian cannot become perfect in a moment, and that

---

[1] *Hom. in Ezk.*, II, ii, 8.
[2] *Ib.*, I, v, 12. A full account of S. Gregory's doctrine of the 'mixed' life, C. Butler, *Western Mysticism*, pp. 253-269.

he must be allowed to progress slowly towards such degree of renunciation as may be necessary for the vision and its fruits. The
theory leaves questions unanswered, no doubt ; in particular the
question of *what* renunciations are necessary for the true Christian
life. But for the immediate needs of any particular case it is unnecessary to answer this question as against the rigorist. If the
rigorist urges in respect of any person that he is not exercising the
full Christian renunciation, it can be replied that he may yet come
to it, but is at present in the preliminary stage.

Yet this valid theory made shipwreck just because there was
one question which it would not face—the question, namely, ' Can a
Christian attain *the fullness* of contemplation without becoming a
monk ? ' For the theory of stages of progress to be applicable to
the facts of life at all only one answer was possible, and that answer
was ' Yes.' If everyone is called to the vision of God, and many
obviously cannot leave the secular life, then monasticism is, strictly
speaking, irrelevant to the issue. You may achieve the vision by
the renunciation of wealth and marriage, it is true ; but you may
also achieve it in ways which do not involve those surrenders.
What grounds then are left for preferring monasticism to the secular
life ?

(*b*) A compromise attractive at first sight is to say that the
monastic renunciations make the pursuit of the vision *easier*. This
is the form of the doctrine as it reached S. Thomas Aquinas. By
the life of the counsels ' a man may come more happily and freely ' to
the heights of contemplation.[1] But this involves a fatal paradox.
Monasticism is now an *easier* life in all that affects spiritual issues
than the secular life ; the latter is the more heroic of the two.
There are passages in the Fathers which betray an uneasy feeling

---

[1] *ST.*, i, 2, q. 108, a. 4—' consilia oportet esse de illis, per quæ melius
et expeditius potest homo consequi finem prædictum ' ; cp. ii, 2, q. 184,
a. 3, *ad* 1—' consilia sunt quædam instrumenta perveniendi ad perfectionem.'
Even Luther at one stage admitted as much, *Contra malignum Eccii judicium*
(1519), art. 15 (*Works* (ed. Weimar), ii, p. 644)—tho counsels are ' media
commodiora,' ' viæ et compendia facilius et felicius implendi mandata Dei ' ;
hence, explicitly, they are ' infra precepta ' as means to end. The compromise
is attractive *at first sight* only, for few impartial thinkers would be prepared,
either on *a priori* or on empirical grounds, to assert anything so positive as
that the monastic life is necessarily, or even generally, the more efficacious
way. Cp. A. L. Smith, *Church and State in the Middle Ages*, p. 83—' If
anyone were to argue at the present day that single-minded devotion to a
profession or an art is hindered by matrimony, he would probably be told,
first, that the statement is untrue ; second, that family life is of more vital
importance to a society and to any normal member of it, than is any profession or art ; thirdly, that celibacy, generally speaking, is a condition at
once selfish, unpatriotic and morally dangerous.' (The third proposition is
of course less solid than the first two.) The truth is, as Dr. Rashdall has
pointed out (*Theory of Good and Evil*, ii, pp. 107 ff.), that we are here within
the realm of vocational morality, in which each man's vocation is his duty
for him, and cannot admit of a ' higher ' and ' lower.' See further, however,
infra, p. 520, additional note K. The exposition of the ' two lives ' in
H. Denifle, *Luther u. Luthertum*, i, pp. 141-188, is admirable, provided always
that it is taken exactly at its face-value.

that this is the case. S. Gregory is constantly lamenting the joys, consolations and supports of the monastic life, which he has lost by undertaking the harder labours of the episcopate. Jerome reveals the same spirit in his denunciations of the troubles and trials of marriage, and frankly admits that he took to the desert in flight from temptations which in the world he would have had to fight and overcome.[1] Cassian's ' Collations ' often revert to the idea that the vision of God is more difficult to achieve in the turmoil of secular affairs than in the quiet of the desert.[2] Chrysostom, liberal-minded as always, regards the temptations and activities of the secular life as more severe than those of monks ; [3] even Clement of Alexandria in the early days dared to assert that married life was superior to celibacy as offering more temptations.[4]

(c) But to say explicitly that the monastic life as such was no better than the secular [5]—still more to say that it was the *less* heroic of the two—was almost impossible in the early centuries. The fall of Jovinian and Vigilantius shows how popular opinion would regard such a heresy.[6] And because the theory of stages of progress faltered at this point, it was steadily overcome by a wholly different version of the ' two lives '—a version which was gnostic and Manichæan [7] rather than Christian. The contemplative life (the life,

---

[1] Cp. especially the peroration of the *contra Vigilantium* (cc. 15, 16)—' I retire to the desert . . . that the eyes of wantons may not lead me captive ; that beauty may not engender lust. You answer, " This is not to fight, but to run away ! " . . . I confess my weakness. I dare not fight in the hope of victory, lest perchance I be overcome. If I flee, I avoid the sword ; if I stand my ground, I must either conquer or fall. . . . Flight makes it impossible for me to win the victory ; but at least it ensures me against defeat.'

[2] Cp. especially *Coll.*, xix, 5, on the advantages of the hermit life for the would-be contemplative—at all events until the desert became uncomfortably crowded with visitors.

[3] Chrys., *de sac.*, vi, 1-8—the temptations and difficulties of the secular priesthood a proof of its loftiness ; *adv. opp. vit. mon.*, iii, 14—marriage makes continence easier ; in all other respects the advantage is with the monk. But the worldling must not expect a higher reward because he has the harder task—he chose it for himself !

[4] *Strom.*, vii, 12, 70. Cp. also the praise of marriage and parenthood in *Strom.*, ii, 23 ; and *Strom.*, iii, 9, 67. Basil, *de renunc. saec.*, 2 (*MPG.*, xxxi, col. 629) places the married man ' in the front-line trench of the battle ' against the devil, though he makes it an occasion of warning rather than of commendation.

[5] That a *good* married life was better than a *bad* monastic one was of course a commonplace (see e.g. Aug., *enarr. in Ps.* 99. 13 ; *de bon. conj.*, 10 (10), 23 (30) ; *de virg.*, 1 ; *de civ. Dei*, xvi, 36 ; *serm.*, 354. 9 (9)).

[6] Many interesting and extraordinary examples of the pitch to which the cultus of the hermits might rise are given by K. Holl, *Enthusiasmus u. Bussgewalt*, pp. 182 ff.

[7] On the gnostic distinction between the ' pneumatikoi ' and the ' psychikoi,' ' hylikoi ' or ' choikoi,' *supra*, pp. 211, 217 ; cp. Irenæus, *hær.*, i, 6, 7 (the three classes of the Valentinians) ; Epiphanius, *hær.*, xxiii, 2 (the two classes of Saturnilus). For the Manichees, F. C. Burkitt, *Religion of the Manichees*, pp. 44-48. Among later heretics the distinction still held good ; thus the Cathari had two classes, the *Perfecti* and *Credentes* :—' The life of the former was so strenuous that those who received the rank were

that is to say, which directly offers its votaries the vision of God)
is better than the active life; the monastic life is 'higher' than
the secular (so at least the argument ran), though certainly not
the easier. Therefore the contemplative life *must be* the monas:ic
life, and the active life the secular.[1] The two differ in *kind* rather
than in degree; they are mutually exclusive alternatives, and the
Christian must choose between them. We may still offer the layman
the hope of salvation; [2] but it is salvation of a definitely lower
grade, for he does not, and by virtue of his secular occupation he
cannot, live the life of contemplation.

The doctrine in this form may be traced in Origen; it dominated
the ideas of the hermits; Cassian is full of it; Jerome and Ambrose
fix it in a definite tradition.[3] S. Thomas Aquinas did his best to
stem the torrent. He asserts in effect that the so-called 'state of

advised to commit suicide' ('endura'—see Ducange, *Gloss.*, *s.v.*), although
the stricter Cathari held that for this category alone was salvation possible
(E. Scott-Davison, *Forerunners of S. Francis*, pp. 208, 209).

[1] The argument may be put in another form. The true Christian life is
of course heroic; but heroism is the highest stage in the path to perfection.
Now the monastic life is more spectacular than the secular; and the spectacular is easily mistaken for the heroic (*infra*, p. 519). Hence the way to
the identification of the monastic with the heroic, and consequently the
highest, stage of life is clear; but once the identification is made the secular
life, *in so far as it debars from monasticism*, must be regarded as the lower,
non-heroic way. The non-heroic is no longer a stage to the heroic; they
are alternative paths.

[2] The possibility of his attaining salvation of a sort—the 'lower rewards'
—is of course implied in the constant assertion that he may reject the higher
course 'without actual sin.' For one of the most extreme expressions of
the invalid theory see the propositions of Matthew Grabon condemned at
the Council of Constance, summarized, Pourrat, *SC.*, iii, pp. 116, 117.

[3] The doctrine is implied wherever it is said in effect that, *ceteris paribus*,
virginity is always the better way and will secure the highest rewards.
It may be inferred in many of the passages cited, *supra*, p. 241, n. 2.
The promise of higher reward for the celibate is explicit, for example, in
Hermas, *Pastor, Mand.*, IV, 4; pseudo-Clem., *ep. ad virg.*, i, 4; Athan.,
ep. 48; Ambrose. *ep.* 63. 10; 40; *de virg.*, i, 7 (36, 37); *de vid.*, 12 (74),
14 (84); and of course in Jerome, *passim*. H. Reuter, *Augustinische
Studien*, pp. 408-427, 476 (esp. pp. 424-427) makes a bold attempt to prove
that Augustine accepted the invalid theory only with the greatest reluctance.
He is no doubt right in insisting (pp. 403-404) that Augustine normally
keeps the concepts of *perfectio* and of the *consilia* distinct; and this is important. But neither the fact that Augustine regards martyrs as achieving
'perfection' without necessarily following the 'counsels' (pp. 399, 412),
nor that he insists (pp. 418, 421—*supra*, p. 254, n. 5) that a good married
life is better than an evil ascetic one, is conclusive; both are commonplaces
which do not touch the root of the matter. On the other hand, Augustine
maintains constantly that virginity as such necessarily qualifies for the
higher rewards; see especially *de sanct. virg.*, 12 (12), 14 (14), 18 (18), 19 (19),
etc. J. Mausbach, *Die Ethik des Heiligen Augustinus*, i, pp. 404-412, cp. *ib.*,
363, 390, 402, 422-427, rightly disposes of Reuter's contention, and demon-
strates Augustine in this respect to be simply a child of his time. But
Augustine's spirituality shows itself, for example, in the peculiar turn he
gives to the story of the young man with great possessions (*serm.* 142. 8 (9)):—
What is the 'counsel' which makes perfection possible? 'Sell all thou hast
and give to the poor . . . ?' No: the final clause—'Come, follow Me' in
true humility (followed by Aquinas in *de perf. vit. spir.*, 7). For Cassian's
variations see *infra*, p. 525, additional note M.

perfection ' (the monastic life) is no real *state* at all, but merely a
way by which its adherents profess that they are striving (as all
Christians should strive) [1] after perfection ; [2] and he goes out of his
way to insist that ' some have perfection ' who are not in the ' state
of perfection ' at all.[3] Despite this warning, however, the invalid
theory made headway throughout the middle ages, as Gerson's
tract on the evangelical counsels clearly shows ; [4] and it was stereotyped by the Council of Trent.[5] In post-Tridentine Roman theology
it sometimes results in a reversion to the conceptions of the desert ;
only monks of the most rigorous orders—the Camaldolese, Car-
thusians and Trappists—are capable of the contemplative life and
its fullest fruits—all others occupy a lower plane.[6] Indeed, it may
be conjectured that humanism will have a severe struggle to get
its way here in the Roman Church, for its triumph would mean the
complete downfall of the theory of monastic superiority which is so
firmly established in the tradition of centuries. So long as the
tendency to exalt the celibate over the married life remains, it will
involve the belief that the celibate is doing more for God than the
married, and therefore will receive, *ceteris paribus*, the higher
rewards.

Thus like the lean kine in Pharaoh's dream, and under cover of
the ambiguous title of the ' two lives,' the conception of ' action '

[1] Aquinas, *ST.*, ii, 2, q. 184, a. 3, ad 2—' The perfection [which consists]
in loving God is of precept universally, so that even the perfection of heaven
is not excepted from this precept.'

[2] *Ib.*, a. 5, ad 2—' Men enter the "state" of perfection, not as pro-
fessing to be perfect ; but as professing that they aim at perfection.' *Essentially*, the state of perfection ' consists not in the absolute renunciation of
property, etc., but in the *readiness* to renounce them, if God wills ; by this
argument S. Thomas proves that nothing prevents a bishop from being
essentially in the ' state of perfection.' But obviously the argument might
be extended to cover laymen of whatever category.

[3] *Ib.*, a. 4, *contra et in corp.* S. Thomas deals with the question of the
double standard at greater length in the ' opusculum,' *de perfectione vitæ
spiritualis*, which is particularly interesting, since it puts forward a *mélange*
of all three theories. (a) The *compromise* theory is in the forefront of the
treatment of ' love towards God ' (cc. 6, 7—' liberius,' ' utilius,' ' per consilia
(sc. evangelica) invitamur,' etc.) ; but (b) there are suggestions of the *invalid*
theory—e.g. c. 8 fin. (from Aug., *de bon conj.*)—Abraham achieved perfection
in the married state, but ' propter temporis differentiam ' (i.e. under the
old dispensation) ; we are not therefore entitled to assume that we may
follow his example without blame ; c. 15—to *vow* oneself to perfection is to
make possible a ' double perfection ' ; (c) The *valid* theory is suggested in
relation even to the evangelical counsels by the unqualified ' quædam perfectionis via ' of c. 7 ; it is explicit in c. 6—the virtue of the saint (' compre-
hensor ') is ' consilium,' but ' æmulari tamen *debemus* ' ; and throughout the
treatment of ' love to one's neighbour ' (c. 14), where the counsels (e.g.
loving one's enemies or sacrificing oneself for others ' extra necessitatis casus ')
are frankly called virtues ' exceeding ordinary perfection,' but obviously are
to be *emulated* by the earnest Christian as in c. 6.

[4] Gerson, *de consil. evang. et statu perfectionis;* cp. Pourrat, *SC.*, iii,
p. 116.

[5] *Sess.* xxiv, can. 10 (Denz.-Bann.[15], no. 981).

[6] See *infra*, p. 526, additional note N.

and ' contemplation ' as differing from one another in *kind* swallowed up the conception of the stages of spiritual progress as differing only in *degree*. How completely this was the case may be seen from Cassian's curious restriction of the title ' active ' life to the preliminary ascetic exercises *of the monk*—the secular life is no longer worthy of a name which suggests that it is even so much as a stage towards the life of contemplation.[1] The familiar restriction of the evangelic counsels—once so elastic and adaptable—to the three monastic duties of poverty, celibacy and obedience, was an inevitable consequence. The disastrous results of this victory of the invalid theory will appear when we come to the mediæval penitential books, with their formalist emphasis on the avoidance of sin and the performance of codified duties as the whole compass of the layman's endeavours ; and their almost complete silence on the vision of God as an inspiration and a goal.

But despite its evil consequences something was attained even by the false doctrine of the two lives—a place of sorts was found for the worldling in the Church. And more was attained by the true doctrine of stages of progress, in so far as it survived. It suggested the thought that the faithful performance of secular duties and the ascetic renunciations of the monks were equally methods of preparing for the vision of God. The thought led to the practical assimilation of the two. Active service—the hall-mark of the Christian in the world—was accepted as a necessary virtue of the cloister ; and active service is the same in the cloister as in the world. The gulf between the professed ascetic and the enforced layman was perceptibly diminished ; and a rigorism primarily negative in character began to give way before a self-discipline whose test was that of charitable thoughts and words and deeds. So far at all events the theory of stages of progress, though vanquished on the main issue, contributed to the defeat of rigorism ; and the new outlook which it thus provided was expressed in practice by the considered enactments of the great monastic legislators.

III. The Reform of Monasticism.

The fourth, fifth and sixth centuries of our era witnessed a remarkable series of efforts to bring the monastic life into closer kinship with the secular. It is difficult to exaggerate the courage and the conviction of a Church which thus set out to use the weapons of discipline, not to repress open wickedness, but to prevent those who were universally regarded as most saintly from becoming righteous overmuch.

---

[1] Cassian, *Coll.*, xiv, 3 (*supra*, pp. 201, 250)—although the forms of the active life are said by Nesteros to be manifold, they appear all of them to be monastic.

(a) S. Pachomius.[1]

In lower Egypt, in Palestine and Syria, hermits of the Antonian model lived wholly separate lives; meeting, if at all, only for spiritual intercourse and mutual exhortation. In the Nitrian desert, and the 'lauras' of Palestine in the fifth century, the system was different—or rather, it began to be a system. As late as Cassian's day there was still no common rule, but a central church gathered the brethren together for worship on Saturdays and Sundays.[2] In upper Egypt, however, Pachomius—a younger contemporary of Antony, and a converted pagan soldier—boldly ventured on a new experiment. Gathering a group of male ascetics into a monastery, he gave them a rule and induced them to live in common discipline under an abbot. The system prospered. Other monasteries were founded, with convents for women, all owing allegiance to the mother-house at Tabennisi, or later at Pabou. By Pachomius' death in A.D. 346, nine monasteries and two convents[3] were combined in what it is universally agreed to describe as the first genuine monastic order—indeed the only genuine ' order ' to exist for many centuries.

John Cassian, whose acquaintance was mainly with the monks of lower Egypt, records that even the tending of the little cell-gardens which provided their daily wants appeared to the champions of the hermit life an almost fatal barrier to contemplation.[4] Antony knew of such extremists; he warned his disciples in consequence to keep their hands occupied, and thereby to supply their own needs and those of such neighbours as could not fend for themselves.[5] Pachomius however reversed all this. Instead of the doctrines of ' no work at all ' or ' work, but only of the simplest kind and the smallest amount necessary to existence or occupation,' he substituted the gospel of continued work, and that not mere manual labour but

---

[1] The sources for the life of Pachomius have all been carefully studied by P. Ladeuze, *Étude sur le Cénobitisme Pakhomien* (1898). He gives convincing reasons for the priority of the *Vita* published by the Bollandists (Ladeuze, pp. 4-78) ; and insists on its general reliability (pp. 106, 107) as against the Coptic and Arabic versions preferred by E. Amélineau.

[2] Pall., *Hist. Laus.* (ed. C. Butler), 7. 5.

[3] Ladeuze, *op. cit.*, p. 178. For the complicated chronology of Pachomius' life, and the reasons for prefering the above date to others suggested for his death, *ib.*, pp. 222-241.

[4] Cass., *Coll.*, xix, 5, 9 ; xxiv, 3, 4, 12. The last passage is complicated by a variety of motives. The monk must not live on charity, for that would be laziness ; nor must he live in a fruitful spot, lest he be distracted by the delights of gardening. He is to choose a rocky and barren site—from which, we must suppose, he will be able to wring enough sustenance for life, but only at the cost of hard work.

[5] Ath., *Vit. Ant.*, 3 (reference to 2 Thess. 3[10]), 44 ; Cass., *Coll.*, xxiv, 10-12 ; cp. *Vit. Patr.*, iii, 55, 56, 212 (Rosweyde, *MPL.*, lxxiii, coll. 768, 807). The same principle, Cass., *Inst.*, x, *pass.* (on the dangers of *acedia*), especially 23—' A monk who works is attacked by one devil only ; an idler by innumerable hosts.' Contrast the Euchites, or Messalians, who regarded all work as sinful, Theodoret, *HE.*, iv, 10.

craftsmanship of a high order. Work, which is the rule of the world, must also be the rule for the monk ; it must be schooled to the service of contemplation. Important in itself, the innovation becomes more significant still when it is regarded as an instance of the principle underlying all Pachomius' reforms. The rule of the world—purified, ordered and simplified, but still the rule of the world—must become the rule of the monastery.

Palladius gives detailed accounts both of life at one of these monasteries,[1] and also of the rule alleged to have been received by their founder from an angel, and by him handed on to his subordinates.[2] Different versions of the rule survive, with marked variations, in five distinct languages.[3] That a primitive nucleus underlies all these versions is attested by the occasional and un-codified character of the regulations which they all record. But although only a few points are touched upon, and those almost at haphazard, the effect must have been revolutionary. As against the hermit-ideal of reducing all eating and drinking to a minimum, Pachomius says, ' Let each man eat and drink as he needs ; . . . and hinder him neither from fasting nor from eating '[4]—asceticism in the technical sense is optional, temperate enjoyment of food wholly legitimate. As against the hermit's quest for solitude, sleeplessness, and the rigours of cold nights in the open air, the rule says, ' Set several cells together, and let the monks dwell three in each cell ; whilst all eat together in a common hall. . . . At night let them spread their blankets, and sleep in linen singlets with girdles.'[5] The only ascetic note here is the curious regulation that they may not lie down to sleep, but must recline on home-made chairs.[6]

Silence is commanded at meal-times,[7] from which it would appear that at other times speech was allowed ; and this the Ethiopian version of the rule makes clear by adding ' and when you have

---

[1] Pall., *Hist. Laus.*, 32. 7 ff. ; cp. the charitable monastery at Arsinoë described by Rufinus, *Hist. Mon.*, ii, 18, of which the monks were so generous that ' not all the poor in Egypt sufficed to exhaust their benevolence.'

[2] *Ib.*, 32. 1.

[3] Ladeuze (p. 260) counts seven versions of the original Rule, discarding (p. 266) Amélineau's Coptic fragments, the secondary Ethiopian versions, and several long Greek and Latin recensions, including that of S. Jerome. He deals with these at length (pp. 256-273) ; but while accepting Palladius' version as the original (p. 262), maintains, after comparing it with the *data* of the earliest ' Life,' that even this ' does not represent the primitive form of the Pachomian rule ' (p. 266)—which is indeed ' irrecoverable ' (*ib.*). H. Leclerq, art. *Cénobitisme* in *DALC.*, ii, col. 3111, accepts these conclusions.

[4] Pall., *Hist. Laus.*, *loc. cit.*

[5] *Ib.* Ladeuze (pp. 263, 264), on the evidence of the ' Lives,' regards these anticipations of the monastic dorter as developments ; in Pachomius' time each monk would have had a separate cell. This makes the regulations even less ascetic.

[6] *Ib.* Ladeuze (p. 264) rejects this precept also, on the ground that Pachomius himself did not observe it (*Vita*, c. 9—Boll., *AS.*, Mai., iii, p. 27 *. Pachomius slept ' sitting on a stone in the middle of his cell, without resting his back against anything '). The version of Dionys. Exiguus (Rosweyde, *MPL.*, lxxiii, col. 242) omits the regulation ; but Sozomen (*HE.*, iii, 14) repeats it.

[7] Pall., *Hist. Laus.*, 32. 6.

risen from your meal, be sparing of speech.' [1] As against the countless prayers of the hermits, Pachomius is content with twelve in
the day, twelve at evening, and twelve in the night-offices, with
three at the ninth hour.[2] Further, the sick are to be cared for
almost lavishly, and their fancies in diet to be considered.[3] The
Arabic life of the saint tells how on one occasion, when he himself
was sick, and the more narrow-minded of his monks murmured
because another inmate of the sanatorium asked for meat, Pachomius
said cheerfully, ' To the pure all things are pure,' and ordered a
kidling to be killed and dressed for himself and his fellow-invalid.[4]

Again, instead of the free individualism of the isolated hermit,
Pachomius instituted a strict apprenticeship of three years' servile
labour,[5] and a rigid organization for the whole of the monk's life.[6]
Each monastery was divided into twenty-four courses or companies,
according to the letters of the alphabet; [7] presumably every company had its own internal organization as well. Finally, as has
already been mentioned, every man was required to work, and the
abbot had to see that work was apportioned him up to the measure
of his strength—his capacity for physical endurance being gauged
in rough-and-ready fashion by the size of his appetite at table.[8]

[1] Zöckler, *Askese u. Mönchtum*, p. 208, from the Ethiopian.
[2] Palladius, *ut sup.*
[3] References, Ladeuze, pp. 300, 301 ; Zöckler, p. 209.
[4] E. Amélineau, *Annales du Musée Guimet*, xvii (1889), p. 566. The
story is no doubt apocryphal ; Ladeuze, p. 167, has collected references to
show that the saint did not spare himself even in sickness. That the infirmary
régime was not always so genial is attested by the statement in Jerome's
version (*reg.* 164 ; *MPL.*, xxiii, col. 86) that incorrigible grumblers were
treated as sick, and sent to the infirmary for punishment.
[5] Pall., *ut sup.*, 5. Ladeuze (pp. 281 f.) rejects this prescription, as
neither the ' Lives ' nor Jerome make any mention of it. But it must have
been at all events an early development from the preliminary testing which
took place during the ten days (Cass., *Inst.*, iv, 3) which the postulant was
required to spend *outside* the monastery before admission. Cassian (*loc. cit.*)
and Jerome's version of the Rule (*ubi supr.*, nn. 49, 139) give some account
of the exercises of this period.
[6] Ladeuze (pp. 284, 285), followed by Leclerq (*DALC.*, ii, col. 3117),
regards the rigid obedience required of the monk as Pachomius' greatest
innovation and contribution to the development of monasticism. The monks
were to be ' ready for all obedience, laying aside all wilfulness of heart ' ;
and ' no one could deserve the name of great except by obedience ' (*Vita*, 19,
80—Boll., *AS.*, Mai., iii, pp. 30*, 46*).
[7] The *Greek* alphabet, Palladius says. Ladeuze rejects the whole conception, both on the grounds that it is not mentioned by the ' Lives ' or
Jerome, and because for the greater part of his life Pachomius knew no
Greek. This, however, seems no reason for discarding the fact of organization. Pachomius certainly used the alphabet to some mystical purpose
(*Vita*, 63 ; Hieron., *præf.*, 9—*MPL.*, xxiii, col. 68), and this may have been
confused with the fact of organization to produce the conflate version given
by Palladius.
[8] E.g. Pall., *Hist. Laus.*, 32. 2—' Proportionately to the strength of each
man as he eats appoint to him his labours'; cp. Soz., *HE.*, iii, 14—' Those
who ate heartily were to be subjected to arduous labours ; easier tasks were
assigned to the ascetics.' On *study of the scriptures* as a duty of the monk,
Reitzenstein, *HMHL.*, pp. 159, 163 ; and for various examples of charitable
services performed by the monks, Pall., *Hist. Laus.*, 14. 3 ; 19. 8.

The rule was by tradition received by Pachomius from an angel,[1] and the great pioneer himself complained that it was all too little. The angel replied that the rule was intended only for weaklings and beginners (there is an echo of the phrase in the far more elaborate code of S. Benedict) ; the mature monk might be trusted to make his own discipline for himself.[2] No doubt it was expected that each man, as he advanced in piety, would add to the mild requirements of the rule voluntary acts of self-discipline.[3] In theory, at all events, he was free to adopt the fullest mortifications of the hermit life. Pachomius does not forbid it, and the angel seems to encourage it. But as a matter of fact it is unlikely that under a system so regulated, so apportioned and so far from individualistic (—remember the three monks allotted to each cell—) self-mortification in advance of the rule would prove a very practicable policy. The monk has been brought a long stage back on the way to the life of the world.

Indeed, the general appearance and life of a Pachomian monastery cannot have been very different from that of a well-regulated college, city, or camp. So at least it seemed to Palladius when he visited the monastery at Panopolis. Among its three hundred inhabitants were fifteen tailors—a curiously large proportion for a community which required little in the way of garments—seven smiths, four carpenters, twelve camel-drivers,[4] and fifteen fullers ; but scarcely any other kind of craft went unrepresented. We hear of shoe-makers, gardeners, bakers, tanners, and calligraphists. Palladius was surprised to find the brethren keeping pigs, but was assured that they were useful as scavengers ; and that they not only added to the communal income, but also furnished tit-bits of pork for the sick and aged of the neighbouring countryside. The routine was military, the different companies taking their meals at different hours, presumably to simplify the problem of domestic service.[5]

Regulated and social discipline has thus taken the place of unrelaxed and anti-social self-torture. Many of the Pachomian monks must have found sensible relief on exchanging the hand-to-mouth existence of petty cultivators or labourers for the highly organized life of the cœnobium, with food, shelter and occupation all found for its inhabitants. What theory, if any, lay behind these

---

[1] 'A pure legend,' says Ladeuze, rather gratuitously ; he means that the tradition does not occur in the 'Lives.' Gennadius (*de vir. ill.*, 7) and Palladius (*loc. cit.*) are the first to record it.

[2] Pall., *Hist. Laus.*, 32. 7.

[3] So the *Paralipomena de SS. Pachomio et Theodoro*, 16 (Boll., *AS.*, Mai., iii, pp. 55*)—'*If the food is laid upon the table* and the brethren by God's help exercise abstinence and refuse to taste of it, great shall be their reward.'

[4] Ladeuze, p. 295, translates καμηλάριοι as 'rope-makers'; but this meaning of the word is unknown, and is probably derived from the spurious κάμιλος which was invented to supplant the 'camel' of Mk. 10²⁵ (see Stephanus, *Thesaurus*, *s.v.* κάμηλος).

[5] Pall., *ut sup.*

far-reaching reforms does not transpire ; but their tendency is open
for every eye to read.   That the mildness of the rule was prevented
from falling into laxity by a strict system of discipline and punishment [1] cannot alter the fact of its general humanitarianism.

Pachomius forced on his reforms in the face of opposition from
representatives of the older hermit type.   So much is hinted at in
an anecdote recorded in the Coptic and Arabic ' Vitæ.' [2]   His
first companion in the new venture was his elder brother John ;
and so revolutionary did Pachomius' scheme appear to him, that
with his own hands he tore down the wall with which his brother
was beginning to fence the precincts of the future monastery.
But the cœnobitic system had come to stay, and in upper Egypt,
at least, those who wished for more austerity were content to seek
it within the confines of the rule.   Such, for example, was the
method of Schenoudi,[3] the veteran abbot of the Coptic monastery
of Athripis,[4] near Panopolis, who crowned a life of Christian service
by hurling a copy of the gospels at Nestorius in the Council of
Ephesus [5]—a gesture at once so orthodox and so effective (for the
missile struck its heretical target full in the chest) that Cyril of
Alexandria promptly rewarded the champion with the office of
archimandrite.

For fifty years, till his death in the year 451 or 452 at the age

---

[1] Hieron., *ut sup.*, nn. 147-154, 160-176.   The punishments (only to be
given after monition) included fasting on bread and water, temporary excommunication, degradation, relegation to the infirmary (*supra*, p. 260, n. 4),
corporal chastisement, expulsion.

[2] E. Amélineau, *Histoire de St. Pakhôme* (*Annales du Musée Guimet* (1889)
xvii), p. 361.   In the Bollandist *Vita* (c. 10) John ' was for restricting the
accommodation' and spoke severely to Pachomius about it.   Dionysius
Exiguus, *Vita*, 15 (*MPL.*, lxxiii, col. 238) merely says that John ' habitaculi
diligebat angustias,' and urged Pachomius to abandon his intention.

[3] Schenoudi is not mentioned by any Greek or Latin writer, and his existence was only rediscovered at the beginning of the nineteenth century.   He
is known to history through Coptic and Arabic panegyrics pronounced on
various anniversaries of his death, published by Amélineau in *Mémoires
. . . de la Mission archéologique française au Caire*, vol. iv (1888 and 1895),
and summarized by him in his *Vie de Schenoudi* (1889).   Some letters and
speeches of Schenoudi and his successor Visa, accepted as authentic by
Ladeuze (*op. cit.*, pp. 151-154) as well as by Amélineau, also survive.   The
historical value of the panegyrics is fully discussed by Ladeuze (*op. cit.*, pp.
136-147), as also Schenoudi's importance (*ib.*, pp. 206-221) and his rule (305-
326).   See also *DCB.*, iv, pp. 611, 612 ;   *DALC.*, ii, coll. 3104-3108 ;   E.
Révillout, in *Révue de l'histoire des religions*, viii (1883), pp. 401-467, 545-581 ;
J. Leipoldt, *TU.*, xxv (1903) ;   Ladeuze, *Révue d'histoire ecclésiastique*, vii
(1906), pp. 76-85.   Canon Hannay's brief account of Schenoudi (*Spirit and
Origin*, pp. 123, 124) is much too flattering.   It may be mentioned as a point
of interest that the Arabic version of the principal panegyric has incorporated as a part of Schenoudi's teaching a reminiscence of the ' Two Ways '
in *Didaché* (Iselin in *TU.*, xiii (1895), i ;   Ladeuze, *op. cit.*, pp. 129-131).

[4] This so-called ' White Monastery ' still exists ;   a description in Amélineau, *Vie de Schenoudi*, p. 88.

[5] Amélineau, *Mémoires*, iv, pp. 67-69, 426-428 ;   *Vie de Schenoudi*, p. 347.
Nestorius, of course, was not at the Council, but an encounter may have
taken place at a preliminary meeting (Ladeuze, *op. cit.*, p. 140, from
Révillout,.

of 118,[1] this 'fourteenth apostle,' as he was called—S. Paul himself being the thirteenth—tyrannized over his monastery with an iron hand, welding the unfortunate monks into a compact army whose only contact with the world was an occasional excursion to break down idols, burn heathen temples and massacre their devotees, or harry heretics into submission.[2] In the intervals of these forays, Schenoudi's monks—the first to be bound by a vow of perpetual obedience to their abbot, which, for greater security, was expressed and signed in writing [3]—reverted to many of the austerities of the early hermits. Every detail of monastic discipline was thought out and regulated ; economical management of the kitchen department was one of the abbot's most passionate interests.[4] ' The bonhommie which marked the Pachomian rule,' a French writer has said, ' was superseded at Athripis by a meticulous intransigence . . . . which aimed at panic-stricken obedience in preference to willing loyalty. The smallest faults were punished with a flogging ; Schenoudi admitted having killed a monk for a trifling theft and lie.' [5]

Prayers, fasts and mortifications were exaggerated to the fullest degree. Schenoudi's own ideal was that of the hermit life. He was constantly in retirement in a cave of his own ; and to his other gifts and graces he added the distinction of being one of the most famous of 'weepers '—not, that is to say, penitents, but ascetics whose labours were crowned with the spiritual reward of an unceasing flow of tears.[6] His attitude towards culture was uncompromisingly hostile. ' He knew Greek,' says Ladeuze, one of his principal modern biographers, ' and could quote philosophers and poets ; he was familiar with classical mythology. . . . But he never allowed himself to be influenced by Greek ideas. Science he regarded as useless ; and he was without theology. . . . His piety was wholly practical ; he had no interest in the metaphysical relations of God with man, or the mystical union of man with God.' [7] Nevertheless, he would not cut himself away altogether from the humanizing principles of the cœnobite life as instituted by Pachomius. Their influence is seen in the fact that even his hermits

---

[1] Ladeuze, *op. cit.*, p. 251.

[2] Amélineau, *Vie de Schenoudi*, pp. 310 ff. ; cp. also Ladeuze, *op. cit.*, p. 220—' Schenoudi's invectives developed into massacres, his anathemas degenerated into persecutions.'

[3] Text and translation, J. Leipoldt, *TU.* xxv (1903), pp. 109, 195-196; Leclerq, in *DALC.*, ii, coll. 3116, 3117. Earlier discussions (e.g. Amélineau, *Vie*, p. 44 ; Ladeuze, *op. cit.*, pp. 314, 315) are superseded by the discovery of the original text. Cp. Ladeuze, *Révue d'hist. ecclés.*, vii (1906), p. 79.

[4] Amélineau, *Vie de Schenoudi*, pp. 98 ff.—detailed instructions for the preparation of vegetables, etc.

[5] Leclerq, *DALC.*, ii, col. 3107. Schenoudi's violence even extended to the police officials who came to protect the monks against his assaults—see the anecdote, Leclerq, *op. cit.*, p. 138, from Révillout.

[6] Amélineau, *Vie*, pp. 65 ff.—On the ' weepers ' in general, O. Zöckler, *Askese u. Mönchtum*, pp. 279 ff. ; and on the miraculous in the accounts of Schenoudi, Ladeuze, *op. cit.*, pp. 141-145.

[7] Ladeuze, *Révue d'histoire ecclésiastique*, vii (1906), p. 78.

were still in some sort attached to the society, and their needs supplied from the monastery farm.[1]

(b) S. Basil.

About fifty years before the time of Palladius and Cassian, S. Basil visited Egypt. The purpose of his journey is not quite clear ; but he may quite possibly have hoped to gain first-hand experience of asceticism there, with a view to leading the religious life himself on the best models.[2] He says that he traversed almost the whole of Egypt, as well as Palestine and Mesopotamia,[3] and he came home with very definite and formed impressions. In Asia Minor, as in Palestine and the East generally, the semi-hermit life was the most popular, and uneducated and often profligate itinerant monks presented a genuine problem. In Cappadocia, the dominant influence was the mysterious bishop Eustathius of Sebaste,[4] who attained in the chequered period of the Arian controversy a reputation as unenviable as that of the Vicar of Bray in a later century, —largely due, as modern historians believe, to Basil's invectives against him [5] at a date when their long-standing friendship had been ruptured by a bitter quarrel.

Eustathius' followers had been guilty of excessive austerities which amounted to schismatic disregard of all ecclesiastical organization, and the Council of Gangra exercised discipline against them, probably about A.D. 340.[6]   But it does not appear that Eustathius

---

[1] Amélineau, Mémoires, iv, pp. 75, 450.

[2] This was about the year A.D. 357 ; Weingarten (Ursprung des Mönchtums, p. 54) throws some doubt on the purpose of the journey.

[3] Basil, ep. 223. 2.

[4] For Eustathius see F. Loofs, s.v., PRE., v, 627-630, and Eustathius von Sebaste (1898) ; also W. K. Lowther Clarke, St. Basil the Great, pp. 159 ff. Though born at Cæsarea in Cappadocia he was a pupil of Arius in Alexandria (Basil, ep. 244. 3, 9 ; 263. 3). After various unsuccessful attempts he was ordained at Cæsarea, and was consecrated Bishop of Sebaste before A.D. 357. By this time he had organized a cœnobitic monasticism in Asia Minor, which won Basil's enthusiastic admiration (ep. 223. 3) ;   and he was a frequent and welcome visitor at Basil's hermitage in Pontus (ep. 223. 5). His doctrinal variations were innumerable and erratic ; he seems to have ' signed every creed that went about for signature in his lifetime ' (B. Jackson, St. Basil (LNP-NF.), p. xxvii).   But his personal character was free from suspicion, and it is not at all clear that he was himself involved in the ascetic extravagances of those who called themselves his followers.

[5] Especially in epp. 223, 244, and 263.

[6] One of the principal efforts of the episcopate in the fourth and fifth centuries was to bring the ascetic movement under ecclesiastical control, since, from one point of view, monasticism was always ' a protest against the non-apostolic character of the Church and the over-centralization of power in the hands of the higher clergy ' (E. Scott Davison, Forerunners of St. Francis, p. 17).   A good review of the struggle in L. Duchesne, Early History of the Church (E. tr.), iii, pp. 22-26 ; cp. W. Bright, Canons of the First Four General Councils, pp. 157-165 (on canon 4 of Chalcedon, with numerous illustrative references) ; Reitzenstein, HMHL., c. 9, especially pp. 189-192 ; H. B. Workman, Evolution of the Monastic Ideal, pp. 11-21. Two figures

was implicated in any other way than by name,[1] and everything points to his teaching as a primary source of Basil's asceticism. In one respect, however, there is a crucial difference. Eustathius *may* perhaps have founded monasteries, though the point is in dispute;[2] Basil made the communal life the foundation-stone of his system. ' Man is not a monastic animal,' he proclaims, using the word in its strictest meaning.[3] Quite frankly he declared against the solitaries; and reversing the whole monastic tradition up to his day, maintained that the conditions of their life militated against the achievement of its purpose.

Even if, as a curious passage of Gregory Nazianzen [4] suggests, he tolerated some degree of eremitism in others, his own theory and practice were quite clear. ' In the solitary life,' says Basil,

' the gifts we have from God are useless, and the gifts we lack cannot be supplied. . . . The hermit has only one aim, to be self-sufficient; and this is plainly opposed to the law of love. . . . There are duties easy enough for cœnobites, which cannot be performed by the solitary; to fulfil one he must omit another. If he visits the sick, for example, he cannot entertain the stranger. . . . How can we rejoice with him who rejoices and weep with him who weeps, when no man knows the condition of his neighbour? The Lord Himself gave us an example . . . for He washed His disciples' feet. Whose feet

stand out particularly, both of them Bishops of Alexandria :—Athanasius, whose ' epoch-making work ' (Reitzenstein, *loc. cit.*) it was to reconcile monasticism and the Church; and Theophilus, who, in the period of strained relations a generation later, proceeded against the monks with the same ruthless intolerance which he also displayed against John Chrysostom. The Council of Gangra was directed against the excesses of Eustathius' followers, who decried marriage and forced married women to desert their husbands, shave their heads, and adopt male costume as an ascetic measure (cann. 1, 9, 10, 13, 14, 17); prescribed vegetarianism (can. 2); avoided the ministrations of married clergy (can. 4), and so forth. The date is doubtful: Hefele-Leclerq (i, p. 1029) follow the general modern opinion that it took place about A.D. 340.

[1] The Council professed only to ' enquire into the matters which concern Eustathius ' and the activities of his ' associates ' (οἱ περὶ Εὐστ.). Socrates (*HE.*, ii, 43) attributes the schismatic teachings of the Eustathians to Eustathius himself. Sozomen (*HE.*, iii, 14) is less definite, and mentions that ' many exonerate him '; he also pays a high tribute to Eustathius' moral character. Eustathius is often supposed to be the author of the *Constitutiones Monasticæ*, usually included in editions of S. Basil (e.g. *MPG.*, xxxi, coll. 1321 ff.), and Sozomen, *loc. cit.*, suggests as much, though he does not definitely name the Constitutions (see also Garnier, *Præfatio*, *MPG.*, xxxi, coll. 119-132).

[2] So Garnier, *loc. cit.*, col. 132, on the basis of Sozomen, *ut sup.*; cp. Lowther Clarke, *St. Basil*, p. 47.

[3] *Reg. Fus. Tract.*, 3. 1.

[4] *Or.*, xliii, 62.—' He founded ἀσκητήρια καὶ μοναστήρια, not far from the cœnobia '; see the full discussion, Lowther Clarke, *op. cit.*, pp. 109-113; cp. also Holl, *Enthusiasmus u. Bussgewalt*, p. 169. Holl thinks it out of the question that Basil tolerated eremitism in any form; and Lowther Clarke makes the οὐ πόρρω mean ' not far removed *in spirit*.'

will you wash ?   To whom will you be a servant ?   Compared with whom will you be last of all if you remain a solitary ? ' [1]

After an early experiment with his friends in Pontus,[2] Basil inaugurated his great monastery at Cæsarea between A.D. 365 and A.D. 370.[3] One of his most important deviations from the Pachomian system was to reduce the size of the cœnobium, so that it ceased to be an army and became a family. As against the two thousand monks at Athripis or the three hundred at Panopolis, Basil's monasteries probably contained no more than thirty or forty.[4] Even more than Pachomius he insisted upon work as a first principle. Everyone of his monks must have, or learn, a trade.[5] 'The purpose of work,' he says,

'is not merely to mortify the flesh, but to exhibit love for our neighbour, that God through us may supply the weak and sickly with the necessities of life. The apostle says that if a man will not work he shall not eat ; zealous work is as necessary as daily bread.'[6] 'The monk ought to labour with his hands . . . tend the sick, wash the feet of the saints, give pains to hospitality and brotherly love . . . be busied in good works and speeches.'[7] 'No devotion to prayer must be allowed as an excuse for avoiding work.'[8]

More important still is the fact that the monk's work is not merely directed to the maintenance of himself and his friends in the monastery, but also to the needs of society outside.[9] For the first time the hospital, almshouse, and school become regular adjuncts of a monastic settlement.[10] Basil goes out of his way to prove that the

---

[1] *Reg. Fus. Tract.*, 7.   Jerome (*ep.* 125. 9) takes less high ground against the hermit-life, but he would not have Rusticus attempt it until after long training in a monastery.   A better parallel to Basil's conception is to be found in the life of Nilus of Calabria (*c.* A.D. 980) whose personal predilections were eremitic, but who gave himself up to public service from a sense of duty (Boll., *AS.*, Sept., vii, pp. 299 ff.).

[2] *Infra*, p. 308.

[3] Basil became Archbishop of Cæsarea in A.D. 370 ; two years later his monastery was sufficiently imposing to have excited the suspicions of Elias, governor of Cappadocia (*ep.* 94).

[4] Lowther Clarke, *op. cit.*, p. 117 ; cp. Leclerq in *DALC.*, ii, col. 3149. Basil's main ideals are simply and clearly expressed in his *ep.* 2.

[5] *Reg. Fus. Tract.*, 38—the professions allowed are strictly utilitarian.

[6] *Ib.*, 37.   [7] *Sermo de ascet. discipl.*, 1 (*MPG.*, xxxi, col. 649).

[8] *Reg. Fus. Tract.*, 37. 2.   Basil adds that, so far from allowing the duty of prayer to impede us from work, we should attempt to hallow work by making it (and everything else) as far as possible an occasion of prayer (cp. *hom. in mart. Julitt.*, 2, 3, for the same sentiment).

[9] *Reg. Fus. Tract.*, 37. 1—quoting Eph. 4[28], ' that he may have whereof to give to him that hath need.'

[10] Also a ' retreat-house ' for the laity—*Reg. Fus. Tract.*, 45. 1 :—the prior must be ready to ' answer the (spiritual) questions of retreatants, that they may be edified in a manner appropriate to their problems, and the monastery be not put to shame.'   For the hospitals cp. Soz., *HE.*, vii, 34; Greg. Naz., *Or.*, xliii, 63 ; Basil, *epp.* 142, 143.   It is a moot point how far the schools were available for purposes of purely secular education. ' At the age of

practice of medicine is not inconsistent with the monastic life.[1]
In all these respects, it has been said, ' he was the precursor of
S. Francis de Sales and S. Vincent de Paul ; with him, as with them,
love of God and love of our neighbour are inextricably bound
together.' [2]

Basil was more interested in the spirit than in the outward
observances of asceticism, though he was quite ready to legislate
about the latter. ' We gain little by escaping from city life,' he
says, ' if we cannot escape from ourselves.' [3] ' Temperance does
not consist in abstinence from harmless food, wherein lies the
" neglecting " of the body condemned by the apostle, but in complete departure from one's own wishes.' [4] ' Beware of limiting
fasting to mere abstinence from meats. Real fasting is alienation
from evil.' [5] There remained indeed a distinct element of severity
about his asceticism. One meal a day was his normal rule ; but
it was not to be applied too rigidly.[6] Sleep was to be broken at
midnight for the recitation of the night office.[7] But regulations
which in the Pachomian rule were a minimum, and challenged the
' athlete of Christ ' to advance far beyond them in self-mortification,
are now a maximum. Self-imposed asceticism beyond that prescribed by rule is strongly and pointedly condemned.[8]

Thus though Basil's discipline on paper was severe enough, it
moved a long way from the Egyptian ideal ; and its restraint of
excess must have been strangely and even repellently novel in the
east as a whole. In another respect, also, practice was less rigorous
than theory. His rules prescribe complete poverty ; [9] but in general

discretion ' children were free to choose whether they would proceed to the
monastic, or retire from the institution into secular, life (*Reg. Fus. Tract.*,
15. 4) ; but were any accepted as scholars except those whose parents
proposed, all being well, to dedicate them to religion ? See Lowther Clarke,
op. cit., pp. 101, 102 ; Leclerq, in *DALC.*, ii, coll. 3150, 3151. Some admirable reflections on the spirit and method of Christian education, *Reg. Fus.
Tract.*, 15. 1-3.

[1] *Reg. Fus. Tract.*, 55 ; note also the curious hint, *Reg. Brev. Tract.*, 140,
that where an illness is the outcome of intemperance, remedial measures
should not be applied with too much alacrity, unless it is clear that the sick
man is penitent and proposes to amend his ways.

[2] Fialon, quoted Lowther Clarke, *op. cit.*, p. 124. See *Reg. Fus. Tract.*,
3. 2, for the explicit assertion.

[3] *ep.* 2. 1.

[4] *Reg. Brev. Tract.*, 128 ; cp. *ib.*, 258, where excessive asceticism is called
Manichæan.

[5] *de jejun. hom.*, i, 10 (*MPG.*, xxxi, col. 181).

[6] *ep.* 2. 6 ; *Reg. Brev. Tract.*, 136—the one meal ; *Reg. Fus. Tract.*, 19.
21—deviations allowed from the rule.

[7] *hom. in mart. Julitt.*, 4 (*MPG.*, xxxi, col. 244) ; cp. *ep.* 2. 6 ; *Reg. Fus.
Tract.*, 37. 5.

[8] *Reg. Brev. Tract.*, 137. ' Self-imposed decisions are dangerous '—the
question shows the reference to be to ascetic aspirations ; *ib.*, 138—' to
aspire to greater achievements than those of your companions (in asceticism)
is a temptation of jealousy . . . all such proposals are to be submitted to
authority.'

[9] *Reg. Fus. Tract.*, 8 ; *Reg. Brev. Tract.*, 85—private property is contrary
to the communal principles of Acts 4[32].

monks were allowed to retain some control over their personal property, if they employed the income in almsgiving, and reduced the capital as occasion offered by similar allocations.[1]

The domestic character of the Basilian monastery, its declared opposition to the hermit life, its active works of charity, its restraint of ascetic exaggerations, its situation in or near the great towns— all of these brought it far nearer to the world than the Pachomian rule had done for Egyptian monasticism. If we cannot quite say, with Weingarten,[2] that Basil's ideal, so far from being hostile to nature, was that of a return to nature, the phrase does at least suggest some part of the truth. It has often been questioned how far in effect S. Basil really provided the pattern on which eastern monasticism throughout the centuries has been built. The Council of Chalcedon on the ecclesiastical side, and the Code of Justinian on the civil, gave formal approval to his system ; it was stereotyped in the first eastern monastic rule—that of Theodore of Studium— in the eighth century.[3] Nevertheless, it is not too fanciful to suggest, with Dr. Lowther Clarke,[4] that while the east has continued to obey the letter of S. Basil's rules, their spirit has always been more at home in the west. Few historians fail to recognize in S. Benedict the true spiritual heir of the great Cappadocian.

(c) S. Benedict.

The rule of S. Benedict had to struggle against all the different forms of organized and disorganized asceticism which Basil had inspected and criticized before he developed his own conception.[5]

---

[1] *Reg. Fus. Tract.*, 9—care to be taken in the disposal of goods ; *Reg. Brev. Tract.*, 94—if a monk brings property with him to the monastery, he must pay his own taxes ; *ib.*, 107—provisional permission for a man to become a monk before he has wound up all his secular affairs ; *epp.* 35-37—Basil regards his foster-brother as holding certain property in trust for himself ; *ep.* 284—monks are property-less in the same sense in which they are body-less—i.e. as having given both to God—and so should be exempt from taxation as from military service. See further Leclerq, in *DALC.*, ii, coll. 3151, 3152; Lowther Clarke, *op. cit.*, pp. 82, 83. S. Ambrose, in the same way, expresses doubts on the advisability of immediate surrender of all worldly goods (*de off.*, i, 30 (150)). Immediate alienation of all property on entrance to the monastery seems to have been the invention of Cæsarius of Arles, *Reg.*, c. 1. On the question how far Basil instituted permanent monastic vows, Lowther Clarke, pp. 107-109; Leclerq, col. 3151; E. F. Morison, *St. Basil and His Rule*, pp. 91-95; B. Jackson, *St. Basil (LNP-NF.)*, p. lii, n. 6, with references there.

[2] *Ursprung des Mönchtums*, p. 53.

[3] See J. O. Hannay, *Spirit and Origin of Christian Monasticism*, pp. 195-198 ; Lowther Clarke, pp. 132 ff., 198 f. ; Leclerq, coll. 3156, 3157 ; C. Butler in *C. Med. H.*, i, pp. 529, 530.

[4] *Op. cit.*, c. viii, *pass.* ; cp. Leclerq, col. 3153 ; C. Butler, *loc. cit.* ; E. F. Morison, *St. Basil and His Rule*, pp. 132, 133 ; O. Zöckler, *Askese u. Mönchtum*, pp. 290-296 ; K. Holl, *Enthusiasmus u. Bussgewalt*, pp. 176, 191 ff.

[5] For pre-Benedictine monasticism in the west see generally Leclerq, *DALC.*, ii, coll. 3175-3232 ; E. Spreitzenhofer, *Die Entwicklung des Alten Mönchtums im Italien*, especially pp. 1-35 ; A. Malnory, *Saint Césaire d'Arles*, pp. 244-279 ; T. S. Holmes, *The Christian Church in Gaul*, pp. 274-

Italy was full of monasteries roughly based on eclectic combinations
of the Pachomian rule with other documents. The same system in
a more cultured form found a home at Lerins in S. Honoratus'
great settlement. Cassian [1] probably reproduced the conditions of
Nitria and Skete at Marseilles ; a reformed and disciplined Lerins
grew up at Arles under S. Cæsarius. Northern Gaul, looking to
its heroic saint and missionary Martin, and his foundations of
Ligugé and Marmoutier, teemed with hermits and itinerants of the
Antonian and Syrian kind, whose connexions with the monasteries
were of the sketchiest description.[2] Ireland saw the development
of monasteries which outrivalled Schenoudi's community in bar-
barity, whilst substituting an unquenchable missionary enthusiasm
for his periodic campaign against heresy. Columbanus brought the
Irish system to Luxeuil, whence it spread across northern Europe ;
it is a strange reflection that his ' truly Prussian ' rule,[3] as Leclerq
has called it, with its six strokes of the rod for serving mass un-
shaved, twelve for coughing during divine office, and two hundred
for speaking with a woman,[4] should for decades have proved a
serious obstacle to the spread of the milder Benedictine obedience.[5]

Rufinus in A.D. 397 had brought a free translation of the Basilian
rules to Italy ; [6] it was left to Benedict to make them effective.
In a sense it is true, as Grützmacher suggests, that there is little
of an epoch-making character in the Rule of Benedict,—it is merely
an ' exact codification of developments which monasticism had
already undergone in the west.' [7] He is probably right in insisting
that the ultimate acceptance of the Rule throughout Europe is

300, 488-510 ; W. Bund, *Celtic Church in Wales*, pp. 145-206 ; C. Butler
in *C. Med. H.*, i, pp. 531-535 ; M. Heimbucher, *Die Orden u. Kongregationen*,
i, §§ 12-16 ; O. Zöckler, *Askese u. Mönchtum*, pp. 323-355, 372-381 ; L.
Gougaud, *Les Chrétientés Celtiques*, pp. 60-108, 145-150 ; and other authorities
cited there. For convenience, the following dates are appended :—*Martin*,
c. A.D. 316-396 ; Ligugé founded *c.* A.D. 360. *Honoratus*, d. A.D. 429.
Cassian, *c.* A.D. 360-445. *Cæsarius*, *c.* A.D. 470-542 ; bishop of Arles, A.D.
502. *Benedict*, *c.* A.D. 480-542 ; Monte Cassino founded *c.* A.D. 530. *Cassiodorus*, A.D. 469—*c.* 565 ; Vivarium founded *c.* A.D. 540. *Columbanus*,
A.D. 543-615 ; Luxeuil founded *c.* A.D. 590.

[1] Cassian's rule (as distinct from the *Institutes*) has been recovered by
H. Plenkers, *Untersuchungen zur Ueberlieferungsgeschichte der ältesten lateinis-
chen Mönchsregeln (Quellen u. Untersuchungen zur lat. Philologie des Mittelalters*,
vol. i, 1906), pp. 70-84 ; cp. Leclerq, *DALC.*, ii, col. 3191.

[2] For examples cp. S. Dill, *Roman Society in Gaul in the Merovingian Age*,
pp. 356, 372.

[3] Leclerq, *DALC.*, ii, col. 3217 ; on the problem of the various Irish
rules, *ib.*, col. 3213, with references to authorities. On Columbanus and his
work generally, Zöckler, *op. cit.*, pp. 381-389.

[4] *Reg. Columbani*, 10 (Holsten-Brockie, *Codex*, i, pp. 174 ff.).

[5] And in many monasteries should have syncretized with it ; see Leclerq,
DALC., ii, col. 3213, on the *regula ad virgines*, and cp. G. Grützmacher,
Bedeutung Benedicts von Nursia, p. 62 ; Zöckler, *op. cit.*, pp. 389-390.

[6] See the *Præfatio Rufini in reg. S. Bas.*, in Holsten-Brockie, i, p. 67—
everything is to be done ' secundum instar Cappadociæ.'

[7] G. Grützmacher, *op. cit.*, pp. 51, 71 ; examples in Spreitzenhofer, *op.
cit.*, pp. 42-51 : but contrast Zöckler, *op. cit.*, pp. 359, 360, and C. Butler,
Benedictine Monachism, pp. 163, 164.

in the main due to the accident of the sack of Monte Cassino by the Lombards between A.D. 580 and 590, and the consequent migration of the monks, with their Rule, to Rome, where they attracted the attention of Gregory the Great and subsequent popes.[1] Nevertheless, S. Benedict shifted the emphasis in monastic theory in a manner which was to make a vast difference in practice.

For Antony, Cassian and Basil the purpose of the monastic life had been the vision of God.   The conditions required for the vision were purity of heart, and the way to purity was self-discipline—a discipline varying from the annihilation of the passions in the Antonian system, to the strict obedience or annihilation of the will in Cassian's, and the attainment of respite, whether from external or internal strain, which was S. Basil's ideal.   They did not, indeed, ignore the truth that spiritual attainment issues and must issue in active service of God.   On this account Antony, with the crude realism of his time and race, penetrates further and further into the desert to ' buckle openly with the divils '[2] on their own ground and conquer them there ; whilst such is the spiritual power that radiates from him that his biographer can call him ' the physician of Egypt.'[3]   For this reason also Basil, for all his love of solitude, places his monasteries wherever opportunities offer of service to the world outside, and allows his monks, if need call, to visit relations and friends.[4]   Vision and service—the service both of God and man—go hand in hand.

Yet it is generally admitted that even Basil, its highest representative, could not wean eastern monachism from self-centredness.[5]

[1] Grützmacher, p. 53.   Among the Popes who popularized the Benedictine rule are, of course, S. Gregory the Great (cp. Dial., ii, 36 ; and see F. H. Dudden, Gregory the Great, ii, p. 173) ; Gregory II and III, and Zacharias (Grützmacher, pp. 65-67).   Boniface of Crediton gave great impetus to its use during his missionary journeys (Grützmacher, pp. 67-71 ; Zöckler, ii, pp. 391, 392 ; Heimbucher, i, § 19), and its universalization was the main instrument of Benedict of Aniane's reforms.   Among the seventh and eighth century Councils which order or imply the universal adoption of Benedict's Rule are those of Autun (c. A.D. 670), can. 15 (Mansi, xi, 123 ; Harduin, iii, 1013 ; Labbe, vii, 551) , Liptinæ (A.D. 743), can. 1 ; Soissons (A.D. 744) can. 3 (' regula sancta ' = ' Benedicti ') ; Aix-la-Chapelle (A.D. 789), can. 72 ; and the so-called ' Concilium Germanicum ' of A.D. 742, can. 7. Cp. also Aix-la-Chapelle (A.D. 817), can. 3 (Hefele-Leclerq, iii, pp. 827, 857, 1033, 824 ; iv, p. 26).

[2] Socr., HE., i, 21 (M. Hanmer's translation, 1577).   So also Cass., Coll., xviii, 6.   Compare also S. Martin's struggles with the ' demons,' of whom ' Mercury was specially annoying, whilst Jupiter was simply stupid and obstinate ' (Sulp. Sev., Dial., ii, 13).

[3] Ath., Vit. Ant., 87—the whole chapter is a eulogy of Antony's beneficent activities ; cp. also cc. 44, 55, 67, 84, 93, 94.

[4] Despite the prohibitions of Reg. Fus. Tract., 32, and Reg. Brev. Tract., 188. 311, the monk is allowed to visit friends and relations ' to edify their faith ' (RBT., 189).   Cp. also the modified permissions of RFT., 33 ; RBT., 220.

[5] See authorities cited above, p. 268, n. 4.   Basil's own rationale of asceticism is magnificently expressed in Reg. Fus. Tract., 2. 3.   Starting from Jn. 14²³, ' If ye love Me ye will keep My commandments,' he bases the duty of love wholly on the debt of gratitude we owe to God for mercies

The greater part of the monk's striving is a striving for that self-conquest which makes union with God possible ; the service in which ' union ' should find its expression receives less emphasis. The monk's warfare is more a fighting *to* God than a fighting *for* God ; his interest is not so much in rescuing and conserving a fallen world, as in achieving for himself the fullness of spiritual experience. ' Panhedonism ' is still a danger. There can be little doubt that at this point Benedict showed himself a spiritual genius of the highest order. He keeps the idea of warfare and service in his Rule, underlining it as it had never been underlined before.[1] It is a service of God—the *opus Dei*, or work of worship.[2] In striking contrast, however, to his predecessors, he eliminates practically all reference to the contemplative life or the vision of God.[3] The fact has given his interpreters some anxious moments. Dom Butler, for example, is at pains to explain that, despite this lacuna, Benedict and Benedictinism as a whole are genuinely contemplative.[4] But is there, after all, anything to disturb us ? Contemplation, as a human activity, we found at an earlier stage to consist rather in looking towards God than in enjoying God, and Cassian himself made worship the essential feature of the contemplative life. Prayer cannot but be contemplative, and by his emphasis upon the *opus Dei* Benedict, like the early monastic pioneers, made prayer the central human activity. What is significant is that, at the cost even of surrendering the great phrase ' seeing God,' he eliminated all thought of the monk's own emotions and experiences from his

already received, and not in any way on the expectation of eternal reward. ' Even were Nature to keep silent ' (cp. Plotinus, *Enn.*, v, 1, 2 ; Aug., *Conf.*, ix, 10, 25, and generally on Basil's dependence upon Plotinus, A. Jahn, *Basilius Magnus Plotinizans* (1838)), the facts of redemption cry out for responsive love and service ; and (reg. 3) loyal service or discipleship can only show itself in loving the brethren. Hence, incidentally, the primacy of the cœnobitic life.

[1] E.g. *Reg. Ben.*, Prol.—' militaturus,' ' arma sumere,' ' exsurgamus,' ' succinctis lumbis,' ' bonis actibus currere,' ' præparanda sunt corda et corpora nostra sanctæ præceptorum obedientiæ militanda,' ' currendum et agendum est,' ' constituenda est schola servitii,' (on the military sense of ' schola ' see G. G. Coulton, *Five Centuries of Religion*, i, p. 208), ' inenarrabili dilectionis dulcedine curritur via mandatorum Dei ' ; c. 1—the cœnobite is ' militans sub regulâ vel abbate '; the hermits, ' contra diabolum jam docti pugnare . . . bene instructi fraternâ ex acie ad singularem pugnam eremi . . . pugnare sufficiunt ' ; c. 5—' servitium sanctum quod professi sunt '; c. 7—' non timore gehennæ sed amore Christi '; c. 58—' lex sub quâ militare vis '; c. 61—' in omni loco uni Domino servitur et uni regi militatur '; c. 73— ' ad perfectionem conversationis festinare,' ' ad celsitudinem perfectionis duci,' ' ad majora doctrinæ virtutumque culmina pervenire ' ; and note, c. 4, the 72 ' instrumenta bonorum operum.'—For text and editions of the Rule, see C. Butler, *Benedictine Monachism*, pp. 160-183 ; Id., *Regulæ Ben. editio critico-practica*, pp. ix-xxiv.

[2] *Reg. Ben.*, cc. 19, 22, 43, 44, 47, 50, 52, etc.

[3] The only reference to the vision of God is in the Prologue :—' that we may deserve to see Him who has called us ' ; though notice c. 4 fin., ' the reward which " eye hath not seen," ' etc.   Private prayer is only mentioned three times (cc. 20, 49, 52).

[4] C. Butler, *Benedictine Monachism*, pp. 58-74, 93-110.

idea of prayer.   His Rule offers no possible excuse for panhedonism ;
the prayer he calls for is wholly theocentric.[1]

May it not even have been too theocentric ?   Is there not too
much of God and too little of man in the Rule ?   What of the
service of man ?   Benedict's monasteries are once more isolated.[2]
Apart from the injunction of universal hospitality [3] he neither
institutes nor contemplates those active works of charity which
Basil had made a part of his system.[4]   In this respect it is true to
say that 'his rule was unfitted for a wide arena.' [5]   But the limitation
was a minor one, in which even the Black Monks themselves did
not acquiesce for long.[6]   Though the relationship of prayer and
action in the full Christian life presents problems which we have
yet to consider, we have already seen that the doctrine of the cen-
trality of prayer need not and should not stand in the way of active
benevolence.   That it did not do so in the Benedictine system is
shown by the later history of western monachism.   Cassiodorus,[7]

---

[1] Dr. Coulton has emphasized (*Five Centuries*, i, pp. 458-465) that vulgar
monasticism in the Middle Ages was primarily concerned with the salvation
of the individual's own soul (egocentrism).   No doubt this is true, though
the phenomenon is not distinctive either of mediævalism or of monasticism.
I have already considered its prominence in the tradition of our Lord's
teaching (*supra*, pp. 140 ff.), and must return to it again (*infra*, pp. 442 ff.).
But Benedict's Rule is eminently sane on the point.   The *fear of hell* is
propounded as a motive only four times (Prol. ; c. 4, *instr.* 45 ; c. 5 ;
c. 7 (as the *lowest* Christian motive) ; in c. 7 it is definitely said *not* to be a
motive at all in the highest Christian life).   The *hope of heaven* is spoken
of more often :—Prol. ' in regni tabernaculo habitare,' ' heredes regni caelorum '
(this however is probably spurious—see C. Butler, *Regulæ Benedicti editio
critico-practica*, pp. 6, 128), ' ad vitam pervenire perpetuam,' ' regni esse
consortes ' ; c. 4, *instr.* 46—' vitam æternam desiderare ' ; *ib.*, fin., ' merces
nobis a Domino ' ; c. 5—' propter gloriam æternæ vitæ ' ; c. 7—' ad
exaltationem caelestem pervenire,' ' spes retributionis divinæ ' ; 73—' ad
patriam caelestem festinare,' ' regna patebunt æterna ' (the last perhaps
spurious—see Butler, *ed. crit.-pract.*, p. 124).   These rather conventional
allusions to what is after all a primary doctrine, not merely of Christianity,
but even of natural religion, do not detract from the genuinely disinterested
character of the language summarized, p. 271, n. 1 above.   On Benedict's
' theocentrism ' see also C. Butler, *Benedictine Monachism*, pp. 302, 313, 414.
H. B. Workman, *Evolution of Monastic Ideal*, p. 150, makes the same point
when, in contrasting S. Benedict's ideal with that of his predecessors, he says
that he substituted ' self-surrender ' for ' self-conquest.'

[2] *Reg. Ben.*, c. 66.   [3] *Ib.*, c. 53.

[4] Note, however, the ' good works of the active life ' which ' found a
place in Benedict's own programme,' and to which Gregory's *Dialogues*
witness—C. Butler, *Benedictine Monachism*, p. 95 ; c. 48 of the Rule gives
Benedict's prescriptions for the daily work of the monk, including reading.

[5] W. Gass, *Geschichte der Christl. Ethik*, i, p. 275.

[6] C. Butler, *Benedictine Monachism*, pp. 314-331, gives a sketch of the
stages by which Benedictinism became a missionary and civilizing force.
Cp. also M. Heimbucher, *Orden u. Kongregationen*, i, § 27 ; U. Berlière,
L'Ordre monastique [2], pp. 84-167 ; but the last should be read subject to
the type of reservation inculcated by Dr. Coulton.

[7] Cassiodorus founded his monastery of Vivarium, at the age of seventy,
about the year 540—i.e. shortly after the foundation of Monte Cassino.   It
was ' the first monastery expressly designed to make its inhabitants not
merely holy but happy ' (F. H. Dudden, *Gregory the Great*, ii, p. 170) ; a
good appreciation in W. Gass, *Christl. Ethik*, i, p. 147.   Cassiodorus himself
gives a description of his monastery and its ideals in his *Institutio divinarum
lectionum*, c. 29.   cc. 1-24 deal with reading Scripture ; c. 25 with the value

equipping his monastery library with Hippocrates and Galen, that his monks might become efficient doctors, and with Columella, that they might direct the petty cultivators of the neighbouring country-side, made the first step forward ; whilst later developments of western asceticism—particularly the mendicant orders—drove the ascetic out into the fullest relations with the world.[1]

Developments such as these were not merely not inhibited by the spirit of S. Benedict's rule ; they were actually made possible by its letter. That nothing might distract his monks' attention from the *opus Dei*, he reduced physical austerity to its lowest terms, and also insisted upon this minimum being treated as a maximum as far as the outward life was concerned. ' Nihil asperum, nihil grave,' is his guiding principle.[2] He was influenced, no doubt,—as Cassian,[3] Cæsarius,[4] and Sulpicius Severus[5] had been before him—

of geography ; cc. 27 and 28 commend secular learning in all its branches, especially the science of agriculture : c. 30 speaks of orthography, and describes the self-filling lamps and clocks with which the monastery is equipped ; c. 31 insists upon the importance of medical study ; c. 32 a fine exhortation to the abbot and brethren ; c. 26 is a note on manuscript ab-breviations, and c. 33 a concluding prayer.

[1] C. Pfister, *C. Med. H.*, ii, pp. 147, 148, puts this development down to the initiative of Columbanus and his disciples ; by its victory over the Irish Rule, Benedictinism inherited the missionary spirit. By the end of the tenth century, however, the centre and west of Europe were at least super-ficially evangelized, and monasticism had solved one of its most stimulating problems. The consequent decline in enthusiasm for service, together with the disorganization produced by the raids of Northmen, Huns and Saracens (cp. U. Berlière, *L'Ordre Monastique* [2] (1921), pp. 76, 77), produced on the one hand such reforming movements, in the directions of greater austerity or of greater discipline, as those of Cluny and Cîteaux (following upon the earlier example of Benedict of Aniane) ; on the other, reversions to a more eremitic type of the contemplative life (Camaldoli, Vallombrosa, Grandmont, the Grande Chartreuse—all eleventh century). The institutions of secular canons, inaugurated by Chrodegang of Metz in the eighth century, and of regular canons (Augustinian and Premonstratensian, eleventh and twelfth centuries), were experiments in a new direction towards the ideal of com-bining the ascetic principle with a life of service ; Norbert, the founder of Prémontré, became an actual forerunner of S. Francis when he established his ' Third Order ' for persons of secular estate in A.D. 1122 (E. Scott Davison, *Forerunners of S. Francis*, p. 99; Heimbucher, § 60, 3 g.). S. Gregory's ideal of the ' mixed life ' of action and contemplation seems never, there-fore, to have died out in the centuries which divide him from S. Francis and S. Dominic. The entire development is reviewed by W. Hamilton Thompson, *C. Med. Hist.*, v, pp. 658-696 ; cp. H. B. Workman, *Evolution of the Monastic Ideal*, pp. 219-268 ; O. Zöckler, *op. cit.*, pp. 393-433 ; U. Berlière, *L'Ordre Monastique* [2], pp. 168-197, 224-276 ; M. Heimbucher, *op. cit.*, i, §§ 20-22, 29-36, 54-60 ; E. Sackur, *Die Cluniacenser*, especially i, pp. 1-35 ; ii, pp. 437-465 ; *ERE.*, viii, pp. 792-796 (*s.v.* 'Monasticism ') ; *PRE.*, xiii, pp. 214 ff. (*s.v.* ' Mönchtum ').   [2] *Reg. Ben.*, Prol.

[3] Cass., *Inst.*, *Præf.* (fin.).—What is ' impossible, hard or difficult ' in the Egyptian rules, ' by reason of severity of climate, some other difficulty, or diversity of customs,' must be modified for the west.

[4] A. Malnory, *S. Césaire d'Arles*, p. 266—(Cæsarius' rules for a nunnery diet)—' il n'entendait pas traiter l'estomac de ses filles comme il avait autrefois traité le sien.'

[5] Sulp. Sev., *Dial.*, i, 9—' the love of eating is gluttony among the Greeks, whilst to the Gauls it is natural ' ; and cp. the pleasantries on the same subject, *ib.*, i, 4, 13, 20 ii, 8.

by the fact that western conditions of life cannot support the rigours
of asceticism which are possible in the east; but that was not all.
Dom Butler has insisted that the life of a Benedictine monastery in
the earliest days did not differ to any appreciable extent from that
of the world outside as far as food, clothing and sleep were concerned;[1] and the later reforms or reactions against Benedictinism
show clearly that a more rigorous régime than this would have been
possible had the founder wished it. But he did not wish it, and the
conclusion seems inevitable that his reluctance was due to the intimate connexion which he descried between an asceticism in which
discipline has wholly taken the place of self-annihilation, and a life
of active service. In whatever forms the idea of service be articulated—whether in praise or prayer or preaching or devotion to the
temporal needs of others—it cannot be achieved by a soul whose
immediate attention is absorbed by the warfare against itself. Its
aim is positive and not negative, constructive rather than destructive, self-forgetful rather than self-centred; and to such an aim the
soul which is absorbed in self-culture can never hope to attain.

S. Benedict was working within the limits of a closed system.
He was legislating for men and women to whom poverty, celibacy
and obedience were the unquestioned presuppositions of their lives.
So much asceticism he was bound to have. Discipline he was bound
to have as well; but one of the first aims of his discipline was to
prevent the ascetic minimum—as it must have appeared in his
time—from burdening itself with accretions which would impede
and not assist the life of service. In so doing he adumbrated, if
he did not actually reach, a condition of things in which the distinction between the monk and the world had been reduced to the
smallest possible dimensions compatible with its existence at all.
Within the limits prescribed by the theory of the double standard
he succeeded in all but abolishing the double standard itself. He
put forward his system as a 'very little rule for beginners,'[2] but
behind that modest phrase is the spirit of our Lord's own words:

---

[1] C. Butler, *Benedictine Monachism*, pp. 24-26, 40-45, 148-152, 284—with
the notes in the second edition on pp. 393-396, 413-414.

[2] Prol.—' minima inchoationis regula.' With what has been said above
as to S. Benedict's principles may be compared Reuter's estimate (*August.
Studien*, p. 477) of Augustine's *de opere monachorum*, a work with which
Benedict was acquainted and from which he quotes (Butler, *Reg. Ben. editio
critico-practica*, pp. 11, 83—especially the latter) :—' This is perhaps the
most significant document in the history of sociology ("Wirtschaftslehre ")
since the end of the fourth century. Had its doctrines been put into practice
they would have put an end to the distinction between the secular and the
religious lives, and have wrought a reform, if not a revolution, in the Roman
Empire.' From the fuller estimate of the treatise, *ib.*, pp. 444, 445, it may
be gathered that Reuter sees its significance under two aspects—(1) it
attempts to assimilate the life of the cloister to that of the world ; and (2)
it suggests (though speaking explicitly of monastic labour only) that *all*
work should have as its object the service of humanity, and not personal
gain. Similarly, of the effect of the Benedictine Rule, H. B. Workman,
Monastic Ideal, pp. 157-159.

' Take My yoke upon you ; for My yoke is easy, and My burden is light.'

IV. The Reform of Penance.

(a) Public Discipline.

Little, however, was to be gained by assimilating the condition and activities of the monks to those of the laity, so long as the latter were bound down by an iron and tyrannical discipline. The problem of rigorism was not solved, but only pushed back a stage further. The monastic vanguard could no longer advance too far ahead of the army ; but the army itself was crippled and disorganized by excess of discipline. The Church had to address itself to the question of penance—an institution whose yoke was as yet by no means easy.

By the fifth century the position in the west is as follows. There are no longer any sins irremissible by the Church on earth, but the number of sins for which reconciliation will only be given *in articulo mortis* is considerable. Penance for grave sin after baptism, but one penance only, is still the invariable rule.[1] So severe has the penitential discipline become, both in character and duration, that (with only the rarest possible exceptions)[2] no one can be found to undergo it voluntarily—except indeed at the moment of death,[3] when neither severity nor publicity nor duration can be enforced. It is not the case that public ecclesiastical discipline died out ;[4] but where it survived it became progressively identified with and assimilated to the discipline of the civil power. During the dark ages, the ecclesiastical judge found himself more and more engaged in secular criminal jurisdiction, to which he could contribute additional terrors by the threat of spiritual sanctions.[5] At the same

---

[1] *Infra*, p. 506, additional note I.

[2] The case of Theodosius is of course the classical one—Ambrose, *ep.* 51 ; *de ob. Theodos.*, 54 ; Theodoret, *HE.*, v, 18. Poschmann, pp. 67, 116, rightly notices that the very rarity of such voluntary penance made those who undertook it heroes in the estimation of the ordinary believer.

[3] *Infra*, p. 511, additional note I.

[4] Evidence for the survival of public penance, O. D. Watkins, *op. cit.*, pp. 567, 568 (*Conc. Tolet.*, A.D. 589), 572 (Isidore of Seville, *c.* A.D. 600), 576 (Éloi of Noyon, *c.* A.D. 650) ; for its attempted revival by the reform councils of Charlemagne, *ib.*, pp. 702, 704, 706 ; and by Louis the Debonnair, H. C. Lea, *Auricular Confession and Indulgences*, ii, pp. 74-78 ; *DCA.*, ii, p. 1598 ; in the eleventh century, Lea, *op. cit.*, i, p. 196 ; ii, p. 112. From this period formal discipline fell into two parts—*solemn* penance which could not be repeated (cp. Aquinas, *ST.*, iii, *suppl.*, q. 28, a. 2) ; Lea, ii, pp. 79-81, and *public* penance, which might be, Lea, ii, pp. 82-89. Cp. also Loofs, *Leitfaden*, pp. 475-478. On monastic discipline, especially by corporal punishment, cp. L. Gougaud, *Devotional and Ascetic Practices of the Middle Ages* (E. tr.), pp. 179-183, 198, 199.

[5] See e.g. Lea, *op. cit.*, ii, pp. 108-112 ; W. S. Holdsworth, *History of English Law*³, ii, pp. 22-25 ; F. Pollock and F. W. Maitland, *History of English Law*², i, pp. 18, 40, 75 ; ii, pp. 452, 544 ; W. Makower, *Constitutional History of the Church of England* (E. tr.), pp. 384-388 ; T. P. Oakley, *English Penitential Discipline and Anglo-Saxon Law* (New York, 1923), pp. 78, 137-140 ; G. Grupp, *Kulturgeschichte des Mittelalters*², i, pp. 246 ff.

time the civil arm assisted the spiritual by compelling notorious offenders to public penance.[1] In England, for example, William the Conqueror put an end to what must have been a long-standing practice when he ordained that 'no bishop or archdeacon should introduce any case touching episcopal laws into the hundred-moot; nor bring before a civil tribunal matters concerned with the discipline of souls.'[2] The statement in Theodore's 'Penitential' that 'public reconciliation has never been instituted in this province, because public penance is non-existent,'[3] can only be true in so far as public ecclesiastical jurisdiction was wholly merged in secular procedure.

That the ecclesiastical courts of the middle ages were able to regain so large a measure of independent and yet effective public discipline over the laity is partly due to causes which belong to the general history of the Church. But it would have been impossible without a considerable reformation of the discipline of open penance, which remained the condition of reconciliation. As compared with the system of the fifth century, the burden laid upon the offender had to be lightened, and his hope of mercy increased. The outcome of the earlier discipline is obvious. Where the general tone of the Christian community was lax, little if any attempt was made to deal with notorious offenders in its ranks; [4] where its tone was rigorist, they were expelled without mercy. In either case the loss both to the Church and to the individual must have been disastrous. Tolerance of grave scandal produces widespread deterioration in the Church; final exclusion of offenders [5] removes from her pastoral care those who need it most, and who might become first penitents and ultimately saints. For a time at least, Christian discipline took a road on which all its purposes were defeated; for the sake of a traditional formula it abandoned its true function of helping both the society and its members towards that vision of God which is their goal. Terrorism, rather than edification, became its leading characteristic.

---

[1] Lea, *op. cit.*, ii, p. 110; Makower, pp. 392, 465—the Conqueror's ordinance that if an offender refused the Bishop's summons to appear before an ecclesiastical court, 'fortitudo et justitia regis vel vicecomitis adhibeatur'; Oakley, pp. 141-149, on secular ordinances enacting ecclesiastical penalties.

[2] Text, Makower, *op. cit.*, p. 465.

[3] Theod., *Pen.*, i, 13. 4; A. W. Haddan and W. Stubbs, *Councils and Ecclesiastical Documents*, iii, p. 187. The problem of the accuracy of Theodore's statement is discussed by Oakley, *op. cit.*, pp. 67, 75-78, with references; the probability of the introduction of public penance by Theodore and Egbert, *loc. cit.*, and p. 81; excommunication in pre-Norman England, *ib.*, p. 86.

[4] So Aug., *c. ep. Parm.*, iii, 2 (13, 14, 16) on the impossibility of dealing with offenders who had a strong party in their favour in the Church (other passages to the same effect, Bingham, *Antiquities*, xvi, iii, 6); Cæsarius, [Aug.], *app. serm.*, 288 (5), 289 (5), 309 (4); Pomerius, *de vit. cont.*, ii, 5 (1, 2) (*MPL.*, lix, col. 449).

[5] In view of the rigours of public penance, excommunication in the fifth and following centuries, though it did not in theory mean 'final exclusion,' had this effect in practice: offenders refused to submit themselves to the discipline which was a condition of sharing the pastoral care of the Church.

An early experiment in mitigation, particularly popular in Asia Minor, was that of the 'stations' ('bathmoi'),[1] or grades of penitents. As his discipline proceeded, the offender found himself gradually coming nearer to full communion with the Church once more. He had been a 'weeper' (' prosklaiôn ')—a mere candidate for admission to penance—standing in the narthex of the Church, and asking the faithful for their prayers. On admission to official status he became a 'hearer' ('akroômenos '), and took his place among the catechumens. Later he was promoted to the rank of a 'kneeler' ('hypopiptôn '), and was dismissed, after prayer for his progress towards restitution, before the 'missa fidelium.' Finally he ranked as a 'stander' ('synestôs '), remaining throughout the liturgy, but neither offering nor communicating. The system is first heard of (but as an already well-known practice) in the canonical epistle of Gregory Thaumaturgus, about the middle of the third century; it was based, perhaps, on an earlier division of catechumens into two classes.[2] It disappeared before the end of the sixth century;[3] and its loss is scarcely to be deplored. It must have served as much to discourage penitents as to cheer them.

To this cause, no doubt, must be referred the fact that, although recommended for universal use by the Council of Nicæa (can. 11), the system of 'stations' never spread far beyond Asia Minor. Syria knew nothing of it, if the 'Didascalia' may be trusted as evidence. There the penitent was treated throughout in the same fashion as the devout heathen, and admitted to the 'missa fidelium' but dismissed after the sermon.[4] In the west he was allowed to be present throughout the Mass, though not of course to communicate or to offer.[5] In general, the Church had to discover less complicated means of mitigating the rigours of primitive penance.

---

[1] On this F. E. Brightman, in Swete, *Church and Ministry*, pp. 367-368 ; W. Bright, *Canons of the First Four General Councils*, pp. 43-50.

[2] Greg. Thaum., *Ep. Can.*, especially c. xi (*MPG.*, x, col. 1048). This canon may be later than the others, but the terms which it explains, and which refer to the grades of penance, are found in cc. vii, viii, ix. On the controversy as to alleged classes among the catechumens, O. D. Watkins, *op. cit.*, p. 242, with footnote. On the possible employment of the 'stations' occasionally in the West, *infra*, n. 5.

[3] So J. Morinus, *de pœn.*, vi, 22 (6-10) ; but contrast E. Martène, *de rit. ant.*, i, 6, 4 (1-5).

[4] Brightman, in Swete, *op. cit.*, p. 367 ; Watkins, *op. cit.*, pp. 254, 255.

[5] Brightman, in Swete, *Church and Ministry*, p. 367, cp. Felix iii, *ep.* 7 (*MPL.*, lviii, col. 926), where the principle is stated in reference to flagitious clergy—thus suggesting an exception to the general rule that clerics are not submitted to public penance. (Poschmann's attempt to make the passage conform to the usual custom is not convincing.) This letter of Felix, however, appears to recognize the stations even in the West :—' tribus annis inter *audientes* sint, septem autem annis *subjaceant* inter pœnitentes manibus sacerdotum, duobus autem annis . . . tantummodo in oratione socientur,' etc. Similarly *Conc.* 2. *Arel.* (A.D. 443 or 452), cann. 10, 11 ; *Conc. Lerid.* (A.D. 524), can. 9, and unless we make the improbable assumption that this is merely a 'mechanical taking-over' (H. Koch, quoted Poschmann, p. 32) of the Eastern system, we must infer at all events occasional attempts to introduce the 'stations' in a very simple form in the West.

The variety of the experiments set on foot proves how alert the Christian conscience was to the problem. Sometimes public penance is expressly forbidden in the case of occult sin (even of the gravest character, as adultery or murder), where publication of guilt would involve danger to the offender's life or liberty.[1] The demand for public penance in respect of purely secret sin was steadily allowed to lapse.[2] Sometimes whole classes of penitents— the young, the married, and so forth—are definitely exempted from the discipline;[3] that is to say, are allowed, or even advised,[4] to postpone the undertaking of penance until death approaches, remaining in communion in the meanwhile without disabilities. Indeed, reconciliation, or at all events communion, was extended in his last sickness to every sinner who by the stretch of humane imagination could be regarded as repentant, however dark his past may have been.[5] Somewhere in the sixth century even the caveat against the ordination of penitents became obsolete.[6]

Further mitigations were introduced into the régime for those cases in which postponement till the sinner's last hours could not be allowed. The laudable but severe custom of associating the laity with the bishop in the decision to grant reconciliation was quietly allowed to lapse,[7] with a consequent lessening both of the solemnity and of the rigidity of the occasion. Retirement to a monastery was treated by Gallic canonists as a satisfactory, though less humiliating, substitute for open penance.[8] At Rome, penance was normally made coincident with the period of the Lenten fast; sinners were formally admitted *en masse* to the status of penitents on Ash Wednesday, and formally reconciled on Maundy Thursday.[9] At the beginning and end of his probation, therefore, the penitent's shame was cloaked by numbers; during its course he was scarcely to be distinguished from a devout Christian preparing for his

---

[1] *Infra*, additional note I, p. 505.

[2] Watkins, p. 696 (similarly F. Loofs, *Leitfaden*, p. 477) regards Theodulph of Orleans (*c.* A.D. 800) as perhaps the last writer to require public penance for all capital sins, whether public or private.

[3] *Infra*, additional note I, p. 506.

[4] So Ambrose, *de pœn.*, ii, 11 (99-107) ; Cæsarius, [Aug.], *app. serm.*, 249. 6 (in the case of young married people).

[5] So first the Nicene canon (c. 13), on which see W. Bright, *Canons of First Four Councils*, pp. 50-55 (earlier exceptional cases, p. 53) ; cp. Innocent I (*c.* A.D. 410), *ep.* 6. 2 (*MPL.*, xx, col. 498) ; and other authorities cited, *infra*, p. 512.

[6] The relevant canons, Tixeront, *Histoire des Dogmes*, iii, p. 110.

[7] For the requirement, especially in Cyprian, Brightman in Swete, *op. cit.*, pp. 372, 373.

[8] *Conversio* ; *infra*, p. 509.

[9] For the reconciliation on Maundy Thursday, Innocent I, *ep.* 25. 7 ad Decentium. The earliest evidence for Ash Wednesday as the date on which penance began is the Gelasian Sacramentary (seventh or eighth century—see H. A. Wilson, *The Gelasian Sacramentary*, p. 15 (i, 16)) ; but as Poschmann (p. 34) and others notice, the tone of Leo's Lenten sermons suggests that the practice was known much earlier. The reconciliation seems, at times at least, to have been given *en masse*, H. C. Lea, *op. cit.*, i, pp. 358, 359 ; cp. *ib.*, p. 186, n. 2, of the wicked Bishop Adalbert in the ninth century.

Easter communion. It is even possible that, in some parts of the Christian world where long penances were still the rule, the offender was sometimes readmitted to communion before he had earned official reconciliation by the completion of his appointed discipline.[1]

(b) Private Discipline.

Methods such as these enabled Christendom during the middle ages to regain the exercise of public discipline without too palpable a reliance on secular compulsion ; and to retain it to a considerable extent, for several centuries, in the churches of the Reformation and the counter-Reformation alike.[2] But the problem of corporate discipline was not thereby solved. The discipline of the community over its members, as we have seen,[3] has a double aspect—the pastoral as well as the penal. It should be exercised by the Church not merely for the sake of her own purity and witness, but also *pro salute animæ* in respect of the erring brother. And although the latter purpose was ostensibly within the purview of the public discipline, it could not be effectively realized so long as no real hope of considerate, patient and open-hearted treatment was held out to the offender to induce him to come forward for his own soul's good. For the ordinary direction of the spiritual life of the Christian multitudes, for correction of trifling faults, for co-operation in the personal self-discipline of the individual, further modifications were necessary if the pastoral responsibility of the Church was to be successfully discharged. ' For us moderns,' says M. Batiffol,[4]

' (and we have been " moderns " in this matter since the seventh century) the Church has suppressed the publicity of penance— has suppressed its corporate and disciplinary side, by distinguishing the internal from the external forum. The Church has endowed the institution with personal, moral and intimate characteristics,[5] and penance, though still in essence a second

---

[1] So for example Theodore. *Penitential*, i, 12, § 4 (Haddan and Stubbs, *Councils and Ecclesiastical Documents*, iii, pp. 186, 187) , and elsewhere in the eighth century (F. W. H. Wasserschleben, *Die Bussordnungen der abendländischen Kirche* (1851), pp. 33, 34 ; Lea, *op. cit.*, i, pp. 508-510). There is no doubt that penitents were required to submit to an *impositio manuum* at frequent intervals during their period of penance ; Felix iii, *ep.* 7 (*supra*, p. 277, n. 5) ; Aug., *serm.*, 232, 7 (8) ; *Statt. eccl. antiq.* (probably from Arles, in the fifth century—Hefele-Leclerq, ii, pp. 103-107), can. 80 ; *Conc.* 3 *Tolet.* (A.D. 589), can. 11. But it is doubtful whether this was so much a mitigation of the penalty as an exacerbation of its disgrace ; Augustine at all events suggests the latter (*serm.*, 392, 3 (3)).

[2] Post-Reformation public discipline—in the Roman Church, Lea, *op. cit.*, ii, pp. 89-91 ; the Reformed Churches, *ib.*, p. 91 ; *ERE.*, iv, pp. 718-720 ; and *infra*, pp. 421 ff.

[3] *Supra*, p. 147.

[4] P. Batiffol, *Études d'Histoire*[5], etc., i, p. 213.

[5] ' L'Église a abondé dans le sens individuel, moral, intime.'

baptism, has become in addition a means of progress to perfection for the baptized.   The Church has adapted the primitive
system of penance to new needs and new ideas.'

It was almost by a series of accidents that such a solution to the
problem was found.   Two barriers stood in the way of employing
penance in a ' personal, moral and intimate ' fashion to help forward the self-consecration of the individual.   One was the caveat
against second reconciliations ; the other the publicity and shame
attaching to the formal readmission to communion.   So long as
these survived no mitigations of the system—no degree of privacy
even in the penitential exercises—could modify the primarily penal
character of the rite.   The two barriers both derived their strength
from a single fact—that reconciliation was normally the prerogative
of the bishop.[1]   As soon as it passed from his hands into the ordinary
jurisdiction of the priest, repetition of penance—often secured, no
doubt, by application to different priests at different times—became easy, and privacy easier still.   Consequently the two relaxations went hand in hand in Christian history, as the priesthood
progressively dispossessed the episcopate of one of its most jealously
guarded prerogatives.[2]

Records are too scanty to admit more than the mention of
isolated facts and possibilities.   When S. John Chrysostom said,
as he was accused of doing,[3] that' though a man should sin a thousand times he might repent a thousand times and receive forgiveness,' any reference to the pardon of venial sin by God is out of the
question—it could not have been made the basis of a serious accusation.   Nor can we suppose that he contemplated the complete
abolition of corporate discipline altogether.   The only possible
interpretation is that he was urging the Church to be prepared to
iterate reconciliation for grave sin.   A more pedantic and refined
casuistry sometimes allowed death-bed communion, though not
reconciliation, to the relapsed sinner.[4]   During the fifth and sixth

---

[1] Poschmann, pp. 48, 49; Brightman, in Swete, *op. cit.*, pp. 397-398, for
the earlier references.   In Africa, and probably Rome as well, the presbyters
were associated with the bishop in the laying-on of hands (Brightman, *ib.*,
pp. 373, 398).   The definitive ruling was that of Pope Damasus (*infra*, p. 281,
n. 1).

[2] Cp. on this H. C. Lea, *Auricular Confession and Indulgences*, i, p. 56.

[3] Socrates, *HE.*, vi, 21.   Socrates says that the statement occurred in
Chrysostom's sermons, although a ' council of bishops ' had insisted upon
the rule of one penance only ; and that he was attacked on the point (naturally enough) by Sisinnius, the Novatianist bishop of Constantinople.   The
seventh accusation brought against Chrysostom by Bishop Isaac at the
Synod of the Oak (A.D. 403—Hefele-Leclerq, ii, p. 148) was that he said,
' If thou sin again, repent again ; and as often as thou sinnest come to me
and I will heal thee.'   For discussions see Batiffol, *Études, etc.*, i, p. 190;
Tixeront, *Hist. Dogm.*, ii, pp. 188-190.   Batiffol assumes that Chrysostom
is supporting repeated absolutions on Maundy Thursday, Tixeront that it is
a question of private absolutions.   The ' council of bishops ' was presumably
urging what to them seemed the liberal (and traditional) view against the
Novatianists.

[4] *Infra*, additional note I, p 512.

centuries the rule of one penance only gradually disappeared ; it is probably safe to associate this development with a growing ascendency of the priesthood in the ministry of absolution.[1] An ambiguous phrase of Cæsarius of Arles may perhaps imply that he was prepared to admit two reconciliations after baptism.[2] At all events the last council to attempt to insist upon the rule is that of Toledo (the third) in A.D. 589. From that date it must be supposed to have fallen into obsolescence—there is now always hope for the penitent sinner, however grave or frequent his sin.

The evidence for the exercise of a ministry of reconcilation by the priesthood is fuller. From an early date, sinners were urged to consult a discreet priest about their sins,[3] in case they had made themselves liable to open penance. This fact in itself must have suggested to parish clergy that they had a definite status in the administration of penance, though their actual duty in the matter was merely to send the questioner away reassured if his sin were venial, or to report it to the bishop for formal treatment if it were mortal. But the priest had also the right to absolve on delegated authority from his bishop, if the latter could not discharge the function himself ; and it was his *duty* to absolve in cases of urgency —as for example cases of sudden sickness—when no bishop could be reached in time.[4] Such reconciliations were often enough of

[1] Apart from their *legitimate* exercise of this jurisdiction, by delegation or in emergencies (*infra*, nn. 3 and 4), there is evidence of attempts by the priesthood to usurp the office. Thus Damasus (A.D. 366-384), *ep.* 5, forbids the exercise of absolution both to *chorepiscopoi* and to priests ; cp. *Conc. Agath.* (A.D. 506), can. 44—Damasus' rulings were adopted by *Conc. Cartag.* (A.D. 390), can. 3, and *Conc. Hippon.* (A.D. 393), can. 34, which implies that the African Church was troubled by the matter. Poschmann thinks (p. 216) that Pope Innocent's decree directing the *public* reconciliation of penitents on Maundy Thursday (*supra*, p. 278, n. 9) was intended to suppress a similar usurpation in his own day. Can. 11 of *Conc. 3 Tolet.* (A.D. 589, *infra*, p. 507) attacks the custom of repeated reconciliation of the same offender *by priests*, and goes on to denounce the whole idea of second penance. This clearly shows the relationship between the two movements, but Poschmann is probably right (p. 161) in inferring from canon 12 that ' the delegated jurisdiction of the priesthood (in penance) went without saying by this time in Spain.' We cannot therefore speak of ' usurpation ' here ; ' peaceful penetration ' would be a better phrase.

[2] *Infra*, additional note I, p. 507.

[3] Origen, *in Ps.* 37 *hom.*, 2, 6 (*infra*, p. 510). Holl, *Enthusiasmus u. Bussgewalt*, pp. 236 ff., considers that the reference here is not necessarily to a priest, but to any person of spiritual insight. Similarly Augustine, *de div. quæst.*, lxxxiii, 26, mentions sinners who are ' not to be compelled ' to public penance ' although they confess sins.' The ' non sunt cogendi ' is of the nature of a canonical instruction to some one who hears the confession ; and, therefore, although Augustine calls these sins ' venialia,' the passage must refer to a confession, by way of consultation, to a bishop or priest. Large parts of Gregory's *regula pastoralis* are devoted to the sympathy and understanding which the priest should show in these consultations.

[4] The evidence for this is overwhelming and undisputed—see e.g. Watkins, *op. cit.*, pp. 146, 147, 195, 416, 486, 487, etc. ; Poschmann, pp. 49, 50, 94, n. 4, 161 ; *DCA.*, ii, p. 1763 ; Brightman, in Swete, *op. cit.*, p. 398. But it was very uncertain how far the priest, as distinct from the bishop, had the power of the keys. In the consecration prayer for a bishop in the Church

a private character, though we know that 'bystanders' were some-times present at the bedside.[1]

Other anticipations of the later practice are not altogether lacking. In Constantinople, prior to S. Chrysostom's translation to the see, there had been a penitentiary priest whose business, according to one interpretation of Sozomen,[2] was to 'appoint a penance, and then to absolve the penitent, leaving him to work out his own satisfaction by himself.' The office of penitentiary priest may indeed have been widespread at this time.[3] It probably dated from the Decian persecution, when penitential business was at its height, but nowhere else is there evidence that the whole transaction —including absolution—was purely private. At best, it involved privacy in the initial formalities and penitential exercises. The institution nowhere survived for long, except possibly at Rome.[4] Even at Constantinople it was abolished by Nectarius (A.D. 381-398), Chrysostom's predecessor, as the result of a scandal, the accounts of which are obscure, but which certainly seem to imply that absolution

Orders (e.g. A. J. Maclean, *Ancient Church Orders*, p. 76) there is a petition that he may have 'power to forgive sins.' The earliest Orders imply that the same prayer is used for presbyters (Maclean, p. 69 ; W. H. Frere, in Swete, *Church and Ministry*, pp. 274-276, but contrast *ib.*, p. 284) ; later Orders, however, have a separate prayer for presbyters, and these omit the petition for power to forgive sins (e.g. *Ap. Const.*, viii, 16). According to Martène, *de ant. rit. eccl.*, I, viii, 9, 12, the modern formula ('whose sins thou dost forgive,' etc.) was not used for presbyters till the tenth century at the earliest. Cp. H. C. Lea, *op. cit.*, i, pp. 122-124, and *ib.*, 127-129, on the for-geries of Benedict Levita (ninth century).

[1] E.g. *Statt. Eccl. Ant.*, can. 76.

[2] Sozomen, *Hist. Eccl.*, vii, 16 :—the word translated 'absolve' is ἀπέλυε. Holl (*Enthusiasmus u. Bussgewalt*, p. 251) and Vacandard (quoted Poschmann, p. 55) support this rendering ; Batiffol (*op. cit.*, p. 159) contests it, and assumes that all the priest did was to 'send the penitent away' reassured (if the sin was merely venial), or with the obligation of under-taking public penance, if it was capital. In the absence of other evidence of private absolution by priests in the third and fourth centuries, Batiffol's conclusion is the more natural ; but cp. on the whole incident, *infra*, p. 509, n. I (*h*).

[3] The facts are :—(*a*) Socrates, *HE.*, v. 19, says that penitential priests were instituted, at the time of the Novatianist schism, and that sinners ἐπὶ τούτου τοῦ πρεσβυτέρου ἐξομολογοῦνται (? 'confess *to* him' or 'perform penitential exercises *under* his supervision '—Batiffol (p. 153) without sufficient reason assumes the latter): (*b*) Sozomen (*loc. cit.*) gives as the reason for the institu-tion that sinners could not face the publicity of the ordinary régime. After mentioning that the Novatianists have nothing of the kind, he adds that 'in the West, and especially in Rome, it is carefully retained.' With Batiffol (p. 158) and against Poschmann (pp. 55, 56) I am inclined to think that this indefinite 'it' (φυλάττεται) refers to the office of penitentiary ; but how far Sozomen was right in this respect is another question ; (*c*) Batiffol (pp. 146-149) infers from the notices of Marcellus (A.D. 304-309) and Simplicius (A.D. 468-483) in the *liber pontificalis*, that these popes instituted the same offices, the one in the city, the other in three suburban churches of Rome. Poschmann however (pp. 51-54) is probably right in insisting that nothing more was intended than to have certain clergy detailed at official centres for *emergency* cases of penance. Vacandard (cited Poschmann, p. 54) is also opposed to Batiffol, but his theory does not appear satisfactory.

[4] See previous note, under (*b*).

was being obtained from the penitentiary in cases which would
better have been dealt with by public procedure.[1]

Even S. John Chrysostom's position is obscure, despite the
temerity of the language attributed to him. That he was a protagonist in the movement for relaxing the rule of one reconciliation
only in public discipline has already been suggested. But from
phrases in his homilies it would appear that his main anxiety was
to discourage the demand that secret sin (whether grave or otherwise) should be submitted to this 'intolerable publicity' (as he
calls it),[2] and to substitute instead the private offices of the priest.
This seems a deliberate invasion of the rights of the bishop; but
no other solution fits the fact that it is in the 'de Sacerdotio'—a
treatise as much concerned with the lower dignity as with the higher
—that his most emphatic assertions of the power of the keys occur.[3]

But however much we admit the occasional possibility of private
absolutions in the early centuries,[4] it is clear that—apart from one
special factor—the practice would have had to face a stern fight
before it could secure a permanent foothold. As late as the ninth
century, councils and bishops in Italy are found insisting that
recourse may only be had to a priest for reconciliation in cases of
urgency.[5] The special factor which intervened to popularize the
new custom was monasticism, with the respect which monastic
institutions commanded in the dark ages. One of the features of
organized monasticism from the first had been the regular private
confession of sins (even of thought) either to a spiritual superior or,
following S. James' exhortation, to one of the brethren.[6] Often
enough nothing whatever is said about absolution. Frequently it

---

[1] For the details of this affair, and the probable motives of Nectarius'
action, *infra*, additional note I, p. 509.

[2] *de incompr. Dei nat.*, v. 7 (*MPG.*, xlviii, col. 746) ; and Soz., *HE.*, vii,
16.

[3] E.g. *de sac.*, ii, 3 (*MPG.*, xlviii, col. 634) ; iii, 5 (*ib.*, col. 643), Mt. 18^{18}
and Jn. 20^{22} applied to the priesthood ; iii, 6, Christian priests cure leprosy
of the soul. Watkins, *op. cit.*, pp. 300-313, has collected numerous passages
which taken alone would imply that Chrysostom thought confession solely to
God to be sufficient in all cases (cp. also K. Holl, *Enthusiasmus u. Bussgewalt*,
p. 272). But it is not clear to what type of sin Chrysostom is alluding in
these passages, and more than once he asserts that for true confession it is
necessary to 'come into church' (*de pœn.*, ii, 1 ; iii, 1—*MPG.*, xlix, coll.
285, 292, etc.), which seems to imply a genuine formality. According to
Socrates (*HE.*, vi, 3), Chrysostom was still a deacon when he wrote the *de
sacerdotio* ; J. A. Nairn, in his edition of the treatise (Camb., 1906), pp. xi-
xiv, gives reasons for thinking that it may have been shortly after his ordination to the priesthood.

[4] See *infra*, p. 534, additional note O.

[5] Council of Pavia (A.D. 850), c. 7 (full text, Watkins, *op. cit.*, p. 686) ;
Atto Vercell. (*c.* A.D. 950), *Capitular.*, 90 ; *MPL.*, cxxxiv, col. 45 (*ib.*). On
Rome, *ib.*, pp. 720-722. Later cases, Lea, *op. cit.*, i, pp. 124, 125.

[6] See e.g. Cass., *Inst.*, iv, 10 ; *Coll.*, ii, 10 ; Basil, *Reg. Fus. Tract.*, 26 ;
Reg. Brev. Tract., 229, 288 ; *Vita SS. Epictet. et Astion.*, 11 (Rosweyde, *MPL.*,
lxxiii, col. 400) ; *Vit. Patr.*, iii, 9, 57 (*ib.*, coll. 743, 769), vii, 1, 5 (*ib.*, col.
1027) ; Ben. Nurs., *Reg.*, 46, etc.—Later enactments of the same kind, Lea
(who, however, minimizes the evidence), *op. cit.*, i, pp. 184, 185.

is implied that the confession itself (assisted perhaps by discreet advice from the confessor) is of a sacramental character, and that absolution, if not superfluous, is at best subsidiary. Serapion,[1] as a boy-attendant upon an older hermit, Theon, fell into the childish sin of stealing a biscuit daily from their common store, and eating it in secret. A discourse of the old man on gluttony convicted him of his imminent spiritual danger, and bursting into tears he produced his latest biscuit—which he had not yet had time to eat—and confessed, not so much the sin of theft as that of gluttony, imploring those present to entreat the Lord to free him from this dreadful slavery. ' Have faith, my child,' the old man said, ' without any words of mine [2] your confession frees you from this slavery.' That this was no *obiter dictum* of a kindly monk is shown by the miracle which followed. A burning lamp emerged from the penitent boy's tunic, ' filling the cell with a sulphurous smell so pungent that we could scarcely stay there,' and typifying, as Theon promptly interpreted the portent, the departure of the spirit of gluttony. Forgiveness had been secured.

It may be the case, therefore, that in many of these monastic confessions it was not thought necessary to conclude the matter with absolution. Cassian's twentieth Collation deals wholly with penance and satisfaction without even mentioning reconciliation.[3] Nevertheless, reconciliation must have been quite normal and well understood ; we cannot otherwise account for the way in which the custom of private absolution followed the monks whenever they left their monasteries. In the east, when the iconoclastic controversies of the eighth century brought them out into the world, their supposed excess of sanctity led not merely to the adoption of the practice of confession among devout lay-folk, but also to the choice of monks as confessors, with the result that both penance and reconciliation became private transactions. The prerogative of the bishop was thus completely invaded—and even that of the priest as well, for lay-monks did not hesitate to give absolution. An anonymous monk of the ninth century, writing under the name of Johannes Jejunator, says roundly, ' God has appointed bishops,

---

[1] Cass., *Coll.*, ii, 11 ; also in *Vit. Patr.*, iv, 47 (Rosweyde, *MPL.*, lxxiii, col. 843), and v, 4, 25 (*ib.*, col. 868).

[2] The compiler of *Vit. Patr.*, iv, disliked this phrase (probably as implying too lax a view of absolution) and omitted it ; it is retained in *Vit. Patr.*, v.

[3] Although (c. 8) the ' intercession of holy men ' is mentioned as a means of securing forgiveness, with reference to 1 Jn. 5[16], Jas. 5[15]. But in the same chapter we are even told that earnest contrition will win forgiveness ' without shameful publication' for those who ' blush to reveal their sins before men.' Poschmann (pp. 72-76) thinks the omission to be due either to Cassian's psychological method of approach, or to the fact that only venial sins are here in question ; but betrays uneasiness on the whole matter. On the whole subject of monastic confessions cp. H. C. Lea, *op. cit.*, i, pp. 184 f., 197-204, 465 ; but his argument from the infrequency of formal penance in the monasteries to its infrequency outside is invalidated by the fact that the *conversus*, being regarded as a life-penitent, was not required to submit to further publicity (cp. Poschmann, *op. cit.*, pp. 128 ff.).

priests and doctors for the instruction of the faithful : monks to hear their confessions.'[1]

In the west, also, the system of private reconciliation spread from the monasteries to the Church at large,[2] though here not controversy but evangelistic zeal provided the point of contact. The Irish missionaries spread the custom in Britain, so much so that Archbishop Theodore found it in universal use.[3] Columbanus introduced it, about the year 590, on the Continent, and there also it found increasing favour. Privacy, naturally enough, made repetition possible and easy. Bishop Chrodegang of Metz (c. A.D. 750) laid a rule of biennial confession upon his canons,[4] thus showing how utterly distinct it now was from that public discipline which had originally refused penance to clerics, because the proper punishment for them was degradation.[5] Midway in the seventh century a Council of Chalon declared ' the penance of sinners, which is the medicine of the soul,' to be ' useful to all men ' ;[6] and the eighth century Dialogue of Egbert shows that the devout laity habitually received absolution in the twelve days before Christmas.[7]

[1] *MPG.*, lxxxviii, col. 1920; on the whole of this eastern development see Tixeront, *Hist. Dogm.*, iii, pp. 255, 256 : K. Holl, *Enthusiasmus u. Bussgewalt*, pp. 310-331. Holl, pp. 319-325, makes it clear that for several centuries the eastern Church saw no irregularity in these monastic absolutions of the laity. They were not suppressed until the western scholastic doctrine of the sacraments made itself felt as the result of Michael Palaeologus' negotiations with the west at the Council of Lyons (A.D. 1274). For confession to laity in the west, see A. Teetaert, *La Confession aux Laïques* (Paris, 1926), *pass. ;* Morinus, *de pœnit.*, viii, 24. 3-16 ; J. Bingham, *Antiquities*, xix, iii, 4.

[2] This is generally accepted, despite the arguments of Batiffol and Duchesne (see Batiffol, *op. cit.*[5], pp. 193, 194 ; and contrast Tixeront, *op. cit.*, iii, pp. 400-402, 405 f.; Poschmann, *op. cit.*, pp. 305, 306 ; and *infra*, additional note O, p. 534). On the missionary activities of the Celtic monks, and of S. Columbanus in particular, see L. Gougaud, *Les Chrétientés Celtiques*, pp. 145-161 ; Watkins, *op. cit.*, pp. 613 (where the strictly *evangelistic* motive is treated as doubtful), 620, 654 ; Tixeront, *op. cit.*, iii, pp. 400-402 ; *C. Med. H.*, ii, pp. 533-536. It is important to notice, however, that the Irish Church was perhaps not wholly unacquainted with public penance—see Watkins, *op. cit.*, pp. 603, 615-617 ; Oakley, *op. cit.*, pp. 66, 67. The penances in use among the Irish were of a specially barbarous kind ; sleeping on nettles and nutshells, for example, or with a corpse,—Oakley (who merely calls them ' quaint '), *op. cit.*, p. 66, with refs.; cp. *ib.*, p. 49, and L. Gougaud, *Devotional and Ascetic Practices of the Middle Ages* (E. tr.), pp. 159-178 (on cold water penances). This may account for the crude and violent character of many mediæval penances (see e.g. Lea, *op. cit.*, ii, pp. 109 ff., 117, 121, 155).

[3] *Supra*, p. 276, n. 3. There is little doubt that Theodore undertook the regulation of (private) penance with alacrity, even though the *Penitentiale Theodori* may not be directly from his hand (Haddan and Stubbs, iii, pp. 173-175 ; Oakley, pp. 106, 107).

[4] Chrod., *Reg. Can.*, 14 (*MPL.*, lxxxix, col. 1104). About the same date Bede (*Hom.*, 2, 16—*MPL.*, xciv, col. 223) assigns the power of binding and loosing to bishops and presbyters alike (Tixeront, iii, p. 405).

[5] *Supra*, p. 168, n. 7.

[6] *Conc. Cabil.*, c. 8—the context (priests to assign a penance after hearing confession) shows the reference to be to formal penance. On the date of the Council (between 644 and 656), Hefele-Leclerq, iii, p. 282.

[7] *Dial. Egberti* (Haddan-Stubbs, iii, p. 413).

(c) The Popularizing of Confession.[1]

So far, however, the system of private confession, penance and reconciliation was a matter of personal piety alone. But in the tenth and eleventh centuries authority awoke to the opportunity thus presented to it by voluntary devotion and the accident of circumstances. A vigorous campaign was begun to popularize confession. A marked change now came over both theory and practice. Three factors are clearly involved in the full usage—factors whose coexistence led, particularly in the first five centuries, to considerable ambiguity in the use of the words ' pœnitentia ' or ' exomologesis,' which vaguely covered them all, and might be used for any one of them.[2] In theory, ' pœnitentia,' (' penance ') covers a virtue (' penitence '), a discipline (' penance ' proper) and a sacrament (absolution as the completion of a good ' penance '). In practice it is made up of three corresponding stages—confession, penitential exercises and reconciliation. The idea of discipline had already shrunk to such minor proportions in respect of private penance and reconciliation, that by the middle of the eighth century the penitential exercises (or ' penances ' proper) were postponed to the end of the process.[3] Reconciliation now followed immediately upon confession. The penitential exercises (or ' satisfaction ' as they were technically called), though no longer an antecedent condition of reconciliation, were not allowed to fall into disuse ; but the practice of commutations, of which more will be said in a moment, robbed them of much of their severity. A new theory, however, was required to account for their continued necessity, and this led to the development of the doctrine of purgatorial fires, and many other refinements which do not concern us. It seems certain, however surprising the fact may appear, that Abailard played a leading part in popularizing the idea of purgatory.[4]

As to the respective importance of the other two elements in the rite—confession and absolution—opinion varied ; and had varied

---

[1] A vast amount of material for the history of this question has been presented, not without acrimony, by H. C. Lea, *Auricular Confession, etc.*, i, pp. 105-167, 460-514. For the eleventh and twelfth centuries, P. P. Schmoll, *Die Busslehre der Frühscholastik* (1909) is indispensable ; and although the main thesis of K. Müller's *Der Umschwung in der Lehre von der Busse* (*Th. Abhandlungen Weiszäcker Gewidmet*, 1892) is generally discredited (cp. Schmoll, p. 18 ; Loofs, *Leitfaden*, p. 475, n. 4 ; Harnack, *Hist. of Dogma*, v, pp. 326, 327 ; vi, pp. 243, 244) his researches remain valuable. For earlier penitential doctrine see especially J. Tixeront, *Mélanges de Patrologie* (1919), pp. 237-260 ; Poschmann, pp. 254-258, 269 (both on Gregory the Great) ; Lea, i, pp. 193-196 (tenth century). A general review in Loofs, *op. cit.*, pp. 475-496 ; or Harnack, *op. cit.*, vi, pp. 243-258. In the text above only the fringes of the subject are touched ; thus all reference to the later scholastic discussions, which—important though they are—hardly affect our present purpose, is omitted.

[2] Cp. *supra*, p. 222, n. 1.

[3] Tixeront, *Hist. Dogm.*, iii, p. 407 ; Loofs, pp. 478, 484-487 ; Schmoll, pp. 7, 8 ; K. Müller, p. 298 ; with references in each case.

[4] See *infra*, p. 513, additional note I.

for a long time.[1] In the primitive period—in the days, for example,
of Hermas, Clement, and Polycarp,[2]—little stress was laid upon
absolution, much upon the efficacy of true penitence (' perfect contrition ' as later it came to be called) to win complete forgiveness
from God. The instances of Lazarus,[3] who was called to life again
before the disciples ' unbound ' him, and of the lepers who were
healed before they ' showed themselves to the priests,' [4] were for
long interpreted to mean that divine forgiveness *preceded* official readmission to communion by the Church.[5] So strongly was it felt
that perfect contrition won complete forgiveness without any
intermediary ecclesiastical action, that even the most convinced
churchmen—Jerome, Augustine, Gregory the Great, and Anselm,
—can be quoted as supporters of the position.[6] Importance was

---

[1] This, however, does not quite represent the form in which the problem
presented itself to the mediæval mind. Really it had two stages: (*a*) On
the penitent's side, so Gregory the Great (*Hom. in i Reg.*, vi, 33 ; *MPL.*,
lxxix, col. 439 ; although (Poschmann, p. 275) it is not certain that this
commentary is really the work of Gregory) had asserted, three things were
important—contrition, confession and satisfaction ; the first problem was
to decide which of these three was—if not of sole necessity—at all events
the primary requirement. (*b*) In the second place it had to be decided
whether each or all of these was adequate to secure divine forgiveness without sacerdotal absolution—this is the problem considered in the text, but
I have used the word ' confession ' as a convenient designation for the penitent's share, regardless of a particular writer's preference for this or that
element as constituting the fundamental subjective condition. A further
question was, What constitutes the essence of that ' contrition ' which is
demanded of the penitent—love, or merely fear ?—and if fear, is there any
degree of fear (e.g. ' servile ' as distinct from ' filial ') too selfish to be regarded
as adequate ? This marks the beginning of the ' contrition-attrition ' controversy (*supra*, p. 249), but again lies outside the confines of our subject.
[2] For this cp. H. B. Swete in *JTS.*, iv (1903), pp. 322 ff. Hermas regards
the purpose of penance as the securing of ' healing ' (ἴασις Vis., i, 1. 9 ; 3. 1 ;
Mand., iv, 1. 11 ; xii, 6. 2 ; *Sim.*, v, 7. 3, 4 ; vii, 4 ; viii, 11. 3 ; ix, 23.
5 ; 28. 5) ; but nowhere treats of absolution as a necessary stage in the
process. At best it would be what Batiffol calls (*op. cit.*, p. 201) ' a simple
parade.' This fact would make the action of the ' confessors,' e.g. at Lyons
and Vienne, or in the Decian persecution, less revolutionary than is commonly supposed. They did not claim, perhaps, to forgive sin, nor to reconcile
to the Church, but merely to testify to the apostate's genuine penitence—
thus implying that he *had been* forgiven by God, and *should be* readmitted
to communion.
[3] Jn. 11⁴⁴.   [4] Lk. 17¹⁴.
[5] For Lazarus and the lepers cp. e.g. Ambrose, *de pœn.*, ii, 7. 58 ; Aug.,
serm., 67. 2 ; 98. 6 ; 295. 2 (3) ; 352. 8 ; Hieron., *Comm. in Mt.*, iii, 16
(*MPL.*, xxvi, col. 122) ; Greg. Magn., *in evang. hom.*, ii, 26. 6 ; *Mor. in Hiob*,
xxii, 31 ; Anselm, *hom.*, 13. What, in these circumstances, the exact duty
of the Church was (' Loose him and let him go,' in the Lazarus-story), was
never clearly defined. At best it could merely be the remission of penalties.
On the later exegesis of the texts (the ' coming forth ' merely the awaken-
ing to the need of confession, etc.), see Lea, *op. cit.*, i, pp. 138-140.
[6] So, for example, Cyprian, *de lapsis*, 17—' only God can have mercy
. . . man is not greater than God ' ; Ambrose, *de Sp. Sancto*, iii, 18, 137—
the function of the minister merely to help—' he has neither jurisdiction nor
power ' ; Hieron., *Comm. in Mt.*, iii, 16 (*ut sup.*)—' God considers not the
sentence of the priest, but the life of the penitent ' ; Aug., *serm.*, 99. 8—the
blasphemy of saying, ' I absolve thy sins ' ; for the vacillations of Alcuin,
Lea, *op. cit.*, i, pp. 125, 126 ; for Anselm, Schmoll, pp. 16-18. Origen,

attached, of course, to the presence and co-operation of the bishop or priest. But different views were held as to his function. The form of absolution until the twelfth century was precatory and not declaratory [1]; it might therefore be said that his *prayers* rather than his *absolution* were the necessary adjunct of forgiveness.[2] His presence might be required to ensure the proper depth of contrition, through the shameful necessity of a verbal acknowledgment to man.[3] He might be there merely as a witness to report the offender's contrition to the Church.[4] The significant thing was that he always had *some* part to play in the rite; and therefore from the third century onwards language of a sacramental character is from time to time employed to designate the nature of his functions.[5]

The twelfth century, however, witnessed the rapid development of a sacramental theory [6] of absolution. It cannot be said that this was a deliberate process,[7] though it was quite as much in the interest of ecclesiastical discipline as in that of individual sanctity. Absolution was now presented as something of inestimable value in itself; men were urged to purchase its unique and peculiar benefits by submitting to the humiliation of confession. The root cause of this development is to be found, I believe, in the fuller understanding of the human heart and its processes which marks the earlier cen-

---

Tertullian and Jerome admit the gift of the keys to Peter (or the Apostles), but insist that it is only transmitted, if at all, to those who rival the original recipients in moral character or miraculous powers (Origen, *Comm. in Mt.*, xii, 14; Tert., *de pud.*, 21; cp. Hieron., *Comm. in Mt.*, iii, 16, *ut sup.*). Similarly, S. Gregory says (*in ev. hom.*, 26. 6) that sacerdotal absolution is only valid ('vera') when it follows the judgment of God; and that perverse use of the privilege of absolution deprives its possessor of the power of the keys.

[1] Morinus, viii, 8-10; Loofs, p. 488; Müller, p. 317. Numerous examples of precatory absolution are given by Morinus.

[2] E.g. Leo, *ep.* 108. 2—'indulgentia Dei nisi *supplicationibus* sacerdotum nequeat obtineri'; Aug., *serm.*, 392. 3—'agite pœnitentiam . . . ut *oret* pro vobis ecclesia.'

[3] E.g. [Aug.], *de ver. et fals. pœn.*, 10 (25); Abail., *scito teips.*, 24.

[4] Alcuin, *ep.* 112 (*MPL.*, c, col. 337)—Lazarus and the lepers again; Anselm, *hom.*, 13 (*MPL.*, clviii, col. 662)—the lepers.

[5] E.g. Tert., *de pud.*, 1 (Callistus)—'I remit sins'; *ib.*, 21—'The Church will forgive sins'; Ambrose, *de Cain et Ab.*, ii, 4. 15—'sins are forgiven through the office of the priest and the sacred ministry;' Aug., *de bapt.*, iii, 18 (23); *c. advers. leg.*, i, 17 (36)—the Church can inflict punishment worse than the sword, the stake, or the arena; Chrysostom, *supra*, p. 283, n. 3; Celestine i, *ep.* 4. 2 (3)—(*MPL.*, l, col. 432)—to deny absolution to the penitent is to 'murder his soul'; Greg., *in ev. hom.*, 26. 4—the priests 'vice Dei' retain the sins of some, and remit those of others; *hom. in Ezk.*, ii, 9. 20. Generally, see Poschmann, pp. 36-40, 106-110; and for the eighth century onwards, Lea, i, pp. 127-132.

[6] The gradual use of the word 'sacrament' in this connexion has been traced by Lea, *op. cit.*, i, pp. 470 ff. But it is important to notice, with Schmoll (p. 10), that as late as the eleventh century 'the conception and number of the sacraments were still so vague and undefined as to prevent the use of the word in its later sense' (cp. *ib.*, p. 16).

[7] Schmoll points out the incidental importance of the Crusades (p. 8) and the revival of heresy (pp. 11-13) in focussing attention on the point. Cp. also Morinus, *de pœn.*, x, 22.

turies of the middle ages, and of which Abailard, S. Bernard and the Victorines are such striking examples. The primitive conception, in short, was too naive to fit the facts. That ' perfect contrition ' would win immediate forgiveness from God was never denied. But a truer psychology saw how rare such ' perfect contrition ' must be. Reflection suggested that here was the real ground for the action of the priest in reconciliation—the power of the keys, for so long only dimly understood, would unlock the stores of divine grace as the faulty human heart could not.

Once this was realized, sacramentalism was bound to prevail. Even Abailard, though in general a staunch supporter of the earlier view,[1] was inclined to make terms with the sacramentalist ;[2] and his disciples, Roland (afterwards Pope Alexander III) and the Master of the ' Sentences,' are perhaps the last great writers to resist the sacramental interpretation. We come to confession, says Roland, not because this secures remission, but because it shows remission to be already secured.[3] ' God remits sins through Himself alone,'

[1] See *scito teipsum*, 17, 19 ; *expos. in Rom.*, ii, 4 ; *sermo* 8 (the mere intention to confess and perform satisfaction ' reconciles at once '). K. Müller, *Der Umschwung in der Lehre von der Busse*, *pass.*, especially pp. 304 ff., makes Abailard the inventor of what is called above the ' earlier ' view. This opinion, however, is untenable in the light of the evidence (*supra*, p. 286, n. 1 ; p. 287, notes). Schmoll (p. 29), by a comparison of the *scito teipsum* with cc. 32-37 of the *epitome*, reaches the highly probable conclusion that the former represents the tractate *de caritate*, which with tractates *de fide* and *de sacramentis* would make up Abailard's complete theological scheme (*Introd. ad Theol.*, i, 1). From this emerges the highly important fact that Abailard did not regard absolution as a sacrament. In *scito teips.*, 26, he repeats the arguments of Origen and Tertullian (*supra*, p. 287, n. 6) that only those who emulate Peter's virtues can claim the power of the keys (so giving S. Bernard grounds for his twelfth accusation, ' he says that the power of binding and loosing was given only to the apostles and not to their successors ') ; and adds S. Gregory's admonition that the sentence of the priest must interpret that of God to be valid. But he is obviously less concerned than his authorities with unjust ' loosing ' by the priest than with unjust ' binding ' (a point on which he might well be sensitive) ; and he even goes out of his way to repeat Gregory's warnings (*ib.*) that the penitent should respect the priest's decision even when he disagrees with it. There is little more here, in fact, than the orthodox view that ' an unjust sentence does not bind ' (see my *Conscience and its Problems*, p. 224).

[2] So *epit.*, 36—the priest the ' vicar of God,' with ' delegated ' power to ' heal sin ' ; he adds that the sinner who dies unshriven, ' through his own contempt or neglect,' will most certainly go to hell. Cp. *serm.*, 8, ' priests have the place of God in the Church,' ' confession to God's vicar, the priest, is the same as confession to God ' ; similarly, *scito teips.*, 24, rejects emphatically the view of those who say ' it is enough to confess to God alone ' (though, in curious contrast with the last-quoted passage, he here takes the ground that God knows all our sins already) ; and (as Müller, p. 308, admits) he does *not* say that absolution merely declares God's forgiveness to have been obtained.

[3] For Roland see Müller, p. 309 ; Schmoll, pp. 35-37. The text in A. M. Gietl, *Die Sentenzen Rolands* (Freiburg, 1892), p. 248.—Roland recognizes a double ' remission,' of which however one kind alone is really worthy of the name :—' in cordis contritione remittitur [peccatum], id est, penitus aboletur ; in oris confessione operumque satisfactione remittitur, id est, remissum monstratur.' But he adds that, *where time allows*, confession

says Peter Lombard; 'the power of binding and loosing is the power of showing a man to be bound or loosed. A man may be already loosed by God, but he is not thereby to be held as loosed in the eyes of the Church, before sentence has been given by the priest.' [1]

Utterances such as these grew rarer as the twelfth century went on. Gratian states both theories, and allows the reader ' to choose for himself.' [2] Richard of St. Victor, though he allows himself to echo some of Abailard's sentiments, is in general a strong sacramentalist. [3] Hugh of St. Victor has no doubts: the ' judgment of heaven,' he says, in a passage which Harnack calls a ' novelty in theology,' [4] 'does not precede the judgment of Peter; it is consequent upon it.' [5] The end of the long conflict is in sight. The priest, who was hitherto spoken of, as often as not, as primarily the witness and helper of the sinner's penitence, now becomes definitely the agent of forgiveness; and the declaratory form of absolution is finally adopted. [6]

If one moment can be called more important than another in this development, it must be that which saw, late in the eleventh century, the publication of an anonymous tract on ' True and False Penitence.' [7] Its authorship was almost at once attributed (without any apparent reason, and in face of definite internal evidence to the contrary) [8] to Augustine. From this strange fact comes the definitive influence which it exercised. It is quoted as authoritative

and satisfaction are indispensable. The argument depends on a curious analogy :—the first of the three immersions in baptism suffices to remit sin, ' but the other two immersions are not superfluous ' (ib., p. 249).

[1] Petr. Lomb., Sent., iv, 18. 5, 6. See Müller, p. 314 ; Schmoll, p. 72 ; Lea, pp. 142, 143, 145, on Peter's theory of the two keys (' clavis scientiæ ' and ' clavis potestatis ').

[2] Gratian, Decretum, D.I. de pœn., init. ; ib., c. 89, dict. Grat. Gratian himself inclined strongly towards the sacramental side—see the long ' dicta Gratiani ' on cc. 60 and 87 ; but the question was still an open one. Schmoll (p. 41) attempts unsuccessfully to prove that for Gratian ' the power of the keys was never in question ' ; but this is contrary to the facts. If by any chance contrition alone (the ' prior sententia ') should prove to be sufficient for forgiveness, the value of absolution would be nil.

[3] R. S. Vict., de pot. lig. et solv., 7, 8 (MPL., cxcvi, col. 1165)—true contrition, even though with confession to God alone, saves from hell, but this is only conditional upon the sinner being willing if possible to seek priestly absolution ; and apart from absolution the pains of purgatory are still binding.

[4] Harnack, Hist. of Dogma, vi, pp. 243, 244 ; cp. ib., pp. 222, 223.

[5] Hug. S. Vict., de sacr., ii, 14. 8 (MPL., clxxvi, col. 566). S. Bernard says the same (in fest. SS. Pet. et Pauli, i, 2 ; Mab., i, col. 2124). On the intricacies of Hugh's theology see Schmoll, pp. 47-53.

[6] For such formulæ see Morinus, viii, 9, 23 ff. ; Lea, i, pp. 480 ff.

[7] MPL., xl, coll. 1113-1130. Lea, i, p. 209, regards the treatise as a fifth century document (cc. 1-9, 13, 16, 17) worked over by a sacramentalist of the early twelfth century. This view has not been generally followed.

[8] In de ver. et fals. pœn., 17 (33), as quoted by Gratian, Augustine is mentioned by name. The MSS. omit the ' Augustine,' but a proper name is required by the sense ; and no purpose (except that of grammar) would have been served by inserting it if it had not originally been there.

by Gratian and the Lombard—both of them at considerable length
—and in many confessors' manuals of the middle ages. The tract
is representative of the transition period ; it even enshrines traces
of the non-sacramental view itself.[1] There are still many opponents
of frequent penance whose arguments have to be answered.[2] The
necessity of priestly absolution is emphatically asserted. The
priest is God's 'ambassador'; to whomsoever the priest remits
God also remits (10 (25))—there is no doubt in the author's mind
of the meaning of the power of the keys. Mortal sin, of course,
requires absolution (4 (10)), and as a multiplicity of little sins can be
avoided by no one, and in itself, if left untended, constitutes the
equivalent of mortal sin (8 (20)), we must all have recourse to sacramental confession ;[3] 'for unless the unity of the Church succours
us, the dead soul cannot be rescued from the hand of the enemy'
(12 (27)). No one can complete a worthy penance without the
support of the Church's unity—apart from the Church's help we
are not able to stand (12 (27)). We have to win the Church's
favour by our tears and groans, that she may take us into favour,
and implore life for the dead (14 (31)). Let the Christian then
place himself wholly in the power of his judge, in the judgment of
the priest, and suppress no part of the truth about himself (14 (30)).
The influence of the tract, backed as it was by the authority of
S. Augustine's name, was decisive. Not much more than a century
later, annual confession of all mortal sin is required of all Christians,[4]
and the new system stands fully grown.

[1] E.g. *de v. et f. pœn.*, 10 (25) (cp. 17 (34))—'satisfaction' procures full
forgiveness (Loofs (p. 490) quite arbitrarily assumes that absolution is implied as well as satisfaction. But in that case how could confession to a
layman be tolerated ?) ; 'confession' goes so far in this direction as to make
the sin venial; *ib.*, you must find a priest 'who knows how to bind and
loose '—this implies Origen's position again, that the unworthiness of the
minister *may* affect the validity of the sacrament, and so tends towards the
non-sacramental view. The section proceeds to say that 'confession is so
salutary' that confession to a layman will suffice where a priest cannot be
had, for 'God considers the heart' (the instance of the lepers quoted for
this).

[2] E.g. *de v. et f. pœn.*, 2 (4)—those who object, 'Shall we sin that grace
may abound'; 6 (17, 18)—those who say 'God will forgive without penance';
and on the other hand, 3 (5-10)—those who deny *all* post-baptismal penance;
5 (11-16)—those who admit *one* post-baptismal penance only. Among other
points of interest and value in the treatise may be noted :—14 (29)—on self-
examination (evidently from a penitential book) ; 15 (31)—the characteristics
of a good confession ; 16 (32)—the discussion on freewill ; 17 (33)—the strong
attack on postponement of penance till death ; 17 (34)—the fully-developed
doctrine of purgatory ; 20 (36)—warnings for confessors (in a treatise addressed to a nun !). Loofs (p. 490) rightly notices that the author, though
he insists upon public penance for public sin (11(26)), shows little interest
in the matter. An investigation into the sources used by the author of the
treatise would be of real value.

[3] This, as Loofs notices (p. 489), though a 'leading thought of the
treatise,' is never 'stated in so many words.' It arises more easily, however, out of 8 (20) than out of the two passages in which Loofs finds it.

[4] *Conc.* iv *Later.* (A.D. 1215), c. 21 (*DB.*, no. 437), but *mortal* sin is not
explicitly specified. On the problems raised by this omission, Lea, ii, pp.
271-273.

V. Penance in the Middle Ages.

Thus the missionary efforts of the Irish saints, the sacramental interests of theologians, and last of all the sanction and approval of Rome, evolved out of the old public discipline of ' penance ' the new private discipline of ' confession '—if one may mark the change by the use of a popular though misleading term. The opportunity thus presented to the Church was one of almost unlimited possibilities. The silent but determined reaction of the Christian conscience against the rigours of the older open penance and absolution had brought to birth, almost by accident, a complete reversal of the relations of clergy and people. It was now the desire of the laity—a desire reinforced by spiritual sanctions in which both they and the clergy placed implicit faith—to obtain the benefit of regular absolution,[1] and they were willing to pay the price of opening their hearts and consciences to the confessor. The clergy no longer had to seek out their flock : their flock came to them *proprio motu*. It remains to be seen how the Church made use of this new development.

Although even so severe a critic of the system of private confession as Dr. Lea asserts that its introduction ' cannot but have been salutary,' [2] the results at first sight must be adjudged more than disappointing. The clergy, for the most part themselves of a low standard of breeding and education, were obviously unprepared for the task laid upon them. Penitential books [3] had to be prepared for their guidance, and they expose a sorry state of things. It is not merely that, apparently in all good faith, they reveal the necessity of dealing with sins of almost unbelievable grossness ; the earliest penitentials, contemporary with the very beginnings of the new development, came naturally enough from northern Europe, where the practice of private confession first spread at all widely, and where barbaric modes of life were still common. Far worse is the impression produced upon modern sensibilities by the mentality of the compilers. There is an absolute rule-of-thumb method for dealing with sins ; they are tabulated and assessed with

---

[1] This is true at best of the *devout* only. The Lateran canon was only enforced with difficulty ; see Lea, i, pp. 231-236, 250-252 ; and B. L. Manning, *The People's Faith in the Time of Wyclif*, pp. 29-38.

[2] Lea, ii, pp. 106, 107, cp. *ib.*, p. 412. The judgment is all the more remarkable in that Professor Lea is referring explicitly to the penitential books. The whole passage should be read. Similarly, W. Gass, *Geschichte der Christlichen Ethik*, i, p. 256—' The judge now becomes a mentor, and thus Christian discipline found a way into its happiest field.' Very different is the regretful opinion of Bishop Creighton, *Persecution and Tolerance*, p. 80 —' The object of penance gradually changed from being the maintenance of the purity of the Christian community to being the discipline of the individual character.'

[3] On the penitential books see especially F. W. H. Wasserschleben, *Die Bussordnungen der abendl. Kirche* (1851) ; H. J. Schmitz, *Die Bussbücher u. die Bussdisciplin* (1883) ; *Bussbücher u. d. Bussverfahren* (1898) ; and now T. P. Oakley, *English Penitential Discipline and Anglo-Saxon Law* (New York, 1923).

an appropriate penance as though by mass-production. Something of the kind has met us in the canonical letters of S. Basil and the canons of the early local councils, but nothing there is really comparable with this callous and impersonal enumeration of crimes and penalties. 'Hitherto,' says M. Tixeront, 'sins were never treated in the abstract; there had only been individual sinners whom it was the priest's duty to judge, and above all to heal'—choosing his penances, that is, in relation to the needs of each particular case;—'with the new system all this is changed.'[1] There is an element of exaggeration in this statement, yet in essence it is true enough. In selecting a penance the priest may either aim at finding a medicine to fit the disease, or a punishment to fit the crime; the penitential books of the eighth and ninth centuries betray a very strong tendency towards the second alternative.

A single instance will make this clear. It comes from a penitential ascribed to Egbert of York.[2] The priest is instructed, after the penitent has made a general confession, to address him as follows:—

'Tell me what you have done and thought. Have you sinned in thought, word or deed? have you sworn by the gospel on the altar?—ten years' penance.[3] Have you sworn by your brother's hand, or another's, or by a consecrated cross?—three years' penance. Have you cursed in anger or been envious?—seven years; have you spread slander?—seven years; have you used idle words or entertained hatred?—fast on bread and water for as long a time as that during which the offence continued. Have you been guilty of gluttony, impure thoughts? . . . (here follows a detailed list of sins of the flesh) . . . have you been cruel to the poor? have you failed[4] to visit Christ in prison, to receive strangers in your house, to wash your guests' feet, to visit the sick, to recall the quarrelsome to peace with one another? have you eaten on fastdays before the hour, busied yourself with idle fables, entertained loose thoughts in church . . . spoken lustful words, committed sacrilege?—seven years' penance, three of them on bread and water.'

Sometimes it is true that, even in the most codified passages, there is an attempt to discriminate, though more emphasis is laid

---

[1] Tixeront, *Hist. Dogm.*, iii, p. 406; for the earlier custom as defined by Tixeront, cp. Poschmann, pp. 28, 29; 96, 97.

[2] Morinus, appendix, p. 15; certainly not authentic. For the genuine penitential of Egbert, see Oakley, pp. 121-123; Haddan and Stubbs, iii, pp. 413-416.

[3] Apart from special acts of penance to meet circumstances of particular gravity (*supra*, p. 285, n. 2), and also (later) Crusades, pilgrimages, etc., 'penance' in this period consisted mainly of fasting on bread and water, recitation of psalms, wearing of sombre clothing, etc., with corporal punishment, exile, or (temporary) seclusion in a monastery (Ducange, *s.v.* 'retrusio') in more serious cases. See Oakley, pp. 49, 50; Watkins, pp. 616, 617.

[4] Text here: 'visitasti . . . excepisti . . . lavasti . . . visitasti . . . revocasti.' A 'non,' or a series of 'nons,' has obviously fallen out.

upon the subdivision of particular classes of offence than upon
the motives of the agent. So for example in the pseudonymous
'Excerptions of Egbert':—[1]

> 'Let him who kills a monk, or clerk, lay aside his arms and
> serve the Lord in a monastery, or do penance seven years in
> exile. The doom of him who kills a bishop or priest belongs to
> the King. Let him who kills a layman out of premeditated
> malice, or to get his inheritance, do penance three, five or seven
> years; if it were for the revenge of his brother, one year, and
> three Lents, and the stated weekdays in the two following
> years; if by sudden violence, three or five years; if by chance,
> one year; if in public war, forty days. Let the freeman who
> kills an innocent person at the command of his chief, do penance
> one year, and three Lents and the stated weekdays in the two
> following years. Let him who by striking a man in a fray has
> brought a man to a state of weakness or deformity, pay the
> charge of the physicians, and make amends for his blemish, and
> for the loss of his work, till he be cured, and do penance half a
> year. And if he be not able to make such restitution, then a
> whole year.'

There are obviously enough curious lapses of moral sensibility
in all this, but in general it sounds rigorous enough; and although
confession and absolution may be private, the penitential exercises
are still public, at all events in cases of grave sin. In practice,
however, the system was by no means so exacting, for the customs
of performing penances by proxy and of commuting them with
money payments—harbinger of the sinister system of indulgences
which developed later—were well known. By their means a
further measure of privacy was secured, and the extremes of humiliation avoided. In the earlier centuries these substitutes were only
allowed in cases of ill-health. Later they were widely tolerated,
or even urged upon the penitent with quite indecent frankness.[2]
The following occurs in the tenth century 'Canons of Eadgar':—[3]

> 'One day's fasting may be redeemed with a penny, or
> with 200 psalms. A year's fasting may be redeemed with
> thirty shillings, or with freeing a slave that is worth that
> money. . . . Thus may a very wealthy man, and one that
> abounds in friends, make his satisfaction much more easy by
> the assistance of his friends. . . . Let [a seven years' penance]

---

[1] *Excerp. pseudo-Egb.*, c. 94 : J. Johnson, *Laws and Canons of the Ch. of England* (ed. 1850), i, p. 234. Cp. also *ib.*, p. 221, canon 162 of the Cotton MS. See Haddan and Stubbs, iii, p. 415, on the provenance of these docu-ments.

[2] On this see Oakley, pp. 52-56, 88-103. The Penitential of Egbert allows cash compensation where the sinner 'does not know psalms and cannot fast' (Haddan and Stubbs, iii, p. 429).

[3] *Canones Eadgari*, 72, 74, 75, 77 (Johnson, i, pp. 445-449; Wilkins, *Concilia*, i, p. 229; and see Oakley, pp. 95-97).

thus be completed in three days. . . . Let him by all possible
means procure seven times a hundred and twenty men to fast
for him three days,' (these would presumably be serfs or freed-
men of his estate), ' then are as many fasts kept as there are
days in seven years. . . . This is that softening of penance
which belongs to wealthy men, and such as abound in friends ;
but '—the Canons conclude with a note almost of regret—' one
in a lower condition cannot make such despatch.' [1]

With this cheapening of penance there went a process to which
the only analogy is the depreciation of currency after the war.
The nominal severity of penances had to be multiplied beyond all
recognition, in order still to mark the Church's sense of the gravity
of sin ; but new mitigations kept their actual value as low as ever.
In the time of Peter Damian penances of a hundred years' duration
were being imposed, but even these could be discharged by serious
effort in six days.[2] We seem to have reached the lowest depths
to which formalism can sink. Theologians have spoken scathingly
of the whole system, and with good reason. Roman Catholic writers
of distinction use of it the phrase ' pénitence tarifée ' ; the whole
process is sometimes described as the elaboration of a ready-reckoner
of the wages of sin.[3] Even the not very enlightened reform councils
called by Charlemagne protested against the penitentials, though
it is not wholly clear to which of their characteristics they took
objection.[4] But the picture has a much healthier side. The
sinner who came to the priest with his confession was not always
ticketed there and then with an appropriate (or inappropriate)
penance, and sent away. There are clear indications that in some
cases, at least, he received more salutary treatment ; perhaps even
that the tariffs laid down in the penitentials are to be taken merely
as rough guides, and not in any sense as definite instructions.

Thus some at least of the penitentials insist that the confessor
must not treat his penitent as a mere example of a class, but as a
genuine individual with definite needs of his own. The authentic

---

[1] Oakley notices, in contrast to this, that the *Confessional* of pseudo-
Egbert, dealing with alleviations, expressly says, ' persons of rank (*potentes*)
are to be judged more severely ' ; whilst the *Penitential* of pseudo-Egbert
provides a descending scale of commutations in accordance with the relative
poverty of the penitent (Oakley, pp. 93, 94).

[2] Petr. Dam., *opusc.* 51, 8 ; *de vit. erem.* (*MPL.*, cxlv, col. 757)—a complicated calculation, making, in the end, twenty recitations of the whole
psalter the equivalent of a century's penance. Cp. also *ib., opusc.* 5 (col.
97), the Archbishop of Milan undertakes a century's penance, its ' redemption '
being ' assessed at so much cash for each year.'

[3] Tixeront, *Hist. Dogm.*, iii, p. 406—' des recettes tout indiquées pour
chaque genre de maladies morales, des comptes faits pour chaque péché
commis.'

[4] *Conc.* ii *Cabil.* (A.D. 813), c. 35—penances assigned in the penitentials
are too light ; *Conc.* iii *Turon.* (A.D. 813), c. 22—too much variety in the
penitentials ; one authoritative book should be prescribed ; *Conc.* vi *Paris.*
(A.D. 829), c. 32—irresponsibility of penitential books. Texts in Watkins,
pp. 674-678.

'Penitential of Egbert' begins with the following instruction to the priest :—[1]

> 'Do not generalize ; consider carefully the fact, the place, the duration, the occasion—how you ought to act. Do not mete the same measure to all. All may have committed the same sin, but you must draw distinctions between rich and poor ; freemen and slaves ; children, lads, adolescents, youths and mature ; between the stupid and the intelligent ; between layman, cleric, monk ; between bishop, presbyter, deacon, subdeacon, reader, whether in grade or not; between the married and the unmarried, the stranger, the deaconess, the nun ; [2] between the weak, the ailing, and the whole. . . . ' (Of the sin :—) 'Was it by accident or design, in public or private, by necessity or accident ? ' (Of the penitent :—) 'How much contrition does he shew? You must discern time and place.'

Thus the tariff was not as formal and inelastic as at first sight appears. In the second place, the confessor was instructed to move his penitent to enquire into the causes of sin ; attention was directed to the underlying motive rather than the fact. To this end the tabulation of the seven (or eight) principal vices was used.[3] This formula—which it is careless to speak of as the seven deadly,' and utterly misleading as the seven 'mortal,' sins—was, as we have seen, a commonplace of the hermits of the desert, which came to the knowledge of the west through Cassian's 'Institutes' and 'Collations,' and Gregory's 'Magna Moralia.' It is a code, no doubt, with all the defects of a code ; but a code of the higher order—of dispositions rather than of actions. It is an attempt to classify the 'roots' of sin—the underlying causes in the soul from which its inordinations arise. Furthermore, it is a curiously successful attempt ; it is almost identical with the list of the principal human instincts upon which the most modern psychotherapy bases its practice. No code which included 'acedia ' or 'tristitia ' —the modern 'negative self-feeling,' it may be supposed—in its list of principal or root sins could be accused of undue formalism : the penitent who used it would inevitably be led to a genuine exercise of self-examination.

Such an exercise was certainly expected of him. In the 'Penitential' of Regino of Prüm,[4] (c. A.D. 906) which was es-

---

[1] Haddan and Stubbs, iii, p. 417.

[2] 'femina canonica vel sanctimonialis' (see Ducange, *Gloss.*, *s.v.* 'canonica' ; *DCA.*, i, p. 283, *s.v.* 'canonici' (*fin.*) with references there). Originally the *canonicæ* were apparently very much the same as deaconesses, the *sanctimoniales* consecrated virgins ; later the *canonicæ* were those (whether virgins or widows) who adopted the Augustinian rule.

[3] *Supra*, pp. 201 f.

[4] Regin. Prüm., *de eccles. disc.*, i, 300 (*MPL.*, cxxxii, col. 251). For the use of this classification in earlier Penitentials, Oakley, pp. 64, 65 ; Lea, ii, pp. 235, 236 ; Watkins, pp. 694, 703.

pecially authoritative, the confessor is to address his penitent thus :—

> ' Now will I explain the eight principal vices to you '—(here follows the well-known list). . . . ' So if you have been proud, humble yourself in the sight of God. If you have loved vainglory, reflect that you are hazarding eternal reward for temporal gain. If the rust of envy has eaten you up, . . . try to think of the good fortune of others as though it were your own. If ' tristitia ' has overcome you, meditate on patience and longsuffering. If the disease of avarice weighs you down, remind yourself that it is the root of all evil, and is compared to idolatry, and that a Christian ought to be liberal.'

I have quoted enough to illustrate this side of the system of penance in the dark ages, and it cannot be denied that there is much in it to be commended. It had at least one notable effect, in that it led to an entirely new evaluation of the difference between venial and mortal sin. At the end of the patristic period, mortal or ' criminous ' sin—the sin which is worst in the sight of God and man, the sin which must be submitted to penance—is judged almost wholly by externals ; it consists in the commission of certain tabulated actions. In the middle ages all this has been swept away. True, there are lists of sins which are mortal *ex genere suo*, but even this is not conclusive. S. Thomas specially notes that a sin mortal in itself may be venial in any particular instance, whilst sins venial *ex genere* may take on a mortal character by reason of their circumstances.[1] In general the theory is wholly different, and concerned with psychological conditions alone. A sin is mortal if it is committed deliberately and with full knowledge of its gravity ; only where there has been some degree of inadvertence does the sin become venial.[2]

There is reason to suppose that we owe this quite inestimable advance in ethics, with so much else that is stimulating in the thought of the middle ages, to the genius of Abailard. He certainly discusses the problem in the ' Scito Teipsum,' and the complexity and hesitation of his argument suggests that he is feeling his way to a new idea. He insists quite openly that ' venial ' sins are actions which ' we know to be wrong, but commit in a momentary forgetfulness of their wrongness ' ; which must imply that mortal sin is sin committed with full knowledge and deliberate intent. So clear a statement was epoch-making, and the Schoolmen were quick to take it up and make it authoritative. More than this—Abailard intended, or at all events allowed, his readers to infer from

---

[1] *S.T.*, i, 2, q. 88, a. 2, *corp.*—For a discussion of S. Thomas's teaching on this point, see my *Conscience and its Problems*, p. 328 ; and for mortal and venial sin in the middle ages generally, Lea, ii, pp. 238-263.

[2] So S. Thomas insists wholly upon the degree of alienation from God —*ST.*, i, 2, q. 72, a. 5, complete ' aversion ' is mortal sin, ' less than aversion ' is venial ; cp. *ib.*, q. 77, a. 8 ; q. 88, aa. 2, 6 ; q. 89, aa. 3, 5, 6.

his discussion that mere over-indulgence at table and unnecessary luxury, *although* the Church in the past has not instituted penalties for them, *although* they are certainly not ' crimes,' and *although* in smart circles they actually command a certain amount of applause, are mortal sin if deliberately admitted.[1] It is obvious that the institution of penance is by such a statement rescued from the danger of formalism, and put on a basis on which it will minister to a very true and real conception of the essential character of sin.

That is true enough ; and we have Abailard to thank for it. Yet it may still be said that this extraordinary preoccupation with sin, penitence and confession, gives religion an entirely false orientation. It is untrue, in fact, to the primary purpose of Christianity to draw men upwards to the vision of God. The criticism is in essence fully justified. The morbid interest in death, judgment, purgatory and hell which—as Dr. Coulton has rightly pointed out,[2] and as the relics of mediæval Church art fully evidence— played so large a part in the religion of the middle ages, seems to be a consequence as natural as it was deplorable. Even so, we must beware of a one-sided emphasis. The new institution of private reconciliation brought the layman to his priest, and enabled the latter to give instruction in an intimacy and with a wealth of detail and illustration wholly impossible in the pulpit. Again, side-by-side with the development of penance went a new emphasis upon the old practice of episcopal visitation ;[3] and, to judge by the earliest surviving visitation articles—those, for example, of Regino of Prüm (c. A.D. 906)—these occasions were capable of being employed by the bishops to the outstanding benefit even of the lowest of their people—the ' porcarii et pastores ' who were

---

[1] See further, *infra*, additional note P; and on Abailard's general position that there ' can be no sin except against conscience,' my *Ignorance, Faith and Conformity*, pp. 7-13.

[2] G. G. Coulton, *Five Centuries of Religion*, i, pp. 67 ff., 441 ff.

[3] For episcopal visitation, see *DCA.*, *s.v.* ' Visitation '; W. Gass, *Gesch. d. Christl. Ethik*, i, pp. 257-261. In the early Church metropolitans were required to visit their provinces annually : *Conc. Hippon.* (A.D. 393)—see *cod. can. eccl. Afric.*, cc. 53, 73, 94 ; *Conc.* 3 *Cartag.* (A.D. 397), can. 4 ; *Conc.* 6 *Cartag.* (A.D. 401), c. 8 ; *Conc. Taurin.* (A.D. 401), c. 2 ; cp. Possidius, *Vita Augustini*, c. 8. Episcopal visitation of the diocese is mentioned in connexion with S. Athanasius (Ath., *Apol. c. Ar.*, ii, 74), S. Martin (Sulp. Sev., *Dial.*, ii, 3 *et pass.*), and S. Chad (Bede, *HE.*, iii, 28) ; it was specially frequent, and not altogether popular, in Spain in the sixth and seventh centuries (*Conc. Lucens.* (A.D. 569), *Conc. Bracar.* (A.D. 572), c. 1 ; *Conc.* 4 *Tolet.* (A.D. 633), c. 36 ; *Conc.* 8 *Tolet.* (A.D. 653), c. 16 ; *Conc. Emerit.* (A.D. 666), c. 11). But the great revival of the institution was due to Charlemagne and his reform councils—*Conc. Arel.* (A.D. 813), c. 17 ; *Capit. Carol. Magn.* (refs. in *PRE.*, xviii, p. 209, *s.vv.* ' Send, Sendgericht '). A picturesque account of S. Udalric's visitation-tours (c. A.D. 950) ' in a waggon drawn by oxen, not because he could not ride a horse, but to be alone with his chaplain and sing his psalms at will,' and of the actual visitations ' continued by torchlight after nightfall,' in *Vit. S. Udal.*, 5 (25), *ap.* Mabillon, *ASOSB.*, saec. 5 ; p. 430.

called in from pasture and forest to be reminded of their religious obligations.[1]

What really happened in the best mediæval confessions can only be known from an examination of the equipment of the priest for his task—a knowledge of the manuals which he was required to keep at hand. S. Gregory's writings were among the most popular religious literature of the period ; and it is hard to believe that a confessor's instructions were not largely influenced by their contents. The 'Pastoral Rule' was in universal use. Leander of Seville circulated it in Spain ; the Emperor Maurice had it translated into Greek ; King Alfred himself produced an English version ; numerous synods in Gaul required the bishops to be acquainted with it. According to Hincmar of Rheims, in the ninth century, a copy of it was delivered, together with the book of canons, to every bishop at his consecration, with a charge to him to frame his life according to its precepts.[2] The 'Magna Moralia' and 'Homilies on Ezekiel' also were in high repute ; but even if he were unacquainted with the latter, some of the dominant ideas of the 'Pastoral Rule' must have filtered through to the ordinary confessor.

From it he would learn, in the simplest language, that the pastor's first duty is to be an example to his people ; and that purity of heart, active love to God and one's neighbour, discretion in speech, and wide sympathy are the necessary conditions of its due discharge.[3] He would learn, too, that the mainstay of this virtuous life, and above all of that sympathy which binds men together most closely in singleness of purpose, is the practice of contemplative prayer, of which S. Gregory had so much to say elsewhere :—

> 'True preachers both aspire in contemplation to the holy Head of the Church, that is the Lord, above ; they also '— and thereby—' descend in commiseration downwards to His members. . . . Within they consider the secret things of God ;

---

[1] Regino, de eccl. disc. (MPL., cxxxii, coll. 185-400). The first book gives 95 visitation articles relative to the parish church and its ministers, supported by 443 canonical citations (the penitential occurs in can. 300). The second book contains the visitation of the laity, who are summoned to attend, under pain of excommunication, by the archdeacon a day or two previously (c. 1). Seven of the laity are sworn as ' testes synodales,' and required to answer the questions put to them by the bishop (cc. 2-4). Eighty-nine questions on the general behaviour of parishioners are then submitted (c. 5). The obligation of the ' porcarii et alii pastores ' to hear mass on Sundays and festivals is mentioned in question 64 ; and in c. 416 a pleasant little sermon to their address (' shepherds were the first to hear the news of the Nativity ') is quoted. The special mention of herdsmen in connexion with this requirement seems to come from the Council of Rouen (seventh or ninth century, see Hefele-Leclerq, iii, pp. 287, 288), c. 14. In q. 65 the obligation of annual confession is recalled. Some four hundred canons are quoted in support.

[2] See F. H. Dudden, Gregory the Great, i, p. 239 ; DCB., ii, p. 790, s.v. ' Gregory.'

[3] Greg. Magn., Reg. Past., ii, 1-4.

without they carry the burdens of the worldly. And always concerning doubtful matters—when in the outside world they are uncertain how to order things,—they should return to their own souls, and consult the Lord. . . . Love rises wonderfully to high things when it is compassionately drawn to the lowliness of its neighbours ; and the more kindly it descends to the weak things of the world, the more vigorously it recurs to the things on high.'[1] 'The pastor should not relax his care for the things that are within, in his occupation among the things that are without ; nor yet neglect to provide for the things that are without, through his absorption in the things that are within.'[2]

Gregory could write far more rapturously than this about the joys of communion with God, but for a clear and practical exposition of the relation between that communion and the ordinary duties of daily life, between religion and ethics, there are few passages in Christian writing so concise or so true to the New Testament spirit. It is not without reason that S. Bernard, who has much to say to Pope Eugenius of the same sort, should select Gregory as his example of the true pastor—indeed, of the true Christian—in this respect of seeking in contemplation both relief from, and inspiration for, the harassing duties of life ;[3] and it is unlikely that humbler confessors did not transmit teaching of the same sort to their penitents.[4]

How Gregory himself hoped that his books would be used may be seen from one chapter in the ' Pastoral Rule '—that headed, ' How those are to be advised with whom everything succeeds according to their wish, and those with whom nothing does.'[5] The former he would have told

> ' that they do not fix their heart on the gift, while they neglect to seek the Giver; nor love their pilgrimage rather than their Father's home ; nor turn the supplies for their journey into hindrances to its progress ; nor so delight in the light of the moon as to shrink from the brilliance of the sun.'

To the latter we ought to say :—

> ' God deals with you as a doctor with a convalescent, who for his future health's sake must be refused many dainties now ; as a father with his son, whom he limits in his present expenditure whilst reserving for his inheritance the whole of the estate. . . . Divine providence would not curb and educate you now under the rule of discipline, unless it designed that you should be saved for ever.'

---

[1] Greg. Magn., *Reg. Past.*, ii, 5.   [2] *Ib.*, ii, 7.
[3] Bernardus Clarevall., *de consid.*, i, 9 (12).
[4] See *infra*, p. 544, additional note Q.
[5] Greg. Magn., *Reg. Past.*, iii, 26.

Every earthly problem, difficulty, circumstance, is to be tested and judged in the light of the vision of God ; that is the whole of the story. If the confessor did not transmit teaching of this character to the multitude of Christians with whom the new system brought him into contact, it can scarcely be said that the system was to blame. However faultily or mechanically it may have been administered, it made possible a wise exercise of pastoral discipline, whose essential secrecy was proof against the danger of rigorism.

LECTURE VI.

THE REPLY TO RIGORISM.

(II.—DOCTRINE.)

Is. lvii. 15—'Thus saith the High and Lofty One that inhabiteth eternity, whose name is Holy, I dwell in the high and holy place : with him also that is of a contrite and humble spirit.'

I. NATURALISM AND CHRISTIANITY.

THE strength of that rigorism, against which the measures considered in the last lecture were directed, lay in the consistency with which it invaded the ethical, the empirical and the theological sphere alike. William James's analysis, already cited,[1] of the psychological attractions of asceticism, gives reasons enough for its triumph in ethics ; on that point no more need be said. The conception of the vision of God as empirically attainable in ecstasy, dream or trance (induced often enough by bodily austerities) was sufficiently corroborated for generations of seekers by the evidence of pathological conditions through which they themselves had passed ; and the hope of further mystic moments of superhuman exhilaration thus offered to the ascetic proved dangerously attractive. And behind or alongside both the ethical and the empirical factors stood a theological formula so ruthlessly simple that it was well-fitted to sweep men off their feet—the formula of the unnatural God.[2] The resultant of all these tendencies in ethics, experience and theology alike was the ' negative way '—that great and tragic accident of Christian thought in which, as the Dean of S. Paul's has justly said,[3]

> ' God can only be *described* by negatives ; He can only be *discovered* by stripping off all the qualities and attributes that veil Him ; He can only be *reached* by divesting ourselves of all the distinctions of personality, and sinking or rising into our ' uncreated nothingness ' ; and He can only be *imitated* by aiming at an abstract spirituality, the passionless ' apathy' of an universal which is nothing in particular.'

[1] *Supra*, p. 194.   [2] *Supra*, p. 213.
[3] *Christian Mysticism*, p. 111. In *Philosophy of Plotinus*, ii, pp. 146, 147, this view of the ' negative way ' is slightly modified.

302

Ideas of this kind had a profound influence upon the language and practice of private devotion. Generation after generation of mystically-minded Christians attempted to obey the instructions of the strange fifth-century writer who called himself Dionysius the Areopagite.[1] ' I counsel thee, dear Timothy,' are his well-known words,

> ' in the earnest exercise of mystic contemplation, to leave the senses and the activities of the intellect, and all things that the senses or the intellect can perceive, and all things that exist not, and all things that exist ; and wholly without understanding (ἀγνώστως) to strain towards union with Him Whom neither being nor understanding can contain. For, by the unceasing and absolute renunciation of thyself and all things else, thou shalt in pureness cast all things aside and be released from all, and so shalt be led upwards to the super-essential Ray of divine Darkness (τὴν ὑπερούσιον τοῦ θείου σκότους ἀκτῖνα). . . . Unto the darkness which is beyond light (κατὰ τοῦτον τὸν ὑπέρφωτον γνόφον) we pray that we may come, and may attain unto vision through the loss of sight and knowledge ; so that, in ceasing thus to see or to know, we may learn to know that which is beyond all seeing and understanding (for this blindness and ignorance is true sight and knowledge) ; and may offer Him That transcends all things the praises of a transcendant hymnody, which we shall do by denying all things that are.'[2]

This is the explicit charter of all those tendencies of thought and behaviour which centre round the conception of the unnatural God. Had Christianity endorsed it, the Church would have dwindled to a tiny sect of anti-social hermits, devoid of all interest in life, art, morality—indeed in everything except what has been called a ' static absorption in an unconditioned Reality.'[3] But the Church knew a better way, and in theology as in discipline her

---

[1] Pseudo-Dionysius figures so largely in all books on mysticism, that I may perhaps be forgiven for passing him over so casually. His date has been fixed by the investigations of J. Stiglmayr (*Das Aufkommen der Pseudo-Dionysischen Schriften*, 1894) between the years 482 and 500 A.D. ; his dependence upon Plotinus as well as upon Proclus seems probable from H. F. Müller, *Dionysius, Proklos, Plotinos* (1918), especially pp. 73-109 ; the fullest exposition of his system is still H. Koch, *Pseudo-Dionysius Areopagita* (1900). C. E. Rolt (*Dionysius the Areopagite on the Divine Names, etc.* (1920), pp. 4-47, and cp. p. 195, n. 1) has defended him against the charge of anti-intellectualism as ably as he can be defended ; but the fact remains that he preferred the *via negationis* (ἀποφατική) to the *via affirmationis* (καταφατική), and in so far as he did not wholly identify ' mystical theology,' which is the way to God, with *negatio*, it was only because the latter still had about it some traces of intellectualism—all negation is still, in some sort, affirmation. Beyond it lay the true way of the mystic (the *via eminentiæ ad Deum*—ὑπὲρ ὅρασιν καὶ γνῶσιν γίγνεσθαι—ep. 5) in which *all* images (affirmative or negative) are laid aside.

[2] Dionys. Areop., *Myst. Theol.*, i, 1, 2.

[3] E. Underhill, *The Mystic Way*, p. 289.

leaders set themselves to eradicate what was false in rigorism whilst retaining what was true.

The task was not an easy one. No mere doctrine of a wholly *natural* God—a God Whose character and lineaments are to be seen indifferently in *all* the processes of nature or *all* the aspirations of the heart and mind—is adequate either to the evidence of conscience, or to the spirit of Christ as revealed in the New Testament. If it be true that God is not far from any one of us (for in Him we live, and move, and have our being) ; it is true also that He dwells in light unapproachable.[1] If He humbleth Himself to behold the things on earth, in His primal nature nevertheless He stands very high above them ; [2] if He finds a home with the contrite and humble, yet His abiding dwelling is the high and holy place.[3] The gnostic, the monks, the rigorist disciplinarian had fastened on a characteristic of the divine nature whose truth no Christian would dare to deny ;— the characteristic of supernatural mystery, of ineffable purity, of all that excites the awe, the sense of nothingness, the self-loathing and world-renunciation of the devotee. The Church was concerned to retain this element of the wholly supernatural in her system of theology, even while she counterbalanced it with the assertion of the witness of nature and conscience to God ; and a great line of Christian theologians laboured to weave the twofold truth into a single harmonious system, with a devotion which cannot fail to excite the admiration of the impartial observer.

Naturalism [4] pure and undisguised, therefore, has never found a place in Christianity. The apologists of the second century came near it, sometimes, with their doctrine of the universal Logos manifest in all the operations of pagan philosophy and pre-Christian religion. The Pelagian glorification of the natural goodness of man

---

[1] 1 Tim. 6[16]. On the doctrine of the *invisibility* of God, as distinct from His *unknowability*, *supra*, pp. 106, 110.

[2] Ps. 113[5, 6].   [3] Is. 57[15].

[4] The different senses in which the word ' naturalism ' can be used are fully dealt with by C. C. J. Webb, *Studies in the History of Natural Theology*, especially pp. 3-11. Here I take it as meaning the identification of God with whatever is visible, or can be explained in terms of the relationships observable between visible objects ; and with nothing that is not so visible or explicable. True or consistent naturalism, therefore, would deny the possibility of ' revelation,' as distinct from ' reason ' so understood ; it would also deny the possibility of moral freedom, as understandable only by the introduction of a principle (that of the autonomy of the will) to which there is no analogy among *visibilia*. A modern expression of consistent naturalism is the following (W. Lippmann, *Preface to Morals*, p. 143). There is a traditional ' disposition to believe that behind the visible world of physical objects and human institutions there is a supernatural kingdom from which ultimately all laws, all judgments, all rewards, all punishments and all compensations are derived. . . . *To the modern spirit . . . the belief in this kingdom must necessarily seem a grandiose fiction projected by human needs and desires.*' Though the author professes to take the ' modern ' view, his use of such phrases as ' the service of an ideal ' (p. 161), ' fulfilling oneself ' (p. 258), ' the meaning and purpose of things outside ourselves ' (p. 183), etc., shows that he has not entirely rid himself of the belief in the ' invisible kingdom ' after all.

approached it very closely. Abailard was not far from it when he all but made the individual untutored conscience the final measure of right and wrong; and eighteenth-century theism echoed much of the naturalistic deism to which it found itself opposed. Christianity never capitulated to these tendencies; indeed the tendencies themselves were at best half-hearted. The apologists, for all their doctrine of Christianity as a republication of natural theology, are unsparing in their condemnation of that same theology as it expressed itself in pagan mythology and folklore. Pelagius reduces supernatural grace to a minimum, but even he will not abolish it; it still remains as a revealed ' law and doctrine ' without which the natural goodness of man must still be at fault. Abailard, by one of the strangest transitions in the whole history of thought, passes on from his great exposition of the autonomy of conscience to what is—for him—a warm championship of the supernatural institution of penance. The reduced Christianity of the eighteenth century is still recognizable as Christianity indeed; there is a wide gulf separating Bishop Butler from Lord Herbert of Cherbury.[1] The truth embodied—distorted, if the word be preferred—in dualism holds its ground against all attacks; it is an unreal simplification of the gospel to suggest that asceticism in all its branches is an invalid accretion to the Christian scheme.

A forgotten controversy of the fourth century emphasizes this rigid determination of the Church to exclude mere naturalism from the sphere of permitted orthodoxy. ' The vision of God ' has in the preceding pages been considered as a phrase whose primary implications are ethical. But not the least aspect of its importance, even in the ethical field, is that it teems with theological problems.[2] For in what sense is God seen, and with what manner of perception; and how far can God ever be seen? Even in the period during which the Old Testament was in formation it was recognized that the tradition of Moses' interview with God embodied problems of this character. Still more, for Christians, the promise ' We shall see Him as He is ' brought up all kinds of questions as to the nature of the resurrection life and experience; questions which seem utterly academic and remote until it is realized that they are only the obverse of the greatest question in the world—that of the being of God.

---

[1] Though, as Professor Webb has pointed out (op. cit., pp. 350, 351), Herbert cannot be accused of naturalism in the fullest sense.

[2] Discussion of the subject was particularly rife in the fourth century: the relevant passages are well collected by D. Petavius, Theol. Dogm. (Paris, 1644), tract. i, l. vii (vol. i, pp. 445 ff.). Three problems were involved: (a) Is God corporeal? (b) Does the incomprehensibility of God limit His powers of revealing Himself to men? (c) How far can the Son be said to know the Father (the Arian controversy)? The discussion therefore goes to the heart of the first two articles of the Creed. How it puzzled patristic writers may be seen from Augustine, de civ. Dei, xxii, 29; de gen. ad lit., xii, 27 ff., epp. 147, 148. For recent discussions see references in J. Mausbach, Die Ethik des hlg. Aug.[2] (1929), ii, p. 401.

But whatever views were taken on questions such as these—
and they were endlessly discussed—or however much it might be
allowed that the saints in heaven shall see God in the day of resurrection (or from the very moment of their release from earthly
tribulation—a matter upon which even Pope John XXII, centuries
later, was caught tripping),[1] one view was utterly unheard-of
until it was put forward by the most extreme wing of the Arians.
The Protean figure of Aetius—'successively a slave, a travelling
tinker, a goldsmith, a physician, a schoolmaster, a theologian, and
at last the apostle of a new Church '[2]— appears for a moment
on the stage of fourth-century controversy with the astounding
declaration, ' I know God as well as I know myself ; nay I do not
know myself as well as I know God ' ; or again, ' We know God as
we know what we see with our eyes or handle with our hands—as we
know a stone or a log or any other material thing.'[3]

This was no claim to special personal illumination. It was a
theological statement designed to strip the conception of the Godhead of every attribute of ineffability, incomprehensibility, transcendence, and other-worldliness. Pressed to its logical extreme—
and there can be little doubt that Aetius, Eunomius, and their
followers, the Anomæans, were willing to accept its fullest implications—this means nothing but the identification of God with the
material universe—a naturalism as complete as any the world has
ever known. Professor Gwatkin found himself able to say of the
Anomæans that they ' betray a directness and firmness of conviction
which gives then a certain dignity ' ;[4] and perhaps sheer atheism
can be dignified. But it was an attempt by simplication to rob
Christianity not merely of all that made it Christian, but of all that
made it a religion at all ; and as such the Church decisively rejected it.

To this abhorrence of naturalism must be attributed the fact
that the threefold reaction of Catholicism against rigorist demands,
which we considered in the last lecture, never went further than
the establishment of a somewhat insecure medial position. The
double standard of counsels and precepts, though it found a place
for the worldling in the Church, left the ascetic his claim to a position of pre-eminence. Monasticism was reformed and controlled,
but not in such a way as to prohibit new movements towards
asceticism if and when they were needed. The rigours of the

---

[1] Cp. H. Rashdall, *Universities of Europe*, i, pp. 529-532 ; H. C. Lea,
History of the Inquisition, iii, pp. 590-595 ; Hefele-Leclerq, vi, pp. 779-783,
825 ; *DTC.*, ii, coll. 657-696 (*s.v.* ' Benoit II ').

[2] Gibbon, *Decline and Fall*, c. 21.

[3] Epiphanius, *hær.*, lxxxvi (*MPG.*, xlii, col. 633). The blasphemy
roused Chrysostom to deliver his five sermons *de incomprehensibili Dei
natura* (see especially ii, 3). It is not clear whether the mediæval mystics
who, in Eckhardt's words (quoted, R. Jones, *Studies in Mystical Religion*,
p. 237), ' were for seeing God with their eyes as they can see a cow,' were
simple visionaries, or rationalists of the Anomæan kind.

[4] H. M. Gwatkin, *Studies in Arianism*, p. 134.

penitential system were mitigated with a free hand ; but the process ended in the fastening of an annual confession upon all the laity, as a new obligation towards Christ and His Church. Most surprising of all is the limited humanism of the Protestant reformers. The cloister is abolished ; but its abolition clears the way for a puritanism as characteristically rigorist as that of the gnostics, though of a different content.

In phenomena such as these, it may be said, are embodied all the characteristic dangers of compromise. Yet in so far as there was compromise, its aim was to retain the essential truths both of rigorism and of humanism, without surrender to either side. What showed itself as compromise in matters of organization took the form of paradox as Christian writers—not theologians alone—laboured to express their thought in terms not wholly unworthy of its subject matter. Clement of Alexandria expounds a doctrine of God[1] clearly akin to the 'negative way'—the 'unnatural God' —of neo-Pythagoreanism and the pseudo-Areopagite ; but Clement is the most humanist in ethics[2] of all the Fathers. Origen's conception of God is far more satisfying to the modern mind than Clement's.[3] The essence of the Godhead to him is not apathy, but love ; nevertheless in practice and theory alike his ethics are dominated by the sternest principles of asceticism. Ambrose is as enthusiastic for virginity and poverty as Jerome himself ; but unlike Jerome he moves in the great world of secular affairs, and his funeral oration over the Emperor Theodosius shows how profoundly he realized the possibility of a secular Christian doing yeoman service for Christ.[4] S. John Chrysostom is a panegyrist of the monastic state ; yet he asserts that, if boys brought up in the world were certain to become good citizens, he would be the first to denounce as an enemy to society whosoever would draw them into the monastery.[5] Instances of this continued attempt to combine humanism and rigorism on equal terms recur throughout the centuries which precede the Reformation. Not least in interest is the story of S. Richard, abbot of Verdun, and the Emperor Henry I, at the very beginning of the eleventh century. Henry, the saintly representative of a saintly family, offered himself to Richard for membership of his abbey. 'Wilt thou then follow the Rule,' the abbot asked, 'and the example of our Lord, and be obedient in all things ? Why then I take thee for a monk. I will charge myself with the care of thy soul ; and so I bid thee go back to govern wisely that empire which God has entrusted to thy hands.'[6]

[1] See C. Bigg, *Christian Platonists of Alexandria*, pp. 92 f.
[2] Thus he recognizes the general superiority of the married life to the celibate as a school of character—*Strom.*, vii, 12, 70. I have given a brief account of Clement's ethics in *Conscience and its Problems*, pp. 178, 179.
[3] Bigg, *nit.*., pp. 196 ff.   [4] *de ob. Theodosii or.* (A.D. 395).
[5] Joann. Chrys., *adv. opp. vit. mon.*, iii, 11 (*MPG.*, xlvii, coll. 366, 367).
[6] *Miracula B. Rich.*, 8 ; ap. Mabillon, *ASOSB.* (Paris, 1701, saecl. vi.; pars 1 ; p. 533.

In no direction is this paradox of the Christian attempt to combine reverence for this world with aspiration for another more marked than in the monastic love of nature. Dr. Coulton, impressed as much by the theoretical rigorism as by the actual laxity of medi- æval monasticism, has recently pointed out the limits of this feature in its composition ; [1] and his evidence is of course of the highest importance. Certainly, we should expect the monk to decry the beauties of nature, or at least to ignore them, as wholly nugatory in comparison with the glories of the heavenly country for which he yearned. No doubt, too, the most earnest preachers of conversion set themselves from time to time to wean men from the joys of this world by deliberately emphasizing its imperfections. But that is only one side of the picture. In east and west alike even the champions of the monastic life vie with one another in their en- joyment of natural beauty, and recognize ' nature-mysticism ' as one of the main avenues to God. In the east, Basil and Gregory dispute the merits of the site for their hermitage in Pontus, as heartily as though they were selecting a spot for a picnic. ' There is a lofty mountain,' Basil writes,[2]

> ' covered with thick woods, watered towards the north with cool and limpid streams. At its foot lie rich water-meadows hedged round by thick-set spinneys. . . . Not Homer's Para- dise, the island of Calypso, can have been more beautiful. Indeed this retreat of mine is itself an island, so cut off it is from all the world. On two sides deep gorges bound it, on the third the rapids of a waterfall; behind is the amphitheatre of the mountain. . . . There is but one pass, and my hermitage is, as it were, its key ; behind me it mounts to a rock-platform with a wide prospect of the meadows and their river . . . the most rapid stream I know, with falls above and deep eddying pools below. . . . And oh ! the redolence of the earth, and the river-breezes, the carpet of flowers, the song of the birds ! . . . Little leisure have I to think upon these things ; but that which charms me most of all the graces of the spot is the peace and quiet that dwell there.'

Gregory of Nazianzus, to whom the panegyric was addressed, was less enthusiastic about the site. He compared it to a desert island, and Basil to a shipwrecked mariner.[3] The hermitage is a mousehole, the woods mere thickets ; the mountains shut out the sun, the river is more menacing than beautiful, the pass a slender path along a precipice. It is a twitter of hunger, not a song of joy,

---

[1] G. G. Coulton, *Five Centuries of Religion*, i, pp. 527-530.
[2] Basil, *ep.* 14. There are, of course, in Basil passages which emphasize the nothingness of natural beauty in comparison with the vision of God ; e.g. *Reg. Fus. Tract.*, ii, 1. So too the very ' negative ' prescription to abandon ' body, senses, land and sea, all that is temporal, all changing things, all the beauty of this world ' in *hom.* 15, *de fide*.
[3] Greg. Naz., *ep.* 5.

to which the birds give utterance.[1]   There is no difference here
other than one of taste in scenery.   Love of nature is apparent as
much in Gregory's humorous depreciation as in Basil's ecstatic
praise.

I take a second illustration from the austere founder of western
monachism.   Five years after the termination of his first great
experiment in the solitary life, Jerome, now in the Imperial city,
sighs not so much for his desert as for the simplicity of country
life ; and his words reveal a new æsthetic quality in the midst of
his ascetic aspirations.[2]   He is writing, apparently, in that moment
of depression which comes to every man on making up his accounts
of domestic expenditure—an occupation, he says, which invariably
stimulates ' either to the anger of a lion, or to anxiety and despair.'
How different would life be in the peaceful haven of the country-
side—

> ' There rural dainties, such as milk and home-made bread,
> with greens watered by our own hands, will supply us with
> rough but harmless fare.   There drowsiness will not blunt our
> prayers, nor gluttony our studies.   In summer the shade of
> the trees will give us privacy ; in autumn the delicate air and
> falling leaves invite us to stop and rest ; in springtime the
> fields will be bright with flowers, and our psalms will find all
> the sweeter accompaniment in the song of birds.   Even in
> the frost and snow of winter, we shall not have to buy fuel . . .
> or at least shall be able to keep ourselves warm at less expense
> than in the city.'

Few passages in S. Jerome's correspondence reveal so human
and natural a sentiment as this.

Still more remarkable is the witness of Irish monasticism—a
movement whose rules and traditions, as was indicated at an earlier
point, attempted to outbid even the austerities of the east.   Professor Kuno Meyer, in his charming collection of ancient Irish poetry,
has more than one example of the hermit's love for the beauty of
his surroundings.   Here are a few lines from a hermit's song of the
ninth century :—[3]

---

[1] Greg. Naz., *ep.* 4.   In a similar connexion, H. B. Workman, *Evolution of
the Monastic Ideal*, p. 34, quotes Antony's reply to the philosopher who asked
how he managed without books—' My book is the nature of created things '
(Rosweyde, *Vit. Patr.*, vi, 4. 16 ; *MPL.*, lxxiii, col. 1018 ; cp. Socr., *HE.*, iv,
23) ; and adds (p. 36) that the constant ' animal-stories ' recounted of the
hermits represent ' a return to the state of the world before the Fall.'   This
last point has not escaped M. Bremond—see J. Bremond, *Les Pères du
Désert*, pref., pp. xxxi, xxxii :—' et puis le désert n'est pas une ménagerie,
pas même un Jardin des Plantes.   Il ressemblerait plutôt aux environs du
Paradis terrestre.'

[2] Hieron., *ep.* 43, *ad Marcellam* (Vallarsi, *MPL.* ;—ed. Ben., *ep.* 45),
A.D. 385.   The Benedictine editors regard the letter as an invitation to
Marcella to join the colony at Bethlehem, and date it thence ' after A.D.
388.'   But it seems clear that Jerome is himself suffering from the distractions
of city life.

[3] K. Meyer, *Ancient Irish Poetry* (1913), p. 30.

' I wish, O son of the living God, O ancient eternal King,
For a hidden little hut in the wilderness that it may be my
    dwelling.

' An all-grey lithe little lark to be by its side,
A clear pool to wash away sins through the grace of the Holy
    Spirit.

' Quite near, a beautiful wood around it on every side,
To nurse many-voiced birds, hiding it with its shelter.

' A southern aspect for warmth, a little brook across its floor.
A choice land with many gracious gifts such as be good for
    every plant. . . .

' Raiment and food enough for me from the King of fair fame,
And I to be sitting for a while praying God in every place.'

With this we may compare a stanza from the ' Deer's Cry,'
better known as ' S. Patrick's Breastplate ' :—[1]

> ' I arise to-day
> Through the strength of heaven ;—
> Light of sun,
> Radiance of moon,
> Splendour of fire,
> Speed of lightning,
> Swiftness of wind,
> Depth of sea,
> Stability of earth,
> Firmness of rock. . . .

Who can deny that there must be a very real love of the natural
world as God's creation, when its forces are thus invoked alongside
the mysteries of Christ's human life, the hierarchies of the unseen
universe, the providence of God, and the abiding presence of the
Redeemer in the soul ? [2]

[1] K. Meyer, *Ancient Irish Poetry* (1913), p. 25 (p. 111—' The hymn in
the form in which it has come down to us cannot be earlier than the eighth
century ').

[2] Compare also the opening stanzas of the tenth-century dialogue between
King Gooary of Connaught, and his hermit-brother, Marvan (Meyer, *op. cit.*,
p. 47) :—

> ' I have a shieling in the wood
> None knows it save my God ;
> An ash tree on the hither side, a hazel-bush beyond,
> A huge old tree encompasses it.

> ' Two heath-clad doorposts for support,
> And a lintel of honeysuckle:
> The forest around its narrowness sheds
> Its mast upon fat swine.

> ' The size of my shieling tiny, not too tiny,
> Many are its familiar paths ;
> From its gable a sweet strain sings
> A she-bird in her cloak of the ousel's hue.'

Marvan's eulogy of his hermitage extends to twenty-four stanzas, all in this
same strain.

The case of S. Bernard of Clairvaux is specially interesting. Taken in its context his famous pleasantry which made the ' oaks and beeches ' of Clairvaux his ' only teachers in the word of God ' [1] does not betray that love of nature which Cotter Morison [2] so confidently finds there.   As the saint used the phrase he intended to convey no more than that he had learnt the salutary art of meditation even whilst engaged in manual labour in the woods.   Bernard's apology to William of S. Thierry, with his bitter attack on such masterpieces of Cluniac ornament as may still be seen in narthex, nave and cloister of Vézelay, exhibits a callousness towards art [3] with which the modern world is out of sympathy.   He could ride for a whole day along the shores of Lake Geneva, and at nightfall—so deep had he been sunk in meditation—betray complete ignorance not merely of its beauties but of its existence ; [4] at first sight this argues as complete indifference towards the beauties of nature as towards those of art.

But these phenomena must be matched with others.   There is a picturesque phrase used of Bernard by Abbot Ernald, that he retired to an ' arbour trellised with sweet peas ' [5] to compose his great sermons on the Canticles ; and the story can scarcely be an invention of that otherwise prosaic biographer.   Bernard himself, in his letter to Henry Murdach, afterwards third Abbot of Fountains and Archbishop of York, can ' scarcely restrain himself ' as he writes of the testimony which Nature bears to God :—[6]

> ' *Experto crede*, you shall find a fuller satisfaction in the woods than in books.   Trees and rocks shall teach you that which you cannot hear from masters.   Surely honey can be drawn from the stone, and oil from the hardest flint ?   Do not our mountains drop sweetness ? the hills flow with milk and honey, and the valleys stand thick with corn ? '

So Bernard revels in the old etymology which interpreted ' Nazareth ' as ' the flower ' ; and of all his many loving sayings about the humanity of Jesus none is more beautiful than this : ' To Christ, Who willed to be conceived and brought up in Nazareth, flowers are very dear.' [7]   One charming little sermon is wholly devoted to eliciting the spiritual lessons which may be derived

---

[1] *Vit.* I, lib. i, *auctore Gullielmo*, c. 4 (23) (Mab., ii, col. 2109).
[2] J. C. Morison, *S. Bernard of Clairvaux*, p. 22.
[3] Cp. G. G. Coulton, *Five Centuries of Religion*, i, p. 291.
[4] *Vit.* I, lib. iii, *auctore Gaufrido*, c. 2 (4) (Mab., ii, col. 2192).
[5] *Vit.* I, lib. ii, *auctore Ernaldo*, c. 6 (40) (Mab., ii, col. 2173).
[6] *ep.* 106 (Mab., i, col. 287).
[7] *de dilig. Deo*, 3 (8) (Mab., i, col. 1335).   It is true that Bernard uses the thought purely for allegorical purposes, but that he should use it at all is significant.   It recurs frequently—see Mabillon's index, *s.v. Nazareth*, and cp. *in annunc. B. Mariæ serm.*, iii, 7 (Mab., i, col. 2110).   The word ' Nazareth ' probably means ' watch-tower ' ; but as S. Matthew brings the ' branch ' prophecy of Is. 11[1] into close connexion with it, there is justification for the mediæval derivation (see *DCG.*, ii, p. 237, *s.v.*).

from cut flowers, garden flowers, and wild flowers in turn.[1] His meditation upon Christ as the Dayspring from on high [2] reveals that he, like Francis, is capable of a Canticle to the Sun, in which his thought passes freely to and fro between the light of nature and the Light of the world.   'The sun is up!' he cries (he is speaking of the dawn of the first Easter, but in mind, I fancy, he is once more for a moment the boy of Fontaines-les-Dijon, looking across the broad plains of Burgundy to sunrise on the Jura) :—

> 'The Sun is up! His earliest rays begin their travels across the globe; stage by stage He pours forth fuller light and greater warmth.   Yet let His heat and strength increase as much as they may,—let Him renew and multiply His rays throughout the days of this our mortal life,—. . . still shall He not shine in mid-day strength, nor be seen in the plenitude He shall at length reveal to those whom He deems worthy of the vision. O true midday! fullness of light and warmth! the Sun shall then stand firm, all shadows shall disappear, and every slough be dried, its exhalations vanquished.   O solstice unending, when night shall fall no more! O midday Light! True balm of spring, true beauty of summer, true bounty of autumn, aye, true rest and silence of winter, all in one!'[3]

II. Irenæus and Clement of Alexandria.

The men who thus rhapsodized over the glory of God's created world were at the same time champions of that life of self-mortification, whose first principle might be supposed to be the vanity of all created things.   Herein is the true paradox, not merely of monasticism, but of the gospel itself; we have seen it in its most baffling form in the life and teaching of Jesus.   It will prove instructive, therefore, to intercept the stream of Christian thought at three or four points in the period before the rise of scholasticism, and to observe the same paradox at work in different spheres—all of them, however, germane to the main problem of Christian ethics, the nature and implications of that vision of God

---

[1] *Serm.* 47, *in cantica* (Mab., i, col. 2951).

[2] *Serm.* 33, *in cantica* (Mab., i, coll. 2876 ff., especially col. 2880).

[3] Further illustrations of this Christian joy in natural beauty may be found in the writings of Ausonius and Sidonius Apollinaris (cp. S. Dill, *Roman Society in the Last Century of the Western Empire*, pp. 167, 178 f., 190, 194, 213, etc.) ; or in the anonymous Irish monk of the seventh century who wrote the *Mirabilia Sacræ Scripturæ* (Appendix to vol. iii of S. Augustine, Benedictine edition ; *MPL.*, xxxv, coll. 2149 ff.)—cp. especially i, c. 7 (reflections on the formation of islands and the problem of the presence of continental animals there, with a catalogue of Irish fauna), and iii, c. 2 (enumeration of supposed cases of parthenogenesis among animals).   Miss Scott Davison (*Forerunners of S. Francis* (1928), p. 44) refers also to the enthusiasm for the beauty of the environment of his hermitage shown by S. Bruno, founder of the Grande Chartreuse (*MPL.*, clii, col. 420).   Cp. G. Grupp, *Kulturgeschichte d. Mittelalters* [2], ii, pp. 374-378 ; iii, p. 283 (the encomium on Clairvaux).

which the testimony of centuries proclaims to be the goal of human life. We shall not expect from our authorities a reasoned synthesis—such an attempt scarcely meets us until we reach the zenith of scholasticism—but at least we shall find them unflinching before the paradox of Christianity.

Before the second century was out, S. Irenæus had crystallized the whole scheme of Christian ethics in a single epigram :—' The glory of God is a living man, and the life of man is the vision of God ';[1] for ' by that vision alone men live ; nay, by it they are made immortal.'[2] At the same time, he emphasized the paradox involved with the words, ' Though He be infinite, incomprehensible and invisible, yet has He made Himself visible, comprehensible and finite to those who believe in Him, that as they receive and see Him by faith He may give them life.'[3] It is through the Incarnation that God has thus accommodated His invisibility to the eyesight, spiritual and physical alike, of mankind ; the ' Father is that which of the Son is unseen ; the Son that of the Father which is seen.'[4] The gnostics held that beyond the god whom the prophets had seen, whose nature (and it was an evil one) was to be inferred from the visible creation, dwelt the invisible God, to Whom access was only possible for them and their illuminates.[5] Irenæus, on the other hand, maintains with the weightiest utterance that the supreme Godhead, though in essence invisible, truly manifested Itself alike in nature, in the prophets, and—last and most of all—in Jesus.[6] Anyone who maintains the contrary is trying to make himself ' wiser than the apostles '—nay, is blasphemously claiming rank as the ' Son of God ' himself, in so far as he professes to bring a new revelation from heaven.[7]

Clement of Alexandria takes up the anti-gnostic polemic.   He

---

[1] Iren., *adv. hær.*, iv, 20. 7.   [2] *Ib.*, iv, 20. 6.
[3] *Ib.*, iv, 20. 5.   [4] *Ib.*, iv, 6. 6.
[5] *Ib.*, i, 19. 2.   Christians hold, in opposition to the gnostics, that the words ' None shall see God and live ' were spoken ' of the Creator ' as much as of the Father, for the Creator *is* the Father—cp. iv, 6. 1, 4 *infra*. E. Norden, *Agnostos Theos*, pp. 65-68, notes that in the Hermetic tract *Koré Kosmou*, of which excerpts are preserved by Stobæus (Scott, *Hermetica*, i, pp. 456 ff.), the (unknown) supreme God is also the Demiurge, as in Christian thought, who chose to reveal Himself to and through Hermes (the relevant passage, Scott, i, p. 458).
[6] *Ib.*, iv, 6. 1, 4.
[7] *Ib.* On Irenæus as evidence for the text of Mt. 11²⁷, A. E. J. Rawlinson, *New Testament Doctrine of the Christ*, p. 254. Bousset, *KC.*, p. 360, has a most suggestive passage on the manner in which Irenæus' humanism (in his view) took the sting out of Pauline dualism, ' inaugurated an exegetically tempered Paulinism,' made it ' ecclesiastically employable,' ' snatched Paul from the gnostics, and so dealt gnosticism its death-blow.'   The view Bousset takes of S. Paul is, of course, perverse ; but he has beyond doubt rightly estimated the importance of Irenæus' contribution to theology.   An interesting pagan humanist contemporary with Irenæus is Galen, who says (*de us. part.*, xvii, 1)—' Among men who worship the gods there is nothing to my mind to compare with the mysteries of Eleusis or Samothrace. Yet the revelations they profess to give are mere twilight compared with the perfect clarity to be seen in Nature.'

recognizes, with Irenæus, that theologically as well as ethically all turns on the conception of what is meant by ' seeing God.' But whereas Irenæus is more interested in *that which is seen* in the beatific vision, Clement's practical mind turns rather to the *process* itself, and to the pre-conditions required by it. At first sight he appears all but a gnostic. He makes little attempt to modify the gnostic conception of a passionless God,[1] Whose very transcendence of natural distinctions makes His nature eternally unknown. He uses all the contemporary ' negative ' phrases for spiritual experience with a careless fervour which in itself is more gnostic than Christian. He borrows the terminology of the mysteries freely, and employs them in a manner only possible to one who knew himself wholly immune from the taint of paganism. ' Theoria,' ' epopteia,' ' gnosis '; initiation, deification, ' being made perfect,' —these are the current coin of his theological traffic.[2] He comes back to the ' magic mirror ' analogy with a zest to which his study of the Scriptures had lent intensity.[3] But these are superficial resemblances only; beneath the surface he is poles apart from gnosticism and its kin.

In three respects particularly does he make this manifest. He is one of the few Christian theologians, for example, to grasp that far-reaching ambiguity besetting the doctrine of the ' double standard ' or the ' two lives ' which has already been noticed; and because the ambiguity is transparent to him he elects for what, in the last lecture, we called the genuinely Christian version of the doctrine, with a whole-heartedness almost unparalleled among other writers. There are, indeed, two lives, two ways, two stages of the Christian journey. But they do not represent two categories of Christians, eternally distinct from one another—the religious and the worldling, the mystic and the uninitiated. They are simply and solely grades, or stages, on the path which all men must tread if they are to come within sight of God. There is only the one road, and all are called to walk by it. A distinction there is between the psychic and the gnostic. But it is not a distinction of vocation, code, and eternal destiny; the psychic is simply the gnostic with wings as yet unfledged.[4] Centuries of error and perversity would have

---

[1] *Supra*, p. 213, n. 1. But for the ' natural ' God cp. *Strom.*, vii, 3. 21— ' Just as tne sun illuminates not only heaven and the whole universe, blazing down upon land and sea, but sends his rays through windows and tiny chinks into the innermost recesses of our homes, so the Word, everywhere poured forth, surveys even the most trivial affairs of life.'

[2] Examples, C. Bigg, *Christian Platonists*, p. 123; G. Anrich, *Das Antike Mysterienwesen*, p. 133; C. Luthardt. *History of Christian Ethics*, (E. tr.), i, p. 142; F. J. A. Hort and J. B. Mayor, *Clement of Alexandria, Miscellanies Book vii*, pp. lv ff.

[3] *Strom.*, vii, 3. 13—' Gnostic souls greet the vision of God, no longer in a mirror or through a mirror, but clearly seen.'

[4] Bigg, *op. cit.*, pp. 119 ff.; J. Tixeront, *Histoire des Dogmes*, i, p. 273. See *Pæd.*, i, 6. 31—' It is not true that some are *gnostic* and some *psychic*, but all, as they put off the lusts of the flesh, are equal and spiritual before the Lord.' Later in the chapter he wrestles with the text, 1 Cor. 3[2], ' I fed

been avoided if the Church had listened to Clement in this matter.

Again, Clement is without doubt, as Dr. Bigg called him, the first of Christian Platonists; that is to say the first Christian philosopher—for, as I have previously suggested, if modern research has established any certainty at all, it is the certainty that Harnack was wrong in claiming this title for the gnostics. The gnostics were not philosophers, nor even sophists. Their ' gnosis ' was not discursive thought or meditation, but a short-cut to heaven by means of theosophical catchwords and thaumaturgic ecstasy. But Clement—for all that he knows and loves his moments of mystic exaltation [1]—will have a sound foundation laid for them in scholarship. The true Christian is the true philosopher. ' He loves and honours the truth,'

> ' and the beginning of [true] knowledge is " wondering at things," as Plato says in the " Theætetus." And Matthias, exhorting in the " Traditions," says, " Wonder at what is before you," laying this down first as the foundation of further knowledge. So also in the " Gospel of the Hebrews " it is written, " He that wonders shall reign, and he that reigns shall rest." It is impossible therefore for an ignorant man, while he remains ignorant, to philosophize, not having grasped the idea of wisdom. For philosophy consists in the attempt to grasp that which truly is, and in the studies which conduce thereto.' [2]

To be a true gnostic, therefore, the Christian must have a liberal education; and Clement, with a fine gesture, is pleased to sketch out his curriculum. Harmony, arithmetic, astronomy and dialectic are all part of the preparation which is to fit the Christian for the vision of God; [3] Greek philosophy shall be his recreation whenever his duties of Christian service have for the moment been discharged.[4] There is something magnificently reckless about this insistence on the need of education for the fullest experiences of Christianity. Obviously enough the doctrine as it stands is dangerously one-sided.

you with milk, not with meat,' and ingeniously makes ' meat ' refer to the nourishment of the saints in heaven. *All* Christians are ' babes in Christ.' But he admits the force of the distinction between ' spiritual ' and ' carnal ' in the preceding verse. In *Strom.*, vi, 12, 13, 14, he allows differences of reward in heaven, but insists that all men are competent to attain the highest degree—it is only voluntary indolence that deprives us of it.

[1] Cp. *Protrept.*, 11, 12—(full of mystery-terminology) ; *Strom.*, iv, 6. 39 ; v, 1. 7 ; vi, 14. 108 (note use of ἐποπτεία) ; vii, 3. 13 (all these on Mt. 5⁸ ; in v, 1. 7 he admits that full vision is not possible in this life) ; vii, 7. 35— a beautiful passage; vii, 11. 63, etc.

[2] *Strom.*, ii, 9. 45. The ' Matthias ' quotation is not otherwise attested, but the *Gospel* or *Traditions* of Matthias are several times mentioned, not only by Clement, but also by other patristic writers (M. R. James, *Apocryphal New Testament*, pp. 12, 13). The ' Hebrews ' quotation is given in a more expanded form in *Strom.*, v, 14. 96, which is repeated almost identically in *Saying I.* of the Oxyrhyncus *Sayings of Jesus* (Evelyn White, *Sayings of Jesus*, pp. 5-8—the *Sayings* were probably excerpts from the *Gospel according to the Hebrews*).

[3] *Ib.*, vi, 10. 80. [4] *Ib.*, vi, 18. 162.

It is too clear an echo of the academic pretensions of the Rabbis not to challenge immediate protest ; and the Schoolmen of S. Victor will betray the limitations inseparable from it even in its finest forms. But at least it asserted, as against the gnostics, that the labours and achievements of the human reason are matters of indifference neither to the destiny of the Christian nor to the will of his Father in heaven. To Clement as much as to any other the Church owes its recognition of the fact that between true religion and sound learning there is a very real connexion, and that intellectual honesty and earnestness are virtues in the sight of God. Narrow, scholastic and aristocratic the conception may be in some of its aspects ; but at its lowest it still asserts that blind faith is only half-faith, where considered faith is possible.

No less important than his reinterpretation of the intellectual content of true ' gnosis ' was Clement's idea of its ethical affinities. As in the one respect he substituted Platonism for Oriental theosophy, so in the other he summoned Stoicism [1] to the rescue of the ascetic element in Christianity from Oriental self-crucifixion. His ' true gnostic ' is wholly alien to gnosticism as we have learnt to understand it. It has been well said of him,[2] that ' his general aim was to moderate the antique rigour in favour of the wealthier classes.' At first sight this seems no very stern ideal ; but the wealthier classes of Alexandria must have found it stern enough. His watchword is moderation ; but it is a moderation which should lead to ' impassivity ' [3]—' the sacrifice which is acceptable to God is unswerving abstraction from the body and its passions.' [4] Martyrdom is the pattern of the Christian life. In a fine passage [5] he describes how the martyr ' goes with good courage to the Lord his friend, for Whom he gave his body (and, as his judges fondly hoped, his soul), to hear from the Saviour the rhythmic words, " Dear brother," because of the similarity of their lives.'

So, though we need not strive after actual martyrdom at the hands of tyrants, we must become ' gnostic martyrs '—' leaving our worldly kindred and wealth and every possession, in order to lead a life free from passion.' [6] Language of this kind could easily be used to champion the most extreme exhibitions of monastic asceticism. But Clement sets it so firmly in a Stoic frame that it cannot thus be interpreted. The body must be treated ' gravely and respectfully,' as a tabernacle given to the soul by God ; ' as the soul is not good by nature, so is not the body by nature bad.' [7] With Plato we are bound to say, ' For the soul's sake, care must be taken of the body ' :—[8]

---

[1] T. C. Hall, *History of Christian Ethics*, p. 149, following P. Wendland (*Quæstiones Musonianæ*, 1886), makes Musonius the source of Clement's Stoicism.

[2] C. Bigg, *op. cit.*, p. 122.

[3] *Strom.*, vii, 3. 13—likeness to God consists in *apatheia*.

[4] *Ib.*, v, 11. 67.

[5] *Ib.*, iv, 4. 14.

[6] *Ib.*, with reference to Mt. 19²⁹.

[7] *Ib.*, iv, 26. 164, 165.

[8] *Ib.*, iv, 4. 18.

'Those then who decry created existence, and vilify the body, are wrong.   They see not that the frame of man was created erect for the contemplation of heaven ; that the harmony of the senses tends to ' gnosis ' ; that the members and parts are constituted, though not for pleasure, most certainly for good.' [1]

If this is Stoicism, then Clement has embraced it because it is nearer to the gospel than that fanatical rigorism with which the Church was so hardly pressed.

That Clement's Stoicism had no other purpose than this becomes transcendently clear when we observe how far he overpassed it in his positive ethical scheme.   Here active love and service at once summarize the four cardinal virtues of Greek philosophy, and transmute them into something wholly Christian.   A contemplation of God which does not issue in love, ' beaming forth from light to light,' is only ' gnosis ' in imperfection ; ' for it is said, " To him that hath shall be given "—to faith " gnosis," to " gnosis " love, to love the inheritance.' [2]   So Clement finds the most compendious description of the Christian gnostic in the 24th Psalm :—' Who shall ascend into the hill of the Lord, or who shall rise up in His holy place ?   Even he that hath clean hands and a pure heart ; and that hath not lift up his mind unto vanity, nor sworn to deceive his neighbour.' [3]   But to blamelessness we must add active benevolence :—

' The gnostic relieves the afflicted, helping them with consolations, encouragement and the necessities of life ; giving to all that need, not indiscriminately but with due consideration— aye, imparting even to those who persecute and hate him, if they require it ; and laughing aloud if it is said that he has given out of fear, if not fear but the desire to help has made him give.' [4]

Nor is his ministry one of temporal succour alone.   He does indeed impoverish himself that he may always help a brother in affliction, and all the more because he knows that he can bear want easier than his brother.   But in another sense ' he fills the vacant place of the apostles, by rectitude of life, by clearness of spiritual intuition, by benefiting those around him, by removing the mountains of his neighbours, by making straight the crooked places of their souls.' [5]   ' He prays that he may bear the sins of his brethren, that they may repent and be converted ; he is eager to give a share of all that is dearest to him to those around him.' [6]   How far Clement has really advanced beyond pagan models may be seen by a single last quotation on this head.   ' The first purification,' he says (he is using the language of the mysteries), ' is abstinence from evil things, which some consider perfection—as indeed it is with the

[1] *Strom.*, iv, 26. 163.   [2] *Ib.*, vii, 10. 55.
[3] *Ib.*, vii, 10. 58 , Ps. 24³⁻⁸.   [4] *Ib.*, vii, 12. 69.
[5] *Ib.*, vii, 12. 77.   [6] *Ib.*, vii, 12. 80.

common believer, Jew and Greek.' But what is the second stage of initiation, the 'higher mystery'? 'Ecstatic absorption in the Godhead,' say the gnostics. 'Complete apathy' is the Stoic answer. Clement will have neither of these: 'With the true gnostic, after he has attained that which is reckoned perfection in others, righteousness advances'—not to ecstasy, not to apathy, but—'to activity in well-doing.'[1]

Two further points in Clement's teaching deserve notice, though we cannot spend more than a moment upon each. More than any other writer of his day he shared in that ingrained tendency of S. Paul and S. John to see the promises of God already fulfilled in the present. Life is still for him a sojourning and a pilgrimage; we are still imprisoned in the flesh. But the bonds are so far loosed that the true gnostic can be spoken of (in another dangerous metaphor borrowed from paganism) as already deified; he walks as a god upon earth.[2] It is this certainty of intimate present communion with God which makes Clement the sunniest of Christian philosophers; but it has a further and more important effect. Clement has a code of Christian behaviour to put before the leisured lads and girls of the Alexandrian Church; a detailed code which in other hands might have become a purely formalist convention. But though it often verges upon a mere routine of good-mannered etiquette, it is never Pharisaic—the stress is always on the spirit rather than on the letter. The reason is clear. Clement is so full of the thought of present possession that he has little attention to spare for the doctrine of future reward;[3] and where the doctrine of reward is absent formalism, as we have seen, has only a barren soil to grow in.

The second point is less evident. Clement's gnostic is to all appearance an isolated individual, with little need for the support given by membership in a Church. He is, in addition, a superior person, independent of the authority of the Church, and ignorant of any obligation to submit his ideals and activities to its control. He has in him, it might be said at first sight, all the makings of heresy, though he is no heretic himself. But this is a misconception of the truth. Clement is as loyal a Churchman as any other. He has a real sense of the function of a divine society, and a real joy in his membership thereof,—a real longing for its consummation.

---

[1] *Strom.*, vi, 7. 60.

[2] *Ib.*, iv, 23. 149; cp. vii,. 1. 3; 10. 57; 16. 95, 101. On the idea of deification generally, *supra*, p. 52; and on the possibility that language of this kind would not endanger theism very seriously, Harnack, *Hist. of Dogma*, i, pp. 119-121. Later history of the idea, *ib.*, iii, pp. 164, 165.

[3] In *Strom.*, iv, 22, Clement puts the problem of disinterestedness in its most famous and most extreme form :—If the gnostic had to choose between 'knowledge of God' and 'attainment of salvation,' which would he choose? The answer is unhesitatingly the former; and from this Clement concludes that the true Christian is he who does good (ἀγαθὸν ποιεῖν—notice how the active ethical interest dominates the discussion) for its own sake without thought either of reward or punishment. For the question, cp. Fénelon, *infra*, p. 459.

In this also he is true to the regulative principles with which the apostolic writers surrounded the thought of the vision of God. I quote one passage only, and that not merely for Clement's sake, but because it looks forward to another Christian Platonist far greater than himself. 'I pray the Spirit of Christ,' he writes,

> 'to wing me to my Jerusalem. For the Stoics say that heaven is properly a city, though places here on earth are not—the latter are called cities, but are none. For a city is an important thing, and its people a decorous body, a multitude of men regulated by law, as the Church (that city on earth impregnable, invulnerable) is ruled by the Word, a product of the divine will on earth as in heaven. Images of this city the poets create with their pens;—the Hyperboreans, the Arimaspian cities, the Elysian plains, are commonwealths of just men. And we all know Plato's city, laid up as a pattern in heaven.' [1]

III. S. AUGUSTINE.

(a) Neo-Platonic influences.

This thought of the city of God leads on inevitably to S. Augustine, who apprehended far more clearly than did Clement that 'the life of the saints is a social one.' [2] Augustine, like Clement, was a Platonist ; indeed, he never ceased to proclaim that it was through the gate of Platonism that he entered the Christian Church. He had long felt a distaste towards the 'vanities' of which he accuses himself in the 'Confessions'—his licentious desires and indulgences ;—his courtship of influential friends, who might find him a 'prefectship';—his search for a rich wife who would not prove a financial responsibility; [3]—his craving for respite from the stress of teaching. [4] He knew of many men, 'great and worthy of imitation,' who 'applied themselves to the study of wisdom in the married state.' [5] But this way, he was convinced, was not the way for him. Why then did he hesitate to turn to the Lord ? His answer is clear. Once he had abandoned his Manichæan errors, he became enmeshed in his horror in the scepticism of the Academy. [6] 'O ye great men, ye Academics,' he cries, 'is it then true that nothing certain for the ordering of life can be attained ? ' [7] Prepared though he was to be counted as a catechumen, [8] he would go no further; 'lest he should come to believe falsehoods,'

---

[1] *Strom.*, iv, 26, *fin.*   [2] *de civ. Dei*, xix, 5.   [3] *Conf.*, vi, 11 (19).
[4] *Ib.* (18).   [5] *Ib.* (19).   [6] *Ib.*, v, 10 (19).
[7] *Ib.*, vi, 11 (18). J. F. Nourrison, *I a Philosophie de Saint Augustin*, ii, pp. 291 ff., puts Augustine's state of mind well :—' In his passion for truth he was never able to drug himself with irony, nor to sink into the slumber of indifference, after the manner of the sceptics. . . . Descartes made of doubt a useful method of enquiry ; to Augustine it was always an intolerable agony.'
[8] *Ib.*, v, 14 (25).

he refused to believe anything at all.[1] He required certainty before he changed his way of life ; he was ready *when he had found wisdom* —but not before—to forsake what he already regarded as empty hopes, lying insanities, and vain desires.[2]

Certainty came to him—a modified certainty [3]—in his first contact with neo-Platonism.[4] Partly, of course, he was moved by the quiet yet firm assurance with which the ' works of the Platonists ' advanced their creed—so different from the flamboyant methods of the Manichees, who ' mocked credulity by the audacious promise of knowledge, and forced upon belief (for they were incapable of demonstration) countless matters at once fabulous and absurd.' [5] Philosophically, the doctrine of the divine Word—not indeed ' made flesh,' [6] nor humbled and obedient to death, but at least as unchangeable, coexistent with His Father, and pouring His fullness into all things—provided him with a decisive weapon against Manichæan dualism.[7] Far more important, however, as an influence in conferring certitude, was the neo-Platonic doctrine of the vision of God, and the way to attain it :—

' I was warned by them to return to myself ; so I entered into my inmost soul under Thy guidance—Thy help enabled me to do so. I entered, and with the eye of my soul (dim though it was) I saw above that eye of my soul, above my mind, the Light unchangeable. Not this common light which we all gaze upon, nor yet a greater light of the same kind . . . not like this was that Light, but different, yea, greatly different, from these . . . He who knows the Truth knows that Light ; and he that knows It knows eternity.' [8]

The experience dispelled for a moment his Academic scruples. ' I heard,' he says, ' as things are heard in the heart ; and room for doubt there was none. I could more readily doubt that I live than believe that the Truth is not—for it is clearly seen, being known by

---

[1] *Conf.*, vi, 4 (6).   [2] *Ib.*, vi, 11 (18, 19), *ut sup.*

[3] Hence the Cassiciacine writings are still full of scepticism, though written after the ' conversion ' had taken place. See W. Thimme, *Augustins geistige Entwickelung*, pp. 17, 18, for further references; and *ib.*, pp. 4, 5, where he cleverly draws attention to Harnack's self-contradictions on the point. Augustine discovered his dissatisfaction with neo-Platonism at all events by A.D. 390 or so (four years after his first contact with it)—*de ver. rel.* 2 (2)—' suavius ad legendum quam potentius ad persuadendum scripsit Plato.' It is perhaps true to say (V. Stegemann, *Augustins Gottesstaat*, p. 65) that he never reached the same degree of certainty as did S. Paul.

[4] *de beat. vit.*, 4—' lectis autem Platonis paucissimis libris '—but five MSS. read ' Plotini,' and this is almost certainly right. Cp. *Conf.*, vii, 9 (13), 20 (26). In vii, 9 (16) he says he read them in a Latin translation—obviously that of Victorinus (*ib.*, viii, 2 (3)).

[5] *Conf.*, vi, 5 (7).   [6] *Ib.*, vii, 9 (14).

[7] The problem of evil occupies the earlier part of *Conf.*, vii ; the neo-Platonic teaching leads up to the solution (evil a perversion of the will) in vii, 16 (22).

[8] *Conf.*, vii, 10 (16). He proceeds ' Love (alone) knows it '—' Caritas novit eam. O æterna veritas, et vera caritas, et cara æternitas—Tu es Deus meus.'

the things that are made.'[1] 'With a flash of a trembling glance, I arrived at Him who Is.'[2] And yet he was not satisfied—the experience was too transitory and precarious :—

'I did not press on to enjoy Thee ; and so—though Thy Beauty caught me to Thee—I was anon torn away from Thee by mine own weight, and fell back with sorrow to a lower sphere. That weight was carnal custom. Yet Thou didst live on still in memory : and I never doubted that there was One to Whom I might cleave, though I was not yet such as to cleave to Him. . . . I could not keep my gaze fixed on Thee. My weakness drew me back, and I was cast back upon my accustomed ways of life, bearing with me naught but a loving memory.'[3]

This neo-Platonic ecstasy, then,—an experience which gave him as his motto for life the words ' It is good for me to cleave to God '[4]— was a foretaste for Augustine of the enraptured certitude of Christian communion with God. But the former could be sublimated into the latter only for a soul more fully turned away from ' carnal custom ' than his. Such conversion of soul neo-Platonism could not give him ; it provided ' the goal, but not the path.'[5] It is not easy to unravel the stages by which Augustine passed from Platonism to Christianity, but it cannot be doubted that he intended the great scene of the ecstasy at Ostia to crown the story, and to give an impression of the greater and enduring certitude conferred upon him, once he had become a Christian, as contrasted with this transient experience of his Platonic days. So much at least is clear from the sublime dignity with which he records the event :—[6]

---

[1] *Conf.*, vii, 10 (16).

[2] *Ib.*, 17 (23)—' in ictu trepidantis aspectus.' Other phrases used by Augustine of the supreme mystical experience are ' rapi in Deum ' (*de op. mon.*, 25 (32)), ' rapi in Deum sicut solet in vehementiori ecstasi ' (*ep.* 147. 13 (31)) ; ' subvehi, volitare ad amplexum Dei ' (*de mor. eccl. cath.*, i, 22 (41)) ; ' contemplatio pulchritudinis Dei ' (*ib.*, i, 31 (66))—cp. Reuter, *Augustinische Studien*, pp. 472-474.

[3] *Ib.*, vii, 17 (23).

[4] *de mor. eccl. cath.*, i, 16 (26) ; *ep.* 155. 3 (12), etc., from Ps. 73²⁸. Harnack, *Hist. of Dogma*, v, p. 62, rightly makes the phrase the centre of all Augustine's thought.

[5] *Conf.*, vii, 20 (26).

[6] *Ib.*, ix, 10 (24 ff.). I have rearranged the passage to exhibit the sequence of thought. The reminiscences of Plotinus are clearer in this passage than at any other point in Augustine's writings. See Gibbs and Montgomery, *Confessions of St. Augustine, ad loc.* ; L. Grandgeorge, *St. Augustin et le Néo-Platonisme, pass.* ; P. Aifaric, *L'Évolution Intellectuelle de St. Augustin*, i, p. 376 (references for parallels) ; W. R. Inge, *Plotinus*, i. p. 206 (*Enn.*, v, 1, in translation). On the comparison between Augustine and Plotinus, with particular reference to their mystical outlook, contrast C. Butler, *Western Mysticism*, pp. 56-70, with V. Stegemann, *op. cit.*, pp. 7, 8. Butler, by putting the question ' Mysticism or Platonism ?,' and answering it ' S. Augustine's contemplations . . . were as fully religious experiences as the highest . . . of the great Christian mystics,' suggests that Augustine is more religious and less intellectualist than Plotinus (cp. also pp. 58, 59, ' the higher operations of the intellect,' ' the cold metaphysical formula ') ;

(25) ' We were saying, then, " Suppose that to any man the tumult of the flesh were silenced—silenced the phantasies of the earth, water and air—silenced, too, the poles ;—yea, the very soul silenced to herself, and gone beyond herself in utter self-forgetfulness ;—silenced fancies and imaginary revelations, every tongue and every sign and whatsoever exists by passing away. [Why should they not be silenced,] since, if any could hearken, they all say, ' We created not ourselves, but were created by Him Who abideth for ever? '—Suppose then that they should now be silenced, having by these words quickened our ears towards Him Who made them; and that thereafter *He* should speak, not by them but by Himself alone, and we should hear Him (Whom in these we love), not by fleshly tongue nor by angelic voice, nor sound of thunder, nor the obscurity of symbols, but without any of these " (as we two now strained ourselves and with rapid thought touched on that eternal Wisdom which remaineth over all). " Why, then," we cried, " if all this could be sustained, and all other visions of far lower kinds be withheld, whilst this one ravished and absorbed and enveloped its beholder amid these inward joys, so that his whole life might be as that one moment of knowledge for which we sighed—would not this be, ' Enter thou into the joy of the Lord'?   When shall it be ? " we cried—" When we all rise again, perchance ? . . . "

(26) ' While we were talking thus, . . . the world with all its delights grew contemptible to us, even as we spake. . . . (24) For as our dialogue reached that point, the very highest pleasures of the bodily senses, though bathed in material light, seemed by reason of the sweetness of that life not merely inconsiderable, but even unworthy so much as of mention.   And with yet more eager longing we rose towards the Self-same.   Little by little we passed beyond all temporal things—beyond the heaven itself, whence sun, moon and stars shine down upon the earth. Aye, further still we soared in this spiritual contemplation and discourse and wonder at Thy works, till we came to our very selves ; and beyond them we passed to reach that region of unfailing plenty, where with the food of truth Thou feedest

---

Stegemann takes the opposite view. W. R. Inge (*op. cit.*, ii, pp. 204-206) utters a warning against overemphasizing the ' intellectualism ' of Plotinus. F. Heiler, *Der Katholizismus*, p. 105, makes Plotinus the more ecstatic of the two.   The real difference seems to lie (*a*) in Augustine's sense of personality, which never allowed him to commit himself to language implying the absorption of the believer in the Godhead ; (*b*) in the fact that although he accepted ' the psychological methods ' (and, we may add, many of the philosophical presuppositions) ' of neo-Platonism . . . these methods are perpetually sweetened and invigorated by the Christian elements of personal love and eager outgoing desire ' (E. Underhill, *The Mystic Way*, p. 298). That the neo-Platonist experienced true communion with God no one is concerned to deny ; but his tendency to suppress emotion and to elevate metaphysics led him to speak of his highest experiences in terms which appeared to rob them of the warmth of personal communion.

Israel for ever, and where life is that Wisdom by Whom all these things are made. . . . And while we thus spake and yearned for her, we slightly touched her with the whole effort of our hearts ; and we sighed and there left bound the firstfruits of the Spirit, and then came back again to the sound of our own voices, where words uttered have both beginning and end. But what is like Thy Word, our Saviour, Who in Himself remains, Who waxeth not old, but maketh all things new ? . . .

(26) ' Then spake my mother :—" Son, for myself I have no further pleasure in this present life. My hopes in this world are satisfied ; and what I need here more, and why I am here, I know not. One thing, indeed, I asked that I might tarry for—to see thee a Catholic ere I died. God has granted me this, and far more beside ; I see thee despising all earthly happiness, —become His bondservant at last. What then do I here ? " '

No one can read the passage without recognizing its significance. Augustine (with Monnica at his side) has at last found the God Who made him for Himself, and for Whom his heart was ever restless till that moment came.[1] He has no longer to wait for fitful moments of illumination, but can with faith and certainty—as in the exordium and in the peroration of the ' Confessions '—call upon God to come ' into himself.' [2]

Between the earlier ecstasies and this final one, Augustine sets a series of outward events to mark the stages in his progress towards Christianity. First comes the conversation with Simplician,[3] with its story of Victorinus and his sacrifice ; then his discovery of the fascinations of monasticism, under the guidance of Pontitian ; [4] the voice in the garden is the climax.[5] Augustine and Alypius make their way to Monnica, and tell her—What ? Apparently that Augustine has finally decided to live the celibate life [6]—the thought underlies the whole development of the eighth book of the ' Confessions,' and no other decision is indicated. We must not (as some authorities do) [7] under-estimate the moral value of this ' conversion,' nor mistake its tenour. No more than any other of the great

[1] Conf., i, 1 (1).
[2] Ib., i, 2 (2)—' in me ipsum Eum vocabo cum invocabo Eum ' ; xiii, 1 (1)—' invoco Te in animam meam.'
[3] Ib., viii, 1 ff.   [4] Ib., viii, 6 (14, 15).   [5] Ib., 12 (29).
[6] Thus ib., 7 (17)—of his prayer from the earliest years up to the moment of conversion—' Give me chastity, but not yet ' ; 11 (25-27)—just before the voice in the garden, the final conflict between the desire for chastity and fleshly temptation ; 12 (34)—after the interview with Monnica—' Thou didst convert me to Thee, that I should not " seek a wife " ' ; cp. Soll., i, 10 (17)— ' For my soul's freedom I have decided not to desire, nor seek, nor marry, a wife.'
[7] So Thimme, op. cit., p. 12 ; Loofs, PRE.³, ii, p. 260—' We are scarcely entitled to speak of Augustine's " wild and dissolute life " ' (' von wildem Lebenstaumel ist kaum je zu reden '), ' at all events he passed out of the short period of indiscretion (" Leichtsinn "), which is all that deserves this stigma, at an age at which our boys are still at school.' Alfaric's minimizing of this moral conversion is particularly unconvincing (op. cit., pp. 392, 393'

Christians of his day did Augustine regard marriage as sinful in the eyes of God, though he never hesitated to set it on a lower plane than celibacy. But—though his sense of honour made it impossible for him to be faithless to a consort, whether mistress or wife [1]—it is clear that sexual indulgence was his besetting temptation, and that he regarded marriage for himself as little more than an opportunity for yielding to it without scandal.[2] The decision against matrimony was therefore for Augustine no mere tribute to conventional ascetic idealism.[3] It was the only way in which he (being what he was) could win victory over the lusts of the flesh ; and the struggle, in its varying forms, had been a long and stern one. Augustine certainly intends us to infer that, without this moral surrender to the divine will, full certitude, mystical and intellectual alike, could never have come to him.

The retreat at Cassiciacum [4] is the next event in the series. To the bishop of Hippo, writing his ' Confessions ' after a lapse of some fourteen years, it must have played the same part as S. Paul's retirement to Arabia.[5] About this time, too, came the decision to resign his professorship of rhetoric.[6] Augustine puts the decision *before* the retreat ; but fails to explain why he did not notify the authorities the moment term was over and he had retired to the country.[7] At Cassiciacum, Augustine says, he was occupied with meditation of the Psalms,[8] and the stress he lays upon the fact suggests that it played a definite part in that conversion of the mind to which reference will be made in a moment. He was in correspondence with Ambrose, but did not find the great bishop's suggestion that he should busy himself with the Book of Isaiah at all congenial.[9]

---

[1] *Conf.*, iv, 2 (2)—of his fidelity to his first mistress.

[2] *Ib.*, vi, 12 (22)—neither he himself nor Alypius recognized anything honourable in marriage as such ; on the contrary, Augustine told Alypius that apart from its ' honourable *name* ' it was merely sustained libertinism. —Monnica evidently took the same point of view. She seems to have acquiesced in the first irregular association with Adeodatus' mother, as a possible defence against worse temptations (*Conf.*, ii, 3 (7)) ; and definitely did not urge him to marriage, as it might interfere with his career (*ib.* (8)) ; cp. ii, 2 (3) (4)—he might have been ' saved from ruin by marriage '. Later (vi, 13 (23)) she takes an active part in urging forward his marriage. It is surprising therefore that she receives the news of his dedication to celibacy so joyfully ; it must mean that although she regarded marriage (with a suitable person) as better than concubinage, and concubinage than unbridled licence, she felt that for Augustine at all events even marriage was a mere excuse for self-indulgence.

[3] O. Scheel, *Die Anschauung Augustins über Christi Person u. Werk*, p. 9—' a conversion to monasticism ' ; Alfaric, *op. cit.*, p. 391—' a simple acceptance of the Christian ideal.'

[4] *Conf.*, ix, 3 (5).

[5] So K. Holl, *Augustins innere Entwickelung (Abh. Berl. Ak. d. Wiss.* (1922), phil.-hist. kl. 4), p. 33.

[6] *Conf.*, ix, 2 (2).

[7] Actually he sent his resignation in some three months later—at the *end* of the vacation, *ib.*, ix, 5 (13,.

[8] *Ib.*, ix, 4 (8).   [9] *Ib.*, ix, 5 (13).

The rest of the story Augustine tells quickly. Somewhere in the following spring he returned with Alypius and Adeodatus to Milan, and the three were baptized at Easter.[1] He notes especially the inspiration he drew from the church services in the cathedral city,[2] and hurries [3] on to his account of the final revelation at Ostia (comparable no doubt, in his mind, with S. Paul's vision in the temple) and his mother's death. With these events the strictly biographical part of the 'Confessions' ends; the story of the conversion is told.

The difficulties of the account are well known. S. Augustine's is the only 'conversion,' other than that of S. Paul, to which the Church has assigned a definite day of observance;[4] but modern writers suggest that we have no right to think of it as a distinct event at all.[5] The 'Confessions' themselves suggest that the retirement to Cassiciacum and the resignation of the chair of rhetoric were inspired, in part at least, by ill-health.[6] The 'retreat,' considered in the light of Augustine's letters and writings of the actual period, was more of a quiet reading-party devoted to philosophical discussions,[7] and varied by country walks and estates business,[8] than the 'Confessions' in any way allow. The Cassiciacine writings reveal the saint as still a sceptic and seeker at heart; [9] the 'conversion' in the garden is mentioned, but its result is summarized in the astounding words, 'So then Philosophy appeared to me so great, so beautiful, that even your worst enemy [10] must at the view have renounced his pleasures, one and all, and thrown himself into her arms.' [11] Even after the 'retreat' Augustine can write a description

---

[1] *Conf.*, ix, 6 (14).   [2] *Ib.*, 7 (15).   [3] *Ib.*, 8 (17).

[4] Boll., *Act. Sanct.*, 28th Aug. (Aug., vi, p. 233); recalled by G. Boissier, *La Fin du Paganisme*, i, p. 291. The 'Conversion of S. Augustine' occurs in the Roman martyrology for May 5th.

[5] See Thimme, Scheel, Alfaric, quoted above.

[6] *Conf.*, ix, 2 (4). *c. Acad.*, i, 1 (3), *de ord.*, i, 2 (5) put the resignation down wholly to the illness, though *de ord.* suggests (*loc. cit.*) that Augustine was thinking of it anyhow.

[7] These discussions are of course embodied in the books written at the time—*contra Acad., de ord., de beat. vit.* (The *Soliloquies* belong to the same period, but, as their title suggests, are of a different genre.) Boissier quite fairly points out, however, that the discussions are not altogether untouched by Augustine's conversion: 'they all lead to Christianity—with a little goodwill we can always descry it in the distance, at the end of every avenue; but we must admit that at first sight it is invisible' (*op. cit.*, pp. 320, 321).

[8] *contr. Acad.*, i, 5 (15); ii, 4 (10); ii, 11 (25).

[9] The passages convincingly collected by Thimme, *op. cit.*, p. 18; cp. Alfaric, p. 382.

[10] A reference to the lawsuit by which the life of his patron and correspondent, Romanianus, was embittered. Boissier entirely mistakes the point, and translates 'l'ennemi le plus résolu de la sagesse' (*op. cit.*, p. 322).

[11] *contr. Acad.*, ii, 2 (6). I follow Boissier (p. 322), with some slight hesitation, in taking the 'titubans, properans, hæsitans, arripio apostolum Paulum' (which immediately precedes the passage quoted) of the 'Tolle, lege' incident, and so equating this passage with the conversion in the garden as a whole. Boissier, although like Bevan (*Hellenism and Christianity*, pp. 142-144) he attempts to mitigate the discrepancies between the 'Confessions' and the Cassiciacine writings, rightly avoids the temptation of giving 'philosophy' here the meaning of 'asceticism.'

of self-training for the vision of God in wholly Platonic terms, with scarcely a sign of Christian influence ; [1] and during the retreat itself he showed himself very uncertain as to the reality of his conversion.[2]   A more difficult problem still is presented by the fact that he describes the ecstasy at Ostia in neo-Platonic terms, more reminiscent of Plotinus even than the account of his earlier ecstasies.   Even if he were still (as is sometimes suggested) a neo-Platonist in all but externals at Ostia, we should have expected his account of the event, written at the height of his ministry (c. A.D. 400), to have been dressed in Christian language, especially as he frankly disclaims any intention of reproducing the exact words of the dialogue.[3]

Has S. Augustine, then, ante-dated his conversion, or compressed into the fictitious dramatic crisis of a few months what actually was a slow and continuous process ?   The problem may be looked at from a different angle.   In the ' Confessions ' Augustine has related a threefold conversion, but although he has suggested, he has never clearly exhibited the interconnexion, either temporal or spiritual, between its parts.   There is the *mystical* conversion— from the partial and transient experiences of the neo-Platonist to the full and enduring communion of the Christian with God—this last typified by the account of the ecstasy at Ostia, for all its Plotinian vocabulary.   There is the *moral* conversion, of which the central factor is that it was a victory—and a decisive victory—over the temptations of the flesh ; [4] though we learn incidentally that in renouncing his bride Augustine renounced a rich alliance,[5] and that his rigorist leanings were so pronounced as at one time to suggest the plan of retirement to the desert.[6]   But alongside both the mystical and the moral conversion, and bound up with them, there went an *intellectual* conversion as well.   Augustine tells us little

---

[1] In the *de quant. animœ*, 33 (70) ff.   The whole passage, which is of extreme importance, is conveniently summarized by C. Butler, *Western Mysticism*, p. 37.   The treatise was written at Rome, A.D. 387-388, perhaps even after the ecstasy at Ostia and his mother's death (Thimme, *op. cit.*, p. 8,.

[2] *Supra*, p. 325, n. 9.

[3] *Conf.*, ix, 10 (26).   It is important to notice that if, as a mature Christian, Augustine could write in so neo-Platonic a manner of the greatest moment in his life, it detracts a little from the arguments for the immaturity of his Christianity at Cassiciacum.   On the other hand, it emphasizes to the full the survival of neo-Platonic enthusiasm even into his ripest period. Unfortunately, as Harnack has observed (*Hist. Dogma*, v, p. 111) he rarely referred to matters of this kind at length after the writing of the ' Confessions ' : so we cannot guess whether he would have given them a more distinctively Christian expression.   See also H. Reuter, *Augustinische Studien*, pp. 471, 472.

[4] *Supra*, p. 324.

[5] *Supra*, p. 319, n. 3, and cp. *Soll.*, i, 10 (17).

[6] *Conf.*, x, 43 (70)—a very different plan from the abortive ' Little Gidding ' proposal of vi, 14 (24).   Augustine accepted at its fullest the contemporary estimate of the monastic life ; see especially H. Reuter, *Augustinische Studien*, pp. 398-447 ; C. Luthardt, *History of Christian Ethics*, pp. 228-231.

of its stages, and gives no hint as to the moment at which it reached
completion, and without this information, which he alone could
give, we are debarred for ever from attempting a full psychological
reconstruction of the conversion.   But he certainly seems to imply
that his whole attitude towards the person of Jesus changed profoundly during the spiritual process recorded in the ' Confessions,'
and that the change was bound up with the mystical and moral
experiences in close causal relationship.[1]

It was the failure to sustain the high neo-Platonic experience of
the vision of God which first turned Augustine's mind seriously to
the person of Christ—a failure due, as he fully recognized, to his
weakness in the face of sensual temptations.   ' I sought a way of
acquiring strength sufficient to enjoy Thee,' he writes, ' but I found
it not till I embraced that mediator between God and man, the
man Christ Jesus, who is over all, God blessed for ever.'[2]   At first,
however, he thought of Him as ' homo dominicus ' alone[3]—no more
than a ' perfect man,' ' a man of excellent wisdom,' ' an example
of despising temporal things for the attainment of immortality.'[4]
Even this fragmentary apprehension of the truth turned him from
one who ' knew whither he would go, but knew not the way ' into
' one who knew the way to the blessed country.'[5]   But the advance
thus made was only partial.   Augustine notes that it did not provide the moral stimulus needed for complete detachment.   ' All
my bones cried out that I should enter into God's will and covenant,
yet entered I not in ';[6] ' Ecce modo fiat, modo fiat—" Do it now "—
urged conscience; and I all but obeyed, yet still held back a little;'[7]
' the way, the Saviour Himself, attracted me, but I could not endure
its straitness.'[8]   It is hard to resist the tempting supposition that
a realization of the full divinity of our Lord must at least have
accompanied Augustine's moral surrender to the will of God, even
if it did not actually condition it ; and in any case must surely
have preceded the illumination at Ostia.   But the evidence is on
the whole unfavourable.   The ' Confessions ' indeed insist that the
recognition of the Incarnation is the coping-stone which completes
the Christian edifice :—[9]

[1] Harnack (*Augustins Konfessionen*, in *Reden u. Aufsätze*, i, p. 74) emphasizes the ' wonderful interconnexion,' in Augustine's development, of
' neo-Platonism, the growing impression made by the person of Christ, the
reading of the Pauline Epistles which corroborated that impression, the
controlling authority of the Church,' and brings the moral conversion into
close relationship with these other motifs.
[2] *Conf.*, vii, 18 (24).   Note the combination of 1 Tim. 2⁵ with Rom. 9⁵.
[3] *de serm. dom.*, ii, 6 (20).   In *Retract.*, i, 19. 8, he deprecates his use of
the term, saying that he borrowed it carelessly from Greek theologians (cp.
Loofs, *Leitfaden*, pp. 274, 286).
[4] *Conf.*, vii, 19 (25).   [5] *Ib.*, vii, 20 (26).
[6] *Ib.*, viii, 8 (19).
[7] *Ib.*, viii, 11 (25) ; *supra*, p. 323, n. 6.   [8] *Ib.*, viii, 1 (1).
[9] *Conf.*, x, 43 (69, 70).   Loofs (*Leitfaden*, pp. 405, 406 ; cp. 359) is inclined
to minimize Augustine's emphasis upon the thought of redemption from sin
through the Atonement.   Thimme (*op. cit.*, p. 21) says, in the same reference,
' the person of Jesus never had the same importance for Augustine as it

'We might think that Thy Word was removed from man, and despair of ourselves, had He not been made flesh and dwelt among us. . . . Thine only Son, in Whom are hid all the treasures of wisdom and knowledge, hath redeemed me with His Blood. . . . I consider my ransom, and eat and drink and distribute: in my poverty, I desire to be satisfied from Him, with those who eat and are satisfied, and they praise the Lord that seek Him.'

Despite this testimony, however, and contrary to all natural expectations, the 'Confessions' do not say explicitly that their author reached his conviction of the full divinity of the Incarnate Christ during the period to which they refer. We can only conclude that this *intellectual* conversion took place later than the other two— later, even, than the illumination at Ostia. This solution explains the curious vagueness of the 'Confessions' on the point. It explains also the hesitations and doubts of the Cassiciacine writings to which we have already referred. And it is fully borne out by the actual references to Christ in those writings. At that early date Augustine did not hesitate to assert either the divinity of Christ or the humanity of Jesus. But his language sounds almost as though he were speaking of two persons, not of one.[1] His 'Christ' is the neo-Platonic 'Son of God' or 'Word';[2] his Jesus is 'a true man,'[3] to Whom we look primarily as an authoritative exemplar of the mystic way[4]—Who 'inflames our minds by His actions as by His

had for Paul or Luther.' It is probably true that the 'evangelical' doctrine of redemption is not one of the 'three great circles of ideas' (Harnack, *Hist. Dogma*, v, p. 4) within whose system Augustine's thought for the most part moves. But this is the accident of history. The controversies in which he was engaged did not concern the *source* of grace, so much as its *sphere* (Donatism) and *mode of operation* (Pelagianism)—and there are ample incidental allusions to show that, if his thought had been turned (as S. Paul's and Luther's were) by practical requirements in this other direction, he would have been both emphatic and illuminating on the atoning death of Christ.

[1] On the affinities (and differences) between Nestorianism and the traditional western Christology, see Harnack, *Hist. of Dogma*, iv, pp. 183-185.

[2] This seems fully established by the arguments and citations of Scheel, *op. cit.*, pp. 27-40; cp. *ib.*, 58, 59.

[3] 'verus homo,' *de ver. rel.*, 16 (30). I am inclined to agree with Scheel (p. 46) that 'in this period (i.e. the Cassiciacine writings), although Augustine held firmly to the true humanity of Christ, the centre of his thought was the Logos-doctrine'; but it is absurd to call this (*ib.*, p. 59) 'an alien conception —religious indeed, but not of the Christian religion,' to which the title 'Christ' is attached as a mere label. Augustine may have *reached* it through neo-Platonism, but his joy at finding the neo-Platonic conception confirmed by the Scriptures was not based upon any mistake.

[4] *de ver. rel.*, 16 (32); 55 (110)—the life of Christ a 'disciplina morum'; *Quæstiones lxxxiii*, 44—the imitation of Christ. Scheel as usual exaggerates (p. 65) in representing this as merely neo-Platonic; Augustine's emphasis, even in this early period, upon the *humility* of Christ as the essential feature in His life to be imitated, is Christian through and through. Cp. *de ver. rel.*, 27 (50); *de ord.*, ii, 9 (27); *Conf.*, vii, 18 (24), with Harnack's fine exposition, *Hist. of Dogma*, v, pp. 131-133, and J. Mausbach, *Die Ethik des hlg. Aug.*, i, pp. 391-394.

words, that they may turn back upon themselves, and look to their Fatherland.'[1] Little importance is attached to the death of Christ except as an example of heroic endurance ;[2] none to the Resurrection ;[3] the Incarnation is spoken of in terms which remind us more of Nestorius than of Catholicism.[4]

The inference is clear.[5] Intellectually at least Augustine was more of a neo-Platonist and less of a Christian, at the date of his baptism and his mother's death, than his reminiscences care to allow. The neo-Platonic influence was slow to lose its grip. The fact is of extreme significance. The danger of Platonism for the Christian Church has always been that, while it insists that all things depend upon God for their existence, it leaves the reader with vague phrases such as ' shadow,' ' copy,' ' mirror,' as the only light it throws upon the character of that dependence.[6] Pantheism, indeed, it finally excludes, as Augustine insisted ;[7] so also the positive dualism of the Manichees.[8] But it lends itself to a seductive doctrine of the relative worthlessness, the vain and illusory character, of the things of this world, which is very difficult to distinguish from dualism itself, and may have the same practical issue in the depreciation of nature and natural society, and the theory of the soul's release from the prison-house of the body by ascetic practices and eremitic self-annihilation. We must remember always that there is here something at least akin to the genius of Christianity ; and we must insist that Augustine saw too clearly the evils and follies of Manicheeism ever to embrace the ' negative way ' as wholeheartedly as did, for example, pseudo-Dionysius.[9] His

[1] *contra Acad.*, iii, 19 (42).

[2] The most explicit passage in *Quæst. lxxxiii*, 25.

[3] Scarcely any reference except *de ver. rel.*, 16 (31)—the resurrection a proof of human immortality.

[4] ' Susceptio hominis ' (*Quæst, lxxxiii*, 25) is the commonest (references, Scheel, p. 47), and notice the extraordinary phrase, ' susceptio inferioris personæ,' which appears to be the original reading in *de gen. c. Man.*, ii, 24 (37)—see note of Benedictine editors *ad loc.*

[5] The best solution of all the problems involved seems to be the following. Shortly after making the acquaintance of neo-Platonism, S. Augustine took up the study of the Pauline epistles. (The ' Tolle, lege ' incident is either symbolical of this, or occurred during the period of study—the book was ready at hand, and *Conf.*, vii, 21 (27) (unless misplaced by Augustine) suggests that the serious reading of S. Paul had already begun.) His Pauline study (1) endorsed the neo-Platonic ' philosophy ' (*c. Acad.*, ii, 2 (5, 6))—probably on the mystical side ; (2) effected the moral conversion (*Conf.*, viii, 12 (29))—later, however, than Augustine suggests, since it is not mentioned in the Cassiciacine *c. Acad.*, ii, 2, but not very much later, since it is referred to in *Soll.*, i, 10 (17) ; (3) last of all, though described (without any particular indication of time) in *Conf.*, vii, 21 (27) (i.e. prior to the account of the ' conversion '), gave him a fully-developed Christology.

[6] Harnack (*Reden u. Aufsätze*, i, p. 72) effectively compares neo-Platonism to a dying man ' who no longer concerns himself with the things of this world except in bare necessities, and sets all his thoughts on the highest and holiest —on God.'

[7] He describes his pantheistic period in *Conf.*, vii, 1 (2).

[8] *Supra*, p. 320.

[9] Augustine's ' negative ' terminology is summarized by Luthardt, *op. cit.*, pp. 222, 223. On this aspect of his thought in general see Reuter, *op. cit.*, pp. 135 ff., 375 ff.

book on the ' Work of the Monks ' is enough to indicate this fact. But centuries later, when for a time Dionysius became the pole-star of western mysticism under the ægis of Scotus Eriugena, it was easy enough for his pupils to support themselves with Augustinian authority.   In S. Augustine's doctrine of the city of this world, for instance, there is at least an element of other-worldliness which sounds harsh and untrue to the modern mind. Dr. Figgis was guilty of a misleading understatement when he attributed to Augustine no more than the pose of ' a modern Etonian condemning the public schools.' [1]

(b) The Two Cities.

For Augustine, as for Clement, there was a city laid up in heaven. But with the same innate tendency to bring the future forward into the present as we noticed in S. Paul, he found the new Jerusalem projected into this world, and traced its fortunes militant here on earth.   Not the mere logic of events—the sack of Rome by Alaric, the cavillings of the heathen—forced him to consider the problem of the relation of this divine commonwealth to the commonwealths of men ; the question is primary for any Christian philosophy of history.   The dualist has an easy answer—the cities of this world, with all their pomp, their pleasures, their culture, are the castles of anti-Christ.   Their story is one of the increase of evil ; their end is destruction ; towards them the Christian can adopt one attitude only—the attitude of flight.   Even within the sphere of orthodoxy a similar attitude was popular—it is one of the many influences to which the rise of monasticism must be referred.

There were times when Augustine himself, still under neo-Platonic influence, felt and said as much. ' The vision of God in the city of God ' was his ideal. ' There we shall rest and gaze, and gaze and love, and love and praise—and to this end no end shall there be.   For what else is our end but to come to that kingdom that hath no end ? ' [2]   But here on earth we dwell also in a city of men.[3] ' That most glorious society and celestial city of God's faithful '— so runs Healy's sixteenth-century translation of the opening words

[1] J. N. Figgis, *The Political Aspects of S. Augustine's City of God*, p. 44.
[2] *de civ. Dei*, xxii, 30 (5) ; cp. *de mor. eccl.*, i, 31 (66), the ' contemplation of the beauty of God.'
[3] Strictly speaking, Augustine distinguishes *three* cities, the ' civitas superna ' or ' cœlestis ' in heaven, the ' civitas Dei ' on earth (the Church) and the ' civitas terrena ' ; e.g. *de civ. Dei*, ii, 29 (2) ; xv, 1 (2), 2 (1)—but *here* the ' civitas sancta ' on earth is the ' shadow-city ' Jerusalem, a ' part of the earthly city,' and the Church is left out altogether.   For the problem involved, which we can leave on one side, see A. Robertson, *Regnum Dei*, pp. 179, 194 ff.; H. Reuter, *Augustinische Studien*, pp. 106-150 ; V. Stegemann, *op. cit.*, pp. 51 ff.; Figgis, *op. cit.*, pp. 68 ff.; H. Leisegang, *Ursprung der Lehre Augustins v. d. Civ. Dei*, in *Archiv. f. Kulturgeschichte*, xvi (1925), *esp.* pp. 133 ff. Boissier (*op. cit.*), ii. p. 329, suggests that Augustine uses the word ' civitas ' in a new sense, but Stegemann (pp. 24 ff.) shows that he was only building with material supplied by Philo, Origen and Ambrose in their commentaries on the Bible. (Leisegang, p. 150, adds the Stoics.)   See also the new *Thesaurus Ling. Lat.*, *s.v.* ' civitas.'

of the ' de Civitate '—' is partly seated in the course of these de-
clining times, wherein he that liveth by faith is a pilgrim amongst
the wicked.'[1] The analogy of the two cities was popular in rigorist
circles—the 'Commentary on the Apocalypse' of Tyconius, the
Donatist,[2] has sometimes been regarded as the source from which
Augustine drew the doctrine—and the saint uses it often enough
in a dualist sense. Ritschl[3] can even assert that he conceived the
' civitas terrena ' (by which he meant all earthly society) to be the
association of men with one another on the basis of sinful purposes.
Even Dr. Figgis[4] is forced to admit that Augustine is 'far more
intransigent than Clement of Alexandria, who would treat Christianity as but the coping-stone of Greek thought,' and the Church,
we might add, as the realization of Greek aspirations towards the
perfect society of men.

The classical passage for this aspect of S. Augustine's thought
is in the 28th chapter of the 14th Book of the ' de Civitate ' :—[5]

> ' Two loves therefore have given original to these two cities
> —self-love in contempt of God unto the earthly ; love of
> God in contempt of one's self to the heavenly. The first
> seeketh the glory of men, and the latter desires God only, as the
> testimony of the conscience, the greatest glory. That glories
> in itself, and this in God. That exalteth itself in its own glory ;
> this saith to God, "My glory, and the lifter-up of my head."
> That boasteth of the ambitious conquerors led by the lust of
> sovereignty ; in this everyone serveth other in charity. . . .
> (In the earthly city) the wise men follow either the goods of the
> body, or mind, or both, living according to the flesh, and such
> as might know God honoured him not as God, but became vain
> in their own imaginations, and their foolish heart was darkened ;
> . . . but in the other, this heavenly city, there is no wisdom of
> man, but only the piety that serveth the true God and ex-
> pecteth a reward in the society of the holy angels and men, that
> God may be all in all.'

The city of this world, Augustine tells us, scarcely deserves the
name of city,[6] for it is compact of injustice only. It was planned

---

[1] *de civ. Dei*, i, 1.   Healy has boldly expanded the first two words
' gloriosissimam civitatem.'

[2] Figgis, pp. 46, 127, with references there. Stegemann (p. 32) shows good
reason for rejecting the view. The Apocalypse of Tyconius had an enormous
influence on mediæval exegesis ; it has survived in large part in the *Commentary* of Beatus of Liébana, whom we shall meet again in an entirely
different connexion (*infra*, p. 442). See T. Hahn, *Tyconius-Studien* (1900), pp.
3-9—for the ' civitas diaboli ' ; ' civitas Dei,' *ib.*, pp. 25-27. Tyconius' seventh
' Rule ' (see the *Liber Regularum*, ed. by F. C. Burkitt, *Texts and Studies*,
iii, 1, pp. 70-85) develops the same idea.

[3] Quoted Figgis, p. 128.   [4] *Op. cit.*, p. 30.

[5] Healy's translation.

[6] Or, more strictly, is unworthy of the name of *populus* or *res publica*,
according to Cicero's definition (*de civ. Dei*, ii, 21 (3) ; xix, 21). Augustine
does not altogether reject this definition ; he merely points out that no

by the apostate angels when they fell from heaven;[1] its ruler is
the devil;[2] it was built by Cain.[3] The carnal peace which it pursues can only be obtained by war;[4] its history is typified by the
carnage, rapine, and ultimate calamity of the Assyrian empire,[5]
and Ninus, the founder of its dynasty, revealed its true nature as
' grande latrocinium '—' flat thievery,' as Healy renders it.[6] ' Thus
the two cities,' Augustine concludes,[7]

> ' are described to be seated, the one in worldly possession, the
> other in heavenly hope; both coming out at the common gate
> of mortality, which was opened in Adam, out of whose con-
> demned progeny, as out of a putrified lump, God made some
> vessels of mercy, and some of wrath; giving due pains unto the
> one, and undue grace unto the other, that the citizens of God
> upon earth may take this lesson from those vessels of wrath
> never to rely on their own election, but hope to call upon the
> name of the Lord.'

All this is in appearance dualist enough to warrant the Christian
in the most drastic flight from the world. But Augustine has another
side,[8] and even if he fails to harmonize the two, it is at least evident
that the latter is no less native to his thought than the former. The
aim of both cities is peace, and peace in whatever form it is secured—
the ' peace of man with man, the peace of a family, the peace of a
city, the peace of the city of God, the peace of all things '—is a
' part of our final good '; it is the ' greatest wish of all the world,'
and a copy of the orderliness which is of the essence of God.[9] So a
man must seek the peace of his children, family, friends and all men
besides; and wish that his neighbour would do as much for him.
His own folk must have the first place in his care, and ' then those
whom his place and order in society affords him more conveniency
to benefit.'[10]

The earthly city, then, may be a *perverse* imitation of the city
of God;[11] but (because its goal is peace) an imitation or copy it
undoubtedly is—a foretaste of, or first step towards, the heavenly
society. As long as the city of God sojourns among men, it need
not scruple to enjoy such peace as the earthly city can afford. It
should be prepared to forward the ends of the earthly city, ' desiring

known society has ever satisfied its conditions except the city of God (ii,
21 (4))—where alone ' true justice' reigns. For human societies—which after
all are more than mere chaos—he discovers ' probabiliores definitiones ' :—
' populus est cœtus multitudinis rationalis, rerum quas diligit *concordi com-
munione* sociatus ' (xix, 24).

[1] *de civ. Dei*, xi, 33.   [2] *enarr. in Ps.*, 61. 6.
[3] *de civ. Dei*, xv, 1 (2)   [4] *Ib.*, 4.
[5] *Ib.*, xviii, 2 (1).   [6] *Ib.*, iv, 6.   [7] *Ib.*, xv, 21 (Healy).
[8] Or perhaps two periods, the latter more humanist than the former
(so Scheel, p. 57, against Willmann). But Scheel proves no more than a free
use of neo-Platonic language in the early period. Augustine's ' this-worldliness ' in this respect is well dealt with by J. Mausbach, *op. cit.*, i, pp. 331-350.
[9] *de civ. Dei*, xix, 11, 13, 14.   [10] *Ib.*, xix, 14.
[11] Just as human pride is ' perversa imitatio ' of the omnipotence of God,
de ver. rel., 45 (84).

and maintaining, as far as it can without injury to faith and godliness, a common agreement among men as to the acquisition of the necessaries of life, and making this earthly peace bear upon the peace of heaven.'[1] Indeed, God Himself had a use for the earthly city. No sooner did it find itself consummated in the Roman empire, than it instituted a world-wide peace, and ' Christ was born in Bethlehem.'[2] God used the Romans to punish the Jews who rejected Christ. They were scattered abroad among the nations, thus fulfilling the prophecies, and proving to the whole world that the Christian dispensation is true.[3] Without the Roman *imperium*, the triumphant victory of the gospel would have been impossible.

With this high valuation of the earthly city goes hand in hand a genuine appreciation of all the good things of life. The marvels of art and science, the harmony of the human body,

> ' the universal gracefulness of the heavens, the earth and the sea, the brightness of the light in the sun, moon and stars, the shades of the woods, the colours and smells of flowers, the numbers of birds, and their varied hues and songs, the many forms of beasts and fishes, whereof the least are the rarest (for the fabric of the bee or pismire is more admired than the whale's) and the strange alterations in the colour of the sea (as being in several garments), now one green, then another, now blue, and then purple '—

all these (with much else that Augustine enumerates) are the infinite ' blessings vouchsafed to man in his misery,' and yet no more than a shadowy foretaste of the glories to be revealed.[4] He cannot doubt for long, therefore, that all good rule on earth, all just sovereignty, and the due enjoyment of the gifts of nature are part of God's will for man ; though reflections of this kind only inflame his longing for the ineffable peace and joys of the heavenly city.

' I love not these things,' he says, after a similar enumeration in the ' Confessions,'[5] ' when I love my God ; and yet I love a certain light and sound and fragrance and food and embracing when I love my God, Who is the light, sound, fragrance, food and embracing of the inner man.' The vast chamber of memory is stored with countless joys of the terrestrial order, and in the summoning and disposal of them one over against another the saint takes an endless delight. Sense-perception, literature, philosophy, geometry all add to the sum of his ecstatic memories ; but the happy life is to rejoice to God and for God and in God, and there is none other.[6]

---

[1] *de civ. Dei*, xix, 17. [2] *Ib.*, xviii, 46. [3] *Ib.*
[4] *Ib.*, xxii, 24 (Healy) ; cp. also the fine catalogue in *de quant. an.*, 72, 73.
[5] *Conf.*, x, 6 (8). The chapter continues with the marvellous interrogatory of the beauties of nature, and their united reply, ' We are not God, but He made us.' Cp. also the fine passage, *de Trin.*, viii, 3.
[6] *Ib.*, 8 (12-15)—the storehouse of memory ; *ib.*, 10 (17)—12 (19)—literature, philosophy, geometry ; 20 (29)—22 (32)—the happy life. The whole section leads up to the ' sero Te amavi, pulchritudo tam antiqua et tam nova ' of 28 (39).

Augustine's mood, indeed, quickly changes. Almost at once he sees in all these positive joys no more than an army of temptations arrayed against his soul. But he has said enough. Rooted firmly in other-worldliness though his thought may be, he is not one to forget the positive goods of nature and human life.[1]

As final evidence of Augustine's willingness to see much that is good outside the strictly limited sphere of revelation and the miraculous, we may consider some of his opinions about pagan philosophy. Socrates he was prepared to call ' illustrious both in his life and in his death.' [2] Plato is ' justly preferred to all the other philosophers of the gentiles ' ; [3] and ' none come nearer to us ' than the Platonists, who have ' recognized the true God as the author of all things, true source of the light of truth, and the beautiful giver of all blessedness.' [4] Plotinus can be quoted as in agreement with the prologue to the Fourth Gospel.[5] Of the Christian's attitude to philosophy as a whole Augustine writes :—

' If those who are called philosophers, and especially the Platonists, have said ought that is true and in harmony with our faith, we must not shrink from it, but claim it for our use as from those who possess it unlawfully. The Egyptians owned not merely idols and heavy burdens, which the children of Israel hated and from which they fled, but also vessels of gold and silver and garments which our fathers, going out from Egypt, took secretly for themselves, designing them for a better use. . . . So, too, heathen learning is not all made up of false and superstitious fancies. . . . It contains also liberal instruction, well fitted for the use of truth, and excellent precepts of morality. Aye, some truths even in regard to the worship of the one God are found among them. . . . These truths therefore the Christian, when he separates himself in spirit from their unhappy company, will bear away with him and put them to their proper use for the proclamation of the gospel. . . . What else have many good and faithful men among our brethren done ? With what a wealth of gold and silver and garments was not Cyprian laden—that eloquent teacher and blessed martyr—when he came out of Egypt ! How much Lactantius brought with him, and Victorinus and Optatus and Hilary—

---

[1] Augustine's ' true worldliness ' (W. Gass, *Geschichte der Christlichen Ethik*, i, p. 174) is well expressed in *de civ. Dei*, xix, 19, in which he says that a man may choose either the active, the contemplative, or the ' mixed ' life. All that matters is that both ' love of the truth ' and ' the duty of charity ' are preserved. Then, dealing with the active life, he says that honour and power should be *used* for the benefit of others. Thus worldly goods are not to be eschewed (that would be mere world-flight), nor to be enjoyed as God is enjoyed (*frui*), but used. The distinction between ' use ' and ' enjoyment ' is fully drawn out, *de doctr. Christ.*, i, 3-5 ; cp. *ib.*, 21-23 (God alone to be ' enjoyed ').

[2] *de civ. Dei*, viii, 3.
[3] *Ib.*, 4.   [4] *Ib.*, 5.
[5] *Ib.*, x, 2 ; cp. also Thimme, *op. cit.*, pp. 35-38.

not to mention living names ! What wealth Greeks without number have borrowed ! ' [1]

(c) *Grace and Freedom.*

It has long been a vexed question whether the doctrine of the Church (the city of God) or the doctrine of grace is the basis and centre of S. Augustine's thought.[2] But the paradox observable in that philosophy of history whereby his doctrine of the Church is framed is no less apparent in his doctrine of grace. It is true, I suppose, that no problem of Christian theology lends itself more readily than this to the perversions associated with the ideas of the ' unnatural ' and the ' natural ' God respectively. The question is not one of merely speculative curiosity ; it is the preliminary to all missionary, evangelistic or pastoral work. There are Christians of whom we do not hesitate to say that they are on the road to salvation. But what is carrying them along that road—their own natural powers alone, or the grace of God alone, or some resultant of the two ? More important still, what is to be said to those not yet ' under grace,' or to those who have fallen from it ? Are we to tell them that all depends upon *themselves*—that if only they bestir themselves they can enter upon or revert to the Christian life without more ado ? Or that all depends upon *God*—that they must wait for the grace of God to stir them, as a ship must wait for a breeze ? Or—if in some way we are able to combine the two conceptions of grace and freewill—of what sort must that combination be to secure the truth of both and still lead men to eternal life ?

Practical common-sense Christianity has usually attempted some such combination, and proclaimed that man is saved by a co-operation of grace with freewill. It was indeed a commonplace of all orthodox Christianity up till the period of the Pelagian controversy ; it has been a commonplace of eastern Christianity at all epochs. ' God did not make men like trees and beasts, without the power of choice,' says Justin Martyr ; [3] ' for if man did not choose the good of his own freewill, he would be worthy neither of praise nor blame.' ' The horse is not expected to plough, nor the ox to gallop. Each has his proper function ; so man is exhorted to strive after knowledge of God, since that is his distinctive and peculiar function ' ; [4]—' no one can be saved against his will ' [5]—writes Clement of Alexandria. But on the other hand the human will to righteousness receives the assistance of divine grace. Clement compares the co-operation of man and God in man's salvation to the co-operation necessary between patient and physician if the former is to be restored to health.[6]

---

[1] *de doctr. Christ.*, ii, 40 (60, 61).
[2] Cp. H. Reuter, *Augustinische Studien*, pp. 45, 47 ff.
[3] Justin, *Apol.*, i, 43.   [4] Clem. Alex., *Protr.*, 10. 100.
[5] Id., *Strom.*, vii, 7. 42. Other references for Eastern libertarianism, Athenag., *leg.*, 31 ; *de resurr.*, 12, 13, 18 ; Theophilus, *ad Autol.*, ii, 27 ; Irenæus, *hær.*, iv, 4, 15, 37, 39 ; v, 27.
[6] Clem. Alex., *Strom.*, vii, 7. 48.

'Some things are given us by God's generosity,' says Tertullian,[1]
'others we acquire by our own efforts ; what God gives us is ruled
by His grace ; what we acquire, we acquire by perseverance.' The
so-called semi-Pelagians in the fifth century ;[2] Gregory the Great
a little later ;[3] the Schoolmen, in particular the Scotists ; the
Council of Trent[4] and the Arminians—all agree in emphasizing this
doctrine of the co-operation of freewill and grace in the process of
sanctification and salvation. The field of activity is mapped out
somehow between the two ; and each has a part to play in bringing
the fruit to harvest.

It is a natural and useful line of thought, no doubt, in dealing
with the unreflective Christian ; and as such it is proclaimed, year
in, year out, from every pulpit. It is useful in keeping a man to
what are often called his ' religious duties '—prayer, communion
and all the ' means of grace ' ; useful in reminding him of a certain
dependence upon God which must keep spiritual pride in check ;
useful also in avoiding the dangers of Quietism. That, however,
is the best that can be said for it. It explains nothing ; it evades
the deepest problems. Put it to the test, and it fails both in theory
and in practice. In theory—for it no more satisfies the demand of
the mind for unity of principle than to say baldly (if we may
glance for a moment at two cognate problems) that truth is given
to man sometimes by reason and sometimes by revelation, each
supplementing the other ; or that the course of events is made up
by the action and interaction of nature and miracle together. In
practice, too, it fails at crucial moments ; above all when brought
to the primary test, What is to be said to the man who has not
strength to begin the Christian pilgrimage, or who has tried to
enter upon it and has failed again and again ? Say to him : ' Arise
and walk ' ; and only too often he answers, ' Lord, I have no
man.' Say to him ' Wait upon the Lord, and He shall renew thy
strength,' and he replies : ' God hideth His face, and forgetteth
mine affliction and oppression.' The theory of co-operation is
helpless here, because as it stands it has not faced a prior question
—the question, ' Which comes first in man's salvation—*grace* to
turn and strengthen the will; or *will* to demand, or merit, or lay
hold on grace ' ?

To this question only two answers seem possible, and if the first
embodies the doctrine of the wholly ' natural,' the second goes far
to assert unequivocally that of the ' unnatural ' God. We may say
that the first movement of the soul towards goodness must come
from the soul itself ; but in that case we can for all practical purposes
abandon the doctrine of grace as a power operative within the soul.
In this matter, as in others, it is the first step which costs. If man

---

[1] Tert., *ad ux.*, i, 8 ; cp. *de patientia*, I ; *adv. Marc.*, ii, 5 ; *adv. Hermog.*, 5.
[2] See especially Cassian, *Coll.*, xiii, 8.
[3] *Magna Mor.*, xvi, 25 (30) ; xxiv, 10 (24) ; xxxiii, 21 (40), etc.
[4] Sess. vi, *Decretum*, cc. 1, 5 ; cann. 4, 5 (Denz.-Bann., nos. 793, 797, 814, 815).

must turn to God unaided, whatever grace he acquires in consequence of that conversion cannot be of vital importance in his salvation. The greatest factor of all in his life is his turning of his own freewill. If he has strength to turn, he has strength to persevere—to go on turning again to God day after day. It will simplify matters to say that all salvation, all progress, depends on the will and the will alone ; ' grace,' if it means anything at all, is merely a pious name for those external things which inspire and encourage to further effort.

This is naturalism undisguised ; but it was adopted none the less by Augustine's pretentious opponents the Pelagians. ' The possibility of goodness was given us by God,' Pelagius is reported to have said, ' but the will and the deed come from ourselves ' ; [1] he exhausted the idea of grace in the phrase ' the law and the doctrine.' [2] Grace, to adapt a phrase which Augustine used in another connexion,[3] is at best an ' adjutorium quo ' ; it is not an ' adjutorium sine quo non.' The law is as good a means of salvation as the gospel ; [4] there were men,[5] even before the coming of Christ, who lived without sin.[6]

Essential Pelagianism, in fact, is no more than an optimistic natural morality.[7] It says to man, ' Do not trouble about doctrine

---

[1] Pel., *ap.* Aug., *de grat. Christi*, 4 (5).

[2] Aug., *de grat. Christi*, 3 (3), 9 (10) ; *de gest. Pel.*, 14 (30)—the last passage suggests that the phrase was coined by Cœlestius, and that Pelagius rejected it.

[3] *de corr. et grat.*, 12 (34).

[4] *de gest. Pel.*, 11 (23), and elsewhere.

[5] *Ib.*, cp. *de pecc. orig.*, 2-10. Perhaps Pelagius had no more in mind originally than to defend certain Old Testament passages ; but he seems to have deduced (or allowed to be deduced) from his statements a doctrine of actual Christian sinlessness (cp. *de gest.*, 7 (20)).

[6] Centuries later, Socinus and his followers adopted the same point of view. ' Nothing is safer and more praiseworthy than to turn to God,' they admitted ; yet all that this appears to have meant is that the recalling to the mind of the doctrine of eternal life, with all that it implies of future reward and punishment, will strengthen a natural disposition to do good. The necessity of the Holy Spirit for the birth of Christian faith and the consequent beginning of true virtue in man, they explicitly denied ; and the ' grace of God in Christ Jesus ' consisted to them simply in the gift of purer and more perfect legislation, with the promise of eternal life to those who observed its precepts (J. A. Möhler, *Symbolism* (E. tr., 1894), pp. 495, 496).

[7] Pelagius himself was a rigorist in ethics. Though he denied ever having said that rich Christians, however good their life might be, could never enter the kingdom unless they renounced their wealth (*de gest. Pel.*, 11 (23)), he certainly said things of the same kind, e.g. *Comm. in 1 Cor.*, i, 27 (*MPL.*, xxx, col. 721)—' Christ condemned riches by being born of a poor mother,' etc. (See also the Pelagian letters published by C. P. Caspari, *Briefe, Abhandlungen u. Predigten*, Christiania, 1890.) But this rigorism no more prevented his outlook being naturalistic than did the laxity of some of the gnostics contradict their dualism. Julian of Eclanum was the Epicurus of Pelagianism but though he liberalized the form of the ethical code (and in this sense may be said to have ' given it a naturalistic tendency ' (Harnack, v, p. 189)) by eliminating its ascetic characteristics, it was naturalistic from the outset, because it was anthropocentric. Anthropocentrism makes strange bedfellows ; Pelagius and Julian, rigorist and humanist, found themselves in

and sacraments unless such ideas appeal to you. You have in yourself the strength to be good ; exert yourself therefore here and now to goodness.' The system may cloak itself in religious language, but it can perfectly well exist and flourish in an atmosphere of atheism or agnosticism. Man is the master of his own fate, the captain of his own soul ; God and grace are unnecessary—' an appendix badly connected with the main theme '.[1]

Opposed to this Pelagian naturalism there stands in history an application of the doctrine of the unnatural God to the problem of grace, which looks back to Augustine as its original begetter. Its essence is expressed in the technical phrase, ' Man cannot merit the first grace '[2]—he cannot, that is, of his own freewill turn himself to God and earn thereby whatever grace and help God is able to give. Grace must come first ; without such prevenient grace man is wholly impotent. No effort of the natural will can therefore have any significance for goodness ; only by an unmediated, super-natural act of God can we enter upon or be maintained in the Christian pilgrimage. The problem as it presented itself to Augus-tine, long before the Pelagian controversy,[3] is envisaged by Bishop Robertson in the following terms :—[4]

> ' If the decision between the effectual operation of grace in the case of one man and its frustration in the case of another ultimately goes back to the different response of the will in the two cases, then it is with the will, not grace, that the crucial decision rests which determines whether grace is to act or no ; freewill, not grace, is the ultimate turning point of a man's relation to God. To the Augustine of the " Confessions " . . . such a conclusion was impossible to rest in. And as in the years following his conversion he gradually exchanged the methods and temper of the Platonic dialectician for the re-sults of deeper study of S. Paul, this assumption appeared to him not only impossible but irreligious also.'

So S. Augustine asserts—and, at first sight, asserts unequi-vocally—the utter nothingness and impotence of man, and the complete irresistibility of God's prevenient grace. He had in earlier days held that the first step by which man was qualified to receive

---

accord against the theocentrism of Augustine ; just as rigorist Pharisees and humanist Sadducees combined against Jesus ; or as, centuries later, the Jansenist Nicole made common cause with Bossuet against theocentric mysticism (Bremond, *HLSR.*, iv, p. 486).

[1] Harnack, *Hist. of Dogma*, v, p. 203 ; and see further, *infra*, pp. 545 ff., additional note, *Augustinism*.

[2] Aquinas, *ST.*, i, 2, q. 114, a. 5; and see further *infra*, pp. 545 ff., additional note, *Augustinism*.

[3] The Pelagian controversy began in A.D. 411 ; but the essential Augus-tinian position is already stated in the *de div. quaest. ad Simplic.*, i, 2 (9) (A.D. 396). Augustine himself draws attention to the fact, *de praedest. sanct.*, 4 (8) ; *de don. persev.*, 20 (52). Cp. Harnack, v, pp. 169, 170.

[4] A. Robertson, *Regnum Dei*, pp. 188, 189.

help—the ' will ' to believe—was taken by his own effort ; [1] but this olive-branch to naturalism he soon withdrew. ' We laboured in the cause of freedom,' he says, ' but the grace of God won the day.' [2] So his mature reflection speaks of mankind as ' una quædam massa peccati ' or ' universa massa perditionis ' ; [3] —' the entire *massa damnata* of the human race lies and wallows in sin, plunging from depth to depth of evil ; and joining in the lot of the fallen angels, pays a worthy penalty for its impious defection.' [4] It may be assumed that much of this terrible phraseology resulted from a theological conception of universal guilt as traceable to Adam's sin. No doubt also, the fidelity of the Church to the practice of infant baptism gave Augustine a stronger bias towards the doctrine. But the real fervour of his statement is quite independent of incidental influences like these. ' Let no man think that he has earned grace by good deeds ; good deeds are impossible till grace through faith has been received.' [5] The very power to believe, or faith itself, cannot come from us ; in this as in all else ' our sufficiency is of God.' [6] ' We cannot even will unless we are called ; and would we will after our call, our will and our running are vain unless God gives strength to the runner and leads him whither He calls him.' [7]

The logical conclusion of this, of course, is that the grace of God is an *irresistible* grace, which saves us whether we will or no. Even Cassian, the practically-minded semi-Pelagian, could contemplate the grace of God as saving men against their will ; [8] though he restricted to a few, such as Paul and Matthew, what Augustine held of all the elect. For though Augustine does not appear to have used the phrase ' irresistible grace,' he is quite familiar with the idea. Before the Council of Carthage (A.D. 418) he was prepared to admit that men could be carried so far along the road by justifying grace as to live, even here upon earth, altogether without sin.[9] Later he modified this daring opinion ; [10] but the retractation is of little real effect. ' He forestalls the unwilling, to make them willing ; He attends the willing, that they will not in vain,' he says in the ' Enchiridion ' ; [11] and elsewhere, ' Grace comes first, good works second.' [12] ' God grants us not only to perceive what we

---

[1] So *div. quæst. lxxxiii*, 68 (4, 5) (even here Augustine tries to safeguard the antecedent grace of God by equating it with ' vocatio,' and saying ' no man can will until he is called thereto ') ; *de lib. arb.*, iii, 19 (53).

[2] *Retract.*, ii, 1 (1) ; cp. *de prædest. sanct.*, 3 (7).

[3] *de pecc. orig.*, 29 (34) ; *de corr. et grat.*, 10 (28).

[4] *enchiridion*, 8 (27)—further illustrations of this type of language, O. Rothmanner, *Der Augustinismus* (1892), pp. 8, 9.

[5] *ad Simpl.*, i, 2 (2) ; cp. *ench.*, 107.

[6] *de prædest. sanct.*, 2, 3, 5, etc. ; *ep.* 194. 3 (9).

[7] *de prædest. sanct.*, 3 (7) ; *de grat. et lib. arb.*, 33.

[8] *Coll.*, xiii, 3 ; cp. *ib.*, xii, 18 ; xiii, 11.

[9] *de dpecc. mer.*, ii, 6 (7) ; *de perf. just. hom.*, 21 (44) ; cp. *supra*, pp. 229-223.

[10] *de nat. et grat.*, 36 (42)—only the Virgin Mary without sin; *de spir. et lit.*, 28 (48)—venial sins, ' sine quibus hæc vita non ducitur'; *c. duas ep. Pel.*, iv, 10 (27), with quotations from Cyprian.

[11] *ench.*, 9 (32). [12] *de div. quæst. ad Simpl.*, i, 2 (3).

should do, but even to do what we perceive.'[1]   The will and grace
of God always attain their end and lead human will as they please ;
grace acts 'indeclinabiliter et insuperabiliter.'[2]

Of those who under the sway of this insuperable grace are led
on from strength to strength, we must therefore say that they are
from the beginning of time *predestined* to receive grace.[3]   'This
is the predestination of the saints,' Augustine says, 'the Divine
foreknowledge and preparation of the gifts by which those who are
freed are freed infallibly.'[4]   Predestinate grace is given unconditionally—not even on the grounds of God's foreknowledge that
it will be well and piously used.[5]   Conversely, those who fail to
bring forth fruits of righteousness fail because they are predestinate,
not to grace and glory, but to eternal damnation.[6]   Modern writers
have attempted to soften the harshness of this doctrine by seeing
in it no more than 'reprobation by pretermission' ; the 'vessels
of wrath' are not predestinate to eternal condemnation, but
'simply left.'[7]   Some of the Augustinian passages which bear on
the subject do indeed admit of this milder interpretation—milder,
that is, only by comparison with Calvin's wild joy in the eternal
torture of the damned—though in one place at least God is praised
as that 'most just punisher of those whom He has predestined
to eternal death.'[8]   Again, it is possible to recognize in the distinction which Augustine very occasionally draws between 'predestination' and 'foreknowledge' an attempt to throw the responsibility for the condemnation of sinners upon themselves.[9]   The

---

[1] *de gratia Christi*, 14 (15), 24 (25) ;   *de corr. et grat.*, 31 (32) ;   *c. duas ep.
Pel.*, i, 37 (38), etc.

[2] *de corr. et grat.*, 12 (38) (but see Mausbach, *op. cit.*, ii, p. 135, on the
interpretation) ;   cp., *ib.*, 14 (43, 45) ;   *de præd. sanct.*, 8 (14) ;   *ench.*, 98, 106 ;
ad Simplic., i, 2 (12) ;   *de grat. et lib. arb.*, 14 (29)—other passages, J. B.
Mozley, *Augustinian Doctrine of Predestination*[3], pp. 143-172 ;   Harnack,
Augustin : Reflexionen und Maximen, pp. 120-122 ;   Rothmanner, *op. cit.*,
pp. 20, 21.

[3] Mozley (*op. cit.*, p. 176) regards Augustine's doctrine of grace as 'no
more than a supplemental one to the doctrine of predestination.'   This,
however, stands in complete contradiction both to Augustine's thought and to
his experience.   Predestination is an inference from the fact of grace, and
not *vice versa*—an answer to the question, 'Why, then, if no man *deserves*
grace, do some receive it and some not ? '

[4] *de don. persev.*, 14 (35) ;   cp. *de prædest. sanct.*, 17 (34).

[5] *de prædest. sanct.*, 18 (36) ;   but contrast *de div. quæst. ad Simplic.*, i,
2 (13), where 'election' is interpreted as 'congruent vocation.'

[6] *de perf. just. hom.*, 13 (31) ;   *ench.*, 26 (100) ;   *de civ. Dei*, xxii, 24 (5).
Generally, cp. *de don. persev.*, 8 (17), 9 (21), 14 (35) ;   *de corr. et grat.*, 7 (13-16),
though these passages might be taken of reprobation by pretermission simply.
In *de don. persev.*, 22 (57-62) he utters a much-needed warning against
careless preaching of the double doctrine.

[7] So J. F. Bethune-Baker, *Early History of Christian Doctrine*, p. 311 ;
Rothmanner, *op. cit.*, pp. 17-20 ;   J. Tixeront, *Hist. Dogm.*, ii, p. 508.

[8] *de an. et ej. or.*, iv, 11 (16).

[9] *de lib. arb.*, iii, 4 (11) ;   *de grat. et lib. arb.*, 21 (43) and elsewhere ;   and
see Cunningham, *St. Austin*, pp. 88 ff. for an attempt at justification.   The
fallacy is clearly brought out by T. A. Lacey, *Nature, Miracle and Sin*,
pp. 62, 63.

attempt was hardly a successful one, as he himself seems to have recognized ; [1] for however much a *man* may ' foreknow ' the failure or sin of another without ' foreordaining ' it, his foreknowledge can only be relative ; whereas *God's* foreknowledge must be absolute, and so identical, in effect, with predestination. But the clearest proof that Augustine was prepared at times to rest, however uneasily, in his conclusion that the failure of sinners is due to God's decision not to give them efficacious grace, lies in his continual struggle with the text, ' God will have all men to be saved.' [2] Sometimes he interprets ' all men ' as ' all the elect,' ' all those who are predestinate to glory ' ; [3] sometimes as ' men representative of every class and condition ' ; [4] sometimes as just ' many men.' [5] He is never willing to give the words their literal and absolute meaning.

No God, we may say, could be more unnatural than the God revealed by such Augustinian passages as these. Even the elementary dictates of natural justice are set at nought by Him. But how far was Augustine genuinely an Augustinian in this matter ? We do not have to read deeply to see that here too—as in his doctrine of the two cities—he attempts to retain alongside his rigorism all that is good in naturalism. He predicates impotence of men freely enough ; but he never says that they are wholly without goodness. Wherever nature remains in any sense at all, there is goodness—there, we may fairly claim, is grace. Grace, in this sense, Augustine chooses to call ' the image of God ' ; [6] but the distinction is so far from necessary that it actually obscures a point of vital importance. And so, though he frequently maintains that works done ' before the coming of faith ' are sinful,[7] yet he speaks of Ahasuerus and Polemon as heathen who, apart from the Christian revelation, received grace for good works.[8] Or again, though infants dying unbaptized are unredeemed from the taint of original sin, and so must go to the ' mitissima pœna ' of limbo, yet he will not say that it were better for them they had never been born.[9] Wherever nature is, there is God's work—' omnis natura in quantum natura est, est bona.' [10] The worst sinner is better off than the beasts

---

[1] F. Loofs, *Leitfaden*, p. 385—' Augustine bases the divine predestination upon the divine foreknowledge, but *it is a foreknowledge of what God Himself will do*, and not of man's future behaviour.' The suggestion that Augustine held a doctrine of predestination *post prævisa merita* is discussed by Tixeront (*op. cit.*, ii, pp. 501-504, based on Petavius), and rejected.

[2] 1 Tim. 2[4]. [3] *ep.* 217. 6 (19) ; *ench.*, 27 (103).

[4] *ench.*, 27 (103) (a fine catalogue of professions, seven lines long).

[5] *c. Julian.*, iv, 8 (44).

[6] *de spir. et lit.*, 28 (48). Augustine is prepared to extend the meaning of ' grace ' widely ; thus in *ep.* 177. 7, 8, he says it can be used ' non immerito ' of that activity of God which makes a man a man, and not a beast or a tree, though he adds that this use is not Scriptural.

[7] *enarr. in Ps.*, 31. 2 (4) ; *c. duas ep. Pel.*, iii, 14 ; *de civ. Dei*, xix, 25.

[8] *de grat. Christi*, 24 (25)—Ahasuerus ; *ep.* 144. 2—Polemon, the reformed (pagan) drunkard ; generally, *de civ. Dei*, xviii, 47.

[9] *c. Julian.*, v, 11 (44).

[10] *de nat. boni*, 1 ; cp. *de civ. Dei*, xii, 5.

of the field, because he still retains the possibility of a higher destiny.[1]
Even the devil's nature, in so far as it is nature, is not an evil
thing.[2]

In the same spirit Augustine insists that although by original
sin man has lost ' freedom ' he still retains ' freewill.'[3] He has
still open to him, for example, the power to pray for grace.[4] His
will is still free to co-operate with grace received, irresistible though
that grace may be.[5] And therefore, despite all that he has said on
the other side—despite God's absolute foreknowledge that the
sinner will most certainly sin—Augustine holds him responsible for
his rejection of grace when offered, or for his lapse from it if once
received.[6] We may well hesitate to accept the arguments by which
Augustine supports this extraordinary conclusion—arguments
which depend for their validity upon fine distinctions, perilously
drawn, as to the exact character of the freewill left to man after
his fall.[7] The real justification (as subsequent paragraphs will
suggest) of his bold attempt lies elsewhere. What is important is
that he attempted to hold the balance between Pelagian naturalism

---

[1] de cat. rud., 18 (30) ; de lib. arb., iii, 5.   [2] de civ. Dei, xix, 13 (2).
[3] The point is made offensively in the early anti-Manichæan writings,
defensively in the later anti-Pelagian ones. For the former, in which it
was sometimes put so strongly as to give the Pelagians ground for accusing
him of inconsistency (c. Julian., vi, 12 (39)), see especially retract., i, 9, where
he collects the very numerous passages from de lib. arb. which were quoted
against him. For the statement in its later form, c. duas ep. Pel., i, 2 (5).
[4] retract., i, 15 (4) ; ep. 157. 2 (10) ; op. imp. c. Jul., iii, 115. Other
references, Mausbach, op. cit., ii, pp. 215, 252.
[5] de spir. et lit., 34 (60).
[6] de duab. an., 14 ; retract., i, 15 (3) ; de grat. et lib. arb., 3 (4), etc.
[7] Augustine has in mind three meanings of the word freedom :—(i) the
freedom of indetermination—posse peccare aut non peccare, de corr. et grat.,
12 (33), ench., 105 ; this, as Cunningham (p. 93) says, comes very near the
' caprice ' of the Pelagians which Augustine attacks, op. imp. c. Jul., vi, 9 ;
ib., i, 78. (ii) Formal freedom—the retention of the faculty to choose good,
without any opportunity for its exercise : as we may say that a man still
' retains his sight ' though he is permanently immured in a dungeon. Thus
he is ' free,' though non potest non peccare, unless the grace of God comes to
his assistance. (iii) Ideal freedom—the non posse peccare of the saints, de
civ. Dei, xxii, 30 (3) ; de corr. et grat., 12 (33).—The freedom of indetermination was Adam's before the Fall. It conveyed responsibility ; but since the
Fall men are no longer free in this sense. Formal freedom men still possess,
and Augustine undoubtedly assumes that it also carries with it responsibility.
This, however, it is difficult, if not impossible to admit ; you cannot blame
a man for not ' using his sight ' in a darkened room if you refuse to open
the shutters. By Adam's sin all men have been placed in darkened rooms,
and for some God refuses to open the shutters—refuses, that is to say, to
set before them any motives for goodness except those which He knows
they will refuse. Cp. the Augustinian position on this point expressed by
E. Portalié, DTC., i, coll. 2389, 2390; but the attempt (ib., col. 2400) to safeguard human responsibility and divine justice is not very successful.
Mausbach (op. cit., ii, p. 224) only saves Augustine by the drastic expedient
of making necessitas peccandi refer ' not to any causal necessity,' but to the
mere empirical fact that all men do sin. Augustine's superficial inconsistency
is well expressed in the summary in N. P. Williams, Doctrine of Original Sin,
p. 369—' We are free to do what we like, but we are not free to like what
we ought to like.'

and Manichæan rigorism—to assert the prevenience of grace and yet the responsibility of man—and that he was not ashamed to face the charge of inconsistency in the attempt.

In his paradoxical emphasis, therefore, both upon divine prevenience and upon human freewill, Augustine followed the true line of Christian development which would allow neither rigorism nor naturalism undisputed sway in theology. But, in the matter of grace at least, he did more than this. He did not hesitate to accept the paradox—'They came of their own will,' he writes of the Philistines who attacked Jehoram ; ' yet " the Lord stirred up their spirits " ; or with equal verity we may say, " The Lord stirred up their spirit, yet they came of their own will." ' [1] His greatness consists in the fact that he attempted to find a solution to the paradox. The solution does not lie, as is often suggested, in his 'skilful analysis' of the psychology of the will ; [2] it is difficult in this regard not to suspect him of ambiguity.[3] It lies in the doctrine that the essence of grace is *love*, and the essence of man's salvation that he should become *loving*. ' Thou tellest of many ways in which God helps us,' Augustine writes against Julian of Eclanum, ' of scriptures, blessings, healings, chastenings, excitations, inspirations ; but that He giveth us *love* and thereby helpeth us, thou sayest not.' [4]

The importance of this conception cannot be over-estimated. Three things are true about love, even in that imperfect form in which we know it. The first is, that it always confers independence upon the object of its love. It gives, compelling no return ; it goes on giving, though no love is given in answer. It is the one force in the world which does not bargain ; which leaves the recipient absolutely free to reject, accept, or repay. So, if God's grace is love, its lovingness consists first of all in giving freedom to men and then in keeping them free, if the phrase may be allowed, without any *arrière pensée*. In creation, providence, redemption, we have no more than three stages of this love of enfranchisement ; God giving men greater freedom, desiring indeed a return, but never demanding or compelling it.

Second, if love endows the *recipient* with formal freedom—with the right to accept or reject at will—it also, and it alone, confers upon the *giver* actual freedom. Of God we can scarcely say this ; for love and freedom exist together from all eternity in the nature of God. But of man it is true. In love and in love alone can he actualize the freedom—the formal right to be free—which God has given him. Passion enslaves its votary ; love enfranchises him from passions. Passion blinds him to the defects of its object till in the end it is repelled and killed by them ; love opens his eyes

---

[1] *de grat. et lib. arb.*, 21 (42). The reference is to 2 Chron. 21[16, 17].

[2] So Cunningham, *op. cit.*, p. 84 ; Portalié, *CE.*, ii, pp. 96, 97 ; *DTC.*, *ut sup.*

[3] *Supra*, p. 342, n. 7.

[4] *op. imp.*, iii, 106—' and by this love,' he adds, ' we understand the power to become sons of God ' ; cp. Mozley, *op. cit.*, pp. 172-176.

to them, but gives at the same time an undying desire for their removal. Passion leads to madness, love to sympathetic understanding; passion destroys personality, love creates it. Man becomes free as he learns to love.

And, finally, love is irresistible; many waters cannot quench it. This is no more than a corollary from the two factors we have just considered. Love is undaunted by opposition, rejection, irresponsiveness; it lives by giving out, not by taking in. Love never faileth. 'Nothing is so hard or iron that love cannot soften it.'[1] And therefore whatever opposes it must in the end give way; 'love is as strong as death.'[2] The same power which confers freedom on its recipients also evokes from them—not by contract, nor by force, but by the invincible suasion of a moral appeal,—an answer of love freely given in return.[3]

God's grace to man, then, because it is a grace of perfect love, endows him with unconditional freedom. But for that freedom to realize itself it must, in loving response, surrender to the irresistible and undying love that called it forth.[4] That this at least was Augustine's dearest thought need not be doubted. It is the very burden of the 'Confessions,' but it rings everywhere in his writings. He saw in man in the abstract—in the state of innocence—a bare indeterminism, a formal freedom both of 'posse peccare' and of 'posse non peccare.'[5] In man in the concrete the same formal freedom remained;[6] but unless it issued in love towards God it was bound to end in slavery to sin. 'Freedom, now made prisoner, can do nought but sin; only if freed and helped by God can it avail for justice.'[7] Sin therefore is voluntary, and yet necessitated by the fact of the situation in which man finds himself—the fact that he has not yet surrendered to the love of God.[8] The truest freedom comes by the death of passion; it is the 'felix necessitas non peccandi,' the 'non posse peccare' of the saints.[9] Augustine never wearies of declaring that God's grace—God's love—has an irresistible power to summon forth this love to God which will make man free in the truest and most actual sense of the word. 'Love is the power that moves me, whithersoever I go.'[10] 'Love, of whatever kind, hath always a living power. Never can love rest

[1] de mor. eccl. cath., i, 22 (41).
[2] enarr. in Ps. 121 [Angl., 122], 10, 12 (with reference to Cant. 8⁶).
[3] ep. 192. 2—the contrast between giving money and giving love in this respect.
[4] serm. 34. 4 (7)—'audi quid tibi dicat ex ore Sapientiæ caritas, Da mihi, Fili, cor tuum (Prov. 23²⁶) . . . totum exigit te, Qui fecit te.'
[5] Supra, p. 342, n. 7.
[6] 'A mode of action, but not a source of action '—Mozley, op. cit., p. 226.
[7] c. duas ep. Pel., iii, 8 (24); cp. ib., i, 2 (5), 3 (7), etc.
[8] de spir. et lit., 3 (5)—love towards God kindled when we 'accept the Holy Spirit'; de nat. et grat., 66 (79)—'sin' the outcome of the 'vice of nature,' not the 'condition of nature.'
[9] Supra, p. 342, n. 7; and cp. de perf. just., 4 (9); de spir. et lit., 30 (52); de civ. Dei, iv, 3; xiv, 11, etc.
[10] Conf., xiii, 9 (10).

idle in the lover's heart; always it moves and drives.'[1] 'God
made Himself lovable, because He knew that would move us to
love Him; by love of the good we become better.'[2] 'That we
might receive the love whereby to love Him, God loved us first
while we loved Him not.'[3] 'It is that which we most delight in to
which we must needs conform.'[4] 'There is no greater incentive
to love than to anticipate in loving.'[5] When grace and salvation
are thought of in terms of love, before everything else, the problem
of freedom and irresistibility is put in a form in which faith can
accept both sides of the antinomy, and hold them firmly together.

Augustine was forced, by circumstance and personal history alike,
to face the dilemma of rigorism and naturalism more frequently
than any other figure in Christian history. His early Manichæan
errors—the labyrinths of later Platonism, leading now to a dualism
almost as acute as that of Mani, now to a naturalistic monism—
the ascendency of monasticism—the puritanism of the Donatists
—the problems forced by the fall of Rome—the final struggle
with Pelagianism, complicated by the excesses of ultra-Augustinian
partizans—under the stress of these conflicting storms his theological
system sways perilously from side to side. In Heiler's effective
phrase,[6] ' he combines in one person Jeremiah and Plato, Paul and
Plotinus, John and Origen, Cyprian and Athanasius; he is the
greatest *complexio oppositorum* of all religious geniuses.' But his
thought remains firmly rooted to the end in the conviction that God
and grace are neither wholly natural nor wholly unnatural. The

[1] *enarr. in Ps.* 121. 1. [2] *Ib.*, 144. 1.
[3] *de grat. Christi*, 26 (27) (with reference to 1 Jn. 4[10, 19]).
[4] *expositio ep. ad Gal.*, 49; cp. *de spir. et lit.*, 3 (5), 4 (6); *de pecc. mer.*,
ii, 18 (33); *c. duas ep. Pel.*, iv, 5 (11).
[5] *de cat. rud.*, 4, 7.
[6] F. Heiler, *Der Katholizismus*, p. 98; cp. p. 100—'What makes Augustine
marvellous and indeed unique is that his character is a microcosm which comprehends the entire range of that macrocosm, the Church.' Harnack, *Hist.
of Dogma*, v, pp. 107-110, has a most illuminating summary of Augustine's
position in the history of thought. Ignoring the degradation and pessimism
into which pagan thought had fallen, Harnack treats Augustine as the
destroyer of the ancient ' classical temper ' with ' its cheerfulness and naïve
objectivity.' But ' nothing was altogether lost,' because Augustine, ' in the
name of God, built up a new world in his own heart and mind ' (that is to
say, he effected a synthesis of naturalism and supernaturalism). Harnack,
however, regards Augustine's system as biassed against naturalism—' something had undoubtedly been lost . . . and that is frank joy in the phenomenal world, in its obvious meaning, and in calm and energetic work. If
it were possible to unite in science and in disposition the piety, spirituality
and introspection of Augustine, with the openness to the world, the restful
and energetic activity, the unclouded cheerfulness of antiquity, we should
have reached the highest level.' Without admitting that the 'cheerfulness'
of antiquity was really as 'unclouded' as Harnack suggests, we can assent
to this criticism in general; and we can add that it was Augustine's neo-
Platonic affinities which watered down the humanist element in his thought.
But it is absurd to maintain, as Harnack does, that the ' great minds who
have been granted us since Luther ' have redressed the balance: if there
was any one person who saw what was needed and supplied it, it was
S. Thomas Aquinas with his doctrine of analogy (*infra*, pp. 379 f.).

conviction is not with him—as with many others it has so often been—a last despairing refusal to surrender to the demands of one or other of the two conflicting philosophies. If he cannot vindicate it triumphantly, he can at least plant his standard on a tower from which to the end it waves, and will always wave, inviolate over all assaults. His analysis of grace is the clue to all his thought. In the greatest of all texts, ' God is love,' he found a truth powerful enough at once to transcend, to embrace, and to reconcile the divergent tendencies into which the Christian interpretation of the universe so constantly finds itself dissolved. By this more than by any other of his services to the Church, his true greatness can be recognized.

IV. S. BERNARD OF CLAIRVAUX.

Very much more might be said of S. Augustine's influence upon the development of western ethics, but it would be impossible even so to over-emphasize his importance. At a time when formalism reigned supreme in the Latin Church,[1] he threw the whole weight of his authority into the balance against it.[2] The purpose of life, in his view, was not to achieve success in measuring oneself against an ethical standard, however refined, but to see God [3]—in Harnack's words, ' he put an end to the possibility that *virtue* was the supreme good, and reduced all virtues to dependence upon God.' [4] Yet dependence upon God was no passive quietism with Him ; it was man's love for God reaching out to God in the fullness of a life of Christian service.

In his conception of the vision of God, again, Augustine mediated between the intellectualist tendencies of Clement of Alexandria and the ecstatic strain to be found in neo-Platonism. He admired the monks of the Egyptian desert more perhaps than any other type of Christian, but he did not follow them blindly in their naïve indifference to culture and education. In all this he conserved what was best in the aspirations of previous centuries (and much

---

[1] For monasticism had so far (as has been suggested above, p. 176, n. 4) made little headway in the west ; and in Africa was probably introduced by Augustine himself (Reuter, *Augustinische Studien*, pp. 428 ff.). An admirable example of fourth-century formalism is to be found in Lactantius, with his insistence that immortality is the reward ' earned ' by virtue (*Div. Inst.*, vi, 12 ; vii, 5) ; his tabulation of duties ; his frank admission of the double standard in its invalid form (*ib.*, vi, 13)—' He who abstains from evil works ' (the lowest of the three stages of righteousness) ' *is sufficiently just* ' ; and his use of the two ways (*ib.*, vi, 3).

[2] By his revived emphasis upon the *love*, rather than upon the *justice*, of God, he ' dethroned the traditional feelings of the baptized, fear and hope —the elements of unrest, and substituted the elements of rest, faith, and love' (Harnack, *Hist. of Dogma*, v, p. 72—see the whole passage). Cp. C. E. Luthardt, *Hist. of Christian Ethics* (E. tr.), p. 227.

[3] *Supra*, pp. 321, 330; cp. also *serm.* 38. 8 (11)—' patria contemplationis angelorum ' ; *de gen. ad lit.*, xii, 26 (54)—' ineffabilis visio veritatis.'

[4] Harnack, *Hist. Dogm.*, v, p. 135 ; cp. *ib.*, pp. 61-66, with the quotation from *ep.* 155, on p. 63.

of it was new to the west), but fought the battle for a theocentric outlook with a zeal unparalleled except in the New Testament.

In another matter, too, Augustine, and Augustine alone of his period, discerned the outline of a New Testament doctrine which the Church was in danger of forgetting ; though his neo-Platonic upbringing made it impossible for him to realize its full importance. It is ' in the face of Jesus Christ,' once again, that men are to see God—' Christus humilis,' ' Christus homo ' is the way to the blessed country.[1] It is this fact above all others which links Augustine with one who drew much from him both in theology [2] and, by way of Gregory the Great,[3] in the language of devotion—one in whose writings, as Harnack justly says, ' the notes of the Christ-mysticism, which Augustine had struck only singly and with uncertainty, became a ravishing melody.' [4] Between the fifth and the eleventh centuries lies the great gulf of the dark ages, when ethics were reduced to little more than formalism and the attempt to impose some element of discipline and decency upon an unruly and chaotic society. The period is one in which pseudo-Dionysius and his Latin translator, John the Scot, were laying the foundations of a new outburst of ' negative' life and doctrine in the middle ages ; but the great saint to whom we come is wholly untouched by their influence. As the greatest of Cistercians—the greatest, that is, of those who strove to recapture the spirit of the Benedictine rule in all its arduous simplicity, where even the Cluniac reform had failed—Bernard of Clairvaux might well have made monasticism a purely centripetal institution, in which each man should be concerned with his own salvation alone. Dr. Coulton, indeed, suggests that he did so, although S. Bernard is one of his heroes ; [5] but the evidence is by no means all on one side.

Take, for example, some sentences from one of the great abbot's sermons on the place of the monks in the world. His text [6] is ' Dentes tui sicut grex tonsarum '—' Thy teeth are like a flock of ewes that are newly shorn.' The word ' tonsæ ' gives him his clue. The passage refers to the tonsured [7] monk, and therefore he is able to say, ' The Holy Spirit commendeth no small mysteries to us by these teeth.' ' Teeth,' he proceeds, ' are white and strong ;

---

[1] de civ. Dei, xi, 2 ; cp. tract. ii, 4, in Joann.; de doctr. Christ., i, 34 (38) ; serm. 81. 6 ; 142. 2. Generally cp. Harnack, Hist. of Dogma, v, pp. 127-133, with Scheel's criticisms, op. cit., pp. 347-380, 411-427. Scheel's rationalization of Augustine's thought about Christ is not convincing.

[2] Mabillon, S. Bernardi opera omnia (Paris, 1839), i, coll. 25, 26 (præfatio, § 25). All the following references are to this edition.

[3] C. Butler, Western Mysticism, p. 277.

[4] Harnack, Hist. of Dogma, vi, p. 9.

[5] G. G. Coulton, Five Centuries of Religion, i, p. 462, in the Appendix headed ' Monks and Personal Salvation.'

[6] Bern., de diversis sermo 93 (Mab., i, col. 2535). The text is from Cant. 4².

[7] I have taken a slight liberty with Bernard's thought ; the point he makes is that the monk is ' shorn ' of all possession—even of his own heart and body.

there is no flesh in their composition; nor have they any cuticle. They brook no foreign body among them; there is no pain so grievous as pain in them; the lips shut them in so that they may remain unseen.' So far of the condition of the teeth; it is allegorical of the monastic life. The monks are 'whiter' than Christians in the world (they have chosen a 'more compendious way' and a 'safer life'); [1] they are not of the flesh, but of the spirit; they have stripped themselves of all worldly integument and outward show. The analogy goes further. The monks are cloistered by their walls, as are the teeth by the lips; dissension within a monastery causes as terrible anguish to the Church as toothache to the body. Above all, just as the teeth can brook no opposition, but crush or reject gritty particles which resist their pressure, so the true monk abhors the tiniest ground of offence, whether in his community or in himself—'nec modicum quidem offendiculum tolerabile reputant.' 'Hence,' Bernard adds, speaking to his own congregation of Clairvaux, and alluding to the almost daily confessions of his monks in half-humorous deprecation,—'hence comes that opportune importunity of yours which tires me so, and which occupies so much of your days—even unnecessarily at times.'

There is nothing here to which Antony, Pachomius, or Benedict would not have subscribed. Nor do the further obvious lessons which Bernard draws from the fact that the teeth are 'orderly disposed in the two jaws, of which the lower is movable, but the upper fixed and firm,' [2] go beyond the conceptions of the older rules. But a new spirit is abroad; what follows is prophetic of the mendicant Orders rather than reminiscent of the older monasticism. 'The teeth are never a pretty sight unless revealed by a smile. They masticate food for the whole body, but themselves enjoy it not. They are not easily worn away.' So nothing is worse than that the monk should be seen abroad, 'posting from village to village and palace to palace,' unless indeed he is driven into public life by that love which covers a multitude of sins. 'For love is like a smile, and full of joy'; and the monk is here to minister true joy ('læta non dissoluta') to the world. His function—his only function—is that of unsparing service; his chief service constant prayer both for living and departed. Like the teeth he must work for others, but he himself should neither gain nor desire ought thereby.

In this trivial conceit, S. Bernard has redressed the balance of monasticism. Nothing is said of the monk saving his own soul. *Sic vos non vobis* is the motto written over the cloister; the whole contemplative life is required to issue in the unmitigated altruism of unwearying intercession, and the love that is like a smile. Prin-

---

[1] 'via compendiosior,' 'securior vita'—the language, like that of S. Thomas, is not incompatible with the valid theory of the double standard (*supra*, pp. 253, 256).

[2] So, though the inferior monks may at times be perturbed, 'the business of prelates is to retain a composed mind.'

ciples of this character were implicit in the rules of Benedict and his predecessors; Basil, Cassiodorus and Gregory the Great had in various ways put them into practice. But here, in the strictest school of reformed Benedictinism, we meet at last with overt expression of that which is to dominate the new ascetic ventures, the Cathari, the Humiliati, and the Waldenses, together with the more orthodox institutions of S. Francis and S. Dominic. Obedience and humility are still high among monastic virtues, but their purpose is merely to fit the monk for service. It is often our duty, Bernard says, to leave spiritual contemplation, however sweet, for the practical labours which minister to men; ' man must live not for himself alone, but for the good of all.' [1] The bridal chamber must be strewn with the flowers of good works before the Bridegroom will visit it.[2] Contemplation without active charity is only an ' inane idleness '; [3] but after a good deed the repose of contemplation may be sought more surely.[4] The more a man can with clear conscience say that inertness and self-love have not hindered him from active service, the more boldly he may strive to learn and understand the deeper and loftier truths.[5] A saint to Bernard is one who has

> ' shown himself benevolent and charitable; who has lived humanely among men, keeping back nothing for himself, but using to the common advantage of all every grace that he possesses; who has regarded himself as a debtor to all men, to friend and foe, to wise and foolish alike. Such as these, being humble at all times, were useful to all. Before all things they showed themselves dear to God and to man; and their fragrance is held in pious memory.' [6]

Naturally enough—for in the main he addresses himself to men of the religious life—the service of which S. Bernard thinks is most commonly that of ministering to the spiritual needs of others; anyone who is called to this must devote himself to it wholeheartedly. With fine allegorism he interprets S. Peter's threefold commission to feed the sheep as a feeding by precept, by example, and by prayer; with an even bolder paraphrase of a text which centuries of Christianity had made sacred, he adds the words: ' Now abideth speech, example, prayer, these three; but the greatest of these is prayer. For forceful speech is work indeed, but prayer wins grace and efficacy both for speech and work.' [7] Nor must a

---

[1] *in cant. sermo* 41 (Mab., i, coll. 2922, 2923); cp. *supra*, p. 145, n. 3.

[2] *Ib., sermo* 46. 7 (Mab., i, col. 2949).   [3] *Ib.,* ' inane otium ' (col. 2948).

[4] *Ib., sermo* 47. 4 (col. 2953).

[5] *Ib.;* cp. *sermm.* 49. 6, 7; 50. 5; 57. 9. In 50. 5 Bernard justifies even absence from Mass where charity requires it—a considerable concession from one who to his dying day scarcely ever omitted attendance (*Vita prima,* v, I—Mab., ii, col. 2249).

[6] *in cant. sermo* 12. 5 (Mab., i, col. 2723).

[7] *ep.* 201. 3 (Mab., i, coll. 430, 431).

man's interest be absorbed by his own prayers and his own work. He must spare loving thought and intercession for the labours of others. In a moving passage of the 49th sermon, whose deep effect upon the monks in Chapter was visible in their expressions and audible in their sighs,[1] he urges them to that highest exercise of Christian charity which can rejoice at the successful accomplishment of great tasks by others, whilst we ourselves are relegated to minor and even menial employments :—' How hard it is, brethren, to praise another's good when we find ourselves surpassed in virtue ! There is still some light left in us if we can feel this truth.' [2]

But though prayer and spiritual ministrations rank first in importance, it would be a misrepresentation of one of the most delicate strains of S. Bernard's thought to suggest that secular life and labour were in his mind a fruitless struggle laid upon us by the mere necessity of physical existence. That the secular life is more irksome, difficult and dangerous than the monastic, he is well aware. With other mediæval moralists he takes the bishop as the type of a man of affairs. His letters and his book ' On Consideration ' show how freely and fully he was prepared to attack episcopal worldliness ; but he will not allow the sheltered monk to criticize the ecclesiastical statesman who bears the real heat and burden of the day. The monk is as the wife who sits at home in ease and comfort ; the bishop as the husband who goes out to fight or labour for her sake :—

' What folly for the woman who spins at home to reproach her man on his return from the field of battle ! If we who dwell in the cloister observe that a prelate, whose daily duties lie among the people, conducts himself with less discretion than he should,—with lack of self-restraint, for example, in speech, in food, in length of slumber, in laughter, in bad temper, in liberty of judgment,—we must not jump to unkind conclusions, but remember what is written, " Better is the wickedness of a man than a pleasant dealing woman " (Ecclus. xlii, 14). For we indeed do well to guard ourselves with vigilance ; but he, in helping many, does better still, and leads the more manly life.' [3]

Bernard, of course, with all the orthodox churchmanship of his day, thinks of the civil State as handmaid to the Church, but in terms of Augustine rather than of Hildebrand—the service of the body has its meaning only as accessory to the salvation of the soul. So regarded, society is a complex and wonderful organism designed to the glory of God—the house in which the Church may finally meet her Bridegroom in the embrace of perfect peace. ' The beams of our houses are cedars, and our rafters are cypresses ' is one of his texts from the Canticles (i, 16), and on it he allegorizes as follows :— [4]

[1] in cant. sermo 49. 7 (Mab., i, col. 2965). [2] Ib.
[3] Ib., sermo 12. 9 (Mab., i, coll. 2725, 2726).
[4] Ib., sermo 45. 2 (Mab., i, col. 2946).

' By " houses " we understand the great mass of Christian people, bound together with the beams of those who hold power and dignity, princes in Church and State. These by wise and firm laws hold them together, lest if each work in his own way and at his own will, the walls should sag and start asunder, and the whole house fall in ruins. By the rafters [1] firmly attached to the beams, and adorning the house in princely fashion, are meant the kindly and regular lives and characters of a clergy properly instructed, and the due administration of the rites of the Church. For how shall the clergy carry out their work, or the Church discharge her duties, if princes do not, like strong and solid beams, protect them by their power, and maintain them by their liberality? '

Rigidly ascetic though his own life was, it is obvious that Bernard's interest in mortification must be modified [2] by thoughts such as these. As with his greatest predecessors, so with him, rigorism and humanism are retained in that paradoxical unanimity which is so distinctive of Christianity. The true preparation for the vision of God is the life of active charity. The same life is its complement and consummation ; asceticism must neither oust service from the preliminary stages, nor impede it in the final. In the ' Apology ' to William of S. Thierry he has much to say against the degenerate licence of Cluny ; but he prefaces it all with a sharp rebuke to the Pharisaism of his own congregation of Cîteaux. ' The kingdom of God is *within* you,' [3] he says, in recollection of another address to Pharisees—

' Ye accuse your brethren in respect of bodily observances ; but the weightier things of the law—its spiritual requirements —ye neglect, straining out the gnat and swallowing the camel . . . as though the cowl made the monk ! Humility in furs is better than pride in a cassock. . . . You blame their eating of flesh ; but you yourselves are gluttons in the matter of beans. . . . These things ought ye to have done, but not to have left the others undone ; if spiritual and bodily observance come into conflict, the latter must give place to the former. For as the spirit is higher than the body, so does spiritual activity bring forth better fruit than bodily mortifications.' [4]

In consonance with this, S. Bernard continually attacks all exaggerations and abnormalities of asceticism. The desire to live

---

[1] ' laquearia '—the word used by the Vulgate implies the ' panels of the ceiling ' rather than ' rafters '—hence they ' adorn ' the house as well as forming part of its structure.

[2] Thus *in cant. sermo* 40. 4, 5, though addressed to the monks, insists that what is required for communion with God is solitude of the spirit, not [necessarily] of the body.' This solitude of the spirit is simply detachment from earthly desires, and ' can be exercised even in a crowd.'

[3] i.e. ' not in external observances.'

[4] *apol. ad Gullielm.*, 6, 7 (12, 13).

a solitary, as distinct from a cloistered, life is a dangerous temptation, against which the monk must at all times be on his guard.[1]
The novice particularly must be warned, and that with severity,
against any tendency to add to the simplicity prescribed by the Rule
by indiscreet and immoderate mortifications.[2]

If S. Bernard hesitates more than a modern might do to praise
and inculcate the life of active service, it is not because he under-
values it. It is rather that it seems to him so high a thing, and
yet so full of dangers—above all the danger of spiritual pride—that
he dare not commend it over-much to any who have not begun by
progress in seeing God to realize their own dependence, weakness,
and need of the Spirit. Hence his first thought is always to direct
his hearers or readers to such an exercise of contemplation as shall
fit them most truly to serve others well. The fullness of the vision
of God is not attainable by any in this life ;[3] even such degree as
can be attained must be reached by stages. The soul must embrace
the feet and kiss the hands of the Bridegroom before it dare aspire
to the kisses of His lips.[4] Of the experience, which, with all other
great Christians, he calls ' seeing God,' and to which he attributes
the origin of whatever is of value in the life of service, he speaks
with bated breath. It is so far beyond all human merit that he
scarcely dare lay claim to it. ' I do not know how it may be for
others,' he says, ' but for myself this is a chamber into which
I have [only] at times been allowed to penetrate—and, alas! how
rare the day, how brief the stay ! '[5] But such as it is, his own
weak experience [6] must serve him as an example whereby to communicate to others that which is the mainspring of the Christian
life.

It would be easy to quote from the sermons on the Canticles
passage after passage descriptive of the psychological effect of that
experience which purifies the soul, and fits and inspires it for the
service of men's needs, spiritual and temporal alike. Bernard is
second to none of the great mystics in these descriptions ; he
recognizes to the full the emotional qualities with which the vision
may be adorned. But his test of its validity is always a moral one.
On the one hand there is the healing effect of contemplation :—

> ' The vision does not terrify but soothe. . . . It tranquil-
> lizes the spirit without wearying it ; here is rest indeed. The
> God of peace makes all things peaceful ; the very sight of His

---

[1] *in cant. sermo* 64. 4 (Mab., i, col. 3050).

[2] *Ib.*, 19. 7 (i, col. 2769).   [3] *Ib.*, 31. 2 (Mab., i, col. 2863).

[4] *Ib.*, 3, *pass. ;* cp. *sermo* 18. 6 (Mab., i, coll. 2764, 2765)—the seven
stages—' compunctio,' ' devotio,' ' poenitentiae labor,' ' pietatis opus,'
' orationis studium,' ' contemplationis otium,' ' plenitudo dilectionis ' ; cp.
de dil. Deo, 8 (23)—10 (29) ; *ep.* 11. 8—the four stages of love ; *de grad.
humilitatis, pass.*—the three stages of humility.

[5] *Ib.*, 23. 15 (Mab., i, col. 2802)—' sed heu ! rara hora, et parva mora ! ' ;
cp. 32. 2—' tempus modicum ' ; 85. 13—' breve momentum et experimen-
tum rarum' ; *de dil. Deo*, 27 ; *de grat. et lib. arb.*, 15 ; and *infra*, p. 392, n. 1.

[6] *Ib.*, 73. 10 ; cp. 74. 1 (Mab., i, coll. 3122, 3123).

repose is repose-conferring. We see Him as a king who, after hearing causes in his court all day long, has dismissed his crowds of attendants, ended the labours of the day, and retired to his palace at nightfall. He enters his chamber with the few friends who share the intimacy of that retreat. Privacy increases his confident tranquillity, and his serenity mounts as he looks calmly round upon the faces of his dearest companions. . . . So (in this inner chamber of contemplation) God deigns to show Himself lovable, serene and peaceful, sweet and gentle, full of mercy towards all who look on Him.' [1]

On the other hand is the power of contemplation to inspire to action and to renew ideals. Of his own experience Bernard says :—

> You will ask how—since the ways of God's coming are past finding out,[2]—could I know that He was present? Why, is living and full of energy. As soon as He comes to me He quickens my sleeping soul, rouses and softens and goads my heart, which was sunk in torpor, hard as stone, stricken with disease. He begins to pluck up and destroy, to plant and build, to water the dry places and illuminate the gloomy, to open shut doors and inflame whatever was cold, to straighten the crooked paths and make the rough places smooth. . . . By the revived activity of my heart I know His presence ; by the sudden victory over vicious desires and carnal joys His power for good. By conviction of secret faults I learn to marvel at the depths of His wisdom. In amendment of life (small though it be) I see His goodness and kindness. In the renewal and recreation of my mind, of my inner man, I glimpse, in some slight degree, the excellence of the divine beauty.' [3]

From true contemplation the soul returns ' fired with an ardent love for God, inflamed with a burning zeal for righteousness, fervent for the pursuit of all spiritual duties and studies.' Intoxication, the sceptic may call this rapture ; but at least, Bernard replies, it is an intoxication whose effects, unlike those of any other, ' are wholly salutary and good.' [4] *Wholly* good, for unless

---

[1] *in cant. sermo* 23. 16 (Mab., i, coll. 2803, 2804).

[2] The passage is very remarkable. (*a*) He has just said that he is unable to discern the *moments* of God's coming and going (' non sensi aliquoties cum intravit. adesse sensi, adfuisse recordor, interdum et præsentire potui introitum ejus ; sentire numquam, sed ne exitum quidem ') ; (*b*) the continuation suggests that what puzzles him is the *way in which* God comes—a purely scientific question (' not by the eyes, not by the ears,' etc.) ; (*c*) but the question put to him is, ' How did you know that God *was present* ? ' (' unde adesse norim ').—The three problems are confused ; but it is the third to which he addresses his answer. His insistence upon the wholly moral tests of God's presence show that he shares in the aversion from panhedonism distinctive of the greatest Christians.

[3] *in cant. sermo* 74. 6 (Mab., i, col. 3126).

[4] *Ib., sermo* 49. 4 (i, col. 2963). The idea is suggested by the text upon which Bernard has to comment, Cant. 2⁴—' He brought me to the house of wine ' (R.V. mg.—Vulg. ' cella vinaria ') ; but the metaphor is pressed too realistically for modern taste.

'discretion,' 'the charioteer of the virtues' which 'orders zeal' so
that it may be truly called Christian charity, is infused into the
soul along with zeal, we cannot claim to have received from the
vision of God all that it has in store for us.[1]

By phrases such as these S. Bernard attempted so to hedge about
the mystical experience of western Christendom with moral safe-
guards—so to set it in the frame of a life of active service—that
the negative and ecstatic implications of the Areopagite tradition
should be kept within their true bounds. In this respect, however,
he made a real advance upon his teachers. In the transition from
Platonism to Christianity, S. Augustine had remoulded the best of
contemporary philosophy to fit the truth of the Word becoming
flesh. He had substituted the ethics of love and humility for the
ethics of self-reliance and self-regard. But he had failed to grasp
that the same Christian standards must be applied to the Church's
mysticism as to her philosophic creed and moral code, if the three
strands of faith, conduct and experience of God are to be woven
into a perfect cord. Hence, as we have seen, his descriptions of
the vision of God, and all that it implies, contain little that is distinctive of Christianity. Beautiful and exalted though they are,
and despite Friedrich Heiler's argument to the contrary, they are
all but wholly Platonic.[2] At this point S. Bernard, infinitely inferior to S. Augustine as a theologian, shows himself the more
truly Christian of the two; the Abbot of Clairvaux completes and
transcends the work of the Bishop of Hippo.

The Bridegroom of the soul—whether the 'soul' be Church or
individual [3]—is to S. Bernard always and only the glorified

---

[1] *in cant. sermo* 49. 5.—Bernard notes that his text (Cant. 2⁴) at once
adds the words ' *ordinavit in me caritatem* '—the immediate sequel of true
contemplation (entry into the 'cella vinaria') is to be moral orderliness,
or 'discretio.' Passages descriptive of ecstasy are *ep.* 11. 8 (the 'fourth
grade' of love); *de consid.*, v, 2 (3); *de dil. Deo*, 27, 28; *in cant. sermm.* 11. 4;
31. 2, 6; 32. 4, 5; 41. 2-4; 52. 3-5; 57. 1, 7, 8; 67. 3; 83. 6; 85. 10-14.
Details of the vocabulary, C. Butler, *Western Mysticism*², pp. 151, 168, 170.
Luthardt, *Christian Ethics*, p. 323 (from Plitt), notices that Bernard only
twice uses the idea of ' deification ' by the vision.

[2] *Supra*, pp. 321, 326; and see F. Heiler, *Der Katholizismus*, pp. 105, 106..

[3] The 'bride' *the Church* :—*in cant. sermm.* 14. 5, 7; 21. 1; 46. 2, 4;
68. 1; 69. 1, etc.; *the individual* :—*ib.*, 46. 5; 68. 4; 69. 1; 73. 10; 74. 3.
The latter series of passages is most instructive. The care with which
Bernard in every case insists upon the temerity of speaking of an individual
soul as the ' bride ' reveals his hesitation to encourage anything of the nature
of erotic imagery in personal religion. Further, his tone in such places
drops almost to a prosaic level. Thus, in *serm.* 67, so long as the Church
is the bride (cp. § 11), 'My Beloved is mine, and I am His' can have the
fullest of meanings (§ 8). But when for a moment he allows it to be applied
to the individual (§ 9) the mystical implication is removed. For ' Dilectus
meus mihi et ego Illi ' we must now read, ' Dilectus meus mihi *intendit*, et
ego Illi '—' God *pays heed* to me, and I to Him '; cp. 69. 7. Bernard is
therefore almost as restrained in this matter as Origen, who commonly
makes the Church the bride (*hom. in cant.*, int. Hieron., i, 7; ii, 3, 10; *comm.
in cant.*, int. Ruf., *prol.*; i; ii (*GCSS.*, 'Origenes,' viii, pp. 39, 45, 55, 61, 90,
113); and only rarely the soul (Hieron., i, 3; Ruf., *prol.*; ii (*ib.*, pp. 32,
61, 125)). On the mystic marriage generally, *supra*, p. 28, n. 2.

Jesus, as known in that humanity in which He walked the earth. The fact is recognized, of course, by writers on S. Bernard or on Christian mysticism as a whole.[1] But few of them—not even Abbot Butler or Miss Underhill—give it the emphasis which it deserves ; whilst for the casual spectator of mediæval piety the glamour of S. Francis has wholly eclipsed the originality of S. Bernard, to whom Christian devotion, whether Catholic or Protestant, owes the rediscovery of its most treasured and evangelical elements.

The majority of S. Bernard's sermons for the Christian year focus loving attention upon the earthly life of Jesus ; but it is in his chapter-house meditations upon the Song of Songs that his deepest aspirations are revealed. With an impressive gesture he sweeps Peter away from heaven's gate, and installs Philip and Andrew in his stead. ' Sir, we would see Jesus,' becomes once more the highest desire of humanity, and to that plea the two apostles are no more deaf to-day than in the days of old.[2]

Eighty years ago, when the supposed ashes of the saint were disinterred from the resting-place to which they were hurried during the Directory of 1792, there was found with them a rude amulet of wood and parchment, with the inscription, ' Fasciculus myrrhæ Dilectus meus mihi ; inter ubera mea commorabitur '—' My beloved is a bundle of myrrh ; he shall lie between my breasts.'[3] That the amulet belonged to Bernard cannot be said, though the characters are alleged to be of the twelfth century. But the text itself was very dear to him, and he built upon it one of his most beautiful sermons. ' The bundle of myrrh ' is the sum-total of the labours and sufferings of Jesus. The Christian will never let them fade from his mind :—

> ' To meditate on these things I have called wisdom ; in them I find the perfection of righteousness, the fullness of know-ledge, the riches of salvation, the abundance of merit. Let Jesus be ever borne, not upon your shoulders as a burden, but before your eyes. . . . Remember how Simeon took Him up, how Mary loved Him . . . how Joseph must often have taken the Child upon his knee, and smiled at Him. . . . Let them be your example. Do ye do likewise ; bear Him with you, and keep Him before your eyes . . . so shall you easily and readily

[1] Cp. C. Butler, *Western Mysticism* [2], p. 138 ; W. R. Inge, *Christian Mysticism*, p. 140, n. (the Appendix on this subject promised in the footnote has apparently never been written) ; F. Heiler, *Der Katholizismus*, p. 132. Fuller appreciations, P. Pourrat, *Spiritualité Chrétienne* [5], ii, pp. 59-76 ; E. Vacandard, *Vie de Saint Bernard*, i, pp. 484-490. On the novelty of the conception, F. Bühler, *Das deutsche Geistesleben im Mittelalter*, p. 522, with reference to pp. 46 and 221.

[2] *in cant. sermo* 15. 3 (Mab., i, col. 2742).

[3] See Ph. Guignard, *Lettre à M. le Comte de Montalembert* (1855), in *MPL.*, clxxxv, col. 1700. E. Vacandard, *Vie de St. Bernard*, ii, p. 528, alludes to the fact, but with appropriate caution. On the disposal of the saint's remains in 1792, *ib.*, pp. 550-553.

bear your burdens, through His help Who is the Bridegroom of the Church, above all, God blessed for ever.'[1]

No lover of S. Bernard will forgive me if I end what I have to say about him without a reference to his sermon on the Name of Jesus —that beautiful piece of mediæval latinity in which his adoring devotion to the Lord he loved so well finds its consummation :—

'The name of Jesus is both light and nourishment. Are you not strengthened in the spirit when you meditate upon it ? What else enriches the mind so much as this name of Jesus ? What so restores our wasted powers, strengthens the soul in virtue, inspires it to good and honourable conduct, fosters in it all pure and saintly characteristics ? . . . No book or writing has any savour for me if I read not therein the name of Jesus ; no colloquy or sermon grips unless the name of Jesus be heard there. As honey to the taste, as melody in the ear, as songs of gladness in the heart, so is the name of Jesus. And medicine it is as well. Is any of you sad ? Let Jesus come into your heart ; let His name leap thence to your lips ; and behold its light disperses the clouds of darkness like the morning sun, and brings back serenity and peace. Is any falling into sin— aye, even the desperate sin of self-murder ? Let him call again upon that saving name ; at once his courage and hope will revive. In the presence of that life-giving name, who has ever remained fast bound by hardness of heart, vulgar idleness, rancour of mind, or dull accidie ? . . . These are the diseases of the soul ; this is their remedy. . . . Naught but the name of Jesus can restrain the impulse of anger, repress the swelling of pride, cure the wound of envy, bridle the onslaught of luxury, extinguish the flame of carnal desire—can temper avarice, and put to flight impure and ignoble thoughts. For when I name the name of Jesus, I call into mind at once a Man meek and lowly of heart, benign, pure, temperate, merciful ; a Man conspicuous for every honourable and saintly quality ; and also in the same Person the Almighty God—so that He both restores me to health by His example and renders me strong by His assistance. No less than this is brought to my mind by the name of Jesus whenever I hear it.'[2]

[1] *in cant. sermo* 43. 4, 5. The text is from Cant. 1[13] (Vulg. 1[12]).

[2] *Ib.,* 15. 6.—It is commonly agreed that the 'Jubilus Rhythmus' (*Jesu dulcis memoria*), though it has a close connexion both of thought and of vocabulary with this sermon, is not by S. Bernard ; for a curious error by which it has recently been supposed to be pre-Bernardine in date, see R. Vaux, *Church Quarterly Review,* cviii (1929), pp. 120-125. An extraordinary example of similar 'Jesus-worship' of a much earlier date is to be found in a hymn attributed to Clement of Alexandria, in which the Saviour is addressed as 'the bridle of colts untamed, the wing of birds that wander not, the infant's helm, the shepherd of the royal flock, the children's guide, the shepherd, husbandman, rudder, bridle, heavenly wing of the holy flock, fisher of men,' etc. (*DALC.,* vi, col. 2843).

Constant recurrence to the name of Jesus, earnest consideration
of all that it stands for—the testing by this standard of our lives
and our whole environment, of things above, and things around,
and things beneath us [1]—this is at once the great mainspring and
the great reward of the Christian life. The result of true ' consideration ' is certain—the flowering of all the graces of Christian
saintliness. Where this result is absent no real union with God
has been attained : where it is present—where the soul is visibly
increasing in saintliness and discretion, in likeness to Jesus our
' brother ' [2]—we need no other test that God has been with us.
Bernard is no theologian ; he remains almost untouched by the
abstract questions of Christian ethics. But of one thing he is
certain. Moral advance is impossible without the vision of God
in Christ ; and moral stagnation is a sure sign that, however much
we claim to know God, our claim is empty and void.

For sanity and saintliness combined—for all the distinctive
lessons of Christianity in ethics—a Christian could scarcely find a
better teacher than S. Bernard. The evangelical character of his
own practice stands out in clear relief, for example, if his attitude
to the problem of discipline is considered. That the whole of his
teaching is a call for *self*-discipline on the part of his hearers—a
self-discipline whose purpose is to fit the soul to see God and to
serve Him—needs no further proof. Beyond this, however, the
exercise of discipline coercively by the authorities of the Church
is wholly repugnant to him. Men cannot be bullied into the way
of seeing God, and that is all that matters. He is enough of a
mediæval man sometimes to set disciplinary machinery in motion
himself. It is his voice that calls, with violence and at times even
with regrettable abuse, for the condemnation of Peter Abailard and
Gilbert de la Porrée ; [3] and the measures which Pope Innocent took
against Louis VII and his partisans had his warm approval.[4]
But how eager he was that charity should overpass justice may
be seen in his attempt (as his biographer says) to ' correct Abailard's
error without confounding its author ' ; [5] in his readiness to accept
Abailard's advance towards a reconciliation through the medium
of Peter of Cluny ; [6] in his own overtures towards a renewal of
friendly theological discussion with Gilbert after the break-up of

---

[1] *de consid.*, ii, 3 (6)—the famous fourfold division is taken from Augustine,
de doctr. Christ., i, 22 ; but whereas Augustine's ' quod infra nos est ' refers
to the body, Bernard's ' quæ sub te ' are the flock of Christ whom the Pope
(herein typical of all Christian pastors) is to tend (*de consid.*, iii, 1), cp. *infra*,
pp. 371 f.

[2] *in cant. sermo* 15. 4.

[3] Good accounts of these two controversies in R. L. Poole, *Studies in
Mediæval Thought and Learning* [2] (1920), pp. 142-145, 160-169; E. Vacandard,
Vie de St. Bernard, ii, pp. 141-162, 337-355.

[4] See Bernard, *epp.* 216, 221.

[5] *Vita prima*, iii, 5 (13) (Mab., ii, col. 2199) ; cp. *ep.* 337. 2 (Mab., i, col.
628).

[6] Petrus Vener., *ep.* iv, 4 (*MPL.*, clxxxix. col. 306).

the Council of Rheims ;[1] and in his schemes for a peace between the pope and the king of France which, while maintaining the dignity of the former, should not humiliate the latter.[2] S. Bernard accuses the heretics of his day of every moral perversion which could well be laid to their charge ;[3] he has no sympathy even with their readiness to die rather than renounce the error which is their faith. But he will not allow force to be used against them except —hypothetically—in the most extreme case ; and he deplores the zealous but misguided outbursts of popular orthodoxy which on occasion led to their deaths. ' Faith can only be produced by persuasion, never imposed by force,' he says ; ' heretics should be taken not by arms but by arguments.'[5] The use of force against the Jews he condemns even more unsparingly ;[6] the synagogue honours his name even to the present day as that of one who in practice as well as in theory was its friend and protector. In this matter (as Cotter Morison pointed out many years ago)[7] even the greatest of his friends, Peter of Cluny. was guilty of the cruellest counsels ; Bernard stands alone in his championship of prayer and preaching as the weapons of the Church against Israel, and in condemnation of the stake and sword.

[1] So R. L. Poole, *Mediæval Thought and Learning*, p. 169 ; Vacandard, ii, p. 353, from John of Salisbury. Gilbert's reply was insulting ; but he had been made to suffer acutely.

[2] Bernard, *epp.* 217, 219, 358.

[3] *in cant. sermones* 65, 66.   [4] *Ib.*, 66. 13.

[5] *in cant. sermo* 66. 12—' fides suadenda est, non imponenda ' ; *ib.*, 64. 8— ' capiantur non armis, sed argumentis.' But in both passages he adds that, if all else fails, force must be used.

[6] *ep.* 365 (Mab., i, col. 667) ; contrast Petr. Ven., *ep.* iv, 36 (*MPL.*, clxxxix, coll. 366-368).

[7] J. C. Morison, *St. Bernard*, pp. 375, 376 ; cp. Vacandard, ii, pp. 288, 289.

LECTURE VII.

CONFUSION AND ORDER.

1 Cor. xiv. 33, 40—' God is not the author of confusion but of peace. . . .
Let all things be done decently and in order.'

I. THE TWELFTH CENTURY.[1]

' THE history of piety in the middle ages,' Harnack has written, ' is
the history of monachism.'[2] Fr. Pourrat rightly takes the phenomenon further back still :—

> ' In the patristic period, no books of devotion were composed
> for Christians living " in the world." The same is true of a great
> part of the middle ages. . . . There were not two " spiritual
> lives," one for the ascetic, the other for ordinary Christians.
> There was only one ; and that was monastic. From the birth
> of monasticism, Christians who proposed to take the quest for
> perfection seriously became monks—either by retiring to the
> desert or cloister, or by practising domestic asceticism of the
> monastic kind. Practically all the saints of the period were,
> or had been, monks. The bishops, the great fathers of the
> Church, had embraced the monastic life prior to their elevation
> to the episcopate. Hence it is not surprising that spiritual
> writers should never have thought of addressing themselves
> to secular Christians; nor that their piety was monastic in
> character.'[3]

There is a sense in which these reflections are no more than plati-
tudes. Why should we expect a difference in character between
lay and monastic piety ? Is Christ divided ? And if there was

---

[1] What follows is a very brief summary of an aspect of mediæval culture
which has often been handled fully ; cp. for example, G. Grupp, *Kulturgeschichte des Mittelalters*[2] (1923-1925), especially vols. iii-vi ; E. Scott-
Davison, *Forerunners of St. Francis* (1928) ; E. Gebhart, *Mystics and
Heretics in Italy* (E. tr. 1922, by E. M. Hulme, of *L'Italie Mystique*, 1890) ;
G. G. Coulton, *Five Centuries of Religion*, vol. ii, especially cc. 7-10 ; Fr.
Cuthbert Hess, O.F.C., *St. Francis of Assisi*[3] (1920) ; *C. Med. H.*, vol. vi
(1929), especially cc. 20 and 21 ; O. Zöckler, *Askese u. Mönchtum*, pp. 471-
537 ; P. Pourrat, *Spiritualité Chrétienne*, vol. ii ; H. O. Taylor, *The Mediæval
Mind ;* and from a different point of view, E. Haskins, *The Renaissance of
the Twelfth Century.*

[2] Harnack, *Hist. of Dogma* (E. tr.), v, p. 10 ; cp. also H. B. Workman,
Evolution of Monastic Ideal, p. 4 ; G. G. Coulton, *op. cit.*, i, p. 89.

[3] Pourrat, *SC.*, i, pp. ix, x.

only to be one kind of piety, nothing could be more natural than that it should radiate outwards from the monastery. As the Church looked to the theologian for the formulation of her doctrine, so she looked to the monk, who had ordered his life in such a way as to find the greatest room for prayer, for expert guidance in the ways of devotion. But here the difficulty began. Monastic piety was bound up with the recitation of ' prayers,' the psalter and the choir offices ; and the time available for these occupations in a secular life was all too restricted. Thus for a period Christian piety, in anything like the full sense of the word, was not merely monastic in character ; it was also the prerogative of the monks, who alone had leisure for it. This factor in pre-Reformation Christianity, purely accidental though it was, reinforced the theory of the double standard in its invalid form, to the practical exclusion of secular persons from all but the most formalist branches of Christian observance.

It is no small testimony, therefore, to the genius of Christianity that the middle ages witnessed a persistent and not entirely unsuccessful demand upon the part of the laity for admission—or re-admission—to the full privileges of religion. As civilization emerged out of the dark ages this tendency showed itself in the curiously pedantic form of ' conversio ad succurrendum ' [1]—the practice by which the layman, at the approach of death, betook himself to a monastery, to meet his end in the monastic habit. The phenomenon, widespread though it was, is no more than a crude manifestation of a tendency whose roots lay very deep, which produced as its fairest fruit the Brothers Minor of S. Francis ; and thence was reborn again in the Third Orders.

The movement has various stages. About the year 1090 Bernold of St. Blaise observed how in Germany groups of pious laymen and laywomen were gathering together to lead a life of evangelical simplicity with community of goods. Often enough they would settle in the neighbourhood of a monastery or convent, and ' offer themselves in service to the monks, after the pattern of Him Who came not to be ministered unto, but to minister '; their pious intentions were rewarded with papal approval.[2] But the first great lay-movement of which history has any clear cognizance is that of the Cathari,[3] who appeared in northern Italy in the middle of the twelfth century, and within a hundred years had acquired innumerable adherents. Almost contemporary were the

---

[1] G. G. Coulton, *op. cit.*, i, pp. 90-94, 382, 383, 476-481 ; cp. also L. Gougaud, *Devotional and Ascetic Practices of the Middle Ages* (E. tr. 1927), pp. 131-145. Gougaud cites the emperor Lothaire, A.D. 855, as among the earliest examples of the practice (*ib.*, p. 135). Eastern examples in K. Holl, *op. cit.*, pp. 321, 322.

[2] Bernold. Const., *Chronicon* (*MGH.*, script. v), pp. 439 (A.D. 1083) ; 452, 453 (A.D. 1091). Grupp, *op. cit.*, iii, pp. 169, 170, sees in this movement the origin of the lay-brothers, or *conversi* in the later sense ; but it seems to have been wider than this, for the groups of women devotees also attached themselves to the monasteries in a ministerial capacity (' more ancillarum ').

[3] Gebhart, pp. 56-58 ; Scott-Davison, pp. 202-225 ; Grupp, iii, pp. 57-59.

Waldenses [1] in southern France ; the Humiliati of Lombardy,[2] of whom some at least received ecclesiastical recognition and never passed into heresy ; and the Béghards and Béguines [3] in the Netherlands. Evangelical poverty, ecclesiastical reform, a strict adherence to the letter of the Sermon on the Mount, study of the scriptures and mission preaching, were the principal ideals held in common by these and similar associations. Inquisitors themselves bore witness to the general purity of their lives, even when their teachings were suspected and condemned :—

> ' Heretics are recognized by their customs and speech, for they are modest and well-regulated. They take no pride in their garments, which are neither costly nor vile. They do not engage in trade, to avoid lies and oaths and fraud ; but live by their labour as mechanics—their teachers are cobblers. They do not accumulate wealth, but are content with necessaries. They are chaste and temperate in meat and drink. They do not frequent taverns or dances or other vanities. They restrain themselves from anger. They are always at work ; they teach and learn, and consequently pray but little. They are to be known by their modesty and precision of speech, avoiding scurrility and detraction, light words, lies and oaths. They do not even say *vere* or *certe*, regarding them as oaths.' [4]

The Penitents of Assisi [5] thus had many forerunners. This in no way detracts from the significance of S. Francis' work. With the establishment and regularization of the two mendicant Orders,[6] the one as a great missionary, the other as an equally great educational machine, the Church took in hand a situation that had been

[1] Gebhart, p. 58 ; Scott-Davison, pp. 241-270 ; Grupp, iv, pp. 379, 380 ; Coulton, ii, pp. 109-112 ; Harnack, *Hist. Dogm.*, vi, pp. 89-92 (notes).

[2] Gebhart, p. 59 ; Scott-Davison, pp. 174-200 ; Grupp, iv, pp. 380, 381 ; Coulton, ii, pp. 113-114.

[3] Grupp, iii, p. 317 ; v, p. 149 ; see also *PRE.*, ii, pp. 516-526 (*s.v.* ' Beginen,' etc.) ; *DTC.*, ii, coll. 528-535 (*s.v.* ' Béghards,' etc.) ; *ERE.*, ii, pp. 842, 843 (*s.v.* ' Brethren of the Free Spirit ').

[4] H. C. Lea, *History of the Inquisition*, i, p. 85. Lea's references here, as often, are sketchy ; but the passage will be found in c. 7 of the thirteenth century *liber contra Waldenses*, formerly ascribed to the Dominican, Rainer Sacchoni, but identified by W. Preger as the work of an inquisitor of the diocese of Passau. (References to Preger's three discussions are given in A. Potthast, *Bibliotheca Hist. Med. Aevi* (*Wegweiser*)², i, p. 109, s.v. ' Anonymus Passaviensis '.) The text was first published, in a garbled form, by Gretser in 1613 ; reprinted thereafter in successive editions of the *Magna* (*Maxima*) *Bibliotheca Vet. Patr.* (e.g. Paris, 1654, vol. iv (2), coll. 745-780). The whole tract is not, of course, so complimentary as Lea's excerpt.

[5] *Leg. III. Soc.*, 37 (Boll., *AS.*, Oct., ii, p. 733)—' viri poenitentiales de civitate Assisii oriundi.'

[6] The rule of S. Francis was approved by Innocent III in A.D. 1210 (Hess, *St. Francis*, pp. 90-108). The Dominicans received episcopal recognition in the diocese of Toulouse in July, 1215 (J. Guiraud, *Vie de S. Dominique*, p. 69) ; but the Lateran Council of the same autumn forbade the foundation of new Orders, and S. Dominic's preachers remained under the Austinian rule until 1218 (*ib.*, p. 97).

full of peril.   Although the Franciscans had still to face the dangers
of heresy and schism during the thirteenth century,[1] the two Orders
played a triumphant part in the stabilization of Christendom.
Organized asceticism received a new impetus to leave the cloister-
garth and minister to the needs of humanity at large.   The monastic
settlement became in ideal a rallying-point rather than a retreat ;
a headquarters rather than a home.   At the same time the aspirations of the laity to a share in that devotion which had hitherto
seemed the peculiar privilege of the monk were recognized by the
establishment of the Tertiaries.[2]   But these principles of a settlement, which, great though it was, was even so not strong enough
to subdue the forces that led ultimately to the Reformation, were
themselves only achieved after a long period of chaos.   The lay-
movements of the twelfth century took the Church entirely unawares.   She could not understand this sudden upheaval of the
established order ; nor was she at that time in a position to guide
the new movements along lines of Catholic thought.

The keynotes of the age were two—restless activity and uncontrolled sentiment.   Of the new zeal for service Bernard, Francis,
Dominic, the military Orders and the lay-movements all alike
provide illustrations.   The quietism which so often went hand in
hand with early monasticism suffered a definite eclipse ; mysticism
and public service formed a new alliance.   The great mystics of
the middle ages are men and women of action ; whilst S. Dominic,
for example—one of the most forceful characters of his day—lived
a spiritual life rich in emotional content.[3]   To him the world owes
as strong an insistence upon the duty of altruism as can well be
asked of any follower of Christ : ' Let our first study be '—so runs
his rule—' to be of service to our neighbours' souls.' [4]   Even the rare
surviving anchorites, it has been suggested,[5] were forced to justify
their existence by performing social duties,—stationing themselves
near ferries or bridges, or in pathless woods and remote valleys, to
offer help and hospitality to the chance wayfarer.

To this passion for neighbourly service was added, especially
by Bernard and Francis, the inspiration of a deep and truly Christian
emotionalism.   The believer's zeal, in their view, must find its
chief source of inspiration in the life and passion of his Lord.[6]

---

[1] For an account of the controversies, see Gebhart, *op. cit.*, pp. 165-219 ;
and cp. Harnack, *Hist. of Dogma*, vi, pp. 93-95, 111, 112.

[2] The Franciscan Third Order, Hess, pp. 320-345 ; K. Müller, *Die Anfänge
des Minoritenordens* (1885), pp. 130 ff.—The Dominican, Guiraud, *op. cit.*,
pp. 180-184 ; generally, Coulton, *op. cit.*, ii, pp. 148-152.   The earlier Premonstratensian Third Order, Scott-Davison, pp. 99, 100.

[3] Grupp, iv, pp. 388-390.

[4] *Constit.*, prol. (in H. Denifle, *Die Constitutionen des Predigerordens*,
ALKG., i (1885), p. 194).

[5] E. L. Cutts, *Scenes and Characters of the Middle Ages* [4], p. 103.

[6] So deeply rooted was this conviction, that even in the heyday of sacramentalist enthusiasm it was still insisted that the sacraments were merely
' instrumenta separata ' of human salvation, whilst the passion of Christ was

Devout reflection on those great themes would inflame the soul with a new desire to imitate in all things the spirit of the Master's life, and in some things at least—as with the Franciscans in the matter of poverty—the letter as well. Strength, however, as well as aspiration, was to be the outcome of contemplation ; the heart which occupied itself with these sacred mysteries knew an exaltation strong enough to triumph over temptation, frailty and self-seeking. In Francis the beauties and simplicities of nature, the gaiety and innocence of beasts and birds, were capable of begetting a like spiritual fervour ; and even Bernard, despite his explicit Cistercian puritanism, was not wholly callous to influences of the kind.

In all this the leaders of orthodox Catholicism were no more than typical of their day. But for all its delicate beauty and real spirituality their emotionalism was subject to the dangers which beset it in every age. Bernard was definitely distrustful of the learning of the schools—witness his action in the matters of Abailard and Gilbert de la Porrée ; Francis was no less on the side of the babes and sucklings against the wise and prudent. He would have no book in the hands of his disciples except the psalter and the gospels, ' lest by reading of the good deeds of others they should find no time for good deeds of their own.' [1] What was needed above all else was a sane yet unflinching theology ; and such a regulative force the twelfth century had yet to find.

S. Bernard's sermons, for example, sometimes betray a chaotic theological background which might well have startled the great writers of the patristic period. Everyone is familiar with the dialogue in heaven which opens the third book of ' Paradise Lost ' ; but its eccentricities are moderate as compared with parallels which can be quoted from the abbot of Clairvaux. In one such passage the Son of God is overheard soliloquizing upon the punishment of mankind—a punishment with which the Father has visited them because (at the instigation of the rebel angels) they sought to steal the Son's prerogative of the knowledge of good and evil. ' Man,' says the Saviour,

> ' grasped at a privilege which is Mine by right. My Father has not pardoned him, His eye hath not spared him. . . . Come then ! that men may know that I love My Father, He shall receive at My hands those whom, for My sake in a sense, He has destroyed. . . . They are jealous of Me, all of them. But lo, I come and so bear Myself on earth that whosoever is indeed jealous, and shall strive to imitate Me, shall do a good work. . . . The rebel angels, I know, cannot be saved : . . . and My Father created man to take their place, and restore the

---

* instrumentum conjunctum ' ; ' unde manifestum est quod sacramenta ecclesiæ specialiter habent virtutem ex passione Christi ' (Aquinas, ST., iii, q. 62, a. 5).

[1] Grupp, iv, p. 389 ; Scott-Davison, pp. 4 ff. ; for a balanced estimate cp. also Hess, *Life of St. Francis*, pp. 346-357.

ruins of Jerusalem. . . . But man can be saved, for no one has been created to take his place.'[1]

The theology of passages such as this does not bear examination ; it is as faulty as it is imaginative. Equally imaginative, and even more insidious, were the glosses with which preachers (mainly Franciscans) adorned the gospel story to make it more attractive. Earliest among surviving examples is a composition called 'Meditations on the Life of Jesus,' owing much to the influence of S. Bernard, which was for long attributed to S. Bonaventura, and certainly dates from his century. Its apocryphal anecdotes,— such as the attempt of Mary the mother of Jesus and Mary Magdalene to dissuade our Lord from the journey to Jerusalem which precipitated His passion, or the incidents of the Via Dolorosa,—had an immediate influence both on the mystery-plays and the religious art of the middle ages.[2] They were incorporated wholesale in the following century into what was probably the first attempt at a biography of Christ since the period of the apocryphal gospels— the 'Vita Christi' of Ludolph the Carthusian.[3] Unlike some more modern literary reconstructions of the gospel story, both these compilations frankly confess that much in them is merely pious fiction ;[4] but their success was enormous. Ludolph's 'Vita' was translated into the vernacular throughout western Europe, and passed through countless editions as soon as the discovery of the printing press made its rapid multiplication possible. The mythological instinct manifested in the 'Legenda Aurea,' the 'Miracles of Mary,' and similar collections of the thirteenth and fourteenth centuries, could not be restrained even when the most sacred life of all was in question.

So long as sentiment predominated over reason, edification

---

[1] *in adv. serm.* 1. 4-5 (Mab., i, col. 1640), cited by Pourrat, *SC.*, ii, p. 61, as an example of Bernard's eloquence, without recognition of its heterodox character. Cp. also the classical and vivacious 'Processus Paradisi' (also quoted by Pourrat), in the exposition of the 85th Psalm (' Mercy and truth are met together ; righteousness and peace have kissed each other '), *serm. in Annunc.*, i (Mab., i, coll. 2099-2101). Truth and Righteousness have fallen out with Mercy and Peace ; for Truth and Righteousness demand man's punishment, whilst Mercy and Peace plead for him. The argument takes place in good forensic fashion before the Father's throne, until a cherub suggests that the case should be transferred, as to a court of final appeal, to the Son, 'to whom all judgment has been given.' Truth and Righteousness demand man's death ; Mercy and Peace his forgiveness. 'Let death win forgiveness, then shall both sides be satisfied' ('fiat bona mors et habet utraque quod petit ') is the Son's decision ; and because no other can be found who is not under the sentence of death for sin, He gives Himself to die. On the influence of this 'Processus' on mediæval art, E. Mâle, *L'art religieux de la fin du M.A.*, pp. 36-38.
[2] *Ib.*, pp. 28-51.—For earlier attempts (mostly in verse, as for example the ninth-century 'Helyand' and Otfrid of Weissenburg's 'gospels book' poem) see *PRE.*, ix, pp. 7-9.
[3] Pourrat, *SC.*, ii, pp. 279, 478-481.
[4] [Bonav.] *medit. vit. Christi*, 9 (quoted Pourrat, ii, p. 278) ; Ludolphus, *vita Christi*, prol. (Pourrat, ii, p. 480).

rather than verisimilitude remained the test of truth. The critical study of the Bible, which had occasionally manifested itself in the patristic period, was now wholly unknown. All that mattered was the allegorical interpretation, and this could be tortured to give any sense which the exegete might wish. Hugh of S. Victor knew of doctors who openly boasted that they recked nothing of the literal meaning of scripture.[1] Secular study for its own sake was discouraged, and that—at heart—for the same reason.[2] The slightest advance towards scientific investigation in connexion with received history, such as Abailard's indiscreet scepticism about the identity of the patron saint of the Abbey of St. Denys,[3] might rouse the stormiest passions. More remarkable, and certainly more fascinating to the ordinary reader, is the indifference to the scientific study of nature bred by this demand for edification. Fostered by the dominant Platonic exemplarism which the authority of S. Augustine rendered supreme at the beginning of the intellectual revival, men saw the world of nature in no other light than as a hieroglyph of spiritual truth; and set themselves to study not so much the composition and characteristics as the symbolical propriety of natural phenomena.[4] None was more than a ' speculum '—a mirror—of some part of the divine nature. It mattered little therefore *what* truth about God could be read into each object, animate or inanimate, so long as *some* truth could be read there ; and once an edifying allegorism had been discovered, further interest in the phenomenon so treated very naturally tended to flag.[5]

Thus numbers, jewels, beasts and birds, were all given their symbolical value. The recitation of the psalter washes away sin, because its 150 psalms recall the 150 days of the flood.[6] Each of the twelve precious stones which made up the wall of the new Jerusalem signified a separate Christian virtue [7] by reason of its colour, its shape or its durability. The natural histories of earlier days were ransacked for animal traits which—whether true or false— might remind the reader or audience of mysteries of the faith ; a popular Bestiary of the twelfth century explicitly avows that these anecdotes about birds and beasts and reptiles are to take the place, in the lives of the uneducated, which scripture fills in the lives of the

---

[1] Hug. S. Vict., *de script. et script. sacr.*, 5 (*MPL.*, clxxv, col. 13).
[2] Cp. generally, Harnack, *Hist. of Dogma*, vi, pp. 31-34.
[3] Abail., *hist. cal.*, 10.
[4] Hug. S. Vict., *didasc.*, vii, 16 (*MPL.*, clxxvi, col. 823)—' simulacra invisibilium ipsa visibilia.'
[5] This matter has been fully studied by E. Mâle, *L'art religieux du XIIIe Siècle*, pp. 23-62 ; cp. also Grupp, *op. cit.*, iii, pp. 327-331 ; H. O. Taylor, *Mediæval Mind*, ii, pp. 67-101 ; G. G. Coulton, *Art and the Reformation*, pp. 242-292. Dr. Coulton insists upon the great variety of meaning attached to individual symbols, but fully recognizes the prevalence of the symbolic atmosphere. The examples quoted in the text above are taken mainly from the *de bestiis et aliis rebus* printed in *MPL.*, clxxvii ; but they occur commonly.
[6] Honor. August., *expos. in psalm.* (*MPL.*, clxxii, col. 272).
[7] [Hug. S. Vict.] *de best. et al. reb.*, iii, 58 (*MPL.*, clxxvii, coll. 115-118).

learned.[1] The guile of the fox, who feigns death till the fledgling comes close enough to be snapped up [2]—the malice of the whale, disguising himself as an island to lure mariners to their doom [3]— these are types of the devil. So is the hedgehog, who shakes the ripe grapes from the vine, and then by rolling upon them impales them on his spines, to carry them away for his young to eat—for the vine is the life of the Christian, the grapes his virtues.[4] The basilisk, too, stands for the devil ; but as the huntsman foils the basilisk by hiding himself behind a mirror, so Christ from the gleaming purity of His mother's innocence came forth to the dis-comfiture of Satan.[5]

The owl, on the other hand, typifies Christ. It loves darkness ; so did Christ love sinners. It has its nest in the ruins ; so Christ was born of the Jewish nation which God had abandoned to its fate. It shuns the daylight ; so Christ sought not His own glory.[6] Another bird, the white caradius, was typical of Christ as well. It possessed the gift of discerning whether the sick should live or not. If they were to die, it turned its head away from them ; if there was hope of life, it sucked out the infection from their lips with its beak, and then soared aloft to lose the taint of disease in the healing rays of the sun. So Christ turned His face from the Jews, but bears away the sins of those who trust in Him.[7]

The lion, again, is a type of Christ, and that for three undoubted reasons. As the beast wanders over the mountain-wastes, the sweep of his tail brushes away his footprints, and so his pursuers are misled. Christ in the same way concealed His real nature from the devil during His earthly life. The lion sleeps with open eyes, thus signifying that our Lord's Godhead was ever alive even when His flesh ' slept ' upon the cross. And lastly, the lion-cub is born dead ; its sire brings it to life on the third day by breathing upon it. This is an obvious type of the resurrection.[8]

If men of no more than normal invention could foster legends such as these, which the commonest diligence in investigation and report might have disproved, there was an unequalled opportunity for the imagination in fields where it could play unchecked. It is

---

[1] *de best. et al. reb.*, prol. (col. 15). The source of all these writings appears to have been the *Physiologus*, by an unknown author of c. II A.D. at the latest—text in D. Pitra, *Spicileg. Solesm.*, iii, pp. 338-372 ; cp. *ib.*, pp. xlvii-lxxv. Though condemned by Gelasius as heretical (*ib.*, p. lxvii), it was in favour even with Gregory the Great (*ib.*, p. lxix), and thereafter had a great vogue. Cp. also E. Mâle, *op. cit.*, pp. 31-34, for mention of other writers indebted to it.

[2] *de best. ct al. reb.*, ii, 5 (col. 59).

[3] *Ib.*, ii, 36 (col. 82)—the ' aspidocheloné.'

[4] *Ib.*, ii, 4 (col. 53). Dr. Coulton reproduces a picture of this hedgehog at its malicious depredations (*Art and the Reformation*, p. 271), with further examples of its symbolical use.

[5] So Grupp, *op. cit.*, iii, p. 329, the source not indicated. Commonly the traits assigned to the basilisk are his death-dealing qualities, and his terror of weasels (so e.g. in the *de bestiis*).

[6] *de best. et al. reb.*, i, 34 (col. 30).

[7] *Ib.*, i, 48 (col. 48).   [8] *Ib.*, ii, 1 (col. 57).

therefore to this period that Christianity owes its first great group of visionary mystics. They are most of them German, and most of them women. Hildegarde of Bingen, whose visions began at the early age of three,[1] and Elizabeth of Schoenau, driven by the physical chastisement of angels to reveal her secrets to the world,[2] are the principal figures of the twelfth century in this respect. S. Gertrude the Great of Helfta, the two Mechtilds, and S. Angela of Foligno belong to the thirteenth century; S. Bridget of Sweden and S. Catherine of Siena carry on the tradition in the fourteenth. The modern enthusiast for mysticism is apt to overlook the bizarre character of many of these ladies' revelations, but Roman Catholic historians are ready to admit that they were not 'authenticated by ecclesiastical authority';[3] and that such approval as they received was 'flattering but vague.'[4] Many of them are eccentric in the extreme, and rival the least disciplined imaginations of the apocalyptists; at other times the metaphor of the mystic marriage is developed in a fashion as dangerous as it is intimate. S. Gertrude initiated a new cult by her adoration of the Sacred Heart of Jesus, through which, in her moments of highest exaltation, she could feel the blood pulsing.[5] S. Bridget was peculiarly subject to ecstatic experiences, and felt herself in consequence empowered to address instructions, remonstrances, and rebukes to popes and bishops, with a freedom equalled only by that of S. Bernard himself.[6]

Not every outstanding mystic was fortunate enough to escape ecclesiastical censure. Joachim, abbot of Flora in Calabria,[7] though treated as a saint in his lifetime, and honoured by Dante with a special place in Paradise,[8] originated a movement so subversive of the established order that sixty years after his death—at the very date, in fact, at which he had fixed the consummation of world history in the coming of the Holy Spirit and the revelation of the Eternal Gospel—his writings were condemned.[9] Communism, asceticism, and evangelical poverty were the burden of his message, framed in an apocalyptic setting of the gloomiest and most menacing

---

[1] *Vita S. Hildegardis*, ii, 1 (16) (*MPL.*, cxcvii, col. 103). Brief accounts of these ladies in E. Underhill, *Mysticism*, pp. 548, 549; Pourrat, *SC.*, ii, pp. 119-146; cp. also M. David-Winstosser, *Deutsche Frauen-mystik im Mittelalter, pass.*; M. Grabmann, *Mittelalterische Geistesleben*, pp. 469-488.

[2] *Vita S. Elizab.*, prol. 4 (*MPL.*, cxcv, col. 121)—her letter to Hildegarde.

[3] Pourrat, *SC.*, ii, p. 123 (of S. Hildegarde).

[4] *Ib.*, p. 142 (of S. Bridget)—'quelque flatteur que soit ce jugement' (of Boniface IX) 'il demeure bien vague.' Cp. Harnack's phrase, of the whole mystical movement, *Hist. of Dogma*, vi, p. 31—'a bold idealism which threatened dogma.'

[5] Pourrat, *SC.*, ii, p. 131; cp. L. Gougaud, *Devotional and Ascetic Practices of the Middle Ages* (E. tr. 1927), pp. 91-104, with notes and references, pp. 121 ff.

[6] Pourrat, *SC.*, ii, pp. 141-145.

[7] Gebhart, *op. cit.*, pp. 70-93; Grupp, iv, pp. 380, 381; Coulton, *Five Centuries*, ii, pp. 114-123. Gebhart's account is particularly fascinating.

[8] *Paradiso*, xii, 139-142.

[9] *Conc. Arel.*, A.D. 1263 (Hefele-Leclerq, vi, pp. 113-115, with references there).

character. In 1155, all but fifty years before the death of Joachim, Arnold of Brescia, probably a pupil of Abailard's, paid the penalty not so much for speculations of this character, as for the revolutionary activities by which he sought to bring about his fantastic millennium.[1]

Even the earliest Schoolmen, who sought to stem the tide of uncontrolled ecstatic speculation by the appeal to reason, were carried away by the intoxication of new ideas—this time of a dogmatic rather than of a visionary order. The undisguised tritheism of Roscelin, the veiled Sabellianism of Abailard, the naked pantheism of Siger of Brabant are all indications of the same phenomenon.[2] In such an atmosphere the errors and superstitions of the dark ages were able to flourish almost if not quite unchecked. Among the northern races heathen beliefs died hard: it would in many cases be truer to say that they never died at all, but survived with only a superficial change of appearance. S. Michael, S. Peter, S. Martin, and S. George took the places of the pagan high gods in popular estimation.[3] Lesser saints succeeded the low gods, inheriting their duties of healing toothache, ophthalmia, and falling sickness, and watching over the cattle.[4] Demons, some of them good-natured, many ridiculous, all irresponsible, abounded;[5] witches were taken more seriously.[6] An effervescence of superstition relatively unknown to the Greek Church beset the west, and grew in intensity as time went on.[7] Even the ancient gods of Greece and Rome had their Christian votaries in the twelfth and thirteenth centuries.[8]

To this same period Catholicism owes a host of new cults, observances, and pious opinions, some of them as edifying as others were the reverse. The Ave Maria was known in the eleventh

[1] Gebhart, *op. cit.*, pp. 62-67.

[2] Roscelin, see R. L. Poole, *Studies in Mediæval Thought and Learning*[2], pp. 90, 128-130; M. de Wulf, *History of Mediæval Philosophy*[5] (E. tr. 1926), i, pp. 110-112 (and references, p. 114);—Abailard, Poole, pp. 116-145; de Wulf, i, pp. 161-166, 200; E. Vacandard, *Vie de S. Bernard*, ii, pp. 118-140, 176-180;—Siger, de Wulf, ii, pp. 101-105; P. Mandonnet, *Siger de Brabant et l'Averroisme latin*, especially pp. clxi-ccvi.

[3] Grupp, iii, pp. 11-14; for the older religions of the North, see *C. Med. Hist.*, ii, pp. 460-495. Many curious examples in P. Saintyves, *Les Saints successeurs des Dieux*, especially pp. 331-354, cp. *ib.*, pp. 10-12.

[4] Grupp, iii, pp. 14-16. The functions ascribed to the saints were sometimes suggested by onomatopœia; thus S. Augustine and S. Ottilia cured diseases of the eyes, S. Zeno toothache, and so forth. The remarkable prominence of animals in Christian hagiography (cp. the collection of anecdotes in W. E. H. Lecky, *History of European Morals*, ii, pp. 168-172) made possible a large selection of saints for the duty of patrons of flocks.

[5] Grupp, iii, pp. 19-25; particularly pleasant is the story from Thomas of Chantimpré of the benevolent demon who smoothed the course of true love by magic.

[6] *Ib.*, pp. 25-31, 40-47, etc.

[7] *Ib.*, p. 28. Grupp notes that Greek theologians were more immune against superstition than Latin ones.

[8] *Ib.*, pp. 64-67.

century ; [1] and from that time forward the ' Miracles of Mary '
received constant new accessions. The invention of the rosary
was attributed to S. Dominic himself ; [2] the dogma of the Immaculate Conception, as the remonstrances of S. Bernard, the Lombard
and S. Thomas show,[3] resisted all attempts at discouragement. The
feast of Corpus Christi received papal approval in the year 1264.[4]
Saints new and old achieved popular recognition—even the uncouth
person of S. Wilgefortis herself (S. Uncumber).[5] The discovery
and bartering of relics became the most profitable of trades.
Splinters of the ark, twigs from the burning bush, the teeth of Amos
the prophet, the stones with which S. Stephen was martyred, all
found a ready sale.[6] The Holy House of Loretto first enters
history towards the end of the thirteenth century.[7]

Alongside this willingness to believe everything, true or false,
which could capture the imagination, there flourished an agnosticism
which was ready to disbelieve anything, however well attested.[8]
Frederick II did not lack either forerunners or imitators. An
anticlericalism, fostered rather than restrained by the known wish
of the better representatives of the papacy for reform, spread into
an antinomianism which refused to pay deference of any kind
to tradition. Other forces contributed to the same result. The
failure of the second Crusade, together with the new respect for the
Moslem world which came in its train, led to a questioning of
traditional Christianity which might go very far. The famous
Dominican explorer, Ricoldo of Monte Croce († 1320), spoke with extraordinary enthusiasm of the piety, altruism, and virtuous lives
of his Arab camel-drivers ; and held them up as an example to the

---

[1] Petrus Dam., *opusc.*, 33. 3—the clerk who, although ' fatuus, frivolus et
ineptus,' was restored to his prebend by the bishop at the Virgin's command,
because he daily said the Angelus.

[2] Erroneously, however ; the story arose out of an alleged revelation
made by the Virgin Mary to Alan de Rupe († 1475), a great enthusiast for
the devotion—Boll., *AS.*, Aug., i, pp. 422-437 ; cp. *PRE.*, xvii, pp. 145-150 ;
DHGE., i, coll. 1306-1312 (*s.v.* ' Alain de la Roche ') ; *ERE.*, x, pp. 853-856.
The practice, in an unsystematic form, is at least as early as the eleventh
century.

[3] Bernard, *ep.* 174 ; Petr. Lomb., *Sent.*, iii, 3. 1 ; Aquinas, *ST.*, iii, q. 27,
a. 2 ; and generally Petavius, *de Incarnatione*, xiv, 2.

[4] *PRE.*, vi, pp. 298-300 ; *ERE.*, v, p. 847.

[5] Grupp, iv, p. 339 ; Coulton. *Five Centuries*, i, pp. 546 ff. ; *Art and the
Reformation*, p. 288. She was a bearded saint whose function was to relieve
wives of their unwanted husbands. The legend of her person arose from a
crucifix (the figure in long Byzantine robes) at Lucca early in the twelfth
century. Further Boll., *AS.*, Jul., v, pp. 50-70.

[6] Grupp, iii, pp. 145-148 ; iv, pp. 340-342.

[7] See *PRE.*, xi, pp. 647-650. The first known documentary reference
dates from the middle of the fifteenth century (Flavius Blondus) ; but
internal evidence associates the story with the end of the period of the
Crusades.

[8] Generally on mediæval unbelief, Grupp, iv, pp. 243-269 ; Coulton,
Five Centuries, i, pp. 465, 466 ;—on Frederick II., particularly Gebnart,
op. cit., pp. 133-164; cp. also H. Reuter, *Geschichte der Rel. Aufklärung*, i,
pp. 152 ff., with reference to the scepticism of pilgrims to Becket's shrine,
to whom the saint refused to appear.

Christian world in a manner which was bound to suggest that the distinctive features of Christianity were superfluities rather than essentials of religion.[1]

In all these ways the bonds of traditional orthodoxy were weakened. Thrown back (as it must have seemed to them) upon their own resources and initiative, the new lay associations came into ever-growing antagonism with the established order ; and movement after movement found itself drawn almost unwittingly into heresy. Some of these aberrations were indigenous to Christianity. The flagellants, for example, attempted to meet the terrors prophesied by Joachim of Flora by popularizing S. Peter Damian's[2] terrible new discipline. Hermann of Altach puts their place of origin as Perugia, and dates them from the first half of the thirteenth century ;[3] and many chroniclers describe their ghastly processions across Europe as they marched two by two, stripped to the waist, their faces veiled, a flag or a cross carried in the van. Their charter was a new gospel written on marble, and delivered ' on the altar of S. Peter at Jerusalem ' by an angel.[4]

Other sects, less revolutionary in general tendency, and animated mainly by the desire for ecclesiastical reform and the ideal of evangelical poverty, were nevertheless led by degrees to discard the ministry and sacraments of the Church, and substitute for them rites of their own. Over against these specifically Christian movements must be set the heresies which owed their origin to the infiltration of Oriental ideas through the channel of the Balkans. The Marcionites ' absorbed the remnants of the Manichæans,'[5] and spread eastward as Paulicians or Bogomils ; allied sects were the Cathari, the Patarini, and probably the Albigenses. All these were puritan and reformist in outlook ; but true to their dualist origin the majority of them stood for universal celibacy and a strict asceticism. As early as 1022 the canons of S. Cross of Orleans were all infected by dualism of this character.[6] Others—the Amalricians, the Béghards and Béguines, the Brethren of the Free Spirit—were more pantheist in outlook ;[7] they revived the gnostic doctrine that the Christian once animated by grace could sin no more.[8] It

---

[1] Grupp, iv, pp. 251, 252.

[2] Petr. Dam., *ep.* v, 8 (*MPL.*, cxliv, coll. 349-352)—a spirited defence of flagellation against those who denounce it as an innovation. Generally, on the practice in this period, L. Gougaud, *Devotional and Ascetic Practices in the Middle Ages*, pp. 184-198, 199-204.

[3] Herm. Altah., *Annales*, ad ann. 1260 ; *MGH.*, script. xvii, p. 402.

[4] J. Bühler, *Das deutsche Geistesleben*, pp. 276, 277 ; from the Strassburg Chronicle (A.D. 1362) of Friedrich Klosener.

[5] R. L. Poole, *Mediæval Thought and Learning*, p. 81.

[6] *Ib.*, pp. 84-86.

[7] Thus the Brethren of the Free Spirit could say, ' If the Saviour had lived longer, He would have reached the same height of the contemplative life as we have attained '—R. Jones, *Studies in Mystical Religion*, p. 213 ; from Ruysbroek.

[8] See the quotations from (?) William of S. Thierry, *epistola ad fratres de monte Dei* (printed by Mabillon, Bernardus Clarevall., *Opera*, ii, coll. 417-492) in Pourrat, *SC.*, ii, pp. 194-196; but contrast on this W. Shewring and J. McCann, *The Golden Epistle of Abbot William*, pp. xl-xlviii.

is certain, of course, that many of the accusations of immorality brought against these sects and their members were not merely exaggerated but false. But one thing is evident. By the beginning of the thirteenth century Christianity was in danger of disruption into groups and movements of every degree of impermanence— a disruption in which all that was distinctive of Christian morality seemed doomed to disappear. Nothing except the centrifugal tendency of the heresies themselves offered any hope of salvation for the Church. As a contemporary German rhymester expressed it,

> ' Heretics untold we see,
> But they always disagree ;
> If together they would stand
> They might conquer every land.' [1]

And the root cause of the danger was the fact that emotionalism had outstripped reason, and the principle of ethical stability and discipline had been lost.

II. The School of St. Victor.

How Innocent III met this perilous situation with the full force of ecclesiastical discipline—how he built on the foundations of Hildebrand with the new instruments of the mendicant Orders, the crusades against the Albigenses, and the all but fully-forged weapon soon to be known as the Inquisition—all this is matter of general history and need not detain us. The greatest minds saw clearly that heresy could never be met successfully except by clear and persuasive argument. Without surrendering the primary conviction that religion is a personal matter between the soul and God, theology must so think out the conditions of that intercourse as to keep it within the bounds of sane reason and sound morality. We naturally think of the great Dominican tradition and its protagonist, S. Thomas, but there were others who bridged the gap between the wild chaos of eleventh-century speculation and the ordered wisdom of scholasticism in its heyday. The new attitude is evident even in S. Bernard. The subjects for meditation which he puts before his pupil Pope Eugenius are very different in scope from those which formed his theme in the chapter-house at Clairvaux. The Pope must rise to ' contemplation ' if he is to achieve his full human dignity : but contemplation is built upon the stepping stones of ' consideration.' [2] And while the objects of

---

[1] Freidank, c. A.D. 1229, quoted J. Bühler, *Das deutsche Geistesleben* p. 258 :—

> ' Wieviel der Ketzer lebend sei,
> ihr keiner steht dem andern bei,
> glaubten alle das gleiche,
> sie bezwängen alle Reiche.'

[2] Bernardus Clarevall., *de consideratione*, ii, 2 (5)—the distinction between ' consideration ' and ' contemplation.' Cp. *ib.*, v, 1-3 (1-6) where the distinction is developed, and ' contemplation ' is spoken of in highly ecstatic terms. ' Consideration ' is called ' philosophy ' in i, 9 (12).

contemplation, properly so-called. are 'things above us '—the angels, the eternal self-existence of God, the Trinity in Unity,[1] the objects of ' consideration ' are things sublunary—myself, ' things around,' even ' things beneath ' me.[2]

The wide field for thought suggested by the formula is no doubt restricted enough in practice. The study of myself is not so much a clear insight into the recesses of the soul, as reflection upon my station and its duties.[3] ' Things below me ' continue the same theme —it is not, as Harnack strangely suggests,[4] that S. Bernard is here inculcating an anti-ascetic attitude towards bodily needs and well-being, but simply that he urges the Pope to care for those to whom, by virtue of his position, he owes oversight and paternal justice.[5] ' Things around ' do not, as we might expect, comprehend the vast world of natural phenomena, but only the immediate social entourage in which I find myself.[6] For all this, the treatment is realist and objective, rather than romantic and subjective ; we must attempt to see things as they are before we can rise to seeing God as He is.

With the theologians of St. Victor, intellectual discipline takes a great stride forward. At the very moment at which Abailard, with an individualism which wrecked his immediate object but after his death secured its purpose, was laying the foundation of that unsparing criticism and accurate dialectic which should serve the thirteenth century so well, the more conservative friends and followers of the teacher he had humbled were entering on a less spectacular, but no less ambitious venture. William of Champeaux, S. Bernard's intimate friend, had been Abailard's master at Paris ; but in 1108 his pupil's triumphant rivalry drove him into retirement at the priory of St. Victor.[7] There, half unwillingly, he resumed his abandoned lectures during the four years which elapsed before he came into public life again as bishop of Châlons-sur-Marne. His brief sojourn at St. Victor, a community of Austin Canons, was far from being fruitless : in the next fifty years the abbey produced writer after writer of renown.

---

[1] Bernardus Clarevall., de consideratione, v, 3-13 (5-19)—' quæ supra nos sunt.'

[2] Ib., ii, 3 (6)—' te, quæ sub te, quæ circa te.'   [3] Ib., ii, 4 (7).

[4] Harnack, Hist. of Dogma, vi, p. 11—a curiously confused passage, in which, after contrasting Bernard with ' the earlier Christians who revered asceticism,' Harnack almost goes on to suggest that the Passion and Cross constitute ' things beneath us.'

[5] Bern., de consid., iii, 1 (1).   [6] Ib., iv, 1 (1).

[7] R. L. Poole, Mediæval Thought and Learning, pp. 118, 119—William and Abailard; p. 96, William at St. Victor. St. Victor became an abbey shortly after William's elevation to the episcopate. Actually, Abailard withdrew from Paris (to Melun) several years before William retired to St. Victor ; this, however, was due mainly to William's hostile influence, which. although it could not succeed in the attempt to suppress Abailard's school at Melun, was strong enough to keep him out of the capital (Abail., hist. cal., 2). William's retirement was also in part due, so report said, to a desire ' to appear more religious, in order to gain preferment ' (ib.). But the movements of the two rivals are not altogether clear.

Of these writers, Hugh and Richard are the two who principally concern us. At first sight their teaching is not revolutionary. Their thought is based upon the Platonic tradition as handed down from Augustine, but seen, in part at least, through the eyes of pseudo-Dionysius. Contemplation—the vision of God—is as always the goal of life. It is an ecstatic experience, or direct intuition, of the divine essence, in which consciousness is raised to such a height that it forgets itself and all around it. In a famous and often-quoted passage Hugh speaks of the coming of contemplation as follows :—

> ' Damp wood kindles slowly under fire, but a strong breeze will fan it into flame, with black clouds of smoke. Little by little the smoke is dissipated as the moisture dries up, and the blaze spreads freely over the whole crackling pile . . . till the wood is wholly changed into the likeness of fire. . . . Then the crackling ceases ; . . . nothing is to be seen save the victorious fire, glowing in the profound peace of great silence. . . . First fire and flame and smoke ; then fire and flame, but smoke no more ; last of all pure fire, with neither flame nor smoke.—As is the damp wood, so are our carnal hearts. . . . Touch them with the spark of the fear of God, or divine love, and great clouds of evil passions and rebellious desires roll upwards. Then the soul grows stronger ; the flame of love burns more hotly and brightly ; the smoke of passion dies down ; and the purified spirit rises to the contemplation of Truth. Last of all triumphant contemplation fills the heart with truth ; we have reached the very source of the Sovereign Truth and been enfolded thereby, and neither trouble nor anxiety touch the heart more. It has found peace and rest.' [1]

The ecstatic character of contemplation is more completely emphasized by Richard of St. Victor. ' Benjamin adolescentulus in excessu mentis ' [2] is the text which he loves above all others. He takes the words of the Vulgate very literally as the final description of the contemplative state. When Benjamin is born, Rachel—who typifies reason in its normal exercise—dies ; ' so when the mind is rapt to contemplation it learns how utterly human reason is at fault. . . . No one should think to reach the purity of that divine light by discursive argument, nor believe that he may grasp it by any exercise of human logic.' [3] In the mystic vision we have passed altogether beyond ' imagination' and ' phantasms ' ; [4] we are carried above ourselves—the mind is alienated,

---

[1] H. S. Vict., *hom. in Eccles.*, i (*MPL.*, clxxv, coll. 117, 118).

[2] Ps. 68[27] (Vulg.), where the English version reads, ' There is little Benjamin their ruler.' The original sense of the phrase is apparently that representatives of the tribe led the procession to the Temple.

[3] *Benj. min.*, 74 (*MPL.*, cxcvi, col. 52).

[4] R. S. Vict., *Benj. maj.*, iv, 4 (col. 138) ; v, 2 (col. 170) ; v, 9 (col. 178) *et pass.*

as in an ecstasy.[1] The ' qualities ' of contemplation are successively
' expansion of mind,' ' elevation,' and ' alienation ' ; [2] and in its
complete realization it is so ineffable that when we return to
normal consciousness we can remember nothing of what we have
learnt.[3]

So far everything is of the ordinary fibre of neo-Platonic mysticism—it has not even a distinctively Christian ring. But even on
this point we must not be unjust to the Victorines. There is one
moment at least at which Richard echoes, with an inimitable and
untranslatable phrase of his own, the most characteristic thoughts
of the New Testament. The purpose of contemplation is not to
achieve a mere ecstatic vacuity. It aims at a genuine vision of
God ' in the face of Jesus Christ.' Its goal is ' Christum clari-
ficatum videre '—' to see Christ in utter clearness.' [4] Still, the
originality of the Victorines lies neither in their description of the
vision of God, nor in their insistence—in which they follow the
genuine Christian tradition—upon purity of heart [5] and intensity
of love [6] as its conditions. God cannot be seen except ' in a clean
mirror.' [7] The real contribution of Hugh and Richard to the
development of Christian thought is their analysis of the intellectual
travail which must accompany moral effort in the process of
advance. It is with them that the word ' meditation,' with all
that it stands for, first comes into prominence as a sign-post for the
Christian pilgrimage.

Contemplation, or seeing God, for all the neo-Platonic language
about ecstasy, is after all apprehension of truth itself—truth as it is
at its very source, as yet unsullied by the perversions of human
imagination. Hugh and Richard observe three stages on the road
upstream to the fountain-head. The last, as we have already
seen, is contemplation; but prior to contemplation come first
' reflection,' and then ' meditation.' ' Reflection '—' cogitatio '—
is described somewhat equivocally. Sometimes its characteristic
is that of simple ideation—' an idea presents itself to the mind
unsought, but makes only a passing impression.' [8] Sometimes, on
the other hand, it is little more than frivolous day-dreaming—' a
casual glance of the mind with a bias towards loitering,' [9] ' a habit
of seeking relaxation among foolish and irresponsible notions ;
a tendency to be attracted by any and every idea, if not to rush
upon it headlong, without any restraint of discretion.' [10] In either
case this reflection—' fancy ' or ' reverie ' would almost give us the
meaning—has no spiritual significance. We need to fasten upon

---

[1] R. S. Vict., *Benj. maj.*, iv, 11 (col. 147) ; iv, 12 (col. 148).
[2] *Ib.*, v, 2 (col. 169)—' dilatatio,' ' sublevatio,' ' alienatio.'
[3] *Ib.*, iv, 23 (col. 167).
[4] *Benj. min.*, 80 (col. 56)—the reference is to the Transfiguration.
[5] *Ib.*, 25 ff. (abstinence, patience, discipline of mind and senses, etc.) ;
68 ff. (Joseph = self-knowledge, discretion) ; *ib.*, iv, 6 (col. 140), etc.
[6] *Ib.*, iv, 16 (col. 154).   [7] *Ib.*, 72 (col. 51).
[8] H. S. Vict., *hom. in Eccles.*, i (*MPL.*, clxxv, col. 116).
[9] *Benj. maj.*, i, 4 (col. 67).   [10] *Ib.*, i, 4 (col. 68).

some part of the content of consciousness, and wrestle with it in the determination to extract matter of real profit. So Richard, with a beautiful rearrangement of a great text from Isaiah, writes of the three stages :—

> ' Reflection wanders up and down with leisurely pace through every byway, heedless of any goal to its journey. Meditation seeks the heights, rugged though they may often be ; and presses on to its destination with intense concentration of purpose. But contemplation rises up with wings in free flight, and flies down the wind with a speed to make men marvel. Reflection can only creep; meditation walks and often runs withal ; contemplation soars throughout the heavens. . . . Reflection wanders from one disconnected impression to another; meditation concentrates on a single subject; contemplation from its place of vantage sees all things in a single glance.' [1]

There is a certain confusion here between philosophic or scientific speculation on the one hand, and what later Catholicism understood by meditation as a mode of prayer on the other. This also (though S. Thomas will be justified in exposing the ambiguity) has its purpose and value, as will appear ; but for the moment it is important to underline the fact that by their conception of ' meditation ' the mystics of St. Victor introduced orderliness into prayer, without quenching individuality. The contribution was one of vast importance. We know little enough of the formulæ by which Christians of the early ages sought to attain the vision of God ; Richard of St. Victor has been called the author of ' the first really theological work which treats of matters of high spirituality.' [2] Yet it seems unquestionable that the strictly monastic tradition had emphasized orderliness—whether in the recitation of set prayers privately, or in the choir office—at the expense of individuality ; whilst neo-Platonism, not least of all in its mediæval representatives, had individualized the ' negative way ' to an extent which made its prescriptions chaotic. The Victorines insist that personal effort is of greater value than traditional methods in meditation ; but they insist as well that what distinguishes meditation from ' reverie ' is just the substitution of order for chaos. They opened up the

---

[1] *Benj. maj.*, i, 3 (coll. 66, 67).—Hugh is at once more explicit and less rigorous about meditation :—' Meditation is thought concentrated in consideration. It makes careful investigation of the cause and origin, the mode and use, of each single matter that it takes in hand. Meditation begins with books ; but it is bound by no rules and principles of reading. *It loves untrammelled space for its wide activity, to fix its gaze freely* upon the contemplation of truth' (*de mod. dic. et med.*, 5—*MPL.*, clxxvi, col. 878). Still, its activities are by nature limited as compared with those of contemplation :—' Meditation is always occupied with piercing to the core of one particular truth ; contemplation is diffused abroad till it grasps many truths, if not the whole. . . . What meditation seeks, contemplation has in possession ' (*ib.*, 8—coll. 879 ; cp. *hom. in Eccl.*, i (*MPL.*, clxxv, col. 117)).

[2] A. Saudreau, *Life of Union with God* [3] (E. tr. E. J. Strickland), p. 132.

way for a manner of prayer which should be at once personal and methodical; and in so doing seized, if we may say so, upon the very essence of prayer as taught by Jesus. Vain repetition meant nothing to Him, however orderly it might be; but His love of order was shown in that He dictated a pattern form of prayer.

So far nothing has been said of the *subjects* of meditation that shall lead to fruitful contemplation. Here again, at first sight, the Victorines are disappointing. S. Bernard had already pointed to the life of Christ as the greatest of all subjects; S. Francis was to repeat the lesson within a few decades. The quasi-philosophic approach of Hugh and Richard is by comparison jejune and un-inspiring. Yet even in this respect, as has just been suggested, they had a definite purpose and performed a real service. They share the Platonic or Augustinian exemplarism with their contemporaries; and yet, in the case of Hugh in particular, there is coming to the surface something akin to a love of natural knowledge not merely as a symbol of the supernatural, but for its own sake as well. A symbol merely quickens the apprehension of something already known; but Hugh of St. Victor suggests that each particular fact acquired by the earnest student is capable of revealing to him something new—something hitherto unknown—as to the ways of God. ' Learn everything; thou shalt find in the end that nothing is super-fluous,' is his motto.[1] He has even a tender thought for those ' who study God's works simply for their marvellous character,' even though they have no intention of allowing the knowledge of God thus acquired to move them to moral effort.[2]

Hence he bids the Christian not to be like the ' illiterates who can only stare at the pictures in an open book, for want of the ability to read.' We are to cast off this ' animal folly,' and seek the ' inner reasons ' of all that goes to make up the visible world. Then, observing the ' organism of the universe,' we shall ' learn how deftly and marvellously the divine wisdom has fashioned it; how fit and congruous is its composition, how fair, how perfect in all its parts '— and learning this, shall come to reverence and adore its Creator [3] For God's wisdom manifest in creation is the ' gate and way ' to a knowledge of His invisible wisdom.[4]

Richard is more interested in ' contemplation,' and less in ' meditation,' than Hugh; but his lesson is the same. After Leah, who represents the moral virtues, comes Rachel—' sapientia '—knowledge; and Benjamin is Rachel's child.[5] After Dan, who in the sacred text prefigures a knowledge of things as they are, comes Naphtali, who rises by allegorism to a knowledge of things invisible.[6] Sometimes Richard uses ' contemplation ' of the whole process of

[1] *erud. didasc.*, vi, 3 (*MPL.*, clxxvi, col. 801), with the account of his own extensive studies (col. 800). Contrast S. Bernard, to whom 'learning for learning's sake' is ' turpis curiositas ' (*in cant. sermo* 36, 3).
[2] *Ib.*, v, 10 (col. 798)—they ought to be ' helped rather than confounded,' their intentions being short-sighted (' improvida ') rather than evil.
[3] *Ib.*, vii, 4 (coll. 814, 815).   [4] *Ib.*, vii, 17 (col. 824)—' janua et via.'
[5] *Benj. min.*, 1.   [6] *Ib.*, 18.

'meditation' and 'contemplation' as well; and then he divides the objects of 'contemplation' into six groups, which he represents as stages in the ascent to God.[1] The beginner studies corporeal entities which are known to him by sense-impression. In the second stage he gains and exploits a knowledge of cause and effect. Then comes the study of law, divine and human; then that of incorporeal subsistences—the soul and the angels. With the fifth and sixth stages we are introduced to contemplation strictly so-called, wherein first 'truths above reason,' and finally 'truths contrary to reason' (such as the mystery of the Trinity!) are perceived and enjoyed.[2] Richard, it will be seen, recognizes no urgent necessity for harmonizing faith and reason; indeed, faith—the acceptance of truths not merely unprovable but even contrary to reason—plays a large part in his scheme.[3] We are led to ask why, in this case, he too should lay such a stress upon 'natural knowledge' as a preliminary to the contemplation of truths known by faith alone. The answer is clear. What the age needs is discipline of mind, even in the soul's highest transports; and discipline of mind can be obtained only in the four 'lower' stages of contemplation.

In comparison with Richard's abstract scheme of subjects for meditation, Hugh's is admirably concrete. He presents his readers with a vast syllabus of encyclopædic self-education—natural theology, psychology,[4] mathematics, physics, ethics, economics, politics—all of them regarded, in Dr. Harris' words, as 'ancillary and propædeutic' to the sacred knowledge of mystical theology.[5] Honorius of Autun has a similar comprehensive articulation of learning into 'ten cities,' through which in succession the soul must pass on its journey back to God.[6] These facts cannot be pressed too far: it is a long stride yet to the independent passion for scientific learning which animated Roger Bacon. Nevertheless, there is something here more than the mere collection of material for pious but unregulated reflection, even though the Victorines have no objection to allegorism. To be beside oneself, other than oneself, absorbed in God, is still indeed the mystic's aim: his highest hope is a condition in which body, mind, and soul alike suffer a complete eclipse. Yet something has been gained—the first step in the ladder is now a recognition of the orderliness of God. And

---

[1] Benj. maj., i, 6, sqq.   [2] Ib.

[3] But contrast de Trin., prol. (col. 889) ; declar. ad Bern. Clarev. (col. 266) —'We must try as far as possible to understand by reason what we believe by faith.'

[4] de med. seu med. art. (MPL., clxxvi, col. 995)—'in moribus meditatio considerationem suam exercet, ut omnes motus qui oriuntur in corde deprehendat, unde veniant et quo tendant'; R. S. Vict., Benj. min., 70—Benjamin is born 'long after' Joseph, because the soul which has not had 'long experience in knowledge of self' (Joseph) can scarcely hope to rise to knowledge of God.

[5] C. R. S. Harris, Duns Scotus, i, p. 51. Hugh's scheme is contained in the first six books of the eruditionis didascalia.

[6] Hon. August., de an. exil. et patriâ (MPL., clxxii, coll. 1241-1246).

this recognition must produce an orderliness of soul as well before the Christian can go further. Humility, self-denial, purity, truthfulness, love, must all precede the nearest approach to that Godhead which burns like a flame.

Perhaps, therefore, it was a gain rather than a loss that the Victorines so far deserted the path taken by S. Bernard as to prefer meditation upon the harmony of the universe to meditation upon the person of Christ. Much indeed would have been lost if later writers upon mental prayer had followed them too closely. But the current set too strongly in the true direction to be diverted for long; and their message of orderliness of mind could not have been more timely. It had to struggle against a legacy of older non-Christian thoughts, as also against the disruptive sentimentalism of the age in which they wrote; the result is a tangle of mystical ejaculation extraordinarily difficult to unravel. But at bottom the Victorines had a new sense of the need for discipline in human life. It is true that this discipline often appears to be demanded only for selfish ends. Richard's passion for ecstasy is panhedonist almost to the core. He is able to suggest that no one who lacks the ecstatic experience is a true Christian ; [1] it almost seems that he believed some Christians at least to have achieved by disciplined effort such power in prayer, that they could command the presence of God as and how they wished.[2]

Yet even here traces of a more fully Christian line of thought can be discerned. The blessings of contemplation are greater than tongue can tell; but the saint is not wholly dependent thereupon. He has still his life of ordered effort to live, and so long as that is before him, his duty is clear :—

> ' The soul seeks to see the invisible ; but nothing presents itself except the appearance of visible things. . . . What then shall she do, and how comport herself ? *Surely it is better for her to meditate upon them in whatever manner she may, than to pass them by in negligence or oblivion.* . . . So we do what we can, and look towards [the things that are invisible] as best we may. . . . For it is better to meditate on the true good *in any fashion whatever,* and thereby inflame the heart's longing for it, than to fix the thoughts on false and deceptive goods.' [3]

[1] *Benj. maj.,* v, 5 (col. 174)—where there is no ecstasy, what else can we feel of ourselves, ' nisi quia minus diligimur, nisi quod minus diligimus ? '—But he had better moments, and from the instance of Bezaleel infers that ' quælibet horum ' (the truths revealed in contemplation) ' absque ullo mentis excessu possunt et solent in contemplationem adduci ' (iv. 22).

[2] *Ib.,* iv, 23 (col. 166)—' alii hoc expectant et accipiunt usque adhuc ex solâ vocante gratiâ, alii vero ut hoc possint sibi comparant (cum gratiæ tamen cooperatione) ex magnâ animi industriâ.'

[3] *Benj. min.,* 14 (col. 10)—' facit tamen quod potest ; intuetur ea quo modo potest.'

III. S. THOMAS AQUINAS.

S. Thomas Aquinas treasured both Hugh and Richard of St. Victor among his authorities, and he uses their thought of the orderliness of nature with startling effect. M. Gilson has rightly called his doctrine a 'Christian humanism' or 'naturalism'; [1] but we miss the point of the epigram unless we realize that the word 'Christian' must here be taken in the sense of 'other-worldly.' An 'other-worldly humanism,' or 'other-worldly naturalism,' is indeed a fair description of the Thomist system. It is a system which champions the dignity of man and nature against those who would decry it, and yet finds the grounds of that dignity in the supernatural order which supplies the abiding source of their being, as well as their only hope of perfection. S. Augustine had found himself obliged at times to emphasize the gulf between nature and God so sternly as to leave no hope of salvation except by the substitution of grace for nature. S. Thomas—equally conscious of the gulf [2]—devoted himself to setting on a firm basis that other aspect of Augustine's thought in which nature, the natural man and natural society, despite their utter difference from God, are yet seen to be in their measure true messengers of the grace of God.

It is necessary for an understanding even of S. Thomas' ethics to see how he approached his task in metaphysics. He conceives reality as an ordered hierarchy of existence,[3] ranging from God at its summit—God Whose being is wholly from Himself,[4] Who is in no sense corporeal,[5] and is perfect actuality and in no degree whatever merely potential [6]—to matter at its base—its existence wholly dependent upon higher orders of being, its essence pure corporeity, its natural mode that of wholly undetermined potency.[7] So much of course is the necessary presupposition of all thought about reality, that there is an ordered something to be thought about, not an undifferentiated chaos nor an insuperable dualism. The novelty of S. Thomas lies in his attempt to avoid the Platonic suggestion that the lower orders of being are mere shadows of the Reality from which they derive existence, and so to eliminate the dangers both

---

[1] E. Gilson, *Saint Thomas d'Aquin* (in the series, *Les Moralistes Chrétiens*, 1925), pp. 7, 10—'entendant par là, non pas une combinaison en proportions quelconques de naturalisme et de christianisme, mais une doctrine où la pure nature exige la foi chrétienne comme garantie de son parfait développement, et où le christianisme exige à son tour une nature distincte qu'il vienne parfaire et sauver.'

[2] Hence he accepts the principle of Dionysius, that we may with equal justice negate the conceptions which we predicate of God (*CG.*, i, 30 ; cp. *ST.*, i, q. 13, aa. 1-3).

[3] On the 'natural priority' of some created things to others, *CG.*, ii, 29 ; *ST.*, i, q. 47, a. 2.

[4] *CG.*, i, 21, 22 ; *ST.*, i, q. 3, aa. 3, 4.

[5] *CG.*, i, 20 ; *ST.*, i, q. 3, a. 1.   [6] *CG.*, i, 16 ; *ST.*, i, q. 2, a. 3.

[7] *CG.*, i, 17—' materia id quod est in potentiâ est '; *ST.*, i, q. 3, a. 2.

of pantheism and of neo-Platonism.[1] This he does—to adopt another phrase of M. Gilson's [2]—by introducing ' discontinuity ' into his system at every point. We have to use the same words— existence, goodness, perfection, activity and the like—of all the entities in the scale of being, from God down to matter itself. But of no two of them can we use these words in the same sense. The higher orders are not merely mirrored in the lower : God is alto- gether different from man writ large, though we use of Him the same words as we use of man.[3]

This is the gist of the famous principle of analogical reasoning [4] which lies at the heart of Thomism. The philosopher cannot transfer direct to any one order of being the operations, functions, characteristics or modes proper to any other order. He can only argue from one to another, on a principle not of identity but of an- alogy, allowing for the differences between them so far as they can be conjectured. By such analogy we can to some extent rise from what we know—' substantial composites—forms interlocked with matter by so indissoluble a bond that this interlocking itself defines their being ' [5]—sensible existence always in potency, always seeking to actualize its true self—to the source and sovereign of existence, Who is pure Being and always in act. What we know of corporeal intelligence can teach us something of incorporeal intelligence, what we know of becoming something about pure Being. The ladder of learning involves a transmutation of knowledge at each rung. But it is a real ladder, not an illusion : not a procession of shadowy allegories, whose meaning is indifferent when once the divine exemplar has been grasped. Every rung in it has a character specifically and uniquely its own, though derived from the one eternal Being towards knowledge of which it leads ; and every rung leads on to the next. Thus, though we cannot know God by the direct operations of reason, nor attribute to Him existence in the sense in which we predicate it of His creation, we are not wholly at a loss. Analogy provides a key for speculation.

The first essential, therefore, for Thomist philosophy is the exact study of the things which our minds are capable of fully appre- hending—mankind and the visible universe—and the principles of being which they make known to us. Hence the importance of physics and psychology in the system ; hence also S. Thomas'

---

[1] *ST.*, i, q. 6, a. 4 *contra*—' non dicuntur omnia entia per esse divinum, sed per esse proprium,' with the criticism of Plato, *in corp. art.* Cp. A. D. Sertillanges, *S. Thomas d'Aquin*, i, pp. 57, 58, for exposition.

[2] E. Gilson, *Philosophy of S. Thomas Aquinas* [3] (E. tr. E. Bullough, 1924), p. 275.

[3] Thus Sertillanges (*op. cit.*, i, p. 188) is justified in saying that S. Thomas set out to discover ' a *via media* between pure agnosticism and anthropo- morphism.'

[4] Or of ' equivocity of being '—see particularly *CG.*, i, 32-34 ; *ST.*, i, q. 13, a. 5.

[5] E. Gilson, *Philosophy of S. Thomas*, p. 269 ; cp. C. C. J. Webb, *Studies in the History of Natural Theology*, pp. 235, 241.

constant discussion of the implications of form and matter, and the nature of their composition. If knowledge of God is in any sense at all possible to man, then such study of nature and nature's laws is the essence, not merely of the preliminaries, but of the process as well. Much will depend thereafter, no doubt, on the right use of analogy. It is sometimes alleged, as for example by M. Rougier,[1] that S. Thomas himself stultified his own application of the principle by mistaking logical for metaphysical distinctions. But no application of the principle will help if a foundation is not laid in the exact knowledge of phenomena ; we must know the truth about the sensible universe if we would rise to the intelligible. This was the Schoolmen's justification for taking over intact the complete Aristotelian system, as an encyclopædic corpus of all that reason had hitherto been able to attain by the observation of nature.

Here, then, is the first of S. Thomas' great contributions to Christianity. He closed the door to all vague phrases, rash generalizations, subjective opinions, and unbalanced speculations in religion. He was convinced that the work of the philosophic theologian can be and must be in essence as discriminating, painstaking and rigorously self-critical as that of the worker in any other field of thought. The conviction dominated his own procedure, not least of all in ethics. He insists that the moralist shall study the implications of man's exact place in the hierarchy of being, before he attempts to estimate the nature and content of human duty. Our whole ethical outlook is to be determined by the fact (which to S. Thomas had as much certainty as any fact could have) that man is intermediate between non-intelligent matter on the one hand, and the angels, who are pure incorporeal intelligence, on the other. His perfection, therefore, must by the root principle of analogy lie in an operation akin to, yet wholly distinct from, the characteristic operations either of brutes or angels. He must not content himself with the life of a brute, but neither must he attempt to be an angel. In either case he will miss his own vocation, which is to be a *man*—a being composed of soul and body—neither more nor less.

Thus S. Thomas is able, as it seems to him, to base his entire ethical system on grounds of coldest reason. Taking earth and sea and sky in one comprehensive glance, he propounds the great Aristotelian thesis that ' whatever acts, whether consciously or unconsciously, acts for an end,' [2] though the end may be, in some cases, the action itself. And the end is ' in some sense appropriate to the agent, and therefore may be called his *good*,' [3] or ' perfection.' [4] That God is the greatest of all goods needs no proof, though S. Thomas argues it briefly, binding up the conclusion with an

---

[1] L. Rougier, *La Scholastique et le Thomisme*, pp. 201-203, 565, 566 *et pass.*; and cp. the difficulties pointed out by Gilson, *Philosophy*, pp. 67, 70.
[2] *CG.*, iii, 2 ; *ST.*, i, 2, q. 1, a. 1.
[3] *CG.*, iii, 3, 4 ; *ST.*, i, 2, q. 1, a. 4 ad 1.
[4] *CG.*, i, 37, 38.

interesting vindication of monotheism.[1] It follows, therefore, that
God is the end to which all things move, that they may achieve the
perfection which He alone can give them,[2] and which ' consists in a
certain likeness to Him ' ; as the perfection of a statue consists in
its likeness to the picture in the sculptor's mind.[3]

So much is true of every created being without distinction.
But here the principle of analogy comes into play again. Each
category of existence has a perfection of its own, and its own
mode of reaching that perfection ; [4] man's business is to discover
wherein consists his own end or perfection, and then to pursue it.
S. Thomas passes in rapid review the possible ' ends ' which have
been suggested for human life.[5] Man's true end cannot be sensual
enjoyment nor bodily well-being ; such enjoyment and well-being
are common to man and the brutes, and man is more than a brute.[6]
It cannot consist in things external to himself—honour, glory,
riches or power. It cannot consist in virtuous acts alone ; for all
such acts have an end beyond themselves.[7] Where then are we to
look for it ? Analogy suggests the answer. Man shares with beings
higher than himself the faculty of intelligence, and unless *that*
achieves its due end, his life remains incomplete ; for in ' every
case the end must consist in an operation distinctive of the particular agent.' [8] So he reaches his conclusion—

' Hence the last end for man is the contemplation of truth.
This alone is distinctive of his nature, and no other [corporeal]
being shares it with him. Nor is there any end beyond it, for
the contemplation of truth is an end in itself. Hereby man is
united in likeness with superior spirits ' (i.e. incorporeal in-
telligences, the angels), ' because this alone of human activities
is an activity of God and the angels as well. . . . And to this
end all other human activities seem to be directed. For perfect
contemplation we require bodily health, which is secured by all
such artificial contrivances as are necessary to life. We require freedom from the perturbation of the passions—a goal
attained by the moral virtues and by prudence. We require
freedom from external perturbations—a freedom at which the
entire organization of civil government aims. So, if you look
at the matter rightly, all human occupations appear to be
directed to the needs of those who contemplate the truth.' [9]

---

[1] *CG.*, i, 40-42.   [2] *CG.*, iii, 17.
[3] *CG.*, iii, 19, 20 ; cp. *ib.*, ii, 46.   [4] *CG.*, iii, 22.
[5] *CG.*, iii, 27-36 ; *ST.*, i, 2, q. 2 ; the whole based on Aristotle, *Eth. Nic.*,
x, 6-8 (*infra*, p. 475, additional note B).
[6] *CG.*, iii, 27 ; cp. *ib.*, 32-33 ; *ST.*, i, 2, q. 2, aa. 5, 6.
[7] *CG.*, iii, 34. S. Thomas rejects that unphilosophical intuitionism which
would make certain types of action ' good in themselves,' as though they
were not subservient to the final good.
[8] *CG.*, iii, 25; cp. *ST.*, i, 2, q. 3, aa. 3-5.
[9] *CG.*, iii, 37 ; cp. *ST.*, i, 2, q. 3, a. 8.

S. Thomas has much more to say about this contemplation of
God which is the end of human life, which we must pass over ; [1]
in particular a delicate little argument which proves that ' knowing
God ' is a more exact description of the end than ' loving God.' [2]
But the picture has another side, to which he devotes equal attention—a side already suggested by the words ' all other human
activities.' Human perfection is akin to the perfection of the angels,
in that it consists in seeing God ; but man is not an angel.[3] By
virtue of his position in the hierarchy of the universe, he is composed
of soul and body ; of reason, that is to say, and passions.[4] There
are those indeed who say that passions are wholly of the body,[5] and
consequently that they are in no way germane, for good or evil,
to the question of human excellence or real being, which concerns
the soul alone.[6] From any such gnostic antinomianism S. Thomas'
study of first principles saves him. Strict argument requires us
to admit, no doubt, that passions are only ' in the soul ' *per accidens.*[7]
Nevertheless, they are ' subject to the command of reason and will '
—more so even than the limbs of the body ; [8] and so are the primary sphere in which moral virtue is exercised.[9] Hence, though
technical excellence of mind is possible without discipline of the
passions, for prudence, which comports that its possessor is ' rightly
disposed towards his true end,' such discipline is essential.[10]

On the other hand, S. Thomas will have nothing to do with the
opposite error, which suggests that all human passions are morally
evil. He goes out of his way to exonerate the Stoics from any such
heresy ; [11] but the point is so clear to him that for once he does not

[1] Thus (*CG.*, iii, 38) the beatific vision is more than the ' communis et
confusa Dei cognitio quæ quasi omnibus hominibus adest ' ; it is more than
demonstrative knowledge, which is possible to few alone (*ib.*, 39 ad *ea enim
quæ sunt*), but it transcends the knowledge which is by faith as well (*ib.*, 40) ;
it is not in its fullness possible in this life (*ib.*, 48) because it is a vision of
God's essence (*ib.*, 51). Consequently neither the ' lumen naturale ' (ordinary
consciousness) nor the ' lumen gratiæ ' (prophetic or angelic consciousness
—see *infra*, p. 548, additional note S) can give it to us ; we need the
' lumen gloriæ ' (beatified consciousness—*ib.*, 53). Even so the divine essence
will not be *comprehended* (*ib.*, 55). Further consequences, *ib.*, 56-63 ; cp. also
ST., i, q. 12, *pass.* ; ii, 2, q. 180, *pass.* ; *de ver.*, qq. 18, 19 ; and on angelic
cognition of God, *CG.*, iii, 49, 50 ; *ST.*, i, q. 56 ; *de ver.*, q. 8.
[2] *CG.*, iii, 26, ad *si aliquis actus ;* but note the concessions of *ST.*, ii, 2,
q. 180, a. 1, ad 1, 2.
[3] Cp. *ST.*, ii, 2, q. 180, a. 3, on the difference between men and angels.
[4] *de ver.*, q. 26, a. 2—' passions ' in the soul by reason of its union with
the body.
[5] *Ib.* ; et *ST.*, i, 2, q. 22, a. 1.
[6] *ST.*, i, 2, q. 56, a. 4, obj. 1 ; cp. *ib.*, q. 24, a. 1.
[7] *de ver.*, q. 26, a. 2 ; *ST.*, i, 2, q. 22, a. 1.   [8] *ST.*, i, 2, q. 24, a. 1.
[9] *ST.*, i, 2, q. 24, a. 1 ; cp. q. 58, a. 1—' non omnis virtus dicitur moralis,
sed solum illa quæ est in vi appetitivâ '; q. 59, a. 1—'virtus . . . inter
passiones medium constituit.'
[10] *ST.*, i, 2, q. 58, a. 5—see *infra*, p. 388, n. 2.
[11] *ST.*, i, 2, q. 24, a. 2—the Stoics indeed said ' omnes passiones esse
malas '; but since they drew no psychological distinction between ' passions '
and ' will,' ' passion ' to them was from the outset an ethical term only, and
meant actions or emotions transgressing the limits of reason. Thus if an
emotion or impulse did not transgress those limits, it did not receive the name
of passion. Cp. *ib.*, a. 3 ; and q. 59, aa. 2. 3.

trouble to argue it. 'The Peripatetics,' he says with finality, 'call the passions good, if they are moderated by reason ; they are bad only when they escape from reason's control.'[1] Hence it adds to the goodness of a good act that it should be done *passionately*— that is with joy, enthusiasm and desire—provided always that the motive is no mere wave of passing emotion.[2]

S. Thomas, therefore, is perhaps the first Christian philosopher to take the corporeal character of human existence calmly. The whole dualist, ascetic school of thought had been frightened of the body and its passions, and had tried to make men 'live like angels' —at best we have met hitherto with mitigations which amount to no more than saying, 'Live like angels if you can ; if you cannot, live as much like them as possible.' S. Thomas, on the other hand, insists on saying, 'Live like men, that is, like embodied souls ; and remember that souls embodied cannot behave as though they were disembodied.' From this it follows, as might be expected, that within a general framework of the double standard and the theoretical preference of the 'religious' to the 'secular' life, his references to the evangelical counsels and the monastic state are relatively cold and brief ; one of his most orthodox modern interpreters is forced regretfully to speak of his 'formula' as being 'incomplete' at this point.[3] The so-called 'religious life' is no more than a 'state of perfection'—a starting-point, perhaps the easiest, but certainly not the only starting-point, for the race which leads to perfection.[4]

Man then, being a little lower than the angels, must remember that he is not an angel—not even an imprisoned one—and must not try to be one. The soul is not entombed in, but endowed with, a body. Bodily emotions and bodily goods, though not the whole of human good, are genuinely and eternally a part of it. Even

---

[1] *ST.*, i, 2, q. 24, a. 2 ; cp. ii, 2, q. 123, a. 10.

[2] *ST.*, i, 2, q. 24, a. 3—' ad perfectionem boni moralis pertinet quod homo ad bonum moveatur non solum secundum voluntatem sed etiam secundum appetitum sensitivum ' (cp. q. 59, a. 5—' quanto magis fuerit perfecta [justitia] tanto magis passionem causat'—and the contrast of man with God and the angels in this respect, *ib.*, ad 3). Then follows a delicate piece of psychological analysis : ' Emotion (passion) can stand in a double relation to the decision of [right] reason. It can precede it ; and in that respect it may cloud the decision of reason (on which depends the moral goodness of the act), and so diminish its worth. For example, an act of charity performed deliberately is more praiseworthy than one performed out of the emotion of pity alone. But emotion can also be consequent upon the decision of the will, and this again in two ways—(*a*) as an epiphenomenon (" per modum redundantiæ ") ; e.g. when the higher part of the soul is intensely moved in a particular direction, and sways the [emotions or] lower part in the same direction—in such a case, emotion consequent upon the decision of the will is evidence of its greater intensity, and so proves greater moral worth ; (*b*) as chosen by right reason—e.g. when a man deliberately and of right reason submits himself to the sway of an emotion, so that by the co-operation of his sensitive appetite he may act the more eagerly. In this case also emotion adds to the moral worth of the action ' (*ib.*, ad 1).

[3] Pourrat, *SC.*, ii, p. 207.

[4] *Supra*, p. 266 ; and cp. *ST.*, ii, 2, qq. 184, aa. 3-8 ; 188.

in the beatified state the body will be necessary for the *bene esse* of the soul, and the joy of the soul will overflow upon the body, so that it too may enter upon the inheritance of its own perfection.[1] This deference to the body and its needs, which allows S. Thomas to sit so lightly in theory to the monastic life, shows itself at all points. Among the lower or bodily desires of human nature to which we are all subject are those for honour, renown, riches and pleasure. The ascetic says, 'These things are evil in themselves, if for no other reason than that they are not the highest.' S. Thomas replies, 'Man's true end, indeed, is to be found in none of these ; but in so far as they are genuine objects of human desire, they are good, and factors in the supreme good.' We find him therefore insisting that the vision of God will confer on those who receive it true honour, true renown, true riches, and perfect joy.[2] The active life, and society as we now know it, will not, of course, continue in the future world, yet even so celestial beatitude, complete though it is in itself, will be further enhanced by eternal friendship.[3] We cannot therefore be wrong if we look for a foretaste here on earth of those eternal joys which will satisfy even our most humble needs. If in the future life the body will be rewarded by the satisfaction of all its legitimate desires, in this life the satisfaction of those desires, each in its own degree, must help towards the vision of God. Hence peace, education, a knowledge of the celestial hierarchies, health, and ' external goods ' are all of them to be regarded as ' instruments ministering to beatitude '— at all events in that as yet imperfect form in which it is possible to man in this life.[4]

Professor Taylor has recently insisted that S. Thomas' use of the principle of analogy stabilized the metaphysic of the middle ages, and reduced it from a chaotic and undisciplined play of opinions to a regulated system.[5] I have dwelt upon the present aspect of S. Thomas' ethics because I believe it had the same effect in this sphere, and for the same reason.[6] It brought back the

[1] *ST.*, i, 2, q. 4, a. 5—the body is relevant to human perfection ' eo quod pertinet ad bene esse ejus' ; a. 6—' ex beatitudine animæ fiet redundantia ad corpus, ut et ipsum suâ perfectione potiatur.' Cp. also C. C. J. Webb, *Studies in Natural Theology*, p. 262 ; and on S. Thomas' use of ' beatitude,' *infra*, p. 551, additional note S.

[2] *CG.*, iii, 63 ; *ST.*, i, 2, q. 4, a. 7, ad 1, 2.   [3] *ST.*, i, 2, q. 4, a. 8.

[4] *ST.*, i, 2, q. 3, a. 4, ad 1 ; a. 6, obj. 1 et ad 1 ; a. 7 ; q. 4, aa. 6, 7. So too of friendship, q. 2, a. 8 ; but here S. Thomas is more rigidly Aristotelian (cp. *Eth. Nic.*, ix, 9. 4) than Aristotle himself. He follows Aristotle in saying that the good man does not need friends for the pleasure of intercourse with them (*Eth. Nic.*, ix, 9. 4 ; *ST.*, i, 2, q. 4, a. 8), but only that he may benefit them and be benefited by them (*Eth. Nic.*, ix, 9. 2, 7 *init.*). But he does not reproduce in this discussion the numerous references to the pleasure wh.ch friendship gives to the good man which are to be found in his source. It is the influence of the idea of Pure Love at work.

[5] A. E. Taylor, *St. Thomas Aquinas as a Philosopher* (Oxford, 1924), pp. 27, 28.

[6] It is arguable of course that by analogy (in his sense of the word) from actual man, S. Thomas has inferred without demonstration the existence of

heroics of ascetic rigorism—always aspiring, often unregulated, sometimes tragically wasteful—to the test of reason, and subordinated them to the supreme rule of the beatific vision as commensurate to human nature. But it would leave an impression of Epicureanism wholly alien to the Angelic Doctor's thought if nothing were said of his positive system of Christian duty. Perhaps his greatest contribution to ethics is the doctrine that the passions are to be ordered and harmonized, rather than extirpated ; and it is from this point [1] that he develops his massive scheme of the cardinal virtues. Its details are so well known that there is no need to dwell upon them ; [2] but the transition deserves a moment's attention.

What manner of acts or habitudes are those which will help the Christian towards his appointed goal ? Granted purity of intention,[3] and eliminating those ' virtues ' or ' excellences ' which are no more than natural aptitudes of mind or body,[4] it is clear that virtue must consist in the direction of the movements of the soul each towards its proper share in the good of the whole. These movements, complex and multiple though they appear to be, have yet one and all been blindly driving man forward towards his true end. They are of two main kinds—action, and passion or emotion.[5] The right direction of emotion is treated under the names of ' temperance ' and ' fortitude '—the one to restrain emotion when it leads us away from our true end ; the other to break down its resistance when it holds us back.[6] But further, the

angels ; and by treating this existence as a certainty and not a mere postulate, has come back again by analogy with limitations and principles for his theory of human virtue. Such a criticism, no doubt, would hold good for any philosopher who, without the mediæval conviction of the existence of angels, were to introduce pure intellectual subsistences into his system, and draw therefrom conclusions as to the relative superiority of man over the brutes. That, however, does not concern us. S. Thomas had his own reasons for believing in the hierarchy of being : and even if the existence of the angels were purely hypothetical, his conclusions as to man would follow from his premises.

[1] Cp. *ST.*, ii, 2, q. 180, a. 2—the relation of the virtues to the contemplative life.

[2] Full accounts in W. H. V. Reade, *Moral System of Dante's Inferno*, pp. 124-161 ; E. Gilson, *La Morale de S. Thomas d'Aquin*, pp. 266-353 ; also T. B. Strong, *Christian Ethics*, pp. 140-142.

[3] Hence the discussion of the obligation of ' ratio (= conscientia) errans ' in *ST.*, i, 2, q. 19, aa. 5, 6 (cp. *Ignorance, Faith and Conformity*, pp. 24-28 ; and *infra*, p. 540) ; and the whole *quæstio*.

[4] *ST.*, i, 2, q. 56, a. 3 ; q. 57, a. 1 ; q. 58, a. 5, ad 2—they are to be called virtues ' secundum quid,' but not ' simpliciter.' On the grounds of the partial confusion involved in this double use of the word ' virtus,' T. B. Strong, *Christian Ethics*, pp. 101-106.

[5] *ST.*, i, 2, q. 59, a. 4 ; q. 60, a. 2.

[6] *ST.*, i, 2, q. 61, a. 2. This is true of ' fortitude ' and ' temperance ' in relation to the passions, ' consideratâ repugnantiâ ipsarum ad rationem.' But considered ' secundum differentiam ab invicem,' the passions are either ' irascibiles ' or ' concupiscibiles ' (i, 2, q. 23, a. 1) ; and fortitude is concerned with the former (i.e. ' circa timores et audacias '), temperance with the latter (' circa delectationes et tristitias ')—q. 60, a. 4. The confusion arises from the fact that virtues can be classified either ' secundum subjecta '

differences between 'action' and 'passion' are twofold. The former (for ethical purposes) operates in the sphere of the will, the latter in that of the emotions ; [1] and again, while the discipline of passion lies mainly in the inner life of man, action in the strict sense is a matter of his external or public life. Thus, whenever an action is in question which will directly affect the world around, we are entitled to ask the agent not merely, 'Are your passions under due control ? ' but also, ' Have you considered the effect which your action will have upon others ? ' If he can answer the first question in the affirmative, we can credit him with temperance and fortitude. But not until he has said 'Yes' to the second—has indicated that in acting he is attempting to give each man (and God as well) his due—can we say that he is exhibiting the virtue of *justice*. Justice, then, falls into line as a cardinal virtue.[2]

Over and above the three 'moral' virtues stands 'prudence,' their 'charioteer'; [3] the one intellectual virtue of the cardinal four. Justice, temperance and fortitude develop generic tendencies in the soul—tendencies towards equity in dealing with others, towards the subjugation of rebellious passions, or the control of reluctant ones :—

> ' But each of these results can be achieved in many different
> ways, varying with different persons ; and the place of prudence
> is to determine the right way in each several case.' [4]   The other
> three cardinal virtues ' dispose us fittingly towards our proper
> end ; but for the [scrutiny and choice of] fit means to be
> employed towards that end we must be disposed by a habitude
> of reason ; for scrutiny and choice are functions of reason. . . .

or 'secundum objecta,' and that unfortunately the passions belong, in one sense, to the 'subjecta,' in another to the 'objecta' (so W. H. V. Reade, *op. cit.*, p. 137, where however this particular point is not discussed).

[1] i.e. the 'rational' and 'sensitive appetites' respectively (*ST.*, i, q. 80, a. 2).

[2] *ST.*, i, 2, q. 60, a. 2. Here again S. Thomas tacitly drops the division ' secundum subjecta ' (' will ' and ' emotion ') and concentrates on that ' secundum objecta ' (the outer and the inner life). Hence he is able to say that justice is justice ' *qualitercumque homo afficiatur ad eam* ' ; a thing which could not be said of ' temperance ' or ' fortitude,' in which the only point to be considered is whether ' homo bene vel male afficitur circa hujus-modi.' I have tried to draw out the distinction in the text above, and as there stated it holds good ; but it is not quite true to the literal implication of S. Thomas' words, which suggest that justice would be justice (assuming that you gave others their due) even if you had not aimed at doing so and regretted the result. As he cannot mean this (he is speaking of justice as a *virtue*), his ' qualitercumque afficiatur ' must be rhetorical only. (Contrast Reade, *op. cit.*, pp. 131, 132, where a different explanation is given.)—In *ST.*, ii, 2, q. 58, a. 5, S. Thomas takes still wider ground, and observes that even a virtue which ' ordinat hominem ad seipsum ' (such as temperance and fortitude, we must suppose, in their regulation of the passions) is not without influence on a man's environment (' est referabile ad bonum com-mune '), and so in a sense comes under the definition of justice. This merely serves to illustrate the artificial character of all such analyses, convenient though they may be.

[3] *in Sent.*, ii, d. 41, q. 1, a. 1, obj. 3.   [4] *de virt. in comm.*, a. 6.

The virtue which effects this is prudence. Prudence therefore is a virtue necessary for the good life.' [1]

A passing illustration makes this clear. A man may have the 'habitudes' of justice, temperance and fortitude. He may have set himself (as we say) to exercise these virtues ; and yet be so completely at a loss in the matter that he has to rely wholly upon the advice of a moral expert. Of such a man S. Thomas says that ' he does well,' but does not as yet ' live well '—for the direction of his activity is not from himself. To ' live well ' he needs to ' do well ' of his own motion ; to add *prudence*, that is to say, to his other virtues.[2]

S. Thomas' discussion of the cardinal virtues, of which the preceding paragraphs have only given the briefest and most superficial review,[3] is no more than one section of his vast treatment of ethics. I have quoted it rather to illustrate the conscientious orderliness of his procedure than for any other purpose ; and we must return to his elucidation of the doctrine of the vision of God. That no aspect of the theological problems attendant upon the doctrine escaped his keen eye has already been suggested. But in two respects at least his advance upon the Victorines is epochmaking. Hugh's unending enumeration of the studies preparatory to the contemplative life at least involves the possibility that the vision of God is the prerogative of the scholarly alone ; Richard had gone a long way towards asserting that true contemplation is only possible in the paroxysms of ecstasy. In neither of these respects does S. Thomas follow them.

At first sight, indeed, he appears to endorse the intellectualism of Hugh of St. Victor. His ' contemplation ' seems to be simply the activity of the mind dealing by demonstration or by analogy with such truths as are accessible to it either by intuition of first principles, or by the observation of natural phenomena. So Dom Chapman, for example, can say that S. Thomas regards contemplation as

[1] *ST*., i, 2, q. 57. a. 5 ; further analysis of prudence, ii, 2, q. 47 *pass.*
[2] *ST*., i, 2, q. 57. a. 5, ad 2. This way of putting the case suggests, however, that prudence is merely ' consideratio '—intelligence—and so not a moral virtue at all. S. Thomas guards against this elsewhere by saying (*ST*., ii, 2, q. 47. a. 1, ad 3 ; cp. *ib.*, a. 4 *corp.*) ' laus prudentiæ non consistit in solâ consideratione, sed in applicatione ad opus '—i.e. he would not credit a man with the virtue of prudence unless, besides being able to *see* the right way of adjusting the respective claims of the other virtues, he had the *will* to enforce them in action. Thus ' prudence ' is more than casuistical ability or technique, however sound ; it involves the formed intention of living a life in which the demands of all our various duties are harmonized on principle. Its principal act is to ' move ' (*ST*., ii, 2, q. 47. a. 6, ad 3) or ' command ' (*ib.*, a. 8) the other virtues. For the same reason, prudence presupposes the other virtues (*supra*, p. 383) ; I could not have the formed intention of harmonizing the claims of justice, say, with those of temperance, unless I had already the intention of being just and temperate. For the basis of this doctrine in Aristotle's account of φρονήσις, cp. *Conscience and its Problems*, p. 126.
[3] For fuller treatment see the authorities cited, *supra*, p. 386 ; cp. also *Some Principles of Moral Theology*, pp. 33-48.

' the brief rest of the mind upon the great verities at which it has arrived by argument and investigation, avoiding any mention of mystical prayer ' ; and that ' he means by the contemplative life the life of study and passion for truth.'[1] It must be allowed that there is much in S. Thomas which corroborates this description. He defines ' wisdom ' as the possession of the most universal principles and the first causes;[2] and wisdom, though it is bound to remain imperfect in this life, is nevertheless ' a participation in our future felicity'—nearer to that felicity even than the prudence which regulates the cardinal virtues.[3] So too contemplation, though in eternity it will be concerned with the being of God alone, must in this life be content to see God as mirrored in His works;[4] and therefore ' some philosophers,' from whom S. Thomas does not dissent, ' thinking of the natural perfection of man, have said that his final happiness is found when the whole order of the universe is displayed to him in his soul.'[5] S. Thomas, then, is the last person to reckon any kind of research or scholarship irrelevant to the vision of God :—

> ' It was a grievous error in those of whom Augustine speaks, to allege that it mattered not what men thought of the created universe, so long as they thought rightly concerning God. For error in the matter of the universe means false opinion about God, and leads men's minds away from God (towards Whom faith would direct them), supplying them with causes other than God.'[6] . . . ' By considering what God has made we can —first of all—catch a glimpse of the divine wisdom which has in some measure impressed a certain likeness to itself upon them. . . . In the second place, such consideration leads to an admiration of God's perfect excellence, and so breeds a reverence for God in the human heart. . . . Thirdly, it inflames the human mind to a love of God's goodness. For whatever goodness or perfection is to be found distributed among particular things, is all united in Him who is the Fount of all goodness. If therefore the goodness, beauty and charm of things created can so gain men's affection, the very Fount of goodness, God Himself, when compared with these rivulets of goodness to be seen in His separate creatures, cannot but inflame our minds and draw them wholly to Himself.'[7]

Despite the emotion which this thought rouses in S. Thomas' heart, it is but cold comfort for the unlearned. They seem to be

---

[1] ERE., ix, p. 96, s.v. ' Mysticism (Roman Catholic).'
[2] CG., i, 94 ; cp. ib., iv, 12 ; ST., i, 2, q. 57, a. 2.
[3] ST., i, 2, q. 66, a. 5, ad 1, 2 (from Eth. Nic., vi, 7) ; cp. ii, 2, q. 45, a. 3, ad 3.
[4] ST., ii, 2, q. 180, a. 4.
[5] de ver., 20, a. 3. It is true that this refers only to man's *natural* perfection ; but as S. Thomas points out in the same place (and it is the first principle of his whole system) supernatural perfection never excludes natural perfection.
[6] CG., ii, 3.   [7] CG., ii, 2.

excluded from any high degree of participation in the vision. But his concessions on the point are singularly graceful and unpedantic. He approaches the question first of all (with a side glance at contemplation) [1] in his discussion of ' religion,' the narrowest of the terms which he knows for the ' direction of a man's whole life ' towards God.[2] The primary act of religion is ' devotion '—the will to give oneself *readily* to all that pertains to the adoration of God.[3] Then comes the crux. ' Meditation or contemplation,' S. Thomas says (and here he uses the two words synonymously),[4] ' is the cause of devotion.' [5] At once the practical directors of souls, remembering his scholastic description of contemplation, rise up in revolt. ' Subtle meditations on intellectual subjects,' they protest,

> ' often impede devotion ; simple matters of faith—the passion of Christ and the mysteries of His humanity—provoke it more readily than the consideration of the divine greatness. It is not those who are most successful in contemplation [as a Schoolman understands the term] who are most devout. On the contrary, the uneducated and womenfolk, who cannot "contemplate," have often the greatest devotion.' [6]

S. Thomas grants it all, yet adheres to his principle. To the first objection he replies that ' some things ' (that is, the ' subtleties ' of which we have heard) ' do not inflame the mind to the love of God, but rather distract from it.' These are not fit subjects for meditation in the spiritual sense of the word, though the scientist, no doubt, must take them into his purview.[7] To the second he

---

[1] *ST.*, ii, 2, q. 81, a. 1, ad 5—the technical restriction of the word ' religion ' to ' those who have given their whole life to the worship of God ' compared to the similar restriction of the word ' contemplative.'

[2] *Ib., corp.*—' religio proprie importat ordinem ad Deum.'

[3] *Ib.*, q. 82, a. 2.

[4] Although (*ST.*, ii, 2, q. 180, a. 3) he recognizes and reproduces the Victorine distinction between ' meditation ' and ' contemplation.' But, significantly enough for his view of contemplation, ' meditation ' is a word which does not enter into his technical vocabulary at all.

[5] *ST.*, ii, 2, q. 82. a. 3—i.e. the ' intrinsic ' cause : the ' extrinsic ' cause, of course, is God.

[6] *Ib.*, objj. 1, 2, 3.

[7] It is to passages such as this (cp. also *ST.*, i, 2, q. 3, a. 6, on the limitations of ' science ' as a mode of approach to God) that we owe the not uncommon statement that the Schoolmen separated speculative science (including of course the articulation of dogma) from mystical theology ; cp. Pourrat, *SC.*, ii, p. 213 (and refer back to *ib.*, p. 154), Chapman, *loc. cit.*, p. 97, on the ' large lines of the scholastic theory '. (Gilson, *Philosophy of S. Thomas*, p. 276, seems to me ambiguous when he says, ' In the Thomistic philosophy mysticism is added to and co-ordinated with natural knowledge ; but without continuing it.') The matter is complicated by the various uses of the word ' mysticism ' ; but I should be inclined rather to summarize the Thomist doctrine as follows : (*a*) Raptures and ecstasies are wholly miraculous, cannot be prepared for, and so are not ' co-ordinated ' in any way with the normal processes of religion in this life ; (*b*) the vision of God in a measure is possible to all men in this life, and is prepared for by contemplation of the works of God (as well as by purity of life); the simple can be perfectly content with the

rejoins that God, in His pity for the frailty of the human mind, provided the earthly life of the Lord as the primary means to excite devout thoughts about Himself.   On the third head, he admits frankly that men of science are often puffed up with their own achievements, in a manner from which the simple and women are exempt.   They have forgotten in their meditations to reflect upon themselves and their own littleness, and so have failed to subordinate their wisdom to God.   Let them ' make a perfect offering of all their attainments,' and thereby their devotion will be increased.[1]

The conclusion is obvious.   No man can afford in his medita-tions to overlook his own position as a dependent, limited, and sinful creature ;   none of us can afford to give the person of Jesus any but primary place there.   As to other subjects of meditation, the higher and wider they are the better ;   but the work of deciding ' subtle problems ' must remain outside the sphere of devotional prayer.   Problems have to be solved, of course ;   but it is at best the solution, and not the intricate analysis by which it is reached, which will afford matter for meditation to the elect few who are able to build it into the fabric of the spiritual life.

The contemplative life therefore is not, as at first appeared, the prerogative of the scholar and the philosopher alone.   The wayfaring man, though a fool, can take his share in it, if by the practice of virtue, and by loving thoughts about the life of Jesus, he is showing himself pure in heart.   Nor need we fear the criticism that even to know the works of God as divine requires an exercise of reason beyond the scope of the simple-minded.   That might be the case if reason were the only road to truth ;   but it is not.   Those who cannot acquire the ' necessary demonstration of the first principles of religion ' (and there are times when S. Thomas in-cludes almost all of us in this category) may have the certainty of them by faith in revelation.[2]   But the second problem still remains. Contemplation is something far more human than the subtleties of the scholar ;   but how does it stand—in S. Thomas' use of the word— in respect of the raptures of the mystic ?   Would Clement, Augustine, Bernard, or Richard of St. Victor find themselves at home within the sober scheme of the ' Summa Theologica ' ?   What has become of the union of the soul with God *sola cum solo*, of the mystic marriage, of the intuitive vision of God in which the soul loses all consciousness of itself and its prayer ?

On this point S. Thomas can speak without a moment's hesita-tion.   The intuitive vision of the divine essence—the sight of God

Incarnation and the Passion as the ' works of God ' supremely suitable for meditation ;   (c) the investigation of subtle problems, if it leads (as it should do where undertaken with humility) to greater appreciation of the works of God, is not irrelevant to contemplation ;   but (d) by reason of its exacting character is hardly the sphere in which contemplative prayer is most likely to be *directly* inspired.   See further, *infra*, p. 548, additional note S.

[1] *ST*. ii, 2, q. 82, a. 3, ad objj.   [2] *ST*., i, q. 1, a. 1.

face to face—is sternly reserved for eternity.[1]   A partial knowledge
of God by ' mental images ' (' phantasmata ') as the result of discursive processes of reason is all that man is allowed here on earth.[2]
Harnack has misrepresented him on this point in quite inexplicable
fashion.[3]   S. Thomas does indeed admit that Moses and S. Paul
received the vision of the divine essence in their ecstasies ; [4] but
the exceptions seem to be made wholly out of deference to scripture,
and cannot be used (as they sometimes are) to insinuate that
S. Thomas was prepared to recognize a whole tract of mystical knowledge alongside the knowledge of God by His creatures.   Actually
he never commits himself to more than the admission that ecstasy
is not impossible, or ' contrary to nature ' ; [5] but for lesser beings
than Moses and S. Paul, such as S. Peter and David, he provides two
kinds of ecstasy in which the contemplation of God is less remote
from that which the ordinary Christian may hope to achieve in this
life.[6] On this point we must take him at his word, and believe that
he had set his face firmly against all exaggerated claims of uncontrolled mysticism.

But that does not mean that his contemplation is an arid, prosaic, or commonplace pursuit.   On the contrary it is set in a context of love towards God,[7] and when we remember all that the
thought of God meant to S. Thomas, we need not fear that the
contemplation of God ' as revealed in His works ' will be anything
but radiant in the fullest degree.   It is daring to speculate in this
matter ; but it is at least possible that to the rare mind of the Angelic

[1] *CG.*, iii, 47, 48; *ST.*, i, q. 12, a. 1; ii, 2, q. 180, a. 5; for S. Bernard's
very similar views cp. *de dil. Deo*, 27-33.

[2] *CG.*, iii, 47.

[3] *Hist. of Dogma*, vi, pp. 105, 106—' According to Thomas, the soul can
already here on earth so receive God into itself that it enjoys in the fullest
sense the vision of His essence. . . . The contemplation that rises to intuition [of the divine essence] suffers thereby no qualitative change.'   Two
blunders here—Harnack ignores altogether (1) that the vision of the divine
essence in this life is rigidly restricted by S. Thomas to Moses and S. Paul—
David, Solomon, Peter and the apostles all being excluded from it ; (2) that
the distinction between the ' lumen gloriæ,' by which the saints see the divine
essence in heaven, the ' lumen gratiæ,' by which the prophets see God ' per
species intelligibiles ' on earth, and the ' lumen naturæ,' which is the normal
method of coming to cognition of God, is emphatically a qualitative one,
and is meticulously sustained by S. Thomas.

[4] *ST.*, i, q. 12, a. 11, ad 2 ; ii, 2, q. 175, a. 3—S. Thomas uses ' raptus '
for ecstasy in the modern sense of the word ; he explains his terminology in
ii, 2, q. 175, a. 2.

[5] *ST.*, i, 2, q. 175, a. 1, ad 2.

[6] The prophets ' see God ' ' per similitudines divino lumine illustratas '
(ii, 2, q. 173, a. 1) ; which may be ' formæ sensibiles ' (as with Daniel),
' formæ imaginariæ ' (Jacob, Jeremiah and Peter), or ' novæ species intelligibiles ' (Solomon, David and the apostles)—q. 173, a. 2 ; q. 175, a. 3,
ad 1 ; q. 180, a. 5, ad 1.   How near the contemplation of the ordinary
Christian can come to this prophetic cognition is not clearly indicated ; see
infra, p. 548, additional note S.

[7] *ST.*, ii, 2, q. 180, a. 1—' Gregorius constituit vitam contemplativam
in caritate Dei, in quantum scilicet aliquis ex dilectione Dei inardescit ad
ejus pulchritudinem conspiciendam '; *ib.*, a. 2, ad 1—' dilectio Dei et proximi
requiritur ad vitam contemplativam.'

Doctor the being of God and the ordered mystery of creation meant as much as the earthly life of Jesus to S. Bernard, or the Passion to S. Francis. Even if this were not the case, there was one mystery of revelation—a mystery focussing for each passing day and moment the eternal truths of the Incarnation and the Passion—which could draw from S. Thomas's contemplation as ardent expressions of prayer, adoration and self-surrender as any that Christian lips have uttered—the mystery of the Eucharist. Where a single soul could combine in itself the passion for truth betrayed in the relentless handling of problem after problem in the ' Summæ ' and the ' Quæstiones Disputatæ,' and the passion for God which inspires the sonorous lines of ' Pange Lingua,' ' Verbum Supernum,' and ' Adoro Te devote,' it would be blind sacrilege to suggest that within its own sphere it lacked any of the fervour of the true Christian mystic.

If S. Thomas is misunderstood on this point, it is because he was the victim of his own high undertaking. He is content to draw a veil over the experiences which contemplation yields, so long as he may be allowed to emphasize its primary function in the divine scheme for human life. Face to face with a riot of religious extravagance of every kind—pantheism, dualism, mysticism, asceticism, heresy, subjectivity and individualism in all its forms—his chosen task was to reduce it all to order, and to find the principles that would lead the world back to sanity and saintliness again. S. Benedict had done the same for monasticism at a similar crisis in its history. The two stand side by side as champions of the every-day against the abnormal ; and (though the ' Contra Gentiles ' is more aspiring) the ' Summa Theologica ' is, by its author's own confession, like the ' Regula Benedicti ' a ' very little rule for beginners.' [1]

It is easy to forget, with men of this calibre, that their passion for orderliness of thought and life must be as great as any which inspires the undisciplined experiments around them. But in the case of S. Thomas the mere facts of his career betray the truth. His exposition is never hurried, never superficial. No stone is left unturned, no avenue unexplored, no problem, objection, criticism undiscussed. Yet the whole vast output (in bulk, no less than in leisureliness, to all appearance the work of a life-time) was compressed within the brief compass of twenty years of teaching and writing—a miracle of concentrated thought sustained at feverish speed. Circumstances have changed, and those who overlook the crucial nature of the intellectual warfare that he waged see in him only a pedant playing with a mosaic of abstract ideas. But if we take from him two thoughts only—that honest intellectual endeavour (impossible, be it remembered, without moral effort of the highest kind) is no less a service of God than any other, and

---

[1] *ST.*, i, prol.—' ad eruditionem incipientium.' Immediately thereafter he says he has been moved to write by a consideration of the difficulties under which ' novices in doctrine' labour.

that ordered discipline is the condition of success in all things, even
in the pursuit of the vision of God—and add to them the lesson of
his life, that he counted the world well lost if he could bring those
two truths home to men in a time of wild and fantastic imaginations,
we shall not think any place too high for him in the roll of Christian
heroes.

IV. S. IGNATIUS OF LOYOLA.

The decline of scholasticism—the break-up of the Thomist syn
thesis—the triumph of formalism and dogma over the free but
ordered exercise of reason,—these things constitute a story which
has been told so often that we may safely pass it by.   And it would
be presumptuous to intrude upon ground covered by one of the
greatest of living Bampton lecturers, and speak of the German
mystics of the fourteenth century—Eckhardt, Tauler, Suso and
Ruysbroek—in whom the solid Dominican tradition [1] is heavily
overweighted by reminiscences of Dionysius the Areopagite.
Through these and other vicissitudes the spirit of S. Thomas lived
on.   More than one effort was made to maintain the spirit of
ordered personal religion and communion with God, in the face
both of growing insistence upon bare obedience to the hierarchy in
externals, and of dying attempts to revive a mysticism unfettered
either by reason or by authority.   A new conception of the practice
of prayer set in steadily.   Contemplation is now approached by
conscious and active reflection upon the great Christian verities—
the ordered hierarchy of creation, the mystery of the Eucharist,
and the stupendous drama of the ministry and Passion of the Lord.
When the mind has worked—not dreamt—upon these data, and
has reached some new aspect of truth not hitherto grasped, it is
free to give emotion play ; or rather, with the termination of the
process, there will come as a natural sequel a sense of joy, peace and
acceptance which will issue in an enhanced purity of life and moral
efficiency.   This is as near to the full vision of God as the Christian
will attain in this life—but it is near enough.   Raptures, ecstasies
and the like, if they come at all, come only to such favoured souls
as Moses and S. Paul ; nor are they any longer held to be of real
significance for the life of the soul. [2]

It seems to have been in Holland that this ordered, disciplined

---

[1] Eckhardt, Tauler and Suso were all three Dominican and German ;
Ruysbroek, a canon regular, and a Fleming, was acquainted with the works
of Eckhardt, and was a friend of Tauler.   Generally, for this group of writers,
see W. R. Inge, *Christian Mysticism*, pp. 148-194 ; Pourrat, *SC.*, ii, pp.
319-378.

[2] The anti-mystical reaction (*infra*, pp. 431 ff., 528) discredited mysticism
by identifying it with pathological phenomena, and some ' mystical ' writers
appear to have accepted and indeed gloried in the identification.   See the
criticism of Ribet. Saudreau, *Life of Union with God* [3], pp. 312, 313 ; and the
remarks of Poulain, *Grâces d'Oraison* [10], p. 311, and Chapman, *ERE.*, ix,
pp. 100, 101.   Hence Dean Inge's criticisms of ' Roman Catholicism ' in
general. *Christian Mysticism*, pp. ix, 143, 144, 264, 265, etc.

and wholly comprehensible system struck its deepest roots.[1] The scholastic element, it is true, has disappeared; the atmosphere of reasoned discipline remains. Towards the end of the fourteenth century, Gerard Groot, a noted professor of Cologne, who after his conversion had spent some years as a lay evangelist, gathered together a group of young students at Deventer into a methodist community known as the Brothers of the Common Life. The society had as its offshoot a congregation of Austin canons at Windesheim. Calligraphy was the principal manual occupation of the brethren, and they achieved a high reputation in this respect. The general movement was known as the 'devotio moderna'; it produced, in addition to the writings of Groot, Petersen and Thomas à Kempis (1380-1471), the 'Imitatio Christi,' a work which can only with difficulty be attributed to à Kempis himself.[2] The central spiritual duty inculcated by this 'modern devotion' was meditation. It took the form of colloquies as between the soul and God, ending in a short ejaculatory prayer, of a character which the 'Imitatio' has made familiar to all; the general non-scholastic tone of the movement made it even possible to speak of a mystic union with God as the terminus of these devotional aspirations in language more akin to that of S. Bernard than that of S. Thomas.

A movement so permeated with the specifically Christian genius as to produce the 'Imitatio Christi' could not fail to exercise lasting influence upon the history of the Church. Nicholas of Cusa, John Gerson and Erasmus himself owed much to its inspiration. But the 'devotio moderna' points onward to a name even greater than any of theirs. In the last years of the fifteenth century John Wessel Gansfort,[3] an eccentric friend of Thomas à Kempis, drew up a 'Rule' or 'Ladder of Meditation,' which, with other writings of the same school, was used as a basis for his 'Exercitatorium Spirituale' by Garcia de Cisneros, abbot of Montserrat in

---

[1] For Groot, the Brethren of the Common Life, the 'devotio moderna' and their influence, see *C. Med. H.*, v, pp. 692, 693; *C. Mod. H.*, i, pp. 434-438, 626-629, 634; C. Ullmann, *Reformers before the Reformation*, ii, pp. 57-184; R. Jones, *Studies in Mystical Religion*, pp. 314 ff.; Pourrat, *SC.*, ii, pp. 379-400; *ERE.*, ii, pp. 839-842; A Hyma, *The 'Devotio Moderna' and the Christian Renaissance* (Michigan, n.d.), etc. Nicholas of Cusa and Erasmus were educated at Deventer; Gerson was a staunch friend of the canons, and defended them against the attacks of Grabon at the Council of Constance. Earlier examples of methodical prayer, Pourrat, *SC.*, iii, pp. 8-13; H. Joly, *S. Ignatius of Loyola* (E. tr.), pp. 49 ff.; A. Poulain, *Grâces d'Oraison*[10], pp. 42 ff.

[2] Bibliography of this controversy, Pourrat, *SC.*, ii, pp. 398-400.

[3] Gansfort's life and writings have recently been studied at length by E. W. Miller and J. W. Scudder, *Wessel Gansfort* (1917) (cp. also C. Ullmann, *Reformers before the Reformation*, ii, pp. 385-567); but they say little of the *Scala Meditationis*. Gansfort's pupils called him 'Lux mundi'; his enemies 'Magister contradictionum,' on account both of his controversial tendencies and of his frequent changes of front. The story of his preferring a manuscript of the Bible in Greek and Hebrew to the offer of a bishopric is well known. Miller and Scudder (i, pp. 160 ff.) make much of his influence on Luther and Melancthon. A more detailed account of the *Scala*, Ullmann, *op. cit.*, pp. 569-576; cp. also Pourrat, *SC.*, iii, pp. 23, 24.

Catalonia.[1] The 'Exercitatorium' was published in 1500, and its use imposed upon all monks of the abbey.[2] Twenty-two years later, one of these monks was chosen as his confessor by a young Spanish pilgrim, Ignatius of Loyola.

Ignatius was now twenty-six years of age, and had been trained to arms. He had fought bravely in the defence of Pampeluna; and it was not till he received the wound which maimed him for life that the garrison lost heart and surrendered the citadel.[3] He was not merely a soldier, but a knight of the old school. As he lay wounded at Loyola,

> ' among the many subjects of vanity which presented themselves to his spirit was one which captivated and monopolized his heart from the outset, so much so that without knowing he would pass two, three, or four hours dreaming thereof. He presented to his fancy the exploits he would fain achieve in the service of a certain lady; the means he would take to come to her manor where she dwelt; the favours he would wear, the words he would speak to her, the doughty deeds he would perform in her service. To such presumption did he attain that he recked not how impossible it was that his dream should be achieved; for this lady was of no ordinary noble blood. She was neither countess nor duchess : her rank was higher than them both.'[4]

To relieve the tedium of his illness, Ignatius asked that the romance of 'Amadis of Gaul' should be brought for him to read. It was not the first time that the ideals of chivalry had influenced the history of Christian devotion. The Crusades, for all their sordidness, had caught a gleam of the possibility of knightly service in the cause of Christianity, and had revived imaginative interest in the earthly life and environment of our Lord. The military Orders made a gallant though in the end unsuccessful attempt to give the ideal a more positive content. S. Francis called his disciples indifferently 'troubadours of God' or 'knights of the

---

[1] The connexion is worked out by H. Watrigant, *Quelques Promoteurs de la Méditation Méthodique* (*Bibliothèque des Exercises* (1919) no. 59), pp. 62-83; cp. Pourrat, *SC.*, ii, pp. 396, 397; iii, pp. 22-28. Gansfort's *Scala* was incorporated by John Mombaer (Mauburnus) in his *Rosetum exercitiorum spiritualium et sacrarum meditationum* (A.D. 1494). This again was used by Cisneros for his *Exercitatorium*. Selections from the *Rosetum* in *Monumenta Ignatiana* (*infra*, p. 401, n. 2), series ii, p. 129; and Watrigant, *op. cit.*, pp. 34-61.

[2] A contemporary manuscript of the *Exercitatorium* insists that every monk of the community is to learn it by heart, ' et donec ea tam practice quam theoretice pleniter noverit seu sciverit non permittetur in aliis libris legere vel studere ' (H. Plenkers, *Un Manuscrit de Montserrat*, *Révue Bénédictine*, xvii (1900), p. 369).

[3] E. Thibaut, *Le Récit du Pèlerin*, p. 33.—This is the critical and annotated French translation of S. Ignatius' autobiography, as dictated by him to Louis Gonzalez in 1553. There is also an English translation, *The Testament of Ignatius Loyola*, by E. M. Rix, with introduction by George Tyrrell (1900).

[4] *Ib.*, pp. 37, 38.

Round Table ' ; [1] Dominic and his friars set out to be ' champions of the faith.' [2] At the very moment that Ignatius was asking for ' Amadis ' at Loyola, and eighty years before Cervantes rang the death-knell of chivalry, a little girl of six, to be known to history later as S. Teresa, was devouring it in the nursery, and ' thought there was no harm in it.' [3] The Society of Jesus and the reformed Carmelites owe more than is sometimes remembered to the romantic fancies of the middle ages.

Ignatius was not so fortunate as Teresa. ' Amadis ' was not in the castle library at Loyola—very few books were. Nothing could be found for his diversion except the ' Life of Christ ' of Ludolph the Carthusian,[4] and the ' Golden Legend.' These two he read, ' with a certain zest for what was told therein.' [5] Then occurred one of the most momentous events in the history of Christendom. Ignatius himself records it in the simplest of sentences : ' But our Lord came to his help, and allowed other thoughts, born of his new reading, to take the place of the former.' Compared with the burning accounts of their conversions given by S. Paul and S. Augustine, the words are prosaic enough ; they justify an imaginative critic in suggesting that the Spanish saint had in him ' something of Sancho Panza as well as of Don Quixote.' [6] But the conversion was complete, or all but complete ; [7] the knight had transferred his allegiance from an earthly princess to a heavenly King :—

> ' He checked his thoughts and said to himself, " How would it be if I were to do as S. Francis did, and as S. Dominic did ? " So he set before his fancy many things that seemed good, and always he set before himself things difficult and painful ; and as he fancied them, he seemed to find within himself the ability to discharge them. And always at the end of his meditations he returned to say to himself, " S. Dominic did this ; I too must do it—S. Francis did that, therefore I too must do it." . . . As he dreamed of walking bare-foot to Jerusalem—of making his diet of herbs alone—of delivering himself to all the other rigours of penitence which he saw the saints to have practised, not only

[1] C. Med. H., vi, p. 728 ; cp. C. Hess, Life of S. Francis, pp. 14-16.
[2] C. Med. H., vi, p. 738 ; cp. J. Guiraud, Saint Dominique, p. 86.
[3] S. Teresa, Life by Herself, ii, 1 (E. tr. D. Lewis (1911), p. 7). Teresa does not mention ' Amadis ' specifically, but it is at least highly probable that it figured among the numerous romances which her mother so imprudently (as the saint thought later) allowed to fall into her hands.
[4] Supra, p. 364.   [5] Thibaut, p. 37.
[6] R. P. Cavallera, La Spiritualité des Exercises, Révue d'ascétique et de mystique, Oct., 1922, p. 367.
[7] There was a period when both the religious and the secular fancies presented themselves to him alternately ; but he notices that, though he enjoyed both types, the latter left him ' arid and discontented ' when he turned from them, whereas after the former he ' remained contented and happy '—Thibaut, pp. 39, 40. The influence of ' Amadis ' remained even during his pilgrimage to Montserrat, and determined the dedication of his armour and his vigil (ib., pp. 50-51).

did he find consolation in these thoughts, but even when he let them be there remained with him joy and contentment.' [1]

It is no part of my purpose to sketch even in outline the history of Ignatius' great foundation. But already, at the very moment of his conversion, it is possible to discern the four great principles which were to dominate the Company from its inception nearly twenty years later. The first is that of militant service—a service so untiring that even the choir-office must be banished to find room for it.[2] The critical ' second week ' of the ' Spiritual Exercises,' preceding the moment at which the postulant's sense of vocation is about to be put to its most searching test, is hedged in by two great meditations, in each of which the same idea is paramount. The week begins with the meditation entitled, ' The Call of the Temporal King helps to the contemplation [3] of the life of the Eternal King ' :—

'The first point is to place before my eyes a human king, elected by our Lord God Himself, whom all princes and all Christians reverence and obey.

' The second is to consider how this king speaks to all his subjects, saying, " My will is to reduce to subjection all the land of the infidels : wherefore, whosoever desires to come with me must be contented with the food that I eat, with the drink and clothing that I have, etc. In like manner he must labour as I do during the day, and watch during the night, etc. ; in order that afterwards he may have part with me in the victory, as he has had in the hard work."

' The third is to consider what good subjects ought to answer to a king so liberal and so kind ; and consequently if anyone did not welcome the request of such a king, how he would deserve to be blamed by all the world, and held as a slothful knight.

' The second part of this Exercise consists in applying the above example of the temporal king to Christ our Lord, in the three aforesaid points. . . .' [4]

The climax of the ' week ' is a meditation developing the same theme. Here the boldness of its author's conception, though commonplace to us nowadays, becomes apparent. The primitive Church had called men to Christian effort in the picture of the two ways ; S. Augustine had thrown his philosophy of history into the

---

[1] Thibaut, pp. 39, 40.

[2] A. Brou, *La Spiritualité de Saint Ignace*, pp. 99-103.

[3] ' Contemplate,' in Loyola's vocabulary, always means ' meditate upon '
— *infra*, pp. 435, 436.

[4] J. Morris, *The Spiritual Exercises of St. Ignatius* (E. tr. London, 1929), pp. 33, 34 (W. H. Longridge, *The Spiritual Exercises, etc.*, pp. 77, 78).—I quote the *Exercises* by the pages and in the translation of Morris's small and handy edition throughout, adding those of Fr. Longridge's annotated edition for convenience of reference.

form of the two cities ; S. Ignatius crowns the work with his meditation on ' two standards ' :—[1]

> ' The meditation on Two Standards, the one of Christ, our Sovereign Leader and Lord ; the other of Lucifer, the mortal enemy of our human nature. . . .
>
> ' The first prelude is the history : it will be here how Christ calls and desires all under His banner : Lucifer on the contrary under his.
>
> ' The second prelude is a composition of place, seeing the spot. It will be here to see a vast plain of all the region round Jerusalem, where the supreme general Leader of all the good is Christ our Lord ; and to imagine another plain in the country of Babylon, where the chief [2] of the enemy is Lucifer. . . .'

There follows a detailed ' consideration ' of Lucifer's army and strategy ; [3] and then

> ' In the same way, on the other hand, we are to consider the sovereign and true Leader, Christ our Lord.
>
> ' The first point is to consider how Christ our Lord, in aspect fair and winning, takes His station in a great plain of the country near Jerusalem, on a lowly spot.
>
> ' The second point is to consider how the Lord of the whole world chooses out so many persons, apostles, disciples, etc., and sends them throughout the whole world diffusing His sacred doctrine through all states and conditions of persons.
>
> ' The third point is to consider the address which Christ our Lord makes to all His servants and friends, whom He sends on this expedition ; recommending to them that they desire to help all.' [4]

Service was not a new ideal for a religious order ; but it had rarely received prominence such as this. The same is true of the second great principle of the Jesuits—that of order, discipline or obedience. With a military leader and a military ideal, the principle of obedience was bound to follow. It is striking to see it

---

[1] It has been suggested (see *Monumenta Ignatiana*, series ii, p. 124) that S. Ignatius drew his conception from S. Bernard's parable ' de pugna spirituali alias de conflictu vitiorum et virtutum ' (Mabillon, i, coll. 2600-2605 ; *MPL.*, clxxxiii, coll. 761-765), or from a similar sermon by Abbot Werner (*MPL.*, clvii, coll. 1144-1146). It is not impossible, though the idea is in itself a commonplace ; but in any case there is a fire and urgency about S. Ignatius' version altogether lacking in the earlier writers. On the possibility of the Turkish menace (Belgrade was captured in 1521, Rhodes in 1522) suggesting a similar crisis in the spiritual world, H. Joly, *S. Ignatius of Loyola* (E. tr.), pp. 39-43.

[2] Longridge (*op. cit.*, p. 101) points out that Lucifer's title ' might be applied to the chief of a band of brigands,' whereas that of our Lord is always a mark of high honour and distinction.'

[3] *Infra*, p. 407.

[4] Morris, pp. 45, 46 ; Longridge, pp. 100-105. Immediately following is an Exercise (' The Three Classes ') in which, by a different ' history ' and ' composition.' the Christian response to Christ's appeal is contrasted with the non-Christian.

foreshadowed even in the vow which Ignatius, Xavier and their five friends—students still, though students already conscious of a preaching apostolate—took on the feast of the Assumption, 1534, in the chapel of S. Denys at Montmartre. 'We formed the resolution, writes le Favre,[1] 'of going, after our return from the Holy Land, to put ourselves under the obedience of the Roman Pontiff.' Just as method, from beginning to end, determines the progress of the 'Spiritual Exercises,' so discipline became the mainstay of the Company of Jesus.[2]

Militancy and discipline—these two characteristics of the new Society arose out of the temperament of Ignatius the soldier. A third—the name itself—recalls Ignatius the Christian. At Loyola he had turned the pages of Ludolph's ' Life of Christ ' ; the ' holy desires and longings ' which it aroused were ' confirmed on a certain night when he could not sleep ' by a vision of the Infant Jesus and His Mother, so that ' from that moment to this month of August, 1555, in which these things are written, he never more for a moment consented to any of the things of the flesh ; '—[3]

> ' and as he began to get up, and walk a little about the house, he decided to write [the life of Christ] in a book ; and he wrote the words of Christ in red ink, and the words of the Virgin in blue. The paper was smooth and ruled with lines, and all was very fairly written out ; for he had a very good handwriting.' [4]

The years that followed his recovery—at best a partial one—and witnessed his attempts to find his final vocation, are confused. He dedicated his secular armour in the chapel at Montserrat, and made his general confession there, but passed almost at once to Manresa,[5] where every day for ten months he read to himself the

---

[1] H. Joly, S. Ignatius of Loyola, p. 133.

[2] It is still more evident in the ' Declaration ' of ' those who wish to bear arms for God in our Society ' drawn up at Rome in 1538 :—' As for the right of commanding, it shall belong altogether to the General. Therefore let all the members of the Society know and remember, not only in the first days of their profession but all the days of their life, that this whole Society and all those who compose it are fighting for God under loyal obedience to our Holy Father the Pope. . . . And though we profess to believe firmly that all the faithful of Jesus Christ are subject to the Roman Pontiff as to their head and the vicar of Jesus Christ, nevertheless . . . we have thought that it would be very useful, in addition to that bond common to all the faithful, to bind ourselves also by a peculiar vow, so that, whatever the present Roman Pontiff and his successors may command us concerning the good of souls and the propagation of the faith, we may be obliged to carry out instantly, without evasion or excuse, in whatever country they may send us. . . . As for the inferior brethren . . . they shall be bound always to obey the General in everything which concerns the Institute, and in his person they shall seem to see Jesus Christ, as if He were really present, and shall revere Him as much as is fitting' (Joly, op. cit., pp. 166-168 ; cp. the 'Constitutions,' ib., p. 216. The 'perinde ac cadaver' article of the Constitutions is given by Pourrat, SC., iii, p. 71).

[3] Thibaut, op. cit., p. 41.

[4] Ib., p. 42. According to another account, the book was of not less than 300 quarto pages, and the miracles were written in gold lettering (Joly, op. cit., p. 18).

[5] Ib., p. 54.

'Passion of Christ,'[1] his life as a whole distinguished by works of charity, by self-mortification, by prayer and ill-health. At Montserrat, as we have noticed, he came under the influence, indirect if not direct, of Cisneros' 'Exercitatorium.'[2] At Manresa there fell into his hands the book which he never ceased to recommend, and which has left its mark on almost every page of the 'Spiritual Exercises'[3]—the 'Imitation of Christ' itself. 'The "Exercises,"' says M. Grandmaison, 'are just the "Imitation," provided with its gospel references, made fragrant by the perpetual presence of the Virgin Mary, enriched by the overwhelming spiritual experience of Ignatius; and then concentrated, organized, and martialled in battle array.'[4]

It is not surprising, therefore, that the 'Exercises' ring with the name of Jesus from beginning to end. Here, as elsewhere, Ignatius is a legatee; but he has used his inheritance to good purpose. He is in the true line of succession from S. Paul, S. Bernard and S. Francis. Whether we read the meditation of the 'Kingdom' or that of the 'Two Standards,' the different exercises of the second, third and fourth 'weeks,' or the fifty-one 'Mysteries of the Life of Christ our Lord,' we are brought back in the most vivid fashion to the earthly life of Jesus. No one has excelled Ignatius in emphasizing the truth that it is through meditation on the Incarnate Lord that the soul is brought nearest to the contemplation of the eternal Godhead.

One more 'principle' of the Ignatian spirituality, and that the most original. It cannot too often be insisted that Ignatius never intended the 'Spiritual Exercises' to be a method of meditation or a school of prayer. They had one purpose, and one purpose only— 'to conquer oneself and regulate one's life, and to avoid coming to a determination through any inordinate affection.'[5] Here *regulate* and *determination* are the all-important words. The 'Exercises' are designed to enable a man 'to find what he wants' ('id quod volo'—a constantly recurring phrase); and 'what he wants' is 'to seek and find the will of God concerning the ordering of life,'[6]

---

[1] Joly, p. 27.
[2] On the extent to which Cisneros' influence is traceable in the *Exercises*, see *Monumenta Ignatiana* (*Mon. Hist. Soc. Jesu*, Madrid, 1919), ii, pp. 94-121; L. de Grandmaison, *Les Exercises de St. Ignace*, in *Recherches de Science Réligieuse*, x (1920), pp. 391-408. At best it was indirect only, as there are no direct quotations in the later book from the earlier.
[3] A. Brou, *La Spiritualité de S. Ignace*, pp. 138-140.
[4] Grandmaison, *ut supra*, p. 396.
[5] From the title to the *Exercises*; Morris, p. 11; Longridge, p. 24.
[6] First Annotation; Morris, p. 1; Longridge, p. 4. The sentence continues, rather unexpectedly, ' for the salvation of one's soul '—thus suggesting a very egocentric aim for the entire *Exercises*. The same impression is conveyed by the opening sentence of the 'Foundation' (Morris, p. 12; Longridge, p. 26)—' Man was created to praise, reverence, and serve God our Lord, and by this means to save his soul.' No very certain conclusion can be drawn from the obvious fact (Longridge, p. 28) that ' my own salvation ' is put by S. Ignatius 'in the second place'; but the whole tone of the *Exercises* makes it clear that this ' end ' is undoubtedly ' secondary and

—to make a 'sound and good election.'[1] They are a handbook
for the Christian who wishes to know *how* he is to serve God.
Here Ignatius shows himself not merely a descendant, but also a
critic, of the mediæval chivalry; he adds the rôle of Cervantes
himself to those of Don Quixote and Sancho Panza. No one has
put this more clearly than M. Bremond :—

> ' Between secular and mystic chivalry there is a profound
> gulf. . . . The knight-errant goes straight ahead, seeking the
> encounter which will give him an opportunity to show his
> prowess, for the greater glory of his lady. But the lady is far
> away, and often silent; and the knight knows little of her
> caprices. So he chooses without hesitation the most spec-
> tacular of such adventures as present themselves. . . . In the
> service of a phantom princess, the cavalier is concerned with
> himself alone. He is his own master; the world is his oyster,
> which he with sword will open. But you may not behave like
> that in the service of God '—[2]

for in the service of God not every adventure that presents itself
may be God's will for the knight-errant; and some, despite their
dazzling attractions, may prove even to be acts of treason to the
King.

The unseen world was very near to Ignatius, and no one was
more on the alert against its illusions—demonic suggestions cloaking
themselves as divine—than he was. Two long sections of the
' Exercises ' are devoted to ' Rules for the Discernment of Spirits '
—rules ' for in some degree perceiving and knowing the various
motions excited in the soul; the good that they may be admitted,
the bad that they may be rejected.'[3] Even the most spiritual of
Christians is in danger of ' making various resolves and plans which
are not inspired immediately by God our Lord; and hence it is necessary that they be thoroughly well examined before they receive
entire credit and are carried out into effect.'[4]

' So the whole idea of chivalry,' M. Bremond comments,

> ' was turned upside down. The fixed idea of the knight-errant
> was, " What new enterprise can I attempt and carry through ? "

subordinate ' (*ib.*, and cp. *infra*, p. 438; and the full discussion Bremond,
HLSR., iii. pp. 29, 30). By mentioning it, Ignatius falls into line with
that sane Christian tradition, going back to our Lord Himself (*supra*, p. 145),
which deprecates fanatical disinterestedness, and will not allow the Christian
to flinch before the thought that service will bring its own reward (*infra*,
p. 554). See also Longridge, *op. cit.*, pp. 205-208.

[1] Morris, pp. 56, 57; Longridge, pp. 127, 129.

[2] *La Vie Spirituelle*, April, 1929 (Supplement), pp. 21-24. M. Bremond
is too good a Shakespearian to object to my rendering his ' il est maître de lui
comme de l'univers ' by a familiar tag. The same point is also well put by
M. de Grandmaison, *ut sup.*, pp. 400, 401.

[3] Morris, pp. 106-111 (first series of ' rules '); pp. 111-114 (second
series); Longridge, pp. 184-190, 190-193. Ignatius' reflections on this
subject began before ever he left Loyola (Thibaut, p. 40).

[4] Conclusion of the Rules, Morris, p. 114; Longridge, p. 193. Cp. also
for commentary, Longridge, pp. 262-267.

Opposed to it is Ignatius' own fixed idea, "What is the enterprise *to which God wills* that I should address myself?" ...
The decision rests with God. From the first lines of the
"Exercises" Ignatius formally abjures, and insists that we shall
abjure with him, the ideal of the knight-errant, the quest of
adventure for adventure's sake.'[1]

Herein lies the importance of Ignatius for the history of the
vision of God. Devoted though he was to the active life of service,
he saw that all its resolutions, as all its achievements, must be the
fruit of an inner communion with God. He is as reticent about this
communion as S. Benedict and S. Thomas,[2] and no doubt for the
same reasons. But its primacy is implied by the 'Foundation'
which stands at the head of the 'Exercises';[3] by the overwhelming
'contemplations,' particularly those of the second week, which are
to precede the 'election'; by the 'colloquy' with which every
exercise ends; and above all by the 'fourth addition'—which all
commentators recognize as the clue to the 'Exercises' as a whole,
as well as to each particular meditation—' in the point in which
I shall find what I desire, there I will rest.'[4] When God has been
found, no further effort of 'method' is needed; and when God has
been found, His purposes will be made clear.

It is a commonplace of history that Ignatius' own Society
scarcely knew for a time what to make of the 'Exercises.' Some
of its members left them altogether on one side; others demanded
more choir offices; others again adopted varied forms of private
devotion.[5] But as the missionary efforts of the Jesuits secured
conversions in all parts of Europe, the question ' How can I pray?'
was raised on every hand; and the missionaries adapted Ignatius'
book to the new need. The 'Directory' of 1591 recognizes its use

---

[1] Bremond, in *La Vie Spirituelle, ut sup.*, p. 24.

[2] *Supra*, pp. 271, 393; cp. also Bernard's unwillingness to dwell on the
subject, p. 352.

[3] ' Man was created to praise, reverence, and serve God our Lord, and
by this means to save his soul ' (on the last clause see *supra*, p. 401, n. 7).
The Foundation goes on to assert (a) that ' the other things on the face
of the earth were created for man's sake, and in order to aid him in the
prosecution of the end for which he was created '; (b) that ' man must make
use of them in so far as they help him to attain his end, and in the same way
he ought to withdraw himself from them in so far as they hinder him from
it '; (c) ' it is therefore necessary that we should make ourselves indifferent
to all created things . . . in such sort that we do not *for our part* wish for
health rather than sickness, etc. . . . . desiring and choosing only those which
most lead us to the end for which we were created ' (Morris, p. 12; Longridge,
p. 27).

[4] Morris, p. 29; Longridge, p. 71—' in puncto in quo invenero id quod
volo, ibi quiescam, sine anxietate progrediendi ulterius '; cp. Second Method
of Prayer, Morris, p. 80; Longridge, p. 163—' If the person considering the
Lord's Prayer find in one or two of the words good matter for thought, and
spiritual relish, and consolation, he should not be anxious to pass on, even
though the hour be spent on that one word which he has found '; cp. also
Longridge, p. 258; A. Brou, *La Spiritualité de St. Ignace*, pp. 49, 50.

[5] Brou. *op. cit.*, pp. 125, 126; Bremond, *HLSR.*, viii, pp. 190, 212.

for and by persons of every class and kind ; [1] representatives of the older Orders adopted it for themselves ; [2] S. Francis de Sales saw at once the genius which had set its seal on every page.[3] Of the differences which arose as to the interpretation of the book more will be said in the next chapter,[4] but differences of interpretation only served to foster its use. Books of devotion beyond number, handbooks for missioners, systems of retreats,[5] have during the last three centuries all of them adopted more or less of the central principle of the 'Exercises.' That principle is one which we have come to recognize as the norm of Christian prayer, understood in terms of worship—the fundamental way by which man approaches God, and so acquires guidance and strength for life. First, such orderly travail of the mind in reflection upon the great mysteries of God's work and being—and above all upon the incarnate life of Christ—as will stimulate, but not overburden, the aspiring soul ; then the quiet looking towards God which sometimes, but not always, finds its consummation in recognized communion with Him ; then as God gives them, new resolutions for the conduct or reformation of every-day life, to be put into effect when the Christian returns to the world once more.

V. S. FRANCIS DE SALES.

It was by an accident of history, or a miracle of providence, that the 'Exercises,' which Ignatius himself hesitated to make obligatory for his own Society,[6] which few of his closest friends could 'give' successfully,[7] and which his disciples found it difficult at first to fit into their missionary scheme, nevertheless came in a short time to dominate the private devotions even of the laity of Catholic Europe. Had there been no such book, the Jesuits would probably have gone about their work of teaching and evangelizing

---

[1] *Directory*, Introduction—' men of every kind and state and condition ' (Longridge, p. 275) ; c. 9—' married persons . . . public functionaries . . . persons of rank and position, heads of families, and the like ' (*ib.*, p. 292). So also the earlier Directory of John of Polanco (A.D. 1575), prologue— ' omnium statuum et utriusque sexus homines seculares immo et ecclesiastici' (*Mon. Ign.*, series ii, p. 796) ; cp. also Boll., *AS.*, Jul. vii, pp. 786-790, for further evidence.

[2] Brou, *op. cit.*, pp. 146-151.

[3] *Treatise on the Love of God*, xii, 8 (Mackey, p. 544) ; cp. Brou, p. 210.

[4] *Infra*, pp. 435-438.

[5] The new Roman canon law (c. 126) requires all secular priests to ' find leisure for the Spiritual Exercises in retreat at least every third year.'

[6] H. Bernard, *Essai historique sur les Exercices*, pp. 152-154 (I owe this reference and the next to M. Bremond's essay in *La Vie Spirituelle ;* I have not been able to consult the original) ; cp. also Watrigant, quoted *HLSR.*, iii, p. 31 n.

[7] So Bernard, *op. cit.*, p. 104. At the end of his life Ignatius could only mention four members of the Company who were able to ' give ' the Exercises well. It must be remembered that ' giving ' them meant taking entire control of the exercitant's spiritual condition over a long period, and so demanded very high personal gifts indeed.

just the same, without ever suspecting the need of it. But though
intended for altogether different purposes, the separate meditations
of the ' Exercises ' proved adaptable to the devotional life even of
secular persons. Thus Catholic ' piety ' took another step in the
direction of becoming non-monastic; just as it also became, as the
result of Ignatius' sense of discipline, more ordered than ever.

The sixteenth century witnessed sporadic attempts by zealous
Catholics of different countries—but especially of Spain—and of
different schools of thought, to convert this accidental process into
a matter of principle. Among them in particular were Azpilcueta
(Doctor Navarrus), the famous casuist and canonist, and the great
Dominican humanist, Louis of Granada.[1] They and others like-
minded were precursors and heralds of a far more influential personality; and their efforts prepared the way for the realization of
one of the dearest, and certainly the most original, of the aspirations
of S. Francis de Sales.[2]

He had been bishop of Geneva some six years or so, when a
budget of his private letters on spiritual matters came into the
hands of an expert, who recognized them as having more than
transitory importance. At his suggestion de Sales incorporated
them in a carefully composed treatise, whose first edition was published the following year (1609). ' The Introduction to the Devout
Life ' is explicitly, directly and enthusiastically addressed to
' persons living in the world.' It was a novelty whose ' hardihood ' we find it difficult to-day to understand; but ' no one
before him had dared to attempt it so resolutely; and almost
everyone thought the project incapable of realisation.'[3] Madame
de Charmoisy, the ' Philothea ' of the ' Devout Life,' was a lady
whose social and family duties made large claims upon her time.[4]
But neither in her case, nor in that of any other reader into whose
hands the book might fall, did its author admit that such claims
need, or ought to, be allowed to debar the soul from the fullest
privileges and responsibilities of the Christian life. In a preface
characteristic not merely in this respect, but also in its quaint
citation of supposed analogies of spiritual law in the natural world,
S. Francis writes :—

> ' Those who have treated of devotion [hitherto] have almost
> all had in mind the instruction of persons very much with-
> drawn from the society of the world ; or at all events they have

[1] Pourrat, SC., iii, pp. 145, 146.
[2] The details of S. Francis' life I take from Hamon's Vie de Saint
François de Sales, citing from the abridged edition of Gonthier and
Letourneau. M. Bremond's appreciation (HLSR., ii, pp. 537-584 ; vii,
pp. 37-111 ; with the chapters on S. Francis as a humanist in i, pp. 55-100
(E. tr.)) is unequalled. There is also an interesting study by Henri Bordeaux
(St. Francis de Sales : Theologian of Love), which has recently been translated. The Introduction to the Devout Life is quoted in the translation of
A. Ross (' Orchard Books ') ; the Love of God in that of H. B. Mackey.
[3] Pourrat, SC., iii, p. 429, cp. 419 ; Bremond, HLSR., i, p. 56 (E. tr.) ;
ii, p. 579.
[4] Hamon, pp. 330-331.

taught a kind of devotion which leads to this complete with-drawal. My intention is to instruct those who live in towns, in households, at the court, and who, by reason of their circumstances, are obliged to lead an ordinary life in outward show : who very often, under colour of an alleged impossibility, are not willing even to think of undertaking the devout life, because they are of opinion that, just as no beast dare taste of the herb called *palma Christi*, so no one ought to aspire to the palm of Christian piety, while living in the midst of the press of worldly occupations. And I show them that, as the mother pearls live in the sea without taking one drop of salt water, and as towards the Chelidonian Isles there are springs of perfectly fresh water in the midst of the sea, and as the flies called *pirastes* fly in the flames without burning their wings, so a vigorous and constant soul can live in the world without receiving any worldly taint, can find springs of sweet piety in the midst of the briny waters of the world, and can fly among the flames of earthly concupiscences without burning the wings of the holy desires of the devout life.' [1]

He recurs to the matter with even greater emphasis in an early page of the book itself :—

' In the creation God commanded the plants to bring forth their fruit, each after its kind ; even so he commands Christians, who are the living plants of His Church, to bring forth fruits of devotion, each one according to his kind and vocation. Devotion ought to be practised differently by the gentleman, by the artisan, by the servant, by the prince, by the widow, by the daughter, by the wife. . . . It is an error, nay rather, a heresy, to wish to banish the devout life from the army, from the workshop, from the courts of princes, from the households of married folk. . . . S. Joseph, Lydia, and S. Crispin were perfectly devout in their workshops; S. Anne, S. Monnica, Aquila, Priscilla, in their households ; Cornelius, S. Sebastian, S. Maurice, in the army ; Constantine, Helen, S. Louis, Blessed Amadeus, S. Edward, on their thrones.' [2]

There is a certain optimism in S. Francis' estimate of Constantine which may surprise the ecclesiastical historian. But the bishop of Geneva was an optimist ; that is to say, a humanist—though in M. Bremond's classic phrase, a ' *devout* humanist,' and the greatest of the devout humanists of his day. This fact alone calls attention to a difference of temperament from Ignatius of Loyola, so striking that it has sometimes obscured their fundamental kinship. It is difficult to imagine any of the ' Spiritual Exercises ' culminating in an instruction to cull a ' bouquet de dévotion ' ; [3] but all S. Francis'

[1] *Devout Life*, introduction (Ross, pp. xxiii, xxiv).

[2] *Ib.*, i, 3 (Ross, pp. 8, 9).

[3] *Ib.*, ii, 7 (Ross, p. 63)—I cannot help feeling that Ross's rendering (' spiritual nosegay,' ' nosegay of devotion ') over-emphasizes the sentimentalism which, at the best, betrays itself in the phrase. On this sentimentalism, which S. Francis shared with his age, see Bremond, *HLSR.*, i, pp. 62, 85.

meditations do. The difference may be crystallized in a single
illuminating parallel. S. Francis has his meditation corresponding
to that of the ' two standards.' But banners and bugles and calls
to arms have all disappeared. We are back in the two cities, or two
kingdoms, once again. Once more we stand on a ' bare plain ', [1]
though this time—a subtle difference—with our ' good angel ' by
our side. Once again we contemplate and contrast Lucifer's servants and the servants of Christ. But there is now no ' summoning
of innumerable devils,' to be ' dispersed throughout the whole world,
omitting not any provinces, places, or states of life, or any persons
in particular.' [2] Satan is the only devil in sight. Whereas, in
Ignatius' imagination, the army of Lucifer is terrible, to S. Francis
it is merely pitiable :—

> ' Observe the bearing of all the miserable courtiers of this
> abominable king : behold some raging with hatred, with envy
> and with anger; others who kill one another; others wasted,
> careworn and intently occupied in gaining riches ; others im-
> mersed in vanity, without any sort of pleasure that is not use-
> less and vain ; others coarse, engrossed and bemired in their
> brutish affections. Observe how they are all without repose,
> without order, and of sorry appearance ; observe how they
> despise one another, and how they do but make a pretence of
> loving one another. In fine, you will see a miserable kingdom,
> tyrannically ruled by this cursed king, which will move you
> to compassion.'

On the other side, no heroic band of knights—' apostles, disciples, etc.'—putting on the cross for death or victory ; but

> ' a great multitude of the devout who are all about [Jesus] with
> their angels. Contemplate the beauty of this kingdom of de-
> votion. . . . Look about over that multitude, and you will see
> that they all have a holy, sweet, and amiable appearance, that
> they listen to our Lord and would all plant Him in the midst of
> their hearts. They rejoice, but it is with a joy that is gracious,
> charitable and well-ordered ; they love one another, but it is
> with a love that is sacred and very pure. Those of this devout
> throng who are in affliction do not distress themselves very
> much, and are not at all disconcerted. In a word, see the
> eyes of the Saviour Who consoles them, and how all of them
> together aspire to them ! '

Without a pause S. Francis proceeds to the astounding sentence : ' *You have now renounced Satan with his sad and miserable
company, by the good affections which you have conceived.*' [3] There

---

[1] *Devout Life*, i, 18 (meditation 10—Ross, pp. 38-40).
[2] Ignatius, *Spiritual Exercises* (tr. Morris), pp. 45, 46.
[3] Cp. Bremond, *HLSR.*, ii, p. 548, on Francis' ' direction ' of Mdme. de
Chantal—' il a libéré tout ensemble et cette âme et la grace à laquelle celle-ci
n'osait pas ou ne savait pas s'abandonner ' ; and *ib.*, i, p. 78 (E. tr.).

is still an ' election ' to be made (S. Francis is about to use the word, as S. Ignatius does at the same point)—we have still to ' reach the King Jesus, and unite ourselves to His blessed and holy company of devout persons.' [1]   But half the work has been done already, and that by the spontaneous ' affections ' of the heart.   One single steady gaze at the two kingdoms—the kingdom of misery and the kingdom of joy—has sufficed for us to renounce the devil and all his works. That is Christian optimism at its highest.   The same trustfulness, good humour, and faith in human nature appear in all S. Francis' life and writings, and radiate calmness and peace round him.   His whimsical treatment of the insatiable borrower who, having nego-tiated a loan of twelve crowns from him one year, and failed to repay it, returned the next for another ten, is no evidence to the contrary.   On the second application, the bishop offered his im-portunate visitor the note-of-hand received from him on the first, saying, ' Why, you ask me for ten crowns only !   Here are twelve good ones ;   and *this* time it is a gift and not a loan.' [2]   The quip pointed the rebuke which S. Francis thought necessary, but at the same time robbed it of all bitterness.   More explicit is the testimony of Mdme. de Chantal's servants :   ' The mistress's former director,' they said, ' only told her to pray three times a day, and it was a nuisance to us all ;   the good bishop makes her pray all the day long, and no one is put to any inconvenience whatever.' [3]

The loving simplicity of S. Francis de Sales, his single-minded belief in the beauty of goodness and the ineradicable excellence of the human heart, need no further emphasis.   He is a true descendant of his namesake of Assisi.   But in both the joyful love of nature and humanity is mingled with a deep other-worldliness.   In one respect S. Francis de Sales' meditation on the two kingdoms strikes a deeper note than any to be heard in Ignatius' ' Two Stan-dards.'   To the latter, Christ is a King arming Himself and His followers for battle ;   the former sees in the centre of the kingdom of light ' *Jesus Christ crucified*, praying with heart-felt love for those poor subjects of the devil, that they may escape from his tyranny: and calling them to Himself.'   De Sales' love for humanity is no mere natural affection and sympathy, any more than that of S. Francis of Assisi.   It finds its heart and soul in the divine love for a lost universe which only the crucifixion could reveal. [4]

The ' Introduction to the Devout Life,' in its final form, com-prises five parts.   In the first, as in the first week of the ' Spiritual Exercises,' the purification of the soul from faults is set before the reader.   The second expounds S. Francis' ' short method for medi-tation.'   The third and fourth contain ' sundry counsels concerning the exercise of virtues and the combating of temptations ' ;   the fifth, dealing mainly with self-examination, proposes ' exercises and

---

[1] Ross, p. 39.   [2] Hamon, p. 417.   [3] Pourrat, *SC.*, iii, p. 444.
[4] This aspect of seventeenth-century religion in France was developed to its highest pitch by Cardinal de Bérulle, on whom see Bremond, *HLSR.*, iii, pp. 3-154.

counsels for renewing the soul and confirming her in devotion.'
As with Ignatius, there is no extended treatment of contemplation
—the 'simple loving look'[1]—as the crowning attitude towards
which the practice of meditation leads. But we are not obliged
here, as we were in the case of Ignatius, to infer from passing though
decisive hints the primacy of the vision of God in the writer's
mind. There are two reasons for this. Francis is not, as Ignatius
was, a man of a single book. 'Philothea' is only a child in respect
of the life of the soul; it is to the nuns of the Visitation that
S. Francis says what he has to say about the heights of spiritual
experience. As Fénelon knew to his unfailing profit, and Bossuet
to his severe discomfiture, the 'Treatise on the Love of God' initiates
its readers into all that they or anyone can ask to know about
union with God, contemplation of the divine being, and the utter
selflessness of pure love which is their distinguishing characteristic.[2]
But though S. Francis de Sales reserves all this for treatment in
his later book[3]—and perhaps when he wrote the 'Introduction'
he was not sure enough of his own spiritual maturity to dare to go
further[4]—even the treatise to Philothea is not reticent as to his
deepest thoughts. 'Above all I recommend to you,' he says,

> 'prayer of the mind and heart, and especially that which
> has for its subject the life and passion of our Lord. For by
> beholding Him often in meditation your whole soul will be
> filled with Him; you will learn His disposition, and you will
> form your actions after the model of His. He is the Light of
> the world, and therefore it is in Him, by Him, and for Him that
> we must be enlightened and illuminated. . . . We must stop
> there, Philothea; and, believe me, we cannot go to God the
> Father but by this door.'[5]

[1] Cp. *Love of God*, vi, 6 (Mackey, pp. 247-250).

[2] *Ib.*, iii, 11-14; vi, 3-10; vii; ix.

[3] S. Francis insists as much in the *Love of God* as in the *Devout Life* that
the full life of contemplation is open to the layman. Thus, x, 3 (Mackey,
p. 414)—'A man may be wholly God's, wholly his father's, wholly his mother's,
wholly his prince's, wholly his commonwealth's, his children's, his friends';
so that being all to each, he is yet all to all'; cp. viii, 9; xii, 4, 5 (Mackey,
346, 538, 540).

[4] Bremond, ii, pp. 551, 577.

[5] *Devout Life*, ii, 1 (Ross, p. 53); cp. also the following: 'In fine, as
men who are in love with a human and natural love have their thoughts
nearly always turned to their beloved one, their heart full of affection for her,
their mouth filled with her praises, and as in her absence they lose no opportunity of showing their love by letters, and meet with no tree upon which
they write not the name of the beloved one; so those who love God cannot
cease to think of Him, long for Him, aspire to Him, and speak of Him: and
they would be willing, were it possible, to engrave the sacred and holy name
of Jesus on the breasts of all persons in the world' (*ib.*, ii, 13—Ross, p. 75).
'You must often repeat with your heart and lips these burning words of
S. Paul, of S. Augustine, of S. Catherine of Genoa and others: "No, I am
no longer my own. Whether I live or die, I belong to my Saviour: I have
no longer any dominion over myself or mine. My *self* is Jesus: my *mine*
is to be His." O world, thou art always thyself, and I have always been
myself, but henceforth I will be myself no longer. No—we will be ourselves

What was the form of meditation which the Jesuits, with the 'Spiritual Exercises' in their hands, and S. Francis de Sales with his 'Introduction,' now commended to the laity as the gate to the vision of God ? S. Ignatius' scheme, as is only natural, is in some degree the more formal of the two. Each meditation (or, as he calls it, 'contemplation') begins with a preparatory prayer, followed by two 'preludes.' The first prelude is a 'composition of place '— that is to say, an imaginative presentation of 'some corporeal place, such as the Temple or the Mountain, where Jesus Christ or our Lady is found, according to what I desire to contemplate.' [1] The second prelude is ' to ask of God our Lord that which I wish and desire '; and this ' petition ought to be according to the subject-matter of the contemplation.' [2] There follows the contemplation proper—the application of the ' three powers of the soul,' memory, understanding, and will,[3] to the subject matter, which is considered in a series of ' points,' usually three in number, but rising sometimes (as in the ' Two Standards ') to six. The exercise concludes with one or more ' colloquies ' between the soul and God (notice here the influence of the ' Imitatio Christi '), or even between the soul and the several persons of the Trinity, or the Virgin Mary ; and the Lord's prayer, perhaps with additional devotions.

The Salesian method [4] is simpler, though not in essentials different. The preparation consists first ' of a lively and attentive apprehension of the omnipresence of God,' and then of an ' invocation.' The meditation is divided into the ' setting forth of the mystery '—Ignatius' ' composition of place,' as S. Francis definitely says ; the ' considerations '—Ignatius' ' points ' ; and the ' affections and resolutions,' in which last definiteness is specially to be aimed at. Finally come thanksgiving for God's goodness and mercy discovered during the meditation ; an offering of the resolution to God ; and S. Francis' own peculiar contribution—the ' bouquet of devotion.' Of this he writes :—

> ' Those who have been walking in a beautiful garden do not leave it willingly without taking away with them four or five flowers, in order to inhale their perfume and carry them about during the day. Even so when we have considered some mystery in meditation, we should choose one or two or three points in which we have found most relish, and which are specially proper to our advancement, in order to remember them throughout the day, and to inhale their perfume spiritually.' [5]

no longer : for we shall have our hearts changed, and the world which has deceived us so often will be deceived in us. For only perceiving our change but little by little, it will think that we are always Esaus ; whereas we shall find ourselves to be Jacobs ' (v, 16 ; Ross, p. 305).

[1] *Spiritual Exercises*, first week, first meditation (Morris, p. 20).

[2] *Ib.*, p. 21. Sometimes there is another prelude before the two first-mentioned—the ' history,' or assembling of the characters who will appear in the ' composition of place.'

[3] *Ib.*, p. 21.   [4] *Devout Life*, ii, 2-8 (Ross, pp. 56-66).

[5] *Ib.*, ii, 7 (Ross, pp. 63, 64).

No one who has glanced through any of the countless manuals of meditation, which for three centuries have been composed on these models, can fail to recognize the type. Its drawbacks are obvious. It involves either a constant dependence upon such manuals themselves, or a ' remote preparation ' sufficiently detailed and extensive to provide the Christian with a scheme of meditation ready for his use, complete with invocation, considerations, colloquies and resolutions. Again, whilst the alert and quick-witted may be tempted by such a scheme to dally in imaginative reflections when they might be aspiring to God, the dull or uneducated recoil from the apparently absurd proposal that they should embark upon so formidable an undertaking.[1] The difficulty is inherent in every attempt to provide ' forms ' of worship, whether public or private, for general use ; and few of the perennial problems which the Church has had to face are more crucial than this. But history and experience alike show that it is not insoluble. From the most ornate and complex liturgy, to the simple daily ' reading a chapter ' in private—we have all known men and women, boys and girls, devoid of any but the slightest advantages of nature and environment, who have been attracted, captured, and transformed by the power of God operating through such a schema-tization of worship. Some element of formalism of course there must be ; but both S. Francis and S. Ignatius wisely insisted that the scheme, though needful, was always the secondary matter. It must be adapted for every different individual ; it might be deserted the moment the soul found ' that which it sought '—' in puncto in quo invenero id quod volo, ibi quiescam.'[2] They would

---

[1] This criticism was voiced in the most trenchant manner by S. Francis' own friend, Camus, Bishop of Belley, in words of whose relevance even to the simple Salesian method he must at least have had some suspicion : ' All this discursiveness, all these " acts " of understanding, will, and memory ; these " preludes," " points," " affections," " resolutions," " compositions of place "—this massive and embarrassing machinery of prayer with which your books on meditation are packed ! . . . Tell a childlike ordinary soul that God became man for our sakes ; he will believe it quite simply, and humbly and gently will accept it as a mystery of grace. Now try to induce him to " make a meditation " on it by these longwinded methods of yours. It is Christmas, for example. Tell your aspirant to build up in his imagina-tion the stable at Bethlehem, complete with ox and ass, till he has a kind of mental picture of it. Next he must invoke the divine grace ; then you will force him to review three " heads of meditation," and show him how to draw out " reasonings " and " discourses," considering, weighing, analysing everything—causes, effects, occasion, place, persons, and the whole series of events, words and actions—for without this spiritual rhetoric, apparently, the art of prayer must fail of its full effect. . . . Thereupon, teach him to " elicit affections " of every kind from this fine exercise of reason ; and on the affections to build " resolutions " of all the colours of the chameleon. And you cannot stop there. He must have forms of " thanksgiving," " oblation," " petition," " colloquy," " union," " elevations " and such like ; with " remote," " near," and " immediate " preparation. . . . Cannot you see that all this will never give him the wings of the dove ? You are simply tying a weight around his neck to prevent him from ever rising at all ' (Bremond, HLSR., vii, pp. 155, 156).

[2] Supra, p. 403 ; and for S. Francis, cp. Devout Life, ii, 8 (Ross, p. 65) It may happen to you sometimes that immediately after the preparation

have been the last to permit handbooks of worship to take the place
of worship itself, or schemes of meditation to alienate the soul from
communion with its Lord.

With S. Ignatius and S. Francis de Sales, and those of every
creed and communion who have followed their pioneer examples,
Christian thought about prayer reaches its high-water mark.[1]
Between the beginning of the twelfth and the end of the sixteenth
centuries Christianity made two startling advances. Piety ceased to
be the prerogative of the cloister: the barriers set up by the invalid
theory of the double standard were broken down for ever. Secular
persons of every kind were invited and exhorted to join the monk
in the life of prayer, not by abandoning their ordinary occupations,
but by using prayer to infuse those occupations with the spirit
of the divine love and self-sacrifice. That was the first advance.
The second, though less final—for it involved no mere abandonment of theoretical error, but the initiation of a new mode of
spiritual warfare—was the discovery that worship need be none the
worse, and may be all the better for being orderly, and the suggestion of methods by which due orderliness could be achieved.
Formalism had at one time proved an obstacle, serious if not fatal,
to the pursuit of the vision of God ; in the matter of prayer, as at
an earlier stage in the matter of penance, it was now converted into
an ally. A dangerous ally it will always be, but an ally with which
no one can dispense ; for as long as men remain disciples they
cannot forgo submission to discipline. By its means all that unbalanced mysticism which sought for communion with God in
ecstasy, visions, and mere emotionalism, was excluded from the
Christian scheme. The new methods of prayer concentrated
devotion upon the life of our Lord, completing by their methodical
approach the work that S. Bernard began. They had the psychological effect—as Loyola and de Sales intended they should—
of stimulating countless souls to the unselfish and unremitting
service of God and man. In their full context of a Christian passion
for orderliness, instinct with the highest zeal—a zeal maintained
at intensity by sane self-discipline—the 'Spiritual Exercises,' the

you will find your affection stirred up towards God ; then, Philothea, you
must give it the reins, without trying to follow the method which I have
given you.'

[1] A friendly critic of the first edition pointed out that the present paragraph was open to misinterpretation, as suggesting that 'methodical, discursive
meditation' was the 'high-water mark of Christian thought about prayer.'
I had hoped it would be sufficiently clear from pp. 436-441 below, and other
passages, that this is a view with which I have no sympathy ; and from
pages 403 and 409 that I am very far from attributing it either to Loyola
or to de Sales. I agree entirely with my critic that to them 'meditation is
but the first degree of prayer, and should commonly issue in contemplation,'
and that no other view is tolerable. In the present paragraph I merely draw
attention to the fact that they were the first, among those who set the vision
of God as the end of life, to help men to achieve an orderly and disciplined
approach towards the vision (cp. *supra*, p. 375) ;—a fact which, *taken in con-
nection with the admitted primacy which they accord to contemplation*, seems to
justify the application of the title 'high-water mark' to their teaching.

' Introduction to the Devout Life.' the ' Treatise on the Love of
God,' and the devotional literature which they have inspired, have
rivalled the Thomist analysis of ethics as contributions of inestimable value to Christianity.

With them, it may be said, the spirit of order won its final
victory over the spirit of confusion. For the writers we have been
considering there was no danger that the defeat of unregulated
individualism would mean any loss either of the rigorist element
in Christianity, or of the spirit of high initiative which alone is
strong enough to resist the sterilizing influences of a code, however
perfect it may be. These defects manifested themselves once more,
no doubt ; they will continue to manifest themselves in every
generation so long as the Church remains militant here in earth.
But when all is said and done, the Catholicism of the sixteenth
century regained one at least of the elements in true Christianity
which had long been lost—the element to which S. Paul alluded
when he spoke of God as the author not of confusion but of peace,
and demanded that all things should be done decently and in order.
And if we enquire for the source of this new acquisition in the
Church, and the reason why men came to accept it not merely on
the commendation of authority but on the witness of conscience
as well, we must look back beyond S. Francis de Sales and
S. Ignatius to the solid basis of sober moral education laid by the
greatest of the Schoolmen.

LECTURE VIII.

LAW AND PROMISE.

Gal. iv. 28—'We brethren, as Isaac was, are the children of promise.

I. THE REVERSAL OF TRADITION.

(a) Protestantism.

CHRISTIANITY is in essence not a law but a promise—the promise of that which, in deference to an unbroken tradition, we have called the vision of God. This truth—fully emphasized by a long line of great Catholic theologians, though obscured for a time in the formalism of the later middle ages—was revived with passionate intensity by the Protestant reformers. But their formulation of the doctrine was characterized by significantly novel traits. To them the test of the Christian was not that he was so living as to secure the promise, but that he had experienced in himself the certain conviction that the promise was indefectibly his. This conviction—the 'assurance' of a status that cannot be lost, conferred upon man with no consequent conditions, and on the sole antecedent condition of faith—is the palladium of orthodox Protestantism. The enunciation of the doctrine, in one at least of its forms, was without doubt the primary work of Luther.[1] It sprang directly from his own personal experience—the conviction of justification by faith which supervened upon his excruciating self-torture in quest of righteousness after the contemporary monastic pattern. Whatever it is which God has in store for man has been given him—almost, if not quite, in its fullest and final degree—here and now; and it has been given him as a possession which cannot be lost.[2]

---

[1] Even Wycliffe failed to anticipate it. Although ' he had just as clear a hold on the principle of justification by faith as any of the later reformers,' he ' emphasizes the fact that we can never be sure of salvation in this life because we may not persevere ' (T. C. Hall, *History of Ethics within Organized Christianity*, p. 382).

[2] Luther, *On Christian Liberty* (H. Wace and C. A. Bucheim, *Luther's Primary Works*, 1883), pp. 109, 112 (with the expansion of the metaphor of the soul as the bride of Christ)—' Since these promises of God are words of holiness, truth, righteousness, liberty and peace, and are full of universal goodness, the soul which cleaves to them with a firm faith is so united to them, nay, thoroughly absorbed by them, that it not only partakes in but is penetrated and saturated by all their virtue. . . . Thus the believing soul, by the pledge of its faith in Christ, becomes free from all sin, fearless

The test of a Christian life, therefore, is on this view the test of subjective assurance. ' He is truly Christian who is solidly persuaded that God is gracious to him ' ; [1] no other is a Christian at all. By statements such as these, which constituted the theological battle-cries of the reformers, Protestantism is committed in its own special fashion to that doctrine of the complete severance of the Christian from the world by grace which characterized one side (but one side only) of Catholic thought ;—the determinism which marks out one aspect of the teaching of S. Paul and S. Augustine, and which animated throughout the illuminism of the gnostics, the sectarian spirit of Marcion and Montanus, and the strict claustration of the most austere monastic congregations. Either a man is ' assured ' or he is not. If he is, he has been transferred from the domain of the devil to the kingdom of God. If he is not, he remains under the divine condemnation. There is no middle way, no bridge, no neutral ground between the two.

Few of us would recognize in this picture the traits of modern Protestantism. Indeed, they are not there to be recognized. But the modern situation is none the less a natural consequence of the reformers' innovation, and cannot be understood apart from its historical causes. Three factors in particular seem to have

---

of death, safe from hell, and endowed with the eternal righteousness, life and salvation of its husband Christ.' It is in this point especially that Luther made his great advance upon Augustinism. As Reuter has shown (*Augustinische Studien*, pp. 57-61, 66-74), Augustine left the Christian uncertain to the last whether he was indeed one of the elect. For all that he could tell he might be unpredestinate to eternal life, and in that case good works, adherence to the Church, perseverance in receiving the sacraments, and even martyrdom itself would be of no avail to secure him salvation. Aquinas had attempted to make good the defect by supplying *tests* of the presence of saving grace :—it may be inferred conjecturally in the man who is conscious of delighting in God, of despising worldly things, and of freedom from mortal sin, but it cannot be directly perceived or demonstrated (*ST.*, i, 2, q. 112, a. 5). Luther, on the other hand, assumed an infallibility impossible in this life ; but even he had qualms on the point—cp. *Table Talk* (quoted J. A. Moehler, *Doctrinal Differences*, p. 150)—' I do not believe S. Paul was able to have so strong a faith on this matter as he asserts. In truth I cannot, alas I believe so firmly as I preach, talk and write, and as other people think I believe.' So also Calvin, *Inst.*, III, 2. 17—' We teach that faith is certain and sure ; but we do not imagine thereby a certainty free from all doubt and care ; the Christian has always to struggle with want of faith '—' perpetuum esse fidelibus certamen cum suâ ipsorum diffidentiâ.'

[1] Cp. Luther, *Shorter Commentary on Galatians* (ed. Weimar, ii, p. 458) —' fabulæ ergo sunt opinatorum scholasticorum hominem esse incertum, in statu salutis sit necne. cave tu, ne aliquando sis incertus'; Calvin, *Inst.*, III, 2. 16—' in summâ, vere fidelis non est, nisi qui solidâ persuasione Deum sibi propitium benevolumque patrem esse persuasus, de ejus benignitate omnia sibi pollicetur ; nisi qui divinæ erga se benevolentiæ promissionibus fretus, indubitatam salutis expectationem præsumit '; *Augsburg Confession*, I, iv—' item docent quod homines . . . justificantur propter Christum per fidem cum credunt se in gratiam recipi et peccata remitti propter Christum.' Loofs (*Leitfaden*, pp. 707, 708) shows, mainly from Denifle, that ' assurance ' was not originally the first principle of Luther's reformed theology.

determined the course of evolution to which the Christianity of the reformed Churches has been subjected.

(1) First of all, the doctrine of the personal assurance of the Christian—of his standing in an inalienable, immediate relationship with God—implies the complete freedom of the individual. As far as the leaders of the reform themselves were concerned, this implication was fully realized from the outset ; though they were not prepared to extend it to their followers, still less to their opponents. Luther, Calvin, Zwingli, Knox all arrogated to themselves a complete independence of authority, and aspired to complete immunity from criticism. They exercised the prophetic office in all its fullness. By precept and example they stimulated others to do the same ; and many of these others, though equally assured of their own prophetic gifts, were by no means their equals in moral intensity. Harnack, who rightly regards this 'subjectivism, individuality, the wish to be oneself, freedom, activity' as a condition rather than a product of the Reformation, has done full justice to its character as a 'two-edged' weapon. 'The age of Savonarola was the age of Machiavelli,' he writes; and again, 'In religion this principle comprehended all forms of individual religiousness, from the right of unbridled imagination and of prophetism, to the right of liberty belonging to the conscience that is bound by the gospel.' [1] The Utopian dreams of academic humanists, no less than the irresponsible vaticinations of innumerable astrologers, [2] all went to swell the resultant torrent of indiscipline.

Thus there came into existence, under cover of the reformed religion, [3] champions of those same moral aberrations as had found earlier expression in gnosticism and the heresies of the middle ages. [4] Luther's own admissions testify to the moral decline which the new liberty of the Christian fostered among his own soi-disant followers, and against which both Anabaptists and Bohemians felt themselves bound to protest. [5] Some communities at least became antinomian

---

[1] *Hist. of Dogma*, vii, p. 18.

[2] T. M. Lindsay, *History of the Reformation*, i, pp. 328, 329, with references there.

[3] Despite the disciplinary tendency about to be noticed (*infra*, p. 421), many of Luther's utterances gave a strong impetus to individualism. Thus, 'We are all priests . . . how then should we not have the power of discerning and judging what is right or wrong in matters of faith ? ' (*To the German Nobility*, Wace and Bucheim, p. 27); 'By "Reformation" I do not mean the *reform* of this human teaching and spiritual authority ; I mean its complete and absolute abrogation, extirpation, and destruction ' (*Reply to Emser*, ed. Weimar, vii, p. 658); 'The gospel and the Church know nothing of jurisdictions, which are tyrannical inventions of men' (*ad librum Ambros. Catharini* (ed. Weimar, vii, p. 721)); 'There can be no supremacy among Christians ; each is subject to the other' (*Of Worldly Supremacy* (ed. Weimar, xi, p. 270)), *et pass.*

[4] For examples see Lindsay, *op. cit.*, ii, pp. 441, 463-468.

[5] The Anabaptists, Moehler, *op. cit.*, p. 373 ; the Bohemian Brothers, *ib.*, p. 428. For Luther's own dismay at the antinomian results of the Reformation, see the passages cited (in part from Döllinger), Denifle, *Luther u.*

almost on principle.[1] This would in any case have been a not unnatural result of a doctrine which endowed the individual conscience with absolutely unqualified autonomy. It was all the more so when that conscience—and that conscience alone—was held to be orthodox, which testified to the valuelessness of law and works as compared with the faith which justifies.[2] It would be absurd to accuse Luther himself of deliberately encouraging, or conniving at, antinomianism in others. 'The highest art, the noblest life, the holiest conduct,' he himself said, ' is love for God and one's neighbour.' [3] He would have the Christian be a ' Christ ' to his fellow-men.[4] But many of Luther's sayings were more capable of the antinomian interpretation than any other. The world does not forget the ' Pecca fortiter.' [5] Once more, to quote Harnack, the greatest modern disciple of the Wittenberg reformer : ' The Lutheran Church had to pay dearly for turning away from legal righteousness. . . By its resolute wish to go back to religion and to religion alone, it neglected far too much the moral

---

Luthertum, i, pp. 19-24, 763-764. Cp. also Luther's letter to Spalatinus, Feb., 1529 (W. M. L. de Wette, *Luthers Briefe, etc.*, iii, p. 424): ' The state of the Church is pitiful ; the peasants learn nothing, know nothing, pray not at all, do nothing—except abuse their liberty. They make neither their confessions nor communions, and behave as if they were completely emancipated from religion.'

[1] *PRE.*, i, pp. 585-592 (*s.v.* ' Antinomistische Streitigkeiten ').

[2] Cp. the strange doctrine of Amsdorf (Moehler, *Symbolism*, p. 166) :— ' Faith does not justify, nay is not faith at all, if accompanied by any works, even the slightest ' ; and the gentle reproof of the Formula of Concord (*Solid. Declar.*, iv, 25)—' It does not follow that we may make the unqualified and naked assertion that good works are pernicious to the salvation of believers.' But in the *Epitome* of the Formula (P. Schaff, *Creeds of Evangelical Protestant Churches*, p. 125) Amsdorf's sentiment is ' repudiated and condemned.'

[3] *Third Sermon for Eighteenth Sunday after Trinity* (*Works*, ed. Erlang., v, p. 163).

[4] *Christian Liberty* (Wace and Bucheim), p. 127—' I will therefore give myself as a sort of Christ to my neighbour, as Christ has given Himself to me ; and will do nothing in this life except what I see will be needful, advantageous and wholesome for my neighbour ' ; *ib.*, p. 123—' We do not then reject good works ; nay, we embrace and teach them in the highest degree.'

[5] *Letter to Melancthon*, from Wartburg, 1st Aug., 1521 (W. M. L. de Wette, *op. cit.*, ii, p. 37)—' esto peccator et pecca fortiter, sed fortius fide et gaude in Christo. . . sufficit quod agnovimus, per divitias gloriæ Dei, Agnum qui tollit peccata mundi ; ab hoc non avellet nos peccatum, etiamsi millies millies uno die fornicemur aut occidamus.' Cp. *Babylonish Captivity* (Wace and Bucheim), p. 185—' We see then how rich a Christian or baptized man is ; since even if he would he cannot lose his salvation by any sin, however great, unless he refuses to believe ; for no sins whatever can condemn him, but unbelief alone.' In a very strange passage Dr. McGiffert contrasts Luther favourably with S. Paul in this matter ; *Protestant Thought before Kant*, p. 25 : ' Paul, too, thought of salvation as a present possession and of the Christian as already saved, but the ground of his salvation was moral transformation, not divine forgiveness . . . Luther broke with the Catholic theory, not by going back to Paul and asserting a present and instantaneous sanctification, but by repudiating altogether the Pauline and Catholic notion of salvation, and making it wholly a matter of divine forgiveness rather than of human character.' Professor Mackinnon (*Luther and the Reformation*, pp. iv, 259) hesitates to accept Dr. McGiffert's contention.

problem—" Be ye holy, even as I am holy." '[1] So when we find
Luther saying, ' There is no one who would not prefer to be without
perfect righteousness than without the grace of God ' ;[2] or ' To a
Christian man his faith suffices for everything; he has no need of
works for justification,' [3] we cannot acquit him of stimulating a
tendency which he himself was one of the first to deplore.

When his friend and fellow-worker, Johannes Agricola (1492-
1566), declared that the decalogue had been wholly abrogated,
Luther promptly denounced him as ' antinomian '—the first use
of the word in history.[4] But Agricola did himself less than justice
in receding from a position which he claimed as a legitimate development of Lutheran doctrine. He did indeed say that works were
wholly indifferent; that man is saved by faith alone without
reference to moral character. He could cry to his hearers, ' Art
thou steeped in sin, an adulterer or a thief? If thou believest
thou art in salvation. All who follow Moses ' (i.e. who obey the
decalogue) ' must go to the devil! To the gallows with Moses !'
But Luther himself said with equal vehemence, ' We do not wish
to see or hear Moses. Moses was given to the Jews, not to Gentiles
and Christians. We have our gospel and New Testament. They
wish to make Jews of us through Moses ; but they shall not.' [5]
Melancthon more curtly proclaimed : ' It must be admitted that the
decalogue is abrogated ' ;[6] and both of them, with Bucer, justified

---

[1] Harnack, *Hist. of Dogma*, vii, p. 167.

[2] Luther, *adv. Latomum* (*Works*, ed. Weimar, viii, p. 106).

[3] *On Christian Liberty* (Wace and Bucheim), p. 110 ; cp. *ib.*, p. 116 : ' The
Christian man is free from all things, so that he needs no works in order to
be justified and saved, but receives these gifts in abundance from faith alone.'
Cp. also Luther's twenty-fifth ' conclusion ' in the *Heidelberg Disputation*,
A.D. 1518 (ed. Weimar, i, pp. 354, 364)—' He is not justified who does many
works, but he who without any work has much faith in Christ.'

[4] *ERE.*, i, pp. 582-584 (*s.v.* ' Antinomianism ') ; *PRE.*, i, pp. 249-253
(*s.v.* ' Agricola ') ; 585-592 (' Antinomistische Streitigkeiten ') ; Loofs, *Leitfaden*, pp. 858-861 ; J. Mackinnon, *Luther and the Reformation*, iv, pp. 161-
179.

[5] So *ERE.*, *ut sup.*, but I cannot identify the reference. But Luther's
attitude to ' Moses ' is sufficiently clear. Denifle has collected the following :
' If Christ were to come, and say to thee as Moses does, " What hast thou
done ? " thou shouldst smite Him dead ' ; ' I will help to stone Moses ;'
' Moses is a hangman, a hideous executioner, who racks and tortures us
with his horrible warnings ' ; ' Moses is like the devil to behold ; his words
might well make the heart quail ; his lips are steeped in hemlock and gall,
yea, in the fires of hell themselves. So away with Moses for ever ! ' (*Luther
u. Luthertum*, i, pp. 651, 652 ; cp. *ib.*, pp. 657, 666 ; Loofs, *Leitfaden*, pp. 744,
771, 772).

[6] So *ERE.*, *ut sup.*, from the first edition of the *Loci*. I have been
unable to identify this reference, and it is noteworthy that Loofs (*op. cit.*,
pp. 786, 787) can only find one antinomian sentence even in this first edition.
Melancthon was always more positive about the obligation of the moral
precepts of the decalogue than Luther, and in later editions of the *Loci*
(Loofs, pp. 850-853), his insistence upon it was intensified. But even in
the 1545 edition (*Opera*, Wittenberg, 1580, foll. 177b, 180a) he calls the suggestion that the Law can be obeyed a ' sarcasm ' and ' irony ' of the devil ;
and in *this* passage (though contrast fol. 187b) the ' tertius usus legis ' (see
Loofs, pp. 850, 861) is merely to remind the Christian of the ' doctrina de
reparatione in promissionibus.'

the bigamy of Philip of Hesse on the ground that ' we are now living under the gospel, which ' (unlike the original ordinance of God) ' has not explicitly prohibited bigamy.' [1] Agricola's antinomianism did no more than carry these principles to their logical conclusion.

The same phenomenon of revolt against the moral law occurs—and that for the same reason—in the history of Methodism two centuries later. Fletcher of Madeley, the saintly friend and disciple of the Wesleys, in his ' Checks to Antinomianism,' says outspokenly :—

> ' Antinomian principles have spread like wildfire among our societies. . . . I have seen them, who pass for believers, follow the strain of corrupt nature ; and when they should have exclaimed against Antinomianism, I have heard them cry out against the *legality* of their wicked hearts ; which, they said, still suggested that they were to *do* something for their salvation. How few of our celebrated pulpits where more has not been said *for sin* than *against* it.' [2]

With no more than a touch of exaggeration—so slight that it was unsafe for his critics to draw attention to it—he paraphrased his eccentric opponent, Richard Hill, as follows :—

> ' Even adultery and murder do not hurt the pleasant children, but rather work for their good.' ' God sees no sin in believers, whatever sins they may commit. . . . Though I should outsin Manasses, I should not be less a pleasant child, because God always views me in Christ. Hence in the midst of adulteries, murders and incests, He can address me with, " Thou art all fair, my love, my undefiled, there is not a spot in thee." Although I highly blame those who say " Let us sin that grace may abound," yet adultery, incest and murder shall, upon the whole, make me holier on earth and merrier in heaven.' [3]

---

[1] The document, T. M. Lindsay, *History of the Reformation*, i, p. 381 ; cp. J. Mackinnon, *Luther and the Reformation*, iv, pp. 265 ff.

[2] J. W. Fletcher, *Second Check against Antinomianism*, 3rd letter (*Works*, Shebbear, Devon, i, p. 63). On the same page Fletcher quotes from Tobias Crisp, a famous antinomian, the following : ' Every elect vessel, from the first instant of his being, is as pure in the eyes of God from the charge of sin as he shall be in glory. . . . A believer may be assured of pardon as soon as he commits any sin, even adultery and murder. . . . There is no sin that ever believers commit that can possibly do them any hurt. Sin is dead, and there is no more terror in it than in a dead lion.' In the *First Check*, 2nd letter (*Works*, i, p. 11), Fletcher says that the antinomians ' have given such shakes to the Ark of the Gospel that had not the Lord interposed it must long ago have been overset.'

[3] *Fourth Check*, 7th letter (*Works*, i, pp. 146, 147). Fletcher's exaggerations consist solely in substituting specific sins for general phrases (' falls,' ' backslidings,' etc.). The passages from which he made up his ' antinomian creed' are these (R. Hill, *Five Letters*, 2nd ed., London, 1772) :—(p. 33) ' When a suitable temptation is permitted to work upon some particular corruption of the heart . . . God for wise reasons (as in the express case of

Augustus Toplady, better known as the author of ' Rock of Ages,' abetted and endorsed all that Hill could say, with even greater emphasis.[1] Wesley, like Luther, registered his emphatic protest against these deductions from his primary doctrines ; but the concise series of propositions which he laid before the London Conference in 1770, though ethically unexceptionable, represents a complete and acknowledged surrender of principle. The banner of ' assurance ' had to be thrown away.[2]

(2) It is fully recognized on all hands that the reformers'

Hezekiah) sometimes leaves His people to themselves in such circumstances ; and then there are no lengths they may not run nor any depths they may not fall into, the sin against the Holy Ghost excepted.' But (p. 35) ' all debts and claims against Christ's people, be they more or. be they less, be they small or be they great, be they before or be they after conversion, are for ever and for ever cancelled. . . . No falls or backslidings in God's children can ever bring them again under condemnation. . . . Black in themselves, they are nevertheless comely through His comeliness put upon them ; and therefore He who is of purer eyes than to behold iniquity can nevertheless address them with "Thou are all fair, etc."' ; (p. 41) God sometimes ' suffers those who have great grace and great experience to fall into sins which, for the matter of them, are perhaps more heinous and scandalous than ever they committed in their natural state ' ; but He does so ' to make them know their place,' ' to make them sing louder to the praise of free sovereign grace ' ; (p. 38) David's faith when he committed adultery ' was still justifying faith, though in a wintry season ' (cp. Fletcher, *Fourth Check*, 2nd letter ; and his quotation from an anonymous writer, *ib.*, 4th letter : ' If a man by the Spirit know himself to be in a state of grace, though he commit murder God sees no sin in him)'. Richard Hill is better known as the author of ' Pietas Oxoniensis,' the defence of the six students of St. Edmund Hall expelled the University for Methodism in 1761.

[1] He had some ground for annoyance, as Wesley had epitomized his creed in the words: ' The sum of all is this : one in twenty (suppose) of mankind are elected ; nineteen in twenty are reprobated. The elect shall be saved, do what they will ; the reprobate shall be damned, do what they can, Reader, believe this or be damned. Witness my hand, A—— T——' (L. Tyerman, *Life and Times of Wesley*, iii, p. 82). He also suspected Wesley's activity behind a pamphlet called ' A letter of thanks to the Rev. Mr. Toplady in the names of all the hardened sinners in London and Westminster' (Toplady, *Works*, (1853), p. 179). But this did not justify him in calling Wesley ' an old fox tarred and feathered,' ' a puny tadpole in divinity' (*Works*, p. 762) ; in speaking of his ' satanic guilt,' ' satanic shamelessness,' and ' deductions truly infernal' (*ib.*, p. 740), or in saying that controversy with him was like ' fighting with chimney-sweepers, or bathing in a mud-pool ' (*Historic Proof*, Advertisement, § 5). A good selection of his language, L. Tyerman, *Wesley's Designated Successor*, pp. 340-342 ; cp. Id., *Life and Times of Wesley*, i, p. 519, for the interesting ' conversation of John Wesley with the Antinomian.'

[2] See the ' Minutes ' in Tyerman's *Life and Times*, iii, p. 73 ; Telford, *Life*, p. 287. In these Wesley insists upon the necessity of works meet for repentance, and then adds, ' Is not this salvation by works ? . . . What then have we been disputing about for these thirty years ? I am afraid *about words*. As to ' merit ' itself, of which we have been so dreadfully afraid, we are rewarded according to our works ; yea, because of our works. . . . Can you split this hair ? I doubt I cannot.' Lady Huntingdon and her friends denounced this retractation as ' Popery unmasked.' Wesley's own doctrine of ' Christian perfection ' did not make his controversy with antinomianism any easier ; but at least it was a ' perfection ' which had to be realized in fact, and did not rest wholly on the assurance of imputation, as did the Calvinist. See *ERE.*, ix, *s.v.* ' Perfection,' esp. pp. 730-733.

practice did not square with their theory of the liberty of the individual. The antinomian results of their own teaching compelled them to rule their several Churches with a rod of iron. As the doctrines of justification and predestination severed the Christian from the worldling, and allowed for none of the lights and shades and gradations of real life, so discipline cut off the Church from the world. The priesthood of all believers was a matter of faith,[1] but it was a priesthood no sooner proclaimed than put into commission. ' Calvin,' it has been well said, ' distrusted not only the natural man, but the Christian man as well ; and believed that he must be held strictly to the observance of the divine law, or he would go astray and fall into sin.' [2] Rudolf Sohm, impressed by Luther's dramatic gesture of committing the ' Decretals ' to the flames, made a vigorous attempt to prove that the Wittenberg reformer consistently refused to incorporate the idea of discipline into his conception of the Church.[3] But the facts are otherwise. ' Only the claim to judge the Church by the Bible,' it has been well said by a modern Protestant, ' rather than the Bible by the Church,' [4] separates Luther and Calvin from the mediæval papacy.

Of the two kinds of corporate discipline to which allusion has previously been made, the reformers chose to retain the penal and relinquish the pastoral. Private confession and absolution, though not wholly condemned, were allowed to fall into the background ; public penance and excommunication were grimly retained. Private confession survived longest among the Lutherans. In the treatise on the ' Babylonish Captivity ' Luther treats it as both useful and necessary,[5] though he would have it entirely voluntary, and allows laymen to give absolution freely.[6] The Augsburg Confession insists that communion is to be allowed only to those who

[1] See *To the German Nobility* throughout, e.g. (Wace and Bucheim), p. 21—' We are all consecrated as priests by baptism ' ; p. 22—' Whatever issues from baptism may boast that it has been consecrated priest, bishop, and pope.' But immediately thereafter—' although it does not beseem everyone to exercise these offices.'

[2] A. C. McGiffert, *Protestant Thought before Kant*, p. 91.

[3] R. Sohm, *Kirchenrecht*, i, pp. 461 ff.—' Nicht bloss das päpstliche Recht, sondern das Kirchenrecht wollte er verbrennen.'

[4] T. C. Hall, *History of Ethics within Organized Christianity*, p. 469 ; cp. *ib.*, pp. 483-485.

[5] Wace and Bucheim, p. 209.

[6] Cp. *Sermon on Mt.* 18[18] (ed. Erlang., xliv, p. 108)—' Not only in the Church is there forgiveness of sin, but wherever two or three are gathered together. . . . So that they may find forgiveness of sin not only in the congregation, but at home, in the field, in the garden ; wherever one meets another he may find comfort and rescue ; and whatsoever comfort my neighbour promises me, that same is confirmed by God in heaven.' Cp. also *Babylonish Captivity* (Wace and Bucheim, pp. 209-211)—' The secret confession which is now practised, though it cannot be proved from Scripture, is in my opinion highly satisfactory, and useful or even necessary. . . . Whosoever voluntarily confesses his sins privately in the presence of any brother . . . is absolved from his secret sins, since Christ has manifestly bestowed the power of absolution on every believer in Him, with whatever violence the pontiffs may rage against this truth.'

have confessed and been absolved, and sets contrition on a level
with faith as a condition of reconciliation.[1]   In the eighteenth
century, however, a general confession in church, with absolution
from the pulpit, became the normal rule ; though private absolution,
with which was bound up the *Beichtpfennig*, or fee paid by the
penitent to the pastor who heard his confession, lingered on in
Prussia even into the early years of the nineteenth century.[2]

On the other hand, all branches of the reformed Churches
retained public excommunication, penance and reconciliation as
matters of principle,[3] though in practice the majority of them
preferred the discipline to be enforced by the civil magistrate.[4]
Luther, dealing with the compulsion exercised by Pope Nicholas II
upon Berengarius in the Eucharistic controversy of the eleventh
century, said wholeheartedly : 'Would to God that all popes had
acted in all matters in as Christian a way.'[5]   None but the Anabaptists[6] and Brownists[7] forbore to appeal to the civil magistrate
to enforce their decisions, whether their conception of Church
polity was Byzantine or theocratic.   Luther would have the civil
government use force against all preachers who opposed the Reformation—'not that one should kill the preachers,' he adds,
'this is unnecessary.   But they should be forbidden to do anything
against the gospel, and should be forcibly prevented from doing
it.'[8]   'They are to be punished for their profanity, for they are not
merely heretics, but open blasphemers.'[9]   To Knox the civil magis-

---

[1] Augsburg Confession, Part II, iv (Kidd, *Documents of the Continental
Reformation*, p. 275).   On faith and contrition, *ib.*, Part I, xii, 2 (Kidd,
p. 265).   Note also the form of confession prescribed in the Shorter Catechism.
with the declaratory form of absolution (' I forgive thee ')—*ib.*, pp. 216, 217.

[2] Cp. L. Pullan, *Religion since the Reformation*, p. 82 ; and see *ERE.*,
iv, pp. 718-720, *s.v.* ' Discipline (Christian) ' ; *PRE.*, x, pp. 483-492 (*s.v.*
' Kirchenzucht ').

[3] The Lutherans, Sohm, *Kirchenrecht*, i, p. 522 ; Confession of Augsburg,
ii, 7 (Kidd, *Documents*, p. 283) ; Calvinists, Sohm, pp. 653-657 ; Lindsay,
Reformation, ii, pp. 107-113.   Sohm, i, p. 522, notes that the Reformers
expressly abandoned the greater excommunication, as partaking too much
of the nature of secular punishment, and retained the lesser only.

[4] Lindsay, *Reformation*, ii, pp. 110, 111.

[5] *Eucharistic Confession* (ed. Weimar, xxvi, p. 443).   Cp. also M. Creighton,
Persecution and Tolerance, pp. 110, 111, for further examples.   Luther had
no hesitation about the doctrine ' extra ecclesiam nulla salus '—e.g. *Kirchen-
postille* (Lk. 2[15-20]—second Mass for Christmas Day—*Works*, ed. Weimar,
x, p. 140)—' Whoever would find Christ must find the Church first. . . . The
Church is not wood and stone, but the faithful people who believe in Christ.
We must turn to them, for they have Christ with them, and see how they
believe and live and teach.   For outside the Church of Christ there is no
truth, no Christ, no salvation.'   On the system of Consistorial Courts by
which the doctrine was put into practice, T. M. Lindsay, *History of the
Reformation*, i, pp. 413-416 ; J. Mackinnon, *Luther and the Reformation*, iv,
pp. 00 ff.

[6] Lindsay, *Reformation*, ii, pp. 443, 446.

[7] McGiffert, *Protestant Thought before Kant*, pp. 130-132.

[8] *True Exhortation* (ed. Weimar, viii, p. 680).   Later, Luther accepted
the death-penalty as warrantable in such cases ; J. Mackinnon, *Luther and
the Reformation*, iv, p. 64.   Cp. *ib.*, pp. 83 ff., on excommunication.

[9] *xpos. of Ps. 82* (ed. Erlang., xxxix, p. 250).

trate is appointed 'to suppress idolatry and superstition'; to abolish all doctrine repugnant to the word of God as 'damnable to man's salvation'; 'to purge the Church of God from all superstition . . . and provide to the uttermost of his powers how it may abide in the same purity to posterities following.'[1] False teachers 'ought not to escape the punishment of the civil magistrate'; and although the Book of Discipline 'dare not prescribe what penalties shall be required of such,' it affirms that 'the one and the other deserve death.'[2]

To Calvin the officers of the Church are schoolmasters to lead us to Christ; but their tutelage is one from which we never escape :—[3]

> 'Man's natural ignorance, indolence and frivolity demand external institutions, and so God appointed pastors and teachers, to instruct his flock. He endowed them with authority; he left nothing undone which might minister to the holy union of the faithful and their proper government.'[4] —'All must conform to this precept, and give themselves up with a mild and docile spirit to teachers so appointed. . . . The more abominable therefore are the apostates who aim at a division in the Church; they chase the sheep away from the fold, to drive them into the jaws of wolves.'[5]

Even the Anabaptists, when they gained possession of Münster in 1533, called upon the magistrates to enforce the complete separation of the Church from the world ; and, by compelling all adults to choose between baptism and expulsion from the city (an expulsion which would inevitably involve capture by a ruthless and bloodthirsty enemy), they achieved more completely than any other of the reformers a position in which discipline was even more effectively used against those without the Church than against those within.[6] Taking the discipline of the Protestant churches as a whole, even Professor Gwatkin, one of their principal apologists, was forced to say : 'The system hardened the saints with formalism and spiritual pride, and drove the sinners to hypocrisy and despair.'[7]

This current of rigid discipline which so soon manifested itself in the Protestant churches is often condoned as no more than a debased mediæval survival, dragging out the last of its evil days in a purer atmosphere where it could not long survive. But it had roots of its own in the new religious outlook. The doctrine of personal assurance—which alone can indemnify the Christian

---

[1] J. Knox, *Book of Discipline* (*Works*, Edinburgh, 1846, ii, pp. 185, 209).
[2] *Ib.*, ii, p. 254.
[3] *Inst.*, IV, 1. 5 ; *ib.*, 1. 13—he attacks 'Cathari, Donatists and Anabaptists' who resent ecclesiastical government 'tamquam aërii quidam dæmones facti essent'; *ib.*, 1. 22—a strong defence of the power of the keys.
[4] Calvin, *Inst.*, IV, 1. 1. [5] *Ib.*, 1. 5.
[6] Lindsay, *op. cit.*, ii, pp. 459-461.
[7] *ERE.*, x, p. 621, *s.v.* 'Reformation.'

against the over-ruling demands of the Church to which he belongs
—was a weapon too delicate and double-edged to meet the requirements of the time. Hardier substitutes had to be found, if
the shock of the Roman counter-attack was to be resisted. So
Melancthon's theology centres upon an enthusiasm for the natural
law which is little more than a quasi-scholastic Aristotelianism ; [1]
Calvin's upon an intellectual conviction of personal predestination,
which is easily transformed into confessional acceptance of the
doctrine of predestination in general.[2] External tests once more
become the hall-mark of Christianity, and with them reappears the
claim of the body to dragoon its members into conformity. Lutheranism itself was not proof against the tendency. Despite all his
personal sense of God, its founder could say, ' By faith we understand that Christ was born and suffered and rose again for us ' [3]—an
intellectual test, that is to say, replaces an empirical one. We
are no longer required to *know* Christ, but only to know *something
about* Him. Acting on hints like these the Augsburg Confession
substitutes for ' assurance ' adherence to a form of doctrine—a
form moreover which it explicitly avows to be ' in no way at variance
with the Catholic Church or the Church of Rome, so far as this
Church is known from the writers of Scripture.' [4]

In so far, therefore, as Christian liberty was the child of the
Reformation, it died in infancy. Friedberg, Richter, Harnack and
Neander are all of the opinion that the true Luther—the Luther who
staked his all upon personal communion with God and assurance
of forgiveness—is only to be found between the years 1519 and
1523. The Eucharistic controversies and the Peasants' War forced
him to insist upon the law at the expense of the gospel in despite
of himself.[5] In any case it is commonly recognized, even by Protestant apologists, that the liberty of thought and action which
characterizes modern Christianity outside the Roman communion
is in no way a direct outcome of the Reformation. That it has
permeated the Protestant churches is due in the main to weakness
resulting from their unhappy divisions, rather than to any welcome
which they themselves offered to the *Aufklärung*.[6]

---

[1] A. C. McGiffert, *op. cit.*, p. 78.

[2] Cp. *ib.*, p. 87—' Calvin gave the doctrine of absolute and unconditioned
predestination an essential place in a system whose controlling principle was
the majesty and might of God. As a result to reject or even to minimize it
seemed to limit God and throw contempt upon Him '; Harnack, *Hist. of
Dogma*, vii, p. 25, on the subservience of the reformers to dogma.

[3] *Commentary on the Psalms* (ed. Weimar, iii, p. 176). For the gradual
supersession of mystical by intellectual apprehension of Christ and His
work in Luther's thought, see Loofs, *Leitfaden*, pp. 701, 723, 724 ; cp. *ib.*,
p. 692 ; passages to the contrary, Lindsay, *op. cit.*, i, pp. 429-431.

[4] *Conf. of Augsburg*, Part I, xxii (Kidd, *Documents*, p. 270).

[5] Harnack, *Hist. of Dogma*, vii, pp. 27, 28, 170, 231 ; Neander, quoted *ib.*,
p. 28 ; for Richter and Friedberg see quotations, Sohm, *op. cit.*, pp. 510,
511, 543 ; cp. Lindsay, *op. cit.*, i, pp. 337, 386.

[6] So McGiffert, *op. cit.*, pp. 99, 187 ; E. Troeltsch, *Protestantism and
Progress*, pp. 87-91, 122 ff. But Troeltsch also insists (pp. 36-39) that this
' individualism ' is ' based upon the idea, which is essentially Christian, of

(3) That the ethics of the reformers should in the main be of a Puritan type was a natural, though not a necessary, outcome of their complete severance of the Church from the world. Much depended, of course, on each teacher's particular aversion. Luther, in his violent reaction against monasticism, stood to a large extent for a humanist, domestic and social type of life, though even he (to use another of Harnack's phrases) was ' far from making the religious man feel at home in this world.' [1] In general, he was tolerant of natural joys and recreations. ' If our Lord God,' he is reported to have said,

> ' may make excellent large pike and good Rhenish wine, I may very well venture to eat and to drink. Thou mayest enjoy every pleasure in the world that is not sinful ; that thy God forbids thee not, but much rather wills it. And it is pleasing to the dear God whenever thou rejoicest and laughest from the bottom of thy heart.' [2]

Zwingli, the one reformer with a full humanist education,[3] llowed Luther in this respect. Calvin, on the other hand, a generation younger than Luther and Zwingli, showed himself more in reaction against contemporary society than against the middle ages, and that although he had been educated in humanist circles.[4] The Christian and the worldling are wholly separate ; whatever, then, the worldling does the Christian must not do. To rigorist discipline is added rigorist ethics. The doctrines of the total depravity of man's fallen nature and the misery of this present life, with the consequent demand for a complete unnaturalness of living, lie over the whole period like a fog. Thus Calvin writes :—

the destination of man to acquire perfected personality through the ascent to God . . . the being laid hold of and moulded by the Divine Spirit.' How far in his opinion the Reformation was directly responsible for a new recognition of this basic idea, Troeltsch does not indicate.

[1] Harnack, *Hist. of Dogma*, vii, p. 191.

[2] C. Beard, *Reformation*, p. 143. Beard refers to Hagen, *Reformations-Zeitalter* for his authority—a book I have not been able to consult. Other examples of ' this-worldliness ' in Luther's teaching, J. Mackinnon, *op. cit.*, iv, pp. 237-239. For Luther's anti-monastic sentiment cp. *Second Sermon for the Fifteenth Sunday after Trinity* (ed. Erlangen, v, p. 100),—' It looks a great thing when a monk renounces everything to go into the cloister and live a life of self-discipline, fasts, vigils and prayer. . . . It looks a small thing when a maid cooks and cleans and does the housework. But the monk has no command of God for what he does, whilst the maid fulfils God's command that one should honour father and mother and help in the care of the home ; and inasmuch as she has such a command, even her small work is to be praised as a service to God far higher than any sanctity or asceticism of monks and nuns '; *ib.*, pp. 84, 87, *First Sermon* ; *ib.*, ii, pp. 133-137, *Sermon for ' Invocavit.'* There is throughout an element of special pleading—it would have been enough to declare the religious and secular lives equally matters of personal vocation alone. But Luther's temper did not allow of this moderation.

[3] Lindsay, *op. cit.*, ii, pp. 10, 37.

[4] Calvin's early training, Lindsay, ii, pp. 12, 96.

' If heaven is our country what is the earth but our place of
exile ?   If to depart out of the world is to enter into life, what
is the world but a sepulchre ?   What is a continuance in it but
absorption in death ?   If deliverance from the body is the
assurance of true freedom, what is the body but a prison ? . . .
We must learn to hate this terrestrial life, that it make us not
prisoners to sin.' [1]   ' Therefore although Christian liberty in
external matters should not be brought to a rigid formula,
nevertheless this one rule is obligatory—believers should in-
dulge themselves as little as possible.   They should perpetually
and resolutely exert themselves to retrench superfluities and
restrain luxury.   They should diligently beware lest they per-
vert into impediments things given for their assistance.' [2]

' I am the enemy of God,' says Hooper, ' the image of the devil,
the library of lies, the friend of the devil, right heir of eternal
death, the child of damnation, a murderer by means of sin, not only
of myself but also of the Son of God that never sinned.' [3]   The
Anabaptist doctrine of the separation of the Christian from the
world was carried to its logical issue, in more than one branch of
the movement, by the enactment that ' believers,' if married, must
even cease to cohabit with unbelieving partners.[4]

So much of the principles which seem to be distinctive of the
first century of the reformed religion.   It can hardly be denied that
they involved what is more truly called a vital contradiction than a
paradox—the contradiction of making a present empirical assurance
of justification the one and only thing that matters, and yet at the
same time of insisting that external conformity to a law—conceived
often enough in highly rigorist terms—matters too.   This contradiction is a new one as compared with Catholic piety.   There,
indeed, there is a paradox ;—the vision of God is the one and only
thing in which the Christian can find his goal, and yet it is his duty
to exhibit love for God and his neighbour in active service.   But the
paradox is not intolerable, for the fruition of the vision is set for
the future.   The path of duty lies in a purity of life which shall make
man worthy to see God.   That the *impure* could ever see God is a
heresy which it is impossible to draw out from the older conception

---

[1] *Inst.*, III, 9. 4.
[2] *Ib.*, III. 10. 4—a specially interesting passage.   Calvin has mentioned
with some enthusiasm the divine bounties in creation—the ' aspectus gratia,
et jucunditas odoris ' of flowers, fruits and so forth.   But whereas he dismisses in three lines the error of that ' inhuman philosophy ' which would
restrict us to the ' necessary use ' of these things, he expatiates for two
columns on the dangers of their abuse.   His sympathies are definitely
rigorist.
[3] Quoted T. C. Hall, *History of Ethics within Organized Christianity*,
p. 394.
[4] Lindsay, *op. cit.*, p. 465.   The rigorist tendency was of course emphasized (and would indeed, apart from any other influence, have been inevitable)
as a result of the rejection of the double standard caused by the revolt against
monasticism and the confessional.   A ' no-compromise ' temper was the
necessary sequel.   Cp. *supra*, p. 234, n. ; *infra*, pp. 520 f., additional note K.

of life ; that the assured and predestinate Christian might live im-
purely without jeopardizing his salvation was a conclusion which—
despite the protests of the reformers—was actually and legitimately
drawn from one at least of their premises.

To this fundamental contradiction it is natural to attribute
the dissolution of historic Protestantism. A brief-lived scholasticism [1] attempted to resolve the inconsistency, but without success ;
thereafter the system fell apart into its constituent though ill-
assorted elements. On the one hand, quietist sects, whose sole
interest was the emotional enjoyment of present religious experience, maintained their existence, though always in limited numbers ;
the tendency has been kept in being by the regular recrudescence
of revivalist evangelicalism. But in the main Protestantism has
settled down to a steady proclamation and inculcation of a sane and
sober type of Christian behaviour. In sheer unconsciousness perhaps, but none the less definitely, it has emphasized the law and
overlooked the promise, thereby breaking away completely from the
theological revolution which gave it birth. The movement in this
direction might well look back to Anabaptism as its source ; for
the Anabaptists, apart from their hysterical excesses at Münster,
laid the greatest stress on purity of life, and inveighed bitterly
against the Lutheran doctrine of justification by faith alone, as
militating against their ideal.[2] Pietism, in its more sober German
form, with Spener and Francke as its founders,[3] carried on the
tradition, and exemplified the ethical character of Christianity by
the impetus it gave to philanthropic activities. In so far as it
failed to hold its own against the rationalism which beset Protestant
Germany in the eighteenth century, its failure is due to the fact
that it made too stringent demands upon its adherents. In a
kindly but yet uncompromising fashion it sought to impose a
rigorist yoke upon the Christian once more.

Little would be gained for our purposes by following the history
of Protestant ethics any further. Kant rescued the idea of the moral
law from the formalist externalism into which rationalism had
brought it,[4] insisting—as few have ever insisted so passionately—
upon the good will as the vital principle of all true conduct. He
gave the moral law inwardness, and in that respect the value of his

[1] C. Beard, *Reformation*, pp. 262-299 ; A. C. McGiffert, *Protestant Thought*,
pp. 141-154.
[2] Lindsay, *Reformation*, ii, pp. 430-443 ; McGiffert, *op. cit.*, pp. 100-107
(esp. p. 105) ; Moehler, *Symbolism*, pp. 365-374.
[3] A useful account of Spener and Francke, in T. C. Hall, *History of
Ethics within Organized Christianity*, pp. 544-553, where Ritschl's under-
valuation of the ethical side of Pietism is dealt with ; cp. also W. Gass,
Geschichte der christl. Ethik, II, i, pp. 285-307 ; *PRE.*, xv, pp. 774-815 ;
C. Mod. H., v, pp. 753-764 ; *ERE.*, x, pp. 6-9.
[4] Cp. E. C. Moore, *Christian Thought since Kant*, p. 34—' Rationalism
had starved the soul, it had minimized and derided feeling. It had suppressed emotion. It had been fatal to art. It was barren of poetry. It
had no sympathy with history and no understanding of history. . . . Rationalism had ended by proving fatal to ideals.'

service cannot be over-estimated ; but a law it remained none the less. Schleiermacher extended the horizon of the law to its uttermost limits ; his ethical scheme forms a network which covers every sphere of human activity,[1] and yet could be summarized by Ritschl in the single thought of the kingdom of God. Both he and Ritschl, acting upon hints conveyed by Kant, revived the sense of religion ; but the place they gave it was one in which it remained uncoordinated with ethics. With Schleiermacher it is a 'feeling' of dependence upon God with which the moral man may console himself during the day's work, or after the day's work is done ; [2] with Ritschl and his disciples the thought of redemption, which might have meant so much, has come to be nothing more than the belief that God has revealed an ideal for man to work towards.[3] Once more the law is primary.

[1] Good accounts of Schleiermacher's ethics in Gass, *Geschichte*, II, ii, pp. 232-247 (esp. pp. 239-245) ; *ERE.*, xi, p. 238 (W. B. Selbie).

[2] See especially Schleiermacher: *On Religion, Speeches to its Cultured Despisers* (E. tr. J. Oman, 1893), pp. 36, 37—' The contemplation of the pious is the immediate consciousness of the universal existence of all finite things in and through the Eternal. Religion is to seek this and find it in all that lives and moves . . . Where this is found, religion is satisfied. . . .' Ethics, on the other hand, seeks ' to distinguish precisely each part of human doing and producing, and at the same time to combine them into a whole, according to natural relationships. *But the pious man confesses that, as pious, he knows nothing about it. He does indeed contemplate human action, but it is not the kind of contemplation from which an ethical system takes its rise.*' Cp. *ib.*, p. 59—' In a healthy state man cannot be represented as acting from religion or being driven to action by religion, but action and religion form each a series by itself and are two different functions of one and the same life. But while man does nothing from religion he should do everything with religion. *Uninterruptedly, like a sacred music, religious feelings should accompany his active life.*' *Ib.*, p. 277—Religion does not, like ethics, ' seek to advance and perfect the universe. . . . It is reverent attention and submission, in childlike passivity to be stirred and filled by the universe's immediate influences.' In all this it is true that Schleiermacher was attempting to emancipate religion from the position of a ' handmaid ' ; but he would never go further than to make it a ' friend ' of ethics (*ib.*, p. 85 f.). The two remain substantially uncoordinated; hence his 'feeling of dependence' is different from the 'spirit of worship' as traditionally understood.

[3] So W. Herrmann, *Communion of the Christian with God*, p. 97—' Jesus gathers together all His powers for the task of redemption, which is His great vocation. This vocation is to *reveal to us* the blessedness of the life of a man who is in fellowship with God.' Later (p. 54) this ' entry of God into communion with us,' which we reach by ' laying hold on the inner life of Jesus in that report which has come down to us,' is identified as ' an invincible certainty that the almighty power of His Father in heaven rules in the boundless world.' This certainty ' makes us feel free from the mastery of the world ' (p. 202), enables us to give ' willing submission to the laws and arrangements by which God works on us on every side ' (p. 207), and to ' carry out love to God in the form of love to our neighbours ' (p. 210). Cp. A. E. Garvie, in *ERE.*, x, pp. 812-820 (*s.v.* ' Ritschlianism ') ; esp. p. 816 : —Ritschl ' speaks of the kingdom of God and redemption as the two foci of Christianity ; but there can be no doubt that in reality he subordinates the doctrine of redemption to the doctrine of the kingdom, as the means to the end.' By the ' kingdom ' Ritschl means ' the moral ideal for the realization of which the members of the community bind themselves to one another by a definite mode of reciprocal action ' (*ib.*).

About a phenomenon so fluid and elusive as that which is summarily called Protestantism it is dangerous, if not impossible, to
generalize.   But it is hard to resist the conclusion, forcibly expressed
by one of the most distinguished of living Bampton lecturers, that
it is in the main responsible for the prevalent modern tendency
to interpret the genius of Christianity wholly in formalist terms—
to exalt the law and to ignore the promise.[1]   That the old terminology of grace, communion and redemption is still in wide use in
orthodox circles goes without saying, but a close testing of the usage
suggests that the words are often employed not so much to designate
experience of supernatural power, illumination, and hope of eternal
life, as to cloak with pious and time-honoured periphrasis the
commendation of an unselfish life of social service.   Christianity
to many Christians has become simply conformity to a code.[2]

The most important result, for our present purpose, of this
post-Reformation development, has been to reverse the entire
traditional doctrine of the character of Christian prayer.   One of
the most remarkable books of the present generation is Friedrich
Heiler's comprehensive survey, under the title ' Das Gebet,' of the
whole range of prayer, Christian and pagan.   As is well known,
Heiler draws the sharpest possible distinction between two forms
of religion, which he calls the ' mystical ' and the ' prophetic '
respectively ; [3]   the latter he identifies with ' biblical ' or ' evangelical ' religion, and especially with the piety of Luther.[4]   He
recognizes frankly that Protestantism has not been wholly lacking in devotees of the contemplative life.[5]   But he regards the

---

[1] T. B. Strong, *Christian Ethics*, pp. 318-339 ; esp. p. 319—' Christianity
is very widely regarded as being merely a name for a particular type of
moral practice . . . (pp. 332, 333).   If there is no authority anywhere in
matters of religion . . . the external ordinary moral life of a man tends to
be separated from his religion.'   The entire argument is of extreme importance.

[2] Or more exactly, perhaps, ' to the *spirit* of a code ' ; for the formalist
is often painfully aware that he does not know what action the code prescribes for his particular circumstances ; his aim is to discover this as far
as possible, and then act upon it (*supra*, p. 133).

[3] *Das Gebet* [5], pp. 233, 248, etc.   Since the publication of his first edition,
Heiler has adopted a more friendly attitude towards mysticism (see *Das
Gebet* [5], pp. x, 587, 588, 593 ; *Der Katholizismus*, pp. 475-555).   He would
no longer be prepared to say ' Mysticism is not Christian in origin, nor is it
in any way distinctive of Christianity ; although Christianity has given it
its finest expressions and most beautiful examples ' (*Das Gebet*, p. 282—the
text of the second edition has not been altered in later ones, but the change
of view is indicated in a new Preface and Appendix).   But he insists thaa
this change of emphasis only serves to intensify the difference between the
' mystical ' and ' prophetic ' types (*ib.*, p. 10).

[4] *Ib.*, pp. 233 f., 257, etc. (' the prophetic religion was restored to its
original strength in the biblical Christianity of the reformers '—p. 233) ;
pp. 244, 245, Luther.

[5] *Ib.*, p. 234—Arndt and Tersteegen ; Zinzendorf is also quoted occat
sionally.   For some extraordinary reason Jacob Böhme does not appearl
either as a mystic, or a Protestant (a passing mention on p. 20) ; Fox only
rarely, Law and Blake not at all.   By these omissions the non-mystic-,
character of Protestantism as a whole, which Heiler is anxious to establish,
is slightly exaggerated.

phenomenon as alien to its genius [1]—an intrusion of mediæval mystical thought into the purer system. Luther, he admits, ' passed through the school of mediæval mysticism,' and never altogether abandoned its teaching, to the ' enrichment ' of his prophetic and biblical piety.[2] But though he regards Luther's blending of the two elements as ' wonderful,' it is clear that he sees the reformer's main importance, in this matter, in his revival of the ' prophetic ' type of prayer.[3] As to that type, there is in Heiler's mind no question. It is not in essence contemplative, but practical. In Luther's hands it lost even the element of ' adoration, praise and thanksgiving,' and was reduced to mere petition.[4]

' Petition,' therefore, is the essence of Protestant, or as Heiler would say, ' prophetic ' prayer. His long analysis of this type of prayer enumerates as its constituents ' complaint,' ' petition,' ' intercession,' ' appeals to God's interests, providence and promises,' ' confession of sin and frailty,' ' expression of confidence,' ' self-dedication,' ' thanksgiving and praise.'[5] Only when all these have been fully explored is a short paragraph allowed to ' longing and seeing ' ; and even here the vision of God is reduced to ' community of purpose ' and ' self-dedication ' once again, in order that the contemplative implication may as far as possible be evaded.[6]

Perhaps Heiler has exaggerated the distinction between mystical and prophetic religion, and over-emphasized the strictly ' prophetic ' character of Protestantism. But in general his estimate seems accurate enough. We may withhold comment for a moment, except in one respect. The elements which Heiler regards as constitutive of prophetic prayer are wholly valid and laudable ; prayer which did not contain them would be less than truly Christian. But in the tradition of the vision of God as the dominant *motif* of Christian prayer they hold a very different position. There they do not stand—they cannot stand—on their own merits ; they are the fruit, the aurora, the coronal of that communion with God towards which the attitude of worship is directed, and which it does not always fail to attain. ' Prophetic ' prayer may or may not be higher than contemplative prayer ; but by giving it pride

---

[1] *Das Gebet*, p. 245—' With a keenness and certainty of which only a great religious genius could be capable, Luther banished the neo-Platonic element which had intruded into the Christian life of prayer, and revealed anew the prophetic type of prayer in its religious purity.'

[2] *Ib.*

[3] See note (1) above ; and cp. p. 585—' Luther's great contribution to the history of Christian prayer was to bring it back to the " biblical " norm.'

[4] *Ib.*, p. 585—' Luther not merely renewed the " biblical " type of prayer, he gave it a particular bias ' (' er hat ihn vielmehr zugleich vereinseitigt ') ' by throwing worship, praise and thanksgiving—weighty elements in Jewish and primitive Christian prayer—into the background. Luther's prayers are dominated, in one-sided fashion, by the prayer of need (" Notgebet "), the request for grace and help ' (here follow examples). ' With extraordinary originality he reduced worship, praise and thanksgiving to petition alone.' Heiler regards this phenomenon with some perplexity, but decides that it is the outcome of the ' unique genius and childlikeness ' of Luther's piety.

[5] *Ib.*, pp. 358-392.   [6] *Ib.*, pp. 392, 393

of place the reformers altered the whole balance of Christian devotion. This is a fact which could not in any case be allowed to pass without consideration ; it becomes of crucial importance when it is set side by side with a parallel, but even more surprising, development in the Catholicism of the counter-Reformation.

(b) Catholicism.

As we have just seen, the primacy, in private devotion, of worship, contemplation, mystical prayer, the vision of God—by whatever name we choose to call it—was allowed to lapse by Protestantism. From having a uniqueness all its own, prayer became a mere auxiliary to effort—a means of securing, or attempting to secure, what lay beyond the immediate reach of the unaided will. Exactly the same phenomenon showed itself in the Catholicism of the sixteenth and seventeenth centuries, with only one difference, and that—though of considerable interest—of no fundamental character. The authority of the Jesuits and the ' Spiritual Exercises,' the personal influence of S. Francis de Sales and the charm of the ' Introduction to the Devout Life,' had given ' mental prayer,' or meditation, a foothold so strong that its right to a place in the Christian life could not very well be challenged. Thus whilst the Protestant tendency was to reduce the idea of prayer to that of petition and intercession only, in Catholicism petition and intercession were always held together in a framework of meditation. But in Catholicism as in Protestantism, contemplation, or the ideal of communion with God as the culmination of approach to Him through worship, suffered a very serious eclipse.

The decade from 1570 to 1580 is of peculiar importance in this connexion.[1] During those years the anti-mystical faction in Spain definitely gained the ascendant. For two generations the suspicions of the hierarchy had been directed by the Inquisition towards a mysterious sect of Alumbrados, or Illuminati, of whom much evil was spoken, but very little proved.[2] If the Illuminati as such had no direct connexion with Lutheranism, at all events mysticism might be accused of it ; both appealed to the inner light as an authority higher than the jurisdiction of ecclesiastical superiors. Thus mysticism of every kind once more became suspect. The feud between Dominicans and Jesuits offered fertile ground for the extension of inquisitorial investigations. Jesuit teachers had shown themselves favourable to mystical thought ; and both within and without the Society there was growing up a strong

[1] For the following paragraphs I am indebted in the main to H. Bremond, HLSR., viii, pp. 185-288 ; A. Saudreau, Life of Union with God [3] (E. tr.), pp. 216-313 ; Mystical State (E. tr.), pp. 110-141, 179-198 ; P. Pourrat, SC., iii, pp. 121-186 ; J. Chapman, in ERE., ix, pp. 100-101, s.v. ' Mysticism (Roman Catholic) ' ; H. C. Lea, History of the Inquisition of Spain, esp. vol. iv, pass.

[2] Bremond, op. cit., pp. 198, 220-223 ; DHGE., ii, coll. 849-853 (s.v. ' Alumbrados ') ; PRE., i, pp. 388-390 ; Lea, iv, pp. 1-34.

feeling that their activities should be exerted in less equivocal directions. The Carmelites, again, had produced two great mystics in S. Teresa and S. John of the Cross ; and no one was prepared to say whether their teaching as a whole was to be commended or deplored. In all the circumstances it is perhaps not surprising that authority took fright.

The evil genius of the reactionaries was the Dominican Melchior Cano,—pre-eminent as a theologian, but with little sense of personal religion, less sympathy, and no restraint whatever. At the right hand of the Grand Inquisitor, de Valdes, he began to move him to vigorous action as early as 1556.[1] Within three years he had won his first spectacular success. Carranza, Cardinal Archbishop of Toledo, a brother Dominican and the greatest ecclesiastic in Spain, was committed to prison, whence he emerged seventeen years later, censured but submissive, only to die on regaining his liberty. In 1559—the year of Carranza's impeachment—de Valdes published the Inquisition's ' Index ' of prohibited books, in which not only the Bible in the vulgar tongue, which had been prohibited earlier,[2] but orthodox mystical writings of every kind were forbidden to the faithful.[3] In 1572[4] Louis de Leon, pre-eminent among contemporary Spanish poets, and a devoted Catholic, spent five years in the dungeons of the Inquisition for the offence of translating the ' Song of Songs ' for the spiritual edification of a devout nun. The campaign against the Alumbrados culminated in a great auto-da-fé at Llerena in 1579.[5] Louis of Granada, the greatest of Spanish ascetical writers, was impeached by Cano, and only escaped condemnation by personal appeal to the Council of Trent.[6] S. Teresa escaped serious molestation, though perhaps for no other reason than that no published work of hers could be made the basis of an accusation. But in 1575 her own confessor was forced by the Inquisitors to make a formal enquiry into her manuscript writings, and his report, though exonerating her in general from suspicion, is weighty with reservations.[7] S. John of the Cross was less fortunate. Before he had published—apparently even before he had written— anything at all, he spent the greater part of a year (1578) in prison, under conditions of the extremest squalor.[8]

The mystical strain among the Jesuits did not escape the vigilant eye of Melchior Cano. He protested publicly that Ignatius Loyola had fled from Spain to avoid trial for heresy,[9] that the ' Spiritual

[1] Pourrat, SC., iii, p. 164 ; Lea, ii, pp. 48-84 ; C. Mod. H., ii, pp. 409, 410.

[2] Pourrat, iii, p. 164 ; Lea, iii, p. 485 (Index of 1551).

[3] Pourrat, iii, p. 166 ; Lea, iii, pp. 486-488.

[4] PRE., xi, p. 394 ; Pourrat, iii, p. 181 ; Lea, iv, pp. 149-162.

[5] Bremond, viii, p. 220 ; Lea, iv, pp. 23-25. The impression created by this auto-da-fé was out of all proportion to its severity, which was not exceptionally noticeable.

[6] Saudreau, Life of Union, p. 250.

[7] An abstract in Pourrat, SC., iii, pp. 158, 159.

[8] Pourrat, SC., iii, pp. 274, 275, 311.

[9] Saudreau, Life of Union, p. 251.

Exercises ' were ' artifices of the devil ' and redolent of illuminism, and that the Jesuits as a whole were ' those false prophets of the last age who should deceive the world.' [1] Something had to be done to repel the attack of the reactionary and all-powerful Dominicans. In 1573, therefore. Mercurian, General of the Jesuits, signalized his elevation to office by banishing from the libraries of the Society practically every mystical writing that was known. ' They are not appropriate to the spirit of our Order,' he maintained, ' and are not to be allowed in any of our colleges, except by the express permission of the provincial.' [2] Worse was to follow. The rector of Salamanca, Balthasar Alvarez, one of the most glorious lights of the Society and a former spiritual director of S. Teresa herself, was suspected of illuminism by his provincial, John Suarez. In 1577 Mercurian ordered a further enquiry. The result was a ' categorical condemnation ' [3] of Alvarez' attempt to keep the contemplative tradition in being. ' He must show more affection and esteem for the method of prayer taught in the ' Exercises '; he must prefer it to all other kinds of prayer, and must follow it absolutely, both he and those whom he directs ; for the Company allows no other.' [4]

What, then, it will very naturally be asked, was Mercurian's conception of the method of prayer taught in the ' Exercises ' ? Were we wrong, at the end of the last lecture, in treating Ignatius as a representative of the classical tradition which makes communion with God through worship the end to which all prayer, and all methods of prayer, aspire ? The question may wait for a moment, while we observe how the Carmelites in their turn defended the challenged orthodoxy of their saints.[5]

S. John of the Cross and S. Teresa were mystics first, psychologists second, and logicians only third. To a wealth of spiritual experience they brought an incomparable sensitiveness of analysis and observation, extending even to the minutest shades of difference in the life of the spirit. They possessed again, in common with many modern psychologists, a romantic taste in terminology ; the innumerable states of the soul of which they speak are all illuminated by the glamour of poetry. It is not for the non-mystical to decide whether they were over-acute in their analysis, and thereby complicated a relatively simple matter (simple, though mysterious beyond comparison) by cataloguing many states where only a few have any outstanding characteristics. Logicians, at all events, Teresa and John were not, and this has made them at once the most

---

[1] Pourrat, *SC.*, iii, p. 168 ; Lea, iv, p. 18.
[2] Bremond, *HLSR.*, viii, p. 231.   [3] *Ib.*, p. 252.
[4] *Ib.*, p. 252 ; Pourrat, *SC.*, iii, p. 178 ; Saudreau, *Life of Union*, p. 254.
[5] But especially S. John of the Cross, for S. Teresa ' already enjoyed an incontestable authority, and needed no defence ' (A. Saudreau, *Mystical State*, p. 117). Good accounts of S. Teresa and S. John are available in all the principal modern writers on mysticism, and their own writings are easily accessible. I have therefore thought it unnecessary to give any further account of them than is required for the general development of the subject.

fascinating and the most elusive of mystics.   No two commentators
interpret them alike.[1]   The same words—'contemplation' and
'union,' for example—are used both in generic and specific senses ;
and subdivisions of a general conception are often alluded to (or
'may be,' for nothing is certain here), without differentiation, by
the very term employed to denote the original conception itself.
Of the 'states' so constantly enumerated it is often quite uncertain
whether they are to be regarded as in the main successive or alter-
nating.   Thus different series can be made out of the rich *data*
supplied, or all but the most elementary series denied.   For all
these reasons the writings of the two saints have become a fruitful
source of controversy ; but their very obscurities and inconsistencies
provided a means of escape from the dangerous situation in which
mysticism found itself at the beginning of the seventeenth century.

Certain features in the Carmelite doctrine were clear.   The two
saints recognized meditation as the appropriate spiritual activity
for the beginning of the soul's approach to God.   They recognized
'contemplation' as the atmosphere in which the mature Christian
should normally move ; and they knew besides of 'extraordinary'
gifts and favours—ecstasies, visions and the like—which, for all the
divine and excellent character they attributed to them, no Christian
was entitled to desire or to pursue.   They recognized, further,—
though here we are on delicate ground—that in contemplation God
and the soul each play an active part.   Contemplation is 'infused'
in so far as it comes from God, and the soul is 'passive' ; 'acquired,'
in so far as the soul prepares for it, or achieves it by its own activity.[2]
This is the point of principal difficulty ; it is also the point at which
escape from the *impasse* proved feasible.

For it is not clear at all whether S. Teresa and S. John of the
Cross meant that *all* contemplation was at once 'infused' and
'acquired,' or not.   If they did, there was for them only *one* 'contemplative state,' though it might have many non-essential differentiations.   If they did not, then there were *two* contemplative

---

[1] On the ambiguities of expression in S. Teresa, Pourrat, *SC.*, iii, pp.
210-230 ; A. Poulain, *Des Grâces d'Oraison*[10], pp. 563-569 ; in S. John of the
Cross, Poulain, pp. 208-228 ; cp. also J. Chapman, *ERE.*, ix, pp. 98, 99.
For differences of interpretation, note that Pourrat and Poulain, *locc. citt.*,
treat the prayers of retirement, quietude, sleep of the powers, union, spiritual
marriage, ecstasy and visions as no more than successive stages of 'extraordinary' or 'mystical' prayer, whilst Saudreau (*Life of Union with God*,
pp. 221, 223, 234) draws a strong line of demarcation after 'slumber of the
powers,' treating what precedes as 'ordinary supernatural prayer,' what
follows as 'extraordinary favours, outside the common way, not to be
desired,' etc. (cp. also Id., *Degrees of the Spiritual Life*, ii, p. 266 ; *Mystical
State*, pp. 35-43). As to S. John of the Cross, Pourrat (iii, pp. 294-296) inter-
calates between the active and passive nights a stage of 'active' contemplation (wholly different from 'passive' contemplation (*ib.*, pp. 305-308)) ;
whilst Saudreau ignores (or rather denies) this distinction, recognizing only
a 'progressive advance in contemplation' (pp. 242-244) running parallel
with the two 'nights' (cp. Id., *Mystical State*, pp. 47-62).

[2] Though the phrase 'acquired contemplation' is not employed until
the seventeenth century—Saudreau, *Mystical State*, p. 118 ; cp. Poulain,
Grâces d'Oraison, p. 66.

states—the less divine, or ' active,' or ' acquired ' ; and the more divine, or ' passive,' or ' infused.' What is certain is that mystical writers who wished both to save themselves from condemnation, and mysticism from oblivion, began at once to speak of two such states.[1] Further, they tended to identify ' acquired ' contemplation with that meditation pure and simple which all should practice ; and ' infused ' contemplation with those ' extraordinary ' states which few will ever experience and none must ever desire. By this means, though the toleration of a mystic here and there was still allowed, for the mass of Christians the vision of God—now an ' extraordinary ' state—became something not merely inaccessible but even taboo. They were condemned to an endless round of ' preludes,' ' compositions of place,' ' considerations,' and ' resolutions,' on carefully prepared subjects of meditation ; and must aspire to nothing higher.[2] The mildest name that can be given to this procedure is Dom Chapman's ' reversal of tradition.'[3] It was even more than that ; it was the virtual denial of almost all that is distinctive in the Christian life of prayer.

The Jesuit problem was in some respects simpler. There is no explicit allusion to contemplation in the ' Spiritual Exercises,' though a consistent tradition in the Company, endorsed by no less a theologian than Francis Suarez,[4] has insisted throughout that they imply contemplation as the goal of meditation on every page. When the storm blew over, the Society was able to admit in official terms [5] that ' contemplation ' was not in itself an iniquity. This

---

[1] On this whole development, Saudreau, *Life of Union*, p. 252 ; *Mystical State*, pp. 115-127, 180-198 ; Pourrat, iii, pp. 309-314 (but he attributes the distinction between active and passive contemplation, which are ' totally different from one another ' (p. 310), to S. John of the Cross) ; Chapman, *ERE.*, ix, p. 100 ; and for its modern repercussions, *infra*, pp. 528 ff., additional note N.

[2] Cp. the criticisms of Camus, *supra*, p. 411, n. 1.

[3] *ERE.*, ix, p. 100.

[4] Saudreau, *Life of Union*, pp. 255, 256, 265-273. Chapman (*loc. cit.*) agrees with Saudreau that to Suarez there is a complete continuity between ' supernatural contemplation ' and ' vulgar mental prayer,' yet cites him as an example of the ' reversal of tradition.' The fact is that the tradition was ' reversed ' both in practice and in theory. All writers are agreed that the reversion *in practice* consisted in the confinement of most Christians to discursive meditation, and this would be a legitimate practical deduction from all authorities who made (like Suarez) meditation and contemplation continuous—though not the only legitimate deduction ; for it would be equally allowable (and more sensible) to follow the general modern practice and encourage Christians to look forward to contemplation. As to reversion *in theory*, experts are not yet agreed as to what the traditional theory was. If, as I have followed Saudreau and Bremond in suggesting, it was that meditation and contemplation are continuous, the passages quoted by the former from Suarez make it clear that there was no ' reversal ' in his case. On a theory more akin to that of Poulain, such as Dom Chapman's appears to be, Suarez would of course appear an innovator.

[5] The decree of Aquaviva, 8th May, 1599—' We must not go to extremes, or presume, in opposition to the constant experience of the Fathers, to despise contemplation, or prohibit it to our members ; . . . true and perfect contemplation is stronger and more powerful than any other method of prayer to subdue human pride,' etc.—Bremond, *HLSR.*, viii, p. 256 ; Saudreau, *Life of Union*, p. 259.

made it possible for many of the French Jesuits to rally to the spiritual standard of S. Francis de Sales,[1] and for a strong mystical school to flourish in the French province,[2] at all events until the condemnation of Molinos, and the consequent extinction of Quietism, seemed to herald a new reign of terror. But, as with the Carmelites, the general Jesuit view now treated contemplatives as few and far between. For the world as a whole, meditation was the highest mode of prayer. Here, however, the Jesuits took a step forward. They provided an answer to the obvious question, ' What is the meaning and purpose of this ceaseless round of meditation if it is not to lead us on to the vision of God ? ' In that answer they made explicit what Mercurian had insinuated, when he spoke of ' the method of prayer taught in the " Exercises." '

The facts are well known and undisputed. One of the most famous Jesuit manuals of devotion is the ' Practice of Christian Perfection,' by Alphonso Rodriguez. It was published in 1614, at a time when S. Francis de Sales was on the point of completing his ' Treatise on the Love of God.' The difference between the two books is startling. Rodriguez knows two kinds of prayer. The one—which earlier writers would have called contemplation, and would have regarded as the normal occupation of all earnest-minded Christians—he treats as ' extraordinary and sublime,' and in no way to be sought for. To ' presume ' so much as to attempt it deserves as its punishment even the loss of the grace of ' ordinary prayer.'[3] And ' ordinary prayer,' with which all ought to be content, is explicitly identified with, and confined to, the ' practice of virtues and a lively sorrow for sin.'[4] If we ' meditate ' at all in the course of it, our ' only aim and end ' must be to ' excite the will to acts of reflection and holy resolutions.'[5] So in prayer we ' apply ourselves only to bewail our sins, to mortify our passions, to root out all evil habits '; we ' employ ourselves in considering exactly our defects and weaknesses.'[6] For ' prayer is not the chief

[1] Bremond, HLSR., ii, p. 582.

[2] Bremond, v, *pass.*, on Lallemant (†1635) and his disciples; iii, pp. 275-279, on Guilloré ; cp. also Saudreau, *Life of Union*, pp. 259-261 ; A. Brou, *La Spiritualité de St. Ignace*, pp. 114, 129, 151. A controversy between M. Bremond and Fr. Cavallera, as to which of the two schools of Jesuit thought represents the mind of Loyola most fully, has generated a vivacious interchange of pamphlets. A brief review of the points at issue by J. Chapman, in *The Downside Review*, xlviii (Jan., 1930), pp. 4-18, can be supplemented by reference to HLSR., iii, pp. 29-32, notes (Bremond's interpretation of the ' Spiritual Exercises ') ; *ib.*, pp. 679-683 (hesitations of a Jesuit critic) ; Cavallera, *Révue d'ascetique et de mystique*, iii (1922), pp. 301-311 ; Bremond, *Ascèse ou Prière ?* (originally published in *Révue des Sciences Religieuses*, 1927 ; now republished in *La Philosophie de la Prière*—see esp. pp. 42-46, 84-90, 102-111); Cavallera, *Révue d'ascetique, etc.*, Jan., 1928 ; Bremond, *R. P. Cavallera et la Philosophie de la Prière*, 1928 (republished in *La Philosophie de la Prière*, pp. 125-186).

[3] A. Rodriguez, *Christian Perfection* (E. tr. R. Coyne, Dublin, 1840), v, 4 (i, p. 240) ; v, 5 (p. 248).

[4] *Ib.*, v, 5 (p. 244) ; 20 (pp. 300, 301).

[5] *Ib.*, v, 11 (pp. 262-265).   [6] *Ib.*, v, 5 ; 8 (pp. 248, 254).

end we propose to ourselves in the spiritual life, but only a means and help we make use of to advance ourselves in perfection.'

Judged by this test, the ' higher ' prayer of contemplation is altogether otiose ; ' ordinary ' prayer—as Rodriguez understands it—is the only kind of prayer which is ' profitable ' and ' practical.' [1] So we reach a wholly novel view of the vision of God, which is yet advanced in all seriousness. The Christian must never have more than *one eye* fixed upon God—the other must always be sternly and critically gazing at himself :—

> ' For if we content ourselves with barely attending to the presence of God, and so become negligent in our actions,[2] and commit thereby several faults in them, this attention [to God] would be no profitable devotion, but a very hurtful illusion. Whilst therefore we have one eye engaged in contemplating God, we must engage the other in seeing how to do all things well for His love, so that the consideration of being in His presence may be a means to oblige us to do all our actions better.' [3]

Two interpretations can be put upon these passages. One is that contemplation of any kind—the ' simple loving look at God '— is wholly ineffective and unpractical ; but how then should it be allowable at all to Christians living in a world where much wrong has to be righted, and much evil attacked ? The other is, that while orthodox ' contemplation '—as distinguished from false contemplation, quietism, or illuminism—may have a residual value for the active life, and therefore is not to be condemned outright, its value is negligible as compared with ' ordinary ' prayer. And this ' ordinary ' prayer is nothing but meditation *per se*— the discursive consideration of the example and commands of Jesus, ending with resolutions and self-dedication, but eschewing altogether the ' simple loving look.' No other kind of prayer is of value for the Christian warfare. I do not know that any writer, however fanatically anti-mystical in temperament, ventured to say

---

[1] A. Rodriguez, *Christian Perfection* (E. tr. R. Coyne, Dublin, 1840), v, 14 (i, p. 270).

[2] The special pleading is obvious—why should attention to God in *prayer* produce negligence in *action ?*

[3] Rodriguez, *Christian Perfection*, vi, 5 (i, p. 348). For Lallemant's implicit criticism of Rodriguez see Bremond, *HLSR.*, v, pp. 33-36, 58-60. The metaphor of the two eyes of the soul is an old one. It occurs in the *Theologia Germanica* (c. 1350), in a somewhat equivocal passage, which seems to derive from the invalid doctrine of the double standard in its most extreme form. The one eye is the ' power of seeing into eternity,' the other ' that of seeing into time and the creatures, . . . of giving life and needful things to the body, and ordering and governing it for the best.' ' But these two eyes of the soul of man cannot both perform their work at once . . . therefore whosoever will have the one must let the other go ' (*Theol. Germ.*, 7 ; tr. S. Winkworth, pp. 21, 22). Subject to whatever reservations we may choose to make, this at least implies that contemplation must be wholehearted and self-forgetful—exactly the doctrine which Rodriguez denies. The *Theologia Germanica* was the main source of such mysticism as Luther valued.

as much in black and white. But the tendency is evident. This
is the unexpressed conception of the ' form of prayer ' which many
of the Jesuits regarded as distinctive of their Society. They did
not fail to commend it far and wide to secular Christians ; and hence,
from another point of view, the ' reversal of tradition,' which belittled contemplation and mysticism of every kind, received added
impetus.[1]

(c) ' Practical ' prayer.

For the purpose of any fair estimate of this new attitude of
Christendom, Catholic and Protestant alike, towards prayer, the
two theories, ' prayer is petition ' and ' prayer is self-training in
virtue,' must be taken separately. Intercession and petition, valid,
necessary and excellent though they are if they take their place
within an atmosphere of worship or communion with God, become
frankly pagan or magical if the element of communion is belittled,
ignored or relegated to the background. The criticism has been
admirably put by Canon Lilley in his delightful book on ' Prayer
in Christian Theology.' Commenting on what he calls ' pagan
prayer,' as exemplified by the theology of Cicero, he says :—

> ' [This] prayer is a request to God for those things, and for
> those things only, which man cannot provide and acquire for
> himself . . . a means of persuading the gods to satisfy our
> desires, to provide for our necessities. . . . In such prayer . . .
> it is mere man that prays. Man presents himself before God
> in and from the midst of his natural desires and necessities.'[2]

The implication is obvious. Man's mind is fixed upon some
object of desire which seems beyond his own unaided attainment ;
he therefore seeks either to cajole the good nature of God, or to
bribe His reluctance, into granting the boon demanded. Such
' prayer,' of course, as Canon Lilley at once proceeds to suggest,
is simply and solely the ' development of the *spell*—i.e. of some
formula having magical significance, by which the invisible powers

---

[1] The dominant Jesuit view is fully stated by A. Brou, *La Spiritualité
de St. Ignace*, esp. pp. 107-110, 130-132. Other famous statements to the
same effect :—by Gagliardi : ' Our prayer is not content merely with meditation on the virtues, nor with asking them of God. We make a *use* of this
prayer of ours : treating it as the most infallible instrument both of exercising and acquiring virtue. *Our* prayer is laborious, practical, buying up
virtue. It is Martha rather than Mary—efficacious or productive. It is
not content with thinking about virtues—it sets itself to exercise them :
and by that very exercise puts us in possession of them ' (Bremond, viii,
pp. 262-263 ; cp. Brou, p. 108). By Alvarez de Paz : ' Contemplation is
excellent ; it can be sought even for its own sake. . . . But the wiser
and healthier way of seeking it is to subordinate its excellence to another
[i.e. a moral] excellence ; seeking it not so much for union with God as for
a genuinely efficacious love which will stimulate us to the practice of virtue '
(Bremond, viii, p. 271 ; cp. le Gaudier, *ib.*, p. 272 ; le Fèvre, Brou, p. 108).
[2] A. L. Lilley, *Prayer in Christian Theology*, pp. 5-8. Canon Lilley notes
that Cicero excludes ' virtue ' from the idea of things prayed for ; but this
makes no difference to the argument as a whole.

could be forced to accomplish the results which men desired.'[1] Very different is the doctrine of prayer as consisting primarily in *worship*, which we have had under constant review. Even in relation to human needs,

> ' the uniform Christian tradition, on the other hand, condemns as of the nature of blasphemy every attempt or desire to bend the divine will to our own. . . . It therefore requires as an indispensable antecedent of all acts of prayer an anxious desire to learn with the highest possible degree of certitude what is the will of God.'[2]

But God's will can only be ' learnt ' by those who are in communion and intercourse with Him ; and, therefore,—

> ' the consistently characteristic Christian view has been that mere man cannot pray at all, that no movement of desire on the part of the natural man can constitute real prayer. It is God in us that prays. It is our nature penetrated by the divine Spirit, and assisted by the divine grace, that is alone capable of prayer in the full Christian sense. . . . [And, therefore, prayer] for Christianity is a continuous spiritual state, within which separate acts, indeed, find their place, and to the support and even the gradual formation of which they can contribute. The simplest act of prayer of the Christian type is already an effect of divine inspiration ; and it is not their mere repetition, however frequent, *but their separate and varied representation of a continuously inspired state of soul* that constitutes them authentic instances of prayer.'[3]

This inherent ' paganism ' of prayer without worship—of ' prophetic ' or Protestant prayer in fact—is recognized by Heiler with almost disarming frankness. He insists on the ' continuity ' of prophetic prayer with ' primitive ' prayer,[4] and on the childlike ' naivety ' which they have in common. His tabulations of their respective features present virtually identical schemes.[5] So far, there is nothing to deplore ; affinities between paganism and Christianity may redound to the credit of the former rather than to the disgrace of the latter. But what is disconcerting is to find this champion of ' prophetic ' prayer recognizing as among its predominant characteristics—even in the case of Luther, his hero— elements which can only be described as frankly superstitious and

---

[1] A. L. Lilley, *Prayer in Christian Theology*, pp. 4, 5 ; cp. pp. 117-119, on the survival of this naively superstitious spirit.
[2] *Ib.*, p. 7.
[3] *Ib.*, pp. 8, 9, and cp. the fine peroration, pp. 122-128. Canon Lilley's philosophy of prayer is identical with that of M. Bremond—in each case the doctrine of prayer is seen to be dependent upon that of habitual or sanctifying grace (cp. Bremond, *HLSR.*, vii, pp. 59-62 ; *La Philosophie de la Prière*, pp. 113-116, 359, 360).
[4] *Das Gebet*, p. 408.
[5] *Ib.*, pp. 38-98 (primitive prayer) ; 347-392 (prophetic prayer).

magical. Prophetic prayer 'appeals to God's interest'[1] (—and surely this is near akin to bribery ?—); ' it attempts by every conceivable means and argument to move God to fulfil its own wishes '; it uses threats and objurgations ;[2] it pleads the fact that God has commanded prayer as a ground for securing His complacency; it converts the name of Jesus into something almost indistinguishable from an incantation ;[3] it attempts to weary God into granting its requests, as though He were indeed the unjust judge of the parable.[4] Phrases which Heiler quotes without the slightest disapproval from Luther's prayers and teaching seem to belong to a circle of ideas the very reverse of Christian :—

> ' Grant me my prayer. Thou must grant it '; ' I am an unworthy sinner, but I *must* have what I want.'   ' Do not provoke us to extremes ; if Thou move us to anger so that we withhold our reverence and tithes, what will become of Thee ? ' ' We must *compel* God to come ; we must *force* Him to grant our wishes with stern and hostile siege ' ; ' A time comes when God cannot endure our cries any longer and answers, " So be it ; have it as ye will." '[5]

When every allowance has been made, every mitigation accepted, every exaggeration condoned, must not these utterances still be adjudged pagan to the core ?

If then the idea of prayer as primarily *petition* comes into competition with that which treats it primarily as communion with God through *worship*, there is a clear issue between paganism and Christianity. If, on the contrary, the primacy of worship or contemplation is challenged (as in sixteenth and seventeenth century Roman Catholicism) by the conception of prayer as, in essence, *meditation with a view to progress in virtue*, the issue is one between Christian prayer and no prayer at all. Here M. Bremond has said all that need be said.   Meditation, with its discursive acts of the reason, and its resolutions—

> ' Is it prayer at all, in the normal sense of the word ?   I realize, of course, that at the beginning and during the course of this series of operations, the divine help is invoked.   That indeed is prayer—but concomitant, or even adventitious, alone : something quite distinct from the reasoning and the resolutions which it ushers in.   And in *them*, apart from these few and sparse interruptions . . . we are immersed in naturalism up to the neck. . . . Nor do these operations deserve all the praise that has been showered upon them as ' practical ' and ' efficacious.'   They are *directed towards* the practical life, I admit, but they are not the practical life itself.   You may learn

---

[1] *Das Gebet*, p. 373 and for primitive prayer, pp. 82, 83.
[2] *Ib.*, pp. 373, 374 ; primitive prayer, pp. 83-85.
[3] *Ib.*, pp. 375, 376.   [4] *Ib.*, pp. 376-378 ; primitive prayer, p. 89.
[5] *Ib.*, pp. 377, 378.

Baedeker by heart, you may book your cabin on the next boat, register your luggage, even get halfway up the gang-plank ; but in no language in the world does that make you a traveller. Why all these complications—preludes, application of faculties, discernment of spirits and the rest—if you are merely going to meditate on the excellence of zeal, and train yourself for the practice of your apostolate ? Have done with these whimsical exercises. Rise from your knees. Get off at once to your desk and write your sermon, or to the hospital and care for your patients.' [1]

It is scarcely necessary to emphasize the point. If meditation without contemplation—practical self-exhortation to activity—is the essence of prayer, why call it prayer at all? Sensitive and æsthetic natures will find it helpful, no doubt, to employ such practices to equip them for the distasteful life of muscular Christianity. But the more they become muscular Christians the more they will learn to despise and to dispense with reveries of this kind. Those of us, on the other hand, who pride ourselves on our muscular Christianity already (as who does not ?) will never feel the need of such exercises at all. We shall go about our daily tasks without them, as enthusiastically as if the name of prayer had never been mentioned in our ears. That prayer will only rise truly from a life given to the service of God is universally agreed ; that it must issue, if it is true prayer, in enhanced capacity for service is self-evident. But call it a mere auxiliary to activity, and you have made it an eccentricity with which, if you are logical, you must allow the majority of Christians to dispense altogether. Its character has been hopelessly compromised. It has degenerated into an optional epiphenomenon of the moral life, a pietistic form of self-suggestion proper only for sick souls.

II. 'WORSHIP' AND 'SERVICE.'

Post-Reformation developments of thought, both in Protestant and in Catholic circles, combined, therefore, to challenge the traditional primacy of the doctrine of the vision of God. By evacuating prayer of all but its 'practical' aspect, by denying (in effect) that communion with God through worship can be an end in itself for human life, they voiced in the most pointed manner a criticism—or, rather, two alternative criticisms—of which many Christians catch an echo in the secrecy of their own reflections. (i) Against that traditional development of thought which, from New Testament or even from pre-Christian times, has taught that the goal of human life is to see God, it is urged, in the first place, that such an ideal is essentially and pre-eminently selfish, in that it proposes a course of life devoted solely to the attainment of personal satisfaction. But (ii) even if it could be shown that the

[1] Bremond, *HLSR.*, viii, pp. 275, 276.

ideal of the vision of God is no more selfish than one of explicit altruism, it might yet be said that on utilitarian grounds alone the latter is the higher of the two. The doctrine of the vision of God makes worship the primary human activity ; and as compared with the ideal of service worship has all the appearance of a barren, limited and anti-social aspiration. If, then, we are to estimate the value of that vast concentration of Christian thought upon worship to which the preceding chapters bear witness, we must be prepared to explore these criticisms, each in its turn, and to ask how far they can be met satisfactorily.

(a) *Is the quest for the vision of God a selfish ideal?*

It would be foolish to deny that the desire to see God in pre-Christian religious thought [1] appealed often enough to motives rightly deserving the adjectives ' selfish ' or ' interested.' In the main it seems to have been animated by a passion for a personal experience—for the attaining of a particular state of consciousness, or indeed, in some cases, of unconsciousness. The special character-istics of this state, as conceived or experienced by different persons or groups, do not affect the question of principle—whether God was ' seen ' in ecstasy, or in dreams, or in a calm untroubled communion with nature, matters nothing. At heart, in all these aspirations, the believer was in pursuit of something *for himself*—regardless, it may almost be said, of the interests of any other, whether God or his neighbour.

Large parts of Christendom, again, in every generation have adopted this same ideal, and can without hesitation be accused of selfishness for that reason. But here the accusation holds at best only within certain limits. The Christian seeker after God was rarely content with solitary enjoyment of the vision. Even the Rabbis, as we have seen, insisted that its attainment is in truth a corporate experience. To S. Paul and S. John it could have no other context than that of the Church—now militant, but in eternity triumphant. Clement's gnostic—a person at first sight wholly self-contained—longs for a city like Plato's ' set up as a pattern in heaven '—an ' ordered multitude ' of the blessed ; to Augustine the vision of God in the city of God was an ideal from which the one member could no more be subtracted than the other.

Christian art and Christian literature tell the same story. In the last quarter of the eighth century an obscure Asturian recluse, Beatus, abbot of Liébana,[2] composed a commentary on the ' Apoca-lypse ' which achieved wide popularity, and was circulated in manu-scripts adorned by miniatures copied from Oriental sources.

---

[1] *Supra*, pp. 54, 104, 110.

[2] This is the same Beatus, and the same Commentary, as transmitted the fragments of Tyconius and what survives of his doctrine of the two cities (*supra*, p. 331). It would be interesting to know whether it was the subject-matter, or the illustrations, of the manuscripts which most of all gave them this double importance for history.

M. Émile Mâle has traced out the epoch-making influence of this forgotten book.[1] The manuscripts travelled into northern Europe by the great pilgrim roads which led to and from St. James of Compostela ; one of them found a home at Moissac, a Cluniac priory not far north of Toulouse. There for the first time (as its seems) the beatific vision of Christ in glory, surrounded by the four beasts and the four and twenty elders, was translated from a coloured miniature to the stone tympanum of a Romance church. Thence also the craftsmen of Moissac and their copyists spread the theme far and wide—back southward to Santiago's Porch of Glory itself ; northwards to Chartres, Le Mans, and Cluny, and from Chartres south again to St. Trophime at Arles. Elsewhere the same school of artists varied the picture. Sometimes it becomes an Ascension ; sometimes a Last Supper or a Pentecost ; sometimes a Day of Judgment—the theme which was to prevail in the thirteenth and following centuries. But in every one of these compositions it is the artist's joy to introduce more and more figures into his scene— angels, apostles, the Blessed Virgin, saints and martyrs, the risen dead (some of them rapt in contemplation from the moment of leaving the tomb), the nations of the world—as in the vast tympanum of Vézelay—real and fabulous alike,—as though to emphasize in the enduring material of stone this primary Christian conviction, that the vision of God is not for the isolated believer, but for the believer in communion with the whole vast animate universe and all its denizens.

Christian poetry tells the same tale. No account of the vision of God and its influence upon the history of Christian ideals could be complete without some allusion to the ' Divina Commedia.' But the reference is specially appropriate at this point. In the final cantos of the ' Purgatorio ' the animated crowds which hitherto have marked the poet's journey have gradually been withdrawn, and on the threshold of the ' Paradiso ' he stands alone with Beatrice in the terrestrial Paradise. As they rise towards the empyrean, heaven grows radiant around them with the spirits of the blest—the myriad splendours,[2] living and victorious ; the ' jewels dear and fair '[3] of the celestial court. The final vision portrays the great Rose of God and His innumerable saints, word-painted as no other poet has ever found it possible to depict them :—

> ' Thus in the form of a white rose revealed itself to me that
> saintly host, which Christ espoused in His own blood. There
> with that other host—the angels—which as it soars, contem-

---

[1] E. Mâle, *L'art religieux du xii⁰ siècle en France, pass. ; L'art religieux du xiii⁰ siècle*, p. 362 ; *ib.*, pp. 369-393, later developments. The Ascension is at Toulouse, Cahors, and Angoulême ; the Last Supper at St. Bénigne, and St. Gilles ; the Pentecost at Vézelay ; the Judgment at Beaulieu, St. Denis, and Autun.

[2] *Paradiso*, v, 104, 105 ; *ib.*, x, 64-66.

[3] *Ib.*, x, 71—of the circle of Doctors in the Sun. Similarly cantos xv, xviii—the Cross of warrior-saints ; xviii, 70 ff. ; xix—the Alphabet and Eagle of just men in Jupiter ; xxii—the contemplatives in the seventh heaven.

plates and chants the glory of Him Who fills it with love, and
the goodness which made it so great—like as a swarm of bees,
which one while settles within the flowers and anon returns
to th. hive where its work is stored in sweetness—now lighted
down upon the great flower with its coronal of many petals ;
now again soared aloft to the place where its love doth for ever
dwell.   And all their faces were of living flame, and of gold
their wings ; and for the rest they were all white beyond
the whiteness of snow. . . . This realm of security and joy,
peopled by folk alike of old time and of new, centred its looks
and its love upon one mark alone. O threefold light, whose
bright radiance, shed in a single beam upon their eyes, doth so
content them, look hither down upon our storm-tossed lives.' [1]

The vision then is to be a corporate one ; and this makes the
quest for it, in any case, something less than wholly selfish. But this
is only half the truth.   The greatest saints have always recognized
that to make enjoyment, even though it be a communal enjoyment,
the goal of life, is to import a motive less than the purest into ethics.
The emphatic protests against ' panhedonism ' in any one of its
different forms, which we have noticed at different stages,[2] are
evidence that Christianity was alive to the danger ; and that however much lesser minds succumbed to it, the greatest figures in
the history of the Church knew that it represented something in
essence at once immoral and un-Christian.

It has recently been suggested [3] that the protests grew in vigour
and intensity with the passage of the centuries; that Cardinal de
Bérulle, for example, the founder of the French Oratorians, realized
the danger more fully than S. Augustine.   It would require a far
wider survey of the available evidence than any we have made
before we could either endorse or rebut this suggestion.   What,
however, is beyond all question is that no century went by without
a few prophetic voices to declare the solid truth.   S. Paul's great
insistence, that the *disposition* appropriate to one who sees God is
of greater importance, here on earth, than the vision itself, is never
without an echo for long.   Divine favours, though they cannot be
treasured too highly if they come unasked, are not to be sought for
themselves.   When they come, they are to be tested lest they
should prove to be sentimental and subjective illusions ;   when
they do not come, and the heart remains dry and the spirit sad,
it must not be concluded either that God is displeased, or that the
yearning soul has given Him cause for displeasure.

The doctrine that the ' end of man is the vision of God,' as a
practical maxim for life, implies that the Christian should set himself first of all to focus his thought upon God in the spirit of worship.

---

[1] *Paradiso*, xxxi, 1-30.   [2] *Supra*, pp. 104, 202 f., 271 f., 352, etc.
[3] Bremond, *HLSR.*, iii, pp. 23-33, with footnotes—a most illuminating
passage.   On Bérulle, whose importance in this respect M. Bremond marks
by crediting him with a ' Copernican revolution ' to theocentrism, *ib.*, pp.
3-279.

It implies this of necessity, and of necessity it implies nothing more —nothing whatever as to the achieving of pleasures, rapture, exaltation in the act of worship. The only achievement man has the right to hope for is that of greater Christian saintliness—greater zeal for service—coming from this direction of the heart and mind to God. It can hardly be denied that in so far as unselfishness is possible in this life at all (to anticipate for a moment another question), this is an unselfish ideal. To look towards God, and from that 'look' to acquire insight both into the follies of one's own heart and the needs of one's neighbours, with power to correct the one no less than to serve the other—this is something very remote from any quest for 'religious experience' for its own sake. Yet this, and nothing else, is what the vision of God has meant in the fully developed thought of historic Christianity.

(b) Is 'worship' a higher ideal than 'service'?

The second question prompted by this review of Christian thought has many aspects. Granted that 'worship' is unselfish, it may be said, surely 'service' may be unselfish too?[1] And further, a comparison of worship and service, viewed in relation to the world's deepest needs, both spiritual and temporal, suggests that service—the unremitting service of God and man—is the more urgently needed of the two. The protagonist of the 'active' as against the 'contemplative' life is often prepared to make very large concessions. He will admit that in some mysterious way God —though He *needs* neither worship nor service—can and does take pleasure in both when they are freely given. He will admit, on occasion, that intercession for others is in itself a genuine form of service, and *where no other service can be rendered them* fulfils the Christian law of love in their regard. He frankly and fully believes (and appeals for support to the most modern developments of psychology) that for many the exercise of worship is a stimulus to better service, so that the man who prays is normally more alert to help his fellows, and to take the initiative against evil in the world, than he who does not. Thus he can admit a 'mixed' life, like that of S. Gregory, in which worship and service—contemplation and activity—are joined in due proportions. By these concessions many Christians of goodwill feel that they have done all that can be demanded of them, or of anyone, to make room for the doctrine of the vision of God, among the multiple calls and responsibilities which their neighbours' welfare lays upon them.

On the other side the advocates of contemplation make overtures of equal importance. They insist, as a matter of sound theology, that the beatific vision implies the seeing of all things in

---

[1] To put the argument at its highest we must concentrate upon *unselfconscious* service—e.g. the spontaneous benevolence of a naturally altruistic person; for the egocentrism of self-conscious service has been considered previously (*supra*, pp. 132-135). On the equation 'self-centredness = selfishness,' *infra*, p. 554, additional note T.

God--as with the eyes of God—*sub specie æternitatis*. So they have no difficulty in denying outright that any worship can be of value unless it rises in a heart which at least desires the well-being of God's whole creation, and issues in the resolution to promote that well-being when and as opportunity allows. In practice, therefore, no less than their interlocutors, they recognize that every life must be a ' mixed ' life. They may be prepared, even, to surrender the idea of the ' primacy ' of worship, as it has been traditionally held ; and content themselves with a scheme in which worship and service stand side by side as equal and co-ordinate goals. So that worship be not put definitely in a lower grade, they will not claim for it the first place unequivocally. Hereby they too hold that they have done their share in bringing the rival ideals to terms.

But the two ideals are not even so in accord, nor will the utmost goodwill on either side avail to reconcile them. One point of view or the other must in the end prevail. The least that the champion of contemplation demands is that worship shall be recognized as one of two co-ordinate ends which it is man's duty and privilege to pursue—as a *part* of his true end, and not merely a means thereto. But the most that the champion of action dare allow is that worship is a means, and only a means, to better service. He will not give it independent value. He claims that the true Christian must set before himself as the goal of his efforts the realization of the kingdom of God or the brotherhood of man ; must form his thought and centre his activity upon these ideals. Prayer and meditation, if they are to have a place in life at all, must make no such claim as will seriously detract from the time available for service. Every hour they monopolize must show fruit in enhanced efficiency if it is to be accounted anything but wasted. Virile, philanthropic, restless in his zeal to do good, the humanitarian is jealous of every moment given to prayer ; he tolerates it simply as a tonic or stimulant to fit him for new ventures of heroic service. That in its own nature worship is a service no less heroic than any other, is a sentiment from which his whole being recoils.

If this conclusion of the apostles of energy is accepted, the whole development of Christian thought about the vision of God must be adjudged a wasteful, if not a tragic, mistake. Selfish the ideal of seeing God may not be ; erroneous it is. It mistakes the means for the end, and in so doing veils the true end from men's eyes. It diverts them from the king's highway of loving energy into a maze of contemplative prayer wholly remote from God's purposes. Unless I am wholly at fault, that is how robust commonsense, even among Christians, has always regarded, and to-day more than ever regards, those who insist that worship or contemplation has the primary place in the ideal life. Its test is wholly pragmatic. If it uplifts, then, but only then, is worship commendable ; if it strengthens and purifies, so far, but only so far, has it a place. But it has no value for its own sake, or apart from these possible influences which it may exert. And in any case, a little of it goes a long way; it must never be allowed to oust positive benevolence from its position as the Christian's first, final, and only genuine duty.

Is it possible, then, to defend the traditional doctrine any longer? We may leave on one side the scholastic arguments with which Aristotle, for example, outside the Christian Church, and S. Thomas within it, have maintained the thesis that contemplation is man's true end.[1] A day may come when abstract reasoning is once more allowed its full weight, and then the Stagyrite and the Angel of the Schools will receive their due reward. For the present the question must be approached from a different angle. The Christian tradition of the vision of God seems, even so, to have a message for the restless energizers of the modern world, with their problems, programmes, and calls to discipleship. The concept of service embraces two very different ideas. Only one of these is Christian—indeed, only one of them realizes the ideal of service at all; for service of the other kind is self-destructive and nugatory. For the purposes of the present discussion, they may be called the *service of humility*, and the *service of patronage*. It should not be difficult to see that only the former of these two has real worth. Once this is recognized, it becomes not unreasonable to suggest that worship alone guarantees to service that quality of humility without which it is no service at all; and therefore that worship may claim and must be allowed a substantive position in the Christian ideal once more. So far from being a selfish goal, worship is the only way to unselfishness which the Christian has at his command.

To serve humanity in the spirit of patronage—as a genius condescending to stupidity, as an expert coming to the help of the inefficient, as a millionaire lavishing gifts upon the destitute—is there anything in the world which breeds more dissension, discontent, just resentment and open revolt than this? The question has only to be asked to be answered; every generation has writhed under the well-meant patronage of Ladies Bountiful. Yet apart from an atmosphere of worship, every act of service avails only to inflate the agent's sense of patronage. He is the doctor, humanity is his patient: he is the Samaritan, his neighbour the crippled wayfarer: he is the instructor, others are merely his pupils. Gratitude (if they show gratitude) only confirms his conviction of his own importance; resentment (if they resent his services) only ministers to the glow of self-esteem with which he comforts himself in secret. The phenomenon has been the commonplace of satirists since the world began. Not only so—we recognize in it as well a principal cause of the divisions of Christendom, of the stultifying of effort, of the disillusionment of enthusiasts. The experts quarrel over rival panaceas; the hierophants jostle each other at the altar; and the more there is of such 'service,' the less the cause of humanity is in truth served at all.

---

[1] *Supra*, p. 382 (S. Thomas); *infra*, pp. 475 f. (Aristotle).

A man must be blind not to recognize something of himself in this picture ; he must be no less callous if he fails to long for the spirit of humility. But humility cannot be acquired by taking thought for oneself ; that way, as S. Paul's condemnation of the law has once for all made clear, lie only the alternatives of pride and despair. The way of worship is the only way left open. Even worship is not altogether exempt from the dangers of pride and despair. But in so far as contemplation, or worship, is to be distinguished from service—and the distinction is one which the world has agreed to make—it is surely true to say that contemplation ministers to humility just as service ministers to patronage.[1] The man who ' serves '—who plans, and organizes, and issues instructions, advice or exhortations—is doing so from the vantage ground of independence. He thinks of himself as a free agent, dowered with talents to be employed for the benefit of others. In worship, on the contrary, the worshipper puts himself in an attitude of dependence. In looking towards God, who is All in All, he sees himself to be nothing ; in worshipping his Redeemer, he knows himself incapable of redeeming even the least of God's creatures. The most he can hope for is that God will deign to use him for the forwarding of His high designs. Worship tells us much good of God, but little good of ourselves, except that we are the work of God's hands. For that we may praise Him, but it leaves us nothing upon which to pride ourselves.

The contrast must not be pressed too far. There are dilettantes of worship who rise from their knees with a self-complacency rivalling the worst conceits of men of action. On the other hand, there are those who—though they make little if any use of the time-honoured forms of worship—yet serve their fellows with a humility which puts the ordinary Christian to shame. The former need not disturb us. They are at best beginners in the art of worship. It is more than likely that their aim is not to look towards God, but to secure private and personal joys in religion. The latter, again, though they set an example which we may despair ever to follow

---

[1] M. Bremond puts this far better than I can (*Philosophie de la Prière*, pp. 50-54). As between ' service ' (' ascèse ') and ' worship,' he says, ' la première se prodigue, la seconde reçoit ; l'une se porte de l'avant, s'affirme, l'autre voudrait s'effacer, s'éteindre. L'une et l'autre comptent sur le concours divin . . . mais la première, sûre que ne lui manquera pas ce concours indispensable, que d'ailleurs elle a demandé, se gouverne comme si elle n'avait plus à compter que sur elle-même. . . . Dans la première, Dieu paraît être comme l'instrument de notre énergie. Dans la seconde, toute notre énergie tend à devenir l'instrument de Dieu. La première, de toute la force dont elle dispose, dit "Volo," elle semble dire à Dieu, "Laissez-moi faire"; la seconde lui dit: "Faites " . . . Dans les activités d'ascèse se déploie une energie toujours consciente, critique, aux aguets, craignant toujours ou de mollir ou de s'appliquer où il ne faut pas ; se surveillant, et s'examinant sans relâche, se demandant des comptes à chaque pas ; tandis que les activités de prière s'oublient, s'abandonnent les yeux fermés à la grâce qui les porte, à la présence qui se donne, à l'union qui se consomme.' Cp. *ib.*, pp. 64, 65, and the whole passage ; and Lallemant, as quoted in *HLSR.*, v, pp. 26-36. Similarly, G. R. Owst, *Preaching in Mediæval England*, pp. 114 ff., on Richard Rolle.

worthily, themselves go far to establish the principle in view. Their unselfish service is in itself proof that—whether by accident or natural gift—they are already in the attitude of worship towards their ideal. The ideal is their All, and they—their needs, their sufferings, their lives—are nothing in comparison with it. They are ready to sacrifice all that they have in its service ; and the spirit of worship is betrayed in the very fact that they would be the last to claim that they had sacrificed anything at all, or to accept the title of heroes. They are beyond the criticism of Christian people ; we can only recognize in them the very type of Christian service itself, and thank God for their example.

But with these exceptions the principle stands true. The danger of 'service,' as an ideal, is that it fosters the spirit of patronage : the glory of worship is to elicit the grace of humility. Without humility there can be no service worth the name ; patronizing service is self-destructive—it may be the greatest of all disservices. Hence to serve his fellows *at all*—to avoid doing them harm greater even than the good he proposed to confer on them—a man must find a place for worship in his life. The truth is not that worship (as the advocate of action allowed us to assert) will help him to serve *better*. The alternative lies not between service of a better and a worse kind ; it lies between service and no service at all. If we would attempt to do good with any sure hope that it will prove good and not evil, we must act in the spirit of humility ; and worship alone can make us humble. There is no other course.

This is no more than to carry to its conclusion what we have noticed already on more than one occasion, that a system of thought which is primarily moralistic, in so far as it sets before men a rule of conduct by which it is their first duty to measure themselves, is in essence egocentric. It is only one of the many forms which selfishness can take, even though its rule appear superficially altruistic. It is not without surprise that one finds Heiler, in the book to which reference has already been made, endorsing this judgment in respect of that 'prophetic' religion of which Luther is the supreme exponent, without the slightest recognition of its seriousness. The adjectives which he employs to illustrate the superiority of 'evangelic' or 'prophetic' religion over its rival, ring out, one after another, with a sound as ominous as it is triumphant. The 'prophetic' religion, Heiler says, is 'self-assertive' and 'voluntaristic.'[1] It enshrines 'an irresistible will to live, an uncontrollable impulse towards the expression, mastery and exaltation of the sense of living.'[2] It 'believes in life, affirms life, and throws itself with joy and resolution into the arms of life.'[3] 'One of the weightiest aspirations of "prophetic" personalities is the vindication of their personal worth.'[4] Most emphatic and illuminating is the following

---

[1] F. Heiler, *Das Gebet*, p. 248 ; cp. p. 283.
[2] *Ib.*, p. 255.   [3] *Ib.*, p. 257.
[4] *Ib.*, p. 361—' Die Behauptung des eigenen Wertes ist der wichtigsten Bitten der prophetischen Persönlichkeiten ' ; cp. *ib.*, p. 376—' Among the

contrast: 'The exclusive object to which "mystical" prayer is directed is God, the one Reality, the highest value ; the object to which "prophetic" prayer is directed is man's own joy and sorrow, his troubles and fears, his plans and confidences.'[1]

I hope I have not misrepresented by these extracts one who has few equals in the sphere of historical theology which he has made his own. But it is hard to resist the conclusion that the 'prophetic' prayer commended in this last contrast is frankly pagan and selfish ; whilst the adjectives and phrases descriptive of prophetic religion quoted in the lines immediately preceding seem to be more applicable to the ethics of Nietzsche than to those of Luther, and certainly to have little if anything in common with the self-denying, self-forgetful genius of Christianity.

But if Heiler is right, and Protestantism—with its rejection of mystical prayer—is as self-assertive as he suggests, the fact is further evidence of our general contention. Where God ceases to be 'the exclusive object towards which prayer is directed,' life and thought at once become patronizing ; it matters little that their patronage expresses itself in the form of what the world calls benevolence. The ultimate purpose which the agent has in view is not the well-being of others, but the 'vindication of his own personal worth.'

means [employed in 'prophetic' prayer] to make God listen, is to appeal to one's own piety and righteousness ' (' die Berufung auf die eigene Frömmigkeit und Gerechtigkeit ') ; so Luther, ' Thou knowest that I have diligently taught Thy word ' (*ib.*,—the same phenomenon in primitive prayer, *ib.*, p. 85).

[1] F. Heiler, *Das Gebet*, p. 359.—It is interesting to compare with this the almost identical phrases in which a modern Roman Catholic commends the 'practical' prayer of the Jesuits. Unlike Heiler, he associates Judaism with 'worship' rather than with 'practice'; apart from this difference his 'Jesuit' prayer is identical with the 'prophetic.' F. Vincent, *S. François de Sales, directeur d'âmes* (1923), p. 113—A contrast is drawn between 'Jesuit prayer' and the older tradition (which is called 'Benedictine'—p. 117) ; the latter is treated as being in essence purely un-Christian. Thus ' if God appears to us, as He did to the Jews, in all His disconcerting majesty, we shall be compelled to abase ourselves before Him, and therefore to subordinate all our other religious duties to that of worship. If we conceive of God after the Jewish pattern we shall tend to forget ourselves, to lose sight of ourselves, to perceive no one except the all-powerful King. . . . But if God is regarded as a father, an indulgent teacher, anxious for the advancement of our souls, we shall be led infallibly *to fix in ourselves the centre of our preoccupations.*' *Ib.*, p. 102—This is the real service which the Jesuits have done to humanity. Till they appeared ' the spirit of worship in the Church, going back behind the gospel to the Mosaic law, and resting upon an awed and frightened idea of the Deity, was dominant.' But the Jesuits, ' with a higher conception of religion,' ' tore Christianity from its age-long habits,' and ' *identified it with moral progress.*' Their ' dominant and invariable preoccupation has been to honour God first by self-culture, then by the cultivation of the service of others.' *Ib.*, p. 117—'The Benedictine's gaze is fixed primarily upon God ; that of the Salesian ' (taken as a type of the Jesuit) ' is above all upon himself.' *Ib.*, p. 128—' Religion has [rightly] become identified with self-culture,' etc. It ought to be added that there is much of value in M. Vincent's book, and that its main purpose (though confused in the working out) is simply to denounce ceremonial formalism unaccompanied by moral effort ; but it has given M. Bremond an opportunity for lively and not unjustified comment (cp. Bremond, *HLSR.*, vii, pp. 27-39, with notes ; *Philosophie de la Prière*, pp. 178-186).

This gives us material for a conclusion. ' Your ideal of service,'—
so we may imagine traditional Christianity answering robust commonsense—' necessarily leads up to the ideal of worship as its consummation. Without the latter you cannot achieve the former ;
and, if worship languishes, service will once more degenerate into
mere self-assertion. The two are, at least, co-ordinate parts of
the same ideal whole.'

It is not likely that such an apologia would satisfy the heroes
of Christian saintliness whose ideals have been considered in preceding chapters. With a faith which the modern world finds it
hard to share they started from the conviction that the life of
heaven would be more akin to adoration than to labour. ' Ubi
non prævenit rem desiderium ' is their definition of heaven ; and
where desire and achievement are simultaneous, there is no longer
any place for effort, as we understand it. But there is still, and
always, a place for contemplation. Service here on earth is no more
than a preparation for the contemplation of heaven, and in heaven
contemplation is the only service required of the redeemed. In
earthly worship man does not merely secure for service that which
alone can make it serviceable ; he anticipates the essential and
all-engrossing activity of eternal life.

Something after the fashion of the last paragraph would run the
full Christian defence of the primacy of worship. But for the
present it is enough, perhaps, to have pressed a less ambitious
argument, urging that without the spirit of worship no service
can be worth the name. Disinterested service is the only service
that is serviceable ; and disinterestedness comes by the life of worship alone. But at once a further criticism presents itself. Christianity has taken the way of the Cross as its example ; it has made
disinterestedness the test of all ideals. By that test worship is
vindicated as being indeed an integral part of the full Christian
life, and the vision of God may still be proclaimed as the goal.
But is the test a fair one—is it, indeed, a test that has any meaning
at all ? The criticism strikes at the very heart of the gospel of
self-sacrifice : but it cannot on that account be disallowed. It
claims that all a man's actions are dominated by self-interest, and
that in consequence the whole quest for disinterestedness, for the
' good will,' for ' Pure Love,' is a meaningless chimera. Outside
organized Christianity the controversy has centred round the ethical
idealism of Immanuel Kant ; within the Church it provided a
dramatic setting for the classical encounter between Bossuet and
Fénelon.

III. DISINTERESTEDNESS AND PURE LOVE.

(a) Bossuet and Fénelon.

The assumption that man is wholly the creature of his impulses,
and that, in consequence, any attempt to escape from the bonds of

self-interest is to strive after the impossible, is one which may fairly be described as ' naturalistic.' By such an assumption the Christian ideal of unselfishness is directly challenged ; it can no longer have any relevance to life. It is not, indeed, suggested that rules of conduct can no longer be propounded ; but they will have no effect unless they appeal directly to self-interest. Purity of motive, unselfishness, duty for duty's sake—these become now the most meaningless of paradoxes ; what could it mean to say to a man that disinterestedness is in his own best interest ?

Two conclusions follow from such a position. The first is, that we cannot commend worship any longer by alleging that it fosters unselfishness ; no man can ever worship except to achieve some curious self-satisfaction of his own. The second conclusion takes up ground we have already reviewed. Worship is as selfish as any other form of activity, but it is the least useful of all activities to society as a whole. Banish it, then, from the programme of life. Urge men to obey God (if you still believe in God), but certainly to serve their neighbours [1]—for that is the obvious and only form of social life ; and promise them gratification here or hereafter (if you and they still believe in a hereafter) as a reward for their service—for so and so only will you induce them to adopt it as their standard of behaviour. Above all, if you are honest, do not perplex them by commending unselfishness; it will only result in their wasting time, temper and effort in the attempt to attain a purity of motive which is for ever unattainable.

Here is a clear issue, clearly recognized by Christians of many schools of thought, but most of all by the Christian mystics. They have protested that disinterestedness is possible to man,[2] and

---

[1] On the assumption, that is, that you find your own curious self-satisfaction (as Bentham did) in contemplating and promoting the mutual exchange of services by members of society. This, however, is an assumption made by all except the most cynical supporters of naturalism. Holding, for example, the view that one's own pleasure is the only end, they find their own pleasure in indicating to others how *they* too may obtain the maximum of pleasure.

[2] Not indeed in this life a continuous *state* of disinterestedness—that is the doctrine of the One Act (cp. von Hügel, *Mystical Element of Religion*, ii, pp. 165-169 ; *ERE.*, x, pp. 532-538 ; H. Bremond, *Bossuet, Maître d'oraison*, pp. xxiv ff.), with its concomitants of Christian sinlessness and the permanence of the contemplative state even in sleep (cp. the alleged errors of Molinos, nos. 25, 55, 57, 61, 62 (D.-B., nos. 1245, 1275, 1277, 1281, 1282)). Even in the first edition of the *Maxims of the Saints* Fénelon expressly repudiated this heresy (see e.g. artt. V *faux* (' la sainte indifference est une suspension absoluë de volonté ') ; VII *faux* (' ne connoissent plus aucun desir même désintéressé ') ; XXV *faux* (' la contemplation pure et directe est absolument perpetuelle ')— ed. Cherel (Paris, 1911), pp. 166, 174, 253. In the *Exposition des (cinq) divers amours* (Cherel, pp. 118-130) he scarcely ever uses the word ' state' at all, and never of the fifth degree of pure or disinterested love. In the MS. corrections for the second edition he uses the word ' state ' less charily, but makes it clear that he means by it a condition habitual, but by no means continuous. Thus in the fifth ' state,' acts of pure love are merely ' more frequent and more intense ' than in the fourth state (Cherel, p. 124) ; and the words

indeed is the essential condition which alone gives any action eternal
worth. The protest is not the easiest in the world to make good.
One of its greatest difficulties has always been presented by that
promise of reward in heaven which (as we saw at an earlier stage)
occupies so large a place in New Testament thought. Not that the
Church, nor indeed moralists as a whole, deny the truth that virtue
will be rewarded and sin punished; not even that they forbid the
truth to be proclaimed. The truth is, indeed, indispensable if God's
justice is in any sense to be recognized; [1] and its proclamation may
from time to time be necessary to attract the attention of the care-
less-minded to the sovereign demands of morality.[2] The problem
arises when the hope of heaven or the fear of hell are ' proposed ' or
treated, as according to the Council of Trent [3] they legitimately
may be, as motives of right conduct. At once the idealist rises
in revolt. The essence of right action, he tells us, is that it should
not be performed out of regard for the agent's own interests, even
the highest ;—action so animated is indistinguishable from the
purest selfishness.

For various reasons the protest attained its greatest volume in
the seventeenth century, and among those who, because of the allied
tenets of their system, came to be called Quietists. But its history
reaches far back into the earlier ages of the Christian Church. Thus
among the alleged errors of Eckhardt condemned by Pope John
XXII was the proposition, ' God is honoured [only] among those
who aim neither at property, nor honour, nor expediency, nor
inner devotion, nor sanctity, nor reward, nor the kingdom of
heaven, but have abjured them all.' [4] Certainly Eckhardt himself,
commenting on the text, ' Blessed are the poor in spirit,' had said :
' A man shall become as truly poor and as free from his creature
will as he was when he was born. And I say to you by the eternal
truth that as long as ye desire to fulfil the will of God, and have
any desire after eternity and God, so long are ye not truly poor.

' d'ordinaire ' are continually inserted, with other modifications, not only in
the *Exposition* but throughout the book. Specially illuminating are the
corrections indicated on pp. 124-128, 130, 135, 152-159, of Cherel's edition,
though it is unfortunate that the editor's manner of noting them does not
make comparison as easy as could be wished.

[1] Or the moral law vindicated. So, of course, Kant ; see particularly the
definition of virtue as ' worthiness to be happy ' in *Critique of Practical
Reason*, I, ii, 2, and the whole discussion (T. K. Abbott, *Kant's Theory of
Ethics*, pp. 206, 221, 227, etc.) ; cp. C. C. J. Webb, *Kant's Philosophy of
Religion*, pp. 63-67. Interesting modern discussions of the whole question
will be found in F. von Hügel, *Mystical Element of Religion*, ii, pp. 152-181 ;
G. F. Barbour, *Philosophical Study of Christian Ethics*, pp. 208-225 ; F. A. M.
Spencer, *Theory of Christ's Ethics*, pp. 179-186.

[2] Cp. my *Ignorance, Faith and Conformity*, pp. 36, 37.

[3] Sess. vi, decretum de justif. 11 (fin.), 16—' bene operantibus . . .
proponenda vita æterna . . . tamquam merces ' ; can. 26—' si quis dixerit
justos non debere . . . expectare et sperare æternam retributionem . . .
A.S.' ; 31—' si quis dixerit justificatum peccare dum intuitu æternæ mercedis
bene operatur, A.S.' (Denz.-Bann., nos. 804, 809, 836, 841.)

[4] Denz.-Bann., no. 508.

He alone hath true spiritual poverty who wills nothing, knows nothing, desires nothing.' [1]

The apostles of Pure Love were often no less unguarded than Eckhardt in their expressions. Bossuet had no difficulty in pla-carding sentence after sentence of a very ominous ring. From Molinos he quotes the maxim : ' He who is nought must close the door on all that is not God ' ; and glosses it in words from which (as he confidently assumes) the Quietist would not have shrunk—' The desire for God is not God ; therefore we close the door on that as well.' [2] ' Holy indifference,' according to the unhappy Spanish heresiarch, ' brings us back to the innocence of our first parents before the fall '—an innocence in which we are sublimely uncon-scious of needs either physical or spiritual.[3] From Lacombe, Bossuet quotes the repeated assertion that the Lord's prayer, because it aspires to gifts and graces from God, represents an imperfect Christianity alone.[4] Madame Guyon provided him with a rare mine in which to quarry. ' We must suppress all desire,' she says, ' even the desire for the joys of Paradise ' ; [5] and again—

> ' We must renounce all particular inclinations, even the noblest, the moment they betray themselves. Only so can we reach that indifference towards all goods, whether of body or soul, whether temporal or eternal, which is the Christian's aim.' [6]
> . . . ' We must be ready, as S. Paul was, to be anathema for the salvation of our brethren. Yet while we work throughout for that salvation we must be indifferent to success or failure in

[1] R. Jones, *Studies in Mystical Religion*, p. 230. Similarly Tauler, of some Beghards among his contemporaries (I rearrange the passage to show the two ideas of *disinterestedness* and *antinomianism*) :—(a) ' They stand exempt from all subjection, without any activity upward or downward, just as a tool is passive and waits until its master wishes to use it. For it seems to them that if they do anything then God will be hindered in His work ; there-fore they count themselves above all virtues. *They wish to be so free that they do not think, nor praise God, nor have anything, nor love nor ask nor desire anything . . . and they also think that they are poor in spirit because they are without any will* of their own and have renounced all possessions. They say publicly that so long as a man strives after virtues, so long is he imperfect and knows nothing of spiritual poverty, nor of this spiritual freedom.' (b) ' They wish to be free of all practice of virtue and obedient to no one, whether pope or bishop or priest. . . . They consider themselves to be higher than the angels and above the stage of human merit and human faith, so that they cannot increase in virtue nor yet commit sin. What-ever nature desires, according to their notion, they can do freely without sin, because they have reached the highest innocence, and no law or com-mandment is put upon them. Whenever their nature urges them in any direction they follow the impulse, so that the freedom of the spirit may be unhindered ' (R. Jones, *op. cit.*, p. 209).

[2] Bossuet, *Instruction sur les états d'oraison*, 3 (Œuvres, Lefévre, Paris, 1836, viii, p. 34) ; cp. Pourrat, *SC.*, iv, p. 211.

[3] *Ib.* So also ' the soul must be dead to every desire, effort, perception ; willing as though it willed not, understanding as though it understood not ; void even of the desire for its own annihilation.' In such annihilation ' consists the life, the repose, and the joy of the soul.'

[4] *Ib.*, p. 39.   [5] *Ib.*, p. 34.   [6] *Ib.*, p. 36.

the effort; we must be such that neither our own damnation nor that of any other creature can cause us a moment's pang, so it be in the will of God.' . . . 'Such is our indifference of soul, that we feel no motions either of joy or of privation; and though our love be stronger than ever before, it can have no desire for Paradise.'[1]

Passages of similar import can be quoted from Fénelon himself, —a fact which shows how dangerous in such a matter it is to judge without the context. 'All generosity,' he says in a letter to Madame de Maintenon, ' all natural affection, is only self-love of a specially subtle, delusive and diabolic quality. We must wholly die to all friendship.'[2] Even in the 'Spiritual Letters' occurs the famous 'sacristan' passage :—

'As the sacristan snuffs out the candles one by one when Mass is over, so must grace put out our natural life; and as his extinguisher, if carelessly employed, leaves behind a smouldering wick to melt away the wax, so will it be with us if a single spark of natural life remains.'[3]

The circumstances which brought Bossuet, Bishop of Meaux, into the field against Quietism in general and Madame Guyon in particular, were as complex as they were discreditable.[4] Perhaps, as M. Bremond suggests, all the protagonists in this minor drama were no more than pawns in the great battle between the Jesuits and Port Royal.[5] Fénelon, again, though a mere priest, was in a position of unequalled power. As early as 1693 an attempt was made at the Sorbonne to discredit him in his position as tutor to the young duke of Burgundy;[6] and thenceforward his influence and that of his friends at Court became steadily more unpopular in high circles. Against Madame Guyon, at the moment in high favour with Madame de Maintenon, rumour had long been active; she had even been confined for the greater part of a year (1688) in

[1] Bossuet, *Instruction sur les états d'oraison*, 3 (*Œuvres*, Lefévre, Paris, 1836, viii, p. 38).

[2] *ERE.*, x, p. 534 (*s.v.* ' Quietism ').   [3] *Ib.*

[4] H. Heppe, *Geschichte der Quietistischen Mystik* (1875), is still valuable for the outline, though it is absurdly sentimental in tone, and elusive as to the real point at issue. A. Delplanque, *Fénelon et la doctrine de l'amour pur* (1907), is of first-class importance, especially for the negotiations at Rome. F. Brunetière, *La querelle du quiétisme*, and *Fénelon* (in *Études critiques sur l'histoire de la litterature Francaise*, 2ᵉ serie (8th ed., 1922), pp. 25-62, 305-334, is readable and incisive, though biassed against Fénelon. M. Bremond's *Apologie pour Fénelon* remains in a class by itself for its exposition of motives and ideals. Miss E. K. Sanders' *Bossuet*, pp. 270-304, gives a very good account for English readers; better than that in her much earlier book on Fénelon. See also F. von Hügel, *Mystical Element, ut sup.*; L. Crouslé, *Fénelon et Bossuet, pass.*; Pourrat, *SC.*, iv, pp. 231-295.

[5] *Apologie*, pp. 55-63.

[6] *Ib.*, p. 50—a problem of casuistry was proposed in the terms, ' Whether a prince may allow his children to be taught by a tutor suspected of quietism ? '

the Convent of the Visitandines, whilst her orthodoxy was under review.

There were many reasons, therefore, why Madame de Maintenon should withdraw her ægis from the lady whose esoteric doctrines had set Paris talking. But it is even now not apparent why Bossuet —whose ignorance of these matters was profound—should have been called upon to take up the affair of Pure Love. In January, 1694, he made his first interrogatory of Madame Guyon ; the nine months' series of conferences at Issy began in July. In the spring of 1695 an accord was patched up between Fénelon and Bossuet in the thirty-four articles, and Fénelon became Archbishop of Cambrai. At the end of the year Madame Guyon was imprisoned at Vincennes, and remained there for the greater part of 1696. The intervening period was spent by Bossuet in preparing an ' Instruction on the States of Prayer,' by Fénelon in writing his ' Explanation of the Maxims of the Saints.' The latter book was published in January, 1697, the former some few weeks later. The two protagonists had taken up their final positions.

Bossuet's problem was not so easy as might be supposed. The ' false mystics ' had committed themselves to many extreme statements ; but word for word parallels could be quoted—and were being quoted, as he knew to his cost—from writers, some of them canonized, and all of them of unquestionable orthodoxy.[1] Two possibilities were open to him. One was to admit the supremacy of disinterestedness in the Christian life, but to assert that it was much more common than the ' new mystics ' suggested.[2] This, however, had its difficulties. It cast some measure of criticism upon the ' saints ' who, like the ' new mystics,' had emphasized the rarity of complete disinterestedness. Further, it might appear to involve the bishop in the extreme and inhuman admission that, for supreme disinterestedness, even the hope of salvation must cease to be a ' motive.' And, finally, it came into conflict with what M. Bremond has called Bossuet's ' fixed idea ' that Fénelon and his friends were a danger to Christianity.[3] In spite of these difficulties, Bossuet's good angel often guided his pen. He himself had recorded for the

---

[1] See particularly books 8 and 9 of the *Instruction sur les États*.

[2] Thus P. de Caussade, who represented himself as a disciple of Bossuet, in his *Instructions spirituelles en forme de dialogues* (1741)—' Q. What was the error of the new mystics on the subject of disinterested love ? ' A. ' They refused to admit this pure love except in a certain state of their so-called " perfect " Christians. But it is present even in beginners . . . for there is only one kind of love ' (Bremond, *HLSR.*, ii, p. 598—the whole passage is important). Caussade is so resolute to read this doctrine into Bossuet, that he can even represent the entire controversy as an amiable conspiracy between Bossuet and Fénelon to provide the public with a collection of sound mystical texts. Bossuet ' was well equipped with information on the subject, because a great Archbishop ' (i.e. Fénelon), ' equally cognizant of mystical theology both in practice and in theory, had previously furnished him with long quotations and beautiful comments on contemplative writers ' (Bremond, *Apologie*, pp. 437-441 ; cp. *ib.*, pp. 450-452 ; and Id., *Bossuet, Maître d'oraison* (Caussade's text in full), pp. xvii, 56).

[3] *Ib.*, pp. 114-123 (' L'idée fixe de M. de Meaux').

Dauphin's edification S. Louis' wonderful anecdote of the woman
who proposed to ' burn up heaven and quench the flames of hell,'
that men might serve God out of pure love alone.   One of Fénelon's
deadliest thrusts was to remind Bossuet of the fact at the very
height of their duel :—

> ' Voila néanmoins l'amour que vous avez enseigné à Mon-
> seigneur le Dauphin, comme étant *plus precieux* que la couronne
> de S. Louis.   Lui enseigniez-vous alors *l'erreur* fondamentale
> du quiétisme ?   Vous perdiez-vous en lui enseignant cette
> erreur ?   Pour moi, je n'ai jamais proposé ce pur amour à
> Monseigneur le duc de Bourgoyne ' [1]—

but it was not a brilliant piece of controversy alone ; it was no
less Fénelon's heart-felt lament for a lost leader.

M. Bremond [2] and Miss Sanders [3] have both shown how the
doctrine of pure love shines through the non-controversial writings
of Bossuet.   Even in controversy he was not always untrue to
his better self.   More often, however, his arguments took another
and less pleasing path.   Again and again he repeats that ' pure
love,' or perfect disinterestedness, is a dangerous and deceptive
illusion, a chimera, a jest, a presumption, a cloud in which the
mystics lose themselves, a shadow for which they abandon the substance of religion, an impious blasphemy.[4] ' Everything we do,'
he says, ' we do to be happy.' [5] ' We wish to be happy ; we cannot
wish anything else.   Theology and philosophy alike recognize
in this man's ultimate goal.' [6] He does not shrink from saying
that the most perfect Christian is he who ' loves ' most absolutely,

[1] *3me lettre en réponse à celle de M. de Meaux*, 13 (*Œuvres*, Didot, Paris
(1838), ii, p. 144).
[2] *Apologie pour Fénelon*, pp. 469-476 ; *Bossuet, Maître d'oraison*, pp.
xxxii-xli.
[3] *Bossuet*, pp. 305-321 ; cp. particularly p. 309—' Desire must be for God
and not for delight in Him ; for His truth, and not for the satisfaction of
possessing it ' ; and the five citations on pp. 319, 320.   Also the ' Instruction
on the Love of God,' *ib.*, p. 131.   Cp. Pourrat, *SC.*, iv, pp. 313, 315-317.
Similarly, Spinoza, *Eth.*, v. 19—' qui Deum amat, conari non potest ut Deus
ipsum contra amet.'
[4] E.g. *Réponse à une lettre de M. de Cambrai* (*Œuvres*, viii, p. 219)—
' L'état des parfaits n'est plus qu'un fantôme ' ; *Second écrit ou mémoire*, 17
(*ib.*, p. 268)—' En poussant l'effort de l'esprit jusqu'au cinquième [degré] on
sort de mesure, on donne dans l'illusion, dans l'amusement, dans la présomp-
tion, et on se perd dans les nues, où l'on n'embrasse qu'une ombre au préjudice
du corps de la religion ' ; *Réponse à quatre lettres* (*ib.*, p. 383)—' Les chimères ne
sont plus chimères, puisqu'on les fait servir à l'impieté et au blasphème ' ;
et pass.
[5] *Préface sur l'instruction pastorale*, 10 (*ib.*, p. 335)—' Il faut remarquer
qu'à la vérité on fait tout pour être heureux, et que c'est là pour ainsi parler
le fond de la nature, que la grace suppose toujours.'   Cp. Fénelon's criticism
of this passage, *infra*, p. 459, n. 2.
[6] *Préface*, 4 (*ib.*, p. 309) ; cp. *5me ecrit ou memoire* (*ib.*, p. 296)—' Rien
ne nous peut arracher du cœur le désir d'être heureux ' ; *Réponse à quatre
lettres* (*ib.*, p. 370, reinforced by a quotation from S. Augustine)—' C'est non
seulement qu'on veut être heureux, mais encore qu' on ne veut que cela, et
qu'on veut tout pour cela,' *et pass.*

whatever his motive may be.[1] 'We wish to be happy,' he writes in the peroration of the 'Instruction,'

> 'and we cannot do otherwise. We cannot banish this motive from any one of our rational actions. . . . Love cannot be disinterested as far as beatitude is concerned. . . . It is an illusion to subtract the motive of personal happiness from our love towards God. . . . To love God is simply to love our own beatitude more distinctly. . . . The desire of reward (where God is the reward) is far from detracting from love, is a quest for love's perfection ; it is indeed love's adequate and perfect motive.'[2]

Stripped of its subtleties and disguises, this is the position which Bossuet attempts to maintain. Our actions are bound to be interested ; but the Christian will strive to concentrate that interest upon gaining the joys of heaven, rather than upon lesser and lower satisfactions.[3] At first sight the doctrine is at least specious. Why should not the moralist say, ' You will always be selfish, but make sure that your selfishness is of a refined order ' ? But the answer is obvious, and Fénelon presses it home remorselessly. Why does the moral man choose ' refined ' forms of happiness ? Because they offer *more* joy than any other object of choice ?—In that case he is as much a hedonist as any other, and the doctrine of universal selfishness is simply reinforced. Or because he regards ' refinement ' as essential in every choice ?—In that case you have admitted the possibility of disinterestedness—the moral man will refuse happiness if it presents itself in ' unrefined ' forms. Thus between the doctrine that some actions may be ethically disinterested, and

---

[1] *Réponse à une lettre de M. de Cambrai* (*ib.*, p. 218)—'Celui-là est le plus parfait qui absolument aime le plus, par quelque motif que ce soit.' This terrible sentence can only imply that by ' loving ' Bossuet means no more than ' performing actions which the true Christian would perform out of love for God.' It involves the corollary that a believer who fulfilled the *whole* law solely with a view to his temporal well-being would be more perfect than one who set himself to do good out of love for God, but occasionally failed under the attack of temptation.

[2] *Instruction sur les états*, 10 (*ib.*, pp. 130, 131).

[3] This seems to be the meaning of the curious passage, *Instruction*, 10 (*ib.*, p. 130)—' Il faut entendre la béatitude comme quelque chose au-dessus de ce qu'on appelle intérêt, encore qu'elle le comprenne, puisque elle comprend tout le bien, et que l'intérêt en est une sorte.' Bossuet reaches the limits of confusion in this passage. He attempts to interpret S. Paul's ' It is more blessed (" heureux ") to give than to receive '—' *non pas précisement* qu'il est plus utile, mais outre cela principalement qu'il est meilleur, qu'il est plus noble, plus excellent, et plus pur.' Why not say frankly, ' it is more disinterested ' (—which of course is what Bossuet, and no doubt S. Paul, means—), instead of suggesting by the ' précisement ' that it is both ' more noble ' *and* a form of self-interest. There follows a curious historical point :—Bossuet suggests (forgetting his ' précisement ') that Anselm was the first writer to ' define beatitude in terms of utility and interest ' ; but in view of Augustine's ' *gaudium* de veritate,' which gave S. Thomas so much difficulty (*infra*, p. 551), this can hardly be true—except perhaps in a very narrow sense.

the doctrine that all actions are equally selfish, there can be no half-way house.[1] Bossuet refused assent to the former of these two propositions; and Fénelon was right in treating him as an adherent —disguised indeed, and all the more dangerous because disguised —of the second. His teaching led straight to naturalism unashamed, and as such was in flat contradiction of all that Christianity stands for.

Fénelon's 'Explanation of the Maxims' is dull and difficult reading; the failure of the book to convince the public occasions no surprise. Yet it has high merits. Not the least of them is that it recognizes—as its title implies—how much 'maxims,' 'epigrams,' 'obiter dicta,' are in need of explanation. A man in the midst of a heroic and selfless career may say, 'I could not be happy were I doing anything else'; but though his maxim sounds selfish, the world judges, and judges rightly, that his life is the very reverse. Or, again, a Christian, intent on his own self-culture, may indeed assert that he is doing all to the glory of God; yet sometimes at least we have good reason to think him none the less 'interested' for that. Bossuet attempted to explain away the maxims of the saints—to force them all into the categories of his own system, which, in so far as he had one, was the very reverse of their's. Fénelon's aim was to analyse their language till he had discerned to a nicety the system of thought which really lay behind. It is not surprising that the result was an arid piece of scholastic exposition.

Elsewhere, however, even in the heat of controversy, Fénelon is almost always lucid, exact, and inspiring. He has one final question with which he counters all Bossuet's arguments. It is the question, 'Granted that we wish to be happy, can we ever wish to be happy in order to glorify God; or do we invariably wish to glorify God only in order to be happy?'[2] To that question the unanimous testimony of the saints—the saints whom Bossuet relegates

---

[1] 3me lettre en réponse à divers écrits, 3 (Fénelon, Œuvres, ut sup., ii, p. 66)—'Vous appelez cet objet spécifique (i.e. "la perfection de Dieu en lui-même") l'objet essentiel; mais est-il le seul essentiel? S'il n'est pas le seul essentiel, c'est en vain que vous nous éblouissez par un si grand terme.' —Fénelon's point is that only one factor is entitled to the adjective 'essential' in any given choice. If 'happiness' is (as Bossuet says) an invariable 'essential,' neither the moral man nor the voluptuary can have any other 'essential'—for what would happen if the two 'essentials' came into conflict? Bossuet's fallacy will be recognized as the same as that with which Mill attempts to reinforce utilitarianism, and Fénelon's answer as the criticism which has universally been directed against Mill. The point is simply and clearly put by E. F. Carritt, Theory of Morals, p. 21, when he exposes the absurdity of saying 'I care for nothing but money; but it must be honestly come by.' If a chance of making money dishonestly occurred, either a man would refuse it—in which case 'money' is not an invariable essential with him; or he would accept it, in which case honesty is not.

[2] 3me Lettre, 4 (ib., p. 66)—'On fait tout pour être heureux. Veut-on glorifier Dieu pour être heureux, on bien veut-on être heureux pour glorifier Dieu?'—or, in the terms of the preceding footnote—if my happiness and the glory of God came into conflict, should I be free to choose the latter?

into oblivion with the scandalous phrase 'four or five mystics whom nobody reads '[1]—gives him an irresistible answer :—

> 'No, Monseigneur, theology does not speak like this. Beatitude is the most perfect means, no doubt ; but the glory of God is man's ultimate goal.'[2]

In a masterpiece of compressed analysis,[3] M. Cherel has shown that the ideal of disinterestedness dominates Fénelon's secular writings—the ' Télèmaque ' or the ' Dialogues on Eloquence,' for instance—as much as his religious treatises. M. Delplanque[4] has subjected to microscopic analysis his most intimate reactions to the condemnation of the ' Maxims ' ; and if here and there traces of pique and rebellion are to be discovered, the general impression is one of a saintly self-forgetfulness which few could hope to emulate in analogous circumstances. We may add that Fénelon's loyalty to the friendless lady in whose inspiration he had come to believe only after genuine and dispassionate enquiry,[5] and his persistence in the cause of what he conceived to be the truth when it must clearly drive him into exile from Versailles, are no less examples of what was the ruling ideal of his life. He knew, as well as anyone can know, that no man can perform a conscious action without being interested in it, or desiring, in some sense, to do it ; and he recognized the philosophical puzzle arising out of this fact.[6] But he insisted in season and out of season that this ' natural inclination ' must not be confused with ' grace '—or, as we may paraphrase it, with the moral question.[7] Within the sphere of the actions which

---

[1] *Préface sur l'instruction pastorale*, 4 (*ib.*, p. 308). S. Francis de Sales, whom Bossuet treats (as Fénelon says, 5*me* *Lettre*, 17, *Œuvres*, ii, p. 99) as 'an author rather to be excused than to be followed,' is included. Cp. Bremond, *Bossuet, Maître d' oraison*, pp. xxix, xxx.

[2] 3*me* *Lettre*, 13 (*ib.*, p. 71)—a reply to Bossuet's ' theology and philosophy alike,' *supra*, p. 457.

[3] *Fénelon : Explication des Maximes*, introduction, pp. 90-93 ; cp. E. K. Sanders, *Bossuet*, pp. 163-165.

[4] A. Delplanque, *Fénelon et la doctrine de l'amour pur*, pp. 427-443. M. Delplanque conducts the same meticulous examination of Fénelon's private correspondence with his friends at all periods of his life (*ib.*, pp. 32-170). He misunderstands the idea of pure love so far as to suggest that Fénelon's friendships were not wholly disinterested, because he was ' happy in them ' (*ib.*, p. 450 ; cp. p. 41) ; but concludes that neither Fénelon nor his friends ' sought their own,' and that the great Archbishop had ' one of the most loving natures there has ever been ' (*ib.*, p. 446).

[5] E. K. Sanders, *Fénelon*, pp. 104, 106, 124 ; Pourrat, *SC.*, iv, p. 253.

[6] 3*me* *Lettre* (*Œuvres*), ii. p. 66)—We have ' une inclination naturelle ' which ' ne peut regarder qu'une beatitude naturelle, c'est à dire un contentement imparfait et passager.'

[7] *Ib.*—Bossuet had said (*Préface*, 10 ; p. 335)—' Cette inclination naturelle se confond avec la grâce, qui en fixe les mouvements généraux . . . il n'y a rien là que dans l'ordre.' Fénelon replies : ' Cette inclination ne peut *se confondre avec la grâce ;* car l'un tend à un objet très différent de l'autre. La nature demande, par une inclination aveugle et nécessaire, un contentement passager. La grâce . . . fait désirer librement une béatitude pleine, permanente et surnaturelle. Peut ou jamais confondre des objets si différents et des affections si diverses ? '—The point lies in the opposition

we desire to do, or which ' interest ' us, there are some whose performance would beyond question constitute a definite menace to
our neighbour's legitimate well-being; such actions we do not
hesitate to call selfish, or 'interested.'[1]   In other actions our
neighbour's interests, if not actually promoted, are at least respected; here (even though the action may in some cases be self-
regarding)[2] we can fairly claim that it is ' disinterested.'[3] The
essence of Christian morality lies in the conviction that Jesus only
desired to do, and only did, actions of this disinterested character;
and that the true follower of Jesus will aspire, at however great a
distance, to imitate Him in this respect.

This was the truth which Fénelon asserted in the controversial
letters following upon the publication of the ' Maxims.' But the
' Maxims' themselves are inspired by a different purpose.   They
are an attack upon the ' false mystics' as implacable as any which
Bossuet launched against Fénelon. He deals with many different
Quietist aberrations in the course of his forty-five chapters; but
only one concerns us here.   It is the Quietist principle that disinterestedness can be and must be achieved by a process of willed,
reflective, or conscious self-annihilation. Here Fénelon stands forward as the champion of a position we have noticed more than once
already; indeed, it may be said that few Christians have ever
asserted it more emphatically than he does. The Quietists set out
to acquire disinterestedness by the methods of formalism, training
themselves *not* to think of themselves, trying even to *desire* the pains
of hell that they might stifle all longing for the joys of heaven. Few
forms of egocentrism are more dangerous than this; mere self-
centredness can never lead to self-forgetfulness. Fénelon at least
has no doubt on the subject. Disinterestedness cannot be acquired
by human effort except as the outcome of worship; God gives it

between ' nécessaire ' and ' librement.' Does Bossuet's ' se confond ' eliminate this opposition or not ? If it does (as Fénelon thinks it must do), the
result is naturalism pure and simple—we do what we do (even in the sphere
of ' grace ') because we cannot do otherwise. If it does not, the possibility
of disinterested actions distinct from, though within the sphere of, ' natural
inclination ' is admitted. See further *infra*, p. 553, additional note T.
Cp. also a most instructive primitive discussion of the same problem in
Hermas, *Sim.* VI, 5⁵⁻⁷. The Similitude as a whole is directed against
gluttony (τρυφή) ; but the definition of ' gluttony ' only comes at the end—it
comprises ' every action which a man finds pleasure in doing.' The inevitable logical conclusion would be that a good act done with pleasure would be
sinful—or at least worthless. To avoid this Hermas quite frankly says—
' There are gluttonies which save men. For many who do good are carried
away by the pleasure thereof, and [therefore] are gluttonous. But this
gluttony is expedient to the servants of God, and gains life for such men.'
  [1] For other possible meanings of the word ' interested ' see *infra*, p. 552,
additional note T).
  [2] E.g. a self-regarding *duty* (such as care for one's health) might in many
cases be performed solely from morally disinterested motives (*infra*, p. 554;
additional note T.
  [3] Or at least (if we admit that what is not wrong may be either ' indifferent ' (allowable) or ' right ') it will be ' not-interested ' ' not-selfish,' or
innocent. See further, *infra*, p. 554, additional note T.

to the worshipping soul.[1] Therefore he takes up the full theocentric position. We are to give ourselves to contemplation as and how we can, and leave the rest to God. From contemplation we shall derive the zest for service, the policy of service, and the selflessness which gives service its only worth. Worship alone will ' disinfect our service from egoism.'

The Quietist may say :—

' We must force on the souls [of those whom we influence] to feel disgust at any love which is mingled with self-interest. We must from the outset make them aspire to a love which is completely disinterested. We must wrest from them the fear of death, of judgment, and of hell—these are servile motives. We must wrest from them the desire for their heavenly home, and cut off every motive of Christian hope.'

Fénelon's answer is immediate :—

' This is to close one's eyes to the ways of God and the operations of His grace. It is to force the wind to blow where we list, and not allow it to blow where it listeth. It makes havoc of all the stages of the inner life.'[2] ' Souls should be left in the activities of a love still mingled with self-interest, so long as the grace of God leaves them there . . . They should try to use these interested motives to subdue the passions, to confirm the virtues, and to detach the soul from all that the present life connotes. . . . It is useless and unwise to suggest to them a higher love to which they cannot attain, because they are lacking in inner enlightenment and in the special influence of grace.'[3]

---

[1] Cp. Cherel, *Fénelon, etc.*, pp. 49-51, with references there ; and S. Bernard's ' tepida omnis oratio quam non prævenerit inspiratio' (*de dil. Deo*, 7 (22)).

[2] *Explication des Maximes*, art. III *faux* (Cherel, p. 143) ; cp. Pourrat, *SC,*, iv, p. 302.

[3] *Ib.*, *vrai* (p. 141). The ' to which they cannot attain ' suggests the double standard in its psychological form (*infra*, p. 531), but the sequel (' we must follow grace step by step patiently,' Cherel, p. 142) makes it clear that Fénelon merely meant ' cannot *at present* attain ' ; and this is emphasized by a MS. correction for art. XI *vrai* of the second edition :—
' We must beware not to press forward impatiently and indiscreetly towards activities which grace does not yet demand of us, and rightly reserves for more suitable occasions. God has His occasions for everything. We should submit patiently to the programme which His grace dictates, and not force Him to conform to ours. . . . We should like always to be fervent and always conscious of vivid love, explicit faith, virtues in abundance : but all that grace demands of us at times is a love that is scarcely felt, and is obscured by the mists of temptation. We should like here and now to rouse ourselves to make such and such a sacrifice, to overcome such and such a temptation, even though the possibility is extraordinarily remote and may never arise at all. . . . We disquiet, we trouble, we torment ourselves in the hope of feeling something we do not feel, and in this distraction of mind we miss the opportunity of doing that which God's grace actually demands of us . . . and so we hinder our spiritual progress instead of forwarding it ' (Cherel, pp. 199, 200). On the rarity of full disinterestedness, cp. Bernard, *de dil. Deo*, 10 (29), 15 (39).

Much more to the same purpose might be quoted, but the point is surely clear. In the beautiful apologue of the pilgrim on the mountains with which Fénelon closes his book,[1] the reader is reminded that complete disinterestedness is a very distant ideal, and very difficult to reach ; there is no short cut to it. It is dangerous to allow the mirage to flatter us that we are nearly at our goal,—to persuade us to behave as though we were there, when we are still far away.[2] Only by discharging the immediate duties honestly and without presumption shall we become disinterested, not by close scrutiny of our spiritual attainments. The rare souls who have achieved the ideal are wholly unconscious—and by the very nature of the case must remain unconscious—that they have succeeded.[3] It is a grace which God alone gives ; not one which man can deliberately compass.

(b) The Spirit of Worship.

The ' Explanation of the Maxims ' was condemned at Rome, after a history of intrigue which it would be difficult to outrival. But at the bar of Christian thought Fénelon's main position has been decisively vindicated. To say that unselfishness is impossible, and therefore cannot be made a test of behaviour, Christian or otherwise, is to deny the crucial principle of the gospel ethics. If we accept the Christian revelation at all, we must accept this as one of its cardinal doctrines. The test of disinterestedness, therefore, can validly be applied in that comparison between worship and activity which was instituted a few paragraphs ago. So tested, worship stands out as the only means by which service can be purged of a self-centredness which renders it all but unserviceable ; and the doctrine that man's first duty is to look towards God in the spirit of worship, which is the fundamental truth implied in the Christian thought of the vision of God, receives its vindication. But the mind still hesitates before this conclusion. It may still be urged that the effort to assure and maintain the attitude of worship is itself a self-centred effort, and therefore bound to defeat its own ends.

Worship is, after all, a form of activity. Its exercise can be sedulously or carelessly practised. Does it not therefore open the door to self-criticism, self-applause, and self-depreciation in the same way, if not to the same degree, as ' service ' does ? It may be *less* self-centred than ' activity ' in the ordinary sense, but if it ministers to thoughts of self at all, does it not share in the same condemnation ? We may defer consideration of this problem for a moment in order to glance at another; for a single answer would appear to suffice for both.

[1] Art. XLV *vrai* (Cherel, pp. 297-300).
[2] *Ib.*—' Rien n'est si dangereux que de se flatter de cette belle idée, et de se croire dans la pratique où l'on n'est point . . . Il faut bien se garder de croire qu'on en a la réalité aussi tost qu on en a la lumière et l'attrait.'
[3] *Ib.*—' Le très petit nombre de celles qui y sont, ne sçavent si elles y sont toutes les fois qu'elles refléchissent sur elles mêmes.'

Where the best Christian thought about the vision of God has differed from non-Christian aspiration is in its emphasis upon the *attitude* rather than upon the *experiences* of worship. What matters, it has said, is that we should look towards God, rather than that we should here and now receive the vision. But that there *is* such a vision, and that it is attainable, theology no less than experience affirms. Not only do the saints see God in heaven—not only has the Church seen Him in the face of Jesus Christ on earth ; for the inspiration and renewal of the individual it has been insisted that the pure in heart shall from time to time have personal experience of God and intercourse with Him, both in their prayers and even in the ordinary activities of life. This provokes the second question,— a question difficult at all times to answer ; but most of all when it comes from those who have sought earnestly for God, and yet seem to themselves never to have found Him. It is often said that to dwell upon the promise of seeing God, of communion with Him, is not so much selfish (—that criticism we have already dismissed—) as idle and unmeaning to the world of to-day. Such phrases, we are told, with all that they imply of personal intercourse with the divine, of spiritual illumination, of inbreathing of grace, as possible sources of strength and consolation in this present life, will to most men never be more than the meaningless and irritating jargon of the pulpit. The reason alleged is that only the very few are endowed with a temperament apt to receive the mystical experience which the words connote. If that were true, the ' practical ' Christian would be right as against the mystic ; and the whole doctrine of the vision of God as the supreme focus of religion, here and here- after alike, would have to be relegated to the lumber-room of for- gotten shibboleths and esoteric cults.

But so far from allowing this opinion to be true, we are entitled to regard it as supremely false. What is the vision of God which Christ promised, in this world in its measure, in the next in its fullness, to the pure in heart ? It is confined—so we should have learnt from Bernard, Francis, Hugh of St. Victor and Thomas Aquinas—within no narrow limits. Wherever a man's mind has been uplifted, his temptations thwarted, his sorrows comforted, his resolutions strengthened, his aberrations controlled, by the sight of purity, innocence, love or beauty,—indeed, wherever he has, even for a moment, recognized and responded to the distinction between good and evil, between better and worse,—such a man has had in part the mystical experience. Dim though his mirror may have been, he has yet seen God. Where he has seen God once there he may see Him again. Purity, innocence, love and beauty are to be seen no doubt most fully in the gospel. But they are to be seen elsewhere as well ; and seeing them elsewhere we can discern their delicacies and refinements in the gospel better even than before.

So far then from being rare, the mystical experience is at once the commonest and the greatest of human accidents. There is not one of us to whom it does not come daily. It is only carelessness or custom that prevents our realizing how divine it is in essence ; only timidity which checks us from proclaiming that we too at such moments have seen God, even if as in a glass darkly ; only folly which blinds us to the fact that these moments of vision are our surest safeguard and our best resource in every temptation, sorrow or selfishness. In every such contact with whatever is true and honourable and just and pure and lovely and of good report the true Christian tradition allows, and indeed constrains, us to recognize the first traces of the vision of God. What Christianity offers, with its fellowship and sacraments, its life of prayer and service, its preaching of the Incarnate Son of God, is the same vision in ever-increasing plenitude ; vouchsafed in such measure as will avail against the worst temptations, the deepest sorrow, the most in-grained self-seeking, and will give constant and daily increase of strength, encouragement and illumination.[1]

There is therefore no need for us to ask whether we are psycho-logically capable of seeing God ; we have already seen Him. Nor is there any need for us to make an effort to assume the attitude of worship ; it is an attitude which has already been imposed upon us—it may be even without our consent—by the God Whom we have come to know in nature, in art, or in friendship. The spirit of worship is not a remote prize. It is an actual endowment, pos-sessed by all men. We are born into a world where we cannot but worship ; even if we learn to worship the devil and his works, we shall still retain some trace of the worship of God to the very end. Wherever goodness has attracted the soul, it has evoked the spirit of worship ; and it will continue to attract. We may resist, deny or betray ; we may welcome, co-operate, and adore ; but we shall never be masters of the situation. Worship depends not upon our own activities, but upon the activities which God brings to bear upon us ; to them we are forced to react as worshippers. If without self-scrutiny and self-torment a man can remain alive to the goodness in his environment, it will draw out all that is best in him, leading him nearer to the perfect goodness revealed in the

---

[1] Further on this continuity between the most primitive and the most perfect attainments in religion, cp. Athanas., *c. gentes*, 30. 3—' Nor . . . is the road to God afar off or outside ourselves ; but it is in us, and it is possible to find it from ourselves . . . And let not the Greeks make excuses . . . pro-fessing to have no such road . . . for we all have set foot upon it and have it ' ; Basil, *hom. in Ps.* 32, 1 (*MPG.*, xxix, col. 324)—' If ever a kind of light piercing thy heart has brought thee unawares the thought of God, and so illumined thy soul as to make thee love Him . . . that dim and fleeting vision can make thee comprehend the state of the blessed who enjoy with God a beatitude without end ' ; Bernard, *de dil. Deo*, 7 (22)—' nemo Te quærere valet, nisi qui prius invenerit ' ; Pascal, *Le Mystère de Jésus*, 6—' Tu ne Me chercherais pas, si tu ne Me possédais.' On this matter, again, Fénelon represented the or-thodox view, which sees ' religious experience ' as a single continuity from its most rudimentary beginnings to its final climax ; Bossuet regarded ' passive contemplation ' as purely miraculous (*Instruction sur les états*, 7 (*Œuvres*, viii, pp. 75, 76) ; cp. von Hügel, *Mystical Element*, ii, pp. 173, 174 ; *Essays and Addresses*, i, p. 279). Generally cp. Bremond, *HLSR.*, vii, pp. 12, 157, 162, where the title ' pan-mysticism ' is given to the doctrine expressed above.

Incarnate Lord. If self-scrutiny and the discipline of struggle with temptation are demanded as conditions of his worship, they will no doubt throw him back upon himself for a time ; but it will be for a time only. And even if he refuse to worship, and turn his back upon all that he knows to be good, the irresistible pressure of goodness will still be upon him. For what we mean by ' goodness ' is the invincible grace of God's love, of which Augustine, rightly discerning the deepest secret of the New Testament, never hesitated to proclaim that it was stronger than death itself.

IV. CONCLUSION.

If what has been said is true, there is no need to admit of that tradition which, so far from merely asserting a moral law, sets the vision of God before the Christian as his promised goal, that it proposes a selfish, unworthy, or meaningless ideal. Further. if it be necessary that the gospel should embody some such promise of an infinitely desirable consummation, it seems true to say that no metaphor employed for the purpose in the New Testament expresses the thought more worthily than this. It was a sound instinct which led Christian theology to select the blessing promised to the pure in heart as the highest blessing offered by God to man. There are many other phrases in which the consummation can be expressed—salvation, membership of the kingdom, eternal life; and each of them is capable of animating devotion and inflaming zeal. But all that is of value in them, and something more besides, is expressed by the thought of the vision of God. The transition from darkness to light, from the incomplete to the complete, from the illusory to the true, envisaged by the word ' salvation '; the thought of fullness of personal activity conveyed by the phrase ' eternal life '; the joy, companionship, orderliness and conformity to the divine will implied by membership of ' the kingdom ' ;—not one of these is lacking when we speak of ' seeing God.'

But something more is present. In this chance phrase of Christian spirituality there is expressed, first of all, the sense that personal contact or intercourse with God is of the essence of that towards which the good life is directed. Next, we find expressed there, more fully than in the other phrases, the sense of the Christian's dependence upon God—the conviction that all attainment is of God's merciful giving. We can speak, as S. Paul does, of working out our own salvation—but the words, out of their context, have a dangerously egoistic ring. We can speak of bringing in the kingdom or building the new Jerusalem—though the New Testament certainly does not sanction either of these modes of speech, and they come near to suggesting that it is man who disposes where God can only propose. Eternal life—the enjoyment of timeless values—can be spoken of as though to be acquired by the simple reorganization of our temporal life and modes of living. None of these inferences would be authenticated by Christian thought at its best ; the unanimous testimony of the saints is that perfection comes not of him that willeth, nor of him that runneth, but of God Who showeth mercy. But this cardinal Christian truth is nowhere more clearly implied than in the doctrine of the vision of God. We may cast out the beam from the eye of the soul ; we may (in Augustine's phrase) [1] ' cleanse ' it by all the actions of a virtuous life ; we may direct it towards God by the processes of prayer and meditation ; but all that is as nothing, unless God of His own free beneficence presents Himself to the clarified vision and supplies the light where- with He may be seen. On any other conception of the goal of man's endeavour Pelagianism may, however invalidly, deflect us from the thought of divine prevenience, but within the doctrine of the vision of God, as we have come to understand it, it cannot find a foothold.

One further point may be noticed. ' Salvation,' ' the kingdom,' ' eternal life,'—these phrases cannot be rightly understood apart from the fact of Christ. But they do not carry the mind in- evitably back to Him. With the vision of God it is otherwise. No Christian can reflect upon it for a moment without remembering that the Church has already seen God in the face of Jesus Christ. At once the whole scheme of the Christian life springs into view. Like can only be seen by like—it is therefore only as worship creates in him some likeness to the character of Jesus that the Christian can achieve his goal. Whatever schematization of virtues or duties may be forced upon us, in the course of our life of worship, as our standard of self-examination or of effort, its content must be filled out and enriched by constant reference to the person of Jesus ; otherwise the scheme may produce nothing but the perversions of formalism. Again, true vision—comprehending, apprehending, understanding vision—demands intelligence as well as will. It is therefore only by studying the nature of God as revealed in Jesus,—by plunging into the depths of that nature till our alien souls find themselves at home there in the end, and thought moves naturally upon lines akin to those discernible in the thought and speech of Jesus,—that we can effectively prepare ourselves for the glory that is to be.[2]

[1] Aug., *serm.*, 88. 6.

[2] For completeness it may be added that ' the vision of God ' seems a more adequate phrase for the expression of the *summum bonum* than either of the two other phrases of technical dogmatic theology, ' perfection ' and ' beatitude ' ; and in exactly the same way it is preferable to the phrases of technical mystical theology—*unio mystica, via unitiva,* etc. ' Perfection ' implies a formalist approach—a comparison of oneself with an established standard ; ' beatitude ' or ' felicity ' is akin to panhedonism (*supra,* p. 141 ; *infra,* p. 551). The mystical phrases, besides being panhedonist in tendency, suggest that one particular mode of experience can be taken as a safe test of whether the Christian is advancing along the true way of life or not ; hence the reticence of the greatest writers on the subject (*supra,* pp. 271, 352, 354, 435, *infra,* p. 550). There is of course no shadow of contradiction be- tween the various phrases. ' Perfection ' (' purity of heart ') and ' beatitude ' are combined with ' vision,' in the archetypal statement of Mt. 5[8], as the con- ditions and the effect of ' vision ' respectively ; and no Christian would wish

Hence comes the importance of ' meditation ' in the Christian scheme of prayer. ' Meditation ' is not the same as contemplative worship ; but it is a stage on the path. There is nothing monastic, pietistic or abnormal about it ; nothing from which one should shrink as though from an effeminate habit or narcotic day-dream. It is essentially virile and stimulating. It has no formal rules ; it is simplicity itself. It means no more and no less than to go back to the gospels, and daily with them in hand to spend some moments of retirement in reverent but definite thought about the person, character and actions of the Lord as there revealed. If the history of Christian thought on ethics has any meaning at all, this must be the first, and indeed the greatest practical lesson to be drawn from it ; a lesson which comes with the glowing commendation of the Christian saints whom we have passed in review, and on the invitation of Him who said ' Learn of Me.' To the personality of Ignatius Loyola, and his initiative, Christendom owes more both of good and of evil than can very well be enumerated ; but the greatest and the best of his achievements was to help Christians of every school of thought to realize how far even the simplest can go in the path of loving Jesus which S. Bernard and S. Francis trod.

With such a background to his life, the Christian may feel himself not altogether at a loss in face of the questions proposed at the outset of the present enquiry—the questions of institutional-ism, formalism, and rigorism. The Church's aim is to help men to see God, and God has already been seen on earth in the face of Jesus Christ. On that truth, as has just been said, depends the whole scheme of Christian ethics ; we must answer our three questions in the light of what the Church knows of the life of Jesus of Nazareth. The first question was that of institutionalism, or corporate disci-pline. At a much earlier stage a distinction was drawn between two aspects of discipline—the pastoral and the penal. By the former we meant such uses of discipline as are designed to comfort, strengthen, and inspire the weakling ; by the latter, such usages as have for their purpose to cut off the Church from the world by cutting off the weakling from the Church. It is almost superfluous to ask which of these two methods conforms most closely to the mind of the good Shepherd. He Who broke not the bruised reed, nor quenched the smoking flax, Who consorted with publicans and sinners, Who bade the apostle forgive even to seventy times seven ;—whosoever came to Him, though they fell away and came back again time after time, He would in no wise cast out. How He could do this without lowering His standards, abating His demands, or compromising with evil, is His own peculiar secret. The Church must learn it if

to deny either the possibility of mystical experience, or the legitimacy of regarding it as an anticipation of the full vision. The only question that arises is, which of these allied and kindred phrases is the best to be used as the determinant of Christian conduct ? For the reasons indicated above, the phrase ' to see God ' seems most of all to answer the requirements of the case.

and as she can ; but her best efforts to put it into effect in the face of the complex demands of the world and the specious allurements of the devil have been blundering and blind compared with His.

Still, the lesson of history, as we have tried to read it, repeats the lesson of the gospel. Penal discipline has always defeated its own ends. Sometimes it has failed openly, lapsing into almost total disuse, as it did in the early Church and with the Reformers. That perhaps is the best that can be hoped for ; at least the ground is kept clear for the emergence of a pastoral discipline adequate to cope with the needs of human souls. Sometimes it has to appearance succeeded, taking a loathsome toll of human consciences, honesties and lives ; and its end has been the greater failure of secret hypocrisy and open schism. The Church must always and everywhere set before men the highest standard she knows in conduct, the truest forms of worship and of creed. But she must be very slow indeed to enforce them even by the threat of confining her membership to those who acquiesce. The shepherd's staff and not the tyrant's sword must be her true weapon. The whole flock is to be led into the fold, not the few harried into it whilst the many are left to their fate.

Much more could be said on the subject of corporate discipline ; but we must pass on. As far as the problem of formalism is concerned, S. Benedict and S. Thomas stand out as guides to a solution. Their principles dictate the conclusion that a reasoned orderliness, rather than an arbitrary and rigid rule, must be the Christian's best safeguard against the cyclones of temptation, the gusts of passion which beset his soul. He must indeed have rules of life. But he does not go out into the void to seek them ; they are forced upon him by the exigencies of his worship. From the first moment that his thoughts are turned to God, a spontaneous orderliness begins to grapple with the chaos of his passions ; and as the demand for orderliness presses outward into consciousness, it brings with it precepts for the mind to grasp and the will to put into effect. Thus law helps forward worship, and worship law ; but worship is both the beginning and the end. The promulgation, the revision, the purification of principles of conduct—these can have no sure foundation except in a soul whose primary interest is to keep its eyes directed towards God.

The progress of worship, therefore, evolves along with itself the rules of a Christian life. They are rules such as those on which Jesus lived His earthly life ; their value will be attested by increased purity of heart, renewed fervour for God's purposes, and more open love for men. Many of the rules we accept unthinkingly, to set before ourselves or commend to others, ring false when this test is applied to them. Yet there are few who, in a very short space of sober and honest reflection animated by the spirit of worship, could not set out for themselves other rules which they do not observe, which could scarcely fail to win approval if

judged by this test.   Communion with God will reveal what rules
we need, and nothing else can serve that purpose.   It is not by
unthinking revival of the laws of other days, but only by wise
adaptation of their underlying principles to the needs of to-day, that
the moral upheaval of the modern world and the modern soul can
properly be met ; and to such wise adaptation only loving adoration
of the nature of God in Christ can be the Church's guide.

So we come to the last and most difficult question.[1]   Are
rigorism, self-abnegation and world-flight no more than obsolete
ideals of other days, or have they too an underlying principle of
which the Church and the Christian are still in need ?   Is the vast
and complex history of the monastic movement no more than a
matter of purely antiquarian interest, or has it a message for the
present time ?   And if it has, how shall the Christian embody that
message in his life from day to day ?   It has proved impossible, in
the course of these chapters, to attribute the other-worldly element
in the gospel and the asceticism of the apostolic Church to any other
source than the personal intuition of Jesus and the influence which
He had upon his followers.   The emergence of monasticism in the
fourth century as a feature in world history finds no explanation
except in the genius of Christianity itself ;   even Protestantism—
despite its revolt from all that savoured of ' monkery '—retained,
at least in its earlier days, the rigorist element in ethics.

Throughout Christian history, again, this rigorism in ethics has
been bound up with a theological formula which—though far from
the whole of the Christian doctrine of God—is an integral part
thereof ;   the formula, not of the unnatural, but of the supernatural,
God.   In recent years, under the influence of Professor Otto's
important study of religion, it has come to be supposed that this
formula, and the attitude of awe, humility and self-contempt with
which it is naturally associated, are the basic factors in religion.
That conclusion is one which Christian history does not substantiate ;
the other-worldly and the this-worldly seem to have equal claims
both upon theological statement and upon Christian behaviour.
But at least the thought of a transcendence of God over His creation,
so infinite that in comparison all creation is as nothing, represents
one factor in the Christian revelation as to which there can be no
question.   It is to this factor that asceticism, or world-flight, in all
its varied forms, has borne consistent witness.

No true scheme of Christian ethics, therefore, can be without its
permanent element of rigorism.   How to incorporate that element
in an individual life is another and more difficult question.   Monasticism, clearly, is by no means the only possible way ; though it

---

[1] What follows is far too superficial a treatment of this vitally important
question ; but it would require another chapter if not another volume to
deal with it adequately.   I can only refer to the well-known passages in
von Hügel, *Eternal Life*, pp. 58, 65, 66, and *Essays and Addresses*, i, pp. 164-
169, 190-194, as indicating the principles upon which alone the question can
be satisfactorily answered.   Cp. also A. E. Taylor, *Faith of a Moralist*, i, pp.
132 ff.

may claim, at its best, to have presented the ideal in a simpler and more cogent manifestation than has been realized anywhere else. But alongside monasticism there has always run some form of lay asceticism, which the greatest theologians have seen to rival it in worth, whilst all have admitted its adequacy and value. Renunciation, detachment, self-denial must have their permanent place in every Christian life, however much at the same time we set ourselves to live in the joyous fellowship of human society, and as the beneficiaries of God in things both great and small. Other-worldliness is no mere *pis aller* of fallen humanity—a last desperate expedient to subdue rebellious passions; still less is it a temporary course of self-training for greater efficiency in humanitarian service. Only at our peril could we confuse it with self-discipline.[1] It must stand, alongside humanism, as a permanent witness to an aspect of the doctrine of God which separates Christianity for all time from naturalism and pantheism.

But if any man presses the question, *What* should I renounce? or, *How* am I to deny myself? he must expect no other reply than to be directed to that life of prayer which consists in seeing God—in meditating upon the person of Jesus. Sympathetic understanding —always partial, but always progressive—of *His* renunciations and self-denials will help the Christian to know what he too must renounce, and wherein he too must exercise self-denial. The exigencies of life—ill-health, misfortune, claims beyond the ordinary upon his time, patience, initiative or endurance,—will appear to him no longer as burdens to be borne with resignation, but as providential calls for the heroic renunciation of joys and liberties which would otherwise be legitimate enough.[2] He will not often have to look further afield. The light of divine knowledge vouchsafed to him in the life of meditation will throw into high relief these opportunities for other-worldliness which God sets in his daily path. The excellency of the knowledge of Christ Jesus the Lord will be for him a gaining Christ, a seeing God; and thereby

---

[1] Cp. a remarkably concentrated sentence of Professor Troeltsch's, which in the briefest possible compass suggests (*a*) that there is a clear distinction between ' asceticism ' and ' self-discipline ' (' limitation by reflection '); (*b*) that the modern world, ignoring the distinction, believes that the only permanent value in ' asceticism ' is that of ' self-discipline,' and so has preserved the latter and abandoned the former; (*c*) that something is in danger of being lost thereby :—' Religious asceticism, in the form of negation of the world, has disappeared from the modern world ; . . . however much the simple life of natural impulse has been limited by reflection and purposeful work ' (*Protestantism and Progress*, p. 24).

[2] Cp. again Troeltsch (*op. cit.*, p. 83, where Lutheranism is contrasted unfavourably, in this matter, with Calvinism)—' Lutheranism endures the world in suffering, pain and martyrdom ; Calvinism masters it for the glory of God.' Note also the curious passage, p. 136, in which the doctrine of ' work for work's sake ' is traced back to Calvinism, and made the modern equivalent of true asceticism, because ' the produce of the work serves, not to be consumed in enjoyment, but to the constant reproduction of the capital employed.'

he will attain a righteousness not of his own, not of an arbitrary law, but of God through faith. Through the power of the Risen Christ he will come to that fellowship in His sufferings and conformity to His death, in which the highest Christian self-renunciation must always consist. The spirit of worship will carry him forward along the *via crucis* so revealed to him, until through a spiritual death gladly accepted he attains, with the saints of God, to the resurrection from the dead.

ADDITIONAL NOTES.

A. The so-called ' Mithras-liturgy.'
B. Aristotle and the ' bios theoretikos.'
C. The original text of Mark 10²³⁻²⁶.
D. Pagan asceticism.
E. The use of ' psychikos ' in early 'gnostic' literature.
F. ' Panhedonism.'
G. The alleged pagan origin of Christian monasticism.
H. Marcion.
I. Public penance in the first five centuries.
J. Tertullian's theory of penance.
K. The double standard and works of supererogation.
L. Gregory the Great on the contemplative life.
M. Cassian on the double standard.
N. Modern versions of the double standard.
O. The question of private absolution in the early Church.
P. Abailard on mortal and venial sin.
Q. Mediæval homiles.
R. Augustinism.
S. S. Thomas on mystical experience and beatitude.
T. Disinterestedness and allied ideas.

Note A.—The So-Called ' Mithras-Liturgy ' (*supra*, p. 32).

As further illustration of the popularity of the conception of ' seeing God ' in the Græco-Roman world, I append a selection from the so-called ' Mithras-liturgy,' published by Dieterich [1] from Par. Pap. 574, a magic papyrus of the beginning of the fourth century A.D. (Dieterich, p. 43), but probably embodying earlier material. There is considerable doubt as to the correctness of Dieterich's suggestion that the passage is a genuine Mithraic liturgy ; the various arguments are summarized in the third edition of Dieterich's book, pp. 234 ff. Cumont regards it as the work of a conjuror with Hermetic interests ; Reitzenstein as a free literary invention, originally in the form of a vision or series of visions (*ib.*, p. 236) ; Gruppe as an instruction prior to a mystic initiation. In any case the Mithraic elements, whatever they may be, have been subjected to drastic syncretistic rewriting.

The text (purged of nonsensical elements) begins with an invocation by the writer, who professes to be setting down a ' dynamis ' given to him by the ' great God Helios Mithras ' through an archangel, ' that I alone may tread heaven and see all things.' A prayer of the initiand follows, in which he addresses the gods as ' first origin of my origin, first beginning of my beginning, spirit of spirit, first of the spirit in me,' and so forth. He proceeds : ' If it seem good to ye to return me, bound as I am by the nature given to me, to an immortal

---

[1] A. Dieterich, *Eine Mithras-Liturgie*, 3rd ed., revised by O. Weinreich, Berlin, 1923.

473

birth, that after my present distress that weighs me down I may see the immortal Beginning (ἐποπτεύσω τὴν ἀθάνατον ἀρχήν) . . . that I may be reborn in mind, and be initiated (ἐνάρχωμαι) and the holy spirit may blow in me ; that I may marvel at the holy fire, and see the abysmal shuddering water of the Rising, and that the lifegiving enveloping æther may hear me—for to-day I am to see with immortal eyes, mortal though I am of mortal mother ' . . . etc.[1]

First Instruction (p. 6) : ' Draw breath from the rays three times as hard as thou canst, and thou shalt see thyself raised aloft and borne upwards, till thou find thyself in mid-air.' Here the initiand is to see ' the divine ordering of that day and that hour,' ' the ascending and descending of the gods,' ' the way of the visible gods,' ' the origin of the ministering wind,' and so forth. The planets here denoted are hostile ; they are to be warded off with the words ' Silence, silence, silence ! '—' the symbol of God living and incorruptible,' and with a hiss and whistling. A prayer (the second), ' I am your fellow wandering star shining upward from the depth ' (ἐγώ εἰμι σύμπλανος ὑμῖν ἀστὴρ καὶ ἐκ τοῦ βάθους ἀναλάμπων), is also recommended. The sun's disc now unfolds, and five-rayed stars fill the air.

Third prayer (p. 8), with eyes closed, to ' him that hath with his spirit sealed the fiery bars of heaven,' addressed by a long catalogue of titles asking him to 'open' to the initiand. (p. 10) : ' Then open thine eyes and thou shalt see the gates opened, and the world of the gods, which lies behind the gates ; and for joy and gladness of that sight thy spirit shall draw into itself and rise upward.'

Fourth prayer : ' Come, Lord.' ' Then shalt thou see a fair young god with locks of fire, in white tunic and scarlet cloak, with a fiery chaplet. Greet him anon with the greeting of fire : " Hail, Lord of might, powerful monarch, greatest of the gods, Helios, lord of heaven and earth, god of gods, mighty is thy breath, mighty thy power. Lord, if it be thy will, announce me to the greatest God . . . as one who, made immortal this very hour by the will of God supremely good, desires and strives to worship as best man can." '

Fifth prayer (p. 12), to be uttered ' as with the bellowing of a horn ' : ' Defend me.' ' Seven virgins in linen raiment with serpent-faces ' appear (the seven Τύχαι, Fates—Dieterich, p. 70).

Sixth prayer : The initiand greets the seven Fates one by one. Seven gods with faces of black bulls and golden diadems appear—' the so-called rulers of the sky ' (πολοκράτορες).

Seventh prayer : Greeting of the polokratores. Then Mithra (?) appears : ' When those have set themselves hither and thither in order, look up into the air, and thou shalt see lightnings flashing down, and the gleam of lights and the earth quaking, and a great god coming down, with a shining countenance, young and golden-haired, in tunic white and golden crown and buskins, with the golden shoulder-blade of an ox in his right hand.[2] . . . Then shalt thou see lightnings glance from his eyes and stars from his body. Then beat upon thy belly, to rouse thy five senses, and bellow loud and long till thou canst no more ; and kiss thine amulets and say, " Abide with me in my soul ; leave me not, for . . . *(text corrupt)* . . . commands thee." Then gaze upon the god, and bellow long, and greet him thus : " Hail,

---

[1] A continuation of this passage in translation is given by W. R. Halliday, *Pagan Background of Early Christianity,* p. 210.

[2] On the significance of this, Dieterich, pp. 76 ff.

Lord, master of the water ; hail, founder of earth ; hail, ruler of the spirit. Lord, born again am I, and so in my exaltation depart ; and being exalted die. Born in life-giving birth and dissolved in death, I go my way as thou hast ordained, as thou has commanded and hast made the mystery." '

What follows is regarded by Dieterich (p. 82) as the magician's addition. The text is corrupt and in parts nonsensical, but may be represented as follows :—

' And when thou hast thus spoken he shall prophesy to thee straightway. And thy spirit shall be weakened, and thou shalt no longer be in thyself, when he answereth thee. So he speaketh to thee his oracle verse by verse ; and when he hath spoken he shall depart ; and thou art left standing as one dumb. Yet thou shalt grasp it all involuntarily (αὐτομάτως) ; and then shalt thou bear in mind unchangeably all that the great god sayeth, were his oracle even a thousand verses long. But if thou wouldest have a fellow-initiate to be alone with thee and hear what is said, let him purify himself with thee [seven] days, and hold aloof from flesh diet and baths. But if thou art alone and wouldest attempt what the god sayeth, speak as one uttering oracles in an ecstasy. And if thou wilt show him aught,[1] judge whether he is a man worthy [to receive it] safely ; using this way as one who prays on his behalf, and whisper to him the first word in the " Deification " ('Αποθανατισμός—apparently the title of the foregoing tract) where it begins " First origin of my origin." What follows speak as an initiate in a whisper above his head, that he hear not, anointing his sight with the mystery.[2] Now this " Deification " happeneth thrice a year ; and if any would hear the rite amiss, my son, for him it shall avail nothing.'

What follows is a jargon of magic prescriptions, incantations and the like : it contains one significant phrase only (p. 21) ἐξάφες ὃ ἔχεις καὶ τότε λήψει—' Lay aside what thou hast, and then shalt thou receive.'

Note B.—Aristotle and the Bios Theoretikos (*supra*, pp. 21, 33).

Aristotle, who begins the *Metaphysics* with the words, ' all men naturally wish to know . . . ,' makes (*Eth. Nic.*, x, 7) ' speculation or contemplation ' the highest activity of which human nature is capable. It would have been enough for his purpose to remind his readers that ' reason is the ruling and guiding principle in human nature ' (§ 1) ; but he supports his assertion by further arguments. Some of these are *a priori*—' of all knowable things,' he says, ' those with which reason deals are the highest.' Other arguments are empirical :—thus (*a*) ' Contemplation is capable of being a more continuous activity than any other ' (§ 2) ; (*b*) ' it is admittedly ' the pleasantest of activities, for ' philosophy purveys pleasures of marvellous purity and stedfastness ; and we may reasonably suppose that those who *know* are more pleasantly employed than those who still seek to know ' (§ 3) ; (*c*) it is more self-sufficient (§ 4) ; (*d*) it is the one activity pursued for its own sake, not for what it brings (§ 5) ; and (*e*) it is the most leisurely (§ 6). (Summary in § 7.) Thus, given only

---

[1] i.e. ' initiate a second person into the mystery.'

[2] Presumably a magic unguent of which the text goes on to speak.

length of life, contemplation must be the true beatitude (§ 7). As such it is more than human—the exercise of a faculty which in comparison with our other faculties may fairly be called divine. So Aristotle comes to his inspiring peroration: 'They tell us we are mortal men alone, and so should confine our thought to what is human and mortal. But I say, that we should play the immortal as much as may be, and strive to live up to the best that is in us—to our true self, which, though small in proportion to the whole self, yet surpasses all the rest in dignity and value' (§ 8).

In the following chapter Aristotle emphasizes—so strongly indeed as to introduce an element of positive depreciation—the inferiority of moral virtue to 'contemplation'; nor does he remind himself, as a more religious writer would have done, that right conduct is essential to true contemplation. He then (x, 8. 7) reverts to his thesis that contemplation is the only 'divine' activity, and the one which most commends a man to the gods (§ 13).

In an admirable little pamphlet of less than forty pages (*Vita Contemplativa*, Heidelberg, 1922), Franz Boll has investigated the genesis and affinities of this ideal of the *bios theoretikos*, as found in Aristotle and his partisans. The employment of the word *theoretikos*, and the Latin word *contemplativa* selected as its equivalent, inevitably carried with it a religious colouring. This result the philosophers must be supposed to have encouraged deliberately; the simplest change of terminology (*philosophikos*, for example, for *theoretikos*, or *speculativa* for *contemplativa*) would have avoided it (p. 7). The vulgar etymology which connected *theorein* with *theos*, perhaps with the sanction of the Aristotelian school (p. 26; Boesch, Θεωρός, *Züricher Diss.*, Gött., 1908, pp. 1 ff.), is of course to be rejected; but the word certainly meant an official delegate sent as representative of a city to a religious festival, an oracle, or a temple (pp. 6, 26).[1] It was synonymous with *epoptes* (cp. Æsch., *PV.*, 118, 298, where the two words are treated as identical), which had a strongly mystical flavour. Especially was it used of the semi-scientific, semi-religious observation of the stars, the visible gods, which the approach of astrology from the East rendered so popular (p. 27, especially the reference to Philo, *spec. leg.*, ii, 3, 45; (*C-W.*, v, 97).[2] *Theorides* was occasionally at least a synonym for the Bacchæ. The Greek philosophers thus accepted and even emphasized this kinship of their craft with the mysteries. Platonic examples of this are well known;[3] Pythagoras imposed the same silence upon his disciples at the beginning of their course as was demanded of the initiand in the mysteries (Hippol., *Philos.*, i, 2, 3; Boll, p. 32); Empedocles used the word *epopteuein* of philosophy (H. Diels, *Fragmente der Vorsocratiker*, i, p. 204—fr. 110, 2). Hence Aristophanes was more than justified in introducing a parody of initiation into his attack on the Socratic school (*Clouds*, 252 ff.; cp. 143; cp. generally Lobeck, *Aglaophamus*, i, 123 ff., Rohde, *Psyche* [8] (E. tr.), p. 384, etc.).

With *contemplatio* and its cognates the case is even clearer. The

---

[1] Cp. Aristoph., *Pax*, 342; *Vesp.*, 1187 f.; Thuc., iii, 104; v, 18; viii, 10; etc.

[2] Cp. F. Cumont, *Astrology and Religion among the Greeks and Romans*, pp. 40-41, 100-104, 135-138, 143-148, 200-202; Pauly Wissowa, i, 1802-1828; vi, 2373.

[3] *Gorgias*, 497 c; *Sympos.*, 209 E, and *supra*, pp. 23-26.

associations with *templum* and the cultus generally could not be avoided, even had it been wished to keep them apart. So in the *Somnium Scipionis* and elsewhere Cicero continually plays with the idea that the universe is God's temple ; philosophy, astrology and religion, therefore, are inseparably linked (Boll, pp. 29-30, similar examples from Seneca, Pliny, etc.; cp. Aug., *d.c.D.*, vii, 31).[1] But despite these curious affinities of the terminology, Boll insists rightly that the ' contemplative life ' for pagan philosophy always consisted primarily in the active investigation of strictly intellectual problems. He distinguishes it both from the ' quietism ' of nature-worship (of which he produces some beautiful classical examples—pp. 23-25), and from the ecstatic experiences of the mysteries. Only in Plato (whose influence Boll (p. 8) is inclined to treat somewhat cursorily) is the ecstatic element in philosophy at all marked.

Boll is peculiarly happy in putting together passages illustrative of the intense respect felt, not so much towards the philosopher, as towards knowledge for its own sake. The ' Felix qui potuit ' of Virgil was of course inevitable (*Georg.*, ii, 490) ; but to it can be added countless passages from Plato (pp. 18, 19, 36, 37-40)—a fragment from Euripides (Nauck, fr. 910), an epigram of Democritus (' I would rather solve one problem of causation than be king of Persia,' Diels, *Fragmente der Vorsocratiker*, i, p. 407—fr. 118) ; Posidonius of course ; a paragraph from Cicero's *Hortensius*, preserved by Augustine (*de Trin.*, xiv, 9) and so forth.[2] If many could not be found to endorse Socrates' contention that ' a life without enquiry is unliveable,'[3] at least Thucydides did not hesitate to represent the greatest of his fellow-citizens as saying, ' We are philosophers without effeminacy,'[4] in his panegyric on Athens.

This conception of the value of knowledge *for its own sake*, the attempt at a ' purely objective ' apprehension of the universe, Boll regards as wholly Greek (p. 8 ; following J. Burckhardt, *Griech. Kulturgeschichte*, i, p. 11) ; other nations had eyes only for ' their own kingdoms, temples and gods.' Not that it was the earliest Greek conception of the highest life. Herodotus (i, 30) makes Solon tell Crœsus in what that consists—to live prosperously in a prosperous city, to see one's sons and grandsons growing up virtuously round one, and at last to fall gloriously in a victorious battle. Boll rightly contrasts this ideal with the later one as exemplified in the legend of Plato who, shipwrecked once on a barren shore, set at nought the merely material evidences of human occupation which it exhibited, but, on observing geometrical figures traced upon the sand, cried to his companions—' Be of good cheer, here be men like us ' (Cic., *de rep.*, i, 17, 29).

The development was the fine flower of the Greek genius. Boll traces the growth of this passion for knowledge from the seven mythical Wise Men and Solon, through the great physicists of the Ionian coast, Thales, Heraclitus and Anaxagoras (who brought the new ideal to Athens), to Socrates, Plato, Aristotle and Archimedes (pp. 8-11). One feature common to the classical philosophers and their disciples—a feature linking them closely to the ascetic element in Christianity—was

---

[1] Generally see *contemplatio*, etc., in Berlin *Thesaurus Ling. Lat.*
[2] Cp. also G. L. Dirichlet, *de veterum macarismis*, pp. 66-69.
[3] Plato, *Apol.*, 38 A. [4] Thuc., ii, 40.

their sense of detachment from the phenomenal world of change around them. The characteristic was heightened by popular fancy which, while it often gave the philosopher the 'nimbus of a demi-god' and expected miracles of him (p. 9), could also insist upon the nebulous character of his speculations and the unpractical dreaminess of his life. So of Thales, who was really (Hdt., i, 170) an active and states-man-like person—Plato, *Theæt.*, 174A; Arist., *Eth. Nic.*, vi, 7 (quoted, p. 36) ; Protagoras (Eupolis, *Kolakes*, fr. 146 (Th. Kock, *Com. Att. Fragm.*, i, p. 297), quoted, p. 36).

The detachment or other-worldliness of the philosophers was not simply the consequence of their preoccupation with abstract interests. It was also deliberately adopted as a principal means of securing not merely the necessary leisure, but also the appropriate outlook, for the prosecution of their studies. Heraclitus' retirement to the mountains (p. 10) ; Anaxagoras, who endured the 'loss of property, the death of his sons, and his own banishment from Athens with equanimity,' provided only that he might continue his contemplation of the uni-verse (pp. 10, 31) ; Socrates, deliberately withdrawing himself from public life, and scarcely ever venturing beyond the city walls,—are well-known instances.

It is scarcely surprising that this deliberate 'misanthropy' [1] (as it must have seemed), as well as the unconscious aloofness of many of the philosophers, was turned into grounds of accusation against them. Christianity in general, and monasticism in particular, have often had to meet the same charges for the same reasons. The 'active life' was championed as against the 'contemplative,' and the arguments on either side became bitter and pointed. In Euripides' lost *Antiope*, Zethos takes the part of the active life against Amphion, his brother, the representative of the contemplative (fr. 183-227 (Nauck, i, pp. 413-450) ; cp. *Gorgias*, 484E, 506B ; Cic., *de Rep.*, i, 30—Boll, p. 33). The comic dramatists, of course, found here a fruitful subject for their wit ; naturally enough they are for the most part on the side of the 'active life' (refs. Boll, p. 33). The most usual accusations against the philosophers are those of effeminacy, useless pedantry, sophistry, dogmatism, pride, laziness, want of patriotism, and the like (Boll, pp. 14, 15, 33-36, with references). The philosophers are no less trenchant in their attacks upon the sordid and immoral shifts which alone make for success in the active (i.e. political) life ; upon its ten-dency to forsake or ignore the higher interests of the soul ; and upon its ultimate disappointment and disillusionment.

Although, therefore, the Aristotelian *bios theoretikos* is, strictly speaking, something quite different from the pursuit of the vision of God, it provided theology with countless analogies, themes, and argu-ments whereby to fill out the conception of the Christian 'contempla-tive life.' Indeed, as is indicated in the text (*supra*, pp. 376 f., 380 f.), under the influence of the rediscovery of Aristotle in the early middle ages, scholastic theology in some of its branches went far to reduce Christian 'contemplation' to something little more than philoso-phizing about the data of revelation and science. When it is said, as it often is, that 'mystical theology was first separated from systematic theology in the thirteenth century,' what is really meant is that the enthusiasm for dialectic, for a short period, almost arrogated to itself

---

[1] So Philo, *de vit. cont.*, 20. *M.* 474 = *C-W.*, vi, 51.

the title 'contemplation,' and that it required a definite effort to
recognize that the Aristotelian *theoria*, which only men of wealth,
leisure, intelligence and worldly culture could undertake, while it
might lead to genuine contemplation, was by no means essential to
it in all cases, and might in some at least prove a positive hindrance
(*supra*, pp. 390, 391).

NOTE C.—THE ORIGINAL TEXT OF MK. 10²³⁻²⁶ (*supra*, p. 69).

The discussion on page 69 does not cover the whole history of the
text. The significant points are :—

(*a*) Both Mt. and Lk. omit Mk. 10²⁴ altogether (Mt. shows a slight
reminiscence of it in the πάλιν δὲ λέγω ὑμῖν, 19²⁴). It is possible that
Mt. and Lk. also agree in the following verse against Mk.—reading
τρήματος for τρυμαλιᾶς, and εἰσελθεῖν for διελθεῖν—but 'assimilation
has run riot here' (B. H. Streeter, *Four Gospels*, p. 317), and it is
impossible to recover the original text. Still, it is not inconceivable
that the story stood originally in Q as it runs in Mt. and Lk., and that
Mk. 10²⁴ is secondary. In this connexion the transposition of verse 24
in D, etc., is not without significance, for (Streeter, *Four Gospels*,
p. 250) 'transposition occurs when a sentence written in the margin'
(not necessarily by the original author) 'is inserted in the wrong place
by the next copyist' (or, better, is inserted in *different* places by
different copyists). So verse 24 (in one or other of its forms) may
be a pious accidental interpolation in the original Mk. But if so it
must have occurred at a very early stage ; how otherwise account for
the reminiscence of it in Mt. 19²⁴ (' And again I say unto you ') ?

(*b*) Assuming, however, that Mk. 10²⁴ (without 'those who trust
in riches ') is authentic, we notice that even the אBk text leaves the
story still unintelligible. With this text the saying exhibits the
sequence (i) 'How hard it is *for the rich* . . . '; (ii) 'How hard it is
[*for anyone*] '; (iii) ' It is easier for a camel than *for the rich* . . . '—a
meaningless order. I am inclined to think that a πῶς has crept into
verse 24 before δύσκολον from the πῶς δυσκόλως of verse 23.[1] The
original sequence would then be (i) ' How hard it is for the rich . . . '
(amazement) ; (ii) ' It is hard [indeed] for anyone; [but] (iii) in the case
of the rich it is easier for a camel . . . ' (exceeding astonishment).

This gives a natural sequence ; and (even assuming that there was
no Q version, and that verse 24 is not an interpolation) it still leaves
reasons why Mt. and Lk. should independently have eliminated Mk.
10²⁴. Mt. left it out because he was dealing specifically with the case
of the rich alone (see *supra*, p. 69, for the distinction between ' enter
into life ' and ' be perfect ') and did not wish to confuse the issue by
discussing the problem of how men *as a whole* are to enter the kingdom. Lk. omits it because it blunts the edge of the ascetic tone of
the passage.

(*c*) Another possibility is that verse 24 originally read ' How hard it
is *for a rich man* to enter the kingdom ' (a mere repetition of 23). This
was felt to be redundant. Mt. and Lk. both independently therefore
omitted it. One text of Mark (אBk) removed the redundancy by

---

[1] Or the πῶς of v. 24 may be, as Euthymius suggests, 'affirmatory'—the
equivalent of ἀληθῶς (H. B. Swete, *St. Mark*, p. 228). The text would then
as it stands give the meaning just suggested.

omitting the ' for a rich man.'   Another (ACθ etc.) both removed
the redundancy and altered the sentiment by writing (with a reminiscence of Prov. 12²⁸) ' for them that trust in riches.'   In this case the
reading of D is an attempt to correct the confusion of ACθ by trans-
posing verses 24 and 25, without noticing that this attached greater
amazement to the difficulty of those who *trusted* in riches entering the
kingdom, than to that of rich men in general.   A further attempt to
correct the ACθ reading is that of Syr.-Sin., which reads ' those that
trust in riches ' in 23 as well as in 24, and so is the least rigorist of all.
—Further suggestions, A. E. J. Rawlinson, *St. Mark*, p. 140.

Note D.—Pagan Asceticism (*supra*, pp. 41, 86, 87, etc.).

It will be convenient to distinguish cult-asceticism—that is to say,
ascetic practices undertaken as a preliminary to ritual approach to the
godhead—from asceticism based upon philosophic theories as to the
nature of the ' flesh,' the passions, and so forth.   It is often maintained that, if one could trace them to their ultimate sources, both
types would be found to have the same origin—a conception of an
evil, or at least a dangerous, *mana* localized in such a way that its
presence can be suspected, detected and guarded against.   It will be
suggested below that such a theory scarcely covers every type of
philosophical asceticism.   But in so far as it holds good, the distinction between cult-asceticism and philosophic asceticism will be found
to lie in the fact that the former localizes the *mana* in specific holy
places and rites, which may therefore be approached only after spiritual
prophylaxis has been employed, but which are only approached intermittently ;   the latter, on the other hand, finds *mana* resident in everyday activities of a particular character, and therefore rules out all such
activities as dangerous at all times for the man who would be, in
Dr. Bevan's striking phrase, ' at home in the universe.' [1]

(A) The distinguishing characteristics of cult-asceticism are therefore (*a*) that it is particularly required of the priesthood, (*b*) that it is
of temporary duration only ;   although in the case of those attached
to the temple-service it lasted, no doubt, throughout the period of
their attachment, or at all events of their turns of duty.   Should they
withdraw to secular occupations, however, the prohibitions were no
longer enforced ;   even the Vestal Virgins might retire into married
life after thirty years' service of the sacred fire.[2]

The principal phenomena concerned have been studied in detail
by E. Fehrle, *Kultische Keuschheit im Altertum* (Giessen, 1910), and
Th. Wächter, *Reinheitsvorschriften im Griechischen Kult* (Giessen, 1910).
Further material is added by H. Strathmann, *Geschichte der früh-
christlichen Askese* (1914—only vol. i published).[3]   A brief resumé of
the main types of ascetic injunctions current in the Græco-Roman
world, drawn principally from these collections, serves at least to
show that, however much philosophical conceptions may have influenced Christian asceticism, the latter held itself singularly aloof
from anything akin to cult-asceticism.

[1] E. R. Bevan, *Stoics and Sceptics*, p. 98.
[2] O. Zöckler, *Askese u. Mönchtum*, p. 102 ; Fehrle, *op. cit.*, pp. 218, 219.
[3] Cp. also P. Wendland, *HRK.*, pp 234-238 ; A. D. Nock in (ed.)
A. E. J. Rawlinson, *Essays on Trinity and Incarnation*, pp. 69-75 ; H.
Hepding, *Attis*, pp. 182 ff.

(i) *Sexual Prohibitions.*—Abstinence was required of both priests and laity before their approach to or participation in the cultus. Little distinction was made between conjugal and extraconjugal intercourse ; [1] the basis of the prohibition therefore was other than moral. The usual period for abstinence was two, three, or ten days (Fehrle, pp. 157-159) ; very occasionally as much as a year is demanded of the priest or priestess (*ib.*, pp. 159-160). More rarely still there are references which may be interpreted as a demand for life-long celibacy (*ib.*, p. 162) ; though, as a rule, where uninterrupted abstinence was required, the most intimate attendants of the deity were selected from the ranks either of children below the age of puberty, or of old men and women (*ib.*, p. 160), who might be expected to comply with the requirement without difficulty.

The basis of these prohibitions is found by Fehrle to be twofold : (*a*) the conception that intimacy with the god precludes intimacy with man (pp. 8 ff.) ; (*b*) that the mysterious associations of procreation made it an activity of peculiar danger, subject to interference by demons, and consequently ritually ' unclean ' (pp. 25 ff.). Strathmann (p. 214) rejects the first of these two bases on the grounds that the *hieros gamos* was rare in Greek thought. This enables him to associate sexual with dietary and other prohibitions ; all of which he regards (with Rohde, *Psyché* [8] (E. tr.), pp. 296, 297, 338, etc.) as springing from the idea of ' demonic infection,' due to their associations with gods of the earth and the underworld (Strathmann, pp. 221, 222, 254, 255, and cp. Wächter, pp. 2-5, with references there). Thus all cult-asceticism was due to an implicit theory of conflict between the cultus-god and demons—the latter standing in some kind of association with the mysterious forces of earth. The almost incredible disorder in which sexual, dietary, and purely ritual prohibitions are jumbled together in some enactments (Nock, pp. 69, 70, 73, for examples) bears out Strathmann's view.

(ii) *Diet.*—Here the prescriptions are innumerable.[2] In the case of flesh, the motive was to avoid infection from the animal's ' demon ' ; the heart and the brain were specially forbidden as being its particular dwelling-place (Wächter, pp. 80, 81). Exceptionally ' demonic ' animals were swine and goats ; beef was often forbidden because of the mythological connexions of the bull with various deities (*ib.*, p. 90) ; birds, except the domestic cock and hen, were generally allowed (*ib.*, p. 93), though the Pythagoreans and Orphics extended their prohibition to the eating of any living thing (*infra*, p. 482), including even eggs (Wächter, p. 81). Fish were sometimes forbidden (*ib.*, p. 95), probably because they were originally assigned to the same genus as snakes, whose ' chthonian ' character was obvious (*ib.*, p. 99). Of vegetables, beans were those most commonly forbidden (*ib.*, p. 105), being reserved for offerings to the dead (Rohde, p. 357). The danger of intoxication made wine specially ' demonic,' and led to very general regulations against partaking of it before entering a temple (Wächter, pp. 109-115 ; cp. generally Strathmann, pp. 234-256).

(iii) *Disease or Death.*—Contact with a diseased person or a corpse rendered unclean (Wächter, pp. 39-62), although the sick themselves were constantly allowed access to temple precincts, in order to be

---

[1] But contrast the Pergamene inscription, Ditt., *Syll.*[3], 982 ; Diog. Laert., viii, 43 (Theano's epigram) ; Strathmann, p. 213 ; Nock, p. 70.

[2] A useful review by H. Lietzmann (on Rom. 14) in *HNT.*, iii, p. 109.

cured by the power of the indwelling god (*ib.*, p. 43). The length of
ritual impurity consequent upon contact with death varied in different cults from one to forty days (*ib.*, pp. 61, 62 ; cp. Rohde, pp.
167, 194, 295).

In all this there is evidently little if any interaction with Christian
asceticism. In particular there is nothing to correspond with the
voluntary adoption of poverty which was so distinctive a mark of
the latter. Nor do any of the prescriptions appear to be lifelong,
except occasionally in the case of the priests, or where (as in Orphic
circles) the cult-idea is reinforced by philosophical considerations.

(B) *Philosophic asceticism* is more closely allied to the Christian
spirit. Setting aside Reitzenstein's theory (*infra*, pp. 495-503), which
stands by itself, the following examples of philosophic asceticism may
be noticed.

Orphism owes its existence to a great revival of religion in Greece
in the seventh and sixth centuries B.C., under the wing of Dionysus-
worship (Rohde, p. 335, cp. Bevan, *Stoics and Sceptics*, pp. 99, 100).
Its complicated mythology embraced the primary dualistic *sôma-sêma*
belief—' the body a tomb '; the ' Orphic life ' of asceticism offered a
way of escape to the believer even while still in the flesh (Rohde,
p. 342). Rohde notes with emphasis, however, that this asceticism
did not involve any ' fierce determination to tear the will away from
life ':—' abstention from the eating of flesh was the strongest and most
striking species of self-denial practised by the Orphic ascetics ' (*ib.*,
p. 343). For the rest we are simply dealing with cult-asceticism once
more. The underlying theory alone is different, in that the body *as
such* is the primary source of spiritual danger ; and naturally enough
the ordinances are not of temporary but of life-long duration
(Strathmann, p. 226).

Pythagoreanism probably owes its ascetic characteristics to Orphic
influence (Rohde, pp. 337, 375). Ultimate escape from transmigration
through an endless series of alien bodies is only possible to the soul by
asceticism (*ib.*) ; but there is no clear evidence that the abstentions
prescribed were other than of the usual ritual character (*ib.*, pp. 397,
398). The same conclusions seem to hold good of the later revival of
the system in what is known as neo-Pythagoreanism ; although the
widespread use of terms familiar also in the early history of Christian
monasticism—' apotaxis,' ' anachoresis,' ' athletes,' ' askesis,' and so
forth [1]—suggests that here as elsewhere, the cultivation of a certain
atmosphere of philosophic detachment [2] from the affairs of this world
was recommended.

Neo-Pythagoreanism, however, developed the less spiritual side of
Orphism, and allied itself more with divination and magic.[3] Its relations with Christian asceticism, therefore, in so far as they can be
established, lie wholly within the crude and superstitious periphery
of that movement, and are anything but central. From Iamblichus
may be quoted frequent verbal repetitions of such phrases as ' com-

[1] Reitzenstein, *HMHL.*, pp. 96 ff., 104 ff. ; and index.
[2] Or even, as with Posidonius (Bevan, pp. 100-105), ' a more urgent
note.' Cp. also W. Warde Fowler, *Religious Experience of the Roman People*,
pp. 380 ff., on Pythagoreanism, Panætius and Posidonius; Dill, *Roman Society
from Nero to M. Aurelius*, pp. 398, 399.
[3] Cp. Posidonius, Bevan, pp. 114-116 ; Cumont, *Astrology and Religion*,
pp. 87-89.

munion with God,' but the interpretation he puts on them is that of revelations and heaven-sent dreams (Strathmann, pp. 310, 315). Similarly, Apollonius of Tyana foresaw the plague at Ephesus before others because of his severe asceticism ; and definitely assured Domitian (a *mauvais sujet* for his instructions) that on the same account he could anticipate the future ' not as soon as the gods but before other men ' (*ib.*, p. 311). But even Iamblichus sets marriage forward as a moral duty ; for ' we must leave behind us a posterity to serve the god.' [1] It is noticeable that the Hermetic texts are practically silent on the whole matter of asceticism.[2]

Neo-Platonism modified the Orphic system under the deeper influence of Plato's philosophy.[3] In the first place, it superseded the bare idea of immortality by that of ' seeing God,' [4] and allowed mortals to experience this vision in their lifetime. ' That which we desire to behold is the Light which gives us light, and by its own light to see it,' says Plotinus (*Enn.*, v, 3, 17) ; and again, ' What is this Bacchic frenzy that thrills through us ; this longing to depart from the body and sink into the depths of the soul ? It is the passion of the true lover. . . . Let us ascend again then to the good, for which every soul thirsteth. For whoever hath seen it knoweth what I speak of, how fair it is. . . . He that hath seen it—what passion of love is his ! What ecstasy of longing ! He prays to be molten into one with it ; he is distraught with joy ! Why even those who have never seen it long for it as their only good ' (*Enn.*, i, 6. 5-7 ; and the whole tractate). Plotinus received this experience four times during the seven years that Porphyry was associated with him.[5]

In the second place, neo-Platonism admitted a certain element of ' world-embracing ' or humanist morality alongside its dualist asceticism. Porphyry's life of Plotinus begins, indeed, with the words, ' The philosopher Plotinus, a contemporary of ours, resembled one who is ashamed because he dwells in the body. For this reason he could never speak of his family or parents or birthplace ' [6]—nor did he keep his birthday for similar reasons. But Porphyry was an enthusiastic champion of asceticism for its own sake,[7] as the *de abstinentia* shows ; and his evidence on the point is open to suspicion.[8] Plotinus, as a matter of fact, led an active busy life. He was always ready to undertake the duty of a guardian or trustee, and his businesslike methods in this capacity gained general approval. His plan for founding and ruling a new city of philosophers is very different from the world-evading principles of the hermit of the desert. His affinities, if any, are with the later, not the earlier developments of Christian monasticism.

Again, Plotinus was no dualist. His attack on the gnostics on

---

[1] *Vit. Pyth.*, 18 (83) ; cp. Diog. Laert., viii, 42 ; and H. Kroll, *Die Lehren des Hermes Trismegistus*, p. 349.

[2] Cp. Kroll, p. 348. But see *Corp. Herm.*, i, 19, 22, for exceptions.

[3] Rohde, pp. 472, 473.

[4] Plotinus, *Enn.*, iv, 8. 1 ; v, 3. 4 ; v, 4. 2 ; vi, 7. 35 ; vi, 9. 10 f. ; Strathm., p. 330 ; Reitzenstein, *HMR.*, pp. 135, 136.

[5] *Vit. Plot.*, 23. [6] *Ib.*, 1.

[7] Reitzenstein, *HMHL.*, p. 98 ; cp. pp. 102, 103 (with quotations) ; contrast p. 227, n. 3.

[8] Strathm., p. 341 ' Porphyry was less enthusiastic about the vision of God than Plotinus ' ; but note Reitzenstein's rather severe criticism of Strathmann on this point, *HMHL.*, p. 98, n. 3,

this point was thorough and incisive ; the witness of nature and history
to God is one of his dearest themes. ' Never say,' he writes, ' that the
world was made evil because there is evil to be seen in it. That would
be to pay too much thought to the world, to confuse it with that ideal
world of which it is but a copy. And can there be a better copy than
this ? What fire more truly reproduces the fire of heaven than earthly
fires ; . . . what sun could be more beautiful than our sun, the sun
in the ideal world only excepted ? ' [1] ' Is there another, better world
than this ? Why, then, if there be none, and yet a world must be,
this world is a true copy of the world of ideas.' [2] ' 'Tis madness,' he
adds, ' to call the soul immortal and divine, even in wicked men, and
then deny the heavens and stars their share in the immortal soul of
all.' [3] History, too, is a sure evidence of providence—no other faith
is possible to a god-fearing man. The so-called ' negative way ' appears
in Plotinus, of course.[4] ' Strip thyself of everything ' [5] is his prescription for the life of contemplation, but the passages just quoted show
that its dangerous tendencies were mitigated by a very real sanity.

The sanity or humanism which characterizes neo-Platonic asceticism
derives quite obviously from a different source than the half superstitious, half cultus *sôma-sêma* conception at work in Orphism and its
descendants. It belongs to the genuine Greek strain of thought [6]
which thinks of ' askesis ' in terms of self-training in virtue, and
requires the body and the passions to be controlled, rather than
mortified or extirpated. The distinction between the two methods of
approach (which might, of course, for all their radical difference, produce
and even merge in identical manifestations), is well brought out by
W. Capelle in *ERE.*, ii, pp. 83 ff. (*s.v.* ' Asceticism (Greek) ') from the
results of earlier investigators. He finds the humanist strain manifest
in the later writings of Plato, but attributes it primarily to Socrates
himself. The basic Socratic doctrine in ethics is not that of self-
immolation, but of moderation, temperance, or self-control ; the
object of this self-control is ' autarkeia,' or freedom from dependence
upon external things.

With the *Cynic* school of philosophy (founded by Antisthenes,
† c. B.C. 370), ' autarkeia ' was rigorously conceived, and led to an
extreme of world-renunciation which took not merely an ascetic but
even an anti-social colouring. But it does not appear to have lent
itself (as for example in Christian Syrian monasticism) to unnatural
forms of self-crucifixion. Curiously enough, it did not include sexual
prohibitions (Capelle, p. 84). The inconsistencies of Cynicism, and its
tendency to rest content with modes of life designed mainly to shock
comfortable society out of its habitual complacencies,[7] were rectified
by the *Stoics*, who in two respects at least introduced modifications of
real importance.

In the first place, the Stoics developed a conception of moral
advance by means of self-discipline, thus making asceticism merely a

---

[1] *Enn.*, ii, 9. 4.
[2] *Ib.*, ii, 9. 8 ; cp. W. R. Inge, *Philosophy of Plotinus*, i, pp. 194-199.
[3] *Enn.*, ii, 9. 5.
[4] See W. R. Inge, *Philosophy of Plotinus*, ii, pp. 133 ff., 165-174 ; cp.
G. S. Brett, *History of Psychology* (*Ancient and Patristic*), pp. 301-305.
[5] *Enn.*, v, 3. 17 ; ἄφελε πάντα.
[6] Cp. Wendland, *HRK.*, pp. 234, 235.
[7] Cp. Dill, *Roman Society from Nero to M. Aurelius*, pp. 350, 351.

means to the good life. In other words, they introduced Greek thought to the doctrine of the two lives in its valid form (*supra*, pp. 243, 248). The distinction between the 'incipientes,' the 'proficientes' and the 'perfecti' goes back to Zeno himself (Capelle, p. 84) ; but it was in Roman Stoicism, under the influence of Panætius, that it achieved its height. In the second place, the doctrine of moral progress made possible a far more flexible treatment of material well-being.[1] On the one hand, beginners and 'proficients' might be excused if they showed some attachment to the comforts of everyday life : on the other hand, the 'wise man' having attained complete detachment ('ataraxia,' 'apatheia'), and consequently being incapable of abusing worldly goods, might be trusted to use them. It is possible of course to quote even from the later Stoics (as Reitzenstein does from Epictetus)[2] passages which seem to imply an extreme rigorism. In one such passage[3] Epictetus insists that persecution or banishment enables the philosopher to 'witness' to God ; in another[4] that asceticism is his great weapon for convincing men of the beauty of Stoicism. 'That ye may see, brethren,' the philosopher cries, 'how ye seek happiness and calm from the wrong quarters, here I come, an example sent you by God, without lands, house, wife or children ;—nay without pallet, coat or vessels. Yet see, how well I fare. Test me and note my calmness ; listen to my prescription ; hear how I have been cured.'

The Stoic literature, like the neo-Pythagorean, is full of the technical terms of early monasticism.[5] But in spite of this, the general principle stands true that Stoic asceticism was of a temporary and adaptable character—once the 'wise man' had achieved his state of 'passionlessness,' he could enjoy the goods of the world, nor were they absolutely forbidden him in the course of his quest. The missionary might find married life, as Epictetus suggests,[6] an obstacle in the way of his championship of 'true cynicism' ; but to the ordinary Stoic marriage was allowable and natural.[7] The same applies to wealth : 'The wise man does not love money, but he prefers (" mavult ") it,' Seneca writes to Gallio ; 'he welcomes it to his home, though not to his heart. . . . His riches excite and exhilarate him, as a favouring breeze affects a sailor.'[8] Seneca could never rid himself of the thought that asceticism was in essence unnatural, and therefore wrong, and on these grounds he condemned the 'unkempt appearance, long hair, neglected beards, ostentatious hatred of riches, and humble mattress' which distinguished the 'perverse way' of some contemporary philosophers.[9]

From this brief review the following points emerge in connexion with the problem of the relation between Christian and pagan asceticism :—

[1] Cp. Bevan, *Stoics and Sceptics*, pp. 58 ff., 63-68.
[2] *HMHL.*, pp. 86, 87.
[3] *Diss.*, III, 24, 111 f. ; and for this aspect of Stoic ethics, Wendland, *HRK.*, pp. 238, 239.
[4] *Diss.*, IV, 8, 30 f.
[5] Reitzenstein (*ut sup.*, p. 482, n. 1).
[6] Epict., *Diss.*, III, 22, 69 ; cp. Dill, *Roman Society from Nero to Marcus Aurelius*, p. 326 ; for more dualistic terminology in Seneca, *ib.*, pp. 308, 513.
[7] Kroll, *Hermes Trismegistus*, p. 348.
[8] Sen., *Dial.*, vii, 21, 22 ; cp. Dill, *Roman Society from Nero to M. Aurelius*, p. 314.
[9] *Ad Lucil. ep.* i, 5. 2.

(1) Nowhere in the pagan world can anything be found akin to the widespread and popular enthusiasm for the early Christian ascetic movement ; nowhere is there anything so thorough-going in character ; nowhere is there any real insistence upon the life-long vocation to asceticism which was felt by the Christian monk or hermit.

(2) Christianity rejected without hesitation the cultus-' tabus ' which marked the pagan movement in all its branches, except Stoicism and the best neo-Platonism.

(3) At the same time it diverged from Stoicism by retaining the dualistic atmosphere in the doctrine of the contrast between nature and the supernatural ; this divergence carries with it (*supra*, p. 470) a recognition that the ascetic *motif* must be a permanent element in ethics, not simply a means to the attainment of moral freedom.

(4) Thus, while the points of resemblance between Christian and pagan asceticism are numerous, the Christian movement exhibits a grasp of principle which brings all subordinate or eccentric manifestations under control ; and at the same time retains all the essential elements of rigorism, which, in so far as they are found in paganism, are there as a rule isolated, over-emphasized, or distorted. In other words, the contribution of Christianity to the world's philosophy of asceticism is unique and epoch-making : its borrowings, if any, are secondary and unimportant. Zöckler has summed up the situation accurately in his *Askese und Mönchtum* (p. 136). ' Asceticism,' he says, ' first achieves its significance as a power in world-history within the sphere of the Christian development. Everything that went before was the merest preliminary. The history, the full development of its nature and potency, its international influence, its constructive yet revolutionary control of the whole process of human civilization— these achievements of asceticism only date from the moment when the spirit of Christianity took possession of it.'

(C) A note may be added on the asceticism of *Philo*. In him a strong theoretical dualism comes to the fore. ' He introduced,' as Bousset says, ' into Plato's thought of the vision of God an opposition where there was none before. For him the ecstatic experience is something new and different, essentially opposed to all activities of the personality, even the highest.' [1] Once again the divine is the wholly abnormal. Conformably with this, Philo is strongly ascetic. He gives an account of his own spiritual wanderings : ' Once on a time, I found room for philosophy and the observation of nature and nature's ways, and plucked fruit from the beautiful and truth-giving tree of contemplation. I busied myself with divine words and thoughts ; and no earthly distractions came near me. No temptation of fame or riches or bodily enjoyment could wean me from my purpose ; my soul was full of the divine, and I wandered with sun and moon and the whole body of heaven. . . . But some envious demon lay in wait for me and plunged me into the great sea of political cares, till the waves all but passed over my head. . . . Moments come when I struggle to the surface and with eyes dimmed by these alien preoccupations look up in hot longing to that pure and happy life once more ; sometimes a calm and halcyon period comes when the waves of civic life are still ; then I take wings and fly to heaven and drink in the air of wisdom

---

[1] Bousset, *RJ.*, p. 449 ; but Bousset seems to under-estimate the dualistic element in Plato's thought for the sake of his contrast. The *Phædo* has after all been called the source of all Western dualism.

once again. Fain would I escape from my harsh servitude; for not men alone, but circumstances too, overwhelm me like a torrent from all sides, and I can only thank God that I am not utterly submerged.' [1]

There can be few who have exploited the resources of the human vocabulary to elaborate the *sôma-sêma* doctrine more successfully than Philo. The body is to him a 'foul dungeon,' a prison cell, a cage, a burden, a fetter, a coffin.[2] His call to the ascetic life is therefore unqualified.[3] But it remains at best an academic appeal. Strathmann has summed it up adequately, if not altogether charitably, in the words: 'Philo's demand for other-worldliness is, like that of other ancient philosophers, purely theoretical and abstract. This is due partly to his Jewish descent, partly to experience that asceticism is not always successful . . . but partly also to the fact that he was a hedonist at heart. He praises the Essenes, but does not join them; he reveres the Therapeutæ, but does not go to the Mareotic sea; his affection for both sects is more or less platonic. . . . His real goal is himself and his own happiness; and therefore his service of virtue and God is at best half-hearted. Despite many fine phrases he is far away from the spirit of "Whom have I in heaven but Thee" . . . because he can never forget himself. . . . He is the picture of a professor of ethics, well-meaning, anxious, rather pedagogic and dry, repeating himself over and other again; shielding his frail constitution from the raw air of Reality. . . . He is a man who has taken diplomas in every branch of his subject, that is why he is so boring. And therefore he has had many readers, but no disciples.' [4]

NOTE E.—THE USE OF 'PSYCHIKOS' IN EARLY 'GNOSTIC' LITERA-TURE (*supra*, p. 93).

As indicated in the text (*supra*, p. 93), Reitzenstein (*HMR.*, p. 74) takes for granted that in early gnostic literature 'psychikos' is invariably used of the element in man hostile to the spirit. But even on the assumption that 'gnostic' is a sufficiently wide term to cover, *inter alia*, the whole of primitive Christianity, this may still be an exaggeration. The relevant facts as to the use of 'psyché' and 'psychikos' at the beginning of our era appear to be as follows:

A. (i) On the one hand, 'psychikos' is used in a derogatory sense in Jude [19], Jas. 3[14].

(ii) From the '*Mithras-liturgy*' (Dieterich, p. 4, l. 23) *as emended by Reitzenstein* (*HMR.*, p. 176, l. 1—ἀρτίας ὑπεστώσης μου πρὸς ὀλίγον τῆς ἀνθρωπίνης μου ψυχικῆς δυνάμεως), Bousset, who accepts Reitzenstein's reading without stating that at the crucial point it has been emended (as he does also with the famous ἀπεθέωσας ἡμᾶς, *KC.*,

---

[1] *de leg. spec.*, iii, 1 (*M.*, ii, p. 299; *C-W.*, v, p. 150).
[2] Bousset, *RJ.*, p. 442, for refs.
[3] Cp. *supra*, p. 41; Strathmann, pp. 134-143; Conybeare, *Philo on the Contemplative Life*, pp. 265-273; Bousset, *RJ.*, p. 444; *KC.*, p. 131. But he approved of marriage—see *de præm. et pœn.*, 108 (*M.*, ii, p. 425; *C-W.*, v, p. 361):—'Neither man nor woman should be without offspring: all servants of God should 'keep the true law of nature, which is to have children.' Other humanist elements in Philo, Strathmann, p. 144.
[4] Strathmann, pp. 145, 146.

p. 166, *supra*, p. 52),[1] infers that the 'gnostic' who wishes to rise to the 'pneumatic' life must 'leave his soul behind' (*KC.*, p. 134; the same inference, Reitzenstein, *HMR.*, pp. 70, 71, 178).

(iii) Lucan, *Phars.*, v, 161 ff., seems to employ *mens* in a derogatory sense (*HMR.*, pp. 73, 74, 323).

These are the only passages which Reitzenstein can quote prior to the great gnostic writers of the second century ; and even there, as he admits, the tendency is to elevate the conceptions of ' psyché ' and ' psychikos,' though traces of the ' older usage ' remain (*HMR.*, pp. 326, 327).

B. (i) On the other hand, the *actual* reading of the ' *Mithras-liturgy* ' (ἁγίας ὑπεστώσης κτλ.) conforms to other passages in the same text (Dieterich, p. 10, l. 25 ; p. 14, l. 25), in representing the soul as the *higher* element in man ; it is the ὑποκειμένη φύσις (p. 4, l. 8), or φθρατὴ (= φθαρτὴ) βροτῶν φύσις (*ib.*, l. 30), which is the lower element—see Dieterich, p. 59.

(ii) As Reitzenstein admits, constant passages in Philo (*HMR.*, pp. 317-320, 324) and other writers of the period (*ib.*, pp. 308, 311, 314, 321, 326, 408, 411) equate ' psyché ' with ' pneuma,' use ' psyché ' of the Godhead, or represent it as ' the spiritual and divine in man.' This is fully confirmed by H. de Witt Burton, *Spirit, Soul and Flesh*, pp. 169, 174, 175, 176, 191 (though on pp. 161, 162, he is prepared to admit traces of the beginning of a distinction between ' pneuma ' and ' psyché ' in Philo; similarly, Bousset, *KC.*, pp. 130, 131 ; Weiss, *Das Urchristentum*, p. 477) ; cp. H. A. A. Kennedy, *S. Paul and the Mystery Religions*, pp. 142-144. Moulton-Milligan, *Vocabulary*, part viii (1929), *s.vv.* ψυχή, ψυχικός, makes it abundantly clear that in ' koiné ' Greek the words bore not a trace of evil significance.

(iii) As I have pointed out in the text (*supra*, p. 93), S. Paul's use of ψυχή betrays no hint of any derogatory meaning attached to the word.

(iv) In the Lucan passage it is not ' mens,' but ' *prior* mens,' which is decried—the *former* state of mind as distinct from the present. Thus there is no taint ascribed to the ' mens ' as such.

(v) In James and Jude, the word may simply have a neutral sense— ' unilluminated ' or ' natural ' man ; and thus be distinct from ' fallen ' or ' sinful ' man. In Jude [19] it is characterized negatively as ' having not the spirit ' : positively as ἀποδιορίζοντες, which may mean either ' wranglers ' or ' separatists,' but does not in itself imply positive aversion from good. In James 3[15] it appears to be identified with ἐπιγείος (' earthly '), as contrasted with οὐράνιος (' heavenly ') ; and the merely psychic man is said to be liable to demonic assaults—δαιμονιώδης —the result again being an anti-social tendency (ζῆλος καὶ ἐριθεία). But in neither passage is there any suggestion that the ' psychikos ' is incapable of redemption ; and this alone could make the use of the word genuinely dualistic.

It seems therefore that the case for an early, widespread, and fundamental antithesis between ' pneuma ' and ' psyché,' whether in Christian or in ' gnostic ' thought, needs a great deal more support than it has hitherto obtained. Failing such support the antithesis

---

[1] In the first case he merely speaks of Reitzenstein's ' revised text ' (*KC.*, p. 133) ; in the second he says the text has been ' reconstructed ' (p. 166). In neither case does he mention that his argument depends *entirely* upon the correctness of the ' revision ' or ' reconstruction.'

remains exceedingly hypothetical, and cannot possibly be employed
to bear the full strain of the theory of Pauline dualism.   On the rare
occasions on which Reitzenstein directly faces the question, ' How
could S. Paul conceive the idea of speaking of the physical and
material element in man by the term " psychikos," when in an infinite
number of expressions " psyché " and " pneuma " must have had the
same meaning for him ? ' (HMR., p. 72 ; cp. ib., p. 412), he is compelled to have recourse to vague allusions to ' Oriental texts ' (p. 72)
and ' circles of thought ' (p. 316), whose contact with Paulinism he
fails to establish.   Somewhere in the second century, no doubt, the
term ' psychikos ' came for a time to be used for the completely unilluminated (examples, Bousset, KC., pp. 197-199, notes).   Later,
however, its fortunes improved once more.   ' Choikos ' (earthly),
' hylikos ' (material), or ' sarkikos ' retained the wholly evil meaning ;
but the Valentinians (desiring, so Bousset says, to ' mitigate the stark
Pauline dualism ') elevated the ' psychikos ' into a third class in between
the ' pneumatikos ' and the ' hylikos,' and spoke of the ordinary
Christian by that name in a spirit of conciliation and compromise
(Bousset, KC., p. 198 ; Reitzenstein, HMR., p. 326, and supra,
p. 217, n. 2).

NOTE F.—' PANHEDONISM ' (supra, pp. 104, 198).

M. Bremond would scarcely object, I believe, if we said that the
unmasking of panhedonism is one of the tasks to which he finds himself specially called.   As long ago as 1906, he had fixed upon ' autocentrism ' as the clue to the complexities of Newman's character.[1]   In
1910, in his Apologie pour Fénelon, his attention reverted to the question, which—when we remember how the psychology of religion, with
its inherent temptation to make ' experience of God,' rather than God
Himself, the central objective both of theological speculation and of
active striving, was at that date just achieving its present widespread
popularity [2]—we can see now to have deserved his epithets ' at
once interesting and novel ' (Apologie, p. 458).   In the Apologie,
pp. 459-468, he insists upon the panhedonist strain in Bossuet, ' concerned as he was to defend the emotional apprehension of God, the
treasury of enjoyment, and illumination in prayer, against the new
mystics.'   ' To him,' M. Bremond says, ' Christian faith and good will
are naturally accompanied by sensation, exhilaration, acceptance,
chaste raptures ' (Bossuet, Instruction sur les États—see especially
Books V-VI, pass.).   ' From his all-but-infallible pen that " naturally "
is worth more than a volume of theories and confidences.   Bossuet
" abhors a vacuum " in prayer.'   The inevitable corollary of this
' naturally ' (which comes near to meaning ' normally ') is that where
no exhilaration accompanies prayer, the purity of prayer itself is suspect
—' pas de plaisir, pas de prière.'   This doctrine M. Bremond finds in
Bossuet (ut supra), Pascal (HLSR., iv, pp. 336-382 ; note especially
p. 360—for Pascal, ' salvation ' is not so much ' sanctification ' as

[1] Newman : Essai de biographie psychologique, p. 347 ; cp. ib., pp. 258-271,
314-326, for the struggle between ' autocentrism ' and ' theocentrism ' in
Newman.

[2] William James's Varieties of Religious Experience was first published
in 1902.

'sense of God'; p. 363, 'In a sense, in Pascal's conversion, it is God who is converted rather than Pascal. . . . He was imperceptible, now He is perceived,' and the criticism of William James in the footnote; p. 373, on the 'sign.' But contrast pp. 404 ff. on 'le meilleur Pascal'), and Nicole (*Apologie*, p. 461; *HLSR.*, i (E. tr.), p. 405; iv, pp. 569-572—note especially the quotation from Nicole on p. 569: 'Spiritual dryness indicates an absence of grace, and therefore a state in which love (towards God) is deficient'). The 'logical consequences of the doctrine for the spiritual life,' M. Bremond truly says (*Apologie*, p. 461), 'are abominable. For nine souls out of ten, it is the short cut to despair.' It should be mentioned that in *HLSR.*, vii, pp. 65-67, M. Bremond cites passages to show that Bossuet (like Pascal) could at times be better than his creed.

The great mystical writers have unanimously asserted, against this 'panhedonism,' or spiritual Epicureanism, that divine graces, though to be accepted with joy (after they have been 'tested'), are not to be sought after; and that their absence (= the well-known mystical phenomenon of 'dryness' or the 'dark night') is indicative neither of moral lapse nor of divine disapproval. In vol. vii of *HLSR.*, M. Bremond has collected a catena of passages, emphasizing the true Christian position, from S. Francis de Sales. The following are noteworthy (for the *Treatise on the Love of God* I add references to Dom Mackey's English translation (1884); but I have not always followed his rendering) :—

P. 78 (from *Entretiens*, p. 150)—' I have observed that many draw no distinction between *God* and the *feeling of God*, between *faith* and the *feeling of faith*. It is a terrible mistake. They fancy that if they cannot *feel* God, they are not in His presence'; p. 80 (from *Treatise*, i, 12, Mackey, p. 50) :—' That holy love, whereby we acquiesce in the union of our spirit with God's—a union of which *we have scarcely any feeling*'; p. 83 (from *Treatise*, vii, 2, Mackey, p. 286) :—'Sometimes, too, as He has drawn us *imperceptibly* into union, He continues *imperceptibly* to help us'; p. 85 (from *Treatise*, ix, 2, Mackey, p. 370) :— ' The love that desires to walk the way of God's will *by the road of spiritual pleasure* ("parmi les consolations") walks ever in fear of taking the wrong path, and of loving the spiritual pleasure more than the will of God '; p. 104 (from *Treatise*, vi, 10'; Mackey, p. 259) :— ' There are souls who continually double back upon themselves, who wish to see and scrutinize their inward sensations, ever gazing in upon themselves to discover the progress they make. Others, again, are not content to be content unless they feel, see and relish their contentment. . . . If God grant them the sacred repose of His presence, they voluntarily forsake it to note their own deportment, to examine whether they are really content, disquieting themselves to ascertain whether their tranquillity is really tranquil and their quietude quiet. . . . *There is no small difference between occupying oneself with the God Who gives contentment, and amusing oneself with the contentment which God gives.* The soul to whom God gives holy, loving quiet in prayer, should refrain as far as possible from the consideration of herself and her repose, which to be preserved must not be curiously observed (*gardé . . . regardé*); for he who loves it too much loses it. The right rule to possess this love is not to be obsessed by it' ('la juste reigle de la bien affectioner, c'est de ne point l'affecter'). Cp. also the beautiful parables of the deaf musician (pp. 89 ff.; *Treatise*, ix,

9, 11 ; Mackey, pp. 388 ff.) ; the statue (pp. 106, 107 ; *Treatise*, vi, 11 ; Mackey, pp. 263 ff.) ; and the sleeping saints (p. 108 ; Mackey, p. 262).—For passages in which Fénelon expresses exactly the same doctrine, see the quotations and references in H. Bremond, *Apologie pour Fénelon*, pp. 458, 459 ; similarly for Guilloré, *ib.*, pp. 464-466, *HLSR.*, iv, pp. 568, 569.   Cp. also the passages quoted from Hilton, Madame Guyon, and other mystics, E. Underhill, *Mysticism*, pp. 335-338 ; *Mystic Way*, pp. 59-62 ; S. Teresa, Vinet and Goodwin, Bremond, *HLSR.*, vii, p. 67 ; Bérulle, *ib.*, iii, pp. 38 ff. ; Camus, *ib.*, viii, pp. 393-397 ; and especially S. John of the Cross, F. von Hügel, *Mystical Element*, ii, p. 51 ; A. Saudreau, *Life of Union with God*, pp. 246, 247.   The whole question is so fundamental, and M. Bremond's analysis so piercing, that no apology is necessary for drawing attention to it even at some length.   On the whole subject A. Saudreau, *The Mystical State*, pp. 72-82, 100-102, is also excellent.

NOTE G.—THE ALLEGED PAGAN ORIGIN OF CHRISTIAN MONASTICISM
(*supra*, pp. 179, 192).

Although, as has been suggested in a previous note, Christian asceticism as a whole cannot be assigned a pagan origin, theories are still current which would attribute the specific variant of *monasticism* to this source.   Two main types of theory may be noticed :— (i) those which connect the Pachomian institution with the Egyptian cult of Serapis ; (ii) Reitzenstein's theory, in which it is suggested that monasticism evolved or crystallized out of a general doctrine of the supremacy of the ' spiritual man ' in the Græco-Roman world.

I. Four facts combine to lend a certain speciousness to the first theory, which attempts to derive the whole of Christian monasticism from the pagan cult of Serapis in Egypt :—

(*a*) The treatise on the ' Contemplative Life ' attributed to Philo, which describes the ascetic practices of an Egypto-Jewish community known as the Therapeutæ, was supposed by Eusebius and the fathers generally (with the exception of Photius) to refer to an otherwise unknown primitive sect of Christian ascetics.   On this fact, which implies a doubt in the fourth century as to the existence of any *Jewish* Therapeutæ, E. Lucius (*Die Therapeuten*, 1879) elaborated the startling theory that the document was a Christian forgery dating from the end of the third century, designed to give nascent monasticism of the Pachomian order a respectable ancestry in popular opinion.   The hypothesis was strengthened by a second theory—that of Weingarten (*Ursprung des Mönchtums* (1877) esp. pp. 15 ff.)— which assumed a similar lack of authenticity for Athanasius' *Life of Antony*.   Both theories had a momentary popularity ; but can fairly be said to have fallen into complete disrepute.   Lucius' thesis was completely demolished by the brilliant destructive criticism of F. C. Conybeare (*Philo about the Contemplative Life* (1895), esp. pp. 362-435).[1]

[1] Conybeare addresses himself to five main points : (*a*) Why did *cenobitism* in particular need a defence ?   (*b*) Why should the treatise be fathered on Philo especially ?   (*c*) How did the forger manage to insert his treatise into the archetype of all MSS. of Philo, whether in the Greek version or in translations ?   (*d*) Why did he refrain from asserting his identity with Philo ? (*e*) Why did he credit the Therapeutæ with ideas and institutions which the fourth century would unhesitatingly brand as heretical ?   There are no satisfactory answers to these questions.

The authenticity of the *Life of Antony* cannot be defended quite so satisfactorily, but enough can be done in this direction to allow it to be regarded as a reasonably trustworthy source—see especially the replies to Weingarten in O. Zöckler, *Askese und Mönchtum*, pp. 188-192 ; and A. Robertson, *Athanasius* (Nicene and Post-Nicene Library of the Fathers), pp. 188-193.

In view of what has been said, these attempts to show that Pachomian monasticism was an alien intrusion into Church history, and did not evolve out of earlier Christian customs or ideas, must be adjudged failures.

(b) Nevertheless, efforts have been made to relate Pachomius to an alleged pagan monasticism in Egypt connected with the Serapis-cult. Only a single slender link can be adduced as evidence, and the investigations of M. Ladeuze (*Étude sur le Cénobitisme Pakhomien* (1898)) make it a very precarious one.

Pachomius founded his first monastery at Tabennesi about A.D. 320, but he had been a Christian and an ascetic for some years (the Memphitic 'Life' says ten) before that date. It is his earlier history that is of special importance. Born a heathen and recruited for military service, he was discharged from barracks about A.D. 314-315.[1] He broke his journey home at a spot called Chenoboskion, and there was baptized, attaching himself a little later to an anchorite of the name of Palæmon, in order to learn the rudiments of asceticism. So far the best Greek version of the life (the Bollandist text). According to a Coptic life of the Saint (published by Amélineau, *Annales du Musée Guimet*, xvii (1889), pp. 1-294), he stopped at the village (here apparantly called Schenesit) ' because he saw there were only a few persons there.' ' He went to the river bank, to a little temple called by the ancients a temple of Serapis, and there he stopped and prayed. The Spirit of God moved him, saying "Strive and remain in this place." And this pleased him, and he stayed there, cultivating a few vegetables and a few palm trees for his own needs, for the poor of the villages, or for strangers who passed by water or road.'[2] Then follows the account of the baptism. The Arabic life gives the same details.[3]

Even if Amélineau were right in holding the Coptic and Arabic lives to be more authentic than the Greek (and Ladeuze has argued convincingly in the opposite sense), there is nothing here on which to base the theory that Pachomius was for a time (between his arrival at Chenoboskion and his baptism) a monk of Serapis. This theory, however, was frankly stated by Grützmacher (*Pachomius u. das älteste Klosterleben* (1896), pp. 39 ff.), and has been accepted by such admitted authorities as Zöckler (*Askese u. Mönchtum* (1897), i, pp. 194, 195), and Batiffol (*Anciennes Littératures Chrétiennes* (1897), i, p. 252—see Ladeuze, pp. 87, 158)—Zöckler with quite amazing inaccuracies. Ladeuze's arguments (pp. 159-162) amply disprove the whole hypothesis, and no more need be said about it.

(c) The 'monks of Serapis,' however, have had a long history as putative parents of Egyptian monasticism, and the theory is not by any means dependent merely upon the trivial mention of an (aban-

---

[1] So Rosweyde (*MPL.*, lxxiii, col. 274) and Ladeuze (*op. cit.*, p. 239). The Bollandists (*AS.*, Mai., iii, pp. 290 ff.) put the date nearly twenty years earlier ; Grützmacher and Zöckler split the difference. Further details, Ladeuze, p. 222.
[2] Amélineau, *ut supr.*, p. 7.   [3] *Ib.*, p. 344.

doned ?) temple of Serapis in two (secondary ?) biographies of Pachomius. Apart, however, from one possibility—that of the so-called
κάτοχοι (see paragraph (d) below)—there is little evidence for any
Serapis-monasticism other than the normal cult-asceticism of the
priests.

The third century tract de abstinentiâ of Porphyry quotes from the
Stoic Chæremon (temp. Nero) an account of the Egyptian priesthood [1]
in which is described their complete isolation during the six weeks
before their principal ceremonies, an isolation which, Chæremon says,
helped them to achieve an askesis ethôn—a 'moral asceticism.' It is
more than probable that Chæremon (and Porphyry after him) is
generalizing or idealizing ; Reitzenstein himself asserts that the picture
is based upon neo-Pythagorean philosophy rather than upon actual
fact.[2] Cumont [3] is even more outspoken. He writes of the 'fluidity'
and 'inextricable confusion' of Egyptian religion in the following
terms :—'The scribe Chæremon, Nero's tutor, recognized in the sacerdotal traditions of his country the Stoic theories. But when the
eclectic Plutarch speaks of the character of the Egyptian gods, it accords
marvellously with the philosophy of Plutarch—when it is the neo-
Platonist Iamblichus, with that of Iamblichus. The nebulous (fum-
euses) ideas of the oriental priesthood allow everyone to see in them
the phantoms he is pursuing ; individual imagination can give itself
free rein, and literary dilettantism please itself by moulding these
malleable doctrines to its taste.'

At best, therefore, it can only be said that the Serapic priesthood
practised cult-asceticism of a kind normal among temple-attendants
in the Oriental world ; and that from such asceticism to the world-
flight of the first Egyptian hermits is a very far cry indeed.

(d) Since the time of Weingarten,[4] however, attention has been
directed to a number of persons who dwelt around the Serapeum at
Memphis about 160 B.C. Their existence is known from a series of
papyrus fragments discovered about the year 1820, and recently re-
edited by U. Wilcken.[5] These persons are in some sense confined
within the temple-precincts by external compulsion ; they date their
letters by the length of their κατοχή ; they cannot leave of their own
freewill but must wait for 'release'—a consummation for which they
long, and which they greet with joy.[6] One at least of them even
appears to communicate with the outside world only through a window
or grating (θυρίς).[7] The four who figure most freely in the documents are two brothers Ptolemæus and Apollonius, and two girl-
twins (αἱ δίδυμαι), Thaues and Taūs, in whom Ptolemæus is specially
interested.[8] They are commonly referred to by modern writers as
the κάτοχοι, and the word goes back to Vettius Valens,[9] by whom it
is used of temple residents of an ecstatic kind ; but the title is not
actually used in the documents. The writers designate themselves

[1] Porphyry, de abst., iv, 6.
[2] Reitzenstein, HMHL., p. 111.
[3] Religions Orientales [4], pp. 81, 82.   [4] Op. cit., pp. 31 ff.
[5] Urkunden aus der Ptolemäerzeit, vol. i (1921) ; cp. also K. Sethe, Serapis
u. die sogenannten Katochoi (1913).
[6] Wilcken, pp. 69 (Pap. 59. 25), 74, 360 (Pap. 78. 39)—[ἄφ]εσις μοι
γίνεται τάχυ.
[7] Sethe, p. 37.
[8] The twins, however, do not appear to have been officially ἐν κατοχῇ.
[9] Wilcken, pp. 70-71.

by such phrsaes as ὁ ὢν ἐν κατοχῇ, οἱ παρακατεχόμενοι, and (once) οἱ ἐγκάτοχοι ; [1] and speak of their condition as ἐγκλείεσθαι or ἐγκατέχεσθα.

Philologically,[2] the words concerned could be used either of pathological 'possession' (by a god, by ecstasy, etc.), or of physical incarceration.[3] Reitzenstein's arguments for the latter meaning here are convincing,[4] and are supported by the evidence of inscriptions elsewhere. The same evidence seems also to rule out Sethe's theory of any *merely* secular imprisonment. The confinement is one intimately associated with a temple, and only the god can give release.[5] On the other hand, the κάτοχοι show no very particular interest in religion.[6] What then was the purpose of their confinement ? Were they refugees from justice who had taken sanctuary in the temple ? or invalids waiting (as in the *incubatio* at other shrines) to be cured ? [7] Were they ecstatics attached to the temple, like the *fanatici* of Bellona ? [8] None of the suggestions seems to fit the facts ; and Wilcken, who gets no further than assigning them 'some kind of religious incarceration by the Deity' ends with the remark that the whole problem gives him a headache.[9] Reitzenstein [10] revives Weingarten's view that 'we have to do with a kind of asceticism' (understanding this in a special sense of his own to which allusion is about to be made), but admits [11] that we have 'no clear evidence as to the character of their asceticism.' He supplies the defect by the statement that 'the confinement itself was an ascetic practice.'

But the facts on this head are much more baffling than Reitzenstein admits. So far from its being the case that we have 'no clear evidence' as to the ascetic life of the κάτοχοι, we have clear evidence that they partook in no respects of any asceticism with which early Christianity was familiar. Ptolemæus holds property both at home and in the Serapeum ; [12] he is continually engaged in its management ; he complains of the irregularity of his remittances ; he has to borrow money, and sometimes falls so deeply into debt that the priests put the bailiffs in.[13] He has legal rights for the redress of which he is continually drawing up petitions. His friendship with the twins, despite their sex, is unrestricted. So far from inflicting pain on himself, he manifests extreme annoyance when he suffers it at the hands of others. Whatever be the truth about the κάτοχοι, one thing is certain. Quite apart from the fact of their temple residence (in itself enough to distinguish them completely from the Christian hermit), they manifest not a single one of the ascetic characteristics which were to be the marks of Christian asceticism five hundred years

[1] Wilcken, p. 52 ; traces of κάτοχοι elsewhere, Sethe, pp. 68 ff.

[2] Reitzenstein, *HMR.*, pp. 200, 201 ; cp. Ganschinietz, *PW.*, x, 2526 f., this last a very disappointing discussion.

[3] Sethe, *Serapis u. die sogenannten Katochoi*, Abh. d. Kais. Ges. d. Wissensch. z. Göttigen ; Phil. Hist. Kl. ; N.F., xiv (Berlin, 1913), pp. 71-82 ; cp. Wilcken, p. 54.

[4] *Op. cit.*, pp. 202, 203.

[5] Wilcken, p. 74 ; Reitzenstein, p. 203. [6] Sethe, p. 83.

[7] Apparently Preuschen's suggestion (Sethe, pp. 21, 22) ; but I have not been able to see his *Mönchtum u. Serapis-kult* (1903).

[8] Reitzenstein, p. 212. [9] Wilcken, pp. 55, 75.

[10] *HMR.*, p. 203.

[11] *Ib.*, p. 199. But this is an understatement ; Wilcken very properly points out that there is no evidence of their having any ascetic practices at all (*op. cit.*, p. 69).

[12] Wilcken, p. 108. [13] *Ib.*, p. 109.

later. It may be impossible to say of what nature their puzzling confinement really was, but every new fact that can be learnt about it distinguishes them even more finally from the monks.

II. The second theory reverts to that conception of Christian origins dominant in Germany to which reference has frequently been made above (see pp. 87, 88, 210). On this hypothesis, pagan religion as a whole was ruled by a single conviction. Two classes of men existed in the world—the *pneumatikos*—the spiritual man, or super-man, often called also the *gnostikos*, or gnostic ; and the natural man—the *psychikos*, later to be known as *sarkikos* as well.[1] To the ' pneumatic' all things were possible ;[2] neither external constraint nor direction had any further power over him. He was endowed with a spiritual body, free from the passions and almost from the needs of the natural body ;[3] he was capable of miracles and wonders, he lived in intercourse with the divine, and could foretell the future. To this condition he had attained through the vision of God by which true *gnosis* was reached. The vision itself might be achieved in various ways ; most important were initiation into a mystery cult, as in the case of Apuleius, or illumination by means of esoteric teaching, as in the Hermetic writings.

To this system Reitzenstein attempts to link up the entire development of Christian asceticism. That S. Paul was by no means wedded to convictions of this character has been suggested earlier (*supra*, pp. 81, 93) ; and it is perhaps because of the weakness of evidence in relation to him that Reitzenstein has attempted to find stronger links at a later point in Christian history.[4] Even so his problem is not an easy one. On the one hand, although, as we have seen, cult-asceticism was common in the Hellenistic world (as for centuries earlier), there is little if any trace that it was based on the ' pneumatic' conception just mentioned ; whilst philosophic asceticism was confined to circles too narrow to admit of its exercising a very wide influence. On the other hand, there does not appear in Christian asceticism any frequent recognition of the fact that after what, on this theory, must have been the culminating moment of ' askesis '—the reception of the vision,—the need for ' askesis ' itself is over, and the life of freedom and wonder-working begins. To the overcoming of this difficulty Reitzenstein accordingly devotes his great and—it must be confessed—involved critique of the ' Historia Monachorum ' of Rufinus

---

[1] Reitzenstein notices (*HMHL.*, pp. 127 ff.) that in Evagrius Ponticus the distinction is between two kinds of *gnosis*—the ' natural ' and ' spiritual.' Generally, of course, *gnosis* is possible to the ' spiritual ' man only.

[2] For this cp. *HMR.*, p. 33—' By rights anyone counted worthy of union with God is autonomous. . . . The vision confers freedom ' ; *ib.*, pp. 78, 200—' As soon as the goal (becoming " pneumatikos ") is reached, the vow of service (i.e. self-discipline and asceticism) is discharged. According to the primitive gnostic view, the ascetic can now do any of the things which formerly were forbidden ; he can even return to the world.' *HMHL.*, pp. 22, 156 (' The gnostic has God within, and so is above the Law ').

[3] Hence the stories of the ' heavenly food,' *HMHL.*, pp. 121 ff., 156 ff., etc.

[4] He does not, of course, surrender his belief in ' Paul the pneumatikos ' ; but it is clear that since (as he assumes) Paul and the hermits shared the same circle of ideas, there would have been no need to deal with the later evidence if the ' gnostic ' character of Pauline thought had been safely established.

and the 'Historia Lausiaca' of Palladius;—a critique which perhaps has not received as much attention as it deserves.[1]

To effect a synthesis between two systems at first sight so alien to one another except in verbal parallels Reitzenstein is forced to make great play with the Greek ' fairy stories ' of *theioi anthropoi*,[2] who go about working miracles without any apparent moral or religious significance. He suggests that we do not possess these stories in their original form. The public was more interested in the miracles than in the ascetic preparation which made the ' pneumatikos ' fit to perform them ; this latter element therefore was quietly dropped.[3] The modern critic must restore it if he would have the stories as they originally ran. Hence Reitzenstein requires us to add to the cult-asceticism and philosophic-asceticism of the pagan world a third—we may call it gnosis-asceticism. We are to think of it as far wider in extent than the other two—it was the preparation for that life of wandering, preaching and miracle-working which was so commonly embraced in the Hellenistic world. But for the reason just mentioned, the necessity of the preparation was forgotten in wonder at the finished product.

On the other hand—and this requires more elaboration—the fairy-story influence has almost entirely obscured the beginnings of Christian asceticism. Originally the latter was wholly akin to the pagan development. There was first of all a testing of the would-be initiate ; then a period of training in purely bodily asceticism,[4] sometimes under a spiritual guide ; finally the postulant is found to be ' perfect ' or pneumatic, his life of visions and wonders begins ; and he is free from all superior control.[5]

---

[1] An important review of *Historia Monachorum u. Historia Lausiaca* (by Dom. C. Butler) appeared in the *Journal of Theological Studies*, vol. xxii (1921) ; but it dealt with the details of Reitzenstein's criticism of the Lausiac History, rather than with the theory as a whole. Fr. Lebreton's essay, *Recherches de Science Religieuse*, 1924, I have not seen.

[2] Dealt with at length in his *Hellenistische Wundererzählungen* (1906), and continually alluded to in *HMR.* and *HMHL.*

[3] *Hell. Wund.*, p. 17 : ' The Oriental teller of moral stories (" Aretaloge "), as he wandered through Greece and Rome, allowed the religious element to fall more and more into the background in comparison with the merely entertaining; the gay imaginative strain, which even to-day reminds us of the Arabian Nights, captivated the audience.' Similarly, p. 34. It follows that although Reitzenstein can describe ' what the original tales must have been like ' (p. 72—emphasis upon the hero giving away all he possessed, retiring from the world, and performing amazing feats of heroism) he cannot quote a single example of a pagan story following this model. Indeed, the conclusion that they *did* follow this model is inferred only from those Christian stories, which—on the assumption that the pagan tales were originally of the kind suggested—he holds to be derived from them (*ib.*, p. 54). The argument obviously involves a vicious circle. Generally it may be said that the main outlines of all Reitzenstein's theories depend upon the vast assumption that community of vocabulary (e.g. between Christian and pagan thought) must imply identity of outlook.

[4] Slightly modified (*HMHL.*, p. 21) by the words : ' No doubt he was told that it was not a matter of mere bodily self-denial alone ; the appetite must be mortified as well.' The modification is however strictly limited : ' Of a training of the soul in the later sense we hear nothing in the earliest ascetic literature.'

[5] So the ' fellaheen,' in the *Hist. Laus.* version of the Paul-Antony story, ' regard Antony with mockery and contempt ; they feel themselves to be

This primitive scheme has been modified, Reitzenstein suggests, in various ways. The earliest in time is one which derives its motive from Greek philosophy [1]—to bodily asceticism must be added a discipline of the soul, or mortification of the personality; and the means to this is blind obedience.[2] This conception represents a transition stage between the earliest and the latest types. On the one hand, it introduces the idea of spiritual self-mortification—'the direct reverse of anything which the hermit could contemplate'[3]—for the aim of the hermit is to be free;[4] at the same time it still allows the postulant freedom after he has become 'perfect'—a conception against which the cloister fought bitterly later. But its general effect is to suggest that not spiritual experience so much as mere self-abnegation is the central point in the ascetic life—'blind obedience without knowledge or talent will bring a simple ordinary man to that deification of personality which Rufinus understands by "perfection."'[5]

Far more drastic are two further modifications, representing two contradictory tendencies.[6] The influence of the fairy-story, on the one hand, has carried the miracles back to the earlier stages of the would-be monk's career, whilst his real asceticism or self-mortification has either been ignored, or so modified as to be in itself miraculous.[7] Thus from his first appearance as a novice he is represented as a 'pneumatikos,' endowed with spiritual power; the crucial moment of achievement is antedated. It is not, however, merely antedated, it is also reduced in importance. It would be absurd to suggest that the newly-admitted novice should *ipso facto* receive the vision of God; therefore the connexion of the vision with the reception of the pneumatic life is broken, and as miracles are more popular with novel-readers than spiritual experience, the *only* change in the monk's life becomes that at which he starts his career as a miracle-worker—that is, the moment he is accepted as a novice.[8]

his superiors both in outward achievement and in greater prowess of faith '—but this *motif* is concealed under later colouring (*HMHL.*, p. 20). Similarly, the Amon story in Athanasius' *Vita Antonii* (*HMHL.*, p. 24).

[1] *HMHL.*, pp. 21, 22.

[2] This is represented by the Latin *Hist. Mon.* version of Paul-Antony (*HMHL.*, pp. 16, 22; other instances, *ib.*, pp. 22, 130); and cc. 1-4 of *Hist. Laus.* (*HMHL.*, p. 154).

[3] Based on Cassian, *Coll.*, xix, 8, with its distinction between the mutually exclusive lives of the hermit, whose aim is *gnosis* or *theoria*, and the coenobite, whose aim is *obedience*. This distinction, however, occurs only here, and cannot be taken as typical (see *infra*, p. 525, additional note M).

[4] *HMHL.*, pp. 20, 155, 156, 191, etc.; cp. *ib.*, p. 189—'Completed asceticism makes the sacraments superfluous and meaningless; the "perfect" man is already risen from the dead'; *ib.*, p. 190—the 'perfect' monk is honoured with sacerdotal titles, i.e. assumes himself to be free from ecclesiastical control.

[5] *Ib.*, pp. 16, 17, 22.   [6] *Ib.*, p. 23.

[7] So the Greek *Hist. Mon.* and *Hist. Laus.* versions of Paul-Antony (*HMHL.*, pp. 14, 16, 17)—'a purposeless fairy-tale of the most outrageous ("grobschlächtig") kind'; and tendencies in Greek *Hist. Mon.* and *Hist. Laus.* versions of Amon (*HMHL.*, pp. 27-29).

[8] The Greek *Hist. Mon.* versions of Paul-Antony (*HMHL.*, pp. 13, 14) and Amon (*ib.*, p. 27); so also the Latin *Hist. Mon.* (c. 9) story of Patermutius—'the raw heathen robber is converted by a miracle and at once called to the *cælestis angelicaque militia*' (*HMHL.*, p. 163).

On the other hand, the ambition both of monastic superiors [1] and of prelates [2] combined to combat any theory which allowed the monk, after he had achieved ' perfection,' to be ' free ' and his own master ; and thus the crucial moment is now not antedated, but postponed till it vanishes from the story.[3] The ' motif ' of obedience, of the annihilation of personality and the individual will, is taken up with new emphasis and made a lifelong obligation. Wonders, therefore, must similarly be reduced in number, for only the free pneumatikos may perform them, and the essence of askesis, which thus becomes lifelong and leads up to nothing, is obedience alone [4]—the obedience of the cloister of later days. By this second influence—an influence which in the terminology we are employing, we should call predominantly formalist—the original character of Christian monasticism has been wholly obscured.

To achieve these results Reitzenstein has to search a wide area for evidence. For pagan asceticism as leading to freedom, he quotes freely from philosophers, theosophists and magic texts ; [5] and lays stress upon the theory that initiation into the mystery qualified the initiate for priesthood, and so required of him conformity to the full priestly rules of abstinence.[6] For this Apuleius is of course his strongest evidence.[7] With it he combines the ' katochoi,' whom—though with more hesitation than Weingarten—he still regards as ascetics waiting for illumination, and other examples of temple ascetics—the ' fanatics,' or those who, though not priests, were attached to a temple and behaved in an extraordinary way.[8] Naturally enough, he uses neo-Pythagoreanism [9] a good deal, though he does not deal with the problem presented by the fact that this system does not appear to show any moment at which natural asceticism as such comes to an end, and miraculous asceticism, or wonder-working, begins.[10]

On the Christian side Reitzenstein avails himself of an elaborate source-criticism which must be adjudged, on examination, to be in the main based upon the theory, and therefore to involve a vicious circle.[11] He divides the complicated sources and versions of the *Hist.*

---

[1] The ' abbot '-motif in the Greek *Hist. Mon.* Paul-Antony story (HMHL., p. 15) and *Hist. Laus.* version (*ib.*, p. 20)—other *Hist. Laus.* illustrations, pp. 193, 194.

[2] HMHL., pp. 117 ff.—Theophilus of Alexandria ; cp. *ib.*, p. 185.

[3] So *Hist. Laus.* reduces the idea of *gnosis* to nothing more than a ' richer store of what is required of every cleric, and indeed of every Christian—a knowledge of Holy Scripture ' (HMHL., p. 159).

[4] *Ib.*, p. 142—with Diadochus of Photiké ' the claim of the ascetic to a higher form of existence is abandoned ' ; *ib.*, pp. 21, 22.

[5] *Ib.*, pp. 86 (Epictetus), 98 (Porphyry), 103 ff. (Philo), 108 (magic); HMR., p. 302 (Hermetica).

[6] HMR., p. 20. [7] HMR., pp. 196, 197.

[8] HMR., p. 212. [9] HMHL., pp. 95, 102.

[10] Reitzenstein seems to be conscious that the historic connexion between Christian and pagan asceticism has scarcely been established by his arguments. He says (*ib.*, p. 96), ' Where definite historical evidence is lacking, vocabulary itself is sometimes a witness.' He then adds in a far more emphatic tone—' the powerful influence which Greek philosophy exercised upon the development of monasticism is *established beyond question* (' steht schon dadurch ausser allem Zweifel ') by the fact that practically all the technical terms of asceticism are borrowed from it.'

[11] The whole theory depends upon the priority of the Latin *Hist. Mon.* (Rufinus) to the Greek ; otherwise it could not be established that the high

Mon., Hist. Laus., Vit. Ant., and *Apoph. Patrum* into those which show the earlier system of testing, training and full illumination; those which are wholly dominated by the fairy-tale motive, and make the monk a wonder-worker from the outset; and those which show later ecclesiastical formalism, insist upon obedience as the dominant characteristic of monasticism, and tend to rob the monk of his vision. Further evidence for the alleged ' freedom ' of the ' perfect ' monk in the earliest period is obtained from the journey-stories told of certain at least of the apparently free ascetics; [1] and from the prominence attached to ' vision ' as the reward of confession or (less often) martyrdom—an experience to which, *faute de mieux*, asceticism affords a second-best initiation.[2] The confessor, at the moment of his imprisonment, is rewarded by visions and revelations, and thereafter and on that account deems himself ' pneumatikos,' and free from any higher ecclesiastical control.[3] The hermit, ambitious for the confessor's privileges, but in the absence of the necessary persecutor unable to attain them by the same means, claims to receive visions or revelations as the reward of voluntary asceticism, and thereby to have the right to regard himself as a spiritual superman of equal rank with those who have suffered for the faith.[4]

I have tried to represent Reitzenstein's connexion of thought and train of argument in the fairest possible manner. No one acquainted with the great German scholar's mannerisms—his discursive arguments, his interminable paragraphs, his constant side-issues and long-delayed reversions to the main problem, his subjective selection and treatment of evidence, his trick of presenting a single fact in constantly changing dress till it becomes a veritable stage-army of proof—will think this an easy task. Perhaps many of the niceties of the argument have been missed; but even if it has only been possible to reproduce it in its crudest form, a formidable number of points are evident in which the theory appears to be expugnable. To the *circulus in probando* of the source-criticism allusion has already been made; two further illustrations of its weakness will suffice. On Reitzenstein's theory any ' late ' monastic source should emphasize ' obedience ' strongly; and where it does so, all is well for his purposes. Sometimes, however, a passage which for other reasons he wishes to treat as ' late ' in origin omits any reference to this feature of obedience.

valuation of the ' pneumatic ' life was the *earliest* motive of monasticism (for though ὁ πνευματικός, *spiritalis homo*, is rare with Rufinus (*HMHL.*, p. 115), he uses the allied words freely enough (pp. 119, 120), whilst the Greek *Hist. Mon.* avoids them all wherever possible (*ib.*, pp. 115-117)). But the priority of the Latin is argued on occasion by assuming that the theory can be used as a decisive test; e.g. p. 13—' Supernatural endurance of hunger and thirst is in this literature a gift only vouchsafed to the perfect '—hence the Greek, which vouchsafes it to Paul at the outset, must be later. Similarly, it is freely assumed that, where Rufinus shows motive and order, and the Greek naive romancing, the latter must be dependent upon the former, because the fairy-tale tendency destroyed the theological balance of the narrative. The possibility of Rufinus imposing theological canons upon chaotic material is not considered. Facts which conflict with the theory are either explained away (e.g. pp. 75, 76—the Greek version is ' more original ' than Rufinus; but ' doubtless the Greek translator had access to an earlier source as well '), or dismissed in a footnote (e.g. p. 20, n. 2, ' Cassian here contradicts himself,' similarly p. 38, n. 3, of Rufinus; cp. *infra*, p. 500, n. 2).

[1] *HMHL.*, c. 4, cp. also Montanism, *ib.*, p. 230, n. 2.
[2] *Ib.*, pp. 79 ff.   [3] *Ib.*, pp. 88 ff.   [4] *Ib.*, p. 87.

But the critic remains undaunted. Without further ado he alleges (in a footnote) that there is no mention of 'obedience' in the anecdote in question, because, being of late origin, it took obedience for granted.[1] Similarly with the word 'pneumatikos'—if it does *not* occur where it might normally have been expected, it must have been removed by an editor to whom the idea was repugnant.[2] With methods such as these, any passage may be persuaded to produce any conclusion that may be desired of it.

What is to be thought, however, of the theory as a whole ? It turns entirely on the suggestion that the ascetic in earliest times, whether Christian or pagan, at a certain moment—perhaps indicated by a vision occurring to him, a miracle performed by him, or a revelation vouchsafed to his spiritual director—becomes 'pneumatikos' and free.[3] On the pagan side, the evidence, taken in bulk, is impressive ; but considered separately, the principal passages are far from producing conviction. Reitzenstein's principal evidence on the Christian side is drawn from the *Acts* of confessors.[4] He suggests that at the moment of their 'confession' (i.e. imprisonment or arrest), they were expected to receive a vision, and thereafter were endowed with all the powers and privileges of a spiritual person. There is no doubt, of course, that the confessor was a distinguished figure in the first three centuries, and that he made the most of his position ; and it is probable enough that, for want of persecution, the voluntary sufferings of the monks were undertaken (in part at least) as a substitute for martyrdom. By a *tour de force* of exegesis, which is palpably fallacious, Reitzenstein suggests[5] that even the Neronian

---

[1] *HMHL.*, p. 23, n. 1.

[2] The Greek *Hist. Mon.*, which rejoices in naive fairy-stories alone, should have had no objection to the phrase *pneumatikos* ; as a matter of fact it avoids it even more than Rufinus does (*HMHL.*, pp. 117-119)—the reason is given as in the text above. A further illustration : in the Paphnutius-story both Rufinus and the Greek retain (at different points) phrases which suggest (contrary to the main outlook of *both*) that there is no distinction before God between the monk and the worldling. In the case of Rufinus, this is put down to the preservation of an older conception—'he cannot have inserted it himself, as it was in direct contradiction to his own view.' (*HMHL.*, p. 38). But in the case of the Greek translator (though the idea was no less repugnant to *him*) we are to suppose that he *could* and *did* insert it, merely to 'exaggerate' the marvel (p. 36, n. 2). This preserves the priority of the Latin perhaps ; but why should Rufinus' poison be his translator's meat ?

[3] Summary, *HMR.*, p. 200.

[4] Note 'confessors' rather than 'martyrs' ; the martyr was exceptional, and in any case his death made it impossible to think of him as belonging to an 'order' in the Church on earth (*HMHL.*, p. 79).

[5] The argument is sufficiently remarkable to deserve reproduction. Livy, xxxix, 14, 10, says that after the discovery of the Bacchanalian mysteries at Rome it was decided to police the city *ne qui nocturni cœtus fierent utque ab incendiis caveretur*. Contrary to the entire structure of the sentence (*ne qui* with the active, *ut* with the passive) Reitzenstein brackets these two purposes of the regulation as though they were one only—'Confederacies' of this kind 'were expected to attempt arson' (*HMR.*, p. 117). And the Christians actually *did* talk about a conflagration—the destruction of the universe in the Day of the Lord (*ib.*). They were moreover a secret cult. When the fire occurred, therefore, nothing was more natural than to accuse them, one and all, of complicity. They were the most suspicious mystery-cult available, and everything else followed (*HMR.*, p. 110).

persecution was stimulated by the belief that Christianity partook of all the ordinary features of a mystery-cult ; but this matters little. The main evidence must come from Christian sources. And the evidence is slight. It consists, in the first place, of a *Passio Montani*, whose original form emphasized the horrors of a confessor's fate ; a later interpolator has added passages telling of the spiritual illumination and joys experienced by the narrators in prison.[1] But nothing is said of their becoming spiritually ' free ' ; and Reitzenstein fails to notice that the fact that the passages which emphasize illumination are (on his own showing) interpolations, invalidates the whole argument for his purposes. It shows that the *earliest* conception of ' confession ' was not that which he wishes to establish.

Further evidence, of no very convincing character, is found in Cyprian, Tertullian and even the New Testament.[2] We may notice particularly the treatment of Ignatius.[3] ' Because Ignatius has become a confessor,' Reitzenstein writes, ' and is in chains for Christ's sake, he can read the heart and is " pneumatikos " (*Phil.* 7[1, 2]) ; he can expect visions (*Eph.* 20[1]).' Specially important to Reitzenstein is a passage in the letter to the Trallians (5[2])—' I am in bonds and am able to understand (νοεῖν) heavenly things and the ordering of angels and the musterings of heavenly rulers, things visible and invisible.' ' As a prisoner,' Reitzenstein infers, ' Ignatius has complete *gnosis*, because his mere imprisonment makes him pneumatikos.'

Exact references are given for these statements ; and the attempt to verify them brings curious facts to light. Ignatius does *not* attribute any or all of his spiritual powers to his imprisonment ; the latter fact is never mentioned as the cause of the former. He does *not* read the hearts of others, he does not even say that anyone thought he did, but implies very definitely on the contrary that he did not.[4] That he claims spiritual insight and authority for his words is true ; but so, for example, does Hermas, and Hermas is no confessor.[5] Ignatius may be resting on his position as a bishop quite as much as on the dignity of his confession ; more probably he speaks simply as a Christian, conscious—quite apart from his temporal or ecclesiastical circumstances—of his intimate communion with God.

Most significant of all, however, is the passage from the Epistle to the Trallians. I have quoted it exactly as Reitzenstein gives it ; but the words bear a very different sense as they stand in their full context. What Ignatius says is ' *even though* I am in bonds and am

---

[1] *HMHL.*, pp. 81-84.

[2] *Ib.*, pp. 79-81, 84 f. Generally, I am inclined to believe that the majority of accounts of ' confession ' are without the crucial vision. Cp. also the humility of the confessors of Lyons and Vienne, Eus., *HE.*, v, 2. 2, 3.

[3] *HMHL.*, p. 80.

[4] At Philadelphia, where Ignatius preached strongly the duty of obedience to the hierarchy, the dissidents suspected that he ' knew beforehand ' the circumstances which made such a message peculiarly appropriate. He answers that he knew the circumstances ' not from human flesh,' i.e. that no one had told him of them. This makes it clear that all they suspected was a leakage of information. Nor does he say that he ' knew beforehand ' of the circumstances at all : he suggests rather that it was by a miraculous dispensation that he was led by the Spirit to proclaim (without himself knowing why): ' Do nothing without the bishop ' (*Phil.*, 7[2]).

[5] Hermas, *Past.*, Vis. iii, 1, 9.

able to understand heavenly things, etc. . . . *yet am I not thereby a disciple.*'[1] The omission of the crucial words alters the whole sense of the passage. Ignatius does not take his stand upon his confession or his visions ; things of this character—which Reitzenstein wishes to regard as the be-all and end-all of Christian ambition in the early centuries—are to the bishop-martyr so unimportant that they do not even constitute discipleship.

We are not done yet with Reitzenstein's account of Ignatius. Its omissions are as instructive as its assertions. We are indeed told (in a cursory footnote) that ' Ignatius seems to expect a far higher dignity to come from his martyrdom';[2] we are not told (though the same passage in the letter to Rome makes it perfectly clear) that Ignatius holds he will not ' attain to Jesus Christ' unless and until he is martyred.[3] ' Confession ' is as nothing to him, either in its implications or its rewards, as compared with martyrdom ; yet ' confession ' is, on Reitzenstein's theory, the moment of all others in the life of the would-be ' pneumatikos.' Ignatius fails his client at the most crucial moment.

But, more than this, the actual contents of Ignatius' revelations are the complete reverse of anything Reitzenstein would have him utter. As protagonist of the primitive freedom of the ' pneumatikos ' his actual allusions to the shackles of the ecclesiastical hierarchy and organization ought to be militantly hostile. But as a fact they are all on the side of order. Throughout the epistles his principal message is ' Do nothing without the bishop,' ' The bishop is in the place of Christ.' But nowhere does he proclaim it more emphatically than in the passage[4] where he specially appeals to the direct authority of the Spirit. ' Even if after the flesh some wished to lead me astray,' he says, ' yet the Spirit is not deceived, since it is from God. . . . I cried aloud when I was among you, I spake with a loud voice, with the voice of God : " Give heed unto the bishop and the presbyters and the deacons ". . . . It was the Spirit who kept preaching in these words " Do nothing without the bishop ; keep your flesh as a shrine of God. Love union. Flee divisions. Become followers of Jesus Christ as He also was of the Father."'

There is no evidence, therefore, that the primitive confessor thought of himself as ' pneumatikos ' by virtue of his confession. The same seems to be true of the primitive ascetic. Cassian expressly notices[5] that though miracles were the appropriate characteristics of saintliness, ' the monks, who by grace possessed these powers, would never use them unless extreme and unavoidable necessity drove them to do so.' Therefore the suggestion that a moment came at which his asceticism procured ' perfection ' or ' initiation ' for the ascetic, after which he was free to abandon it or not as he wished, is wholly fanciful. That the confessors came into conflict with the hierarchy in the third century, as did the monks, whether in hermitage or cloister, for many centuries thereafter, is a fact of history, but it does not bear upon the problem. Let us assume that the theory of ' gnosis '-asceticism, as described by Reitzenstein, was as current in contemporary paganism

---

[1] Ign., *Trall.*, 5[2]. Cp. also *Eph.*, 3[1]—' Even though I be bound in the Name, I have not yet become perfected in Jesus Christ. I am only now making a beginning of discipleship ' ; *Magn.*, 12[1]—' Even though I be bound, I am naught in comparison with any one of you who are free.'
[2] *HMHL.*, p. 80.   [3] *Rom.*, 5[3].   [4] *Phil.*, 7.   [5] *Coll.*, xv, 2.

as he would have us suppose. Even so, unless it can be shown that primitive Christian asceticism was temporary in character, its essential contact with, or dependence upon, pagan asceticism, remains unproved.

NOTE H.—MARCION (*supra*, p. 218).

Bousset's views are expressed, *Hauptprobleme*, pp. 109, 130, 329; *KC.*, pp. 187-191, 361. Harnack's attack on the theory that Marcion was the typical gnostic has two phases. (*a*) In *Dogmengeschichte* ⁴, i, p. 292, he says, ' Marcion was not a gnostic in the strict sense,' and gives as his reasons that (i) his interests were soteriological, not speculative or apologetic ; (ii) his emphasis was on faith not knowledge; (iii) he discarded not only the Semitic cultus but also the Greek philosophical method ; (iv) he made no distinction of esoteric and exoteric. As it is now generally admitted that (i), (ii), and (iii), so far from being anti-gnostic, are specifically gnostic traits (and even Harnack admits this for all except the ' top storey '—*supra*, pp. 210, 212), his case is considerably weakened. (iv) is undoubtedly peculiar to Marcion ; I have suggested above that it is due to Marcion's drawing the dividing line between good and evil at a different point from that adopted by the gnostics generally.

(*b*) In *Marcion* ² (1926) and *Neue Studien zum Marcion* (1923), he emphasizes details of Marcion's theory which blur its sharp dualism, and accuses Bousset of ignoring them : e.g. (*Marcion*, pp. 350 ff.)— Bousset cuts out the ' just God ' altogether, and either introduces a ' God of darkness ' in his stead, or (by eliminating ' evil matter ') converts the ' just God ' into the author of evil, and so identifies him with the ' devil.' On this it may be observed : (i) Harnack himself admits that Marcion makes no use of the devil and evil matter in his system (*Marcion*, p. 140), that he speaks in strong terms of the wickedness of the demiurge (*ib.*, p. 95, ' conditor malorum,' ' sævitia Creatoris,' etc.), and that no evidence, except the bare epithet ' just,' can be produced for his having thought well of the demiurge (*ib.*, p. 143).

(ii) E. de Faye, despite his high opinion of Harnack's work on Marcion (*Gnostiques et Gnosticisme* ², pp. 143, 530), admits Irenæus' account of the evil nature of the just God (p. 156) ; insists that Marcion's belief in the evilness of matter was ' more central ' than Harnack allows (p. 534) ; emphasizes the significance of Marcion's tenet that Cain was saved, whilst Abraham was not (pp. 534-535— but on p. 149 he appears to deny that Marcion ever said this) ; and only rescues Marcion from dualism by adopting a definition which reduces dualism to an absurdity (*supra*, p. 212).

(iii) Finally, it is amazing to find that after doing all in his power to *reduce* the dualistic element in Marcion, Harnack ends with an impassioned plea for a dualism akin to his—e.g. (*Marcion*, p. 253), ' We need to realize the *uniqueness* of the revelation of God in Christ ' ; (*ib.*, pp. 255, 256)—Marcion's rejection of the Old Testament and the Law the most important feature in his system ; (*ib.*, pp. 258 ff.), Marcion's dualism emphasized and upheld : Tolstoy and Maxim Gorki his disciples ; (*ib.*, p. 264—concluding paragraphs of the book)— ' Must not the philosophy of religion treat the dualism of " grace " and the "world" as ultimate? . . . Would that there were still Marcionites to be found among the train of seekers after God!'

It should be added that Bousset does not, of course, ignore the fact that at times Marcion's demiurge, or 'just God,' is a third term between the good and evil principles. He only suggests, and the weight of the evidence seems to be on his side, that this is of the nature of a transient compromise, and does not belong to the strict rigour of Marcion's thought. See especially *PW.*, vii, col. 1508.

NOTE I.—PUBLIC PENANCE IN THE FIRST FIVE CENTURIES.

To relieve the footnotes, I append here the principal authorities for some of the more detailed matters mentioned in chapters iv and v above. Papal rescripts are quoted with the numeration as in *MPL*.

(a) Public penance urged even for secret sin (supra, p. 227).

So Origen, *hom.* xiv *in Lev.*, 4 (*GCSS.*, 'Origenes,' vi, p. 486)—'si quis forte nostrum recordatur in semetipso alicujus peccati conscientiam . . . confugiat ad pœnitentiam'; *hom.* xvii *in Luc.* (*MPG.*, xiii, col. 1846)—'si *revelaverimus* peccata non solum Deo, sed et his qui possunt mederi, etc.'

Ambrose, *de pœnit.*, i, 16 (19)—'si quis igitur occulta crimina habens . . . pœnitentiam egerit,' etc.; Augustine, *serm.* 392, 3—the adulterer may not take refuge in private confession to God ('occulte ago, apud Deum ago'—this implies that his sin is occult, for otherwise he would have been forced to public penance) : Augustine urges public penance upon him. Similarly S. Basil's ruling (*ep.* 199 (*canonica* ii), c. 34), that a confessed adulteress should not be 'publicly exposed' (δημοσιεύειν) implies that her sin was secret, and that he is making an exception to a general rule that secret sin (of a mortal kind) demands public penance. Pacian's insistence that the 'capital' sins can be committed in the heart (*parœn.*, 5 : *MPL.*, xiii, col. 1084), implies that even for such secret offences public penance is required.—B. Poschmann, *Die Abendländische Kirchenbusse*, pp. 8, 87 (following Morinus), establishes the same principle for Leo and Cæsarius of Arles. But Aug., *serm.* 82, 7 (10); 8 (11); 9 (12), makes it clear that by Augustine's time the principle of 'public penance for public sin alone' was making itself felt ('ipsa corripienda sunt coram omnibus, quæ peccantur coram omnibus; ipsa corripienda secretius, quæ peccantur secretius . . . nos non prodimus palam, sed in secreto arguimus. ubi contigit malum, ibi moriatur malum' *infra*, p. 537), and by the time of Gregory the Great little trace of the earlier custom remains (Poschmann, pp. 265-275). For the similar development in the east, see K. Holl, *Enthusiasmus u. Bussgewalt*, p. 250.

(b) Public penance required for the three grave sins only.

By the middle of the fifth century, public penance, though still required for the three grave (formerly irremissible) sins, is apparently required for these only—Leo, *ep.* 167, inq. 19 :—'si autem idola adoraverunt aut homicidiis vel fornicationibus contaminati sunt, ad communionem eos nisi per pœnitentiam publicam non opportet admitti' (but as Leo is dealing with the special case of Christians who have fallen into sin *while in captivity*, it cannot be inferred that in the absence of such mitigating circumstances he would be content with penance in the matter of the three sins *par excellence* alone) ; Pacian, *paræn.*, 4 ; Aug., *de fid. et op.*, 19 (34). Augustine, however, though he mentions this point of view, does not agree with it, and demands public penance for all sins in S. Paul's catalogue, 1 Cor. 6¹⁰ (*speculum de Act. Apost.*). Similarly Cæsarius ([Aug.], *app. serm.* 257, 2) insists that a multitude of venial sins makes public penance as necessary as does mortal sin :—' si . . . in unum colligantur, etiamsi capitalia crimina non addantur, quantis et qualibus bonorum operum copiis redimi poterunt, nisi . . . per humilem et compunctam pœnitentiam. . . . Dei severitas vel justicia fuerit mitigata ? ' The adjectives, and the allusion to capital sins, make it practically certain that public penance is here intended.

Public penance could still of course be undertaken *voluntarily* for lesser sins, as in the earlier period (cp. Cyprian, *de laps.*, 28—people who had merely *thought* of apostasy ' exomologesim conscientiæ faciant et . . . salutarem medellam parvis licet et modicis vulneribus exquirant '). So Inn. I, *ep.* 25, 7 (10) ad Decentium (*MPL.*, xx, col. 559)—' sive ex gravioribus commissis *sive ex levioribus* pœnitentiam gerunt,' but see *infra*, p. 534, on the difficulties of this passage). Where such an obligation was undertaken in sickness, and the penitent recovered, the fact that no mortal sin was involved was taken into account, and the usual disabilities of public penance modified (references, Poschmann, pp. 150, 151 ; but in view of the explicit ' *quamdiu* probabilem sacerdos eorum approbaverit vitam ' of *Conc. Barc.* (A.D. 540), c. 8, I cannot accept Poschmann's unqualified conclusion that ' the convalescent was *thenceforward* (' fürderhin ') pledged to a penitential mode of life ').

(c) *Public penance excused when danger to the penitent's life, etc., might be feared* (*supra*, p. 278).

So Basil, *ep. can.*, c. 34 ; Aug., *serm.* 82, 7 (10) ; 8 (11) ; 9, (12) (*supra*, p. 504). It cannot certainly be inferred from these passages that *no* penalty was exacted from the offender ; but any kind of open denunciation (e.g. Aug., *loc. cit.*, 9 (12), ' tu, adulter, corrige te ! ') was eschewed. In some cases, also, abstention from the Eucharist, without any other mark of public penance, was all that was demanded (perhaps the ἀφορισμός of *Ap. Can.*, cc. 6, 9, 10, 11, etc., as contrasted with the ἐξ ἐκκλησίας ἐκκύπτεσθαι of cc. 29, 30, etc.) ; after a given period the offender was publicly reconciled—though even this publicity was considerably mitigated (*supra*, p. 278).—So *Conc. Illib.*, can. 14 — ' post annum sine pœnitentiâ reconciliari debebunt ' (the variant reading ' post pœnitentiam unius anni ' seems untrustworthy) ; *ib.*, c. 79—' placuit eum abstineri [a communione] ; et si emendatus cessaverit, post annum poterit communioni reconciliari,' *et pass.* Further possible instances in Cyprian, Basil, Ambrose, etc., are collected and discussed by Poschmann, *Kirchenbusse u. ' correptio secreta' bei Augustinus* (Braunsberg, 1923), pp. 67-72 ; but I doubt whether he reckons sufficiently with the possibility that many of the injunctions concerned merely advise voluntary abstention from communion for a period as a practice of private penitence (Cæs. Arel. [Aug.], *app. sermm.* 229, 2 ; 257, 4 ; cp. Loofs, *Leitfaden*, p. 340, n. 4 and refs.), and are not canonical regulations at all. In that case there would be *no* reconciliation (not even, as is sometimes suggested, a private one) ; after the agreed period had elapsed the penitent

would spontaneously return to communion. For an *official* reconciliation after such ' private ' penance the only certain evidence seems
to be the two canons of Elvira just quoted. The same problem in
Gregory, Poschmann, *Abendländ. Kirchenb.*, pp. 260-262.—In the case
of Avitus of Vienne and the ' homo nimis crudus ' whom, having
excommunicated, he exempts from public penance, public reconciliation seems certain (Avitus, *ep.* 16, ad Victorium ; *MPL.*, lix, col.
234) ; but the facts were exceptional.

(d) *Mitigations of public penance in the fifth century (supra, p. 278).*

The most important evidence is Leo, *ep.* 167—directed mainly to
the relaxation of the life-long disabilities which remained even after
reconciliation (*supra*, p. 228). Thus § 10 now allows one who has
done penance to engage in legal business ; § 11 suggests that honest
commerce may be undertaken ; § 13, a young man who, with honourable intent, marries after penance is guilty of venial sin alone.
(Similarly *Conc.* vi. *Tolet.*, can. 8). The concessions are made with
a certain hesitation and reluctance. But (§ 12) return to military
service after penance remains absolutely forbidden.

It may be assumed that in most of these cases the ' penance '
was undertaken during an illness from which, against his expectation,
the sick man ultimately recovered. Several Gallic councils *forbid* the
admission of young people to penitence (i.e. during health)—e.g. *Conc.
Agath.* (A.D. 506), can. 15 ; *Conc.* iii. *Aurel.* (A.D. 538), can. 24. The
phraseology of the Council of Agde suggests further that (to avoid
possible inconvenience arising from the recovery of a penitent who
undertook the status on his presumed death-bed) the sick shall receive
the viaticum *without* official penance at all—' juvenibus poenitentia
non facile committenda est . . . viaticum tamen omnibus in morte
positis non negandum' (cp. *infra*, p. 512). Similarly, the married
are forbidden to undertake penance (with its obligation of lifelong
continence) without the consent of the other party to the marriage :—
Conc. ii. *Arel.* (A.D. 443 or 452—see Hefele-Leclerq, ii, pp. 460 ff.),
can. 22 ; *Conc.* iii. *Aurel.* (A.D. 538), can. 24 ; cp. Fulgentius, *ep.* 1, 9
(18) (*MPL.*, lxv, col. 309).

In view of the general condemnation of military service for Christians no similar relaxations appear to have been officially suggested
or allowed in favour of soldiers ; but a supposed sermon of Cæsarius
([Aug.] *app. serm.* 258, 2) deals with the matter by insisting that the
important thing is to abandon sin, and that in comparison the assumption of penitential garb is a trivial matter (cp. *ib.*, 249, 6—the same
advice for a young married man).

(e) *The rule of one penance only (supra, pp. 171, 227, 275).*

For the rule of one penance (or rather one reconciliation) only
after baptism, cp. Ambrose, *de pœn.*, ii, 10 (95)—' sicut unum baptisma
ita una pœnitentia, quæ tamen publice agatur ' ; Siricius, *ep.* 1, 5
(6) ad Himerium (*MPL.*, xiii, col. 1137), ' suffugium non habent pœnitendi ' ; Aug., *ep.* 153, 3 (7)—' locus humillimæ pœnitentiæ non con-
cedatur ' (the last two citations of relapsed sinners). Augustine
appears in this sentence to refuse even second *penance* (without reconciliation) to the relapsed. But he is clearly speaking of penance *with
hope of reconciliation*, for he urges that they are to be exhorted to
acts of penance, and insists that such acts ' proderunt in posterum.'

It is the position of Tertullian (even in his Montanist days) again (*supra*, p. 225). On Batiffol's suggestion (*Études d'Histoire, etc.*[5], pp. 189, 190) that Leo's sermons imply the possibility for minor sins of second penance *with reconciliation* (which Batiffol regards as ' une sorte de coulpe publique '—public, indeed, but not to be confused with ' la cérémonie solennelle de la reconciliation ' for grave sins, although the two take place on the same occasion), *infra*, p. 534.

(*f*) *Disappearance of the rule of one penance* (*supra*, p. 281).

(i) O. D. Watkins, *op. cit.*, pp. 510, 560-561, suggests that Cæsarius allowed two or more penances in certain cases. But the inference seems a mistaken one. Cæsarius is urging ([Aug.] *app. serm.* 258, 1) that sinners should not delay their ' penitence '; the divine mercy is available ' if we do not put off our conversion, nor add sin to sin.' A single fracture of a limb is easy to heal ; if it is broken ' secundo ac tertio ' the cure is much more difficult. And so ' si semel aliquis *vel secundo* peccaverit et . . . ad pœnitentiæ medicamenta confugerit, pristinam incolumitatem sine aliquâ morâ recipiet.' But if he adds sin to sin, and allows the wound to putrefy, he will fulfil the apostolic prediction of treasuring up wrath for himself in the day of judgment. A few lines later (overlooked by Watkins) Cæsarius makes his meaning quite clear—' if you once contract the *habit* of sin (' consuetudinem peccandi facere ') you may be unable to escape the devil's net, even if you wish to do so.'—The message is simply, Come to penance before you become a hardened sinner ; every delay will make it harder and less possible for you to face it. It may be added that Cæsarius would never have introduced so startling a novelty in discipline, if at all, in so haphazard a fashion.

(ii) *Conc.* iii. *Tolet.* (A.D. 589), can. 11, *supra*, p. 281, n. 1. After condemning the ' execrable presumption ' of those who attempt to obtain second absolution, the council insists upon full publicity of penance (cp. also can. 12), and dismisses all hope for relapsing sinners with the words ' secundum priorum canonum severitatem damnentur.' This proves attempts to introduce the practice of repeated penance and absolution. ' What the council condemns is nothing else than private ecclesiastical penance, such as later became universal in the Church ' (Poschmann, p. 159). But, as Poschmann points out, this is also the *first* council to take any explicit notice of a *custom* of repeating absolution ; hence the custom must have been of local and recent growth (*ib.*, p. 223).

(iii) A writer, often supposed to be Victor of Tunenna († A.D. 567), if not Victor of Cartenna (*c.* A.D. 450), uses language which suggests the abandonment of the rule of one penance by the contemporary African Church.[1] [Ambr.] *de pœnit.*, 12 (*MPL.*, xvii, col. 1073)— ' sed ais mihi, peccata peccatis adjeci, et qui jam cadens erectus fueram, iterum cecidi . . . quid trepidas ? quid vereris ? idem semper est qui ante curavit ; medicum non mutabis . . . noto te sanabit antidoto . . . unde dudum curatus fueras, inde iterum curaberis . . . qui naufragavit, non iterum navigat ? ' Poschmann's arguments against the natural and obvious meaning of the passage (*op. cit.*, pp. 167-171), though not without weight, are unconvincing. — On

---

[1] In the seventh edition of his *Études* (p. 224), Batiffol rejects *both* attributions, as also this interpretation of the passage ; but does not state how he understands it.

the other hand, the passage from S. Éloi of Noyon († A.D. 658), which Watkins, pp. 527, 578, cites as admission of repeated penance (Eligius, *hom.* 15; *MPL.*, lxxxvii, col. 648), is a mere *rechauffé* of Cæsarius (*supra*), and has the same meaning.

(g) *Excommunication and imposition of penance* (*supra*, p. 227).

The details relative to excommunication and imposition of penance are well put together by Brightman, in Swete, *Church and Ministry*, pp. 355, 363-365, 366, 372-373 (cp. for reconciliation, Poschmann, pp. 46-48). As regards *exclusion*, or *excommunication*, we may notice the following :—

(i) The ideal was that the sinner should voluntarily denounce himself (not necessarily in public) and accept loss of communion, at the same time petitioning for admission to the status of penitent (' sponte confessi,'—' qui sibi ipsi pœnitentiæ locum petierunt '— Aug., *sermm.* 351, 4 (10) ; 232, 7 (8)). To this end, if the bishop knew of the offence, he was bound, by entreaty, exhortation and monition to try to bring the sinner to the appropriate state of mind (see *infra*, p. 537, on Augustine's *correptio secreta*; cp. Ambrose, *de off.*, ii, 27; Pomerius, *de vit. contempl.*, ii, 7, 2 (*MPL.*, lix, col. 451)—' diu hortati et salubriter objurgati.'

(ii) The sinner might deny the offence, but be willing to recognize the jurisdiction of the Church. Then would take place the process of investigation of *Didascalia*, ii, 47 ff., summarized by Brightman, *op. cit.*, p. 364. Cp. also J. Bingham, *Antiq.*, XVI, iii, 9, 10.

(iii) If private exhortation proved useless, and the sinner refused to appear for the public investigation, or resisted an adverse decision, the bishop would proceed to formal excommunication ; even so he was still bound to do what he could to induce the offender to ask for penance. But formal excommunication was only allowable if there was some degree of notoriety about the sin ; if it was known to the bishop only, he could not denounce the offender publicly (Aug., *serm.* 351, 4 (10)).

(iv) A penitent was still excommunicate, but under the *lesser excommunication* only (separation from the sacraments). So probably were offenders who had been forcibly excommunicated, but of whose return there was still some hope. Where, however, an offender remained fully recalcitrant, the bishop (if he had the moral support of his flock) sooner or later had recourse to the *greater excommunication*, which forbade any kind of intercourse, even social (' a colloquio et convivio '), with the offender. So the formulæ in Synesius, *ep.* 58 (*MPG.*, lxvi, coll. 1400-1404) ; cp. *Conc. i. Tolet.* (A.D. 400), cc. 7, 15, 16, 18 ; *Conc. iv. Cart.* (398), c. 73 ; *Conc. ii. Arel.* (A.D. 443-452), c. 49 ; *Conc. Angev.* (A.D. 453), c. 4 ; *Conc. i. Aurel.* (A.D. 511), cc. 1, 3 ; *Conc. iii. Aurel.* (A.D. 538), c. 6 ; *Can. Apost.*, 30, etc., Basil *epp.* 61, 288, etc.

(v) But in many cases, especially of notorious sin, a bishop acted much more precipitately than the strict letter of the canons allowed. So the story of the excommunication of the Emperor Philip, Euseb., *HE.*, vi, 34 ; and the excommunication of Theodosius.

(vi) The bishop was normally empowered to remit part of the sentence either in view of extenuating circumstances, or on account of manifest zeal shown during the penitential exercises ; see, e.g. *Conc. Anc.*, c. 5 ; *Conc. Laod.*, c. 2 ; *Conc. Nic.*, c. 12 ; *Didascalia Apost.*,

c. 6 (E. tr. M. D. Gibson, p. 32) ; Basil, *ep. can.*, cc. 74, 84 ; Greg.
Nyss., *ep. can. ad Letoïum, pass.*, e.g. can. 5 ; *cod. can. eccl. Afr.*, c. 43 ;
Innocent I, *ep.* 25, 7 (10) ; Leo, *epp.* 10, 8 ; 159, 6.

(vii) Voluntary confession was almost always regarded as a ground
for mitigation of penalty ; e.g. Greg. Thaum., *ep. can.*, 8, 9 ; *Conc.
Illib.*, c. 76 ; Basil, *ep. can.*, c. 61 ; Greg. Nyss., *ep. can. ad Let.*, 4.
One of the rare explicit exceptions to this rule is *Conc.* iii. *Aurel.*
(A.D. 538), can. 7, where the penalty for confession and for conceal-
ment is the same.

(*h*) *The abolition of the penitentiary priests by Nectarius* (*supra*,
p. 282).

The details of this affair are inextricably confused. Three questions arise :—

(i) What jurisdiction had the penitentiary ? (ii) What was the
exact occasion of scandal ? (iii) What did Nectarius hope to gain by
abolishing the office ?—Neither Sozomen nor Socrates is clear on any
of these points ; together they are quite unintelligible. References
to the recent discussions will be found, Poschmann, p. 57, n. 1. He
and Galtier hold that the penitentiary had plenary judicial functions
which, when they led to the degradation of a deacon, were deemed
excessive. For this, however, there appears to be no other evidence.
Batiffol, (*Études d'Histoire, etc.*, p. 157) holds that the scandal consisted
in the degradation of the deacon on the testimony of one witness only,
and that an accomplice ; others think that the penitentiary broke
the seal of confession by denouncing the deacon. But none of these
theories accounts for the abolition of the *office*.—I am inclined to think
that the penitentiary (legally or illegally) was giving absolutions on
easy terms, and absolved the lady ; but when the deacon's crime was
discovered (not necessarily by any violation of the seal) and he was
degraded, the disproportion between the treatment received by the
two accomplices respectively was so great as to cause dissatisfaction
and scandal in the Church. Thus, whilst Sozomen's highly-coloured
picture of the cause of the scandal is an unjustifiable piece of fiction,
designed to make Socrates' account intelligible, he is probably right
in saying ἀπέλυεν—the penitentiary, whether with legitimate or with
usurped jurisdiction, *did* give absolution (*supra*, p. 282). Nectarius'
suppression of the office was designed, on this hypothesis, to bring the
entire control of discipline back into the bishop's hands and prevent,
if not priestly usurpation, at all events irresponsible absolutions :
both Socrates and Sozomen assert that (although it may have had
this result) the general effect on morality was bad. The texts will
be found in full in Watkins, *op. cit.*, pp. 315-317. W. Bright, *Age of
the Fathers*, i, p. 527, says wisely, ' Nectarius' action neither prohibited confession nor abrogated penance . . . but it removed a great
stimulus and threw the whole subject into the background.' Somewhat similarly, K. Holl, *Enthusiasmus u. Bussgewalt*, pp. 274, 275.
On the later history of public penance in the East, Holl, pp. 277-291.

(*i*) *Retirement to a monastery* (' *conversio* ') *a substitute for public
penance* (*supra*, p. 278).

The popularity of this custom has been established, principally for
the fifth-century Church in Gaul, by the researches of B. Poschmann,
Die Abendländ. Kirchenbusse, pp. 128-142, 280 f. ; its frequency revived

a kind of domestic asceticism as well (*ib.*, pp. 131, 132), so that penance for grave sin became indistinguishable from saintliness. Cæsarius ([Aug.] *append. serm.* 261, 1) says, ' et ille quidem, qui pœnitentiam publice accepit, poterat eam secretius agere '—one of the passages which have been taken to imply the existence in the fifth century of private penance with *private absolution* (Poschmann, *op. cit.*, pp. 139, 140 ; *see infra*, p. 536). But Gennadius (*de eccl. dogm.*, 53 ; *MPL.*, lviii, col. 994) makes the point quite clear—' sed et *secretâ satisfactione* solvi mortalia crimina non negamus, sed *mutato prius sæculari habitu et confesso religionis studio* per vitæ correctionem et jugi imo perpetuo luctu miserante Deo veniam consequatur.'—In the ' appendix ' to the late eighth century *Codex Regularum* of Benedict of Aniane occurs an *ad monachos de pœnitentia* ascribed to ' S. Paulinus ' (Holsten-Brockie (1759), i, p. 130), which Morin and Poschmann (*op. cit.*, p. 128) date from the fifth century. (Watkins, p. 504, following *MPL.*, lviii, col. 875, wrongly assigns it to Faustus of Riez.) It says explicitly, ' abrenuncianti publica pœnitentia non est necessaria, quia conversus ingemuit et cum Deo æternum pactum inivit.' It is a curious coincidence of name that Paulinus of Aquileia in A.D. 794 should embody the principle in a letter to Heistulf, a Lombard who had killed his wife, whom he enjoins either to enter a monastery or to do public penance (*MPL.*, xcix, col. 183 ; Watkins, *op. cit.*, p. 685). The practice was called *conversio* (see Ducange and *Thes. Ling. Lat.*, s.v.) ; and must be distinguished from *intrusio, retrusio* (confinement in a monastery—see Ducange, s.vv., and *D.C.A.*, s.v. ' seclusion ' ; cp. *supra*, p. 293, n. 3), which was compulsory, and not necessarily lifelong ; cf. for this Poschmann, p. 259.

(*j*) *The attempt to introduce public confession of details of sin* (*supra*, p. 228).

Leo, *ep.* 168, 2—' illam etiam contra apostolicam regulam præsumptionem, quam nuper agnovi a quibusdam illicitâ usurpatione committi, modis omnibus constituo submoveri. de pœnitentiâ scilicet quæ a fidelibus postulatur ne de singulorum peccatorum genere libello scripta professio publice recitetur, cum reatus conscientiarum sufficiat solis sacerdotibus indicari confessione secretâ . . . removeatur tam improbabilis consuetudo . . . sufficit enim illa confessio quæ primum Deo offertur, tum etiam sacerdoti, qui pro delictis pœnitentium precator accedit.'—The custom, prior to this attempted innovation, is quite certain. The would-be penitent laid bare his case before the bishop, or a priest delegated for the purpose (Origen, with his advice as to the importance of *choosing* the right recipient for such confidences, is obviously thinking of an even earlier stage—in *Ps.* 37 *hom.* ii, 6 ; *MPG.*, xii, col. 1386). He was then told whether public penance was or was not required. If it was, his public entry into the *status pœnitentiæ* would be all the notification which the other members of the Church received either of the fact or the character of his sin. This private statement of the details of the case to the bishop is of course implied in many of the passages where public penance for private sin is demanded or excused (*supra*, pp. 504 f.). Similarly Origen, *hom. in Lev.*, ii, 4 ; (*GCSS.*, ' Origenes,' vi, p. 296)—' per pœnitentiam remissio peccatorum, cum peccator . . . non erubescit sacerdoti Domini indicare peccatum suum ' ; Cyprian, *de lapsis*, 28—' apud sacerdotes Dei dolenter et simpliciter confitentes ', etc. It is unnecessary to add that at this date, even though private *penance* may

have been occasionally allowed, private *reconciliation* was wholly
unknown. *At some point* the process was bound to be public, and so
to involve the acknowledgment that grave sin had been committed.
But the detailed confession of the sin was *not* that point (*infra*,
pp. 534 ff., for further considerations).

(k) *Popularity of death-bed penance* (*supra*, pp. 227, 275).

Cp. Cæsarius, [Aug.] *app. serm.* 256, 4—' cum enim omnes homines
pœnitentiam velint in finem vitæ suæ accipere ' ; and the innumerable
canons of councils regulating the practice. Cæsarius warns his hearers
of the danger of such postponement—you may be shipwrecked,
drowned, murdered, or stricken with apoplexy ; and suggests as a
compromise, not immediate public penance, but ' illa pœnitentia quæ
per omnem vitam a bonis Christianis agitur '—i.e. daily acts of self-
mortification. Of this he says, ' per quam omnia capitalia crimina
damnantur et minora peccata jugiter redimuntur ' ; where ' damnantur ' seems to mean that such a life expresses the penitent's self-
condemnation on account of his ' capital' sins (and will avail, *faute de
mieux*, with God).—Poschmann, pp. 52, 53, gives reasons for supposing
that the penitentiary priests at Rome (*supra*, p. 282) were appointed
to be at hand for emergency death-bed cases where the bishop could
not be informed in time.—On the postponement of *baptism* for the
same reasons as that of penance, cp. Tertullian, *de bapt.*, 18—' si
qui pondus intelligant baptismi, magis timebunt consecutionem quam
dilatationem ' ; Aug., *Conf.*, i, 11, (17).

(l) *Efficacy of death-bed penance.*

Where a sinner had recourse to death-bed penance after a careless
life, theologians took a pessimistic view of its efficacy. So Aug.,
serm. 393—' si quis autem positus in ultimâ necessitate ægritudinis
suæ voluerit accipere pœnitentiam . . . fateor vobis non illi negamus
quod petit, sed non præsumimus quia bene hinc exit . . . si securus
hinc exit, ego non sum securus.' The doubt was specially strong in
southern Gaul. Faustus of Riez († A.D. 492) in his public utterances
expressed the gravest doubts ([Aug.] *append. sermo* 255—assigned to
him by Malnory, *S. Césaire d'Arles*, p. 190—' pœnitentia quæ ab
infirmo petitur, infirma est. pœnitentia quæ a moriente tantum petitur,
timeo ne ipsa moriatur ') ; in his correspondence he frankly denies
that this ' momentanea pœnitentia ' can obtain remission of capital
sins (*ep.* 5 ad Paulinum, *CSEL.*, xxi, p. 184).

Cæsarius says the same ([Aug.] *append. sermo* 256, 3—' pœnitentiam illi dare possum, integram securitatem dare non possum ').
Avitus of Vienne († 533), however, denounced Faustus' view as
' contrary to the truth ' (*ep.* 4, *MPL.*, lix, coll. 219 ff.). The best exposition of the facts is in Poschmann, pp. 107-115.

(m) *Refusal of absolution to death-bed penitents* (*supra*, p. 227).

Prior to canon 13 of Nicæa, which enjoined that all who could
possibly be regarded as penitents should receive the viaticum in their
last hours (*supra*, p. 278), though *after* the disappearance of the *tria
irremissibilia*, absolution was sometimes withheld from sinners *etiam
in fine*. Thus *Conc. Illib.* (A.D. 306—presided over by Hosius of
Cordova), cann. 1, 2, 6, 7, 8, etc. (in some cases there is confusion
between ' nec in finem ' and etiam in fine,' which makes it difficult

to decide exactly. On the supposed Novatianism of the council, Poschmann, p. 143.) Batiffol compares with this the attitude of popes Marcellus (A.D. 308), and Eusebius (A.D. 309), to the *lapsi*, which may be inferred from the Damasian epitaphs (*Études d'Histoire*[5], pp. 142, 143).

Brightman (Swete, *Church and Ministry*, p. 377), notes only two other cases of the refusal of death-bed absolution, Neo-Cæsarea (A.D. (?) 315), can. 2, and Arles (A.D. 314), can. 22. To these must be added Sardica (A.D. 343), can. 2 (drafted by Hosius of Cordova), and Saragossa (A.D. 380), can. 3—the latter Spanish, the former under Spanish influence ; and both later than the Nicene canon. But in the fifth century, Gallic rigorists attempted to reintroduce the practice in a new and more limited form by denying absolution *to those who deferred penance till the hour of death.* They were rebuked by Innocent I (A.D. 402-417), *ep.* 6, 2 (6) ad Exsuperium (*MPL.*, xx, col. 498), who recognizes that in the times of ' crebræ persecutiones ' lifelong penance without reconciliation was imposed, but maintains that the Church is now right in prescribing that the dying shall receive communion. In A.D. 428 Pope Cœlestine writes sternly to the bishops of Vienne and Narbonne (*ep.* 4, 2 (3) ; *MPL.*, l, col. 431)—' agnovimus pœnitentiam morientibus denegari, nec illorum desideriis annui, qui obitus sui tempore hoc animæ suæ cupiunt remedio subveniri. horremus, fateor, tantæ impietatis aliquem reperiri.' So also Leo, *ep.* 108, 4 ad Theodor. Forojul. In spite of these Papal decisions, there are numerous western canons of the fifth and sixth centuries (Poschmann, pp. 98, 99) against relapsing sinners, or penitents who have disregarded the obligations of the status, none of which say anything about conceding them the viaticum in their last hours. But *Conc. Ilerd.* (A.D. 524 or 546; see Hef.-Lecl. *ad loc.*), can. 5, is explicitly in favour of leniency—' sanctam communionem *nisi in exitu* non percipiant.' The council of Elvira, by regulating the practice (cann. 3, 9, 10, 13, etc.), in some cases, and forbidding it in others, shows it to have been well-known at that date (' in fine habere communionem ' etc.) See also Morinus, *de pæn.* V, c. 30. 9, 10 ; X, 1-14. Note esp. *ib.*, X, 1, 4—the occasional survival of this rigorism in France up till the late fourteenth century.

(*n*) *The recovery of death-bed penitents.*

(i) Sometimes a penitent who received absolution on his (presumed) death-bed recovered unexpectedly. The earliest custom, in these cases, was to hold him exempt from further penance. So Cyprian, *ep.* 64, 1—' pacem quomodocumque a sacerdote Dei semel datam non putavimus auferendam ' ; cp. *ib.*, 55, 13 ; Dionysius Alex., *ep. ad Conon.* (ed. Feltoe (1905), pp. 59-62).

(ii) *Conc. Nic.*, can. 13 (*supra*, pp. 278, 511), whilst insisting that all sinners who desired it must be reconciled on their death-beds, enacted that if they recovered they must complete their appointed course of penance : εἰ δὲ ἀπογνωσθεὶς καὶ κοινωνίας πάλιν τυχὼν πάλιν ἐν τοῖς ζῶσιν ἐξετασθῇ, μετὰ τῶν κοινωνούντων τῆς εὐχῆς μόνης ἔστω. So also Greg. Nyss., *ep. ad Letoïum*, 5 ; and commonly. Hence (Leo, *ep.* 167, 9 ad Rust.), a sick man who had sent for a priest prematurely, and on his arrival found himself a little better, would rather naturally plead for a postponement of the rite.

(iii) The Nicene canon had not actually said that sinners were to be *absolved*, but only that they were to receive the viaticum (ἐφόδιον—but see Bright, *Canons of First Four General Councils*, p. 51, for wide usages of the term which would easily allow of its covering absolution). To resolve the ambiguity, Gallic canonists at the Synod of Orange (A.D. 441) (can. 3) made a definite distinction between the *viaticum* and *plenary reconciliation*, deciding that death-bed penitents might receive the former but not the latter. Such penitents, if they recovered, had consequently no ground for refusing to accept the Nicene ruling, which the canon therefore repeats. The text runs :—' qui recedunt de corpore pœnitentiâ acceptâ placuit *sine reconciliatoriâ manu* eis communicari, quod morientis sufficit consolationi secundum definitiones patrum, qui hujus modi communionem *viaticum* nominarunt. *Quod si supervixerint, stent in ordine pœnitentium* et ostensis necessariis pœnitentiæ fructibus communionem *cum reconciliatoriâ manus impositione* percipiant.' Similarly *statt. eccl. ant.*, cc. 76-78 (sometimes called canons of an alleged fourth Council of Carthage, A.D. 398—see Hefele-Leclerq, ii, pp. 102-108) ; Felix iii, *ep.* 7, ad univ. ep. (= *Conc. Rom.*, A.D. 487) can. 3, 5 ; *MPL.*, lviii, coll. 926, 927 ; Siricius, *ep.* 1, 5 ad Himerium—' viatico munere . . . per communionis gratiam volumus sublevari ' (Poschmann (p. 61) points out with justice that the explicit reference here is only to sinners, who, after reconciliation (suffugium non habent pœnitendi '), break one or more of the lifelong obligations imposed even upon reconciled penitents) ; *Conc. Barc.* (A.D. 540), c. 8 ; and frequently. Batiffol (p. 181) appears to take the Orange canon in connexion with the relapsed only, but it obviously applies to all who have begun their penance but not completed it. Poschmann's attempt (pp. 108, 109, cp. also Hefele-Leclerq, ii, p. 1030, n. 1) to show, in the face of the ' sine reconciliatoriâ manu,' that the viaticum included absolution of a sort, is not at all convincing (cp. Morinus, *de pœn.*, VI, 21, 6). In Rome the principle that the sinner restored to health must complete his penance was maintained by Leo (*ep.* 167, 7), though sick-bed absolution was not refused (*ep.* 108, 4, 5—' nec satisfactio interdicenda est, *nec reconciliatio deneganda* '). In Spain, at all events, all traces of this rigorism had vanished by the sixth century (Poschmann, pp. 150 ff., 289 ff.).

(o) *Penance and Purgatory* (*supra*, p. 286).

See *Cath. Encycl.*, i, p. 599, s.v. ' Apocatastasis ' (Batiffol) ; *PRE.*, v, p. 788, s.v. ' Fegfeuer ' ; *ib.*, ix, p. 81, s.v. ' Indulgenzen ' ; Loofs, *Leitfaden*, pp. 449 ff. ; Tixeront, *HD.*, i, ii, iii, indices s.v. ' Purgatoire ' ; etc.—Two doctrines must be distinguished—(*a*) that of purgatory as a ' second chance '—a place where all, or almost all sinners, however impenitent they may have been at death, may submit to purification and so achieve ultimate salvation. This Origenistic or universalistic view, though popular nowadays, had only a temporary footing in the early Church—though from Origen (*de princ.*, ii, 10, 4 ; *c. Cels.*, v, 15) it spread even to Jerome and Ambrose (Tixeront, ii, pp. 335, 341 f., 345-350). Clem. Alex., *Strom.*, vi, 14, seems to hold the same view, though it is not clear whether he extends the ' second chance ' to sinners as widely as Origen does.

(*b*) The ' Catholic ' doctrine—in purgatory sinners who *die in a state of grace*, and are consequently assured of salvation, are cleansed from minor faults, and expiate sins already repented of and forgiven. Hints of this view are found in Tertullian (*de resurr.*, 43 ; *de an.*, 58) and Cyprian (*ep.* 55, 20) ; Augustine, whilst not prepared absolutely to condemn the Origenistic view (Tixeront, ii, p. 433), nor absolutely to affirm the other (*ench.*, 69—' tale aliquid post vitam fieri incredibile non est '), is generally ' Catholic ' on the point (Tixeront, ii, pp. 433, 434 ; Loofs, p. 450). In Cæsarius and Gregory the Great the Catholic position is quite explicit (Tixeront, iii, pp. 426-428 ; Loofs, p. 450). Cæsarius asserts that the fires of purgatory will be necessary to complete the redemption of such sins as have not been fully redeemed by good works (i.e. penitential satisfactions)—' quicquid enim de istis peccatis [minutis] a nobis redemptum non est, illo igne purgandum est,' [Aug.] *app. serm.* 104, 4 ; the same principle applies to capital sins, but here the redemptive exercises are more severe, and include public penance (*ib.*, 7, 8—' digna pœnitentia '). Hence the danger of postponing good works in the case of minor sins, and penance in the case of ' capitalia ' ;—the former postponement will involve greater purgatorial punishment, the latter *may* involve (if the sinner die unexpectedly without absolution) forfeiting the chance of attaining to heaven even through purgatory (*ib.*, 9—cp. Greg. Magn., *dial.* iv, 25, 39).

But as absolution was normally given only after the necessary satisfactions, or temporal penalties, were discharged, the number of sinners destined for purgatory was (in the view of the early centuries) relatively small—the alternatives for most were simply heaven and hell. When, however, absolution came to precede satisfaction the case was altered ; it was no longer a guarantee that purgatory would be avoided. Purgatory, therefore, became a normal stage in the heavenward progress of all redeemed Christians, except those whose penitential exercises, whether before or after absolution, had been so exhaustive as to appear a sufficient substitute. Hence Abailard's insistence upon the subject (*scito teips.*, 19, 25 ; *expos. in Rom.*, iv (*MPL.*, clxxvii, col. 840) ; cp. Loofs, p. 593 ; K. Müller, *Umschwung i. d. Lehre v. d. Busse*, pp. 306-308—but see the criticism of Müller, Loofs, p. 476) ; cp. also Ric. S. Vict., *de pot. lig.*, cc. 2-8. There was thus no difference of principle, but only the breaking up of one equation into two. On the earlier theory confession plus satisfaction (plus absolution) cancelled the pains both of hell and of purgatory ; in the later theory confession (plus absolution) cancelled the pains of hell, satisfaction those of purgatory. The many theological problems raised by the doctrine do not concern us here. For mediæval crudities on the subject, see G. G. Coulton, *Five Centuries of Religion*, i, pp. 73-77.

NOTE J.—TERTULLIAN'S THEORY OF PENANCE (*supra*, p. 225).

We may notice in greater detail some problems connected with Tertullian's doctrine of penance. The first two arise out of the curious passage (*de pœn.*, 10[8]), in which, dealing with the reluctance of sinners to come to exomologesis, he asks ' an melius est damnatum latere, quam palam absolvi ? '

(a) Preuschen, *Tertullians Schriften ' de pœn.' u. ' de pud.'*, pp. 12-13, takes ' palam absolvi ' of the day of judgment. He holds that Tertullian's purpose is to provide a status of lifelong penance (without absolution on earth), which shall win absolution in heaven, as in *de pud.*, 3. He supports this by referring to the phrase ' in vestibulo collocavit ' of *de pœn.*, 7[10], which he takes literally—' has placed in the narthex of the Church '—i.e. has assigned penitent post-baptismal sinners a permanent place there, with consequent permanent exclusion from communion. The difficulty of this is that not even *de pud.* assigns lifelong penance without absolution to any except the three ' irremissibilia ' ; whilst the sins for which second penance is available in *de pœn.*, 7⁹, are enumerated as giving way to ' carnal concupiscence, worldly entanglements, the subversion of faith by fear of earthly power, wandering from the sure way by perverse traditions, scandals and temptations '—a much wider list. On Preuschen's theory, Tertullian Catholic would be more severe than Tertullian Montanist.

(*b*) Batiffol, *Études d'Histoire*, p. 75, building on ' damnatum latere,' thinks that Tertullian is urging open penance for *secret* sin. This is possible ; but since ' damnatum ' is rhetorical (one is not finally 'damned ' till the last judgment, and then one's damnation is anything but ' latent '), ' latere ' is probably so too ; and the phrase need mean no more than ' skulk about in sin.' But further, in *de pud.*, 2¹³⁻¹⁵—(' omne delictum aut venia dispungit aut pœna ; venia ex castigatione, pœna ex damnatione . . . alia [delictorum pars] erit quæ veniam consequi possit, in delicto scilicet remissibilli ; alia quæ consequi nullo modo possit, in delicto scilicet irremissibili ')—' damnatio' means ' excommunication,'[1] not ' damnation.' For in 3⁴ we are to learn that the irremissible sins do *not* necessarily involve ' damnation ' in the literal sense ; and ' pœna ex damnatione '—i.e. the acceptance of lifelong penance—is explicitly said to ' expunge' sin,[2] just as does ' venia ex castigatione '—i.e. the acceptance of temporary penance, with absolution (' venia ')[3] as its sequel—for ' remissible ' sins. So ' damnatum latere ' probably means ' skulk about in a state of excommunication,' and has no reference to secret sin.

(*c*) *de pud.*, 19 ²³⁻²⁵—An involved argument about 1 John 4¹⁶·¹⁷ ; then—' [distinctionem delictorum a qua digressi sumus] hîc enim Joannes commendavit, quod sint *quædam delicta quotidianæ incursionis*, quibus omnes simus objecti. cui enim non accidit, aut irasci inique, et ultra solis occasum ; aut et manum immittere, aut facile maledicere, aut temere jurare, aut fidem pacti destruere, aut verecundiâ aut necessitate mentiri ? in negotiis, in officiis, in quæstu, in victu, in auditu quanta tentamur, ut si nulla sit venia istorum, nemini salus competat ! horum ergo erit venia per *exoratorem Patris Christum. sunt autem et contraria istis ut graviora et exitiosa quæ veniam non capiunt*, homicidium, idolatria, fraus, negatio, blasphemia, utique et mœchia et fornicatio, et si qua alia violatio templi Dei. *horum ultra exorator non erit Christus ;* hæc non admittet omnino qui natus ex Deo fuerit, non futurus Dei filius, si admiserit.'

The difficulty here is as follows. The Church of the period recognized three classes of sins ((i) venial, (ii) grave—requiring penance, but not irremissible, (iii) irremissible) ; Tertullian in this passage mentions two groups only, and it is not clear how they are to be harmonized with the normal three-fold scheme. His groups are :—

---

[1] Generally lifelong, without hope of ecclesiastical absolution (cp. P. de Labriolle, *Tertullien, de pœn., de pud.* (Paris, 1906), p. xxviii) ; but contrast the loose usage of *de pud.*, 18¹, where it does not exclude *venia* (absolution).

[2] I.e. by winning divine forgiveness in heaven , *supra*, p. 225.

[3] That this is the normal meaning of *venia* is amply proved by G. Esser, *Die Bussschriften Tertullians* (Bonn, 1905), p. 23.

(i) ' sins of daily occurrence.' These are in fact mostly trivial ; though
one does not care to think that breaking promises ('fidem pacti
destruere ') was quite so common as he suggests. These ' will receive
pardon through the intercession of Christ ' ; (ii) ' graver and destructive
sins, which do not admit of pardon.' The list that follows gives seven
sins, which may or may not be a mere expansion of the three irremissibilia ;[1] and then adds ' for these Christ will no longer intercede.'

Presumably ' venia ' means absolution by the Church, as in de
pud., 2[18] (supra, (b)). Then ' horum ultra exorator non erit Christus '
means, Christ will not ask for them to be pardoned on earth (though
pardon is available for them in heaven, if lifelong penance is done on
earth, as in de pud., 3[4], supra, p. 225, n. 2). But the phrase is an odd
one for the purpose ; and this interpretation has the further inconvenience that it appears to demand (penance and formal) absolution
(' venia ') for daily and trivial sins (such as Augustine later will repeatedly declare to be expunged by repentance and the Lord's prayer),[2]
whereas the lists of sins for which penance is required (but absolution
allowed) in de pœn., 7[9], de pud., 7[15], are of a much more serious character.[3]
This of course may be another piece of Montanist rigorism.[4]

On the other hand, ' venia ' may perhaps mean ' immediate forgiveness (by God) here and now by the direct intervention of Christ's
intercession, without formal penance, reconciliation, etc.' This would
suit list (i) ; it would allow us to take list (ii) either as referring to the
three ' irremissibilia ' alone, or as including in addition the sins of
de pœn., 7[9], de pud., 7[15]; it would give a point to the ' ex ' of ' exorator '
—' Christ will decline to plead for them effectively,' i.e. without the
addition of penitential exercises on the part of the sinner.[5] And it
would say enough for Tertullian's purposes in this chapter, in which
he is merely proving that we all recognize some distinction between
sins. But it involves reading a great deal into ' exoratio,' and taking
' venia ' in a very specialized sense, neither as ' absolution ' as in
c. 2, nor ' pardon ' generally, as in c. 18, fin. And it either makes list
(ii) include two classes of sins (' grave ' and ' mortal ') without differentiation, or ignores the grave sins altogether. Nevertheless this
seems to be perhaps the best solution.

---

[1] Blasphemy, denial and idolatry of course go together as forms of
' apostasy ' ; ' fraud ' may belong to them as meaning the fraudulent
obtaining of a certificate of having sacrificed (as commonly in the Decian
persecution), which Tertullian would regard in the same light as actually
having sacrificed. A similar list of ' capital ' sins in adv. Marc., iv, 9 (in
relation to baptismal remission) gives ' falsum testimonium ' for ' negatio,'
which may refer to a lying pretence of not being a Christian. On the other
hand, ' fraus, negatio ' in the one list and ' falsum testimonium, fraus ' in
the other would naturally seem to refer to sins in business-life.

[2] Aug., ench., 71 ; de symb., 7 (15) ; serm. 56, 8 (12) ; 58, 7 (8) ; de
nupt. et con., i, 33 (38), etc. ; and cp. supra, p. 339, n. 10.

[3] de pœn., 7 : supra, p. 515 ; de pud., 7, enumerates attendance at
theatrical and gladiatorial shows, etc. ; undertaking of civil office ; performing duties in connexion with idolatrous worship, and so forth (cp.
Brightman, in Swete, Early History of the Church and Ministry, pp. 321-330,
for other lists of this character).

[4] So de Labriolle (op. cit., p. xxviii) appears to take it. On the other
hand, Esser (op. cit., p. 16) takes list (i) to include both venial sins and remissible sins for which penance is required. But this involves a double meaning
both for venia and for exorator, and appears highly artificial.

[5] So apparently Prümmer, Theol. Mor., i, p. 228—' sensus videtur esse :
hæc non possunt deleri oratione solâ.'

The possibility suggested in the text (*supra*, p. 225), that 'horum ultra exorator non erit Christus' means that certain sins will *never* be forgiven in this world or the next and are in fact inadmissible to penance, is of course contrary to the general tone of *de pudicitia;* but it may be an ultra-rigorist aspiration which Tertullian lets slip by the way. He certainly recognized some sins for which even life-long penance without absolution was refused—the 'monstra' of *de pud.*, 4[5], which are banished not merely from the threshold ('limen') but even from the shelter ('tectum') of the Church (cp. *ib.*, 13[11], on incest). The rendering would fit the immediate context—some sins we all recognize to be forgivable, some sins we all agree to be unforgivable; but in view of the main emphasis of the *de pud.* it cannot be regarded as more than a possibility.

NOTE K.—THE DOUBLE STANDARD AND WORKS OF
SUPEREROGATION (*supra*, p. 240).

A.—In two important essays (*The Spirit and Origin of Christian Monasticism*, pp. 287-301, and *ERE.*, iv, pp. 203-205; s.v. 'Counsels and Precepts'), Canon Hannay approaches the whole question of the double standard with an admirably judicious impartiality. He does not appear to consider that what has been called above the 'valid' view has any bearing upon the matter; but addresses himself entirely to the 'invalid' view. Its essence, he observes, is contained in two 'judgments'—

(i) Some ways of life are 'higher' (e.g. 'more heroic') than others, and merit greater heavenly reward: (ii) 'A Christian may without sin refuse' a higher way of life, 'even when it has been presented to him' (*Spirit and Origin*, p. 296).[1]

Both these judgments Canon Hannay regards as 'entirely natural'; in the former (not necessarily or commonly, however, with reference to monasticism), the Protestant reformers and controversialists implicitly concurred 'even when they did not say so' (p. 297). Protestantism, however, rejected the second judgment; the Christian is no longer free to refuse the higher (more heroic, though not necessarily monastic), way of life without sin, if he is 'called' to it.[2]

This 'Protestant' view Canon Hannay hesitates to accept. It would involve him (he suggests) in the conclusion that a man who 'receives the call' to virginity and, marrying, 'refuses to obey the

---

[1] This judgment is of course involved in the assertion that the worldling, though debarred from the higher reward offered to the monk, is not debarred from salvation altogether—as he would be if he were guilty of 'actual' sin in refusing, and maintaining his refusal of, the higher life (*supra*, p. 255). But the judgment is not always of the essence of the invalid theory, for that theory still persists, in a modified form, wherever it is held that some Christians *are by divine providence debarred* from the higher life (*infra*, pp. 531 f.). Of these it would of course be absurd to say that they 'may refuse' the higher life, for they are not in a position to 'accept' it; but they are still debarred, on the invalid theory, from the highest rewards.

[2] In addition to the passage quoted by Canon Hannay from Rothe, the 'Protestant' view is well expressed in Martensen, *Christian Ethics*, i, pp. 424 f. ('the counsels are precepts for single individuals under special circumstances'), R. L. Ottley, *Christian Ideas and Ideals*, pp. 65-67, and generally *PRE.*, iv, pp. 274 ff. (s.v. 'consilia'), where full references to the controversial post-Tridentine documents on both sides are given.

call,' and 'to the end of his life does not repent,' is 'in the same position as the unrepentant adulterer.' Such a thought, Canon Hannay says, is 'intolerable ; state it nakedly, and all consciences revolt against it ' (p. 299).

Several curious confusions are involved in this statement of the case :—

(a) Even the invalid theory never held that a genuine *call* (duty, obligation) might be refused without sin, though no doubt Protestantism has often accused it of doing so. Nor does Canon Hannay really defend this position, though his language seems to suggest it. The misunderstandings are due to an ambiguity between the words 'call' and 'opportunity,' which Canon Hannay perpetuates in his vague phrase ' presented to him.' If the word ' call ' be taken in its strict sense, as a definite obligation clearly recognized by conscience as absolutely and immediately laid upon it by God, two conclusions follow : (i) No moralist, Catholic or Protestant, would ever admit for a moment that *such* a call might be refused without sin ; (ii) the thought by which the rejection of such a call is put on the same plane as the gravest mortal sin is no longer ' intolerable.' If Jonah had persisted in his refusal to preach at Nineveh, or S. Paul had refused to go to the Gentiles, no one would have hesitated to regard them as traitors against conscience to the most flagrant degree.

Canon Hannay's hesitations are due simply to the fact that ' calls ' as unequivocal as Jonah's or S. Paul's are extremely rare. What we usually speak of as ' calls ' are no more than ' opportunities ' or ' possibilities ' entering into competition with other ' opportunities ' or ' possibilities.' The rejection of them, bound up as it may well be with the acceptance of an alternative ' opportunity ' of doing good, may be (in any given case) a mistaken choice, but it is in no sense on a par with the deliberate violation of an unquestioned moral obligation. Canon Hannay, however, after recognizing that Protestant controversialists are using the word ' call ' in the strict sense (see his summary of Rothe, p. 298), proceeds to argue as though it meant no more than ' opportunity.' If the ' call to virginity ' in his example were an unquestionable ' call ' (e.g. if the man who proposed to marry knew himself to be suffering from an incurable and highly contagious disease) no words could be too strong in insisting that to disregard it was to be guilty of mortal sin. Obviously, therefore, the words ' call to virginity ' to Canon Hannay mean no more than the ' opportunity ' or, at best, the ' advisability of remaining single.'

(b) What the theory of the double standard held, even in its invalid form, and what Canon Hannay really defends, is the perfectly sound probabilist view that where either of two ways of life is ' safe,' a Christian is not bound to take the generally safer (' higher,' ' more heroic ') way, or ' opportunity,' *merely by virtue of* this generally ' safer ' character.[1] I have argued in support of this position else-

---

[1] This is true, even if ' generally safer ' or ' higher' means ' safer or higher for all Christians without exception.' Universal obligation would only begin if it seemed at least possible that the ' safer or higher ' course was also *essential* for all Christians. On probabilist principles it would then begin (*Conscience and its Problems*, p. 282) unless simultaneously it appeared also possible that the ' generally safer ' course might be *wrong* for some Christians. The case would then be one of ' perplexity,' to be solved along different lines (*ib.*, pp. 288, 331-336, 395-399).

where,[1] and have nothing to add on the point. The valid theory in no way impugned this principle. All it did was to insist that the principle could not be applied to the contemplative life, or vision of God, because properly understood this 'life' is *not* the 'safer' of two 'safe' ways, but the universally obligatory goal of the Christian pilgrimage.

(c) What, then, were in fact the errors of the invalid theory ? The first, though less important, was that of hardening a particular way of life (monasticism) into a universally 'higher,' 'safer,' or 'more heroic' one—of mistaking, in short, the *spectacular* for the *heroic*. The heroic is, of course, as Canon Hannay suggests, always higher than the non-heroic. But neither monasticism, nor any other spectacular way of life, is to be identified with heroism *sans phrase*. Curiously enough, Canon Hannay seems to echo this mistake when, by way of analogy, he treats the life of the soldier in battle as one 'of greater sacrifice' than that of the sergeant 'who throughout the course of a long war drills recruits at the depôt.' The former is without doubt infinitely the more spectacular, or dramatic (using these words without the slightest derogatory implication), but the degree of heroism involved in the respective instances is wholly independent of the external circumstances. The soldier *may* be merely a reckless adventurer, the sergeant *may* be breaking his heart because duty prevents his going to the front ; if so, the latter is the true hero, not the former. The 'invalid' theory of the double-standard elevated one particular kind of spectacular life into the heroic life *per se ;* Protestantism rightly maintained that neither this particular kind of spectacular life, nor *any* spectacular life merely because it was spectacular, could be regarded as necessarily heroic. Any form of life can call for the display of the fullest heroism, if God so ordains it. One 'opportunity' may be more spectacular than another ; but all 'opportunities' open the door to the highest exhibitions of Christian self-sacrifice.

Whether Protestant writers, as Canon Hannay suggests, implicitly deny this conclusion, I cannot say. But without doubt it is accepted by the best Roman Catholic thought unhesitatingly. Baron von Hügel (*Essays and Addresses*, i, p. 282) insists that when the Reformation 'dug up the very roots of all and any monasticism' (i.e. abolished, for Protestantism, the 'invalid' theory of the double standard) it destroyed the conception of the 'supernatural' as distinct from the 'natural' good. But when he proceeds to restore the conception of 'supernatural good,' even in its 'massively heroic' form (as we might say, a form at once heroic *and* spectacular), he chooses his crucial instances not merely (as the 'invalid' theory did) from the monastic or celibate life, but also from among army chaplains and officers, schoolboys, historians, astronomers, and washerwomen (pp. 284-291). And he is careful to observe that although the supernatural good is 'more striking, more easily seized' in such examples, they do not by any means exhaust its possibilities—' the material of the supernatural is not only the heroic, but also, indeed mostly, the homely ' (p. 284). With such a conception of the heroic, or higher life, no Protestant can quarrel.

[1] *Conscience and its Problems*, pp. 261-265, 269-275, and especially p. 282. Cp. also H. Rashdall, *Theory of Good and Evil*, ii, pp. 122-130, where the same result is reached on different premises.

(d) Still, no great principle of ethics was violated by reducing the life of the counsels to the three monastic vows. There may well be ' generally higher ' courses of action—i.e. courses which in the majority of normal cases are more likely than others to produce the highest flowers of Christian perfection [1]—even though monasticism is not necessarily one, or the highest one, among them (*supra*, p. 253). The great error of the invalid theory (at which Canon Hannay only glances in passing) was the suggestion that anyone who for whatever reason refused [2] this ' generally higher ' way of life was *ipso facto* debarred from the highest rewards or attainments of Christianity. It suggested to the man who found himself in the lower way that he was only capable there of limited progress ; and thus inspired the lax or conventional Christian to limit the possibilities of progress still further, till a mere routine of casual conformity seemed to be all that was demanded of him for the attainment of salvation of the lower grade. Thus it gave an immense stimulus to formalism of the most outrageous type, the result of which is to be seen (as I have suggested) in the repellent *pénitence tarifée* of the early middle ages. In rejecting the double standard, Protestantism rejected, *inter alia*, this erroneous implication ; although, as will be seen, it readmitted it in another form by rejecting the valid theory at the same time as the invalid.

B.—I cannot therefore agree with Canon Hannay's implied suggestion that the rejection of the ' invalid ' theory of the double standard (i.e. the doctrine that one particular mode of life alone qualified for the highest rewards), was anything but right and Christian. Nevertheless, something was undoubtedly lost by the Protestant campaign against monasticism. Baron von Hügel calls it the conception of the ' supernatural good,' or the ' heroic ' (*op. cit.*, pp. 282, 284) ; Canon Hannay agrees (*ERE.*, iv, p. 205) :—' Protestantism is less rich than Catholicism in examples of heroic Christianity. The general tendency of Protestantism has been to raise to a high level the common Christian life, and to develop certain virtues of a kind suitable to the lives of citizens. It has not made for, and except in comparatively rare instances, has not achieved, the production of unique saints. . . . This failure must be attributed to the denial of the doctrine of ' counsels ' and ' precepts,' and the consequent unwillingness of Protestant teachers to hold up for admiration lives which must always be rare, and are never imitable except by those who realize the peculiar glory of very great kinds of renunciation. . . . Thus Protestant theologians . . . have deprived Protestants of an incentive to a lofty kind of life ; and have risked and actually suffered the loss to organized Protestant Churches of souls who have felt the need of heroic self-sacrifice for the sake of Christ.'

---

[1] Cp. Rashdall, *Theory of Good and Evil*, ii, p. 116—' Without denying to every honourable and worthy calling either its characteristic virtues or its characteristic vices, it is surely undeniable that some professions are as a rule more favourable to the development of character than others.' This would be analogous to the doctrine of sins ' mortal *ex genere*,' which is only intelligible if it is taken as ' a rough and ready guide as to what sins usually connote a sinful disposition ' (see *Conscience and its Problems*, especially p. 328 n. ; *ib.*, pp. 72-78, 329-332 ; and *supra*, p. 297). But we must remind ourselves that the vision of God is not a ' generally higher way,' but the universally obligatory goal.

[2] Or *was debarred from* the ' higher ' life by temperament, or by other obstacles sufficiently involuntary to make the word ' refuse ' inappropriate ; see further, *infra*, p. 531.

Similarly Dr. H. B. Workman, in his admirable *Evolution of the Monastic Ideal*, p. 334 : ' Protestantism has too often driven out the eagle to save the sparrows.' [1] Above all, Dr. Rashdall (*Theory of Good and Evil*, ii, p. 137) says, ' If we look to the practical effects of the two one-sided doctrines, it would seem that Protestantism [2] . . . in its periods of dullness and spiritual lethargy has reduced its moral ideal for all men to one of mere respectability, and tended to discourage acts or careers of exceptional self-denial and devotion. Catholicism, on the other hand, has at no period of its history failed to give all due encouragement to exceptional missions and high religious or social enthusiasms.' [3]

But the origin of this defect in Protestant ethics must be sought not in the rejection of the ' invalid theory,' which, as I have attempted to show, was too faulty to have any except evil effects, but in the rejection of the ' valid theory ' of counsels and precepts—that is, of the doctrine of Christian progress. And this is to be found not in the depreciation of monasticism, but in the rejection of the distinction between mortal and venial sin. [4] This distinction can and does, indeed, take on an ' invalid ' form, whenever it treats the avoidance of venial sin as optional. [5] But if it is rejected in its valid form, as explained above, [6] it involves us at once in the doctrine of the equal depravity of all sin—a Stoic formula which Christian ethics has always reprobated. [7]

The consequences of the theory of the equality of all sins are obvious. It leads to rigorism and despair on the one hand ; on the other it induces even the earnest Christian to concern himself with the everyday at the expense of the abnormal. He will be *no more* at fault if he refuses to obey the call to be a missionary than if he loses his temper in the home ; it is not certain whether he has the call to be a missionary, but he certainly does lose his temper. To conquer the latter will involve less disturbance of his ordinary life than to obey the former ; he therefore sets himself to become good-tempered at home and ignores the possibility of a missionary vocation. I am not aware that anyone has ever argued explicitly in this sense, but its psychological inevitability is obvious. If all sins are equal there can be no logical approach to their conquest. They may be taken in any order, and naturally enough the nearest and easiest is taken first, and preoccupies attention to the virtual exclusion of more important matters of duty. The rejection of the double standard in its valid form led

[1] The sentence continues ' or sought to exterminate the sparrows because of their inferiority to the eagles ' ;—repeated the evil, in fact, which the double standard was originally designed to avert. The reference, of course, is to Ambrose, *de fug. sec.*, 5—' qui non potest volitare ut aquila, volitet ut passer.' Dr. Workman's general position is akin to that of Canon Hannay ; he pleads for the double standard in its invalid form, and appears to make the same confusion between the heroic and the spectacular (pp. 335, 336).

[2] Here, again, for purposes of simplification, I have omitted a sentence asserting (as Dr. Workman in the preceding note) that ' Protestantism has in its periods of austerity and enthusiasm imposed upon all men a standard too rigid,' etc.

[3] Dr. Rashdall adds, in the same sense in which I have criticized the invalid theory (*supra*, p. 257) that Catholicism, as the result of its ' one-sided doctrine,' ' has at times relaxed the minimum standard of morality required as '' necessary to salvation '' to a dangerous and deplorable degree.'

[4] For Luther's rejection of this distinction see H. Denifle, *Luther u. Luthertum*, i, pp. 501 ff. ; further references, Hannay in *ERE.*, iv, p. 204.

[5] *Supra*, p. 249. [6] *Ib.* [7] *Ib.*

to the same result as the invalid theory had stereotyped for the lower or secular life—it tended to stultify the whole idea of constant and unlimited moral progress.

C.—A difficult question remains. If sound moral theory does not make it a duty to embrace the ' generally higher ' course on the mere grounds that it is ' generally higher,' what is to be said of the man who nevertheless embraces that course ? Is he, as vulgar mediæval thought supposed, to be praised for doing more than his duty, or a work of supererogation ? The answer must be ' No,' for the following reason. *Praise* is possible only where actions are done from a good motive. Presumably the man is praised for doing his duty (as well as for doing the ' something more than his duty ') ; and this can only mean that he is doing what he conceives to be his duty because he conceives it to be his duty. But what was his motive for doing the ' something more ' ? It may have been a mere whim or fancy—in that case we certainly do not praise him ; and if the matter is a grave one he is even to be blamed for treating it in a flippant spirit. It may have been a selfish motive ; in that case he is certainly to blame. Only one motive is left—he did it because, after weighing all the circumstances, he came to the conclusion that it was the right thing for him to do—was in fact *an additional duty*.[1]

Consequently in respect of the ' something more,' we are justified in praising him on exactly the same grounds as those which entitled us to praise him for ' doing his duty '—namely, that he is doing what he conceives to be his duty. We may also, in certain cases, praise him for having become by moral effort the sort of man who is capable of recognizing a duty where we should have seen none. But that is in any case praising him for the *past* and not for the *present ;* and sometimes at least, on this score, we may feel obliged to blame him if he has culpably allowed himself to become a victim to hyper-conscientiousness, so that he imagines duties where we see only scruples, and attempts the foolhardy or impossible.

Again, we may praise him for doing his duty ' so well ' or ' so cheerfully,' or ' in the face of such and such odds and difficulties ' ; i.e. we may recognize that he has succeeded where most men would have failed miserably ; or has done the *whole* of his duty where few would have been able to do more than *a part*. But always we shall come back to the fact that we can only praise him for doing ' more than his duty ' (whatever that phrase may mean) [2] *if he conceived it to be his duty ;* that is, the only praise to which he is entitled is that due to all who do successfully what they conceive to be their duty because they so conceive it. Thus no one can be praised for doing more than he thinks to be his duty ; there is no merit in so-called ' works of supererogation ' other than the merit of having done what you believed you were bound to do.

The idea of ' special merit ' attaching to ' works of supererogation '

---

[1] The grounds on which he reached this conclusion do not affect the point (though see the following sentences) ; nor does the character of the problem (whether ' doubt ' or ' perplexity ') which he had to solve.

[2] It may mean, I suppose, ' something more than *we* conceived to be his duty before he made it clear that *he* conceived it to be his duty '; or again, ' a duty only perceived by him, in a case of *primâ facie* doubtful obligation, after the application of (e.g. probabilist) principles designed to resolve such cases.'

is therefore wholly illusory. Still more so are the ideas of the treasury and transference of merit, in so far as they depend upon it.[1] Most illegitimate of all was the sale of indulgences which was grafted upon the theory. On these matters, though the grounds on which he reaches his conclusion are not made evident, Canon Hannay's views are entirely acceptable.[2]

NOTE L.—GREGORY THE GREAT ON THE CONTEMPLATIVE LIFE
(*supra*, p. 244).

In *Benedictine Monachism*, p. 96, Dom C. Butler opens a summary of S. Gregory's teaching on the double standard with the words : ' The active life is by necessity, the contemplative by choice ; because one may enter the heavenly kingdom without having exercised the contemplative life, but no one can enter it without having exercised the good works of the active life.' A footnote gives references to *Hom. in Ezk.*, I, iii, 9, 10 ; II, ii, 8, 9, 10 ; *Mor. in Hiob.*, vi, 60, 61 ; xxx, 53 ; xxxi, 102. Similarly in *Western Mysticism*, p. 249 : ' The active life is necessary, the contemplative optional.' Here a part of *Hom. in Ezk.*, I, iii, 10, is quoted in translation ; and it is to be noticed first, that this is the only one of the passages cited which appears to make contemplation ' optional ' at all ; second, that if the remainder of § 10, and with it §§ 11-13, which expand it, are taken into account, the purpose of the passage is by no means so explicit.

The translation given by Dom Butler is quite accurate, and there is no need to reproduce Gregory's simple Latin. The English runs :

' Though each life is by the gift of grace, yet as long as we live among our neighbours one is by necessity ("in necessitate ") the other by choice ("in voluntate "). For who that knows God enters into His kingdom unless he first works well ? *Without the contemplative life, therefore, those can enter into the heavenly kingdom who neglect not to do the good they can ;* but without the active life they cannot enter, if they neglect to do the good they can. Therefore the active life is by necessity, the contemplative by choice.'

The passage cannot be separated from its sequel. Gregory at once repeats his aphorism in a new form : ' The active life is in slavery, the contemplative in liberty,' and illustrates his meaning by quoting Ex. 21[2-6]—the passage about the manumission of the Hebrew slave

---

[1] There are, of course, innumerable ways in which a saint can help a sinner, and if this is all that is meant by the ' treasury and transference of merit ' no objection can be taken to the idea. But much objection can be taken to the *phrase ;* for a literal ' transference of merit ' is exactly one of the ways in which the saint *cannot* help the sinner.

[2] *Spirit and Origin*, pp. 300, 301. Dr. Rashdall's discussion (*Theory of Good and Evil*, ii, pp. 130-138) does not seem to go to the heart of the problem. While insisting that ' no man can do more than his duty,' he goes on to say (p. 135), ' It is good for a rich man to sell all he has and give to the poor . . . but this only becomes a *duty* in persons endowed with a sufficient love of the poor to do this not grudgingly or of necessity.' But he does not discuss the case of the person who, although *not* ' endowed with a sufficient love, etc.,' nevertheless divests himself of his wealth, and so has done a ' good ' thing which apparently was not his duty. Yet this is a type of case in which a man appears to have done more than his duty. What would Dr. Rashdall have thought of such an action ? If not *duty*, is it *sinful* (if for no other reason than that it is temerarious or scrupulous) ? Or is it a work of supererogation ? Or was it the rich man's duty after all ?

in the seventh year.   He continues : ' The six years' slavery represents
the perfection of the active life : the seventh year is the contemplative
life.   So by perfect performance of the active life we reach the freedom
of the contemplative ' (§ 11).   But (§ 12, from Ex. 21⁵) the servant
may say, ' I love my master, my wife and my children ; I will not
go out free ' ; he may then, of his own will, decide to remain in slavery,
and if he does so ' he shall serve his master for ever.'   The interpretation is easy : ' Loving the active life and its fruits ' (which we
remember, he has achieved *in perfection*) ' he does not wish to pass
on to contemplation.   He sees that he has good works in the servitude
of his ministry, and so shrinks from passing on to the quiet of contemplation.'

Here the Vulgate gives S. Gregory an opportunity which the
English version does not provide.   Our ' for ever ' is in Latin ' in
seculum,' and the Pope takes this to mean ' for this life.'   *Erit servus
in seculum, ut esse post seculum liber possit*—' He shall be a slave for
this life in order that after this life he may be free.   For he is a
" slave for this life " who has decided to serve men by the active life,
in order that after this life he may be able (" valeat ") to come to the
true liberty' of the contemplative life (§ 13).   For, as Gregory says elsewhere (*Hom. in Ezk.*, II, ii, 8), after death there can be no place for the
active life.

S. Gregory's theory is therefore clear.   The active and contemplative lives are not alternatives ; the former has meaning only as a
preliminary to the latter.   The earnest Christian will certainly
enter upon the contemplative life at death.   The only thing that is
a matter of ' choice ' (' voluntas ') is the *moment at which the transition
from the former to the latter shall be made*.   This may be postponed
until death, and if so, and if we have been ' perfect in the active life,'
we shall then ' enter the kingdom of heaven,' and there begin the life
of contemplation.

Here is a position resembling in certain respects that of the Abbot
John (*infra*, pp. 525, 526).   But the two are not the same.   John draws
a distinction between the ' higher goal ' of contemplation and the
' lower goal ' of action, whereas in S. Gregory there is only the *one*
goal—that of contemplation in the life to come.   Gregory's theory
here is indeed a little pedantic, since it stereotypes the active and
contemplative ' lives ' much more rigidly than he does elsewhere :
but it does not seem to entitle us to say that with him contemplation
is ' optional.'   So far is this from being the case, that he continually
insists that pastors and preachers, at all events, are under an *obligation*
in *this* life to practise contemplation as well as action (passages collected, Butler, *Western Mysticism*, pp. 253-257, 260, 265) ; and warns
them against the danger of subordinating contemplation to action
(*ib.*) ; though with equal wisdom, he warns against ' adopting the
contemplative life to an extent beyond one's powers ' (*Mor. in Hiob.*,
vi, 57).   He recognized to the full the temperamental disabilities
which for many will make progress in contemplation slow, arduous
and even distasteful (*ib.*) ; and because in this world they will never
get far beyond the normal confines of the active life, he is able to
say (*ib.*, xxxii, 4), that the ' active life ' (again, ' in this world ' is to
be understood) ' is the lot of many, the contemplative of few alone.'

Dom Butler's exposition of S. Gregory's thought (*Western Mysticism*, pp. 91-133, 245-273), apart from the single passage in respect

of which I have ventured to differ from his interpretation, is admirably lucid, exact and inspiring. I add one further reference, mainly because of its quaintness. On Ezk. 44[20]: ' Neither shall [the priests] shave their heads nor suffer their locks to grow long ; they shall only poll their heads,' the Pope comments as follows : The eyes are the symbol of spiritual vision, or the contemplative life ; the hairs of the head, which may grow so long as to veil the eyes, the cares of the active life. The priest or bishop immersed in worldly responsibility is not to break away from its cares altogether (i.e. shaving the head), but he must not let them grow so thick that they distract him from the primary duty of quiet contemplative prayer.[1]

NOTE M.—CASSIAN ON THE DOUBLE STANDARD (*supra*, p. 255).

Cassian is not always quite consistent in his view. (*a*) His interlocutors were almost entirely anchorites ; we are not therefore surprised that in *Coll.*, xiv, 9 ; xviii, 4 ; 6 ; 16 (*fin.*) ; and xix, 3, 4, strict equations are drawn. The cœnobium = the active life, or lower stage ; the desert = the contemplative life, or higher stage ; the ideal is to pass from the cœnobium to the desert. Thus no one who cannot *first* live the cœnobite life, and *then* pass to the desert, can hope to contemplate at all.

(*b*) A variant of this view is that of *Coll.*, xiv, 2-4. Here contemplation, the goal, is only possible in solitude (c. 10—' It is impossible for the soul which is taken up even to a slight extent with worldly cares to achieve spiritual knowledge ') ; but the preliminary stage may be passed either as an anchorite, or in the cœnobium, or in works of active mercy (the guest-house, the hospital, etc., c. 4). Apparently not all of these possible preliminaries are monastic in the strict sense.

(*c*) On the other hand, numerous passages refer to contemplation without suggesting that solitude is essential for its pursuit. Note especially *Coll.*, i, 12-15 : Germanus enquires how the contemplative life can be lived amid everyday cares. Moses, instead of answering, as Nesteros (xiv), Piamun (xviii), John (xix), and Abraham (xxiv), would have answered, ' It cannot,' proceeds to give rules for retaining the presence of God among the distractions of life. Further, Cassian recognized, as S. Gregory later insisted, that in fact the ' active ' and ' contemplative ' lives must always be mixed, both because ' the poor are always with us ' and demand our care and attention (i, 10, 13), and because even in the desert there are sufficient distractions to impair (xxiv, 3), if not to make impossible (xix, 3, 5), the ' contemplative science.' On this view, therefore, contemplation, though still perhaps only possible to the *monk*, is not confined to the *hermit*.

(*d*) A wholly unique point of view is expressed in *Coll.*, xix, esp. cc. 8, 9. Here a clear and mutually exclusive distinction is drawn between the life of the hermit, whose aim is *contemplation*, and that of the cœnobite, whose aim is *self-mortification*. (A similar recognition of the two lives as alternatives in xxiv, 8 ; but the difference of aim is not stated, nor even suggested, there.) This apparently implies that after the preliminary stage of cœnobite life (cc. 2, 10, 11), or its equivalent (cc. 12-14), there is a choice between (*a*) more cœnobitism, (*b*) the hermit life ; and that those who choose the former must

[1] *Reg. Past.*, i, 7 ; *ep.* vii, 4.

abandon the aspiration to contemplate—the 'higher goal' (c. 3). They correspond to the worldlings of the ordinary invalid theory.

But the theory is biassed by the fact that it is bound up with Abbot John's personal experience. He found it impossible (because of the 'crowd' in the desert) to exercise *theoria* there, and so gave up the attempt. He retired to the cœnobium, there to exercise the lower virtues once more. If he tends to represent the obedience of the cœnobite life as a parallel and separate goal from the contemplation of the hermit, and not as a stage on the road, it is no more than a transparent subterfuge with which to cloak the truth that he is content with the lower attainment when he might have pressed forward to the higher. (Cassian specially adduces him as an instance of extreme humility, xix, 1, 2.) He did not enter a new vocation : he merely went back to the earlier stages of his chosen mode of life. We may think him pusillanimous in resting content with an elementary grade of perfection ; but at least he is not adopting a theory different from that of the *Collations* generally, except in so far as he suggests that for *him* personally 'contemplation' was as impossible in the desert as in the cœnobium.

(*e*) What does not appear in the *Collations* at all, so far as I can see, is any suggestion that contemplation is open to others than the monks.

Note N.—Modern Versions of the Double Standard
(*supra*, p. 256).

The 'invalid' theory of the double standard shows itself in post-Tridentine Roman Catholic thought in various forms :—

(*a*) Despite S. Thomas' insistence (*supra*, p. 256) that the monastic life, or *status perfectionis*, is in effect no more than one among many 'ways' to perfection, there are those who still suggest, with many hesitations and ambiguities, that it is a way which *per se* alone makes possible the highest attainments and the highest rewards. The ambiguity of the word 'state'—which can be taken to mean either 'mode' or 'achievement'—helps, of course, very considerably to this end. Thus Dr. Koch, while insisting that the counsels are 'merely surer and more effective means of attaining perfection,'[1] proceeds to derive from Mt. 19[16 ff.] a 'clear distinction between obedience to the commandments, and poverty as a *state of higher perfection*,'[2] without observing that a 'state of higher perfection' and 'a more effective means of attaining perfection' are two very different things—there is now a distinction not between the *efficacy of respective means*, but between *the degrees of perfection which respective means make possible*. With this new distinction he parallels one between 'eternal life as the reward of *ordinary good conduct*, and a treasure in heaven laid up for those who *sacrifice everything* to serve God.' Here we have a distinction between two ways of serving God—'ordinary good con-

---

[1] A. Koch and A. Preuss, *Handbook of Moral Theology*, i, p. 237 ; cp. *ib.*, p. 241—'All good works are means of attaining perfection, but some are more effective than others.' These are the 'evangelical counsels in the narrower sense,' which have a '*relatively* higher value' (i.e. *not* an absolutely higher value). For a criticism of this form of statement, but at the same time a recognition that it is not so objectionable as the sharp and final distinction between the 'lower' and 'higher' life, *supra*, p. 253.
[2] *Ib.*, p. 239.

duct' and 'complete sacrifice.' The Christian may choose between them, but if he chooses the former he cannot hope for 'treasure in heaven.' We are thus still further from the fundamental Thomist conception of the counsels as merely the most *effective* means of attaining the perfection (and consequently the treasure in heaven) which is open to all.

Similarly P. Pourrat, in his admirable *Spiritualité Chrétienne*, says that 'merely to abstain (*s'abstenir uniquement*) from what is forbidden by the law of Christ under pain of grave sin, is to respect the *precepts* of the gospel morality, and to assure that minimum of the Christian life which is absolutely necessary for salvation, *but it is not to follow perfection.*'[1] That it is not a following of perfection is obvious—but does such a 'minimum' life, deliberately chosen, really merit salvation at all? Is not the 'following of perfection' a precept of the gospel? That there is a clear and absolute distinction as regards both merit and rewards between the way of the counsels—interpreted in the narrowest sense of the monastic life and that alone—which alone can open the door to the highest degree of perfection, and all other 'ways,' however self-sacrificing and heroic, is asserted in the sentences— 'Merely to be spiritually detached (*détaché de cœur*) from the things of this world *would not suffice* for the attainment of the supreme degree of perfection; *they must be actually abandoned*' ('il faut les abandonner en fait');[2] 'The *highest degree* of evangelical perfection, in so far as it implies that *universal effective renunciation*, is undoubtedly the privilege of a tiny number of Christians.'[3] The implication is clear— those who cannot (for any reason however laudable or compelling) *actually abandon* the things of this world, are finally precluded from attaining the *highest degree of perfection;* and so must forfeit the 'recompense reserved for the apostles and those who, following their example, abandon all.'[4]

Again, U. Berlière, *L'Ordre Monastique*[2] (1921), p. 18, speaking of the 'unique ideal imposed upon all Christians,' says that 'the reproduction of this model is effected ("s'opère") by the imitation of the life of Christ as perfectly as possible.' That of course is true. But on p. 10 he writes 'the *raison d'être* of monasticism is the imitation of the life of Christ as perfectly as possible.' If the phrase 'raison d'être' is to be taken seriously, the only conclusion is that the life of Christ cannot be 'imitated as perfectly as possible' in any other way; if it could be, monasticism would have no *raison d'être* left. On p. 23, M. Berlière says :—'Life in the world and the religious life are two parallel vocations leading to the same end, both willed by God, both in possession of the means of grace necessary for the attainment of eternal salvation by the imitation of the life of Christ'—a wholly admirable statement. What then is meant by calling (p. 23) the evangelical counsels 'a special vocation to perfection' ('un appel spécial à la perfection')?—The word 'special' is vague, no doubt; but whether it means 'a call more urgent than the call implied in life in the world' (which contradicts the idea that 'perfection' is a 'unique ideal *imposed upon all* Christians'), or 'a call attended by the promise of more grace than that given to life in the world,' it insinuates the invalid theory once again. Only if 'special' meant merely

---

[1] P. Pourrat, *Spiritualité Chrétienne*, i, p. 3.
[2] *Ib.*, p. 5.   [3] *Ib.*, p. 9.   [4] *Ib.*, p. 7.

one of two parallel and equal calls ' (which it could scarcely mean) should we still be within the confines of the valid theory.

(b) A distinction between what may be called *simple perfection* (with *meditation* as its normal form of prayer) and *mystic union* (with the practice of *contemplative* prayer). This was common in the seventeenth and eighteenth centuries, when ' mystic union ' was generally equated with ' ecstasy,' and therefore—though it could not safely be regarded as a heterodox aspiration and was still by courtesy treated as the ' higher ' way—was in considerable disrepute.[1] In practice, it led to a system in which spiritual directors forced their penitents as far as possible to be content with ' meditation ' along fixed and approved lines ; and its general depreciation of ' contemplation ' has led Dom Chapman to call it ' the reversal of tradition ' (*ERE.*, ix, p. 100). A brisk and biting attack upon the whole conception may be read in Camus (see H. Bremond, *HLSR.*, vii, pp. 154-162, for quotations).

Three lines of reasoning, all of them wholly valid, have led to the abandonment of the distinction in this form :—(i) a distaste for the strict equation between ecstatic or pathological phenomena (now once again admitted to be irrevelant to the spiritual life), and ' mystic union '[2] (readers of Dean Inge's *Christian Mysticism* will remember his repeated and emphatic protests on this head) ; (ii) a recognition that the claim to genuine experience of God (i.e. ' contemplation ' in the theological sense) can be fairly made by a very large number of earnest-minded Christians ;[3] (iii) the empirical observation that ' meditation ' in the strict sense is not congenial to many whose spirituality is in no way open to doubt; whilst conversely, genuine ' contemplation ' of a high kind, and with results admittedly of the most Christian character, is far more accessible to the ordinary believer than was once supposed.[4]

(c) The ground of debate has therefore shifted. The distinction is still made, but this time *within* the sphere of ' contemplation ' itself, and so at a point sufficiently remote from the preoccupations of nine

---

[1] For the history of this development (which is briefly recounted above, pp. 434 f.) see J. V. Bainvel, in A. Poulain, *Des Grâces d'Oraison* [10], pp. xxxii f. ; and Poulain, *ib.*, p. 66 ; P. Pourrat, *Spiritualité Chrétienne*, iii, pp. 310-314 ; C. Butler, *Western Mysticism* [2], pp. xii, li, 308, 309 ; H. Bremond, *HLSR.*, vols. v, vi and viii ; Dom Chapman, *ERE.*, *ut sup.*, and especially A. Saudreau, *Mystical State* (E. tr.), pp. 116-129, 180 ff.; cp. also his *Life of Union with God*, p. 252. It was in defence of S. John of the Cross that Carmelite writers introduced the term ' acquired contemplation ' (Saudreau, *Mystical State*, pp. 118 f. ; Poulain, *op. cit.*, pp. 66, 659 f.) to insinuate the idea that there was nothing extra-human about the ' contemplation ' which he taught. Simultaneously (Saudreau, *op. cit.*, p. 119) came the further defensive step which drew an equation between ' acquired prayer ' and ' meditation,' and so tied almost all earnest Christians down to the latter. The higher stages of prayer—i.e. contemplation, mystic union, and so forth—which, although vindicated by the authority of S. Teresa, were henceforth to be treated as suspect and dangerous for ordinary Christians to aspire to—were now called ' infused ' or ' passive contemplation,' as distinct from ' acquired.'—On the alleged recognition of ' acquired contemplation ' in Richard of S. Victor, contrast Saudreau, *Mystical State*, p. 115, with Poulain, *op. cit.*, p. 67 ; on the distinction between meditation and contemplation in general, *supra*, pp. 374, 375.

[2] Cp. C. Butler, *Western Mysticism* [2], pp xlv, liii.

[3] *Ib.*, p. xii.   [4] *Ib.*, p. li.

Christians out of ten to enable it to escape general attention. 'Contemplation' is now held to be open to every earnest Christian ; but we are told of two kinds of 'contemplation'—'active' and 'passive' —the former within the reach of every 'contemplative' in virtue of his own efforts (reinforced by habitual or ordinary grace), the latter reserved for those to whom God of His own motion grants it dy 'extraordinary' grace, and independent of all human effort and industry.[1] Theologians who hold that this distinction between 'ordinary' and 'extraordinary' grace is dualistic and unsound, have attempted to break it down by suggesting that in *all* contemplation there is both a human ('active') and a divine ('passive') element, and that this can be best expressed by speaking of all contemplation as 'infused.'[2] But the upholders of the double standard have met this suggestion in advance by opposing to 'infused' contemplation a lower type which they call 'acquired,' so that the distinction between 'acquired' and 'infused' corresponds to that between 'active' and 'passive' which the word 'infused' might otherwise have eliminated.[3]

I do not propose to pursue the theological question further ; and that for the following reason. If the writers who say that 'infused' or 'passive contemplation' cannot 'even in the slightest degree or for a single moment' be promoted by our 'acts and industry' *really mean what their words imply*, their theological outlook may be dualist, but it has not forced them so far into the invalid theory of the double standard. 'Infused' or 'passive' contemplation is now something irrelevant to the normal development of the spiritual life—as irrelevant as visions and revelations of the Lord. It cannot be aimed at, prepared for, or ministered to ; it is as likely to occur, or not to occur, if I choose the profession of a dentist as if I choose that of a Trappist.

But very few of the writers concerned appear ready to accept any such interpretation of their words. Even Dom Butler has occasional hesitations on the point. In *Western Mysticism*[2], p. 314, though his language is not absolutely definite, its natural implication is that 'infused, passive or extraordinary contemplation' is 'entirely beyond the power of the soul to prepare for or to bring about, being, according to theologians, wholly the operation of God, working on the soul by an extraordinary grace.' But on p. 319 he defines a 'contemplative' as 'one who practices contemplation' and

---

[1] Poulain, *op. cit.*, pp. 1-3, *et pass.* As what is here concerned is 'contemplation,' and not ecstatic experience, there is no prohibition against desiring it.

[2] So H. Bremond, *HLSR.*, vii, p. 152.

[3] So C. Butler, *Western Mysticism*, p. 314 : 'Modern writers on mystical theology commonly distinguish two kinds of contemplation, the one *acquired, active, ordinary ;* the other *infused, passive, extraordinary*.' Although on p. 315 Dom Butler refers to his 'Afterthoughts' as though correcting his approval of this distinction, I cannot find there anything bearing strictly upon the point except the suggestion (p. lxxxiv) that the phrase 'acquired contemplation' should be abandoned, with the implication that all contemplative prayer, even the initial grades, is 'infused,' though in these grades at least the will is active (cp. *ib.*, pp. lxxx, lxxxi). *Primâ facie*, this suggestion is identical with that of M. Bremond ; and Dom Butler insists that 'in the abstract, it cannot be said that anyone is debarred from the higher and even highest grades of contemplation' (p. lxxxi). But the reservations about to be noticed (*infra*, pp. 530 f.) suggest that the proposal cannot be taken absolutely at its face value.

adds ' but if there be two kinds of contemplation, ordinary (acquired, active) and extraordinary (infused, passive), it follows that there will be two kinds of contemplatives.' The only fair inference is that the ' higher kind of contemplation ' can be *practised*—which is obviously inconsistent with its being ' beyond the power of the soul to prepare for or to bring about.'

Immediately thereafter, adapting the language of Austin Baker, Dom Butler says that the ' perfect ' contemplatives (who ' experience the higher mystic states and extraordinary contemplation ') are those who ' in the midst of business *can keep the mind in singleness and fixed on God*'—surely a contributory activity of the soul. Similarly (pp. 321, 322), the ' contemplative state ' is one ' wherein is the obligation of *aiming* at contemplation and of taking *reasonable measures* calculated to bring the soul to it, first in the lower grade, *and then*, if the call and enablement come, *in the higher*.' This implies that ' reasonable measures ' can be taken by the soul to attain the higher grade of contemplation. How then is it true to say that this grade ' cannot be prepared for ' ? Dom Butler further insists (p. lviii), that the higher states are ordinarily the result of a ' prolonged systematic course of prayer,' which again is a form of preparation ; there are ' states of life,' he says, ' some of them even the holiest, the conditions of which render practically impossible, even for a saint, the higher grades of contemplation ' (*ib.*)—thus to avoid if possible the choice of such a ' state of life ' would undoubtedly be to ' prepare for ' the higher grades.

Similarly, A. Poulain, who identifies (*op. cit.*, p. 66) ' infused, passive, extraordinary, or eminent contemplation' with those ' mystic states ' which ' our efforts and industry cannot avail to produce even feebly or for an instant ' (*ib.*, p. 1), insists nevertheless that we ' can dispose ourselves for them ' (p. 121), and gives instructions (pp. 559, 560) for such ' dispositions '—including in most cases ' long hours of prayer ' (' la longue oraison ').

If then even the higher grades can be to some extent ' prepared for,' the question at once arises, is anyone *ex hypothesi* debarred by his state of life from the activities necessary for the highest stage of contemplation ? Once again we meet with ambiguities and hesitations. Poulain says (p. 561) : ' Are there any obstacles of a purely natural kind, independent of our will—for example, psychological incapacity (" le genre de mentalité ") ? *I have no answer to give to this question*, interesting though it is ; so far as I know, no one has ever discussed it.' But he goes on to observe, as a fact repeatedly verified in his own experience, that ' multiplicity of occupations and especially overwork (" surmenage ") produce a notable weakening of the mystic union ' ; and concludes with what is all but a clear statement that only under the conditions of certain religious orders is ' infused contemplation ' possible—' Il semble donc que, dans ce degré ' (*sc.* ' l'union mystique ') ' Dieu *exige*, au moins à certains jours ou heures, une vie calme et recueillie.' The juxtaposition of the sentences suggests very forcibly that the Christian engaged in a ' multiplicity of occupations ' is incapable of the necessary ' vie calme et recueillie,' and therefore debarred from the highest stages of prayer.

Dom Butler says definitely : ' Contemplation, even the *high* ' (*not* here, explicitly, the ' highest '—but this is probably an oversight) ' kinds of it . . . in theory lies open to all, and may be found and exercised in any state of life whatsoever ' ; [1] and again, ' Speaking in the abstract, it cannot be said that anyone is debarred from the higher, and even highest, grades of contemplation.' [2]   But almost at once he adds, ' The life of the vast majority of the devout servants of God is cast . . . in conditions of this workaday world wherein the very performance of God's will in the duties of their state *renders impossible* those opportunities for such prayer and recollection as are the ordinary means of attaining to [the higher] grades of contempla- tion.' [3]   Again ' there are states of life . . . the conditions of which *render practically impossible*, even for a saint, the higher grades of contemplation.' [4]

These statements are not indeed absolute ; the words ' ordinary ' in the first, and ' practically ' in the second, leave an obvious loophole open. [5]   But the suggestion that only in certain vocations are the highest aspirations of the Christian realizable is not quite excluded.   The corollary must be that a Christian is entitled to choose a vocation which he knows will render it (' normally ' or ' practically,' if you wish) impossible for him to attain the highest goal ; and may do so without blame.   It is the invalid theory again, in a refined form.

(*d*) In the forms considered hitherto, the invalid theory has in- volved the doctrine that the Christian may without sin refuse the higher way of life.   Not that in every case in which a man remained ' in the world ' the reason was that he had ' refused ' to be a monk.   Often his inferior position appeared to have been thrust upon him by provi- dence—e.g. he might not be able, in given circumstances, to embrace the life of the counsels without actually breaking a precept, such as that of discharging his necessary duties as a husband, parent or son. But a new turn is given to the theory by the introduction of psycho- logical considerations, which would make the adoption of the lower life not a matter of free choice, but one of divine decree ; and so would avoid the dangerous corollary that we are not always bound to do the most that is within our power.   The idea is suggested by Poulain's ' genre de mentalité ' (*supra*, p. 530) ; it is implied by Dom Butler when he says that to be a ' perfect contemplative ' a man must have a ' strong interior spirit and propensity ' for contemplation, and be one who ' in the midst of business can keep the mind in singleness and fixed on God.' [6]   In the absence of such qualities, the soul might appear to be doomed for ever to the lower life.

This change of emphasis would not make the theory any less attrac- tive, nor any less dangerous, for the ordinary man.   He does not wish himself to enter into the highest grades of communion with God ; and he knows many (himself included) of whom he would say without hesitation, on psychological grounds, that it is ' practically impossible ' that they should ever attain such heights.   He might even go further, and say without qualification that such a consummation was *absolutely* impossible.   Nor does the change from a vocational to a psychological barrier make the theory acceptable theologically.   It does indeed eliminate the ambiguous statement that a ' Christian may without

---

[1] *Western Mysticism*, p. lxxx.   [2] *Ib.*, p. lxxxi.   [3] *Ib.*   [4] *Ib.*, p. lviii.
[5] On p. lix the two are conjoined—the duties of a pastoral priest in a modern town parish ' *make practically impossible* that tranquillity of mind and those long hours of prayer which are the *normal conditions* of the higher mystical experiences.'
[6] *Op. cit.*, p. 319.

sin refuse the higher life' (*supra*, pp. 517 f.) ; for a man cannot ' refuse ' that which he is psychologically incapable of attaining. Nevertheless if the new form of the theory were pressed to its logical conclusions we should have to say of it that it was theologically erroneous, for it limits the mercy of God to an almost unheard-of degree.

To say that an individual is psychologically incapable *here and now* [1] of the highest developments of character, is of course no more than to assert the valid theory that the Christian life is one of stages. To say that he may fail to attain ' perfection ' within the space of life allotted to him on earth is simply to state the obvious. But it is quite a different thing to say that he is *for ever* incapable of perfection in the fullest sense, and therefore is not called upon to aspire to it at all ; it implies that for all eternity God has decreed a ' Thus far and no farther ' in his case. For such a view no justification whatever can be quoted. Who shall say of what even the meanest soul is capable, once it comes under the sphere of grace ?

And lastly, as has just been suggested, the theory would be practically disastrous. It would encourage the lazy and insincere Christian to vindicate his refusal to attempt to make progress by appealing to a conviction that he is one of those who are psychologically debarred from going further—and he would certainly not hesitate to narrow the confines beyond which lies that ' infused contemplation ' from which he is permanently excluded. I do not say that these conclusions must any of them be drawn inevitably from the books of Fr. Poulain or Dom Butler—which, indeed, are both of them storehouses of true Christian sentiment ; but what makes the conclusions less than inevitable is only a vagueness of statement and an atmosphere of hesitation which leave the reader in doubt upon the vital point.

More satisfying is the tone of the ' pan-mystical ' [2] writers who are aligned against the doctrine of ' passive ' or ' extraordinary ' contemplation—notably A. Saudreau, L. de Besse, R. Garrigou-Lagrange and Henri Bremond.[3] I am so wholly in agreement with their main contentions that I content myself with a minimum of quotation :—

Canon Saudreau :

' Union with God—this then is the end to which those who are truly spiritual incessantly tend. It is to be considered as a gift depending on the divine bounty, that no human effort is sufficient to produce. At the same time it must not be forgotten that God only bestows it on those who are well prepared, and that to these God hardly ever refuses it. . . . Do all that depends on yourself, and sooner or later the Lord will grant it to you.' [4]

---

[1] Cp. Gregory the Great, *supra*, p. 524.   [2] *Supra*, p. 465, n.

[3] For a general history of the whole controversy in modern times, see C. Butler, *Western Mysticism*[2], pp. i-lxxxv ; J. V. Bainvel, in A. Poulain, *Grâces d'Oraison*[10], pp. xlvii-xciv ; cp. *ib.*, pp. 652-653 ; and Pourrat, *SC.*, iv, pp. 645 f., 650 f.

[4] *Life of Union with God*[3] (E. tr.), p. 318. Saudreau identifies ' union with God ' with ' perfection ' (p. 2), ' perfect conformity to the divine will ' (*ib.*), ' contemplation ' or the ' contemplative life ' (p. 14). At the same time, while admitting the term ' extraordinary contemplation ' (p. 13) as a synonym for ' revelations, visions and alienation of the senses ' (p. 11), he denies all distinction between ' acquired or active ' and ' infused or passive ' contemplation (p. 15), thus making contemplation of the highest kind (exclusive of course of pathological phenomena) the ' usual crowning point of the spiritual life ' (pp. 15, 16 ; cp. also Id., *The Mystical State* (E. tr.), especially pp. 60-61, 130-141, 179-201).—Some doubt may arise as to the

Fr. R. Garrigou-Lagrange :

' There are not two ways of perfection, the ordinary (intended for all), and an extraordinary (by way of contemplation and mystical life), a special vocation to which not all fervent souls may aspire. There is only one unitive way which, by docility to the Holy Spirit growing ever more and more perfect, leads to a mystic union more and more intimate. This . . . is not of itself or by its nature extraordinary, but the perfect order, the full development of charity, realized actually in souls truly generous, at least towards the end of life, if they live long enough. It may well be that owing to lack of proper guidance, or of favourable surroundings, or as the result of a nature strongly carried to exterior activities, some generous souls may not arrive at the mystic life until after a time longer than the usual span of life. But this is accidental; however often it may occur it does not touch the essential law of the full development of the life of grace.' [1]

M. Bremond :

' The mystic is the [ordinary] worshipper perfected ; the worshipper is the mystic in swaddling bands, the mystic in orientation and desire.' [2] ' No one is absolutely incapable of mystic experience.' [3] ' The heights which modern speculative mysticism seems to put before us as exceptional experiences, are set within our grasp by ' ordinary grace '—we are invited to them thereby. In bidding us love Him with all our strength, God makes the mystic life a duty for us.' [4] ' Nowadays ' (as distinct from the seventeenth and eighteenth centuries) ' tactics have changed, but the battle goes on as before. The mystics are not decried, they are exalted beyond all recognition—treated as supermen who have nothing in common with us. We bow low when they appear on the stairs ; but by dexterous elbowings we show them the door just the same, and then up with the drawbridge ! As if there were two Christs, or rather as if the mystics had a monopoly of union with God ! No doubt their prayer is more perfect, more *prayerful* than ours . . . but why imagine between their prayers and ours a gulf so wide that one or the other must be treated as falling

completeness of Saudreau's pan-mysticism from the 'hardly ever' of the above passage, as also from the hesitating ' God does not *usually* refuse this gift to those who are really faithful ' on p. 10. This doubt is greatly enhanced by a passage on p. 17, which seems not to have had a place in the first edition :—' Perfection as described by theologians in connexion with the unitive way supposes a degree of virtue *to which only a few are called, and at which the greater number of human beings cannot arrive. . . . The great majority of men* do not receive the mystical graces of light and love that are necessary for the life of union with God, *either because God does not call them to such a high degree of virtue. . . .*' The general tenour of M. Saudreau's books makes it hard to believe that this is a complete surrender to the invalid theory ; the passages fall into line if they are taken to mean simply that few Christians will attain perfection within the span of this present life, and that in this sense they may be said ' not to be called ' to it.

[1] *Perfection Chrétienne et Contemplation*, pp. 191, 192 ; and in *La Vie Spirituelle*, April, 1921, p. 5 ; quoted in apparently different versions, C. Butler, *Western Mysticism* [2], p. lv ; J. V. Bainvel, in A. Poulain, *Des Grâces d'Oraison*, p. lii. The words ' however often it may occur ' (*si fréquentes soient-elles*) do not appear in Dom Butler's version. An even stronger statement by a Spanish Dominican, J. G. Arintero, Butler, *loc. cit.* ; Poulain, p. l. Some exaggerations in Lagrange are criticized by Butler, pp. lvi, lxxxi.

[2] *HLSR.*, i (E. tr.), p. 398.

[3] *Ib.*, p. 401 ; cp. p. 404.   [4] *Ib.*, vii, p. 149 ; cp. *ib.*, p. 153.

outside the definition of prayer altogether ?   With us there is only a spark, whilst with them it is a living flame ; but in us and in them alike the same fire burns.' [1]

NOTE O.—THE QUESTION OF PRIVATE ABSOLUTION IN THE EARLY CHURCH (*supra*, p. 283).

This problem has been raised again in recent years. The ground is clearer than it used to be, for it is generally admitted now that public confession of the details of sin was never required in the early Church, whilst excommunication and penitential exercises were also allowed a considerable amount of privacy on occasion (*supra*, pp. 228, 278, 505). The question then is, simply, *Was absolution ever given privately* prior to the spread of the Scoto-British system on the continent ? If it was, we shall have to admit, in Batiffol's phrase (*Études d'Histoire, etc.*[5], p. 216), that the early Church knew an 'escalier de service' to reconciliation, as well as an 'escalier d'apparat.' The passages in which (apart from cases of emergency death-bed absolution) private absolution has been suspected have recently been re-examined by B. Poschmann, *Die Abendländische Kirchenbusse* (1928), esp. ch. iii ; see also his *Kirchenbusse u. 'correptio secreta' bei Augustinus* (Braunsberg, 1923).[2] I summarize the arguments, adding a few points by the way.

(*a*) Innocent I, *ep*. 25, 7 ad Decentium (*MPL.*, xx, col. 559—the Maundy Thursday decree, *supra*, pp. 278, 505), speaks of those ' qui sive ex gravioribus commissis sive ex levioribus pœnitentiam gerunt.' Batiffol (*Études d'Histoire, etc.*[5], pp. 163-164, 189-191), by a judicious blend of this and the two following testimonia, produces the theory that the ' leviora ' were sins for which, though not subject to canonical penance, the sinner voluntarily and without formality undertook penance during Lent. He then mingled with the official penitents at the Maundy Thursday reconciliation, and so received absolution, not as a rite which could not be repeated, but as ' une sorte de coulpe publique ' which might be renewed each 'Holy Week. This reconciliation was not in itself private, but probably led to private reconciliations by delegated priests under Leo's approval (*ib.*, pp. 192, 217).

Against this it is to be urged (i) that ' pœnitentiam gerunt ' in *this* context must mean ' formal penance ' ; (ii) that ' leviora ' need not mean ' sins for which no canonical penance ' was required. They might be either (*a*) ' lighter ' relative to the ' graviora ' alone, but not in relation to anything else—i.e. a survival of the old distinction (*supra*, pp. 223, etc.), between sins for which penance was necessary *and reconciliation allowed* (' minora ' and ' leviora ' in Cyprian and Tertullian), and the three sins *par excellence* for which, in the earliest

---

[1] H. Bremond, *La Philosophie de la Prière* (1929), p. 96. Cp. also M. Bremond's examples of ' pan-mysticism' from S. Francis de Sales, *HLSR.*, vii, p. 84; and from Camus, *ib.*, pp. 148, 151, 155, 158, 160; his list of modern writers who support the same view, *ib.*, p. 162 ; and M. Ledoux's fine appreciation of M. Bremond's work in this respect, Bremond, *La Phil. de la Prière*, pp. 359, 360, with quotations from de la Taille, Wehrlé, and Blondel. On the doctrine that contemplation is open to all, in S. Augustine, S. Gregory, and S. Bernard, see C. Butler, *Western Mysticism*, pp. 240-242, 269-273, 286-287; and for Dom Butler's own ' pan-mysticism,' *supra*, p. 531 (top).

[2] For the purposes of this note I abbreviate the first of these books as *AK.*, the second *KB.*

system, though penance was allowed, absolution could not be given ;
(β) ' occult ' sins voluntarily brought forward as matter for penance
by a conscientious Christian.

(b) Leo i, *ep.* 167 ad Rustic., *inquis.* 19 (*MPL.*, liv, col. 1209) :—
persons guilty of the three sins *par excellence* ' ad communionem nisi
per pœnitentiam publicam non oportet admittere ' ; minor (specified)
sins ' possunt jejuniis et manus impositione purgari.' Batiffol (pp.
163, 164) takes this ' manus impositio,' again, of his supposed secondary
purpose of the Maundy Thursday reconciliation—the ' coulpe publique,' which he regards as renewable. But there is no suggestion
of *renewability* anywhere in the text ; we are probably dealing simply
with public reconciliation without any *public* penitential exercises (cp.
supra, p. 505). Poschmann's suggestion (*KB.*, pp. 73, 74) that this
' manus impositio ' is simply the rite of laying-on of hands on penitents
during the course of their penitential exercises (*supra*, p. 279), and
that therefore Leo here enjoins the sinners, without becoming official
penitents or requiring official (unrenewable) reconciliation, to submit
to some of the humiliations of public penance as a temporary discipline,
is possible ; but seems untenable for lack of other evidence.

(c) *Leo's Lenten sermons* (Batiffol, pp. 183-187 ; Poschmann, *AK.*,
217-222) are full of exhortations to ' pœnitentia.' They are addressed
to general congregations, among whom he mentions particularly the
catechumens, the penitents, Christians who are living ' chastely and
soberly ' together with sinners of various degrees (*serm.* 43, 3). But
nothing is said about their requiring, as a whole, formal reconciliation
whether public or private. The call to ' pœnitentia ' is therefore
simply one to ' repentance ' as a spiritual state or activity—which in
some cases, indeed, might waken the conscience to the need for formal
' penance ' ; but in the majority (where capital sin was not in question)
would lead only to works of charity and private self-discipline, as
for ' venial ' sin. (So Poschmann, *AK.*, pp. 219, 220 ; Vacandard,
in *DTC.*, iii, col. 853).

Batiffol can only convey verisimilitude to his theory, that we
have here a call to (private) penitential exercises to be rewarded by
the (public but renewable) Maundy Thursday reconciliation, by
printing and reading, almost as if it was one of the sermons (pp. 187,
188), Leo, *ep.* 108 (ad Theodor.), 3. Here Leo sets out to describe
canonical public penance—' quid de pœnitentium statu ecclesiastica
habeat regula non tacebo,'—and bases it on the dogma that for
' remissio *criminum* ' ' indulgentia Dei nisi supplicationibus sacerdotum nequeat obtineri.' In a later paragraph of the letter, he says :
' *Every* Christian ought to examine his conscience lest he be putting
off his conversion from day to day, and postponing his satisfaction
to his last moments : for it is dangerous, in our frail and ignorant
human life . . . to depend for the hope of divine mercy upon those
few moments in which there may scarcely be time either for the
penitent's confession or the priest's absolution.'

This passage is irrelevant for the matter of the Lenten sermons,
and even so does not establish the case. It merely says, at best,
that since all ' crimina ' require formal penance and reconciliation,
every Christian ought to examine himself to see whether he has committed any, and *if so* whether he is deliberately postponing his reconciliation. Batiffol, by ignoring the reference to ' crimina,' suggests
that *all* Christians need official reconciliation ; and by inserting the

letter into the context of the sermons, that such reconciliation should be (or may be) an annually renewable one on Maundy Thursday. In none of the three ' testimonia ' hitherto considered is there any evidence for this renewable reconciliation ; still less, therefore, for the private reconciliation by the priest which Batiffol very sketchily (pp. 192, 193)[1] suggests grew out of it.

(d) Cæsarius Arel., [Aug.] *app. serm.* 261, 1—on the heroism of one who undertakes public penance—' et ille quidem qui pœnitentiam publice accepit, poterat eam secretius agere ; sed credo, considerans multitudinem peccatorum suorum videt se contra tam gravia mala solum non posse sufficere ; ideo adjutorium totius populi cupit expetere.'

Tixeront (*Hist. Dogm.*, iii, pp. 397-399 ; but contrast Watkins, *op. cit.*, p. 557 ; Poschmann, *AK.*, pp. 138, 225) thinks that this refers to private penitential exercises with (? renewable) Maundy Thursday absolution (as Batiffol). Poschmann (*loc. cit.*), on the other hand, holds that it refers to the possibility of retiring to a monastery (' conversio '—*supra*, p. 510). Even this is not necessary. Cæsarius may be referring to the heroic act of a conscientious person who does public penance for non-canonical sins (for which such penance would not normally be required) out of personal humility and sense of weakness. Or the ' agere pœnitentiam ' may be used, as in other instances from Cæsarius (see next paragraph, *e*), of private penitential exercises, where in good faith, and on grounds of severe inconvenience alone, formal penance has been postponed to a later occasion. It is even possible that the ' credo ' and the ' poterat eam secretius agere ' are both sarcastic, and that what Cæsarius means is ' he might have *tried* to satisfy God and his conscience by private penance '—like Augustine's adulterer (*supra*, p. 504) who says, ' occulte ago, apud Deum ago.'

(e) Cæsarius more than once deals with hard cases of persons who have made themselves liable to public penance, but find it morally impossible to undertake it (soldiers, young married persons, etc.). In general he allows them to postpone formal penance (' accipere pœnitentiam ') till their death-beds, provided that they ' agunt pœnitentiam ' daily throughout their lives. So *serm.* 256, 1—the Christian guilty of capital sins may discipline himself and perform works of charity ;—' qui hæc fideliter implere voluerit, etiamsi *pœnitentiam non accipiat*, quia semper illam fructuose et fideliter *egit* bene hinc exiet ; et si eo tempore, quo moriturus est, *eam acceperit* . . . non solum eum veniam peccatorum credimus obtinere, sed etiam præmia æterna percipere ' ; *ib.*, 4, of ' illa pœnitentia quæ per omnem vitam a bonis Christianis *agitur*, per quam omnia et *capitalia crimina damnantur* et *minora peccata jugiter redimuntur* ' . . . ' cum enim omnes homines pœnitentiam velint in finem vitæ suæ *accipere* . . . quare non quotidie *ipsam pœnitentiam agimus ?* . . .' (The same advice also given explicitly to the young, *serm.* 249, 6 ; implicitly to soldiers, *serm.* 258, 2 ; but in neither case is the distinction between ' accipere ' and ' agere ' employed.)

Tixeront (in *L'Université Catholique*, cited Poschmann, *AK.*, pp. 117, 224)[2] here also appears to assume a private penance for capital sin. But the inference is out of the question ; for (i) *this* ' pœnitentia '

---

[1] In the *seventh* edition, pp. 190, 191.
[2] I have not seen the original.

is performed by *all* good Christians ; (ii) *daily* or *throughout their lives ;* and (iii) leads to no specific absolution (other than that of death-bed penance) ; for capital sins can only be 'redeemed' by absolution after public penance (*serm.* 104, 7 ; 262, 1) ; whilst this 'daily' penance (of self-discipline, love and almsgiving) avails only to 're-deem' *lesser* sins, and can only *condemn* capital sins—i.e. bring the offender into a state of mind in which he realizes their heinousness (*supra*, p. 511).

(*f*) A long and wearisome controversy between B. Poschmann and K. Adam on the subject of St. Augustine's teaching must be mentioned. A full list of the *acta* of the controversy is given by Poschmann, *AK.,* p. 5 ; beside Poschmann, *KB.,* the reader should also consult K. Adam, *Die Geheime Kirchenbusse nach dem Heiligen Augustin* (Kempten, 1921).[1] The discussion has raged over a wide field, but the problem turns in the main on Augustine's conception of 'correptio secreta.' The principal passages are the following ;—

(i) *Serm.* 82, 7 (10) f.—'ipsa corripienda sunt coram omnibus, quæ peccantur coram omnibus, ipsa corripienda sunt secretius quæ peccantur secretius.' . . . Then follow two instances of secret sin (murder and adultery) of which the bishop obtains cognizance, and he proceeds, 'corripio in secreto ; . . . persuadeo pœnitentiam . . nos non prodimus palam, sed in secreto arguimus. ubi contigit malum, ibi moriatur malum' (*GKA.,* pp. 17-27 ; *KB.,* pp. 22-26).

From the insistence upon secrecy Adam assumes that a secret penitential discipline took place ; this is possible, though Poschmann denies it. In an earlier pamphlet Adam deduced further from the 'ibi moriatur malum' that there was a private absolution following immediately upon this secret discipline (*KB.,* p. 2 ; *GKA.,* p. 18) ; he still holds to this private absolution (*GKA.,* p. 58), though he eliminates the idea of immediacy.[2]—But Augustine's point is a different one. What has to be kept secret is not so much *that* the offender has sinned, but the *exact character* of his sin. Hence he cannot even be publicly rebuked ('Tu, adulterer, corrige te' (*ib.,* 9 (12)) ; private expostulation (which, the bishop hopes, will lead the sinner to volun-tary public penance), is all that is possible. The 'ibi moriatur malum' is obviously rhetorical only. Nothing whatever is said or implied even as to private penance, still less as to private reconciliation.

(ii) *Ep.* 95, 3—A bishop's difficulties in the discharge of disciplinary responsibility :—'quid cum sæpe accidat, ut si in quemquam vindi-caveris, ipse pereat : si inultum reliqueris, alter pereat ? ego in his quotidie peccare me fateor, et ignoro quando quove modo custodiam id quod scriptum est ; *peccantes coram omnibus argue ut ceteri timorem habeant* (1 Tim. 5[20]), et quod scriptum est : *corripe eum inter te et ipsum solum* (Mt. 18[15]) . . .' (*GKA.,* pp. 27-30 ; *KB.,* pp. 28-31).

Two questions are involved, distinguished by the '*et* ignoro'— (*a*) 'When shall I " punish " and when not ? ' (*b*) '(If I decide to attempt to " punish ") shall I proceed by " correptio publica " or " cor-reptio secreta " ? ' Adam takes 'vindicta' from the first question and applies it to 'correptio' in the second ; 'correptio' whether public or private, must be not merely an exhortation to penitence,

---

[1] I cite this as *GKA.*

[2] In the *seventh* edition of *Études d'Histoire,* pp. 211-214, Batiffol holds to the theory of private penitential exercises in this case, but does not ex-plicitly advocate private absolution.

but a ' vindicta '—a full disciplinary process. Hence (*GKA*., p. 29)
' correptio privata ' = ' vindicta privata.' I can see no justification
for this procedure. Poschmann agrees in rejecting Adam's conclusion,
but makes the second question explanatory of the first :—(*a*) ' Shall
I punish or not ? '; *that is* (*b*) ' Shall I excommunicate openly, or by
using private monition only, and eschewing public excommunication,
run the risk of appearing not to have taken any notice of the offence ? '
(*KB*., p. 30).

(iii) *Serm*., 351, 4 (9)[1]—on penance for sins against the decalogue
(3 (4)) :—the sinner has both to exercise discipline on himself *and*
to submit to ecclesiastical authority—' et cum ipse in se protulerit
severissimæ medicinæ, sed tamen medicinæ, sententiam, veniat ad
antistites per quos illi in ecclesiâ claves ministrantur, et . . . a præ-
positis sacramentorum accipiat satisfactionis suæ modum . . . ut si
peccatum ejus non solum in gravi ejus malo, sed etiam in tanto scan-
dalo aliorum est atque hoc expediri utilitati ecclesiæ videtur antis-
titi, in notitiâ multorum vel etiam totius plebis agere pœnitentiam
non recuset ' (*GKA*., pp. 30-36 ; *KB*., pp. 32-40).

The sins here referred to, being forbidden by the decalogue, certainly demand penance and absolution ; and the last sentence implies
at first sight that public penance will only be required for public sin.
So Adam takes it, adding the corollary that for private sin private
penance is available and necessary—presumably (on Adam's theory)
with private reconciliation, as in (i). Poschmann, on the other hand,
by laying all the emphasis upon ' in notitiâ,' and insisting that it must
be distinguished from ' coram ' or ' in conspectu,' apparently would
render ' do penance with full advertence, on the part of the people,
as to the nature of his sin '—i.e. with public ' correptio ' or denunciation—(as distinct from a penance, in the case of slightly lesser sins,
with public penitential exercises only, but no denunciation). This,
however, is very forced. The meaning of the passage is, after all,
clear. ' Crimina ' require penance and absolution ; in some cases
(as for example, in those of great scandal at least) the whole process
will be public ; in others some part of the process (not necessarily
all, as Adam suggests ; nor necessarily the ' correptio ' *only*, as Poschmann) may perhaps be private. Nothing whatever is said or suggested
as to private absolution, nor is it implied that public penance is *confined* to notorious ' crimina '—we are merely told that in the case of
such open sin public penance will certainly be demanded.[2]

(iv) *de fid. et op*., 26 (48). A tabulation of sins into three classes :
(*a*) there are some sins ' ita gravia ut etiam excommunicatione plec-
tenda sint '; (*b*) others ' non eâ humilitate pœnitentiæ sananda
qualis in ecclesiâ datur eis qui proprie pœnitentes vocantur, sed
quibusdam correptionum medicamentis '—this last category is referred to in Mt. 18[15] : —' corripe eum inter te et ipsum solum.' (*c*)

---

[1] Batiffol, in the *seventh* edition of *Études d'Histoire, etc*., pp. 337-362,
rejects the Augustinian authorship of this sermon, though he regards it as
the work of a contemporary African bishop, which reveals a ' system of penance
corresponding point for point with S. Augustine's '. He concludes that it
shows ' that public penance was only demanded on exceptional occasions ;
but it gives no hint of the rite of private absolution ' (p. 362).

[2] A further though minor problem lies in the distinction of two further
grades of publicity which can be inferred from ' in notitiâ *multorum* vel
totius plebis ' (*GKA*., p. 35 ; *KB*., p. 34). But no question of principle is
involved here, and the phrase may be merely rhetorical.

There is also a third class of venial sin (*GKA.*, pp. 39-62 ; *KB.*, pp. 41-53).

Adam treats this as the ' classical evidence ' for a private penitential procedure in Augustine. He attempts to show (*GKA.*, pp. 46-47) that ' correptio ' (especially in the plural) in Augustine always means some kind of disciplinary procedure (= ' vindicta '; *supra*, pp. 537 f,), and that he has a settled use of ' medicamenta ' in the sense of ecclesiastical sacraments (p. 48). Poschmann, *KB.*, pp. 23, 24, disposes of the first of these points ; and the qualifications which Adam himself has to make on the second point (*GKA.*, p. 48) are enough to render it unconvincing. Still, *per se* the passage is difficult. If there were any other real evidence for private penance *with private absolution* the second category of sins here mentioned would fit in very well with it.[1] As it is, I think we must agree with Poschmann (p. 47) that Augustine is not here making a strictly logical classification. The sins referred to in the second category are sins which, like those of the third class, prayer and almsgiving will heal ; but because the sinner is for some reason or another blind to them, they need the admonition of the bishop (or indeed of any other Christian) to bring them before the sinner's conscience, so that he will take the necessary steps for dealing with them.

(v) *Conc. Hippon.* (A.D. 393), can. 3. The canon contains three regulations : (i) The duration of penance to be decided by the bishop with reference to the gravity of the offence. (ii) Presbyters not to reconcile except in the bishop's absence and in case of necessity (*supra*, p. 281). (iii) ' cujuscumque autem pœnitentis publicum et vulgatissimum crimen est, quod universa ecclesia noverit, ante apsidem manus ei imponatur.'

Is this an *extraordinary* regulation for *specially* grave ' crimina,' or an *ordinary* regulation for *ordinary* ' crimina ' ?—i.e. What other course is a possible alternative to ' ante apsidem ' ? Public absolution in a less conspicuous place ? or *private* absolution ? Poschmann originally took the first alternative—the regulation is intended merely to import additional disgrace into the punishment of specially grave sin. Later (*KB.*, p. 37) he veered to the second alternative ; the opposite of ' ante apsidem ' is ' in strict privacy,' and we have (by implication) a case of definite private reconciliation for grave sin. In *AK.* he makes no allusion to this interpretation, from which I infer that he is still doubtful about it.

In general it would seem that Poschmann's first interpretation is quite valid. But even if it be rejected :

(*a*) The canon need not imply ' occult grave sins *must* be reconciled ; but they may be reconciled privately.' It may simply mean that *at this moment* at Hippo the practice was that only notorious grave sin should be officially submitted to public penance, all other sin being left to the conscience of the individual, stimulated no doubt

---

[1] Batiffol, in the *seventh* edition of *Études d'Histoire*, pp. 213, 214, is not prepared to see more than private penitential exercises here. His general conclusion (p. 224) is that *if* a prisoner, lying under sentence of death, confessed mortal sin and showed due penitence, Augustine would have absolved him privately. As this would be a case of necessity, analogous to death-bed penance, the conclusion is a safe one ; but when Batiffol adds that ' it opens up a perspective of a penitence with private reconciliation,' we can scarcely avoid asking how distant that ' perspective ' is supposed to be.

by the ' correptio privata ' of the bishop.   If under this stimulus he took the heroic course of offering himself for public penance, his discipline would take place ' ante apsidem ' too.

(b) The fact that the regulation follows one about reconciliation does not necessarily imply that the ' manus impositio ' here must mean reconciliation.   There is no continuity of thought between the second and first clauses of the canon ; and so need be none between the third and second.   Hence the ' manus impositio ' may refer either to admission to penitential status, or to the exercises of that status (*supra*, p. 279, n. 1), and not to reconciliation ; and if the implication is that notorious sinners and occult sinners are to be treated differently, it is hazardous to infer more than that for the latter private penitential exercises, or private admission to penitential status alone, will sometimes be accepted.

(c) It may merely be a piece of local rigorism in the matter of death-bed reconciliations (suggested by the ' necessity ' of the preceding regulation) :—notorious sinners may not be reconciled in the semi-privacy of the sick room, but must either (if they recover) submit to the full public discipline, or be allowed to die unshriven (cp. *supra*, pp. 229, 512).

If a single case of private reconciliation (other than sick-bed cases) could be quoted from the first five centuries, the evidence just reviewed might take on a very different character.   As it is, any assumption of private penance *with private absolution*, running parallel to the public institution as a recognized alternative, involves the hypothesis of a conspiracy of silence on the part of patristic authorities (so Boudinhon, and Poschmann, *AK.*, p. 226) ; and flies in the face of the vast bulk of contemporary evidence.

NOTE P.—ABAILARD ON MORTAL AND VENIAL SIN (*supra*, p. 297).

The importance of Abailard's contribution in this respect has not been generally recognized by writers on his ethics.   Often it is altogether ignored.   J. Schiller, *Abälards Ethik im Vergleich zur Ethik seiner Zeit* (1906), p. 37, glances at it, but attributes too much insight to Abailard's contemporaries.   ' Other schoolmen of the period,' he says, ' recognized, like Abailard, the importance of subjective considerations ; but at the same time they insisted upon the gravity of legal obligation ' (i.e. the law of God), ' and so allowed objective considerations to have the decisive voice in determining the gravity of sin.'   The facts, however, warrant a much more definite distinction between Abailard and his contemporaries.   The degree of an author's moral sensitiveness in this matter may be judged by the following tests :

(a) How far is he prepared to deny that there are sins which are *always* mortal, or (conversely) to assert that (e.g.) ignorance of the moral law exempts from condemnation ?   The test question here was that of the Jewish authorities who put to death Christ and the apostles, ' thinking to do God a service,'—how far did their (presumably) good intentions make them blameless in the matter ?

(b) How far is he anxious to assert that ' venial ' sin can only too readily be turned into ' mortal ' ?

On (a) Abailard is far more explicit than his contemporaries.

have analysed his views as expressed in the *Scito teipsum* in *Ignorance, Faith and Conformity*, pp. 8-12.   He definitely exempts the Jews from blame (c. 13), and insists that there can be *no* sin except where a man consents to that to which he believes he ought not to consent.—Peter Damian, on the other hand (*opusc.* 10, 1 ; *MPL.*, cxlv, col. 223), enumerates seven ' criminalia vitia ' (adultery, homicide, theft, perjury, false witness, ' rapine,' blasphemy), and says—' ut si quisquis in quolibet horum deprehensus obierit, evadere damnationis æternæ sententiam nullatenus possit '—thus admitting no excuse in these cases.—Anselm (*cur Deus homo*, ii, 15) admits that the offence of the Jews may have been ' venial ' only ; but maintains (*de conceptu virg.*, 4), that there are some actions, ' such as perjury and certain others,' which are bound always to be sinful (' quæ numquam nisi injusta possunt esse '— ' injusta ' here being subjective as well as objective).—Bernard is prepared also to make allowances for those who slew the Lord, though he insists that they were ' magni peccatores ' (*de præc. et disp.*, 10 (20)) ;   but on the more general question says ' siquidem adulterium *quocumque modo, quocumque perpetres animo*, turpe flagitium est ac criminale peccatum ' (*ib.*, 8 (18)).   He is extremely unwilling to admit that a conscience in good faith can ever prescribe an erroneous course of action (this of course would make it impossible to exculpate the Jews—they cannot have acted in good faith), and does not shrink from the absurd corollary that the man who does evil believing it to be good is therefore more worthy of the title ' wicked ' (' nequam ') than he who does evil believing it to be evil (*op. cit.*, 14, 35-41).[1] Hugh of St. Victor says that there are actions which ' non possunt nisi mali esse ' (*Sent.*, iii, 15 ; cp. also the discussion *de sacr.*, ii, 13, 1).— Richard of St. Victor defines mortal sin by wholly objective characteristics, without reference to subjective considerations (unless the *contemptus* of the last clause is subjective) : ' mortale est quod a quovis non potest committi sine grandi corruptione sui ; item, mortale est quod non potest committi sine grandi læsione proximi ; mortale nihilominus quod non potest committi sine magno contemptu Dei ' (*de diff. pecc. mort. et ven.* ; *MPL.*, cxcvi, col. 1193).   Peter Lombard, with the air of one who makes a proclamation (' intende, lector, propositis verbis totâ mentis consideratione '—did he wish to dissociate himself publicly from Abailard's known position ?), and basing himself on Aug., *c. mend.*, 8 (18, 19), says that there are some actions which, however *bonâ fide* (' etsi bonam habeant causam '), are always sin ; and instances the Jews as a case in point (P. Lomb., *Sent.*, ii, 40. 3).— The only writer to echo Abailard's position uncompromisingly is Robert Pullus, who had a pretty taste in casuistical problems (*Sent.*, vi, 7-11), and so knew the difficulties—' is ex eo quod ignorans aut facit aut dimittit, reatum nequaquam trahit ' (*ib.*, vi, 2).

(*b*) Abailard's treatment of *venial sin* betrays novelty in emphasis rather than in matter.   All his contemporaries allow that venial sin can become mortal ; but they are most commonly concerned to show that this is unusual.   So Bernard, *de præc. et disp.*, 11 (25, 26)—' cibo exsaturari ' and even ' irasci fratri ' are venial *ex genere*, and only become mortal ' cum per contemptum vertuntur in usum et consuetudinem.'   Abailard on the contrary, goes out of his way to insist

---

[1] Each does evil ; but the former is in error as well as to its real nature— and this error increases his culpability '   The fact that the former meant well and the latter did not is wholly ignored.

that *even the most trivial offence* can only too easily become mortal. Thus the *epitome* c. 33 (Cousin, *Opp. P. Ab.*, ii, p. 588 ; *MPL.*, clxxviii, col. 1754), which, if not from Abailard's pen, certainly reproduces his teaching :—' quantumcumque igitur, ut ait Augustinus,[1] in se leve sit peccatum, dum placet et ex industriâ perpetratur, mortale est.' More remarkable is a highly characteristic passage, *Scito teipsum*, 15. I give the Latin abbreviated as far as possible, followed by an English version, in which the necessary connections of thought are indicated by [   ] (Cousin, ii, pp. 620, 621 ; *MPL.*, clxxviii, coll. 658, 659 ; the punctuation as given here corresponds exactly with neither of these texts) :

' peccatorum autem alia *venialia* dicuntur et quasi levia, alia *damnabilia sive gravia*. rursus damnabilium quædam *criminalia* dicuntur, quæ in illis personam infamem vel criminosam facere habent, si in audientiam veniant ; quædam vero minime. *venialia* quidem [vel][2] talia peccata sunt, quando in eo consentimus cui non consentiendum esse scimus, sed tunc tamen non occurrit memoriæ illud quod scimus[3] . . . quandoque itaque vel in vaniloquium, vel in superfluum esum vel potum consentimus, quod tamen nequaquam esse faciendum scimus ; sed tunc minime recordabamur quod non esset faciendum. tales itaque consensus, quos per oblivionem incurrimus, venialia aut levia dicuntur peccata. . . .[4]

' quae *damnabilia et graviora* dicuntur peccata[5] . . . non per oblivionem, sicut illa, incurrimus, sed tamquam ex studio et deliberatione committimus[6] . . . horum autem alia *criminalia dicuntur*, quæ per effectum cognita nævo magnæ culpæ hominem detrahunt— ut consensus perjurii, homicidii, adulterii, quæ plurimum ecclesiam scandalizant. cum vero supra quam necesse est cibo indulgemus, vel non mediocri cultu ex vanâ gloriâ nos adornamus, etsi hoc scienter præsumimus, *non hæc crimini ascribuntur*, et apud multos plus laudis habent quam vituperationis.'

In so far as the meaning of this passage is doubtful, it is because Abailard has conjoined in it two discussions : (*a*) the distinction between mortal and venial sin ; (*b*) the distinction, among mortal sins, between criminous and non-criminous. Both discussions were urgent at the period, the former because the priest must know what sins called for official cognizance by the Church ; the latter, because he must know which of the sins calling for formal cognizance could be dealt with by private penance, and which must be sent forward for public canonical procedure (cp. *epit.*, 33 : ' horum mortalium est aliud criminale, aliud non ' etc., and commonly in the period). Hence the passage may be rendered as follows :—

---

[1] I cannot trace the source of this, and neither Cousin nor Migne gives any reference ; but the idea is obvious.

[2] Both Cousin and Migne print this *vel*, but it is meaningless, since there is no other *vel* to correspond.

[3] Here a short digression on the distinction between forgetfulness and ignorance.

[4] Here a digression on the ' satisfaction ' necessary for venial sin—the ' quotidiana confessio ' (of the Lord's prayer). This digression merges into the beginning of the next paragraph, which consequently opens informally. In the text I have retained only the significant words.

[5] He has just indicated, in the digression, ' perjury,' ' homicide,' and ' adultery,' under this head.

[6] Here a Scriptural proof text (Ps. 13[2]).

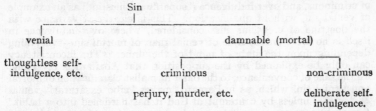

'Of sins some are called *venial* or light, others *damnable* or grave. Again of these damnable sins some are called *criminous*, viz. those which have it in them to make their agents infamous or criminous if they become known ; others are not criminous, [but the distinction between criminous and non-criminous, as it affects merely a man's external status, has no bearing upon the true character of his sin]. *Venial* sins are those which we commit when we consent to something which we know should not be consented to, but do not happen to remember our knowledge. . . . Sometimes, for example, we consent to idle speech or excessive eating or drinking, which we know to be wrong, but forget the fact at the time of indulgence—such "consents" as these, into which we fall by forgetfulness, are called venial or light sins. . . . But the so-called *damnable* or *grave* offences, unlike venial sins, are not incurred by forgetfulness ; we commit them, as it were, of intention and malice prepense. . . . Of these some are *criminous*, viz. those which, as recognized by their results, dishonour the agent with the scandal of grave culpability—e.g. consent to perjury, homicide, and adultery, which create the greatest scandal in the Church. But [many other actions, not in any sense criminous, are damnable, grave or mortal too. Thus] excessive indulgence in food, or immoderate luxury in clothing designed to administer to vanity, even if deliberately indulged in, are not criminous, and many people are inclined to praise rather than to blame them ; [but deliberate indulgence in them obviously makes them mortal too.']

This interpretation is rendered necessary by the facts that (*a*) Abailard specifically makes over-indulgence in food venial *if and when it is absent-minded ;* (*b*) states that some mortal sins are not criminous. Hence the reference to *deliberate* over-indulgence at the end is only intelligible if it implies that such over-indulgence is (*a*) mortal, in contrast with *absent-minded* over-indulgence ; and (*b*) (as he says), non-criminous, though mortal, in opposition to perjury, etc., which are criminous as well as mortal. The thought is a very real contribution to the proper understanding of 'sin,' and Abailard recognizes his temerity both by pointing out that the very offences which he is selecting as typical of non-criminous mortal sin are commonly more praised than blamed ; and also by avoiding the direct statement that they are damnable or mortal, though leaving it as the only possible inference from the passage.

Apart from the boldness of the conception, the only objection to this interpretation is that in chapter 16, in discussing the rather hyper-critical question, 'Whether it is better to aim at avoiding criminous or venial sin ? '[1] Abailard quotes perjury, etc., as examples

[1] On this curious dichotomy of ' sin ' into ' criminous ' and ' venial,' see the final paragraph of this note. For the moment we may assume that here he identifies ' criminous ' with ' mortal.'

of criminous, and over-indulgence ('superflua comestio ') as an example
of venial sin, without qualification. This is clearly at variance with
the doctrine of c. 15, as just considered, where over-indulgence in
itself is no more an example of venial than of mortal sin—everything
depending upon the state of mind of the sinner. The inconsistency
can only be explained by the supposition that Abailard is reverting,
for the sake of convenience, to the older formalist classification of mortal
and venial sin, which, as in Bernard, makes ' cibo exsaturari ' venial
ex genere, ' unless by contempt of God it has hardened into a habit'
(' excepto cum per contemptum vertuntur in usum et consuetudinem '
—*de præc. et disp.*, 11 (26)).

Indeed, on Abailard's definition of mortal and venial sin, the
question of c. 16 is pointless ; venial (or absent-minded) sin could
only be avoided by first avoiding mortal (or deliberate) sin in respect
of the same temptations. To a confessor of the old school the question
would mean : ' I am not very likely to commit murder ; shall I then
stop bothering about that possibility, and concentrate on avoiding,
e.g. over-eating ? ' To Abailard (on the basis of c. 15), it would have
to mean : ' I am not very likely to be *deliberately* gluttonous ; shall
I therefore stop bothering about that possibility and concentrate upon
avoiding *thoughtless* gluttony ? ' The answer would be, ' You can
only avoid thoughtless gluttony by being particularly careful first to
avoid deliberate gluttony.' As he does not take this line of argument,
it is legitimate to assume that he is ignoring the thought of c. 15, and
is adopting the old-fashioned premises of his enquirer in order to
answer a question which has no practical value for himself at all.

That Abailard in chapter 16 is arguing an old-fashioned question
on old-fashioned lines is further shown by the fact that the only types
of sin there brought into contrast are ' criminalia ' and ' venialia '—
non-criminous mortal sin does not appear, nor does the word ' damnabilia,' which in chapter 15 he has used throughout to cover both
types of mortal sin. The question therefore belongs to a period in
which ' criminous ' and ' mortal ' were synonymous [1]—a period, that
is, before the distinction of public penance for public (criminous) mortal
sin and private penance for occult (non-criminous) mortal sin had
forced into view the doctrine that not all ' mortal' sin (requiring
penance) was ' criminous ' (requiring *public* penance).[2] Abailard's
purpose in recording the discussion is manifest at the end of the chapter
—it is to exhort Christians first to secure themselves against temptation to grave sin, and then ' to strive to avoid even these lesser sins,
for that is how virtue is brought to perfection.'

NOTE Q.—MEDIÆVAL HOMILIES (*supra*, p. 300).

As further evidence for the better side of popular mediæval thought,
I quote the following passages from the homily called *Vices and Virtues*
(Middle English, twelfth century—trans. by F. Holthausen)—*EETS.*,
no. 89 (1888) :—

(P. 22) Reason speaks to the soul : ' I am a gleam of God's face
that was shaped in thee, dear, dear soul, *Ratio* by name, that is Discernment.'

---

[1] As commonly up to the tenth century—e.g. Aug., *ench.*, 17 (64)—19 (71) ;
de bon. conj., 6 (7) , Isidor. Hisp., *Sent.*, ii, 20. 4 (' peccatum perpetrare
crimen est ') ; Rab. Maur., *de vit. et virt.*, iii, 1 (*MPL.*, cxii, col. 1337).
[2] *Supra*, pp. 278, 504.

(*Ib.*, p. 30) of hope : ' *Dedisti lætitiam in corde meo,* "Thou, O Lord, gavest bliss into my heart, so that to me there is naught of all the world's bliss. And Thou hast given me this as an earnest of that eternal bliss." Dear soul, if thou hast this bliss in thy heart, which does not come from any world's bliss, then thou mayest be sure of God's grace ; and if thou hast not, do not cease neither night nor day ere thou have it ' (followed by a very beautiful allegory based on the phrase ' the oil of gladness ').

(*Ib.*, p. 38) of charity : ' Then wilt thou truly abide in God, if thou thinkest more of Him than thou dost of anything in the world, by day and by night, for thou hast great need that He be always thy shield against all evils and thy helper to all good. If thou hast this thy love in God, it then behooves thee, if thou wilt have charity in thee, to be well aware that thou shouldest love thy neighbour, that is, every man who bears thy likeness. . . . S. Gregory [1] gives us an example of this, that just as no web can be woven without two beams, so charity can never be finished without two loves ; and just as many threads are necessary ere it be made, so is much reflecting of thoughts and words and works needful to charity during all thy lifetime, ere it be ordained in thee as it is necessary.'

(*Ib.*, p. 88) of the Kingdom of God : ' "The Kingdom of God is not meat and drink ; but righteousness and peace and joy in the Holy Ghost." Dear soul, I beg and warn thee to have no hope in thy fasting, nor in thy watching, nor in any other good. Except thou have these three things, God will never reign in thee, nor thou evermore in Him.'

(*Ib.*, p. 124) on purity of heart : ' God cannot be seen with any other eyes but with the heart's. Wash and wipe well clean the eyes because it is true what they tell thee. . . . Of all the blessings which God promised in His preaching, there is none so high as is "who is pure in heart." May he get it whoso can ! I warn thee, thou never gettest it clean whilst thou doest not care what thou thinkest, nor what thou speakest, nor what thou hearest speak. And except thou gladly makest it clean as much as possible, with God's help, thou shalt never see God Almighty with these eyes with which thou seest sun and moon.'

NOTE R.—AUGUSTINISM (*supra*, p. 338).

With Bishop Robertson's statement of the problem (*supra*, p. 338) may be compared the following : ' If grace is the might of omnipotence directed by omniscience, no dubiety can arise respecting the side faith must embrace. Its lot must be cast in with Augustinianism, for there is no faith without, in the end, ascribing everything to God. To-day, as always when we are forced to recognize life's appalling failures, faith must rely not partially, but utterly upon God. Even semi-Pelagianism can provide no satisfactory religious basis. If God will only act when we begin, or continue acting only as we fulfil certain conditions, then in the last issue our reliance is on man and not God. But to the miserable uncertainty and painful anxiety of that trust all experience . . . bears witness. The religious man always has ascribed, and found his whole peace and confidence in ascribing, all things

[1] Pseudo-Gregor., *Hom. in Ev.*, ii, 38.

to God. Any good result, in particular, he does not dream of ascribing in part to God and in part to his own right resolve. He speaks, not of man that runneth, but of God who giveth the victory; and he has only one hymn of praise : " O the depth of the riches both of the wisdom and the knowledge of God ! " ' (J. Oman, *Grace and Personality*, pp. 24, 25).

Particularly important is the sentence ' even semi-Pelagianism provides no solution.' Once the principle that grace must come first has been admitted, nothing is lost by adding that it must also come second, and last as well—that man can never at any point bestir himself in pure freedom to good actions—that he needs, in the language of the Schoolmen, *subsequent* as well as *prevenient* grace. The semi-Pelagian doctrine that, once the first grace has been given, man must co-operate with it of his own freewill, must always lie under the suspicion of inconsistency with its premises. Who shall say whether the will, once it has come, by no activity of its own, ' under grace,' does not continue ' under grace ' thenceforward and always—is not always, that is to say, under the irresistible sway of this new power ?

Thus, in strict logic, the entire Augustinian position is conceded once the Church admits the contention (as to which, as Moehler says, ' all Confessions are agreed ') ' that grace first determines, and consequently goes before, all the truly pious endeavours of man.' [1] In the Reformation and post-Reformation periods, Lutherans and Jansenists, on the one hand, maintained that every such action, to the end of life, was determined by grace and grace alone.[2] Man remains quite passive : a saw in the hand of the Divine workman, ' a pillar of salt, a block, a clod of earth.' ' No human will can resist the grace of God within, once God has decided to save the soul.' [3] Trent and Calvin took the opposite and less consistent view ; so do the English Articles. ' If anyone saith that the freewill once moved and stimulated ("excitatum ") by God, doth not co-operate by assenting to the stimulus and call of God, thereby to dispose and prepare itself to acquire justifying grace ; or that it cannot dissent, if it so will ; but doth nothing at all and remaineth passive like a thing inanimate—*anathema sit*.' [4] Trent indeed came very near to Pelagianism when it asserted that this *prevenient* grace might be resisted (' dissentire '). It is probably true to say that by the ambiguous use of such words as ' gratia excitans ' and ' adjuvans ' the Council evaded our fundamental question : ' Is the first step in salvation taken by grace or by man's unaided will ? ' and kept open the way both for Pelagian and Augustinian interpretations.

It is not unreasonable to ask, however, whether the difference between Augustinism and Pelagianism is not wholly academic. The Augustinian Christian, though under irresistible grace, is required to exercise moral effort as much as though he were not under grace at all—that is to say, is required to exercise all the effort he can. So is the Pelagian. What, then, *in practice*, is the difference between the two ; and why did Augustine take the controversy so much to

---

[1] J. A. Moehler, *Symbolism* (E. tr. 1894), p. 97.
[2] *Ib.*, pp. 86, 88.   [3] *Ib.*, pp. 89, 90.
[4] *Conc. Trid.*, sess. vi, can. 4; D.-B., no. 814. Cp. for Calvin, Moehler, *op. cit.*, pp. 98 ff. (note reservations) ; and for the Church of England, *Articles* xii, xvii.

heart ? [1] He himself, like S. Paul, whose predestinarianism he does no more than inherit and develop (*supra*, pp. 232, 339 f.), is capable of as impassioned moral exhortation as any Pelagian ; can it then be said that any good purpose was served by his insistence upon the primacy of grace ? No doubt, as has been indicated above (*supra*, pp. 337 f.), the elimination of the idea carries with it the elimination of supernaturalism in all its forms, and the denial of all practical value to Christianity, except as a new law ; but the rationalist will ask whether this is any loss, if moral effort is demanded as much by Christianity as by naturalism.

Three points seem to deserve attention :—

(*a*) It has often been observed that, as a mere matter of fact, predestinarianism and the doctrine of irresistible grace—so far from leading, as Pelagius supposed, to moral laxity—have a strong tendency to enhance the impulse to moral effort (cp. C. C. J. Webb, *History of Philosophy*, p. 86, where what is said of the Stoics as ' champions of religion ' is even more applicable to them as champions of ethics). It is difficult at first sight to assign a psychological cause to this phenomenon. But something can be suggested. Among the earnest-minded, the chief occasion of moral sterility is despair—the sense of the futility and inadequacy, in face of the evils of life, even of the highest human effort. Once substitute for despair the certainty of achievement, and activity revives again, to put forth its strongest efforts. We might expect the certainty of achievement to rob effort of all interest, transforming life from an enthralling and splendid adventure into a commonplace progress to a predetermined end. Actually, however, this does not happen, even in the lesser things of life. The moment at which the scholar sees that his problem is *going to be solved*—however distant the solution may still be—is the moment which stimulates him to renewed and better (because care-free) efforts. The moment at which the athlete sees he is going to win his race is the moment at which he is spurred to an even swifter pace. He is no longer under the psychological restraint of keeping something in reserve for the crisis ; the crisis has come and is over—all that remains is to complete the victory. The doctrine of irresistible grace (or rather, as Augustine has taught us to conceive it, of irresistible love) perpetuates for the moral life the victorious tension of these ' moments ' which the scholar and the athlete prize ; it elicits greater effort by dealing a death-blow to anxiety.

(*b*) Thus the doctrine of grace has the highest possible psychological value for the moral pessimist—the ' twice-born ' or ' sick soul ' of James' *Varieties of Religious Experience*. Has it a similar value for the optimist—James' ' once-born ' or ' healthy-minded ' ? Here again the answer is in the affirmative. As has been argued in chapter viii above (pp. 445 ff.), moral effort will only stultify itself unless it is permeated throughout by the spirit of humility. Worship is the psychological instrument for the production of that spirit ; the doctrine of God's prevenient grace is its intellectual correlative. The optimist must learn that he owes all that is good in his life and works to the unmerited grace of God. Without that lesson he will never

---

[1] There is no need to ask why Pelagius took it to heart. He was convinced that the Augustinian man, believing himself to be under irresistible grace, *would* not, and probably *could* not exercise effort as though he were ' not under grace.'

be able to serve in humility, but only in patronage ; and the service of patronage, as has been argued above, may be the worst disservice of all.

(c) We infer, therefore, not only that *worship* occupies an integral place in the Augustinian scheme, whilst in the Pelagian it is purely optional (cp. *supra*, p. 338) ; but also that the whole tenour of Augustinian preaching will be entirely different from that of the Pelagian. Like the Pelagian, the Augustinian will exhort the optimist to humility and the pessimist to courage.   But once that has been done, the Pelagian's bolt is shot ; whilst Augustine has not yet used the most potent weapon in his armoury.   Pelagianism can at best exhort men to love God ; Augustinism tells them of God's gracious love to men, confident that—where exhortation fails, as it so frequently does—that love itself, as well as the subjective recognition of it, will be in the end of unfailing effect.   The immediate practical issue between Augustine and Pelagius was that of the method of the Church's approach to men. Was she to come as a formalist legislator—confirming the pessimist in his pessimism and the optimist in his patronizing outlook ; or could she bring a *gospel* which would convert the pessimist into an optimist, and elicit from the optimist the grace of humility without which all his achievements are at best in vain ?

NOTE S.—S. THOMAS ON MYSTICAL EXPERIENCE AND BEATITUDE
(*supra*, pp. 385, 391, etc.).

1. *Mystical Experience.*

In an important essay (*ERE.*, ix, *s.v.* ' Mysticism (Christian, Roman Catholic),' esp. pp. 95, 96) Dom John Chapman advances a view as to a theory of mysticism ' latent in S. Thomas,' which ' has not been discovered by most of his followers and commentators.' He starts from S. Thomas' well-known distinction between human cognition, in which the ' species intelligibiles ' (pure abstract truths and ideas) cannot be known save in and by constant reference to ' phantasmata ' (' mental images,' including ' verbal images,' A. D. Sertillanges, *St. Thomas d'Aquin*, ii, p. 163—the whole doctrine from Aristotle, *de an.*, iii, 7 ; the Thomist references well put together by L. Schütz, *Thomas-Lexikon* [2] (1895), p. 415, *s.v.* ' intelligere ' (a) 16), and *angelic* cognition, by direct intuition of ' species intelligibiles.' He then points out that, according to S. Thomas, (a) in the state of beatitude man will share in the angelic cognition ; [1] (b) Moses and S. Paul had this gift in their life-time ; [2] (c) one of the means by which God reveals truth to the prophets is ' imprimendo species intelligibiles ipsi menti,' presumably without ' phantasmata ' (*ST.*, ii, 2, q. 173, a. 2) ; (d) Adam in the state of innocence, though he did not know God ' per essentiam,' knew Him ' per intelligibiles effectus ' (*ST.*, i, q. 94, a. 1), somewhat as the angels do (*ib.*, q. 56, a. 3—man since the Fall normally only knows God ' per sensibiles et corporeos effectus,' *ib.*, q. 94, a. 1) ; and this is called ' contemplation '

---

[1] In an *enhanced* form ; for only *as a reward* do either angels or man see the divine *essence* by the infusion of the *lumen gloriæ* (*CG.*, iii, 51-53 ; *ST.*, i, q. 12, aa. 4, 5 ; q. 62, a. 1 ; *de ver.*, q. 8, a. 3.

[2] Also in the enhanced form.   They saw God in His essence (*ST.*, i, q. 12, a. 11, ad 2).   Chapman rightly regards this as an ' incautious admission,' and it does not affect the argument.

(*ib.*; cp. *de ver.*, q. 18, a. 2, ' conformiter angelis '; cp. *ib.*, ad 4, 5);
(*e*) even after the Fall man *by grace* sees God in contemplation by the
same ' light of grace or wisdom ' as Adam,[1] ' quamvis perfectius in
statu innocentiæ ' (*de ver.*, q. 18, a. 1, ad 4). To these might be added
(*f*) that David also was given the gift ' ut contempletur veritatem
divinam per intelligibiles effectus ' in ecstasy (*ST.*, ii, 2, q. 175, a. 3,
ad 1).

On these passages, Dom Chapman comments : ' It follows from
S. Thomas's epistemology that man's intellect in this life is not
radically incapable of receiving pure intellectual *species* such as it
will connaturally receive after death. . . . We should anticipate that
S. Thomas also must regard mystical theology as the angelic consciousness communicated to man, and we might confidently argue to this
from the fact that " intellectual visions " are not peculiar to prophecy,
but are understood by all mediæval writers to be common in the
saints. But as a fact, S. Thomas incidentally confirms our anticipations by a clear statement ' (then follows *de ver.*, q. 18, a. 1, ad 4—see
(*e*) above), ' Therefore contemplation restores to man by grace some
measure of that angelic knowledge which Adam had of God before
the Fall.'

Unless I misinterpret Dom Chapman's argument, S. Thomas'
theory would be that after a period of ' contemplation ' (= Hugh's
' meditation '), the mystic rapture normally supervenes, and the soul
receives angelic knowledge (' species intelligibiles ' without ' phantasmata ')[2] as the prophets have done. Thus a mystical experience
akin to ecstasy would be the normal completion of the activity of
contemplation.

This theory is profoundly impressive, and Dom Chapman has done
great service by eliciting it from his evidence. In the main it is, I
think, to be accepted ; but the following points are of consequence :—

(*a*) Except in *de ver.*, q. 18, a. 1 (to which we must recur), S. Thomas
never asserts angelic knowledge of any human being except specially
favoured Biblical characters—Moses, S. Paul, S. Peter, David, Solomon, and the Apostles.

(*b*) Even in prophecy, what is important is not the presence of
' species intelligibiles,' but of the ' lumen propheticum.' Not only
is the ' impression of new species ' used indiscriminately to cover
' imaginary ' (phantasmic) as well as ' intelligible ' species (*ST.*, ii,
2, q. 173, a. 2 *corp.*) ; but the gift of new intelligible species is confined
to Solomon and the Apostles (*ib.*), who do not of course monopolize
the title of ' prophets ';[3] and it is definitely asserted that the possession
of the necessary ' lumen ' is more important (' principalius ') than
the presence of new species. Thus merely natural phenomena (' ea
quæ cursu naturali homo apprehendit ') can lend themselves to prophetic purposes if we have the right ' lumen ' whereby to look at them.
Similarly in *ST.*, i, q. 43, a. 7, ad 2, the ' visio prophetica ' is identified outright with the ' visio imaginaria,' which is of course ' per
phantasmata ' (cp. *ST.*, i, q. 12, a. 13, ad 3 ; and for the influence

---

[1] Or the angels—' secunda autem visio, quæ est per medium quod est
species, est naturalis angelis ; sed est supra naturam hominis ; unde ad
eam indiget lumine gratiæ.'

[2] Dom Chapman points out rightly that it could not *employ* these *species*
without *phantasmata* when it returned to normal consciousness.

[3] Cp. *supra*, p. 392, nn. 3, 6.

of the ' lumen gratiæ ' in drawing out ' deeper truth ' from ' phantasmata,' *ib.*, obj. 2, et ad 2). The test question therefore is, to whom and when is the ' lumen gratiæ ' (= 'revelationis,' *ST.*, i, q. 1, a. 1, ad 2 ; ' fidei vel prophetiae,' i, 2, q. 109, a. 1 *corp.*) given ? [1]

(*c*) In *de ver.*, q. 18, what S. Thomas says about contemplation is very much determined by the fact that he is interpreting texts of Hugh of St. Victor (see a. 1, ad 4 ; a. 2, ad 3). Where he is not working on these texts (as in *ST.*, ii, 2, q. 180), he does not speak of the ' lumen gratiæ ' supervening upon contemplation.

(*d*) How far are we entitled to assume that S. Thomas shared ' the view of all mediæval writers ' that ' intellectual visions ' (or angelic knowledge) are ' common in the saints ' ? The conclusion cannot be derived from his use of the phrase ' visio intellectualis ' ; for he uses this (of men) even for knowledge ' per phantasmata '—e.g. *ST.*, i, q. 84, a. 1, obj. 1, et ad 1 :—' visio intellectualis ' = ' cognoscere *corpora* intelligendo.' The least we need is an assertion that the ' lumen gratiæ sive sapientiæ,' or ' species intelligibiles ' without ' phantasmata,' are commonly given in contemplation. I can find no such assertion, though the tone of *ST.*, i, q. 12, a. 13, is not unfavourable to it.

(*e*) In *de ver.*, q. 18, a. 1, ad 1, S. Thomas develops a theory which only partially bears out Dom Chapman's contention. He is considering the ' media ' necessary for seeing God,[2] and decides that in his fallen state man needs ' a triple medium ' :—(1) the ' created thing from which he ascends to a knowledge of God ' ; (2) ' the likeness of God Himself which he apprehends from the created thing ' ; (3) ' et [indiget] lumine quo perficitur ad hoc ut in Deum dirigetur, *sive sit lumen naturæ, ut lumen intellectus agentis, sive gratiæ, ut fidei et sapientiæ.*' Now ' ascending from created things to a knowledge of God ' can scarcely be other than a description of the contemplative life. Hence it seems to follow that meditation upon God's universe will sometimes be attended by the ' lumen gratiæ,' or prophetic or mystic (angelic) consciousness ; but often only by the ' lumen naturæ,' or ordinary power of the human mind to see ' intelligible species ' in ' creatures ' by means of ' phantasmata.' Thus the statement of *de ver.*, q. 18, a. 1, ad 4, upon which in the main Dom Chapman depends, is not necessarily intended to be true of all, or even of most, contemplation.

On the whole, then, I should conclude that S. Thomas believed ' angelic knowledge ' would *sometimes* supervene upon contemplation : but perhaps only rarely. In any case he was anxious not to emphasize the point, if not even to avoid it as far as possible. In this he shows himself, as we should expect, to be in the forefront of great Christian writers (*supra*, pp. 105, 202 f., 271, etc.). His business was not, like the panhedonist, to emphasize the joys which come from the vision of God ; but rather to encourage man to look towards God in contemplation, even though no ' consolations ' are found there. The attitude, rather than the reward, was the important thing. And this statement holds good even if Dom Chapman's view be accepted without qualification.

---

[1] I cannot understand why in *ST.*, ii, 2, q. 173, a. 2, the *lumen propheticum* should commonly be spoken of by the wider term of *lumen intelligibile* (which normally covers the *lumen naturale* as well ; Schütz, *op. cit.*, p. 455. *s.v.* ' lumen,' 16 ; and cp. *ST.*, i, 2, q. 109, a. 1 *corp.*).

[2] Not of course in His essence, which is reserved for the blessed.

2. *Beatitude.*

It must however be admitted that S. Thomas' vocabulary was such as to make him peculiarly open to the accusation of panhedonism. Phrases such as ' summum bonum,' ' finis ultimus,' ' perfectio ' and the like, as designations of the goal towards which human life, and indeed all movements of creation tend, are of course wholly unexceptionable. But S. Thomas also calls such movements and tendencies by the term ' appetitus,' and follows tradition in using ' beatitudo ' or ' felicitas ' for the end. But he was more than alert to the problem of the apparently interested character of these phrases ; if for no other reasons than that Augustine (who popularized the word ' beatitudo ' in Latin—*Thes. Ling. Lat.*, s.v.) had defined it as ' *gaudium* de veritate ' (*Conf.*, x, 22—*ST.*, i, 2, q. 4, a. 1, *contra*), and that Aristotle, after raising the question ' whether we desire life for the sake of pleasure or pleasure for the sake of life ' (*Eth. Nic.*, x, 4, 11),—which S. Thomas interprets as ' utrum in beatitudine sit principalius visio quam delectatio,'—had ' left it undecided ' (*ST.*, i, 2, q. 4, a. 2, *corp.*).

S. Thomas has no doubt as to the lines which his answer must follow. In *ST.*, i, 2, q. 2, a. 7, he asks ' whether human beatitude consists in any good of the soul ("in aliquo bono animæ") ? ' Now the ' possession ' of the last end is of course a good of the soul, but the ' possession ' of the end is distinct from the end, or beatitude, itself (*ib., corp.* ad *Respondeo ;* but ad *Res ergo ipsa* he changes the terminology, and confines ' beatitudo ' to ' *adeptio* rei quæ appetitur ut finis ' ; the last end is ' *id in quo* beatitudo consistit.' The sense, however, is clear). The soul is, in itself, in potency only ; it has to be brought into act ; and the bringing of it into act is of course the work of something itself in act, i.e. ultimately of the last end, or God (cp. *ST.*, i, q. 2, a. 3, *corp.*). Hence neither the soul itself, nor its actualization, can be its own last end. No kind of ' delectatio,' being merely the actualization of a potency, is real ' beatitudo ' ; ' delectatio ' can only be produced by ' id quod beatum facit,' and it is this which is the ' end.' Similarly, the last end of *man in general* must be ' bonum universale ' ; whereas any state of any individual soul is ' bonum particulatum ' ; hence *my* ' delectatio ' cannot be my last end.

From these metaphysical arguments S. Thomas descends to a plane on which he is more easily understood. He admits, or rather insists, that ' delectatio ' is necessary to beatitude, but only as a concomitant—as heat is a necessary concomitant (or consequent) of fire ; this result being reached after a consideration of the four possible meanings of the word ' necessary ' (*ST.*, i, 2, q. 4, a. 1, *corp.*). But he maintains emphatically (*ib.*, a. 2) that the ' vision ' is more important than ' delight in the vision ' ; for ' delight consists in quiescence of the will, and such quiescence is the consequence of the excellence of that to which the will has attained.' Hence (ad 2), though animals are directly moved to action by the appeal of particular pleasures, ' the human mind recognizes the good in its universal aspects, and finds pleasure when it has attained it.' Desires are given to man to direct his mind to the vision of God which alone will satisfy them ; not for him to make self-satisfaction the end for which he strives. (Cp. also *CG.*, iii, q. 26, ad *Item, si aliquis actus ;* et seq.).

Hence in his definitions of ' beatitude ' S. Thomas is sedulously careful to avoid panhedonist implications, and usually excludes all mention of ' delectatio '—e.g. *ST.*, i, q. 26, a. 1—' bonum perfectum intellectualis naturæ'; *ib.*, q. 62, a. 1—'ultima perfectio rationalis seu intellectualis naturæ'; etc. In the earlier 'quæstiones' of the 'Prima Secundæ' he mentions 'adeptio' or 'fruitio boni' as a second term included in the meaning of 'beatitude' (e.g. i, 2, q. 1, a. 8; q. 2, a. 7; q. 3, aa. 1, 3; q. 5, aa. 1, 2); but all this is with a view to the cardinal distinction of q. 4, a. 2 (*supra*), which relegates enjoyment to a wholly secondary place. It is because man can distinguish the *end* from the *pleasure of the end*, that of him alone among corporeal beings can the word 'beatitude' be used. Animals have an 'end,' but being creatures of sensitive appetite alone, it can present itself to them only in the form of particular pleasures; hence their end cannot be more than 'delectatio,' and, as we have seen, 'delectatio' is something much less than true 'beatitude.'

It may be added that many of the attacks on the alleged 'interested' character of Christianity (*supra*, pp. 142, 442) would have been avoided if theology, whether expert or popular, had insisted more that in so far as words like 'beatitude' are used to designate the goal of life, they exclude from the primary place any idea of self-satisfaction or the gratification of desire.[1]

NOTE T.—DISINTERESTEDNESS AND ALLIED IDEAS (*supra*, p. 461).

It is only possible here to deal with the problems raised by the words 'disinterestedness' and 'selfishness' in the most superficial manner. Three questions, however, seem important :—

(A) *Definitions.*—From what may be called a 'teleological' point of view (i.e. in respect of the end intended) an 'interested' action is an action performed not for its own sake, but with some ulterior purpose; 'disinterested' actions are those done for their own sake alone. But in ethics the word 'interested' commonly means 'selfish' (both words carrying with them an atmosphere of blame); whilst 'disinterested' and 'unselfish' are more or less akin, and are both used with the implication of praiseworthiness. If there is a difference between them, it is perhaps that 'unselfish' is more commonly used where the action concerned is seen directly to benefit some particular individual other than the agent, 'disinterested' where the beneficiary cannot, for some reason, be thus identified with a particular person. It is 'unselfish' of me to give up my chair to another person : it is 'disinterested' of me to provide a garden seat for the use of the public in general. There are other shades of difference between the two words, but they do not appear to affect the question as a whole.

It is when we attempt to define 'interestedness' or 'selfishness' and their opposites that our difficulties begin. An obvious definition would be, 'Selfishness consists in the pursuit of my own interests'; meaning by my 'interests,' my desires, purposes, 'ends' or the like. But such a definition implies (as naturalism has commonly insinuated)[2] that the 'moral' man, who desires to do what is right, is as selfish as any other, in so far as he is merely pursuing his dominant 'interest';

---

[1] An important essay by Fr. R. Garrigou-Lagrange on 'Pure Love and the Principles of St. Thomas,' drawing conclusions similar to those suggested above from other passages in the *Summa Theologica*, appeared in *La Vie Spirituelle*, xx (1929), Supplement, pp. 229-279; but came to my notice too late for me to use it in the text.

[2] *Supra*, p. 452.

in fact, that as we are always interested in doing what we set out to do, there can be no such thing as ' disinterestedness ' at all. All actions are ' interested '; there is no distinction except between different varieties of interest. Here however we are evidently using the word ' interested ' in a psychological and not an ethical sense ; ' interestedness ' is no longer a blameworthy characteristic which distinguishes some actions from others, but a non-moral characteristic of all actions. This definition, therefore, would be quite misleading ; and the ambiguity between the psychological and the ethical meanings of the word ' interested ' suggests that it is advisable to avoid any attempt to build up a definition round the phrase ' my own interests.'

There is an alternative approach which promises better things. Among our interests—possible if not actual—is the interest in the well-being of others. May we, then, define ' selfishness ' as a ' lack of due regard for the well-being of others'? We must insist upon the adjective ' due,' for it is possible to pay *undue* regard to the well-being of others, and to refuse such undue regard cannot be called selfish. If a starving man refrained from taking food in order to perform an unimportant act of courtesy towards some one who in no way needed it, we should say that he exhibited *undue* regard for his neighbour in the circumstances (Quixotism) ; nor should we consider it selfish of him to postpone the act of courtesy until he had appeased his hunger. Unselfishness, in the same way, is the payment of due regard to the well-being of others ; though where by the ' others ' concerned we mean no less than the community as a whole, or the ideal society whose realization is the object of the moral law as such, we should more naturally use the word ' disinterestedness.' [1]

It might however be objected that when the unjust judge redressed the widow's wrongs he was paying a due regard to her well-being, but that we should call him selfish none the less. But here there seems to be a certain confusion of thought. How much regard was due to the widow's well-being in the circumstances ? Most of us would say, ' At least so much that the mere recital of her wrongs would induce the judge, apart from all other considerations, to intervene on her behalf.' But so much regard as this the judge refused to show her ; apart from the consideration that she would cease to importune him thereafter, he refused, and would have continued to refuse, to help her. It is true that his action *promoted* her well-being, but it promoted it out of regard for *some other* interest, not out of regard for that well-being itself.

It seems practicable then to define selfishness as a failure or refusal [2] to pay due regard to the well-being of others, and unselfishness or ' disinterestedness ' as the reverse of this. How much regard is ' due ' to others in any set of circumstances is of course a question for the casuist, as is also the question of discriminating between the different claims made by ' others ' upon us at any given moment. This latter question, however, seems only to be capable of a true solution in so far as all the

---

[1] And in cases where no particular regard could be said to be due to others at all, we should most naturally speak of the action as ' not-selfish,' ' innocent,' or ' legitimate,' since ' unselfish ' and ' disinterested ' have to some extent assumed the positive meaning of ' altruistic.'

[2] Where it was a *failure*, though we should call the act ' selfish,' we might exempt the agent from the charge of ' selfishness ' (e.g. he might not realise that his action is ' selfish ') ; in the case of a *refusal* the agent of course would be blamed for selfishness.

' others ' can be subsumed under a single ' other ' of whose claim at any particular moment their claims are aspects or fragments ; in so far, that is to say, as we attempt to unify their claims in the all-inclusive claim of God. This consideration by itself reinforces the general contention that the problem of disinterestedness can only be solved by those whose primary attention is to the vision of God.

A first consequence of this manner of defining ' disinterestedness ' and kindred ideas is, that the amount of pleasure which we take (or anticipate) in the performance of an action has nothing to do with the question of its selfishness. All that matters is the payment of due regard to the well-being of others. It is no longer necessary to treat enjoyment (as the Quietists did) as in itself a mark of selfishness.[1] Similarly with the expectation of reward, either here or hereafter : if *due* regard is being paid to the claims of others—that is, if those claims would be honoured to the same extent were no reward promised or anticipated—the mere presence of such an expectation, even in a lively form, does not convert an essentially unselfish act into a selfish one.[2] Nor is it necessary to ignore (as Kant was compelled by his theory to do) the fact that some virtues at least require for their merest exercise the presence of enjoyable emotion in the agent. Without such emotion we may speak, for example, of philanthropy, but scarcely of kindness ; of compensatory justice, but not of gratitude ; of the discharge of paternal obligations, but not of fatherly love. Yet kindness, gratitude, and fatherly love appear to be specific virtues, akin to, yet distinct from, philanthropy and the other two. A good act performed gladly and spontaneously has at all events in certain respects more moral worth than the same act done regretfully and with effort ; and this truth is secured by eliminating all reference to pleasure from the definition of selfishness.

Similarly, to define selfishness as a lack of due regard for the well-being of others, makes it possible to treat both what are called ' self-regarding virtues,' and what are called ' innocent amusements,' as not necessarily selfish ; even though we might prefer to call them ' *not*-selfish ' or ' *not*-interested ' rather than *un*selfish or ' *dis*interested.' [3] This judgment again is one which the normal Christian conscience would endorse as against the Puritan.

(B) *Ethical self-centredness.*—At various points in the preceding chapters it has been suggested that among recognizably *selfish* states of mind is one in which the individual is unduly preoccupied with doing right.[4] Although this seems to correspond with a general and valid judgment of conscience, it is not at first sight altogether concordant with our definition of selfishness. To put the case in its most extreme form, it seems absurd to say of a person who is preoccupied with promoting the well-being of others, that he can ever be lacking in due regard for that well-being.

But such a condition of things is neither impossible nor uncommon. Actually the type of person with whom ' benevolence ' becomes a form of selfishness is one whose only concern with the well-being of others is that *he himself* should promote it ; he is not interested in that well-being as such, but only in his own activity in promotion of it. His attitude is that of the patron, the benefactor, the expert.[5] If another

---

[1] *Supra*, pp. 453-455.   [2] *Supra*, p. 145.   [3] *Supra*, pp. 461, 553.
[4] *Supra*, pp. 96, 133, 447-449.   [5] *Supra*, p. 447.

philanthropist anticipates him in some charitable act, he is capable of resentment ; if no one appears as a recipient of his favours, he feels baulked of his proper opportunities of ' service ' ; and he has no interest whatever in any human beings except the ' unfortunates ' on whom he may shower his benevolence.

Each of these reactions betrays a want of due regard for the well-being of others. If he had such a regard he would frankly rejoice that his neighbours were so well endowed with temporal and spiritual blessings, or at all events so well provided with benefactors, as to need no help from him. The absence or paucity of such joy in the well-being of others, *except when it is the result of his own efforts*, is at once the proof and the measure of his selfishness, however altruistic in appearance his activities may be. Once again a state of mind which conscience naturally proclaims to be selfish betrays as its distinguishing characteristic a lack of due regard for the well-being of others ; and we are justified in treating ethical self-centredness as a form of selfishness.

The test employed in the preceding example, to expose the selfishness of some types of character preoccupied with doing right, may be called a competitive one. It put the question, ' How does such a person regard the efforts of fellow-workers in the same field ? ' The same test can also be employed in cases where the competitive element is less immediately noticeable—e.g. where there is no recognizable and determinate body of potential beneficiaries. A man may state his ideal to be the upholding of the moral law, or obedience to the will of God, or may find his chief preoccupation in carrying out what he conceives to be some particular precept of the divine legislation. But we can still discern whether his regard is primarily fixed upon the vindication of the law (and so disinterested), or upon his own success in relation to it, by asking whether he rejoices when he finds others fulfilling it and mourns when they violate it, or whether he ignores their efforts, even if he does not secretly take some pleasure in their failures. Elijah's supreme ignorance of the seven thousand in Israel who had not bowed unto Baal is the culminating evidence of the self-centredness of his state of mind before the theophany at Horeb—a self-centredness to which the whole incident bears witness (' I am not better than my fathers,' etc.). ' I have been very jealous for the Lord, the God of hosts ' meant—at this stage of his development—little more than, ' I have been very eager to plume myself on carrying the campaign against Baal-worship to a successful issue.' Not every preoccupation with doing right is self-centred, of course ; but the danger is always there, and self-centredness and disregard for the well-being of others as such (even when by ' others ' we mean something as abstract or ideal as ' the moral law ') seem to grow simultaneously and with equal pace.

(C) *Self-forgetfulness and disinterestedness.*—The phrases ' self-forgetful,' ' unselfconscious,' have been used above from time to time as characteristic of the ideal Christian life.[1] The usage is more or less of a commonplace, but it cannot be allowed to pass altogether without criticism. In particular it raises two problems : (1) Are the words ' unselfconscious,' ' self-forgetful ' mere paraphrases for disinterestedness ? (2) How far, if at all, is self-forgetfulness in fact a distinguishing mark of the ideal Christian character ?

' Self-consciousness ' is a term capable of analysis into various elements. Psychologically, a man is self-conscious when he recognizes

[1] *Supra*, pp. 96, 133, 197 f., 204, etc.

the fact that he is doing whatever he is doing. In this sense, self-consciousness seems to be very little more than bare consciousness, and unselfconsciousness comes near to simple automatism. To this psychological self-consciousness, however, which for practical purposes we may regard as present in every awareness,[1] may be superadded two other elements, for which we must find names, however inadequate they may be :—

(1) *The critical self-consciousness :* This adds to the recognition that I am doing something an awareness of the character of the act ; as for example, that I am doing a wrongful or a notable act. Or again the critical self-consciousness may apply itself to the parts or stages of the act, or to the act (or series of acts) considered as means to an end ; in such a case it will ask, for example, ' Am I doing this as I have been taught to do it ? ' or ' Am I doing it in the most economical, tactful, or effective manner ? ' and in reply will record judgment on the facts before it.

(2) *The emotional self-consciousness* records emotions roused in and by the process of doing the act. These emotions, though they may sometimes appear to be spontaneous, are often consequent upon a judgment of the critical self-consciousness, and may arouse not merely further emotions but also further judgments in turn. Thus a state of self-consciousness with which most of us are familiar is made up of (*a*) the judgment, ' This is a wrongful act ' ; (*b*) the emotion of shame at finding oneself doing what is wrong ; (*c*) a certain pride in the fact that one is ashamed of doing what is wrong ; (*d*) a judgment that one is wrong in feeling such pride ; and so forth. But of each emotion it can be decided whether it is disinterested, not-interested, or interested, in so far as it is or is not compatible with a due regard for the well-being of others, understood as in the previous paragraphs.

In a completely self-forgetful or unselfconscious state it would seem that there would be neither critical nor emotional elements present to consciousness as being in any way associated with the self.[2] Approximations to such a state (other than sleep or anæsthesia) are to be seen on those occasions when we speak of a person being ' absorbed ' or ' engrossed ' in what he is doing.[3] But it is an obvious truth that one can be thus engrossed in activities which no stretch of imagination could call ethically disinterested ; this purely psychological self-forgetfulness is very far from being the exclusive prerogative of virtue. Again, especially with those in whom disinterestedness is not as yet habitual, a strong exercise of critical self-consciousness may be necessary to enable them to do a disinterested action—they will be forced to reflect seriously

---

[1] Cp. J. Laird, *Idea of the Soul*, p. 73—' Even when we do not turn back (upon ourselves) in this determined and reflective fashion, it seems still to be true that in an unavowed, half-explicit fashion we are aware, all the time, of the personal togetherness of our knowing.'

[2] The critical consciousness might conceivably be alert, with the judgment, ' That is the wrong way to do the thing ' ; but it would not be the *self*-consciousness : ' *I am doing* the thing in the wrong way.' Similarly, there might be a pronounced emotional tension, but in the extreme case (perhaps because of the tension itself) the soul would not at the moment be consciously self-registering in respect of it (*supra*, pp. 198, 199). How far in fact such states are completely realizable is of course another question.

[3] The psychological distinction between 'absorption,' ' attention,' and ' abstraction '—in all of which self-consciousness is reduced to a minimum—is a side issue into which there is no need to enter.

both before and during the process of acting. And finally, as we have seen, there appear to be certain ' disinterested ' actions which only achieve their highest value if they are performed with joy, and it would be absurd to say that the consciousness of this joy detracted from the disinterestedness of the action.

For all these reasons it is evidently impossible to equate ' self-forgetfulness ' and ' disinterestedness ' unconditionally. Nevertheless, there appears to be a certain propriety in using the phrase ' self-forgetful ' of the disinterested man, and that for several reasons :—

(a) Human nature being what it is, of all the emotions which an action tends to rouse in the soul the ' interested ' ones are commonly those which manifest themselves first and in greatest strength. Where these emotions are not present (i.e. when, so far as his motives are concerned, a man is showing himself ' disinterested ' or at all events ' not selfish ') the emotional tension is often so slight as to justify us, for practical purposes, in treating the case as one of emotional unselfconsciousness. It is sad but true that often enough, in our present ethical state, the most we can hope for is that we should be able to do the disinterested thing without noticeable reluctance and regret. In this sense, therefore, and to this extent, self-forgetfulness is a genuine *differentia* of disinterestedness.

(b) Where the critical self-consciousness is acutely alert, a part of the self is, if we may say so, detached for the special duty of observing the self in its activity. The consequent psychological dislocation, or dissociation, results in a loss of concentration, and so in a lack of complete spontaneity or effectiveness in the action performed. The action is to some extent studied, laboured, clumsy or tactless ; like the efforts of a musician, athlete or craftsman who is striving to achieve, though he has not achieved, complete mastery over his instrument and perfect technique in his execution. So long as a habit is being acquired or an aptitude perfected this state of affairs is inevitable ; but the nearer we approach to a spontaneous efficiency the more we can dispense with the critical self-consciousness.

The same appears to be true of perfect saintliness, so far as we are able to conceive it. We credit the saint with having achieved the aptitude of a spontaneously disinterested life. He is able to see the unselfish course without reflection, and to follow it without effort. There is here, therefore, a further element of ' self-forgetfulness ' in the character of the fully disinterested man ; though it cannot be regarded as anything more than a psychological condition which he shares with the perfect technician in any sphere of activity.[1]

(c) Thus of the perfectly disinterested man we should perhaps be justified in predicating ' self-forgetfulness ' in two ways: (1) in that he no longer experienced interested emotions, (2) in that he had achieved a spontaneity of disinterested service which rendered the critical self-consciousness superfluous. Of these two, it is the former which is really distinctive of disinterestedness as such. In any case we should be wrong if we suggested that he was on all occasions ' self-forgetful ' in the sense of being free from ' disinterested ' or ' not-selfish '

---

[1] Nor is it to be expected that a ' saintly ' character will ever attain this automatism of technique in all spheres of perfection during the course of this earthly life. But he may attain or be endowed with it in *certain* spheres (e.g. in respect of resisting temptations of a particular kind), and so be free to turn his critical self-consciousness to the conquest of other provinces of virtue.

emotions : that would be to substitute Nirvana for Heaven, and to identify spiritual fullness with complete psychological vacuity.

These considerations, incidentally, throw some light on the problems of mysticism. Once again an ambiguous phrase ('self-forgetfulness') allows invalid theories to borrow a specious justification from a valid theory. The valid theory is that the disinterested life must of necessity be self-forgetful in sense (*a*) above—i.e. that it is free from interested emotions (together with the interested thoughts which naturally go with them). But of the invalid theories, that of some among the ecstatic mystics identified the disinterested life with nothing short of self-forgetfulness in sense (*b*) (i.e. 'critical unselfconsciousness'); whilst the doctrines of passivity, or quietism, made the self-forgetfulness of absorption the only genuine disinterestedness (cp. *supra*, p. 454), even if they did not go further still and insist that there was no true communion with God except in 'purely interruptive' states (*supra*, p. 197, n. 6). The ambiguity of the word ' self-forgetfulness ' forms a bridge by which a variety of phrases from the invalid theories, and others like them, have been allowed almost without protest to pass over into the vocabulary of mystics whose general orthodoxy is above question (*supra*, p. 199, n. 5), and justifies Fénelon in his insistence that the ' maxims ' of the saints cannot be accepted uncritically (*supra*, p 459).

INDICES.

I. PERSONS, DOCUMENTS, AND COUNCILS.

(For heresies, sects, and monastic orders, see Subject Index.)

AARON, 11, 41.
Abailard, 249, 288-290, 297, 298, 305, 357, 363, 365, 368, 372, 473, 514, 540-544.
Abbott, T. K., 453.
Abraham, 11, 45, 116, 403.
Abrahams, I., 2, 11, 21, 22.
Acesius, 226.
Acher, Testament of, 19.
Acts of the Apostles, 85, 100, 156, 172, 174, 267.
Adalbert (Bishop), 278.
Adam, 42, 331, 332, 339, 342, 548, 549.
Adam, K., 537-539.
Adeimantus, 25.
Adeodatus, 325.
Adlington, W., 31.
Aeschylus, 476.
Aetius, 306.
Agde, Council of (A.D. 506), 281, 506.
Agricola, Johannes, 418, 419.
Ahasuerus, 341.
Aix-la-Chapelle, Council of (A.D. 817), 207.
Akiba, Rabbi, 82.
Alan de Rupe, 369.
Alaric, 330.
Alcuin, 288.
Alexander, 156.
Alexander the Great, 35, 103.
Alexander III, 289.
Alexander VIII, 7.
Alfaric, P., 321, 323-325.
Alfred, King, 299.
Alvarez, Balthasar, 433.
Alypius, 323-325.
Amalric, 220.
Ambrose, S., 131, 139, 176, 221, 226, 238, 241, 248, 255, 268, 275, 278, 287, 288, 307, 324, 330, 504, 506-508, 513, 521.
'Ambrosiaster,' 225.
Amélineau, E., 258-260, 262-264, 492.
Ammon, 176.

Amos, Book of, 11.
Amos, 369.
Amsdorf, N., 417.
Amun, 208.
Ananias, 158.
Anastasius Sinaita, 132.
Anaxagoras, 477.
Ancyra, Council of (A.D. 314), 227, 508.
Andocides, 29.
Andrew, S., 355.
Andrew, Acts of, 215.
Angela of Foligno, S., 367.
Angers, Council of (A.D. 453), 508.
Anrich, G., 27, 209, 314.
Anselm, S., 458, 541.
Antiochus Epiphanes, 15.
Antisthenes, 484.
Antony, S., 180, 182-184, 187, 192, 199, 202, 203, 258, 270, 348.
Anz, W., 209.
Aphraates, 185, 193.
Apollinaris, Sidonius, 312.
Apollonius of Nitria, 200.
Apollonius of Tyana, 483.
Apophthegmata Patrum, 195, 200.
Apostolic Canons, 508.
Apostolic Church Order, 113, 114.
Apostolic Constitutions, 112-114, 131, 229.
Apostolic Teaching, the, 111.
Apuleius, 30, 32, 231, 495, 498.
Aquila, 406.
Archimedes, 477.
Arintero, J. G., 533.
Aristides, Apology of, 36, 119, 146, 229.
Aristippus, 77.
Aristophanes, 27, 29, 30, 476.
Aristotle, 2, 21, 33, 242, 381, 382, 385, 388, 447, 473, 475-478, 548.
Arius, 159, 264.
Arles, Councils of (A.D. 314), 512; (A.D. 443 or 452), 226, 228, 277, 506, 508; (A.D. 813), 298; (A.D. 1263), 367.

Dispositions. *See Motives.*

Doctrine, Christian, and ethics, 10, 95, 96.

Domestic Codes. *See Codes.*

Dominicans, the, 361, 397, 431, 433.

Donatism, Donatists, 234, 242, 328, 345, 423.

Double standard, doctrine of the, 274, 306, 314, 346, 360, 384, 412, 426, 437, 462, 473, 523; Matthæan doctrine of, 69, 115, 240; growth and validity of, 240; valid theory of, 217, 242-253, 519, 520, 528, 532, 558, compromise theory, 253, 256; invalid theory of, 242-244, 254-257, 346, 359, 412, 437, 517-534, 558; works of supererogation and, 240, 517-532; modern versions of, 526-534.

Dryness, spiritual, 490.

Dualism, 58, 212, 213, 379, 393 in apocalyptic, 59; relation of asceticism to, 67; in the Fourth Gospel, 82-84, 210; Oriental, 86; Pauline, 92-94, 210, 313; gnostic, 209, 210, 213, 216, 217, 337; Marcion, 218, 503; Tertullian, 220, Manichæism, 320, 329; S. Augustine, 332, 345; mediæval sects, 370; Philo, 486.

EBIONISM of the Third Gospel, 69-74.

Ecstasy, ecstatic experience, 211, 475, 477, 483, 494, 529, 549, in apocalyptic, 15, 16, 21; in paganism, 36, 56; in Philo, 44, 45, 486; as the whole end of human endeavour, 104, 197, 302, 373, 378, 388; knowledge of God through, 100; monastic quest for, 196, 197; Pauline view of, 197, 'passivity' in, 197-199; dangers of, 202; in Christian prayer, 205; in gnosticism, 214, 315, 318; in S. Augustine, 321, 322, 326; in S. Bernard, 354; in German mystics, 367; in Richard of S. Victor, 373, 374, 378, 388; Thomist view of, 390, 392; reaction against, 394; and *see Experience, Religious.*

Egoism, Egocentrism, 96, 133, 134, 145, 146, 445, 461, 462.

Emotionalism, 362, 371, 412.

Enthousiasmos, 86.

Epicureanism, 33, 34, 386; spiritual, 490.

Epopteia, the, 27, 28, 211, 314.

Eremetism, 7, 41, 181, 191, 208, 265, 273, 329; and *see Hermits.*

Eschatology, of Jesus, 58; Jewish, 61-63; of the Baptist, 63; Pauline, 63, 77, 101.

Essenes, the, 41, 60, 487.

Eternal life, 19, 94, 337, 429, 466, 467.

Ethics, Christian, 1, 2, 6, 7, 10, 57, 67, 68, 76-78, 85, 123, 129, 139, 203, 206, 242, 313, 337, 346, 357, 468, 470; fundamental problem of, 3; variations in, 10; pagan, 41, 54; of Jesus, 56; in the Gospels, 66, 68, 140, 141, 146, 463; double standard in, 69 (*see Double Standard*); Pauline, 78, 233; humanist, 80, 81; rigorist perversions, 165; and religion, 97, 300; Jewish, 61, 95, 123; irrationalism in, 138; and vision of God, 312, 313; of S. Thomas Aquinas, 379, 385, 386, 388, 412; Protestant, 425, 427, 520, 521.

Eulabeia, Eulabeis, the, 133.

Eupatheia, 42.

Eustathians, the, 265.

Excommunication, in Judaism, 148, 149; in the New Testament, 153, 154, 160, 161, 165, 166; permanent, 165, 168, 170; in Hermas, 170; in the fifth and following centuries, 276, 299, 508, 515, 534, 538.

Exomologesis. See Penance, Pœnitentia.

Experience, Religious (Mystical, Spiritual, etc.), 4, 188, 220, 302, 303, 367, 401; relation to creed and conduct, 9, 10; in Judaism, 15, 22, 38, 46; in paganism, 27, 37, 49, 53, 110, 473-475; quest for, 53, 54, 201, 203; in the New Testament, 94, 104-108; absence of, in formalism, 135, 139, 167; and ecstasy, 197, 198; and panhedonism, 198, 199, 271, 427, 442, 444, 489; in monasticism, 202, 205, 271; in gnosticism, 210; and the response of God, 207, 214; stages of, 243, 531; and disinterestedness, 318, 464; and action, 362; necessity of, 465; as contemplation, 528; and the double standard, 533. *See also Contemplation, Ecstasy.*

FAITH, 116, 230, 339, 345, 462, 472, 497, 515, 545; and gnosis, 128, 318, 316, 317, 383; and alms as a remedy for sin, 131; Pauline view of, 134, 135; and reason, 377; and contrition, 422; justification by, 414-421.

Fasting, 61, 115, 125, 130, 131, 180.

184-188 ; austerities of, 189-191 ; attitude to the Church, 191, 192 ; and the vision of God, 193-207, 270, 497 ; and Christian charity, 201-202 ; doctrine of prayer in, 203-205 ; and contemplation, 206, 207 ; and the secular life, 235-239, 253-254 ; rule of Pachomius, 258-262, 267-269 ; Schenoudi, 263, 264 ; S. Basil, 264-270 ; S. Benedict, 268-275, 347, 349 ; confession of sins in, 283-285, 348 ; love of nature in, 308-312 ; S. Bernard, 347-350, 393 ; lay adoption of, at approach of death, 360 ; active service in, *see Service ;* Protestant revolt against, 425, 426 ; Serapis-, 492, 493, 494 ; as a substitute for public penance (*Conversio*), 278, 509, 510, 536.

Monism, 58, 83, 84, 210, 212, 213, 345.

Monophysites, the, 195.

Monotheism, 38.

Montanism, Montanists, 220, 221, 224, 225, 234, 499.

Morality. *See Ethics.*

Mortification, Christian, 76, 89, 90, 195, 220, 263, 351, 352, 497.

Motives, disregard of, 132, 172, 174 ; and danger of anthropocentrism, 133, 134 ; of reward, *see Reward ;* examination of, 296 ; purity of, 452, 522 ; and disinterestedness, 455, 456, 458, 461, 462.

Murder, 112, 113, 115, 171, 223, 224, 227, 228, 419, 420, 537, 541-543.

Mysteries, the, 16, 23, 24, 27, 29-33, 38, 46, 47, 50, 54, 102, 107, 108, 110, 150, 210, 231, 314, 476, 498, 500, 501 ; of Eleusis, 27-30, 313 ; ' lesser ' and ' greater,' 28 ; Mithraism, 28, 30, 32 ; Attis-Cybele, 28, 30, 32 ; Orphic, 30 ; Isis-Osiris, 30-32.

Mysticism, 27, 38, 94, 100, 106, 107, 108, 110, 205, 220, 251, 303, 321, 330, 338, 347, 354, 355, 362, 387, 473, 533, 549. *See Experience, Religious,* etc.

Mystics, Greek, 27, 29, 43 ; Jewish, 32 ; ecstatic, 45, 214, 391, 558 ; spiritual self-importance in, 205 ; mediæval, 306, 362, 367, 368, 394 ; the great Christian, 321, 352, 393, 452 ; of S. Victor, 375, 377 ; the Carmelite, 432-435 ; the ' false,' 456, 457, 460, 461, 489 ; and ' ordinary ' Christians, 464, 533.

NATURAL God, doctrine of the. *See God.*

Naturalism, 8, 304-306, 337-339, 341-345, 379, 440, 452, 461, 471, 547, 552.

Nature-mysticism, 308-312.

Negative Way, the, 196, 302, 303, 307, 329, 347.

Neo-Platonism, 208, 210, 320-322, 327-329, 346, 375, 380, 483, 486.

Neo-Pythagoreanism, 211, 482, 483, 498.

Nestorianism, 328.

Nezîfa, 149.

Niddûi, 149.

Nirvana, 558.

Novatianism, 225-227, 234, 512.

OBEDIENCE, 141, 248, 501 ; absolute—to the will of God, 65-67 ; motive for, 117 ; ceremonial, 138, 172, 394 ; monastic, 140, 497-500, 526.

Optimism, Christian, 406, 408.

Oratorians, the French, 444.

Orderliness, spiritual, 375-379, 412, 469.

Orders, Mendicant, 273, 348, 361, 362, 368, 371 ; military, 140, 396 ; the Third, *see Tertiaries.*

Origenist heresy, 238.

Orphism, Orphics, 34, 86, 214, 481, 482, 484.

Orthodoxy, 2, 370, 433, 456, 558.

Other-worldliness, 7, 63, 85, 86, 240, 330, 332, 334, 408, 470, 471, 478, 487.

PAGANISM, 4, 5, 8, 44, 45, 77, 87, 88, 107, 212, 314, 318, 439, 440, 486, 502.

Panhedonism,' 104, 198, 271, 272, 353, 378, 444, 467, 473, 489, 490, 550, 551.

Pan-mysticism, 465, 532, 533.

Pannuchides, the, 27.

Pantheism, 38, 329, 368, 380, 393, 471.

Parousia, the, 85.

Passion, the, 391, 393, 394, 401, 409.

Passions, the, 386, 387, 436, 462, 469, 480, 484.

Passivity, 197, 198.

Patarini, the, 370.

Paulicians, the, 370.

Paulinism. *See S. Paul.*

Peasants' War, the, 424.

Pelagianism, Pelagians, 328, 335-338, 342, 345, 467, 546-548.

Penance, 222, 223, 226, 229, 242, 277, 279, 284, 285, 307, 412 ; commutation of, 13, 294, 295 ; restoration after, 153, 159, 167, 179,

Scrupulosity, 133, 134, 145, 522.

Secular life, the, 81, 82, 235, 237, 242, 253-255, 257, 267, 274, 350, 360, 384, 522.

Self-abnegation, 7, 470, 497; -annihilation, 274; -centredness, 97, 133, 141-143, 145, 198, 270, 274, 442-445, 461, 463, 552-555; -consciousness, 555-557; -control, 484; -crucifixion, 54, 484; -examination, 97, 145, 296, 408, 465-467; -forgetfulness, 96, 133, 135, 142, 143, 145, 197-199, 204, 207, 274, 322, 460-462, 555-558; -humiliation, 57; -love, 201, 331, 349, 451, 452, 455, 462; -mortification, 7, 41, 48, 61, 80, 146, 261, 267, 312, 401, 497; -torture, 261, 414, 465.

Selfishness. *See Self-centredness.*

Selflessness. *See Self-forgetfulness.*

Semi-Pelagianism, Semi-Pelagians, 336, 545, 546.

Sentimentalism, 364, 378, 406.

Serapis, cult of, 491-494.

Sermon on the Mount, the, 64, 65, 71-73, 112, 125, 361.

Service, Active, and Worship, 54, 199, 257, 354, 363, 429, 441-452, 462, 463, 471; in monasticism, 199-204, 266, 271-274, 348-352, 362, 398, 399, 403; resulting from the love of God, 199, 346, 412, 426; of the Christian Gnostic, 315, 317; of humility and of patronage, 447-450, 548; disinterested, 199, 451, 452, 557.

Shekinah, the, 11, 20-22, 100.

Sin(s), *Didaché* on, 112-115; 'Grave,' 113, 223, 227, 229, 280, 504-507, 510, 511, 515, 516, 534, 538, 539, 542, 544; 'Capital,' 114, 201, 202, 278, 282, 504, 505, 514, 536, 537; relief by alms, 131, 138, 139; *Hebrews* on, 154; 'unto death,' 161, 162; against the Holy Spirit, 162-165; Hermas on, 167-171; 'Venial,' 170, 249, 280, 282, 284, 297, 339, 505, 507, 514-516, 534-537, 539-544; 'Mortal,' 171, 226, 229, 249, 291, 296-298, 515, 516, 535, 540-543; post-baptismal, 226, 275; secret, 151, 278, 283, 504, 510, 515, 535, 537, 540; Abailard on, 473, 540-544.

Sinlessness of the Christian, 229-233, 237, 246, 337, 339, 370, 452.

Solitude, Solitaries, 2, 180, 184, 250, 265, 266.

Sôma-sêma, 41, 47, 86, 482, 487.

Sotêr (Saviour), 84.

Speculation, religious, 368, 371, 375, 380, 475, 478, 489.

Stoicism, Stoics, 34, 37, 38, 81, 120, 136, 210, 231, 248, 249, 316, 317, 319, 330, 383, 484-486.

Stylites, the, 189, 190.

Subjectivism, Subjectivity, 393, 416.

Supererogation, works of, 131, 138, 240-242, 473, 517-523.

Supernaturalism, 234, 345, 547.

Superstition, 45, 104, 368, 423.

TEACHING of Jesus, the humanist interpretation of, 55; eschatological interpretation of, 56-58; on asceticism, 63-68, 109; on God, 95, 96, 141; on the kingdom, 66, 95, 99, 141; on human conduct, 66, 96; on the 'Two Ways,' 125; on recompense, 140-146.

Teleioi, 86.

Tertiaries, 273, 360, 362.

Theia thea, the, 27.

Theism, 35, 318.

Theocentrism, 64, 96, 97, 142, 198, 272, 338, 444.

Theodicy, 44.

Theology, moral, 7, 250; Jewish, 15; the Egyptian and Asiatic cycles of, 30; Aristotle on, 33; ascetic, 36; Philo's, 40, 43, 44; of the mysteries, 47; pagan, 54, 88; New Testament, 55, 94, 137; Christian, 54, 68, 210, 304; German eschatological school of, 57; German *religionsgeschichtliche* school of, 86, 87; Pauline, 91, 92, 104; danger of rhetoric in, 129; results of codification in, 139; dualist, 210, 212, 213; sect,' 234; post-Tridentine Roman, 256; rigorist, 302, 343; natural, 305, 343; mystical, 377, 390; Melancthon's, 424; witness of, to the vision of God, 464.

Theophany, 23, 99, 219, 555; Jewish, 11, 100; the Fourth Gospel as a, 105.

Theosophy, 54, 208, 211, 212, 214, 219, 316, 498.

Therapeutæ, the, 40, 41, 44, 45, 60, 487, 491.

This-worldliness, 55, 332, 425, 470.

Thomism. *See S. Thomas Aquinas.*

Tolerance, 5.

Tradition, the ignoring of, 369.

Trances, 12, 15, 21, 54, 59, 110, 302.

Transfiguration, the, 97-101, 106, 374.

Trappists, the, 256.

harper ✦ torchbooks

† The New American Nation Series, edited by Henry Steele Commager and Richard B. Morris.
‡ American Perspectives series, edited by Bernard Wishy and William E. Leuchtenburg.
* The Rise of Modern Europe series, edited by William L. Langer.
¶ Researches in the Social, Cultural, and Behavioral Sciences, edited by Benjamin Nelson.
§ The Library of Religion and Culture, edited by Benjamin Nelson.
Σ Harper Modern Science Series, edited by James R. Newman.
o Not for sale in Canada.
△ Not for sale in the U. K.